DRYDEN'S

OUTLINES OF

CHEMICAL TECHNOLOGY

—FOR THE 21ST CENTURY

THIRD EDITION

EDITED AND REVISED BY

M. GOPALA RAO
Professor of Chemical Engineering
Howard University, Washington, D.C.

Professor (1971-74) and Head (1968-73)
Department of Chemical Engineering
Indian Institute of Technology, Kanpur, India

AND

MARSHALL SITTIG
Now resident in
Charlottesville, Virginia

On loan from Princeton University
Princeton, New Jersey, U.S.A. to
I.I.T.-Kanpur under the Kanpur Indo-American Program
sponsored by the
U.S. Agency for International Development (1968-1970)

EWP

AFFILIATED EAST-WEST PRESS PVT LTD
New Delhi

2022

Published by Affiliated East-West Press Private Limited
G-1/16, Ansari Road, Darya Ganj, New Delhi-110002
e-mail: aewp.pub@gmail.com

ISBN 10: 81-85938-79-2
ISBN 13: 978-81-85938-79-0

Dedicated
to the memory of
Charles E. Dryden (1917–1967)
a great engineer, a great teacher,
a great person.

Visiting Professor of Chemical Engineering
Indian Institute of Technology
Kanpur, India
On loan from Ohio State University
Columbus, Ohio, U.S.A.
1963–65

TABLE OF CONTENTS

PREFACE TO THE SECOND AND THIRD EDITIONS (1973 & 1997)

The two editors who have twice revised Professor Dryden's work started with a sense of deep respect for the uniqueness and the thoroughness of the original edition.

The book "Outlines of Chemical Technology" was unusual in that it was essentially two intertwined books—one dealing with the state of chemical process technology on a worldwide basis, and the second dealing with the particular relevance of each specific process or industry to the Indian scene.

The first edition was comprehensive and very timely when it was published. The second edition was revised in India in 1968-71 by M. Gopala Rao and Marshall Sittig and was published in 1973.

The good work of D.S. Panesar in drawing flow diagrams and graphs is hereby acknowledged. Although this book has continued to be used, it is clearly time for a wholly revised edition to carry into the 21st century. In addition to checking and updating, the editors of the revised editions have broadened the coverage of the book to include new material on pollution control and on applications of the computer to the chemical industry.

Particular thanks are due to:

Professor A.K. Gupta, Department of Chemical Engineering, I.I.T.-Delhi, and Mr. G.D. Kamat of Sci-Tech Books and Periodicals in Bombay for their help in making this Third Edition possible. Elaine Anderson of Barboursville, Virginia, U.S.A. performed all the word processing for this volume.

Washington, D.C. and Charlottesville, Virginia 1997

* * *

In preparation of this Third Edition, the editors have:

- removed out-of-date material
- added recent material in its place
- placed products in a world perspective where possible, giving comparisons with Europe and the U.S.A.
- indicated the locations of major manufacturing plants in India
- and, where possible, shown target development figures for India for the year 2000 in keeping with the new title: "Dryden's Outlines of Chemical Technology—for the 21st Century."

PREFACE TO THE FIRST EDITION (1965)

The curriculum in Chemical Engineering at the Indian Institute of Technology, Kanpur, was arranged so that a comprehensive study of the chemical process industries was given in the second semester of the fourth year. By then the students have had a suitable background in stoichiometry, thermodynamics, kinetics, rate processes, chemical engineering operations, organic and physical chemistry so that industrial chemical processes can be studied with the use of these fundamentals. Such a course thus furnishes adequate preparation for a more meaningful summer industrial experience and for the Ch.E. synthesis courses in process and plant design which may follow in the fifth year.

A one-semester course which encompasses three one-hour lectures per week is so short that only the essential features of chemical process industries can be stressed. Standard industrial chemistry reference books are too detailed for reading assignments to obtain essential facts. Furthermore, there are no texts available which relate to the emerging chemical process industries of India. For these reasons, an outline series of notes was prepared for the course which analyze processes from industries classified as inorganic, natural products, synthetic organics, polymers and metals. Selection of industries and processes was necessary to keep within the time limits of one semester. The ones chosen are representative of each type of industry and furnish the basic principles of a particular technology.

A portion of these notes was originally prepared by C.E. Dryden in 1961-62 for a similar course at Ohio State University. Supplementary material, plus revision and adaptation for Indian conditions, was done while working at the IIT-Kanpur. A preliminary edition under the title "Chemical Technology Outline Series," Indian Edition, was printed at the IIT-Kanpur in October 1964.

Professor Dryden resisted the temptation to write these notes in text prose style. Both this style and the outline form have been classroom tested. The results were strongly in favor of the outline form which stresses only the essential facts for students to comprehend, a necessary criterion for a short, concise study of a broad spectrum of industries. The most successful method of study is that of assigning material from these notes on an advanced schedule basis. The students are not expected to memorize factual material but should obtain general impression and observe how chemical and engineering principles are used in each process and industry. They are given a ten minute quiz on this assignment at the start of the class. The instructor then expands on material covered in the notes, preferably by introducing the latest developments with the knowledge that students have the necessary background.

A shorter course than envisioned in this book can be set up by selecting topics from within the framework of the text. The book can also serve as introductory reading to become familiar with the scope and problems of a particular chemical process before making a detailed study of numerous sources.

NOTES FOR TEACHERS

While this book is directed both to the student and to the practicing engineer, it was felt that some specific notes to teachers, based on classroom experience at the Indian Institute of Technology, Kanpur, would be helpful.

It has been the custom to start each lecture period with a ten minute quiz. This helps to insure that a student does the assigned reading on which the quiz is based; furthermore it helps to insure prompt arrival of students at the start of the class hour.

Now there is presented A Possible Course Outline. It is one which has been used successfully at IIT-Kanpur. It involves 3 lectures per week for 15 weeks.

Following the course outline is a discussion of Plant Inspection Trips which are viewed as a desirable and necessary adjunct to the proper teaching of this course.

In preparing the Third Edition of the book, much emphasis has been placed on listings of manufacturers and plant locations so that the student can see where these factories are, where their raw materials sources might be, where their products might go, and consider these plants as possible sources of summer employment or of permanent employment.

A POSSIBLE COURSE OUTLINE

	Topic	Class Lecture Number
I.	**Introduction**	1
II.	**Inorganic Chemical Industries**	
	Sulfur and Sulfuric Acid	2
	Fuel and Industrial Gases	3
	Cryogenics in Chemical Technology	4
	Fertilizer Industry	5
	Nitrogen Industry	6-7
	Phosphorus Industry	8
	Electrochemical Industries	9-10
	Chlor-Alkali Industry	11
	Chemicals from the Sea	12
	Cement and Lime	13
	Water and Air	14
	Nuclear Materials	15-16
	Explosives and Propellants	17
III.	**Natural Product Industries**	
	Soaps and Detergents; Glycerin	18
	Paints and Varnishes (including Pigments)	19
	Carbohydrates and Fermentation	20-21
	Food Industry	22
	Pulp and Paper	23
	Coal and Coal Chemicals	24
	Petroleum	25-26
IV.	**Synthetic Organic Chemical Industries**	
	Petrochemicals and Chemicals from C_1 Compounds	27-28
	Chemicals from C_2 Compounds	29-30
	Chemicals from C_3 Compounds	31
	Chemicals from C_4 Compounds	32
	Chemicals from Aromatics (including Dyes)	33
	Pesticides	34
	Pharmaceutical Industry	35
	Biotechnology	
V.	**Polymerization Industry**	
	Fundamentals	36
	Polymerization Technology	37-38-39-40-41
VI.	**Metallurgical Industries**	42-43
VII.	**Pollution Control & Toxic Chemicals**	44
VIII.	**Applications of the Computer to the Chemical Industry**	45

PLANT INSPECTION TRIPS

Visual observation of actual chemical plant operations is one of the best ways of learning what goes on in a typical chemical industry. For this reason, several well-planned and coordinated plant trips should be taken to supplement the reading assignments and classroom discussions. Hard hats and safety glasses should be required for these trips.

The major test of knowledge acquired on a plant visit is the report submitted within the time limit of one week after the plant is visited. To insure good reports, familiarize yourself with the industrial processes to be seen and study the suggestions given next.

Report Form

Type of Report: The instructor will discuss the type of report to be submitted. One type of report can be based on the assignment given to a typical engineer inspecting industrial facilities for possible purchase by his company.

The student is free to submit the report in any style he desires. However, the important information must be included.

Type of Material to be Included in Report:

Introduction
- Name of plant
- Address
- Inspection date
- Person(s) contacted and titles, and important phone numbers
- Type of plant, history of plant & industry

Description of process(es)
- Flow sheet
- Raw materials
- Chemical reactions
- Process controls
- Products
- Unusual engineering features
- Safety aspects
- Environmental pollution aspects

Economics
- Cost of raw materials
- Products (manufacturing cost and selling price)
- Labor
- Capital investment
- Competitive aspects locally and nationally

Summary
- Potential of the plant and the industry
- Engineering improvements required
- Recommendations for purchase

Hints when making inspection trip
- Study the industry ahead of time
- Ask questions in a loud voice so all can benefit from the discussion
- Take plenty of notes

I

ORIENTATION

IA. INTRODUCTION

The chemical and allied industries in India rank amongst the top of all manufacturing industries both in capital assets and importance to the nation. A great number of their products are used in manufacturing industries in India. These chemical industries also supply vital materials for preparation of drugs and growth of agricultural food products.

The nature of the chemical industry is different from much of the rest of industry. Its basic purpose is to start from an ore or other chemical raw material and end up with a consumer product through series of chemical and physical changes. In this, it differs from many manufacturing industries which are assembly industries and not creative industries in the same sense as are the chemical and allied industries.

Chemical engineers are trained primarily to work in chemical industries. Of those having technology and graduate degrees in chemical engineering, approximately 95% work in some phase of the industrial chemical business: for example—research, design, development, production, technical sales and service, or management, both in the private and public sector.

It is essential that chemical engineering students have a comprehensive picture of the chemical industries, particularly as to the reasons and the basis for the many and diverse operations which are carried on. It will be shown in the study of a number of types of chemical industries that the fundamentals of chemistry, thermodynamics, kinetics, engineering, and economics are always valid, even though the operations may appear complex at times.

A selected series of outline notes will be used to show how these fundamentals have been applied. These will be divided into five categories for ease of study:

1. Inorganic chemical industries
2. Natural product industries
3. Synthetic organic chemical industries
4. Polymerization industries
5. Metallurgical industries

with added material on

6. Pollution control and toxic chemicals
7. Applications of the computer to the chemical industry

Additional study is recommended in terms of plant inspection trips and a computation laboratory in which detailed material, energy, and equilibrium calculations are submitted with flow sheets for several industrial processes.

As an aid to the description of some of the various positions which a chemical engineer may assume, and as an aid to the reader of this book in helping him to fit the position to his own personality and capabilities, Table IA-1 is presented:

Table IA-1
Qualifications Required for Various Jobs

Qualifications / *Jobs*	*Verbal Ability*	*Social Intelligence*	*Analytical Mindedness*	*Numerical Ability*	*Mechanical Interest*	*Forcefulness*	*Self-sufficiency*	*Sociability*	*Self-confidence*	*Imagination Resourcefulness*	*Frustration Perseverance*	*Supervising*	*Persuading*	*Helping Others*	*Working with Data*	*Working with Instruments*
Teaching	××	×				×				×		×		××		
Pure research			××		×		××		×	××	××				×	××
Commercial research			××		×	×				××					×	××
Applied research	×	×	××		××		×	×		××	×			×	×	××
Pilot plant		×	××	×	××					×	×	×	×		×	××
Design			××	××	××			×		×	×	×	×		××	×
Production	×	×			××	××	×					××	×		×	××
Market research	×	×	××	××		××	×		×	×	×				××	
Market development	××	×	×			××	×	×	×	××	××		××	×	×	
Sales	××	××				××	××	×	××	××	××		××	××		
Technical service	×	×	××		××	×			×	×				××		×
Analytical			××	×	×		×									××
Patents—Law	×	×	××						×	××			×		×	
Personnel	×	×	×					×					×	××		
Purchasing	×	×						×	×	×				×	×	
Accounting			××	××			×		×							

Column heads originally suggested by Arthur Atkin, psychologist and specialist in aptitude testing. (*By permission of Chem. & Eng. News.*) Taken from the article "Happiness as a Goal" by Carl Pacifico, *Chem. & Eng. News*, **37** (4): 1–13 (Jan. 26, 1959).

Check your talent against the needs of the job and see what the future may hold for you.

IB. CHEMICAL INDUSTRIES—FACTS AND FIGURES

1. The Production Picture for India

The Chemical Industry's share in the nation's gross industrial output is estimated to have risen from a mere eight percent in 1970-71 to about forty percent in 1995. The country has become self-sufficient in almost all major heavy chemicals which form building blocks for several downstream products like drugs, dyestuffs, pesticides, plastics, paint, etc. See Table IB-1.

Table IB-1
Annual Production/Use of Chemicals, Fertilizers and Pesticides
(In Thousands of Tons)

Item	Production		
	1990-91	1991-92	1992-93
(a) Chemicals			
1. Inorganic Chemicals	3,217.9	3,191.5	3,257.8
2. Organic Chemicals	567.6	678.2	716.0
3. Dyestuffs	27.0	27.0	25.7
4. Pesticides	70.9	72.8	76.9
(b) Fertilizers	22,221.2	23,308.0	22,712.8

Source: "Kothari's Industrial Directory of India" (1994)

The Indian chemical industry can catapult itself into one of the leaders in some selected sectors notably all types of fertilizers, synthetic fibers and specialty chemicals. Research and development in India in this field is expected to make an impact on the global scenario and India is likely to enter the world market significantly to design, commission and operate plants and provide services for them.

Actually, the time of preparation of the third edition of this book—in 1995-96—is a most exciting time to review the prospects of the Indian chemical industry.

Whereas for many years after independence in 1947, India had been a closely controlled economy with very limited encouragement for foreign investment, a marked change occurred in about 1992 with the advent of a new government.

Indian economy has undergone a transformation within a short span of three years. As a result of the policy of economic reforms, launched by the government, India has shed the goal of attaining self-sufficiency in a closed economy and adopted the model of a free market, aiming at globalization. The results are already visible. Today, the granaries are full. The recessionary phase of the economy is over and the industry is well on the road to revival. Exports are booming and foreign exchange reserves surging. A large number of foreign investors have taken advantage of the situation to come to India. These include multinational giants, like Enron Corporation of the United States, General Motors, Motorola, Daimler Benz of Germany, Toshiba of Japan and

View of Chambal Fertilizers and Chemicals Plant at Kota in Rajasthan

*****

From "The Hindu Survey of Indian Industry" (1994)

*****

Note open location of piping in steel structure characteristic of most modern chemical plants. This permits ease of access for maintenance and prevents accumulation of explosive vapors in an enclosed building.

Daewoo Corporation of South Korea, to mention only a few. Hundreds of others are queuing up with investment proposals, seeking government approval.

The international economy has also undergone major changes—some of them very significant to India.

One major change has been the emergence of the Gulf States as suppliers not only of petroleum raw materials, but of petrochemical products. In the raw material area there are the prospects of an Oman-to-India pipeline and possible liquefied natural gas (LNG) shipments from Qatar to Maharashtra.

Also on the international scene, the fall of the Soviet Union and the re-unification of Germany have had major effects on the worldwide chemical industry.

2. The Raw Materials Picture for India

India is well endowed with a large variety of minerals. Coal and iron are the country's principal mineral assets, while mica and manganese deposits are of world importance. Except for aluminum, however, the country is deficient in ore deposits of other major non-ferrous minerals. Bihar State is the major source of mineral wealth in India, but mineral deposits exist in almost all sections of the country.

Petroleum is the major raw material lacking in adequate quantity in India. The total demand for petroleum products by the terminal year of the Seventh Plan is projected at 55 million tons and is expected to increase to 90 million tons by the turn of the century. The western offshore is expected to contribute between 27 and 30 million tons of oil annually by the end of the Eighth Plan. The present production level is 20 million tons. According to ONGC sources, the increased production would be contributed by fields other than the Bombay High.

Indian coal reserves are estimated at over 40 billion tons, but this is hard to qualify. Coking coal reserves are probably about 23,000 million tons. Iron ore reserves are estimated at about 20 billion tons or 5% of total world reserves; India ranks third in world deposits of manganese; India is the major world producer of mica, supplying 80% of world output. New and sophisticated methods of mineral surveying may yield other mineral deposits now unknown. Considering the size of India's population, an industrially developed India will require much effort in uncovering new mineral sources to support its industries in the future.

India is one of the few countries endowed with abundant natural mineral resources. The resources potential offers good growth prospects for rapid industrial progress, employment and exports. The country's mining operations presently pertain to the extraction of nearly 58 minerals from 4,000 mines. It produces three fuel minerals, about a dozen metallic minerals and the balance of minerals are of non-metallic types. India is one of the largest producers of iron ore, chromite, manganese ore, mica, barytes, etc. in the world. It is a matter of satisfaction that the country is self-sufficient in as many as thirty odd minerals which would otherwise have to be imported.

These minerals form the primary raw materials for such diversified industries as iron and steel, ferro alloys, power, aluminum, cement, etc.

Fig. IB-1. Map of India.

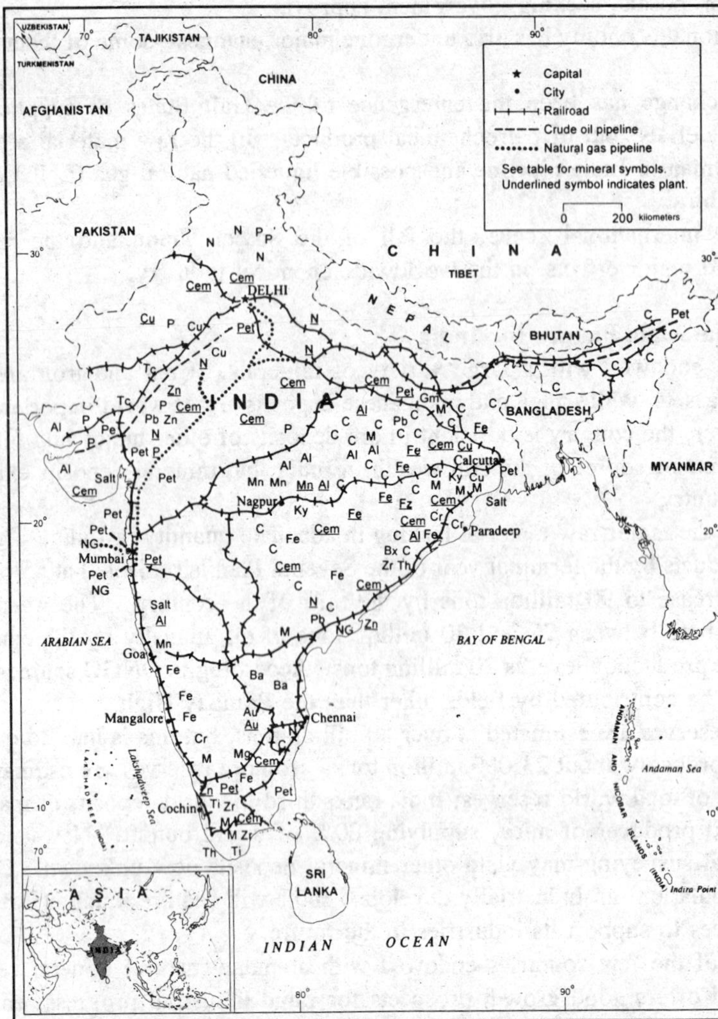

Based on a map in "Mineral Industries of Asia & the Pacific," U.S. Bureau of Mines (1992)

Legend for Map of India

Commodity	Symbol	Commodity	Symbol	Commodity	Symbol
Aluminum	Al	Kyanite	Ky	Phosphates	P
Barite	Ba	Lead	Pb	Salt	Salt
Bauxite	Bx	Manganese	Mn	Talc	Tc
Cement Plants	Cem	Mica	M	Thorium	Th
Coal	C	Natural gas	NG	Titanium (rutile or ilmenite)	Ti
Copper	Cu	Nitrogen (ammonia plants)	N	Zinc	Zn
Fertilizer	Fz	Petroleum, crude	Pet	Zirconium	Zr
Gold	Au				
Iron & Steel	Fe				

Figure IB-1 shows the map of India with the approximate locations of mineral resources from a report by the U.S. Bureau of Mines on worldwide mineral resources. The legend to symbols is shown below the map.

Fuels represent 90% by value of all minerals produced. Yet despite one of the lowest energy usages, India is import dependent for 45% of its oil requirement. It is only marginally self-sufficient in natural gas and coal. The oil refining industry has been thrown open to foreign investors as a step towards privatization of the state controlled monopoly. Nationwide exploration will be necessary to reduce the dependence on the offshore Bombay High field.

Coal remains the principal fuel. Reserves are vast and the country is the world's fifth largest producer. Quality is generally poor and coking coal deposits limited, however. Output will need to rise to keep the energy balance; more if the oil search fails. Aluminum output is rising rapidly, the bauxite reserves are almost 5% of world total. Iron ore production is below capacity because of stagnant domestic demand and reduced export orders, but the reserve base is large and of high quality and could compete in the Far East with Australia and Brazil. Known copper reserves contain over 6 mt metal. They support an industry of 45,000 tpy, all produced by Hindustan Copper Limited, whilst demand is 140,000 tpy. The forecast for 2,025 is 350,000 tpy. Lead is also a deficit metal with a high growth profile. Domestic reserves (2 mt metal) could support significant expansion. Zinc supply is closer to balance and expanding more rapidly because of the higher Zn content of the Pb-Zn ores.

Table IB-2 summarizes the picture on the mineral reserves of India.

Table IB-2
Mineral Reserves of India

	Unit	Reserves	% World Total
Bauxite	mt	1,080	4.5
Beryllium	t	64,000	17.0
Chromite	mt	18.1	4.3
Iron Ore	mt	3,300	5.1
Manganese	mt	17	2.1
Rare Earths	mt	2.3	2.7
Titanium	mt	43.0	15.0
Zinc	mt	11.0	7.3
Zirconium	mt	2.1	4.3

t = tons mt = millions of tons

Source: "World Index of Resources and Population" (1994)

3. The Energy Picture for India

This topic includes the exploration and exploitation of the primary energy resources (coal, crude oil, natural gas, uranium, water, biomass, etc.), the transportation of these resources (if necessary) to the locations of conversion, the conversion of the resources into energy products, the transportation of the energy products to the consumption points and finally the pattern of consumption.

Since independence electricity generation capacity has multiplied by over fifty times from a meager 1,362 MW in 1947 to about 70,000 MW in 1994. Though the average annual growth rate has been maintained at 10.3 percent, there is always a shortfall in meeting the target. The shortage in capacity is as much as 10,000 MW.

Nearly 70 percent of the total installed capacity is thermal-based. In order to meet the continuous growth, the unit sizes have grown in stages from 30 MW, 60 MW, 110/120 MW, 200/210/250 MW to 500 MW. While this is the scenario in power sector, in the industrial side, India has embarked upon massive expansions in steel, sponge iron, fertilizer and refineries which all call for steam generation for process as well as co-generation. Industries have resorted to use of waste heat from different processes for steam generation.

On a national basis, the quantity availability of power has limited expansion in the chemical industry and the quality of available power (power tripping and reduced voltages) has caused severe economic problems; in some cases this has led to the necessity for in-house power generation which increases cost severely.

The following tabulation from the Planning Commission gives a panoramic view of the energy future in India.

Table IB-3
Projected Energy Consumption in the Indian Economy in 1999-2000 and 2004-05

Unit: mill Gcal

Items	1984-85 Gross Energy	1984-85 Share (%)	1999-2000 Gross Energy	1999-2000 Share (%)	2004-05 Gross Energy	2004-05 Share (%)
I. Commercial Energy:						
(a) Coal and Lignite	729	31	2,194	42	3,372	48
(b) Nuclear Energy (uranium)	12	1	187	4	187	3
(c) Hydroelectric	46	2	102	2	137	2
(d) Hydrocarbons	458	20	1,574	30	2,057	29
Total Commercial Energy	1,245	54	4,057	78	5,753	82
II. Non-Commercial Energy:						
(a) Fuelwood	696	30	732	14	805	11
(b) Dungcake and Agr. Waste	382	16	479	9	527	7
Total Non-Commercial Energy	1,078	46	1,211	23	1,332	18
III. GRAND TOTAL:	2,323	100	5,268	100	7,085	100

Source: "Energy Modelling For India," Planning Commission (1993)

Against the Eighth 5-Year Plan (1992-1997) target of capacity addition of 27,728 MW in the government sector, only 17,000 MW is likely to be commissioned during the plan period as per the estimate of Ministry of Power in October 1993. Among the eight government cleared foreign power projects, only two are likely to be commissioned during this plan period: Enron Phase-1 (695 MW) and GVK industries (235 MW), a total of 930 MW. Additional capacity from private Indian power projects is likely to be 1,290 MW. The major projects being 500 MW each of Bombay Suburban Electric Supply (BSES) and CESC.

Table IB-4 is a tabulation of power projects involving foreign participation which were cleared by the Central Government as of 1994. These will hopefully be phased in the period 1995-2000.

Table IB-4
Seven Foreign Projects Cleared by the Central Government

Project and State	Promoters	Capacity (MW)	Cost (Rs crore)
Jegurupadu GBPP *Andhra Pradesh*	GVK Industries	235	827
Kakinada GBPP *Andhra Pradesh*	Spectrum Power Generation Ltd	208	748
Visakhapatnam Thermal Power Project *Andhra Pradesh*	Ashok Leyland, National Power plc, UK	1,000	3,000
Mangalore Thermal Power Project *Karnataka*	Cogentrix, Inc	1,000	5,088
IB Valley Thermal Project *Orissa*	AES Corp.	420	2,025
Dabhol Combined Cycle Gas-based Power Project *Maharashtra*	Enron Power	2,015	9,051
Zero Unit Power Project *Tamil Nadu*	ST Power Systems	210	750

Source: "Energy Scenario & Energy Magazine" (1994)

The importance of nuclear energy in meeting the country's long term energy needs was understood by the planners, right from the beginning. Recognizing that nuclear technology would be subject to a progressively restrictive technology central regime and also that the long term strategies for exploitation of the country's vast thorium resources are bound to be somewhat different from those of most other countries engaged in nuclear power development, tremendous emphasis was placed on achieving self-reliance in technology development. This policy has yielded rich dividends and today one can proudly use the realization of indigenous capability in all aspects of the nuclear fuel cycle.

The following projects are providing nuclear power according to *"Kothari's Industrial Directory of India" (1994)*:

1) Tarapur Atomic Power Station (TAPS):

The station comprising two BWR (Boiling Water Reactor) units, each rated at 160 MW, has completed twenty-two years of successful commercial operation. Since the date of its commencement of commercial operation, the cumulative electricity generated from this station is nearly 40,000 MUs (million British thermal units). It provides electricity to Maharashtra and Gujarat.

2) Rajasthan Atomic Power Station (RAPS):

This station has two units, each rated at 220 MW. It generated 1,087 MUs last year. This low MU is due to RAPS I unit operating at restricted power level of 100 MW. It provides electricity to Rajasthan.

3) Madras Atomic Power Station (MAPS):

With two PHWR (Pressurized Heavy Water Reactor) units, each rated at 235 MW, this station generated 2,161 MUs last year in spite of both the units running at 75% of full power levels. It provides electricity to Madras.

4) Narora Atomic Power Station (NAPS):

It has two PHWR units, each of 235 MW and generated 538 MUs only, since the unit 2 started functioning only from January, 1992 and operated only at 50 percent full power. It provides electricity to UP and Delhi.

At present there are four major projects under construction to give a total capacity of 2,320 MW. The projects are at Kadrapar Atomic Power Projects (KAPP) 1 and 2, Kaiga 1 and 2, RAPP 3 and 4, TAPS 3 and 4.

Nuclear source is clean, compact and concentrated. Nuclear is economical. A unit of electricity from the nuclear power stations at Tarapur and Kalpakkam cost 40 to 58 paise per KWH compared with 60 to 90 paise per KWH from thermal stations in the respective regions. The greatest advantage of nuclear power is that it can be installed in location even remote from hydel and coal resources (Hydel and Coal resources are not being evenly distributed geographically).

In spite of mishaps like Chernobyl in the Ukraine and Three Mile Island in the U.S.A. which are very rare occurrences, the nuclear power industry has an excellent track record of safety and at present seems to be the viable solution for the deteriorating conventional sources in the long run.

For a discussion of the effects of energy costs on the economics of one energy-intensive chemical (chlorine), the reader is referred to Chapter II which compares power costs in India, China, U.S.A., and Saudi Arabia.

4. The Transportation Picture for India

Transport is an integral part of the economic picture in the production of chemicals. The relative volumes and densities of various raw materials and products and the relative freight rates by rail, sea, etc., go far to determine the desirable location of any chemical manufacturing enterprise and the profitability of its operation.

4.1. Rail Transport

The Indian railway system is the largest in Asia and the fourth largest in the world. The railway system comprises 33,600 km of broad-gauge 1.676-m track, 24,000 km of meter-gauge (1.00-m) track, and 4,250 km of narrow-gauge, 0.762-m and 0.610-m track. The total track length of all gauges is approximately 61,850 km, of which 12,617 is double track and 6,500 km is electrified. The mixed-gauge trackage introduces complexities, such as loss of time in transshipment and multiple stockage of spare parts. The rail system has considerable old equipment that is unreliable and expensive to maintain. At year end 1992, detailed plans were revealed to upgrade the railroads through the use of heavier rails of higher tensile strength, welded rails, and prestressed concrete sleepers to improve track structure. Modern electronic devices were expected to improve reliability of signals and telecommunications. In addition, locomotives were to be upgraded to higher horsepower and greater fuel efficiency, coaches would be built of lighter weight and greater speed potential, and freight cars would be constructed of better payload-to-weight ratio. During 1993-94, railways carried 362.1 million tons of revenue-earning traffic, a growth of 3.6% over the previous year.

Table IB-5 summarizes statistics on goods traffic on Indian railways.

Table IB-5
Goods Traffic on Indian Railways (In Net M. Tons) (Estimated)

Commodity	1988-89	1989-90	1990-91	1991-92
(1) Coal	128.01	131.10	139.00	145.30
(2) Raw Material for Steel Plant	26.18	28.00	28.50	31.00
(3) Pig Iron & Finished Steel	10.68	10.20	11.25	11.9
(4) Iron ore	13.64	15.00	15.00	16.1
(5) Cement	25.91	27.50	28.50	29.60
(6) Foodgrain	24.00	23.50	25.00	25.10
(7) Fertilizer	16.10	17.20	18.75	19.10
(8) Mineral Oil	22.60	24.50	25.00	25.00

Source: "S.I.R.I. Directory of Industries in India" (1995)

4.2. Road Transport

India's road network includes 515,000 km of hard-surface two-lane roads and approximately 1.12 Mkm of gravel, loose-surface, or prepared-earth routes having at least one lane and, in many stretches, two lanes. This secondary system is not well drained in all places, but generally can accommodate passing of vehicles headed in opposite directions. As in many Asian countries, access to some remote areas is by cart tracks, current or abandoned.

Road transport at present accounts for 50% of total freight movement and 80% of passenger traffic. As industrial development and automobile production grow, this will obviously be a priority item for growth as well.

4.3. Water Transport

India has an extensive coastline of some 5,700 km and a large domestic shipping industry with total tonnage at 6 million as at the end of December, 1991. Among eleven major ports, Bombay is the biggest port in India handling more than 25% of the total trade through Indian ports. There are 139 minor ports and more than 13 million tons of cargo is handled by all the existing ports. During the Eighth Plan 1992-97, capacity of the major ports is proposed to be increased from 169.23 MT to 237.09 MT. The commodity-wise breakup of the capacity is given below.

Iron Ore	30%
Fertilizers (Raw and Finished)	6%
Coal	30%
General Bulk Cargo	25%
Containers	8%

The country has about 16,200 km of inland waterways, with 3,630 km navigable by large vessels. Principal seaports are Bombay, Calcutta, Cochin, Kandla, Madras, New Mangalore, and Port Blair in the Andaman Islands. A newer port at Visakhapatnam is growing rapidly and likely will become India's most active port in the next 5 to 10 years. Cochin Port has endured labor problems and suffered losses of traffic to other ports. Madras Port has recently earned a reputation as the cleanest and most efficient port in India.

4.4. Pipelines

Pipelines, relatively new to India, consist of 3,497 km for petroleum crude, 1,703 km for refined products, and 902 km for natural gas, in all totalling 6,102 km. Pipelines are undergoing further development and expansion as new routes and terminals are being proposed with increasing urgency.

4.5. Air Transport

India has a total of 345 airports, 292 of which are presently usable. Of these, 203 have paved runways, 2 of them with runways more than 3,659 m long, 59 of them with runways 2,440 to 3,659 miles, and 87 of them with runways 1,220 to 2,439 m in length. Air service utilizes about 93 large transport aircrafts.

5. The Automobile Industry as a Major Consumer of Chemicals

In the developed countries, such as the U.S., the automobile industry may be thought of as a big "engine" which drives a number of supplier industries such as:

- Steel for bodies and frames

- Glass for windows
- Rubber for tires
- Petroleum as a fuel
- Plastics for parts and fittings
- Lead for batteries
- Copper for wiring and radiators
- Zinc for die cast handles
- Polymers for insulation and finishes
- Platinum for pollution control devices
- Aluminum for engine and body parts and wheels
- Ceramics for insulation and brake linings

As an example of this effect, "Chemical Weekly Annual" for August 15, 1995 has reported on the possible implications of automotive industry growth for the paint industry.

First, they have surveyed possible projections in production of various types of vehicles as follows:

FUTURE PROJECTIONS

(Sales in Lakhs)

Category	Sales 1994-95	Sales 2000-1	Annual Growth rate %
Medium/Heavy Com. vehicles	1.03	1.75	9%
Light Commercial vehicles	0.8	1.75	13%
Cars	2.65	7.5	19%
Scooters	10.33	17.94	9.5%
Motorcycles	6.52	13.26	13%
Mopeds	5.23	7.8	7%

In 2000-01 out of 7.5 lakh cars, luxury cars will amount to 2.5 lakhs or about 33%. These have huge implications for the paint industry. First of all, an economy car consumes about 10 to 12 liters of paint as opposed to about only 1.8 liters for a scooter. Further, a luxury car will consume a larger quantity of paint than the economy car. Last but not the least, the car finishes are the highest quality paints and hence it will upgrade the quality of paints in general and automotive paints in particular. This should do a lot of good to the paint industry.

There are a number of foreign participations in the automobile industry in the process of development. These include:

Car	Foreign Company	Indian Company
Cielo	Daewoo, S. Korea	DCM
Ford Fiesta	Ford, USA	Mahindra & Mahindra
Maruti Esteem	Suzuki, Japan	Maruti Udyog
Mercedes	Mercedes-Benz, Germany	TELCO
Opel Astra	General Motors, USA	General Motors (India)

Peugot 309	Peugot, France	Premier Auto
Rover Montego	Rover, UK	Sipani Automobiles
Uno	Fiat, Italy	Premier Auto

It will be appreciated that the above are renowned international companies and they have the highest standards for car finishing paints and so the standards of automotive paints made in India will have to attain international standards. This will also have a spill over effect and the quality of other paints will also improve. So the growth and boom in the automotive industry is going to be a boon for the paint industry in more ways than one!

IC. UNIT OPERATION AND UNIT PROCESS CONCEPTS

A formula for successful chemical industries production can be expressed as the equation:

$$\text{Commercial Production} = f\,(\text{Chemical Changes} + \text{Physical Changes}).$$

For solving this equation, chemical engineering applies fundamental knowledge of unit processes and unit operations in a coordinated pattern for successful commercialization of chemical processes and products.

The unit operation approach is already familiar to chemical engineering students. By a combination of science and engineering principles, a series of unit operations for handling problems of physical changes has been developed by the chemical engineering profession. These unit operations can be applied to widely divergent manufacturing procedures with no change in concept, merely a change in conditions. In like manner, the unit process concept can be used in systematizing chemical reactions which are found in many types of chemical industries. A chemical engineer, thinking in terms of unit processes, can apply previous chemical reaction performance knowledge to a new type of chemical produced from one or more unit process steps. For example, nitrations are almost always exothermic and all of the physical-chemical principles of equilibrium and reaction rates are similar. The selection of construction materials and equipment for unit processes can also be categorized. Liquid phase nitrations require a well-agitated reactor design with provision for heat removal. Materials of construction are cast iron.

Tables IC-1 & IC-2 list and briefly illustrate most of the unit processes and unit operations respectively encountered in the chemical industries. The application of these unit building blocks will be amply demonstrated throughout the book.

From the previous discussion one might think that it is a relatively easy job to commercialize a chemical process. However, the permutations and combinations of the host of physical and chemical variables required to successfully produce chemical products mean that each process studied will have important differences as well as similarities to other chemical processes. It is often the novelty of the approach which is the key to a better process. We must be keenly aware of these differences as well as unitizing approaches.

Table IC-1 Outline of Unit Processes

	Unit Process	*Typical Industry Using Process*
1	Alkylation Addition of alkyl radical (—CH_3) with side chain final product 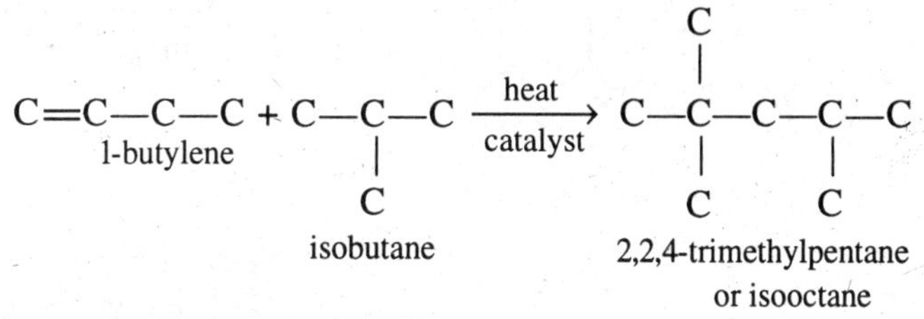	Petroleum Organic chemicals
2	Amination by Ammonolysis $Cl\cdot CH_2\cdot CH_2\cdot Cl + 4NH_3 \rightarrow NH_2\cdot CH_2\cdot CH_2\cdot NH_2$ ethylene dichloride → ethylene diamine $HO_2C(CH_2)_4CO_2H + 2NH_3 \rightarrow NC\cdot(CH_2)_4CN$ adipic acid → adiponitrile	Dyestuffs Organic chemicals Synthetic fibers
3	Amination by Reduction $CH_3\cdot CH\cdot NO_2\cdot CH_3 + 3H_2 \rightarrow CH_3\cdot CH\cdot NH_2\cdot CH_3$ 2-nitroparaffin → isopropylamine	Dyestuffs Organic chemicals
4	Ammonoxidation $CH_3{:}CH_2\cdot CH_3 + NH_3 + 1.5O_2 \rightarrow CH_2{:}CH\cdot CN + H_2O$ propylene, ammonia, air → acrylonitrile	Plastics Synthetic fibers
5	Calcination $CaCO_3 + \text{heat} \rightarrow CaO + CO_2$ limestone → lime	Cement
6	Carbonylation $CH_3OH + CO \rightarrow CH_3COOH$ methanol, carbon monoxide → acetic acid	Organic chemicals
7	Carboxylation 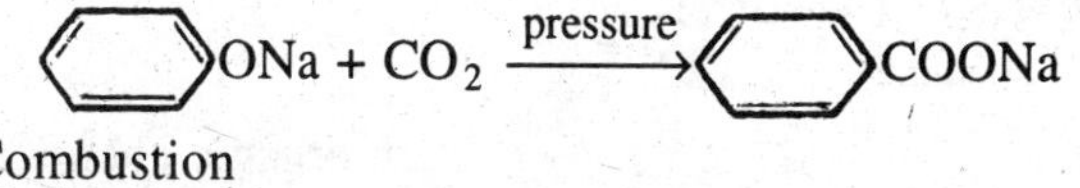	Organic chemicals
8	Combustion $CH_4 + 2O_2 \rightarrow CO_2 + 2H_2O$	Process heating

	Unit Process	Typical Industry Using Process
9	Condensation	Synthetic perfumes
	$C_6H_5CHO + CH_3CHO \xrightarrow{NaOH} C_6H_5CH{:}CHCHO + H_2O$ benzaldehyde, acetaldehyde → cinnamaldehyde	
	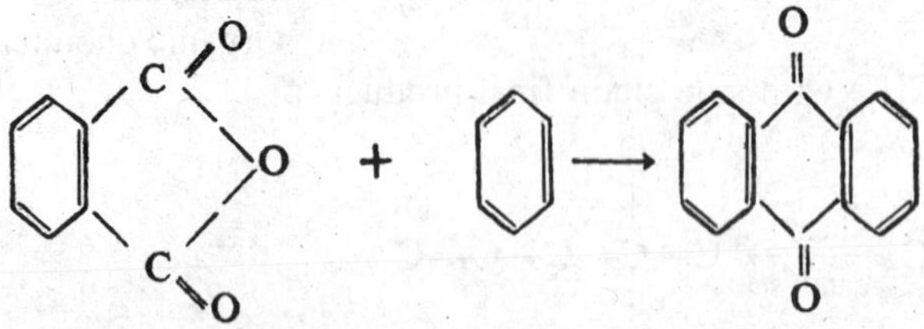 phthalic anhydride → anthroquinone	Organic chemicals Dyestuffs
10	Cracking or Pyrolysis	Petroleum Destruction distillation of coal
	C—C—C—C—C—C—C → C—C—C + C=C—C—C	
11	Cyanidation or Cyanation	Organic chemicals
	$HC{:}CH + HCN \rightarrow CH_2{:}CH{\cdot}CN$ acetylene → acrylonitrile	
12	Cyclization 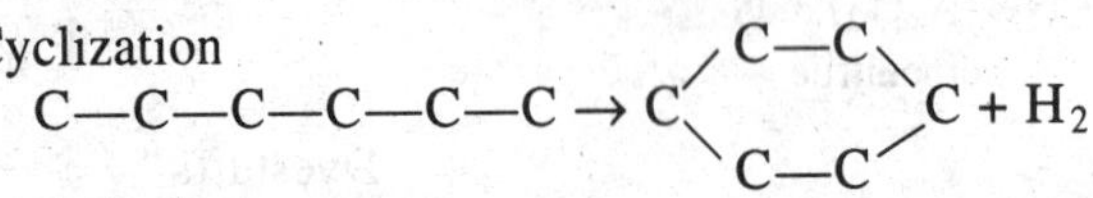	Petroleum
13	Dehydration	Organic chemicals Inorganic chemicals
	$CH_3CH_2OH \rightarrow H_2C{:}CH_2 + H_2O$ ethyl alcohol → ethylene	
	$Ca(OH)_2 \rightarrow CaO + H_2O$ calcium hydroxide → calcium oxide	
14	Dehydrogenation	Synthetic rubber
	$CH_3{\cdot}CH_2{\cdot}CH{:}CH_2 \rightarrow CH_2{:}CH\,CH{:}CH_2 + H_2$ 1-butene → 1,3-butadiene	
15	Diazotization and Coupling	Dyestuffs
	(a) $R{-}NH_2 + HCl + HNO_2 \rightarrow R{-}N_2Cl + 2H_2O$	
	(b) 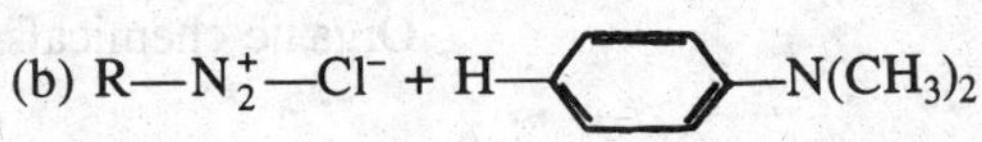 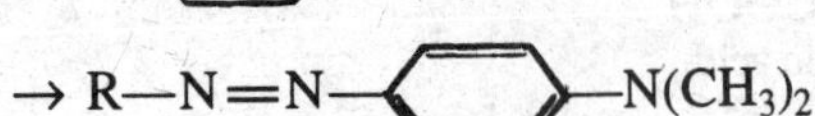	
16	Disproportionation	Organic chemicals
	$2CH_2{:}CHCH_3 \rightarrow H_2C{:}CH_2 + CH_3CH_2CH{=}CH_2$ propylene → ethylene + butylene	
17	Double Decomposition (metathesis)	Inorganic chemicals
	$Ca(OH)_2 + H_2SO_4 \rightarrow CaSO_4 + 2H_2O$	

	Unit Process	*Typical Industry Using Process*
18	Esterification Alc + Acid $ROH + R'COOH \rightarrow R'COOR + H_2O$ $ROH + H_2SO_4 \rightarrow RHSO_4 + H_2O$	Oils and fats Soaps Organic chemicals
19	Halogenation $CH_2{=}CH_2 + Cl_2 \rightarrow ClCH_2{\cdot}CH_2Cl$ ethylene → ethylene dichloride 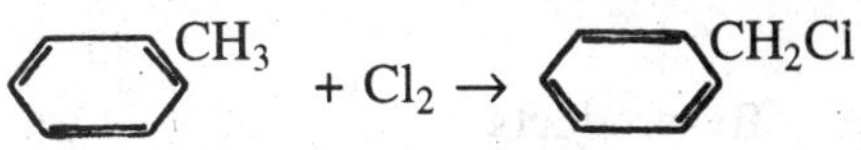 toluene → benzyl chloride	Organic chemicals
20	Hydration $H_2C{:}CH_2 + H_2O \rightarrow CH_3CH_2OH$ $CaO + H_2O \rightarrow Ca(OH)_2$	Organic chemicals Inorganic chemicals
21	Hydroformylation Olefin → aldehyde with additional C $RCH{=}CH_2 + CO + H_2 \rightarrow R(CH_2)_2{-}CHO$	Organic chemicals
22	Hydrogenation $R{=}R' + H_2 \rightarrow RH{-}HR'$	Fats + waxes Coal hydrogenation Petroleum
23	Hydrolysis $C_6H_5Cl + H_2O \rightarrow C_6H_5OH + HCl$ chlorobenzene → phenol	Organic chemicals
24	Hydroxylation $RCH_2OH + CH_2{-}CH_2$ (bridged by O, ethylene oxide) $\rightarrow RCH_2(OCH_2\ CH_2)_nOH$	Detergent manufacture
25	Isomerization $C{-}C{-}C{-}C \xrightarrow[\text{catalyst}]{\text{heat}} C{-}C(C){-}C$	Petroleum
26	Nitration 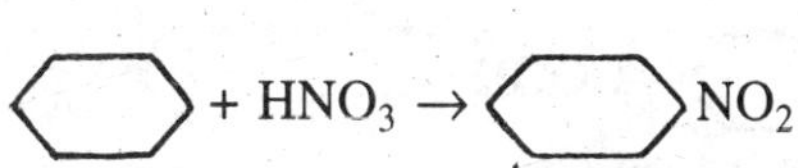 nitrobenzene $CH_3{\cdot}CH_2{\cdot}CH_3 + HNO_3 \rightarrow$ $CH_3{\cdot}CH_2{\cdot}CH_2{\cdot}NO_2$; $CH_3{\cdot}CHNO_2{\cdot}CH_3$; $CH_3{\cdot}CH_2{\cdot}NO_2$; $CH_3{\cdot}NO_2$ nitroparaffins	Explosives Dyestuffs Organic chemicals

	Unit Process	Typical Industry Using Process
27	Oligomerization	Organic chemicals

$3CH_2{:}CH\,CH{:}CH_2 \rightarrow$

1,3-butadiene

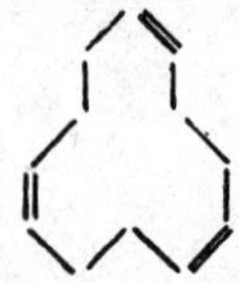

1,5,9-cyclododecatriene

28 Oxidation — Organic chemicals

$RCH_2OH + O_2 \rightarrow RCHO + RCOOH$

$CH_3 \cdot CH_2 \cdot CH_2 \cdot CH_3 + O_2 \rightarrow 2CH_3COOH + \text{By-products}$

$2CH_4 + 3/2O_2 \rightarrow HC{\vdots}CH + 3H_2O$

29 Polymerization — Petroleum, Plastics, Elastomers, Synthetic fibers

(a) Addition polymerization

$$\underset{\text{ethylene monomer}}{H_2C{=}CH_2} + H_2C{=}CH_2 \rightarrow \underset{\text{dimer}}{—CH_2—CH_2—CH_2—CH_2—}$$

$$\xrightarrow{C_2H_4} \text{etc.} \rightarrow \underset{\text{polyethylene}}{(CH_2)_n}$$

$$\underset{\text{polyvinyl monomer}}{H_2C{=}CHX} + H_2C{=}CHX \rightarrow H_3C—CHX—CH{=}CHX$$

$$\xrightarrow{H_2C{=}CHX} \text{etc.} \rightarrow \underset{\text{polyvinyl polymer}}{(C_2H_3X)_n}$$

X = chloride, acetate

(b) Condensation polymerization

—splitting off of small molecules such as H_2O, NH_3, CH_2O, NaCl

(1) $n(HO—R_1—\underset{\underset{O}{\|}}{C}—OH) \rightarrow H(—O—R_1—\underset{\underset{O}{\|}}{C}—)_n—OH + (n-1)H_2O$

(2) HO—CH_2—CH_2OH + HOOC——COOH

ethylene glycol   terephthalic acid

$\rightarrow$ Alkyd resins + H_2O

30 Reduction — Polymer catalyst manufacture

$3TiCl_4 + Al \rightarrow 3TiCl_3 + AlCl_3$

	Unit Process	*Typical Industry Using Process*
31	Sulfonation 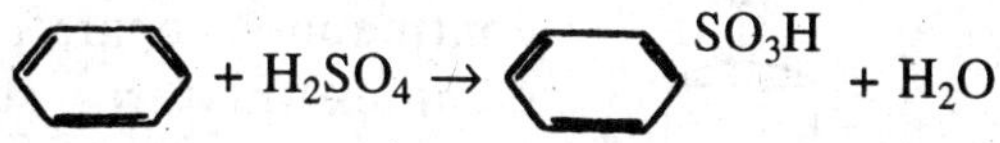	Dyestuffs Surface active agents
32	Thionation 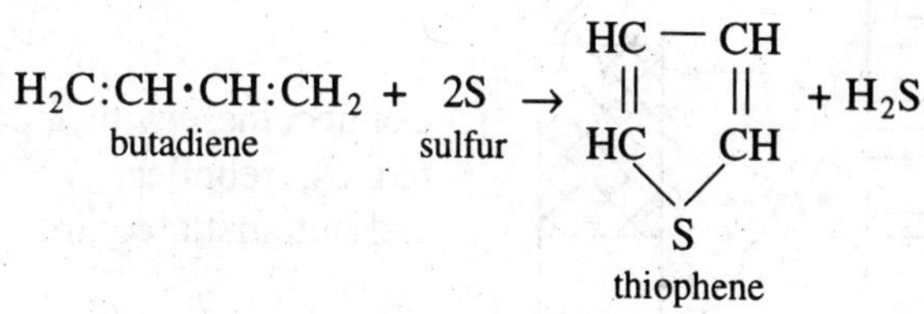 $CH_3OH + H_2S \rightarrow CH_3SH + H_2O$	Organic chemicals

Table IC-2 Outline of Unit Operations

	Unit Operation	*Schematic Representation*	*Comments*
1	Distillation		
	(a) Batch	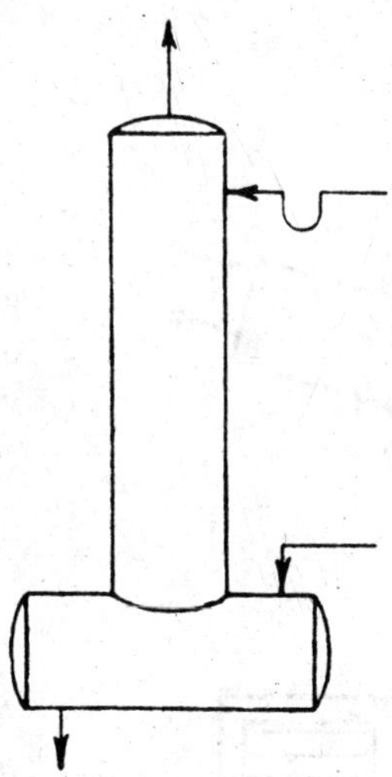	Used for intermittent operation and handling small volumes of feed and product

Unit Operation	*Schematic Representation*	*Comments*
(b) Continuous fractionator	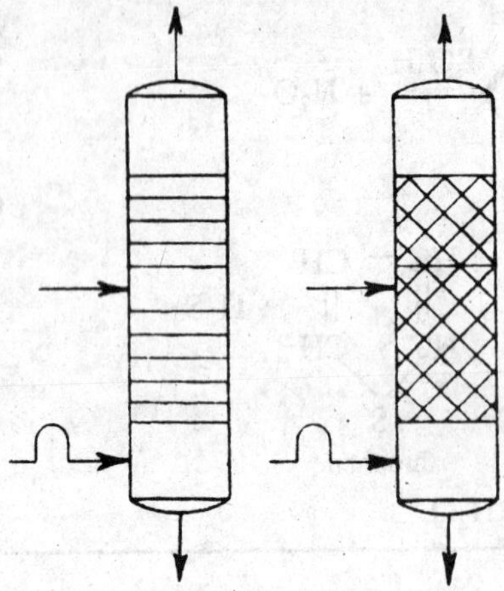	Used for high volume continuous separation of complex mixtures such as petroleum fractions Connect these with appropriate pumps, reboilers, condensers and automatic controls
2 Drying of Solids		
(a) Spray drier	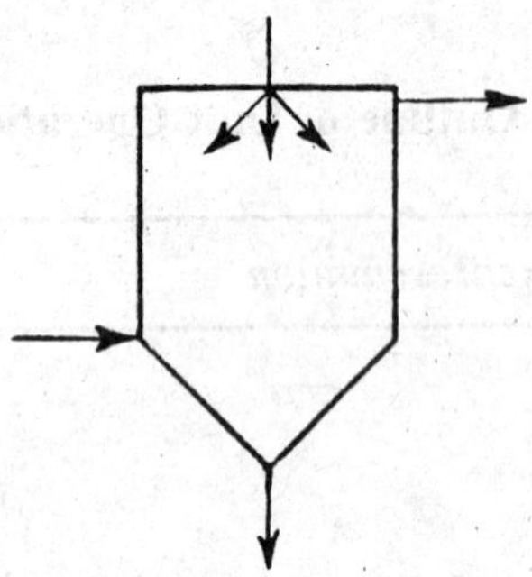	Suitable for large capacity operation on liquid feed to give powdered, spherical, free-flowing product; used in production of pigments, detergents, synthetic resins, and misc. inorganic salts
(b) Rotary drier	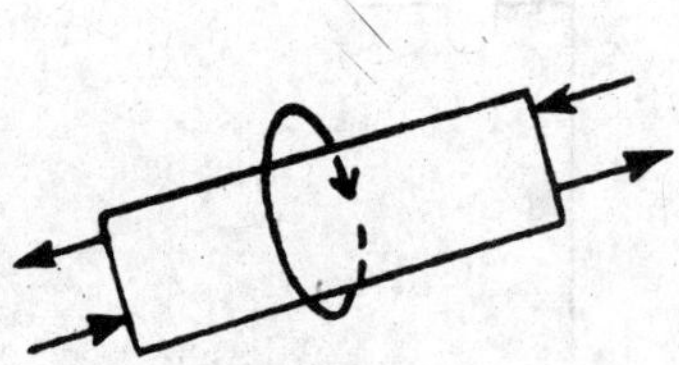	Suitable for drying free-flowing granular solids which do not dust or stick; high-temp. versions are kilns for calcining cement, lime, etc.
(c) Tunnel drier	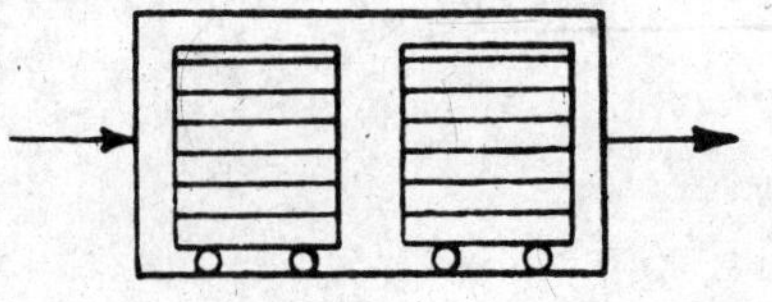	Applicable to drying pastes or powders in trays; also used to dry pottery, lumber, leather, etc., in sheet or shaped forms

Unit Operation	*Schematic Representation*	*Comments*
3 Evaporation		
(a) Open pan	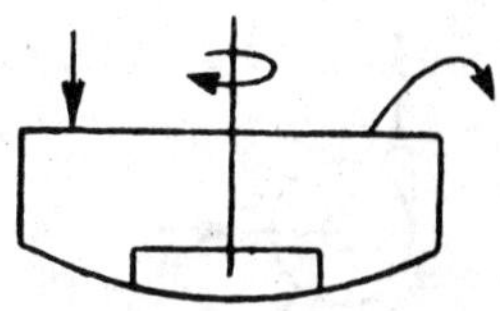	Used for small batches; often of viscous mat'ls; such designs are easy to clean
(b) Multiple effect	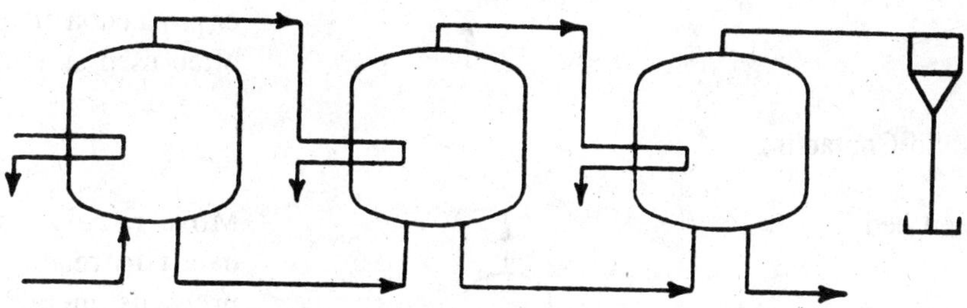	Used to achieve max. heat economy in evap'n of paper mill black liquor, sugar syrups and sol'ns of inorganic chemicals
4 Extraction		
(a) Liquid-liquid	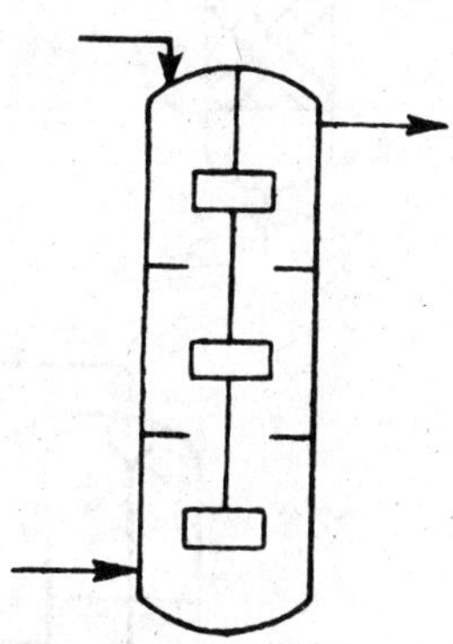	Used to contact solvent and feed to give raffinate and extract; widely adapted to removal of naphthenes from lube oil fractions using solvents such as furfural
(b) Solid-liquid (leaching)	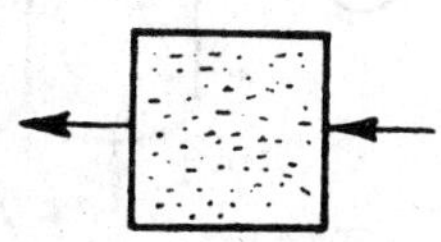	Involves removal of a solute from a solid by means of a liquid solvent; often used in ore treatment to recover metal values

Unit Operation	*Schematic Representation*	*Comments*
5 Fluid Handling		
(a) Centrifugal pump	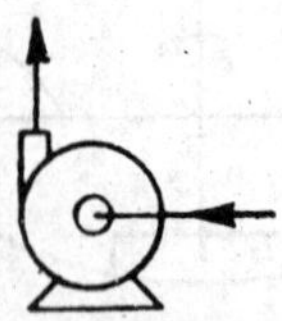	Most widely used for liquids of all types; simple in construction and maintenance
(b) Reciprocating pump or compressor	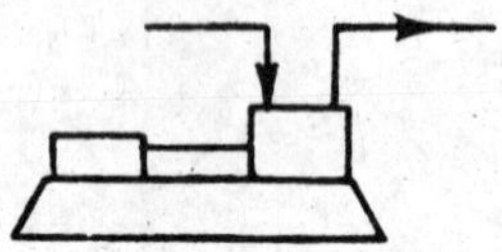	Generally used for higher pressure delivery; may be used for metering or proportioning
(c) Jet ejector	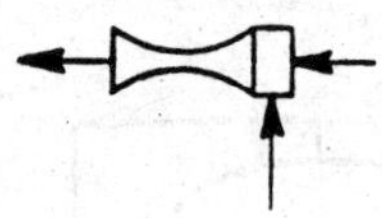	Used for low pressure operation or production of vacuum; steam often used as motive fluid
6 Fluid-solid Contacting		
(a) Fixed bed		Most widely used type of catalytic reactor; used with precious metal catalysts to minimize attrition losses; catalyst usually in form of pellets
(b) Fluid bed	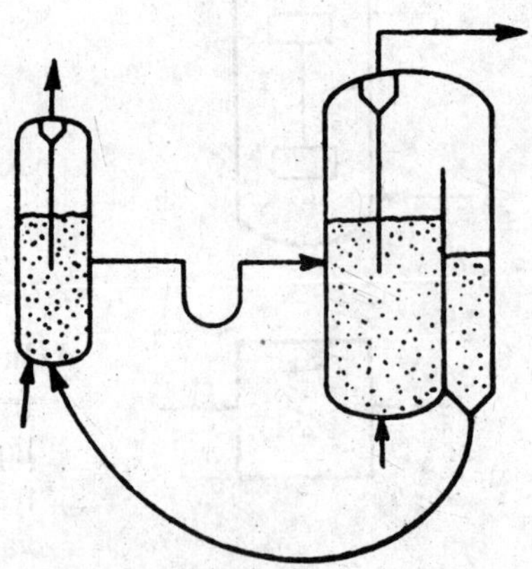	Used to contact finely divided solids with reactant gases, *e.g.*, cracking catalyst with oil vapors and then with air; also used in roasting of sulfide ores to give oxides and SO_2

Unit Operation	Schematic Representation	Comments
(c) Moving bed	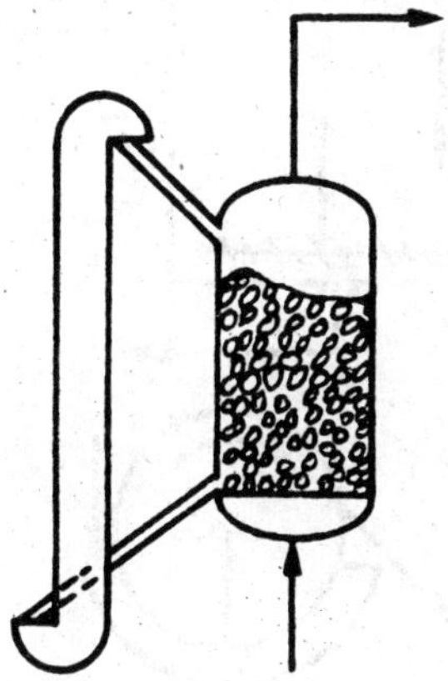	Combines virtues of fixed bed reactor with ability to regenerate catalyst by movement to separate regeneration zone
7 Fluid-solid Separation		
(a) Centrifugation	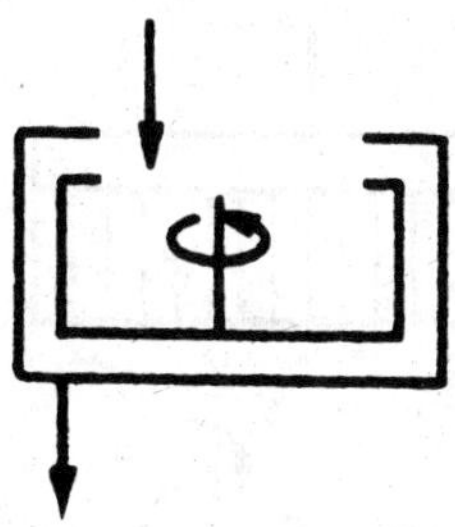	Used to separate very finely divided solids from liquid or liquids from liquid emulsions
(b) Settling tank	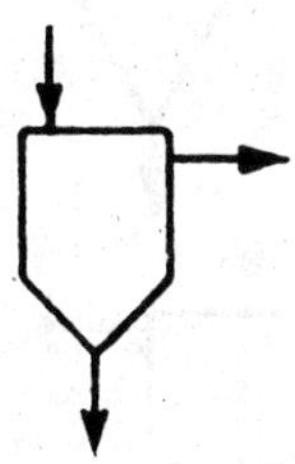	Simple device used to remove large particles from gas stream by simple settling in low-velocity zone
(c) Wet scrubber	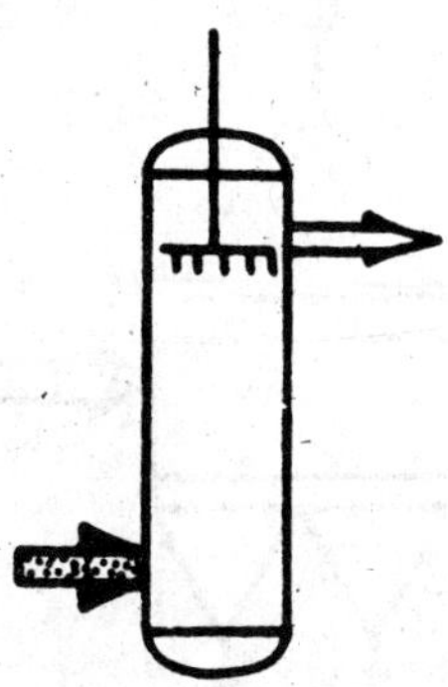	Effective means of removing suspended particles from gas stream by contact with liquid shower

Unit Operation	*Schematic Representation*	*Comments*
(d), Crystallizer	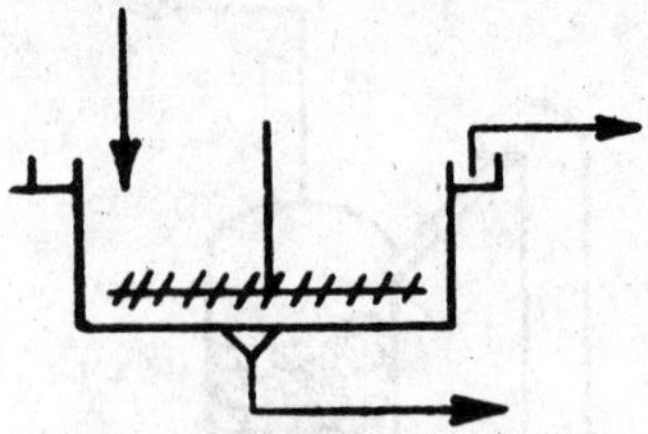	Hot, nearly-saturated solutions are stirred and cooled to effect nucleation and crystal growth; widely used with inorganic salts
(e) Filter (rotary)	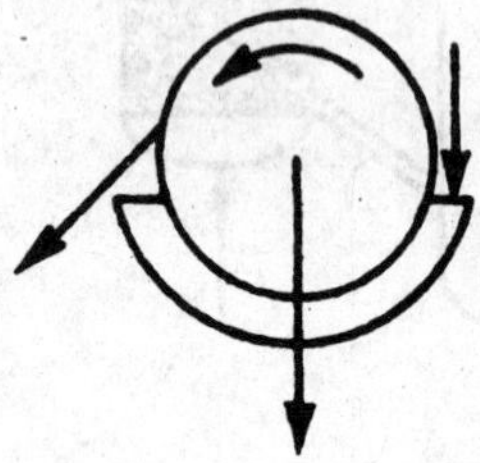	Vacuum applied to interior of drum pulls filtrate out of cake; used to separate minerals from slurries, pulp fibers from water, etc.
(f) Filter press	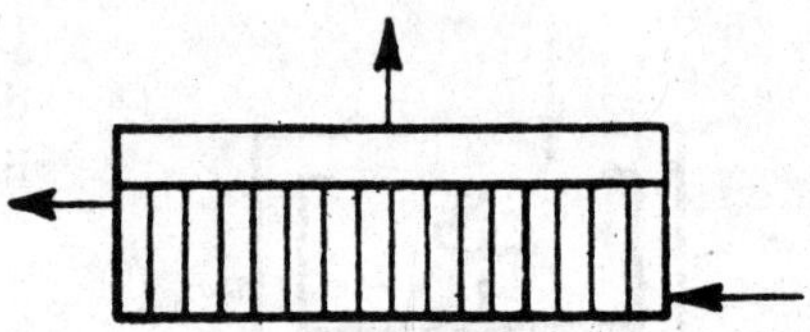	Simplest type of pressure filter; widely used; plates and fabric filter media may be made of a variety of corrosion-resistant materials
(g) Cyclone separator	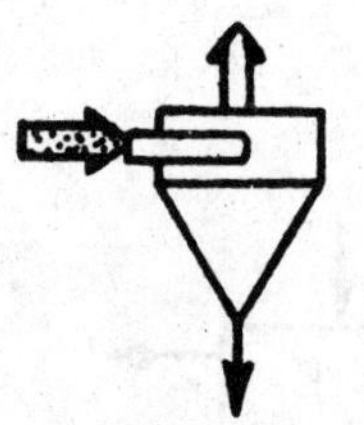	Used to separate solid particles or liquid droplets from gases to permit product recovery or to cut down product loss and air pollution
(h) Electrostatic precipitator	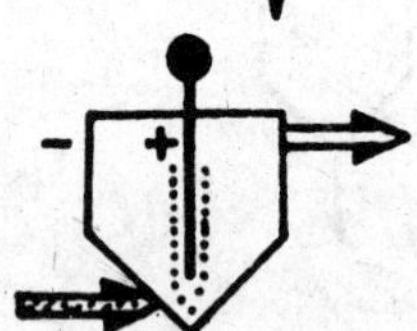	Used to remove fine dusts or mists suspended in gases; features high collection efficiency at wide variety of operating conditions
(i) Bag filter	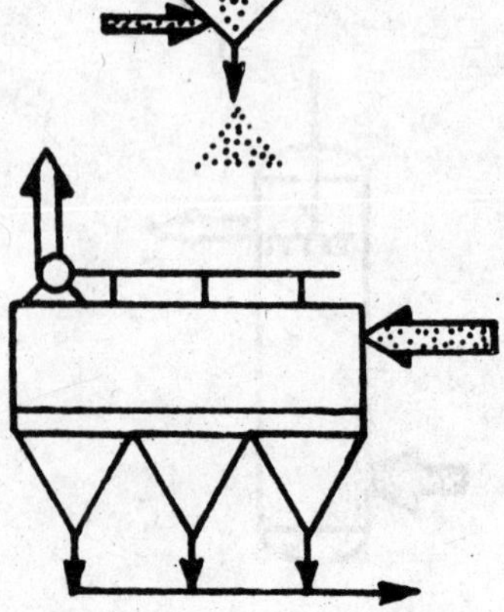	Batteries of tubular fabric bags are mounted so solids may be removed continuously by flow reversal and mechanical shaking

Unit Operation	*Schematic Representation*	*Comments*
(j) Thickener-classifier	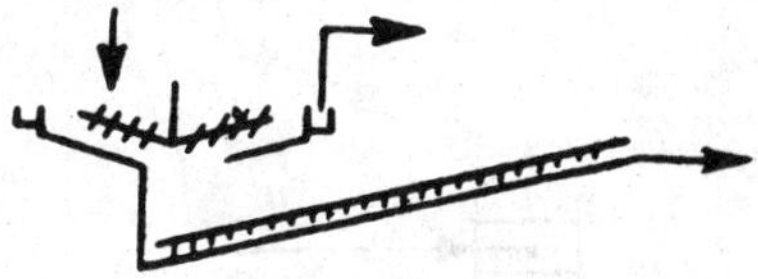	Used to separate slurry into sludges and clear liquid; used widely in mineral industries and in sewage effluent clarification
8 Fluid Storage		
(a) Gas holders	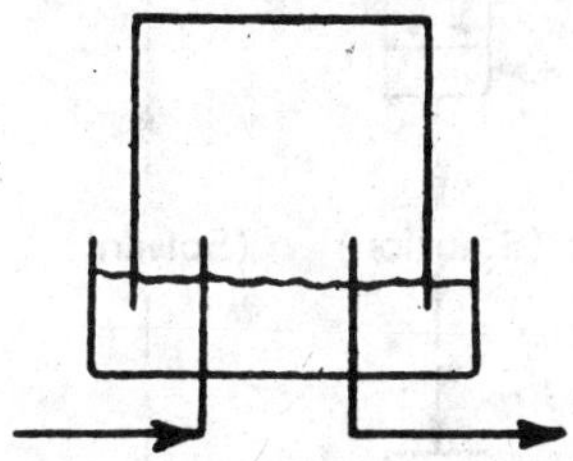	Used for low pressure storages of gases at constant pressure using liquid seal (usually water)
(b) Tanks	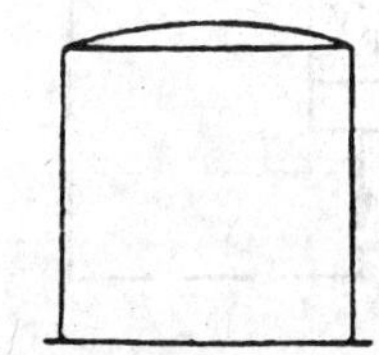	Widely used for storage of liquids of all types, usually at atmospheric pressure; may have floating roof
(c) Pressurized spheres		Used for pressurized storage of liquefied gases or high vapor pressure liquids to permit safe storage with no vapor losses
(d) Underground caverns	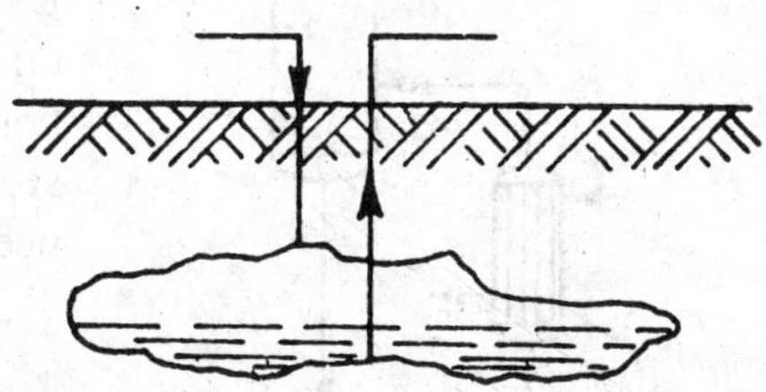	Used for large volume storage of liquids or of liquefied gases

Unit Operation	Schematic Representation	Comments
9 Gas-liquid Contacting		
(a) Absorption	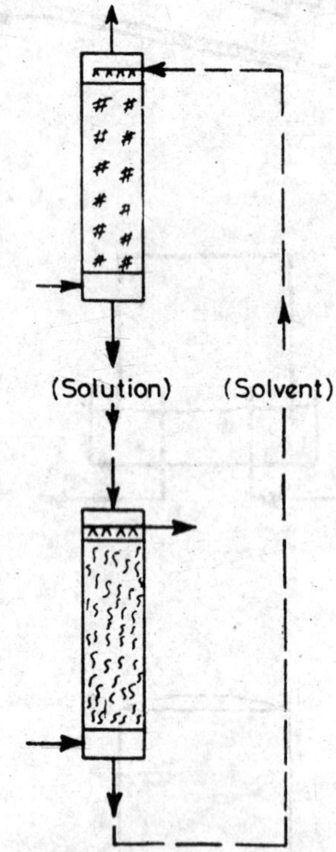	Used for taking up a soluble gas in a solvent liquid and producing a solution plus a lean exit gas; *e.g.*, used in H_2S removal from hydrocarbons
(b) Stripping		Used for removing a soluble gas from solution by counter-current contact with an inert gas; used to recover solute gas and regenerate solvent for subsequent absorption step
10 Heat Exchange		
(a) Fired heater	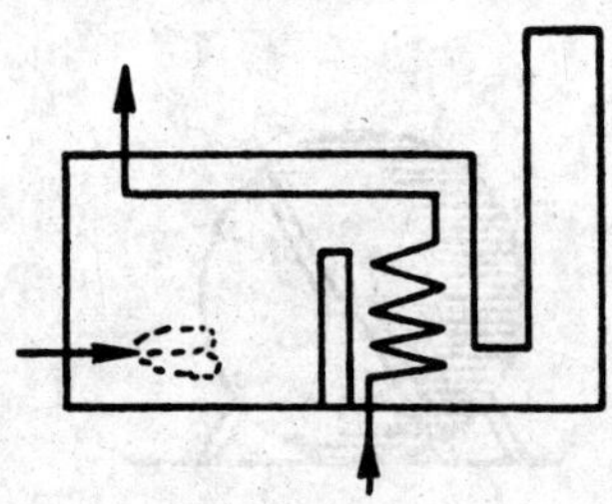	Used to heat petroleum fractions to distillation or cracking temperatures in direct-fired tubes
(b) Reboiler	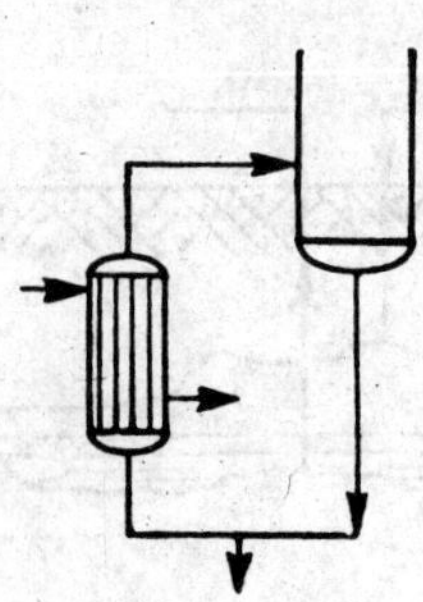	Uses natural circulation to circulate fractionating tower bottom in heat exchange with steam, *e.g.*, to provide necessary heat for fractionation

Unit Operation	*Schematic Representation*	*Comments*
(c) Condenser	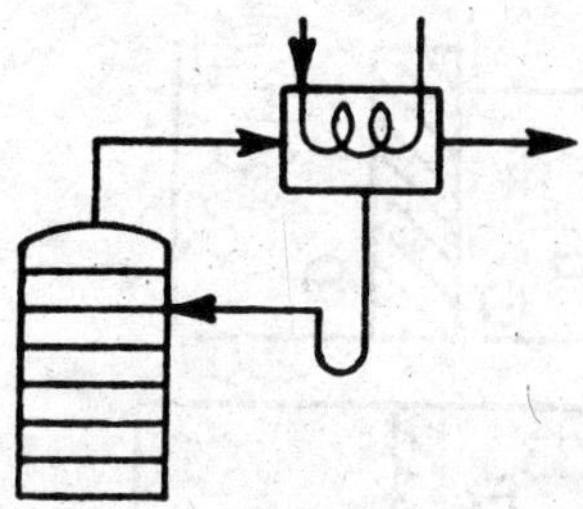	Usually water-cooled tubular construction to provide reflux and overhead product from fractionating column
(d) Shell and tube exchanger	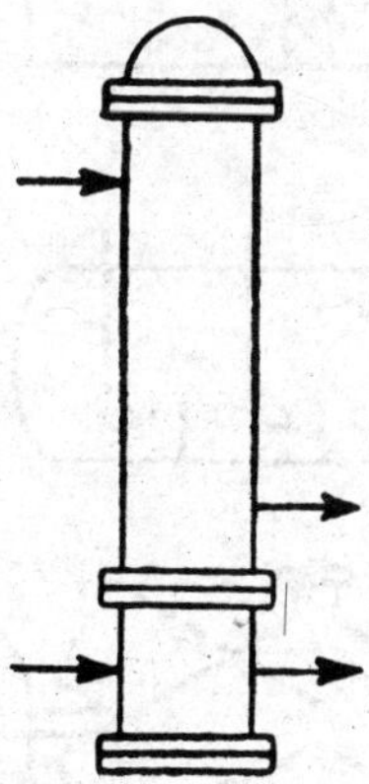	Common type of device for process heat exchange
(e) Jacketed kettle	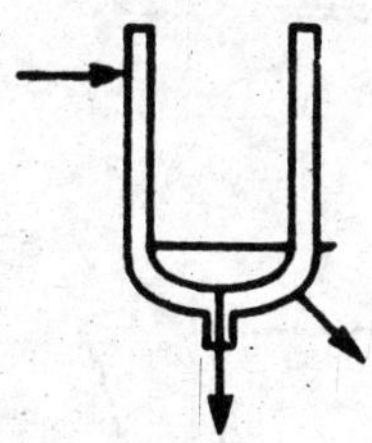	Common construction for reaction kettles; water or brine may be used for cooling; hot water, oil or Dowtherm for heating
(f) Direct mixing (quenching)	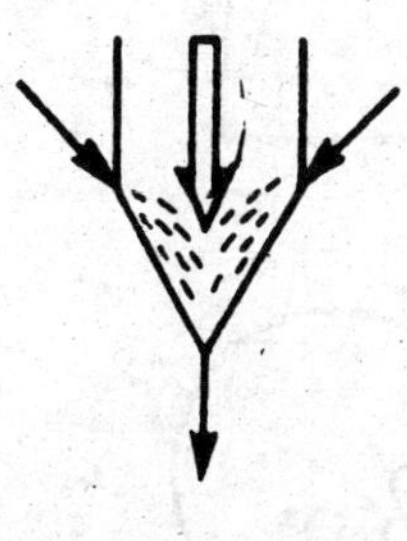	Features intimate contact of coolant fluid (*e.g.*, water) with process gases to give quick quench, *e.g.*, in hydrocarbon pyrolysis to acetylene

Unit Operation	Schematic Representation	Comments
11 Membrane Separation		
(a) Dialysis	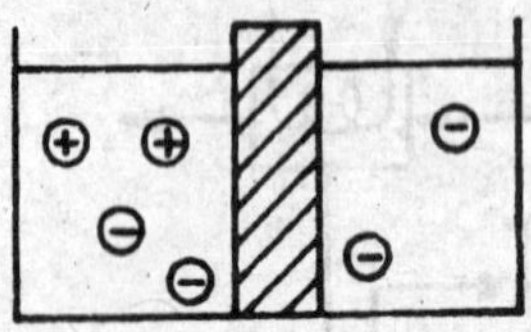	Used to separate mat'ls in sol'n having widely different mole. wts., *e.g.*, caustic from sugar or cellulose
(b) Gaseous diffusion	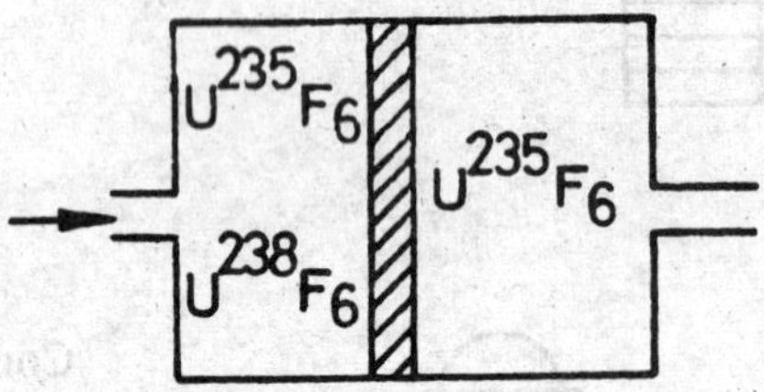	Uses microporous (*e.g.*, Ni) barriers in multistage operations to separate light (*e.g.*, $U^{235}F_6$) from heavy (*e.g.*, $U^{238}F_6$) components
12 Mixing		
(a) Agitation	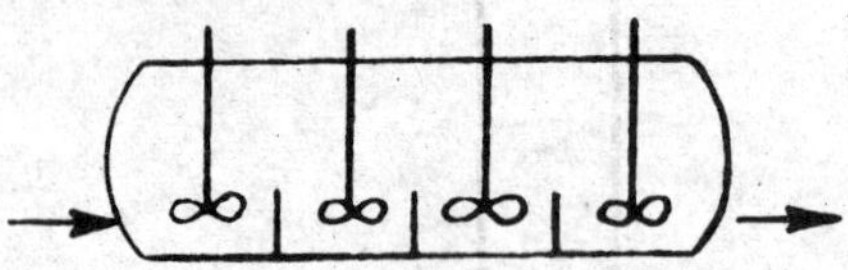	May be used for liquid-liquid or solid-liquid mixing in single or multiple compartments; widely used in process industries
(b) Solids blending	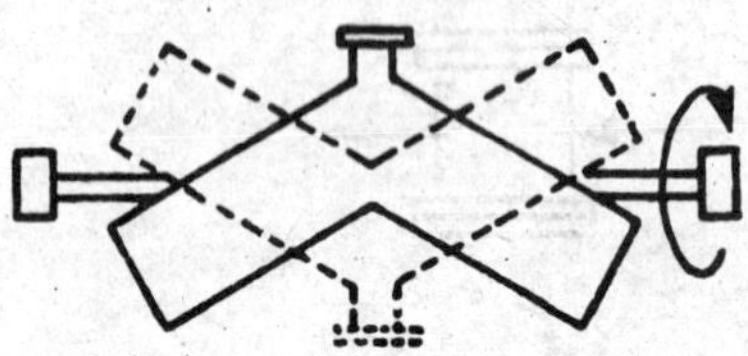	The device shown divides and recombines a granular mass over and over again to effect uniformity
13 Size Reduction and Enlargement		
(a) Crushing	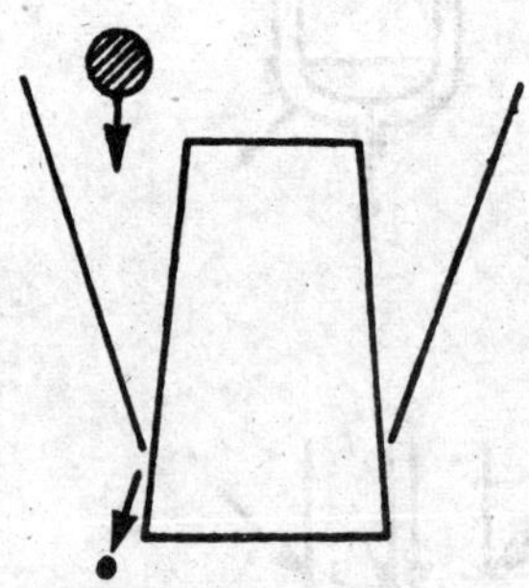	Used typically in 4 : 1 size reduction of hard materials from –5 to –20 mesh or –1 to –4 mesh
(b) Grinding	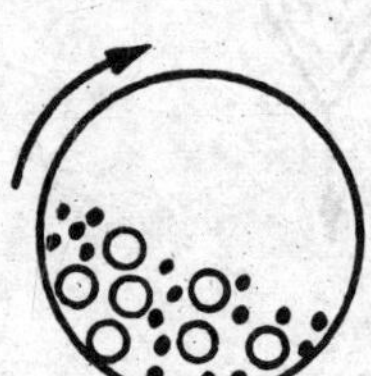	Wet or dry grinding may be carried out in presence of balls, pebbles or rods; feed may be –4 to –100 mesh and reduction ratio 10-15 to 1

Unit Operation	*Schematic Representation*	*Comments*
(c) Pelletizing	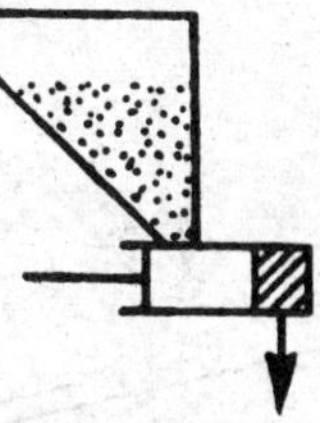	Used to make tablets from powders of medicinals, catalysts, etc.
14 Solids Handling		
(a) Pneumatic conveying	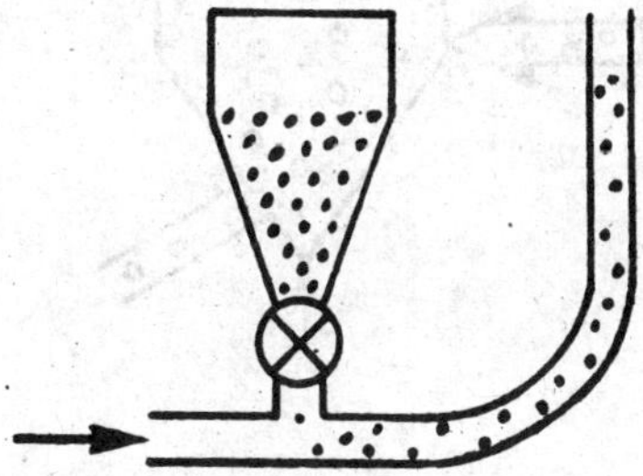	Used originally for grain; now used widely for cement, catalysts, coke and powdered chemicals
(b) Bucket elevators	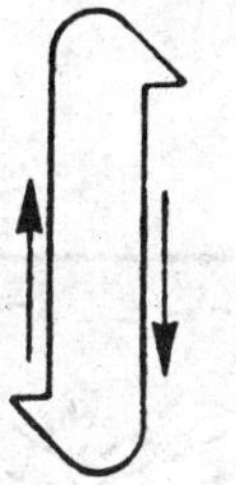	Used for elevating materials; can be used for moving powdered or granular mat'ls to and from storage or between reaction vessels as in moving-bed catalytic processes
(c) Screw conveyor		Versatile; can be used to mix and heat or cool; can be operated under pressure; useful for powders or sticky materials
(d) Belt conveyor		Can be used to handle large volumes over long distances economically; used near horizontal; belting may be fabric or rubber

Unit Operation	*Schematic Representation*	*Comments*
15 Solid/solid Separation		
(a) Screening	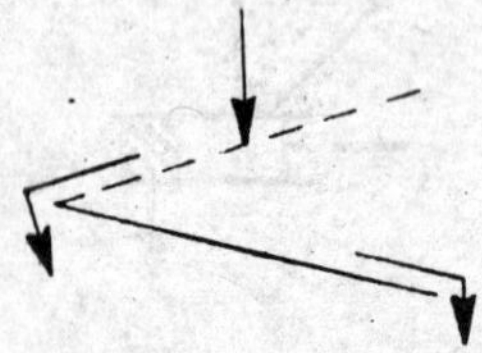	Wire, plastic or fabric screens are used to separate solids of varying sizes
(b) Elutriation	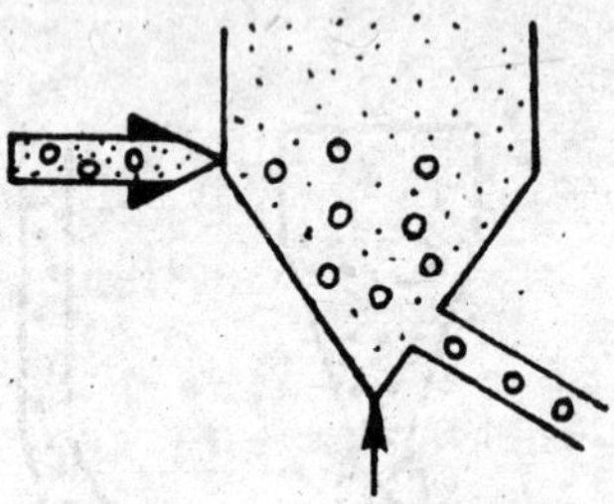	May be used to remove fines from a solid by passage of a gas to fluidize and transport the fines
(c) Froth flotation	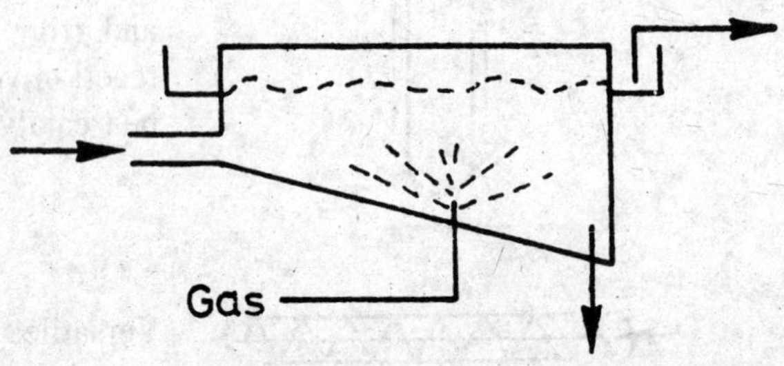	Finely ground (–50 mesh) ores are suspended in water in presence of flotation reagents (*e.g.*, RCOONa) and blown with air; desired product collects in froth
(d) Jigging	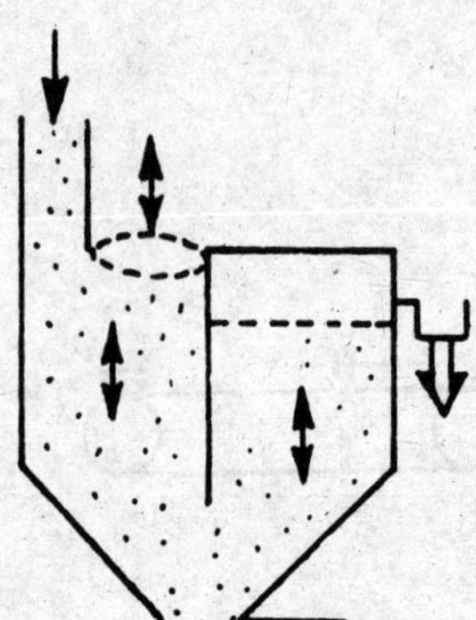	One of the oldest processes used for separation of heavy minerals from lighter gangues as well as for separating coal from heavier contaminants

Unit Operation	Schematic Representation	Comments
(e) Magnetic separation	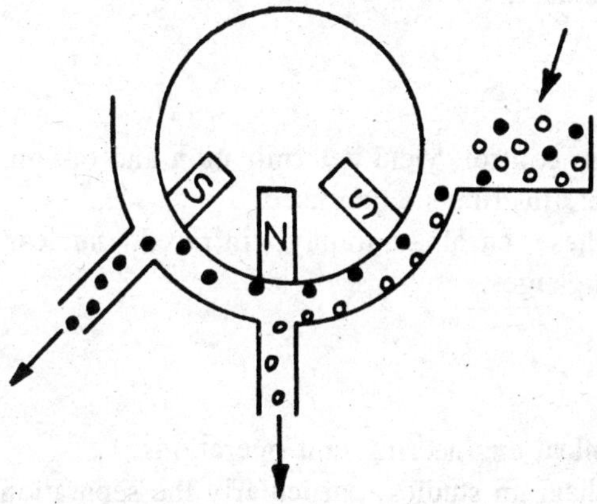	Used to remove tramp iron from feed to subsequent grinding and pulverizing steps; also used to concentrate magnetic iron ores

ID. GENERAL PRINCIPLES APPLIED IN STUDYING AN INDUSTRY

Within any chemical industry there is an inconceivable number of principles of science and engineering which are continually being used. We cannot possibly look at all of these principles and their specific applications, even for one industry. Only the essential features can be pointed out in a discussion of these topics:

1. Market and Sales—Justification of the Industry
2. Methods of Production
   (a) Chemical reactions
   (b) Process flow diagrams—flow sheets
   (c) Material requirements
3. Chemical Engineering Problems
   (a) Manufacturing
   (b) Economics

The complexities which exist in studying the interrelationships of these items can be reduced to problems which have been solved on the basis of science and engineering principles learned in chemical engineering degree curricula, principally the following:

1. Chemistry
2. Thermodynamics
3. Reaction Kinetics
4. Process and Mechanical Design
5. Economics
6. Unit Operations and Unit Process Concepts

A brief review of these principles with emphasis on their general usages in the process industries will be given next. (Unit operations and unit process concepts have already been discussed in Section IC.) The reader is referred to standard texts for a more complete review and further study.

1. Chemistry

All phases of chemistry are usually involved. Chemical equations are particularly important to establish conversion and yield data.

(a) Analytical Chemistry

(1) Necessary for process control, yield determination and optimization.
(2) Modern and electronic instrumentation used.
Examples—vapor phase chromatography, infrared, nuclear magnetic resonance, radiation attenuation gauges.

(b) Physical Chemistry

(1) Integrated with chemical engineering unit operations.
(2) Important in phase diagram studies, particularly the separation processes.
(3) Involves use of chemical kinetics and catalysis.

(c) Inorganic Chemistry

(1) Involves one or more reactions which do not contain combinations of C, H, and O with or without other non-metallic elements.
(2) Principles of theoretical inorganic chemistry are currently being discovered and applied in a manner formerly used only in organic chemistry.
- Types of bonding, metal-organic complexes, reaction chemistry predictions.

(d) Organic Chemistry

(1) Usually involves combinations of C, H, and O with or without other non-metallic elements.
(2) Large portion of commercial organic chemicals derived from aliphatic and aromatic compounds of petroleum.

2. Thermodynamics

(a) Definition

Science which deals with relationships amongst the various forms of energy.

(b) Examples of Applications of Chemical Engineering Thermodynamics

(1) Chemical equilibria.
- Ideal systems: low pressure, variable temperature
- Non-ideal systems: high pressure, variable temperature

(2) Energy applications.
- Heat of reaction
- Work of compression and expansion of real gases

(c) Laws of Thermodynamics

(1) First law—total energy of a system entering a process, plus any addition during the process, must equal the total energy of the system leaving the process.

(2) Examples of first law usage.
- Heat of reaction and its temperature coefficient
- Sensible heat transfer in preheating and cooling
- Heats of solution and absorption
- Heat effects in phase changes

(3) Second law—heat (q) and work (w) as forms of energy are only interchangeable under ideal reversible conditions as predicted by definite thermodynamic property functions. For irreversible events, the heat/work ratio will always be greater than under ideal conditions.

(4) Examples of second law usage.
- Calculation of equilibrium constants of various reactions in a chemical converter
- Calculation of the effect of temperature on equilibrium constants
- Calculation of extent of reaction and equilibrium yields
- Predicting the effect of solvents, inert diluents, and recycle streams

(d) Thermodynamic Functions

H = enthalpy, U = internal energy, PV = external work

$$H = U + PV;\ \Delta H = \Delta U + \Delta(PV) \quad \text{(d.1)}$$

A = total useful work, T = absolute temperature, S = enthalpy

TS = unavailable energy or work loss

$$A = U - TS;\ \Delta A = \Delta U - \Delta(TS) \quad \text{(d.2)}$$

$$U = q - w \quad \text{(d.3)}$$

$$S = dq/T \quad \text{(d.4)}$$

G = free energy

$$G = H - TS;\ \Delta G = \Delta H - \Delta TS \quad \text{(d.5)}$$

These relations are shown graphically below.

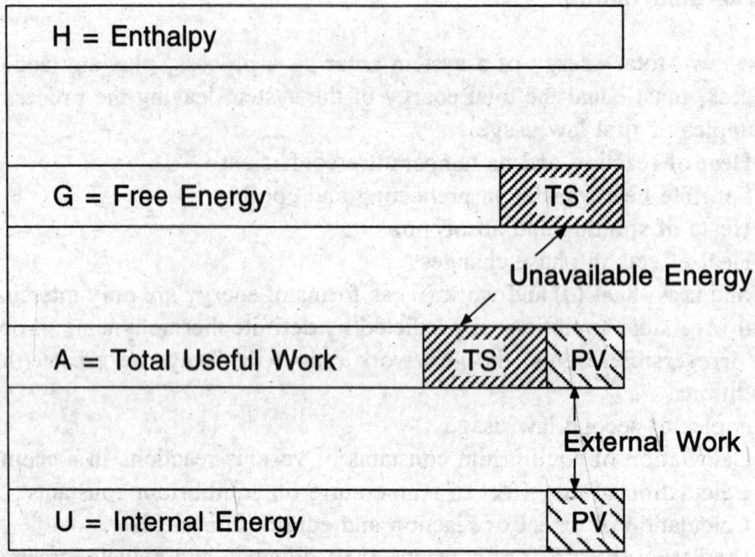

(e) Quantitative Expressions for First and Second Laws

(1) Chemical reaction: $mM + nN \rightarrow xX + zZ$

(2) Heat effects: $\Delta H_R = \Delta H_{reaction} = \Sigma H_{products} - \Sigma H_{reactants}$

ΔH_R – when system liberates heat; exothermic reaction

ΔH_R + when system absorbs heat; endothermic reaction

Equilibrium effects:

ΔG_f^o = standard free energy of formation of a compound

= 0 for an element

(3) $\Delta G_f^o = \Sigma (G_f^o)_{products} - \Sigma (G_f^o)_{reactants}$

K = equilibrium constant based on forward reaction

(4) $-\Delta G_f^o = RT \ln K$

(5) a = activity of component = γC; γ = activity coefficient; C = concentration

(6) $$K = \frac{a_X^x \cdot a_Z^z}{a_M^m \cdot a_N^n} = \underbrace{\frac{C_X^x \cdot C_Z^z}{C_M^m \cdot C_N^n}}_{\text{(ideal portion)}} \cdot \underbrace{\frac{\gamma_X^x \cdot \gamma_Z^z}{\gamma_M^m \cdot \gamma_N^n}}_{\text{(non-ideal portion)}}$$

For gas systems $C = \pi Y$, π = total pressure,

Y = mole fraction, f = fugacity coefficient

(7) $$K_p = \pi^{x+z-m-n} \cdot \frac{Y_X^x \cdot Y_Z^z}{Y_M^m \cdot Y_N^n} \cdot \frac{f_X^x \cdot f_Z^z}{f_M^m \cdot f_N^n}$$

(f) Some Useful Qualitative Concepts of First and Second Laws

The expressions (e)3 and (e)7 can be used to predict the effect of temperature and pressure on equilibrium conversions. However, some predictions of chemical reaction behavior can be made through use of the Le Chatelier principle of physical chemistry which is a qualitative statement of the first two laws of thermodynamics.

(1) Le Chatelier principle
A reaction always shifts in such a manner as to restore the initial conditions.

(2) Example using a change of temperature.

$$SO_2 + \tfrac{1}{2}\, O_2 \underset{r}{\overset{f}{\rightleftharpoons}} SO_3;\ \Delta H_R = -23.49 \text{ Kcal}$$

- Lower the temperature and reaction f will occur since heat is liberated, tending to compensate for the temperature lowering and attempting to achieve the original temperature condition.
- Raise the temperature by adding heat energy. Reaction r takes place since the system will attempt to restore the original lower temperature state by absorbing the energy added to the system.
- *Summary*: Low temperature favors high conversion in an exothermic process.

(3) Example using a change of pressure in a constant volume system:
Reaction f results in a decrease in the number of moles and therefore is favored by an increase in pressure as the system

$$2H_2 + O_2 \underset{r}{\overset{f}{\rightleftharpoons}} 2H_2O(g);\ \Delta H_R = -115.59 \text{ Kcal}$$

attempts to maintain the original lower pressure condition. Reaction r will take place if the pressure is decreased as there is a net molar increase.

- *Summary*: High pressure favors high conversion in a reaction where there is a decrease in the number of total moles.

(4) Graphical illustration of temperature effects
Typical equilibrium conversion curves and conditions within a reactor depending on type of heat removal are shown below.

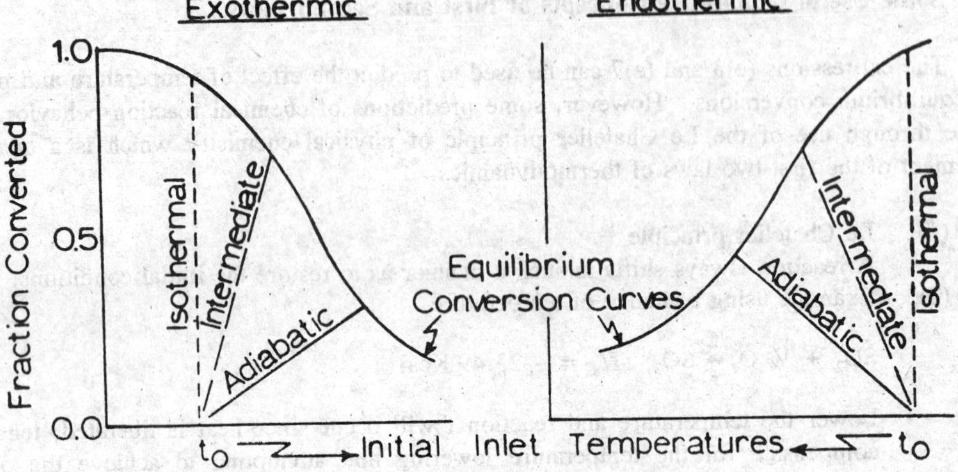

In both types of reactions illustrated, the maximum equilibrium yield is obtained under isothermal conditions which is practically impossible to attain infinite volume reactor systems. An intermediate condition between the isothermal and adiabatic cases is achieved. Reaction kinetics as a function of temperature is also an important design consideration and very often stage-wise operation with heat exchange is practiced. This is illustrated below for a three-stage process with exothermic reaction. The corollary exists for an endothermic reaction.

FLOW DIAGRAM

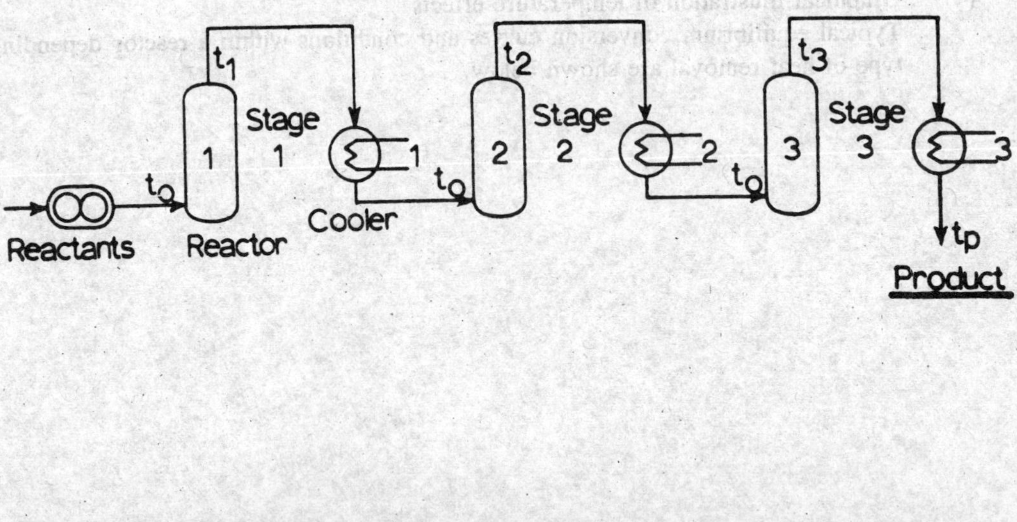

CONVERSION DIAGRAM

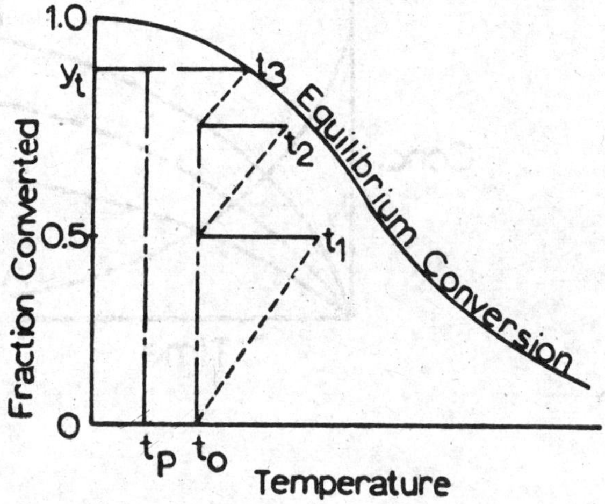

Note : **Reactions 1 and 2 are operated at higher average temperatures to attain higher reaction rates per unit volume.**

3. Reaction Kinetics

(a) Definition

The study of chemical kinetics and application to the design of processes.

(b) Classification of Reactions

(1) Reacting Phases

- Homogeneous—reaction takes place in one phase only
- Heterogeneous—reaction involves more than one phase

(2) Mechanism—molecular, chain initiated, photochemical initiated

(3) Catalysis—catalytic, non-catalytic

(4) Energy Transfer—adiabatic, isothermal or intermediate (non-adiabatic—non-isothermal)

(5) Chemical Equations

- Simple reaction equation

$$A \longrightarrow R$$
$$A + B \longrightarrow R$$
$$A \longrightarrow R + S$$
$$A + B \longrightarrow R + S$$
$$2A \longrightarrow R$$
$$A \longrightarrow 2R$$

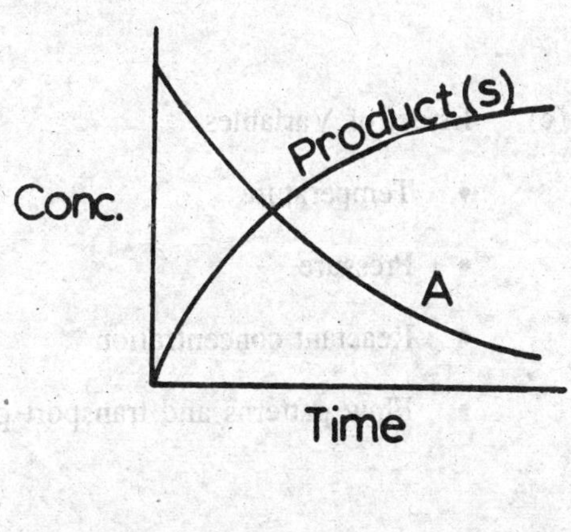

- Parallel reaction equations

$$\begin{cases} A \rightarrow R \\ A \rightarrow S \end{cases}$$

$$\begin{cases} A + B \rightarrow R \\ A + B \rightarrow S \\ A + B \rightarrow T \end{cases}$$

$$\begin{cases} A \rightarrow R \\ A + B \rightarrow T \end{cases}$$

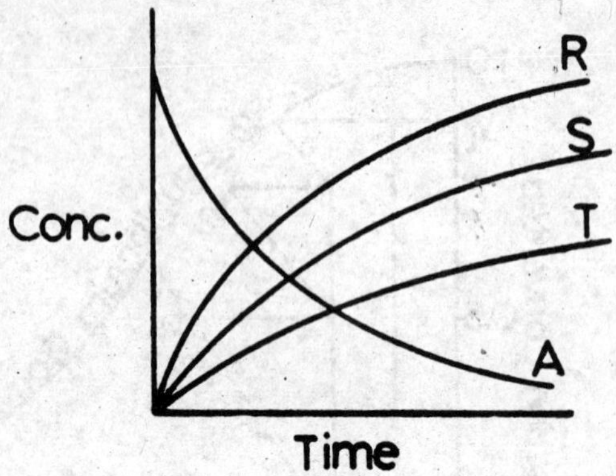

- Series reaction equations

$$A \rightarrow R \rightarrow S$$

- Complex series

$$A + B \rightarrow R$$

$$A + R \rightarrow S$$

$$A + S \rightarrow T$$

- Reversible reaction

$$aA \rightleftharpoons rR$$

$$mM + nN \rightleftharpoons xX + zZ$$

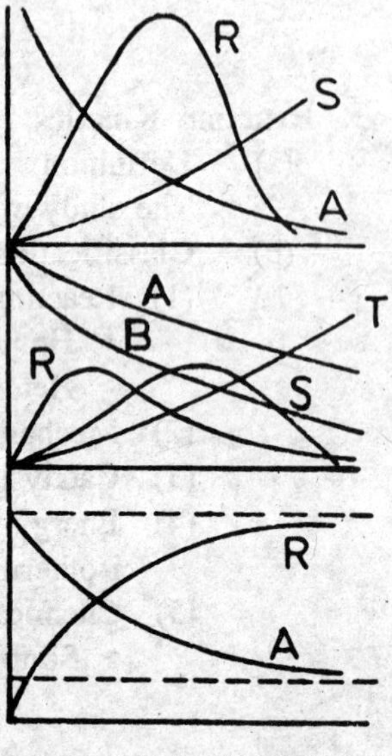

(c) Effect of Variables

- Temperature
- Pressure
- Reactant concentration
- Flow patterns and transport properties

(d) Reaction Rate Equations

For the reaction $aA + bB \rightarrow R$

$$-\frac{dC_A}{dt} = r = kC_A^m \cdot C_B^n.$$

Molecularity $= a + b.$

Order of reaction $= m + n.$

Simple order reaction : molecularity = order of reaction.

For the reaction $aA + bB \underset{r}{\overset{f}{\rightleftharpoons}} rR + sS$

$$-\frac{dC_A}{dt} = k(C_A^a C_B^b - \frac{C_R^r C_S^s}{K_f}).$$

For the reactions $A \xrightarrow{1} R$

$A \xrightarrow{2} S$

$$\frac{dC_R}{dt} = +k_1 C_A^m,$$

$$\frac{dC_S}{dt} = +k_2 C_A^n,$$

$$-\frac{dC_A}{dt} = (k_1 C_A^m + k_2 C_A^n).$$

For the reaction $A \rightarrow R \rightarrow S$

$$-\frac{dC_A}{dt} = k_1 C_A^m,$$

$$\frac{dC_R}{dt} = k_1 C_A^m - k_2 C_R^n,$$

$$\frac{dC_S}{dt} = k_2 C_R^n.$$

Differential rate equations for other systems can be formed in like manner. Integration is required for useful design computations. Typical curves of concentration versus time are pictured in Section (b) 5.

(1) Specific reaction rate constant, k

- Units depend on order of reaction
- Effect of temperature on reaction appears only in k

$$k = je—E/RT \quad \text{(d.1)}$$

E = activation energy, R = universal constant, T = absolute temperature,
j = proportionality constant

The exponential effect of temperature on reaction rate is very important in process considerations.

(2) Examples of process design using temperature effect of reaction kinetics

- Producing a high yield from an endothermic reaction

Chemical reaction: $2CH_4 \underset{r}{\overset{f}{\rightleftharpoons}} C_2H_2 + 3H_2;\ \Delta H = +$

Flow Diagram

(See also Wulff Process, Fig. IIB-9)

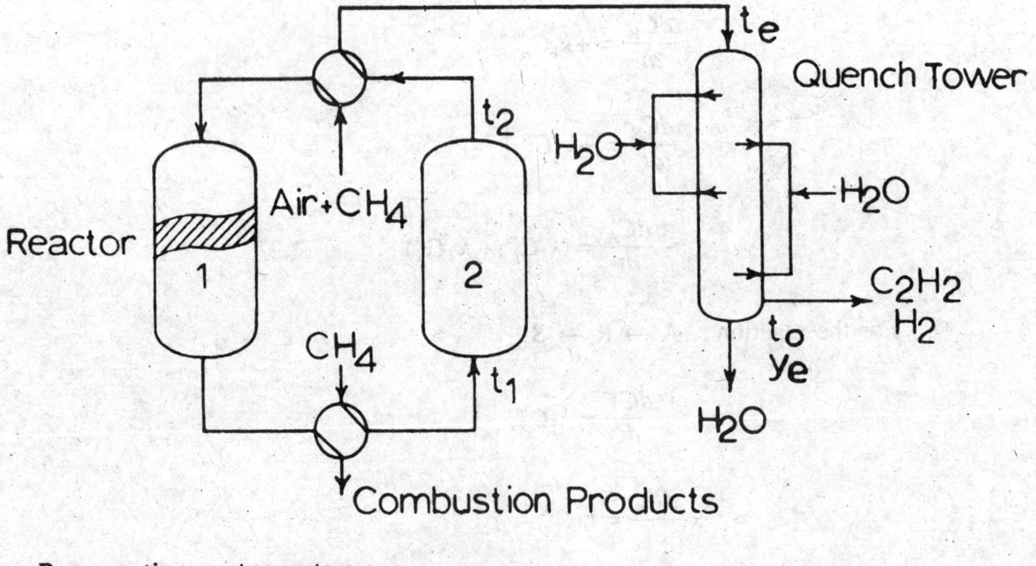

Regenerative reactor system
Reactor 1 is on "Heat-up"
Reactor 2 is on "Make"

Conversion Diagram

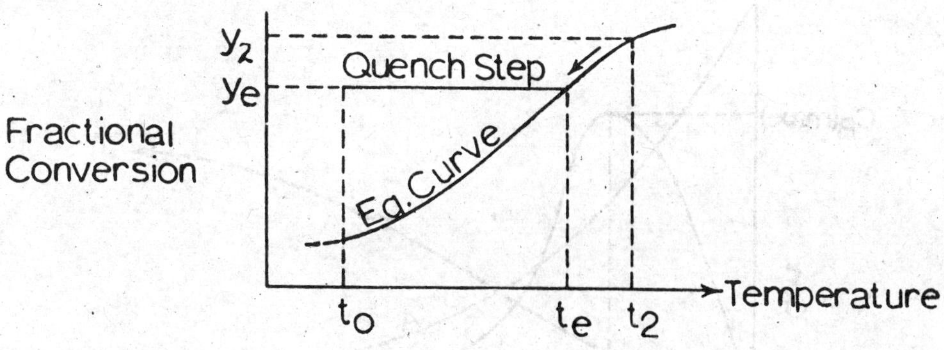

The product gases leave the reactor at t_2 and with an equilibrium conversion of y_2. If the cooling process were gradual, as from t_2 to t_0, the composition of the gases would be that predicted by the equilibrium curve and the conversion would decrease. By using a water quench, the gas temperature is dropped so rapidly from t_e to t_0 that the rate of the reverse reaction,

$$r_r = je^{-E_r/RT} \cdot C^m_{C_2H_2} \cdot C^n_{H_2}$$

is essentially zero by the $e^{-1/T}$ effect, with conversion at y_e.

- Producing a high yield from a reversible series chemical reaction
  Chemical reaction:

  $$A \rightleftharpoons B \rightleftharpoons C$$

FLOW DIAGRAM

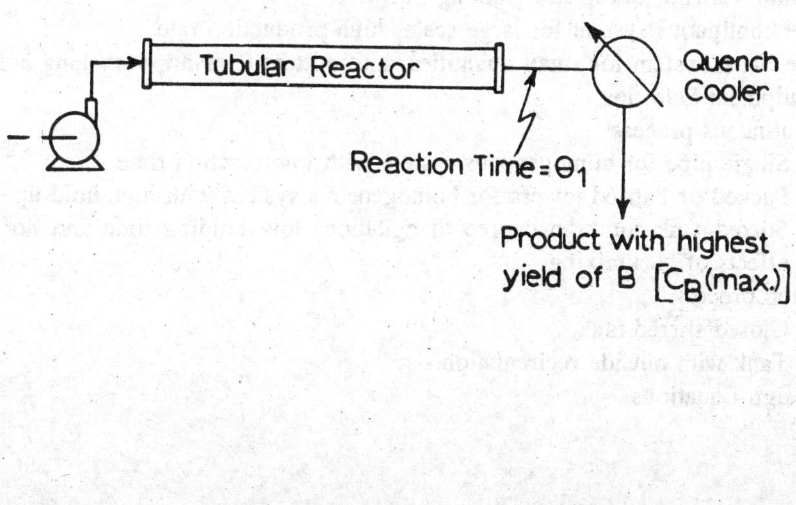

CONVERSION DIAGRAM

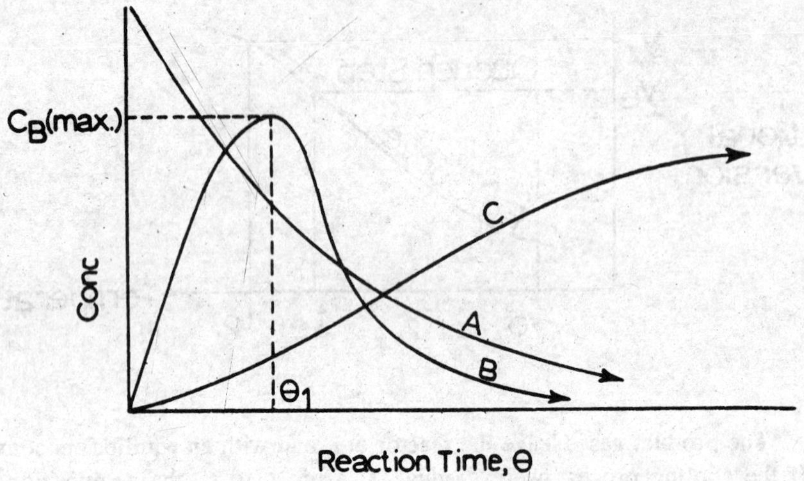

Thermodynamic calculations show a very low yield of B. However, by studying the reaction kinetics, it was determined that the reaction path pictured in the above conversion diagram was such that an economic yield of B could be obtained by quenching the reaction after time θ_1.

(e) Classification of Chemical Reactors
- (1) Simple batch homogeneous reactors
  No addition or removal during reaction time interval
- (2) Semi-batch reactors
  Addition and/or removal of one or more constituents
- (3) Continuous homogeneous reactors
- (4) Continuous heterogeneous reactors
  Example—fluid bed catalytic reactor

(f) Design Criteria for Reactor Systems

(1) Economic Considerations are Guiding Factor
- Use continuous system for large scale, high production rate
- Use batch system for small quantities, intermittent demand, very long holding times

(2) Equipment Selection
- Continuous process
  * Single pipe for homogeneous system with low reaction time
  * Packed or baffled towers for homogeneous system with high hold-up time
  * Stirred tank for high degree of agitation, low holding time and no detrimental effects of backmixing
- Batch process
  * Closed stirred tank
  * Tank with outside recirculation

(3) Design Equations

- Homogeneous systems

  Batch reactors—use integrated rate equations of the type listed in Section (d)

  Flow reactors

$$\frac{V_R}{F} = \int_0^x \frac{dx}{r} = \theta \tag{f.1}$$

x = fraction conversion desired; V_R = reactor volume;
F = feed rate, volume/time; θ = holding time

The backmixing effects should be considered, particularly for large diameter equipment.

- Heterogeneous systems

  Used mostly for catalytic systems

$$\frac{W}{F} = \int_0^x \frac{dx}{r} \tag{f.2}$$

W/F = kg of catalyst to kg-moles of feed/time

The rate equations for catalytic systems are largely empirical.

- Space velocity specifications

  Reactor designs frequently are based on space velocity (SV). For homogeneous reactors, SV is the reciprocal of equation (f.1)

$$\text{SV} = \frac{1}{\theta} = \frac{F}{V_R}, \text{ reciprocal time units} \tag{f.3}$$

Space velocities for heterogeneous reactor design are more arbitrary, but all are based in principle on the reciprocal of equation (f.2)

$$\text{VHSV} = \text{volume hourly space velocity}$$

$$= \frac{\text{gas volume (specify inlet or exit) at STP}}{\text{hr} \times \text{void volume of reactor}} \tag{f.4}$$

$$\text{WHSV} = \text{weight hourly space velocity}$$

$$= \frac{\text{kg of feed}}{\text{hr} \times \text{weight of catalyst in kg}} \tag{f.5}$$

4. Process and Mechanical Design

The design phase of commercialization requires the synthesis or combination of all of the principles we have discussed in Sections IC & ID 1-3. This is probably the broadest and most important area of endeavor for the chemical engineer.

The design of chemical plants is often divided into two parts: (1) process design, and (2) mechanical design. Process design is concerned with unit operations and processes, whereas mechanical design deals with construction details of equipment, foundations, buildings, process auxiliaries, installation, operation and maintenance details. There is considerable overlapping between these two divisions with chemical engineers taking the major role in solving the process design problems.

(a) Process Design

Research and development work on a chemical process is usually completed to the point where sufficient information is available to prepare a series of flow diagrams or flow sheets which incorporate unit operations and unit processes to achieve the desired production.

(1) *Types of Flow Sheets*

A. Block Diagrams. These are simple rectangular box diagrams which give a graphic layout of the various steps in a process. An example is given in Figure ID-1.

B. Simplified Engineering Flow Sheets. Visualization of the process in terms of possible physical equipment to carry out the operations of the chemical process is one of the essential steps in formulating a process design. A typical example of this type of flow sheet is shown in Figure IIA-4. Such flow sheets exist in all degrees of complexity, giving stream quantities, specifications, material and energy balances, instrumentation details, and process auxiliaries requirements.

C. Other Design Flow Sheets. A complete plant design requires a vast number of intricate and detailed flow sheets for such things as piping layout, electrical layout, instrumentation details, plant layout, etc.

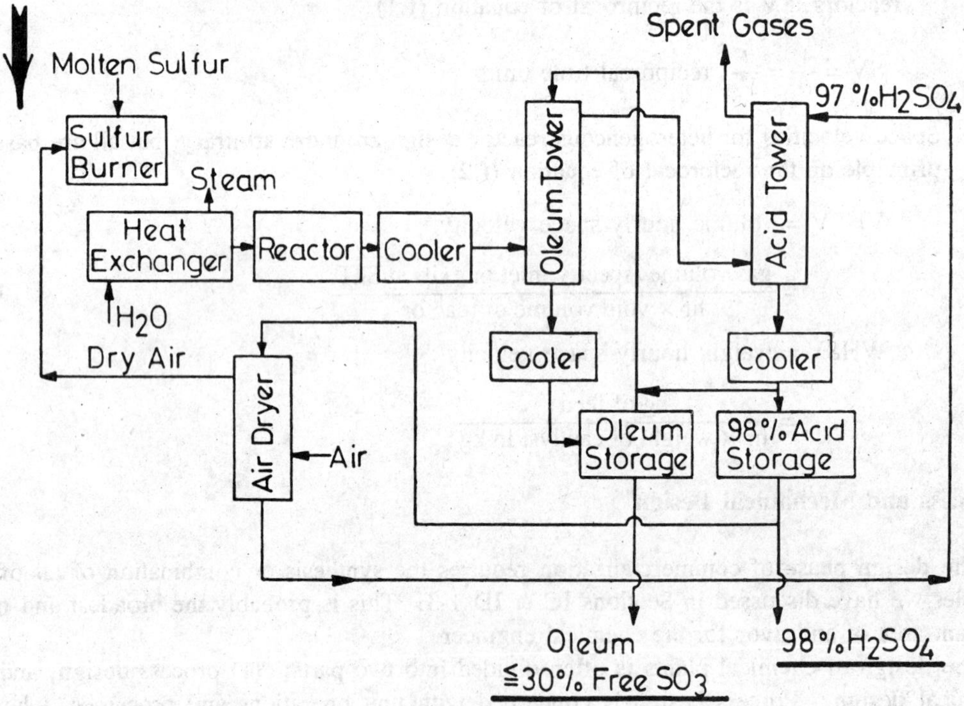

Chemical Reactions

Oxidation:	$S + O_2 \rightarrow SO_2$;	$\Delta H = -70.9$ Kcal
Oxidation:	$SO_2 + \frac{1}{2}O_2 \rightarrow SO_3$;	$\Delta H = -23.0$ Kcal
Hydration:	$SO_3 + H_2O \rightarrow H_2SO_4$ (aq);	$\Delta H = -31.6$ Kcal

Fig. ID-1. Block diagram for manufacture of sulfuric acid and oleum by contact process.

Only block diagrams and simplified engineering flow sheets will be used to understand the process design principles of chemical technology. Heat exchangers for optimum heat recovery are not usually shown. An arrow points out the start of the process and the products are underlined.

(2) *Process Steps*

As an elementary approach to most chemical processes, the following broad steps can usually be considered:

- Prepare the reactants
- React them
- Separate the products
- Purify the products

These involve unit operations and unit processes with the latter most important in any chemical reactor design problems.

(3) *Design Steps*

- Collect all laboratory and process development information
- Prepare flow sheets
- Choose conventional design procedures for equipment designated on flow sheets as unit operations oriented
- Design the reactors; this is one of the major problems of the plant design job; optimum design is critical
- Select control instrumentation for process monitoring and analysis
- Select and size materials handling equipment—pumps, piping, conveyors, etc.
- Design all process auxiliaries
- Make plant layouts
- Itemize all designs for cost estimating

5. Economics

(a) Profitability Analysis of a Projected Chemical Process Venture

(1) Capital Investment

Fixed capital for plant facilities

- Site
- Buildings
- Utilities plants
- Process equipment
- Storage facilities
- Auxiliary utilities and emergency facilities

Working capital

- Raw materials inventory
- In-process inventory
- Product inventory
- Maintenance and repair inventory
- Accounts receivable credit carry-over
- Minimum cash reserve

(2) *Total Product Costs*

(a) Manufacturing costs

- Raw material
- Shipping containers
- Operating costs
  - * Operating labor
  - * Operating supervision
  - * Operating supplies
  - * Utilities
    (1) Electricity
    (2) Steam
    (3) Water
    (4) Fuel
  - * Control laboratory
  - * Miscellaneous
- Overhead costs
  - * Employee benefits
  - * Medical service
  - * Cafeteria
  - * Purchasing
  - * Shops
  - * Property protection
  - * General plant supervision
- Depreciation
- Property taxes and insurance

(b) General expenses

- Freight and delivery
- Administrative expense
- Sales expense
- Research expense

(3) *Economic Analysis*

(a) Selling price

Market analysis

- Price-volume relationship; present and anticipated
- Application of products
- Competition

Income taxes

Net and new earnings

(b) Profitability

Return on investment

Cost and profit charts

Other methods of economic analysis

- Pay-out time
- Interest rate of return on discounted cash flow method
- Project present worth

The capital and total product costs are estimated from process and mechanical design flow sheets and specifications, once a market and sales analysis has been conducted to establish the annual plant capacity.

This latter is a function of a marketing analysis group composed of engineers and economists who have developed methods of forecasting production statistics and demands for chemicals under consideration for manufacture. To fully appreciate the problems encountered in marketing and sales forecasting, a study of any process industry must include a discussion of competition and use patterns characteristic of that industry.

(b) Principles of Economic Balance

The engineer is concerned with the selection of conditions which will yield a maximum return on investment for the plant he is designing. The reason why one finds a set of variables chosen in a given process or one process favored over another is frequently based on optimizing the economic balance. As an example of economic balance, we can look at the optimum design of a heat exchanger as a familiar equipment sizing problem. Increasing the fluid velocity in the tubes of a shell-and-tube exchanger will increase the heat transfer coefficient and reduce the size of the exchanger for a given capacity. This will reduce the annual charges on the fixed investment of the heat exchanger. As a counter-balancing effect, the increased velocity will call for increased pumping costs. A minimum operating cost is found which fixes the conditions for design of the heat exchanger as seen below:

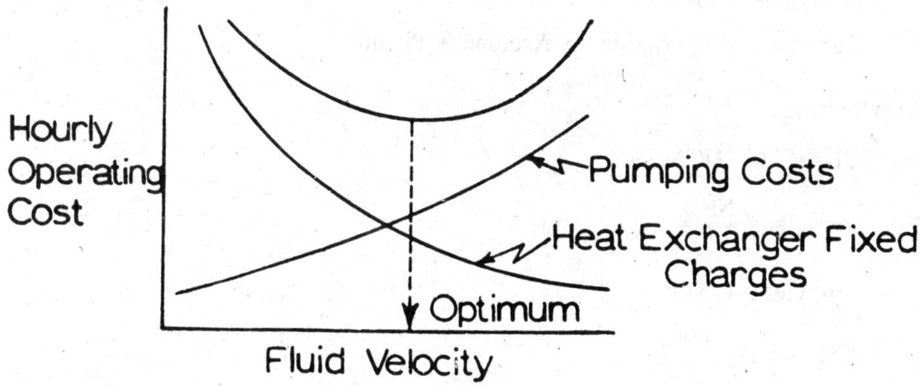

This same principle applies to choice of alternates for a complete plan and economic operation of plants as well as equipment and process design. The use of computers in such systems studies aids materially in solving such decision-making problems.

The principles of economic balance will show up repeatedly in our study of the chemical process industries.

(c) Choice Between Alternative Processes

In the case of many major chemical products there is a variety of alternative routes available to a potential producer depending on the cost and availability of raw materials, power, etc. Some specific examples of products which may be made by a number of competing routes are as follows:

(1) Acetaldehyde

(a) $CH{\equiv}CH + H_2O \rightarrow$

(b) $LPG + O_2 \rightarrow$

(c) $C_2H_5OH + O_2 \rightarrow$

(d) $H_2C{=}CH_2 + O_2 \rightarrow$

(2) Acetone

(a) $Ca(Ac)_2$ + heat $\rightarrow$ (Obsolete)

(b) Fermentation $\rightarrow$

(c) Isopropyl alcohol $- H_2 \rightarrow$

(d) Isopropyl alcohol $+ O_2 \rightarrow$

(e) Propylene $+ O_2 \rightarrow$

(f) Cumene hydroperoxide $\rightarrow$ Acetone + Phenol

(3) Acrylonitrile

(a) $CH{\equiv}CH + HCN \rightarrow$

(b) Propylene $\xrightarrow[O_2]{NH_3}$

(c) Propylene + NO $\rightarrow$

(d) $\underset{O}{CH_2{-}CH_2} \xrightarrow[-H_2O]{+HCN}$

(e) $CH_3CHO \xrightarrow[-H_2O]{+HCN}$

(4) Butadiene

(a) Ethyl alcohol $\xrightarrow{-H_2O}$

(b) Acetaldehyde $\rightarrow$ 1,3-butanediol $\xrightarrow{-H_2O}$

(c) $CH{\equiv}CH + CH_2O \xrightarrow{H_2}$ 1,4-butanediol $\xrightarrow{-H_2O}$

(d) $C_4H_8 - H_2 \rightarrow$

(e) $C_4H_{10} - 2H_2 \rightarrow$

(f) $C_4H_8 + O_2 \rightarrow$

(g) $C_3H_6 \rightarrow C_2H_4 + C_4H_8 \rightarrow$

(h) $C_3H_6 \xrightarrow{CH_2O}$ Methyldioxane →

(i) $C_2H_4 \rightarrow C_4H_8 \rightarrow$

(5) Caprolactam

(a) Cyclohexane $\xrightarrow{O_2}$ Cyclohexanone $\xrightarrow{NH_2OH}$ Oxime →

(b) Cyclohexane $\xrightarrow{NOCl}$ Cyclohexanone Oxime →

(c) Cyclohexane $\xrightarrow{HNO_3H_2}$ Cyclohexanone Oxime →

(d) Cyclohexane $\xrightarrow[\text{acid}]{\text{peracetic}}$ Caprolactone →

(e) Toluene $\xrightarrow{O_2}$ C_6H_5 COOH $\xrightarrow{H_2}$ C_6H_{11} COOH $\xrightarrow{HOSO_2ONO}$

(f) Phenol $\xrightarrow{H_2}$ Cyclohexanol → Oxime →

(6) Glycerin

See Figure ID-2 for a graphic representation of alternative routes to glycerol from propylene alone. There are also:

(a) Fermentation →

(b) Hydrogenolysis of dextrose →

(c) Fat splitting in soap mfg. →

(7) Isoprene

(a) Isopentane – H_2 →

(b) Isopentane + O_2 →

(c) Propylene → Dimer $\xrightarrow{-CH_4}$

(d) Isobutylene $\xrightarrow{CH_2O}$ Dimethyldioxane →

(e) CH≡CH + Acetone $\xrightarrow{H_2}$ $\xrightarrow{-H_2O}$

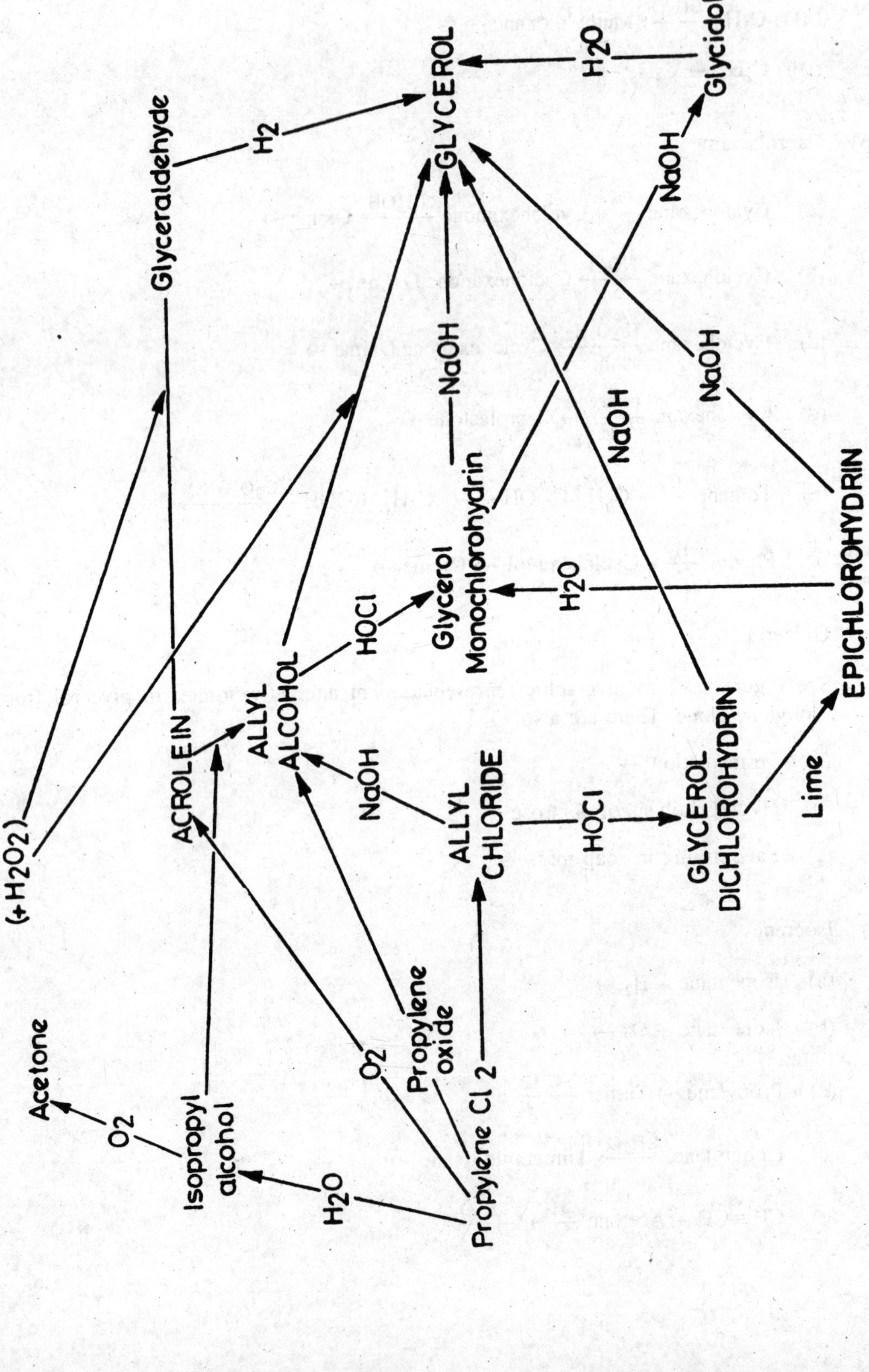

Fig. ID-2. Alternative process routes to glycerol from propylene.

(8) Phenol

(a) Coal tar distillation

(b) $C_6H_6 + H_2SO_4 \xrightarrow{NaOH}$

(c) $C_6H_6 + Cl_2 \xrightarrow{NaOH}$

(d) $\text{Cumene} \xrightarrow{\text{air}} \xrightarrow{H_2SO_4}$ (+ Acetone)

(e) $\text{Toluene} \xrightarrow{O_2} \text{Benzoic acid} \xrightarrow[Cu]{O_2}$

(f) $C_6H_6 + \xrightarrow[O_2]{HCl} C_6H_5Cl \xrightarrow{H_2O}$ (+ HCl-recycled)

(g) $C_6H_6 \xrightarrow{H_2} C_6H_{12} \xrightarrow{O_2} C_6H_{11}OH \xrightarrow{-3H_2}$

II

INORGANIC CHEMICAL INDUSTRIES

Processes for the industrial production of inorganic chemicals are historically the oldest of the commercial chemical field. A typical example was decarbonation of limestone ($CaCO_3$) to produce quicklime (CaO) in the Egyptian, Greek and Roman civilizations. As knowledge of chemistry was increased, processes became more complicated than just a simple preparation from naturally-occurring minerals. Today several of the inorganic processes are equally as complex as many of the processes found in the natural product or organic chemical industries.

As a general rule, inorganic processes are simpler and more easily developed than those classified as organic processes. Inorganic processes are usually one or two simple reaction steps with no side reactions, irreversible for maximum yields, and with no danger of thermal decomposition. A major problem of the inorganic industry is to obtain economic raw materials sufficiently pure to give good yields of refined inorganic chemical products. Whereas the unit processes employed are relatively simple, e.g., neutralization or calcination, the development of suitable unit operation sequences to produce high purity inorganic chemicals with economical yields is the major task of the chemical engineer in the inorganic chemical industries.

Only a representative few of inorganic chemicals will be discussed in this book. Details of processes for the production of other inorganic chemicals can be found in the chemical technology literature.

Factors which are responsible for such high costs in the Indian chemical industries as a whole are made up of a combination of the following factors:

- Low capacity plants, often not operating at full capacity
- Higher fixed capital investment since many of the plants are foreign built and/or Indian mechanical equipment is expensive
- Scarcity of raw materials, sometimes involving imports
- Technological problems, particularly maintenance and repair
- High cost of electric power, utilities and transportation

These factors make it difficult to compete in the world market at the present time. A gradual reduction in costs is expected as the industries grow and gain more experience.

IIA. SULFUR AND SULFURIC ACID

Sulfur

Sulfur is the basic raw material for manufacture of sulfuric acid, which is considered the barometer of India's industrial progress. In more advanced countries this rule is no longer valid as the overall industry grows rapidly with sulfuric acid virtually stable. Current production is at the same level as that of the USA in about 1900 and the per capita consumption of acid in India is only 4% of that in the USA. These figures give indication of the immense development possibilities for India.

1. Pertinent Properties of Sulfur

Sulfur has the chemical formula S and an atomic weight of 32.07. It exists as rhombic crystals, m.p. 112.8°C and as monoclinic crystals, m.p. 119°C and it boils at 444.6°C. The specific gravity at 18°C of the rhombic form is 2.07 and of the monoclinic form is 1.96. The liquid has a specific gravity of 1.803. It is insoluble in water, but soluble in organic solvents and liquid ammonia. Sulfur exists in the following forms: rock, lump, molten, ground powder and sublimed powder (flowers of sulfur).

2. Consumption Pattern

2.1. 80-90% of sulfur-containing raw materials are converted to these commercial oxidized forms:

Sulfur dioxide	(SO_2)
Sulfur trioxide	(SO_3)
Sulfuric acid	(H_2SO_4)
Oleum	($H_2SO_4+SO_3$)

2.2. End uses for elemental sulfur are:

- 85 to 90% for sulfuric acid manufacture
- Rest for production of:
  SO_2, SO_3, CS_2, and P_2S_5;
  rubber vulcanization agents;
  gunpowder, sulfur dyes;
  putties, sulfur concrete;
  paper. Divided approximately: 7% to paper and pulp, 3% to CS_2 manufacture.

2.3. The applications spectrum for sulfuric acid is in U.S.A.:

• Phosphate fertilizers	70
• Petroleum refining	5
• Inorganic chemicals and pigments	4
• Copper leaching	3
• Synthetic rubbers and plastics	2.5
• Industrial organic chemicals	2.5
• Pulp and paper	2
• Others	11

3. Raw Materials Sources

Sulfuric acid may be produced from elemental sulfur, pyrites (sulfides of iron), hydrogen sulfide as contained in sour gas and petroleum, waste gases from the burning of fuel and smelting operations such as pyrites of copper, iron, zinc and lead. Elemental sulfur, pyrites and sulfides are the basic raw materials for production of sulfuric acid in India. Sulfuric acid produced by burning of fuel and smelting operations is called by-product sulfuric acid.

In India, all the factories are based on elemental sulfur except for Hindustan Copper Ltd., Khetri and Ghatsila and Hindustan Zinc Ltd., Udaipur and Cominco Binani, Alwaye which are based on smelter gases from copper and zinc smelters respectively. One plant based on iron pyrites (PPCL-Amjhore) is operating satisfactorily.

India is practically devoid of deposits of elemental sulfur. The important deposits of pyrites are those of Amjhore in Rohtas district of Bihar and Saladipura in the Sikar district of Rajasthan.

The only deposits of sulfur are found in the Puga valley of Kashmir, but due to difficult terrain conditions, these deposits have not acquired due economic importance. Three alternative sources of recovering sulfur for reducing the dependence on import have been adopted: (1) recovery of elemental sulfur from petroleum refineries; (2) production of by-product sulfuric acid from zinc and copper smelters; and (3) production of sulfuric acid from pyrites. Madras Refinery Ltd. is the only plant from which elemental sulfur is recovered during the refining of crude petroleum. Sulfuric acid, however, is produced on a large scale, as a by-product in the production of fertilizers and in the smelters of zinc, copper, and other non-ferrous metals. Pyrites and Phosphate Chemicals Ltd. operates with a capacity of 400 tons of pyrite ores per day. Based on these pyrites, two sulfuric acid plants have been set up in Sindri. In order to meet their requirements fully, the PPCL has embarked on a new scheme to produce 90 tons of pyrites per day.

3.1. Classification of Processes:

- Elemental sulfur mining from salt domes (USA, Sicily)
- Hydrogen sulfide conversion from natural gas and industrial gases (Indian refineries and many U.S. refineries)
- Iron pyrites from Amjhore in Bihar State

3.2. Elemental Sulfur Mining (Frasch Process)

3.2.1. Reference flow sheet: Figure IIA-1

3.2.2. Chemical reactions: None

3.2.3. Raw materials

- Sulfur deposits in salt domes
- Large supply of hot water

3.2.4. Quantitative requirements

(a) Basis: 1 metric ton of sulfur
Water (160°C) 6 tons

(b) Dome operating capacity: 500-8,000 tons/day of sulfur

3.2.5. Process description

Wells drilled into free sulfur-bearing salt domes. These are found in the USA along the Gulf Coast. Treated hot water is pumped into deposit melt sulfur; water moves upward and outward to bleeder wells on outer periphery of area where it is aerated and discharged. Molten sulfur sinks to bottom of casing and is jet pumped with compressed air to sump-separation units and shipment or storage. Filtration is sometimes used to remove carbonaceous and mineral matter.

3.2.6. Major engineering problems

(a) Heat transfer in melting and shipping operations
(b) Finding suitable sources of treated water
(c) Corrosion

3.3. Oxidation-reduction of H_2S

3.3.1. Reference flow sheet: Figure IIA-2

3.3.2. Chemical reactions

(a) $2H_2S + 3O_2 \rightarrow 2SO_2 + 2H_2O;\quad \Delta H^\circ = -247.89$ Kcal

(b) $4H_2S + 2SO_2 \xrightarrow{Al_2O_3} S_6(g) + 4H_2O;\quad \Delta H^\circ = -42.24$ Kcal

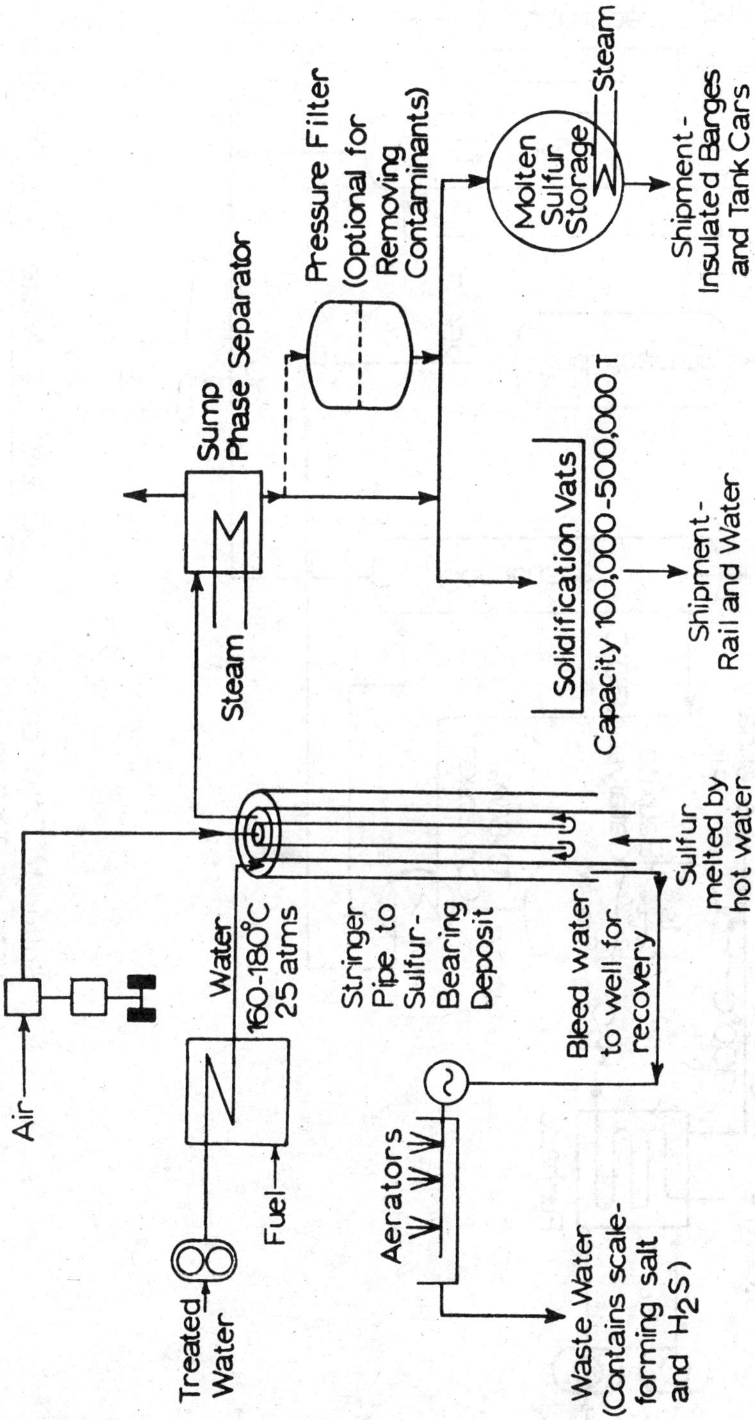

Fig. IIA-1. Elemental sulfur mining by Frasch process.

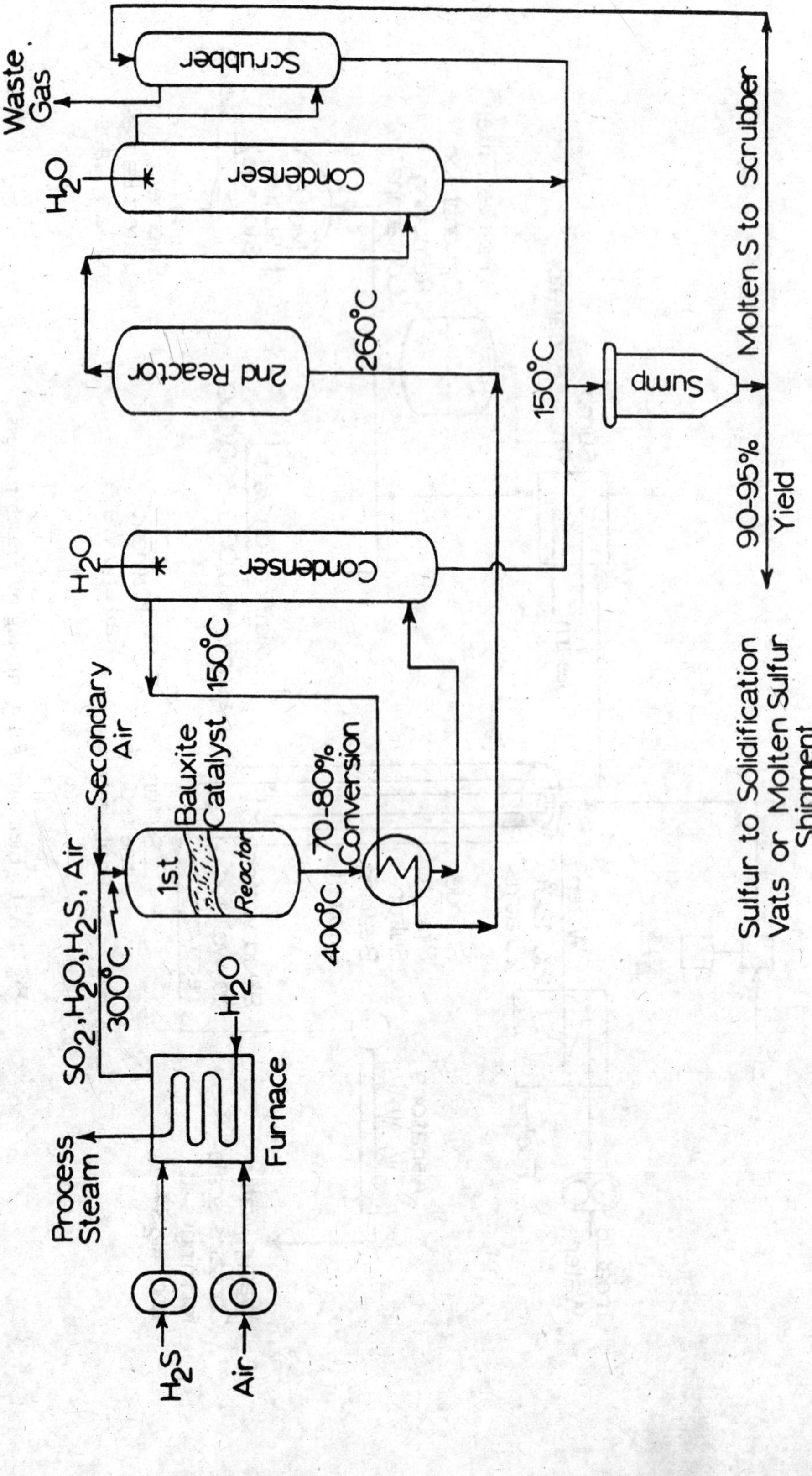

Fig. IIA-2. Sulfur production by oxidation-reduction of H_2S.

3.3.3. Raw materials

- H_2S from natural (sour) gas and petroleum refinery streams. Recovered by scrubbing with ethanolamines and high-temperature stripping.

3.3.4. Quantitative requirements

(a) Basis: 1 metric ton of sulfur and 100% yield
H_2S 1.2 tons; Air 1,700 Nm^3

(b) Plant capacities: 20-600 tons/day

3.3.5. Process description

H_2S and air burned in reaction 3.3.2(a). The product SO_2 oxidizes H_2S by reaction 3.3.2(b) in a two-stage catalytic converter with intercooling and condensing. Final waste gas is scrubbed with molten sulfur.

3.3.6. Major engineering problems

(a) Two-stage reactor design for exothermic SO_2 oxidation of H_2S. 70-80% conversion in first stage at 300-400°C range followed by 250-300°C operation in second reactor to obtain favorable equilibrium.

(b) Heat exchange for molten sulfur handling

(c) Corrosion

(d) Final clean-up of stack gases

3.4. Elemental Sulfur from Pyrites (Finnish Process)

3.4.1. Reference flow sheet: Figure IIA-3

3.4.2. Chemical reactions

(a) Thermal dissociation

$$FeS_2 \xrightarrow[1,300^\circ C]{1 \text{ atm.}} \tfrac{1}{2}S_2(g) + FeS(l); \quad \Delta H = +15.98 \text{ Kcal}$$

(b) General combustion reaction

$$C + H + S + O_2 \rightarrow SO_2, H_2S, CO, H_2CO_2, H_2O$$

(c) Sulfur recovery from gases—Hot stage

$$2COS + CS_2 + 2SO_2 \xrightarrow[600^\circ C]{\text{catalyst}} S_6 + 3CO_2$$

(d) Sulfur recovery from gases—Cold stage

$$4H_2S + 2SO_2 \xrightarrow[280^\circ C]{Al_2O_3} 4H_2O + S_6$$

(e) Roasting of FeS (pyrrhotite) for SO_2 recovery

$$2FeS + 3\tfrac{1}{2}O_2 \xrightarrow[1,000^\circ C]{1 \text{ atm.}} Fe_2O_3 + 2SO_2; \quad \Delta H = -295.02 \text{ Kcal}$$

3.4.3. Quantitative requirements

(a) Basis: 1 ton of elemental sulfur (99+ % purity, 92% total S recovery)

Pyrites ore (Amjhore)	4.4 tons
Limestone	0.65 ton
Fuel oil	0.76 ton
Water	25 tons
Electricity	1,800 KWH

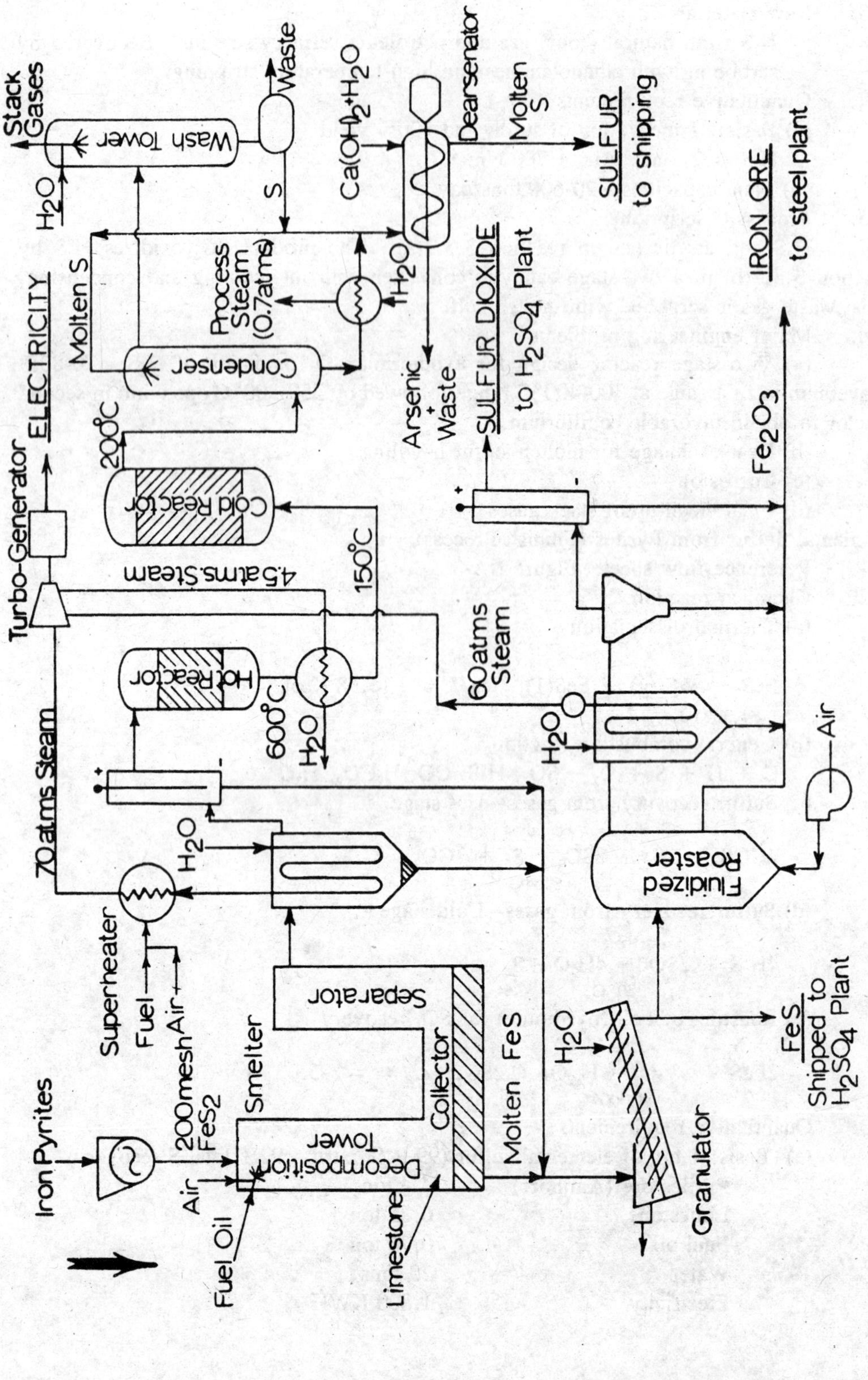

Fig. IIA-3. Sulfur and sulfur dioxide from pyrites.

Co-products:

SO_2 from FeS roasting = 1.2 tons

Fe_2O_3 from FeS roasting = 2.8 tons

Electricity = 3,200 KWH total or 1,400 KWH net

(b) Plant capacities: 250 tons/day as elemental sulfur

3.4.4. Process description

Pyrites ore is dried in a rotary kiln with flue gases and ground to —200 mesh. It is dispersed with hot combustion gases from oil burners at the top of a vertical circular shaft furnace (5.5m diameter x 10m height). Heat of dissociation and fusion is transferred to the FeS_2 as it moves downward in the suspension. At the bottom of the vertical shaft the gases change 90° and move horizontally. The liquid droplets of FeS are caught in the molten horizontal batch and any silica gangue is trapped and fluxed with lime, floating on top of the molten FeS matte. The liquid FeS is tapped periodically and granulated in water to produce ~4 mm grains for further roasting operations.

Hot gases at 1,300°C move through a high-pressure heat recovery boiler section (70 atms. steam), cooling to 300°C. Dust is next separated by electrostatic precipitation.

The first step in combined S recovery is done in a high temperature catalytic reactor [see reaction 3.4.2(c)] where carbon compounds with S are eliminated. The reaction gases, still containing SO_2 and H_2S, are cooled to 150°C by passing through a low-pressure heat recovery boiler (4.5 atms. gage). This is followed by "cold stage" catalytic reaction [see 3.4.2(d)] where aluminum oxide catalyzes the H_2S+SO_2 reaction to produce S_6 vapor.

After catalysis, sulfur gas is condensed on molten sulfur droplets in a spray condenser. The heat of fusion is recovered via low-pressure steam boiler (0.7 atm. gage). The exit gases are next washed with water in another tower to further recover entrained and uncondensed sulfur.

The sulfur usually contains arsenic which attacks the vanadium or platinum catalyst in the $SO_2 \rightarrow SO_3$ contact process for H_2SO_4. It can be removed by contacting molten sulfur with milk of lime in a continuous autoclave.

Sulfur as SO_2 for sulfuric acid can be obtained by roasting the granulated FeS from the smelting furnace. Fluidized roasting at 1,000°C produces SO_2 gas which is cooled in waste heat boiler, cleaned by cyclones and electrostatic precipitation. The hot cinders of iron oxide, suitable for blast furnace sinter cake, are cooled on conveyors and shipped to steel plants.

3.4.5. Major engineering problems

(a) Pyrites ore beneficiation

The process was developed for pyrites ores of Finland which have 1.5% SiO_2. Indian ore at Amjhore has 5-7% SiO_2 and requires either flotation initially or extra limestone to flux out the silica. The latter is preferred since there is a 30% loss of ore in beneficiation.

(b) Grinding

The particle size range of —200 mesh was an economic balance between heat transfer rate from combustion gases plus residence time, as dictated by rate of fall of particles, tower height, and grinding costs.

(c) Substitution of coal for fuel oil

Low-grade fuel oil is only available at the Amjhore site at high costs. Smelting with coal would represent a savings of 20% in the cost of sulfur produced. Use of coal is being considered for pilot plant development in India. The question of using pulverized coal directly in the smelter burners or working with secondary combustion gases after ash has been removed must be resolved.

(d) Gaseous reactions in the smelting furnace

Complete combustion of fuel without excess air is desirable to avoid unbalance of the H_2S-SO_2 ratio which can be shifted with only minor changes in the oxygen/fuel ratio. The smelter feed system requires close instrumental control.

(e) Two-stage catalytic reactor design

Plant first operated only with cold stage so that COS and CS_2 remained unconverted to free sulfur. By first using a high-temperature catalyst, these compounds can also be oxidized and the sulfur yield increased from 85 to 92%. Design of the cold stage is similar to Process 3.3.

(f) Heat recovery and generation of electric energy

Despite the initial endothermic smelting step and the high electrical energy usage for grinding, the overall process has excess heat energy which is converted via three stages of steam boiler heat recovery to electric energy with a net production of 1,400 KWH/ton of S.

4. Economics

4.1. Elemental Sulfur Deposits and Supply

- USA furnishes about 60% of world sulfur
- Increasing quantities expected from Mexico via Frasch process and from Canada and Europe via natural (sour) gas process

The panorama of world sulfur production is shown in Table IIA-1.

Table IIA-1
1985 World Sulfur Production (in 10^6 t)

Country Sources	USA	CIS	Canada	Poland	PR China	Japan
Sulfur—all forms	11.4	9.8	6.7	5.1	0.9	1.5
—Frasch	5.0	0.9	-	4.4	-	-
—Native (mined)	-	1.7	-	0.5	0.3	-
—Pyrites	withheld	3.4	-	-	0.2	0.3
—By-products*	6.4 (C,N)	3.8 (N)	6.7 (N)	0.2 (M)	0.4	1.2 (M,C)

*Primarily: N = natural gas, M = metallurgy, C = crude oil

Source: "Industrial Inorganic Chemistry" by Buchner et al (1989)

Sulfuric Acid

1. Pertinent Properties of Sulfuric Acid

- Pure 100% H_2SO_4:

Mol. wt. 98.08   M.P. 10.5°C   B.P. 340°C (decomposition)

Solubility: Completely miscible with H_2O with large heat of solution. SO_3 soluble in H_2SO_4 to give varying percentage of oleum.

- Grades of acid

Grades of acid	$\%H_2SO_4$	Sp. gr. at 18°C
50° Be (Fertilizer acid)	62.2	1.525
60° Be (Oil of vitriol)	93.2	1.833
95% acid	95.0	1.840
98% acid	98.0	1.843
Monohydrate acid (H_2SO_4)	100.0	1.834
20% oleum (fuming)	104.5—20% Free SO_3	1.924
40% oleum (fuming)	109.0—40% Free SO_3	1.963
65%	114.6—65% Free SO_3	1.987

2. Methods of Production

2.1. Classification of Processes

- Contact process
- Chamber process

Both processes are based on SO_2. Chamber process was developed first (1746) but produced acid of concentration less than 80%. Contact process yields 98% H_2SO_4 and higher which can be diluted, if necessary. Chamber process is virtually obsolete.

2.2. Contact H_2SO_4 Process

2.2.1. Reference flow sheets: Figures ID-1, IIA-4

2.2.2. Chemical reactions

(a) $S(s) + O_2(g) \rightarrow SO_2(g)$; $\Delta H = -70.9$ Kcal

(b) $SO_2(g) + \frac{1}{2}O_2(g) \underset{}{\overset{V_2O_5}{\rightleftharpoons}} SO_3(g)$; $\Delta H = -23.0$ Kcal

2.2.3. Raw materials

- SO_2 is obtained from the following sources:

	W. Europe	USA
(a) Sulfur	47	82
(b) Pyrites	35	2
(c) CuS, ZnS, PbS, MoS_2	17	1.5
(d) Waste H_2SO_4	7	5.6
(e) H_2S sources		

(a) Sulfur source

Combustion yields very pure SO_2 which requires only filtration and drying.

(b) Pyrites source

Iron pyrites containing 40-45% S are roasted and must be purified by dust removal, cooling, scrubbing, filtering and drying by conc. acid scrubbing to remove dust, moisture, and catalyst poisons (As, Cl, F).

(c) Smelter sources

SO_2 obtained by roasting non-ferrous sulfide ores such as zinc, lead, and copper; given same treatment as pyrites gas. (See Chapter VI on Metallurgical Industries for further information.)

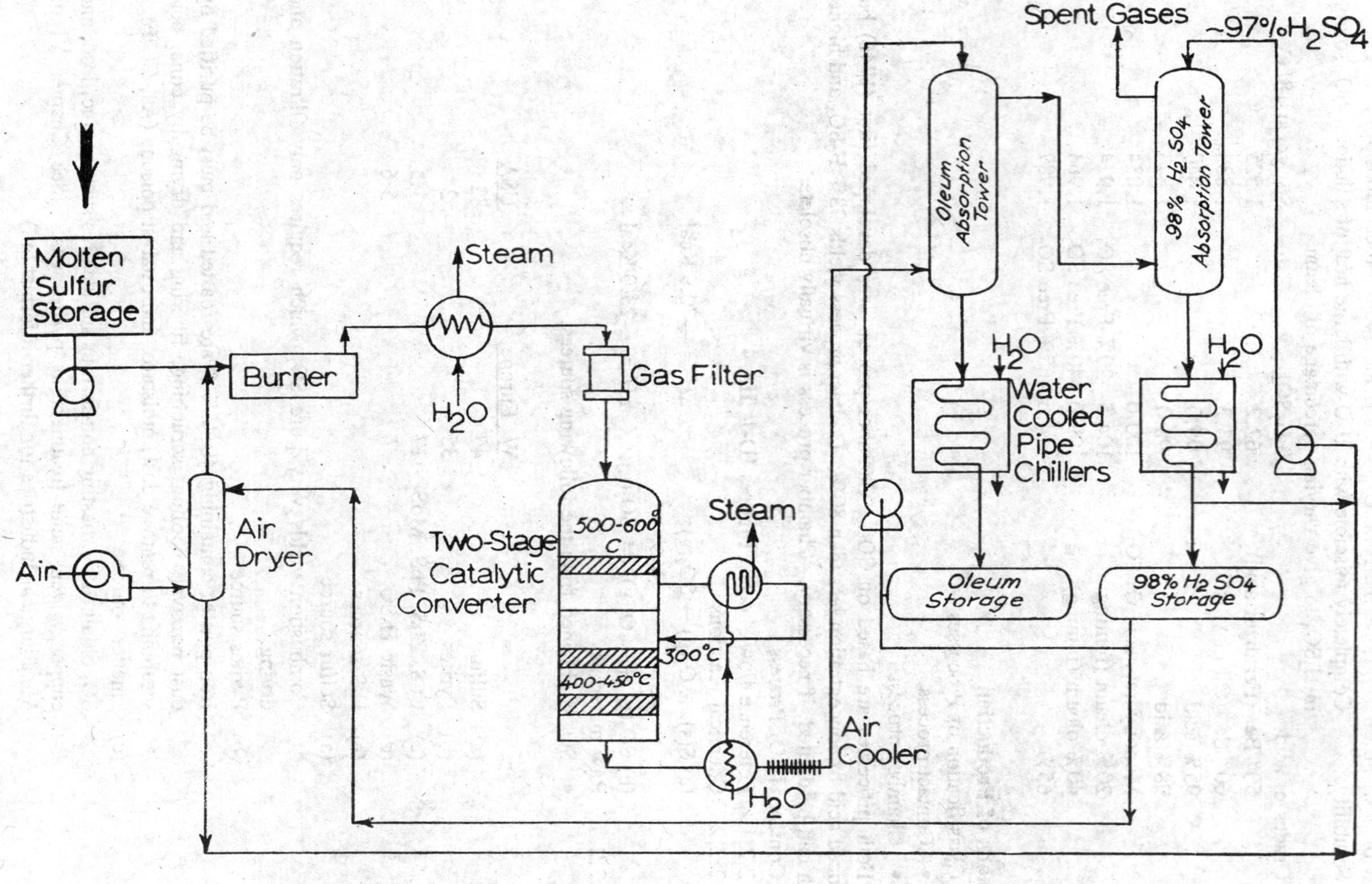

Fig. IIA-4. Simplified engineering flow sheet for manufacture of sulfuric acid and oleum by contact process.

(d) Waste H_2SO_4
$FeSO_4$ from iron and steel pickle liquors and H_2SO_4 from petroleum refinery operations are roasted to recover SO_2.

(e) H_2S sources
H_2S is recovered by scrubbing various fuel and refinery gases with ethanolamines followed by hot stripping. The sulfide gas is burned as in reaction 3.3.2(a) under Sulfur.

- Catalyst
Most widely used catalyst is vanadium pentoxide dispersed on a porous carrier in pellet form. Platinum catalyst was previously used but suffers from easy poisoning, fragility, rapid heat deactivation, high initial investment.

* Characteristics of catalysts

(1) *Porous carrier* having large surface area, controlled pore size, and resistance to process gases at high temperature: in pellet form if used in fixed beds, powdered form for fluidized beds. Examples—alumina, silica gel, kieselguhr, zeolite.

(2) *Active catalytic agent*—V_2O_5 in this case. Preparations are secret for competitive reasons; usually consist of adding H_2O soluble compounds to gels or porous substrates and firing at temperatures below sintering point.

(3) *Promoter*—alkali, and/or metallic compounds added in trace amounts to enhance activity of catalytic agent.

* Advantages of V_2O_5 catalyst
— Relatively immune to poisons
— Low initial investment and only 5% replacement per year
— Requires only 10 kg of catalyst mass containing 7-8% V_2O_5 per daily ton of 100% acid

* Disadvantages of V_2O_5 catalyst
Must use dilute SO_2 input (7-10%); as catalyst is less active and requires high O_2/SO_2 to give economic conversion. Larger converters and higher initial investment are necessary.

2.2.4. Quantitative requirements

(a) Basis: 1 ton of 100% H_2SO_4

SO_2	0.67 ton
Air	1,450-2,200 Nm^3

(b) Plant capacities: 50-1,000 tons/day of 100% acid

2.2.5. Process description

Air-SO_2, gas containing 7-10% SO_2 and 11-14% O_2 is preheated by converter gas, if necessary, and sent to first stage reactors of steel construction. This is the high temperature (500-600°C) stage, contains 30% of total catalyst and converts about 80% of SO_2. The converter product is cooled by heat exchange at 300°C and fed to a second stage where total yield is increased to 97% by operating at 400-450°C for favorable equilibrium.

High yield product gases are cooled to 150°C by water and air heat exchangers and absorbed in oleum fed at a rate to allow not over a 1% rise in acid strength. Final scrubbing is done with a lower strength (97%) acid. Oleum concentrations up to 40% can be made by tower absorption. Higher strength oleum up to 65% is prepared by distilling 20% oleum.

2.2.6. Major engineering problems

(a) Design of multistage catalytic converter for a highly exothermic reaction: Some designs contain 3 or 4 stages rather than the conventional two-stage operation for large capacity plants. For equilibrium design information, see Table IIA-2 and Figure IIA-5.

(b) Optimization of space velocity in catalyst chamber: Pumping costs versus fixed charges of reactor.

(c) Corrosion problems: Optimization studies show that equilibrium yield can be increased by square root of system pressure p_T at a given temperature:

$$Y_{SO_3} = K_p Y_{SO_2} \cdot (Y_{O_2})^{1/2} \cdot (p_T)^{1/2}$$

but increasing compression costs & corrosion problems dictate low pressure (1 atm.) operation.

(d) Adaptation of process to various types of gas feeds.

(e) As the result of considering problems (a) and (b) above, thin catalyst beds result (30-50 cm height). Yield can drop due to longitudinal mixing if the convective gas velocity through the bed is too low.

(f) Removal of heat of absorption of SO_3 in acid. Pipe coolers with water dripping over external surface have been replaced by cast iron pipe with internal fins to promote better heat transfer. Pressure drop must be low so 8 cm stacked packing is often used.

Table IIA-2 Thermodynamic Data for SO_2 Oxidation

$$\text{Basis:} \quad K_p = \frac{P_{SO_3}}{P_{SO_2} \cdot (P_{O_2})^{1/2}} = \frac{Y_{SO_3}}{Y_{SO_2} \cdot (Y_{O_2})^{1/2} \cdot (p_T)^{1/2}}$$

Temperature °*K*	°*C*	*Heat Evolved Kcal/g mole.*	K_p
600	327	23.42	4,170
700	427	23.27	257
800	527	23.08	32.0
900	627	22.87	6.47
1,000	727	22.63	2.03

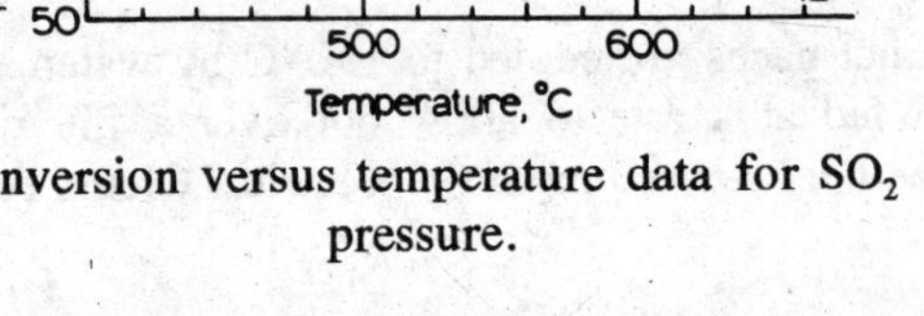

Fig. IIA-5. Equilibrium conversion versus temperature data for $SO_2 + \frac{1}{2}O_2 \rightleftharpoons SO_3$ at 1 atm. pressure.

3. Economics

3.1. Type of Process

Prior to 1947, a number of chamber process plants were installed. Since that date only contact plants are being licensed with minimum capacity set at 50 tons per day. The superiority of the contact process results from:

- Engineering improvement to contact plant, particularly the catalyst performance
- High strength acid which reduces costs & increases the economic allowable market area
- High SO_3 acids applicable to newer uses such as sulfonation and sulfation reactions

3.2. Production Units

Largest single users in the range of 100-800 tons of 100% H_2SO_4 per day are fertilizer manufacturers who operate their own acid plant to avoid high shipping costs of low bulk value acid.

3.3. Plant Location and Production in India

Sulfuric acid tends to be made in India at locations near to acid consumption, often in small plants. Initially, plants were built near seaports but it is more economical to transport sulfur from the seaport to an inland plant adjacent to the point of consumption, then to transport acid from a plant near a seaport.

Table IIA-3 summarizes data on world production of sulfuric acid.

Table IIA-3
World Production of Sulfuric Acid (in 10^6 tons of 100% H_2SO_4)

	World	USA/ Canada	Latin America	Western Europe	Eastern Europe	Asia/ Oceania	Africa
1975	109.2	32.1	4.1	25.1	28.1	16.0	3.8
1980	142.0	44.4	6.1	27.8	32.6	22.5	8.6
1986	145.4	34.8	7.7	24.8	38.5	26.5	13.1

Source: "Industrial Inorganic Chemistry" by Buchner et al (1989)

Regionally the evolution in sulfuric acid production is very different. In Western Europe a decline in production is predicted, whereas further high growth rates are expected in Latin America and Africa. The USA and Russia produce the highest quantities followed by the People's Republic of China, Japan, France, West Germany and Canada.

Locations and installed capacities of sulfuric acid plants in India are listed in Table IIA-4. This is an interesting table to reflect on for a moment in view of:

1. The large numbers of plants spread around India.
2. The large variation in sizes of plants at individual locations. There is, however, apparently, a "standard" design of about 33,000 tons/year which is widely utilized.
3. The association of plants with products. Thus they may be associated with sulfur sources (as in the case of zinc smelters, for example) or with consuming industries (fertilizer plants, for example). In the latter case, the production may be partially or totally captive production.

Table IIA-4
Locations and Capacities of Sulfuric Acid Plants in India

	Installed Capacity Tons/Year
Adarsh Chemicals & Fertilizers Ltd.	
Udhna, Surat, Gujarat	49,000
Agro Chem Punjab, Ltd.	
Singhpura, Patiala, Punjab	33,000
Albright, Morarji & Pandit Ltd.	
Ambarnath, Maharashtra	45,000
Andhra Fertilizers	
Tadepalli, A.P.	16,500
Andhra Sugars	
Tanuku, A.P.	30,900
Anil Starch Products	
Bhavnagar, Gujarat	18,000
Ahmedabad, Gujarat	12,600
Asian Fertilizers	
Gorakhpur, U.P.	33,000
Assam State Fertilizers & Chemicals	
Chandrapur, Assam	16,500
Atic Industries Ltd.	
Post Atul, Gujarat	16,500
Atul Products Ltd.	
Dist. Valsad, Gujarat	32,050
Baroda Rayon Corporation Ltd.	
Surat, Gujarat	21,600
Bengal Chemicals & Pharmaceuticals Ltd.	
Panihati, West Bengal	33,185
Bharat Fertilizer Industries	
Kharivali, Maharashtra	33,000
Bharat Fertilizers & Chemicals	
Alwar, Rajasthan	39,600
Bhatinda Heavy Allied Chemicals	
Bhatinda, Punjab	16,500
Bhilai Engineering Corporation	
Bilaspur, M.P.	33,000
Bihar State Superphosphate Factory	
Dhanbad, Bihar	8,380
Cawnpore Chemical Works	
Kanpur, U.P.	9,000
Century Textiles & Industries Ltd.	
Bombay, Maharashtra	29,700
Chloride Industries Ltd.	
Haldia, West Bengal	33,000
Coimbatore Pioneer Fertilizers	
Coimbatore, Tamil Nadu	18,000

Cominco Binani Zinc	
Binanipuram, Kerala	38,000
Coromandel Fertilizers	
Visakhapatnam, A.P.	297,000
Dharamsi Morarji Chemical	
Ambernath, Maharashtra	220,000
Kumhari, M.P.	102,000
Divya Chemicals	
Raigarh, Maharashtra	36,500
East Coast Fertilizers & Chemicals	
Mayurbhanj, Orissa	33,000
EID Parry (India)	
Ennore, Tamil Nadu	16,500
Ranipet, Tamil Nadu	16,500
Fertilizers & Chemicals Travancore	
Ambalamedu, Kerala	330,000
Udyogamandal, Kerala	308,550
Fertilizer Corporation of India	
Sindri, Bihar	264,000
Gammon Fer-Chems	
Belagula, Karnataka	20,800
Grasim Industries	
Kumarpatnam, Dharwar, Karnataka	20,800
Gujarat State Fertilizers Company	
Vadodara, Gujarat	155,100
Harshvardan Chemicals & Minerals	
Antravalia, M.P.	155,100
Hindustan Copper	
Khetri, Rajasthan	182,000
Ghatsila, Bihar	54,000
Hindustan Fertilizer Corporation	
Namrup, Assam	82,500
Hindustan Heavy Chemicals	
Khardah, West Bengal	8,550
Hindustan Lever	
Haldia, West Bengal	136,950
Hindustan Organic Chemicals	
Rasayani, Maharashtra	43,800
Hindustan Zinc	
Debari, Udaipur, Rajasthan	87,000
Indag Products	
Cuddalore, Tamil Nadu	16,500
India Ceroils	
Dharuhera, Haryana	49,500
Indian Dyestuff Industries	
Kalyan, Thane, Maharashtra	33,000

Indian Iron & Steel Company Burnpur, West Bengal	31,020
Indian Link Chain Mfg. Co. Thane, Maharashtra	16,500
Indian Oil Corporation Digboi, Assam	7,300
Indian Rayon & Industries Ltd. Veraval, Gujarat	20,625
Indian Sulph Acids Industries Shahabad, Kurukshetra, Haryana	33,000
Jayshree Chemicals & Fertilizers Pataudi, Haryana	33,000
Kesoram Industries Ltd. Tribeni, Hooghly, West Bengal	16,500
Khaitan Chemicals & Fertilizers Nimrani, Khargone, M.P.	33,000
Khetawat Chemicals & Fertilizers Haldia, West Bengal	33,000
Kothari Industrial Corporation Ennore, Madras	33,000
Krishna Industrial Corporation Nidadavole, A.P.	16,760
Kumar Chemicals & Industries N. Arcot, Tamil Nadu	33,000
Madras Petro-Chem Ltd. Manali, Tamil Nadu	16,500
Mahadeo Fertilizers Fatehpur, U.P.	33,000
Meta Zinc (India) Thane, Maharashtra	41,250
Mittal Fertilizers Rae Bareli, U.P.	33,000
Munak Chemicals Bhatinda, Punjab	56,100
National Rayon Corporation Kalyan, Thane, Maharashtra	48,000
Navin Fluorine Industries Udhna, Gujarat	31,040
Nirma Pvt. Ltd. Mehsana, Gujarat	100,000
Oriental Carbon & Chemicals Dharuhera, Haryana	33,000
Paradeep Phosphates Paradeep, Orissa	660,000

Company / Location	Capacity
Paushak	
Baroda, Gujarat	18,000
Phosphate Company	
Rishra, West Bengal	64,350
Punjab Sulfur Products	
Hoshiarpur, Punjab	16,500
Pyrites, Phosphates & Chemicals	
Amjhore, Bihar	105,600
Rama Industrial Chemicals	
Vapi, Gujarat	100,000
Rama Krishi Rasayan	
Loni Kalbhor, Maharashtra	24,750
Rama Phosphates	
Indore, M.P.	33,000
Ramganga Fertilizers	
Bharatigram, U.P.	33,000
Rampur Distillery Chemicals	
Rampur, U.P.	33,000
Ranjan Chemicals	
Barauni, Bihar	16,500
Rashtriya Chemicals & Fertilizers	
Trombay, Maharashtra	99,000
Rohtas Industries	
Rohtas, Bihar	3,000
Sarada Fertilizers	
Bankura, West Bengal	33,000
SFL Industries	
Rail Majra, Punjab	82,500
Sahibabad Chemicals & Fertilizers	
Sahibabad, U.P.	20,000
Shaw Wallace & Company	
Avadi, Tamil Nadu	41,250
Shree Acids & Chemicals	
Gajruala, U.P.	33,000
Shriram Rayons	
Kota, Rajasthan	16,500
Shri Sulfurics	
Bharuch, Gujarat	33,000
Shriniwas Fertilizers	
Jhansi, U.P.	33,000
Solar Chemicals	
Chandrapur, Maharashtra	16,500
Sonawala Chemicals	
Kalyan, Bombay, Maharashtra	3,300
South India Viscose	
Coimbatore, Tamil Nadu	29,100

Southern Petrochemical Industries Corporation	
Tuticorin, Tamil Nadu	154,770
Sri Durga Bansal	
Faizabad, U.P.	33,000
Steel Authority of India	
Bhilai, M.P.	48,390
Bokaro, Bihar	84,000
Rourkela, Orissa	18,000
Durgapur, West Bengal	19,750
Sundarsan Industries	
Jamshedpur, Bihar	33,000
Tamil Nadu Fluorine & Allied Chemicals	
Cuddalore, Tamil Nadu	21,780
Tarapur Acids and Alkali	
Thane, Maharashtra	39,600
Tata Iron & Steel Company	
Jamshedpur, Bihar	31,500
C.D. Thakkar & Company	
Burdwan, West Bengal	12,000
Tinplate Company of India	
Golmuri, Bihar	3,300
Travancore Rayons Ltd.	
Rayonpuram, Kerala	18,290
Travancore Titanium Products	
Trivandrum, Kerala	108,000
Trimurtee Fertilizers	
Kanpur Dehat, U.P.	33,000
Udaipur Phosphates & Fertilizers	
Khemli, Rajasthan	33,000
Unialkem Fertilizers	
Raisen, M.P.	23,760
Uranium Corporation of India	
Jaduguda Mines, Sinhbhum, Bihar	16,500
Varinder Agro Chemicals	
Sanghera, Punjab	100,000
Vidarbha Phosphates & Fertilizers	
Pulgaon, Maharashtra	33,000
Vidula Chemicals & Manufacturing Industries	
Parganas, West Bengal	16,500
Western Chemical Industries	
Goregaon, East Bombay, Maharashtra	3,900
Total	Approx. 6,000,000 tons per year

Source: "Fertiliser Statistics" Annual (1993-94)

IIB. FUEL AND INDUSTRIAL GASES

The chemical industries depend to a major extent on gases composed of one or more of the chemical elements carbon, hydrogen, oxygen, and nitrogen. These gases are used for fuel and for synthesis of important inorganic and organic chemical compounds. Raw materials for supplying these gases are such cheap sources as water, air, coal, natural gas, and petroleum. The last two are presently found as natural resources in the Indian states of Assam and Gujarat and only in small quantities. Consequently, the manufacture of fuel gas is limited to coal as a source of carbon with very low production compared to the USA.

The discussion in this section is limited to fuel gases, chemical synthesis gases, and acetylene. Oxygen and nitrogen are covered in the next Section on "Cryogenics in Chemical Technology."

Fuel Gases

1. Classification

Type	*Kcal/cu m*	*Principal Use*
Producer gas [CO, N_2, H_2 with steam added to reduce ΔH (net) to zero]	1,200-1,600	Steel industry's heating requirements (heat treat, coke ovens)
Water gas (CO, H_2)	2,500-2,700	Heating, Chemical synthesis
Coke oven gas (H_2, CH_4, CO)	4,500-8,000	Heating, Chemical synthesis
Carburetted or Oil gas (water gas and pyrolyzed oil)	4,000-9,000	Heating
Natural gas and LPG (Liquefied Petroleum Gas)	6,000-14,000	Heating, Chemical synthesis

2. Chemical Reactions

(a) $C(s) + O_2(g)$ (excess air) $\rightarrow CO_2(g)$; $\Delta H° = -96.5$ Kcal

(b) $2C(s) + O_2(g)$ (limited air) $\rightarrow 2CO(g)$; $\Delta H° = -57.8$ Kcal

(c) $C(s) + CO_2(g) \rightarrow 2CO(g)$; $\Delta H° = +38.7$ Kcal

(d) $C(s) + H_2O(1) \rightarrow CO(g) + H_2(g)$; $\Delta H° = +38.9$ Kcal

(e) $CO(g) + H_2O(1) \rightarrow CO_2(g) + H_2(g)$; $\Delta H° = +0.4$ Kcal

3. Methods of Production

3.1. Producer Gas

3.1.1. Reference flow sheet: Figure IIB-1

3.1.2. Raw materials

- Coal or blast furnace coke
- Air

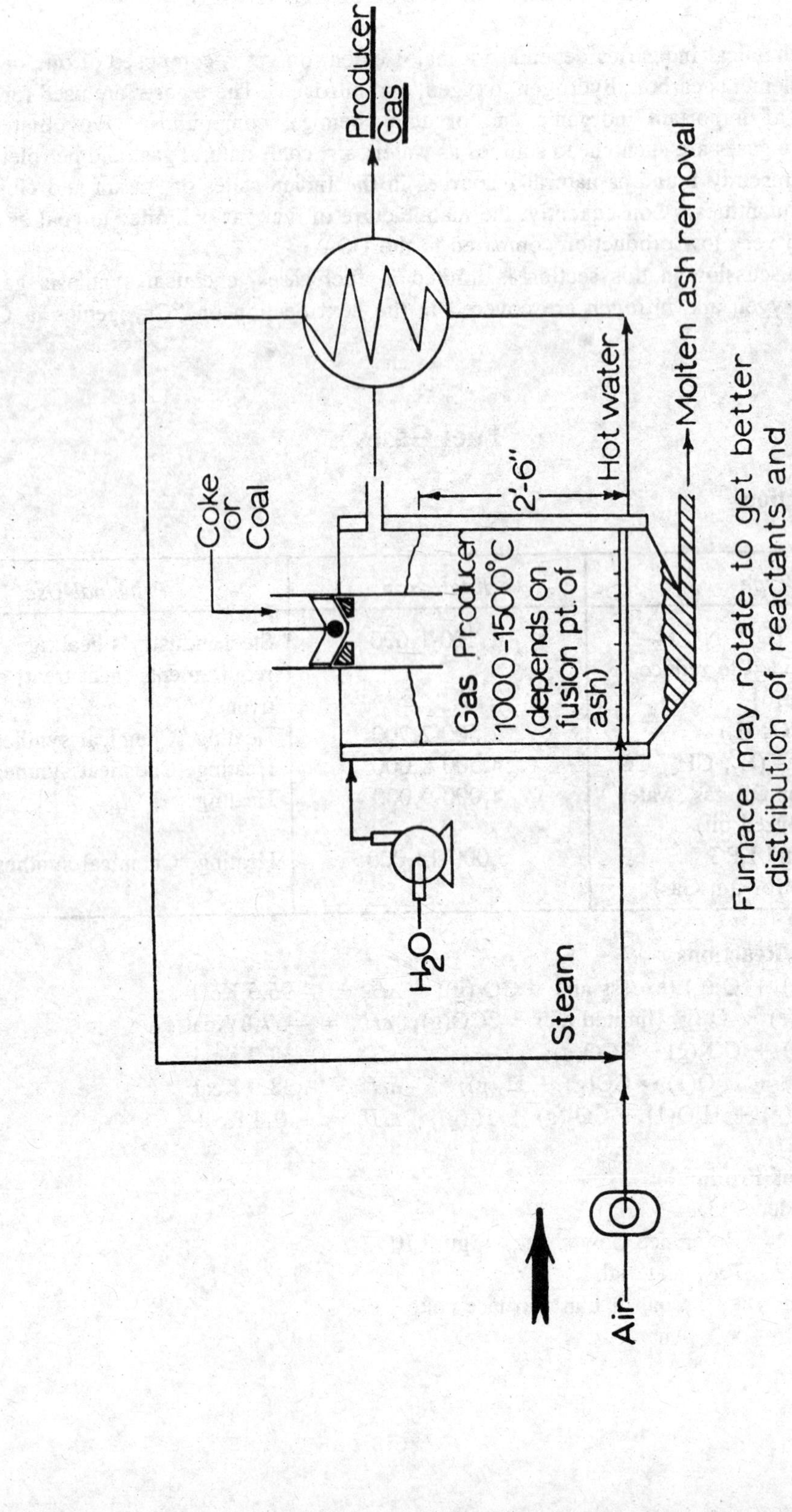

Fig. IIB-1. Manufacture of producer gas.

3.1.3. Quantitative requirements

(a) Basis: 100 Nm^3 of producer gas

Coke	20-25 kg
or Coal	25-30 kg
Air	60-80 Nm^3
Steam	8-10 kg

(b) Plant capacities: 25,000-250,000 cubic meters/day

3.1.4. Process description

Steam and air mixture injected in bottom of a water-cooled jacketed steel furnace equipped with a rotating grate to remove fusible ash. Solid fuel is added from hopper valve on top of furnace. Producer gas is cooled by passing through a waste heat boiler.

3.1.5. Major engineering problems

(a) Design of suitable gas producer furnace to:
- Keep uniform fuel surface
- Provide adequate gas-fuel contact time at high temperature
- Avoid clinkering and provide for proper fused ash removal

(b) Addition of correct steam quantities to supply net heat of reaction near zero on a continuous once-through process

3.2. Water Gas

3.2.1. Reference flow sheet: Figure IIB-2

3.2.2. Raw materials

Bituminous, anthracite coal, or coke

3.2.3. Quantitative requirements

(a) Basis: 100 cu m of water gas from C

C as coke	55 kg
or C as coal	58 kg
Air	220 Nm^3
Steam	80 kg

(b) Plant capacities: 250,000-1,500,000 Nm^3/day

3.2.4. Process description

- *Regenerative process*—older process consisting of two reactors, one operates on blow period which heats carbon by reaction 2(a), the other on a run period where endothermic reaction 2(d) occurs. The cycle of 4-6 minutes is divided as:

Blow or heat-up	35%	Downrun	33%
Uprun	30%	Short purge uprun	2%

Reactors or generators are steel with refractory lining. If higher BTU gas is required, an additional high-temperature carburetor section is required for pyrolyzing oil spray and mixing.

- *Continuous process*—newer process invented in 1940's by Germans. Based on use of tonnage or low purity grade oxygen made by air separation procedure. The correct ratio of steam, oxygen, and coal is added to the reactor to yield a self-sustaining reaction of approximately zero heat release. Subsequent innovations allow for ash content >30% so Indian coal can be used.

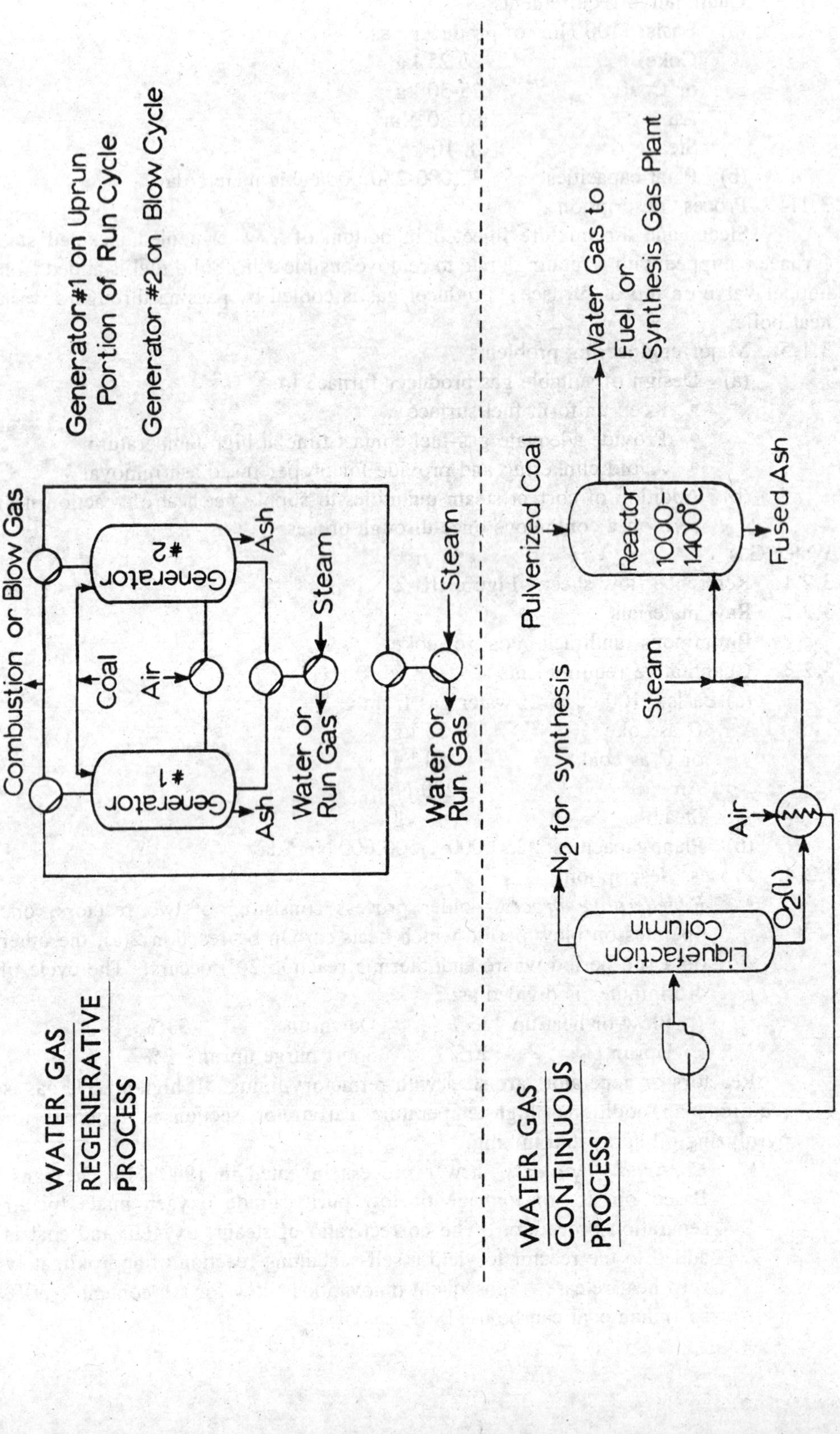

Fig. IIB-2. Water gas manufacturing processes.

3.2.5. Major engineering problems

(a) Designing suitable ash removal systems for various grades of coal in continuous processing

(b) Optimizing cycle for regenerative process

3.3. Coke Oven Gas

Because of a shortage of natural gas in India and the great demand for steel and chemical fertilizers, a combination plant producing these two products can be erected as done at Rourkela. The net result is a coke requirement for the blast furnace yielding coke oven gas which can be converted to NH_3 synthesis gas.

3.3.1. Reference flow sheet: Figure IIB-3

3.3.2. Process description

Upgraded coal for coking purposes is fed to a by-product coke oven which uses producer gas for heating the batch chamber to 1,000°C for 12-20 hours. Gas is removed continuously and put through a series of purification steps as shown in the flow sheet to produce coke oven gas.

If NH_3 synthesis gas is required, further purification including scrubbing with alkali to remove CO_2, liquefaction to remove light hydrocarbons and finally scrubbing with liquid N_2 to take out CO. The N_2 for scrubbing and make-up is obtained from a liquid air fractionation plant, the oxygen being used to purify pig iron and make high grade steel by the Linz and Donowitz (L and D) process.

3.3.3. Major engineering problems

- Obtaining suitable grades of coking coal in India. Washing, preroasting, and solvent extraction are some of the schemes used.
- Choice of scrubbing liquors for CO_2 and CO.

In the latter case, copper formate was too expensive so liquid N_2, already available, was specified even though it meant cryogenic design features (insulation, avoidance of moisture).

3.3.4. Economics of coke oven gas

The use of 1.8 x 10^6 m^3 of coke oven gas for ammonia synthesis plant to give about 500 tons of NH_3 per day at Rourkela is an indication of the importance of this type of gas in the Indian economy. This is so because of a lack of cheap natural gas. In the USA where the reverse is true, coke oven gas is used mostly as a heating source within the steel plant complex.

3.4. Natural Gas

The major portion of natural gas is used as an important raw material in the industrial chemical field. The subject will be discussed further under "Synthesis Gases."

3.4.1. Reference flow sheet: Figure IIB-4

3.4.2. Process description

Gas is pumped from natural gas and petroleum wells to drying units (absorption, adsorption or refrigerated compression). Separation of the heavy ends done by either absorption or liquefaction. Adsorption is not competitive for this operation.

The natural gas, containing over 95% CH_4 with the balance as ethane is next sent to purification units for removal of H_2S and other sulfides. Various absorption and chemical reaction methods are available with the ethanolamine absorption process in current favor.

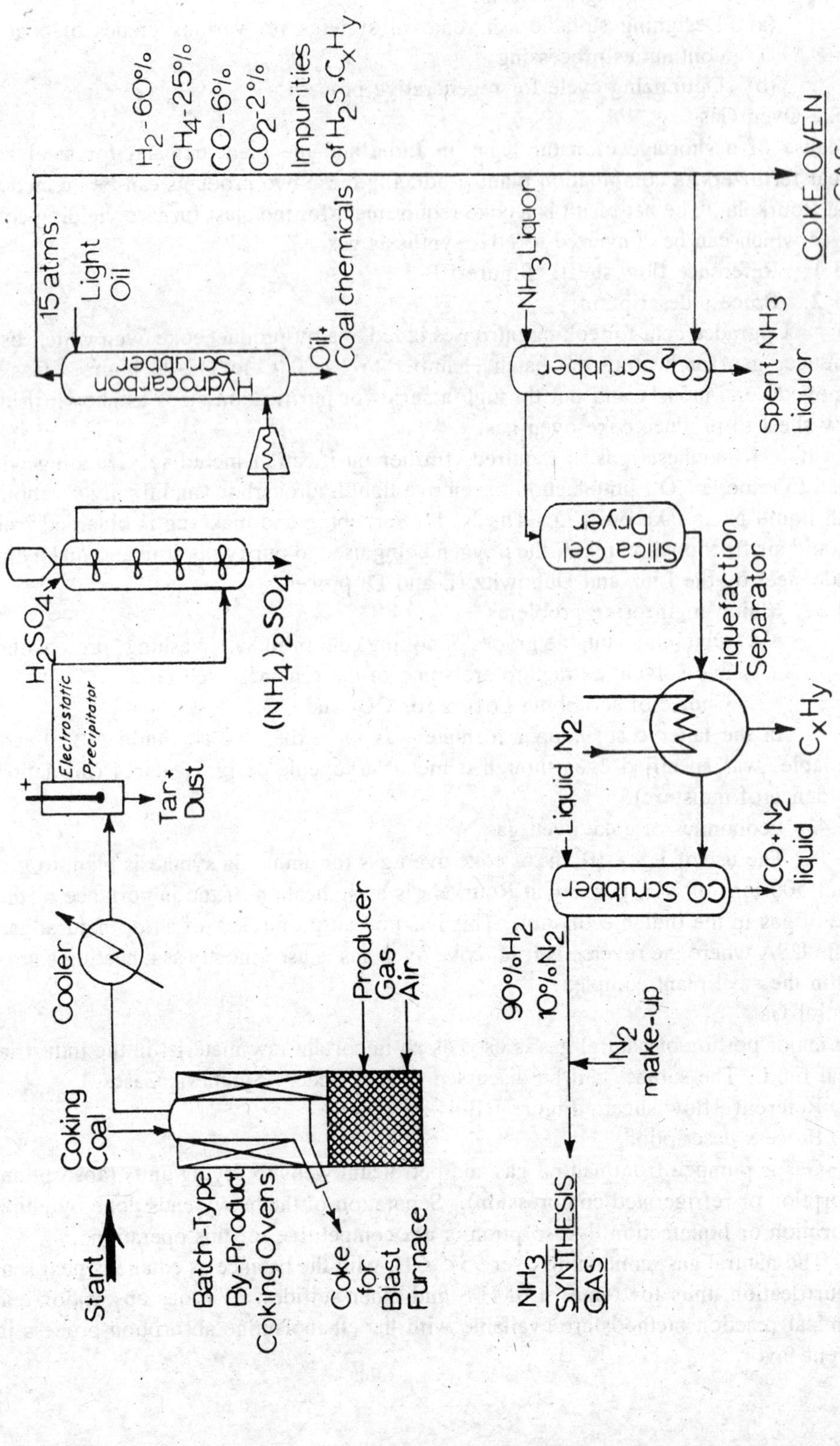

Fig. IIB-3. Coke oven gas plus derived NH_3 synthesis gas.

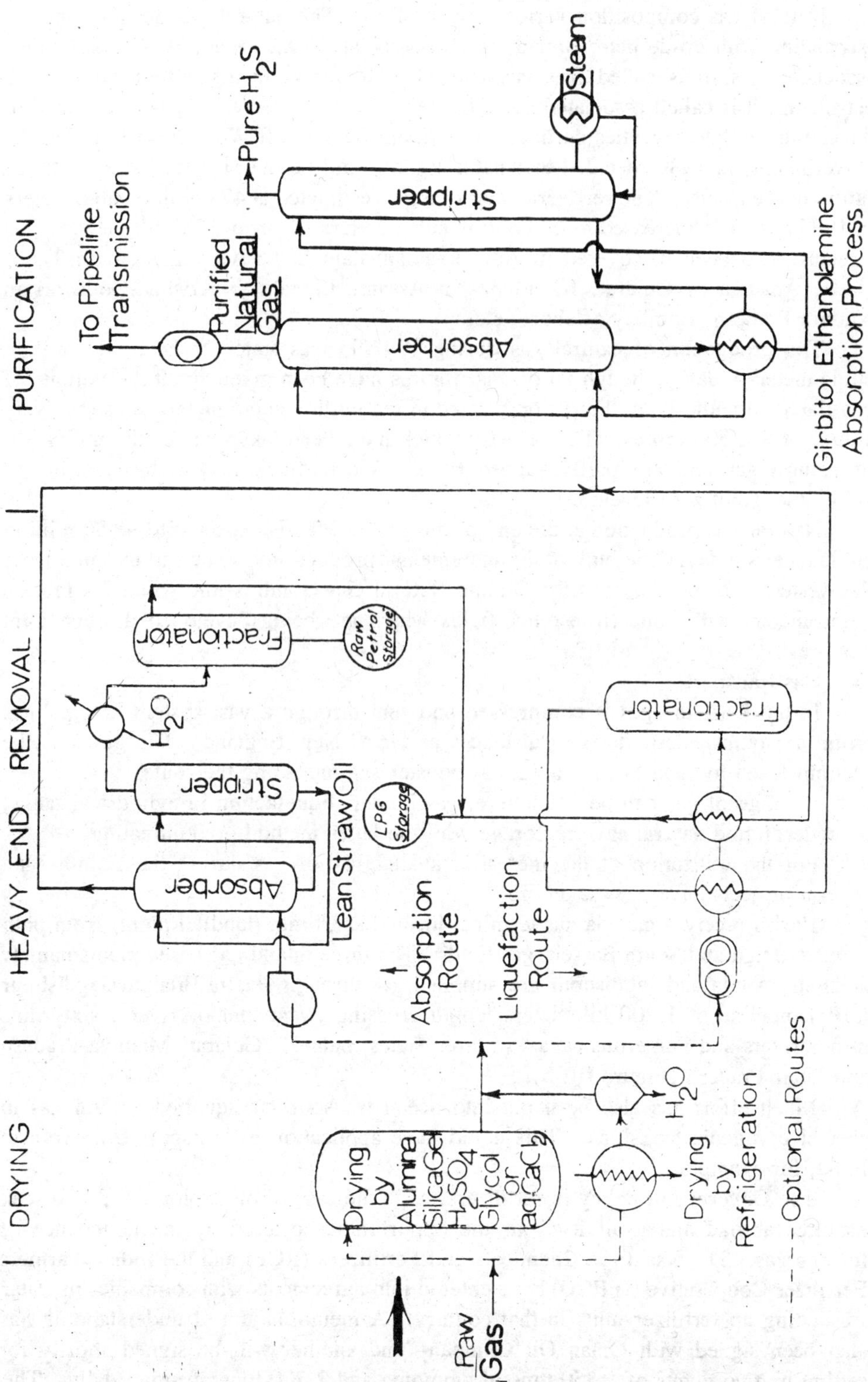

Fig. IIB-4. Natural gas and LPG treatment processes.

Natural gas composition varies with location. The natural gas occurs either in association with crude petroleum or as non-associated gas. When it occurs as non-associated gas, it is called free gas and when it occurs in association with crude petroleum, it is called associated gas. In view of large reserves of gas established in the country in late seventies particularly in South Bassein off West Coast in India, the Government, in 1980, decided that natural gas would be the preferred feedstock for future new capacity. The recoverable gas reserve estimated at 479 billion cubic meters in 1985 has since increased to 686 billion cubic meters. During 1989-90, new oil/gas structure had been discovered in Adiyakkamangalam in Cauvery Bassein in Tamil Nadu, Anadala in Gujarat, Khoraghot in Assam, Lingala in Krishna-Godavari in Andhra Pradesh, Bombay offshore, etc.

The production of natural gas during 1992-93 was stated to be 50.04 million cubic meters a day. Though no official figures have been given about the volume of gas flared, it could be in the region of nine to ten million cubic meters conservatively valued at Rs. 500 crores. The projects which have been taken up for the utilization of natural gas and are partly funded by the World Bank may reduce flaring to negligible if not zero levels.

Natural gas production at the end of the Eighth Plan is expected to be 80 million cubic meters a day. The bulk of the incremental production is expected to come from the western offshore fields of the Oil and Natural Gas Commission, while 7.4 million cubic meters will come from other fields which are being developed through joint ventures.

3.4.3. Gas transport

In the USA the gas is compressed and sent through a vast system of pipelines from the southwestern states to distances as far as New England. The gas must be recompressed by natural gas engines at booster stations along the route.

Storage of gas can be via sphere, gas holder, liquefaction in cylindrical tanks, or underground natural cavern storage with the latter method predominating.

For the utilization of the increased availability of gas during the Eighth Plan several projects have been taken up.

Hazira receives gas via gas terminal located at Ubrath (landfall point) from both Bombay High and South Bassein gas fields. The three inland gas-based plants namely Bijaipur, Aonla and Jagdishpur are supplied gas through Hazira-Bijaipur-Jagdishpur (HBJ) pipeline of 1,700 kilometers length crossing twenty major rivers, sixty-nine minor rivers and numerous canals in three states, namely, Gujarat, Madhya Pradesh and Uttar Pradesh (Figure IIB-5).

Much effort has also been put into ocean transport of liquefied natural gas in special cryogenic tankships. This could have application to transport from Iran to India, for example.

The Government policy in fertilizers, as in the case of oil exploration, is to seek pastures abroad and avail itself of the opportunities offered by the abundance of foreign gas. The Rashtriya Chemicals and Fertilizers (RCF) and the Indian Farmers Fertilizer Cooperative (IFFCO) have entered into agreements with companies in Qatar for setting up fertilizer units in that country. A memorandum of understanding has also been signed with Oman Oil Company and another will be signed shortly for setting up two plants of 1,350 tons of ammonia and 2,200 tons of urea daily. The

Center is also thinking of reaching an agreement with Iran for setting up plants of the same capacity. The foreign ventures will be financed by funds raised abroad.

3.5. Liquefied Petroleum Gases (LPG)

3.5.1. Reference flow sheet: Figure IIB-4

3.5.2. Process description

These gases are by-products from natural gas separation plants and petroleum refineries. They consist essentially of purified propane and butane in various mixtures. The propane fraction only is supplied for residential fuel in northern winter climates because of its lower boiling point.

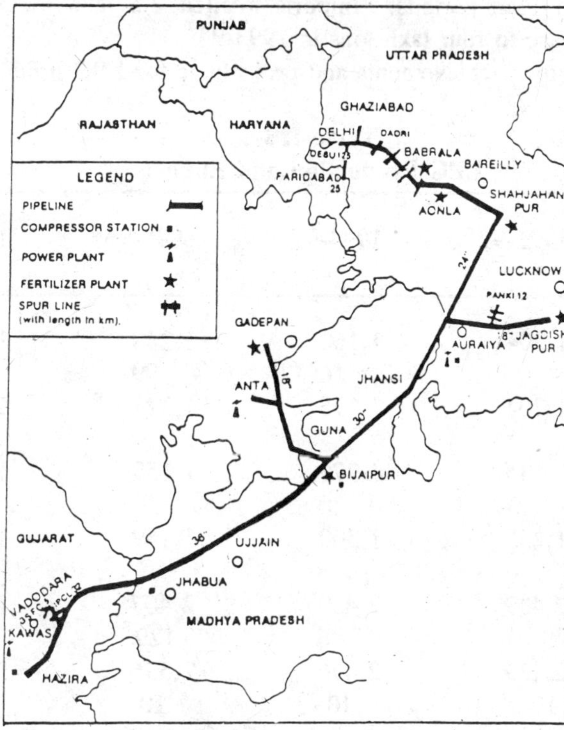

Fig. IIB-5. Hazira-Bijaipur-Jagdishpur pipeline from South Bassein.
Source: "Handbook on Fertiliser Technology" (1992)

The flow sheet indicates the possible physical steps used for separating moisture, H_2S and petrol. Drying can be either by adsorption or refrigeration; the heavy end removal by either absorption or refrigerated liquefaction. The choice depends on location and power costs. Natural gas as the overhead is stripped of H_2S in an ethanolamine absorption process.

3.5.3. LPG production

The indigenous availability of LPG is expected to increase from 2.57 million tons in 1992-93 to 2.83 million tons by 1996-97 and further to 3.89 million tons by 1999-2000. The additional availability is expected from new sources and augmentation of production capacity at some of the existing sources.

The demand is projected to increase to around 6.23 million tons by the turn of the century. There are plans to enroll twelve lakh new customers in 1993-94 and ten lakhs in 1994-95. During 1992-97 (Eighth Plan) it is proposed to enroll eighty lakh new customers. Apart from stepping up indigenous availability port facilities are also being expanded to facilitate imports.

LPG is now imported at Bombay and Visakhapatnam. In addition, two new import facilities of six lakh tons each will be set up at Kandla and Mangalore by the end of the Eighth Plan.

It is also proposed to build new import facilities at Haldia in West Bengal, Nhava-Sheva in Maharashtra, Okha/Sikka in Gujarat and Ennore in Tamil Nadu during the Eighth and Ninth Plan periods. Imports totalled 2.5 lakh tons in 1991-92 and are projected to increase to four lakh tons in 1993-94.

Table IIB-1 shows achievements and projections for LPG production and imports.

Table IIB-1
LPG Production and Imports

LPG Production	1991-92	1994-95*	1995-96*	1996-97 *(thousand tons)*
Refineries				
Existing	1,204	1,160	1,248	1,322
New	-	16	99	196
Subtotal	1,204	1,176	1,347	1,518
Fractionators				
Existing	1,235	1,270	1,159	1,212
New	0	30	30	102
Subtotal	1,235	1,300	1,189	1,314
Grand Total				
Existing	2,439	2,430	2,407	2,534
New	0	46	129	298
Total	2,439	2,476	2,536	2,832
Enrollment (in lakhs)	10.2	10	10	40
Resultant Demand (Packed + Bulk)	2,650	3,271	3,347	3,726
Possible Imports	215	600	600	900
Surplus/Deficit	4	−195	−211	6

*LPG production estimates for 1994-95 and 1995-96 are as per projections tabled by production sources. However, actual production is expected at higher level as per past experience.

Source: "The Hindu Survey of Indian Industry" (1994)

Synthesis Gases

1. Definition

Synthesis gas is generally considered to be a variable mixture of CO and H_2 for synthesis of organic compounds (see Table IIB-2). There are cases where CO is not needed and these specific cases are so labelled:

- Ammonia synthesis gas ($3H_2 + 1N_2$)
- Hydrogenation of coal (H_2 only)

Note that all synthesis gases contain hydrogen.

Table IIB-2
Reactions Using CO-H_2 Synthesis Gas

Synthesis Process	*CO/H_2 Ratio*	*Catalysts*	*Temp. °C*	*Press. atms.*	*Products*
Methane	-	Ni	250-500	1	CH_4
Fischer-Tropsch	0.5-2.0	Co, Ni, Fe	180-300	1-30	Paraffinic and olefinic hydrocarbons varying from methane to waxes, plus small quantities of oxygenated products
Synol	0.3-0.5	Fe	185-225	15-30	Chiefly straight chain normal alcohols
Methanol	0.3	ZnO, CuO, Cr_2O_3	250-350	100-300	Methanol (CH_3OH)
Higher alcohol synthesis		Fe+alkali	400-500	100-300	Alcohols from C_1 to C_n
Isosynthesis	0.5	ThO_2, ZnO, Al_2O_3	400-450	100-300	Saturated branched hydrocarbons
Oxosynthesis (uses olefins as additional starting material)	1.2	Cobalt $[Co(CO)_4]_2$	150-200	150-200	Oxygenated hydrocarbons, aldehydes and alcohols

2. Consumption Pattern

- Table IIB-2 illustrates some of the products from synthesis gas in addition to a major production of ammonia and hydrogenation compounds. Over 90% of all H_2 manufactured in India is used for NH_3 production.
- A number of specific uses for synthesis gases will be discussed in the sections which follow (*e.g.*, ammonia, petrochemicals).

3. Methods of Production

3.1. Classification of Processes

3.1.1. From petroleum hydrocarbons

- Reforming
- Partial combustion

3.1.2. From coal or coke

- Water gas
- Coke oven gas

} see Fuel Gas Section

Refinery operations in India are such that large quantities of naphtha are available for synthesis gas and petrochemical primary materials such as acetylene, ethylene, propylene, butylene, and butadiene. We will discuss processes which produce high yields of definite compounds in Chapter IV. These processes involve thermal pyrolysis of C_2 and higher saturates in the presence of steam, with or without O_2. The term cracking has also been applied to such processes, *e.g.*, naphtha cracking.

3.2. Reforming of Hydrocarbons by Steam

3.2.1. Reference flow sheet: Figure IIB-6

Based on ICI steam-naphtha reforming process

3.2.2. Chemical reactions

- Reforming reactions

(a) $C_nH_{2n+2} + nH_2O \overset{Ni}{\rightleftharpoons} nCO + (2n+1)\,H_2;\quad \Delta H° = +\,52$ Kcal for $n = 1$, $+\,238$ Kcal for $n = 6$

(b) $CO + 3H_2 \rightleftharpoons CH_4 + H_2O;\quad \Delta H° = -52.0$ Kcal

- Water gas shift reaction

(c) $CO + 3H_2 \overset{FeO}{\rightleftharpoons} CO_2 + H_2;\quad \Delta H = -9.806$ Kcal

3.2.3. Raw materials

- Refinery naphtha or off-gases
- Air (optional)
- Steam
- Small make-up quantities of nickel and promoted iron oxide catalyst, ethanolamines, and ammoniacal cuprous formate

3.2.4. Quantitative requirements

(a) Basis: 100 Nm^3 of hydrogen of 99.+ % purity

Naphtha	21.9 kg
Steam	560 kg

(A) Reforming for preparation of synthesis gas containing H_2 with or without CO.

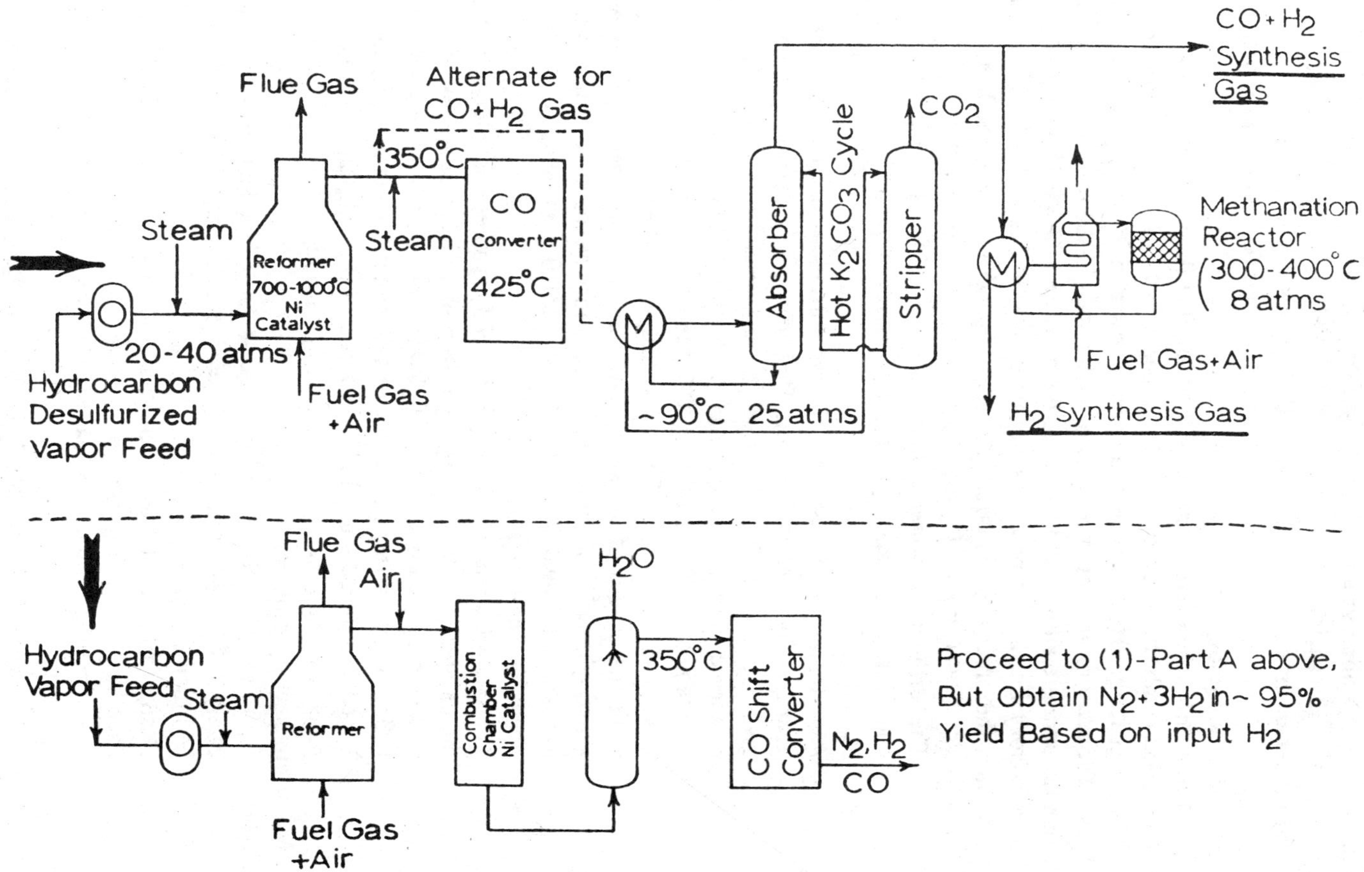

(B) Reforming for preparation of ammonia synthesis gas.

Fig. IIB-6. Steam reforming process for synthesis gas.

Fuel (as naphtha)	22.3 kg
Cooling water	6.5 tons
Electricity	1.4 KWH
(b) Plant capacities:	10-200 tons/day of H_2
	80,000-1,680,000 Nm^3/day of synthesis gas

3.2.5. Process description

The hydrocarbon feed is mixed with steam and fed to the reforming furnace. The nickel catalyst is packed in vertical tubes of 3-4 inches in diameter and about 20-25 feet long. Heat for the endothermic reaction is supplied by combustion gas. The reaction temperature must be maintained in the range of 700-1,000°C; high temperature alloy steel is used for the tubes and the steel wall of the furnace is refractory lined. A space velocity of 500-600/hr is maintained. After the reformer, the process takes three alternates depending on end-products.

- *For CO-H_2 synthesis gas*
  The effluent reformer gas is cooled to 35°C and pumped to a hot potassium carbonate scrubbing system to remove CO_2.
- *For H_2 gas*
  A water-gas shift converter is used to remove CO and form more hydrogen by reaction 3.2.2(c). Reformer gas is quenched with steam to give 350°C input gas to a catalytic converter using iron oxide catalyst promoted with chromium oxide. A space velocity of 100-200/hr is maintained. After scrubbing CO_2, the traces of CO are removed by methanation reaction. For high purity hydrogen (99.9%), one or two additional stages of the shift converter, CO_2 absorber combination are added with either ammoniacal cuprous formate or molecular sieves used to remove residual CO and CO_2 down to 10 ppm or less.
- *For NH_3 synthesis gas*
  The correct amount of nitrogen for NH_3 synthesis is added via air and the oxygen is burned out by hydrogen in a nickel catalyzed combustion chamber inserted immediately following the reformer. Gases are cooled to 350°C by a water quench tower and then passed to the shift converter. Except for the additional N_2 which passes through, the remainder of the process is the same as for hydrogen preparation.

3.2.6. Major engineering problems

(a) Sulfur contamination of reforming catalyst. Naphtha must be purified by catalytic hydrogen treatment to remove sulfur to yield a vapor feed of less than 5 ppm sulfur.

(b) Design of an efficient reformer furnace to economically supply endothermic heat of reaction.

(c) Avoid carbon formation on catalyst by use of highly specific catalyst (ICI patents).

(d) Removal of CO_2 and CO. The bulk of the CO_2 is absorbed by either potassium carbonate or monoethanolamine (MEA). The latter requires more heat, but has higher driving force for absorption giving smaller towers.

Final traces of CO and CO_2 can be removed by methanation reactions, the reverse of reforming.

$$\left.\begin{array}{l} CO_2 + 4H_2 \rightleftharpoons CH_4 + 2H_2O \\ CO + 3H_2 \rightleftharpoons CH_4 + H_2O \end{array}\right\} \begin{array}{l} \text{300-400°C, 8-10 atms.} \\ \text{Nickel catalyst} \end{array}$$

The disadvantage is use of H_2 and generation of methane impurity. For higher purity hydrogen, use ammonium cuprous formate or molecular sieves at increased cost.

3.3. Partial Combustion

3.3.1. Reference flow sheet: Figure IIB-7

3.3.2. Chemical reactions

$$CH_4 + 2O_2 \rightarrow CO_2 + 2H_2O$$
$$CH_4 + H_2O \rightarrow CO + 3H_2$$
$$CH_4 + CO_2 \rightarrow 2CO + 2H_2$$

Net reaction : $3CH_4 + 2O_2 \rightarrow 3CO + H_2O + 5H_2;\ \Delta H \cong 0$

The CO : H_2 ratio can be lowered by adding extra steam to give the water gas shift reaction:

$$CO + H_2O \rightleftharpoons CO_2 + H_2$$

3.3.3. Raw materials

- Lower purity natural gas than required for steam reforming; can use cheap liquid hydrocarbons also
- Tonnage oxygen (low-purity grade)
- Steam
- Small make-up quantities of promoted iron oxide shift converter catalyst, ethanolamines, and ammoniacal cuprous formate

3.3.4. Quantitative requirements

(a) Basis: 100 Nm^3 of hydrogen of 99.+ % purity

Naphtha	29.2 kg or methane (35 Nm^3)
Steam	104 kg
Oxygen	26 Nm^3
Cooling water	8 tons
Electricity	0.7 KWH

(b) Plant capacities: 10-200 tons/day of H_2
100,000-1,600,000 Nm^3/day of synthesis gas

3.3.5. Process description

Hydrocarbon feed and oxygen are preheated separately, mixed at 550°C and fed to a burner in a refractory-lined furnace labelled gas generator. After water quench from 1,100°C to 430°C, the gas can take three alternate routes:

- *H_2 route*

Steam is mixed with product gas and fed to shift converter to produce more H_2 from CO. Amine absorption of CO_2 is followed by caustic scrubbing. Traces of CO and CO_2 can be removed by either ammoniacal cuprous formate or liquid nitrogen scrubbing. The purified hydrogen can be used as is or mixed with gaseous nitrogen from the air separation plant for NH_3 synthesis.

- *CO + H_2 route*

The shift converter is bypassed and only amine scrubbing to remove CO_2 is utilized.

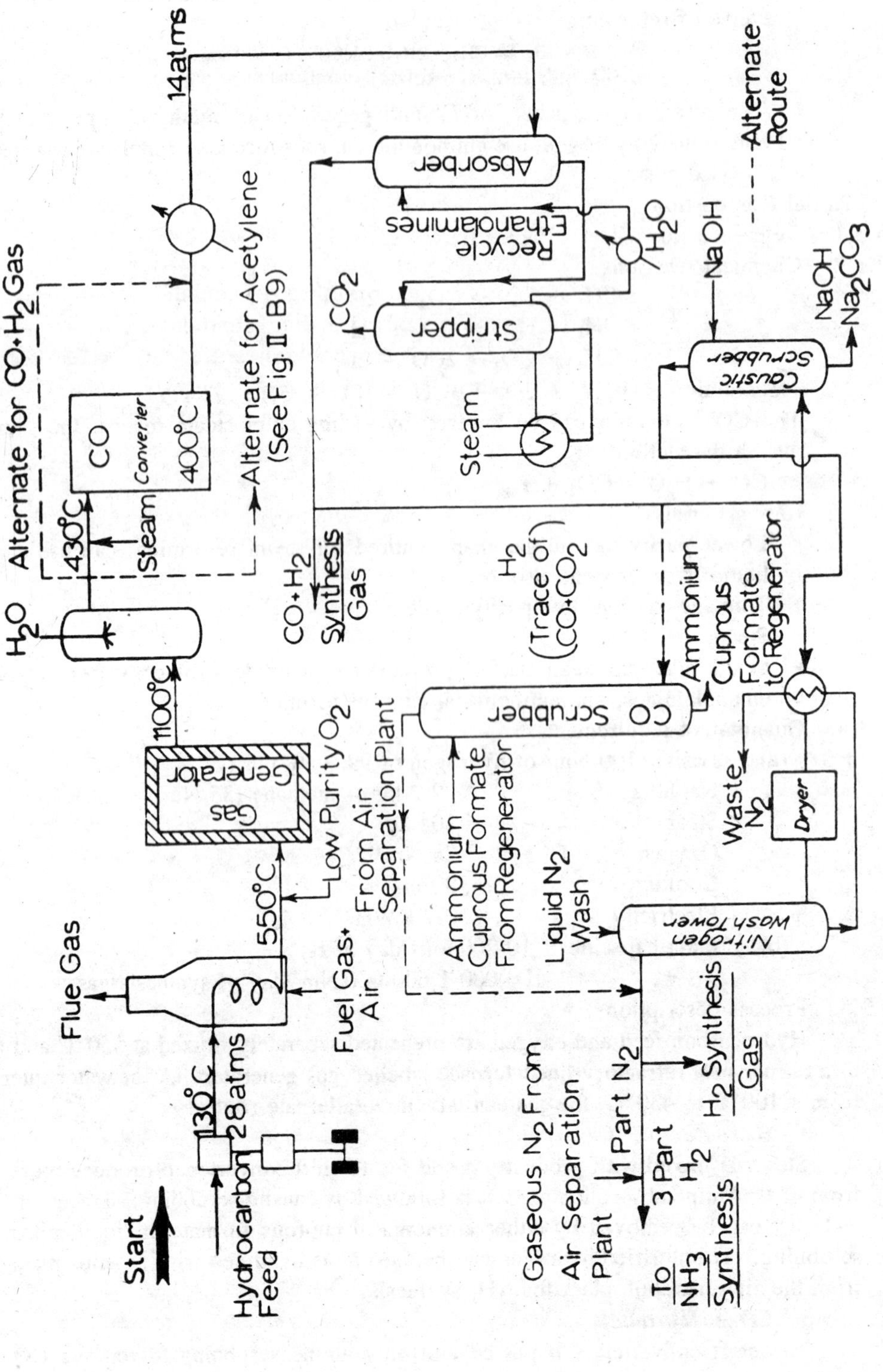

Fig. IIB-7. Partial combustion process for synthesis gas.

- *Acetylene route*

In some cases the gas generator is optimized for acetylene production. In this case the product gas is treated with dimethyl formamide to remove acetylene and polymers before further CO-H_2 processing.

3.3.6. Major engineering problems

(a) Correct design of burner for flame stabilization in gas generator

(b) Removal of trace impurities of CO and CO_2

(c) Handling deposited carbon

4. **Economics**

4.1. CO-H_2 synthesis gas plants by either steam reforming or partial combustion are competitive. The trend in the USA now favors partial combustion because of the high cost of hydrocarbon fuel and inefficient heat transfer in the reforming furnace. The continually lowered cost of tonnage oxygen and the production of acetylene as valuable by-product are additional incentives.

Steam reforming is making a strong comeback with improved metallurgy of reformer tubes permitting advantageous use of pressurized feeds. This process is favored in India at present when using naphtha feedstock.

4.2. By-product H_2 from petroleum refinery catalytic reforming units is now considered competitive with processes already discussed. As much as 1,400 tons (15 x 10^6 Nm^3) of H_2 per day are produced from a total available catalytic reformer capacity of 1 x 10^6 bbl. per day; much of this hydrogen is being used for captive ammonia synthesis at refinery locations.

Acetylene

1. **Pertinent Properties of Acetylene**

Mol. wt.	26.02	
Triple point	—80.6°C and 961.5 mm Hg pressure	
B.P.	—84°C	
Ignition point	305°C	
Explosive limits:	Lower = 2.3% volume in air	(The widest limits for any
	Upper = 80% volume in air	hydrocarbon)

Acetylene, either as liquid or as gas, is highly explosive since it is an endothermic compound and decomposition into the elements ($C_2H_2 \rightarrow 2C + H_2$) can be initiated even in the absence of air by heat or mechanical shock; once initiated, decomposition proceeds with explosive violence. Gas cylinder storage requires the addition of a mutual solvent (*e.g.*, acetone) and a porous inert material (*e.g.*, asbestos) as a safe release carrier.

2. **Consumption Pattern** (see Table IIB-3)

Table IIB-3
Acetylene Use in the USA and Western Europe (in wt.%)

Product	USA			Western Europe	
	1982	1985	1989	1982	1987
Vinyl chloride	43	31	45	33	31
1,4-Butanediol	28	47	40	12	13
Vinyl acetate	17	-	-	10	18
Acetylene	8	14	15	45	38
Miscellaneous (*e.g.*, trichloroethylene, etc.)	4	8	15	45	38
Total use (in '000 tons)	115	80	122	ca. 320	330

Neoprene and acrylonitrile have decreased in importance as consumers of acetylene.
Source: "Industrial Organic Chemistry" by Weissermel et al (1993)

3. Methods of Production

3.1. Classification of Processes

3.1.1. From petroleum hydrocarbons

- Partial or stage-wise combustion
- Pyrolysis
- Arc process

3.1.2. From calcium carbide

The classic manufacture of acetylene based on calcium carbide is of significantly decreasing importance.

Calcium carbide production (in '000 tons) has been as follows:

	1985	1987	1989
Russia	609	591	532
Japan	445	354	344
USA	209	209	242

3.2. Acetylene from Partial or Stage-wise Combustion of Hydrocarbons

3.2.1. Reference flow sheet: Figure IIB-8

3.2.2. Chemical reactions

- Exothermic heat supply

  (a) $CH_4 + 2O_2 \rightarrow CO_2 + 2H_2O$; $\Delta H° = -212.798$ Kcal
- Endothermic production reaction

  (b) $2CH_4 \rightarrow C_2H_2 + 3H_2$; $\Delta H° = +89.97$ Kcal
- Undesirable side reaction

  (c) $C_2H_2 \rightarrow 2C + H_2$; $\Delta H° = -54.194$ Kcal

3.2.3. Raw materials

- Low purity natural gas or higher mol. wt. hydrocarbons

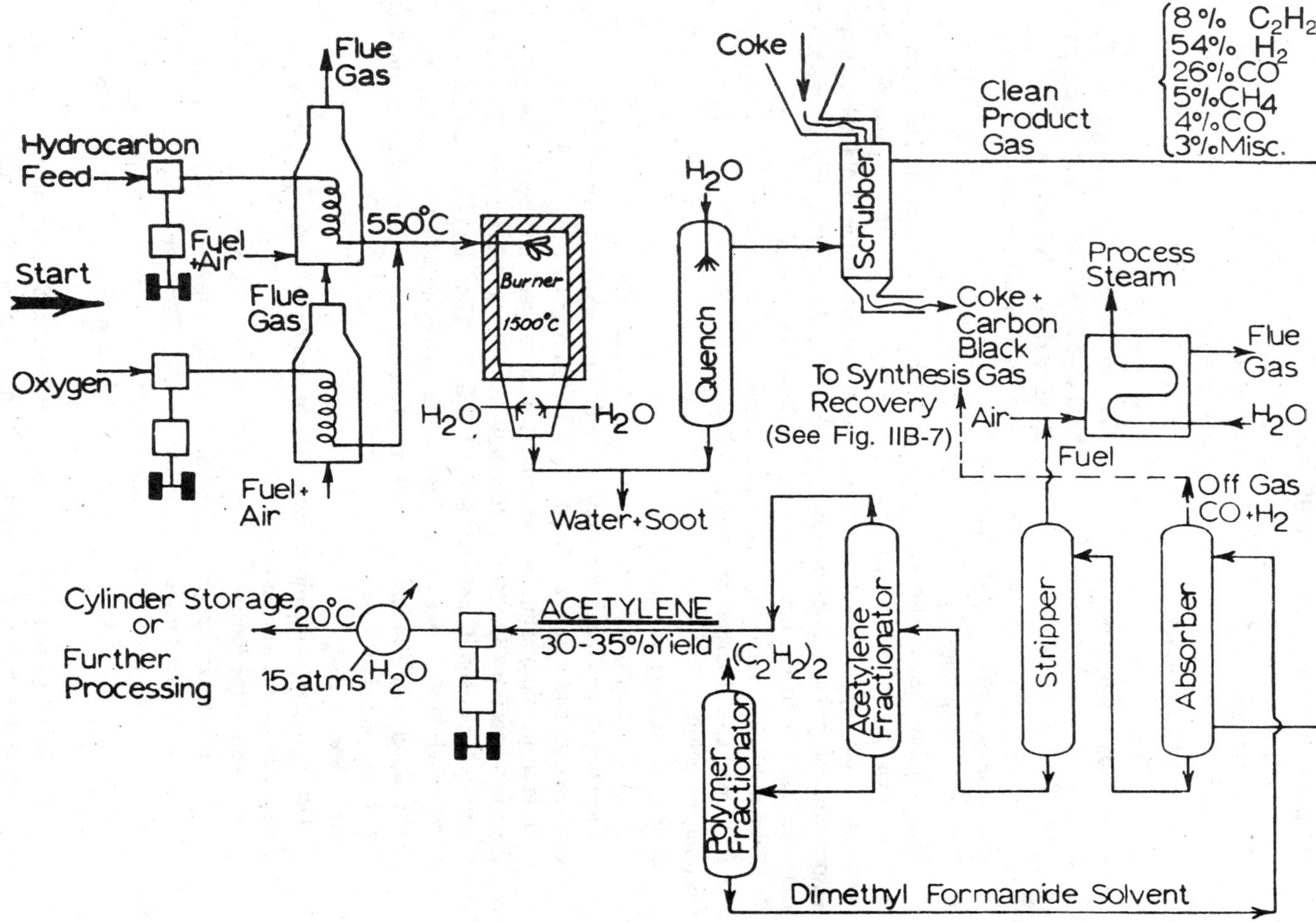

Fig. IIB-8. Acetylene from partial combustion of hydrocarbons (Sachsse process).

- Tonnage low-purity grade oxygen

3.2.4. Quantitative requirements

(a) Basis: 1 ton of acetylene (99% purity—35% yield)

Natural gas	5,200 cu m (STP) or naphtha = 4.1 tons
Oxygen (95%)	4.7 tons
Electricity	350 KWH
Process steam	12 tons
Water	1,100 tons
By-product yields:	900 cu m (STP) of off-gas @ 3,000 Kcal/cu m—can be used for synthesis gas
	20 kg carbon polymers
	5 kg acetylene polymers

(b) Plant capacities: 10-60 tons/day

3.2.5. Process description

Hydrocarbon feed and low purity oxygen are heated separately to 550°C and fed to an acetylene production burner which can be designed for one-stage or two-stage operation. The hydrocarbon is cracked to acetylene at the 1,500°C operating temperature and product gases are quenched immediately to avoid undue pyrolysis of acetylene. The residence time is less than 100 milliseconds.

Carbon black is removed in the water quench and on a moving bed. Acetylene and its dimer are absorbed in cold dimethyl formamide and then stripped in a fractionating column.

3.2.6. Major engineering problems

(a) Thermodynamic and kinetic considerations

The clue to obtaining commercial yields of acetylene to provide the correct environment and time scale for the series reactions 3.2.2(b) and 3.2.2(c).

From a thermodynamic equilibrium standpoint, the endothermic hydrocarbon pyrolysis reaction 3.2.2(b) is favorable at high temperatures. The rate of pyrolysis is not significant until about 1,300°C. Thus the clue to a good design is to provide rapid heat-up to induce the pyrolysis and then quench to low temperatures again before the back reaction and the side reaction to produce $C+H_2$ become significant.

(b) Burner design

Developing a workable burner was the major engineering problem. Two basic designs are currently used:

- *One-stage burner*

The entire hydrocarbon feed and oxygen, preheated to 550°C, are mixed and fed to the burner throat at high velocities. Flame stabilization is important, *i.e.*, the flame must have positioned, intense combustion to produce correct temperature, and the high temperature residence time must be uniform for all molecules.

The amount of oxygen is kept below that needed for complete combustion; only combustion takes place to the extent necessary to provide sensible heat and endothermic heat of formation for acetylene at reaction.

- *Two-stage burner*

A portion of the hydrocarbon is mixed with sufficient oxygen for complete combustion to supply heat requirements. As hot gases leave the flame zone to enter the reaction chamber, the balance of the hydrocarbon is injected into the hot gases which heat and pyrolyze the hydrocarbon molecules to acetylene and side products. The sensible heat of the combustion gas is thus used from combustion temperature of 2,000°C down to the lower cracking limit of 1,300°C.

The combustion fuel can be different from the reactant fuel and steam may be injected to increase equilibrium yield possibilities.

Individual burner capacities are rated for as much as 15 tons of acetylene per hour.

(c) Separation of polymers and purification of acetylene

(d) Design for explosion-proof plant operation

3.3. Pyrolysis of Hydrocarbons (Wulff Process)

3.3.1. Reference flow sheet: Figure IIB-9

3.3.2. Chemical reactions

- For several commercial hydrocarbon feeds

Propane

(a) $C_3H_8 \xrightarrow{\text{steam}} CH = CH + C_2H_4 + CH_4 + CO + H_2 + CO_2$

Ethylene

(b) $C_2H_4 \xrightarrow{\text{steam}} CH = CH + H_2 + CO + CO_2 + CH_4$

Methane

(c) $2CH_4 \xrightarrow{\text{steam}} CH = CH + 3H_2 + CO + CH_4$

3.3.3. Raw materials

- Low purity natural gas or higher mol. wt. hydrocarbons
- Steam for dilution and process heat

3.3.4. Quantitative requirements

(a) Basis: 1 ton of acetylene (99% purity—35% yield)

Natural gas	4,700 Nm^3
Steam (40 atms.)	27 tons
Electricity	400 KWH
Cooling water	900 tons
Make-up solvent in absorbers	3 kg
By-product yields:	4,500 Nm^3 of off-gas @ 2,650 Kcal/m^3
	0.17 ton of tar

By changing operating conditions, appreciable yields of ethylene for petrochemical processing can be obtained in place of acetylene.

(b) Plant capacities: 10-40 tons/day

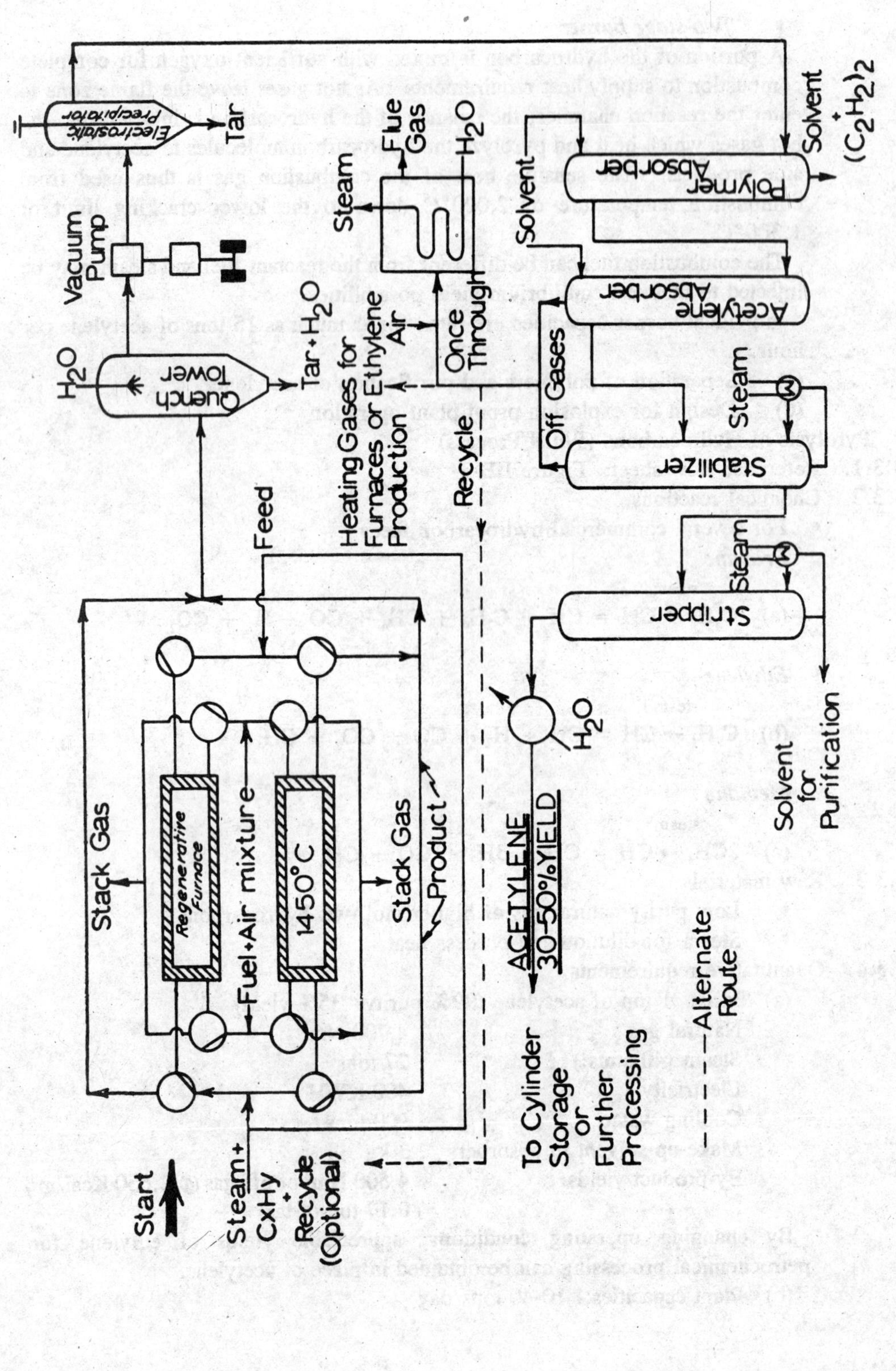

Fig. IIB-9. Acetylene from pyrolysis of hydrocarbons (Wulff process).

3.3.5. Process description

Hydrocarbon feed plus diluent steam (~$7H_2O/1$ ratio) to improve equilibrium yield is fed to a set of regenerative furnaces operating in pairs on a 1-1.5 minute cycle.

The furnace is designed with brick refractory walls and internal checkwork. The furnace is heated on the "blow run" with fuel-air mixture. After this heat-up period, the valves are switched to the "make run" position, and pyrolysis feedstock is vaporized into the same end of the furnace for the 1-1.5 minute period. The cycle is repeated again using the other end of the furnace so all flows are reversed from the previous cycle. The other furnace in the paired system operates on a staggered cycle so continuous production of acetylene is possible.

Pressure maintained in the furnace is 0.5-0.6 atmosphere by means of vacuum pumps after the quench tower. Note that a better equilibrium yield is obtained at low pressure. Residence time in the furnace is 0.02-0.04 second.

Separation of off-gases and polymers from acetylene is similar to the partial combustion operation.

3.3.6. Major engineering problems

(a) Optimizing yield by correct furnace design and operation. Same thermodynamic and kinetic problems as in partial combustion process. Steam dilution more feasible in the Wulff process because of the independent heat-up cycle.

(b) Purification of acetylene

(c) Design for explosion-proof plant

3.4. Acetylene from Calcium Carbide

3.4.1. Reference flow sheet: Figure IIB-10

3.4.2. Chemical reactions

(a) $CaO + 3C \rightarrow CaC_2 + CO;$ $\Delta H = +111$ Kcal

(b) $CaC_2 + H_2O \rightarrow Ca(OH)_2 + CH \equiv CH;$ $\Delta H = -30$ Kcal

(c) $CaCO_3 \rightarrow CaO + CO_2;$ $\Delta H = +44$ Kcal

(d) $2CO + O_2 \rightarrow 2CO_2;$ $\Delta H = -135$ Kcal

3.4.3. Raw materials

For calcium carbide production, a stable supply of limestone, coke and cheap electric power are required in addition to process water to complete the reaction to acetylene. The lime should be low in S and P, otherwise H_2S and phosphine are produced with acetylene and these give trouble in subsequent processing.

3.4.4. Quantitative requirements

(a) Basis: 1 ton of acetylene (99% purity)

$CaCO_3$	5.5 tons
Water	33 tons (wet process)
	3 tons (dry process)

(b) Plant capacities: 3-30 tons/day of acetylene

3.4.5. Process description

Lime is produced in a fuel-fired limestone kiln. The lump product is ground with coke in a 60/40 ratio to about 5 cm lump size and reacted in an electric furnace at 2,100°C. The gaseous effluent, mostly CO, is recovered for lime kiln fuel. The molten CaC_2 is solidified and ground under nitrogen to avoid explosion of acetylene

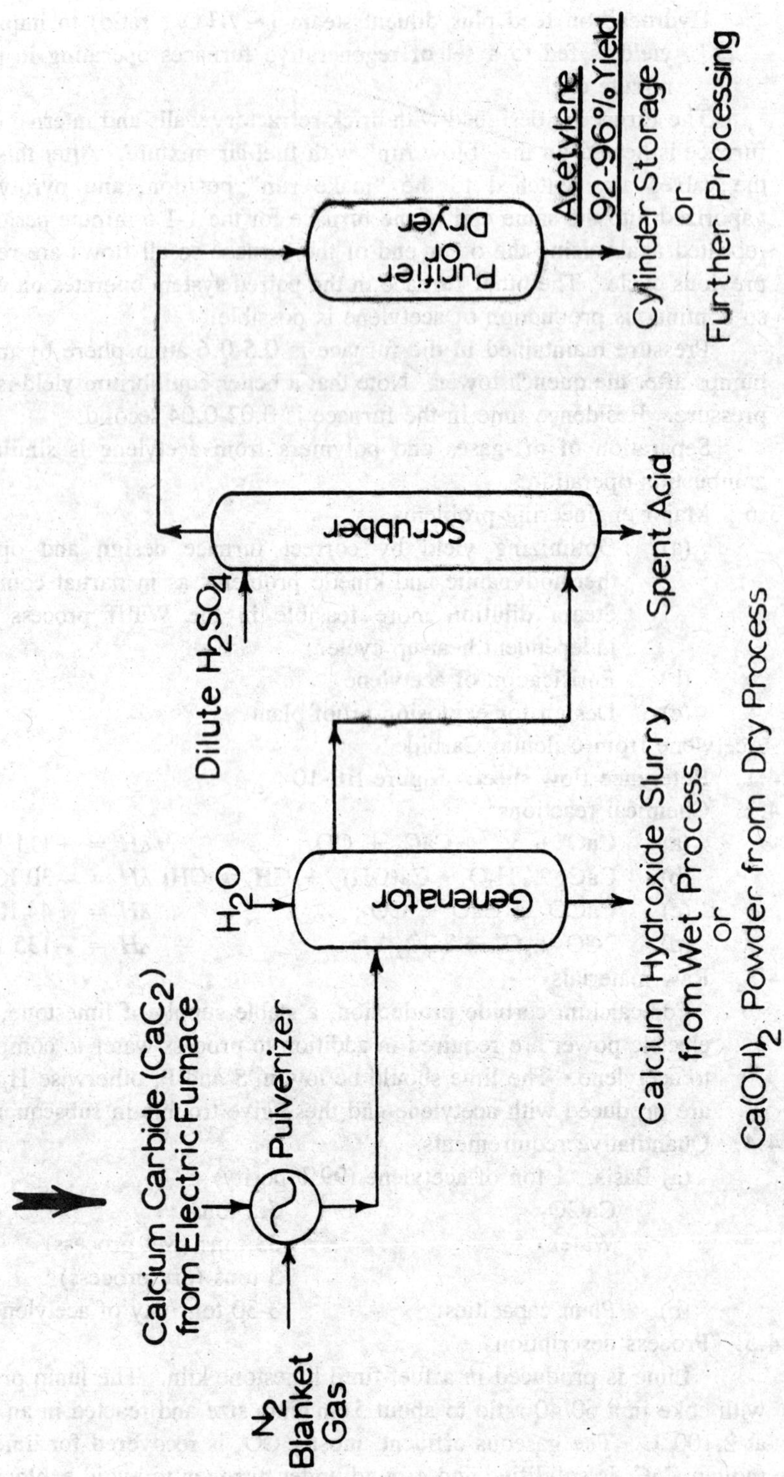

Fig. IIB-10. Acetylene from calcium carbide.

released by moist air.

Two methods for release of acetylene from CaC_2 by water are currently in use:

- *Wet process*

  Pulverized carbide is added through a gas tight hopper valve arrangement to the acetylene gas generator in which the quantity of water used is sufficient to discharge the calcium hydroxide as a lime slurry containing 85-90% water which is usually lagooned. The temperature is kept below 90°C and 2 atms. in the gas generator.

  The impure C_2H_2 from the generator, which contains traces of ammonia, sulfides, and phosgene, is scrubbed with acid solution. It is then further purified and dried with iron-oxide and alumina or silica gel.

- *Dry process*

  To eliminate the waste disposal problem with lime slurry, the dry process uses only equal weight quantities of H_2O to CaC_2. This 80% excess water over stoichiometric equivalent is removed by the heat of reaction to produce acetylene. An essentially dry lime is available for reuse as a lime source.

  The dry process is inherently more dangerous because of temperature control in the generator, particularly as regards local hot spots. The average generator conditions are maintained below 150°C and 30 cm of water pressure. Local temperature rise is avoided by good distribution and mixing.

3.4.6. Major engineering problems

(a) Choice of lime
(b) Avoidance of contact of CaC_2 with moisture or moist air during storage and grinding
(c) Temperature and pressure control in generators, especially in the dry process
(d) Purification of generator gas before further use
(e) Waste disposal of lime residue from generator

4. Economics

4.1. Choice of Process

- Carbide plants are only economical at a plant location supplying cheap power, ample limestone, and adequate waste disposal facilities. This is particularly true for Indian conditions at present.
- Hydrocarbon processes not subject to above limitations. Choice among processes using hydrocarbons is very close.
  (1) Slight advantage to partial combustion where off-gases can be used for high-value synthetic chemical manufacture.
  (2) All thermal processes presently suffer from high cost of recovery and purification of acetylene in low concentration product gas. This is not true of the arc process where steam dilution is avoided and high C_2H_2 yields occur. Commercial development of the arc process by Huels in Germany and DuPont in USA has proven possibly competitive in areas of cheap electric power.

4.2. Market and Sales Problems

- Many chemicals can be made from alternate starting materials, particularly ethylene.
  - (1) Ultimate cost by the various routes dictates the choice with ethylene-based processes moving well ahead
  - (2) Ethylene preferred for acetaldehyde, acetic acid, and vinyl acetate; propylene preferred for acrylonitrile
  - (3) Acetylene now used for chlorinated compounds: tri- and perchlorethylene, vinyl chloride and neoprene
- New product chemicals developing, including butyrolactone and vinyl pyrrolidone and its polymers.

Olefins have replaced acetylene as a raw material, especially for numerous monomers. The olefins are more available (and thus more economical) and easier to handle than acetylene.

By way of example, the large decrease in the fraction of important industrial chemicals derived from acetylene between 1965 and 1980 in the USA is shown in the following table:

Table IIB-4
Production of Industrial Chemicals Based on Acetylene and Olefins in the USA (in '000 tons)

	Acetylene Based				Olefin Based		
	1965	1974	1980	1987	1974	1980	1987
Vinyl chloride	159	59	50	73	2,490	2,890	3,657
Acrylonitrile	91	-	-	-	640	830	1,157
Chloroprene	82	-	-	-	144	200	110
Vinyl acetate	64	32	23	-	604	848	1,137
Miscellaneous (1,4-Butanediol, THF, acrylic acid/esters, etc.)	68	91	46	60			

Source: "Industrial Organic Chemistry" by Weissermel et al (1993)

IIC. CRYOGENICS IN CHEMICAL TECHNOLOGY

Cryogenics deals with the production and utilization of low temperatures in the region from absolute zero to 123°K. Oxygen and nitrogen form a major portion of the cryogenics industry; other gases of commercial purity prepared by cryogenic methods are:

- Noble gases (helium, argon, krypton, xenon, neon)
- Hydrogen

Cryogenic engineering has received a big boost in past years due to large scale inputs of funds into the development of intercontinental ballistic missile systems, and into space exploration, by the two super powers, USA and Russia. Cryogenic phenomena are applied to computers, gyroscopes, superconductors, nuclear fusion power, etc. Applications are also found in food preservation, preservation of blood, marrow, and even human organs. Cryogenic products are used in chemical and metallurgical process industries.

Liquefaction of Gases

Vapors of substances which are liquid around room temperature and atmospheric pressure, are condensed by cooling. For substances which are liquid at lower temperatures, liquefaction is possible by compression, or a combination of compression and cooling. Examples of such gases are: ammonia, sulfur dioxide, methyl chloride, fluorocarbons, chlorine and hydrogen sulfide. Cooling reduces the pressure required for liquefaction. In the case of so-called "permanent" gases such as oxygen, nitrogen, hydrogen, and helium, more involved methods of cooling, compression and even expansion may be necessary for liquefaction. Compressed gases must be cooled by one or more of the following three ways to produce liquid:

(1) Exchange of heat with a colder stream
(2) Expansion through a throttle valve (Joule-Thomson expansion) adiabatically
(3) Adiabatic expansion against a piston or in a turbine

Work for a reversible liquefaction may be calculated from availability increase:

$$-W_n = \Delta B = \Delta H - T_0\, \Delta S$$

Linde Cycles

The elements of gas liquefaction may be discussed by considering the liquefaction of methane gas which is available at 800 psia and 60°F, for example. From the data given in Mollier chart (*P-H* diagram), it can be seen that by simple expansion to 1 atm., the temperature of the gas will drop to 10°F, but no liquid will be obtained. The gases must be cooled to some point over the liquid vapor dome in the *P-H* diagram before expansion.

In the flow diagram of the simple Linde cycle shown in Figure IIC-1, gases are cooled to a temperature T_2 by the cold gases separated from the gas liquid mixture in the liquid reservoir, 4, and then throttled to a lower pressure at 3. The uncondensed gases from the reservoir, after exchanging heat with the incoming gases, are compressed and water-cooled to 800 psia and 60°F, and are recycled. The process is also shown on the *P-H* diagram in Figure IIC-1.

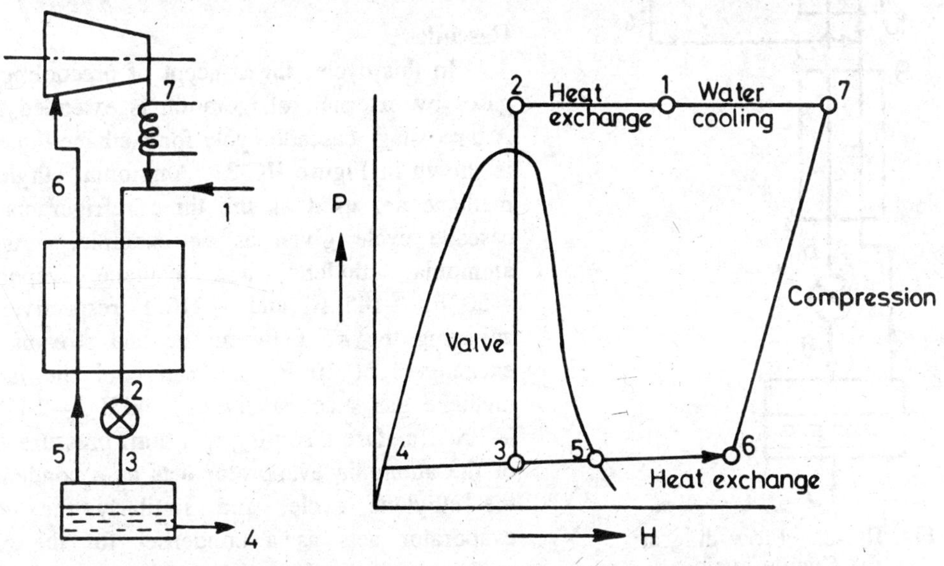

Fig. IIC-1. Flow diagram and *P-H* diagram for simple Linde cycle.

One variation in the simple Linde cycle is the high-pressure cycle in which more than one compressor is used, and the gas is expanded twice. The intermediate pressure is a design variable. The power requirement for liquefaction is reduced by this arrangement. Another possible variation in the simple Linde cycle is the use of ammonia (or any suitable refrigerant) for precooling of the feed stream. Auxiliary refrigeration is applied to increase the temperature drop of Joule-Thomson expansion. An ammonia evaporator in the ammonia refrigeration cycle acts as a cold box to cool the incoming warm gases (between 1 and 2), and the cold exit gases are further cooled before expansion in another heat exchanger by means of cold (low pressure) saturated vapor from the liquid receiver. The power requirement for liquefaction is again reduced by this arrangement.

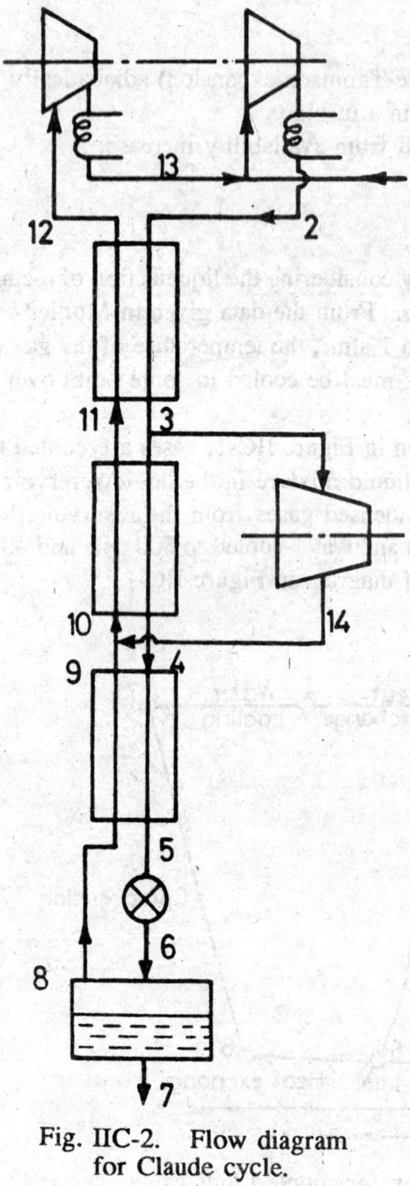

Fig. IIC-2. Flow diagram for Claude cycle.

Claude Cycle

In this cycle, a fraction of the gas is expanded in a high-speed expander. If appreciable amounts of liquid are allowed to form in the expander, the efficiency of the expansion process decreases due to irreversibilities. Therefore, final liquefaction is still done in this cycle, by a Joule-Thomson expansion. The flow sheet of the cycle is shown in Figure IIC-2.

The theoretical work per pound of liquid decreases rapidly as more and more gas is expanded through the turbine. Non-isentropic expansion and compression would increase the work considerably. Gas going into the expander could be cooled some more by auxiliary refrigeration.

However, difficulties will be encountered in the design of compressors and expanders to operate at low temperatures and with wet gas.

Cascades

In this cycle, the concept of precooling of the gases by external refrigeration is extended further. A three-stage cascade cycle for methane liquefaction is shown in Figure IIC-3. Ammonia, ethylene and methane are used as the three refrigerants in the cascade cycle given as an example. Assuming ammonia, ethylene, and methane evaporate at —50°F, —145°F, and —210°F respectively, and adjusting the ΔT between the end streams of the exchangers at 10°F, one can cool the incoming methane gas successively to —40°F, —135°F and —200°F before throttling to 1 atm. pressure. A part of the ammonia evaporator acts as a condenser for the ethylene cycle, and similarly the ethylene evaporator acts as a condenser for the external methane refrigeration cycle, while ammonia is con-

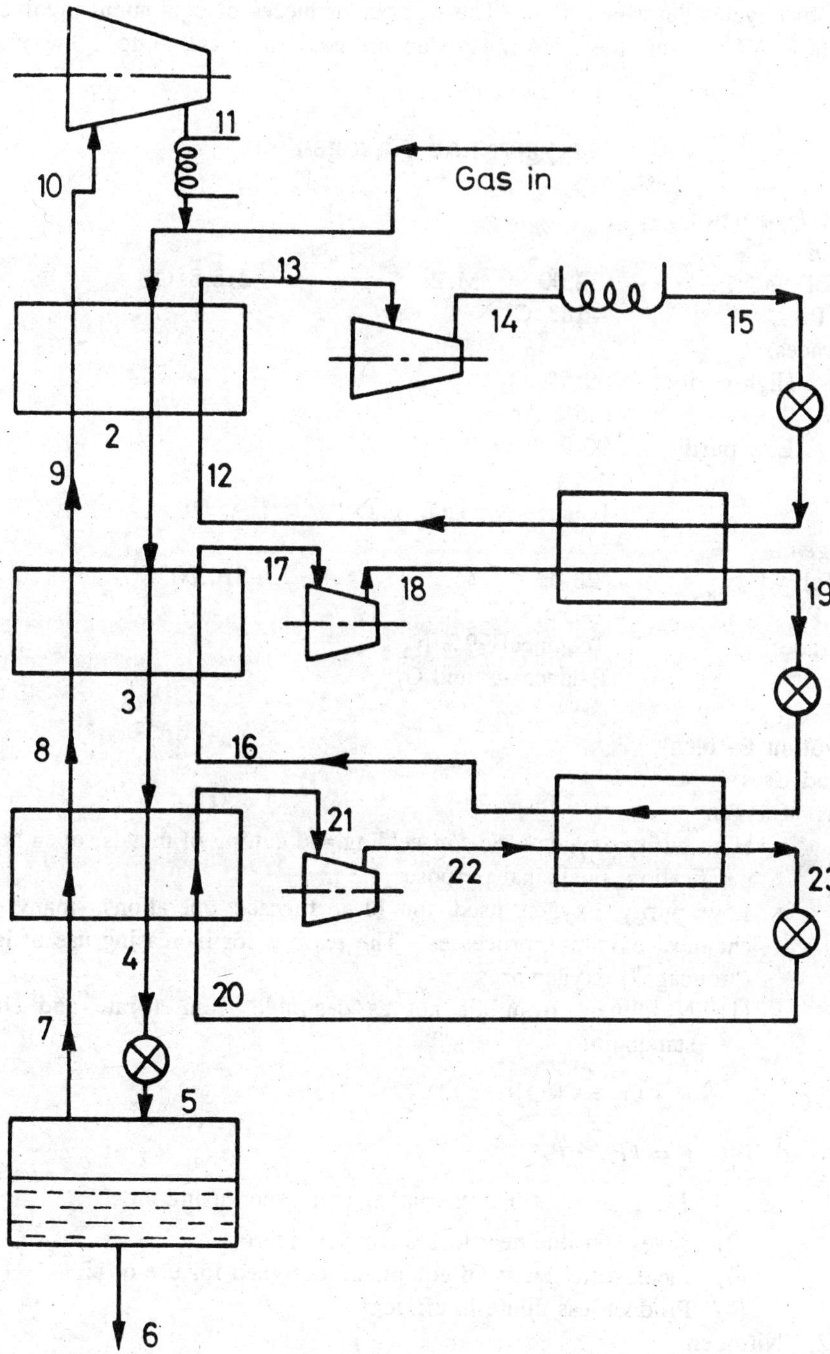

Fig. IIC-3. Cascade cycle.

densed in water-cooled tubes. The total theoretical work requirement for this cycle is the least among the various cycles described here. The number of pieces of equipment involved in this cycle is quite large. However, these are fairly standard equipment and quite a few of them are repeated.

Oxygen and Nitrogen

1. Pertinent Properties

Oxygen

Mol. wt.	32.00	M.P.	–218.8°C
B.P.	–183°C		
Grades:			
High purity	99.5% O_2		
	0.5% Ar		
Low purity	90-95% O_2		
	4-5% Ar		
	Balance N_2, CO_2, H_2O		

Nitrogen

Mol. wt.	28.02	M.P.	–210.00°C
B.P.	–195.8°C		
Grades:	Technical 99% N_2		
	Balance Ar and O_2		

2. Consumption Pattern

2.1. End Uses

2.1.1. Oxygen

- High purity oxygen used for welding and cutting of metals, open hearth steel purification, medicinal purposes
- Low purity oxygen used for blast furnace operations, many industrial chemical oxidation processes. The reasons for increasing use of low purity ("tonnage") oxygen are:
  (1) N_2 diluent from air not as desirable from a rate and equilibrium standpoint

  $$R + O_2 \underset{r}{\overset{f}{\rightleftharpoons}} RO_2$$

  $$r_f = kP_{O_2} \cdot P_R$$

  P_{O_2} is at least 5 times larger than when using air

  (2) Saves sensible heat losses from N_2 inert
  (3) Increases capacity of equipment designed for use of air
  (4) Product less dilute in effluent

2.1.2. Nitrogen

- Protective atmosphere to prevent oxidation in metal working and food preservation
- Captive usage in NH_3 and nitrogen chemicals
- Liquid N_2 used for refrigerative cooling in transportation industry

3. Methods of Production

3.1. Classification

All major production methods are based on liquefaction and subsequent fractionation of air.

Process modifications include:

- Variations in compression, purification, and refrigeration cycles
- Variations in equipment design for all major unit operations such as heat exchange, rectification, gas compression and expansion

3.1.1. Specific process cycle nomenclature

The two basic cycles are:

- Linde—uses refrigeration by Joule-Thomson cooling
- Claude—obtains refrigeration by adiabatic expansion of compressed air in a turbo-reciprocating or rotating expansion machine

The process to be described in detail is the conventional Linde-Frankl cycle.

3.2. Conventional Linde-Frankl Cycle

3.2.1. Reference flow sheet: Figure IIC-4

3.2.2. Chemical reaction

For CO_2 scrubbing tower $2NaOH + CO_2 \rightarrow Na_2CO_3 + H_2O$

3.2.3. Raw materials

Air of usual composition by volume

N_2	78.03	H_2	10^{-4}
O_2	20.97	CO_2	$0.02 \rightarrow 0.07$
Ar	0.94	H_2O	$0.01 \rightarrow 0.03$

Minor quantities of NaOH, NH_3 and silica gel

3.2.4. Quantitative requirements

(a) Basis: 1 ton of 95% oxygen in 300 tons/day plant

Air	3,600 Nm^3
Steam	1.75 tons
Cooling water	5 tons
Electricity	450-480 KWH

(b) Plant capacities: 50-500 tons/day

3.2.5. Process description

Air is compressed to 4-5 atms., cooled with H_2O and passed into regenerative exchangers. These are cylindrical pressure vessels packed with aluminum spirals and operating in pairs. Air is cooled in one, while cold product gas (O_2 or N_2) is removing sensible heat from the packing in the other. After 2-4 minutes, the cycle is reversed by automatic valves.

Air entering the cold exchanger contains both H_2O and CO_2 which must be removed before entering the fractionation section operated at —183 to —195°C to prevent plugging. These impurities are removed on the cold packing throughout the exchanger and then reevaporated by the product gas which starts with zero concentration of H_2O and CO_2 and thus provides an equilibrium driving force for the vaporization process. Both the O_2 and N_2 product gas necessarily contain H_2O and CO_2 impurities in this type of cycle design and only low purity oxygen can be obtained.

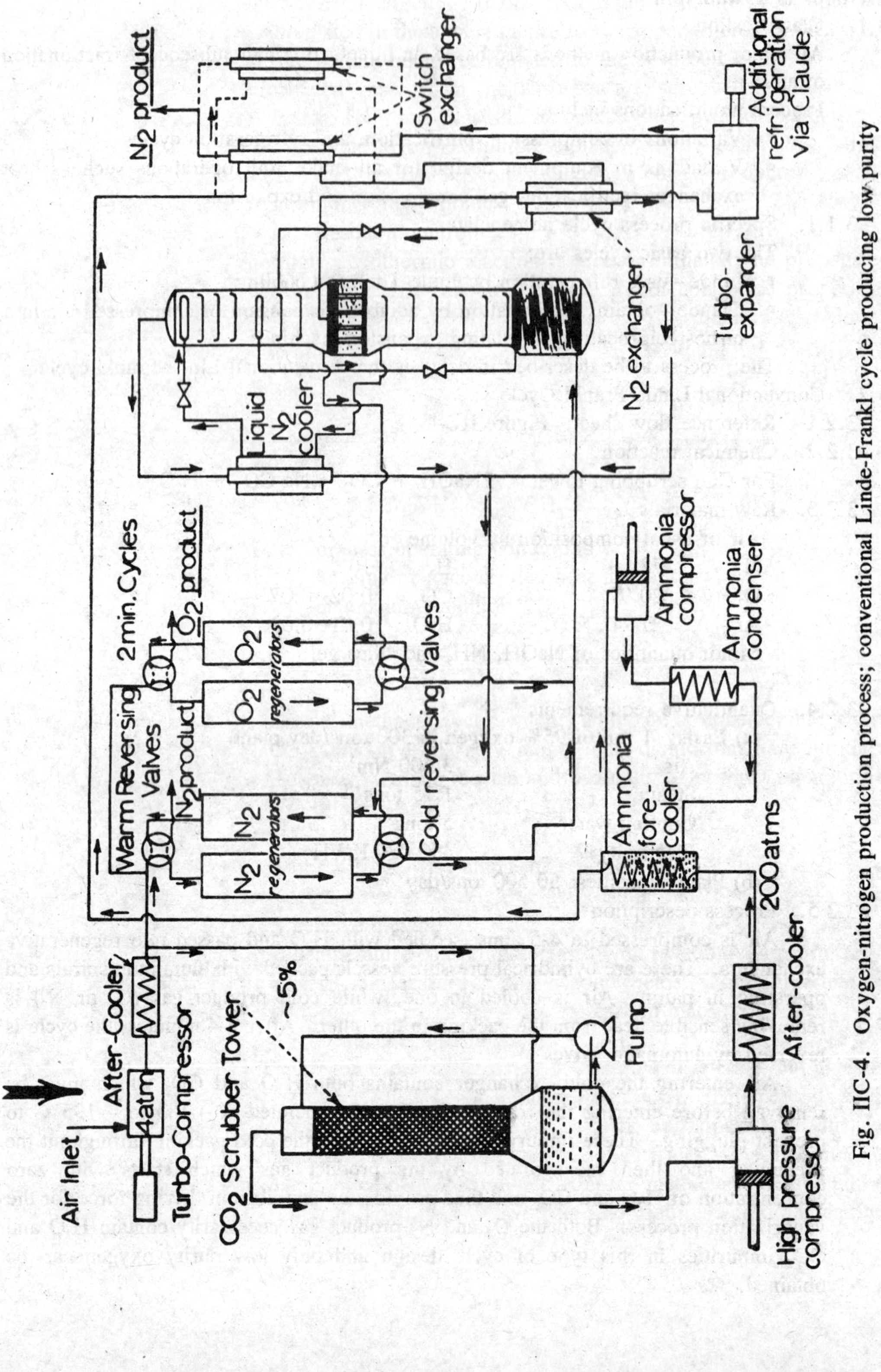

Fig. IIC-4. Oxygen-nitrogen production process; conventional Linde-Frankl cycle producing low purity tonnage oxygen.

The air leaving the regenerative heat exchangers is cooled to −170°C and fed to the reboiler section of the double column where further cooling takes place. The double column is, in fact, two distillation columns with a low pressure (1.4 atms.) column standing on the top of the high pressure (5.7 atms.) column, the reboiler of the upper column working as the condenser of the vapors from the lower column. In the high pressure section, the more volatile nitrogen works its way to the top of the column and is condensed inside the tubes of the reboiler section of the low pressure column by the liquid oxygen surrounding the tubes. This is accomplished because the temperature of liquid oxygen at 1.4 atms. is lower than the condensation temperature of the saturated nitrogen vapor at 5.7 atms. This condensed nitrogen is then sprayed into the top of the low pressure column for reflux. The less volatile oxygen still containing 50% N_2 is pumped to the middle of the low pressure column where final rectification takes place.

The removal of argon, which boils 2.9°C lower than oxygen, requires a much larger number of plates in the columns. Such designs are used only for high purity O_2 product (see Section 3.3).

To provide heat balance and flow control, a 3-6% side stream is drawn from the compressed air before entering the regenerators. This air is dried and freed of CO_2 by the NaOH scrubbing tower. The purified air is next compressed to 200 atms., cooled by H_2O, NH_3 refrigeration, and N_2 product heat exchange before entering a turbo-expander operating on the Claude principle. This balancing stream of cold air is fed near the bottom of the low pressure column.

3.3. Cycles for Producing High Purity Oxygen

3.3.1. Reference flow sheet: Figure IIC-5 (Kellogg process)

3.3.2. Process description

The major difference between the Kellogg and Linde-Frankl cycle is the use of a recuperative-reversing heat exchanger. These are built in a concentric triple-tube design with high purity oxygen moving through the inner tube, never contacting the incoming air. This is known as recuperative heat exchange. The reversing principle is used to remove CO_2 and H_2O from the incoming air stream by switching the flow of the N_2 product stream and the air stream in the outer two annuli.

Other purification details include:

- A catalytic oxidation chamber inserted after the initial compression to 70 psig to convert hydrocarbons to CO_2 and H_2O.
- Silica gel filter ahead of the double column.

3.4. Other Cycles

Various modifications have been incorporated since Linde first invented the basic cycle with Joule-Thomson cooling about 1900. These include various chemical methods for removing (1) water and carbon dioxide and (2) operating at pressures as high as 200 atms.

A novel process (Elliott) does not use air expansion for refrigeration, but sets up heat exchange with nitrogen coolant in strictly recuperative heat exchangers. This design eliminates the heat balance control stream, but requires cleaning the heat exchangers by melt-down every 3-5 hours.

A strictly Claude-operated process uses adiabatic expansion of 70-80% of the incoming air from 25-50 atms. to the 5.7 atms. column pressure.

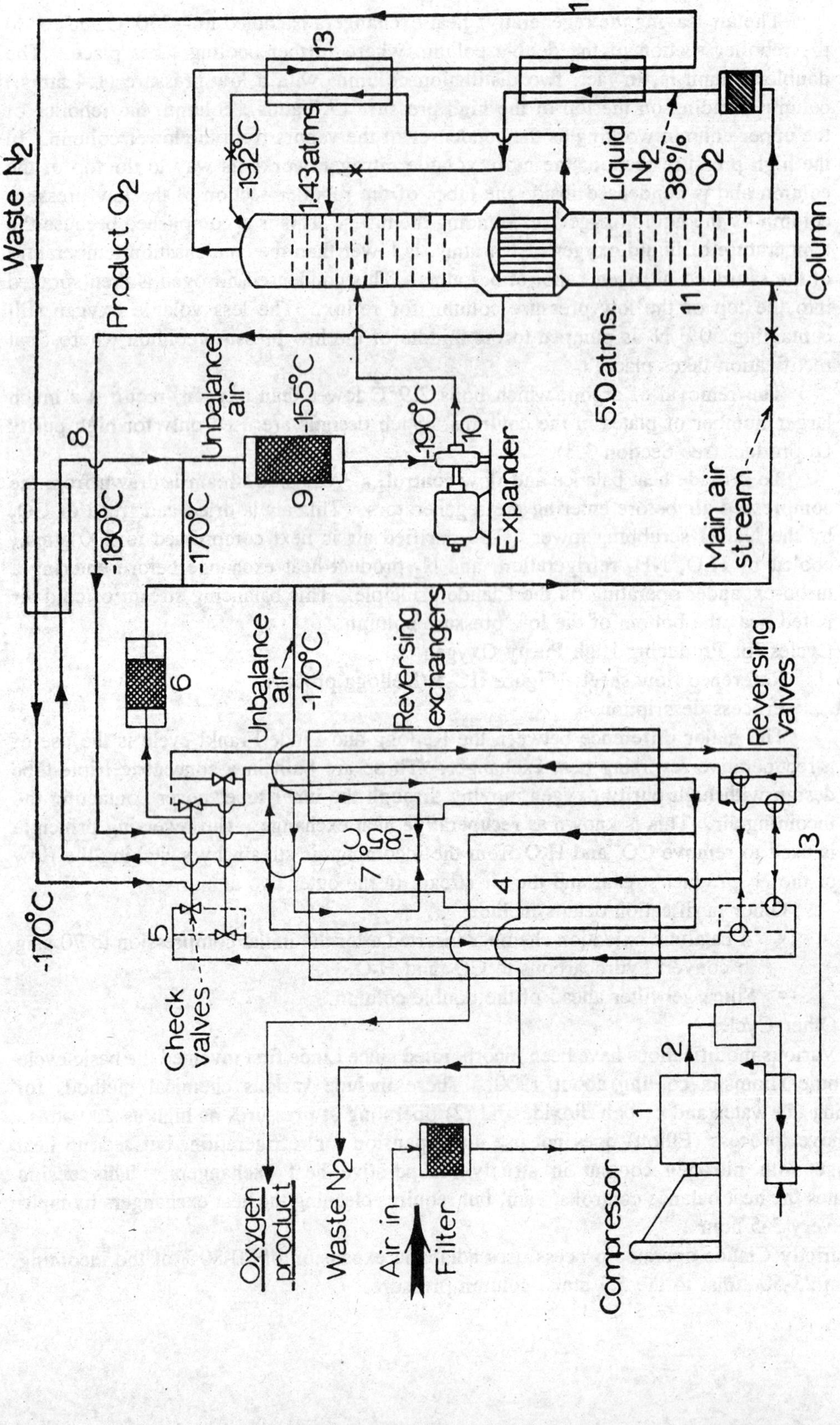

Fig. IIC-5. Oxygen-nitrogen production process; Kellogg low-pressure cycle producing high purity oxygen.

Cycles differ also in detail of separation of products. Liquid products can be drawn directly from the column. Rare gases can also be separated, *i.e.*,

- Argon side-streamed for fractionation from residual N_2 and O_2 in separate column
- Neon-helium from N_2 product by venting from top of main condenser
- Krypton-xenon from O_2 product by adsorption from top of main condenser

3.5. Major Engineering Problems

(a) Complete removal of H_2O, CO_2 and hydrocarbons to prevent plugging in the low temperature sections of the plant
(b) Developing effective low temperature insulation and lubricants
(c) Complex heat balancing designs
(d) Prevention of explosive mixtures in oxygen-rich regions

4. U.S. Economics

4.1. Major increase in low purity oxygen since 1950 has been in application to chemical processing such as:

- Blast furnace operation
- Oxidation of hydrocarbons

The decision to use oxygen is an economic one, balancing process savings and product quality improvement against additional cost of O_2 over compressed air.

U.S. uses of oxygen have been tabulated by P.J. Chenier in "Survey of Industrial Chemistry" (1992) as follows:

Primary Metals Manufacturing	55%
Chemicals Manufacturing	20%
Partial Oxidation Processes	10%
Metals Fabrication	5%
Miscellaneous	10%

U.S. production of oxygen has risen from some 25 billion pounds in 1970 to about 40 billion pounds in 1990. The price in dollars per hundred cubic feet is about 45 cents as of the period 1985-1990.

5. Indian Economics

The cryogenic industry is in its infancy. Nearly all of the oxygen produced is high purity and used largely for oxy-acetylene welding and cutting. The steel industry is experimenting with enriched air and pressurized blast furnace operations so some use of O_2 in this area is expected. The oxygenated Linz and Donowitz (L & D) furnace operation to produce higher quality steel is already in use and with more adoptions, tonnage oxygen production is expected to grow steadily.

Note that the L & D process uses 0.07-0.08 ton of O_2/ton of steel.

Another major use for oxygen is for the production of synthesis gas by partial oxidation. Although present economics favors the reforming process which requires no oxygen, the two processes are competing so some tonnage oxygen requirement is likely to arise from the petrochemical and fertilizer industries.

The Indian oxygen industry is in a period of rapid expansion as of 1995. The major producers are:

Praxair (which used to be the Linde Division of Union Carbide Corp.).

BOC India Ltd. (which used to be IOL Ltd.) which is associated with the worldwide British-based British Oxygen or BOC.

Praxair is stated to be building the world's largest air separation plant to supply the Jindal Iron & Steel Plant in Karnataka State. The plant will increase India's total oxygen production capacity by 25%.

Praxair plans to build a second plant in Haldia in West Bengal to supply a petrochemical complex with oxygen.

6. Non-cryogenic Alternatives

Systems can also be improved with the increasing availability of less expensive packaged pressure swing adsorption systems based on molecular sieves for oxygen supply compared to cryogenic systems.

Manufacturing technologies for high-volume industrial air gases have been reviewed by the Technology Information, Forecasting & Assessment Council (TIFAC). (See Section IX—References.)

IID. FERTILIZER INDUSTRY

The fertilizer industry is the major component of the agricultural chemicals industry which in turn is a major chemical engineering contribution to agro-business or the overall coordinated food production, distribution and delivery industry. Other important chemical engineering contributions are in pesticides manufacture and in the chemical engineering operations in the food industry such as freeze drying.

The production of nitrogen fertilizers should be given the highest national priority next only to defense and family planning.

Proper application of 1 ton of balanced fertilizer to soil will produce about 10 tons of additional foodgrain or even more for high yielding varieties of seeds. Therefore, a nitrogenous fertilizer plant producing 1 lakh tons per year may be considered as a factory indirectly producing 1 million tons of foodgrains.

Three major components are necessary in fertilizers:

(1) Nitrogen (N)—required during early stages of plant growth to promote development of stems and leaves.

(2) Phosphorus (P)—which stimulates early growth and accelerates seeding or fruit formation in later stages of growth.

(3) Potassium (K)—essential to the development of the starches of potatoes and grains, the sugar of fruits and vegetables and the fibrous material of plants; an ample supply of potassium in the soil sometimes helps to prevent disease and to lessen the effects of excessive nitrogen application.

Potassium, along with nitrogen and phosphorus, is one of the primary nutrients considered essential for plant growth. Both muriate of potash (potassium chloride) and sulphate of potash are used as fertilizers, the former being more common occurrence. Potassium occurs in nature as insoluble potash bearing silicates and as highly soluble salts like potassium chloride in underground deposits and in sea water. The earlier source of potassium was ashes from the burning of wood and plant wastes. The principal potash minerals are sylvinite, a mixture of sylvite (KCl) and halite (NaCl) in different proportions, carnalite ($KCl.MgCl_26H_2O$), kainite ($KCl.MgSO_43H_2O$), langbeinite ($K_2SO_4.2MgSO_4$) and to a limited extent as nitrate (KNO_3). India has no exploitable deposits of potassium. Two possible sources of potash in the country are the bitterns left over salt recovery and molasses/distillery slop. Consequently, present requirements are met entirely through imports.

India has made great strides in the development of fertilizer industry and ranks as the 4th largest producer in the world. Despite several odds, the industry fared extremely well during 1991-92 with higher capacity utilization in both nitrogenous and phosphatic units. There was an impressive pick up in capacity utilization during 1991-92. In the case of Nitrogen (N) the ratio rose to 89% from 86% earlier and in the case of Phosphate (P) to 93% from 75%.

Consumption of fertilizers went up marginally to 12.7 million tons in 1991-92. The unsatisfactory off-take of fertilizers during 1991-92 was due to erratic monsoon during 1991 and to some extent an increase in fertilizer prices.

Production of nitrogenous and phosphatic fertilizers during 1991-92 stood at about 9.9 million tons registering about a ten percent increase over the previous year. The gap in domestic demand was met through imports, according to *"Kothari's Industrial Directory of India" (1994)*.

These materials are constantly being added to, and subtracted from the soil. Fertilizers offer only one form of addition of these elements to the soil, as shown in the following tables:

Nitrogen Balance for the U.S.

		Tons
Losses:		
	Harvested crops	5,500,000
	Pasturage (animal feed)	1,500,000
	Drainage	900,000
	Erosion	500,000
		8,400,000
Gains:		
	Bacterial fixation	3,000,000
	Rainfall	1,300,000
	Fertilizers	400,000
		4,700,000

Potash Balance for the U.S.

Losses:		
	Harvested crops	3,800,000
	Grazing	11,400,000
	Leaching	10,000,000
	Erosion	35,000,000
		60,200,000
Additions:		
	Rainfall (dust)	1,800,000
	Fertilizers	360,000
	Manures	3,330,000
	Irrigation	590,000
	Seeds	60,000
		6,140,000

Growing plants in various areas have widely differing requirements for N, P & K, depending on the nature of the plant, the composition of the soil, the physical type of soil and whether or not the area in question is irrigated. Details of such requirements for different crops in different states in India are given annually in "Fertiliser Statistics" published by the Fertilizer Association of India, New Delhi.

A major problem in India is that only nitrogen is present as an indigenous raw material—in the air. Phosphorus and potassium must, on the whole, be imported although intensive searches are being conducted for indigenous sources of these materials.

The sections of this book which follow, treat, in order, the nitrogen industries and the phosphorus industries as major contributors to fertilizer production.

To give an idea of the overall fertilizer factory picture in India, Table IID-1 is adapted from "Fertiliser Statistics, 1993-94." It shows both nitrogenous and complex fertilizer plants in operation and those planned for the near future.

Figure IID-1 then shows the locations of these factories in India. Table IID-2 shows phosphate fertilizer plants in operation and planned. This is followed by Figure IID-2 which shows phosphate fertilizer plant locations on the map of India.

Table IID-1
Locations of Nitrogenous and Complex Fertilizer Factories Throughout India

No.	State/Name of Factory & Location	End Product
I. In Production		
Andhra Pradesh		
1.	Coromandel Fertilizers, Visakhapatnam	Urea, NP
2.	Fertilizer Corporation of India (FCI), Ramagundam	Urea
3.	Godavari Fertilizers & Chemicals, Kakinada	DAP
4.	Nagarjuna Fertilizers & Chemicals, Kakinada	Urea
5.	Rashtriya Ispat Nigam, Visakhapatnam	AS
Assam		
6.	Hindustan Fertilizer Corporation (HFCL), Namrup (I, II & III)	AS, Urea
Bihar		
7.	SAIL, Bokaro	AS
8.	HFCL, Barauni	Urea
9.	FCI, Sindri (M)	AS, Urea
10.	TISCO, Jamshedpur	AS
Goa		
11.	Zuari Agro Chemicals (ZACL), Zuarinagar	Urea, NPK, DAP
Gujarat		
12.	Cyanides & Chemicals, Surat	AS
13.	Gujarat Narmada Valley Fertilizers Co. (GNFC), Bharuch	Urea, CAN Nitrophosphate
14.	Gujarat State Fertilizers Co. (GSFC), Vadodara	Urea, AS, DAP
15.	Gujarat State Fertilizers Co., Sikka	DAP
16.	GSFC-Polymer Unit, Vadodara	AS

Fig. IID-1. Location of nitrogenous and complex fertilizer factories (as of 1-10-1995).
Source: The Fertilizer Association of India

17.	Indian Farmers Fertilizer Coop. (IFFCO), Kalol	Urea
18.	IFFCO, Kandla	NPK, DAP
19.	Krishak Bharati Coop. (KRIBHCO) (2 plants) Hazira	Urea
Haryana		
20.	National Fertilizers (NFL), Panipat	Urea
Karnataka		
21.	Mangalore Chemicals & Fertilizers (MCFL), Mangalore	Urea, DAP
Kerala		
22.	Fertilizers & Chemicals Travancore (FACT) Udyogamandal (I to V)	AS, APS
23.	FACT, Ambalamedu (I & II)	Urea, NPK, DAP
Madhya Pradesh		
24.	SAIL, Bhilai	AS
25.	NFL, Vijaipur	Urea
Maharashtra		
26.	Deepak Fertilizers & Petrochemicals Corp. Taloja	Ammonium Nitrophosphate
27.	Rashtriya Chemicals & Fertilizers (RCFL), Trombay (I to V)	Urea Nitrophosphate Ammonium Nitrophosphate
28.	RCFL, Thal Vaishet (2 plants)	Urea
Orissa		
29.	SAIL (Fert. Plant) Rourkela	CAN
30.	SAIL, Rourkela	AS
31.	FCI, Talcher	Urea
32.	Paradeep Phosphates, Paradeep (I & II) (National Fertilizers Ltd.)	DAP
Punjab		
33.	NFL, Nangal (I & II)	CAN, Urea
34.	NFL, Bhatinda	Urea
35.	Punjab National Fertilizers & Chemicals, Naya Nangal	ACI
Rajasthan		
36.	Chambal Fertilizers & Chemicals Ltd., Gadepan	Urea
37.	Shriram Fertilizers & Chemicals (SFC), Kota	Urea
Tamil Nadu		
38.	EID-Parry (India), Ennore	APS, APS
39.	Madras Fertilizers (MFL), Manali	Urea, DAP, NPK Urea
40.	Neyveli Lignite Corp., Neyveli	Urea
41.	Southern Petrochemical Industries Corp. (SPIC), Tuticorin	Urea, DAP, NPK
42.	Tuticorin Alkali Chemicals and Fertilizers, Tuticorin	ACI
Uttar Pradesh		
43.	FCI, Gorakhpur	Urea
44.	Duncans Industries, Panki	Urea
45.	IFFCO, Aonla	Urea
46.	IFFCO, Phulpur	Urea

47.	Indo Gulf Fertilizers & Chemicals Corp., Jagdishpur	Urea
West Bengal		
48.	HFCL, Durgapur	Urea
49.	Hindustan Lever, Haldia	DAP
50.	IISCO, Burnpur-Kulti	AS
51.	SAIL, Durgapur	AS
II. Under Implementation		
Maharashtra		
52.	Aarali Drugs, Thane	AS
Uttar Pradesh		
53.	Oswal Chems. & Fertilizers, Shahjahanpur	Urea
54.	Tata Chemicals, Babrala	Urea
West Bengal		
55.	HFCL, Haldia	Urea, NP/NPKs

Note: In addition to the plants mentioned above, the existing ammonia plant of FACT Udyogamandal (22) and GSFC, Vadodara (14) will be replaced with enhanced capacity.

Code to abbreviations used above:

APS = Ammonium Phosphate Sulfate
AS = Ammonium Sulfate
CAN = Calcium Ammonium Nitrate
DAP = Diammonium Phosphate
NP = Nitrophosphate
NPK = NPK complexes

Table IID-2
Locations of Phosphate Fertilizer Factories Throughout India

No.	State/Name of Factory & Location
I. In Production	
Andhra Pradesh	
1.	Andhra Sugars, Tanuku
2.	Krishna Industrial Corporation, Nidadavole
3.	Pragati Fertilizers, Visakhapatnam
Assam	
4.	Assam State Fertilizer & Chemicals, Chandrapur (Formerly Chemical Unit of AIA)
Bihar	
5.	Pyrites, Phosphates & Chemicals Ltd., Amjhore
6.	Sri Krishna Fertilizers, Muzaffarpur
7.	Tulsi Fertilizers & Chemicals, Patna

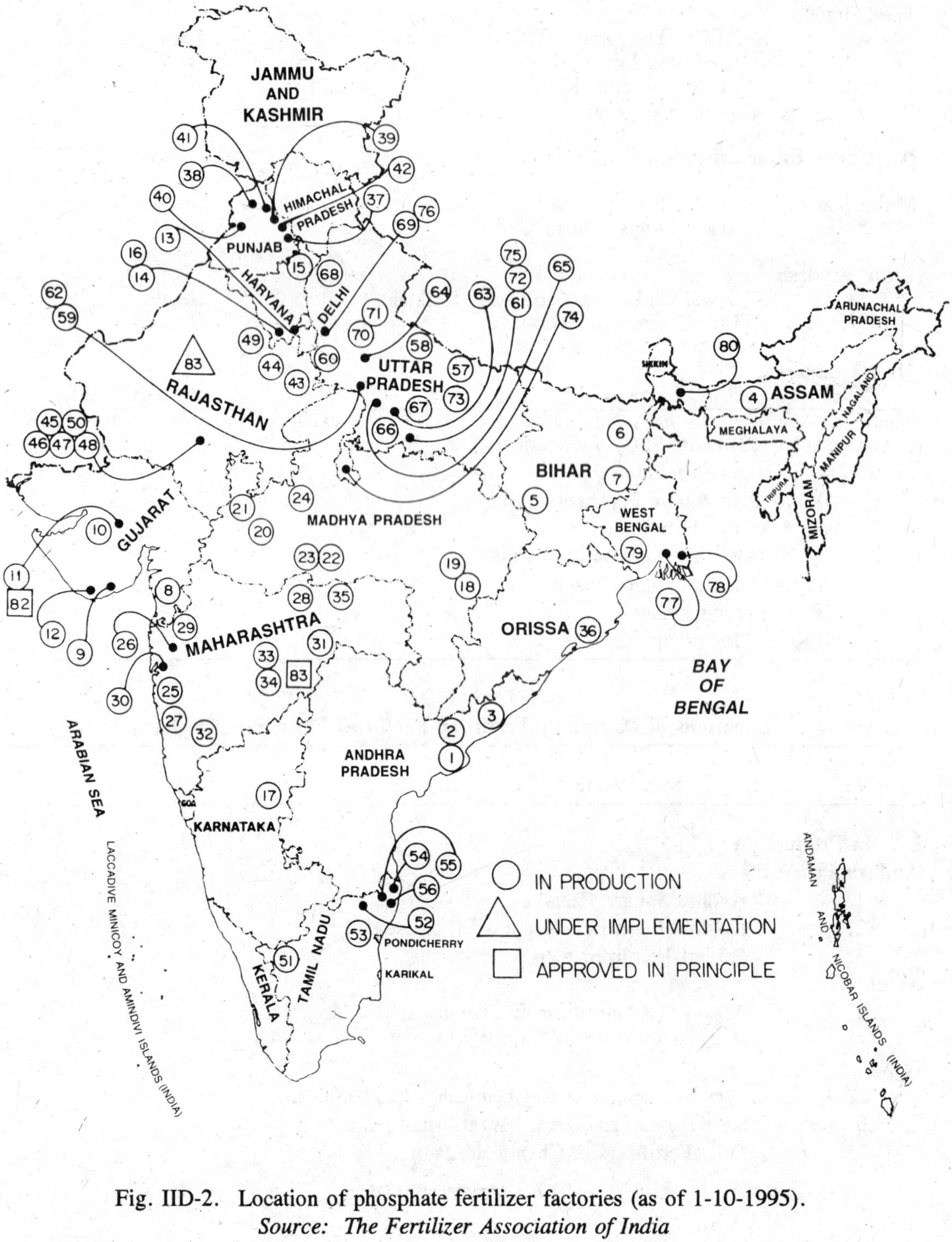

Fig. IID-2. Location of phosphate fertilizer factories (as of 1-10-1995).
Source: The Fertilizer Association of India

Gujarat

8. Adarsh Chemicals & Fertilizers, Udhna
9. Anil Starch Products, Bhavnagar
10. Dharamsi Morarji Chemical Co., Amreli
11. Growmore Fertilizers, Nandesari (Formerly Viraj Chemicals)
12. Mardia Chemicals, Surendranagar
13. Rama Fertilizers, Junagadh

Haryana

14. Jayshree Chemicals & Fertilizers (Unit III), Pataudi
15. India Ceroils, Dharuhera (Formerly Multitech International)
16. Nitin Chemicals & Fertilizers, Rukri
17. Oriental Carbon & Chemicals, Dharuhera

Madhya Pradesh

18. BEC Fertilizers, Bilaspur
19. Dharamsi Morarji Chemical Co. (DMCC), Kumhari
20. Harshvardan Chemicals & Minerals, Antravalia
21. Khaitan Chemicals & Fertilizers, Nimrani
22. Rama Phosphates, Indore
23. Swastic Fertilizer & Chemicals, Indore
24. Unialkem Fertilizers, Raisen

Maharashtra

25. Bharat Fertilizer Industries, Kharivali (II & III)
26. DMCC, Ambernath (SSP)
27. Hindustan Farms & Fertilizers, Raigad
28. Maharashtra Agro Ind. Dev. Corp., Panvel
29. Noble Fertilizers, Taloja
30. Patel Narayan Das Bhagwan Das Fertilizers, Jalgaon
31. Rama Krishi Rasayan, Loni-Kalbhor
32. Raashi Fertilizers, Lakhmapur
33. Vidarbha Phosphates & Fertilizers, Pulgaon

Orissa

34. East Coast Fertilizers & Chemicals, Kalma

Punjab

35. Agro Chemical Punjab, Dera Bassi
36. H.S.B. Fertilizers, Shahpur
37. Modern Agro Chemicals, Alawalpur
38. Munak Chemicals, Bhatinda
39. SFC Industries, Rail Majra
40. Varinder Agro Chemicals, Sanghera

Rajasthan

41. Bharat Chemicals & Fertilizers, Alwar
42. Hindustan Copper (HCL), Khetri
43. Liberty Pesticides & Fertilizers, Madri, Udaipur
44. Madhuvan Chemicals & Fertilizers, Dabok, Udaipur
45. Phosphates India, Bichhadi
46. Shurvi Colour Chemicals, Udaipur

47. Surajgarh Chemical & Fertilizer, Surajgarh
48. Udaipur Phosphates & Fertilizers, Khemli

Tamil Nadu

49. Coimbatore Pioneer Fertilizers, Coimbatore
50. EID Parry (India), Ranipet
51. Indag Products, Cuddalore
52. Kothari Industrial Corporation, Ennore
53. Shaw Wallace & Company, Avadi

Uttar Pradesh

54. Asian Fertilizers, Gorakhpur
55. Awadh Fertilizers, Baharaich
56. Brij Fertilizers, Shikohabad
57. Ganges Fertilizers, Farrukhabad
58. S.D. Fertilizers, Kanpur Dehat
59. Girraj Fertilizers & Chemicals, Shikohabad
60. Kaashi Urvarak, Lucknow
61. Khaitan Fertilizers, Rampur
62. Madan Madhav Fertilizers & Chemicals, Fatehgarh
63. Mahadeo Fertilizers, Fatehpur
64. Mittal Fertilizers, Rae Bareli
65. Natraj Organics, Muzaffarnagar
66. Neera Chemicals & Fertilizers, Ghaziabad
67. Ramganga Fertilizers, Gajruala
68. Shree Acids & Chemicals, Gajruala
69. Shree Behariji Fertilizers, Kanpur Dehat
70. Sri Durga Bansal, Faizabad
71. Shrinivas Fertilizers, Jhansi
72. Trimurtee Fertilizers, Kanpur Dehat
73. Vijay Fertilizers, Ghaziabad

West Bengal

74. Jay Shree Chemicals & Fertilizers, Khardah (Plants I & II)
75. Phosphate Company, Rishra
76. Sarada Fertilizers, Bankura
77. Sunderban Fertilizers & Chemicals, Jalpaiguri

II. Under Implementation

Madhya Pradesh

78. Rama Phosphates, Indore

Maharashtra

79. Ganga Fertilizers, Yavatmal
80. Shiva Fertilizers, Nanded

III. Approved in Principle

Bihar

81. Ranjan Chemicals, Begusarai

Gujarat

82. Mardia Chemicals, Surendranagar

Maharashtra

83. Parbhani Farmers Coop. Factory, Parbhani

IV. Under Consideration

Rajasthan

84. Pyrites, Phosphates & Chemicals, Saladipura

IIE. NITROGEN INDUSTRIES

Abundant nitrogen in the air is commercially fixed by reaction with low-cost hydrogen to give ammonia. This low-cost chemical is used for supplying:

- Nitrogen fertilizers in the form of liquid and aqueous NH_3 solutions, ammonium salts, and urea
- Nitric acid
- Most nitrogen chemical compounds

About 90% of ammonia production is used in India for fertilizers. In this country, agriculture plays a predominant role with about 60% of the population employed therein. Exports of agricultural products will be the principal source of foreign exchange needed to import capital goods for industrialization for some years to come. Thus the attainment of a higher national income is closely linked to agriculture. The soils have become highly deficient in growth elements (N, P, K) from continual cropping without replenishment and heavy monsoon rains cause rapid leaching. Thus, fertilizer addition on a planned basis is the only way to increase agricultural productivity. The emphasis and priority on fertilizer production and the importance of nitrogen industries should be obvious.

Ammonia

1. Pertinent Properties of Ammonia

Mol. wt.	17.03
M.P.	−77.7°C
B.P.	−33.4°C
Solubility	Very soluble in water

Grades: Anhydrous or liquefied NH_3, stored at 80°F with a pressure of 175 psig. Aqueous grade (28 wt.% NH_3).

2. Consumption Pattern

2.1. End Uses

The end uses for ammonia worldwide are as follows:

Direct application as fertilizer	25%
Urea (for both fertilizers & plastics)	21%
Ammonium phosphates	16%

Nitric acid	12%
Miscellaneous	12%
Ammonium nitrate	8%
Ammonium sulfate	3%
Acrylonitrile	3%

2.2. Nitrogen Consumption in Fertilizer

2.2.1. Fertilizers supplying nitrogen are prepared in two basic types:

- Mixed fertilizers—these contain three principal elements (nitrogen, phosphorus, and potassium). The composition is expressed as wt.% total N, available P_2O_5 and soluble K_2O (e.g., 5-10-5 is 5 wt.% N, 10% P_2O_5, 5% K_2O). These are generally granular solids.
- Chemical nitrogen fertilizers—chemical compounds used separately where direct application is required.

3. Methods of Production

3.1. Classification of Processes

All processes for synthetic NH_3 are based on the pressure-catalytic reaction of N_2 and H_2. The principal variation is in the operating pressure.

3.2. Process for NH_3 Production

3.2.1. Reference flow sheet: Figure IIE-1

3.2.2. Chemical reaction

$$N_2 + 3H_2 \overset{Fe}{\rightleftharpoons} 2NH_3; \quad \Delta H^\circ = -22.0 \text{ Kcal}$$

3.2.3. Raw materials

- H_2 from synthesis gas (see Figures IIB-6 & IIB-7)
- N_2 from air addition in synthesis gas process or from air liquefaction process (see Figures IIC-4 & IIC-5)

3.2.4. Quantitative requirements

(a) Basis: 1 ton NH_3—85% yield

H_2	0.21 ton or 2,000 Nm^3
N_2	0.96 ton or 1,400 Nm^3
Synthesis catalyst	0.2 kg
Power	850 KWH
Fuel gas for compressors	3,800 Kcal
Cooling water	12.5 tons

(b) Plant capacities: 100-1,500 tons/day of NH_3

3.2.5. Process description

Ammonia synthesis gas (3 moles pure H_2 : 1 mole pure N_2) is compressed to the operating pressure (100-1,000 atms. depending on conversion required). It is sent through a filter to remove compression oil and additionally through a high temperature guard converter (converts CO and CO_2 to CH_4 and removes traces of H_2O, H_2S, P and As). This is done by catalyst and suitable getter materials.

The relatively cool gas is added along the outside of converter tube walls to provide cooling so that carbon steel can be used for the thick wall pressure vessel and internal tubes. The preheated gas flows next through the inside of the tube which contains promoted porous iron catalyst at 500-550°C. The NH_3 product, with an 8-

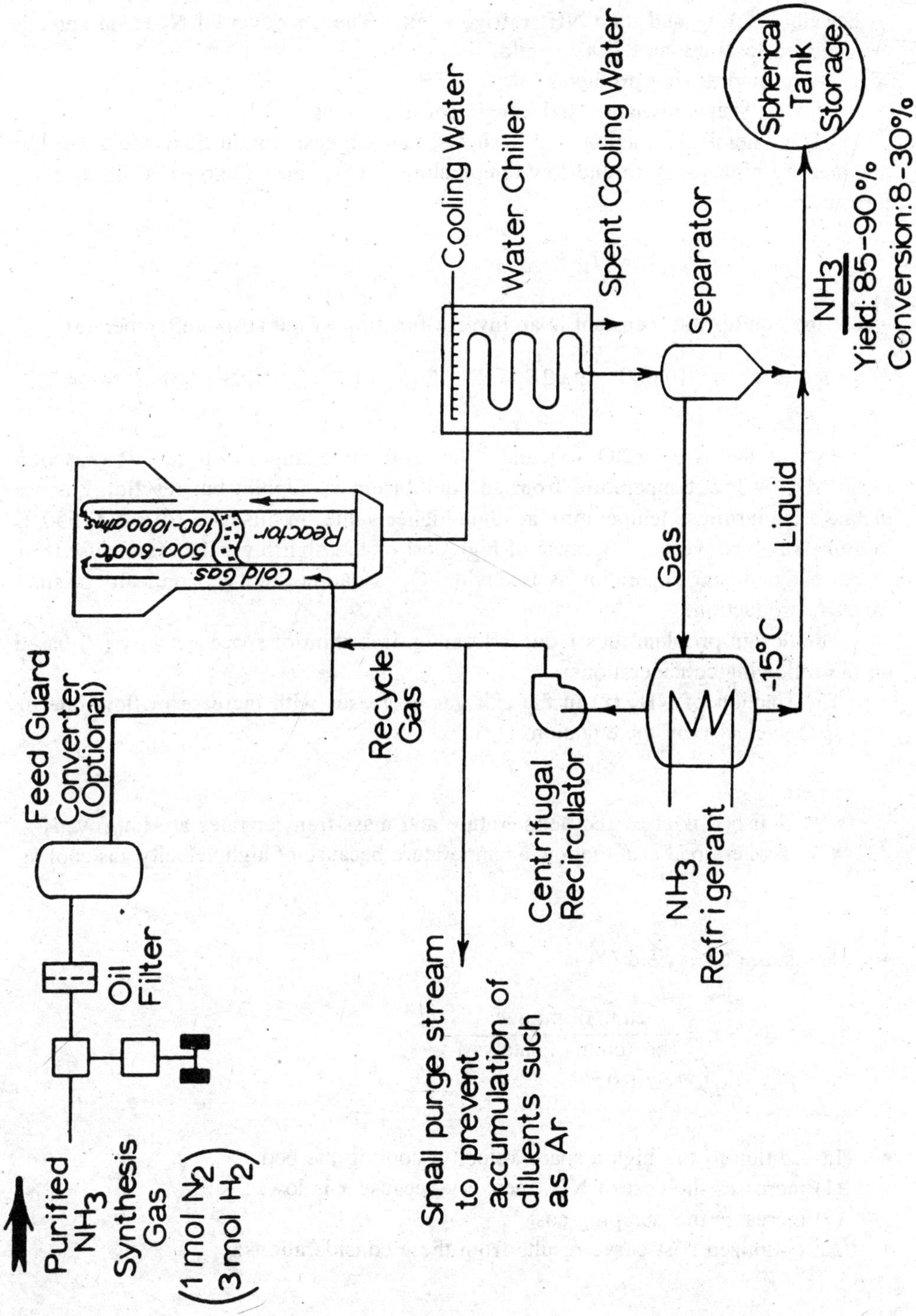

Fig. IIE-1. Synthetic ammonia process.

30% conversion depending on process conditions, is removed by condensation, first with water cooling and then NH_3 refrigeration. The unconverted N_2-H_2 mixture is recirculated to allow an 85-90% yield.

3.2.6. Major engineering problems

(a) Thermodynamic and kinetic considerations

The chemical reaction 3.2.2 shows that highest equilibrium yield can be obtained by high pressure and low temperature. This can be expressed in equation form as

$$Y_{NH_3} = \sqrt{K_p \cdot Y_{N_2} \cdot Y_{H_2}^3 \cdot p_T}$$

where the equilibrium constant is an inverse function of the absolute temperature:

$$\Delta F^\circ = -RT \ln K_p = -19{,}000 + 9.92T \ln T + 1.15 \times 10^{-3}T^2 - 1.63 \times 10^{-6}T^3 - 18.32T$$

As with the case for SO_2 oxidation, the exothermic ammonia production reaction is favored by low temperature from an equilibrium standpoint but reaction kinetics dictate a compromise temperature at some higher value, in this case from 500-550°C in a one-stage converter. Because of high cost of the high pressure vessels used for reactors, a multistage operation as used with SO_2 oxidation is not economically feasible for NH_3 production.

The design problem thus reduces to an optimization of space velocity (V) based on the following considerations:

- The fraction of NH_3 (x) in the exit gas decreases with increase in flow rate or space velocity by the equation

$$x = fV^{-n}$$

  where

  $n < 1$ if bed is at correct temperature and mass transfer rates are improved

  $n > 1$ where bed is at too low a temperature because of high velocity gas cooling

- The space time yield (Y) is

$$Y = V \cdot x = \frac{\text{cu m of product}}{\text{(hr) (cu m of catalyst)}}$$

$$Y = V \cdot V^{-n} = V^{(1-n)}$$

- In addition to too high a space velocity, cooling the bed
  (1) increases the cost of NH_3 recovery because x is lower
  (2) increases the pumping cost
- An optimized cost curve results from these considerations:

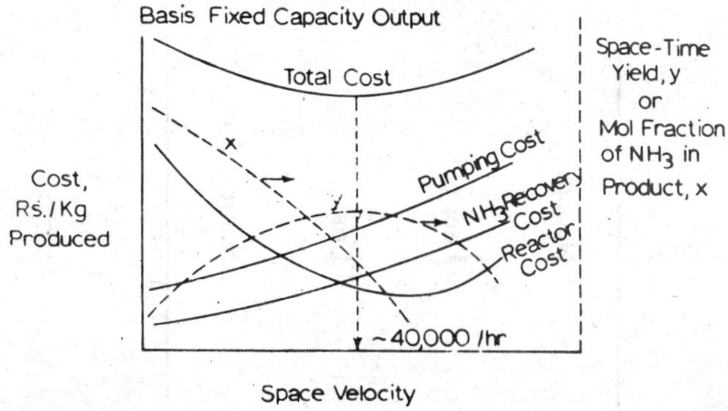

(b) Catalyst development

The preparation and use of active catalysts for ammonia synthesis has been the subject of years of research. The principal aim, of course, is to develop catalysts that will allow improved yields at lower temperature and pressures and thus lower production costs.

To date all NH_3 synthesis catalysts are based on iron oxide promoted by alkali or nonferrous metal oxides such as K_2O (1-2%) and Al_2O_3 (2-5%). The iron oxide is fused in an electric furnace and the promoters added. The solidified mass is ground to desired particle size. The iron oxide is reduced to porous iron in the start-up phases of operation in the synthesis reactor. There is a maximum operating temperature of about 620°C, above which the catalyst fuses.

A promoted iron catalyst has been developed in Europe (Mont Cenis process) which allows for very low temperature (400°C) and low pressure operation (100 atms.). The life of the catalyst is not firmly established.

(c) Process design modifications

The above considerations have resulted in a number of design modifications, particularly as to the pressure used which affects conversion, recirculation rates and refrigeration. The processes have been named as follows:

- Very high pressure (900-1,000 atms., 500-600°C, 40-80% conversion)—Claude, DuPont, L'Air Liquide
- High pressure (600 atms., 5,000°C, 15-25% conversion)—Casale
- Moderate pressure (200-300 atms., 500-550°C, 10-30% conversion)—Haber-Bosch, Kellogg, Fauser, Nitrogen Engineering Corporation
- Low pressure (100 atms., 400-425°C, 8-20% conversion)

Mont Cenis: This process uses a new type of iron catalyst promoted iron cyanide.

The modern trend is towards lower pressure and increased recirculation loads because of the relatively high cost of pressure vessels. The trend is also to large single-train plants using centrifugal compressors and having capacities as high as 1,000 tons/day from a single reactor at low production cost.

4. Process Choices

Table IIE-1 shows the cost of production for various Indian fertilizer plants using various feedstocks.

Table IIE-2 shows a list of Indian ammonia plants showing feedstock choice and sources of process know-how.

Table IIE-1

Cost of Production of Fertilizer Plants Based on Different Feedstock—India

Name of Unit	Plant Capacity	Year of Establishment/Date of Commercial Production	Capital Cost of Project in Rs. crores	Cost of Production Rs./ton of ammonia 1989-90	Feedstock
IFFCO, Phulpur	Ammonia-900, Urea-1,500	March 1981	205.00	3,268.74	Naphtha
NFL, Panipat	Ammonia-900 Urea-1,500	Sept. 1, 1979	223.50	4,042.89	Fuel Oil
FCI, Ramagundam	Ammonia-900 Urea-1,500	Nov. 1, 1980	217.90	11,601.19	Coal
RCF, Trombay-V	Ammonia-900 Urea-1,000	July 1, 1982	166.09	4,133.00	Natural Gas

Source: "Global Trends in Chemical Products," Nandini (1994)

Table IIE-2 List of Ammonia Plants, Feedstock, Capacity and Licensors (as on 31.3.1991)

Name of Plant	Feedstock	Ammonia Capacity tons/day	Licensor			
			Gasification	H_2S, CO_2 removal	Synthesis	Engineering
1. Fertilizer Corp. of India Ltd.						
(a) Sindri (M)	Fuel Oil	900	Shell-partial oxidation	Lurgi-Rectisol	Topsoe	PDIL
(b) Gorakhpur	Naphtha	550	Shell-partial oxidation	Hot Potash MEA Benfield	Chemico/ TEC	TEC/ PDIL
(c) Ramagundam	Coal	900	Krupp-Koppers coal gasification	Lurgi-Rectisol	Montedison	PDIL
(d) Talcher	Coal	900	Krupp-Koppers coal gasification	Lurgi-Rectisol	Montedison	PDIL
2. Hindustan Fertilizer Corp. Ltd.						
(a) Durgapur	Naphtha	600	ICL, steam re-forming	Vetrocoke	Montedison	FEDO/ PDIL
(b) Barauni	Naphtha	600	Selas-steam reforming	Vetrocoke	Montedison	PDIL
(c) Namrup I	Natural Gas	200	Chemico steam reforming	Hot Potash MEA	Chemico	Chemico/ PDIL
Namrup II	Natural Gas	600	KTI Selas	Vetrocoke	Montedison	PDIL
Namrup III	Natural Gas	600	Haldor Topsoe	Benfield	Haldor Topsoe	PDIL

Table IIE-2 (cont'd)

Name of Plant	Feedstock	Ammonia Capacity tons/day	Licensor			
			Gasification	H_2S, CO_2 removal	Synthesis	Engineering
3. Rashtriya Chemicals and Fertilizers Ltd.						
(a) Trombay I	Natural Gas	350	Topsoe-steam reforming	BASF/ MDEA	Chemico	PDIL
Trombay V	Natural Gas	900	Topsoe-steam reforming	Benfield	Topsoe	Topsoe/ PDIL
(b) Thal-Vaishet	Asso-ciated gas/ Natural Gas	1,350 x 2	Topsoe-steam reforming	Benfield	Topsoe	Topsoe/ PDIL
4. National Fertilizers Ltd.						
(a) Nangal	Naphtha	300	Topsoe-steam reforming	Linde-PSA	Grande paroisse	PDIL
Nangal (Expn)	Fuel Oil	600	Shell-partial oxidation	Lurgi-Rectisol	Topsoe	PDIL
(b) Bhatinda	Fuel Oil	900	Shell-partial oxidation	Lurgi-Rectisol	Topsoe	EIL
(c) Panipat	Fuel Oil	900			Topsoe	EIL
(d) Vijaipur	Asso-ciated Gas	1,350	Topsoe-steam reforming	Benfield	Topsoe	Topsoe/ PDIL
5. Indian Farmers Fertilizer Cooperative Ltd.						
(a) Kalol	Natural Gas	910	Kellogg-steam reforming	UCAR-MEA	Kellogg	Kellogg
(b) Phulpur	Naphtha	900	Kellogg-steam reforming	Benfield	Kellogg	Kellogg

Table IIE-2 (cont'd)

Name of Plant	Feedstock	Ammonia Capacity tons/day	Licensor			
			Gasification	H_2S, CO_2 removal	Synthesis	Engineering
(c) Aonla	Associated gas	1,350	Topsoe-steam reforming	Benfield	Topsoe	Topsoe PDIL
6. Krishak Bharati Coop. Ltd. Hazira	Natural gas/ Associated gas	1,350 x 2	Kellogg-steam reforming	Benfield	Kellogg	Kellogg FEDO
7. Fertilizers & Chemicals Travancore Ltd.						
(a) Alwaye	Naphtha	355	Texaco-partial oxidation, ICI-steam reforming	MEA	Werksur ICI	PGC/ FEDO
(b) Ambalamedu (Cochin I)	Naphtha	600	ICI-steam reforming	Vetro-coke	Montedison	FEDO/ PDIL
8. Coromandel Fertilizers Ltd. Visakhapatnam	Naphtha	357	Kellogg-steam reforming	Dow Chemical MEA	Kellogg	Kellogg
9. Gujarat State Fertilizers Co. Ltd. Baroda	Naphtha and natural gas (in two streams)	500 + 450	ICI-steam reforming	Vetro-coke/ glycine	Casale	Toyo
10. ICI-India Ltd.	Naphtha	830	ICI-steam reforming	Benfield	ICI	ICI
Kanpur Expansion	"	415	TEC	Benfield	-do-	H&G (I)

Table IIE-2 (cont'd)

Name of Plant	Feedstock	Ammonia Capacity tons/day	Licensor			
			Gasification	H_2S, CO_2 removal	Synthesis	Engineering
11. Madras Fertilizers Ltd., Manali	Naphtha	750	Topsoe-steam reforming	Cata-carb	ICI	Chemico
12. Mangalore Chemicals & Fertilizers Ltd., Mangalore	Naphtha	660	ICI-steam reforming	Benfield	ICI	H&G (I)
13. Neyveli Lignite Corp. Ltd., Neyveli	Fuel Oil	285	Shell-partial oxidation	Benfield	Montedison	PDIL
14. Shriram Fertilizers & Chemicals, Kota	Naphtha	600	Topsoe-steam reforming	Benfield	Topsoe	Chiyoda
15. Zuari Agro Chemicals Ltd., Goa	Naphtha	660	ICI-steam reforming	Benfield	TEC	TEC
16. Southern Petro-chemical Industries Corp. Ltd., Tuticorin	Naphtha	1,100	ICI-steam reforming	Vetrocoke	ICI	Davy Power Gas
17. Steel Authority of India Ltd., Rourkela	Naphtha/ Coke oven gas	450	Topsoe-steam reforming	Benfield	Uhde	Uhde
18. Gujarat Narmada Valley Fertilizers Co. Ltd., Bharuch	Fuel Oil	1,350	Texaco-partial oxidation	Linde-Rectisol	Topsoe	Linde
19. Deepak Fertilizers & Petrochemicals Corp., Taloja	Associ-ated gas	272	Selas-steam reforming	UCAR-MEA	Topsoe	EIL

Table IIE-2 (cont'd)

Name of Plant	Feedstock	Ammonia Capacity tons/day	Licensor			
			Gasification	H_2S, CO_2 removal	Synthesis	Engineering
20. Indo-Gulf Fertilizers & Chemicals, Jagdishpur	Asso-ciated gas	1,350	Topsoe-steam reforming	G.V. (glycine)	Topsoe	PDIL/Topsoe
Under Construction						
1. Nagarjuna Fertilizers & Chemicals Ltd., Kakinada	Natural gas	900	Topsoe-steam reforming	G.V. (glycine)	Topsoe	PDIL/ Topsoe
2. Chambal Ferts. & Chem. Ltd., Gadepan	Asso-ciated gas (HBJ pipeline)	1,350	Topsoe-steam reforming	G.V. (glycine)	Topsoe	PDIL/ Topsoe
3. Tata Chemicals Ltd., Babrala	Asso-ciated gas (HBJ pipeline)	1,350	Topsoe-steam reforming	G.V. (glycine)	Topsoe	PDIL/ Topsoe
4. Bindal Agro, Shahjahanpur	Asso-ciated gas (HBJ pipeline)	1,350	Topsoe-steam reforming	G.V. (glycine)	Topsoe	PDIL/Topsoe

Source: "Handbook on Fertiliser Technology" (1992)

5. Worldwide Distribution of Ammonia Production Capacity

The production capacity for synthetic ammonia has increased strongly in recent decades despite the stagnating consumption in the western industrialized countries since the end of the 1970's. New plants have been installed in the USSR, India, the People's Republic of China and Mexico in particular, increasing the worldwide capacity from 72.2×10^6 t/a in 1975 to 128×10^6 t/a ammonia in 1985 (see Table IIE-3).

Table IIE-3 Ammonia Capacities in the World Regions in 10^6 t NH_3

	North America	USA	Central & South America	Western Europe	Eastern Europe	USSR	Asia & Oceania	Africa
1975	18.3	14.3	2.6	17.2	8.5	10.9	18.5	1.1
1980	21.4	18.6	4.5	17.8	11.2	20.0	32.4	2.3
1985*	20.7	16.4	7.3	17.3	13.9	25.3	40.6	3.4

*estimated

Source: "Industrial Inorganic Chemistry" by Buchner et al (1989)

The countries producing the largest quantities are the USSR, the People's Republic of China and the USA. The 1985 world demand was 108 x 10^6 t and this was expected to rise to ca. 125 x 10^6 t ammonia by 1990.

Nitric Acid

1. Pertinent Properties

Mol. wt.	63.03
M.P.	—42°C
B.P.	86°C with decomposition
Sp. gr. 18°/4	1.502

Completely miscible with H_2O; forms a constant boiling mixture at 110°C and 760 mm which contains 68 wt.% HNO_3.

Grades: Concentrated (95%) as technical, C.P. or USP, commercial (52-68%); Fuming (>86%); Red Fuming (>95% with 10-15% excess dissolved oxides of nitrogen); Nitrating or mixed acid (80% HNO_3-15% H_2SO_4 to 50% HNO_3-48% H_2SO_4)

2. Consumption Pattern

2.1. End Uses

Estimated USA applications spectrum for nitric acid in 1985:

- 76% for ammonium nitrate of which
  —80% was for fertilizers
  —19% was for explosives
  —ca. 1% was for N_2O
- 9% for adipic acid (fiber and plastics precursor)
- 3.5% for dinitrotoluene (for toluene-diisocyanate)

- 3.5% for nitrobenzene (for aniline)
- 2% for sodium, potassium and calcium nitrates
- 1% for nitro-compounds for explosives
- ca. 5% for miscellaneous purposes

3. Methods of Production

3.1. Classification of Processes

3.1.1. Ammonia oxidation process

Accounts for 90% production. Process is divided into four fundamental steps:

- Oxidation of NH_3 to NO
- Oxidation of NO to NO_2
- Absorption of NO_2 in water
- Concentration of HNO_3

Variations are in (1) pressure levels in oxidation and absorption, (2) power recovery, and (3) methods of dehydrating the 60% acid formed on absorption.

3.1.2. $NaNO_3 + H_2SO_4$ process

Oldest process used exclusively prior to 1920.

3.1.3. N_2 fixation from air (Wisconsin process)

Production of NO and NO_2 by high temperature (2,200°C) reaction using air in a gas-fired pebble bed heater followed by quick quench. Effluent contains 2% NO_2 which was too dilute to recover economically.

3.1.4. Nitrogen fixation by nuclear fission fragments

Air exposed to radiation in a nuclear reactor to form NO. Present economics give too high a plant investment.

3.2. Ammonia Oxidation Process for Nitric Acid

3.2.1. Reference flow sheet: Figure IIE-2

3.2.2. Chemical reactions

- Ammonia oxidation—major reactions
  - (a) $NH_3 + 5/4\ O_2 \rightleftharpoons NO + 3/4\ H_2O(g)$; $\Delta H° = -54.0$ Kcal
  - (b) $2NO_2 + O_2 \rightleftharpoons 2NO_2$; $\Delta H° = -27.2$ Kcal
- Ammonia oxidation—side reactions
  - (c) $NH_3 + 3/4O_2 \rightleftharpoons 1/2N_2 + 3/2H_2O(g)$; $\Delta H° = -75.7$ Kcal
  - (d) $NH_3 \rightleftharpoons 1/2N_2 + 3/2H_2$; $\Delta H° = -11$ Kcal
  - (e) $NH_3 + O_2 \rightleftharpoons 1/2N_2O + 3/2H_2O(g)$
  - (f) $NH_3 + 3/2NO \rightleftharpoons 5/4N_2 + 3/2H_2O(g)$; $\Delta H° = -107.9$ Kcal
- Nitrous oxide oxidation and absorption
  - (g) $2NO + O_2 \rightleftharpoons 2NO_2$; $\Delta H° = -27.2$ Kcal
  - (h) $3NO_2(g) + H_2O(1) \rightleftharpoons 2HNO_3(aq) + NO$; $\Delta H° = -32.2$ Kcal
  - (i) $2NO_2 \rightleftharpoons N_2O_4$; $\Delta H° = -11.46$ Kcal
  - (j) $2NO_2 + H_2O \rightleftharpoons HNO_3(aq) + HNO_2$
  - (k) $2HNO_2 \rightleftharpoons H_2O + NO + NO_2$

3.2.3. Raw materials

- NH_3 from synthetic ammonia process
- Filtered air
- Platinum-rhodium make-up catalyst

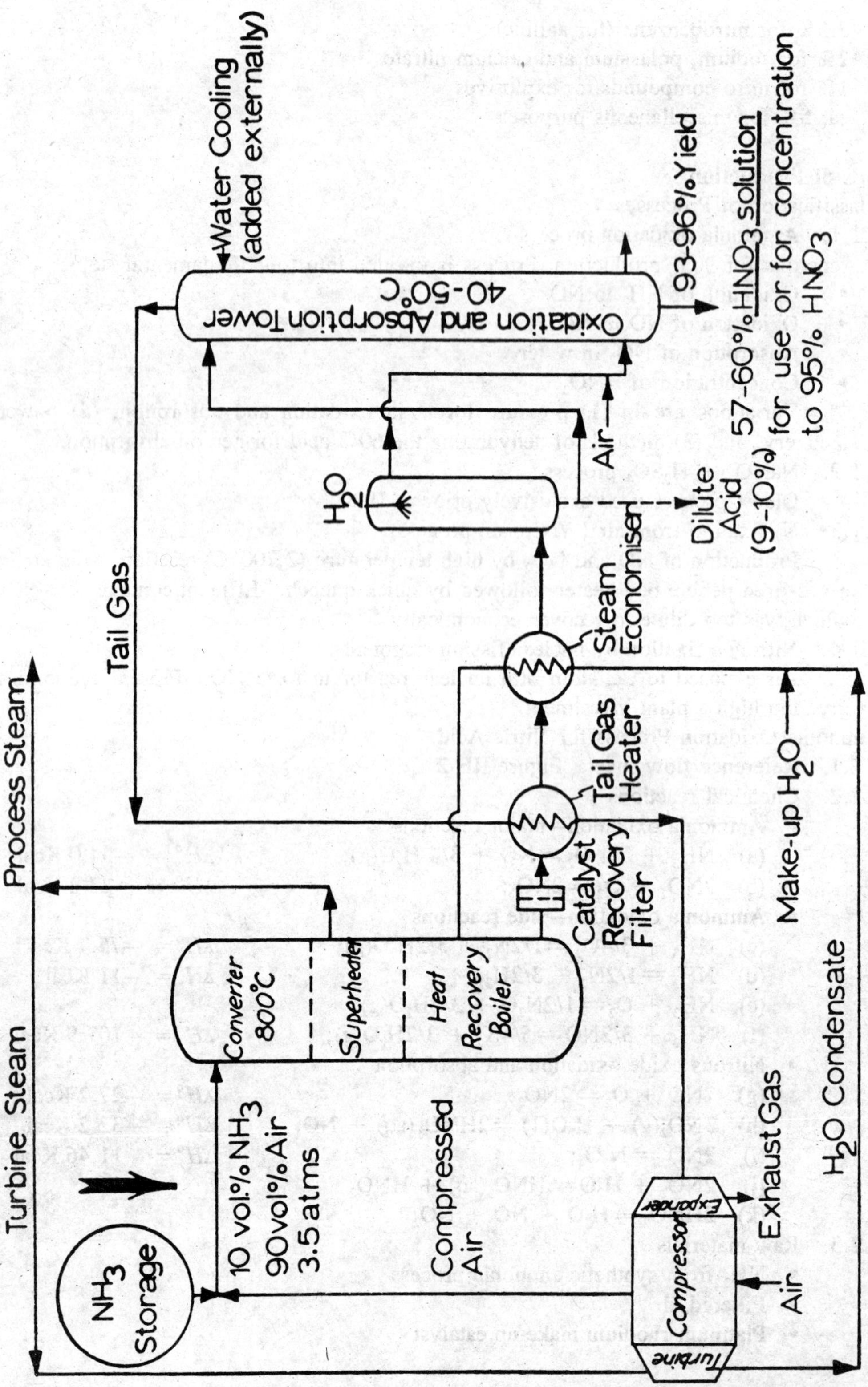

Fig. IIE-2. Nitric acid by ammonia oxidation process.

3.2.4. Quantitative requirements

(a) Basis: 1 ton HNO_3 (100%)

Anhydrous NH_3	0.287-0.290 ton
Air	3,000 Nm^3
Platinum (2-10% Rh promoted)	0.1 gm
Process water	120 tons
Steam credit	1 ton @ 200 psig
Power	10-30 KWH

(b) Plant capacities: 50-250 tons/day in individual units with 3-5 units per plant

3.2.5. Process description (Montecatini intermediate pressure process)

Compressed air is mixed with anhydrous ammonia; fed to a shell and tube converter designed so that the preheater and a steam heat recovery boiler-superheater are within the same reactor shell. The converter section consists of 10-30 sheets of Pt-Rh alloy in the form of 60-80 mesh wire gage packed in layers inside the tube. Gas passes downward with a velocity designed to give a contact time of about 2.5 x 10^{-4} sec in the catalyst zone at 800°C.

Product gases from the reactor, containing 10-12% NO, are sent through heat recovery units, a quench unit for rapid cooling to remove a large fraction of the product heat, and into the oxidizer-absorber system. Air is added to convert NO to NO_2 at the more favorable low temperature (40-50°C) environment of the absorption system.

The equipment in the absorption train may be a series of packed or sieve tray vertical towers or a series of horizontal cascade absorbers. The product from this water absorption system is 57-60% HNO_3 solution which can be sold as is or concentrated as discussed next.

Concentration of the nitric acid to 95% can be done by one of several processes:

- Concentration by H_2SO_4

Rectification by 93% H_2SO_4 (66°Be) in silicon-iron or stoneware towers produces concentrated nitric acid and 70% H_2SO_4 which can be reevaporated to 93% or used elsewhere in the plant.

- Concentration by $Mg(NO_3)_2$

Developed in 1958 by Hercules Powder Company. Magnesium nitrate solution containing 70-75% $Mg(NO_3)_2$ is fed to a dehydrating tray tower along with the dilute HNO_3 from the absorption system. The salt solution acts as an extractive distillation agent, removing water at 100°C or higher, thus allowing rectification without azeotropic formation. The dilute $Mg(NO_3)_2$ solution is reconcentrated by evaporation.

Advantages of $Mg(NO_3)_2$ process are:

(1) Operating costs about half of those encountered with H_2SO_4 concentration
(2) Capital requirements are only 70% as great
(3) Acid quality and yield is improved

3.2.6. Major engineering problems

(a) Thermodynamic and kinetic considerations

All of the important oxidation reactions in 3.2.2 are exothermic. Reaction 3.2.2(a) has an extremely favorable equilibrium constant so that a one-step, high-temperature converter design may be used.

There is a slight equilibrium advantage to operation at low pressure (1 atm.). This is more than offset by increased capacity in a given reactor volume with subsequent catalyst and reactor savings when operating at higher pressures (3-8 atms.).

The NO oxidation reaction 3.2.2(b) does not have as large an equilibrium constant. Hence, this reaction predominates in the water cooling and absorption portions of the process, which operate at 40-50°C. Note that all of the NO which is liberated on absorption of NO_2 must also be reoxidized in the absorption tower [see reaction 3.2.2(g)].

Reaction kinetics in the NH_3 oxidation stage can be summarized as:

(1) The reaction to form NO is favored by increasing temperature until an optimum is reached which increases with higher gas velocities. This results from the prevention of back diffusion of NO into the higher NH_3 concentration region. If this occurs, reaction 3.2.2(f) is quite probable and should be avoided for high NO yield.

(2) Alloying platinum with rhodium improves yield at a given set of conditions.

(3) Rate of NO formation very nearly corresponds to diffusional transport of NH_3 molecules to the catalyst surface.

(4) Reaction rate is directly proportional to the system pressure.

The absorption of nitrogen oxides from gaseous mixtures by chemical reaction with water has the following design criteria:

(1) Low temperatures are beneficial for absorber operation efficiency.

(2) Increasing pressure favors physical absorption rates and shifts chemical equilibrium to produce higher acid strengths.

(3) The rate of absorption is dependent on concentration of NO_2 in gas phase. In commercial absorbers where the concentration of NO_2 is greater than 5%, the controlling reaction is solution of N_2O_4 accompanied by hydrolysis to HNO_3 and HNO_2.

(b) Process design modification

Most plants use intermediate (3-4 atms.) or high pressure (8 atms.) processes rather than the complete atmosphere process or a combination of 1 atm. pressure oxidation and high pressure absorption. Top pressure is limited by pressure vessel costs.

The reasons for elevated pressure processes are:

- High reaction rates and lower volumes in both oxidation and absorption equipment
- Higher acid strength
- Lower investment costs

The disadvantages of higher pressures:

- Lower oxidation yields
- Higher catalyst losses unless good filtering procedures are used
- High power requirements if power recovery units are not specified

4. Economics

4.1. Market and Sales

Nitric acid finds its largest end use in the fertilizer industry, both as an acidulant for phosphate rock to produce nitrophosphate for mixed fertilizers and in the production of ammonium nitrate, a synthetic nitrogen fertilizer containing 35% N. This is expected to increase in line with the population growth and increased standard of living.

New uses have been found for ammonium nitrate-oil mixtures as a cheap open-pit explosive for quarrying, mining, and construction. The market for other nitrate-base explosives is considered stable with very little growth.

Rocket propellant compositions may ultimately provide a small but increasing market for such products as fuming red nitric acid (conc. HNO_3 with N_2O_4 solubilized), N_2O_4 and monopropellants such as tetranitromethane.

4.2. Plant Capacity

The Indian scenario for nitric acid is as follows:

Major Producers	Concentrated Nitric Acid In TPD	Dilute Nitric Acid In TPD
Deepak Fertilizers & Petrochemicals Corporation Ltd.	100	
Deepak Nitrite Ltd.	100	660
GNFC (Gujarat Narmada Valley Fertilizers Corp.)	100	630
Hindustan Organic Chemicals Ltd.	100	
Rashtriya Chemicals & Fertilizers Ltd.	66	1,070
VBC Industries Ltd.	80	
Rourkela Fertilizer Plant		1,000

Demand for concentrated nitric acid is estimated to be around 84,000 tons per annum.

Source: "Global Trends in Chemical Products," Nandini (1994)

Urea

1. Pertinent Properties of Urea ($NH_2 \cdot CO \cdot NH_2$)

Mol. wt.	60.05	M.P.	132.7°C
B.P.	Decomposes	Sp. gr. 20°/4°C	= 1.335

Fairly soluble in water (110 g per 100 g @ 20°C, 135 g per 100 g at 100°C)

Grades:
- C.P., technical (containing 46% N)
- Fertilizer: granular—coated with non-hygroscopic dust such as phosphate rock or limestone (40-42% N)
- Liquor—mixtures of urea in NH_3 solution (*e.g.*, 45% total N, 30% as free NH_3, 15% as urea)
- Slow release—contains low mol. wt. urea polymers

2. Consumption Pattern

2.1. End Uses

Urea is used in solid fertilizer (53%), liquid fertilizer (31%), and miscellaneous applications such as animal feed, urea, formaldehyde resins, melamine and adhesives. Presently, the most popular nitrogen fertilizer is a urea-ammonium nitrate solution. Urea-formaldehyde resins have large use as a plywood adhesive. Melamine-formaldehyde resins are used as dinnerware and for extra-hard surfaces (Formica®). The melamine is synthesized by condensation of urea molecules.

2.2. Production Patterns

Urea is the nitrogen compound with the largest production volume in the world. Its utilization is increasing steadily, it being the preferred nitrogen fertilizer worldwide. (Urea is also used in much smaller quantities for the manufacture of industrial products. The following statistics relate to total urea manufacture.) The production and consumption of urea for 1983/84 are shown in Table IIE-4.

Table IIE-4 Production and Consumption of Urea in the Different Regions in 1983/84 in 10^6 t N

	World	North America	South America	Western Europe	Eastern Europe	Africa	Asia	Oceania
Production	23.045	2.302	1.015	1.829	6.438	0.619	10.743	0.099
Consumption	21.842	1.532	1.118	1.176	3.822	0.803	13.318	0.073

Source: "Industrial Inorganic Chemistry," Buchner et al (1989)

The major reason for the rapid growth of urea (doubling time—3 years) is the worldwide shift to the high nutrient-high nitrogen fertilizers provided by urea in solid or aqueous solution form. Urea is replacing the highly acidic ammonium salts in regions where soil is already too acid and lime is scarce.

Urea can be easily granulated. It also provides a medium for a slow release variety of fertilizer by forming a low molecular weight urea-formaldehyde polymer.

2.3. Plant capacities and process licensors and engineering firms involved in India. Table IIE-5 gives a summary of data on Indian urea plants.

Table IIE-5 List of Urea Plants, Capacity and Licensors (as on 31 March 1991)

	Name of Plant	Urea capacity tons/day	Licensor
1.	Fertilizer Corp. of India		
	(a) Sindri (M)	1,000	Montedison
	(b) Gorakhpur	950	Mitsui Toatsu
	(c) Ramagundam	1,500	Montedison

	(d) Talcher	1,500	Montedison
2.	Hindustan Fertilizer Corp.		
	(a) Durgapur	1,000	Montedison
	(b) Barauni	1,000	Montedison
	(c) Namrup I & II	1,000	Montedison
	(d) Namrup III	1,167	PDIL
3.	Rashtriya Chemicals & Fertilizers		
	(a) Trombay I	300	Chemico/UTI
	(b) Trombay V	1,000	Snam Progetti
	(c) Thal Vaishet	1,500 × 3	Snam Progetti
4.	National Fertilizers Ltd.		
	(a) Nangal	1,000	Montedison
	(b) Bhatinda	1,550	Mitsui Toatsu
	(c) Panipat	1,550	Mitsui Toatsu
	(d) Vijaipur	2,200	Snam Progetti
5.	Indian Farmers Fertilizer Coop. Ltd.		
	(a) Kalol	1,200	Stamicarbon
	(b) Phulpur	1,500	Snam Progetti
	(c) Aonla	2,200	Snam Progetti
6.	Fertilizers & Chemicals Travancore Ltd. Ambalamedu (Cochin Phase I)	1,000	Montedison
7.	Coromandel Fertilizers Ltd. Visakhapatnam	400	CPI Allied
8.	Gujarat State Fertilizers Co. Ltd., Baroda	1,100	Mitsui Toatsu
9.	ICI-India Ltd.		
	Kanpur	1,364	Mitsui Toatsu
	Expansion	682	Power Gas Corp.
10.	Madras Fertilizers Ltd. Madras	640	Chemico
11.	Mangalore Chemicals & Fertilizers Ltd., Mangalore	1,000	Stamicarbon
12.	Neyveli Lignite Corp. Neyveli	465	Montedison
13.	Shriram Fertilizers & Chemicals, Kota	1,000	Stamicarbon
14.	Zuari Agro Chemicals, Goa	1,140	Mitsui Toatsu
15.	Southern Petrochemical Industries Corp. Ltd., Tuticorin	1,530	Mitsui Toatsu

16.	Gujarat Narmada Valley Fertilizers Co. Ltd. Bharuch	1,800	Snam Progetti
17.	KRIBHCO, Hazira	1,100 × 4	Snam Progetti
18.	Indo Gulf Fertilizers and Chemicals Ltd., Jagdishpur	2,200	Snam Progetti
Under Construction			
1.	Nagarjuna Fertilizers & Chemicals Kakinada	1,500	Snam
2.	Chambal Fertilizers and Chemicals Ltd. Gadepan	2,200	Snam
3.	Tata Chemicals Ltd., Babrala	2,200	Snam
4.	Bindal Agro, Shahjahanpur	2,200	Snam

Source: "Handbook on Fertiliser Technology" (1992)

3. Methods of Production

3.1. Classification of Processes

3.1.1. Ammonium carbamate decomposition

Ammonia and CO_2 are compressed and reacted at 100-200 atms., and 170°-190°C in an autoclave to form ammonium carbamate ($NH_4 \cdot COO \cdot NH_2$). Urea is formed by dehydration in a low-pressure stripping operation. Process modifications occur in recycle of unreacted NH_3-CO_2 and percentage excess NH_3 in reactants.

3.2. Urea by Ammonium Carbamate Decomposition

3.2.1. Reference flow sheet: Figure IIE-3

3.2.2. Chemical reactions

(a) $CO_2 + 2NH_3 \rightarrow \underset{\text{ammonium carbamate}}{NH_4 \cdot COO \cdot NH_2}$; $\Delta H° = -37.4$ Kcal

(b) $NH_4 \cdot COO \cdot NH_2 \rightarrow \underset{\text{urea}}{NH_2 \cdot CO \cdot NH_2} + H_2O$; $\Delta H° = +6.3$ Kcal

Undesirable side reaction

(c) $2NH_2 \cdot CO \cdot NH_2 \rightarrow \underset{\text{biuret}}{NH_2 \cdot CO \cdot NH \cdot CO \cdot NH_2} + NH_3$

3.2.3. Raw materials

The principal raw materials required for this purpose are CO_2 from synthesis gas manufacture, and NH_3.

3.2.4. Quantitative requirements

(a) Basis: 1 ton of prilled urea (99+%)

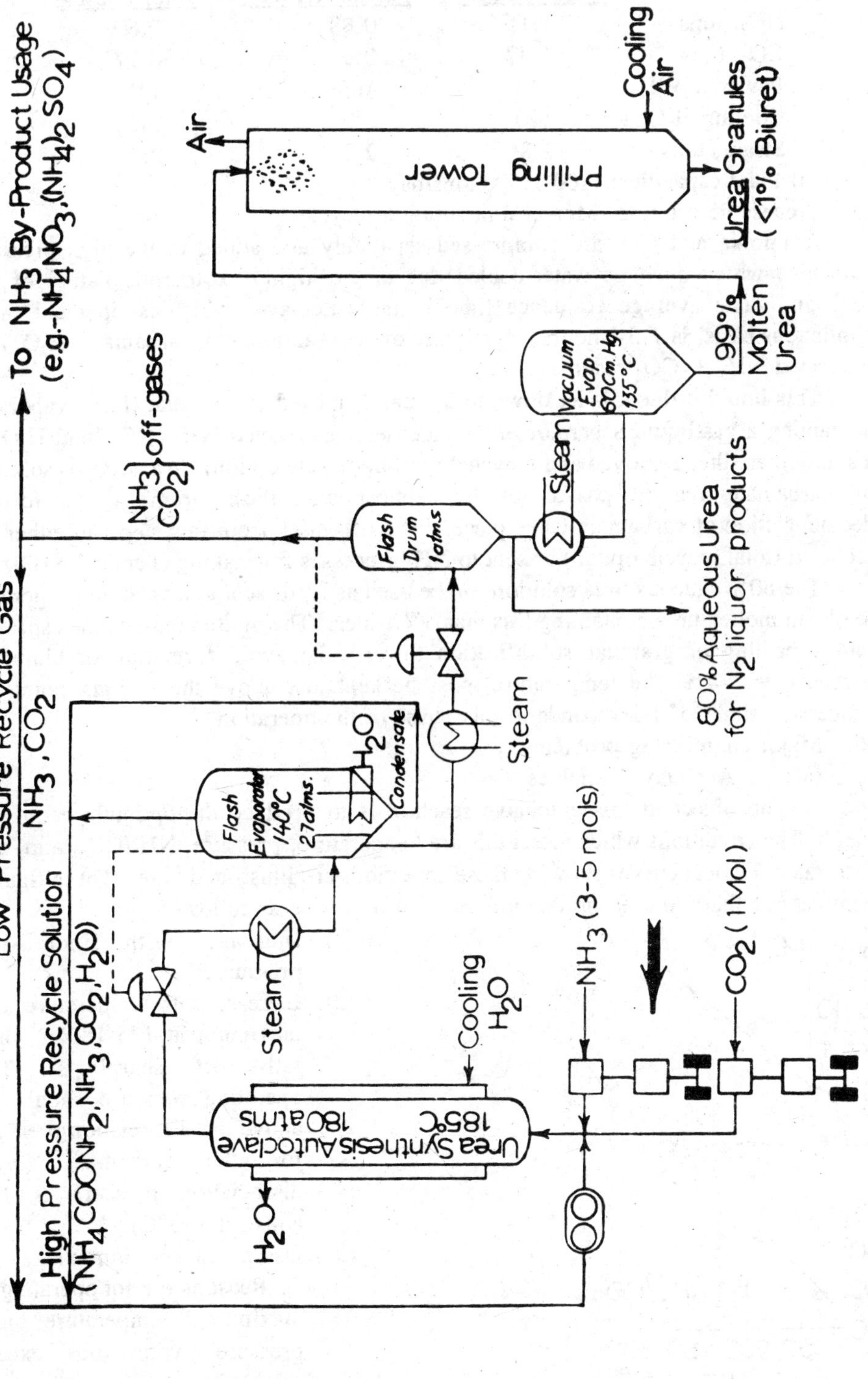

Fig. IIE-3. Urea from ammonium carbamate.

	Once-through	*Partial Recycle*	*Total Recycle*
NH_3, tons	1.15	0.88	0.60
CO_2, tons	1.47	0.91	0.77
Power, KWH	210	165	145
Cooling H_2O, tons	120	70	110
Steam, tons	1.8	2.0	2.4

(b) Plant capacities: 100-1,500 tons/day

3.2.5. Process description (Montecatini solution recycle)

Ammonia and CO_2 are compressed separately and added to the high pressure autoclave which must be water-cooled due to the highly exothermic nature of the reaction. The average residence time in the autoclave, which is operated on a continuous basis, is 1.5-2 hours. A mixture of urea, ammonium carbamate, H_2O, and unreacted $NH_3 + CO_2$ results.

This liquid effluent is let down to 27 atms. and fed to a special flash-evaporator containing a gas-liquid separator and condenser. Unreacted NH_3, CO_2, and H_2O as a solution are thus removed and recycled (partial recycle option). An aqueous solution of carbamate-urea is passed to the atmospheric flash drum where further decomposition of carbamate takes place. The off-gases from this step can either be recycled (total recycle option) or sent to NH_3 processes for making chemical fertilizer.

The 80% aqueous urea solution can be used as is, or sent to a vacuum evaporator to obtain molten urea containing less than 1% water. The molten mass is then sprayed into a prilling or granular solidification tower. To avoid formation of biuret in percentages >1%, the temperature must be kept just above the melting point for processing times of 1-2 seconds in this phase of the operation.

3.2.6. Major engineering problems

(a) Autoclave variables

The object in this autoclave reaction is to produce the optimum economic yield. The conditions which affect this are temperature, pressure, NH_3/CO_2 ratio, and feed rate. Typical curves showing these conditions are illustrated here. These figures demonstrate that the urea production rate can be varied as follows:

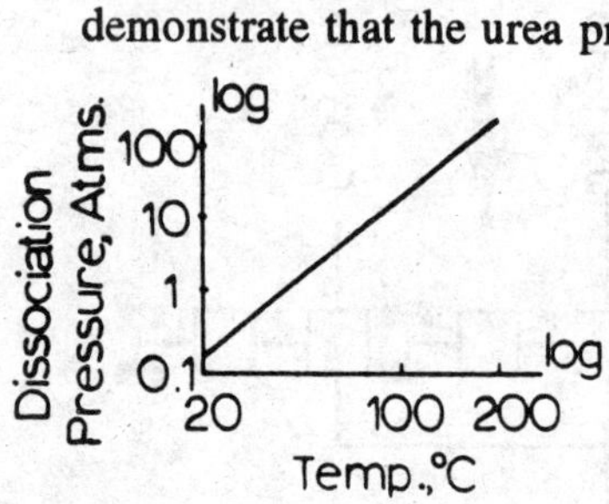

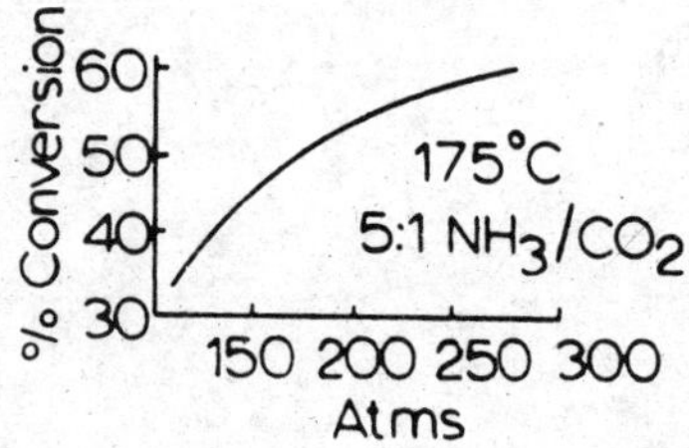

(1) Increase with increasing pressure.
(2) Increase with temperature to a maximum at 175-180°C, then falls off sharply. The operating pressure should be above the dissociation pressure for the carbamate (*e.g.*, dissociation pressure is 180 atms. at 190°C).
(3) Use no excess ammonia.

Reasons for not operating at maximum temperature and pressure with no excess ammonia are:

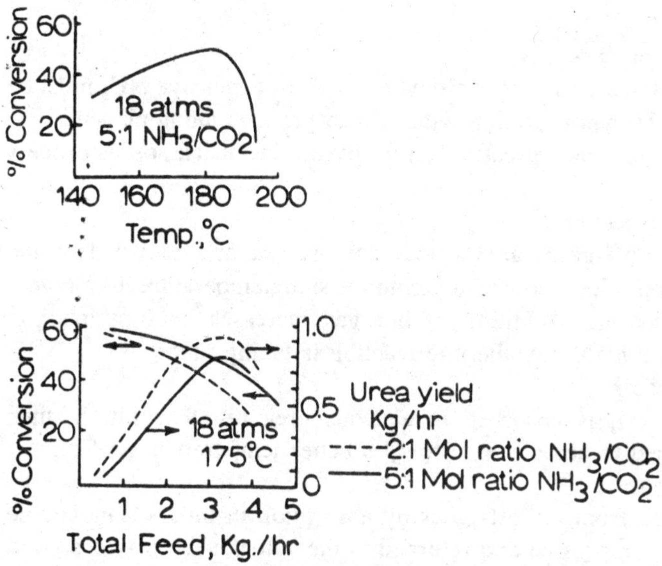

Reproduced with permission from *Chem. Eng. Progress*, **54** (4) : 56-57 (1958).

(1) Increased pressure increases capital and operating costs of compression and reaction equipment.

(2) Increased temperature accelerates decomposition of urea to biuret, a compound detrimental to germinating seeds and toxic to animals.

(3) The above stipulated conditions produce intolerable corrosion rates, and a compromise design must be chosen.

(b) Carbamate decomposition and recycle

Optimized by short residence times in a stripping column operating at conditions favorable for dissociation—low pressure and high temperature. The latter should be below 110°C if hold-up time exceeds 1-2 seconds to avoid biuret formation. Use of millisecond contact time in a flash evaporator allows 140°C operating temperatures in the high recycle design shown in Figure IIE-3.

Main difference in competing processes (see below) is in the recycle design. Since conversion is only 40-50% per pass, the unreacted off-gases must be recirculated or used economically elsewhere. Recompression of off-gases is virtually impossible because of corrosion and formation of solid carbamate in compressors. In the flow sheet of Figure IIE-3, a solution is formed and pumped into the autoclave.

(c) Production of granular urea (Prilling)

Problem again is biuret formation. Vacuum drying of 80% urea to 99+% and spraying to air cool and solidify must be done just above the melting point of urea and with a minimum residence time in the range of several seconds.

(d) Heat dissipation in the autoclave

The exothermic heat of reaction can be removed by coils, wall cooling, or by adding excess reactants to provide sensible heat pick-up.

(e) Corrosion

This has been the major reason why the NH_3-CO_2 process was slow to develop. High cost silver or tantalum liners are used in the autoclaves with Hastelloy C, titanium, stainless steel (321 SS), and aluminum alloys used in other parts of the plant. Minimum temperature and pressure conditions with excess NH_3 are desirable to reduce the severe corrosion rates. Under these conditions, stainless steel can be used in the autoclave.

(f) Process design modifications

Only major differences are in off-gas treatment and their effect on the remainder of process:

(1) Once-through process

Simplest, as off-gases are used elsewhere. More expensive NH_3 must be reclaimed, usually by neutralization with acid to produce ammonia salts.

Demand for urea is now greater than for by-product salts; so this process is unattractive.

(2) Hot-recycle process

CO_2 and NH_3 off-gases are heated, compressed and recycled to the autoclave. Requires close control of compression temperature to prevent carbamate solidification. Addition of hot gas increases cooling load on autoclave in which a highly exothermic reaction is taking place.

(3) "Inventa" process

Unconverted NH_3 is absorbed in aqueous urea nitrate solution, then stripped and returned to autoclave. Provides better temperature control.

(4) "Chemico" process

CO_2 is stripped from the off-gases by absorption in monoethanolamine (MEA). NH_3 is recompressed and returned to the autoclave. Provides good temperature control.

(5) Solution recycle (Montecatini)

This is essentially described by Figure IIE-3. Recycle gases are absorbed in reaction product water and pumped back to the autoclave. Its advantage is in optimum autoclave temperature control, but requires higher pressures, temperatures, and excess NH_3 to obtain good conversion per pass.

(6) "Pechiney" process

Uses mineral oil as a carrier for temperature control and to minimize corrosion problems. Mineral oil-urea liquid is passed to a carbamate stripper. Urea solution is withdrawn from the bottom and the oil is pumped to a carbamate slurry tank where off-gases are mixed with cool oil to form a slurry of oil-carbamate crystals which is returned to the autoclave.

(7) Dutch State Mines (Stamicarbon) process

Reactor effluent is not expanded to a lower pressure, as in the conventional urea process, but is stripped at synthesis pressure by CO_2 feed gas in a special heated stripper.

(8) Allied Chemical high pressure process

This process is operated in India at Visakhapatnam. It has been licensed by Allied Chemical to Vulcan-Cincinnati who built the Vizag plant. The process operates at about 275 atmospheres pressure and 400°F. It features a high conversion of 75% per pass and does not recycle carbamates. Reactor effluent is flashed to recover NH_3 and CO_2 and the urea-water mixture remaining is fed to an evaporator at the top of the urea prill tower. A zirconium-lined reactor is used to minimize corrosion.

(9) Toyo Koatsu process

This type of plant combines an ammonia and urea process with consequent substantial savings in capital investment and utility requirements. The essence of the process is that the carbon dioxide formed in the ammonia plant by the shift reaction is absorbed by a mixture of hot carbamate solution (from the urea plant) and ammonia (from the ammonia synthesis loop). The resulting mixture is passed straight to the urea reactor.

The process used in India's largest single fertilizer plant—that of Indian Explosives Ltd. at Kanpur in Uttar Pradesh—is a version of the Toyo Koatsu process employing total recycle.

4. **Economics**

4.1. Market and Sales

4.1.1. Fertilizer

The major reason for the rapid growth of urea (doubling time—3 years) is the worldwide shift to the high nutrient-high nitrogen fertilizers provided by urea in solid or aqueous solution form. Urea is replacing the highly acidic ammonium salts in regions where soil is already too acid and lime is scarce.

Urea can be easily granulated. It also provides a medium for a slow-release variety of fertilizer by forming a low molecular weight urea-formaldehyde polymer.

4.1.2. Industrial chemicals

Major uses in plastics, particularly urea-formaldehyde and urea-melamine types.

4.1.3. Animal feed

Ruminants such as cattle and sheep are capable of digesting urea up to 40% of their total protein requirements. The balance can be provided with low-cost carbohydrate feeds containing low protein. Such supplements are only practical in countries where urea is abundant and cheap. This is not the case for India.

4.2. Investments

Urea plants are adjuncts to ammonia production complexes so that the major investments in utilities have already been made.

Ammonium Nitrate

1. **Pertinent Properties**

Mol. wt.	80.05
M.P.	170°C
B.P.	Decomposes at 200°C or higher
Solubility:	Soluble in water (900 gm/liter at 20°C), alcohol and NH_3
Grades:	C.P.—white hygroscopic crystals or granules; fertilizer—93-95% containing 33% N

Explosive when mixed with combustible materials or exposed to high temperatures.

2. **Consumption Pattern**

The increased use of nitrogen as agricultural fertilizer has placed a heavy demand for ammonium nitrate salts in mixed fertilizers. Little is used for direct application in India because nitrate nitrogen is inferior to ammoniacal nitrogen, particularly in rice paddies. It is converted to nitrolime or nitrochalk (calcium ammonium nitrate) and ammonium sulfate nitrate.

2.1. End Uses

	USA	*India*
Fertilizer	85%	>90%
Explosives	12	
Misc. chemicals	3	

The chief use of ammonium nitrate until after World War II was as an explosive. Although it still accounts for more than 75% of all explosives, its major use is now as a fertilizer because of its high nitrogen content, 33.5% N.

3. Methods of Production

3.1. Classification of Processes

All processes are based on the reaction of nitric acid and ammonia with principal variations in methods of producing the product in solid form as pellets, crystals or flakes.

3.2. Reference Flow Sheet: Figure IIE-4

3.3. Chemical Reaction

$$NH_3 + HNO_3 \rightarrow NH_4NO_3; \qquad \Delta H = -20.6 \text{ Kcal}$$

3.4. Raw Materials

- 57-60% HNO_3 from oxidation-absorption tower
- Liquid NH_3
- Clay such as diatomaceous earth, kieselguhr for coating on end-product to avoid explosions

3.5. Quantitative Requirements

(a) Basis: 1 ton of ammonium nitrate (98% yield)

Ammonia	0.22 ton
60% HNO_3	1.38

(b) Plant capacities: 100-500 tons/day

3.6. Process Description

The process flow sheet shows three or four modifications now in use in different plants, all based on ammonia-nitric acid reaction.

3.6.1. Prilling process

The ammonia vapor is reacted with aqueous nitric acid in a stainless steel reaction vessel with agitation. The heat of reaction causes water to boil off and the final salt solution is 75% and 140°C when pumped to a vacuum evaporator to concentrate further to 95% solids. The hot liquor is sprayed from the top of a prilling tower (60-75 meters high) counter-current to conditioned air flow. The solidified spherical pellets or prills are about 1.5 mm in diameter and must be screened and dried before coating with clay. Fines and oversized material are redissolved and sent to the neutralizing reactor for recycle.

Development work has been done on a centrifugal oil-quenching process for prill production which may result in replacement of large and costly prilling towers with more compact equipment.

3.6.2. Crystallization process (not shown on flow sheet)

This process is similar to the prilling process up to the point of spraying. The liquor from the vacuum evaporator contains 80-85% solids and is fed to a vacuum

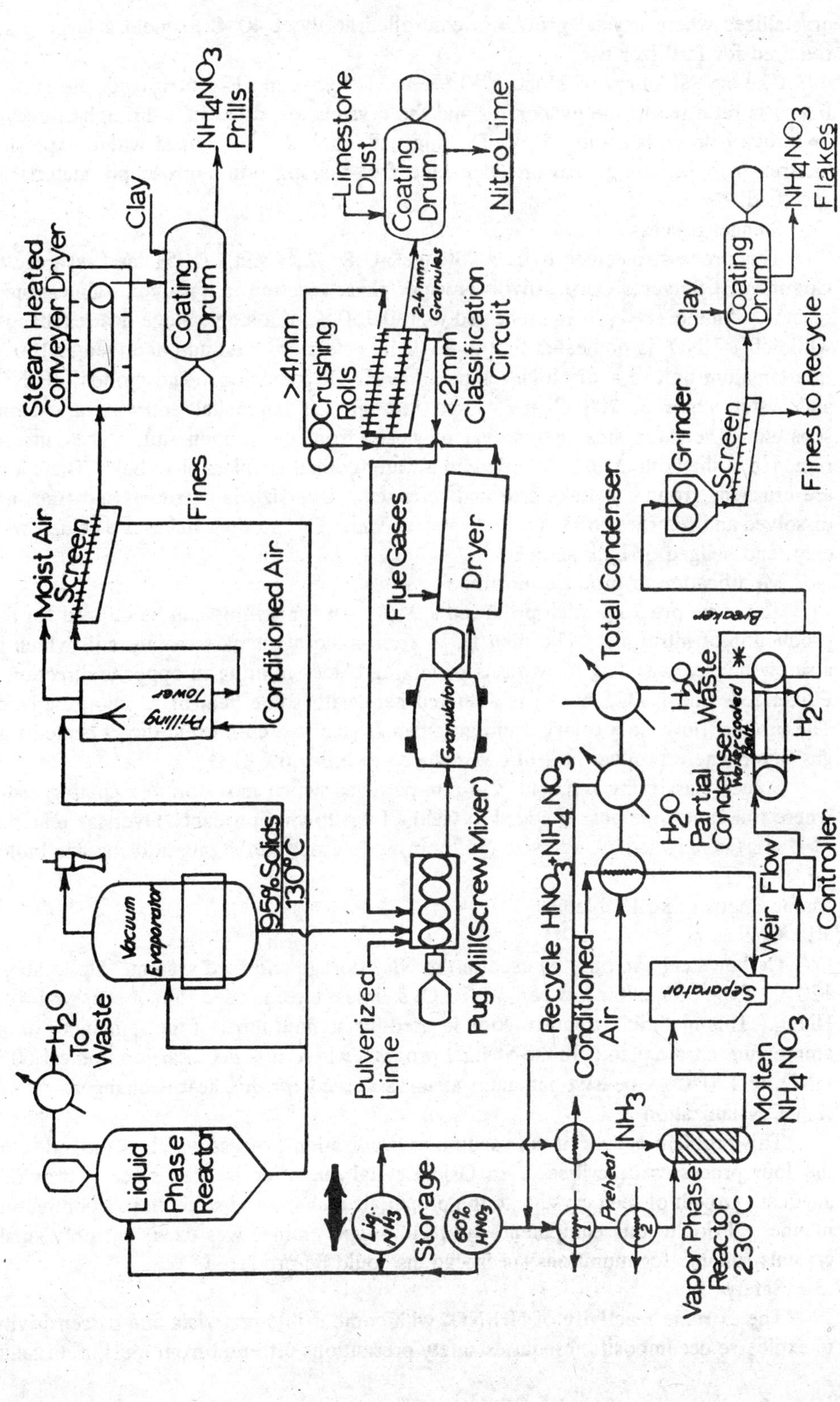

Fig. IIE-4. Production of ammonium nitrate and nitrolime.

crystallizer where crystal growth is controlled at about 40°C to yield a large grain required for fertilizer use.

The crystal slurry with about 40% crystals by weight is centrifuged; the mother liquor is returned to the evaporator and the crystals are dried in a through-conveyor or a rotary dryer at about 15°C. Dusting with clay (2-4%) is used where explosion hazards in bulk storage are prevalent and free-flowing non-hygroscopic material is specified.

3.6.3. Stengel process

This process, patented by L.A. Stengel, U.S., 2,568,901 (1951) and assigned to Commercial Solvents Corp., involves vapor phase reaction in a packed stainless steel reactor. Ammonia vapor is preheated to 140-150°C in a single stage heat exchanger while 60% HNO_3 is preheated first to 95°C in a stainless steel unit and then to 160°C in a tantalum unit to avoid high temperature HNO_3 corrosion. The molten NH_4NO_3 and water vapor at 200°C are passed through the tangential entry of a cyclone separator where air aids in removal of steam from the molten salt. The latter is removed at the bottom and solidified on a water-cooled stainless steel belt. The solids are crushed, ground to flake size and screened. Oversize is reground and fines are dissolved and returned to HNO_3 preheater stream. The product flakes are coated with clay, and bagged or bulk shipped.

3.6.4. Modification to produce nitrolime

The same process which produced a 95% melt for prilling can be utilized for the production of nitrolime. The melt flows from a storage tank to a pug mill which is a screw mixer consisting of two sets of mixing blades rotating in opposite directions. Pulverized lime (—325 mesh) is admixed here with some heat of reaction evolved. The product flows to a rotary drum granulator, then to a co-current direct heated flue gas dryer where product moisture is reduced to 0.5-0.6% H_2O.

Screen classifying separates 2-4 mm particles which move on to a coating drum where fine limestone dust is added to yield a free-flowing product. Oversize material (>4 mm) is recycled. Undersize (<2 mm) is returned to the pug mill for size build-up.

3.7. Major Engineering Problems

3.7.1. Corrosion

Carbon steel can only be used in the NH_3 storage and feed system. Up to about 120°C, Type 304, extra-low carbon (ELC) stainless steel is used for aqueous or 100% HNO_3. This material of construction is used throughout most of the remainder of an ammonium nitrate plant. In the Stengel process, where it is necessary to preheat 60% HNO_3 to 170°C, expensive tantalum metal is needed for this heat exchanger.

3.7.2. Crystallization

This problem occurs in the vacuum crystallization process which is the oldest of the four processes described. An Oslo-Krystal classifier is used since it provides adequate growth of seed crystals to the proper size, shape and strength in a continuous manner. Prior to this equipment, the paddle type grainer was used, but only small crystals suitable for munitions specifications could be produced.

3.7.3. Safety

The extreme reactivity of NH_4NO_3 with combustible materials and its sensitivity to explosive decomposition requires safety precautions different from most in organic processing. Any air used in drying must be free of oil and other combustibles. The Stengel process has the greatest inherent safety in its design since the equipment is designed for short residence times and low hold-up.

3.7.4. Conditioned air requirements

Both NH_4NO_3 and nitrolime are hygroscopic so that humidity and temperature requirements of the air in the materials handling area are critical. Air conditioning is requisite; for example, at Rourkela a 1,200 ton refrigeration unit is required.

Economics

4.1. Ammonium nitrate *per se* as a fertilizer end-product has no application in India because it has too high a leaching rate on soil application. Consequently, it is strictly an intermediate in the manufacture of nitrolime and ammonium sulfate nitrate.

4.2. Plant Location

Only captive production in an ammonia-nitric acid plant complex is competitive. It is especially desirable if a balanced plant production-sales for urea and mixed fertilizers can be achieved. The ammonia off-gases from the once-through urea can be used to make ammonium nitrate or nitrolime. The 1,800 ton per day nitrolime fertilizer plant at Rourkela is strictly an ammonium nitrate processing plant with no urea facilities. Built at a cost of Rs. 21 crores, this plant is one of the largest fertilizer plants in the world. It was located at Rourkela to utilize the gases from the by-product coke ovens of the steel plant. The proximity of coal and iron has thus dictated the site location for fertilizer plant.

Plants producing prilled ammonium nitrate in India include the following:

1. Anil Chemicals Ltd.,
   J-18, MIDC Area, Chikalthana - 431 210, Dist. Aurangabad (Maharashtra)
2. Atash Industries India Ltd.,
   Village Lohop Patalganga, Taluk Khalapur, Dist. Raigad (Maharashtra)
3. Deepak Nitrite Ltd.,
   Nandesari, Baroda (Gujarat)
4. Fertilizer Corporation of India Ltd.,
   P.O. Sindri, Dist. Dhanbad (Bihar)
5. ICI (India) Ltd.,
   Gomia, Dist. Giridih (Bihar)
6. Steel Authority of India Ltd.,
   Rourkela Steel Plant, Rourkela (Orissa)
7. Sterling Nitrochem Ltd.
8. VBC Industries Ltd.

4.3. Choice of Processes for NH_4NO_3 as the End-product

The Stengel process is considered the cheapest for new investment money. It is also the safest from a hazard standpoint.

4.4. Investment Statistics

The incremental capital required to expand a nitric acid-ammonia complex to include NH_4NO_3 manufacture varies with the degree of integration and relative size of the various plants in the complex. As a rough figure, use 10% of the cost of a nitric acid plant investment.

Ammonium Chloride

Ammonium chloride is used as a fertilizer for rice and some other crops in a limited way since it may increase the residual chloride content of some soils.

Besides its use as fertilizer, pure ammonium chloride (technical grade) is also used in the manufacture of dry cells, and as a flux in galvanizing and tinning industries.

IIF. PHOSPHORUS INDUSTRIES

1. Introduction

Phosphorus in elemental form and in its many products is derived from commercial deposits of phosphate rock in the mineral form fluorapatite $[Ca_{10}(PO_4)_6F_2]$.

Major products of a fully-developed phosphate industry are:

- Phosphorus
- Phosphoric acid
- Ammonium phosphate (largely as fertilizers)
- Calcium phosphate (largely as fertilizers)
- Nitrophosphate (largely as fertilizers)
- Sodium phosphate
- Organic phosphates

2. Consumption Pattern

The phosphorus industry of India is at present tied nearly 100% to fertilizer planning and production. Consequently, it has grown at the same pace as the nitrogen industries.

2.1. Rock Phosphates

Phosphorus content of rock phosphate is expressed as percentage P_2O_5. In trade, it is expressed as bone phosphate of lime (BPL) which chemically means the tricalcium phosphate content, i.e., $Ca_3(PO_4)_2$.

The high grade rock phosphate from Jhamarkotra containing +30 percent P_2O_5 is used for superphosphate manufacture. The rock phosphate from Jhabua and Chattarpur is used for the production of elemental phosphorus and in fertilizer mixtures. Mussoorie rock phosphate is used for direct application.

About 75 percent of known phosphate occurrences in India are low grade ore with 10 to 25 percent P_2O_5 and requires prior beneficiation to upgrade P_2O_5 content to about 30 percent to make it acceptable as feedstock for fertilizer manufacture.

A commercial beneficiation plant installed by Hindustan Zinc, of 600 tpd capacity, to treat the ore from Maton deposit containing 20-25 percent P_2O_5 and SiO_2 varying up to 30 percent is in operation since 1975. A 200 tpd mobile semi-industrial plant has been installed by RSMML at Udaipur. Based on its experience, a large commercial beneficiation plant of 2,700 tpd capacity was being installed at Jhamarkotra for beneficiating low grade (18-20 percent) Jhamarkotra rock containing high dolomite. The commercial plant was expected to be operative during the end of 1991. For the Jhabua and Lalitpur silicious rock phosphate setting up of a moderate sized commercial beneficiation plant is under consideration.

Domestic production of rock phosphate during 1990-91 was about 5.5 lakh tons. As the demand for rock phosphate outstrips the domestic supply, bulk of India's rock phosphate requirements is met through imports from Jordan, Morocco, Senegal, Florida and Togo. About 3.5 million tons of rock phosphate was imported during 1990-91.

World phosphate ore reserves are estimated as shown in Table IIF-1.

Table IIF-1 Reserves of Phosphate Ores in 10^9 tons

World	North America	South America	Western Europe	Eastern Europe	Africa	Western Asia	Eastern Asia	Oceania
67.1	12.9	2.8	1.0	4.0	33.7	2.9	7.1	2.7

Source: "Industrial Inorganic Chemistry" by Buchner et al (1989)

World phosphate ore production figures are as shown in Table IIF-2.

Table IIF-2. World Phosphate Ore Production 1982-1984 in 10^6 t

	1982	1983	1984
USA	37.4	42.6	48.4
Mexico	0.4	0.4	0.4
Central and South America	2.8	3.2	3.5
Africa	30.1	33.7	35.5
—Morocco	17.9	20.1	21.2
—Tunisia	4.2	5.9	5.3
Western Asia	9.0	10.2	12.4
—Jordan	4.4	4.7	6.3
Eastern Asia	14.1	14.1	15.0
Western Europe	0.4	0.5	0.5
Australia and Oceania	2.9	2.8	2.8
Eastern Europe	26.6	27.7	28.0

Source: "Industrial Inorganic Chemistry" by Buchner et al (1989)

Phosphorus

1. Pertinent Properties

1.1. Yellow Phosphorus (P_4)

Mol. wt.	123.9
M.P.	44.1°C
B.P.	280°C
Density (gm/cc):	
Solid	1.82
Liquid	1.74 (45°C)

Ignites spontaneously in air, must be stored under water. Possesses disagreeable odor with extreme toxicity.

1.2. Red Phosphorus (P_4)

Mol. wt.	123.9
M.P.	593°C
Density of solid	2.36 gm/cc

Exists in at least six different crystal modifications. Formed by heating yellow phosphorus to give a higher degree of oxidation resistance and stability.

2. Consumption Pattern

Approximately 18-20% of the phosphate rock processed in the U.S. is initially converted to elementary phosphorus. The principal derivative of phosphorus is high purity phosphoric acid in a whole range of concentrations from 50% aqueous grade up to superphosphoric acid (85% P_2O_5 = 100% H_3PO_4 + 11% free P_2O_5). These acids go largely to the food and detergent industries.

2.1. End Uses of Elemental Phosphorus in the USA

Phosphoric acid (high purity and strength for detergents and food chemicals)	90%
Phosphorus oxychloride ($POCl_3$)	3
Phosphorus trichloride (PCl_3)	3
Phosphorus pentoxide, red phosphorus for matches and incendiaries and otherwise	4

3. Methods of Production

3.1. Reference Flow Sheet: Figure IIF-1

3.2. Chemical Reactions

(a) $2Ca_3(PO_4)_2 + 10C + 6SiO_2 \rightarrow P_4$ (yellow grade) + $6CaSiO_3 + 10CO$

(b) P_4 (yellow grade) $\xrightarrow[250\text{-}450°C]{}$ P_4 (red grade)

3.3. Raw Materials

Low grade, crushed phosphate rock, coke as reductant, and sand as flux

3.4. Quantitative Requirements

(a) Basis: 1 ton of yellow phosphorus (93% yield)

Phosphate rock	7.5 tons at 32% P_2O_5 to 9.6 tons at 25% P_2O_5
Sand	3.3-3.8 tons
Coke	1.6-1.8 tons
Carbon electrode consumption	18-25 kg
Electricity	12,000-15,000 KWH
Cooling water	200-250 tons

(b) Plant capacities: 25-70 tons/day of P per furnace, 2-5 furnaces per plant

3.5. Process Description

Phosphate rock is ground, mixed with a portion of the coke requirement, then sintered into nodules to obtain better electrical resistivity characteristics and to avoid entrainment of fines in the released P_4 and CO vapors. Screening is necessary to maintain size control with the fines recycled to the sintering operation. Coke breeze (relatively small particles produced in the coking of coal) and sand are mixed in controlled quantities based on phosphate rock analysis.

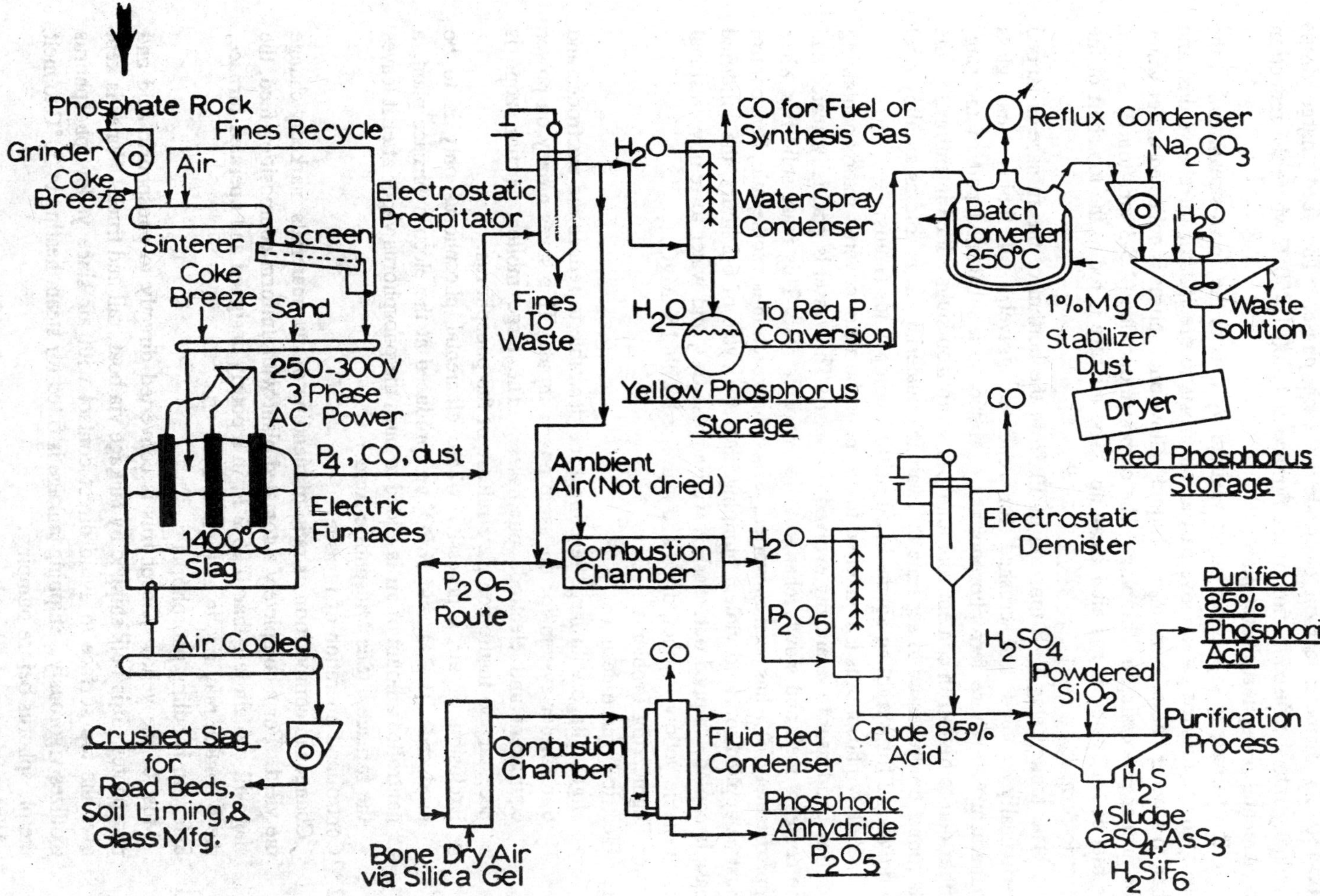

Fig. IIF-1. Production of elemental phosphorus, phosphorus pentoxide and phosphoric acid by electric furnace method.

The electric furnace is 250-300 volt AC-three phase design with power fed to one 100-150 cm diameter carbon electrode on each phase. The feed charge drops gradually into the fused section of the furnace at 1,400-1,450°C where the reduction to elemental phosphorus takes place.

The furnace is kept under slight vacuum by fans in the down-stream end of the plant, so the furnace gases move past an electrostatic precipitator to remove dust and then to a water-cooled condenser. Liquid yellow phosphorus is collected under water for further processing or shipping. The carbon monoxide (2.5-3 tons/ton P) is used as fuel or for synthesis gas after clean-up. The mixture is fed to the top shaft of the electric furnace.

The molten slag (~8 tons/ton of P) from the bottom of the furnace is tapped periodically, cooled and crushed for road-bed gravel, soil liming, and glass manufacture. Where ferrophosphorus by-product is a substantial part of the slag, either due to high-iron content rock or from scrap iron slugs added intentionally, the slag must be processed to separate this valuable material. It is sold as an alloy steel additive and for weighting agents in oil drilling compounds (muds).

Yellow phosphorus is converted to red phosphorus in covered retorts containing a reflux condenser to retain any evolved P_4 vapor. The vessel is gradually heated and the contents melt and slowly change to red phosphorus. This mass solidifies when approximately 70% has been converted. Since this reaction is exothermic, heat control must be applied to avoid violent bumping. After a cycle of 6-8 hours, the solidified mass is cooled, chipped out, washed with aq. Na_2CO_3 and water to remove residual and unstable yellow P_4, then dried and stabilized with 1% MgO.

3.6. Major Engineering Problems

3.6.1. Electric furnace design

- High voltage with large reaction zone desirable to reduce the electrodes and transformer system for the same power input. This saves money on power equipment and electrode purchases. The large molten reaction zone is necessary to insure complete release of the phosphorus.
- Exclusion of air a necessity where elemental phosphorus only is to be produced. If P_2O_5 and H_3PO_4 are produced at the electric furnace plant, a controlled amount of air is added to burn the phosphorus vapor after it leaves the furnace. (See Phosphoric Acid.)

3.6.2. Control and operation of furnace

Changes in composition or ratio of blending of raw materials markedly change the yield. For a completely automated plant with uniform composition feed, the slag will contain less than 0.25% P; in a poorly designed and operated furnace, the P content may rise to as high as 2%.

3.6.3. Safety in handling phosphorus

Most of the yellow phosphorus is converted directly to phosphoric acid and phosphates. It is bulk shipped by tankage via boat, rail and truck. Water is kept over the top surface to avoid direct contact with air since yellow phosphorus oxidizes vigorously. Shipping tankage is fitted for steam heating to 50°C to melt the phosphorus before pumping.

Where elemental phosphorus must be used directly, as in incendiaries and matches, conversion to the less poisonous red allotropic form with improved oxidation resistance is required.

4. Economics

4.1. Plant Location

The usual economic balance is between shipping large tonnage of raw materials (~15 tons/ton of P) and the cost of electric power. Market locations of phosphorus and derivatives are of secondary importance. In India, seaport locations will be best with shipping of P or H_3PO_4 inland to fertilizer plants. In the USA, elemental phosphorus is shipped as far as 1,000 miles for conversion to pure phosphoric acid and phosphates for food and detergent industry.

4.2. Selection of Raw Materials and By-product Usage

P_2O_5 content of imported rock should be high, (35-40%) to avoid excessive shipping costs and increased by-products disposal. In a typical plant, several hundred tons per day of slag, CO, and ferrosilicon are difficult to dispose of. Much of the slag is dumped on waste piles with the only proven use as a road-bed material.

4.3. Capital Investment

Plant costs would be about Rs. 5 crores for a 75 ton/day plant in India with the electric furnace requiring 40-50% of this cost, depending on size.

4.4. Competition

The main end use of electric furnace phosphorus is phosphoric acid. A wet process using strong sulfuric acid for the H_3PO_4 was originally developed in the USA (see following pages). In 1920, the electric furnace was developed to the point where it could use lower grades of rock and produce low-cost acid of high purity. In the late 1950's, improvement in the wet process flow diagram and cheaper equipment have produced acid of reasonably good purity at costs below that produced via electric furnace. In countries where there is excess Cl_2 and HCl, a wet process using HCl may be utilized. Such is the case in India. The future growth of the elemental phosphorus business will depend on developing non-H_3PO_4 products of high purity such as organic phosphates for engine additives and lubricants.

The USA production of elemental phosphorus was ca. 570 x 10^3 t in 1969, 332 x 10^3 t in 1983 and 348 x 10^3 t in 1984. This decline has been mainly caused by increasing energy costs, which make the production of phosphoric acid for fertilizer from elemental phosphorus increasingly uneconomic. In addition, the incorporation of phosphates in household detergents has decreased due to ecological reasons.

Table IIF-3 gives a survey of elemental phosphorus production capacities in different countries and regions.

Table IIF-3
Phosphorus Capacities in 1984 in 10^3 t/a

USA	412
Canada	90
Mexico	10
Western Europe	200
West Germany	80
The Netherlands	90
Comecon	715
Russia	615
South Africa	6
India	10

Source: "Industrial Inorganic Chemistry" by Buchner et al (1989)

Phosphoric Acid

1. Pertinent Properties of Orthophosphoric Acid (H_3PO_4)

Mol. wt.	98; forms $(H_3PO_4)_2 \cdot H_2O$ in water solutions
M.P.	42.4°C
B.P.	Loses water of hydration from $(H_3PO_4)_2 \cdot H_2O$ at 213°C
Density	1.83 gm/cc at 20°C

Completely miscible with water

Grades: Shipped in concentrations from 50% H_3PO_4 in H_2O up to an equivalent 118% solid (100% H_3PO_4 + 11% P_2O_5) as technical, commercial, USP and food grades. Shipping containers are made from rubber-lined steel, or glass.

2. Consumption Pattern

Virtually all of the annual phosphate rock processing in India is attributed to the manufacture of phosphoric acid. This in turn is converted largely to calcium and ammonium phosphates for concentrated fertilizers at the production site.

2.1. End Uses

	USA	*India*
Fertilizers	42%	>90%
Soaps and detergents	37	
Food chemicals	12	

3. Methods of Production

3.1. Wet Process—accounts for 2/3 of production in USA
- 3.1.1. Strong sulfuric acid leaching
- 3.1.2. Hydrochloric acid leaching (Israel Mining Industries = IMI process)

3.2. Electric Furnace Processes
- 3.2.1. Direct conversion at plant site
- 3.2.2. Oxidation and hydration of phosphorus near consumers' market

3.3. Blast Furnace—no longer competitive

4. Wet Process (Strong Sulfuric Acid)

4.1. Reference Flow Sheet: Figure IIF-2

4.2. Chemical Reactions

(a) $Ca_3(PO_4)_2 + 3H_2SO_4 + 6H_2O \rightarrow 2H_3PO_4 + 3(\underbrace{CaSO_4 \cdot 2H_2O}_{\text{gypsum}})$

(b) Side reactions

$$CaF_2 + H_2SO_4 + 2H_2O \rightarrow 2HF + CaSO_4 \cdot 2H_2O$$
$$6HF + SiO_2 \rightarrow H_2SiF_6 + 2H_2O$$

4.3. Raw Materials

The high grade of imported ore is necessary to avoid solubilization of mined rock impurities such as aluminum, silicon, iron oxides, and alkali minerals. In USA a beneficiation process is used on low-grade ore which involves milling, screening, hydroseparation, classification, and flotation.

The only other raw material required is strong sulfuric acid which comes from a contact sulfuric acid plant located at or near the phosphoric acid plant.

4.4. Quantitative Requirements

(a) Basis: 1 ton of 100% H_3PO_4 in 90% yield 2.7 tons of gypsum

Phosphate rock (32% P_2O_5)	2.5 tons
Sulfuric acid (93-98%)	2.0 tons

(b) Plant capacities: 100-150 tons/day of 100% H_3PO_4

4.5. Process Description

Phosphate rock is ground to 65% —200 mesh and fed to a chute where a recycle stream of weak H_3PO_4 washes it into a reaction tank. Strong H_2SO_4 is metered with automatic control which keeps the acid and rock feed ratio at the desired setting.

A single reactor can be designed by proper baffling and residence time capacitance to permit a 98% conversion in 4-6 hours. In other designs, a series of 4-5 continuous mixing tanks can be used with slightly better efficiency of extraction by minimizing backmixing. Heat of reaction is controlled by pulling cooling air across.

The gypsum-phosphoric acid slurry goes to a travelling pan vacuum filter where the 40% acid is removed and the cake washed with water. Filtrate from the latter is returned to the reactor. The gypsum is free-filtering and cake thicknesses of about two inches can be readily obtained. The gypsum can either be dried for use in plaster, paints and cements, or reacted with ammonium carbonates to give ammonium sulfate (fertilizer ingredient) and calcium carbonate (Merseberg process).

The dilute acid is concentrated in a single effect evaporator to any grades $>50\%$ acid. Most of the wet process acid is being converted to high concentration chemical fertilizers.

Pyrophosphoric acid ($H_4P_2O_7$) can be made by heating the orthophosphoric acid to 250°C. By increasing the temperature to red heat (~900°C), metaphosphoric acid (HPO_3) results.

4.6. Major Engineering Problems

4.6.1. Process design

- Fineness of grind—Economic balance between grinding costs and reactor fixed charges as shown by the curves below:

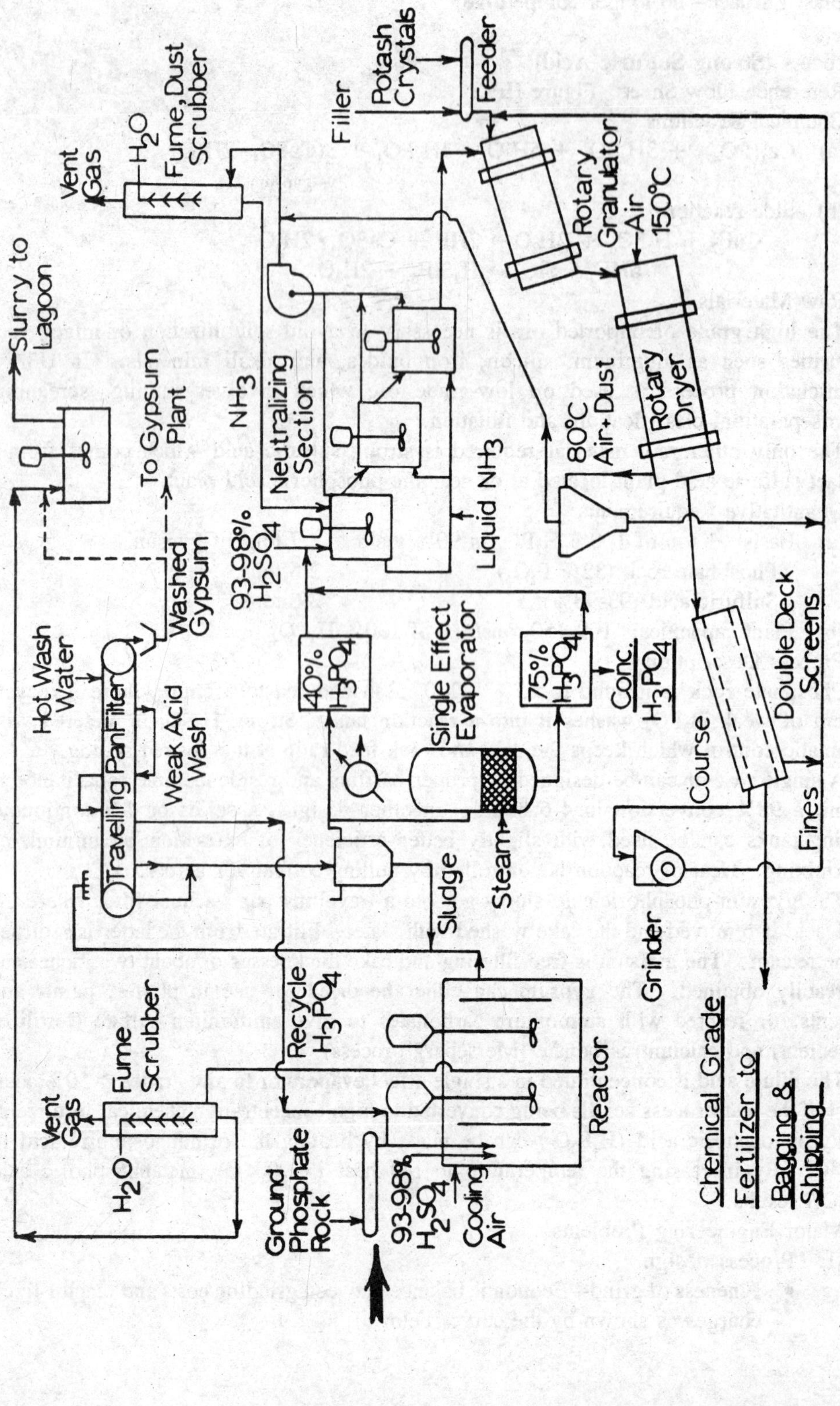

Fig. IIF-2. Production of phosphoric acid and chemical fertilizer from phosphate rock by strong acid process.

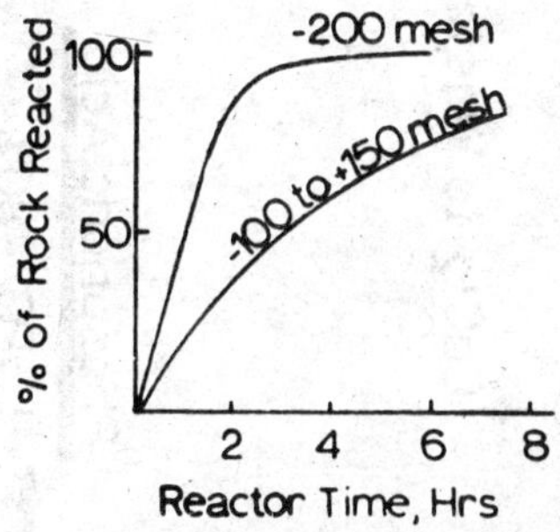

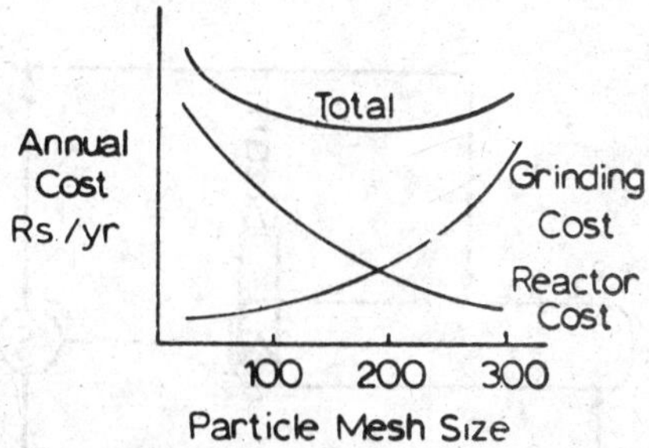

- Temperature—If the temperature is kept above 100°C, undesirable semi-hydrate ($CaSO_4 \cdot 1/2H_2O$) and anhydrate ($CaSO_4$) crystals are formed which are difficult to filter. By digesting at 80°C, the gypsum ($CaSO_4 \cdot 2H_2O$) rhombic crystals predominate and these can be filtered and washed easily.
- Control of sulfuric acid—1-1.5% residual H_2SO_4 is left in the slurry going to the filter, again to produce a more filterable gypsum. Small percentages of sulfuric acid can be tolerated for fertilizer-grade acid. If a purer product is desired, the excess H_2SO_4 is eliminated with a slower filtration rate resulting.

4.6.2. Materials of construction

- Reaction tanks constructed of steel and lined with acid-proof brick
- All air vent systems are polyvinyl chloride (PVC) coated steel
- Filter is Type 316 stainless steel with polypropylene filter cloth and rubber-lined vacuum receivers of steel
- Storage tanks of rubber-lined steel

5. Wet Process (Hydrochloric Acid Leaching) (IMI Process)

5.1. Reference Flow Sheet: Figure IIF-3

5.2. Chemical Reactions

(a) $Ca_3(PO_4)_2 + 6HCl + 6H_2O \rightarrow 2H_3PO_4 + 3CaCl_2$

(b) Side reactions

$CaF_2 + 2HCl \rightarrow 2HF + CaCl_2$

$6HF + SiO_2 \rightarrow H_2SiF_6 + 2H_2O$

5.3. Raw Materials

Phosphate rock of high P_2O_5 content (>30%) is preferred to avoid excessive acid consumption. Hydrogen chloride gas or concentrated aqueous HCl (>30%) as waste or by-product acid is used. Organic C_4 and/or C_5 alcohol solvents are used to extract H_3PO_4 from $CaCl_2$ solution.

5.4. Quantitative Requirements

(a) Basis: 1 ton of 100% H_3PO_4 in 98% yield

Phosphate rock (32% P_2O_5) 2.3 tons

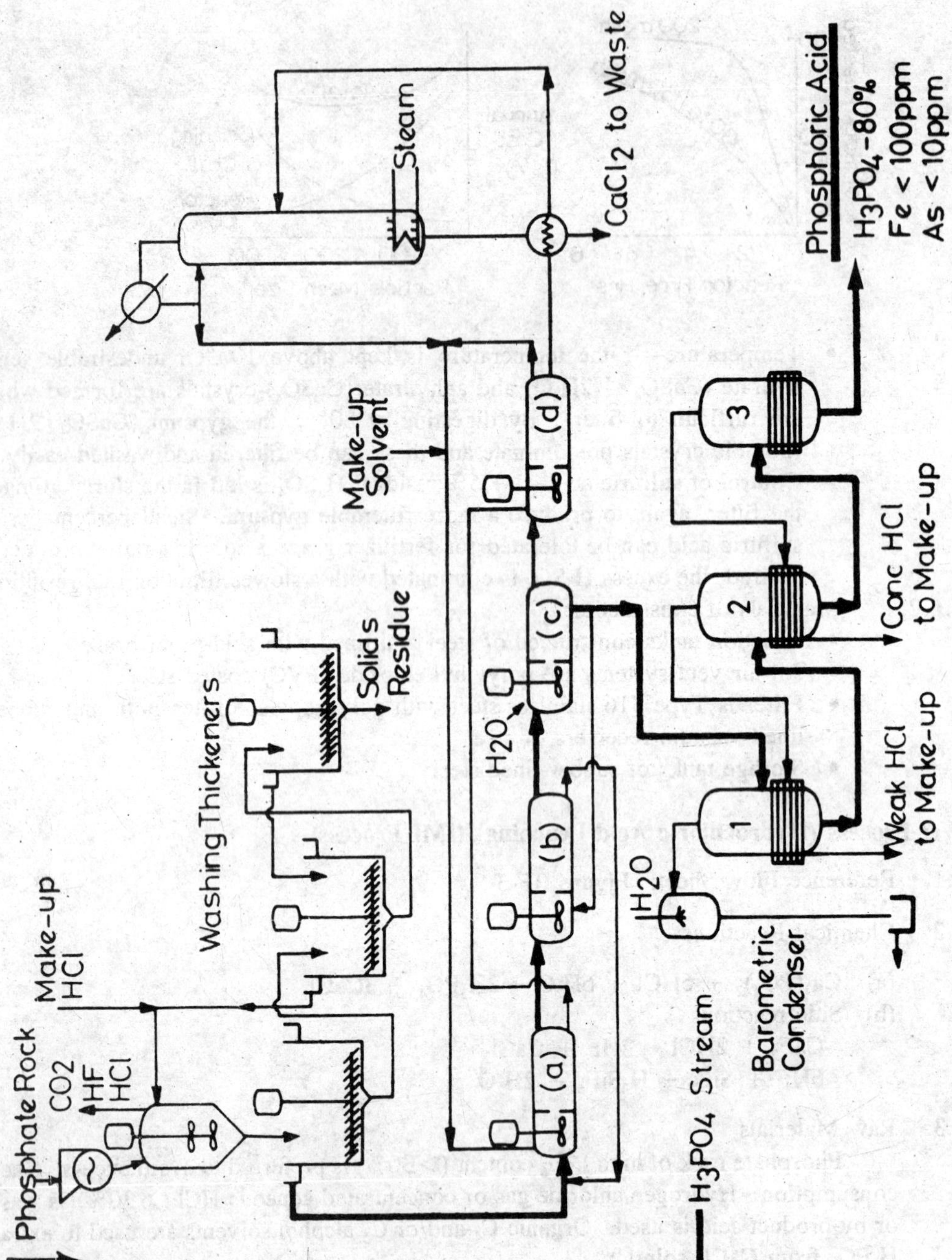

Fig. IIF-3. Production of phosphoric acid by HCl leaching.

HCl (100%)	1.4 tons
Solvent make-up (Butanol or Amyl Alcohol)	3 kg
Flocculating agent	0.4 kg

(b) Plant capacities: 15-150 tons/day of 100% H_3PO_4

5.5. Process Description

Phosphate rock is ground to pass a 20 mesh screen and fed into a dissolver where an acid stream of conc. HCl plus make-up wash water from the counter-current decantation system is added. Fumes of CO_2, HF and HCl are scrubbed for acid recovery.

The mixture is fed to a series of decantation units with overflow from the first settler moving to the counter-current solvent extraction operations. The solids underflow goes to 2-3 washing thickeners.

Extraction of H_3PO_4 plus some free HCl is done in a battery of mixer-settlers (a) with $CaCl_2$ + CaF_2 retained in aqueous phase. The extract is again passed through several more mixer-settlers (b) for removal of trace impurities of Ca^{++} which are co-extracted. The extractant is aqueous reflux from the next unit—transfer extractors (c) where water extracts H_3PO_4 and HCl from solvent phase.

The washed solvent is recycled to a final series of mixer-settlers (d) where the balance of HCl is extracted from raffinate phase of extractors (a). The acid-free brine is sent to steam stripping for solvent recovery.

The aqueous acid raffinate from (c) is separated and concentrated in a triple effect evaporator to give three different overhead streams:

(1) Alcohol—water overhead flash from the first effect which is condensed and returned to extractors (a)

(2) Dilute HCl from the second effect

(3) Conc. HCl from the third effect

The HCl is returned to acid make-up. The bottoms from the third effect is product phosphoric acid (80% H_3PO_4).

5.6. Major Engineering Problems

5.6.1. Solvent recovery

The use of relatively expensive solvent in producing low-cost acid means careful attention to design and operation of solvent-handling equipment.

5.6.2. Materials of construction

All sections of the plant must be HCl resistant which requires rubber-lined or PVC-lined mild steel or rigid PVC equipment. The latter is recommended. For evaporation and steam stripping equipment, impervious graphite (*e.g.*, Karbate, Diabon) is specified.

5.6.3. Waste disposal

Problems of disposing of $CaCl_2$ aqueous effluent and siliceous rock residue become acute where lagooning is not allowable.

6. Electric Furnace Process (Direct Conversion at Plant Site)

6.1. Reference Flow Sheet: Figure IIF-1

6.2. Chemical Reactions

(a) $2Ca_3(PO_4)_2 + 6SiO_2 + 10C \rightarrow P_4 + 10CO + 6CaSiO_3$

(b) $P_4 + 10CO + 10O_2 \rightarrow 2P_2O_5 + 10CO_2$

(c) $P_2O_5 + xH_2O \rightarrow 2H_3PO_4 + (x-3)H_2O$

6.3. Raw Materials

Low grade crushed phosphate rock, coke as reductant, and sand as flux

6.4. Quantitative Requirements

(a) Basis: 1 ton of 100% H_3PO_4 in 90% yield; 2.3 tons of by-product slag

Phosphate rock (28% P_2O_5)	2.9 tons
Sand	0.85 ton
Coke breeze	0.5 ton
Air	3,600 Nm^3
Electricity	4,800 KWH
Carbon electrode consumption	8 kg

(b) Plant capacities: 60-200 tons/day of 100% H_3PO_4 per furnace, 1-4 furnaces per plant

6.5. Process Description

The first part of the electric furnace process is identical with that described under Phosphorus until the vapors leave the furnace. The oxidation of these gases is accomplished by an air combustion section down-stream from the furnace exit. The P_2O_5 thus formed is removed by spraying the hot gases with water. Some mist is formed which is next removed by a scrubbing system discussed below.

The crude 85% acid is given (1) an H_2SO_4 treatment to remove entrained calcium salts as $CaSO_4$, (2) a powdered silica addition to remove HF, and (3) a counter-current scrubbing with H_2S to remove arsenic as AsS_3. The sludge is removed in a sand filter and the acid can be sold as is or diluted to 50 or 75% grades.

6.6. Major Engineering Problems (see also Section 3.6 under Phosphorus)

6.6.1. Complete removal of acid mist

A number of methods have been tried to solve this difficult engineering problem. By purely fluid mechanics designs, a system which includes a Pease-Anthony venturi scrubber, screens and final water spray has been successfully adopted. The weak acid recovered from the last two units is used as the knock-down spray fluid for hydration of P_2O_5. A second method, which is probably more successful, uses only a high voltage electrostatic precipitator after the initial hydrating spray tower.

6.6.2. Materials of construction

High temperature acid brick is used in the furnace and combustion chamber areas. The hydration tower and other aqueous units are either stainless steel or lead-lined steel. The electrostatic precipitator element is graphite to resist the action of the free HF steel present.

7. Electric Furnace Process (Oxidation and Hydration of Elemental Phosphorus)

7.1. Reference Flow Sheet: Figure IIF-1

7.2. Chemical Reactions

(a) $2P + 2\frac{1}{2}O_2 \rightarrow P_2O_5$

(b) $P_2O_5 + 3H_2O \rightarrow 2H_3PO_4$

7.3. Raw Materials

Elemental phosphorus, air and steam

7.4. Quantitative Requirements

Basis: 1 ton of 100% H_3PO_4 in 96% yield

Phosphorus	0.33 ton
Air	1,260 Nm^3
Water and steam	Not definite

7.5. Process Description

This method of production is used mainly for smaller customer requirement capacities remote from major phosphoric acid manufacturing facilities.

Phosphorus is melted at 50°C and metered by water displacement to a steam ejector and atomization section of the combustion nozzle. Compressed air is injected around the steam atomized phosphorus droplets and the exothermic reaction raises the gas temperature to 2,000°C. The entire chamber is about 1.2 m in diameter and 3.0 m long and is built of stainless steel with water-cooled walls. Both vertical and horizontal units are used.

The gaseous oxides, partially hydrated, are treated in the same manner as described in the previous section on conversion of electric furnace gas to 85% H_3PO_4. Purification is still required to remove arsenic via H_2S for making food-grade acid derivatives.

7.6. Process Modification to Produce Phosphorus Anhydride

The burner designed is changed so that no steam is admitted. The air must also be dried by silica gel or alumina fixed bed adsorption towers. The P_2O_5 can be condensed as a solid in a large air-cooled tower about 3 m in diameter and 12 m tall. Revolving chains clean off the needles which accumulate on the sides of the vessel. A new method employs self-agglomeration on small spheroids of P_2O_5 in a fluidized bed operation. Condenser size is about 5% of the air-cooled tower unit for the same capacity.

7.7. Major Engineering Problems

In addition to the ones described in Section 5.6, the combustion chamber design and operation for molten P_4 feed required a great deal of development. Under improper operation, a glassy type of metaphosphoric acid and its polymers can form and drop to the bottom of the chamber, necessitating frequent shut-down and clean-out. By placing the combustion chamber near the bottom a great deal of the metaphosphoric acid can be vaporized and passed overhead.

8. Economic Evaluation of Phosphoric Acid

8.1. Capital Investment Comparison for Acid Versus Electric Furnace Processes

After losing out to the electric furnace process for nearly 35 years, both the acid processes are now used almost exclusively for new additions to the growing demand for phosphoric acid, particularly in fertilizers. The reasons are:

- Capital investments compared to an electric furnace plant. This more than offsets the price differential for the high grade rock required by the wet process.
- The lack of need for the high purity acid produced by the electric furnace method in the fertilizer market.
- Possibility of producing ammonium sulfate from gypsum by-product in the H_2SO_4 process.
- Use of cheap HCl or excess Cl_2 in India.

8.2. H_2SO_4 Versus HCl Acid Processes

The HCl process is only economical where there is excess chlorine and a scarcity of native sulfur. Such is the case for India. Since the processing costs are approximately the same for either process, the selection can be made on the basis of parity price of HCl versus H_2SO_4.

8.3. Plant Location Comparison

With the exception of acid produced from P_4 at or near consumer plants, both wet process and electric furnace acid plants are located in the region of phosphate rock, *i.e.*, USA—Southeastern and Rocky Mountain states. Rock beneficiation is required for upgrading low P_2O_5 rock in the wet process where high purity acid is required for all uses except triple superphosphate fertilizer.

8.4. By-product Usage

The extraction of uranium at rates of 0.1-0.2 kg per ton of rock is potentially attractive for the wet process. This appears as an impurity salt in the H_3PO_4 liquor from the gypsum filter and can be extracted by precipitation or solvent extraction methods. To date, the Atomic Energy Establishment has found more economic sources of supply for uranium.

8.5. Production Capacities

Comparative data on phosphoric acid production capacities worldwide are given in Table IIF-4.

Table IIF-4 Phosphoric Acid Capacities in 10^3 t/a P_2O_5 (1985)

Area	Capacity Available	Capacity Available and Planned
North America	13,091	14,136
—USA	11,109	11,802
—Canada	1,262	1,310
—Mexico	720	1,120
West Europe	4,734	4,994
—West Germany	330	330
Central and South America	961	1,301
—Brazil	832	952
Africa	4,374	6,049
—Morocco	1,520	2,840
—Tunisia	1,100	1,430
—South Africa	882	907
Middle East	1,326	1,506
Asia and Australia	2,708	3,906
—Japan	500	500
Comecon Countries	9,918	10,610
—USSR	6,746	6,876
India	726	759

Source: "Industrial Inorganic Chemistry" by Buchner et al (1989)

A summary of Indian phosphoric acid capacities is given in Table IIF-5.

Table IIF-5 Manufacturers and Licensed Capacity of Phosphoric Acid (As of October 1, 1994)

Name of Factory	Sector	Date of Commissioning	Per annum capacity of acid as P_2O_5 ('000 tons)
1. Albright, Morarji & Pandit Ambarnath (Mah.)	Private	January 1968	17.4
2. Coromandel Fertilizers Vizag (A.P.)	Private	February 1968	112.0
3. EID Parry (India) Ennore (T.N.)	Private	March 1963/ Modn. 1988-89	19.0
4. Fertilizers & Chemicals Travancore Alwaye (Kerala)	Public	December 1960 Expn. March 1972	33.0
5. Fertilizers & Chemicals Travancore Ambalamedu (Cochin Phase II) Kerala	Public	December 1976	115.2
6. Fertilizer Corp. of India Sindri (Bihar) (Rationalization)	Public	April 1979	119.0
7. Gujarat State Fertilizers Co. Baroda (Gujarat)	Private	May 1967	54.0
8. Hindustan Copper, Khetri (Rajasthan)	Public	October 1976 (Closed since April '85)	69.0
9. Hindustan Lever, Haldia (West Bengal)	Private	October 1979	41.7
10. Hindustan Zinc, Debari (Rajasthan)	Public	February 1979	26.0
11. Paradeep Phos., Paradeep (Phase II) (Orissa)	Public	June 1992	225.0
12. Rashtriya Chemicals & Fertilizers Trombay (Mah.)	Public	June 1975	30.0
13. Southern Petrochemical Industries Corp. Tuticorin (Tamil Nadu)	Private	July 1976	52.8

Source: "Fertiliser Statistics" (1993-94)

Calcium Phosphates

Large tonnages of low-grade calcium phosphates are made as fertilizers. There are two distinct grades possible based on the method of production from phosphate rock:

- Superphosphate—made by reacting phosphate rock with sulfuric acid; contains 16-20% P_2O_5
- Triple superphosphate—made by reacting phosphate rock with phosphoric acid; contains 42-50% P_2O_5

Only superphosphate is produced in India for economic reasons discussed later. After 1962, no further licensing of superphosphate plants was permitted to promote the growth of mixed chemical fertilizers which contain various percentages of N-P_2O_5-K_2O. This move was to force agriculturists to work with higher cost, balanced ingredient fertilizers which ultimately yield better crops with larger profits.

1. Superphosphate

1.1. Reference Flow Sheet: Figure IIF-4

1.2. Chemical Reactions

(a) Acidulation

$$\underset{\text{phosphate rock}}{[Ca_3(PO_4)_2]_3 \cdot CaF_2} + 7H_2SO_4(aq) \rightarrow \underset{\text{superphosphate}}{3CaH_4(PO_4)_2 \cdot 7CaSO_4} + 2HF$$

(b) SiO_2 impurity removal

$$4HF + SiO_2 \rightarrow SiF_4 + 2H_2O$$
$$3SiF_4 + 2H_2O \rightarrow 2H_2SiF_6 + SiO_2$$
$$H_2SiF_6 + NaCl \rightarrow Na_2SiF_6 + 2HCl$$

1.3. Raw Materials

A high (30-35% P_2O_5) grade of natural or beneficiated phosphate rock is ordinarily specified, since the demand is for high P_2O_5 content product. Dilute sulfuric acid (50°-55° Be or 62-70% H_2SO_4) is the only other chemical involved.

1.4. Quantitative Requirements

(a) Basis: 1 ton of superphosphate

Phosphate rock	0.5-0.6 ton
Sulfuric acid	0.3-0.4 ton

(b) Plant capacities: 100-1,400 tons/day

1.5. Process Description

Phosphate rock lumps are crushed in a jaw crusher and ground to —100 mesh in a hammer or ring mill. A continuous feed of dilute sulfuric acid (65-70%) and powdered rock phosphate is monitored by automatic control into a steel trough, lead-lined and brick-lined, covered with a hood to collect SiF_4 and HF fumes. The rotating mechanism, made of cast iron blades on a square shaft, moves the product gradually forward at the rate of 0.2 to 0.5 meter per minute through the 12-15 meters reactor-conveyor unit. With proper grinding and acid control, the reaction is effectively complete and can be sent directly to a granulator. The older method was to store for a nominal 24-hour period to insure complete reaction.

The SiF_4 and HF fumes along with CO_2 are scrubbed in water and the silica is removed by NaCl according to chemical equations in 1.2(b).

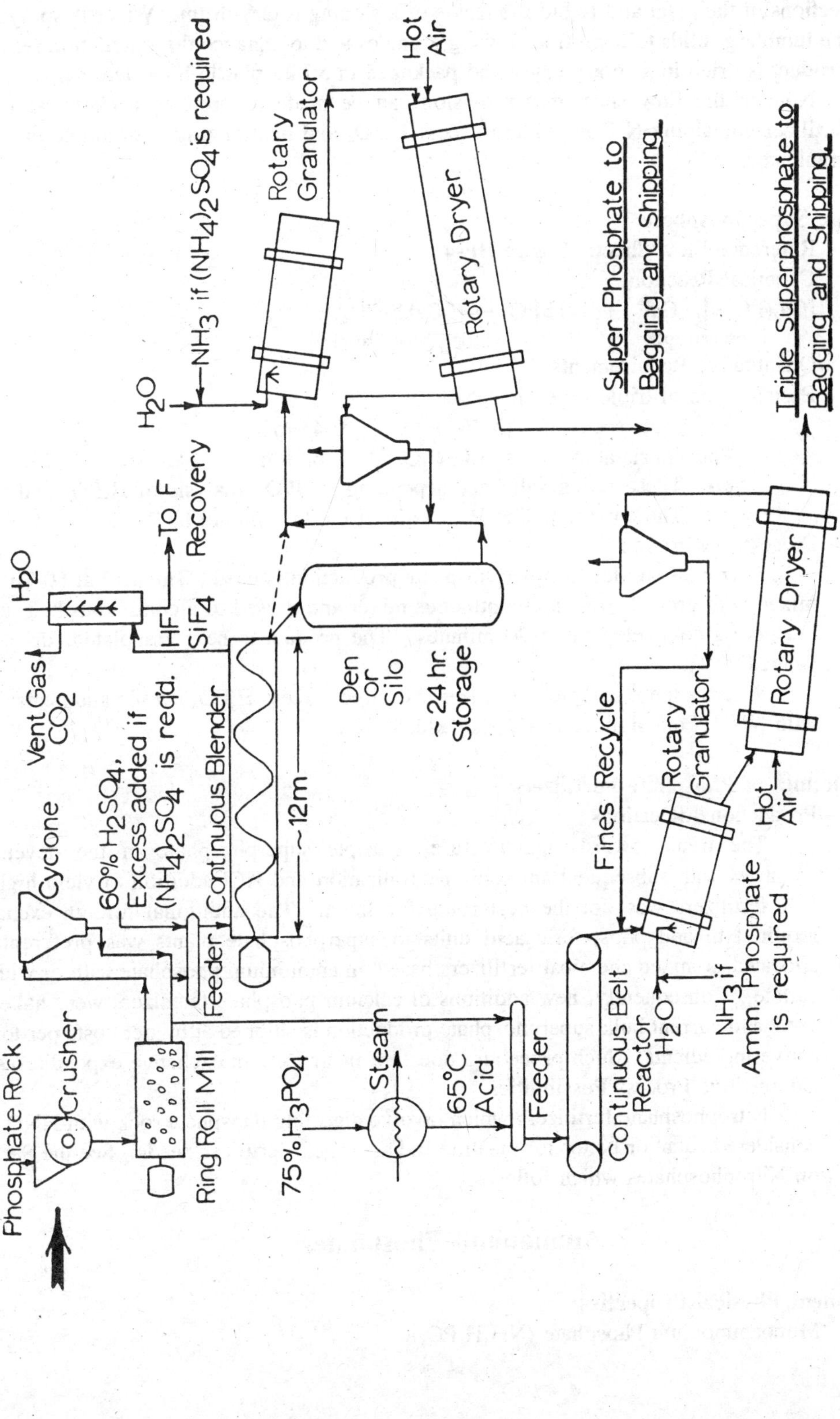

Fig. IIF-4. Superphosphate and triple superphosphate fertilizer production methods.

The porous, crumbly material from the den is mixed with rock dust from the grinding sections of the plant and fed to the inside of a sloping rotary drum. Water is sprayed on the tumbling solids to form free-flowing granules and to enhance the acidulation reaction. Product is dried in a rotary dryer and packaged in 50 kg plastic-lined jute bags.

Note in the flow sheet that provision can be made to produce a chemical mixed fertilizer containing N-P by adding excess H_2SO_4 and neutralizing with ammonia in the granulator.

2. Triple Superphosphate

2.1. Reference Flow Sheet: Figure IIF-4

2.2. Chemical Reaction

$$\underset{\text{phosphate rock}}{[Ca_3(PO_4)_2]_3 \cdot CaF_2} + 14H_3PO_4 \rightarrow \underset{\text{triple superphosphate}}{10CaH_4(PO_4)_2} + 2HF$$

2.3. Quantitative Requirements

Basis: 1 ton of triple superphosphate

Phosphate rock	(32%, P_2O_5)	0.45 ton
Phosphoric acid	(56%, P_2O_5)	0.62 ton

Note: These ratios will vary depending on P_2O_5 analysis of H_3PO_4 and rock. The corresponding P_2O_5 ratio of the two should be 2-2.5.

2.4. Process Description

A process similar to superphosphate production is used. The acid at 60-70°C is mixed with ground rock in a continuous mixer and passed to a continuous belt where reaction is completed in 15-20 minutes. The product is next granulated, dried and bagged.

Where a more complete fertilizer is desired, excess H_3PO_4 is used and neutralized with NH_3. Potassium salts are also added.

3. Economics of Phosphate Fertilizers

3.1. Production Allocations

The trend towards manufacture of triple superphosphate in the developed countries with subsequent ammonia neutralization and KCl addition to yield high N-P-K fertilizers was not the best route for India. The additional foreign exchange required to add phosphoric acid units to superphosphate plants was preferentially allocated to mixed chemical fertilizers based on ammonium phosphate with or without sulfate. Consequently, new additions of calcium phosphate fertilizers were halted in 1962 and current bulk superphosphate production is shipped at higher costs per ton of active ingredients. Such procedure does not incur foreign exchange expenditures.

3.2. Competitive Process Possibilities

Nitrophosphate fertilizers which involve digesting phosphate rock with HNO_3 are considered equal or better for meeting India's urgent fertilizer needs. See the Section on Nitrophosphates which follows.

Ammonium Phosphates

1. Pertinent Physical Properties

1.1. Monoammonium Phosphate ($NH_4H_2PO_4$)

Mol. wt.	115
M.P.	Decomposes
Density	1.80 gm/cc
Solubility in water	32 gm/100 cc at 15°C

1.2. Diammonium Phosphate $(NH_4)_2HPO_4$

Mol. wt.	132
M.P.	Decomposes
Density	1.62 gm/cc
Solubility	131 gm/100 cc at 15°C

2. Consumption Pattern

The only major use is for chemical fertilizers. Minor uses are in fire-retardants, nutrient yeast culture, ammoniated dentrifices.

3. Chemical Fertilizer

A mixture of ammonium phosphate and sulfate plus potash (KCl)

3.1. Reference Flow Sheet: Figure IIF-2

3.2. Chemical Reactions

$NH_3 + H_3PO_4 \rightarrow NH_4H_2HPO_4$

$NH_3 + NH_4H_2PO_4 \rightarrow (NH_4)_2HPO_4$

$NH_3 + H_2SO_4 \rightarrow NH_4HSO_4$

$NH_3 + NH_4HSO_4 \rightarrow (NH_4)_2SO_4$

3.3. Quantitative Requirements

Depends on grade of material. Compute stoichiometric ratios and allow 99% yield and 3% NH_3 handling loss.

3.4. Process Description

The two principal steps are neutralization and granulation. For neutralization, phosphoric and sulfuric acids are added to the first of three continuous mixed reactors. Anhydrous liquid ammonia is added beneath the slurry level in the first neutralizer in an amount equivalent to 80% neutralization. Further ammonia is added in the 2nd and 3rd tanks to obtain conversion to the diammonium salt if a higher N fertilizer is needed.

The exothermic reaction heats the slurry nearly to the boiling point (130°C). Unreacted and excess NH_3 vapor is collected from the top of each tank and recharged below the liquid level. This cuts NH_3 losses to less than 3%.

Slurry from the third neutralizer is mixed with KCl and absorbed in a bed of dry recycle fertilizer moving through a rotating drum granulator. This provides a tumbling action to coat recycle material with a slurry film.

A rotary adiabatic drier reduces the moisture to less than 1%, with a 10 minute contact time with air initially at 150°C. Dried product is separated into three fractions on a double deck screen. A portion of the product from the deck of the lower screen (—6 +12) is sent to bagging operations. The balance, together with pulverized oversize and fines, is returned to the granulator. The weight ratio of recycle to product is 6 : 1-15 : 1 depending on the grade produced.

3.5. Major Engineering Problems

- NH_3 losses

- Corrosion—use Type 316 for hot acid and fume ducts; carbon steel for granulation, drying and screening

3.6. Economics

3.6.1. Raw material requirements

A completely integrated fertilizer complex produces NH_3 and H_3PO_4. Potash (KCl) has to be imported as India has only small reserves in terms of sea bitterns which have not yet been developed.

3.6.2. Plant investment and production costs

The decision to allocate licenses to mixed chemical fertilizer plants rather than augmented triple superphosphate plants was taken after examining capital investment, production, and shipping costs. The latter was less for the higher percentage N and P possible with chemical fertilizers, the other two items being comparable.

Nitrophosphates

Nitrophosphates are mixtures of ammonium nitrate and various phosphates made by acidulation of phosphate rock with nitric acid alone or in combination with sulfuric acid. This method of making fertilizers is widely used in Europe and has been adopted for the Trombay operation. It does not necessarily require sulfuric acid, so it may be attractive for countries lacking indigenous sulfur.

1. Reference Flow Sheet: None

2. Chemical Reactions

2.1. Nitric Acid Digestion—Ammonia Neutralization

$$Ca_3(PO_4)_2 + 6HNO_3 + 4NH_3 \rightarrow Ca(NO_3)_2 + \underset{\text{acid soluble}}{2CaHPO_4} + 4NH_4NO_3$$

2.2. Nitric Acid-Sulfuric Acid Digestion—Ammonia Neutralization

$$Ca_3(PO_4)_2 + 6HNO_3 + 6NH_3 + H_2SO_4 \rightarrow 2CaHPO_4 + 6NH_4NO_3 + CaSO_4$$

2.3. Conversion to Monocalcium Phosphate

$$2CaHPO_4 + H_2SO_4 \rightarrow \underset{\text{water soluble}}{Ca(H_2PO_4)_2} + CaSO_4$$

2.4. Carbonitric Process

$$Ca_3(PO_4)_2 + 6HNO_3 + 6NH_3 + CO_2 + H_2O \rightarrow 2CaHPO_4 + 6NH_4NO_3 + CaCO_3$$

The chemistry is more complex than these reactions would indicate and is not well known. Ratios of constituents can be varied to produce different types of products.

These simplified reactions neglect the fluorine in phosphate rock.

3. Process Description

Rock phosphate is pulverized and digested with nitric or mixed acid in equipment similar to the wet process for producing phosphoric acid. Acid strength is 25-40% HNO_3. The digested slurry is pumped to an ammoniating tank where chemical reactions are completed. The slurry is granulated and dried in rotary equipment, and screened in a conventional classifying circuit.

4. **Major Engineering Problems**

4.1. Removal of Calcium Nitrate

$Ca(NO_3)_2$ is extremely hygroscopic and will cause the product to lump. For HNO_3 (reaction 2.1) the digested liquor must be chilled to remove calcium nitrate by crystallization. The mixed acid process (reaction 2.2) or carbonitric process (reaction 2.4) avoids the problem by conversion to $CaSO_4$ or $CaCO_3$.

4.2. Corrosion

Digestion and neutralization equipment require 18-8 stainless steel because of HNO_3 corrosiveness. Plant costs are higher than in the wet process phosphoric acid plant which has a larger percentage of mild-steel equipment.

Sodium Phosphate

Numerous combinations of Na with P and O exist; many of the structures are not definite.

1. **Classification of Structure**

(X = monovalent alkali metal such as Na)

- Metaphosphate PO^{-3}
- Hexametaphosphate $(XPO_3)_6$
- Polyphosphate $X_5P_3O_{10}$
- Pyrophosphate $X_4P_2O_7 \cdot YH_2O$
- Orthophosphate $H_2PO_4^{-1}$, HPO_4^{-2}, PO_4^{-3}

2. **Consumption Pattern**

The principal use of alkali phosphates in the USA has been in detergent formulation.

However, ecological considerations have forced the reduction in phosphate content of detergents in the U.S.A. in particular in favor of other builder material in detergent formulations.

Phosphates are still widely used, however, in metal cleaning, boiler water treatment, in the textiles industry and in foodstuffs.

3. **Methods of Production**

Ortho- and polyphosphate are made from varying ratios of sodium carbonate, sodium hydroxide, and orthophosphoric acid. The other salts are made from the corresponding phosphoric acids (meta- and pyro-).

3.1. Sodium Tripolyphosphate ($Na_5P_3O_{10}$ or STPP)

3.1.1. Reference flow sheet: Figure IIF-5

3.1.2. Chemical reaction

$$5Na_2CO_3 + 6H_3PO_4 \rightarrow 2Na_5P_3O_{10} + 9H_2O + 5CO_2$$

3.1.3. Properties of $Na_5P_3O_{10}$

Mol. wt.	368
Form	White powder
Solubility	12.8 gm/100 cc H_2O at 20°C
	33 gm/100 cc H_2O at 100°C
pH of 1% solution	9.7

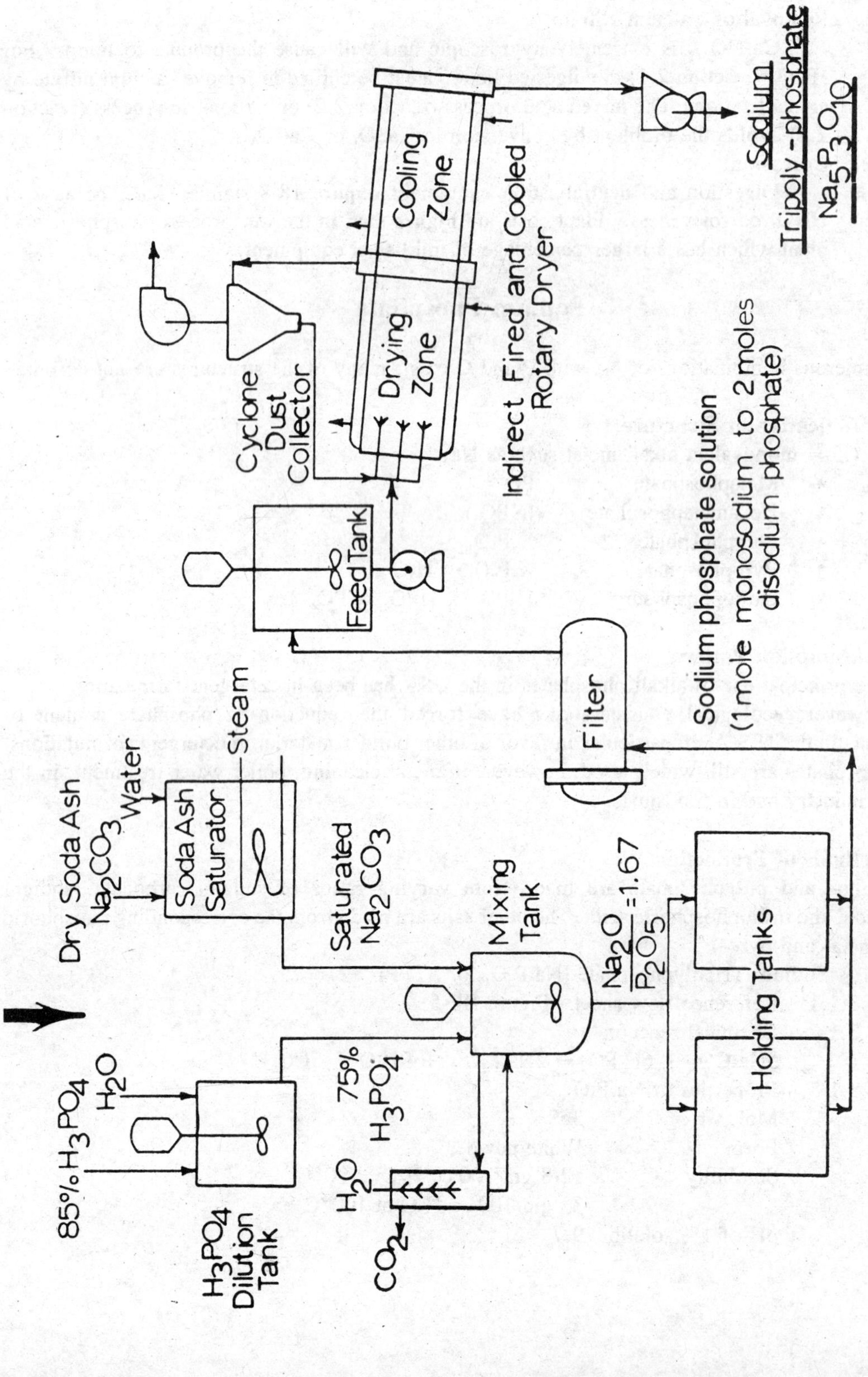

Fig. IIF-5. Manufacture of sodium tripolyphosphate ($Na_5P_3O_{10}$ or STPP).

3.1.4. Quantitative requirements

(a) Basis: 1 ton of STPP at 99% yield

Sodium carbonate (58% Na_2O)	8.81 tons
Phosphoric acid (75% H_3PO_4)	1.0 ton

(b) Plant capacities: Quite varied as phosphoric acid is made from P_4 and converted to STPP at consumers' plants to save freight costs; 20-150 tons/day is the size range.

3.1.5. Process description

Saturated soda ash solution and technical grade concentrated H_3PO_4 are diluted with water and steam in a batch mixing tank. A 1.67 ratio of Na_2O/P_2O_5 must be attained to form 1 mole of monosodium to 2 moles of disodium phosphate. Carbon dioxide comes off and is scrubbed by the incoming water to return entrained solids.

The solution is filtered to remove impurities and dried, dehydrated, annealed, and cooled along the length of an indirect-fired rotary kiln. Grinding, storage, and packaging complete the process.

IIG. ELECTROCHEMICAL INDUSTRIES

1. Definition of Electrochemistry

Electrochemistry deals with:

- Chemical changes produced by electric current
- Electrical energy produced by chemical changes

2. Classification of Electrochemical Industries (with examples)

2.1. Aqueous Electrolytic

2.1.1. Electroseparation (chlorine-caustic)

2.1.2. Electrowinning (low purity copper from ore leachings)

2.1.3. Electrorefining (high purity copper from crude copper anodes)

2.1.4. Electroplating (nickel and chrome plating on steel)

2.2. Fused Electrolytic (aluminum, magnesium and sodium cells)

2.3. Electrothermal (calcium carbide, calcium cyanide, graphite, synthetic abrasives such as silicon carbide, arc processes)

2.4. Electric Furnacing (alloy steels)

2.5. Chemical to Electrical Conversion (batteries, fuel cells)

2.6. Gas Phase Electric Discharge (ozone)

2.7. Electroorganic Chemical Processes (adiponitrile, tetraethyl lead)

In addition to the above classification, the chemical engineer uses electrochemical principles in dealing with corrosion phenomena.

3. Fundamental Concepts for Electrolytic Processes

One of the most difficult tasks in learning electrochemistry is to understand and use the nomenclature properly. In particular + and — signs on potentials and EMF's must be watched carefully.

The system to be used is that adopted by the National Bureau of Standards, the Electrochemical Society of USA and most applied electrochemical plants. It is sometimes called the "European System" and is that adopted by applied electrochemistry texts.

3.1. Types of Electrodes

- Anode

  $A^- - e \rightarrow A^\circ$ (Production of element from anion)

  $M^\circ - e \rightarrow M^+$ (Solution of metal cation)

Since loss of electrons implies oxidation, the *anode* is where oxidation takes place.

- Cathode

  $M^+ + e \rightarrow M^\circ$

  $A^\circ + e \rightarrow A^-$

Since gain of electrons implies reduction, the *cathode* is where reduction takes place.

3.2. Flow of Current

3.2.1. Electron flow can usually be established from the chemistry of the cell. The flow of current, however, is exactly opposite to the flow of electrons as current was originally designated as going in one direction, and later on in the history of electrochemistry, it was found that electrons were travelling in the opposite direction. However, the original designation, now known as positive current, was not changed.

3.2.2. Symbols used for direction of current flow

$\longrightarrow$ Positive current flow

$\leftarrow\cdots\cdots$ Electron flow

3.3. Electrolysis Cell

- This cell uses electrical energy to produce endothermic chemical changes
- Typical electrolysis cell
- In the electrolytic or electrolysis cell, the positive current flows from the positive electrode (+) to the negative electrode (—) inside the cell

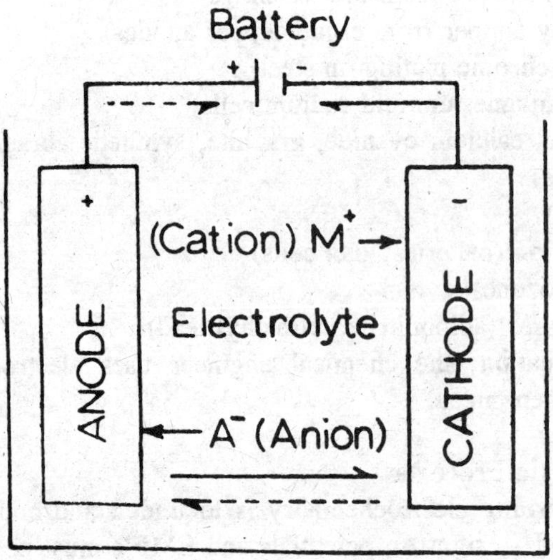

Example

$A^- - e \longrightarrow A^\circ$

$M^+ + e \longrightarrow M^\circ$

3.4. Voltaic Cell

- **This cell uses exothermic chemical reactions to produce electrical energy, *e.g.*, fuel cell**
- **Also designated as galvanic cell**
- **Typical voltaic cell (see the figure which follows)**
- **In the voltaic cell, the positive current flows from the positive electrode (+) to the negative electrode (—) outside the cell**
- **A voltaic cell can become an electrolysis cell by use of an external voltage greater than the voltaic cell voltage and imposed in the opposite directions**

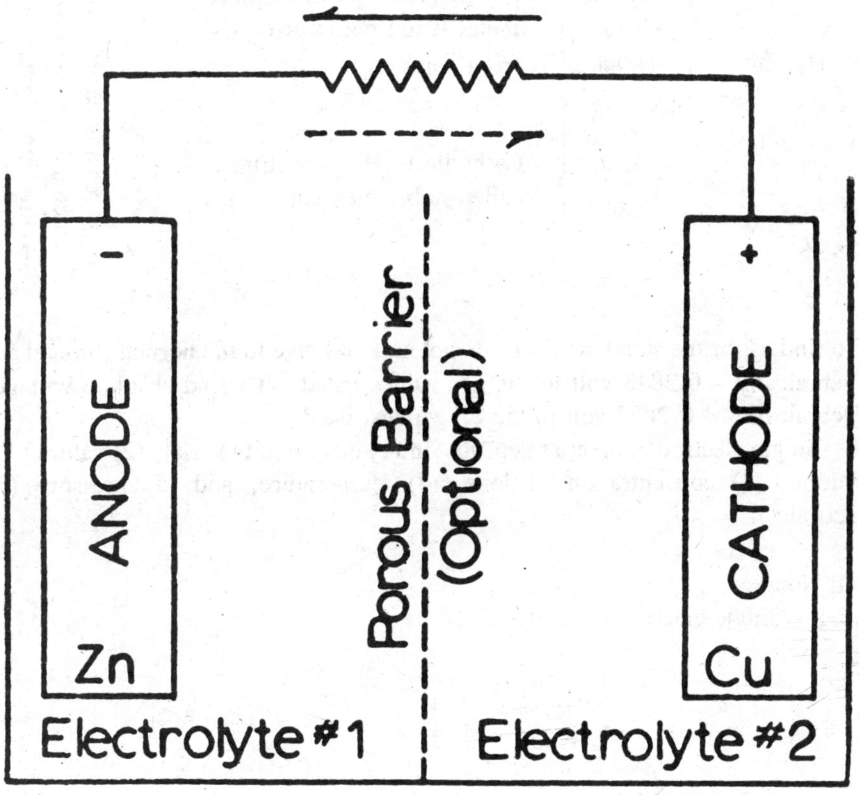

Example

Anode

$$Zn^{\circ} - 2e \rightarrow Zn^{++}$$

Cathode

$$Cu^{++} + 2e \rightarrow Cu^{\circ}$$

$$Zn^{\circ} + Cu^{++} \rightarrow Zn^{++} + Cu^{\circ}$$

3.5. Single Electrode Potentials

The single electrode potential is a measure of the potential difference existing between the electrode and the solution in which it is immersed. This is where the confusion of the algebraic sign convention enters. A typical standard electrode potential or EMF series, using the sign convention as discussed above, is given below. Other elements in the series can be found in standard texts. These are based on solutions of unit ion activity = 1N in solution and are relative to hydrogen.

Reaction (Written cathodically)	e_h° = volts at 25°C*	
$Li^+ + e \rightarrow Li$	–2.959	Anodic to H^+; will displace metal listed below it or H_2 from solution
$Zn^{++} + 2e \rightarrow Zn$	–0.761	
$H^+ + e \rightarrow \frac{1}{2}H_2$	0.0000	
$Hg^+ + e \rightarrow Hg$ (Normal calomel cell)	+0.2848	Cathodic to H^+, sometimes called noble elements
$Cu^{++} + 2e \rightarrow Cu$	+0.344	
$Ag^+ + e \rightarrow Ag$	+0.797	
$Cl_2 + 2e \rightarrow 2Cl^-$	+1.36	

←Increasing ease of reduction←
→Increasing ease of oxidation→
→Direction of external current flow when hooked up as voltaic cell
\+ ——→ –

*To find e_c° or the standard electrode potential relative to the normal calomel cell, add algebraically —0.2848 volt to the e_h° values listed. To find absolute voltages, add algebraically +0.2822 volt to the e_h° values listed.

Single electrode potential depends on (1) electrode material, (2) nature of ions in solution, (3) concentration of ions, (4) temperature, and (5) pressure (for gas electrodes).

3.6. Cell Notation

3.6.1. Single electrode potentials

$$M_1^\circ \mid M_1^+ (aq)$$
$$M_2^+ (aq) \mid M_2^\circ$$

3.6.2. Conventional cell notation

←—— Outside cell

$$M_1^\circ \mid M_1^+ (aq) \parallel M_2^+ (aq) \mid M_2^\circ$$

Anode   Cathode

– Inside cell ——→ +

3.6.3. Example of voltaic cell (Daniell cell)

$$-0.522\text{v} \longleftarrow +0.581\text{v}$$

$$\overset{-}{Zn} \mid ZnSO_4\ (aq) \parallel CuSO_4\ (aq) \mid \overset{+}{Cu}$$

Anode — Cathode

The EMF of this cell is computed by subtracting algebraically the less positive from the more positive single electrode potential. These electrode potentials are based on a solution different than 1N or $e°$ values.

$$E = +0.581 - (-0.522) = +1.103 \text{ volts}$$

Electrode reactions

Anode: $Zn° - 2e \rightarrow Zn^{++}$

Cathode: $Cu^{++} + 2e \rightarrow Cu°$

3.6.4. Example of electrolysis cell

(a) First set up as conventional voltaic cell

$$+0.344\text{v} \longleftarrow +0.797\text{v}$$

$$Cu \mid CuSO_4\ (1N) \parallel AgNO_3\ (1N) \mid Ag$$

Anode (−) — Cathode (+)

According to EMF table, external current will flow from the more positive to the less positive potential and the cell voltage will be 0.797 — 0.344 = 0.453 volt.

Electrode reactions

Anode: $Cu° - 2e \rightarrow Cu^{++}$

Cathode: $Ag^{+} + e \rightarrow Ag°$

(b) To make an electrolytic cell and reverse the reaction, a back EMF of at least 0.453 volt must be applied to the cell with the following results:

$$Ag \mid AgNO_3\ (1N) \parallel CuSO_4\ (1N) \mid Cu$$

Anode (+) ⟶ Cathode (−)

Electrode reactions

Anode: $Ag° - e \rightarrow Ag^{+}$

Cathode: $Cu^{++} + 2e \rightarrow Cu°$

3.7. Electrode and Cell Potentials from Thermodynamic Properties

3.7.1. Single electrode potentials

$$e = e° + 2.3\frac{RT}{nF} \cdot \log (a_x^i)$$

where R = 8.32 joules/°K

T = °K

F = 96,500 coulombs

$e°$ = standard electrode potential at 25°C and unit activity

n = number of equivalents involved

a_x = activity of anion, cation, gas, or solid involved in reaction, gm equiv. ions/liter

i = number of atoms of the xth element involved in reaction

All of these electrode potentials must be written cathodically, *e.g.*,

$$Cu^{++} + 2e \rightarrow Cu^{\circ}$$

3.7.2. Electromotive force of cell, EMF

This is the algebraic difference between two single electrode potentials composing the cell, generally set up as the cathode potential minus the anode potential.

$$E = E^{\circ} + \frac{2.3RT}{nF} \cdot \log \left(\frac{a^i_C}{a^i_A}\right)$$ C stands for cathode, A stands for anode

3.7.3. Example of calculation of cell EMF

$$\underset{\text{Anode}}{Zn \mid Zn\,(a_{Zn^{++}})} \quad \| \quad \underset{\text{Cathode}}{Ag^{+}\,(a_{Ag^{+}}) \mid Ag}$$

Electrode reactions

Anode: $Zn^{\circ} - 2e \rightarrow Zn^{++}$

Cathode: $2Ag^{+} + 2e \rightarrow 2Ag^{\circ}$

Overall reaction

$$Zn^{\circ} + 2Ag^{+} + 2e \rightarrow 2Ag^{\circ}$$

For this case $n = 2$ and activity $a_{Zn^{\circ}}$ and $a_{Ag^{\circ}}$ solids are unity.

For the anode, the single electrode potential is

$$e_{Zn} = e^{\circ}_{Zn} + \frac{2.3RT}{nF} \log a_{Zn^{++}}$$

when written cathodically as

$$Zn^{++} + 2e \rightarrow Zn^{\circ}$$

For the cathode, the single electrode potential is

$$e_{Ag} = e^{\circ}_{Ag} + \frac{2.3RT}{nF} \log (a_{Ag^{+}})^2$$

when written cathodically as

$$Ag^{+} + e \rightarrow Ag^{\circ}$$

To determine the EMF of the cell, subtract algebraically the anode voltage from the cathode voltage:

$$E = e^{\circ}_{Ag} - e^{\circ}_{Zn} + \frac{2.3RT}{nF} \log \frac{(a_{Ag^{+}})^2}{a_{Zn^{++}}}$$

Define $E^{o}_{Ag, Zn} = e^{o}_{Ag} - e^{o}_{Zn}$; then, for the overall reaction

$$E = E^{o}_{Ag, Zn} + \frac{2.3RT}{nF} \log \frac{(a_{Ag^{+}})^{2}}{a_{Zn^{++}}}$$

3.7.4. Effect of temperature on reversible cell potentials

The net work done by the system for a reversible process is its free energy (ΔG),

(3.1) $-\Delta G = nE_{r}F = -\Delta H + T\Delta S$ All terms in joules: 4.182 joules/calorie

r = reversible

Differentiation of Eq. (3.1) with temperature gives

(3.2) $$(\frac{\partial E_{r}}{\partial T})_{p} = \frac{1}{nF} \cdot (\frac{\partial G}{\partial T})_{p}$$

(3.3) $$= -\frac{1}{nF}[(\frac{\partial \Delta H}{\partial T})_{p} - T(\frac{\Delta S}{T})_{p} - \Delta S]$$

But

$$(\frac{\partial \Delta S}{\partial T})_{p} = \frac{C_{p}}{T}; \quad p(\frac{\partial \Delta H}{\partial T})_{p} = C_{p},$$

so that substituting in Eq. (3.3) gives

(3.4) $$\Delta S = nF(\frac{\partial E_{r}}{\partial T})_{p}$$

This leads to the basic equation relating cell potential to enthalpy of reaction

(3.5) $$E_{r} = -\frac{\Delta H}{nF} + T(\frac{\partial E_{r}}{\partial T})_{p}$$

For many reactions the $T(\partial E_{r}/\partial T)$ term can be neglected within an accuracy of ±10% in computing E from ΔH or vice-versa.

4. Some Practical Problems in Using Electrochemical Theory

4.1. Actual Voltage and Voltage Efficiency

4.1.1. Polarization

The theoretical cell voltage was shown as the algebraic difference of the two single electrode potentials which make up the cell. This voltage is always different than the actual voltage (E_{a}) used or observed because of irreversible effects, particularly polarization. A graph of this effect is shown here for an electrolysis cell.

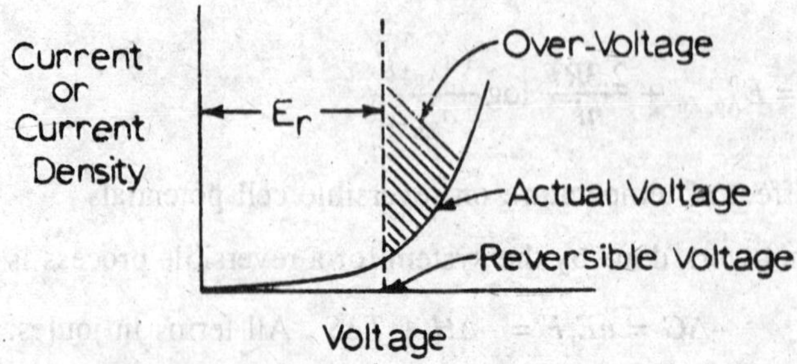

Polarization is caused by gas absorption, concentration gradients, and electrode impurities which form on the surface during electrolysis, giving a high resistance and inefficiency in terms of I^2R losses.

4.1.2. Voltage efficiency (η_v)

$$\eta_v = \frac{E_r}{E_a} \times 100 = \frac{\text{theoretical voltage}}{\text{actual voltage}} \times 100 \quad (4.1)$$

Usually runs 40-70%, largely caused by polarization.

4.2. Current Efficiency (η_I)

$$\eta_I = \frac{\text{theoretical current to produce one gm equiv.} \times 100}{\text{actual current to produce one gm equiv.}} \quad (4.2)$$

The product of current x time is related to theoretical gram equivalent by:

1 Faraday = 96,500 coulombs = 96,500 ampere-seconds to deposit one gram equivalent of any substance under ideal conditions.

The inefficiency of the cell is measured by values greater than 96,500 ampere-seconds to deposit one gram equivalent of a desired substance. It is caused by

- Cell short circuiting
- Electrolytic side reactions
- Instability of primary cell products

η_I is usually 95-98%.

4.3. Energy Efficiency (η_w)

$$\eta_w = \eta_I \cdot \eta_v \quad (4.3)$$
$$= (95 \rightarrow 98) \cdot (40 \rightarrow 70)$$

4.4. Decomposition Efficiency (η_D)

This is similar to conversion efficiency in a chemical reactor.

$$\eta_D = \frac{\text{equivalents produced}}{\text{equivalents charged}} \times 100$$

Example: η_D is about 50% for aqueous caustic-chlorine cells. Attempts at higher efficiencies result in undesirable side products such as ClO^- in a caustic-chlorine cell.

5. Examples of Electrochemical Industries

The electrochemical industries became an important factor in the Indian economy just prior to World War II. They use simple, rather pure raw materials and are located at sites of cheap electric power (hydroelectric and thermal).

The three best known industries in this classification (see Section 2) are chlorine-caustic, aluminum and phosphorus. The first will be discussed in Section IIH under Chlor-Alkali Industry. Aluminum will be discussed in Chapter VI under Metallurgical Industries. Phosphorus manufacture has been discussed in Section IIF. Graphite furnishes an excellent example of the electrothermal phase of the industry.

Two developmental areas in electrochemical industries are fuel cells and high temperature arc processes.

Graphite

1. Consumption Pattern

Graphite is an allotropic form of carbon which has unusual properties, particularly as a high temperature lubricant, as a corrosion and heat resistant material for the chemical industry, and as an electrical conductor for electrodes, brushes, and contact points. It has excellent moderating characteristics for thermalizing fission neutrons and is used extensively in nuclear reactors. A high purity grade of graphite is required for this latter usage.

2. Reference Flow Sheet: None required

3. Chemical Reaction

C (amorphous) → C (graphite); $\Delta H = -2.5$ Kcal

4. Raw Materials

The major materials are graphitizing grade coke and pitch binder. Furnacing sand for covering the reactants is used repeatedly and the sawdust for a final insulation cover is generally burned out, requiring replacement.

5. Quantitative Requirements

(a) Basis: 1 ton of graphite

Coke	1.1-1.5 tons
Pitch binder	0.15-0.17 ton
Electricity	7-10,000 KWH

(b) Furnace capacity: 10-25 tons

6. Process Description

Artificial graphite is prepared in electric resistance furnaces in which the charge forms the resistor. The furnace is built up in a rectangular shape with loosely-piled refractory brick on the

sides, concrete ends and floor have cooling pipe embedded in them to cool the projecting electrodes.

The coke is calcined at 1,400°C to volatilize impurities, ground and mixed with pitch, then extruded into various shapes (*e.g.*, rods, tubing for graphite pipe, crucibles). These are prebaked at 1,100°C and packed in the graphitizing furnace with finely carbonaceous material to give electrical continuity.

The graphitizing furnace is heated to about 3,000°C with a 200 volt-4,000 ampere starting characteristic, dropping to 40 volts-9,000 amperes as the material graphitizes. A run requires 2-4 days of heating, one day each to load and unload, and 15-20 days to cool. The furnace side walls must be rebuilt each time.

Fuel Cells

The concept of a fuel cell is quite similar to that of batteries as chemical energy is converted to electrical energy. A fuel cell differs from a battery in that the electrical output is maintained by a continuous supply of chemical reactants (oxidant and reductant). The fuel cell has become of major interest in view of its inherently high efficiency and the rising cost of fuel.

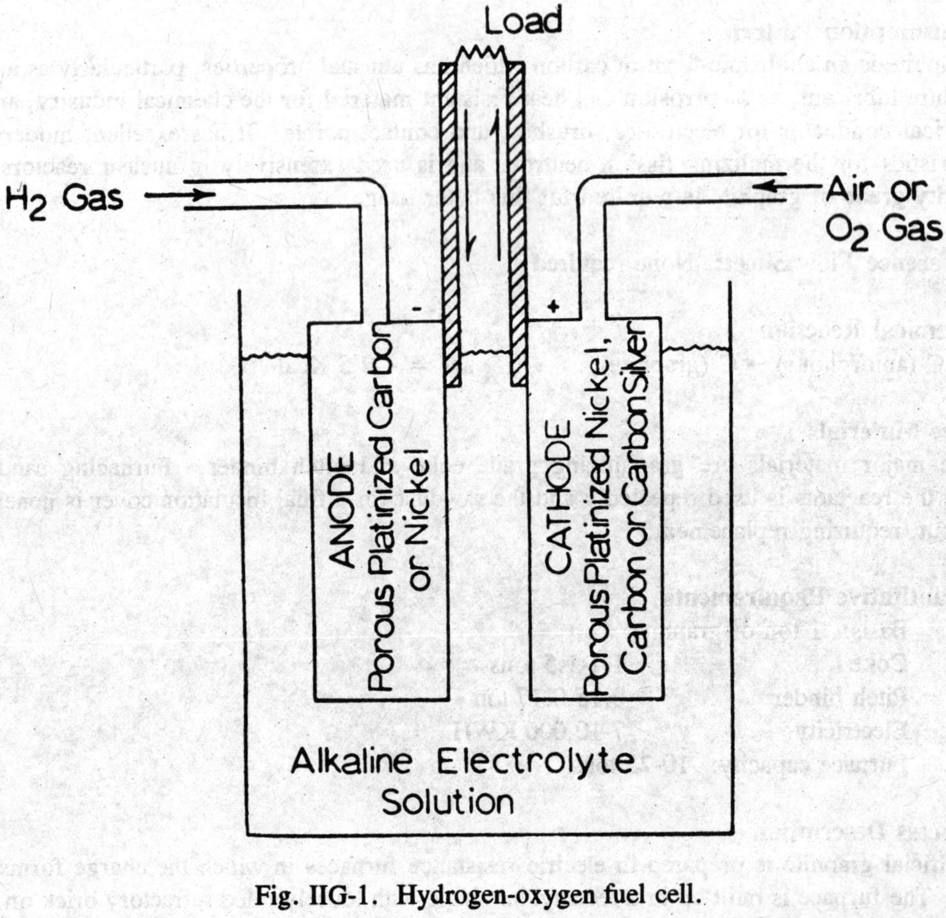

Fig. IIG-1. Hydrogen-oxygen fuel cell.

Cell Reactions

(1) Anode:

$$H_2 + 2OH^- \rightarrow 2H_2O + 2e$$

(2) Cathode:

$$O_2 + H_2O + 2e \rightarrow HO_2^- + OH^-$$

(3) Overall cell reaction:

$$H_2 + ½O_2 \rightarrow H_2O$$

1. Fuel Cell Efficiency

We are interested in the efficiency of conversion of ΔH to useful electrical energy, which would be ΔG or nEF. The ideal or reversible efficiency (η_r) would be

$$\eta_r = \frac{\Delta G}{\Delta H} = 1 - \frac{T\Delta S}{\Delta H}$$

$T\Delta S/\Delta H$ term is usually less than 0.1 so the ideal fractional efficiency for conversion of chemical energy to electrical energy is greater than 0.9.

Comparing this with the same chemical reaction energy ΔH going into heat and then to electrical energy via the steam boiler-turbine generator system:

$$\text{Ideal Carnot cycle efficiency} = \frac{T_1 - T_2}{T_2}$$

Such efficiencies are practically always less than 0.5 and so commercial interest in fuel cell is certainly justified.

The overall efficiency (η_o) of a fuel cell power unit is the fraction of the heat reaction of the primary fuel which is converted to useful electrical work at the terminals of the device.

$$\eta_o = \frac{EIT}{\Delta H}$$

(where E = delivered voltage at the terminals, I = current delivered for period of time T) will always be less than η_r for these reasons:

- No cell ever operates at infinitesimally small current required for reversibility.
- I^2R losses from polarizability and cell resistances. Some of this can be recovered in volatilizing the primary fuel.
- Chemical reaction used to compute ΔH may not be the correct one at the electrodes.

2. Characteristics of a Hydrogen-Oxygen Fuel Cell

The schematic for this elementary cell is shown in Figure IIG-1 together with the cell reactions. Even though this cell is now operating satisfactorily, there are some economic problems encountered in using it commercially. These cells may be employed for special purpose, low power packs in remote locations.

A major technical difficulty is increasing current density at the electrodes and hence decreasing fixed charges per KWH. Electrode kinetics is connected with the study of suitable catalysts and their incorporation in electrode materials. The fuel element (anode) is the major concern with hydrogen fuel giving the least trouble of all of the potential hydrocarbon type fuels.

3. Development of Commercial Fuel Cell

Use of cheaper fuels is required. A power pack for transportation purposes has been developed, using propane-air. In general, any attempts to use cheaper fuels have not met with any degree of success because of the accumulation of non-reactive impurities and carbon formation at the electrodes.

A suggested method of avoiding some of these problems is that proposed by Pittsburgh Consolidated Coal Corporation, USA (see Figure IIG-2).

Coal volatiles are supplied to a high temperature fused K_2CO_3 electrolyte fuel cell from a retort. CO is generated by feeding the CO_2 from the cells to the retort after removal via reaction

$$C + CO_2 \rightarrow 2CO; \quad \Delta H = +41.22$$

High temperature cells are desirable to reduce the I^2R and polarization losses.

Typical Cell Reactions

- **Cathode reaction**

$$1/2O_2 + CO_2 + 2e \rightarrow CO_3^{=}$$

- **Anode reactions**

(1) *For* H_2

$$H_2 + CO_3^{=} - 2e \rightarrow H_2O + CO_2$$

(2) *For CO*

$$CO + CO_3^{=} - 2e \rightarrow 2CO_2$$

(3) *For* CH_4

$$CH_4 \rightarrow C + 4H$$

$$C + 2CO_3^{=} - 4e \rightarrow 3CO_2$$

$$4H + CO_3^{=} - 4e \rightarrow H_2O + CO_2$$

Data below referring to Figure IIG-2:

Stream compositions @ 55.5% fuel gas burned per pass

Stream No.	(1)		(2)		(3)		(4)		(5)	(6)	(7)
CH_4	1.75 moles	25.2%	1.75	25.1%	0.0	0.0	0.00	0.0%			
CO	0.95	13.8	1.15	16.9	2.68	16.1	0.60	10.6			
CO_2	0.42	6.1	0.22	3.2	6.80	41.0	0.38	6.7		8.50	2.14
H_2	3.51	51.1	3.31	48.0	2.43	14.5	4.50	79.6			
H_2O	0.27	3.9	0.47	6.8	4.86	29.2	0.19	3.3	2.58		
N_2										15.95	15.95
O_2										4.14	0.96

Analysis of solids

Stream No.		H	C	N	O	S	Kcal/kg
(8)	Coal	5.74	82.26	1.31	8.13	2.56	7970
(9)	Char	0.92	0.92	97.10		1.08	8060

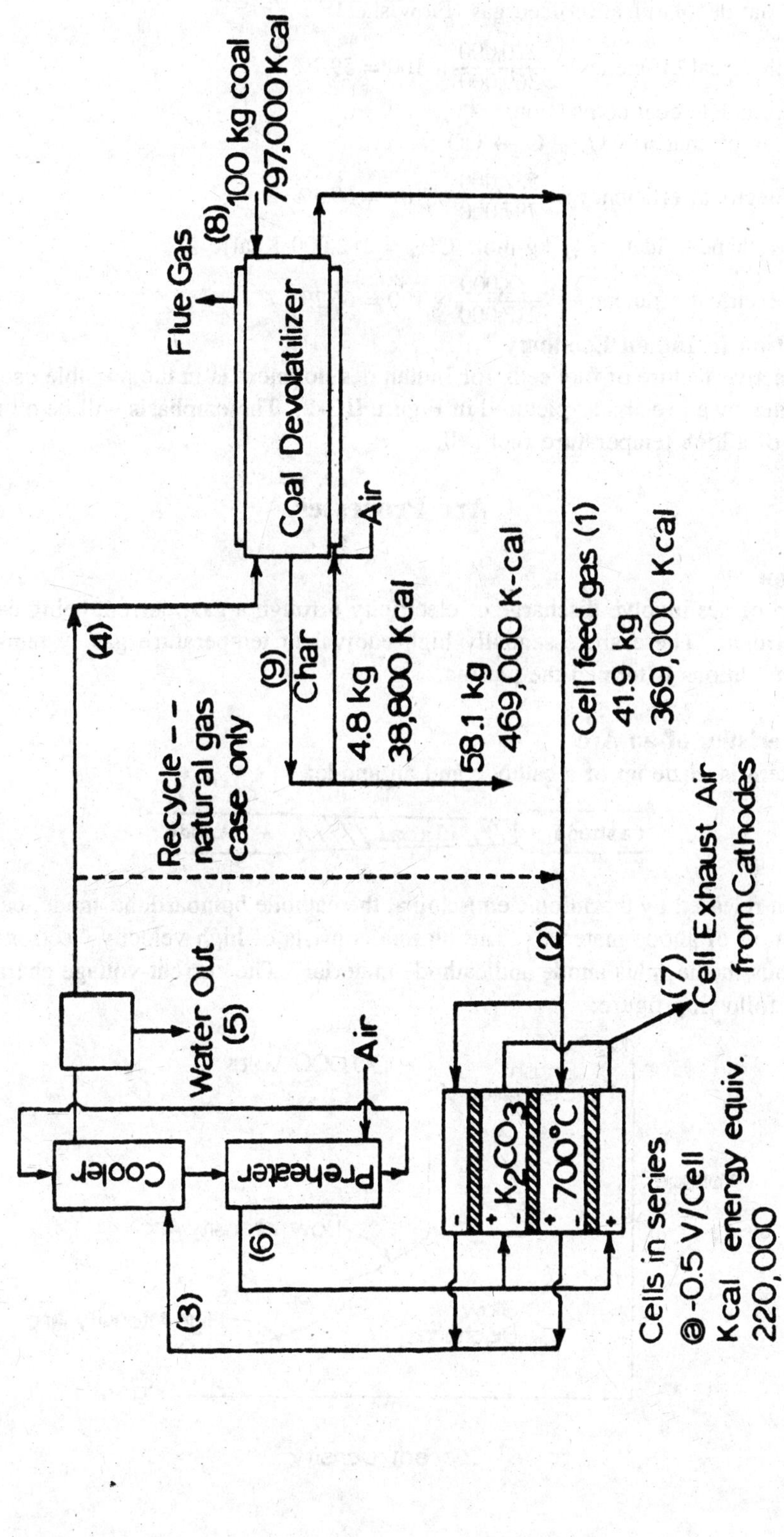

Fig. IIG-2. High temperature fuel cell using coal.

Efficiency of fuel cell system for electrical energy output

- Coal devolatilization feed gas (Flow sheet)
- Electrical efficiency $= \dfrac{220{,}000}{369{,}000} \times 100 = 59.7\%$
- Complete coal conversion
  Use of char as $CO_2 + C \rightarrow CO$

  Electrical efficiency $= \dfrac{552{,}000}{797{,}000} \times 100 = 69.5\%$

  Methane oxidation (1 kg-mole CH_4 = 212,000 Kcal)

  Electrical efficiency $= \dfrac{138{,}000}{212{,}000} \times 100 = 65.2\%$

4. Application in Indian Economy

The attractive feature of fuel cells for Indian development is in the possible use of low-grade coal and lignites by a process as pictured in Figure IIG-2. The emphasis will be on the successful development of a high temperature fuel cell.

Arc Processes

1. Definition

These processes involve discharge of electricity through a gas, current being carried by ions and free electrons. These are essentially high equivalent temperature gas systems and the gas under these conditions is termed the plasma.

2. Characteristics of an Arc

The system is made up of a cathode and an anode:

Electrons released by thermionic emission at the cathode bombard the anode, causing heating and volatilization of anode material. The plasma consists of high velocity electrons, ions of the original gaseous media, plus anode and cathode material. The current-voltage characteristics are shown in the following figure:

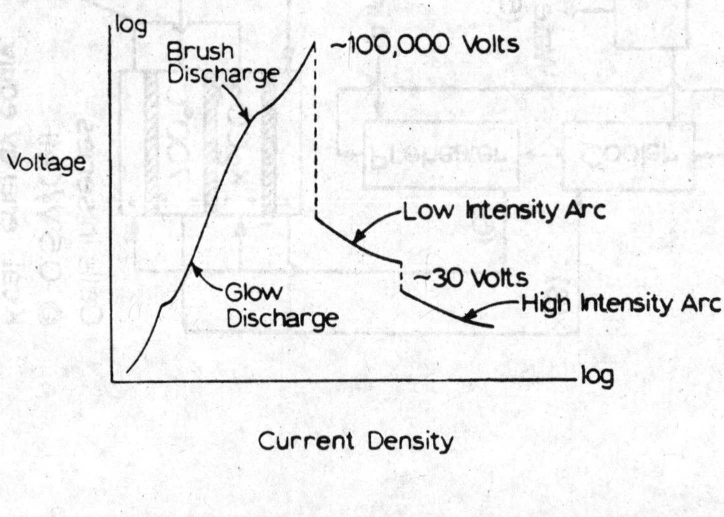

For high temperature work, only the low voltage-high current conditions on the right hand side of the diagram are of interest.

3. Applications of High Intensity Arc to Chemical Processing

By proper design of the arc injection system, almost any material (solid, liquid, or gas) can be heated to temperatures over 7,000°C with a power consumption of less than 20 KWH/kg.

Some of the applications which are possible with devices based on the high intensity arc principle are

Chemical processing for endothermic reactions

- Pyrolysis of hydrocarbons to unsaturates
- Fixation of atmospheric nitrogen to yield NO_2
- Production of hydrogen cyanide
- Reduction of phosphates to elemental phosphorus
- Reduction of oxides to elements
- Preparation of refractory nitrides

Mechanical applications

- Simulation of high stagnation temperatures in ablation studies
- Cutting, welding, and flame hardening of metals
- Flame spray coating of materials with refractories or ceramics
- Spheroidizing high-melting refractories
- New design of wind tunnels

Radiation and photochemical applications

- Arc image furnace
- Laser pumping component
- Photochemical conversions based on 2,000 to 4,000 Å

Electroorganic Chemical Processes

Although electroorganic chemistry is at least sixty years old and much literature exists on laboratory investigations, commercial applications have come only in the last few years. The organic chemist has been interested only in preparative processes without any economic considerations. Application of the chemical engineering viewpoint to the manufacture of commercially desirable compounds (acrylonitrile and tetraethyl lead, for example) has combined some of this laboratory art with new materials and new technology to give new practical processes. These afford alternative routes to tonnage chemicals bypassing present patented processes.

1. Adiponitrile from Acrylonitrile

1.1. Reference Flow Sheet: Figure IIG-3

1.2. Raw Materials

This process uses low-cost acrylonitrile made in one step from propylene, ammonia and air to give adiponitrile in a second step. Alternatively, one must go in four steps from benzene to cyclohexane to adipic acid to adiponitrile.

1.3. Chemical Reactions

Cathode: $2CH_2{=}CHCN + 2H_2O + 2e \rightarrow NC(CH_2)_4CN + 2OH^-$

Anode: $H_2O \rightarrow 2H^+ + \frac{1}{2}O_2 + 2e$

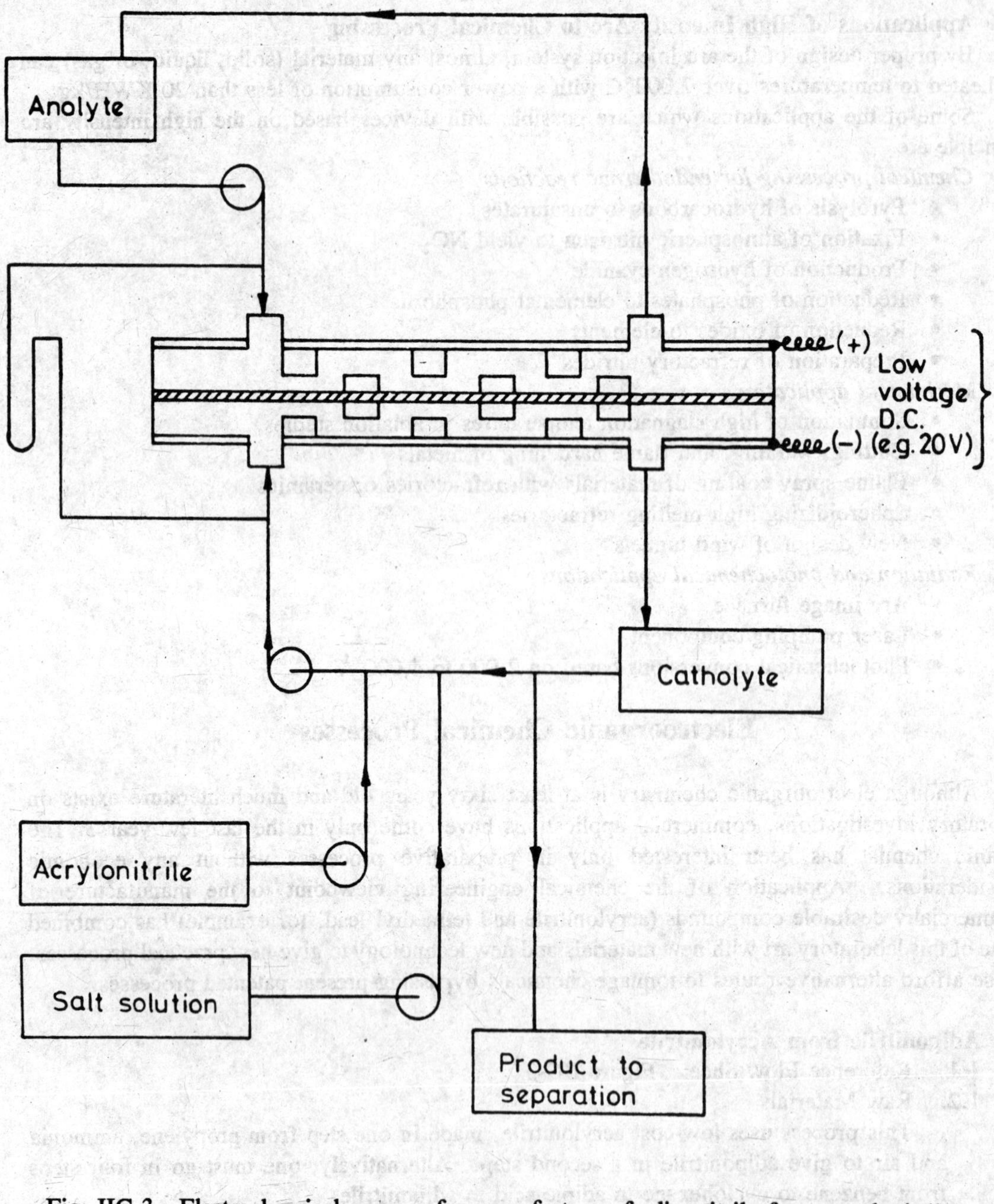

Fig. IIG-3. Electrochemical process for manufacture of adiponitrile from acrylonitrile.

1.4. Process Description

The electrolytic cell uses a lead cathode and a platinum-coated carbon or titanium anode. The anode and cathode are separated by a permeable membrane and separate fluid circulating systems are maintained for the sulfuric acid anolyte and for the quaternary ammonium salt solution which is the catholyte and which acts as an ionic solvent for acrylonitrile. The cell is operated at about 70°C and atmospheric pressure.

For adiponitrile product recovery, a stream is bled from the catholyte circulating loop and sent first to an extraction column where it is extracted with acrylonitrile. The organic phase is then contacted with water to remove the salt for recirculation to the cathode liquor. The extracted organic layer is then stripped of acrylonitrile and finally distilled. Yields of adiponitrile are 90%.

1.5. Major Engineering Problems

(a) Provision of a catholyte material giving adequate electrical conductivity and acrylonitrile solubility and also able to be subsequently separated from the adiponitrile product.

(b) Control of concentration of acrylonitrile in the catholyte; if concentration is too high, by-product polymerization products are formed; if too low, propionitrile is formed by reduction of acrylonitrile.

(c) Provision of good agitation or turbulence within the cell to minimize local ion concentrations and keep reaction rate, and the use of high current densities from being limited by slow diffusion rates.

(d) Development of special on-stream gas chromatograph to measure concentrations of acrylonitrile and by-products in the catholyte rapidly and continuously.

2. Tetra Ethyl Lead (TEL)

2.1. Reference Flow Sheet: Figure IIG-4

2.2. Raw Materials

- Ethyl magnesium chloride (Grignard reagent)
- Ethyl chloride
- Lead metal

(The lead metal is wholly consumed and need not be recycled as in the conventional process.)

2.3. Chemical Reactions

$$2C_2H_5MgCl + 2C_2H_5Cl + Pb \rightarrow Pb(C_2H_5)_4 + 2MgCl_2;$$

compare with older process

$$4NaPb + 4C_2H_5Cl \rightarrow Pb(C_2H_5)_4 + 4NaCl + 3Pb$$

2.4. Process Description

The electrolytic cell uses a sacrificial lead anode and a stainless steel cathode. The electrolyte comprises the Grignard reagent together with appropriate solvents. The solvent mixture includes diethyl ether, tetrahydrofuran to increase conductivity and an aromatic hydrocarbon. Excess alkyl halide present reacts with any magnesium plating out at the cathode to convert it to additional Grignard reagent. The cell is operated at about 70°C and atmospheric pressure. The lead metal is added to the cell in the form of pellets' which enter a compartment separated from the rest of the cell by a porous membrane.

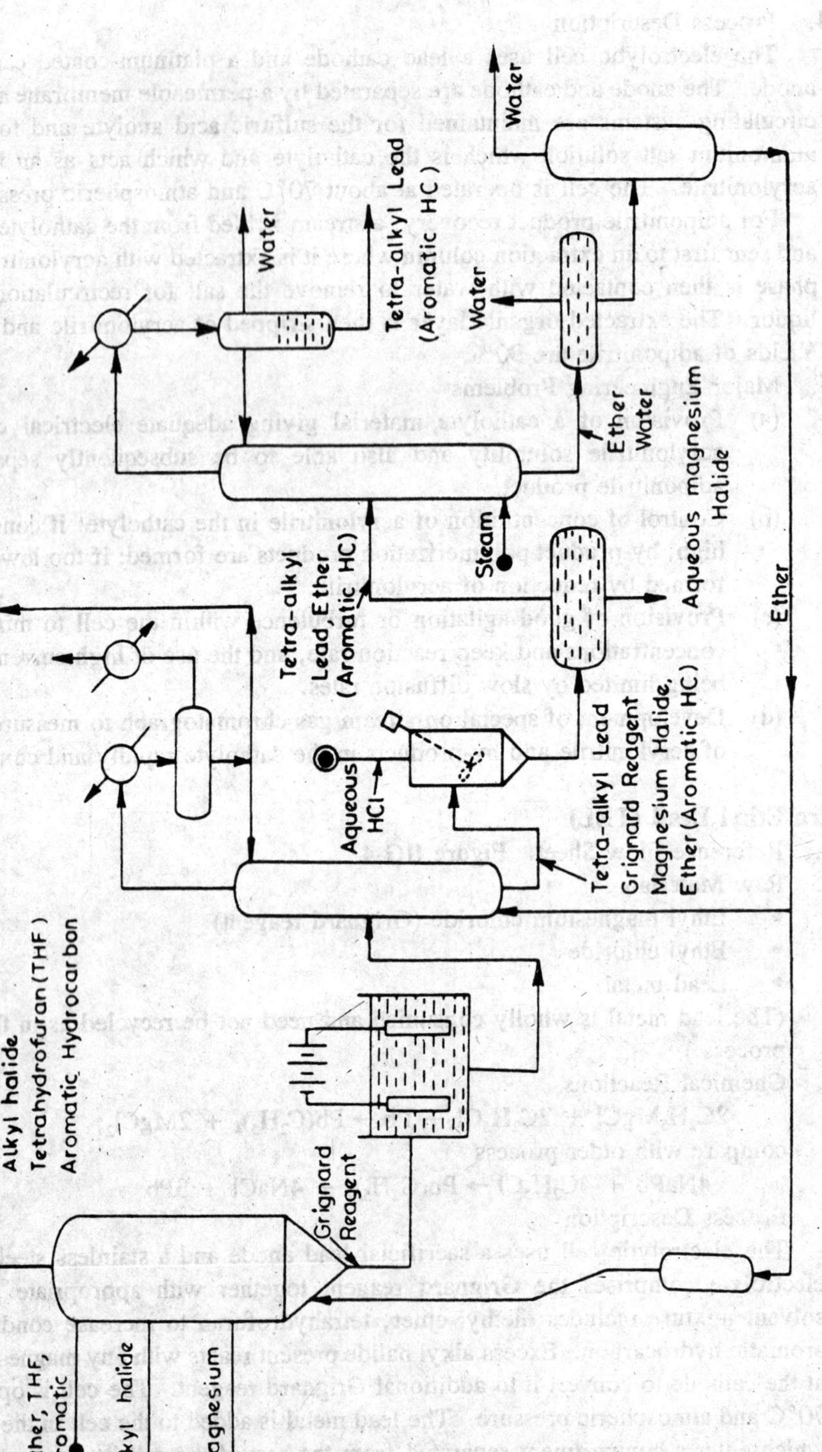

Fig. IIG-4. TEL recovery from an alkyl Grignard-containing electrolyte.

TEL recovery is accomplished as shown in Figure IIG-4 by HCl washing followed by steam distillation. TEL yield is over 96%; this is higher than in the older non-electrolytic process.

2.5. Major Engineering Problems

(a) Elimination of the magnesium metal which would be deposited at the cathode and bridge the gap between the electrodes, shorting out the cell. This is accomplished by providing excess C_2H_5Cl to react with the magnesium as it is formed.

(b) Precise temperature control. Increased temperatures caused by the heating effect of the electrolytic current increase the conductivity of the electrolyte but lead to side reactions. The aromatic hydrocarbon present acts as a thermal stabilizer for the TEL present. However, the cell is cooled by a jacket fluid and/or recirculation of electrolyte through an external cooler.

IIH. CHLOR-ALKALI INDUSTRY

The chlor-alkali industry represents production of three major industrial chemicals:

- Soda ash (sodium carbonate—Na_2CO_3)
- Caustic soda (sodium hydroxide—NaOH)
- Chlorine (Cl_2)

These chemicals have as widespread distribution in industry as does sulfuric acid.

The electrolysis of NaCl brine furnishes over 90% of the chlorine produced plus its co-product sodium hydroxide. This alkali is competitive in many areas with soda ash also produced from brine by a non-electrolytic process.

The use of a common raw material, NaCl, together with similarities in alkalinity and/or co-production of chlorine, is the reason why the above-outlined chemicals form the basis for the chlor-alkali industry. This industry is worthy of study because of these production achievements.

- Quarries and transports vast quantities of limestone (for soda ash production)
- Extracts NaCl mineral from open-water brine or deep wells
- Processes products to exceptional purity
- Operates 100% indigenously—no imports required
- Walks an economic tightrope shipping products such as low-priced soda ash

Soda Ash (Sodium Carbonate—Na_2CO_3)

1. Pertinent Properties

Mol. wt.	106.00
M.P.	851°C
B.P.	Decomposes
Soluble in water	(8.9 gm per 100 g 20°C)

Grades:

- 99% sodium carbonate (58% Na_2O) as light (solids density 1.86, bulk density 0.6) and dense (solids density 1.91, bulk density 1.0) grades of granular product
- Washing soda ($Na_2CO_3 \cdot 10H_2O$)

2. Consumption Pattern

Soda ash is the most available high-tonnage, low-cost, reasonably pure, soluble alkali on the market. Consequently, it is found in numerous industries.

2.1. End Uses

In the U.S., glass is the biggest industry using soda ash. The 36% used by this industry is divided into 60% bottles and containers, 29% flat glass, 7% fiberglass, and 4% other. Other soda ash uses are:

Chemical manufacture	17%
Soaps/detergents	9%
Miscellaneous	7%
Pulp and paper	2%
Desulfurization	2%
Export from the U.S.	27%

In India, the breakdown of soda ash use is given by the *IRIS Investor's Guide to Indian Corporates (1995)* as:

Soaps/detergents	40%
Glass	18%
Sodium silicate	15%
Trade	9%
Chemical industry	12%
Miscellaneous	6%
Total	100%

The LeBlanc process for the manufacture of soda ash was discovered in 1773 and was used universally for many years in Europe. Salt cake (sodium sulfate) reacts with limestone to give soda ash and a troublesome side product gypsum (calcium sulfate). The process is no longer used.

$$Na_2SO_4 + CaCO_3 \rightarrow Na_2CO_3 + CaSO_4$$

In 1864, Ernest Solvay, a Belgian chemist, invented his ammonia-soda process. A few years later the soda ash price was reduced one third. The Solvay process had completely replaced the LeBlanc method by 1915. The Solvay method is still very popular worldwide. However, in the U.S. large deposits of natural trona ore were found in the 1940's in Green River, Wyoming. In the last few years, there has been a tremendous conversion from synthetic to natural soda ash. The first and last Solvay plant in the United States (a large Allied Chemical plant in Solvay, NY) closed in 1986. Trona ore is found about 500 meters below the surface. It is called sodium sesquicarbonate and is mostly $2Na_2CO_3 \cdot NaHCO_3 \cdot 2H_2O$ (45% Na_2CO_3, 36% $NaHCO_3$, 15% water + impurities). Heating this ore gives soda ash. The conversion from the Solvay process to natural soda ash has been called one of the most successful U.S. chemical industry transformations of the late 1970's and early 1980's. The ratio of production for selected years certainly proves this point.

	1948	1974	1981	1985	1986
Solvay	94	46	9	6	0
Natural	6	54	91	94	100

A new solution mining method that is claimed to be 25% cheaper may take over in the 1990's. Despite the fact that no new Solvay plants have been started since 1934 in the U.S., it is still an important method worldwide. There is some fascinating chemistry in this involved process and we will discuss it in detail.

Since the shutting down of the last synthetic sodium carbonate manufacturing unit in the USA in 1985, USA production has been exclusively derived from natural sodium carbonate deposits. Other producers of "natural" sodium carbonate are Kenya, Mexico and Russia. In 1985, 30% of the world production was from natural deposits. This figure is expected to rise still further due to the low energy requirements and low pollution of "natural" sodium carbonate production together with innovative developments in the recovery of sodium carbonate from brines (solution mining). Total sodium carbonate consumption will rise still further, despite much lower consumption in the glass industry due to increased glass recycling and increased use of plastic containers. Increased sodium carbonate demand is particularly forecast for the plate glass and glass fiber industries.

The world production of sodium carbonate doubled between 1960 and 1975, but this growth had petered out by 1985 at which time the production at 28.7×10^6 t was similar to that for sodium hydroxide. Table IIH-1 gives the regional distribution of sodium carbonate production in 1985.

Table IIH-1 1985 Production of Sodium Carbonate by Region in 10^6 t

World	28.7
North America	8.6
South America	0.3
Western Europe	5.2
Eastern Europe	9.5
Asia/Oceania	4.8
Africa	0.3

Source: "Industrial Inorganic Chemistry" by Buchner et al (1989)

The country with the largest production is the USA with 7.7×10^6 t. It is also the most important sodium carbonate exporter with 1.5×10^6 t in 1985. Then come Russia, China, Bulgaria and West Germany.

Soda ash is used in the manufacture of glass and glassware, sodium silicate, paper and pulp, textiles, detergents and a number of other chemicals. There are seven units in the organized sector in India manufacturing soda ash. The estimated demand for soda ash during 1989-90 was 9 lakh tons which would go up to 13.40 lakh tons during 1990-91. The installed capacity was 14.60 lakh tons during 1988-89 and the production figure was 12.03 lakh tons. The government has delicensed the soda ash industry to facilitate new entrants.

Authoritative estimates indicate an expected growth rate of 8% per annum in the consumption of soda ash in the next ten years. Accordingly, the demand estimated for 1994-95 is 19.2 lakh tons as against the present capacity of 15.5 lakh tons. As per the information available on the progress of implementation of soda ash projects, production capacity was expected to reach 20 lakh tons by 1992-93.

3. Methods of Production

3.1. Classification of Processes

- Solvay or ammonia-soda
- Dual process (Na_2CO_3 + NH_4Cl)
- Natural soda ash from deposits

3.2. Solvay or Ammonia-soda Process

3.2.1. Reference flow sheet: Figure IIH-1

3.2.2. Chemical reactions

(a) Overall reaction

$$CaCO_3\ (s) + 2NaCl\ (aq) \rightarrow Na_2CO_3 + CaCl_2$$

This reaction takes place in a number of steps:

(b) $CaCO_3\ (s) \rightarrow CaO\ (s) + CO_2\ (g)$; $\Delta H = +43.4$ Kcal

(c) $C\ (s) + O_2\ (g) \rightarrow CO_2\ (g)$; $\Delta H = -96.5$ Kcal

(d) $CaO\ (s) + H_2O\ (1) \rightarrow Ca(OH)_2\ (aq)$; $\Delta H = -15.9$ Kcal

(e) $NH_3\ (g) + H_2O \rightleftharpoons NH_4^+OH^-$; $\Delta H = -22.1$ Kcal

(f) $CO_2\ (g) + OH^- \rightleftharpoons HCO_3^-$

(g) $CO_2\ (g) + H_2O \rightleftharpoons HCO_3^- + H^+$

(h) $Na^+ + Cl^- + NH_4^+ + HCO_3^- \rightarrow NH_4^+Cl^-\ (aq) + NaHCO_3 \downarrow$

(i) $2NaHCO_3\ (s) \rightarrow Na_2CO_3\ (s) + CO_2\ (g) + H_2O\ (g)$; $\Delta H = +30.7$ Kcal

(j) $2NH_4Cl\ (aq) + Ca(OH)_2\ (s) \rightarrow 2NH_3\ (g) + CaCl_2\ (aq) + 2H_2O\ (1)$; $\Delta H = +10.7$ Kcal

3.2.3. Raw materials

Input bulk requirements for the Solvay process are salt, coal, and limestone. Salt is used as brine pumped from deep wells or as crystalline salt via evaporation procedures. NH_3 make-up in the recirculation load amounts to about 1.5 kg/ton of Na_2CO_3, or greater than 99.8% recovery.

3.2.4. Quantitative requirements

(a) Basis: 1 ton of Na_2CO_3 (58% NaO)

Salt	1.55 tons
Limestone	1.2 tons
Coke	0.09 ton
High pressure steam	1.35 tons
Low pressure steam	1.60 tons
Ammonia losses	1.5 kg
Cooling water	40-60 tons
Electric power	210 KWH

(b) Plant capacities: 200-2,000 tons/day

3.2.5. Process description

The principal discovery of Solvay in 1869 was that NH_3 dissolved in an NaCl solution and then reacted with CO_2. A precipitate of $NaHCO_3$ was obtained which could be calcined to produce high purity Na_2CO_3.

Saturated salt brine is purified in a series of wash towers with NH_3 and then with CO_2 to remove Ca, Mg and Fe as a sludge.

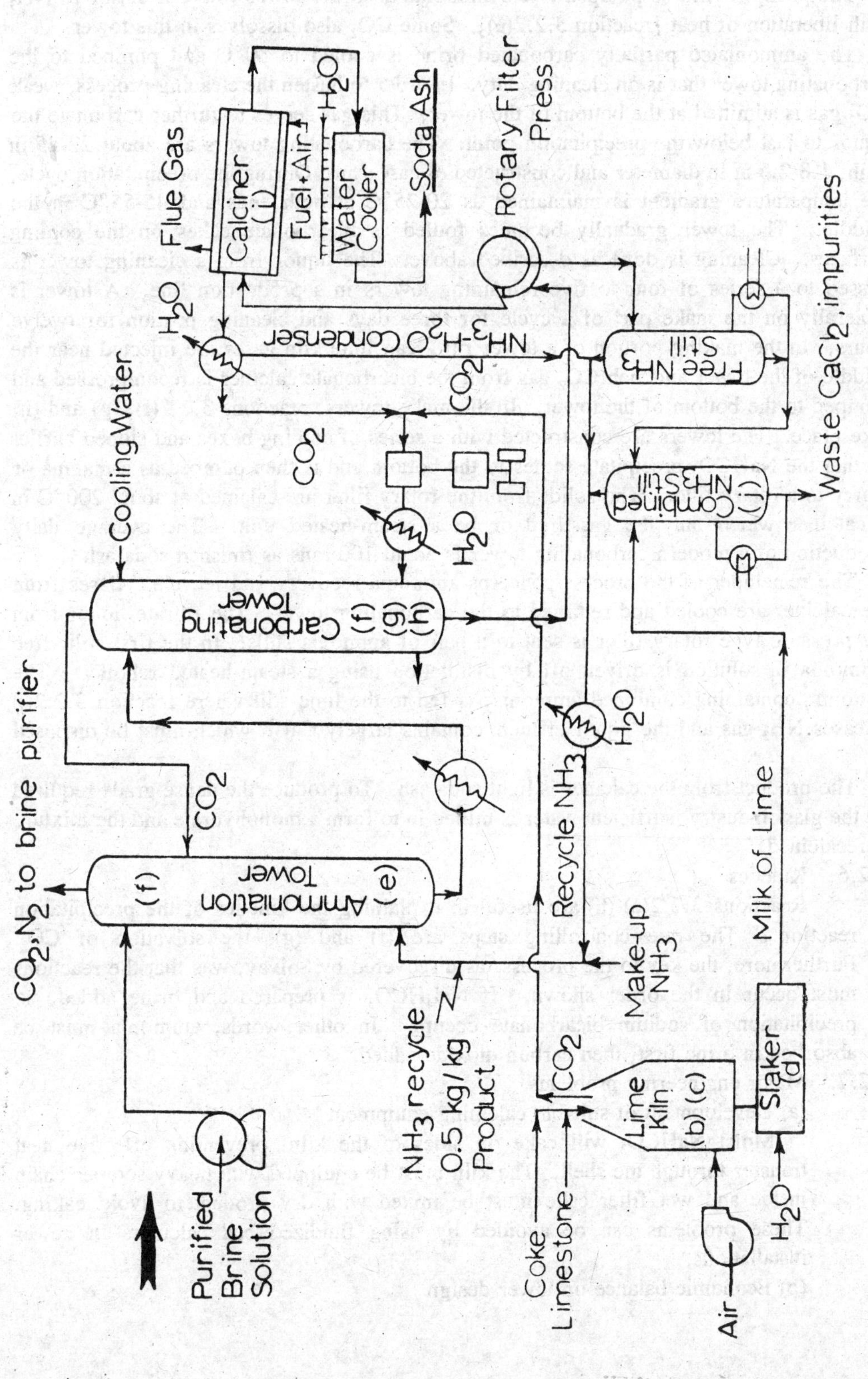

Fig. IIH-1. Manufacture of soda ash by Solvay process.

The purified brine is pumped to the ammonia absorber tower where it dissolves NH_3 with liberation of heat [reaction 3.2.2(e)]. Some CO_2 also dissolves in this tower.

The ammoniated partially carbonated brine is cooled to 30°C and pumped to the carbonating tower that is on cleaning duty. In order to hasten the cleaning process, weak CO_2 gas is admitted at the bottom of the tower. This gas serves to further carbonate the liquor to just below the precipitation point. The carbonating towers are about 22-25 m high, 1.8-2.5 m in diameter and constructed of cast iron. During the precipitation cycle, the temperature gradient is maintained as 20-25°C at both ends and 45-55°C in the middle. The tower gradually becomes fouled as bicarbonate cakes on the cooling surfaces. Cleaning is done as described above. The liquor from a cleaning tower is passed to a series of four to five remaining towers in a production line. A tower is generally on the make part of a cycle for three days and cleaning portion for twelve hours. In the making portion of a tower run, lean lime kiln gases are injected near the middle of the tower and rich CO_2 gas from the bicarbonate calciner is recompressed and pumped to the bottom of the tower. In the make towers, reactions 3.2.2(f), (g) and (h) take place. The towers are constructed with a series of cooling boxes and sloped baffles so that the $NaHCO_3$ precipitate settles to the bottom and is then pumped as a magma or slurry to a rotary filter. The solids from the rotary filter are calcined at about 200°C in a calciner which may be gas-fired or be a steam-heated unit. The average daily production of a modern carbonating tower is about 100 tons as finished soda ash.

The remainder of the process concerns ammonia recovery and recycle. Gases from the calciner are cooled and returned to the carbonating tower. The filtrate liquor from the pressure type rotary filter is sent to a pair of ammonia stills. In the first still, free ammonia in solution is driven off by distillation using a steam-heated reboiler. The bottoms, containing combined ammonia, is fed to the lime still where reaction 3.2.2(j) releases NH_3 gas and the liquor effluent contains largely $CaCl_2$ which must be disposed of.

The product from the calciner is light soda ash. To produce the dense grade required by the glass industry, sufficient water is milled in to form a monohydrate and the mixture is recalcined.

3.2.6. Kinetics

Reactions 3.2.2(e)-(h) are useful in explaining the kinetics of the precipitation reaction. The rate controlling steps are (f) and (g), the solvation of CO_2. Furthermore, the key to the process, as discovered by Solvay, was that the reactions must occur in the order shown. If NH_4HCO_3 is prepared and brine added, no precipitation of sodium bicarbonate occurs. In other words, ammonia must be absorbed in brine first, then carbon dioxide added.

3.2.7. Major engineering problems

(a) Development of suitable calcining equipment

Moist $NaHCO_3$ will cake on sides of the kiln, preventing effective heat transfer through the shell. The kiln must be equipped with heavy scraper chain inside and wet filter cake must be mixed with dry product to avoid caking. These problems can be avoided by using fluidized bed calciners in newer installations.

(b) Economic balance on tower design

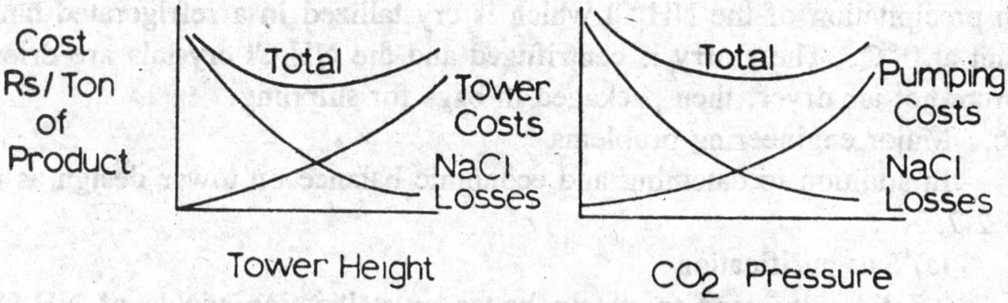

The tower height, pressure and temperature are optimized, giving approximately 75% yield of $NaHCO_3$ from NaCl.

(c) Ammonia recovery

NH_3 inventory costs 4-5 times that of Na_2CO_3 inventory so losses must be kept low. By proper choice of equipment design and maintenance, losses are less than 0.2% of recycle load (0.5 kg/kg product) or about 1 kg/ton of Na_2CO_3.

(d) Plant modernization

Three Solvay plants were built prior to 1947 in India. These had to be modernized:

- Substituting better materials of construction in replacement maintenance
- Use of automatic control

(e) Waste disposal

Find uses for large quantities of $CaCl_2$-NaCl liquor or dispose as waste.

3.3. Dual Process (Modified Solvay)

3.3.1. Reference flow sheet: Figure IIH-1

3.3.2. Chemical reactions

(a) $C\ (s) + O_2\ (g) \rightarrow CO_2\ (g)$

(b) $NH_3\ (g) + H_2O \rightleftharpoons NH_4^+OH^-$

(c) $CO_2\ (g) + OH^- \rightleftharpoons HCO_3^-$

(d) $CO_2\ (g) + H_2O \rightleftharpoons HCO_3^- + H^+$

(e) $Na^+ + Cl^- + NH_4^+ + HCO_3^- \rightarrow NH_4^+Cl^-\ (aq) + NaHCO_2 \downarrow$

(f) $2NaHCO_3 \rightarrow Na_2CO_3 + CO_2 + H_2O$

3.3.3. Raw materials

Input bulk requirements are crystalline salt, fuel, and ammonia since NH_4Cl is a co-product.

3.3.4. Quantitative requirements

(a) Basis: 1 ton of Na_2CO_3 (58% Na_2O)

Salt	1.26 tons
NH_3	0.323 ton
High pressure steam	1.35 tons
Low pressure steam	0.10 ton
Cooling water	50-80 tons
Electric power	450 KWH
Co-product	0.62 ton of NH_4Cl

(b) Plant capacities: 30-500 tons/day

3.3.5. Process description

The principal modification of the dual process is the recovery of NH_4Cl as a co-product rather than liberation of the contained ammonia for recycle as in the Solvay process. The liquor from the bicarbonate filters is mixed with washed salt feed to aid in precipitation of the NH_4Cl which is crystallized in a refrigerated tank-continuous unit at 0°C. The slurry is centrifuged and the NH_4Cl crystals are dried in a rotary drum hot air dryer, then packaged in bags for shipping.

3.3.6. Major engineering problems

In addition to calcining and economic balance on tower design as mentioned in 3.2.7:

(a) Salt purification

Solid salt, used to obtain better crystallization yields of NH_4Cl, cannot be purified as with brine feeds in Solvay. Only purification is mechanical washing and dewatering.

(b) Corrosion

NH_4Cl solution is quite corrosive in equipment involved in crystallization and solids recovery. Durmet 20 or rubber-lined units specified.

(c) Refrigeration

Economic balance on yield of NH_4Cl versus refrigeration costs with temperature of crystallization as a variable. Note that at economic temperature of around 0°C the electric requirements are still twice that of the Solvay operation.

4. Economics

4.1. Marketing and Sales

Soda ash is still the cheapest alkali, but competition from NH_3 for weak alkali requirements can be expected as NH_3 costs continue to drop relative to soda ash. Price reduction for soda ash must come by erecting plants in the 1,000 ton per day size compared to present sizes of about 1/5 this figure. Note that Indian f.o.b. prices are over twice U.S. prices despite lower-cost labor and all-indigenous operations.

4.2. Choice of Processes

(a) Advantages of Solvay

- Can use low-grade brine
- Less electric power
- Less corrosion problems
- No co-products to dispose of
- Does not require NH_3 plant investment

(b) Disadvantages of Solvay

- Higher salt consumption
- Higher investment in NH_3 recovery units versus crystallization units for NH_4Cl
- Waste disposal of $CaCl_2$-brine stream
- More steam consumption
- Higher capacity plant for economic break-even operation (100 versus 55 tons/day)
- With current fertilizer shortages, all of the NH_4Cl will be used as a mixed chemical fertilizer ingredient, so co-product disposal no problem

4.3. Plant Location Factors

One ton of Na_2CO_3 requires eight tons of brine, limestone and coal so proximity to raw materials is prime consideration. Salt sources are usually the key factor as they are less widely distributed than limestone or coal.

4.4. Industry Diversification

Most companies have gone or should go into production of caustic, chlorine and sodium bicarbonate with the NaCl brine available. Plants for glass manufacture (to use dense or heavy soda ash), cement (to obtain lime sludge), and solid carbon dioxide are closely tied into the vast manufacturing complex which characterizes the chlor-alkali industry.

Producers of sodium carbonate (soda ash) in India are shown in Table IIH-2.

Table IIH-2
Units Manufacturing Soda Ash in India

Name and Address	*Product Range*
Atul Products Ltd. 297, GIDC Industrial Estate, Ankleshwar PIN-393 002, Dist. Bharuch (Gujarat)	By-product
DCW Ltd. Dhrangadhra (Gujarat)	Standard Solvay process
Gujarat Alkalies & Chemicals Ltd. Baroda (Gujarat)	Caustic soda conversion process
Gujarat Heavy Chemicals Ltd. Sutrapada (Gujarat)	Akzo dry lime (modified Solvay process)
Orissa Cement Ltd. Unit Hari Fertilizers, Sahupuri - 221 009 Varanasi (U.P.)	Modified dual process
Punjab National Fertilizers & Chemicals Ltd. Naya Nangal, Tehsil Anandpur Sahib Dist. Ropar (Punjab)	Modified dual process
Saurashtra Chemicals (Unit of VXL Ltd.) Porbander (Gujarat)	Standard Solvay process
Tata Chemicals Ltd. Mithapur, Jamnagar (Gujarat)	Standard Solvay process
Tuticorin Alkali Chemicals & Fertilizers Ltd. Harbour Construction Road, Tuticorin - 628 005 (T.N.)	Modified dual process

Source: "SBP Handbook of Projects for Corporate Diversification" (1992)

Chlorine-Caustic Soda

These two chemicals are being discussed in combination as they are produced as co-products in the electrolysis of brine. This process accounts for 80% of caustic soda and >95% of chlorine production in India.

1. Pertinent Properties of Chlorine (Cl_2)

Mol. wt.	70.9		
M.P.	−101.6°C	Critical temp.	146°C
B.P.	−34.6°C	Critical pressure	93.5 atms.
Liquefaction point	5.7 atms. and 15°C		
Toxic gas	0.35-2.0 ppm is max. conc.		
Grades	Technical (99.0%)		

2. Pertinent Properties of Sodium Hydroxide (NaOH)

Mol. wt.	40.00
B.P.	1,390°C
M.P.	318°C

Very soluble in water with high exothermic heat of solution

Grades: Available in solid form of flakes, granules, sticks, lumps, pellets and aqueous solutions (50 and 73% NaOH). Purity of solid forms ranges from 60% Na_2O (77.4% NaOH) to 76% Na_2O (98% NaOH).

3. Consumption Pattern

The start of the chlorine industry in the 1920's was the result of successful development of the electrolytic brine decomposition process. Caustic soda, formed in the ratio of 1.1 tons per ton of chlorine in the electrolytic process, had previously been solely manufactured by a lime-soda ash process which is gradually being replaced.

Virtually all the basic discoveries and inventions necessary for the development of both the diaphragm and mercury cell processes for the brine electrolysis were made during the period from 1883 to 1893. The first diaphragm plant in the USA was built in 1893 in Rumford Falls, NY. The first mercury cell of industrial significance was invented in 1892 to make pure caustic soda. With the development of the LeBlanc and Solvay processes for making sodium carbonate, sodium hydroxide became a relatively common chemical. Soda ash was converted to caustic soda by the well known lime-soda reaction. Even though electrolytic caustic soda was produced in the 1890's, the lime-soda process remained dominant until the late 1940's. Caustic soda is no longer produced for sale by this process. However, small amounts continue to be made by the method, largely for captive consumption.

There were thirty-eight caustic soda units in the organized sector at the end of 1989. Caustic soda is produced through four processes: the mercury process (88% of total), diaphragm process (7%), membrane process (4%) and chemical process (hardly 1%). The installed capacity in 1989-90 was 11.03 lakh tons while production amounted to Rs. 8.92 lakh tons.

The estimated production of caustic soda during 1991-92 is 10.23 lakh tons as against 9.99 lakh tons in 1990-91.

Authoritative estimate shows that the demand for caustic soda would spurt to 10 lakh tons by 1991-92 and to 14 lakh tons by 1994-95.

These statistics were presented by Kothari in the "Industrial Directory of India" (1994).

3.1. End uses for chlorine are shown in Tables IIH-3, IIH-4 and IIH-5.

Table IIH-3
Present and Projected Chlorine Use Pattern for India

Use	1990	1995	2000
			('000 tons)
Pulp and paper	140	170	210
PVC	115	150	200
Chlorinated paraffin wax	72	80	100
Inorganic chemicals	65	70	75
Organic chemicals	40	45	55
Pesticides & Insecticides	38	45	50
Miscellaneous	30	40	50
Water treatment	16	25	42
Pharmaceuticals	15	18	20
Rayon grade wood pulp	10	10	10
Total	541	653	812

Source: "Hindu Survey of Indian Industry" (1995)

Table IIH-4
Quantities of Chlorine Consumed in the USA in 1982 for Different Applications in 10^6 t

All Organic Chemicals	Only C_2 Chemicals	Paper & Pulp	Inorganic Chemicals	$TiCl_4$	Water Treatment	Cleaning & Sanitation
5.922	3.304*	1.240	0.714	0.357	0.400	0.304

*mainly vinyl chloride

Source: "Industrial Inorganic Chemistry" by Buchner et al (1989)

Table IIH-5
Chlorine—Projected Demand Pattern in USA (%)

User Sector	1994	2000	2010
PVC	34	41	55
Organic Chemicals	32	27	17
Inorganic Chemicals	12	13	15
Pulp & Paper	9	6	-
Water Treatment	5	5	5
Others	8	8	8
Total	100	100	100
Total Demand	**12.4 million TPA**		

(Source: C&EN, 21 Nov. 1994)

The use of chlorine for pulp and paper bleaching, blamed for dioxin contamination through wastewater, is expected to be virtually eliminated by 2010. Pulp and paper bleachers have already voluntarily cut chlorine use by about 60%, leading to closure of several chlorine plants in the logging regions of Pacific Northwest of USA.

3.2. End Uses for Sodium Hydroxide

These are summarized worldwide in Table IIH-6 and for India in Table IIH-7.

Table IIH-6
World Caustic Soda Demand 1993-2000 ('000 ton/year)

	1993	1994	1996	2000
Consumption				
Organic Chemicals	7,619	7,636	7,902	8,467
Textile Industry	2,321	2,344	2,471	2,783
Paper and Pulp	6,545	6,578	6,898	7,411
Alumina	3,213	3,163	3,367	3,742
Soaps and Detergents	2,072	2,094	2,204	2,431
Inorganic Chemicals	7,083	7,135	7,354	7,869
Neutralization	1,845	1,944	2,083	2,222
Dye	231	231	238	251
Miscellaneous	8,013	8,141	8,210	8,314
Total	**38,942**	**39,266**	**40,727**	**43,490**

Source: *"Chemical Weekly," Bombay (1995)*

Table IIH-7
Indian Caustic Soda Demand—Present and Projected ('000 tons)

Use	1990	1995	2000
Paper/paperboard	160	235	300
Miscellaneous	113	133	160
Soaps and detergents	110	115	130
Chemicals	90	105	120
Aluminum	86	110	110
Exports	15	35	93
Rayon grade wood pulp/ viscose yard/VSF	89	89	89
Cotton textiles	77	77	77
Fertilizers	40	50	72
Dyes and intermediates	35	42	50
Pharmaceuticals	31	34	38
Petrochemicals	13	22	35
Demineralization	16	20	26
Power	16	20	26
Oil drilling	8	10	12
Vegetable oils	8	9	10
Rayon tire cord	9	9	9
Minerals and metals	4	5	6
Total	920	1,120	1,363

Source: *"Hindu Survey of Indian Industry" (1995)*

4. Methods of Production

For many years since its discovery in 1853, the "lime causticization" method of manufacturing caustic soda was used which involves reaction of slaked lime and soda ash.

$$Na_2CO_3 + Ca(OH)_2 \rightarrow 2NaOH + CaCO_3$$

In 1892, the electrolysis of brine was discovered as a method for making both sodium hydroxide and chlorine. This rapidly grew in importance and since the 1960's it has been the only method of manufacture. Among electrolytic industries it is the second largest consumer of electricity, aluminum manufacturing being the largest.

Year	*% of NaOH by Electrolysis*
1935	44
1940	50
1954	85
1962	100

Up to the beginning of the 1980's, the chlorine production of a region was an indicator of the strength of its chemical industry, since the evolution of chlorine production paralleled that of the total chemical production. Chlorine production appears to have reached the zenith of its growth or is even in decline. Chlorine is being displaced from its largest application fields such as plastics, solvents and pulp bleaching for a number of reasons, some ecological. The world chlorine production capacity fell ca. 4% between 1980 and 1986 and a further fall is expected in the USA (despite the >90% utilization of the effective USA capacity and ca. 90% utilization of the European capacity in the summer of 1986). The chlorine capacities on January 1, 1986 in 10^6 t/a are given in Table IIH-8.

Table IIH-8
Chlorine Capacities on January 1, 1986 in 10^6 t/a

USA	12.140	EEC	9.345
W. Europe excl. EEC	1.409	North America	14.195
South America	1.296	Africa	0.382
Near East	0.520	Asia/Oceania	5.445
Japan	3.248	Eastern Europe	5.780
USSR	3.400	India	1.2

The demand for chlorine in India is expected to increase from about 10 lakh tons in 1993-94 to about 19 lakh tons by 2002-03. Since chlorine is a co-product of caustic soda manufacture, the availability of chlorine to ensure the growth of the chlorine end use industry is possible only by ensuring that the caustic soda industry remains healthy and continues to grow. See Table IIH-7.

4.1. Classification of Processes

4.1.1. Electrolytic process producing chlorine, sodium hydroxide, and hydrogen as co-products; accounts for 80% of production.

(a) Diaphragm electrolytic cell—uses saturated NaCl solution and produces 10-12% caustic which must be concentrated. Being replaced by membrane cells.

(b) Mercury electrolytic cell—uses saturated NaCl solution with solid salt make-up, gives 70% caustic solutions directly.

4.1.2. Chlorine processes without co-products

(a) HCl-air oxidation with Fe_2O_3 catalyst

(b) HCl-air-Cl_2 oxychlorination processes, *e.g.*, production of ethylene dichloride from ethylene

(c) HNO_3-NaCl-air process

4.1.3. NaOH process with no Cl_2 co-product

Na_2CO_3-$Ca(OH)_2$; no further investments allocated as process not competitive.

4.2. Electrolytic Process

4.2.1. Reference flow sheet: Figure IIH-2

4.2.2. Electrolysis reactions

(a) Diaphragm cell type

Cell notation

$$\uparrow Cl_2, C \mid NaCl\,(aq) \quad \underset{\text{Anode}}{+} \xrightarrow{\hspace{6em}} \underset{\text{Cathode}}{-} \quad NaOH\,(aq) \mid Fe, H_2 \uparrow$$

Cell reaction

- Anode : $Cl^- - e \rightarrow \frac{1}{2}Cl_2$
- Cathode : $Na^+ + H_2O + e \rightarrow Na^+ + OH^- + \frac{1}{2}H_2$
- Overall : $NaCl + H_2O \rightarrow NaOH + \frac{1}{2}H_2 + \frac{1}{2}Cl_2$; $\Delta H = +53.4$ Kcal

(b) Mercury cell

Cell notation

$$Cl_2 \uparrow \mid C \quad NaCl \quad (\text{sat'd}) \quad \underset{\text{Anode}}{+} \xrightarrow{\hspace{6em}} \underset{\text{Cathode}}{-} \quad Na^\circ \mid NaHg\ (\text{amalgam})$$

Cell reaction

- Anode : $Cl^- - e \rightarrow \frac{1}{2}Cl_2$
- Cathode : $Na^+ + e \rightarrow Na^\circ$
  : $Na^\circ + Hg \rightarrow NaHg$ (amalgam)
- Denuding : $NaHg + H_2O \rightarrow NaOH + \frac{1}{2}H_2 + Hg$
- Overall : $NaCl + H_2O \rightarrow NaOH + \frac{1}{2}H_2 + \frac{1}{2}Cl_2$

4.2.3. Raw materials

The principal raw material is a purified solution of 10-15% NaCl or solid salt depending on the type of electrolysis cell used. Minor quantities of Na_2CO_3 and NaOH for salt purification, and H_2SO_4 for Cl_2 drying are required.

4.2.4. Quantitative requirements

(a) Basis: 1 ton of Cl_2; 1.15 tons of NaOH (98%); 283 Nm^3 of H_2 (26 kg)

Salt	**1.3 tons**
Soda ash (58% Na_2O)	**26 kg**

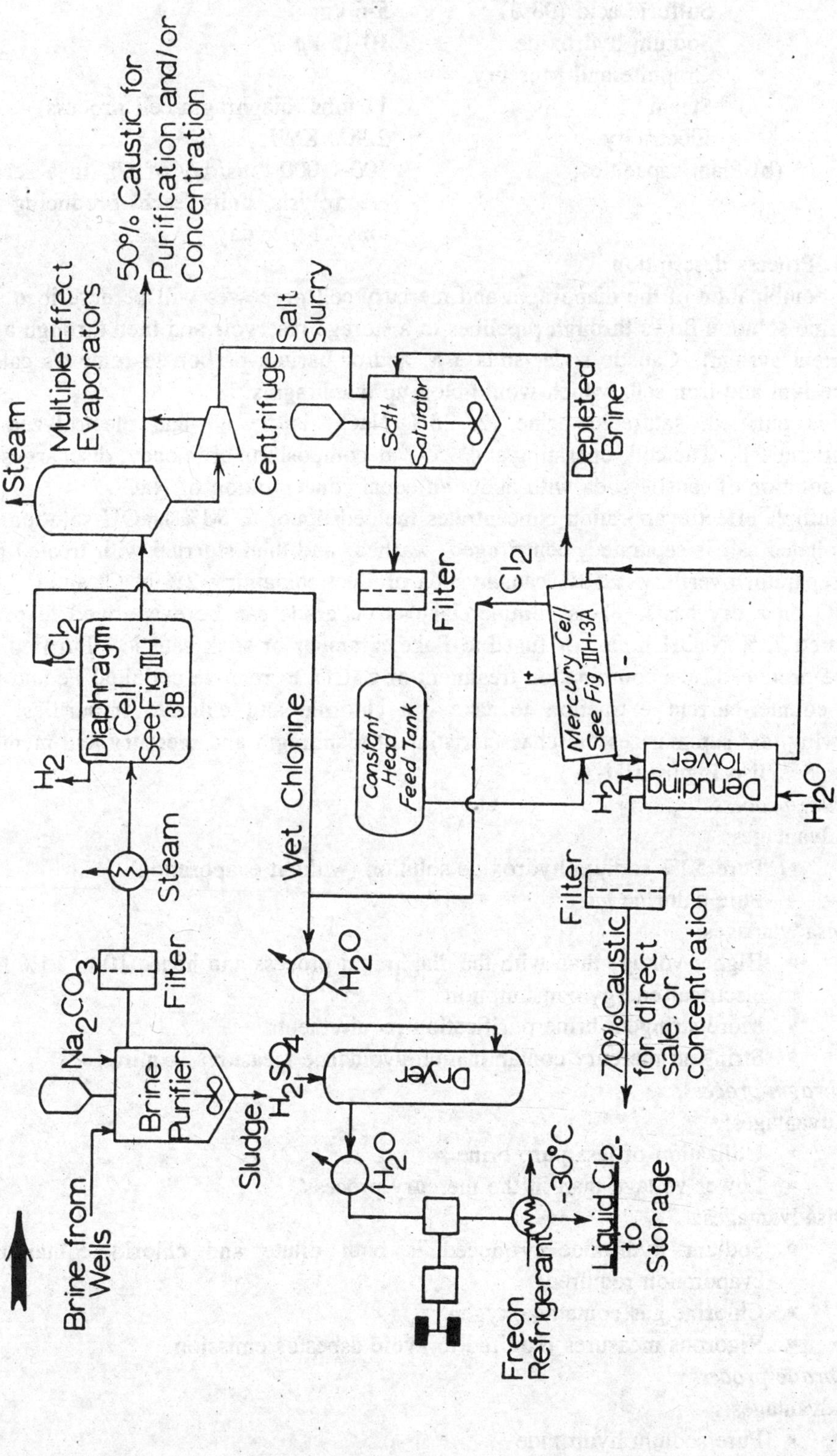

Fig. IIH-2. Electrolytic process for chlorine-caustic soda production.

Sulfuric acid (98%)	5-6 kg
Sodium hydroxide	10-15 kg
Graphite and Mercury	
Steam	11 tons (diaphragm cell process)
Electricity	2,900 KWH
(b) Plant capacities:	100-1,000 tons/day of Cl_2 in a series of electrolysis units each producing 0.5-2 tons Cl_2 per day

4.2.5. Process description

A combination of the diaphragm and mercury cell processes will be described.

Brine solution flows through pipelines to a storage reservoir and then through a brine treatment system. Caustic soda, soda ash, and/or barium carbonate removes calcium, magnesium and iron salts which would clog up diaphragms.

This purified, saturated brine (25-28% NaCl) is heated and electrolyzed in a diaphragm cell. The cell, operating at 45-55% decomposition efficiency, discharges a 10-12% solution of caustic soda with about an equal concentration of NaCl.

Multiple effect evaporation concentrates the cell liquor to 50% NaOH solution. The precipitated salt is separated, centrifuged, washed, and then slurried with treated brine. Salt separator overflow is 50% caustic soda product containing 2% NaCl and 0.1-0.5% NaClO on a dry basis. This commercial caustic grade can be evaporated to produce saturated 73% NaOH liquor or fused to flake, granular or stick caustic. Purified grade can be produced by a combination treatment of $CaCO_3$ to remove colloidal Fe and liquid NH_3 counter-current extraction to take out chloride and chlorate impurities. The following text summarizes the characteristics of diaphragm and mercury and membrane cells. See also Figure IIH-3.

Mercury process:

Advantages:

- Pure 50% sodium hydroxide solution (without evaporation)
- Pure chlorine gas

Disadvantages:

- Higher voltage than with the diaphragm process and hence 10 to 15% higher electrical energy consumption
- More stringent brine purification requirements
- Stringent mercury contamination avoidance measures required

Diaphragm process:

Advantages:

- Utilization of less pure brine
- Lower voltage than in the mercury process

Disadvantages:

- Sodium hydroxide produced is both dilute and chloride-contaminated, evaporation required
- Chlorine gas contains oxygen
- Rigorous measures required to avoid asbestos emission

Membrane process:

Advantages:

- Pure sodium hydroxide

- Electrical energy consumption only about 77% of that of the mercury process
- No mercury or asbestos used

Disadvantages:

- Sodium hydroxide content only ca. 33% by weight
- Chlorine gas contains oxygen
- Very high purity brine required
- Present high cost and short lifetime of the membranes

Fig. IIH-3. Various caustic/chlorine cell configurations.

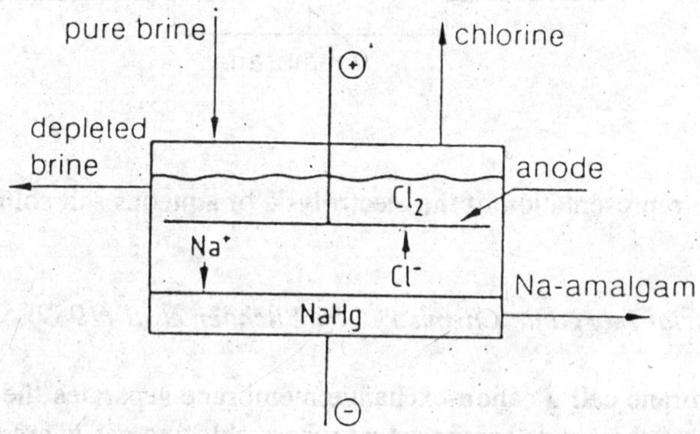

A. Schematic representation of the electrolysis of aqueous salt solutions by the mercury process.

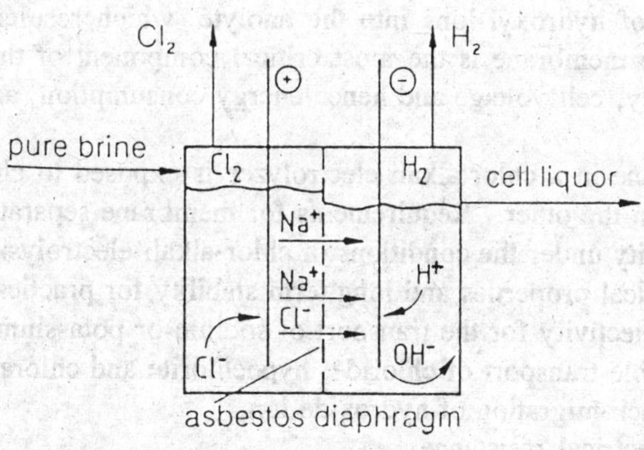

B. Schematic representation of the electrolysis of aqueous salt solutions by the diaphragm process.

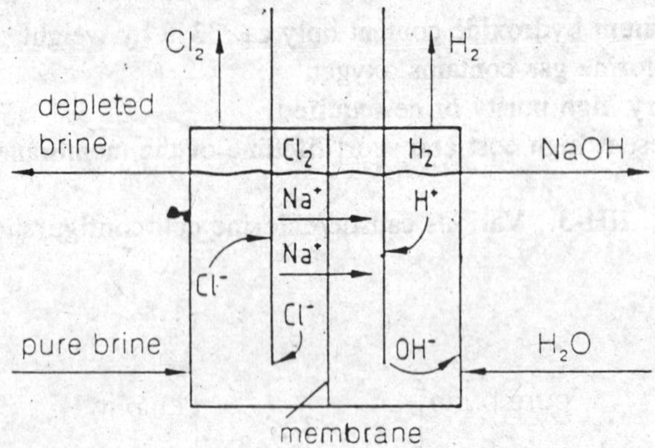

C. Schematic representation of the electrolysis of aqueous salt solutions by the membrane process.

Source: "Industrial Inorganic Chemistry" by Buchner et al (1989)

In a membrane cell a cation-exchange membrane separates the anolyte and catholyte. Brine is fed into the anode compartment where chlorine gas is created and the sodium ion and associated water of hydration migrate through the membrane into the catholyte. Unlike the diaphragm cell process, the cation-exchange membrane prevents the migration of chloride ions into the catholyte. Depleted brine is discharged from the anolyte to maintain a minimum NaCl concentration. Water is electrolyzed at the cathode and strong caustic (32-35 wt.%) is produced either by controlling the water addition rate directly to the catholyte or by recirculating caustic to which water has been added. There is some back-migration of hydroxyl ions into the anolyte, which results in the loss of current efficiency. The membrane is the most critical component of this cell technology, and current efficiency, cell voltage and hence energy consumption, are greatly dependent on its quality.

The membrane in a chlor-alkali electrolyzer is exposed to chlorine on one side and strong caustic on the other. Requirements for membrane separators are as follows:

(a) Durability under the conditions of chlor-alkali electrolysis. It should have good mechanical properties and long term stability for practical use.
(b) High selectivity for the transport of sodium or potassium ions.
(c) Negligible transport of chloride, hypochlorite and chlorate ions.
(d) Zero back-migration of hydroxide ion.
(e) Low electrical resistance.

Today's membranes consist of a film of perfluorosulfonate polymer, a Teflon reinforcing fabric, and a perfluorocarboxylate polymer all bonded together.

For a new plant, the membrane process is the first choice since both the capital investment and the operating cost are the least. The advantage increases as the energy prices increase. Because of environmental regulations as well as cost consideration, the mercury and diaphragm plants are being converted to or replaced by membrane plants.

The catholyte from diaphragm cells typically analyzes as 10-12% NaOH and 15-17% NaCl. This cell liquor is concentrated to 50% NaOH in a series of steps primarily involving three or four evaporators. Membrane cells, on the other hand, produce 30-33% NaOH which is evaporated in a single stage to produce 50% NaOH. Seventy percent caustic containing very little salt is made directly in mercury cell production by reaction of the sodium amalgam from the electrolytic cells with water in denuders.

The electrical energy consumed during the electrolysis of brine to produce chlorine gas and sodium amalgam is greater than that used to generate Cl_2 and H_2 in the diaphragm or membrane cell. However, the latter processes also use energy in the form of steam for evaporation of the cell liquor. The minimum energy required to convert salt to Cl_2, H_2 and 50% NaOH (6.05 GJ/T of Cl_2) is the same in all of these processes. The flow diagrams of all the three processes are given in Figure IIH-3.

To produce the solid salt needed for the mercury cells, the centrifuged salt is added to a salt saturator where depleted cell brine contacts the salt and provides a replenished feed to the electrolyzing compartment of the mercury cell.

The wet chlorine gas from the anodes is cooled to remove water and further dried in a sulfuric acid scrubber. The gas is condensed by one of the following pressure-temperature combinations:

- High pressure (7-10 atms.), water cooling
- Medium pressure (2-3 atms.), refrigeration at —20°C
- Low pressure (5-10 cm H_2O), refrigeration at —40°C

Rotary compressors with sulfuric acid seals are specified for this liquefaction process.

Hydrogen evolved at the cathode is either burned for boiler fuel or used as a hydrogen source at plant locations where diversification of processes can utilize the hydrogen in chemical synthesis.

4.2.6. Major engineering problems

(a) Choice of cell design

All the main technologies—mercury cell, membrane cell, and diaphragm cell—are in use in India for the manufacture of caustic soda and the dominance in capacity and production is in that order.

While the membrane cell process is the most modern, energy efficient and pollution free, the conversion cost of existing mercury cells and diaphragm cells has become prohibitive. This is due to high cost of capital equipment, high technology transfer fees, compounded by an import duty of 35 percent on capital equipment. This has impeded the progress of adopting the membrane cell technology at a faster rate.

(b) Corrosion

Handling wet chlorine requires stoneware, plastic, glass, or rubber-lined equipment. After drying with H_2SO_4 it can be handled in mild steel or iron.

Brine solutions are also very corrosive at elevated temperatures. Evaporators for cell liquor must be nickel-lined to avoid iron contamination. The remainder of the plant can be constructed of cast iron, steel and wood. Mercury cells are also made with rubber-lined steel.

5. Economics

5.1. Plant Location

Need careful analysis of such factors as cheap power and salt sources, coupled with the rising cost of transportation. In some cases, it was more advantageous to locate within a plant complex or near the product market because of the relative costs of transporting salt and finished products. For example, one-third of caustic plants are attached to paper and rayon mills.

5.2. Caustic-chlorine-hydrogen Balance

The utilization of chlorine at a rate of around 65% of production as was the case in India in 1964 is not considered economic. The excess Cl_2 has to be burned to HCl or otherwise destroyed. Hydrogen disposal is a much easier problem.

Outlets for saleable chlorine must be developed to balance caustic-chlorine co-production. A substantial new usage of Cl_2 will be polyvinyl chloride and chlorinated hydrocarbons prepared from petrochemical intermediates.

In the developed countries, the balance is in the reverse, with caustic soda being the disposal problem. This explains why other chlorine processes are important (Section 4.1.2).

5.3. Lime-soda Process

Since this process (Section 4.1.3) produces no chlorine, it might appear attractive for Indian conditions. The cost of soda ash is too high and the electrolytic process is the choice until Na_2CO_3 costs drop to less than one-half that of NaOH per unit weight. The situation is even more favorable for electrolysis as more Cl_2 co-product is utilized.

5.4. Choice of Electrolytic Cell

Production costs at a given location must be compared. Mercury cells are desirable for rayon grade caustic if fuel costs are high relative to mercury costs. Mercury must be imported, but so must asbestos for the diaphragm units, yet this advantage may diminish as newer installations favor mercury cells to meet the demand for high purity, high conc. NaOH and take advantage of coupling procedure illustrated in Figure IIH-2. The chief concern in using mercury is its shortage and continuously rising price.

Recently, concern over pollution of waterways by mercury has become another powerful factor influencing the choice of diaphragm cells; it has been discovered that waste mercury is converted by bacteria to soluble methylmercury which is ingested by fish leading to hazardous mercury concentrations in food fish.

5.5. Power Costs

The Indian caustic soda industry does not have a level playing field vis-a-vis international competitors due to the following facts:

The present average power cost for the Indian industry is over Rs. 2.2/KWH with some of the states which have a larger concentration of caustic soda plants like Gujarat, Maharashtra and Tamil Nadu charging even more for power supplies. The cost of power constitutes nearly 70 percent of the total cost of production.

Apart from cost, in many States, the quality of power supplied is poor and power tripping and cuts are the order of the day. This has forced the caustic soda industry to invest heavily on self power generation. The cost of such power is high due to the administered price of fuel oil.

Electrical power cost in India is substantially higher than those in other countries. Power cost constitutes about 70% of the total production cost while other raw materials account for 11% and overheads are 19%. Table IIH-9 gives comparison of power costs in India and other countries.

Table IIH-9 Comparison of Power Costs

Country	Power Cost, Rs./KWH
India	2.40
China	1.26
USA	0.60
Saudi Arabia	0.40

Source: "Chemical Weekly," 27 Dec. 1994

The indexed production costs of caustic soda in India and some other countries are given in Table IIH-10.

Table IIH-10 Indexed Caustic Soda Production Costs

Country	Indexed Production Cost
India	100
China	66
USA	46
Saudi Arabia	40

Source: "Chemical Weekly," 27 Dec. 1994

This clearly indicates the disadvantage of Indian alkali industry vis-a-vis other international producers. Apart from cost, in many States, the quality of power supplied is poor and power tripping and cuts are very common. This has forced the caustic soda industry to invest heavily on in-house power generation. Some units like DCW favor this approach since the cost of one unit of power generated in-house is claimed to be 60 to 70 paise less.

Producers of caustic and chlorine in India are shown in Table IIH-11.

Table IIH-11
Locations of Caustic Soda Manufacturing Units in India

Name and Address	Process Used
Ahmedabad Mfg. & Calico Printing Co. Ltd.	
(i) Ahmedabad (Gujarat)	Diaphragm cell
(ii) Anik-Chembur, Bombay (Maharashtra)	Mercury cell
Andhra Sugars Ltd. Kovvur - 534 350, Dist. West Godavari (A.P.)	Mercury cell

Atul Products Ltd. P.O. Atul, Dist. Valsad (Gujarat)	Mercury cell
Ballarpur Industries Ltd.	
(i) Yamunanagar, Dist. Ambala (Haryana)	Diaphragm cell
(ii) Ballarpur, Dist. Chandrapur (Maharashtra)	Diaphragm cell
(iii) Binaga, Karwar, North Kanara (Karnataka)	Mercury cell
Bihar Caustic & Chemicals Ltd. Garhwa Road, Rehla - 822 124 Dist. Palamau (Bihar)	Mercury cell
Century Chemicals (Unit of Century Textiles & Industries Ltd.) Murbad Road, Kalyan (Maharashtra)	Mercury cell
Chemfab Alkalies Ltd. Kalapet, Pondicherry	Membrane cell
Durgapur Chemicals Ltd. Durgapur (W.B.)	Mercury cell
Grasim Industries Ltd. Nagda, Birlagram (M.P.)	Mercury cell
Gujarat Alkalies & Chemicals Ltd. P.O. Box Petrochemicals 391 346, Dist. Vadodara (Gujarat)	Mercury cell
Hindustan Heavy Chemicals Khardah - 24-Parganas (W.B.)	Mercury cell
Hukumchand Jute & Industries Ltd. Amlai, Dist. Shahdol (M.P.)	Mercury cell
ICI (India) Ltd. Rishra, Dist. Hooghly (W.B.)	Data not available
Indian Aluminum Co. Ltd. Haldia (W.B.)	Data not available
Jayshree Chemicals Ltd. Ganjam (Orissa)	Mercury cell
J.K. Chemicals Ltd. Panchakadi, Thane (Maharashtra)	Mercury cell

Kanoria Chemicals & Industries Ltd. Renukoot, Dist. Sonebhadra (U.P.)	Mercury cell
Modi Alkalies & Chemicals Ltd. SP-460, Matsya Industrial Area Alwar - 301 030 (Rajasthan)	Mercury cell
National Rayon Corp. Ltd. Mohone - 421 102, Kalyan, Dist. Thane (Maharashtra)	Mercury cell
Nepa Ltd. Nepanagar - 450 221 Dist. East Nimar (M.P.)	Mercury cell
Orient Paper & Industries Ltd. Brajrajnagar, Sambalpur (Orissa)	Mercury cell
Punjab Alkalies & Chemicals Ltd. Nangal-Una Road, Naya Nangal - 140 126 Dist. Ropar (Punjab)	Mercury cell
Rohtas Industries Ltd. Dalmianagar (Bihar)	Mercury cell
Saurashtra Chemicals (Unit of VXL India Ltd.) Birlasagar, Porbander (Gujarat)	Chemical process
Shriram Industrial Enterprises Ltd.	
(i) Shriram Foods & Fertilizers Ltd. Najafgarh Road, New Delhi	Diaphragm cell
(ii) Shriram Vinyls, Kota (Rajasthan)	Mercury cell
Sirpur Paper Mills Ltd. Sirpur, Kaghaz Nagar - 504 296 (A.P.)	Diaphragm cell
Southern Petrochemical Industries Corp. Ltd. SPIC Nagar, Tuticorin - 628 005 (T.N.)	Mercury cell
Sree Rayalaseema Alks. & Allied Chems. Ltd. Vasant Nagar, Gondiparla Village - 518 004 Kurnool Dist. (A.P.)	Membrane cell
Standard Mills Co. Ltd. Ghandsoli, Thane (Maharashtra)	Mercury cell

Tata Chemicals Ltd. Mithapur, Jamnagar (Gujarat)	Diaphragm cell
Titaghur Paper Mills Co. Ltd. (i) Titaghur, 24-Parganas (W.B.) (ii) Kakinara, 24-Parganas (W.B.) (iii) Chowdwar (Orissa)	Diaphragm cell
Travancore Cochin Chemicals Ltd. Eloor, Alwaye (Kerala)	Mercury cell

Source: "SBP Handbook of Projects for Corporate Diversification" (1992)

IIJ. CHEMICALS FROM THE SEA

Oceans cover over 70% of the earth's surface. The sea is still our important source of food but it is also a dumping ground for sewage, radioactive wastes and a supplier of raw materials for a host of chemical industries.

The oceans contain on an average about 35 parts per 1,000 (3.5%) dissolved salts. Table IIJ-1 gives the known abundances of elements in sea water. Sea is a source for fresh water (desalination), food (50 million tons of fish), and salts that contain in some measure all the elements present on earth.

Table IIJ-1 Known Abundances in Sea Water

The large number of known elements in sea water indicates that probably all of earth's naturally occurring elements exist in the sea

Element	Milligrams per liter	Element	Milligrams per liter
Chlorine	19,000	Thorium	0.0007
Sodium	10,600	Cobalt	0.0005
Magnesium	1,300	Nickel	0.0005
Sulfur	900	Gallium	0.0005
Calcium	400	Cesium	0.0005
Potassium	380	Antimony	0.0005
Bromine	65	Cerium	0.0004
Carbon	28	Yttrium	0.0003
Oxygen	8	Neon	0.0003
Strontium	8	Krypton	0.0003
		Lanthanum	0.0003
Boron	4.8	Silver	0.0003
Silicon	3.0	Bismuth	0.0002
Fluorine	1.3	Cadmium	0.0001
Nitrogen	0.8	Tungsten	1×10^{-4}
Argon	0.6	Germanium	1×10^{-4}
Lithium	0.2	Xenon	1×10^{-4}
		Chromium	5×10^{-5}

Rubidium	0.12	Beryllium	5×10^{-5}
Phosphorus	0.07	Scandium	4×10^{-5}
Iodine	0.05	Mercury	3×10^{-5}
Barium	0.03	Niobium	1×10^{-5}
Indium	0.02	Thallium	1×10^{-5}
Aluminum	0.01	Helium	5×10^{-6}
Iron	0.01	Gold	4×10^{-6}
Zinc	0.01	Praseodymium	2×10^{-7}
Molybdenum	0.01	Gadolinium	2×10^{-7}
Selenium	0.004	Dysprosium	2×10^{-7}
Copper	0.003	Erbium	2×10^{-7}
Arsenic	0.003	Ytterbium	2×10^{-7}
Tin	0.003	Samarium	2×10^{-7}
Lead	0.003	Holmium	8×10^{-8}
Uranium	0.003	Europium	4×10^{-8}
Vanadium	0.002	Thulium	4×10^{-8}
Manganese	0.002	Lutetium	4×10^{-8}
Titanium	0.001	Radium	3×10^{-11}
		Protactinium	2×10^{-12}
		Radon	9×10^{-15}

The important commercial products obtained from sea water are common salt, magnesium compounds, potassium compounds, and bromine. Also potentially important are placer deposits of a host of minerals on sea beaches; phosphorite and calcareous deposits from the continental shelves; oil, gas, sulfur and coal, iron, etc., from the subsea floor rocks; and clays, manganese nodules and calcareous oozes from the deep sea floor.

Salt Industry

Man has been producing salt from time immemorial. Salt is being made in India from sea water all along its coastline—from Kutch and Saurashtra in the west, down to Kanyakumari in the south, along the coastlines of Tamil Nadu and Andhra Pradesh, and up to Sundarbans and the Central Coast in West Bengal.

Salt is also produced in India from subsoil brine (Kutch and Saurashtra area), from Sambhar and Didwana lakes in Rajasthan, and from the Mandi mines (rock salt) of Himachal Pradesh.

Salt forms an important part of our diet. Sodium chloride is the starting material for the production of a good number of sodium compounds. It is used in chlor-alkali industry, water softening, soaps, dyes, food preservation and in a host of other industries.

1. Process Description

Solar evaporation of sea water is used extensively for the manufacture of salt in India. Sea water is drawn into reservoirs where all suspended matter settles down and the brine density is allowed to raise to 10°Be. Then the brine is fed through a number of condensers where further concentration takes place to 22-23°Be. Calcium carbonate and bicarbonates are precipitated out in the first condenser where the density increases from 10°-14°Be. Gypsum is precipitated from brine between 14° to 18°Be. The brine from the condensers goes to crystallizer beds and sodium chloride crystallizes out from 25° to 29°Be. The mother liquor when it reaches 29°Be is discharged from the crystallizers and fresh brine is fed in again. Salt is removed, collected, and dried. A single crop is obtained anywhere between 3 to 15 days depending upon the seasonal conditions. The mother liquor from the crystallizers is called bitterns (29°Be). Upon further concentration to 36°Be, bitterns yield several fractions of salt containing other salts of magnesium and potassium as impurities.

2. Major Engineering Problems

Some of the factors that influence solar evaporation are: solar energy absorbed, air humidity and temperature, and the wind velocity. Suitable dyes or black sands are used to increase the rate of absorption of solar energy and thereby increase the evaporation rate. Suitable soil stabilization is necessary for the open brine condensers and crystallizers to reduce seepage and to increase their bearing strength for mechanical harvesting of salt crystals. In modern salt farms soil is stabilized by blending the soil with salt, gypsum and bentonite, and is lined with bricks, bituminous plaster and plastic films. Heavy mechanical salt harvesters are used in western countries for gathering salt.

3. Production and Consumption of Salt

Nearly 30% of the salt produced in the world is recovered from sea water and most of it by natural solar evaporation. Indian salt industry is an age-old industry and salt production has been mainly by solar evaporation. It has not been fully mechanized which probably limits the individual salt works capacity to reach maximum of 1 to 1.5 lakh TPA. There are very few salt works in that capacity range in India. Most of them are in Gujarat. For the membrane cells in caustic soda industry, high-quality salt is necessary and to produce this salt is a challenge for the Indian salt industry.

The 1982 production of salt in the world and in several selected countries is given in Table IIJ-2.

Table IIJ-2
1982 Sodium Chloride Production in 10^6 t

World	North America	USA	West Germany	USSR	P.R. China	India	Australia
168.7	50.3	34.2	11.5	15.4	16	10	5.6

Source: "Industrial Inorganic Chemistry" by Buchner et al (1989)

As to the uses of salt, half is consumed in the important electrolysis of brine to form two top fifty chemicals, sodium hydroxide and chlorine. One-fifth is used on highways for deicing and competes with calcium chloride in this application. The food industry and animal feeds make up a third important use. Salt is surpassed only by phosphate rock in total production of all minerals. Salt has decreased somewhat in the last few years. It is still one of the cheapest chemicals at 3¢/lb in 1991. Its current production is 77 billion lb, giving a commercial value of $2.3 billion.

The marine chemicals industry is yet to be developed in India. The important minerals dissolved in sea water are sodium chloride, magnesium chloride, magnesium sulfate, calcium sulfate, potassium chloride and various bromides. Of these, common salt (sodium chloride) is the only one produced in sizable quantities in India. The present annual production of salts from sea and subsoil brine is about 6.5 million tons. The inorganic chemical industry, which produces mainly Caustic Soda, Chlorine and Soda Ash, depends on salt from the sea as raw material. Thirty-eight units, producing 70 lakh tons of Caustic Soda every year and four big factories making an equal quantity of Soda Ash, together use about 20 lakh tons of common salt, according to Kothari's "Industrial Directory of India" (1994).

Production of Magnesium Compounds from Sea Water

Magnesium is one of the most abundant elements found in the earth's crust (nearly 1.9%). Magnesium ion is the third most abundant element present in sea water (at a concentration of 1,272 ppm). Other important sources of magnesium salts in addition to sea water are dolomite ($MgCO_3 \cdot CaCO_3$), and magnetite ($MgCO_3$). Most of the magnesium compounds are consumed in the production of metallic magnesium. Other uses of magnesium compounds are found in refractories, insulating compounds, manufacture of rubber, pharmaceuticals, printing ink and toilet goods. Magnesium compounds are manufactured from sea water using lime treatment. This process was adopted by the Dow Chemical Company, Freeport and Velasco, Texas, and by Merck & Company at South San Francisco. Again, these compounds can also be manufactured from bitterns or from sea water and dolomite.

Sea water has normally 4.176 gm/liter of $MgCl_2$, 1.668 gm/liter of $MgSO_4$ and 0.076 gm/liter of $MgBr_2$.

1. Reference Flow Sheet: Figure IIJ-1

2. Chemical Reactions

$$MgCl_2(aq) + Ca(OH)_2(c) \rightarrow Mg(OH)_2(c) + CaCl_2(aq); \Delta H = +2.26 \text{ Kcal}$$

$$MgSO_4(aq) + Ca(OH)_2(c) + 2H_2O(1) \rightarrow Mg(OH)_2(c) + CaSO_4 2H_2O(c); \Delta H = -3.170 \text{ Kcal}$$

3. Engineering Problems

Magnesium hydroxides are completely insoluble in sea water. Preparation of purified lime or calcined dolomite slurry of proper characteristics is important. Slow settling and precipitation rates give rise to problems. Magnesium hydroxide has to be removed from large volumes of sea water. Purification of hydrous precipitates and filtration of the slimes also pose some problems.

Crystalline Magnesium Chloride from Bitterns

Crystalline magnesium chloride from bitterns is produced by solar evaporation. This method is used in Italy. The method has promise in Kutch and on the Saurashtra Coast.

1. Process Description

Deposition of a pure variety of magnesium chloride hexahydrate takes place between 38 and 39.5°Be densities from low sulfate containing bitterns, and a crude variety between 36.5 and 39.5°Be densities from high sulfate containing bitterns. Sulfate-free bitterns are obtained in inland salt works off the little Rann of Kutch.

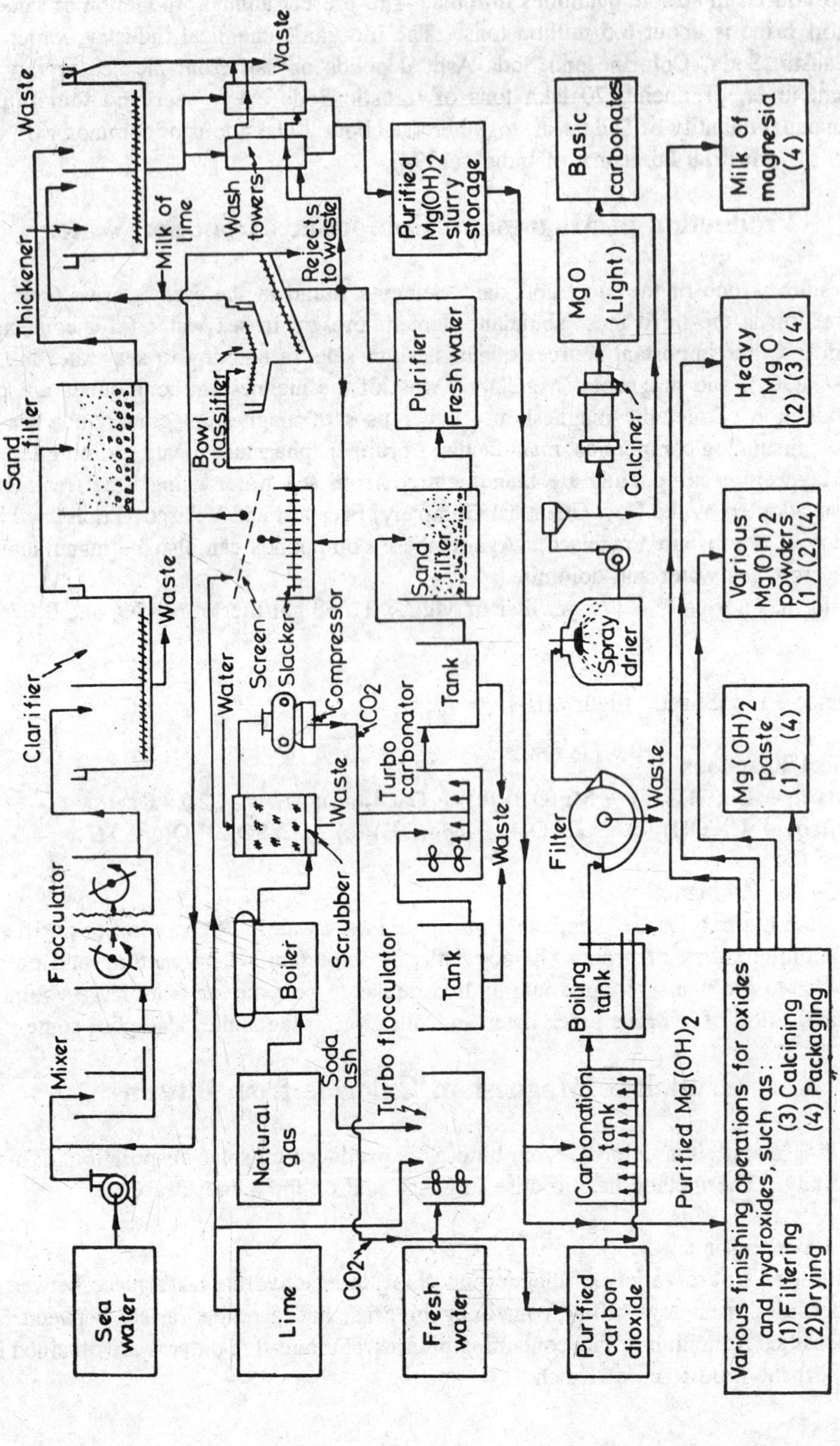

Fig. III-1. Flow sheet for production of magnesium compounds from sea water.

Bittern, also known as Mother liquor, is left after the recovery of salt and it is the only source for the recovery and manufacture of other marine chemicals like potash in the form of potassium schoenite, potassium chloride, potassium sulfate, magnesium sulfate, magnesium chloride, bromine, magnesium carbonate and magnesium oxide.

2. Production Prospects in India

Assuming 40% recovery of magnesium chloride from bitterns as crystalline product, the potential for production of magnesium chloride crystals in Kutch (inland salt works) is 47,000 tons per annum and in Saurashtra (marine salt works) 160,000 tons per annum. Demand of magnesium chloride is likely to go up to 1,500 tons per annum in the future. Excess production can go into export markets.

3. Product Uses

$MgCl_2$ is used in the textile industry, in the production of magnesium metal, in the extraction of plutonium from irradiated nuclear fuels, in the manufacture of other magnesium compounds, in magnesium oxychloride cement, etc.

4. Future Trends

The Central Salt and Marine Chemical Institute has developed processes now available for commercial purposes for the following marine chemicals: Free flowing table salt, dairy salt, iodized salt, cattle licks, potassium chloride, potassium schoenite, refractory grade magnesia, light and heavy magnesium carbonate, magnesium oxide, bromine, sodium alginate and agar-agar.

Being endowed with plentiful resources of sea and inland brine, India is in an advantageous position to make great strides in the manufacture of salt and marine chemicals.

Magnesium Oxide

On heating magnesium hydroxide obtained from the processing of sea water, magnesium oxide is formed. Magnesium carbonates can also be used for the production of MgO. Magnesium oxide is used as a refractory material, as an abrasive and as an insulating material, and also in the vulcanization of rubber.

Magnesium Sulfate

1. Process Description

Epsom salt ($MgSO_4 \cdot 7H_2O$) is made by treating magnesium carbonate or hydroxide with sulfuric acid. A mixture (known as Sels mixture) of varying compositions of magnesium sulfate (35-38%) and sodium chloride (45-50%) crystallizes during the solar evaporation of the sea bitterns. Six tons of "Sels mixture" is obtained for every 100 tons of salt. "Sels mixture" is chilled to 10°C to crystallize out $MgSO_4 \cdot 7H_2O$ which is centrifuged and dried. A slurry containing "mixed salt" (details given in the following section) and 36°Be bitterns is stirred in a steam jacketed dissolver at 110°C for fifteen to twenty minutes and allowed to settle for ten minutes. A suspended slurry of kieserite is filtered hot at 110°C through a sparkler pressure filter. The cake obtained mainly consists of kieserite 32-37%, magnesium sulfate 13-15%, magnesium chloride 5-7%, and sodium chloride 2-3%. The cake is dissolved with the requisite amount of water and the solution is heated to 60°C and cooled to the room temperature to crystallize out Epsom salt. On further chilling the mother liquor to 10°C, another crop of Epsom salt is obtained.

2. Production in India

Total existing capacity for magnesium sulfate in India is 9,500 tons, 6,000 tons based upon sulfuric acid and 3,500 tons associated with sea bitterns. The Kandla unit manufactures 2,000 tons/year of Epsom salt as a co-product of potassium chloride from salt bitterns.

Mixed Salt Recovery Processes

Most of the mixed salt processes were developed as a part of integrated multi-product processes. The processes have great economic potential, but the markets will have to be developed. Mixed salts contain various degrees of impurities, along with chlorides of sodium and potassium, sulfates of calcium, magnesium and potassium. Most of the processes involve precipitation whether by heating or cooling or adding chemicals. Phase diagrams and data on enthalpy concentration diagrams have a great bearing on the development of processes in this area.

The Central Salt and Marine Chemical Research Institute (CSMCRI) at Bhavnagar developed a process in which bitterns are pretreated by the addition of excess calcium chloride to remove sulfates. When the treated hot bitterns are cooled, mixtures of magnesium sulfate and potassium chloride are separated. The mother liquor is concentrated and cooled for crystallization of carnallite, a chloride of magnesium and potassium. There are several processes reported in literature for production of mixed salts.

Potassium Recovery

Potassium is the sixth most abundant element in sea water. There are no deposits of potash in India. Large quantities of potassium salts are needed in the manufacture of mixed fertilizers. CSMCRI estimates that 40,000 tons of potassium chloride can be manufactured annually on the basis of present production of common salt in this country.

Fractional crystallization of sea bitterns usually results in recovery of potassium in the chloride form, carnallite ($KCl \cdot MgCl_2 \cdot 6H_2O$). CSMCRI has developed a process for recovery of potassium from carnallite. A concentrated aqueous solution of carnallite at 115°C, upon cooling, yields potassium chloride.

Other methods for recovery of potassium involve the use of a highly selective chelating or sequestering agent such as dipterylamine which forms a stable and insoluble complex with potassium.

Bromine

Bromine, a dark red, low-boiling and high-density liquid of intensely irritating odor, is very reactive chemically, and belongs to the halogen group of elements. In sea water, Br_2 occurs in concentrations between 60-70 ppm. In bitterns, bromine is concentrated up to 2,500 ppm.

1. Pertinent Properties

M.P.	7.2°C	
B.P. (at 760 mm of Hg)	58.78°C	
Sp. gr. at 20/4°C	3.1193	
Specific heat:		
Liquid at 0°C:	0.107 cal/gm°C	
Vapor between 83-228°C:	0.0553 cal/gm°C	
Heat of fusion at M.P.	16.14 cal/gm	
Heat of vap. at B.P.	44.8 cal/gm;	$T_c = 311°C$

2. Uses

Most of the bromine is converted into inorganic and organic compounds. Ethylene dibromide and methyl bromide are used for fumigation of foodgrains, fruits, seeds and soil and for scavengers anti-knock fluids in aviation petrol. The requirements for these compounds are EDB 250 tons and MB 750 tons annually in India. Bromine in small dosages (1 ppm) sterilizes water in swimming pools. Bromine is used in the preparation of fire extinguishing compounds and fire proofing agents, and also dyes.

3. Production from Sea Water

3.1. Reference Flow Sheet: Figure IIJ-2

3.2. Chemical Reactions

$$Cl_2 + 2Br^- \rightarrow 2Cl^- + Br_2$$
$$SO_2 + Br_2 + H_2O \rightarrow 2HBr + H_2SO_4$$
$$2HBr + Cl_2 \rightarrow 2HCl + Br_2$$

3.3. Process Description

The process involves oxidation of bromide ions in sea water or brines to free elemental bromine which is vaporized by air or steam. When sea water is used, bromine is first concentrated by vaporizing chlorinated sea water with air, and then SO_2 is introduced into dilute bromine laden air and is sent to an absorption tower counter-current to water. The resulting hydrobromic acid solution is chlorinated and is steamed to vaporize Br_2 which is later condensed to liquid bromine. By-product acids HCl and H_2SO_4 are used to acidify the incoming sea water.

Absorption of bromine laden air is also possible by using sodium carbonate solution, but the end-products are sodium bromide and sodium bromate. When bitterns (30°Be) are used as raw material source, preheated bitterns can be directly steamed out.

Sea Floor Minerals

Discovery of huge, high grade deposits of a number of industrially important minerals on the ocean floor has opened up possibilities of large scale mining of the ocean floor. Mining and processing of hard minerals from the ocean floor are the important problems, in which processing falls clearly in the area of chemical engineer. It is likely within the next few decades, that the bulk of the world's consumption of manganese, nickel, cobalt, and copper will be met by the sea-floor mining.

The nature of the mineral deposits of the sea and their mineral contents are given in Table IIJ-3. Minerals are presently mined from all these environments except from the deep sea floor area

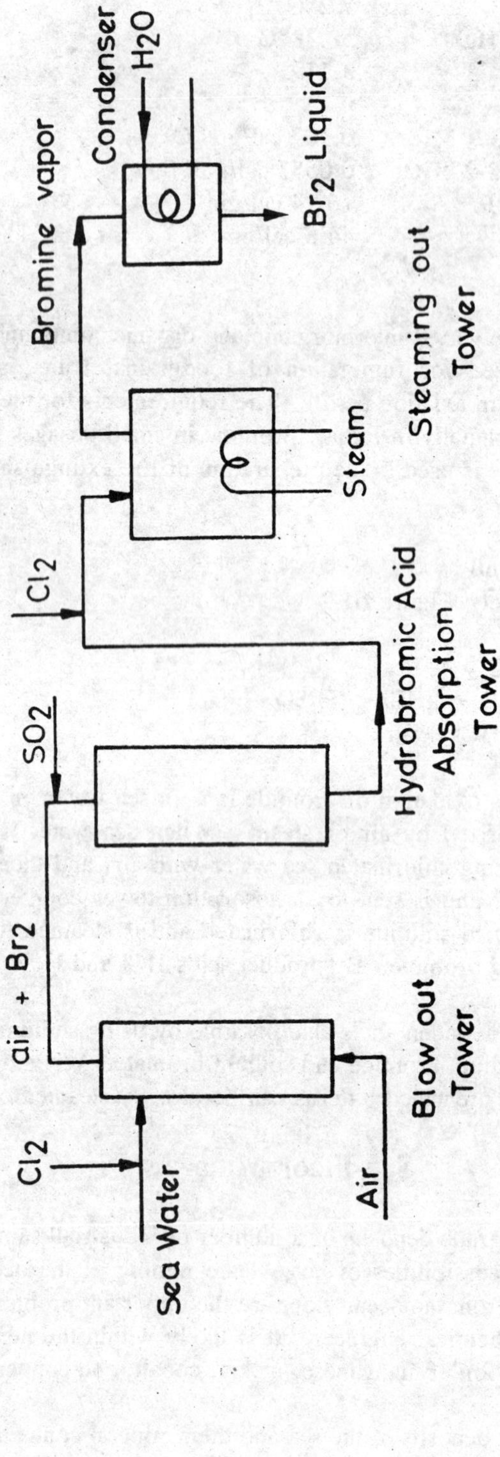

Fig. IIJ-2. Flow diagram of plant for the production of bromine from sea water.

which contains unbelievably large mineral deposits.

Table IIJ-3
Mineral Deposits of the Sea

Region	*Minerals*
Ocean beaches	Placer deposits of platinum, gold, diamonds, ilmenite, magnetite, zircon, rutile, columbite, chromite, cassiterite, scheelite, wolframite, monazite, quartz, calcium carbonate
Continental shelves	Phosphorite, barium, sulfate nodules, tin, platinum, gold, iron, manganese, copper, zinc, silver, lead
Subsea floor rocks	Oil, gas, sulfur, salt, coal, iron ore and other mineral deposits
Deep sea floor	Clays, calcareous and siliceous oozes, animal remains, zeolites bearing potash, manganese nodules also containing iron, cobalt, nickel, copper, molybdenum, vanadium

1. Recovery from Off-shore Placer Deposits

The mined clays are dumped into a revolving trommel which separates oversize pebbles and undersize clay particles. The middling product from the screens goes to jigs where heavy minerals are concentrated. In the case of minerals such as rutile and tin, Humphrey spirals or shaking tables may also be used. If the mineral product is a mixture of ilmenite, zircon and monazite sands, further processing in magnetic and electrostatic separators will be necessary. In such cases, the material is dried in a rotary kiln and heated to 300°F before it is fed to the above-mentioned separators.

Some of the beach sands of Kerala and Tamil Nadu have the following composition: 55.4% ilmenite, 4.1% rutile, 7% zircon, 5% monazite, 5.9% garnet, 13.9% quartz. At present 89% of ilmenite, 25.3% rutile, 93% of zircon, and 88% of monazite are being recovered from sands of the above compositions.

2. Off-shore Mining and Processing

The major difficulty is in removing the ore from the sea floor to the deck of the process barge. Of considerable interest are sea floor phosphorite deposits on the shelves off the coasts of many nations. In order that the off-shore phosphorite nodules are saleable, the nodules are crushed, ground and calcined (at 1,800°F). The above processing boosts the P_2O_5 contents from an average value of about 29% to 33%.

3. Deep Sea Sediments

Most important of these sediments is easily manganese nodules. Also, calcareous oozes (almost pure $CaCO_3$ in unconsolidated and fine grained form) are found within a few hundred miles off the coast of many nations. It should cost less than $0.50/ton to pump them into the hold of a vessel. Similarly, siliceous oozes can be found, and could serve in most of the applications in which diatomaceous earth is used.

Manganese nodules also contain in varying quantities impurities such as copper, cobalt, nickel, molybdenum and iron. A differential leaching process can be used for processing these nodules. The nodules are crushed to 50 mesh size, H_2SO_4 is used as solvent and at a pH of 2.0 and temperature of 77°F, copper is preferentially put into solution. The copper solution is separated and the solid phase is washed and is then subjected to second leaching with sulfuric acid at a pH of 2.0 and a temperature of 120°F, at which point nickel goes into solution. By similar manipulation of temperature and pH, cobalt also can be put into the solution. After nickel, cobalt and copper are removed, the remaining mixture of manganese and iron oxides can be charged into a furnace for the manufacture of ferromanganese. The individual solutions separated from the solid phases can be purified, concentrated and electrochemically converted to nickel, copper and cobalt metals.

IIK. CEMENT AND LIME

The processes and products discussed in this section are based on limestone which is predominantly calcium carbonate ($CaCO_3$). This material is distributed rather uniformly in 3-4 wt.% throughout the earth's crust, coming largely from igneous rock formations. Consequently it is well distributed throughout India, being sparse only in W. Bengal, northern Bihar, Assam and certain areas of Punjab, Rajasthan, Andhra Pradesh, and Tamil Nadu States. Limestone rock is usually available at the surface and can be collected by open-pit quarrying methods. Certain deposits are low-grade and must be treated by beneficiation methods, largely froth flotation, to remove excess silica and alumina.

The limestone-based industries of cement and lime are characterized by high tonnage low cost-low margin operations which require efficient management to create a profitable venture.

Cement

1. Definition

Cement is a generic name for powdered materials which initially have plastic flow when mixed with water or other liquid, but form a solid structure in several hours with varying degree of strength and bonding properties which continue to improve with age. The most common is Portland cement which is the basis for a number of cement products. Specifically, Portland cement is defined as finely ground calcium aluminates and silicates of varying compositions which hydrate when mixed with water to form a rigid continuous structure with good compressive strength.

2. Properties of Cement

2.1. Constituents of Cement

	Code	Chemical Formula	Type	%
(a) Portland				
	C_2S	$2CaO \cdot SiO_2$	Silicate	Major
	C_3S	$3CaO \cdot SiO_2$	Silicate	Major
	C_3A	$3CaO \cdot Al_2O_3$	Aluminate	Major
	C_4AF	$4CaO \cdot Al_2O_3 \cdot Fe_2O_3$	Aluminate	Minor
	—	MgO		Minor
	—	CaO		Minor

(b) High alumina

C_3A	$3CaO \cdot Al_2O_3$	Aluminate	Major
C_2S	$2CaO \cdot SiO_2$	Silicate	Minor
C_2AS	$2CaO \cdot Al_2O_3 \cdot SiO_2$	Mixed	Minor

(c) Hydraulic hydrated lime

—	$Ca(OH)_2$	Hydroxide	Major
C_2S	$2CaO \cdot SiO_2$	Silicate	Minor
C_3A	$3CaO \cdot Al_2O_3$	Aluminate	Minor

2.2. Types of Portland Cement

Varying the percentage of constituents changes the rate of setting, heat evolution, and strength characteristics.

- Type I - Regular: 40-60% C_3S, 10-30% Ca_2S, 7-13% Ca_3A; hardens to full strength in 28 days
- Type II - Modified: Higher C_2S/C_3S to resist sulfate attack
- Type III - High Early Strength: Attains strength of Type I in only 3 days; high heat rates—useless on massive structures; higher C_3S and C_3A percentage with finer grinding to increase hydration rate
- Type IV - Low Heat: Designed for massive structure work; low C_3S and C_3A which are largest contributors to heat of hydration
- Type V - Sulfate Resistant: Good for sea water contact; $C_3A < 4\%$

2.3. Other Types of Cement

2.3.1. High alumina—manufactured by fusing limestone and bauxite; rapid rate of strength development to high values but with high heat rate liberation; superior resistance to sea and sulfate waters.

2.3.2. Pozzolana—mixture of volcanic ash, burnt clay or shale in 2-4 parts with hydrated lime. Mixed with Portland cement as a cheap extender.

2.3.3. Hydraulic lime—used only for brick mortar composition, low price and strength.

2.3.4. Magnesium oxychloride—lightly calcined MgO mixed with $MgCl_2$ forms excellent high-strength, spark-proof, wear-resistant flooring; high bonding strength to wood fibers so useful in forming indoor construction material with only fair resistance to water.

2.4. Relative Compressive Strength Characteristics

Cement when mixed with other ingredients such as sand and gravel is used for structural purposes under compressive loading since it has very poor tensile strength. Some comparative data give a general idea of comparative strength properties:

Mortar composition (1 cement : 3 sand + H_2O)

Type		*Compressive Strength, kg/cm²* 1 day	3 days	28 days
Portland	Type I	37	120	340
	Type II	28	83	260
	Type III	103	240	440
	Type IV	20	49	177
	Type V	28	88	214

Hydrated lime		14	30
Aluminous	280	480	690

3. History of the Cement Industry

India ranks as the fourth largest producer of cement in the world after China, Japan and the United States and is poised to emerge as a leader among cement producing countries.

The cement industry has come a long way since the first bag of cement was packed in the year 1914 at Porbundar. A mere 945 mts. was produced in that year throughout India compared to the production of about 48.75 million tons in the year 1990-91 as against the target of 49.00 million tons from an installed capacity of 63.96 million tons.

Broadly the progress of cement industry falls into five phases. The first period beginning from 1947 till 1980 is the period during which government exercised strict control over the entire industry by various policies and legislations. The cement industry experienced a period of price and distribution controls. The years from 1980 to 1989 mark the second phase of partial decontrol. The third period could be considered as beginning from 1989 to 1992 when the industry functioned free from price and distribution controls, but remained still under a regime of controlled economic decision making. The fourth period beginning from 1992 onward is the period when cement industry has been free from all price, distribution and licensing controls. However, it would still have to face pangs of transitional period of structural reform process. The fifth and decisive period will commence from 1995 onwards when free market conditions in cement would work within a reformed economic system.

Cement factories in India are mainly concentrated in Madhya Pradesh, Tamil Nadu, Andhra Pradesh, Rajasthan, Gujarat, Bihar and Karnataka. The limestone reserves of these states account for 90 percent of the reserves in India. Location of a cement factory near limestone resources has its own advantages. The different varieties of cement produced in India may be described as ordinary portland, portland, pozzolana, portland blast furnace slag, special high strength cement, low heat cement, oil well cement, colored cement and white cement.

4. Methods of Production

4.1. Classification of Processes

- Cement rock beneficiation
- Portland cement production

4.2. Cement Rock Beneficiation

Much of the locally available limestone has too high a silica and iron content for direct use in cement manufacture. These undesirable constituents can be removed by ore dressing or beneficiation methods which are based on fluid mechanics and adsorption.

4.2.1. Reference flow sheet: Figure IIK-1

4.2.2. Quantitative requirements

(a) Basis: 1 ton of low-grade limestone

Water	2-3 tons
Reagents	50-200 grams
Electricity	2.5 KWH

(b) Plant capacities: 300-1,000 tons/day

4.2.3. Process description

The operations are grinding, classification, flotation and thickening.

Rock is wet-ground, fed to a hydroseparator where the overflow goes directly to the

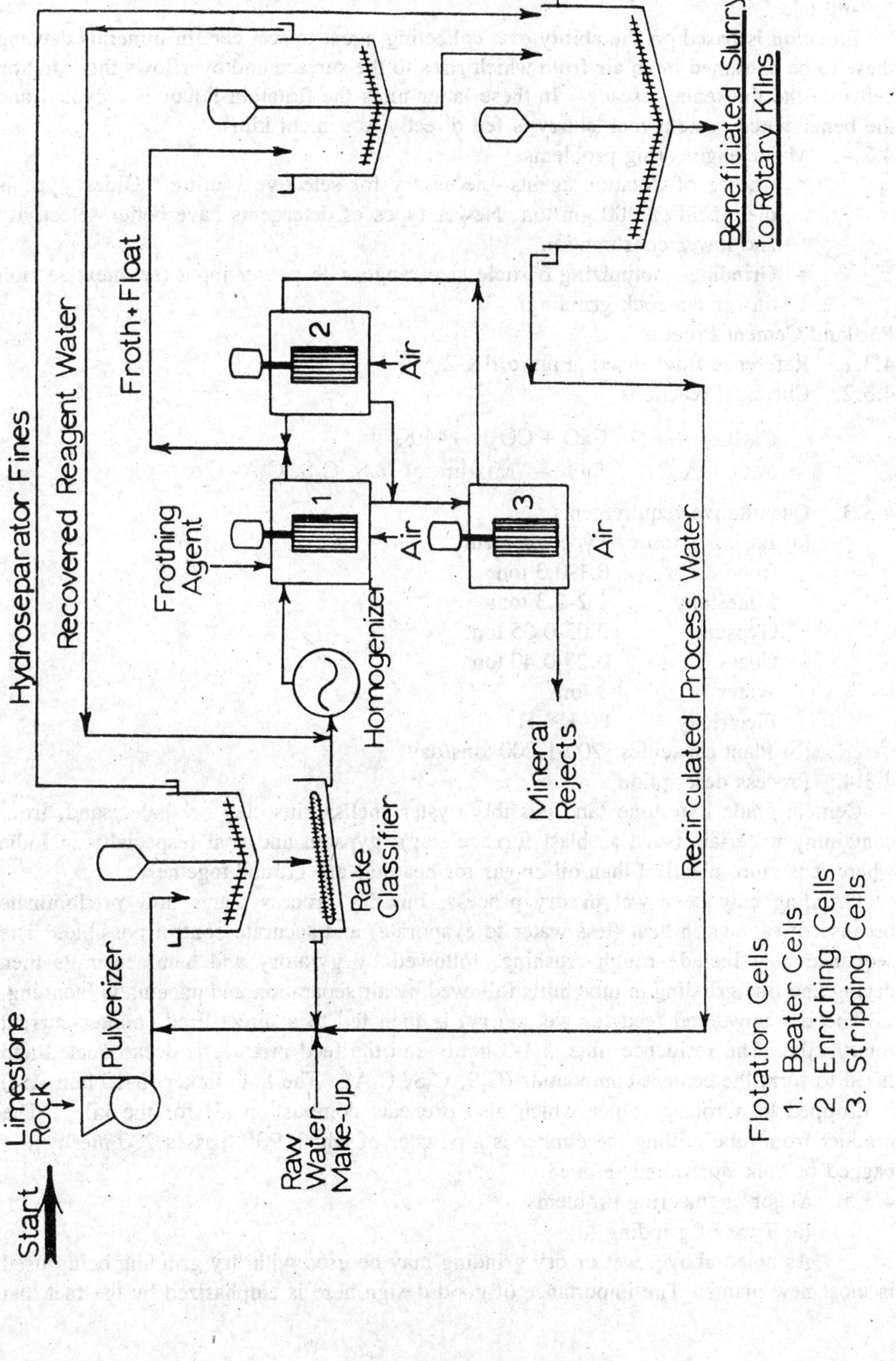

Fig. IIK-1. Limestone beneficiation.

final thickener, being of satisfactory composition. If not, it is subjected to flotation separation as well as the coarse material which must be floated to remove silica, mica and talc.

Flotation is based on the ability of a collecting agent to wet certain minerals causing these to be entrained in an air froth which rises to the surface and overflows the flotation cell into the thickener cascade. In these latter units the flotation liquor is recycled and the beneficiated cement rock slurry is fed directly to cement kilns.

4.2.4. Major engineering problems

- Choice of flotation agents—necessary for selective wetting. Oldest type is oleic acid @ 200 gm/ton. Newer types of detergents have better selectivity and lower consumption.
- Grinding—optimizing particle size range with power input (see next section on cement rock grinding).

4.3. Portland Cement Process

4.3.1. Reference flow sheet: Figure IIK-2

4.3.2. Chemical reactions

$$CaCO_3 \xrightarrow{1,000°C} CaO + CO_2; \quad +44 \text{ Kcal}$$

$$CaO + Al_2O_3 + SiO_2 \rightarrow \text{Mixture of } C_3S, C_2S, C_3A$$

4.3.3. Quantitative requirements

(a) Basis: 1 ton of Type I cement

Clay	0.1-0.3 ton
Limestone	1.2-1.3 tons
Gypsum	0.03-0.05 ton
Coal	0.25-0.40 ton
Water	3 tons
Electricity	80 KWH

(b) Plant capacities: 200-1,200 tons/day

4.3.4. Process description

Cement-grade limestone (and possibly oyster shells) plus clay or shale, sand, iron-containing materials (such as blast furnace slag), gypsum and coal (especially in India where it is more plentiful than oil or gas for heating) are ground together.

Grinding may be a wet or dry process, but dry process plants now predominate because of savings in heat (less water to evaporate) and accurate control possible. The sequence may include rough crushing, followed by gyratory and hammer mills then drying and fine grinding in tube mills followed by air separation and pneumatic blending.

The dry powdered feed (or wet slurry) is then fed to a direct-fired counter-current rotary kiln. The residence time is 1-3 hours and the feed mixture is decarbonated and fused to form the cement compounds (C_2S, C_3S, C_3A). The hot clinker (3-10 mm size) is dropped to a rotary cooler which also preheats combustion air for the kiln. The product from tube milling the clinker is a powder of which 90% passes 200 mesh; it is bagged or bulk stored and shipped.

4.3.5. Major engineering problems

(a) Type of grinding

As noted above, wet or dry grinding may be used with dry grinding being used in most new plants. The importance of good design here is emphasized by the fact that

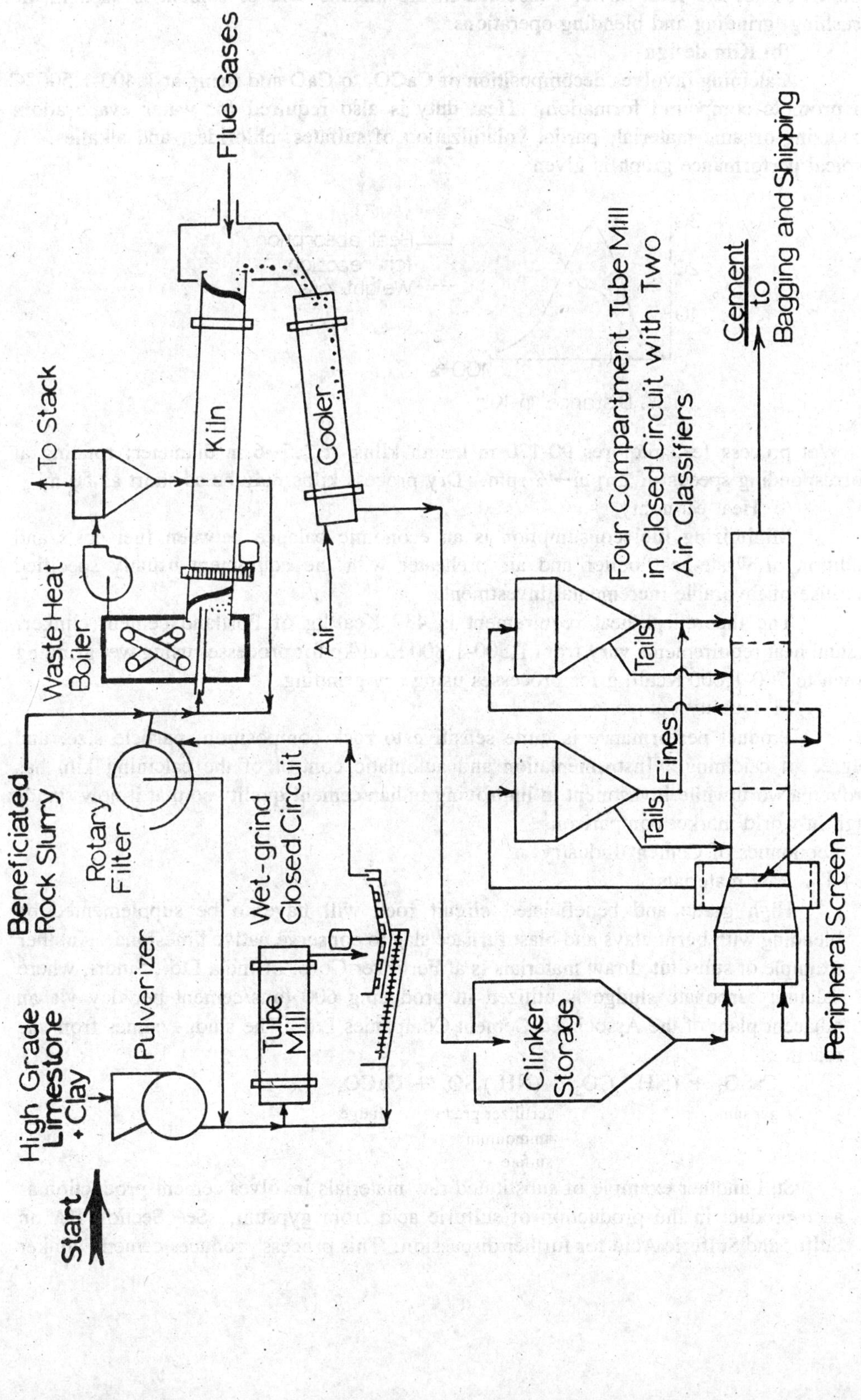

Fig. IIK-2. Portland cement manufacture.

about 80% of the total power consumed in the manufacture of cement is used in the crushing, grinding and blending operations.

(b) Kiln design

Calcining involves decomposition of $CaCO_3$ to CaO and firing at 1,400-1,500°C to promote compound formation. Heat duty is also required for water evaporation, oxidizing organic material, partial volatilization of sulfates, chlorides, and alkalies. A typical performance graph is given:

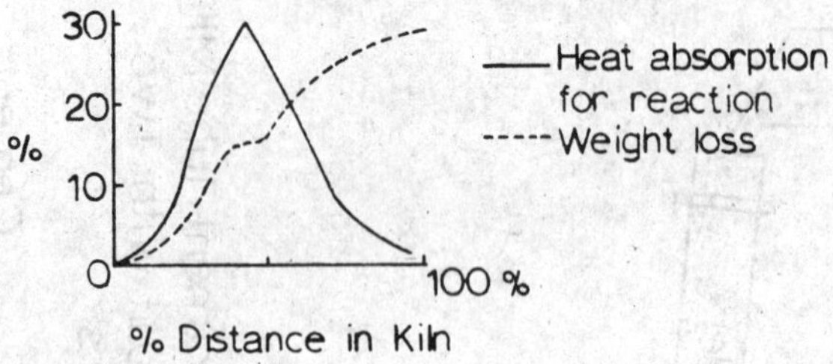

Wet process feed requires 90-170 m length kilns of 2.5→6 m diameter; rotating at corresponding speeds of 2 rpm→½ rpm. Dry process kilns may be as short as 50 m.

(c) Heat economy

Minimizing fuel consumption is an economic balance between fuel costs and addition of waste-heat boiler and air preheater with the equipment usually specified because of favorable incremental investment.

The theoretical heat requirement is 430 Kcal/kg of Portland cement clinker. Actual heat requirements vary from 1,300-1,800 Kcal/kg for processes using wet grinding down to 700-1,000 Kcal/kg for processes using dry grinding.

(d) Quality control

Product performance is quite sensitive to rock composition, particle size, and degree of calcining. Instrumentation and automatic control of the calcining kiln has proven a worthwhile investment in improving Indian cement quality so that it now stands high in world market comparisons.

4.4. Economics of Cement Industry

4.4.1. Raw materials

High grade and beneficiated circuit rock will have to be supplemented by blending with burnt clays and blast furnace slag to conserve native limestone. Another example of substituted raw materials is at Fertilizer Corp. of India Ltd., Sindri, where calcium carbonate sludge is utilized in producing 600 tons/cement per day via an adjacent plant of the Associated Cement Companies Ltd. The sludge comes from the reaction:

$$\underset{\text{gypsum}}{CaSO_4} + (NH_4)_2CO_3 \rightarrow \underset{\text{fertilizer grade ammonium sulfate}}{(NH_4)_2SO_4} + \underset{\text{sludge}}{CaCO_3}$$

Still another example of substituted raw materials involves cement production as a co-product in the production of sulfuric acid from gypsum. See Section IIA on Sulfur and Sulfuric Acid for further discussion. This process produces cement clinker and a gas containing 9% SO_2 as co-products. The process is carried out by heating gypsum, coke and shale in a coal-fired kiln at 2,500°F. The following are some of the reactions which occur:

$$CaSO_4 + 2C \rightarrow 2CO_2 + CaS$$
$$CaS + 3CaSO_4 \rightarrow 4CaO + 4SO_2$$
$$3CaS + CaSO_4 \rightarrow 4CaO + 2S_2$$
$$2CaSO_4 + C \rightarrow 2CaO + CO_2 + 2SO_2$$
$$8CaO + Al_2SiO_7 \rightarrow 2Ca_3SiO_5 + Ca_2Al_2O_5$$

5. Overall Factors to be Considered in Cement Industry

The manufacture of cement will be discussed in some detail here because there are so many factors which could be applicable to almost any other industrial chemical product, including reviews of

1. Process technology
2. Industry problems including
   a. Capital availability
   b. Power
   c. Locational problems
   d. Raw material problems
   e. Transport problems
   f. Export problems
3. The advent of mini-plants
4. The impact of research and development
5. Future market influences and trends

A review of the cement industry has been provided in "Kothari's Industrial Directory of India" published in Madras in 1994 which could serve as a pattern for the consideration of many industrial chemical processes—sort of an outline for considering processes in general. Thus the Kothari treatment of the cement industry has been abstracted at length here as a study aid to Indian students. It is a good case history of the factors involved in considering an industry.

Several salient features characterize the cement industry and it is imperative to bear them in mind while discussing the industry. It is a core sector industry and cement is an infrastructural product. Any increase in its price would have a cascading effect on many other sectors, especially that of construction. It is a capital-intensive industry. A new one million ton plant would cost between Rs. 180-200 crore, with its gestation period ranging between 2 and 3 years. It is also a power-intensive industry and is therefore highly susceptible to power cuts.

Incidentally power is considered to be a major cost of production in the manufacture of cement. Besides it is an industry which depends heavily on the policies of the government.

5.1. Production

Global cement production has surpassed one thousand million tons and the Indian cement industry is marching towards the 100 million milestone in the production capacity by the turn of the century.

For 1992-93, the center set a production target of 56.5 million tons for the cement industry. Going by this, the industry would have to achieve a production target of 4.9 million tons per month. Cement production during 1991-92 was of the order of 50.61 million tons. The capacity utilization of the large cement plants showed an improvement during 1991-92 at 87.9 percent against 83.7 percent in 1990-91. For the Eighth Five

Year Plan, the Planning Commission has indicated a production target of 78 million tons by the terminal year of the plan.

5.2. Consumption

The per capita consumption of cement in India is 43 kg as compared with world average of about 200 kg in 1989. The demand for cement is expected to be around 65.00 million tons during 1994-95 and around 87.00 million tons during the years 1995-2000 as per the demand projection made by the working group on cement industry. The cement manufacturers association has taken steps to boost the use of cement in techno-economically superior sectors like housing, precast and prefab construction, cement concrete roads and cement canal lining. These sectors have remained untapped so far due to the scarcity of cement.

Per Capita Cement Consumption

Country	Per Capita Consumption in kgs
Japan	561
U.K.	242
Korea	533
Malaysia	268
China	135
India	43

5.3. Technology

Cement may be manufactured employing three alternative technologies: (a) the largely outmoded wet process technology, (b) the more modern dry process that requires only 19 percent coal utilization (as against 30 percent for the wet process) and (c) the latest precalcinator technology through which optimum power utilization may be achieved. Here the calcination of raw material is partly or completely carried out before the feed enters the rotary kiln, thus reducing the thermal load on the kiln. Precalciners can be fitted on to existing dry process kiln. Besides saving power, the adoption of this technology enables an increase in installed capacity by 30-50 percent. The 3,000 tons per day plants being set up in the country use this technology.

Modernization provides the key to the problem of technology obsolescence in the industry. This may be done by closing down uneconomic units and converting the others to semi-dry or completely dry process. Process conversion costs less than the cost associated with the setting up of green field units of similar capacity. Modernization and rehabilitation by way of conversion of wet to dry process and addition of precalciners to existing dry process units are long overdue in the country. The conversion program in all would require an investment of Rs. 1,500 crore. Since the cement units are not in a position to generate funds of this dimension from their own resources, the government should think in terms of a modernization fund as has been done for the textile industry. Financial institutions should also dovetail their soft loan schemes to meet the cost of modernization and companies should earmark adequate funds for R and D programs for improving existing technologies and adapting foreign knowhow to Indian conditions. The industry's present commitment to R and D is almost negligible.

5.4. Problems

The main impediments to the growth of the cement industry in India may be broadly listed as follows:

1. Shortage of Capital
   The cement industry is capital-intensive in nature. On account of its record of declining profitability, it is unable to raise the required finance from the capital market.
2. Power Shortage
   Cement industry is also power-intensive, frequent power cut affects the production. Though many units try to tide over the power crisis by installing their own generators, they seem to suffer loss due to high cost of such an effort. It is estimated that 50-55 percent of total manufacturing cost relates to power. In 1989-90 nearly 17% of total cement production within the country was captive power at high cost.
3. Locational Problems
   Cement industries are mainly situated in Western and Southern regions producing about 71 percent of the total output, while the Northern and Eastern regions account for 29 percent of the total output. The Southern and Western regions consume only 57 percent of their total output, while the Northern and Eastern regions consume 43 percent of their total production. There is excess production in the South and Western regions while there is excess demand from Northern and Eastern regions. These factors lead to heavy transport cost.
4. Shortage of Coal
   Coal shortage affects production of cement industry resulting in idle capacity and under utilization of capacity. The impurities and low quality of coal affects the furnaces and quality of cement. Coal supplied to cement units has reportedly an ash content up to 57 percent and a calorific value of 3,000 and even less against the calorific value of 4,500 to 6,500 of imported coal.
5. Non-availability of Railway Wagons
   Non-availability of railway wagons leads to considerable delay in bringing in the raw materials and in dispatching the cement to various potential markets. Sending cement by open railway wagons leads to pilferage and damage by rain. Fifty-five percent of cement is dispatched by rail and 45% by road.
6. Defective Method of Transport
   Methods of cement bagging and its transportation in India are primitive which make marketing inefficient and uneconomical. Hardly any quantity of cement at present is handled by bulk.
7. Negligible Share in World Trade
   India's share in world trade is negligible. Currently, India exports only about 3.5 lakh tons in a year.
8. Technological Obsolescence
   The industry is in need of change in the production process. There is a need for conversion from wet process to dry process. It needs an investment exceeding Rs. 200 crore. If the industry does not earn reasonable profit, institutional finance also becomes difficult.

   The other factors that affect the cost of production and the profitability of the industry are (1) price increases in critical energy inputs such as coal, power, lignite, etc., (2) higher wages and lower labor productivity, (3) royalty and other levies—public levies of royalty and mineral rights tax constituted 60 to 70 percent of limestone cost in Andhra Pradesh, (4) lower capacity utilization where higher capacity utilization has been achieved, with captive power generated at twice the cost of grid power, (5) high capital and financing cost of the new plants owing to high import duty for plant and machinery as well as high cost of steel and (6) increases in freight charges over the period.

5.5. Mini Cement Plants

Mini cement plants play a vital role in socio-economic development. In India, sizeable deposits of limestone, which is the main raw material required for the production of cement, are spread over the country. In those places where there are limited quantities of limestone available, and it is not possible to set up large plants, the Government has decided to start mini plants.

The Government encourages the setting up of mini cement plants due to the following reasons:

(1) They help utilization of limestone reserves.
(2) The gestation period in commissioning these units is just about half of that of larger units.
(3) The infrastructural requirements of the mini cement plants are much less.
(4) The cement produced may be locally distributed thus easing the complicated distribution problem and transport bottleneck.
(5) There is an inherent rural development and employment potential in these plants.
(6) The mini plants are having advantage of lower cost per installed ton capacity. It is less than 75 percent of the capital costs of the large units.
(7) Mini plant wages are not regulated by the cement wage board. As a result the minimum wage paid by the large unit is nearly Rs. 1,100/-p.m., while the wage in the mini plants is Rs. 350/-p.m. only.
(8) The cost involved in having captive power unit is less in the case of mini plants.
(9) As the mini plants produce lesser quantity of cement, it is possible to have better quality control and effective distribution system.
(10) Distribution control was not exercised in the case of mini cement plants whereas major cement plants were under control for distribution and levy obligation.
(11) Fifty percent relief in excise duty was offered to offset the higher cost of production due to lack of rail head and rail linkage facilities for coal and also to offset the high cost of labor which is about five to seven times more when compared to major cement plants. Keeping in mind all these advantages, the government is providing all help to the mini plants. The mini plants are very successful in China. At present there are about eighty plants of different sizes in India. There is very good scope for starting new units in Orissa and Northern and Eastern parts and in many hilly regions. Like the large and medium cement plants, most of the mini cement plants are situated in Andhra Pradesh, Karnataka, Madhya Pradesh, Gujarat and Rajasthan. The total capacity of the mini cement plants is estimated at around 2,400,000 tons per annum which is just 4 percent of the country's total production capacity of 60,000,000 tons per annum.

5.6. Export Prospects

Indian cement is exported mainly to Nepal, Bangladesh and a small portion to Sri Lanka. Though export enquiries for about 1 million tons are on hand with India, with the huge domestic demand exports have taken a back seat. Substantial export can be achieved if 100% EOU are set up in the coastal area. These units would have the benefit of low project cost due to the concessional import duty and could afford to import coal against export earnings.

It was believed that the post-gulf war would lead to massive requirements of cement once the reconstruction of Kuwait and Iraq was commenced. It was estimated a good deal of Iraq's 7 million ton capacity has been destroyed. Cement is one of the extreme focus items for exports, the target being 5 million tons by the end of the Eighth Five Year Plan.

In addition to commercial marketing of cement export, the following measures could be considered: (a) supply of cement to Indian construction companies working abroad; (b) cement to be included as one of the commodities, while giving aid to other countries; (c) while going in for large imports to include cement as one of the items to be exported from India as counter trade.

At the global level, given the present scenario, prospects for cement exports are deemed to be favorable in the coming years. There is good potential for export, what is required is adequate infrastructural facilities.

5.7. Research and Development

Research and Development work in the field of cement technology is being carried on by the Cement Research Institute, several universities and also by various organizations in public and private sectors. The gamut of their activities includes use of industrial waste such as flyash, pozzolana in the manufacture of cement, productivity enhancement programs, development of mini cement plant technology and a host of other programs.

The I.I.T. Kanpur and the Regional Research Institute, Jorhat had developed a technology for the manufacture of cement from paddy husk. Already a factory in Shimoga, Karnataka has been making successful application of this technology to produce cement. The states of Uttar Pradesh, Punjab and Haryana are taking speedy action to establish similar plants. The cement from paddy husk may be utilized for any construction work.

5.8. The Future

The future of the cement industry should be potentially good. Cement concrete roads cost more, but they have longer life. All over the world cement roads have proved their superiority over bituminous ones. Concrete gains in strength with age unlike other construction materials, which deteriorate. The Municipal Corporation of Bombay has gone in for concrete roads, in spite of their higher initial cost, in roundabouts and junctions. There are 2,280 major bridges to be constructed, thirty-three submersible bridges to be built, 400 level crossings to be replaced by roads overbridges, and 300 bypasses to be constructed. The private sector has been permitted to construct express highways of 2,000 km length. The government is considering a proposal to privatize the 65 lakh km length of National Highways. If the proposal materializes there will be a boost to the demand for cement. The housing shortage is likely to go up to 39.1 million units by the turn of the century. Water is becoming a scarce resource and need for better water management is keenly felt. Advantages of lining of the canals must be taken note of. Water loss in a cement concrete lined canal can be only 0.03% of an unlined canal. The carrying capacity of water increases by over 75 percent and alkalinity of land adjoining the canal area is avoided. All these, together with rapid industrialization, are bound to create additional demand and augur an excellent future for the cement industry.

The producers and capacities of Indian cement plants are given in Table IIK-1.

Table IIK-1
Producers and Capacities of Indian Cement Plants

	Tons/Yr.
Associated Cement Companies Ltd.	7,983,000
Birla Jute & Industries Ltd.	3,250,000
Century Textiles & Industries Ltd.	3,200,000
Chettinad Cement Corporation Ltd.	600,000
Dalmia Cement (Bharat) Ltd.	591,000
DCM Shriram Consolidated Ltd.	200,000
Grasim Industries Ltd.	2,500,000
Gujarat Ambuja Cements Ltd.	2,000,000
Gujarat Sidhee Cement Ltd.	1,200,000
India Cements Ltd.	2,600,000
Indian Rayon & Industries Ltd.	1,800,000
Jaiprakash Industries Ltd.	2,500,000
J.K. Corporation (formerly Straw Products Ltd.)	583,000
J.K. Synthetics Ltd.	1,540,000
Kesoram Industries Ltd.	1,326,000
Larsen & Toubro Limited	5,350,000
Madras Cements Ltd.	1,710,000
Modi Cement Ltd.	1,146,000
Mysore Cements Ltd.	2,095,000
Narmada Cement Company Ltd.	1,000,000
Orient Paper & Industries Ltd.	900,000
Orissa Cement Company Ltd.	800,000
Panyam Cements & Mineral Industries Ltd.	531,000
Priyadarshini Cement Company Ltd.	600,000
Raasi Cement Ltd.	1,100,000
Saurashtra Cement & Chemical Industries Ltd.	863,000
Shree Cement Ltd.	600,000
Shree Digvijay Cement Company Ltd.	1,075,000
Total	49,643,000

In addition, there are reported to be a number of mini plants (less than 300 T/D) with capacities totalling 5,700,000.

Source: "The Investor's Guide to Indian Corporates," I.R.I.S. (1994)

Lime

1. Physical Properties

1.1. CaO: Quicklime

Mol. wt.	56.08
M.P.	2,570°C

B.P. 2,850°C
Density 3.32 gm/cc
Soluble in water and acids

1.2. $Ca(OH)_2$: Hydrated or slaked lime

Mol. wt.	74.10
Density	2.2 gm/cc
Decomposition to CaO	580°C
Slightly soluble in water	(0.18% at 0°C, 0.08% at 100°C)

Grades: Commercial lime is not 100% CaO or $Ca(OH)_2$ but mixtures with MgO and/or $Mg(OH)_2$.

- Quicklime: high-calcium (>90% CaO); low-magnesium (5-25% MgO), dolomitic (25-40% MgO).
- Hydraulic lime and slaked lime $Ca(OH)_2$ plus MgO-$Mg(OH)_2$ in varying percentage.

2. Consumption Pattern

Lime is used as a basic flux in the manufacture of steel. Silicon dioxide is a common impurity in iron ore which cannot be melted unless it combines with another substance first to convert it to a more fluid lava called slag. Silicon dioxide is a Lewis acid and therefore it reacts with the Lewis base lime. The molten silicate slag is less dense than the molten iron and collects at the top of the reactor, where it can be drawn off. Over 100 lbs of lime must be used to manufacture a ton of steel.

$$CaO + SiO_2 \rightarrow CaSiO_3$$

The uses of lime in chemical manufacture are too numerous to discuss since over 150 important chemicals are made with this basic material. In fact, only five other raw materials are used more frequently than lime for chemical manufacture: salt, coal, sulfur, air and water.

3. Methods of Production

3.1. Classification of Processes

- Calcining limestone to yield quicklime
- Hydration of quicklime

3.2. Quicklime Process

3.2.1. Reference flow sheet: Figure IIK-3

3.2.2. Chemical reaction

$$CaCO_3(s) \rightarrow CaO(s) + CO_2(g); \quad \Delta H = +44 \text{ Kcal}$$

3.2.3. Quantitative requirements

(a) Basis: 1 ton CaO

Limestone (Pure)	1.87 tons
Coal	0.3 ton

(b) Plant capacities: 100-500 tons/day

3.2.4. Process description

Limestone is quarried or mixed and put on conveyors feeding the mill crushing unit. Limestone of several sizes is produced, with jaw or gyratory crushers used for hard rock and hammer or roll mills used for soft rock. The size depends on type of calciner as follows:

- Vertical shaft 10-20 cm
- Moving bed 1-10 cm
- Rotary kiln 0.5-5 cm
- Fluidized bed 0.5-0.05 cm

Vertical shaft or rotary kilns are usually specified.

A vertical shaft kiln is 3-8 meters in diameter and 10-25 meters high, lined with refractory brick and covered with sheet steel outside for strength and prevention of gas leakage. Operation is of two types:

- Unmixed—coal is fired in separate combustion chamber and flue gases supply heat of decomposition
- Mixed—coal is mixed with limestone lump; simplifies kiln design, but coal ash is added to product

Feed is from top of furnace where combustion gas preheats the stone as it gradually slides down the shaft into the calcining zone. This section of the shaft kiln operates at 1,000-1,100°C ($CaCO_3$ decomposes at 898°C). The lime lump moves to the cooling section where heat exchange occurs between the secondary air and hot lime particles.

After further cooling in a conveyor, the lime is either packaged as lump lime or crushed and screened to yield pulverized lime. Containers are jute bags with inner seal lining of polyethylene to prevent moisture contact.

A rotary lime kiln operates in a similar manner to that described for cement calcining.

3.3. Hydrated Lime Process

3.3.1. Reference flow sheet: Figure IIK-3

3.3.2. Chemical reaction

$$CaO(s) + H_2O\ (1\ \text{or}\ v) \rightarrow Ca(OH)_2(s); \quad \Delta H = 15.9\ \text{Kcal}$$

3.3.3. Quantitative requirements

(a) Basis: 1 ton of $Ca(OH)_2$

Quicklime (Pure)	0.787 ton
Water	0.242 ton

(b) Plant capacities: 50-100 tons/day

3.3.4. Process description

Quicklime lump, crushed to 2 cm or less, is added along with water or steam to a vertical cylindrical pug mill containing 18-24 extended horizontal arms. Operation is usually continuous. Product from complete reaction is light, dry slaked lime which is classified by screen or air separators to remove any overburned (unreactive) lime that did not hydrate. The finely divided product is packaged in bags for shipping.

Steam under pressure is used to more rapidly convert MgO where dolomitic lime is used. The product is known as hydraulic lime.

3.4. Major Engineering Problems

3.4.1. Choice of kiln

Rotary kilns are favored for large production rates of quality product. The degree of calcining is more readily controlled. For example, overburned lime requires a higher temperature-residence time to produce partially fused unreactive CaO-MgO for refractory sales. This degree of overburning is usually more easily

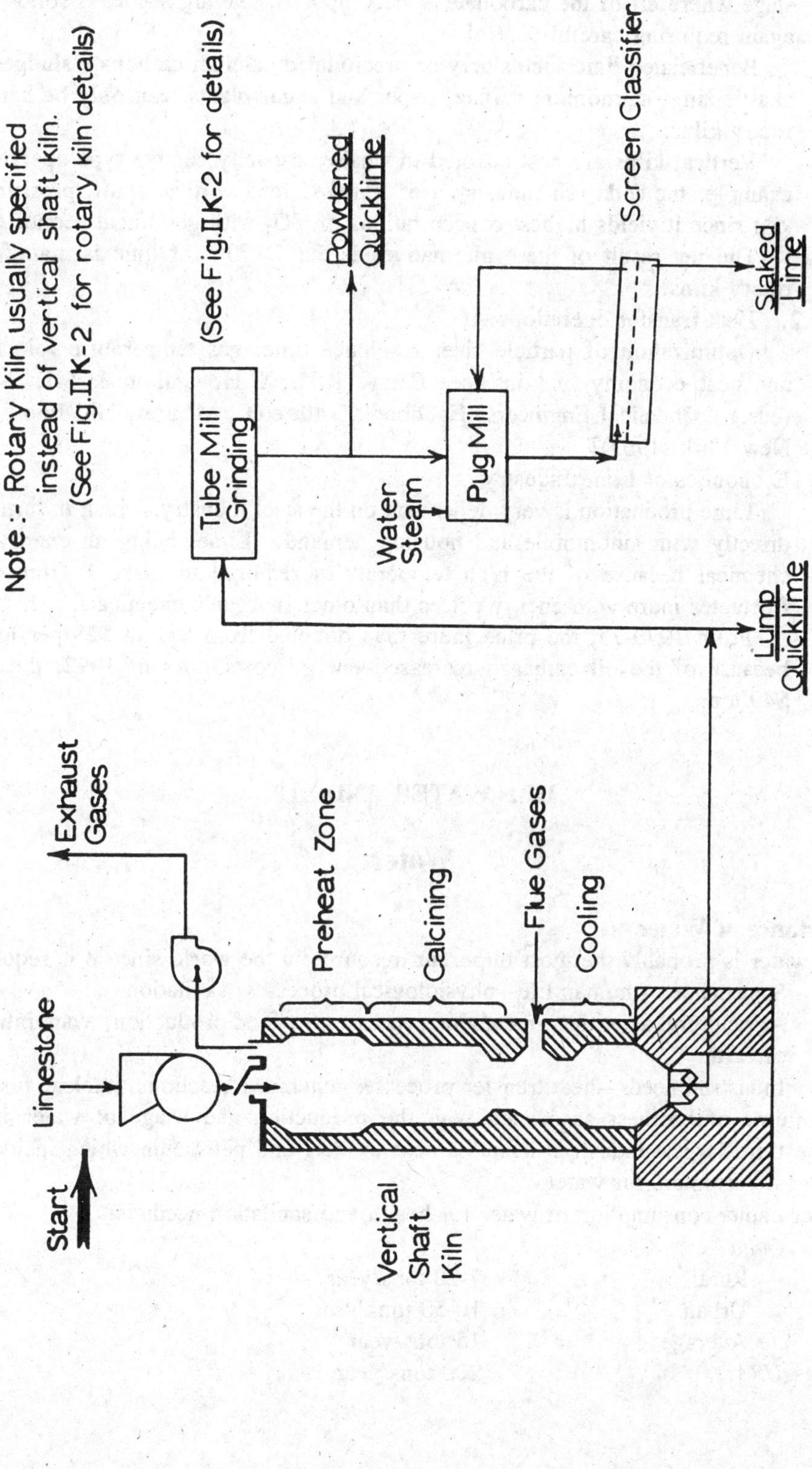

Fig. IIK-3. Lime manufacture.

controlled in a rotary kiln. Conversely, lime for hydration must be calcined to a stage where all of the carbonate is decomposed, leaving a porous solids structure, again requiring careful control.

Beneficiated limestone slurry or precipitated calcium carbonate sludges, as from causticizing, ammonium sulfate, paper and sugar plants, can only be handled with rotary kilns.

Vertical kilns are best adapted to smaller capacity captive type operations. For example, the soda ash industry uses a mixed feed vertical shaft, pressurized draft kiln since it yields highest concentrations of CO_2 with good heat economy.

The net result of these alternatives is that >70% of lime is manufactured in rotary kilns.

3.4.2. Heat transfer operations

Optimization of particle size, residence time, gas temperature-velocity profile and heat economy in kilns [see Perry, R.H., C.H. Chilton & S.D. Kirkpatrick (eds.), "Chemical Engineers' Handbook," 4th edn., McGraw-Hill Book Co., Inc., New York (1963)].

3.5. Economics of Lime Industry

Lime production is very dependent on the steel industry, which in turn fluctuates directly with automobile and housing demand. Lime, being an energy intensive chemical because of the high temperatures required to make it from limestone, fluctuates more with energy prices than other inorganic chemicals.

From 1970-75, the price more than doubled from $12 to $28 per ton, mainly because of the oil embargo increased energy costs. As of 1992, the price was $49/ton.

III. WATER AND AIR

Water

1. Importance of Water

Fresh water is probably the most important resource in the world since it is required for:

- Sustenance of human life—physiological processes, sanitation
- Agricultural activities—metabolic processes for food production, evaporative cooling of earth
- Industrial needs—heat transfer processes, chemical reactions, nuclear fusion power

The volume of business associated with the production and usage of water in India is probably the third largest industrial business next to steel and petroleum which incidentally are also the largest customers for water.

The per capita consumption of water for health and sanitation needs is:

India	
Rural	7-20 tons/year
Urban	10-50 tons/year
Average	15 tons/year
USA	200 tons/year

2. Sources of Water

All of the water supplies at present come from precipitation which averages 115 cm of water over the entire 806 million acres of India. This is compared with 75 cm average for the USA. The rainfall is largely confined to a period of 2-3 months during the monsoons except in the northwestern region of the Himalayan mountains where the snows of winter gradually melt throughout the remainder of the year. This predominant highly seasonable rainfall requires storage reservoirs such as dams to aid in levelling surface flow throughout the year.

The precipitation varies from essentially zero in the northeastern section near Pakistan to over 250 cm along the southwestern coast of India.

2.1. Steady-state Yearly Cycle of Water in India

Input	35×10^{11} tons/year
Output	
Evaporation losses	11.5×10^{11} tons/year
Soil seepage	7.5×10^{11} tons/year
Surface flow into rivers, dams, lakes	16.0×10^{11} tons/year

3. Consumption Pattern

3.1. Water usage in 1985 in India with estimates for the year 2025 are shown in the following table:

Water Use by Purpose	Utilization: 1985			Future estimated requirement: 2025		
	Surface Water	Ground Water	Total	Surface Water	Ground Water	Total
1. Irrigation	33.14	17.34	50.48	61.17	24.37	85.54
2. Net Consumption for	0.79	0.06	0.85	3.53	0.43	3.96
(a) Domestic and Municipal Supply	0.22	0.08	0.30	1.21	0.43	1.64
(b) Industrial Use	0.14	--	0.14	0.82	--	0.82
(c) Thermal Power Generation	0.43	--	0.43	1.50	--	1.50
3. Pisciculture	--	--	--	2.79	--	2.79
4. Forestry	--	--	--	2.21	--	2.21
5. Livestock Need	0.49	--	0.49	1.18	--	1.18
Total Demand	34.42	17.40	51.82	70.88	24.80	95.68
Total Utilizable Flow	68.41	35.58	103.99	68.41	35.58	103.99
Demand as Percent of Utilizable Flow	50.3	48.9	49.8	103.6	69.7	92.0

(figures in million hectare meters)

Source: "India 1993-94," Indian Express Publication (1993)

- In 1985, irrigation alone accounted for 97% of the total demand for water, two-thirds of which was met from surface water resources. Including other uses, total demand for water was about half of the utilizable flow.
- By projections for 2025 AD, almost 92% of the utilizable flow of water is likely to be consumed. Share of irrigation in total demand is likely to diminish to 68%. But three-fourths of the irrigation needs would be drawn from surface resources. Therefore, including increased claims of other users, the total demand for surface water may exceed the total utilizable flow, as estimated way back in 1974.
- Even for ground water, a large claim would be for minor irrigation purposes. It is obvious that industrial uses of water will not severely tax the water resources. Note carefully that these are average figures. In all of the intensely populated and industrialized urban locations, however, water shortages exist because of poor planning.

3.2. Industries' Typical Water Needs

Reference flow sheet: Figure IIL-1

- Cooling
- Processing—entering into or contacting manufactured products
- Power generation—surface condensers and feed water
- Sanitary services
- Fire protection
- Miscellaneous—air conditioning, landscape maintenance

3.3. The Largest Users of Water by Industry Classification are:

- Steel
- Oil refineries
- Pulp and paper

3.4. Types of Water Used by Chemical Industries in Order of Increasing Cost

(*Note:* 1 cubic meter = 1 metric ton of water)

<u>*Type of Usage*</u>

Irrigation water

Raw water from lakes, rivers, etc., pumped and filtered

Adiabatic cooling towers

Softened or cation exchange removal; particularly useful in textile or pharmaceutical industries

Municipal processed water—softened by lime soda process, decolorized and deodorized, then chlorinated

Double deionization (anion and cation exchange); used in place of distilled water

Distilled water

4. Plant Location Factors Related to Water

4.1. Plants requiring cooling water should be preferably located on lakes, rivers, or oceans

- Examples—power generating stations, nuclear processing plants, oil refineries, steel plants.

4.2. Use of tube wells should be considered if other factors favor inland off-water site.

4.3. Regions in the vicinity of hydroelectric installations have ample water for industrial usage. Transportation of other raw materials may be a problem, however.

4.4. Expensive cooling towers may be required to conserve water and make a possible plant site feasible from a water use standpoint.

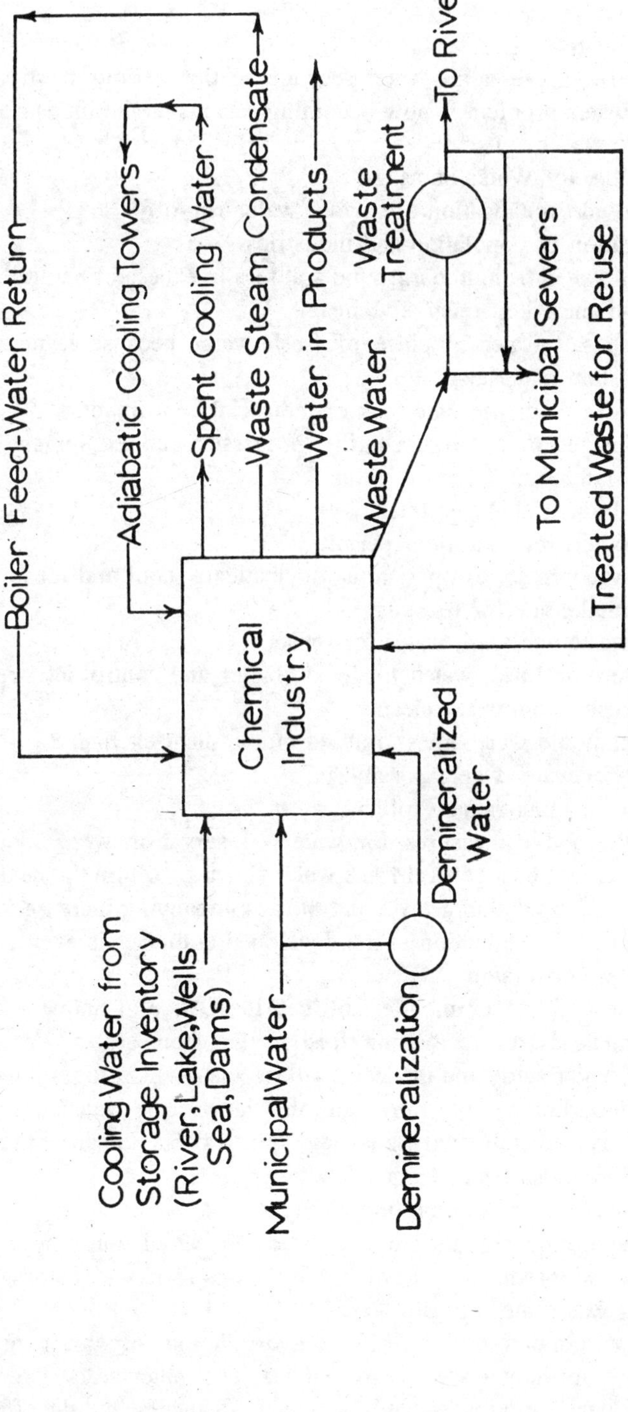

Fig. III-1. Flow sheet for industrial use of water.

4.5. Temperature of water is a factor. Wide extremes of water temperatures throughout the year are undesirable, particularly on high-temperature end of scale.

4.6. Waste disposal of contaminated aqueous streams to be state-regulated.

5. Water Shortage Problems

Parts of India are arid or have saline water seepage so that serious fresh water shortages exist. In other areas, the water problem is now becoming serious as the industrial concentration in a given area increases.

5.1. Factors Responsible for Water Shortages

- Failure to provide equalization of surface water run-off
- Overconcentration of population and industries
- Withdrawal of water from underground aquifers in excess of natural recharging rate
- Water wastage since it is relatively cheap
- Failure to use salt water in place of fresh water because it requires expensive corrosion-resistant materials
- Poor selection of plant sites and lack of industrial coordination
- Inadequate design of water-consuming processes and equipment from a water conservation standpoint

5.2. Steps to Reduce Industrial Water Intake

- Reuse water wherever conditions permit
- Use cooling water in series operations, adiabatically cool and reuse
- Treat waste condensate for reuse
- Recondition waste and wash water for reuse
- Reduce pressure on lines, watch for leaks, meter and control all streams
- Keep heat transfer equipment clean
- Insulate hot and cold water lines to avoid mutual heat exchange
- Substitute air for water where possible

5.3. Water Shortage as a Long-range Problem

Even if all of the above measures for water conservation were adopted, it is still anticipated that there will be a general fresh water shortage within the next few centuries. This is because of the population growth and the accompanying increase in industrial and agricultural activities. The situation in the developed countries is even more serious.

5.3.1. Saline water conversion

In 1952 the U.S. government established the Office of Saline Water to develop economical methods for recovering fresh water from sea water. A number of processes are under study and the technical aspects of this program will be discussed later. It is important to note, however, that large-scale transportation of water is expensive. This means that only areas less than 400-600 km from the sea coasts will be able to afford fresh water from salt water.

5.3.2. Prevention of natural evaporation losses

Water evaporation amounts to 3-4 times the actual consumption in the water balance cycle. Any reduction in evaporation losses from water storage facilities will aid in solving water shortage problems.

The use of monomolecular films of hydrophobic, organic compounds of low vapor pressure on the surface of lakes, dams, and water storage reservoirs is now under test. Evaporation losses can be reduced drastically, but the effects on natural purification processes and water wildlife are uncertain. The principal problem is a substantial reduction in the amount of oxygen diffusing at the water-air interface.

6. Methods of Treating Fresh Water

6.1. Impurities to be Removed

Water treating or conditioning for general use in a community is usually a municipal function serving both residential and industrial needs. The impurities which must be removed from water will vary according to geographical location. These impurities are classified as:

6.1.1. Hardness impurities—dissolved salts of Ca and Mg

- Temporary or carbonate hardness
  Ca and Mg bicarbonates—reduced by boiling to precipitate insoluble carbonates, but forms sediments
- Permanent or non-carbonate hardness
  Ca and Mg sulfates or chlorides—must be removed by chemical reaction or ion exchange

6.1.2. Other water impurities

- Gases—air, CO_2, H_2S
- Insoluble matter causing turbidity
- Soluble color compounds
- Pathogenic organisms

6.2. Conditioning Methods

To remove or reduce a portion or all of the above impurities, several basic processes are available to municipalities or industrial plants. The choice depends on the nature of the raw water input and the desired end usage of the conditioned water. Most frequently a combination of processes is employed.

6.2.1. Classification of conditioning methods

- Lime-soda process
- Filtration—usually done on sand filters
- Decolorization and deodorization—activated carbon adsorption
- Chlorination
- Ion exchange
  (a) Zeolite softening for cation removal
  (b) Synthetic resins—used for cation and/or anion exchange
- Boiler water feed conditioning
  (a) Addition of sodium hexametaphosphate $(NaPO_3)_6$ to form soluble complexes of Ca, Mg, Fe and Al
  (b) Deaeration by means of spraying as hot water or addition of scavenger such as sodium sulfite

6.3. Municipal Water Conditioning

Water conditioning is confined to approximately 10% of India's population with plants existing only in urban areas. The principal processes involved are (1) lime-soda to precipitate Ca and Mg as well as decolorize and remove turbidity agents, (2) activated carbon treatment, (3) filtration, and (4) chlorination.

6.3.1. Reference flow sheet: Figure IIL-2

6.3.2. Chemical reactions

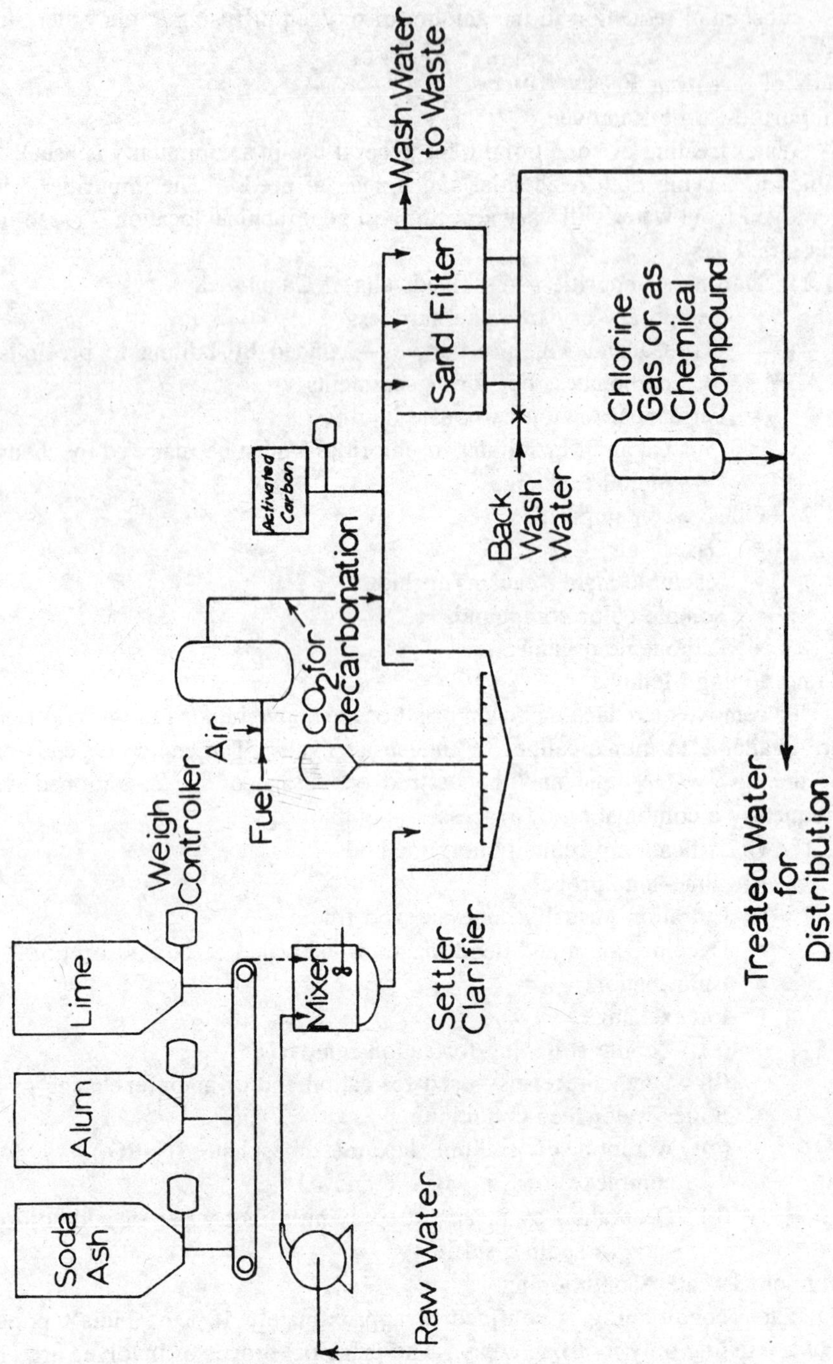

Fig. III-2. Municipal water treatment flow sheet.

- Temporary or carbonate hardness
  - (a) $Ca(HCO_3)_2 + Ca(OH)_2 \rightarrow 2CaCO_3 + 2H_2O$
  - (b) $Mg(HCO_3)_2 + Ca(OH)_2 \rightarrow MgCO_3 + CaCO_3 + 2H_2O$
  - (c) $MgCO_3 + Ca(OH)_2 \rightarrow Mg(OH)_2 + CaCO_3$
- Permanent or non-carbonate hardness
  - (d) $CaCl_2 + Na_2CO_3 \rightarrow CaCO_3 + 2NaCl$
  - (e) $CaSO_4 + Na_2CO_3 \rightarrow CaCO_3 + Na_2SO_4$
  - (f) $MgCl_2 + Ca(OH)_2 \rightarrow Mg(OH)_2 + CaCl_2$
  - (g) $MgSO_4 + Na_2CO_3 + Ca(OH)_2 \rightarrow Mg(OH)_2 + CaCO_3 + Na_2SO_4$
  - (h) $Al_2(SO_4)_3 + 3Na_2CO_3 + 3H_2O \rightarrow 2Al(OH)_3 + 3CO_2 + 3Na_2SO_4$

6.3.3. Raw materials

The three principal chemicals required for the lime-soda process are quicklime (>90% CaO) or hydrated lime [$Ca(OH)_2$], light soda ash (98% Na_2CO_3) and alum [$Al_2(SO_4)_3 \cdot xH_2O$]. Small amounts of activated carbon and chlorine, or chlorine compounds such as sodium hypochlorite (NaOCl) are required for complete conditioning of most raw water supplies.

6.3.4. Quantitative requirements

(a) Basis: 100,000 tons of 100 ppm hardness water (Conditioned product water of 35 ppm)

Hydrated lime	27 tons
Soda ash	24 tons
Alum	1.8 tons
Activated carbon	8.5 kg
Chlorine	6 kg

(b) Plant capacities: Depends on size of municipality and per capita consumption design. One unit may treat as much as 400,000 tons/day.

6.3.5. Process description

Raw water input is metered and pumped to a continuous mixing unit where the requisite amount of chemical reagents are added to remove hardness and defloculate turbidity components. This latter is accomplished by forming a highly absorptive precipitate of aluminum hydroxide from the reaction of alum and soda ash. Supernatant water is removed from clarifiers which follow the mixer.

Because of the high OH^- concentration maintained to kill bacteria and insure a reasonable removal of Mg as $Mg(OH)_2$, this effluent water must be recarbonated to neutralize the excess alkalinity. This is done by spraying with combustion gases.

The remainder of the process is the addition of activated carbon, filtration via sand filters, and controlled addition of chlorine. The sand filters are backwashed periodically to carry off the precipitated materials and clean the filter beds.

6.3.6. Major engineering problems

- Provision of ample raw water supplies.
- Waste disposal of sludge. In some plants this is done by lagooning. Where land is scarce or lime is not plentiful, the sludge can be calcined and sold for agricultural lime.

6.4. Ion Exchange Processes

6.4.1. Reference flow sheet: None

6.4.2. Chemical reactions

- Cation exchange

(a) $MX + HR \underset{r}{\overset{f}{\rightleftharpoons}} HX + MR$ or $MX + NaR \underset{r}{\overset{f}{\rightleftharpoons}} MR + NaX$

where R = resin, M = cation, X = anion

- Anion exchange

(b) $HX + ROH \underset{r}{\overset{f}{\rightleftharpoons}} RX + H^+ + OH^-$

6.4.3. Process description

Water is passed through a fixed bed of cation exchange resin where the forward reaction of 6.4.2(a) takes place. The resultant acidic water is either treated in an anion exchanger or neutralized. This produces water of equal quality with that prepared by distillation. The doubly-deionized process must be used with a highly acid cation exchange resin and a highly basic anion exchange resin either in series or mixed.

When the exchange capacity of the resin has been exceeded, the activity of the ion exchange resin can be readily regenerated by forcing the reverse reactions to occur. Strong acid is added to the cation exchanger in back flow. In like manner, a highly basic solution is added to the anion exchange resin.

Ion exchange processes are used for household conditioning of hard water or where high purity water for certain industrial applications is required.

7. Methods of Obtaining Fresh Water from Saline Waters

Reference: Figure IIL-3

This topic is of lesser importance in Indian technology than the problems of establishing protected fresh water supplies by water treating as described in Section 6. There are locations in India where saline water processing is already being considered. Large sea-coast cities such as Madras are making comparative studies to obtain fresh water from sea water. The other serious problem is brackish and alkaline waters that exist in certain sections of Punjab, Rajasthan and the Ganga Valley. This condition is caused by extreme weathering of igneous rock, poor drainage and high water levels.

The engineering development of processes for desalination gives an informative comparative study. The real problem is one of scale-up and cost reduction.

7.1. Economic Considerations

Industrial and agricultural water currently costs less than Rs. 10 per 1,000 tons for plants larger than 10^4 tpd. The conclusion is that present water prices will increase many fold as present raw water sources diminish. However, even at Rs. 300 per 1,000 tons, water is a cheap process item—only 30 paise per ton.

The two main costs in producing fresh water from sea water are:

- Energy costs
- Fixed charges on investment

These are closely related in an economic balance. If one tries to reduce energy costs, the investment costs are invariably increased, so that an optimum balance for

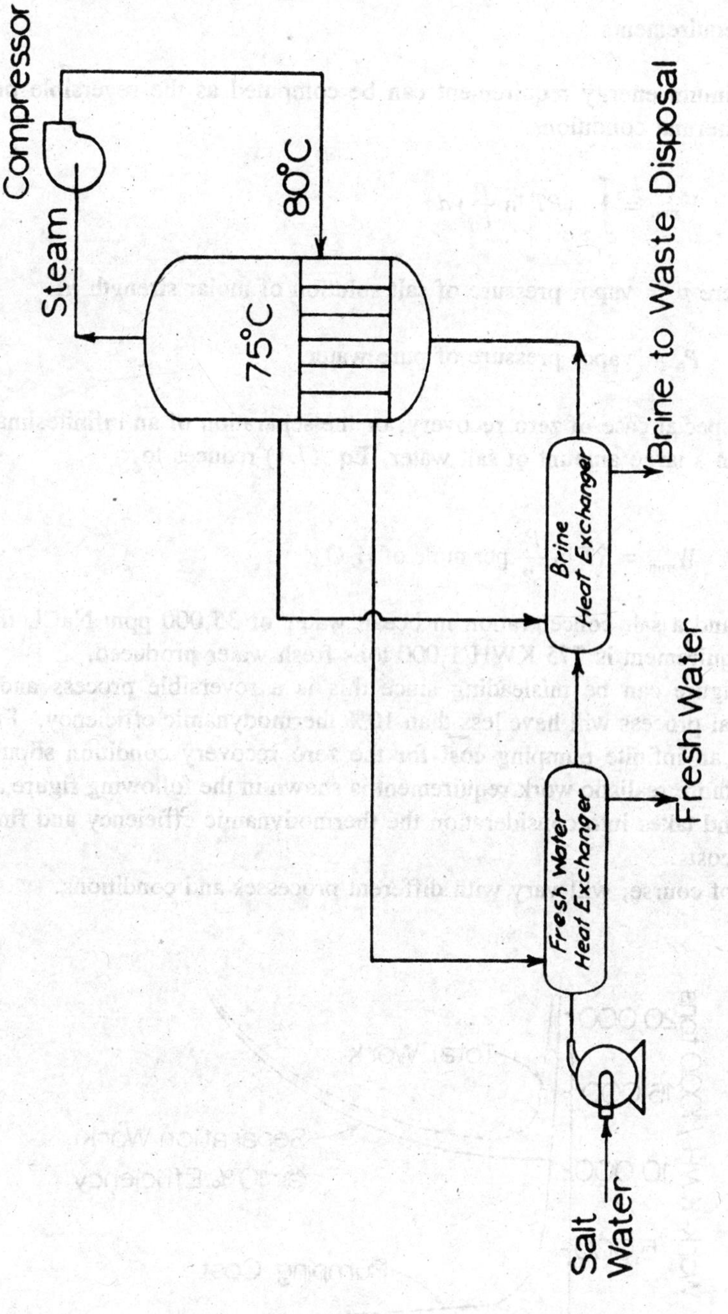

Fig. III-3. Vapor recompression process for recovery of fresh water from salt water.

these opposing tendencies must be determined for minimum cost.

7.2. Energy Requirements

A minimum energy requirement can be computed as the reversible process work under isothermal conditions.

$$W_{min} = \int_{n_2}^{n_1} (RT \ln \frac{p}{P_0})\, dn \tag{7.1}$$

where p = vapor pressure of salt solution of molar strength n,

P_0 = vapor pressure of pure water.

For a special case of zero recovery, or the separation of an infinitesimal amount of water from a large amount of salt water, Eq. (7.1) reduces to

$$W^{\circ}_{min} = RT \ln \frac{P_0}{p} \text{ per mole of } H_2O \tag{7.2}$$

At 70°F and a salt concentration in ocean water of 35,000 ppm NaCl, the minimum energy requirement is 775 KWH/1,000 tons fresh water produced.

This figure can be misleading since this is a reversible process and nearly any commercial process will have less than 10% thermodynamic efficiency. Further, there would be an infinite pumping cost for the zero recovery condition stipulated in Eq. (7.2). A more realistic work requirement is shown in the following figure as a function of yield and takes into consideration the thermodynamic efficiency and finite recovery pumping costs.

This, of course, will vary with different processes and conditions.

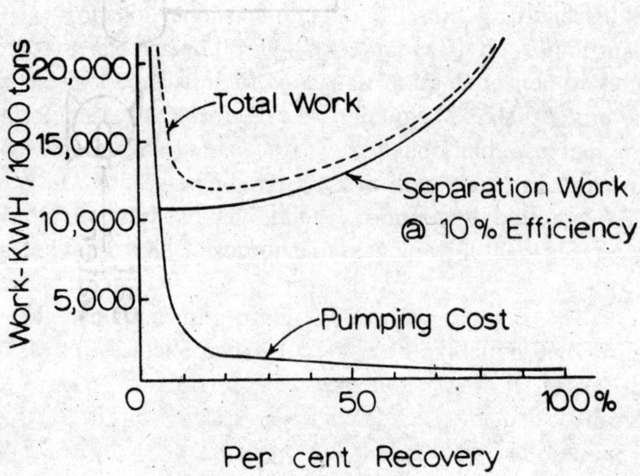

A majority of the presently proposed processes use energy in the form of heat which requires a further look at the relationship between heat energy (Q) and work (W) via the Carnot cycle.

$$W_{min} = Q_{min} \frac{T - T_0}{T} \tag{7.3}$$

where T is the absolute temperature of the heat source, T_0 is the absolute temperature of the heat sink.

With sea water at 20°C and steam at 120°C, Q_{min} is 2.6 kg cal/kg, so 211 kg of water per kg of steam could be produced in an infinite number of stages. The most practical number of stages is between 6 and 15 and hence the effective thermodynamic efficiency for a steam consuming process is 3-7%.

7.2.1. Potential energy sources

- Major importance
  - (a) Direct combustion of fuels
  - (b) Electrolytic fuel cells
  - (c) Waste heat from power plants and industrial processes
  - (d) Nuclear fission
- Minor importance
  - (e) Solar
  - (f) Hydroelectric
  - (g) Winds and tides
  - (h) Geothermal

7.3. Classification of Processes

7.3.1. Processes based on separation of water from brine

(a) Evaporation or distillation

(1) Single-stage flash
*(2) Multistage flash
*(3) Multiple effect submerged tube
*(4) Vapor recompression
(5) Combinations of (3) and (4)
(6) Solar energy
(7) Nuclear energy
(8) Ocean temperature differences
(9) Critical pressure

(b) Freezing or crystallization

(1) Indirect refrigeration
*(2) Direct refrigeration using a special refrigerant
*(3) Direct refrigeration using water
(4) Hydrocarbon hydrates
(5) Zone freezing and melting

(c) Solvent extraction
*(d) Reverse osmosis

7.3.2. Processes based on separation of salt from brine

(a) Ion exchange

*(b) Electrodialysis with ion-selective membranes

A discussion of several of the processes of commercial interest will show some of the problems encountered.

*Means the process is under active commercial development.

7.4. Evaporation Processes

The principles of multiple effect and vapor recompression evaporation are known from study of unit operations. Some of the peculiar engineering problems related to salt/water separation should be pointed out.

7.4.1. Multiple effect evaporation

Multiple effect practice is required to reduce energy costs. A convenient equation for calculating the kgs of water/kg of steam (w) in an effect evaporator is

$$w = \frac{w_1(1 - w_1^n)}{1 - w_1}$$

where w_1 = 0.85-0.95 kg H_2O/kg steam in the first effect and depends on evaporation design.

For $w_1 = 0.93$ and $n = 15$, $w = 8.8$.

The maximum number of effects is limited by the boiling point rise (BPR) av.

$$n_{max} = \frac{t_1 - t_2}{(\text{BPR})\text{ av}}$$

where t_1 = temperature of steam in first effect,

t_2 = temperature of water as heat sink.

A practical number of stages fixed by an economic balance between steam costs and fixed investment charges is between six and fifteen.

A long tube (10-12 m) vertical evaporator with steam on the shell side is usually used. The main engineering problems are:

- Scale formation—this is reduced by internal sludge control where seeds of scale-forming material are added to the evaporating liquor so that any scale will form on seeds rather than on the heat transfer surface
- Corrosion—limited by proper feed deaeration and correct choice of alloys

7.4.2. Multiple flash distillation

This differs from multiple effect evaporation in the pressure-temperature relationships employed. Sea water is preheated under pressure and introduced to a flashing unit where the pressure is lower. A portion of the hot feed water is flash distilled and condensed in a feed water preheater. The remaining water, at a lower temperature, passes to the next effect where the pressure is lower and the cycle repeats.

The major advantage is the lower cost of equipment per unit of capacity, since large shell and tube evaporators are eliminated. Corrosion at the high temperatures employed is the major disadvantage.

7.4.3. Vapor recompression evaporation

A schematic diagram for vapor recompression is shown in Figure IIL-3. The preheated brine solution is fed to the body of conventional evaporator where steam is formed and then compressed before returning to the tubes of the evaporator. The steam condenses, giving up latent heat to the boiling salt solution. Pure condensate water is passed through the feed preheater before being collected as product. This system can also be used in a flash evaporation cycle.

Compression energy is a major cost item so compression ratio must be kept as low as possible. Pressure differences across the compressor are directly related to temperature differences at the heat transfer surface. For low compression ratios and small temperature differences, a large heat transfer surface is required. This dictates an economic balance of the order of 3-5°C temperature difference and a pressure ratio of 1.15 to 1.25. For prevention of scale it is necessary to operate below atmospheric pressure and handle large volumes of vapor against a small head. High speed rotary axial or centrifugal compressors are available for this purpose.

Advantages of vapor recompression

- Requires only one evaporator instead of 5-6 in multiple effect evaporation
- Has lower energy requirements

Disadvantages of vapor recompression

- High priced energy in the form of electricity or high pressure steam is needed for operating the compressor

7.5. Freezing or Crystallization Processes

7.5.1. Direct refrigeration—flash freezing of water

This method, shown in Figure IIL-4, uses direct freezing of water at low pressure. Sea water is sprayed into a flash vacuum chamber at 0.005 atm. This is lower than the vapor pressure of the brine solution. The process is adiabatic and the necessary heat of vaporization removes heat from the solution and forms small ice crystals. The ice-brine slurry is withdrawn from the bottom of the vacuum chamber and moved to a wash column where the ascending ice crystals are washed countercurrently by descending water produced by condensing the water from the compressor. Additional refrigeration must be supplied to discharge some of the heat at ambient temperature.

Modifications of the freeze method include:

(1) Use of inert hydrocarbon such as isobutane as the indirect refrigerant.

(2) Formation of hydrocarbon hydrates such as propane hydrate crystals at about 45°C and 5 atms., followed by washing and decomposition at 1 atm. to recover propane and pure water.

Advantages of freeze methods

- Uses only about 85% of the energy required in evaporation processes
- Low temperature operation avoids scale formation and corrosion

Engineering problems

- Effective method for washing ice crystals—must avoid small size by increasing crystallizing time or supplying nucleation sites
- Building compressors to handle large volumes of water vapor at low pressure—use of LiBr absorption cycle to dissolve water from flash unit may be substituted

7.6. Reverse Osmosis

Osmosis is the process of diffusion through a semi-permeable membrane or barrier. The natural tendency is for fresh water to diffuse into sea water when such materials are

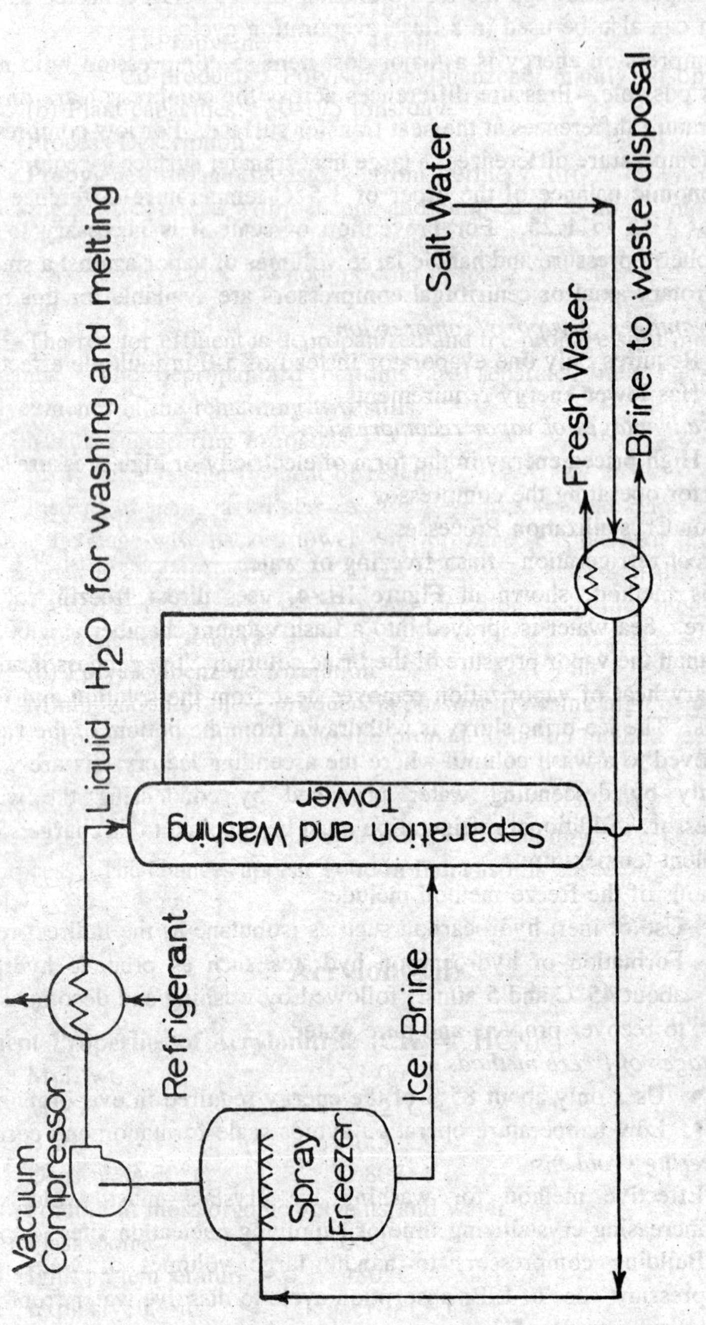

Fig. III-4. Direct refrigeration-flash freezing process for producing fresh water from sea water.

on opposite sides of such a membrane. In reverse osmosis (or ultrafiltration), the natural process is reversed by application of pressure to a body of sea water, thus forcing fresh water through the membrane.

Pressures of the order of 750-1,500 psi are used in this process. The appealing facet of reverse osmosis is that separation efficiencies of the order of 10-30% can be achieved without expensive heat exchange surface.

7.7. Electrodialysis

This process differs from the methods given above in that the salt is removed from water. This is accomplished by a pair of thin membranes, alternately cation- and anion-permeable.

Figure IIL-5 shows the method of operation of an electrolysis cell for accomplishing the separation. Cation membranes (C) contain negatively (—) charged side groups and repel anions but allow cations to permeate. The anion-permeable membranes (A) act via opposite charge. By imposing an EMF, E across a group of membranes, Na^+ ions can move toward the anode (—) but only through C type membranes. Cl^- ions move oppositely. The net result is a removal of NaCl from one compartment to give pure water and a concentrated brine flow from the adjacent compartment.

An electrodialysis unit consists of 200-1,000 of these compartments lined up as in a filter press to allow for use of voltages greater than 110 volts and to reduce Joule heat losses. Fluid flow is parallel through each compartment.

Major engineering problems

- Economic balance between (1) small compartment clearance (0.5-1 mm) to reduce cell resistance and (2) pumping costs for increased friction.
- Development of low-cost membranes with reasonable life.
- Disposal of concentrated brine, particularly from inland brackish water processing
- Limitations on energy requirements

The energy for separation is largely that required to overcome electrical resistance. By combining Ohm's and Faraday's laws:

$$E = \text{KWH/1,000 tons} = k\frac{iARfcF}{ne}$$

where i = current density; A = transfer area per cell; R = total resistance of unit; c = salt concentration; f = fractional transfer of electrolyte from low concentration cell; F = Faraday constant; n = No. of cell pairs in the assembly; e = current efficiency; k = constant dependent on units of measurement.

The equation above shows that the power needed is directly proportional to current density and salt concentration. Reducing current density will increase the number of units required for a fixed fresh water output so a balance must be established between energy costs and fixed charges on the electrodialysis units. For optimum design the energy requirement of 30,000 KWH/1,000 tons when using sea water is 2-3 times larger than any of the other processes. By taking advantage of the direct effect of concentration, the energy requirement can be reduced to 2,500-7,500 KWH/1,000 tons for brackish water of 3,000-8,000 ppm.

7.8. Nuclear Energy

The energy requirements for the desalination processes discussed above can be met by either coal-fired or nuclear-fueled power plants.

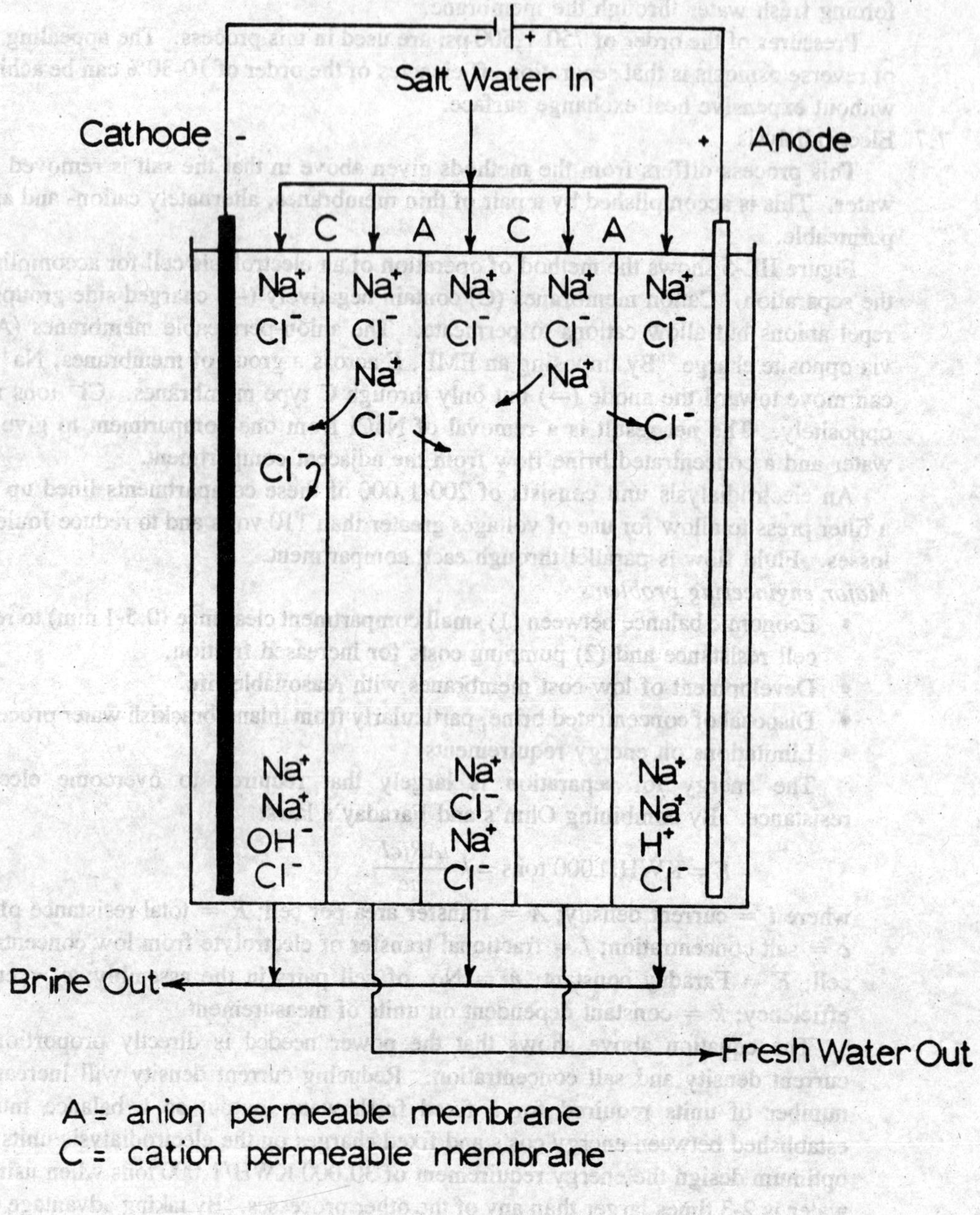

Fig. IIL-5. Schematic drawing of electrodialysis cell for producing fresh water from sea water.

8. Waste Water Treatment and Disposal

In the flow sheet for industrial use of water (Figure IIL-1), the treatment of waste water is indicated. This can be a complex problem for the chemical industries. Increasingly stringent laws prohibit pollution of water sources.

The cost of conditioning water for reuse or disposal may be more than the cost of original water. Much research and development work is necessary to economically solve the problems. Some of the solutions which can be applied are:

8.1. Recovery of Wastes as Valuable Products

Examples

- Refineries—centrifuge waste water to recover hydrocarbon fractions
- Lime sludge from lime-soda water softening process calcined and sold for agricultural lime

8.2. Segregation and Blending of Wastes to Facilitate Treatment

Examples

- Electroplating—solutions to be oxidized (cyanide) must be kept separate from those requiring reduction (chrome-bearing solutions)
- Separate concentrated and dilute wastes
- Blend alkaline and acid wastes to give neutral pH
- Segregate and sell certain wastes to neighboring plant—one refinery sold waste caustic to adjacent pulp mill

Air

1. Air as a Chemical Raw Material

You will read the statement in the literature that nylon is made from coal, air and water. This statement, while slightly oversimplified, emphasizes the simple fact that a source of carbon compounds, combined with ever-necessary water, and air to carry out oxidation processes are the basic essentials for nylon, and indeed for many heavy organic chemicals.

Further, air is the only raw material which is freely available to the chemical industry. Because of its oxygen content, air is the predominating raw material in many chemical processes, a fact which is accepted more than it is appreciated. The tonnage requirements of air for several important chemical process industry applications are as follows:

	Air required
• To produce 1 ton of H_2SO_4 from sulfur by the contact process	2.8 tons
• To burn 1 ton of coal in a modern power station	10-11 tons
• To oxidize ammonia to produce 1 ton of HNO_3	5.3 tons
• To produce 1 ton of pig iron by the blast furnace route	2.5-4 tons

When using air as a chemical raw material one is almost always using it only as a source of oxygen, with the nitrogen present as an adulterant ranging from unnecessary to uneconomic and annoying. There is an economic balance between using pure (or reasonably pure) oxygen made by air separation at some cost premium and simply using the cheaper air.

The availability of pure air as a chemical raw material presents real problems in areas of heavy industrial concentration. The feed to air separation plants must be free of hydrocarbons to avoid explosion hazards and hydrocarbon-containing vapor effluents may make the supply of such pure air both limited and dependent on such factors as wind direction. Thus air pollution control is important, not only as regards the chemical industry's relations with the neighboring community, but also as regards preservation of its own sources of supply.

The question of air pollution control is treated briefly in Section VII at the end of this volume.

IIM. NUCLEAR MATERIALS

1. Power Generation in India

Electric power generation in India is mostly from coal-based thermal and hydroelectric (hydel) plants. Though the nuclear power plants with an installed capacity of 1,720 MWe contribute only about 3 percent of the nation's requirement, theirs is a significant percentage in the regions where they are located. Solar, biogas and other non-conventional sources of energy should continue to be developed to satisfy specific local needs. However, they are not likely to provide, in the near future, the large-packets of power needed for industrial production or for convenient transmission. As we progressively run out of our coal reserves and as setting up of hydel plants becomes more difficult due to problems caused by displacement of large numbers of people, nuclear energy is emerging as the inevitable option for India's future energy needs as pointed out in *"The Hindu Survey of Indian Industry" (1994)*.

The nuclear program has been designed to make maximum use of the limited uranium resources and the five times higher thorium resources. Apart from the first two boiling water reactors, using enriched uranium, all the other reactors are pressurized heavy water reactors (PHWRs) which use natural uranium as fuel and heavy water as moderator and coolant. Based originally on the CANDU design, the first two reactors were set up with Canadian collaboration in Rajasthan. The design of these reactors has been continuously improved and two PHWR units each have been set up at Kalpakam near Madras and at Narora in U.P. and one unit at Kakrapar in Gujarat. The second unit at Kakrapar is nearing completion and two units at Kaiga in Karnataka and two more units in Rajasthan are past the half-way mark and will be commissioned during 1996-97. These PHWRs which are built and operated by the Nuclear Power Corporation of India Ltd., have a capacity of 220 MW each, and have been standardized.

These apart, future nuclear plants have to be of a higher capacity as the Indian electric grids become stronger and of larger capacities. With this in view, the indigenously designed 500 MW PHWR which incorporates many new concepts has now been completed. Construction of the prototype unit shall shortly be started in Tarapur.

A great deal of research and development in various areas like reactor physics, material science, reactor engineering, control systems and instrumentation, have been carried out at the Bhabha Atomic Research Center (BARC) to design the PHWR. Nuclear reactors need remote handling and robotics techniques for many operations such as coolant channel inspection, decontamination, coolant channel replacement and repair. NPCIL has been able to do all these indigenously with the R and D back up of BARC.

The heavy water required for the PHWRs is produced at several plants of the Heavy Water Board and in this area, India is not only self-sufficient, but is in a position to also export the product. The fuel bundles are manufactured by the Nuclear Fuel Complex at Hyderabad. Many Indian companies in the public and private sectors like BHEL, ECIL, Larsen and Toubro and

Walchandnagar Industries have participated in component, system and instrumentation development for these reactors. The Electronics Corporation of India Ltd. (ECIL), a public sector unit of the Department of Atomic Energy, is the country's premier organization in the areas of control systems, instrumentation, computers, electronic components and communication systems.

The nuclear fuel cycle in a nuclear power program starts from prospecting and mining through reactor design and operation to reprocessing and nuclear water management. Prospecting for uranium and other nuclear minerals countrywide is done by the Atomic Minerals Division. Mining and processing of the ores to produce "yellow cake" or uranium oxide is done at the Jaduguda mines in Bihar by the Uranium Corporation of India Ltd. (UCIL). The used fuel needs chemical processing to extract the plutonium produced from uranium during the operation of the reactor. This process is called reprocessing and the high toxicity of plutonium makes it highly complex and demanding. The processing plants and facilities for the safe management of nuclear waste are now built and operated by BARC. India is one of the few countries to have a comprehensive capability over the entire nuclear fuel cycle.

1.1. Economic Justification for Nuclear Power

Cost of power can be broadly divided into fixed and variable costs. The fixed investments for nuclear power plants at about Rs. 1,200-1,500 per installed KW are to be compared with Rs. 900-1,000 for coal-fired power plants. The difference in capital costs is more than offset by the lower fuel costs for nuclear plants in industrial regions of Bombay and Madras, 700-1,000 miles from the nearest coal fields. Nuclear plants require only 1/100,000 the weight of fuel input so transportation costs of 25-50 tons of nuclear fuel per year are insignificant. The net result is power generation at 3 paise/KWH in a nuclear station near Bombay versus 3.7 paise for conventional coal power plants.

The above statistics are sufficient to justify nuclear energy development in India. The status of nuclear energy development in India has been discussed in Section IB-3 at the beginning of this book under "The Energy Picture for India." The role of the chemical engineer in this area of industrialization will now be examined.

1.2. Nuclear Agro-Industrial Complexes (Nuplexes)

India is primarily an agrarian country and forecasted population growth indicates huge future food demands. The utilization of nuclear energy to help feed the country at the same time it is furnishing power to developing industries, is a "natural" for India. Such a combination of service is made possible in the "nuplex."

In a nuclear energy complex or "nuplex," the energy producing power station and all the energy consuming processes are planned and constructed as a single overall system. In such nuclear complexes, many basic industries are grouped and integrated with interchanging of materials around large low-cost nuclear energy centers. There are already in existence around the world a number of economically-sound and well-integrated industrial complexes such as around low-cost gas fields in Texas, and low-cost coal fields in South Africa. Electricity is an important raw material, and large nuclear power stations are important sources of this raw material.

A third of the world's land is arid and relatively unoccupied, whereas half of the entire population of the world occupies a tenth of the land area. Much of this arid land lies close to the sea, and if water and power needs can be met, this desert land can bloom and produce food for the growing population of the world. There are economic advantages of combining desalination of sea water, and production of power in a single

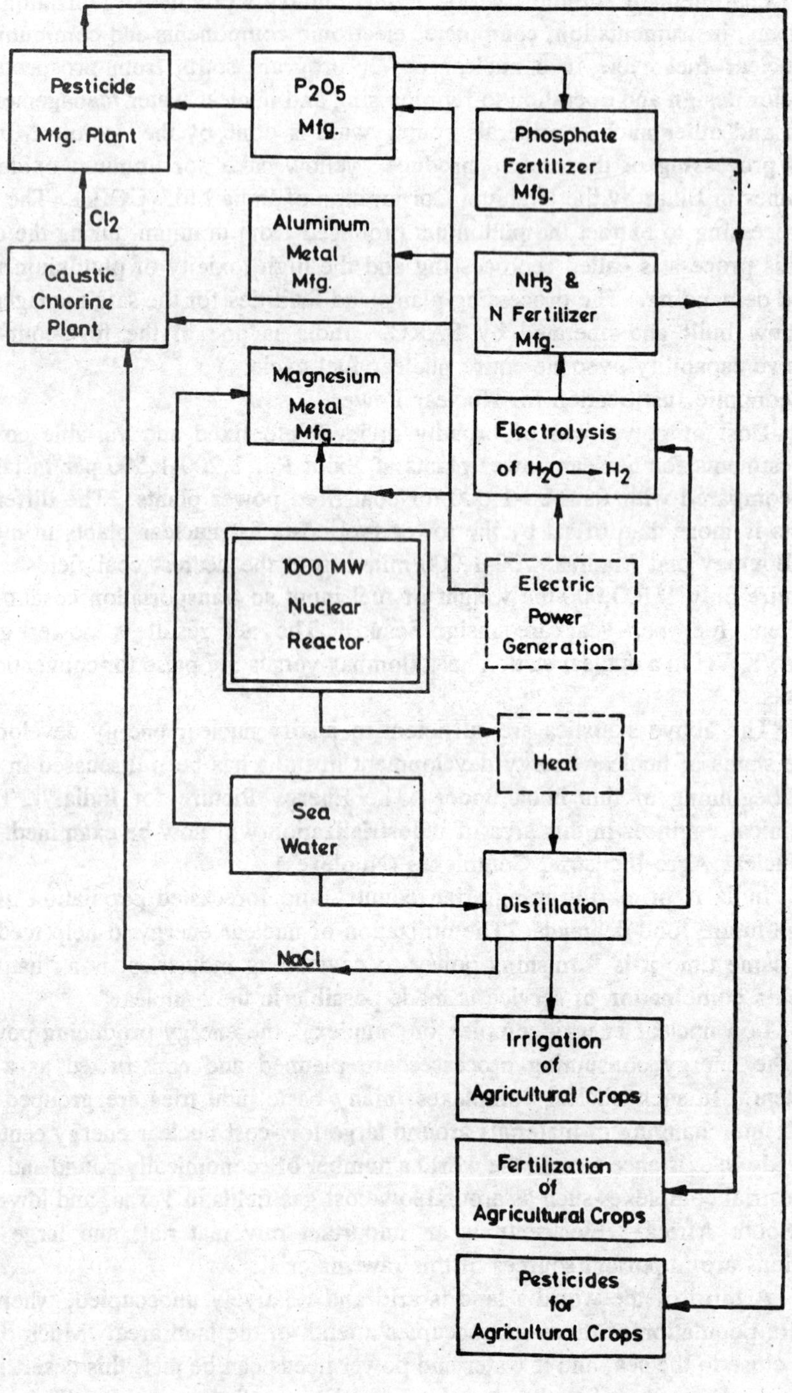

Fig. IIM-1. Block diagram of a "Nuplex."

system. To this system, power consuming processes such as nitrogen fixation, aluminum and chlorine production, etc., can be added. Various inputs and outputs of a nuclear powered agro-industrial complex are presented in Figure IIM-1.

2. Energy via Nuclear Fission Reactors

2.1. The basic nuclear energy equation, based on U^{235}, is

$${}_{92}U^{235} + {}_{0}n^{1} \rightarrow X + Y + 2 \text{ to } 3\ {}_{0}n^{1}$$

where ${}_{0}n^{1}$ = neutron, and X, Y = fission fragments ranging from mass no. 80-160 and highly radioactive.

$-\Delta H$ for this reaction is about 18 million KWH per kg of uranium or two million times the energy released in combustion of an equal weight of coal.

Note that two or three neutrons are produced for every neutron used, giving rise to a nuclear-chain reaction which could be quite destructive (nuclear bomb) unless controlled. The science and engineering involved in handling nuclear reactions of this type is termed nuclear engineering.

3. Role of the Chemical Engineer in Nuclear Engineering

Many chemical engineers specialize in the design and operation of nuclear fission reactors for heat and energy extraction. On a broader basis, nuclear chemical engineering encompasses these areas (see Figure IIM-2):

3.1. Nuclear raw materials separation and preparation of nuclear fuels
3.2. Nuclear fuel "burning" and heat removal
3.3. Spent fuel reprocessing
3.4. Utilization of fission products
3.5. Disposal of radioactive wastes

4. Important Components of a Nuclear Fission Reactor

4.1. Fuels

4.1.1. Fission fuel

Elements or compounds such as oxides, carbides, nitrides, sulfates, chlorides of:

- Uranium (U-233, U-235)
- Plutonium (Pu-239, Pu-241)

4.1.2. Fertile fuels

These contain atomic elements which by nuclear reactions give fission fuels.

- Uranium (U-238)
- Thorium (Th-232)

$${}_{92}U^{238} + {}_{0}n^{1} \rightarrow {}_{92}U^{239} \xrightarrow{\beta^-} {}_{93}Np^{239} \xrightarrow{\beta^-} {}_{94}Pu^{239} \quad \text{(fission fuel)}$$

4.1.3. Structural components

Materials with low absorption for neutrons. Typical examples: zirconium (Zr), aluminum (Al), stainless steel.

4.1.4. Coolants to remove liberated energy

Na, NaK, Bi, purified H_2O, deuterium oxide or heavy water (D_2O).

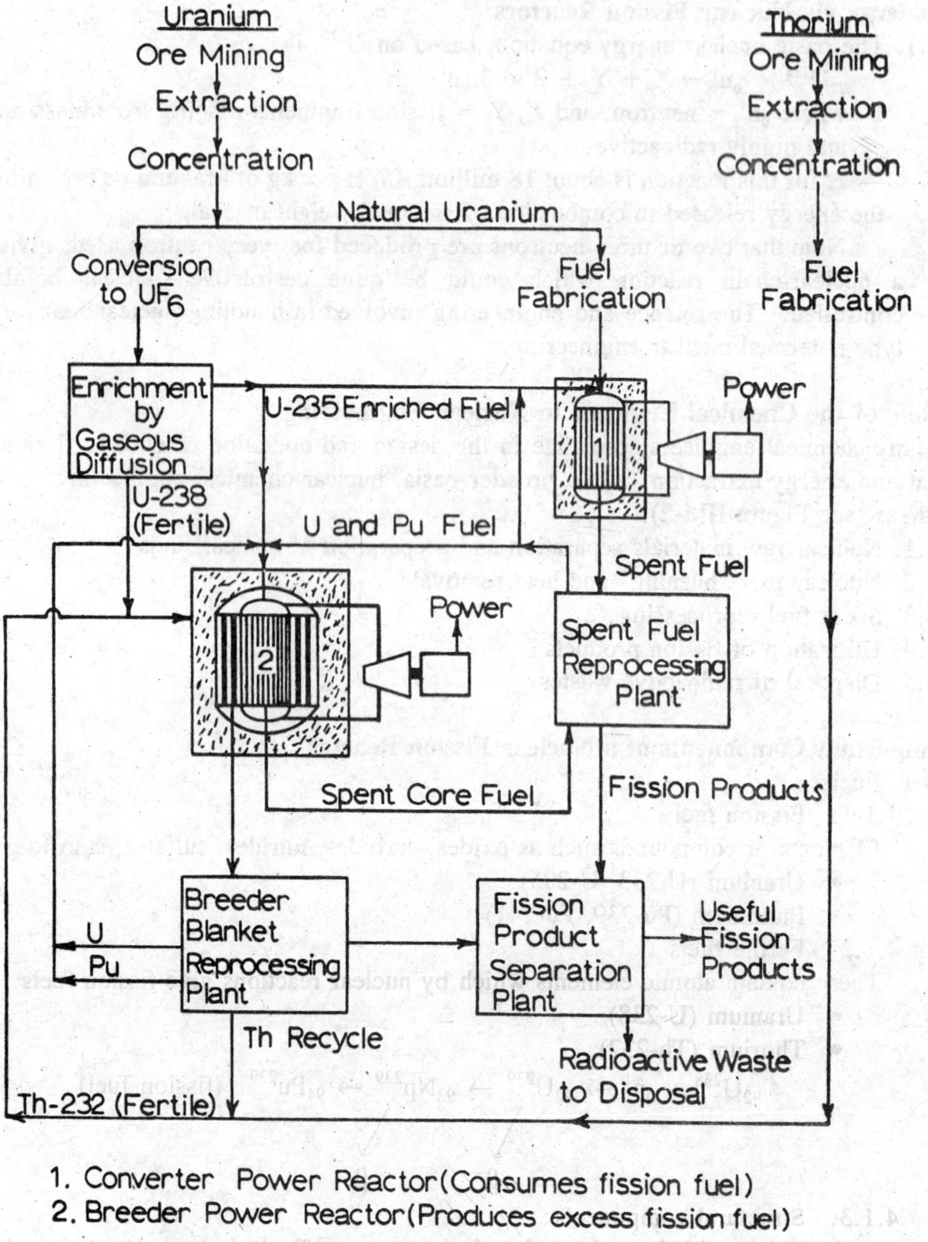

Fig. IIM-2. Nuclear reactor fuel cycles.

4.1.5. Moderators

Moderating materials are required if the absorption of neutrons is to take place at or near the environmental temperature of the reactor. The fission neutrons liberated are of extremely high energy and must be moderated to environmental temperatures by non-absorption type collision with moderating materials.

Typical moderators are: pure graphite, D_2O, H_2O, beryllium.

Examples of unusual chemical technology in preparing these components will be illustrated using uranium and heavy water. Graphite has previously been described in Section IIG. Reactor-grade graphite requires purified coke and only the center of the core will meet the rigid specifications for low neutron absorption. A discussion on the possibilities of using thorium is also included since India has the world's largest deposits of monazite sands.

5. Uranium

5.1. Abundance

In all naturally occurring uranium, the isotopic abundance of fission fuel as U-235 is only 0.714%, the balance being U-238. Enrichment, if necessary, must be done by gaseous diffusion using UF_6.

Sources of uranium contained in ores can be arranged in order of descending concentration:

5.1.1. Pitchblende (1 to >10% U)

A primary mineral found in African Congo and Northern Canada. Dense, black impure form of U_3O_8 mixed with ores of valuable metals such as tantalum, niobium, and vanadium. Not too useful in Indian production because of location.

5.1.2. Carnotite (0.1 to 0.5% U)

Secondary mineral ($K_2O \cdot 2UO_3 \cdot V_2O_5 \cdot 8H_2O$) formed by reaction of uranium-bearing ground waters on sedimentary rocks. Small deposits are being mined in Jaduguda at the rate of 1,000 tons of ore per day of marginal grade.

5.1.3. Monazite sands (0.25% U)

Chief source of thorium (10-11% ThO_2) but contains useful quantities of uranium.

5.1.4. Phosphate rock inclusions (0.01 to 0.03% U)

U_3O_8 can be recovered as by-product of phosphate fertilizer production. Extraction not economic as long as carnotite and pitchblende exist in abundance.

5.2. Pertinent Physical Properties of Uranium and Its Compounds

	U	UO_2	UC	UF_6
M.P. (°C)	1133	2750	2315	64
B.P. (°C at 1 atm.)	3900	-	-	56.5
Density (gm/cc)	18.7	10.5	12.9	gas
Thermal conductivity, Kcal/sec cm^2 °C/cm				
100°C	7.1	1.96	6.6	-
400°C	8.8	1.31	6.6	-
700°C	11.4	0.88	6.6	-

5.3. Methods of Production

5.3.1. Concentration

Removal of non-uranium constituents by:

(a) Leaching
- Acid leach (H_2SO_4 or HCl) on low limestone ores
- Salt roast, soda ash leach
- Salt roast, acid leach

(b) Ion exchange following acid leach

(c) Solvent extraction of acid leach slurries by organic phosphate esters such as tributyl phosphate in kerosene

5.3.2. Purification of concentrates

Solvent extraction of aqueous nitrates with organic phosphates

5.3.3. Conversion

Depends on final form of uranium needed as reactor fuel. Reference flow sheet: Figure IIM-3.

(a) Roasting of nitrate to UO_3 followed by NH_3 or H_2 reduction to UO_2 a preferred compound for reactor fuels because of its radiation stability compared to uranium metal. Reaction with fluorine produces UF_4.

(b) Uranium metal fuel elements by reduction with alkali metals

$UF_4 + 2Ca \rightarrow 2CaF_2 + U \qquad \Delta H = -137.6$ Kcal

(c) Uranium carbide

$UO_2 + 4C \rightarrow UC_2 + 2CO$

Uranium carbide is also preferable to uranium metal from a stability standpoint.

(d) Uranium hexafluoride gas for enrichment via gaseous diffusion

$UO_2 + 4HF \rightarrow UF_4 + 2H_2O \qquad \Delta H = -63.6$ Kcal

$UF_4 + F_2 \rightarrow UF_6 \qquad \Delta H = -60.0$ Kcal

5.4. Application of Fluidized Bed Technique in Uranium Gaseous Conversion Processes

Fluidized beds are fluid-solid systems in which the solid is maintained in suspension by gas flowing through a vertical reactor. Such equipment is being used increasingly throughout the chemical process industries for a number of reasons. A few important ones are:

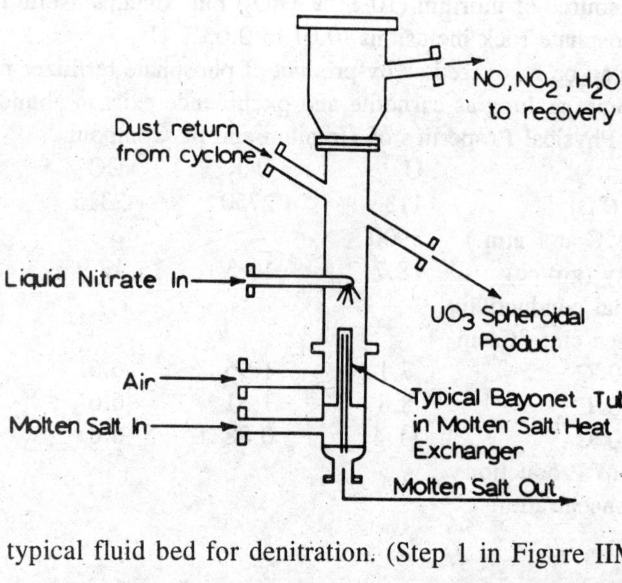

A typical fluid bed for denitration. (Step 1 in Figure IIM-3.)

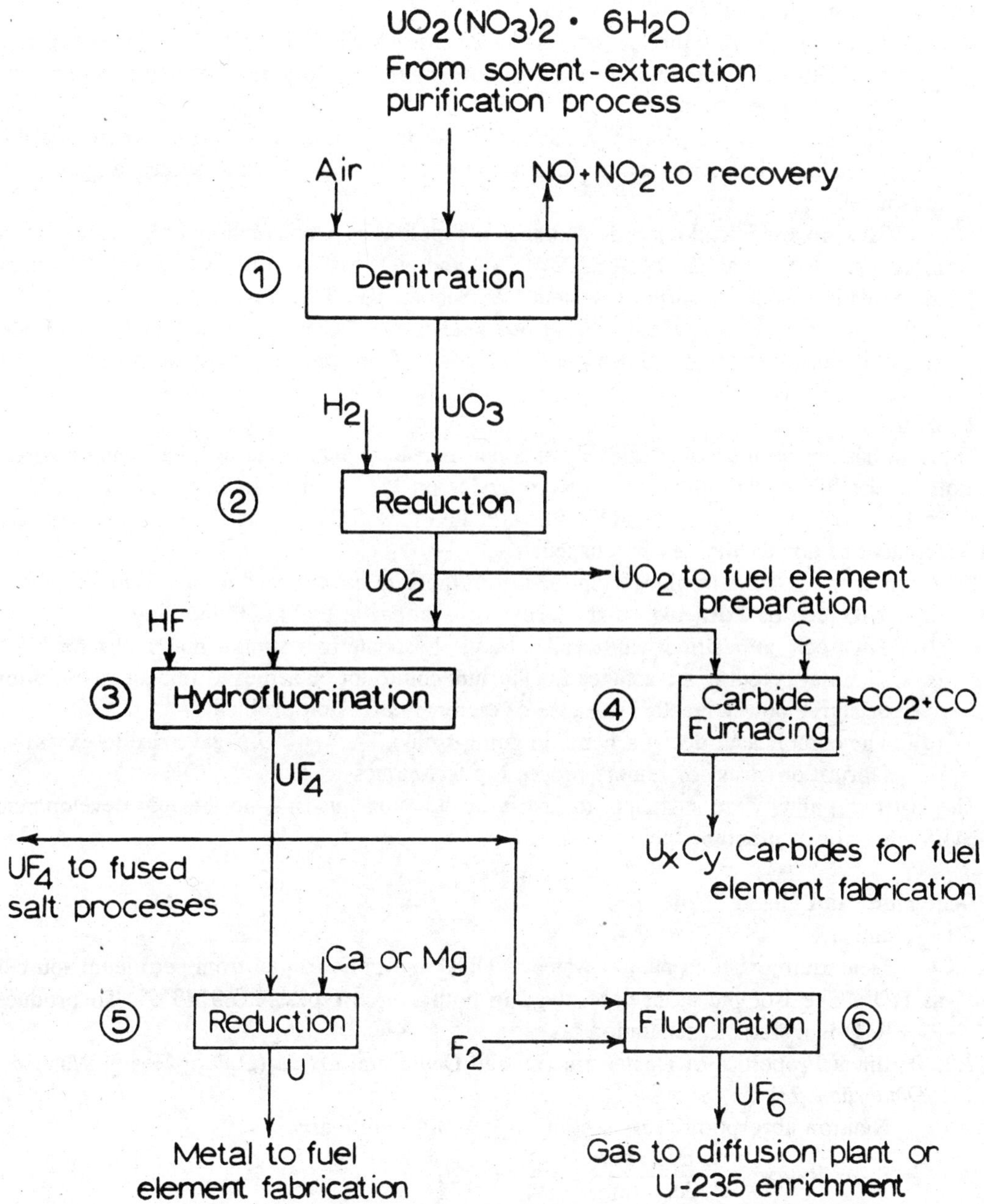

Fig. IIM-3. Uranium conversion processes.

- Highly turbulent mixing insures uniform temperature and ease of temperature control
- Good heat transfer and internal heat exchange surfaces permit high production rates in continuous processing
- A free-flowing product of high bulk density suitable for subsequent process steps
- A closed system with no moving parts minimizes possibility of personal exposure to dust and fumes

This last reason is primarily responsible for the choice of fluid beds where possible in the nuclear industries since all uranium liberates alpha radiation dangerous to personnel.

The process is endothermic and heat is supplied by a conventional high temperature molten salt (45% $NaNO_2$, 55% KNO_2). NO and NO_2 gases are recovered as HNO_3 in an air oxidation, water absorption system (see Section IIE, Nitric Acid).

Other processes now using fluid bed reactors are Steps 2, 3 and 6 in Figure IIM-3 and in the calcination of radioactive liquid wastes from fuel reprocessing plants.

6. Thorium

Thorium has not been used extensively as a power reactor fuel because it has some inherent limitations in the fuel cycle which ultimately operates on U^{233}. Since India possesses monazite sands with 10-11% concentration of ThO_2 in the amount of 200,000 tons of Th, it is important that the development of this technology be pushed.

Experiences in the USA in pioneering the use of thorium have turned up the following facts:

(a) ThO_2 can be extracted satisfactorily from monazite by NaOH leaching

(b) ThO_2 can be purified with tertiary butyl phosphate in a similar manner as for U_3O_8

(c) Thermal breeding advantages for thorium could not be achieved in aqueous solution or slurry power reactors because of extreme corrosion problems

(d) The complicated decay scheme in going from ${}_{90}Th^{232} \rightarrow {}_{92}U^{233}$ gave rise to excessive fabrication costs for remote processing techniques

The last two points were sufficient to justify abandoning most of the thorium development in the U.S. in favor of uranium fuel cycles.

7. Deuterium and Heavy Water

7.1. Abundance

Deuterium exists in natural water as HDO and in hydrogen from petroleum sources as HD. The isotopic atom percentage in both source types is 0.0143%. To produce 99+% D is a sizeable separation task.

7.2. Pertinent Properties of Deuterium (D) and Deuterium Oxide (D_2O or Heavy Water)

Deuterium (D)

Neutron absorption cross section (σ_a) = 0.46 millibarns

$$\text{Ratio}: \frac{\sigma_a \text{ hydrogen}}{\sigma_a \text{ deuterium}} = \frac{330}{0.46} = 720.$$

The low neutron absorption cross section of deuterium relative to hydrogen explains why it is in demand in reactors where neutrons are expensive. It permits the use of natural uranium fuel for reactors, an important point for Indian technology which provides no uranium enrichment facilities.

Relative volatility ratio:

$$\alpha_{H-D} = \sqrt{\frac{P_{H_2}}{P_{D_2}}} = 1.40 \text{ at } 1.6 \text{ atms.}$$

Deuterium oxide (D_2O)

B.P. at 1 atm. = 102.6°C
Vapor pressure at 100°C = 722 mm
Relative volatility ratio:

$$\alpha_{H_2O-D_2O} = \sqrt{\frac{P_{H_2O}}{P_{D_2O}}} = 1.026 \text{ at } 100°C$$

7.3. Separation Processes

The ideal process for concentrating deuterium should have these characteristics:

- Independence from any industrial process
- No by-product given off
- Use natural water as D source
- Have lowest cost

Methods of separating deuterium are tabulated as:

Method	*Material Used*	*Separation Factor*
(1) Dual temperature exchange	H_2S-H_2O	2.2 at 35°C, 1.8 at 135°C
(2) Distillation	H_2O	1.05 at 100 mm
(3) Electrolysis	H_2O	7-8
(4) Distillation	H_2	1.75

Because the economics in making a 6,500 concentration step-up by one type of process is not favorable, a combination of processes as shown in Figure IIM-4 is used for production of heavy water.

7.3.1. Dual temperature exchange

A number of processes involving HD-containing gas can be employed. The best one from a separation factor-low heat input standpoint is the water-H_2S system based on the following exchange:

$$\text{(a)} \quad H_2O + HDS \underset{r\,@\,135°C}{\overset{f\,@\,35°C}{\rightleftharpoons}} HDO + H_2S$$

$$\text{(b)} \quad H_2O + D_2S \underset{r\,@\,135°C}{\overset{f\,@\,35°C}{\rightleftharpoons}} D_2O + H_2S$$

$$\text{(c)} \quad 2HDO \rightleftharpoons D_2O + H_2O$$

At operating concentrations of 0.015 to 15 atom % D, the exchange is predominantly by equation (a) involving HDO and HDS.

The exchange is carried out in conventional gas-liquid contactors of the sieve or bubble tray type. The left-hand portion of Figure IIM-4 is the schematic flow diagram with the stagewise operating graph for a set of stages given next.

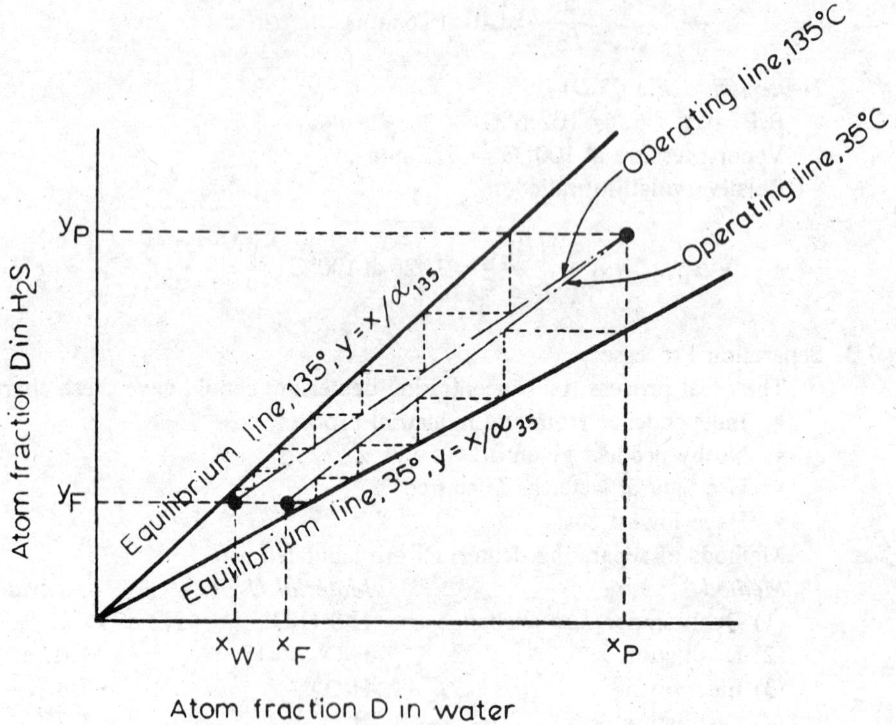

McCabe-Thiele diagram for dual-temperature water-H_2S exchange process.

Natural water at 0.015 atom% D, given as x_F in the operating diagram, is enriched in deuterium by contact with sulfide gas at low temperature where the forward reaction is favored. A portion of the enriched water at concentration x_p is sent to the next concentration unit. The balance is sent through the hot tower where the water is stripped of deuterium by the reverse reaction (r). The exit sulfide gas is enriched in deuterium to provide reboil vapor for the cold tower.

Heat is conserved by heat exchange between stages and within a stage. Modern plants, such as the Savannah River plant of the DuPont at Aiken, South Carolina, USA, use two sets of stages to produce x_p of around 15 atom % D which is fed to the distillation unit.

Major Engineering Problems

- Choice of temperatures and pressures—design principles require the largest possible temperature difference between the hot and cold towers. High pressures are advantageous to attain high mass flows at allowable linear velocities in towers of reasonable diameter. The upper limit of pressure is well-defined as that where the solid hydrate of H_2S forms at a given cold tower temperature. The triple point for the hydrate is 29.5°C and 22.1 atms. It was expedient to choose a class of standard 20 atms. piping pressure fittings for the design. The operating temp-

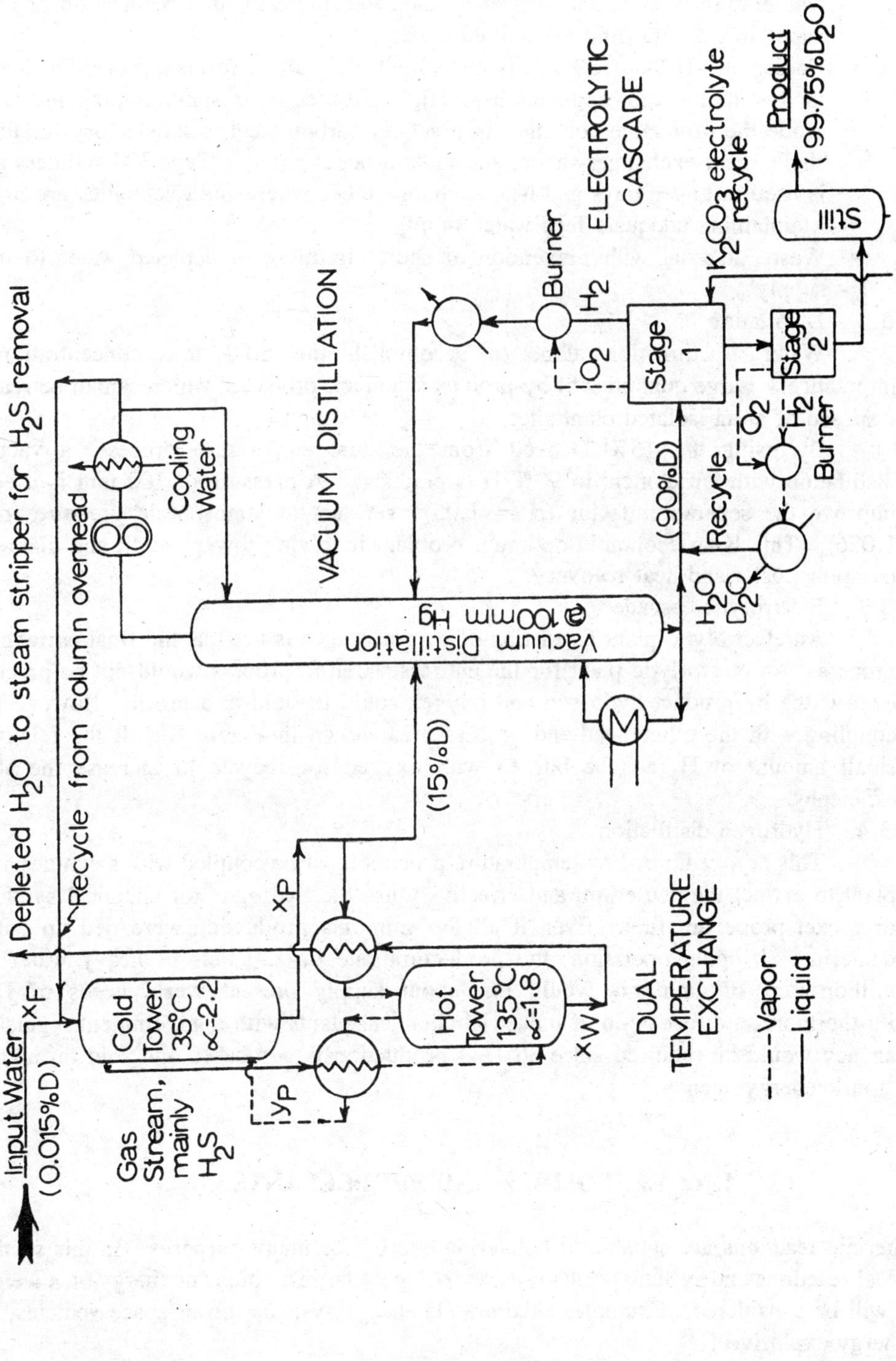

Fig. IIM-4. Heavy water (D_2O) production.

erature was set at 35°C for the cold tower. The optimum temperature in the hot tower is not as well-defined, but above 140°C the gain from increase in temperature is more than offset by the rapid increase in concentration of water vapor in gas returning to the cold tower.

- Corrosion—H_2S corrodes carbon steel but iron sulfide forms a protective coating in low momentum applications. High turbulence or spray impingement will erode the protective coating. In practice, carbon steel is satisfactory for tower shells, heat exchanger shells, and most process piping. Type 304 stainless steel is used in tower trays and heat exchange tubes where fluid velocities are high.
- Maintaining adequate feed water supply.
- Waste disposal with prevention of short circuiting of depleted water to input supply.

7.3.2. Distillation

Water fractionation alone to accomplish the 6,500-fold concentration is impractical. Large quantities of by-product steam are produced which cannot be readily disposed of at an isolated plant site.

By using the 15% D feed from the dual-temperature process, a vacuum distillation with enrichment to 90% D is practical. A pressure of 100 mm is used to improve the separation factor (α = 1.05) over that at atmospheric pressure (α = 1.026). This is an economic optimum problem involving tower height and diameter, pumping costs, and heat recovery.

7.3.3. Electrolytic cascade

An electrolytic plant consisting of several stages is used as the final enrichment process. An electrolytic plant for the entire separation process would not be practical even if the by-product hydrogen and oxygen could be sold at a profit. However, by coupling with the other head-end processes as shown in Figure IIM-4, the relatively small amount of H_2 can be burned with oxygen for recycle to increase the stage efficiency.

7.3.4. Hydrogen distillation

This cryogenic or low-temperature process must be coupled with a synthesis gas plant to extract the deuterium and effectively use the hydrogen for chemical synthesis or rocket propellant fuel. Even if all the ammonia production were tied up with a deuterium stripping operation, the production rate of 230 tons of heavy water per million tons of ammonia would just about supply present world needs of D_2O. Furthermore, a direct tie-in of industrial chemical plants with a government regulatory agency would be required since all D_2O production is purchased and sold through an atomic energy agency.

IIN. EXPLOSIVES AND PROPELLANTS

Exothermic reactions are capable of delivering energy for many purposes. In this section, only chemical reactions and systems which release extremely large amounts of energy on a weight-time basis will be considered. Examples cited are (1) energy systems for air-space vehicles, and (2) high energy explosives.

Indian chemical engineers play a vital role in developing, maintaining safety, and operating such high energy systems. In February 1964, India entered the space age with the firing of the first space rocket at Thumba in Kerala. Since then, a large space research center has been set up here. A rocket launching complex has also been constructed at Sirhari Kota in Andhra Pradesh. The first Indian space satellite was expected to be put in orbit around 1975. India also has plans to put up a communications satellite into a synchronous orbit.

A thorough knowledge of thermodynamics, kinetics, physical properties and behavior of materials under extreme conditions of pressure and temperature is a prime requisite.

Energy Systems for Air-Space Vehicles

1. Introduction

The major interest in developing energy systems for air-space vehicles is centered on rocket propellants although there is still some need for high energy liquid fuel systems for manned aircraft. Thus, a knowledge of propulsion principles is necessary to understand energy systems requirements. The next section is an outline of the important considerations in propulsion needed to guide selection and development of appropriate energy systems.

2. Propulsion Fundamentals

The primary function of a propulsion system is to accelerate a given mass, called payload, from rest to a desired velocity, requiring a force labelled as thrust. Using the chemical rocket as an example, the thrust is developed by a chemical reaction which produces hot gases of mass *dm* in time *dt* inside a chamber which expand through an exhaust nozzle.

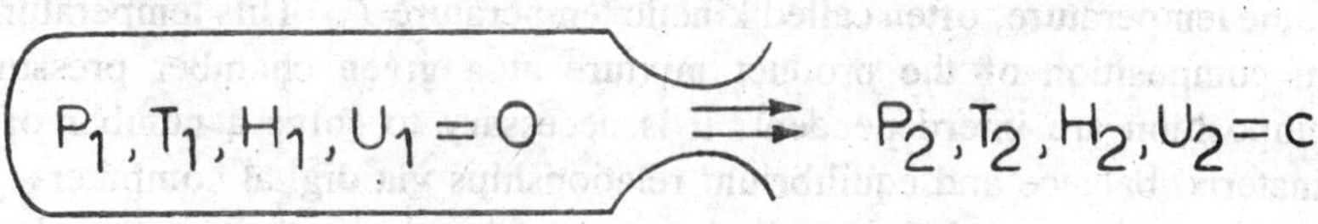

P = pressure H = enthalpy
T = temperature U = velocity
c = velocity of sound

Because of the constricting nozzle, chamber pressure p_1 is created in excess of the ambient pressure which exists at the end of well-designed nozzle section. This excess pressure integrated over the entire inside area A of the chamber is the resultant thrust equal to the time rate of change of momentum of the reaction products.

$$\text{Thrust} = pdA = F = \frac{(U_2 - U_1)}{g_c} \cdot \frac{dm}{dt}, \tag{1}$$

where g_c = gravitational conversion constant = 9.7 kg m-meter/kg f-sec^2. With the knowledge that reaction product jet velocity U is much larger than unreacted propellant velocity

$$U_2 - U_1 \cong U_2 = c, \tag{2}$$

Eq. (1) becomes

$$F = \left(\frac{c}{g_c}\right)\left(\frac{dm}{dt}\right) = \left(\frac{c}{g}\right) \cdot \left(\frac{g}{g_c} \cdot \frac{dm}{dt}\right) = \left(\frac{c}{g}\right) \cdot \left(\frac{dW}{dt}\right), \tag{3}$$

where W = weight of propellant.

Defining the specific impulse I_{sp} as

$$I_{sp} = c/g, \tag{4}$$

there results from (3)

$$I_{sp} = \frac{F}{(dW/dt)} = \frac{\text{kg} \cdot \text{force}}{\frac{\text{kg} \cdot \text{mass}}{\text{sec}}}. \tag{5}$$

The specific impulse of a propellant is thus defined as the kgs of thrust obtained from the reaction of a kg of propellant per second. It is a convenient measure of the effectiveness of a given weight of a material as an energy source.

From energy equations of an adiabatic flow process in the rocket

$$-H = -(H_2 - H_1) = \Delta \text{ (kinetic energy)} = \frac{m}{2Jg_c} \cdot (U_2^2 - U_1^2) = \frac{mc^2}{2Jg_c}, \tag{6}$$

where J = mechanical equivalent of heat, 425 kg f-meters/Kcal.

Define $H' = \frac{H}{(g/g_c) \cdot m}$ = enthalpy (Kcal per kg weight of propellant)

and use in equation (6) along with I_{sp} from equation (4).

$$I_{sp} = \sqrt{\frac{2J}{g} \cdot (H_1' - H_2')} = 9.36\sqrt{H_1' - H_2'}. \tag{7}$$

The initial enthalpy H_1 of the reaction product gases in the rocket chamber is controlled by the adiabatic flame temperature, often called kinetic temperature T_1. This temperature is computed for equilibrium composition of the product mixture at a given chamber pressure p_1. Since temperature-composition are interdependent, it is necessary to solve a number of simultaneous equations for material balance and equilibrium relationships via digital computers.

As the product gas is expanded through the nozzle, the kinetic temperature drops so that the equilibrium composition should change. This is known as the shifting equilibrium case. The enthalpy H_2 at the exit might then be computed on a final kinetic temperature T_2. There is a kinetic lag in producing the equilibrium condition so that the actual enthalpy and composition of expanded gas lies between the extremes of initial chamber composition at T_1 and theoretical exit composition. Conservative estimates of specific impulse are based on the chamber composition existent throughout the expansion process, the so-called frozen equilibrium case.

The adiabatic flow process in the expansion through the nozzle can be analyzed for the ideal gas case, giving rise to a different form of the specific impulse equation:

$$I_{sp} = 9.36\sqrt{\frac{T_1}{M} \cdot \frac{\gamma}{\gamma - 1} \cdot [1 - (\frac{P_2}{P_1})^{(\gamma-1)/\gamma}]}, \tag{8}$$

where Υ = specific heat ratio, and M = average molecular weight of reaction products.

Of the terms involved in equation (8), the dominating ones are the chamber kinetic temperature and the molecular weight of the gases. For high specific impulse fuel systems, reactions with high adiabatic flame temperature and low molecular weight products are most desirable.

3. Classification of Energy Systems

Basis—Type of Energy

Systems	I_{sp}, *sec*
Chemical	200-500
Nuclear fission	500-1,500
Free radicals	1,500-2,000
Arc jet	1,000-5,000
Magnetohydrodynamic plasma	30,000-60,000

Only the first two systems are operational, with chemical rockets by far the most versatile of the two.

4. Classification of Chemical Energy Systems

4.1. Basis—Chemical Reactant Characteristics

- *Monopropellant*—a single chemical compound or a homogeneous mixture of compounds, each of which is capable of sustaining an exothermic reaction when catalyzed.
- *Bipropellant*—consists of an oxidizer and reducer (fuel) which will sustain an exothermic reaction when mixed and ignited. Note that high energy propellant systems exclude air as an oxidizer, thus differing from combustion engines.

4.2. Basis—Physical Characteristics (see Table IIN-1)

4.2.1. Solid propellants

- *Double Base*—monopropellant such as nitrocellulose (50-99%) with diphenylamine stabilizer (1-2%) and nitroglycerine explosive (0-50%) or non-explosive plasticizer such as diethyl phthalate (0-30%).
- *Composite*—a mixture of finely ground oxidizer in a matrix of plastic, resinous, or elastomeric fuel material.

Example—Ammonium perchlorate (75%), synthetic rubber (18%), additives (2%).

4.2.2. Liquid propellants

(a) Monopropellant

- Homogeneous—nitromethane, ethyl nitrate
- Compound—liquid ammonia, ammonium nitrate

(b) Bipropellant

Fuel and oxidizer are stored separately with mixing taking place only in the combustion chamber.

Classification according to ignition characteristics when mixed:

Hypergolic—spontaneously ignited

Non-hypergolic—not self-ignited

Principal oxidizers are H_2O_2, HNO_3, N_2O_4, liquid O_2 and liquid F_2.

Principal fuels are kerosene (JP-4), hydrazine (N_2H_4), liquid H_2.

4.2.3. Hybrid propellants—usually a mixture of solid fuel and liquid oxidizer.

Table IIN-1 Properties of Typical Propellants

Oxidizer	*Fuel*	*Ratio : Wt.*	*Oxidizer/ Fuel Vol.*	*Bulk Density, gm/cc* ρ	*Chamber Temp. °C* T_1	*Av. Mol. Wt. of Combustion Products*	I_{sp}, *Sec.* (P_1/P_2 = *68 atms./ 1 atm.*)	$I_{sp}\cdot\rho$
* *Liquid Bipropellants*								
Liquid	92.5% EtOH	1.73	1.23	0.99	3140	24.1	298	285
Oxygen	Hydrazine	0.90	0.80	1.07	3150	19.3	313	335
(LOX)	Hydrogen	4.02	0.25	0.28	2750	10.0	390	172
(B.P. 183°C)	Kerosene	—	—	—	3210	22.4	290	—
Fluorine	Hydrazine	2.30	1.54	1.31	4420	19.4	363	478
(B.P. 187°C)	Ammonia	3.29	1.48	1.18	4290	19.3	357	422
Hydrogen	(B.P. 252°C)	7.60	0.35	0.45	3600	11.8	410	305
5% H_2O_2	Hydrazine	2.17	1.54	1.26	2580	19.5	282	365
Red fuming	Hydrazine	1.47	0.95	1.28	2820	26.8	283	365
HNO_3 (15% NO_2)	Aniline	3.0	—	—	2830	22.0	258	—
N_2O_4	Hydrazine	1.34	0.93	1.22	2990	20.9	292	357
* *Composite Solid Propellants*								
Ammonium perchlorate (oxidizer)								
Polyester-styrene (fuel)		3.0	1.71	1.64	2110	23.4	215	353
* *Liquid Monopropellants*								
Nitromethane		—	—	1.14	2180	—	218	248
Hydrogen Peroxide (87%)		—	—	1.46	715	—	126	184
* *Double Base Solid Propellants*								
Nitro-cellulose-nitroglycerine (Ballistite)		—	—	1.62	2800-3300	—	210	340

5. Basic Considerations in Developing High Performance Chemical Propellant Systems

5.1. Ideal Performance Criteria for Propellants

- High heat of reaction
- Low molecular weight combustion products
- High density
- Easily stored with no special handling problems
- High reliability over wide storage temperature range
- Non-corrosive
- Low toxicity
- Readily ignitable
- Predicted and controllable burning rates
- Non-detonating when exposed to shock, heat, impact, or trace impurities
- Low-cost and amenable to simple system designs

No system today meets all eleven requirements but the tabulation is valuable in setting forth goals for research and development projects.

5.2. Selection of Fuel Systems

5.2.1. High specific impulse

The first requisite is a high heat of reaction. In Section 2, it was proven that a combination of high flame temperature and low molecular weight of gaseous products will maximize I_{sp}.

The energy generated in combustion reaction is derived from breaking of chemical valence bond forces, constituting energy of formation, in fuel and oxidizer molecules, and forming new and stronger valence bonds in the gaseous product molecules. A tabulation of typical valence bond energies is a useful selection guide.

Bond Energies in Kcal

Typical Compound	*Reactants*		*Combustion Products*	
Alcohol	C—O	224	C=O	256
Hydrocarbon	C—C	137	N=N	225
Cyanogen	C—N	129	N=O	150
Oxygen	O—O	117	H—F	134
Hydrogen	H—H	103	C—F	106
Hydrazine	N—H	85	H—O	103
Hydrocarbon	C—H	80		
Fluorine	F—F	36		

In selecting propellant combinations for high flame temperatures, the choice of fuel and oxidizers will be centered on compounds formed from low strength chemical bonds which will yield stable products of high bond energies. As a further guide, a graph of heat of oxidation versus atomic number (Figure IIN-1) shows that the more promising elements to be used as fuels are H, Li, B, Be, C and compounds thereof. Beryllium is not of any practical use because of its extreme toxicity. High energy fuels of the B_xH_y variety are of some interest for high performance manned aircraft engines.

A second point to consider is the availability of combustion energy in the form of translational energy measured by kinetic chamber temperature T_1, the only energy mode available for propulsion. At temperatures above 3,300°K the reaction energy is robbed by combustion products in the dissociation of molecules → atoms → ions, thus putting an upper limit on T_1. The highest kinetic temperature known is 4,420°C for the fluorine-hydrazine systems, principally because HF is not easily dissociated. Combustion gases of the CO_2-H_2O type are limited to about 3,300°C because of the relatively high degree of dissociation of CO_2 and H_2O.

Specific details for a number of types of propellants are listed in Table IIN-1. The cheapest and most practical liquid bipropellant combination is oxygen-kerosene (JP-4 jet fuel). Solid rockets of the perchlorate-rubber type are also used extensively. If cost is not considered, ultimate high performance rockets will use liquid bipropellants with fluorine as the oxidizer.

5.2.2. Burning rate

In accordance with equation (5) of Section 2, the total force F developed is the product of the specific impulse I_{sp} multiplied by the burning rate. The latter is an important design variable.

- Burning rate control in liquid propellant systems

For bipropellant systems, the oxidizer and fuel are pumped at controlled rates through a premix chamber into the combustion chamber. The combustion rate is fixed by the dimensions of the chamber and the ability to cool the walls of the chamber and the throat. Heat transfer from the chamber walls is accomplished by: (1) regenerative cooling in which one of the propellants is circulated through cooling jackets before ad-

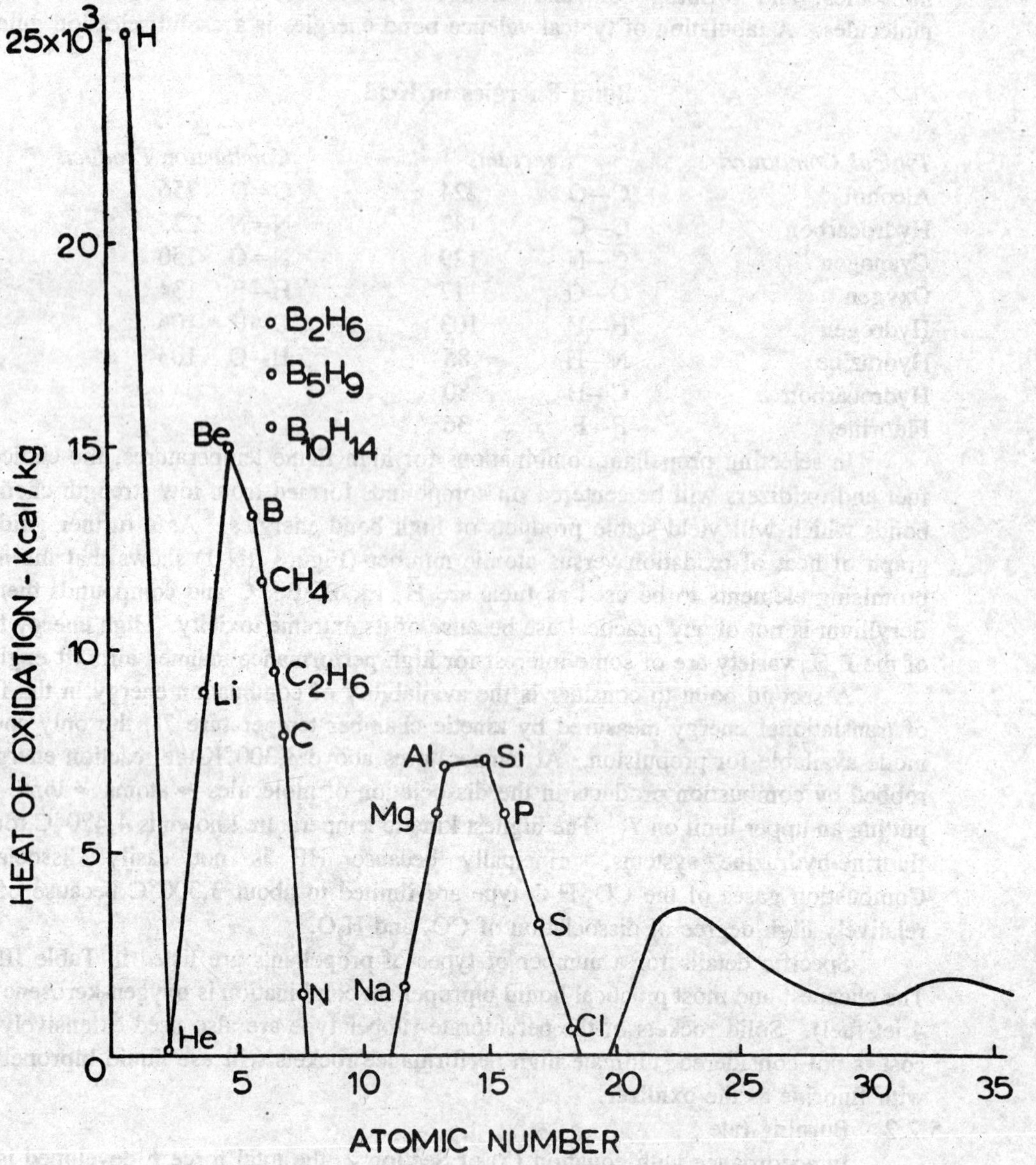

Fig. IIN-1. Heat of oxidation for various chemical elements.

mittance to the premix chamber, (2) film or sweat cooling where the propellant is added through a porous wall to form a cool protective film. Rocket performance is slightly decreased because the coolant film does not burn efficiently.

- Burning rate control in solid propellant systems

The most significant design principle in the burning of solid propellants is that the burning proceeds in a direction perpendicular to the burning surface. For a given chamber diameter and propellant composition, the burning rate is controlled by the free area to solid area configurations. Two common examples are illustrated.

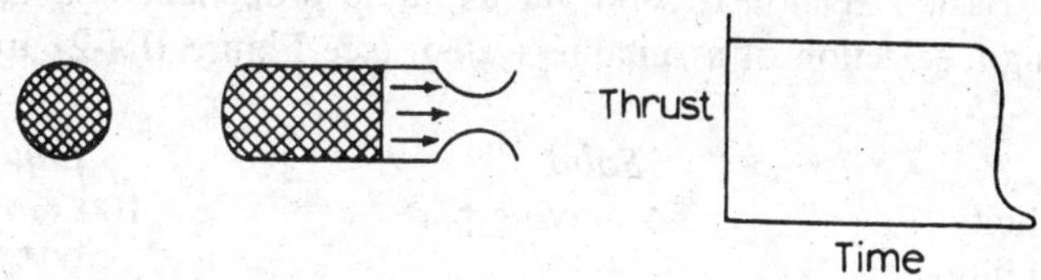

(a) Cigar or end burning

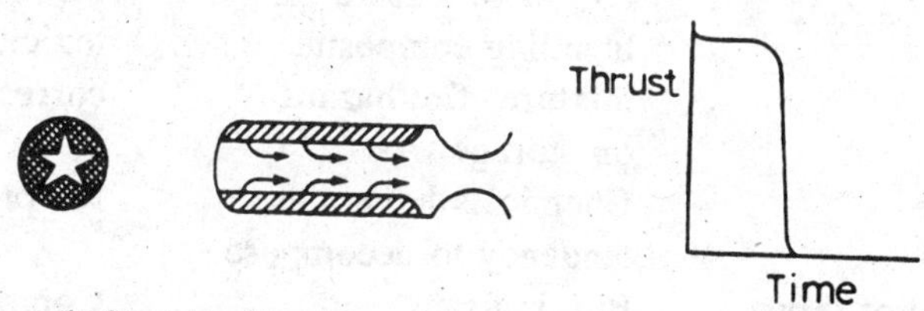

(b) Star internal burning

The internal burning type will give higher thrust for a shorter duration. The burning rate r_s in length/time is pressure sensitive as shown by a typical empirical equation:

$$r_s = bp^n, \tag{9}$$

where n varies from 0 to 0.7 with 0.4 being typical when p is expressed in atms. The coefficient b is dependent on prior storage temperature. This temperature sensitivity is a major disadvantage of solid propellants when compared with liquid propellants.

Besides controlling burning rate by geometry and pressure, the solid propellant characteristics are important. Choice of oxidizers of identical particle size distribution will show $KClO_4$ with the highest burning rate and NH_4NO_3 the lowest.

5.2.3. Handling, storage and utilization of propellants

The propellants listed in Table IIN-1 without B.P. designation are storable without losses in the usual chemical storage equipment at normal temperature.

Those liquid chemicals listed with B.P. designations (oxygen, fluorine, and hydrogen) are in the cryogenic class. As such, they require special vacuum-insulated containers in which significant storage losses may occur, otherwise high pressure storage is needed.

- *Hydrogen*—ideal fuel in terms of I_{sp}; has high diffusivity and chemical reactivity, giving smooth combustion; high cooling capacity for regenerative or sweat cooling of thrust chamber. Its real disadvantages are low storage temperature requirements and low density of the liquid (0.7 gm/cc) or high pressure requirements if H_2 gas is stored at normal temperatures. Useful fuel for nuclear rockets (see Section 6).
- *Fluorine*—most promising of all oxidizers; very toxic, can be transported and stored in aluminum or stainless steel tanks, jacketed for liquid nitrogen and

the whole container insulated with a vacuum jacket. Fluorine-containing combustion products, *e.g.*, HF, are an air pollution problem when emitted from ground take-off rockets. Water reacts with fluorine leakage to produce soluble HF which can be neutralized.

- *Oxygen*—most used cryogenic oxidizer with no corrosion or toxicity problems such as found with fluorine; ultimate specific impulse x density is too low (172 for O_2-H_2 versus 305 for F_2-H_2).

5.2.4. Choice of propellant systems

Basic selection is solid versus liquid propellants. Some of the considerations in making a selection of a suitable system (see Figure IIN-2) are:

Item	*Solid*	*Liquid*
Simplicity	3-4 moving parts	100 moving parts
Reliability	99%	97%
Safety	Explosion hazard on blending composite mixture, fire hazard on storage	Fire hazard, plus toxicity and corrosiveness
Storage	Chemicals have tendency to decompose	No problems
Control of thrust	Burning rate uncontrollable if initial propellant temperature is permitted to vary	Complete
Ultimate I_{sp}	300	412
Cost versus size	Low-cost for small size rockets; launching systems inexpensive	Only adaptable to expensive, large size, long-range rockets; launching systems expensive

5.3. Safety Requirements

In addition to normal chemical plant hazards, the rocket and propellant industry handles potentially high energy materials which can be explosive, toxic and corrosive. For these reasons, safety of personnel and capital investment protection are of paramount importance in design and production. Some of the safety practices encountered include:

- Isolation—individual buildings where dangerous materials are processed are separated by distance (>100 meters) and barricades
- Ventilation and floor drainage—must be considered for corrosive and toxic liquid propellants
- Fire or explosion protection—automatic deluge sprinkler systems installed; buildings are fireproof construction and often barricaded; floors are electrical conducting, all other materials are spark-proof and explosion-proof.
- Size control—for batch operations, particularly in final blending of composite propellants, the amount is limited and operation is isolated and automated; continuous mixing preferred since it minimizes hold-up in processing equipment

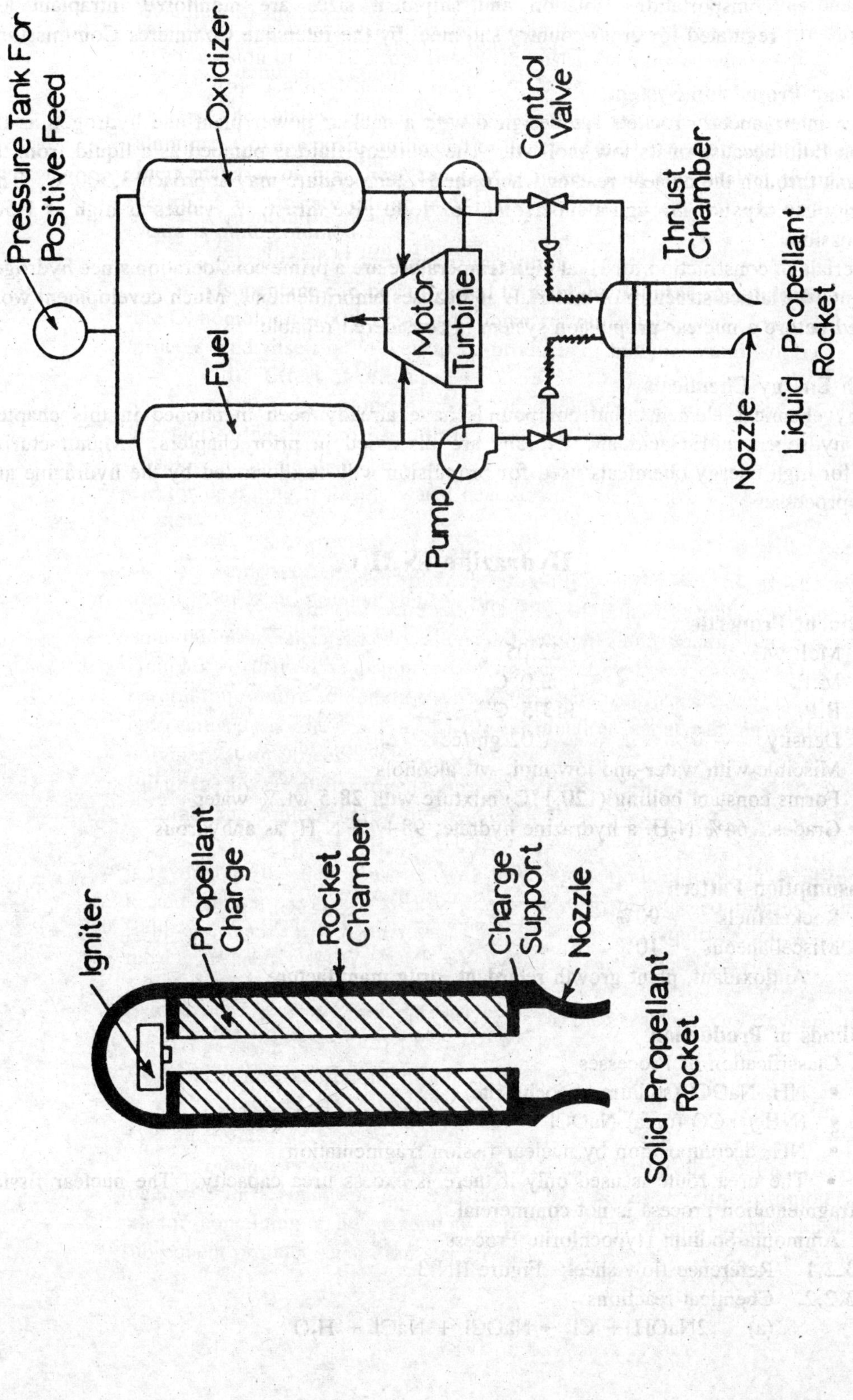

Fig. IIN-2. Characteristics of liquid and solid propellant systems.

- Transportation—isolation and shipment sizes are monitored intraplant and regulated for cross-country shipment by the Interstate Commerce Commission

6. Nuclear Propulsion System

Large interplanetary rockets are designed with a nuclear power plant and hydrogen as the propulsion fluid because of its low mol. wt. The working fluid is pumped as a liquid from the storage tank through the nuclear reactor where the H_2 temperature may approach 3,300°C. This high energy gas expands through a supersonic nozzle to give thrust. I_{sp} values as high as 1,500 sec are possible.

Materials of construction for H_2 at high temperature are a prime consideration since hydrogen diffuses into the lattice structure of materials and causes embrittlement. Much development work is required before a nuclear propulsion system is considered reliable.

7. High Energy Chemicals

Many chemical elements and compounds have already been mentioned in this chapter. Oxygen, hydrogen, nitric acid and its salts are discussed in prior chapters. Manufacturing methods for high energy chemicals used for propulsion will be illustrated by the hydrazine and diborane processes.

Hydrazine (N_2H_4)

1. Pertinent Properties

Mol. wt.	32.05
M.P.	2.0°C
B.P.	113.5°C
Density	1.02 gm/cc

Miscible with water and low mol. wt. alcohols

Forms constant boiling (120.1°C) mixture with 28.5 wt.% water

Grades: 64% N_2H_4 a hydrazine hydrate; 98+ % N_2H_2 as anhydrous

2. Consumption Pattern

Rocket fuels	90%
Miscellaneous	10%

Antioxidant, plant growth retardant, drug manufacture

3. Methods of Production

3.1. Classification of Processes

- NH_3-NaOCl (sodium hypochlorite)
- $(NH_2)_2 \cdot CO$ (urea)-NaOCl
- NH_3 decomposition by nuclear fission fragmentation

The urea route is used only if there is excess urea capacity. The nuclear fission fragmentation process is not commercial.

3.2. Ammonia-Sodium Hypochlorite Process

3.2.1. Reference flow sheet: Figure IIN-3

3.2.2. Chemical reactions

(a) $2NaOH + Cl_2 \rightarrow NaOCl + NaCl + H_2O$

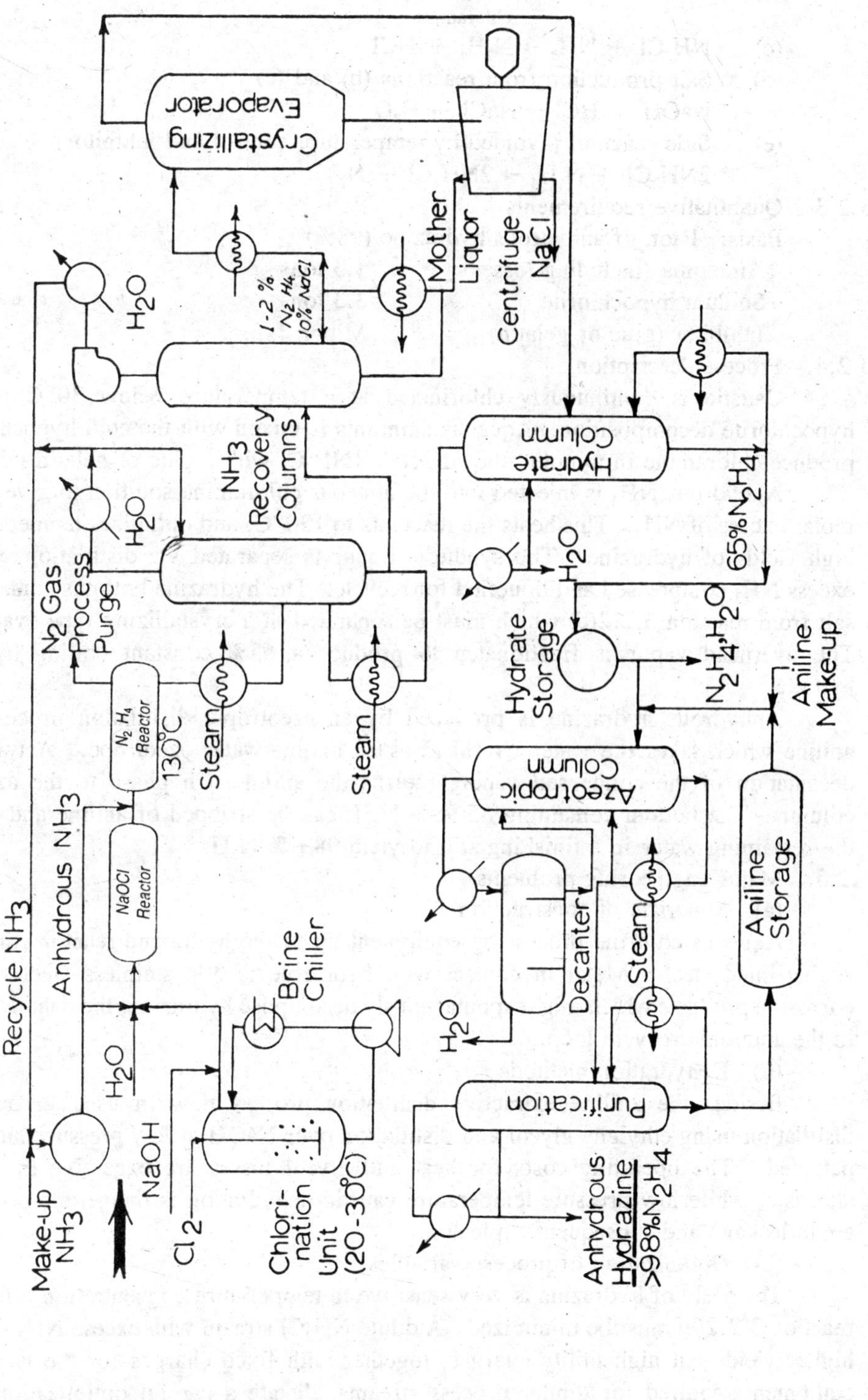

Fig. IIN-3. Production of hydrazine by the ammonia-sodium hypochlorite process.

(b) $NH_3 + NaOCl \rightarrow NH_2Cl + NaOH$
chloramine

(c) $NH_2Cl + NH_3 \rightarrow N_2H_4 + HCl$

(d) Salt production from reactions (b) and (c)
$NaOH + HCl \rightarrow NaCl + H_2O$

(e) Side reaction (avoided by temperature control and inhibitor)
$2NH_2Cl + N_2H_4 \rightarrow 2NH_4Cl + N_2$

3.2.3. Quantitative requirements

Basis: 1 ton of anhydrous hydrazine (98%)

Ammonia (including losses)	1.3 tons
Sodium hypochlorite	3.3 tons
Inhibitor (glue or gelatin)	Minor

3.2.4. Process description

Caustic is continuously chlorinated at a temperature below 30°C to avoid hypochlorite decomposition. Aqueous ammonia is mixed with the cold hypochlorite to produce chloramine in a mole ratio of $3NH_3/1NH_2Cl$ with a glue or gelatin inhibitor.

Anhydrous NH_3 is injected into the aqueous chloramine solution to give a 20-25 molar excess of NH_3. This heats the reactants to 130°C, and optimizes temperature for high yields of hydrazine. The synthesis liquor is separated via distillation, with the excess NH_3 compressed and liquefied for recycle. The hydrazine bottoms contain some salt from reaction 3.2.2(d) which must be separated in a crystallizing type evaporator. The overhead vapor is fractionated to produce a 65% constant boiling hydrazine hydrate.

Anhydrous hydrazine is produced by an azeotropic distillation process using aniline which takes the water overhead as an aniline-water azeotrope. A two-phase decantation of the condensed vapors returns the aniline-rich phase to the azeotrope column. The bottom containing 85-90% N_2H_4 can be stripped of aniline and most of the remaining water in a finishing still to yield 98+% N_2H_4.

3.2.5. Major engineering problems

(a) Materials of construction

Aqueous chlorine processing equipment up to the hydrazine reactor consists of rubber-lined steel. Metal in contact with hydrazine is 304 stainless steel to avoid corrosion products which might spontaneously decompose hydrazine; the balance is steel in the ammonia recycle loop.

(b) Dehydration methods

Besides the aniline extractive distillation process now in use, an extractive distillation using ethylene glycol and distillation over NaOH at low pressure have been patented. The operating costs for heat and glycol losses are excessive in the first alternate, while low pressure-temperature caustic dehydration is dangerous because of air in leakage and subsequent explosion.

(c) Optimization of process variables

The yield of hydrazine is very sensitive to temperature-concentration effects and reaction 3.2.2(e) must be minimized. A dilute NH_2Cl stream with excess NH_3 will give higher yields but high utility charges, together with fixed charges for the large-sized equipment required for diluter process streams, dictate a careful optimization of the process design.

(d) Safety considerations

Contact with air is avoided by operating under N_2 seals at pressures never less than atmospheric. The N_2 gas is obtained from the hydrazine reactor as the result of some decomposition of hydrazine.

Anhydrous N_2H_4 is shipped under N_2 gas in stainless steel drums; a trace of organic inhibitor is added to provide stability.

Outdoor type construction is used throughout for better ventilation and avoidance of explosive mixture in case of leakage.

3.2.6. Economics—U.S.

Hydrazine is largely used as rocket fuel for military purposes, being in commercial development since World War II (1945). At present prices, it is not attractive for commercial jet fuel or other non-fuel purposes. Limited military usage has restricted the production to two suppliers by the chloramine route. A major break-through by fission fragment synthesis or other new processes can occur with an appreciable lowering in price and much greater production demands.

Boron-Hydrogen Compounds

As seen in Figure IIN-1, compounds of boron and hydrogen (boranes) furnish high heats of combustion.

Diborane	B_2H_6	17,800 Kcal/kg	I_{sp} range 280-300 sec
Pentaborane	B_5H_9	16,700	
Decaborane	$B_{10}H_{14}$	15,300	

For this reason, the processes for manufacturing these high energy compounds of extreme toxicity are of interest.

1. Pertinent Physical Properties

1.1. M.P., B.P., Density

Compound	*Normal State*	*M.P., °C*	*B.P., °C*	*Density, gm/cc*
Diborane	Colorless gas	—164	—92	0.43
Pentaborane	Colorless liquid	—47	58	0.61
Decaborane	White solid	103	213	0.94

1.2. Relative Toxicities

Compound	*Max. Permissible Conc., ppm*	*Odor detection, ppm*	*Hazard Index* vap. press./LC_{50}*
Diborane	0.1	3.7	$2 \times 10^6/80 = 25{,}000$
Pentaborane	0.01	2.5	$2.75 \times 10^5/6.8 = 40{,}000$
Decaborane	0.05	0.35	$63/1.4 = 45$
Hydrazine		69.83	$1.9 \times 10^4/570 = 33$
Carbon tetrachloride	100	—	$1.44 \times 10^5/2.39 \times 10^4 = 6$
Benzene	100	—	$1.25 \times 10^5/1.6 \times 10^4 = 7.8$

*Vap. press. in ppm (volume basis @ 20°C)

LC_{50} is ppm dosage for 50% kill cn rats in 4 hours

2. Methods of Production

2.1. Reference Flow Sheet: Figure IIN-4

2.2. Chemical Reactions

(a) $3CH_3OH + H_3BO_3 \rightarrow B(OCH_3)_3 + 3H_2O$
methyl borate

(b) $Na + H \rightarrow NaH$

(c) $7NaH + B(OCH_3)_3 \rightarrow NaBH_4 + 6Na + 3CH_3OH$
sodium borohydride

(d) $3NaBH_4 + BX_3 \rightarrow 2B_2H_6 + 3NaX$; X = F or Cl

(e) $B_2H_6 + xH_2 \rightarrow yB_5H_9 + zB_5H_{11}$

(f) $2B_5H_9 \rightarrow B_{10}H_{14} + 2H_2$

(g) $B_5H_{11} \rightarrow xB_{10}H_{10} + yB_4H_{10} + zH_2$

2.3. Raw Materials

Methanol
Boric Acid
Sodium metal
Industrial grade hydrogen
Boron trifluoride or trichloride
Glycol ether
Mineral oil

2.4. Plant Capacities: 5 tons/day

2.5. Process Description

Methyl borate is prepared by the reaction of methanol with metaboric acid. Sodium hydride is prepared as a dispersion of 5-25 micron crystals in inert mineral oil. This dispersion is added to a jacketed reactor along with methyl borate and the resulting exothermic sodium borohydride reaction is controlled by water-cooling the jacket. The sodium-oil dispersion and methanol vapor are recycled with the sodium borohydride mixed with glycol ether in the diborane reactor. BF_3 or BCl_3 is added to produce diborane gas.

The more desirable pentaborane is prepared by mixing diborane and hydrogen and passing it through a heated catalytic hydrogenerator. If the low vapor pressure decaborane powder is required, a mild pyrolysis of the B_5 boranes accomplishes this.

2.6. Major Engineering Problems

(a) Toxicity control

This problem is acute because of the extremely low maximum permissible concentration of 0.01-0.1 ppm for the boranes. New instrumentation for the required sensitivity had to be developed. In the early development stages, canary birds as monitoring agents were used. By observing such safety precautions as avoidance of inhalation, skin contact, and ingestion, the safety record in the research, development, and production programs since 1947 has been as good as any other chemical industry.

(b) Reactivity control

The explosive nature of reactions of boranes with air or water necessitates extreme care in design and operation of these processes. Reactors are built behind concrete barricades and instrumentation located remotely. All equipment is dried carefully and flushed with nitrogen before adding reaction material.

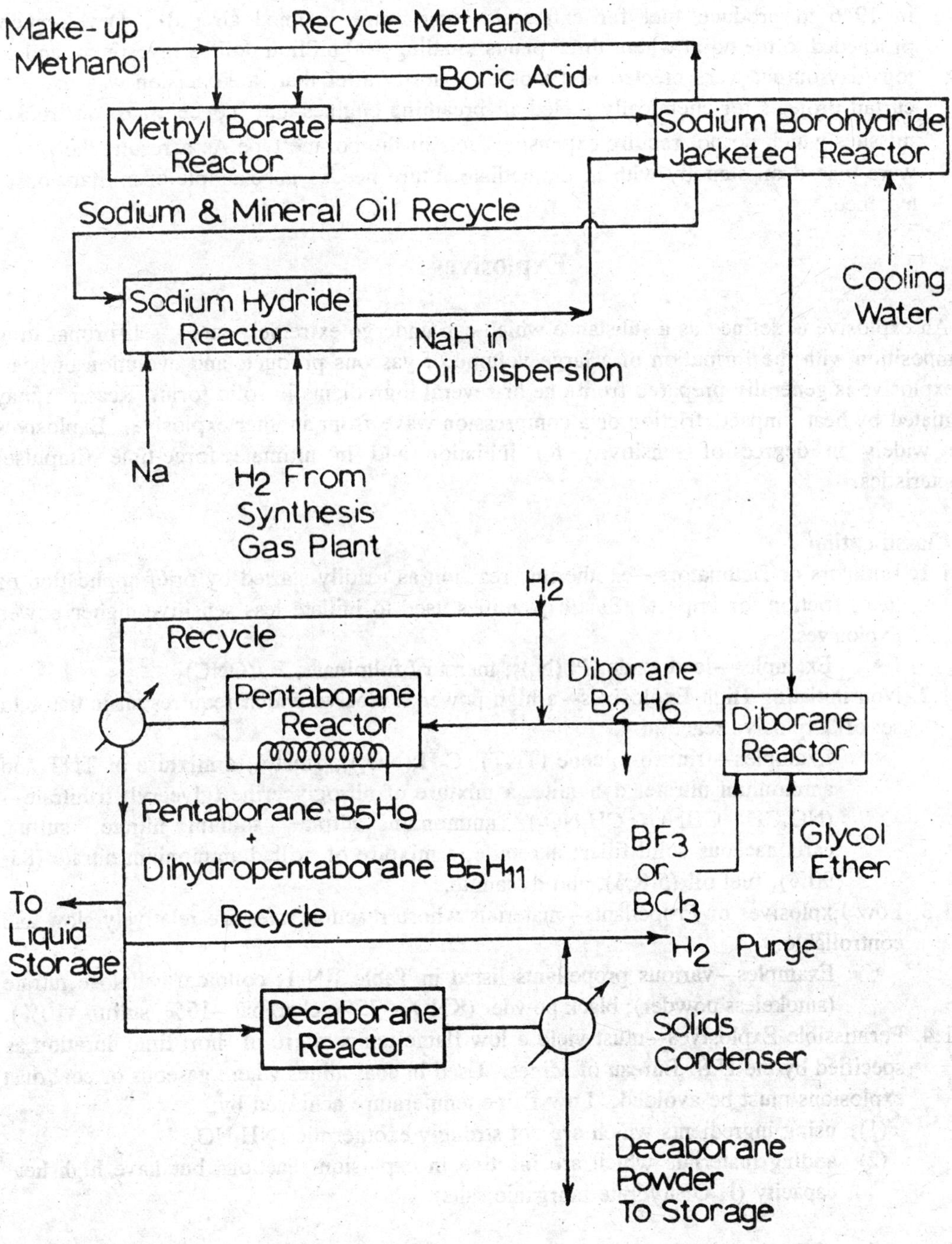

Fig. IIN-4. Production of boranes.

2.7. Economics

The high energy borane fuel program was initiated by the U.S. Department of Defense in 1946 to produce fuel for extremely long range manned aircraft. Development proceeded to the point where three plants totalling 100 million dollars investment and 11 tons/day output were erected in 1956-58. Shortly after that, the decision was made to curtail projects for chemically fueled air-breathing engines and concentrate on rocket missiles which do not require expensive fuels of the borane type.As a result, the plants were placed on standby with no immediate future needs—an example of military obsolescence.

Explosives

An explosive is defined as a substance which can undergo extremely rapid, self-propagating decomposition with the formation of a large volume of gaseous products and evolution of heat. The explosive is generally prepared from one or several ingredients in solid form. Reaction may be initiated by heat, impact, friction or a compression wave from another explosive. Explosives differ widely in degree of sensitivity for initiation and in ultimate force-time (impulse) characteristics.

1. Classification

1.1. Initiators or Detonators—exothermic reaction as readily started by brief application of heat, friction, or impact. Small quantities used to initiate less sensitive higher power explosives.

- Examples—lead azide, $Pb(N_3)_2$; mercury fulminate, $Hg(ONC)_2$

1.2. Non-initiating High Explosives—a high power explosive which requires an initiator to set off explosive reaction.

- Examples—trinitro-toluene (TNT), $C_7H_5(NO_3)_3$; amatol, a mixture of TNT and ammonium nitrate; dynamite, a mixture of nitroglycerine (glyceryl) trinitrate—($NO_3CH_2 \cdot CHNO_3 \cdot CH_2NO_3$), ammonium nitrate, sodium nitrate, sulfur, carbonaceous solid filler; akremite, a mixture of prilled ammonium nitrate (85-90%), fuel oil (5-8%), and dynamite.

1.3. Low Explosives or Propellants—materials whose reaction rates are relatively slow and controllable.

- Examples—various propellants listed in Table IIN-1; colloidal cellulose nitrate (smokeless powder); black powder (KNO_3—75%, charcoal—15%, sulfur—10%).

1.4. Permissible Explosives—must yield a low flame temperature of short time duration as specified by the U.S. Bureau of Mines. Used in coal mines where gaseous or coal dust explosions must be avoided. Low flame temperature achieved by:

(1) using ingredients which are not strongly exothermic (NH_4NO_3)

(2) adding materials which are inactive in explosion reactions but have high heat capacity (H_2O, hydrate inorganic salts).

2. Properties of Explosives

Standard tests are available to measure:

- Power or brisance—combination of force x velocity to achieve shattering characteristics

- Sensitivity—measured by impact loading, friction, and initiating temperature
- Explosion or adiabatic flame temperature
- Velocity of detonation wave

3. Consumption Pattern

The principal uses for explosives of all types can be divided into two broad groups.

3.1. Government Usage

- High explosives for military usage—production depends on war or peace status
- Propellants
  - (a) Military rockets
  - (b) Space travel developments

3.2. Industrial Usage

- High explosives in categories such as:

Coal mining	30%
Metal mining	20
Non-metallic mining and quarrying	23
Construction and road building	25

III

NATURAL PRODUCT INDUSTRIES

Nature synthesizes many organic compounds starting basically from the CO_2-O_2 photosynthesis process. The principal industries based on natural products are:

IIIA Edible and Essential Oils
IIIB Soaps and Detergents; Glycerin
IIIC Paints and Varnishes
IIID Carbohydrates and Fermentation
IIIE Food Industry
IIIF Pulp and Paper Industry
IIIG Coal and Coal Chemicals
IIIH Petroleum

Petroleum ranks near the top in tonnage with paper also high in ranking. The natural product industries are so important in the food and sanitation situation of India that the chemical engineer's role in these industries must not be neglected.

IIIA. EDIBLE AND ESSENTIAL OILS

In this section we deal first with edible oils, with naturally-occurring compounds based on long chain fatty acids and esters (particularly glyceride esters), as well as derivatives such as glycerin, long chain fatty alcohols, sulfates and sulfonates. Products from these compounds are used for food, sanitation, polymers, and in the paint industry. The per capita consumption of all such products is about 7.5 kg per year in India versus 15.5 as a world average.

Another group of organic compounds which are pleasantly odoriferous is the essential oils used in cosmetics, perfumes, soaps, and medicines.

India ranks high among the oilseeds producing countries in the world with, perhaps, the largest number of commercial varieties of oilseeds, such as groundnuts, rape and mustard, sesame, kardiseed, nigerseed, soyabean, sunflower seed, linseed, castor seed, copra, cotton seed and a number of minor seeds of tree origin. Oilseeds take their place, next only to foodgrains, as the second largest agricultural crop. The cultivation of oilseeds in India is spread over various states with a distinct regional pattern covering about 19 to 20 million hectares, which accounts for about 11 percent of the total land under cultivation in the country.

In India where fats of animal origin such as fish oil and lard are seldom used as cooking media, the term "vegetable oils" is used as a synonym for "edible oils." However, it needs to be remembered that there are, on the one hand, vegetable oils such as castor oil and linseed oil which are non-edible and, on the other hand, edible oils like groundnut and coconut oil which are finding increasing industrial applications as in cosmetics, soap making, etc. Edible oils are a major source of nutrition for the people in the country. Oil cakes, which are by-products of the oil extraction process, are important sources of animal nutrition. They can also be processed into protein rich edible flour.

India has a highly developed oil based industry, employing more than 15 million persons. However, it remains an essentially food oil industry, accounting for as much as 83 percent of the total supply of vegetable oil in the country. The major non-food users of oil are the soap, paint and varnish industries. These are the "essential oils."

Solvent extraction is a continuous chemical process for processing oilseeds such as groundnut, soyabean and rapeseed as opposed to physical crushing for oil extraction. Crude vegetable oil, the main product from the solvent extraction process, is primarily used in the manufacture of refined edible oils and vanaspati, and to a lesser extent in glycerols and fatty acids used in soaps and other toiletries. While there are a number of other value-added products for varied applications, the domestic industry and consequently the market for these products is nascent. A by-product of the process is de-oiled cake, which, being high in protein content, is used as cattle feed. A substantial proportion of the domestic production of de-oiled cake is exported to the Middle East and other Asian countries.

Out of the estimated production of 20 million tons, about one million tons is from castor and linseed—non-edible oilseeds. Of the domestic supply of six million tons of edible oils for 1992-93, about five million tons are from the seven major oilseeds and the balance from non-traditional sources such as cotton (3.5 lakh tons), rice bran (2.5 lakh tons) and coconut (1.6 lakh tons) besides various minor oils and solvent extracted oils (2.4 lakh tons). See Table IIIA-1.

Table IIIA-1
Estimate of Oilseeds Production and Oil Availability in India

	Oilseed Production			Oil Available
	1992-93 Trade estimate	1991-92 Official estimate	1992-93 Official estimate	1992-93
				(in million tons)
Edible				
1. Groundnut in shells				
(a) Kharif	5.50	4.85	5.60	-
(b) Rabi	2.40	2.22	2.20	-
Total	7.90	7.07	7.80	1.81
2. Rapeseed and mustard seed	5.85	5.84	5.80	1.99
3. Soyabean	2.90	2.28	2.95	0.45
4. Sunflower				
(a) Kharif	0.70	0.38	0.38	-
(b) Rabi	0.98	0.80	0.80	-
Total	1.68	1.18	1.18	0.35

5. Safflower	0.34	0.20	0.42	0.09
6. Sesame	0.87	0.67	0.69	0.25
7. Nigerseed	0.20	0.19	0.17	0.06
Total edible	19.74	17.43	19.01	5.00
Non-Edible				
8. Linseed	0.05	0.30	0.30	0.12
9. Castorseed	0.70	0.58	0.69	0.22
Total	0.75	0.88	0.99	0.34
Grand Total	20.49	18.31	20.00	5.34

Source: "Kothari's Industrial Directory of India" (1994)

Although India is one of the major oilseeds producing countries in the world accounting for one-tenth of the total world output, her consumption at only 11.24 gm per capita per day is far below that of Brazil (50 gm), South Korea (41), Pakistan (43), China (37) and that of advanced countries whose consumption level is 110-149 gm per day.

The Indian production picture may be contrasted with the worldwide vegetable oil production picture.

Worldwide Vegetable Oil Production
(in 10^6 tons)

	1990
Soya oil	16.9
Palm oil	10.6
Rape oil	8.1
Sunflower oil	8.0
Coconut oil	3.1
	46.7

There are, of course, other oil sources including:

Animal sources:
- Lard from hog fat
- Tallow from beef and mutton fat

Ocean sources:
- Menhaden fish
- Sperm whale
- Codfish

but these are of lesser significance and will not be considered in detail here.

End uses of vegetable oils have been estimated as follows:

Edible	
Liquid oil	57%
Vanaspati (Hydrogenated oil)	19
Soaps and detergents	10
Cosmetics	9
Paints and varnishes	2
Miscellaneous	1

1. Chemical Composition and Physical Properties of Vegetable Oils

1.1. Fats and Oils—mixtures of glycerides of fatty acids where R_1, R_2 and R_3 are not necessarily the same

$$\begin{array}{l} R_1 \cdot CO \cdot O \cdot CH_2 \\ \qquad\qquad\quad | \\ R_2 \cdot CO \cdot O \cdot CH \\ \qquad\qquad\quad | \\ R_3 \cdot CO \cdot O \cdot CH_2 \end{array}$$

By terminology of the industry, oils are all liquid and fats are solid at normal temperatures.

1.2. Waxes—mixed esters of polyhydric alcohols other than glycerin. Usually solid at room temperature.

1.3. Effect of Degree of Saturation—number of double bonds in the fatty acid radical (R) controls the melting point and chemical reactivity as shown in the following table:

R		Number of	Melting	Reactivity to
Name	Composition	Double Bonds	Point, °C	Oxygen
Stearic	$C_{17}H_{35}$	0	69	Nil
Oleic	$C_{17}H_{33}$	1	14	Fair
Linoleic	$C_{17}H_{31}$	2	−5	Rapid
Linolenic	$C_{17}H_{29}$	3	−11	Extremely rapid

The ability to react with oxygen enhances the use of unsaturated fatty acids as film forming vehicles for paints. It also is the cause of rancidity in edible fat products which can be avoided by use of:

- Hydrogenation—removes reactive double bonds
- Antioxidants—compounds which oxidize preferentially to fats without much increase in color or odor

2. Methods of Extracting Vegetable Oils

2.1. Reference Flow Sheet: Figure IIIA-1

2.2. Mechanical

Seeds cleaned and hulled, steam cooked at 220-250°F for 15-20 minutes, then pressed in either:

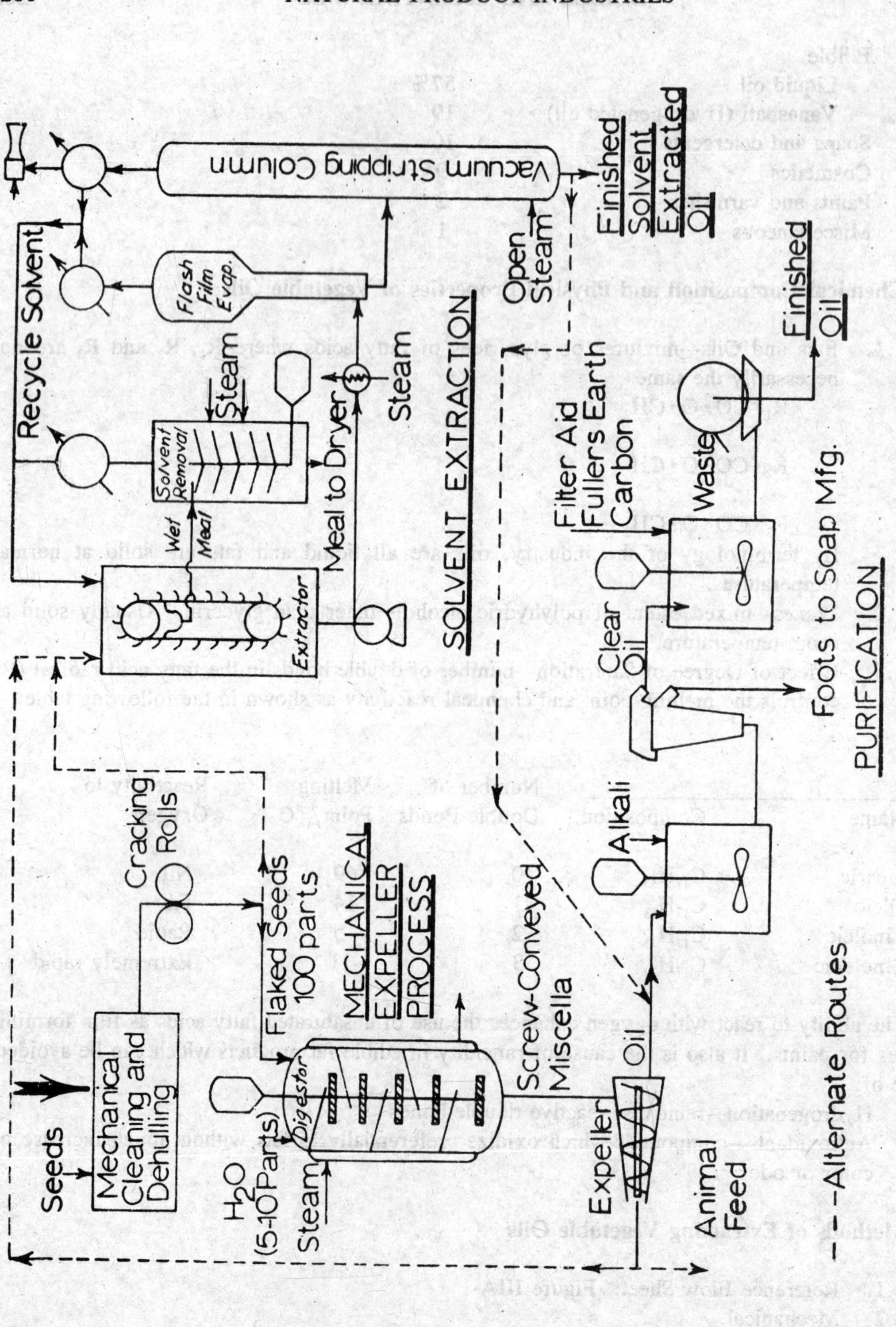

Fig. IIIA-1 Vegetable oil extraction methods.

- Continuous screw extruder or expeller
- Batch hydraulic press

2.3. Solvent Extraction

2.3.1. Characteristics

May be used alone or in combination with mechanical methods. The latter is preferred for most seeds except soyabean since solvent extraction gives

- high yields—98-99% of available oil
- poor quality—dark color, odoriferous, and high free fatty acid content

Combination of expeller and solvent extraction methods yields over 80% as prime quality oil and only 18-19% as the poorer grades.

2.3.2. Types of solvents used

- Petroleum cuts in the hexane range—flammable
- Trichlorethylene—toxic

Despite fire hazards, petroleum solvents are preferred.

2.4. Purification

Alkali such as NaOH or Na_2CO_3 is added to remove free fatty acids as "foots" by centrifugation. Bleaching is done with adsorbent clays such as Fuller's earth and with adsorption carbon. Filtration is done on pre-coat rotary vacuum filters (or plate and frame presses for small capacity plants).

An alternate route is to solvent extract by use of propane. This solvent is miscible with all of the oil below 80°C but is immiscible with fatty acids and color bodies near the critical temperature of propane (96°C). Temperature gradients in an extraction column are used to effect a two-phase separation.

3. Hydrogenation of Oils

Hydrogenation is a unit process which is used in the fat and oil industry to remove double bonds, raise the melting point of the fat, and improve its resistance to rancid oxidation. The major end-product in India is Vanaspati, a solidified household oil for cooking. Other products are vegetable ghee, hardened industrial oils, and partially hydrogenated liquid oil.

3.1. Reference Flow Sheet: Figure IIIA-2

3.2. Chemical Reactions (* indicates activated catalytic state)

(a) $$R_1\,(C = C)_x\,R_2 + (x-y)\,H_2 \xrightarrow{\text{Ni* catalyst}} R_1\,(C = C)_y\,R_2$$

Example:

$$(C_{17}H_{31}COO)_3 \cdot C_3H_5 + 3H_2 \xrightarrow{\text{Ni*}} (C_{17}H_{33}COO)_3 \cdot C_3H_5$$

(b) Nickel catalyst preparation (nickel formate decomposition)

$$Ni(HCOO)_2 \cdot 2H_2O \xrightarrow[\text{(oil base)}]{190^\circ C} Ni^* + 2CO_2 + H_2 + 2H_2O$$

This produces a finely divided catalyst which is preferred for well-stirred hydrogenation reactors.

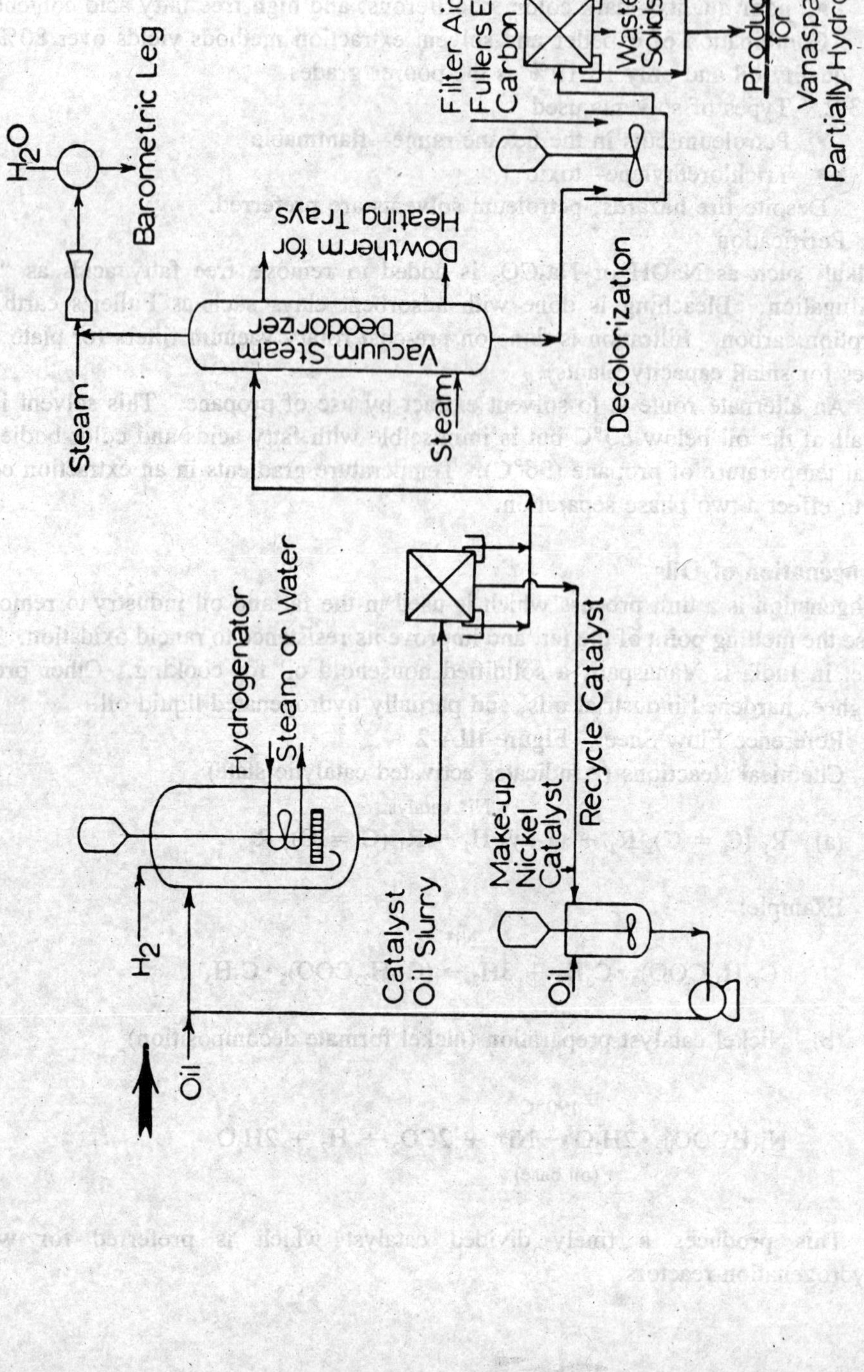

Fig. IIIA-2. Hydrogenation of vegetable oils.

(c) Nickel catalyst preparation (reduced Ni on inert catalyst support)

$$Ni(OH_2) + H_2 \rightarrow Ni^* + H_2O$$
$$NiCO_3 + H_2 \rightarrow Ni^* + H_2O + CO_2$$

Nickel salts are precipitated on inert porous carrier such as kieselguhr or diatomaceous earth and reduced at high temperature in a hydrogen atmosphere.

(d) Nickel catalyst preparation (Raney or spongy nickel method)

$$\underset{\text{alloy}}{2Al \cdot Ni} + 6NaOH \rightarrow \underset{\text{(Raney nickel)}}{Ni^*} + 2NaAlO_3 + 3H_2$$

Produces spongy, high-surface area catalyst when the sodium aluminate is washed out with water.

3.3. Raw Materials

Major raw materials are oils to be hardened, and purified hydrogen which can be obtained from several sources such as:

- Electrolytic H_2O or chlor-alkali
- Steam-iron: reaction of steam on Fe followed by regeneration with water gas
- Synthesis gas processes discussed in IIB

Sulfur containing compounds (SO_2, H_2S) are extreme poisons for the hydrogenation catalyst. These are removed from the last two H_2 processes by cryogenic distillation or a reactive metal guard converter.

3.4. Quantitative Requirements

This depends on the type of oil and extent of saturation desired. A typical example using cottonseed oil is as follows:

(a) Basis: 1 ton hardened oil

Hydrogen	50 Nm^3
Nickel catalyst losses	0.6 kg
Steam	0.5 ton
Cooling water	4.5 tons

(b) Plant capacities: 5-30 ton batch reactors operating on 1-3 hr cycle
Number of reactors will vary from 2 to 10, depending on plant size.

3.5. Process Description

Batch operation is used because of large residence times (1-3 hours) and variation in oil input and product properties from day to day. Batch hydrogenators can treat 5-30 tons of oil per batch; are equipped with coils for heating and cooling, and turbine agitators to disperse the injected hydrogen.

The pressure-temperature relationships are complicated in that the combination controls the selectivity of hydrogenation for certain types of double-bond saturation. For example, ghee-base oil is hydrogenated at low pressures (1-2 atms. gage) and high temperatures (135-180°C) to yield a fat with melting point similar to butter. Vanaspati shortening is produced by hydrogenating at higher pressures (2-3.5 atms. gage) and lower temperatures (120-160°C) to maintain higher melting point fats of maximum stability for cooking purposes.

A typical hydrogenation batch process operates as follows: Oil is charged to the reactor, heated and evacuated to drive off air and water. A catalyst-oil slurry is pumped in;

the catalyst concentration is 5 to 15 kg per ton of oil. Hydrogen is introduced and the steam is turned off since reaction is mildly exothermic. After the desired hydrogenation has ensued as checked by an iodine number iteration, the batch is cooled and filtered to recover the catalyst for reuse.

The hydrogenated oil is next deodorized in a Dowtherm heated, steam sparging vacuum tower which operates on a continuous basis. The oil is next decolorized with Fuller's earth, carbon or similar absorbent, then filtered, mixed with vitamins, and sent to the packaging-storage operations. This involves refrigerated slow-cooling in packaged tins to reproduce the granular structure of ghee. For non-granular products used for confectionery and bakery purposes, rapid chilling in a jacketed cylinder equipped with fast-revolving internal scraper blades is employed.

3.6. Major Engineering Problems

3.6.1. Thermodynamics and kinetics

(a) Heat of reaction

The heat of reaction for hydrogenation of oils is mildly exothermic as shown by the following generalized diagram:

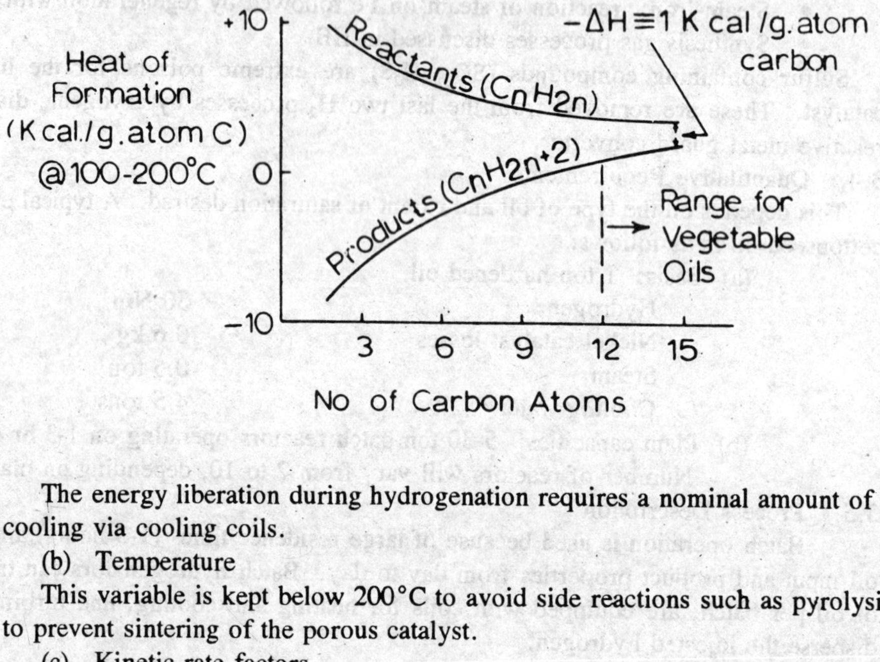

The energy liberation during hydrogenation requires a nominal amount of water cooling via cooling coils.

(b) Temperature

This variable is kept below 200°C to avoid side reactions such as pyrolysis and to prevent sintering of the porous catalyst.

(c) Kinetic rate factors

For a gas-liquid reaction of the hydrogenation type:

$$H_2\,(g) + \text{Oil}\,(1) \rightarrow \text{Fat}\,(1),$$

research has shown that a series of rate processes exist with 8 kinetic resistances pictured by this analog diagram:

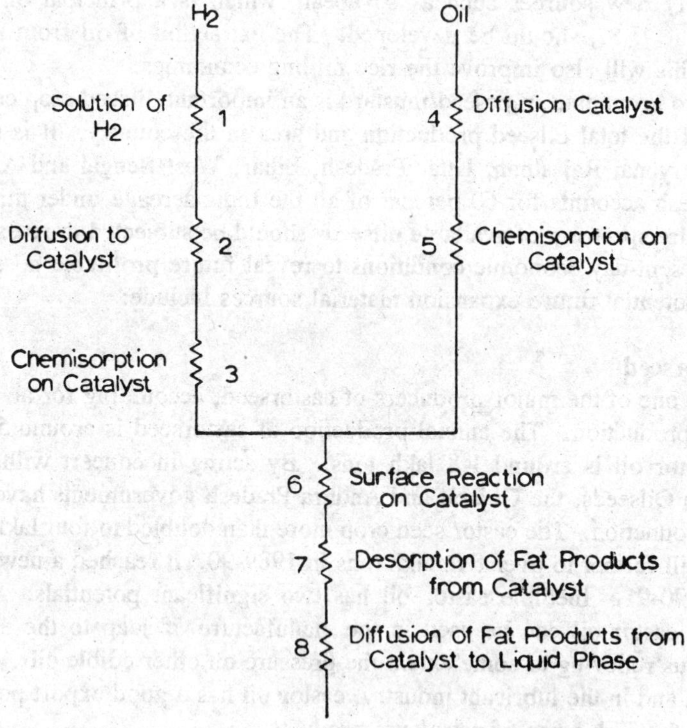

As typically found for many heterogeneous catalytic reactions, the rate behavior was characterized as:

- Surface reaction and adsorption controls reaction rate in the vicinity of 100°C
- Rates are increased by increasing H_2 pressure (maximum pressure of 7 atms. gage used commercially)
- At 180°C, mass transfer for solution of H_2 and diffusion to and from catalyst are the rate-controlling steps

3.6.2. H_2 handling problems

Hydrogen gas has a wide explosive limit range (4.1-74.2%). All equipment should be leak-tested with freon or helium detectors before operating. While hydrogen embrittlement is a problem at high temperatures and pressures such as found in the ammonia synthesis plants, carbon steel can be used throughout for oil hydrogenation.

4. Economics

4.1. Raw Materials

Groundnuts (peanuts) furnish the principal oil stock for India. Although it is possible to expand this type of source, other oils such as cottonseed for better quality Vanaspati, linseed for paints, and coconut for soap should have increased support. The cottonseed crushing industry is not presently an attractive economic venture for a number of reasons, *e.g.*, (1) high price of whole seed because of competition for cattle feed usage, (2) low oil yield, (3) no market for oil cake.

Entirely new sources such as soyabean, which is a principal oil and cattle food source in the U.S., should be developed. The extraction of oil from rice bran will be pushed. This will also improve the rice milling economics.

Next to groundnut, rapeseed/mustard is an important oilseed crop contributing about one-fifth of the total oilseed production and area in the country. It is mainly grown in Punjab, Haryana, Rajasthan, Uttar Pradesh, Bihar, West Bengal and Assam. Of these, Uttar Pradesh accounts for 60 percent of all the India acreage under this crop.

The entire spectrum of available oilseeds should be subjected to re-examination in the light of present-day economic conditions to reveal future profitable possibilities.

Some potential future expansion material sources include:

1. Castorseed

India is one of the major producers of castorseed, accounting for about 28 percent of the world production. The annual production of castorseed is around 5 lakh tons while that of castor oil is around 1.8 lakh tons. By acting in concert with the Technology Mission on Oilseeds, the Gujarat and Andhra Pradesh governments have helped growers increase production. The castor seed crop more than doubled to four lakh tons in 1988-89 and rose still further to over five lakh tons in 1989-90. It reached a new high of 7.5 lakh tons in 1990-91. Inedible castor oil has two significant potentials: (a) with suitable processing castor oil can be used in the manufacture of soap to the extent of over 25 percent, thus relieving to some extent the pressure on other edible oils, (b) being used in conversion and in the lubricant industry, castor oil has a good export potential especially in view of the high price of petroleum products.

2. Soyabean

Soyabean, designated as a miracle crop with over 40 percent protein and 20 percent oil, has now been recognized all over the world as a potential supplementary source of edible oil and nutritious food. Currently the U.S.A., Brazil and China are the three big soyabean producing countries.

Soyabean is not new for India. Black soyabean has been cultivated for ages in the low hills of Kumaon and Garhwal regions of U.P. as well as on the foothills of the Himalayas and in some scattered pockets of Central India. However, strangely enough, the crop has never been popular in the Indian sub-continent and other tropical countries. The importance of soyabean in Indian agriculture as a crop to narrow the oil and protein gap has now been generally appreciated. Studies have indicated that the soyaflour, a by-product, can be used for fortification of wheat or other cereal flour up to 20 percent without detectable difference from the viewpoint of taste or appearance, but can considerably increase nutritional quality.

Besides, soyaflour is known for its value as cattle feed in order to narrow the gap between the availability and increasing requirement of nutritious feed for livestock.

3. Rice Bran Oil

Rice bran is the most important source of edible oil among the unconventional sources. Rice bran is the brown coating around the white starchy rice kernel which is obtained by dehusking paddy and polishing the rice. Despite the impressive growth of rice bran technology in the country, only a third of the available potential has been exploited.

India produces about 80 million tons of paddy annually. This can yield about 5 million tons of rice bran and the extent of 8 lakh tons of rice bran oil. Production of rice bran oil is currently estimated at about 2 lakh tons and hardly 10-15 percent of it is of edible grade, although the potential availability is reckoned at about 8 lakh tons.

4. Linseed

Linseed is mostly used for non-edible purposes. It is a dual purpose crop yielding oil and fiber. The relative contribution of this crop to the country's total oilseed acreage and production are 11.7 percent and 5.2 percent respectively. The crop is grown mainly as a source of oil which is commonly used for cooking in M.P. and U.P., but a major portion is used in industries, as in manufacture of paints and varnishes.

5. Coconuts

Innovative processes have been developed which can improve the quality and quantity of yield from coconuts. Now, India imports coconut oil in spite of being the third largest grower of coconuts in the world. Typically, we only exploit about 10 percent of the coconut. It was reported that Alfa Laval, Pune, is putting up a plant for Regent Agro in Andhra Pradesh. This plant is to use wet processing techniques which use 93 percent of the coconut. India has the potential to export 1.25 lakh tons of coconut powder, 1.2 lakh tons of coconut oil and one lakh ton of other products annually after meeting domestic requirements. Kerala, Tamil Nadu, Karnataka, A.P., West Bengal, Orissa and Maharashtra have adequate amounts of coconuts to sustain about three such plants.

IIIB. SOAPS AND DETERGENTS; GLYCERIN

1. Introduction

These chemical compounds are used for human comfort, cleanliness and for industrial surface active applications. Their action is based on colloidal chemistry principles as pictured:

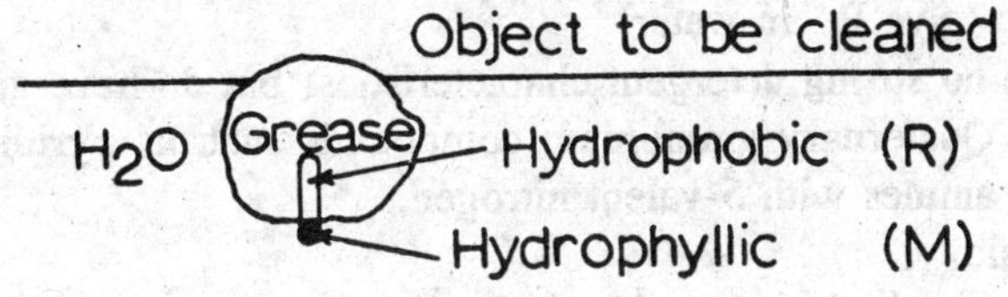

The grease is pulled away from the surface to be cleaned by the "key" mechanism shown. The success of any cleansing agent is to supply compounds with hydrophobic and hydrophyllic groups which will also appreciably decrease surface tension and increase wettability.

2. Classification of Cleansing Compounds

2.1. Soaps—compounds of the type R•COO•M where R•COO• is fatty acid radical representing oleic, stearic, palmitic, lauric, and myristic. These are usually present in soaps as mixtures based on glyceride raw materials. M is an alkali element such as Na or K.

2.2. Detergents—synthetic organic chemicals which promote better surface tension lowering than soaps. These are discussed here because of the competitive position with soaps.

Where the use of detergents increases to the point of creating problems in municipal sewerage plants due to excessive foaming and inability to reduce the organic content of the sewage effluent, biodegradation of detergent compounds becomes an important factor. In the U.S., detergent compounds, which can be oxidized to simple end-products, are known as biologically soft syndets and are preferred in detergent compounding.

2.2.1. Anionic (give R^- in water)

- Sulfated fatty alcohols

$$R{\cdot}OH + HO{\cdot}SO_3H \rightarrow RO{\cdot}SO_3H + H_2O$$

The sulfated compounds are quite stable in alkaline, acid, and hard water.

- Sulfonates

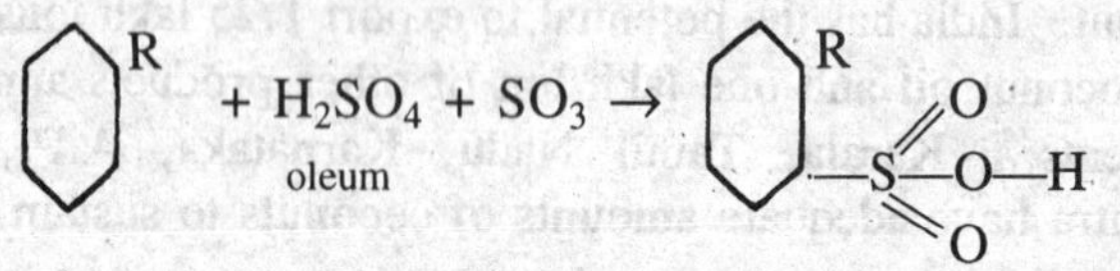

aryl-benzene sulfonate (ABS)

These are low-priced detergents which are not as stable as sulfates and require more additives in final compounding to improve performance. They represent the major ingredient of compounded detergents.

The molecular structure of R is important in determining whether a compound is biologically soft. Straight chain-normal paraffin structure gives a soft ABS whereas a branched or isoparaffin structure resists biodegradation.

- Sulfated esters and acids

Good stability in hard water, but not under acid and alkaline conditions.

2.2.2. Cationic (give R^+ in water)

These have no strong detergent characteristics, but do have germicidal properties.

Example: Quaternary ammonium compounds such as pyridinium derivatives and amines with 5-valent nitrogen.

2.2.3. Non-ionic

- Alkyl-aryl-ethylene oxide derivatives
- Aliphatic polyhydric alcohol esters
- Fatty acid amides

Such compounds produce little foam but possess excellent soil removal and grease emulsification characteristics.

2.2.4. Detergent builders

- Phosphates such as sodium tripolyphosphate and tetrasodium pyrophosphate used as much as 30-50% in detergent formulations to extend foam
- Sodium carboxycellulose (1-3%) to improve soil and dirt suspension
- Fluorescent dyes as brighteners
- Sodium silicate to avoid aluminum corrosion in washing machines
- Zeolites as alternative phosphorus-free builders

3. Use Pattern

A partial list of uses of soaps and detergents is given to show the diversity of applications:

Textile manufacture
Sanitation
Food processing
Shaving soaps
Synthetic rubber and plastics emulsion polymerization
Paints—water emulsion formulations
Paper—application of sizing
Oil production—drilling fluid oils
Inks—water in oil emulsions
Agriculture—emulsifying agents for sprays
Construction—waterproofing cements by formation of insoluble Ca soaps; bituminous emulsions

In 1991-92, the capacity of units manufacturing soaps and detergents in the organized sector of India had reached 500,000 tons each. Thus, together, their capacity was the highest ever, at 1 million tons a year. Production was lower at 480,000 tons for soaps and 280,000 tons for detergents. The Eighth Five Year Plan document projected the capacity of soaps at 600,000 tons and production at 580,000 tons in 1996-97. In the case of detergents, capacity in 1996-97 has been forecast at 580,000 tons and production at 400,000 tons. Thus, production of soaps and detergents was expected to exceed 1 million tons in the late 1990's.

India has made significant progress in the export of soaps and detergents. In 1975-76, the value of total exports of soaps and detergents was hardly Rs. 46 million. By 1991-92, it had risen to Rs. 633 million. Among the countries which imported soaps from India were both developed and developing ones such as Oman, Qatar, Saudi Arabia, United Arab Emirates, Bangladesh, Canada, Japan, Malaysia, Singapore, Thailand, the erstwhile USSR and the Republic of Tanzania.

During the last 2½ years, the economic policies of India have undergone a sea change. The economy is being restructured in a bid to globalize it. The convertibility of the rupee and the exemption of income tax on profits from exports are two measures which have provided a boost to exports. In the current year, total exports are expected to rise by at least 25 percent over 1992-93 and the export of soaps is also anticipated to improve by a wide margin.

The export of soaps and detergents is poised to leap forward owing to two factors. First, quality of Indian soaps is of the international standard and their prices are competitive. Hence, the industry is likely to reach new heights in export earnings in the coming two to three years.

Indian soaps have been made competitive by the recent spurt in the production of edible oils which has been instrumental in making the country self-sufficient, as already stated, in edible oils.

Since 50 percent of the cost of soap—toilet and laundry—is due to oils and fats, this one factor is designed to change the growth pattern of the soap industry.

Understandably, the soap manufacturers are bullish on exports and they are intensifying their efforts in this regard. They are studying the perfumes used abroad and are going in for new brands which conform to the latest trends in foreign countries.

Large manufacturing units for soaps and detergents are using the latest technology, as stated earlier. Their products are, in some cases, superior to the products marketed in developed countries. That is why we can look forward to growing markets for Indian soaps and detergents in foreign countries. See Table IIIB-1.

Table IIIB-1
Production of Soaps and Detergents in India

(In thousand tons)

Year	Soaps		Detergents	
	Capacity	Production	Capacity	Production
1989-90	435	394	440	240
1990-91	435	435	440	263
1991-92	500	480	500	280
1996-97 (Target)	600	580	550	440

Source: S.I.R.I., "Directory of Industries in India" (1995)

India is the largest soap manufacturer in the world. In 1993-94, the production volume for toilet soaps was 1.49 million tons of which the organized sector accounted for 0.42 million tons.

The soap and detergent market is dominated by the Indian affiliate of world majors like Hindustan Lever (HLL), Tata Oil Mills Company (TOMCO), Procter & Gamble, Godrej, Colgate Palmolive, and local players like Nirma, Karnataka Soaps and Calcutta Chemicals.

With a total turnover of more than Rs. 3,000 crore, the industry is poised for a better future. Detergents alone constitute as much as Rs. 2,000 crore, a mammoth 67 percent of the total market, while output of the soaps segment is estimated at Rs. 1,000 crore. The synthetic detergents are basically a new concept in India. It was introduced three decades ago in the late fifties. The Synthetic Detergent Bars (SDBs) constitute about 16 percent of the market for fabric washing. This market is estimated at more than three lakh tons and its growth rate is about 15 percent per annum. See Table IIIB-2.

A new washing segment that has emerged in the last one year or two is the washing machine market. Market sources predict that this particular category will leapfrog into the next decade at a growth rate of 25 percent per annum.

An econometric model, which took into account variables like previous habit formations, growth of real national income as well as the availability of soapery oils, which is likely to be a constraint, projected the total Fabric Washing Products (FWP) demand by 1990 at 22.25 lakh tons. The break-up of this into washing soaps and synthetic detergents are 8.90 and 13.35 lakh tons.

Table IIIB-2
Trends in Fabric Washing Products (FWP) in India

Year	Total FWP	Synthetic Detergents (Lakh tons)	Washing Soaps
1990	22.25	13.35	8.90
1995	30.80	18.48	12.32
2000	42.50	25.50	17.00

Source: "Kothari's Industrial Directory of India" (1994)

At present there are 22 units manufacturing synthetic detergents in the organized sector in India with an installed capacity of 4.4 lakh M.T. per annum. Their names and addresses are given in Table IIIB-3.

Table IIIB-3
Indian Detergent Manufacturers

Name & Address

1. Calcutta Chemical Co. Ltd.
   35, Panchitra Road, Calcutta - 700 029

2. Detergents India Ltd.
   Industrial Development Area, Kodur - 516 101
   Dist. Cuddapah (A.P.)

3. Dai-Ichi-Karkaria
   Bombay (Maharashtra)

4. Dharamsi Morarji Chemical Co. Ltd.
   Roha (Maharashtra)

5. Godrej Soaps Ltd.
   Eastern Express Highway, Vikhroli, Bombay - 400 079

6. Haryana Detergents Ltd.
   Dharuhera (Haryana)

7. Hindustan Lever Ltd.
   (i) Haji Bunder, Sewree, Bombay - 400 033 (Maharashtra)
   (ii) Bari Brahamana, Pampri, Jammu (J&K)
   (iii) Chindwara (M.P.)
   (iv) 63, Garden Beach Road, Calcutta (W.B.)
   (v) Hamirpur Dist. (U.P.)

8. Karnataka Soaps & Detergents Ltd.
Bangalore (Karnataka)

9. Kerala State Detergents & Chemicals Ltd.
Maduratham, Tirur Taluk, Kuthipuram (Kerala)

10. Kusum Products Ltd.
Panchugopal Bhaduri Sarani, Guru Garden Road, Rishra
Dist. Hooghly (W.B.)

11. Pee Cee Cosma Sope Ltd.
Bhind Dist. (M.P.)

12. Procter & Gamble Ltd.
Mandideep (M.P.)

13. Shaw Wallace Ltd. (EOU)
Fatehpur (U.P.)

14. Spic Fine Chemicals Ltd.
Karaikal (T.N.) (under implementation)

15. Stepan Chemicals Ltd.
A-5/11B, Focal Point, Rajpura, Dist. Patiala (Punjab)

16. Swadeshi Detergents Ltd.
Plot No. 37/3, Industrial Area, Site No. 4, Sahibabad
Dist. Ghaziabad (U.P.)

17. Swastic Household & Industrial Products
Saltpan Road, Wadala, Bombay - 400 031 (Maharashtra)

18. Tata Oil Mills Co. Ltd.
(i) Sewree, Bombay (Maharashtra)
(ii) Jasidih, Santhal Parganas (W.B.)
(iii) Pithampur (M.P.)

19. Tata Vashisti Detergents Ltd.
Lote Parshuram, Dist. Ratnagiri (Maharashtra)

20. Ultramarine & Pigments Ltd.
SIPCOT Industrial Complex, Ranipet, North Arcot Dist. (T.N.)

21. Union Home Products Ltd.
Baloor, Mangalore, Dist. South Kanara (Karnataka)

22. Whitco Ltd.
Kalol, Dist. Panchmahal (Gujarat)

Source: "SBP Handbook of Projects for Corporate Diversification" (1992)

4. Methods of Soap Production

4.1. Batch Saponification Process

Acid hydrolysis of glycerides followed by alkali addition (Twitchell process) or direct saponification using strong caustic in batch process operation are the oldest types of soap manufacture.

4.2. Continuous Hydrolysis and Saponification Process

This method is in greater use because it has these advantages over the batch process:

- Flexibility in control of product distribution
- Higher glycerin yields (>80%)
- Less off-color production during the short-time hydrolysis step
- Requires less space and manpower

4.2.1. Reference flow sheet: Figure IIIB-1

4.2.2. Chemical reactions

(a) Fat splitting

$$\underset{\text{triglyceride}}{(R \cdot COO)_3 \cdot C_3H_5} + 3H_2O \rightarrow \underset{\text{fatty acid : glycerin}}{3R \cdot COO \cdot H + C_3H_5(OH)_3}$$

(b) Saponification

$$R \cdot COO \cdot H + M \cdot OH \rightarrow \underset{\text{soap}}{R \cdot COO \cdot M} + H_2O$$

where M is usually an alkali metal such as Na or K.

4.2.3. Raw materials

Refined tallow, recovered and refined grease, coconut and palm oils are the principal fatty constituents. Metal oxides such as ZnO are frequently added as fat splitting catalysts. Alkali for saponification and builder-type additives, mainly rosin, complete the raw material requirements.

Caustic soda and vegetable oil are the two raw materials for the production of toilet soaps as the use of animal tallow is not allowed in India. Distilled fatty acids derived from vegetable oils such as palm oil or other solvent extracted oils and minor oils are an important constituent. Demand supply gap for vegetable oils and its derivatives is met through imports.

4.2.4. Quantitative requirements

(a) Basis: 1 ton of anhydrous soap

Oil or Fat	1.1 tons
50% NaOH	0.3 ton
Sodium silicate	6 kg
H_2O	0.8 ton
Steam	1.5 tons

(b) Plant capacities: 2-15 tons/day

4.2.5. Process description

Glycerides plus catalyst are added at the bottom of the hydrolysis tower where high pressure water at 230-250°C is passed counter-currently to the glycerides. Reaction 4.2.2(a) occurs with a 15-20% glycerin solution being removed from the

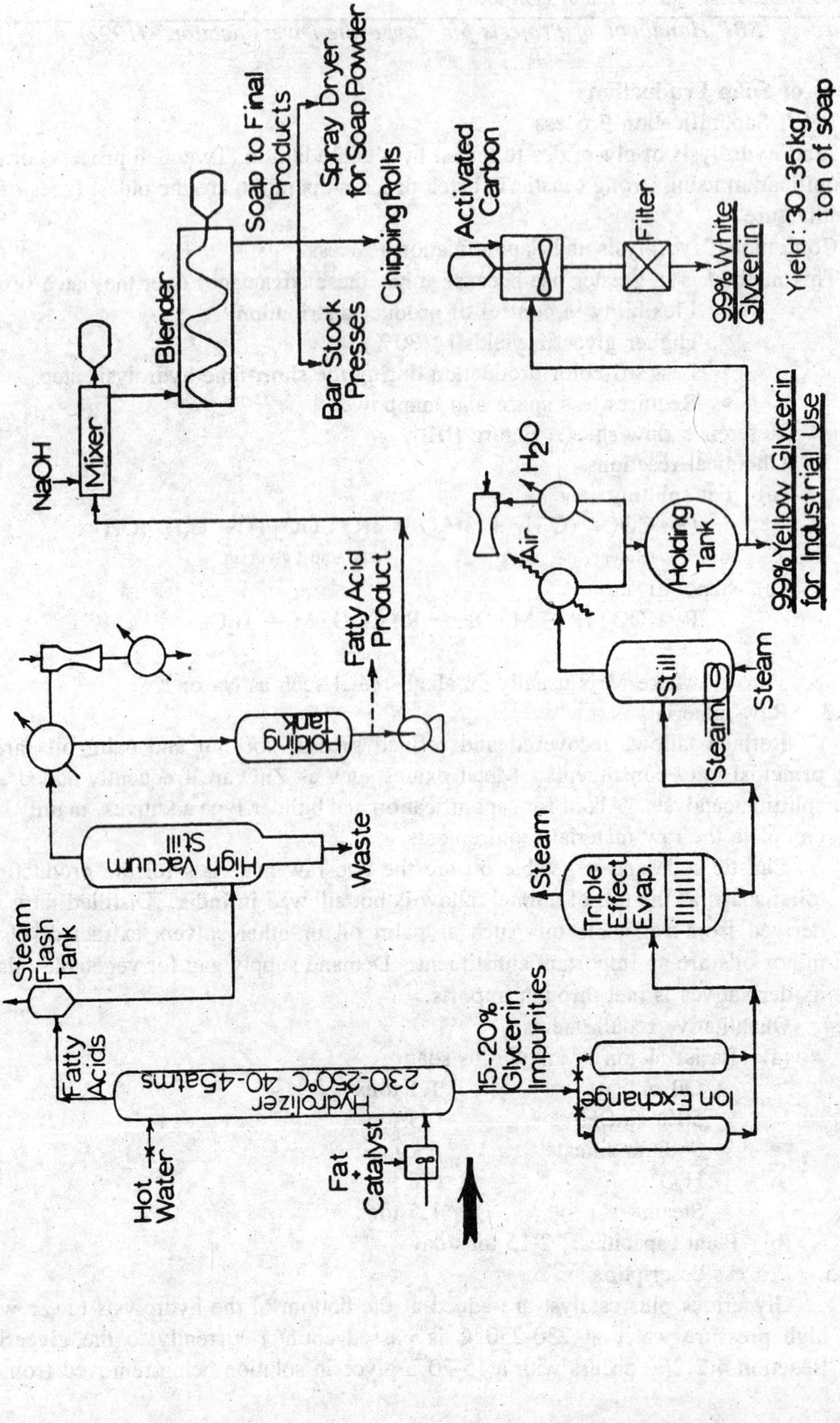

Fig. IIIB-1. Continuous process for fatty acids, soap, and glycerin.

bottom of the tower. The fatty acids are passed overhead to a flash tank to remove excess steam. The crude fatty acids are vacuum distilled and the condensate in the distillate receiver is either available as a marketable product or for soap manufacture.

Caustic soda is added to fatty acids in a continuous high speed mixer and the saponification is completed in a slow speed blender where other ingredients are added if desired. Soap from the blender may be pumped through heated lines to bar soap, flake or spray drying equipment followed by packaging operations.

4.2.6. The soap industry in India

A large percentage of soap production in India is in villages where relatively crude methods are employed and where glycerin is not recovered from the product. Proper future growth of the soap industry will depend on availability of vegetable oil raw materials and decreased reliance on imported tallow and palm oil.

5. Methods of Detergent Manufacture

Two of the most prominent detergents in use today will be discussed.

5.1. Sulfated Fatty Alcohols

High molecular weight alcohols, such as the group from lauryl alcohol ($C_{12}H_{25}OH$) up to oleyl alcohol ($C_{18}H_{35}OH$), are derived from coconut oil by either sodium reduction or catalytic hydrogenation. Sulfation of these alcohols then follows.

5.1.1. Catalytic hydrogenation of coconut oil

Hydrogenation is done at high temperatures (200-300°C) and pressures of 100-200 atms. using copper salts as catalysts. In addition to hydrogenating at the carboxyl linkage, saturation of the double bonds occurs which is not desirable for best detergency action.

5.1.2. Sodium reduction of coconut oil

Molten sodium is added slowly to coconut oil in an aliphatic solvent (xylene or toluene) plus esterifying alcohol such as amyl alcohol. The reactions occurring are:

$$C_5H_{11}\cdot OH + Na \longrightarrow C_5H_{11}\cdot ONa + H^* \quad \text{(* indicates active hydrogen)}$$

$$\begin{array}{l} R_1CO\cdot OCH_2 \\ \quad\;| \\ R_2CO\cdot OCH \\ \quad\;| \\ R_3CO\cdot OCH_2 \end{array} + 6H^* \rightarrow \begin{array}{l} R_1CH_2O.OCH_2 \\ \qquad\;| \\ R_2CH_2O\cdot OCH \\ \qquad\;| \\ R_3CH_2O\cdot OCH_2 \end{array} \xrightarrow{H_2O} \left\{ \begin{array}{l} R_1CH_2OH \\ \\ R_2CH_2OH + C_3H_5(OH)_3 \\ \\ R_3CH_2OH \end{array} \right.$$

After reaction is completed, the batch is pumped into a water tank where the mixture settles into three layers; the top is the high molecular weight alcohol, the intermediate layer contains regenerated reducing alcohol, and the bottoms have caustic soda and glycerin for recovery. The economics of the process compared to hydrogenation involves an economic balance between the higher cost of high-pressure hydrogenation equipment on one hand and higher cost sodium reductant and more complex product separation on the other.

5.1.3. Sulfation of fatty alcohols

Oleum or an excess of 98% H_2SO_4 is added to the purified fatty alcohols; acid sulfate is then converted to sodium salt.

$$R{\cdot}CH_2OH + H_2SO_4 \rightarrow R{\cdot}CH_2O{\cdot}SO_3H \xrightarrow{NaOH} \underset{\text{sodium salt of sulfated fatty alcohols}}{R{\cdot}CH_2O{\cdot}SO_3Na}$$

Any excess sulfuric acid is neutralized and the sodium sulfate is usually left with the entire mixture and dried.

5.2. Alkyl-Aryl Sulfonates

Compounds under this classification are prepared in a three-step process using cheap petroleum raw materials. Kerosene feedstock may be fractionated by a molecular sieve process in vapor phase. Molecular sieve adsorbents are synthetic zeolites of controlled pore size such that normal paraffins are adsorbed internally, but isoparaffins and cyclic hydrocarbons are not adsorbed. Desorption yields the normal paraffin structure required for biologically degradable detergents. Where fractionation is not used, a cheaper mixed aryl compound results with a substantial fraction as isoparaffin (bio-hard).

(a) $$\underset{\text{paraffin}}{C_nH_{2n+2}} + Cl_2 \rightarrow \underset{\text{alkyl chloride}}{C_nH_{2n+1}Cl} + HCl$$

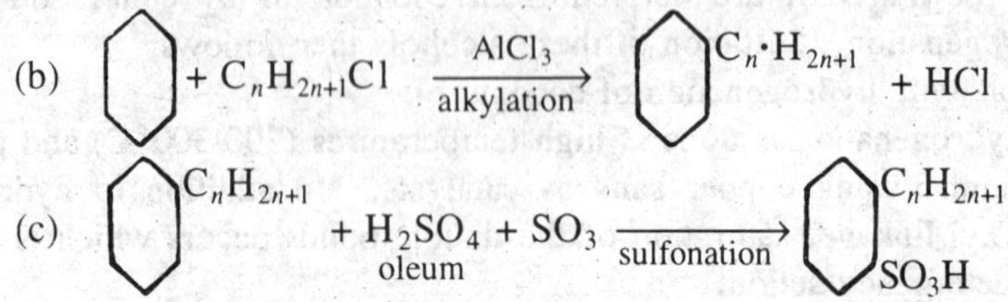

aryl-benzene compound — aryl-benzene sulfonate (ABS)

6. Economics

Detergents made a relatively late entry into the Indian market (dominated by laundry soaps) in 1956. From 1.05 million tons in 1989, the market is currently around 1.71 million tons and is valued at Rs. 30 billion in terms of size. India has the second largest market in the world after the U.S. and the market is growing at the rate of 10% annually. The detergents market is characterized by the presence of a large unorganized sector which specializes in low cost washing products. Manufacture of laundry soaps is reserved for small-scale industry.

The main raw materials for detergents are soda ash and Linear Alkyl Benzene Sulfonate (LABS). LABS is the primary active ingredient. Alpha Olefin Sulfonate (AOS) is a costlier substitute for LABS and is primarily imported. For decades, Sodium Tri-Polyphosphate has been used as builder in detergents. However, phosphate free, environment friendly detergents have recently made an entry into India.

Comparative per capita consumption data for some countries is indicated below. The per capita consumption of washing products and health and personal care products in India is below the regional averages, indicating a large market potential. The demand projections for washing active substances in India from 1990-2005 are given in a second tabulation.

Comparative Per Capita Consumption Data (1992-93)

Country	Population million	Per Capita Consumption			
		Synthetic detergents kg	Soap kg	Toothpaste gm	Shampoo gm
China	1,151	1.3	0.8	190	NA
India	860	1.6	1.4	49	85
W. Europe	348	15.5	NA	629	1,053
Indonesia	179	1.1	2.0	112	70
Philippines	55	3.1	3.4	96	125
Thailand	57	1.6	3.4	288	135
Japan	124	8.1	8.9	441	732
Taiwan	19	4.3	6.2	167	234
Korea	43.2	6.2	3.3	402	547
Malaysia	16	2.2	3.7	375	156
Australia	16	18.5	13.2	354	1,057
Av. SEA	349	2.0	2.3	186	159

Source: "Chemical Weekly Annual" (1995)

Demand Data on Washing Substances in India (1990-2005)

('000 tons)

	Toilet Soap	Laundry Soap	Synthetic Detergents	Total WAS
1990	330	800	1,175	2,305
1992	380	890	1,425	2,695
1994	450	930	1,735	3,115
1996	515	1,075	2,085	3,675
1998	600	1,120	2,470	4,190
2000	690	1,180	2,925	4,795
2005	975	1,425	4,275	6,675

Source: "Chemical Weekly Annual" (1995)

The demand data and projections for surfactants from 1990-2000 are given below.

Demand for Surfactants in India 1990-2000

(metric tons)

	1990	1995	2000
Alkyl/Aryl benzene sulfonates (ABS)	140,000	221,000	310,000
Alcohol sulfates (AS)	1,200	2,650	3,630
Alcohol ethoxylates (AE)	730	1,480	2,280
Alcohol ethoxy sulfates (AES)	940	1,900	2,925
Alpha olefin sulfonates (AOS)	6,500	12,800	35,700

Nonionics, cationics & amphoterics	8,700	10,773	12,980
	158,070	250,603	367,515

Source: "Chemical Weekly Annual" (1995)

Most of the detergent intermediates and raw materials are produced in India with the exception of alpha olefins. The projections and demand data for raw materials like linear alkyl benzene, ethylene oxide, fatty alcohols, and alpha olefins are tabulated below.

Demand for Detergent Raw Materials and Intermediates in India 1990-2005
(metric tons)

	1990	1995	2000	2005
Linear alkyl benzene	150	208	300	490
Ethylene oxide	5.3	6.7	8.4	10.7
Fatty alcohols	3.0	5.1	6.9	9.8
Ethylene oxide condensates	7.5	9.0	11	13.1
Alpha olefins	5	9	25	36
Caustic soda	110	145	195	255
Soda ash	549	868	1,295	1,852
Soapery oils	620	800	1,200	1,350
Sulfuric acid	234	383	585	855

Source: "Chemical Weekly Annual" (1995)

Glycerin

1. Pertinent Properties of Glycerin (Glycerol)

Mol. wt. 92.1
M.P. 17.9°C
B.P. 290°C
Miscible in water and alcohol
Grades: Yellow distilled (99%) for industrial and explosives.
U.S.P. (95-98%) colorless, purified for human consumption.

2. Consumption Pattern

Glycerin has a wide variety of industrial uses based on its physical properties of moistening and lubrication and the chemical reactivity of its OH groups.

2.1. End Uses

Alkyl resins and plastics	35%
Tobacco humidification	15
Cellophane plasticizer	12
Explosives	10
Food and Pharmaceuticals	10

3. Methods of Production

3.1. Classification of Processes

3.1.1. Natural product triglyceride hydrolysis (see soap mfg.)

3.1.2. Synthetic glycerin from propylene (petrochemical processing)

- Allyl chloride route
- Acrolein route

The acrolein route produces acetone co-product.

3.2. By-product Glycerin from Soap and Fatty Acids

3.2.1. Reference flow sheet: Figure IIIB-1

3.2.2. Process description

The dilute glycerin (sweetwater) is put through successive beds of anion and cation exchange resins to remove some color and dissolved salts. The liquid effluent is concentrated by triple effect evaporation and vacuum distilled to produce industrial grade (99%) yellow glycerin. A final purification step is performed using activated carbon to obtain water-white U.S.P. glycerin.

3.3. Synthetic Glycerin from Propylene via Allyl Chloride

3.3.1. Reference flow sheet: None

3.3.2. Chemical reactions

(a) $\underset{\text{propylene}}{CH_2{=}CHCH_3} + Cl_2 \xrightarrow{400\text{-}500°C} \underset{\text{allyl chloride}}{CH_2{=}CHCH_2\cdot Cl} + HCl$

(b) $\underset{\text{chlorhydrin}}{CH_2{=}CHCH_2\cdot Cl} + HOCl \rightarrow \underset{\text{glycerol dichlorhydrin}}{CH_2OH\cdot CHCl\cdot CH_2Cl}$

(c) 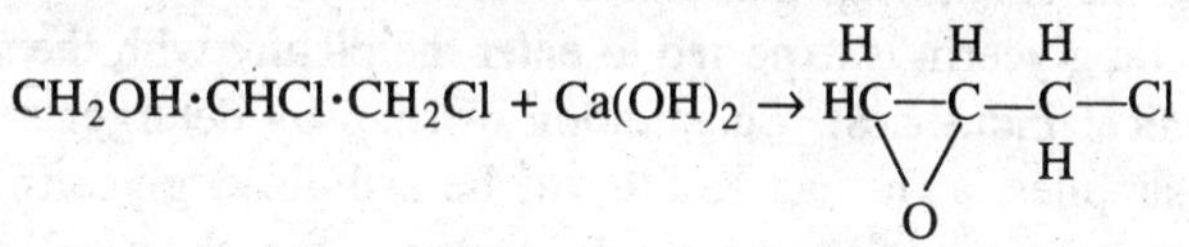

epichlorhydrin

(d) 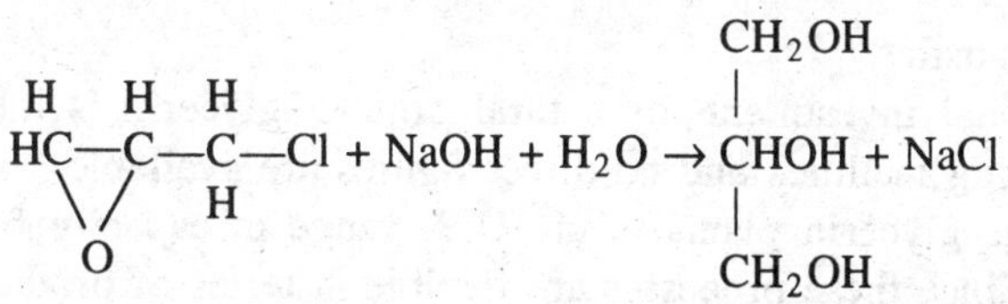

glycerin (75-80% yield)

Note: This process produces the intermediate epichlorhydrin, a basic ingredient of epoxy resin manufacture.

3.4. Synthetic Glycerin from Propylene via Acrolein

3.4.1. Reference flow sheet: None

3.4.2. Chemical reactions

(a) $\underset{\text{propylene}}{CH_3\cdot CH{=}CH_2} + H_2O \rightarrow \underset{\text{isopropanol}}{CH_3\cdot CHOH\cdot CH_3}$

(b) $CH_3\cdot CHOH\cdot CH_3 + O_2 \xrightarrow[120°C,\ 2\ atms.]{\text{liquid phase}} \underset{\text{hydrogen peroxide}}{H_2O_2} + \underset{\text{acetone}}{CH_3\cdot CO\cdot CH_3}$

(c) $$CH_3{\cdot}CH{=}CH_2 + H_2O + O_2 \xrightarrow[\text{Cu}_2\text{O catalyst, 350°C, 1-10 atms.}]{\text{vapor phase}} \underset{\text{acrolein}}{CHO{\cdot}CH{=}CH_2} + H_2O$$

(d) $$CHO{\cdot}CH{=}CH_2 + CH_3{\cdot}CHOH{\cdot}CH_3 \xrightarrow[\text{MgO-ZnO, 400°C}]{\text{vapor phase}} \underset{\text{allyl alcohol}}{CH_2OH{\cdot}CH{=}CH_2} + CH_3{\cdot}CO{\cdot}CH_3$$

(e) $$CH_2OH{\cdot}CH{=}CH_2 + H_2O_2\ (aq) \xrightarrow[\text{WO}_3\text{ catalyst, 60-70°C}]{\text{liquid phase}} \underset{\text{glycerol}}{C_3H_5(OH)_3}$$

Overall yield of glycerol from propylene = 50-60%.

Note: This process also produces acetone co-product, as well as acrolein, allyl alcohol, and hydrogen peroxide as intermediates.

4. Economics

4.1. Synthetic versus Natural Product Glycerin

Only natural product glycerin is currently being produced in India. Because soap plants have such small capacity, central fat-splitting plants have been suggested wherein glycerin can be recovered economically via large capacity throughput and the fatty acids shipped to the small soap manufacturers.

Synthetic glycerin is expected to enter the picture with the successful promotion of the petrochemical industries. Substitution of soap by detergents will further curtail natural glycerin supplies. The net result will be stabilized glycerin supply from both sources which will create an attractive raw material for chemical specialty products such as plastics.

4.2. Plant Statistics

The capital investment for natural product glycerin is inherently tied up with soap manufacturing facilities and no direct figures are available.

Synthetic glycerin plants in the U.S. range in capacity from 33 to 100 tons/day of glycerin. Since these processes are flexible in terms of product output such as hydrogen peroxide, acetone, acrolein and epichlorhydrin, the glycerin production from a given plant will vary considerably depending on the market demand for various products.

Glycerin Production (% synthetic)

	1975	1980	1988
Western Europe	38	29	18
USA	50	47	33
Japan	54	37	30
World	30	28	21

Source: "Industrial Organic Chemistry" by Weissermel et al (1993)

Total Glycerin Production ('000 tons)

	1985	1986	1988
Western Europe	209	195	200
USA	143	146	139
Japan	40	51	51

Source: "Industrial Organic Chemistry" by Weissermel et al (1993)

IIIC. PAINTS AND VARNISHES (INCLUDING PIGMENTS)

1. Introduction

The paint and varnish industry is essentially a compounding industry and hence the coverage given here will be fairly brief.

The manufacture of paints, varnishes, lacquers and enamels involves a few unit operations and no unit processes. Of course, the manufacture of ingredients such as pigments and resins involves chemical reactions and therefore unit processes. Synthetic resins are considered later in the text and only an example of a new process involved in the manufacture of titanium dioxide pigment will be considered in this chapter.

Although the chemical engineer's involvement in paint manufacturing processes is not as extensive as in some other industries, the use of protective coatings for equipment and structures is of obvious importance to the chemical engineer.

The formation of protective coatings by paints, varnishes, lacquers and enamels involves the production of films of the order of one mil (1/1000-inch) thick on surfaces. In general, the requirements for such surface coatings include the following:

(1) Hiding power or covering power
(2) Color
(3) Weather resistance
(4) Washability
(5) Glass
(6) Anticorrosive properties
(7) Consistency suited to application (by brushing, dipping, spraying or roller coating)
(8) Non-toxicity
(9) Low-cost

Table IIIC-1 summarizes some of the components of the various types of surface coatings used today.

Table IIIC-2 gives some information on the manufacture, application and use of the various types of surface coatings.

Table IIIC-1 Components of Various Types of Surface Coatings

Component	*Oil-based Paints*	*Water-based Paints*	*Varnishes*	*Lacquers*	*Enamels*
Pigment	Titanium, lead, zinc oxides and colorants	Titanium, lead, zinc oxides and colorants	-	Optional	Titanium, lead, zinc oxides and colorants
Solvent (vehicle)	Oil	Water	Oil	Ethers, alcohols, esters, ketones	See varnishes
Film-former (resin)	Oil	Butadiene-styrene copolymer resin emulsion	Natural or synthetic resins	Nitrocellulose usually (or phenolic or alkyd resin)	See varnishes
Drier	Heavy metal carboxylates	-	Heavy metal carboxylates	-	Heavy metal carboxylates
Diluent (thinner)	Naphthas, turpentine	None used	Naphthas, turpentine	Naphthas, turpentine	Naphthas, turpentine
Plasticizer	Some oils	-	-	Dibutyl phthalate, tricresyl phosphate, etc.	-
Pigment extender	Clay, talc, etc.	Clay, talc, etc.	-	-	Clay, talc, etc.
Oil	Linseed, soya, tung, castor	-	Linseed, soya, tung, castor	-	Linseed, soya, tung, castor
Antiskinning agent	Polyhydroxy phenols	-	Polyhydroxy phenols	-	Polyhydroxy phenols
Dispersing agent	-	Casein	-	-	-
Antifoam agent	-	Pine oil	-	-	-
Preservative	-	Chlorinated phenols	-	-	-

Table IIIC-2 Summary of Manufacture, Application and Use of Various Types of Surface Coatings

	Oil-based Paints	*Water-based Paints*	*Varnishes*	*Lacquers*	*Enamels*
Major unit operation in manufacture	Grinding or milling	Grinding or milling	Cooking	Mixing	See varnishes
Method of application	Brushing, dipping, spraying, or roller coating	Brushing, dipping, spraying, or roller coating	Brushing and spraying	Brushing, dipping and spraying	Brushing, spraying or baking
Mode of drying	Oxidation and/or polymerization	Evaporation and agglomeration	Oxidation and/or polymerization	Evaporation	See varnishes
Major product uses	General household and industrial applications	General household and industrial applications particularly for do-it-yourself application	Used in finishing furniture, exterior woodwork, marine application; also in electrical impregnation	Used in finishing metals and furniture, in food container linings and in coating fabrics	Used in finishing automobiles and other vehicles; used for small household appliances, lamps, etc.

We will now consider some of the ingredients of surface compositions in somewhat more detail.

2. Pigments and Extenders

Historically, white lead ($2PbCO_3$-$Pb(OH)_2$), zinc oxide and lithopone (ZnS-$BaSO_4$) were the principal white pigments used; colored pigments consisted of Prussian blue ($Fe_4(Fe(CN)_6)_3$), lead chromates, various iron oxides and a few lake colors (a lake being an organic dye on an inorganic adsorbent such as clay).

Now, titanium dioxide is one of the most important of the white pigments. Chromium oxides and hydrates give green, yellow and orange colors. Carbon black is the principal black pigment used. Organic pigments (metal phthalocyanines) are finding an increasingly important place as durable blue pigments. Luminescent pigments are becoming available for use in outdoor advertising display and safety signs.

After independence, the production of pigments was undertaken in India. These pigments included titanium dioxide, phthalocyanine blue, Prussian blue, ultramarine blue, chrome pigments and carbon black.

Besides the above prime pigments, an important group of anticorrosive pigments such as zinc chrome, and basic lead sulfate are now being made in India. The manufacture of metallic pigments such as aluminum paste has also been started.

2.1. Titanium Dioxide

Titanium dioxide features low-cost per unit of hiding power as is widely used in exterior paints, enamels and pigmented lacquers. A typical exterior white paint may actually contain 15% TiO_2, 25% zinc oxide, 50% white lead and 10% of a pigment extender. Such a paint has a self-cleaning feature by a "chalking" process.

The available titanium ores are rutile (TiO_2) and ilmenite (FeO-TiO_2). Titanium dioxide pigments have traditionally been made from these ores by a rather complex wet chemical process involving

- digestion in sulfuric acid
- removal of iron as $FeSO_4$
- concentration in vacuum evaporators
- precipitation of titanium hydrate
- calcination, grinding and bagging

More recently, the flame process has been developed. The pigment product from the flame process has superior qualities and the flame process is potentially a lower cost process than the wet process. In this type of process, the ore is just chlorinated and volatile $FeCl_3$ separated from $TiCl_4$ if iron is present in the ore. Then the $TiCl_4$, which is a liquid at room temperature, is fed to a burner along with oxygen where the following reaction occurs:

$$TiCl_4 + O_2 \rightarrow TiO_2 + 2Cl_2$$

The chlorine is recovered for recycle to the ore chlorination step.

Refractory-lined furnaces of special design are used in the process. The reaction takes place at 1,500°C and the chemical engineering design problems are fairly formidable. Many patents have been issued on various burner designs featuring gas mixing devices, etc.

In India, there are at present four manufacturers of titanium dioxide pigment viz. Travancore Titanium Products Ltd., Kerala (TTP); Kolmak Chemicals Ltd., West Bengal; Kerala Minerals & Metals Ltd., Kerala (KMML) and Kilburn Chemicals Ltd., Tamil Nadu. All companies, with the exception of KMML, use the sulfate route to produce titanium dioxide pigment. Only KMML produces rutile grade titanium dioxide.

TTP was set up in 1951 in collaboration with the then British Titan Products Ltd. (now Tioxide) with technology from National Lead (NL), USA. The details about these titanium dioxide producers are given in Table IIIC-3. Uses are shown in Table IIIC-4.

Internationally, the minimum economic capacity for a titanium dioxide plant is 50,000 TPA. Among the two technologies for titanium dioxide manufacture, the chloride technology is not easily available to new entrepreneurs for medium sized projects of 15,000-20,000 TPA capacity. But the sulfate technology is available from several companies abroad. In India, the elemental sulfur, required to produce sulfuric acid in sulfate route, has to be imported. Therefore, the raw material assembly cost for the sulfate process under Indian conditions is estimated to be about 11% higher than that for the chloride process.

Table IIIC-3
Titanium Dioxide Producers in India

Company	*Technology Route*	*Grade*	*Installed Cap., TPA*
Travancore Titanium Products Ltd.	NL/Tioxide (Sulfate)	Anatase	24,500
Kolmak Chemicals Ltd.	Indigenous (Sulfate)	Anatase	2,400
Kerala Minerals & Metals Ltd.	KMML (Chloride)	Rutile	22,000
Kilburn Chemicals Ltd.	(Sulfate)	Anatase	3,960
Total Capacity			**52,860**

Source: "Chemical Weekly"

Table IIIC-4
Comparison of Consumption Patterns of Titanium Dioxide (%)

Region → *Industry*	*USA*	*Western Europe*	*Rest of World*	*India*
Paints & Coatings	51	62	75	68
Paper	24	9	4	6
Plastics	14	18	8	10
Others	11	11	13	16

Source: "Chemical Weekly"

3. Oils

Oils serve a dual purpose in surface coating formulation—as carriers for the pigments and, importantly, as formers of the protective films.

Hence, reactive oils containing some degree of olefinic unsaturation are used and these are called drying or semi-drying oils, depending on the degree of unsaturation. These are in contrast to the edible oils and the essential oils which are described in the preceding section. However, some of the edible oils (which must be hydrogenated or have antioxidants added to prevent rancidity when used for food purposes) can also be used as drying oils.

Linseed, soyabean, tung oil, castor oil and tall oil are important drying oils.

In the field of drying oils, India has large supplies of basic paint oils such as linseed and castor. Moreover, use is being made of semi-drying oils such as coconut, tobacco seed and kardi-seed.

4. Driers

Metallic salts, particularly heavy metal salts of carboxylic acids, such as cobalt, naphthenate, for example, are used in conjunction with drying oils. The unsaturated drying oils polymerize by a reaction mechanism which involves a peroxide intermediate. The metallic drier salts are oxidation catalysts and promote the oxidation-polymerization process.

Manufacture of naphthenate driers, using imported naphthenic acid, has been well established for some time in India while the production of octoate driers has just started.

5. Resins

A variety of resins are used in various surface coating formulations as shown in Table IIIC-1.

Oil-base paints use essentially no resins. Water-base paints, on the other hand, contain no oils and depend on vinyl acetate, acrylic or butadiene-styrene polymer resins as the film-forming materials.

Varnishes incorporate one or more of a variety of natural or synthetic resins. These may be phenolic, alkyd, urea-formaldehyde, acrylate, vinyl or silicone resins as well as such natural resins as African copal, or rosin.

Lacquers traditionally contained nitrocellulose as the resin constituent but may now be based on phenolic or alkyd resins as well.

In the case of resins, India has indigenous rosin, shellac, cashewnut shell and bhillawanut shell liquids. However, with the advance in paint technology, the emphasis has shifted more and more to the use of synthetic resins. Alkyds, phenolics, maleics, urea-formaldehydes and melamine formaldehyde resins production is now well established in the country.

6. Diluents

Diluents or thinners for paints and varnish compositions may include aliphatic or aromatic naphtha fractions or may contain turpentine.

Lacquers employ aliphatic chemicals such as ethers, esters, ketones and alcohols to provide the desired controlled volatility.

India has virtually only one natural solvent, *viz.*, turpentine. The production of pine oil and dipentene from turpentine has also been started. The commissioning of steel plants has made available aromatic hydrocarbons such as benzene, toluene and xylol. The production of synthetic solvents—butyl alcohol, butyl acetate and ethyl acetate—has commenced in the country.

7. Economics of the Paint and Varnish Industry in India

The paint industry belongs to the category of light chemical industries, using simple machinery and plant. Moreover, its power and fuel consumption forms a minor cost factor. All-in-all, the investment factor is negligible compared to the large chemical industries. The industry is a raw material intensive industry and raw materials account for 70-80% of the total cost of the paint.

India is fortunate in that a number of paint raw materials such as barytes, gypsum, China clay, natural yellow and red oxide of iron, shellac, rosin, linseed oil, castor oil, glycerin, white spirit, vegetable turpentine, solvent naphtha and denatured spirit are available indigenously. Manufactured pigments and colors such as titanium dioxide, zinc and lead pigments, chrome oxide green, synthetic red oxide of iron and coal tar solvents are also available in the country.

The era of paint industry in India started in 1902 when Shalimar Paints, Color and Varnish Co. was set up in Calcutta. But the real growth started after the outbreak of the second World War. At this time several new paint manufacturing units, promoted by foreign companies as well as Indian entrepreneurs, were set up. The present-day giant, Asian Paints, was also started during the same period (in 1942). This fully Indian company became the nation's largest paint producer in the next 25 years (by 1967). After Independence, the paint industry grew steadily both in terms of paint produced and number of manufacturers. The turnover of paint industry has grown from Rs. 20 crore (Rs. 200 million) in 1950 to Rs. 200 crores (Rs. 2 billion) in 1993; a hundredfold increase in only 43 years! See Table IIIC-5.

Table IIIC-5
Installed Capacities of Major Indian Paint Producers (1992)

Company	*Installed Capacity, TPA*
Asian Paints	108,000
Berger Paints	14,000
Garware Paints	8,000
Goodlass Nerolac Paints	20,640
ICI Ltd.	13,550
Jenson & Nicholson Ltd.	35,000
Shalimar Paints	14,204
Total	**213,394**

Source: "*Chemical Weekly*"

Considering the meager per capita paints consumption in India—just 0.23 kg —as compared to USA (25 kg), Germany (21 kg), Sweden (19 kg), France (15 kg), Japan (8 kg), Malaysia (4.8 kg), Philippines (4.2 kg), Thailand (1 kg), it is certain that vast scope exists for the expansion of paints market and industry in India.

In the Indian paints market, the share of industrial paints is about 30% and that of decorative paints is about 70%. In the developed countries the industrial paints account for 70% of the market.

Unfortunately, paint is considered a luxury item even though it can prevent the heavy losses caused by corrosion in the country—estimated to be about Rs. 4,000 crores per year, i.e., every 15 seconds one ton of steel is converted to rust!

IIID. CARBOHYDRATES AND FERMENTATION INDUSTRIES

Naturally-occurring combinations of C, H, and O, with the last two in the same ratio as H_2O, are termed carbohydrates (hydrates of carbon). The most common types are:

sucrose (ordinary sugar)	starch
dextrose	cellulose

Cellulose will be discussed under Pulp and Paper Industry (Section IIIF). The fermentation industries will be presented here since most fermentation processes use carbohydrates as a substrate for production of various chemicals and biologicals.

Sucrose

1. Pertinent Properties of Sucrose

Chemical formula : $C_{12}H_{22}O_{11}$ (disaccharide)

Structural formula :

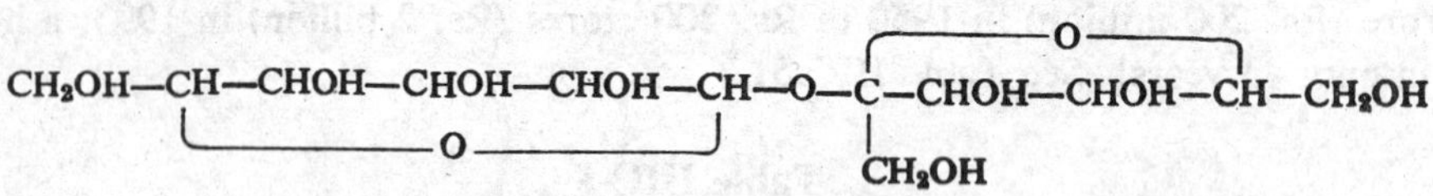

Mol. wt.	342
M.P.	186°C (decomposition)
Density	1.58 gm/cc
Solubility	Very soluble in water, slightly soluble in methyl and ethyl alcohol
Forms	Powdered, granulated

2. The Sugar Industry

The sugar industry was initially concentrated in the subtropical states of Uttar Pradesh and Bihar, but since the Second Plan it has dispersed into the Deccan area and the Southern States.

About 35 million farmers (including their families) constituting about 7 percent of the rural population are engaged in growing sugar cane. The industry absorbs a sizable portion of the cane crop and provides the farmer with resources to meet his commitments. Each sugar factory deals with thousands of cane farmers, ranging from 7,000 to 8,000 in the southern states and Maharashtra to 40,000-45,000 in Northern India.

Sugar cane, being a highly perishable crop, cannot be transported over long distances. Hence, the factories have necessarily to be set up within economic distances. Having regard to this basic characteristic of the industry, the concept of a minimum spatial distance between one factory and another has come to be accepted.

Sugar cane is the main raw material for the sugar industry, accounting for almost 60 percent of the cost of production of sugar. The sugar industry is an important agro-based industry. Its fortunes largely depend on the adequate availability of sugar cane. By the year 2001 AD, the country may require 350 million tons of sugar cane.

The worst handicap crippling the industry is the low level of productivity. This is attributed to inadequate irrigation facilities, untimely supply of quality seeds, etc. The erratic trend in the production of sugar is attributed to the fact that it is an agro-based industry and its output fluctuates with the vagaries of monsoons.

One factor which is of crucial importance to the growth of the sugar industry is the yield of sugar cane per acre. Percentage recovery of sucrose is the second factor which determines the production. In India, both the yield of sugar cane per acre and percentage recovery of sucrose are low.

Indian sugar factories have low milling efficiency and recovery of sugar from sugar cane is very low. One reason for this is the uneconomic character of many of the sugar mills. Further, Indian sugar mills do not have sugar plantations of their own (as in the case of the West Indies) and hence, do not have control over the quantity and quality of sugar cane supplied by innumerable cane growers.

The sugar industry has undergone a significant change since 1992 and India has emerged as a net exporter of sugar which was being imported for many years. In view of the comfortable position in regard to indigenous output, the Government has decided to give boost to sugar exports. Exports have gone up from 20,000 tons/year in 1986-90 to 200,000 tons in 1990-91 to 550,000 tons in 1991-92. This contrasts with internal Indian consumption of some 10-15 million tons.

The level of technology in the Indian sugar industry is quite high and a number of developing countries have borrowed Indian sugar technology. Unfortunately, however, many of India's factories had been set up in the early thirties and had become uneconomic. For these the need of the hour is modernization, rehabilitation and expansion. Attention also needs to be paid to cane development. More profitable utilization of by-products is another avenue that requires attention. Manufacture of paper and newsprint from bagasse, alcohol from molasses would also enable the factories to recover the cost of conversion of cane into sugar.

Sugar Scenario

Year	Area under sugar cane ('000 hectares)	Yield of cane per hectare (tons)	Production of sugar cane ('000 tons)	No. of factories in operation	Average actual capacity (tons) per 24 hours	Total cane crushed ('000 tons)	Recovery of sugar from cane %	Total sugar produced ('000 tons)
1980-81	2,667	57.8	154,248	314	1,707	51,598	9.98	5.147
1985-86	2,862	60.0	171,681	341	1,891	68,576	10.23	7.016
1990-91	3,682	64.3	240,287	385	2,088	122,319	9.85	12.046

Source: "Kothari's Industrial Directory of India" (1994)

A notable feature of the industry's working is that it does not depend on external energy resources, such as coal and firewood. It not only generates its own power, but also produces surplus power for supply to the grid in nearby rural areas, minimizing transmission losses.

If the entire potential is harnessed, the industry can easily provide an additional 2,000 MW at a fairly reasonable cost. The capital cost per megawatt produced by sugar mills, at 80 percent efficiency, would hardly be 40 percent of that of a thermal station.

While in other sectors in the country cooperative movement has either failed or made negligible progress, the success achieved by the cooperative sugar factories had been heartening. They dominate the sugar scene today. Cooperative sugar mills have two positive advantages in their favor. First, they get the maximum supply of sugar cane as almost all the sugar cane farmers are members of the cooperative sugar mills. Secondly, profits of the cooperatives are distributed among farmers instead of going into the hands of a few "sugar barons."

The cooperative factories, particularly those in Maharashtra, have not only brought out the competence of the local entrepreneurs, but have provided gainful employment to the local working class which otherwise might have joined the exodus of job seekers heading towards the urban area. The welfare activities undertaken by these factories have metamorphosed the rural areas surrounding them. They have started 12 colleges of arts and science, two medical colleges and 12 polytechnics. Needless to say, almost all of them have housing complexes for the employees with medical and educational facilities at least up to high school level. They have set up by-product based industries: 22 distilleries, 8 paper mills and 4 chemical plants. Besides six dairies, a number of poultry farms have been sponsored by them. The culmination of the success story was reached when a cooperative sugar machinery manufacturing plant was set up by them near Pune. The National Heavy Engineering Cooperative Ltd., having an annual turnover of about Rs. 2 crore, has introduced a continuous vertical crystallizer of latest design for maximum reduction of sugar losses.

3. Methods of Production

3.1. Classification of Processes

- Extraction of sugar cane to produce crystalline white sugar
- Extraction of sugar cane to produce gur, a dark brown sugar concentrate

3.2. Extraction from Sugar Cane for Crystalline Sugar Production

3.2.1. Reference flow sheet: Figure IIID-1

3.2.2. Chemical reactions—none of any importance

3.2.3. Quantitative requirements

(a) Basis: 1 ton of raw sugar (97% sucrose); yield from cane—95% on sucrose basis, 9.5-15% on cane basis

Sugar cane	6-10.5 tons of 16-10% sucrose content
Water	3-4 tons
Lime	12-17 kg
SO_2	6-10 kg

(b) Plant capacities: 100-400 tons/day of sugar

3.2.4. Process description

Canes are shredded in crushers and then squeezed through a series of pressure mills containing grooved walls. Weak juice and make-up water are added as extractant fluids before squeezing to optimize juice yield at 95-97%.

The juice is treated with calcium phosphate, followed by lime to precipitate the colloids. SO_2 is next bubbled through until the pH is 7.0 to 7.1. This procedure provides maximum flocculation of impurities. The SO_2 also acts as a bleaching agent. Phosphoric acid or CO_2 can be substituted as the acidifying agent depending on the type of extract handled.

Closed steam in a coil is used to heat and further flocculate the impurities in a continuous settler. The clarified liquor overflows to the evaporator. The underflow muds are processed on a continuous rotary press to recover sugar solution which is either passed forward to the evaporator or backward to the thickener again if it is not clear. The filter cake is used for fertilizer.

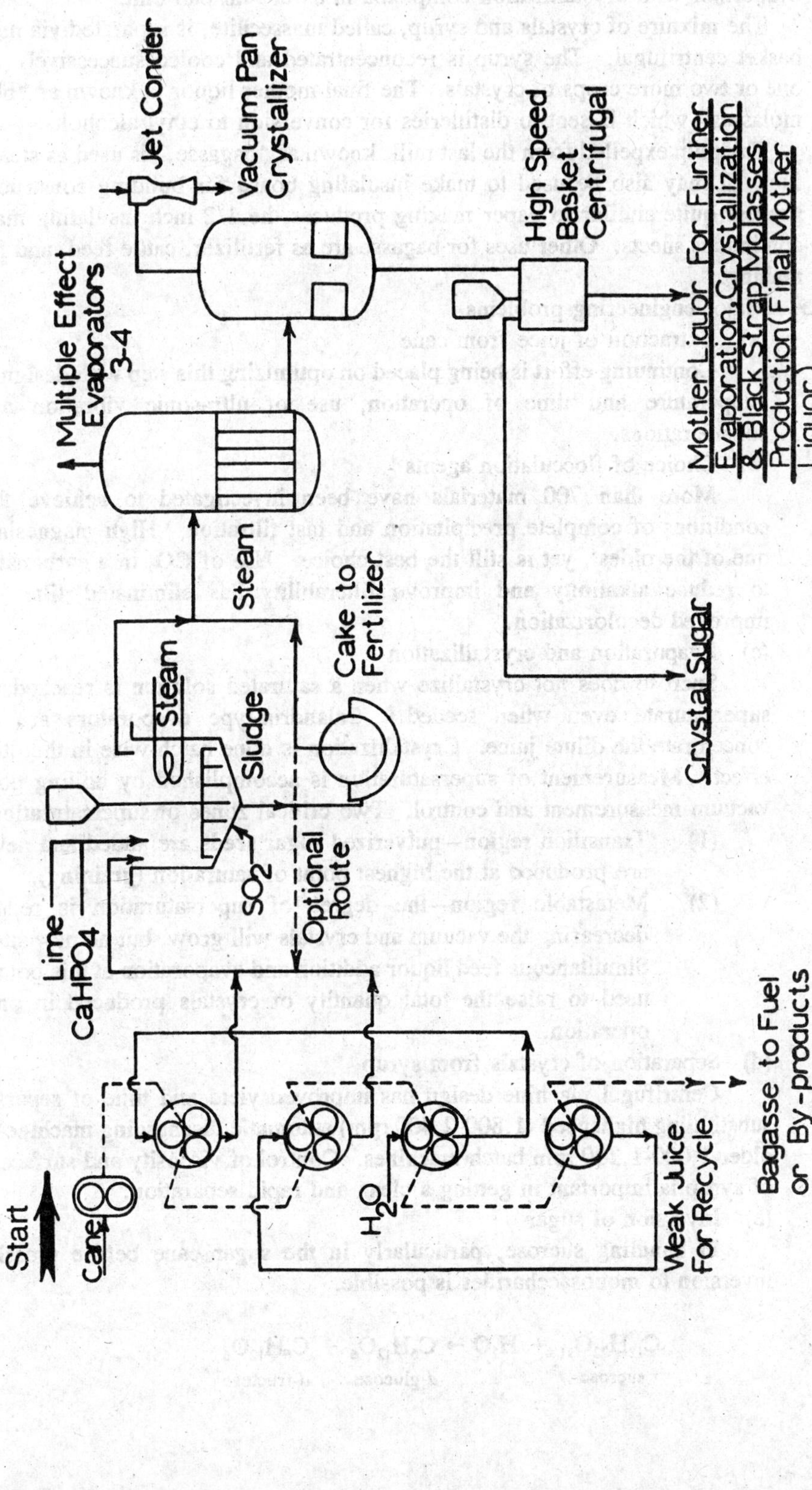

Fig. IIID-1. Extraction of sucrose from sugar cane.

The clarified juice is concentrated from 80-85% water to 40% in a 3 or 4 effect evaporator with crystallization completed in a vacuum pan unit.

The mixture of crystals and syrup, called massecuite, is separated via high-speed basket centrifugal. The syrup is reconcentrated and cooled successively to obtain one or two more crops of crystals. The final mother liquor is known as "blackstrap molasses" which is sent to distilleries for conversion to ethyl alcohol.

The pulp expelled from the last mill, known as "bagasse," is used as steam boiler fuel. It may also be used to make insulating board for building construction. A process quite similar to paper making produces the 1/2 inch insulating material in continuous sheets. Other uses for bagasse are as fertilizer, cattle feed, and for paper making.

3.2.5. Major engineering problems

(a) Extraction of juice from cane

Continuing effort is being placed on optimizing this step with design of rolls, temperature and time of operation, use of ultrasonic vibration as major considerations.

(b) Choice of flocculation agents

More than 700 materials have been investigated to achieve the ideal conditions of complete precipitation and fast filtration. High magnesia lime is one of the oldest, yet is still the best choice. Use of CO_2 in a carbonation step to reduce alkalinity and improve filterability has eliminated filter aid and improved decolorization.

(c) Evaporation and crystallization

Sucrose does not crystallize when a saturated solution is reached and will supersaturate even when seeded. Calandria-type evaporators are used to concentrate the dilute juice. Crystallization is done batch-wise in the 4th or last effect. Measurement of supersaturation is accomplished by boiling point-rise, vacuum measurement and control. Two critical zones of supersaturation exist:

(1) Transition region—pulverized sugar seeds are added and new nuclei are produced at the highest point of saturation (graining).

(2) Metastable region—the degree of supersaturation is reduced by decreasing the vacuum and crystals will grow, but no new sites form. Simultaneous feed liquor addition and evaporation at this point can be used to raise the total quantity of crystals produced in one batch operation.

(d) Separation of crystals from syrup

Centrifugal machine design has improved yield and time of separation by substituting highspeed (1,800-2,400 rpm) automatic discharging machines for the older 1,000-1,200 rpm batch machines. Control of viscosity and surface tension of syrup is important in getting a clean and rapid separation.

(e) Inversion of sugar

In handling sucrose, particularly in the sugar cane before pressing, the inversion to monosaccharides is possible.

$$\underset{\text{sucrose}}{C_{12}H_{22}O_{11}} + H_2O \rightarrow \underset{d\text{-glucose}}{C_6H_{12}O_6} + \underset{d\text{-fructose}}{C_6H_{12}O_6}$$

The extent of inversion is measured by a polarimeter with centrifugal cane sugar with no inversion having +97° polarization and completely invert sugar testing −20°.

The inversion is minimized by shading cuttings and making quick delivery to the sugar cane presses, less than 2 days being a practical goal. During the remainder of operations, the process is designed for low temperature-short time conditions to reduce both inversion and caramelization.

3.3. Extraction from Sugar Cane for Gur Production

Gur is the villager's sugar and represents a low-cost product made by a simple evaporation process. Approximately 60% of the sucrose for edible purposes in India is consumed in the form of gur.

3.3.1. Process description

The sugar cane juice is extracted as described in Section 3.2. Impurities are coagulated by addition of a vegetable base mucilagent and skimmed off the top. The clarified cane juice is then concentrated in open pan evaporators until the correct consistency is achieved by solidification test sampling. This is in the range of 80-85% solids. The product is run out of the bottom of the pan evaporators to can packages. It is a dark brown solidified paste at room temperature and inverts partially to monosaccharides on storage. It does contain nutritionally desirable minerals, particularly iron.

4. By-products of the Sugar Industry

Molasses, bagasse and press mud are the major by-products of the sugar industry. Molasses is an important by-product having strong linkages with the alcohol industry. Seventy percent of the molasses is used for manufacture of industrial alcohol and balance 30% for potable alcohol. Previously the pricing and distribution of molasses was controlled and the prices (at Rs. 140 per ton) were kept artificially low. In April 1993, molasses was decontrolled and prices shot up to levels of Rs.1,000 to 2,000 per ton. This has led to improved profitability of sugar mills with negative effects on alcohol based industries. However, lately prices have stabilized at around Rs. 650 per ton. However, it varies significantly among states.

Bagasse is another by-product which has substantial use as fuel in boilers for generation of steam, raw material for the paper industry as well as cogeneration of power. Usually in a sugar factory 35% of cane crushed would yield into bagasse. Press mud is the residue of the sugar juice after all purification is complete. It is used in the farms as manure. The production of press mud is around 3-7% of cane crushed depending on the process of manufacture.

Starch

Starch is a high polymer carbohydrate occurring in grains and roots in the form of granules of 3-100 μ size. These granules can be extracted from the grains by water hydration of the cells.

1. Pertinent Properties of Starch

1.1. Chemical Formula: $C_6H_{10}O_5$

1.2. Chemical Structure

1.2.1. Amylose or linear polymer

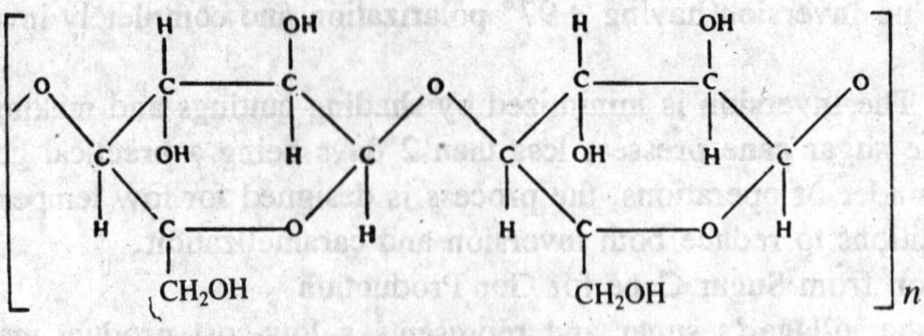

1.2.2. Amylopectin or branched chain polymer

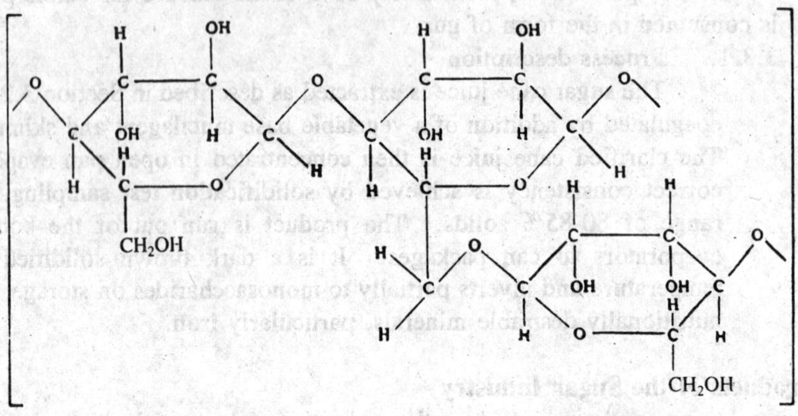

n varies from 200-500. Common industrial starches from maize contain 15-30% amylose and 85-70% amylopectin.

1.3. Chemical Reactivity

Readily hydrolyzed by acids, alkalis, and enzymes to molecules of progressively smaller size, giving soluble starch, dextrin, dextrose (*d*-glucose).

1.4. Reaction with Water

Starch granules (3-20 μ from maize) swell progressively as shorter polymers dissolve until a gel forms, depending on time-temperature of contact. Gels form in several minutes in water at 60-80°C.

2. Consumption Pattern

Unlike sucrose, starch has found considerable usage in industries other than food. Hydrolyzed products (dextrins, syrups, and sugars) go largely to the food industries.

2.1. End Uses

Starch	*USA*	*India*
Paper	12%	10%
Textiles	7	65
Jute	0	4
Food	5	} 1
Adhesives	5	
Laundry products	4	
Beverages	4	

Miscellaneous	3	—
	40	80
Hydrolysis products	60	20

3. Methods of Production

3.1. Reference Flow Sheet: Figure IIID-2
3.2. Chemical Reactions—none of importance
3.3. Process Description

The major source of starch is maize kernels and a wet milling process for the removal of starch will be presented.

Maize kernels containing 60-65% starch are screened and air cleaned, then steeped in 50-55°C water containing 0.15-0.30% SO_2 as a bacteriostatic. The softened grains are passed through coarse grinding mills to rupture the cells and loosen the oil germ which is floated off in a large slurry tank.

The starch portion of the kernel is wet ground on buhrstone mills and passed over nylon cloth where water washes the starch through and leaves the fiber and hulls on the screen.

The starch suspension in the underflow from the screens contains gluten (water insoluble protein) which is separated as the light fraction in a two-stage centrifuge operation.

The starch is recovered as filter cake on a continuous rotary filter. It can be dried, powdered, and sold as pearl starch. Other products can be made by gelatinizing with water or by hydrolysis.

Starch derivatives of higher value than starch itself are important. Some of the more interesting products are discussed next.

Starch Derivatives

1. Dextrin

1.1. Description—heat and acid depolymerization yields a water soluble carbohydrate gum which is used in adhesives and gums.

1.2. Chemical Reaction

$$(C_6H_{10}O_5)_n \xrightarrow[\text{HCl}]{\text{heat}} \frac{n}{x} \cdot (C_6H_{10}O_5)_x$$

1.3. Methods of Production

- Batch heating in scraping-type autoclave units—older inefficient method
- Fluidized hydrolysis—modern method

1.4. Description of Fluidized Hydrolysis

1.4.1. Reference flow sheet: Figure IIID-3

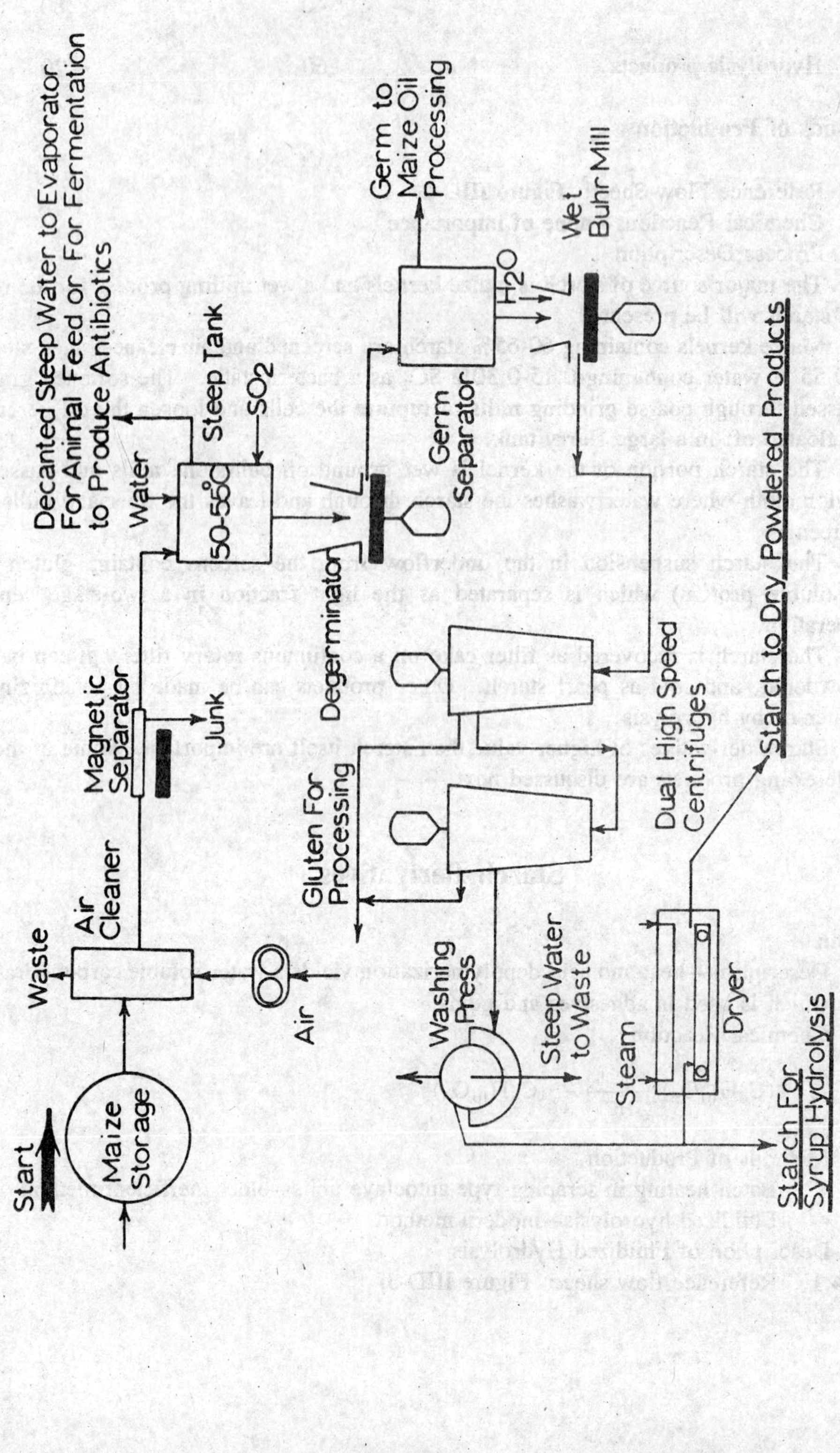

Fig. IIID-2. Starch production from maize.

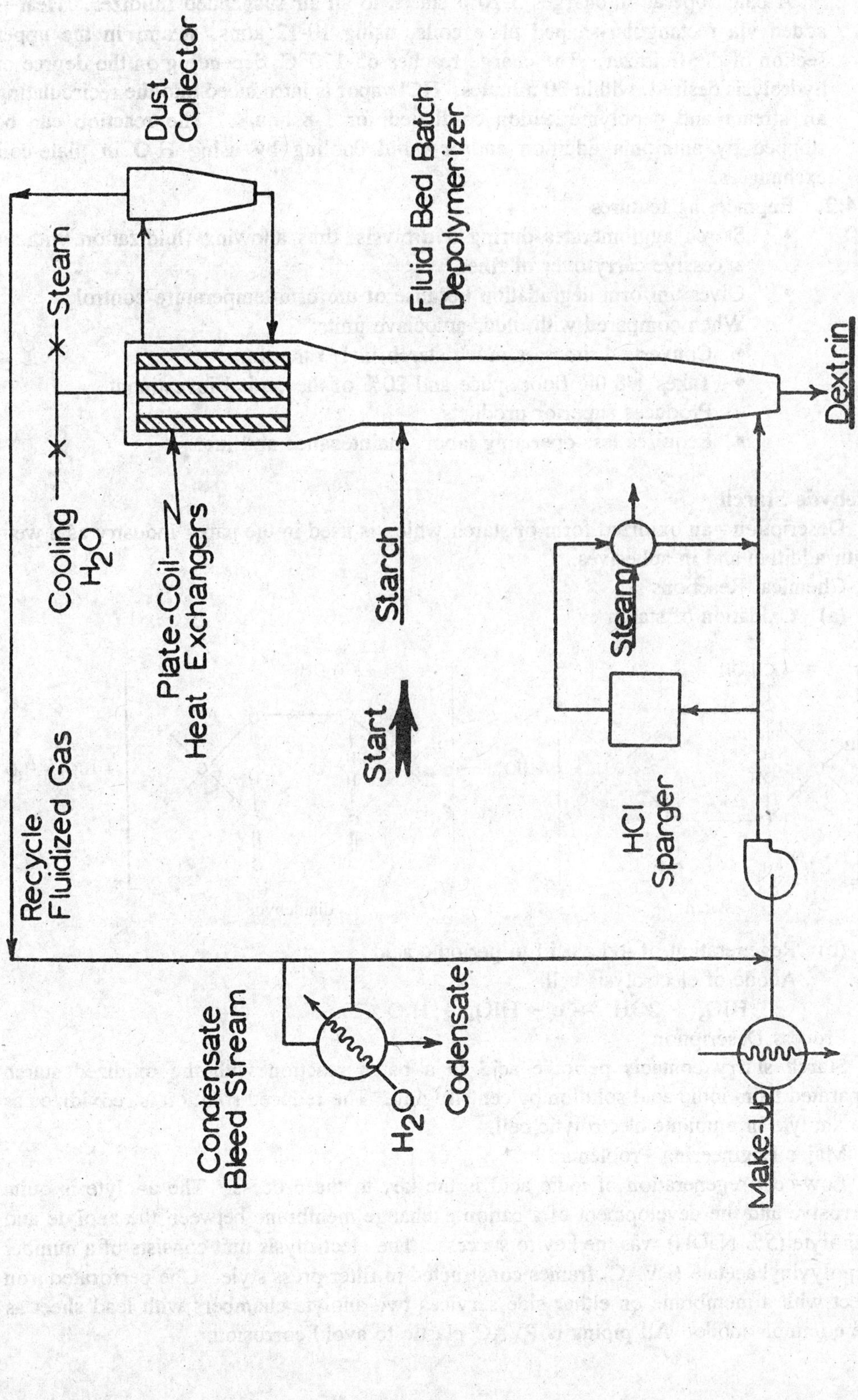

Fig. IIID-3. Production of dextrin by starch hydrolysis in a fluidized bed.

A batch operation charges 5-10 μ starch to an air suspended fluidizer. Heat is added via rectangular-shaped plate coils, using 10-12 atms. steam, in the upper section of the fluidizer. The charge reaches 65-170°C, depending on the degree of hydrolysis desired, within 30 minutes. HCl vapor is introduced into the recirculating air stream and depolymerization continued for 1-8 hours. The reaction can be stopped by ammonia addition and/or rapid cooling by using H_2O in plate-coil exchangers.

1.4.2. Engineering features

- Starch agglomerates during hydrolysis, thus allowing fluidization without excessive carry-over of fines
- Gives uniform degradation because of uniform temperature control

When compared with older autoclave units:

- Converts 4 times as much starch in 1/3 the time
- Takes 1/8 the floor space and 20% of the capital investment
- Produces superior products
- Requires less operating labor, maintenance and fuel

2. Dialdehyde Starch

2.1. Description—an oxidized form of starch which is used in the paper industry as a wet-strength additive and in adhesives.

2.2. Chemical Reactions

(a) Oxidation of starch

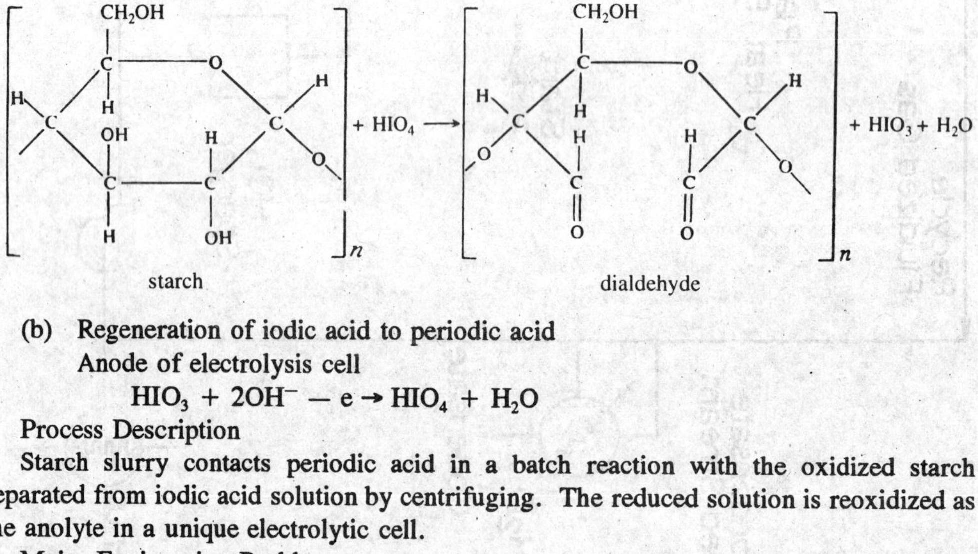

(b) Regeneration of iodic acid to periodic acid

Anode of electrolysis cell

$$HIO_3 + 2OH^- - e \rightarrow HIO_4 + H_2O$$

2.3. Process Description

Starch slurry contacts periodic acid in a batch reaction with the oxidized starch separated from iodic acid solution by centrifuging. The reduced solution is reoxidized as the anolyte in a unique electrolytic cell.

2.4. Major Engineering Problems

Low-cost regeneration of iodic acid is the key to the process. The anolyte is quite corrosive and the development of a cation exchange membrane between the anolyte and catholyte (5% NaOH) was the key to success. The electrolysis unit consists of a number of polyvinyl acetate (PVAC) frames constructed in filter press style. One perforated iron sheet with a membrane on either side services two anolyte chambers with lead sheet as the common anode. All piping is PVAC plastic to avoid corrosion.

3. Starch Phosphate

3.1. Description—a starch ester which is water soluble, has excellent freeze-thaw stability, good thickening power. Expected usage is as thickeners in canned and frozen foods, adhesives, emulsion paint formulations, pharmaceutical filters and binders.

3.2. Chemical Reactions

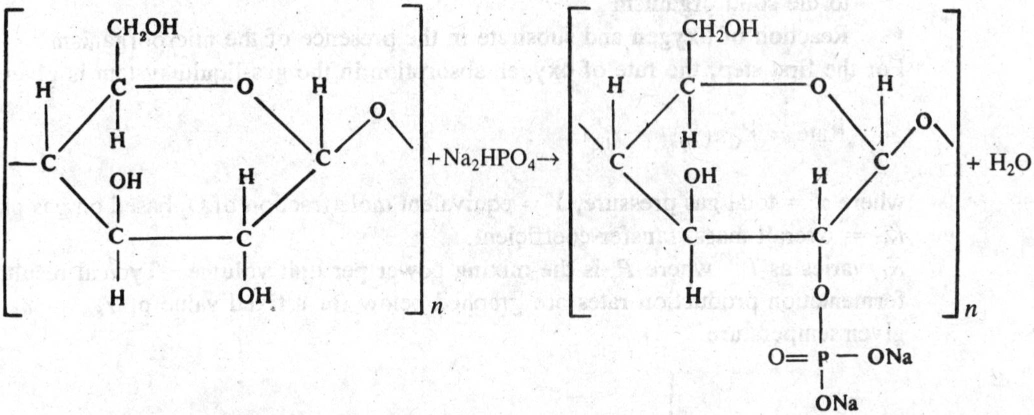

3.3. Process Description

Starch slurry is reacted with alkaline phosphate solutions at various conditions depending on degree of esterification. Control of pH (8.5-9.5), temperature (50-70°C), and time (10-60 minutes) are examples of range of variables used. The water soluble solutions are filtered and the filtrate spray dried.

Fermentation Industries

1. Introduction

Fermentation processes utilize microbiology in producing chemical compounds, but have a history similar to all natural product processing. Those processes yielding simple structural chemicals, *e.g.*, ethanol, butanol, or acetone, are gradually being replaced by synthetic processes with cheap and abundant raw materials. However, fermentation processes are still useful for production of complex organic chemicals such as medicinals, antibiotics, and for chemicals of more complex structure, such as citric and lactic acids derived from low-cost carbohydrate sources.

2. General Characteristics of a Fermentation Process

The action of a specific microorganism on a substrate to produce the desired chemical compound is termed fermentation. The majority of processes require oxygen and are classified as aerobic. The few processes carried out in the absence of air are classified as anaerobic. In general, the process involves addition of a specific culture of microorganisms to a sterilized liquid substrate or broth in a tank (submerged fermentation), addition of air if aerobic in a well-designed gas-liquid contactor, and carrying out the fermentation to grow microorganisms and produce the desired chemicals. This can be done batch-wise or continuously at a given temperature and time, then processing the broth to remove the desired chemical.

Some of the engineering problems in such processes will be discussed next with typical fermentation process examples given last.

3. Major Engineering Problems

3.1. Kinetics of Submerged, Aerobic Fermentation

- Gas-liquid contact by proper dispersion of air in the tank and oxygen transfer between gas bubbles and liquid
- Liquid-solid transfer in which dissolved oxygen and the substrate are transferred to the solid organism
- Reaction of oxygen and substrate in the presence of the microorganism

For the first step, the rate of oxygen absorption in the gas-liquid system is given by:

$$\text{Rate} = K_G\pi(Y_{gas} - Y_{liq}),$$

where π = total gas pressure, Y = equivalent mole fraction of O_2 based on gas phase, K_G = overall mass transfer coefficient.

K_G varies as $P_v^{1/3}$ where P_v is the mixing power per unit volume. Typical results for fermentation production rates are graphed below for a fixed value of $Y_{gas} - Y_{liq}$ at a given temperature.

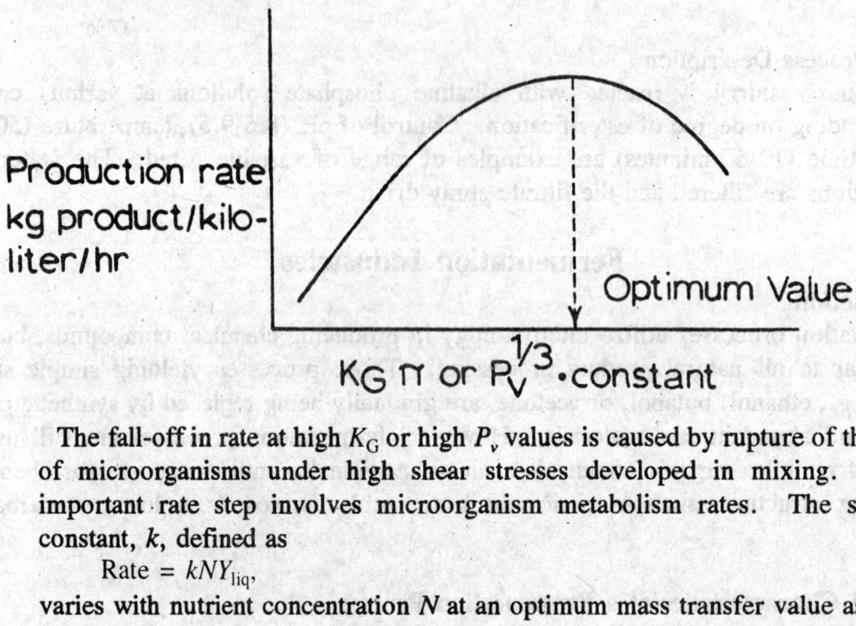

The fall-off in rate at high K_G or high P_v values is caused by rupture of the cell walls of microorganisms under high shear stresses developed in mixing. The other important rate step involves microorganism metabolism rates. The specific rate constant, k, defined as

$$\text{Rate} = kNY_{liq},$$

varies with nutrient concentration N at an optimum mass transfer value as pictured:

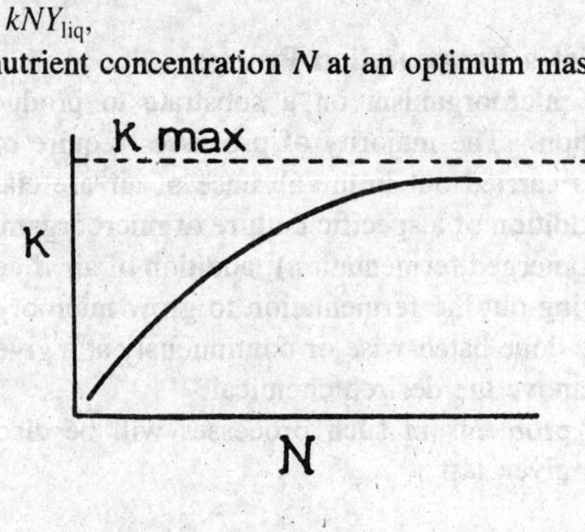

3.2. Scale-up of Submerged Fermentation

Air is generally used to supply the oxygen demand. If the volume of air per unit volume of liquid per unit time, v, is the constant scale-up factor, then severe foaming may result in tank designs of total volume V where the height-diameter ratio ($H : D$) is kept constant.

V varies as HD^2 or as D^3

A_x, the escape area for unused gas, varies as D^2

$$\text{Escape velocity} = \frac{vV}{A_x}, \text{ proportional to } \frac{D^3}{D^2} \text{ or } D$$

Thus the escape velocity increases with tank size, causing increased and possibly unmanageable foaming unless a large diameter, low height tank is used. Mixing in this case may be ill-defined. If the scale-up is done on a fixed linear exit velocity basis, the oxygen supply may be insufficient in large volume systems. Design must be a compromise involving tank shape, optimized mixing of air supplied, and exit velocity. $H : D$ usually works out to be between 2 : 1 and 3 : 1.

3.3. Air Sterilization

Contamination of pure cultures used in fermenters is avoided by heat sterilization of the air. This is most simply accomplished by adiabatic compression to 200°C and removing all dust and oil by passage through fibrous filters.

3.4. Media Sterilization

Temperature sterilization of the substrate feed is still the best method. The more costly ionization radiation becomes important where off-color and odor is traced to heat liable substrates.

3.5. Continuous versus Batch Fermentation

Batch processes are usually preferred for long residence time processes or because of the hazards of contamination and mutation of the specific microorganism. This is so despite the fact that continuous processes provide for easier control, uniformity of product if not contaminated, and reduced labor costs.

3.6. Design Principles for Sterile Operations

- No direct connection between sterile and unsterile parts of system
- All-welded, smooth inside construction
- Smooth joints using Teflon or Kel-F as sealant gasket
- Use Kel-F diaphragm valves
- Maintain sterile areas under positive pressure to avoid back-diffusion of unsterile air
- Independently sterilize each part of system
- Continued use of steam for labile zones

4. Economics of the Fermentation Industry

Prerequisites for a successful fermentation process are:

- Microorganisms must be specific and produce good yield of desired end-product
- Rapid fermentation rates must be achieved
- Use economic raw materials with dependable supply
- Products easily recovered and purified

A great deal of research revolves around the first two points. A new strain of microorganism which can be developed to give high specificity at rapid rates and operate in high end-product concentration will be the key to a new process or a new chemical.

Cheap substrates are difficult to find even if they are by-products from other processes. One interesting development in the worldwide fermentation picture is the use of cheap petroleum hydrocarbons to produce food for human consumption. Japan is actively engaged in this research.

Examples in India of typical fermentation industries presently economic are ethyl alcohol and penicillin. Ethyl alcohol will be discussed next and penicillin will be discussed in Section IVH under Pharmaceutical Industry.

Ethyl Alcohol

1. Pertinent Properties of Ethyl Alcohol (Ethanol)

Mol. wt.	46.07
Density	0.791 @ 20°C
M.P.	—112°C
B.P.	78.3°C
Flash point	21°C
Ignition temperature	372°C
Explosive limits:	Lower = 3.5% by volume
	Upper = 19%
Toxicity limit	1,000 ppm
Grades	Anhydrous, 95%, denatured

2. Consumption Pattern

Ethyl alcohol serves largely as an intermediate for a number of other chemical products. Its original prime use in blended power fuels has virtually disappeared with increased petrol refinery capacity.

2.1. End Use Pattern

	India	*USA*
Synthetic rubber	33%	
Solvent	15	27%
Polyethylene	13	
Potable spirits	10	
Plastics	9	
Acetaldehyde-acetic acid	7	53
Butyl acetate	5	
Other chemicals	—	15
Miscellaneous	8	5

3. Methods of Production

3.1. Classification of Processes

3.1.1. Fermentation

- From sucrose substrate
- From waste sulfite substrate of paper mills
- From starch substrate

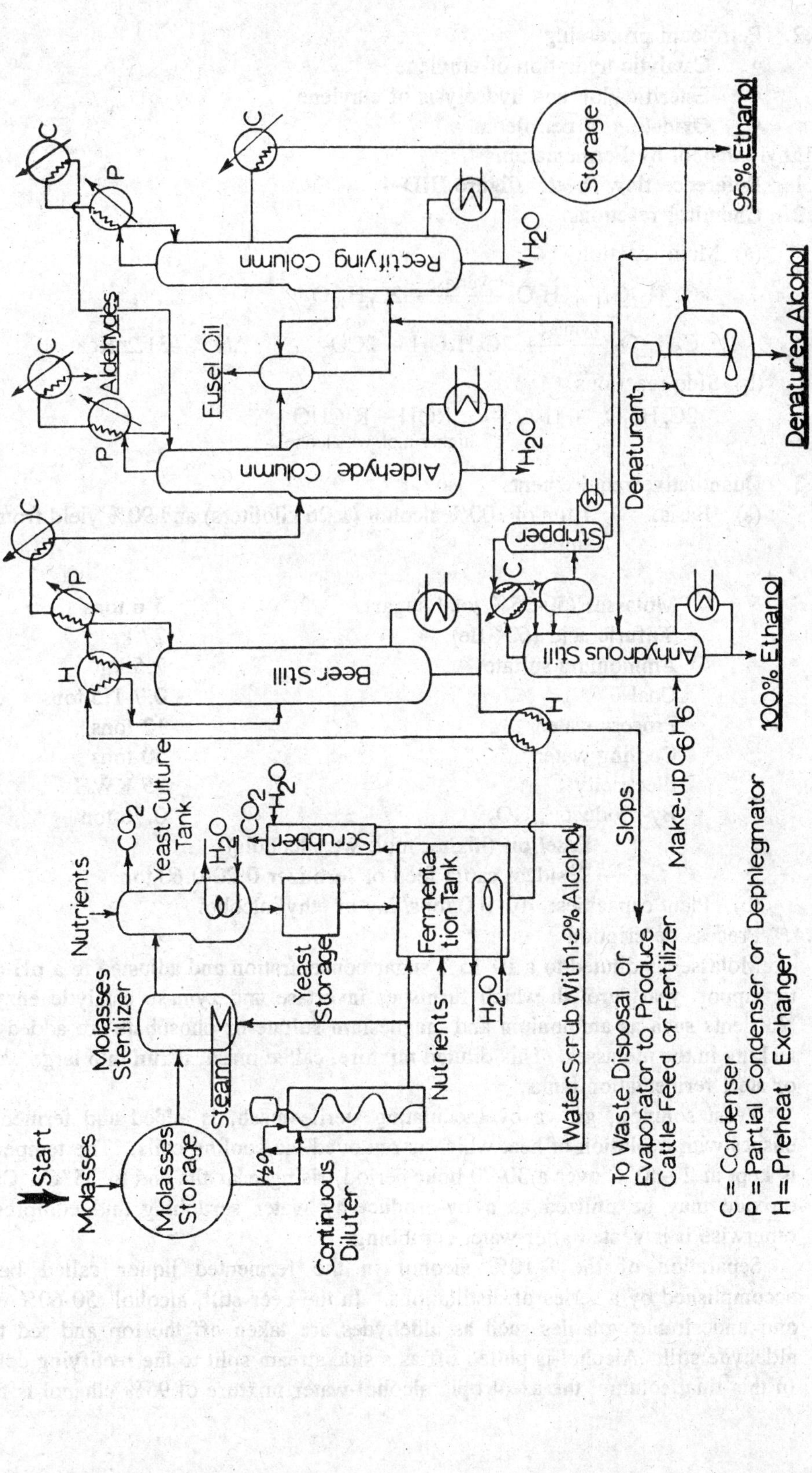

Fig. IIID-4. Ethyl alcohol by fermentation.

3.1.2. Petroleum processing
- Catalytic hydration of ethylene
- Esterification and hydrolysis of ethylene
- Oxidation of petroleum

3.2. Ethyl Alcohol by Fermentation

3.2.1. Reference flow sheet: Figure IIID-4

3.2.2. Chemical reactions

(a) Main reaction

$$C_{12}H_{22}O_{11} + H_2O \xrightarrow{\text{invertase}} 2C_6H_{12}O_6$$

$$C_6H_{12}O_6 \xrightarrow{\text{zymase}} 2C_2H_5OH + 2CO_2; \qquad \Delta H = -31.2 \text{ Kcal}$$

(b) Side reactions

$$2C_6H_{12}O_6 + H_2O \rightarrow \underset{\text{higher mol. wt. alcohols}}{ROH + R'CHO}$$

3.2.3. Quantitative requirements

(a) Basis: 1 ton of 100% alcohol (1.26 kiloliters) and 90% yield from total sugar

Molasses (50-55% total sugar)	5.6 tons
Sulfuric acid (60° Be)	27 kg
Ammonium sulfate	2.5 kg
Coal	0.7-1.5 tons
Process water	12 tons
Cooling water	50 tons
Electricity	35 KWH
By-products: CO_2	0.76 ton
Fusel oil (higher mol. wt. alcohols)	
Residual cattle feed or fertilizer 0.20-0.60 ton	

(b) Plant capacities: 10-100 tons/day of ethyl alcohol

3.2.4. Process description

Molasses is diluted to a 10-15% sugar concentration and adjusted to a pH of 4-5 to support yeast growth which furnishes invertase and zymase catalytic enzymes. Nutrients such as ammonium and magnesium sulfate or phosphate are added when lacking in the molasses. This diluted mixture, called mash, is run into large wooden or steel fermentation tanks.

Yeast solution, grown by inoculating sterile mash, is added and fermentation ensues with evolution of heat which is removed via cooling coils. The temperature is kept at 20-30°C over a 30-70 hour period, rising near the end to 35°C. Carbon dioxide may be utilized as a by-product by water scrubbing and compressing; otherwise it is vented after water scrubbing.

Separation of the 8-10% alcohol in the fermented liquor called beer is accomplished by a series of distillations. In the beer still, alcohol (50-60% conc.) and undesirable volatiles such as aldehydes are taken off the top and fed to the aldehyde still. Alcohol is pulled off as a side-stream split to the rectifying column. In this final column, the azeotropic alcohol-water mixture of 95% ethanol is taken off as a top side-stream, condensed and run to storage where it is split into three parts:

(1) direct sale as potable, government controlled alcohol
(2) denatured by small additions of mildly toxic ingredients and sold for industrial uses
(3) made anhydrous by ternary azeotropic distillation using benzene or extractive distillation using ethylene glycol

When fusel oil recovery is practiced, side-streams are drawn off near the bottom of the aldehyde and rectifying columns and are separated by decantation. These higher molecular weight alcohols are sold directly for solvents or are fractionated to give predominantly amyl alcohol.

The bottoms from the beer still, known as *slops*, are either discharged as waste or concentrated by evaporation to cattle feed depending on fuel and by-product sales economics.

3.2.5. Major engineering problems

- Collection and storage of molasses
- Maintenance of sterile and specific yeast culture conditions
- Batch versus continuous operation: continuous molasses dilution in the head end of the process and continuous distillation are incorporated to save space, equipment and operating costs
- Waste disposal problem: if uneconomic to concentrate for cattle feed, must use trickling filters, activated sludge or anaerobic digestion to lower the biological oxygen demand (BOD) before discharging to water run-off
- Fuel economy in the series of distillations: use of preheat exchangers
- Development of methods to produce anhydrous alcohol from the 95% alcohol azeotrope

4. Economics of Ethyl Alcohol Industry

4.1. Choice of Process

Six possible processes were listed in Section 3.1. Alcohol by fermentation in India is limited to sucrose substrate because of insufficient supplies of starch and paper mill wastes. This type of process furnished the bulk of alcohol requirements until the late 1960's when alcohol from petroleum processing became available in India. The reason for this switchover is that the inherently small ethanol producing plants widely distributed throughout sugar cane producing areas of India cannot compete with the cost of ethanol produced in a large capacity plant of a petrochemical complex. Furthermore, it is impossible to supply the entire future demand for alcohol from agricultural raw material. For example, in 1963, the synthetic rubber plant at Bareilly used nearly all of the alcohol in U.P. State for its preparation of butadiene and ethylene.

Fermentation alcohol served a good purpose in starting off the organic chemical industry of India, saved foreign exchange, and developed technical knowhow to incorporate in the larger plants based on petroleum. This pattern is identified with that recorded in the USA, Japan, and other highly industrialized countries.

4.2. Trends in Ethanol Industry Growth in India

At present there are about 127 units (at the end of 1990-91) manufacturing alcohol with an installed capacity of 744 million liters.

Until now Uttar Pradesh, Maharashtra, Tamil Nadu and Karnataka have been the leading alcohol producing States in the country. It is expected that in the coming years only Uttar Pradesh, Tamil Nadu and Madhya Pradesh will have surplus alcohol availability.

The production and consumption trend of alcohol (for industrial purpose and potable purpose) in the country during the past few years has been as follows:

Production and Consumption Trend of Alcohol (Mill. Liters)

Year	Production	Consumption	
		Industrial	Potable
1985-86	578	234	341
1986-87	616	247	320
1987-88	636	413	392
1988-89	798	381	416
1989-90	927 (Est.)	452	474

Source: *"SBP Handbook of Projects for Corporate Diversification" (1992)*

In the past few years many new sugar units have come up in the country and many existing sugar mills have expanded their capacity. This is expected to increase the availability of molasses in the country.

Further, some new chemical and allied industrial units are coming up in the country which will use alcohol as the main raw material, namely, the SM Dyechem's new glycol unit at Pune will require about 1,000 lakh liters of alcohol per annum. DCW wants to expand its capacity for production of PVC via alcohol route, VAM Organic also wants to go for massive expansion and diversification.

The shortage of alcohol in the country affects alcohol user chemical units and consequent low production of alcohol based chemicals. This results in wastage of precious foreign exchange in the import of these chemicals.

For instance, in the last few years, Reliance has imported about 10,000 tons of acetic acid and IPCL has imported 3,000 tons of *n*-butanol.

As per the "Perspective Plan for Chemical Industry (up to 2000 AD)" the demand for industrial alcohol in the country is expected to rise to about 15,00,000 KL and 24,00,000 KL per annum by 1994-95 and 1999-2000 respectively.

Fermentation Products from Petroleum

Since, as will be discussed in Section IIIE which follows, food production in India is of major importance, all potential food sources must be explored. In his big search for food, modern man is now looking beyond agriculture, animal breeding and fish harvesting. One new potential food source is based on the discovery that it is possible to sustain fermentation processes, not only on conventional carbohydrate media, but also on petroleum hydrocarbon media.

It has been known for some years that bacteria would attack hydrocarbons, undesirable foreign materials having been produced in that way in aircraft fuel tanks, etc. The application of this knowledge to the production of synthetic protein materials containing the essential amino acids by hydrocarbon fermentation dates only from the early 1960's, however.

Microorganisms, in particular yeasts and bacteria, can synthesize proteins from the above C sources in the presence of aqueous nutrient salt solutions containing the essential inorganic sulfur, phosphorus, and nitrogen compounds. The first industrial plants were built by BP in Scotland (4,000 tons per year; basis, *n*-alkanes) and in France (16,000 tons per year; basis, gas oil) for the production of the so-called alkane yeast (Toprina®). The French plant was converted from gas oil to an *n*-alkane basis (30,000 tons per year), and then shut down in 1975. The unit in Scotland discontinued operation in 1978.

N-alkanes are also carbon sources for SCP (single-cell protein) plants in operation in, for example, former East Germany, Rumania, and Russia. For example, in 1990, Russia produced 1.3 x 10^6 tons of SCP. While gaining energy, microorganisms (*e.g.*, Candida yeast) degrade *n*-paraffins step by step to CO_2 and at the same time produce protein-rich cellular substances. Approximately one ton of yeast with an amino acid pattern similar to fish meal results from one ton alkane feed. Industrial SCP manufacture takes place in continuously operated fermentation apparatus under aseptic conditions with good mixing and heat removal.

One of the major stimuli for development work on protein food production from petroleum lies in the rate of food production as compared to conventional means. Thus, bacteria and yeasts that feed on hydrocarbons are capable of doubling their weight in 3 to 5 hours, whereas plants like soyabeans require as much as 1 to 2 weeks and cattle 2 to 4 months to double their weight. Land requirements for protein production by fermentation would be a small fraction of that needed for agriculture or animal raising; also water requirements would be lowered.

Figure IIID-5 shows the essentials of a process for the production of food proteins from petroleum.

The feed material may be a gas oil (as shown) or a pure *n*-paraffin fraction. In any event, the bacteria "eat" only the straight chain waxy materials; thus when a gas oil is fed, it is biologically dewaxed at the same time fermentation occurs, giving an oily co-product having improved pour point and cloud point. Even methane may be used as a substrate in hydrocarbon fermentation.

The approximate chemical reaction which occurs in this process is:

$$2n(CH_2) + 2nO_2 + 0.2NH_4^+ \rightarrow n(CH_{1.7}O_{0.5}N_{0.2}) + nCO_2 + 1.5nH_2O + 200,000\ n\ \text{Kcals}$$

Thus, it may be seen that oxygen from air and ammonia salts are the other essential reactants in the process. The aqueous feed also contains inorganic nutrients for the fermentation such as potassium, sulfur, phosphorus and other mineral salts.

Compressed air bubbled into the fermenter not only serves as a reactant, but assists in heat removal by evaporative cooling. The process takes place at 30-70°C and at atmospheric pressure over a reaction period of 3 to 6 hours.

The product steam is continuously withdrawn from the fermenter and after separation is dried to give a product ready for packaging and shipment.

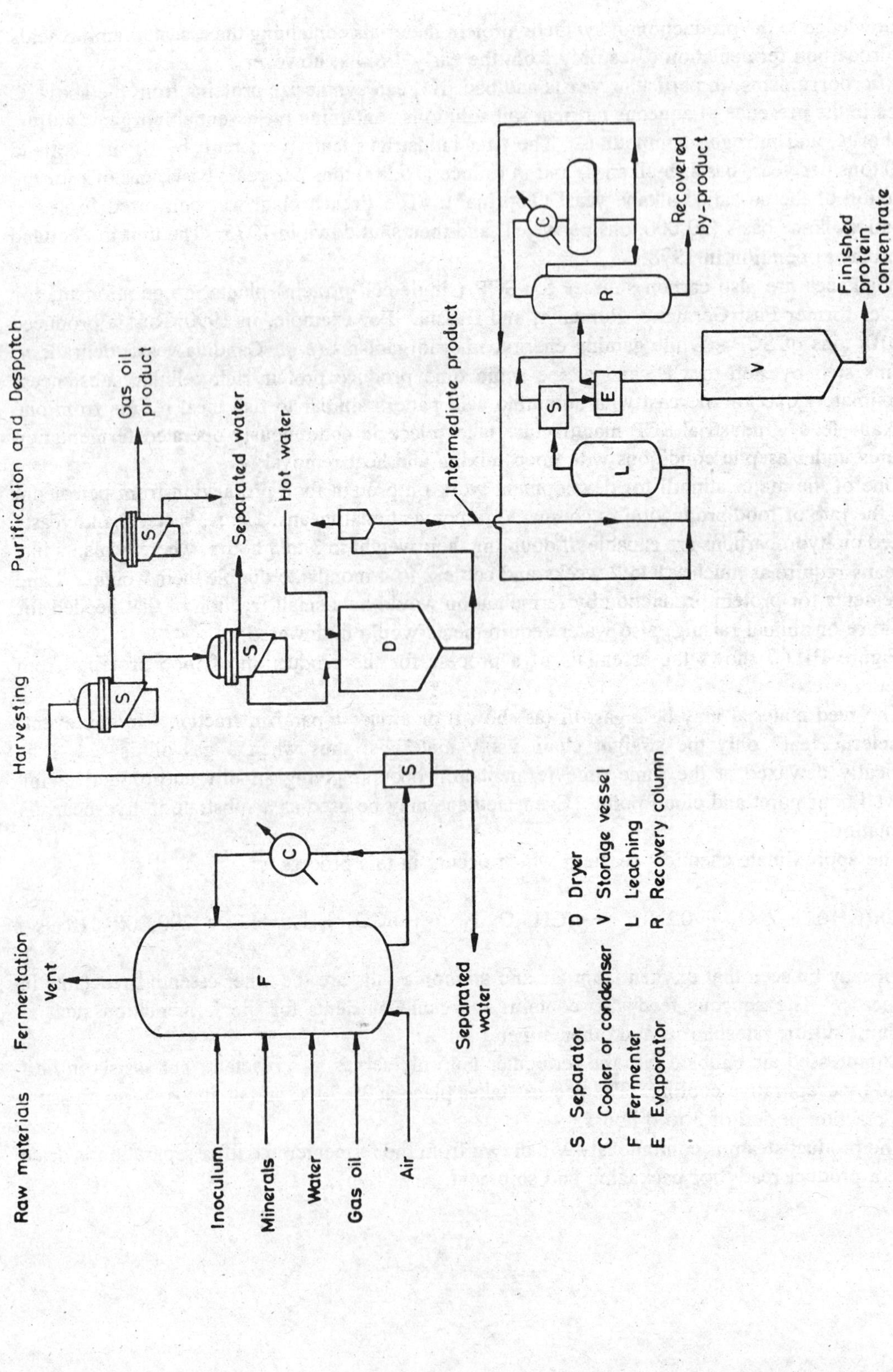

Fig. IIID-5. Flow diagram of petroleum fermentation process.

IIIE. FOOD INDUSTRY

India is primarily an agrarian country. It has a population of nearly a billion people. When one takes these two factors together, one is faced with the handling of a tremendous tonnage of foodstuffs.

Much of the food produced in India today may be consumed within a very few miles of the point where it is grown. Also, the production of certain types of foodstuffs is seasonal. As the preservation facilities existing in the country are not adequate, some foodstuffs are not available year round. As the standard of living increases and as living patterns change, there will be increasing emphasis on

— Food storage
— Food processing
— Food transport
— Food preservation

Food storage may involve chemical engineers in developing improved cold storage facilities—improved refrigeration cycles, new refrigerants, better insulation, improved processes.

Food processing may include freezing, dehydration, freeze drying, and food packaging processes.

Food transport may involve chemical engineers in the design of refrigerated road and rail carriers.

Food preservation may include inert gas blanketing of goods, food freezing and the use of chemical additives.

Food Storage

Vegetables and fruits are generally processed as soon as the raw materials are recovered at the plant, but due to some unavoidable circumstances such as early arrivals, non-availability, market price considerations which change according to time, etc., they may have to be stored prior to processing. During storage products continue to mature; loss of water by chemical and physical breakdown takes place. Respiration produces heat and causes self-heating in the harvested product. The loss of sugar during storage also results in loss of flavor, sweetness and general excellence. During storage, especially at high temperatures and humidities, all fruits and vegetables may be susceptible to molds and other diseases and some vegetables become hard. Thus the storage area should be well ventilated to dissipate the heat generated. Shade, water baths, precooling and even cold storage, when available, should be used. Graded material should be stored and all bruised, shriveled, discolored or soured portions should be removed.

Food Processing

The food processing industry in India consists of basic food industry, processing foodgrains, pulses, oilseeds and sugar cane, etc. Further, the processed food industry produces a wide range of products based on fruits and vegetables and several other products, viz., extruded foods, confectionery, bakery products, beverages (alcoholic and non-alcoholic) and dairy products. India's geographical and climatic advantage to produce a wide range of fruits, vegetables, cereals, edible oilseed, etc., is a strong foundation for the development of food processing industries.

Use of processed food is not new in India, being used in the country for centuries. The forms in which processed foods were prepared however were simple—jams, jellies, vermicelli, papads, pickles, dried and salted fish and meat, etc. These products were prepared as traditional food. What is new is the emergence of processed food preparation on a mass scale for sale on a commercial basis. Processed food as an industry started early in the century with biscuits and bread manufacture. Later, production of confectionery, dairy products, chocolates, dehydrated vegetables, soft drinks, etc., came in vogue. However, compared to western standards, processed food in India is still in its infancy.

The food processing industry has tremendous potential for growth, diversification and export. India is one of the largest producers of fruits and vegetables (29 million tons of fruits and 45 million tons of vegetables in 1991). Out of this very large quantity of raw fruits and vegetables only 8.94 lakh tons were processed and still small 48,900 tons were exported. The per capita income of the producers can only be increased by processing them to value-added products. This leads to increased food availability, because of lesser waste, increased rural employment, increased GNP, increased Government reserve and increased export earning, according to the *SBP Handbook of Export Oriented Food Processing Projects*.

Earlier, the major objective of food processing was food preservation. However, consumer convenience, their tastes, nutrition and their choice of food type and form have been the major determining parameters in today's food processing operation. The convenience in terms of saving in cooking time and effort has gained importance because of small and nuclear family and the wife has also become an earner.

The modern processing of foods as an organized industrial activity started in this country over six decades ago, to meet the needs of the British people living in India. Till 1950, the product range was limited—bread, biscuits, confectioneries, jams, jellies, aerated soft drinks, pork and pork products. Subsequently, the spectrum of food processing industries was widened and in the last few years it has undergone a quantum jump. There is an average more than 8% growth rate predicted for the coming years from Rs. 28,000 crore market in 1991-92.

Besides the commercial production of the traditional convenience food, the production of various snacks and snack mixes increased manifold. The ready-to-eat snack breakfast cereals, extruded snack products and texturized vegetable protein foods have shown large increased production and consumer acceptance. The existence of present fifty-four units offering ready-to-eat snacks, fried snacks, including French fries and potato wafers, etc., also indicates the fast growth of this sector. Besides satisfying the domestic demand, the industry also earns foreign exchange which increased steadily from Rs. 800 crore in 1980-81 to Rs. 2,800 crore in 1990-91.

Over the years, the profile of food processing sector has undergone a change. The new products such as ready-to-eat (RTE) snack foods, breakfast cereals, other extruded snack foods and texturized vegetable protein foods have shown an increased trend in their production, acceptance and consumption as well. The food processing industry has shown tremendous growth over the last 10-15 years. Besides meeting the domestic demand, the Indian processed food industry earns foreign exchange through exports. Exports have steadily risen from Rs. 1,955 lakhs in 1980-81 to Rs. 78,000 lakhs in 1987-88 and 280,000 lakhs in 1990-91.

The eighties have seen a phenomenal expansion of the food processing industry in India attributed mainly to two factors. First, there has been a technological revolution in the Indian food processing industry in terms of processing and packaging. Consequently, a new range of products have come to the market, which have ease in handling, long shelf life under non-air conditioned storage, ready-to-eat or heat-and-eat or ready mixes, etc., according to the *SBP Handbook of Export Oriented Food Processing Projects*.

In India, agriculture contributes to 35% of GDP and employing 70% of the population. The Indian government has therefore consistently laid emphasis on this sector. Moreover, India's productivity in this sector is very low not only when compared to the developed economies of the world, but even compared to some of the less developed countries. Thus, a huge potential exists for exploiting the rich natural resources of this country through technology.

The food industry accounts for only 5.2% of the investment while contributing to 18% of the GDP. However, of late, there has been a surge of interest, particularly from foreign investors, and it is expected that this sector, in view of its attractiveness, will see large investment flows over the next few years. The socio-economic trends visible in the country also suggest a movement away from traditional foods to ready-to-eat and processed foods. This trend, more visible in the eighties and nineties, is likely to gather momentum in the future, resulting in rapid growth of this industry.

It is estimated that current post harvest loss of cereals and legumes is 15-20%, while that for perishable fruits and vegetables, the figure is 20-30%. The loss due to the latter alone is estimated at Rs. 30 billion. Substantial losses also occur in transportation of animals and fish. This is indicative of the huge potential of the market. Add to this the fact that because of the resources at its command, India has a major competitive advantage in this industry over the rest of the world.

If India were to improve its productivity from the dismal level at present, it should be left with a sizable surplus of food produce. Coupled with additions in the food processing capacity, this could lead to the country becoming a major exporter of food products.

Table IIIE-1 indicates some trends in agricultural production in India over the years.

Table IIIE-1 Agricultural Production in India ('000 tons)

Commodity	1985	1986	1987	1988	1989	1990	1991	1992	1993	1994
Beef and veal	876	881	1,010	891	970	1,012	1,016	1,020	1,050	1,060
Coarse grains	25,796	26,573	23,755	31,329	34,559	32,553	26,284	37,230	31,410	36,100
Cotton	1,964	1,579	1,555	1,802	2,308	1,989	2,053	2,380	2,090	2,264
Oilseed meals	5,468	5,318	5,875	8,072	8,175	9,100	9,551	10,685	--	--
Eggs	15,000	16,080	17,470	18,300	21,420	23,320	24,675	26,075	27,570	--
Fluid milk	19,000	19,500	21,200	22,000	24,000	27,500	28,200	29,400	30,500	30,500
Rice	63,825	60,416	56,862	70,489	73,573	74,291	77,680	72,610	78,000	78,000
Sugar (raw value)	7,071	8,149	10,153	10,591	10,177	12,575	13,707	15,249	12,470	11,730
Vegetable oil	2,913	2,915	3,211	4,358	4,260	4,675	4,915	5,215	5,317	5,529
Wheat	44,069	47,052	44,323	46,169	54,110	49,850	55,134	55,690	56,760	57,800

Source: U.S. Department of Agriculture, "Asia and the Pacific Rim" (1994)

The growth momentum was initiated in the eighties when the Central Government constituted a separate ministry for food processing. The result was the induction of modern processing and packaging technology, the entry of new players from all sectors of industry, large corporate houses, multinationals and government sector undertakings besides several small entrepreneurs in the unorganized sector. The decade also saw successful transplanting of freeze drying, soya milk extraction and sophisticated extrusion cooking apart from the increasing use of tetrapacks and multilayered films for packing.

The food processing business in India is currently undergoing rapid transformation into a high tech, high volume, export oriented industry, thanks to the policies of economic liberalization. The Government of India has delicensed almost all food processing industries except for beer, potable alcohol and wines. Automatic approval for foreign investment up to 51 percent has been introduced practically in all fields barring those reserved for the small scale sector, milk products and malted foods. It is most likely that in the next year or two, even these reservations, many of them irrational such as for biscuits and ice cream, will be lifted as the industry matures.

The export of processed food is showing a healthy growth trend. In April-November 1993-94, the exports of $500 million was 20 percent more than the 1992-93 figure of $430 million for the same period. The only category showing a shrinkage in export value was non-Basmati rice. At this rate, it is most likely that the export of processed foods from India will cross the $1 billion mark in 1994-95.

The industry can be divided into the following major segments:

1. Consumer Food Industry (e.g., confectioneries, cocoa products, bakery products, soft drinks, etc.)
2. Grain Processing
3. Marine Products
4. Dairy Products
5. Poultry and Meat Products
6. Fruit and Vegetable Processing

The industry is characterized by a large number of players in the unorganized sector. The organized sector produces a variety of food products valued at Rs. 90 billion.

1. Consumer Food Industry

Processed food as an industry started early in this century with biscuits and bread manufacture. Biscuits and bakery segment make up almost Rs. 2,000 crores of the processed food industry. After the fruit and vegetable category, this is the biggest. Due to the large number of units in the unorganized sector, the bakery industry has been accorded the small scale sector category from as far back as 1977-78. Today biscuits, cookies and buns have become commonplace consumption items in numerous households. Bread also forms an integral part of the day's menu in a large percentage of families. There are 75,000 bakery units in India. Bread and biscuit producers are a major sector responsible for 82% of production. The balance in cake, buns, rolls and pastries products.

After the processed fruit and vegetable sector, the bakery sector is the next largest. However, in this sector only 35% of the output is by organized sector and the rest is by SSI units. Today baked products like breads, biscuits, buns, pastries, and cakes have become commonplace items in most of the houses.

For the customer, a lot of new products will hit the market in the next two years. The Kelloggs breakfast cereals plant near Bombay, reputed to cost around Rs. 60 crores, will be introducing a whole host of coated breakfast cereals not made as yet in the country and totally different from the plain corn, wheat and oat flakes available as of now. Companies like Rishabh Foods have introduced co-extruded snack foods which have proved very popular. Some companies like Haldiram Bhujiawala have started packaging Indian snacks and savories so that they can be conveniently distributed throughout the country. Pepsi has already come up with bottled dilute fruit juices and fruit juice cocktails which are much healthier than the usual carbonated drinks.

A Bangalore-based company called Pep-Sip Wines & Spirits (P) Ltd. has just started manufacturing winecoolers, a low (6 percent) alcohol drink containing fine white wine, fruit juices, fructose, citric acid and preservatives. It is being offered in 335 ml bottles. A whole new range of frozen desserts will be on offer soon from Brooke Bond. Even ready-to-eat preparations in reusable pouches may soon make a comeback, at least in the big cities where homecooking is slowly becoming a weekend pastime rather than a daily routine due to shortage of time.

Many new products have been launched during 1992-93 by various companies. These products include "Top Ramen Noodles" and "Cup O'Noodles," "Everyday Slender," "Peppy," "Milkana, Coconut Milk Concentrate," "Palak Puree," etc.

These developments reflect the changing face of the Indian food market. Snack foods, such as chips and puffs with a market size of just 4,000 tons are valued at Rs. 36.5 crores and projected to grow at 25 percent per annum. The market penetration of breakfast cereals may be quite low—1,200 tons (Rs. 4.8 crores) for cornflakes and 400 tons (Rs. 3 crores) for oats—but the expected growth rate is 10 percent each.

In the modern society ready-to-eat foods are becoming of paramount importance owing to the fact that the career housewife who has the entire responsibility of the family on her shoulders, finds little time to cook the same at home. This eventually boosts up the demand for ready-to-eat foods in the market.

Production and Share (%) of Food Products for the Year 1991

Category	*Rs. (Crores)*	*%*
Bakery Products	664.0	6.5
Confectionery	360.0	3.5
Processed Fruits and Vegetables	132.2	1.3
Beverages (Cold)	1,590.0	15.6
Beverages (Hot)	1,561.0	15.3
Dairy Products	1,929.9	18.9
Indian Foods	144.5	1.4
Western Foods	148.1	1.5
Oils and Fats	3,676.5	3.6
Frozen Foods	27.5	0.3

Source: "SIRI Directory of Industries in India" (1995)

The soft drink segment of the processed food industry is estimated to have a Rs. 1,000 crore market which included organized and unorganized sector. Soft drinks are non-alcoholic carbonated synthetic flavored/sweetened beverages and also fruit-based drinks. Some of the major producers are Parle's, Pepsi, Pure Drinks, McDowell and Dukes. Soft drink concentrates account for Rs. 300 crore market. Rasna brand from Pioneer Industries is the undisputed market leader.

Soft drinks can be classified into two broad categories—carbonated drinks and non-carbonated drinks. Both have an enormous market. In the case of carbonated beverages, the effectiveness of carbon dioxide is the main factor determining the quality. A prolonged, visible and sparkling effervescence is sought after to produce the soda taste in such drinks. The basic constituents of a soft drink are water, sweetener, acidulants, flavorings, colorings, foaming agents and preservatives. The soft drink market is dominated by a few brands. Coca Cola, for example till it was defranchised in the late seventies, had a Rs. 1,000 million complex with 22 bottling plants all over India. Its place was taken up by Thums Up, Campa Cola, etc.

The size of the carbonated soft drink (CSD) market is increasing fast. The growth rate for the last few years has been 10%. The market has been estimated to be 180 million cases in 1991 (each case contains 24 bottles) according to the *SBP Handbook of Export Oriented Food Processing Projects*.

2. Grain Processing

Grain processing forms the largest part of the food sector contributing 40% of the total value. It comprises of three groups:

(a) Primary unorganized sector: rice hullers, flour grinders, oil mills
(b) Cottage scale: bakeries, rice flake making units, etc.
(c) Organized sector

Rice milling forms a large part of this industry. This consists of hulling as well as polishing.

Rice exports have received a major boost ever since the government removed price constraints on basmati as well as non-basmati rice exports. Among the listed companies, Satnam Overseas and R.T. Exports are the major players in this business.

3. Marine Products

It is heartening to note that a blue revolution is taking place in India. It is expected that marine products will be one of the top five foreign exchange earners for the country. Seafood exports from India have already reached Rs. 1,750 crores in 1992-93 from less than Rs. 500 crores a few years ago. It is estimated that exports in 1997-98 are likely to be Rs. 3,500 crores.

With the ever increasing demand for marine products all over the world, but dwindling sea catches with prohibitive cost of catching, aquaculture is becoming the answer. Aquaculture is growing of fishes and crustaceans on land by creating as much natural environment as possible. Essentially, this means converting of waste/unusable protein into highly nutritious human protein. The glamor of fish and crustaceans is mainly due to the fact that they are rich in protein without any injurious cholesterol.

Crustaceans (particularly shrimps) are preferred to fish because the time taken for growing fish into commercially saleable is much longer than shrimp. In a year, on an average, one can get only one harvest of fish as against two harvests of shrimp. The price realization on shrimp is very much higher than on fish.

For growing shrimp the most important input is a proper location. It should have access to unlimited and unpolluted saline water. For setting up a 100-hectare farm which produces about 1,000 tons shrimp, the requirement of water is 250,000 tons every day. Therefore, direct pumping of water from sea/creeks becomes essential. The sea is preferred because it offers chances for proper mixing of water, whereas there is a possibility of letting in used water in a creek. This will be pronounced if there are many farms nearby.

If the temperature goes below the ambient temperature of 25 to 30°C, it will result in stunted growth. This puts the zones beyond the Vindhyas to a disadvantage. In Gujarat and West Bengal coasts, significant winter reduces the number of crops. Prolonged rainy season is not recommended as this will reduce salinity and therefore Maharashtra and the western coast are not preferred. Hence, coastal regions of Andhra Pradesh and Tamil Nadu are found suitable.

India enjoys certain inbuilt advantages to be a leading player in this industry worldwide. Most of the European and American countries are out of the race since the tropical climate is not suitable. Ecuador and Mexico are the two countries in South America which have the potential. Of these, Ecuador has already reached its peak. Mexico does not offer the right industrial climate. Regarding African countries, though it is possible to have a growing aquaculture industry, the political and other environmental factors are not conducive. Madagascar has some aquaculture activities. That really brings Asian countries to the forefront.

Taiwan, Philippines and Thailand are the countries where aquaculture is already practiced, but does not flourish there due to wrong methods and lack of understanding. Therefore, India and China are the two countries which are bestowed with natural supportive factors.

Numerous aquaculture units are coming up around Nellore (Andhra Pradesh), Tuticorin and Mayiladuthurai (Tamil Nadu). Till now out of a potential 1.2 million hectares available, only about 80,000 hectares are being exploited.

Key Success Factors: However, certain relevant factors ensure India's sustained growth. The approach should be to look for sustainable production levels per hectare rather than maximum production per se. It is advisable to maximize return by optimizing production.

Each site has its own peculiarities and therefore it is better to arrive at what production the soil can sustain in the long run.

It is better to realize this industry has a technology to it. It may not be as clear as in the chemical or engineering industry. The technology here is actually good operating practices in relation to water management, farm management and health management of the shrimp. The fallout of disease is a major threat and once disease strikes, one could do very little about it. To prevent diseases, proper water exchange and feeding programs are necessary.

As mentioned earlier, all these units are clustering around a few localities because of their suitability to aquaculture. This industry, being basically a biological one, is not likely to cause any major pollution as the let out water can be treated for avoiding any environmental pollution. But there has to be discipline amongst the aquaculturists since they can pollute themselves and therefore spoil the industry.

Indian products as of now are at a discount in the world markets compared to other countries. It is possible that we can also get a premium price if we improve our production conditions. This increased realization will increase the profitability substantially.

Large industrial houses are entering this industry and therefore we can expect total quality management concepts to be adopted. The list of entrants is very impressive and evokes a lot of confidence. To mention a few: Thapars, in collaboration with Luxe Enterprises, Taiwan at Nellore; ITC in collaboration with Trudina, Singapore at Tuticorin; S&S Industries in collaboration with Hanqua Taiwan at Sirkazhi; Balaji group at Nellore; Spencer in collaboration with Aquatic Farms, the U.S. at Mayiladuthurai; Rank Aqua in collaboration with Hanqua Taiwan at Nellore; Usha Shriram at Mayiladuthurai; DCM near Karaikal; Aquamarine of Nellore; Kings group at Tuticorin and Nellore. Most of these units are of international economic size of 100 hectares each.

4. Dairy Industry

Milk production has been rising in India and has touched 57 million tons a year. This makes India the second or third largest milk producer in the world. It is estimated that 41.6 million tons are consumed as liquid milk and only 2.3 million tons are processed and packed. Only a small portion of the milk is converted into value-added products. It is projected that by 1996-97, the country will produce around 92,000 tons of butter and ghee each, 9,000 tons of cheese and 12,000 tons of flavored milk.

The dairy industry is today capable of pasteurizing the milk or packing it aseptically in laminated containers. The aseptical packing has not caught on, but it could be the solution for overcoming the seasonal variations in the availability of milk. Improved hygienic standards could result in Indian milk becoming acceptable in the export markets. The technical expertise, plant and machinery are available for the manufacture of milk products.

New techniques have not been introduced for the manufacture of lactose and casein. Ice cream making plants capable of continuous freezing, mixing fruits, and creating ripple are also being manufactured. Curd, flavored milk and lassi have also become available in the market. Last year saw greater emphasis being given to automation. Earlier, the targets were to set up higher capacity units, that is of the order of one lakh liters per day or more. The projects nearing completion are the NDDB dairy at Madras, the dairy at Karnal and the Amul project as of 1994.

After the break-up of the Soviet Union, India has become the second largest milk producer in the world, next only to the U.S. The estimated production of milk in India is 55 million tons per annum. The value of the annual output of its dairy industry is Rs. 30,000 crores, which is expected to treble by 2000 AD.

The demand for milk and its products is ever increasing. About 46 percent of the milk produced in India is drunk as liquid milk. This is essentially because, apart from drinking milk directly, the Indian tea and coffee consumers use milk. Another feature contributing to the demand is the consumption of ghee which, as a cooking medium, is used only in the Indian subcontinent. About 34 percent of the milk is converted into ghee. Chhas (buttermilk) and lassi form a part of the Indian meal. The consumer is chasing many more processed food products than it was 10 to 15 years ago.

Rapid growth in the demand for fast foods even in rural areas established the trend for favoring packaged milk and milk products, offering the combined benefit of health, convenience, hygiene and value for the money. The rural market is expected to grow much faster than the urban market in terms of market share in certain milk products.

With high quality technology and expertise available indigenously and the Milk and Milk Products Order announced by the Government enabling the private sector to deal directly with the farmer, at the same time, laying emphasis on plant hygiene, the industry is on the threshold of a new boom.

Several entrants from the corporate sector have gone ahead with speedy implementation of their projects such as Amrut Industries Ltd., Cepham Milk Specialties, Indiana Dairy Specialties Ltd., Lactose India Ltd., Modern Dairies, Ravileela Dairies and Vishal Lactose. Many other entrants are expected, including corporate giants such as Thapars, J.K. Group, Godrej, Gujarat Ambuja Proteins and Mohan Meakin, as well as ice cream makers such as Kwality, Vadilals and Dharnendra.

Unlike other agro-products, milk has the peculiarity of cyclic yield. There are six lean months and six flush months. The yield variance between the lean and the flush is as high as 60-70 percent in the case of buffaloes and 30-40 percent in the case of cows. This necessitates balancing of the procurement and utilization. This leads to conversion of skimmed and whole milk into spray dried powder. Though this is the easiest way of wringing the surplus, it is also open to seasonality of demand, lending a speculative aspect in its trade and also requiring large working capital.

In the developed world, innovations have taken place in converting milk into value-added branded consumer products. Other than butter and cheese, a number of products are on the shelves—cheese and butter spreads (with low fat content), dairy fat and vegetable fat, quark (an intermediate between curd and cheese), and yogurt. All these have contributed to the full and profitable use of milk round the year.

The emerging trends in India are all oriented towards convenience and processed foods and the industry should diversify into innovative dairy products.

Of the three major constituents of milk, fat (cream), protein (casein) and sugar (lactose), isolating protein is emerging as a major industry. The inert nature of dairy proteins and the absence of any peculiar flavor/taste have helped casein get well ahead of other forms of vegetable proteins.

India can play a major role in this segment to use the surplus milk very profitably. The benefits of delicensing can be clearly seen. Indiana Dairy Specialties, a Bangalore-based unit, has taken the lead and is setting up a plant to produce 990 tons of casein per annum for export to Australia.

The production of cheese and casein leaves behind whey which can be further used for extraction of lactose. Lactose India Ltd. has set up a plant for this purpose and has entered into a contract with Amul for cheese whey. Indiana Dairy is in the process of tying up an arrangement to use whey for the extraction of lactic acid and also for whey based instant energy beverages.

5. Poultry and Meat Products

India has a very large livestock population. According to 1982 census, the livestock population was over 600 million. The break-up is given below as published in the *SBP Handbook of Export Oriented Food Processing Projects*:

	Stock in Million
1. Cattle	192
2. Bullock	70
3. Sheep	48
4. Goats	95
5. Pigs	10
6. Poultry	100
Total (1 to 6)	*515*

India ranks first among the livestock holding countries in the world. Fifty-five percent of world's buffaloes, 20% of world's cattle and goats, and 16% of the world's sheep populations are accounted for by India.

The current production of meat and meat products in the country is 1.33 million tons. The value of total meat and meat products including poultry and eggs is Rs. 3,208 crores. The major portion of meat and meat products (54%) is contributed by sheep and goats. Cattle and buffalo meat accounts for 26%. Pig meats contribute 7%. The balance is poultry and others.

Major domestic market is for sheep and goat's meat, although pork products demand (ham, salami, sausage, bacon, etc.) is becoming more and more popular in the urban areas.

The increased demand for hygienic meat in our country has led to the meat production and processing through modernized slaughter houses. At present there are about 2,800 municipal slaughter houses functioning in the country. Most of the slaughter houses, however, lack the minimum basic amenities for the production of hygienic meat. So modernization of old slaughter houses is very essential.

Besides being used as workforce in fields, pulling carts and water wheels, etc., the livestock provide other products such as milk, fiber, meat, dung, etc. An estimate of the output of such products follows:

	Item	*Quantity*
1.	Milk	40 million tons
2.	Fiber	15,000 tons
3.	Dung (Dry)	450 million tons
4.	Meat	4.44 million tons
5.	By-products (hides & skins)	—

Source: "SBP Handbook of Export Oriented Food Processing Projects" (1993)

There is a large potential for export of buffalo meat, particularly in the Middle East countries. Buffalo's meat of the value of more than Rs. 90 crore was exported in 1990-91.

Modern meat processing plants have come up in public and private sectors mainly for export purpose. Foreign collaboration in this respect is encouraged.

6. Fruit and Vegetable Products

India's position is among the top three world producers of fruits and vegetables, yet there is inadequacy to utilize its potential to considerable extent.

Around 28 percent of fruits and vegetables valued at Rs. 2,750 crores is wasted every year due to poor harvesting, lack of storage, transportation and post harvest processing. In addition, inadequate storage destroys around 20 percent of total foodgrains output. These wastages aggravate the food processing industry's problem since the per hectare yield is nowhere near potential.

Only 14 percent of agricultural raw materials and around 10 percent of the annual fruit and vegetable production of over 40 million tons and around 32 million tons are processed.

India accounts for less than one percent of the global trade in fruits and vegetables, although processed food exports have shown a compound growth of over 10 percent a year in the last decade.

India lacks the right management techniques, technologies and enough market information for the post harvesting processing of fruits and vegetables. Not enough money has been invested in processing machinery, grading and packing machinery and cold storage and freezing drying systems. The installed capacity is too small and the technology used too old to be economical.

Having these constraints, the industry has grown at four to six percent annually over the last few years, and has been categorized as a sunrise industry. It is expected to be one of high growth industries of the current decade, given its relatively high profit margin—food processing gross profit margin is estimated at 9.3 percent as against the average of 7.4 percent for all other industries. The changing demographic, sociological and environmental factors—the increasing numbers of urban consumers, estimated at 220 million with an annual growth rate of 4 percent, the gradual breakdown of the joint family system, and the emergence of nuclear families, and the growing number of working women—all point to an emerging boom in processed food industry.

In the world's scenario of horticulture, India ranks second to Brazil so far as production of fruits is concerned and next only to China in case of vegetables as shown in the following table.

Fruits and Vegetables Production—World Leaders ('000 tons)

	Fruits	*Vegetables*	*Total*
1. China	13,623	104,771	118,394
2. India	24,767	48,716	73,483
3. USA	22,906	26,669	49,575
4. Brazil	25,529	5,104	30,633
5. World	*325,806*	*414,101*	*739,907*

Source: "SBP Handbook of Export Oriented Food Processing Projects" (1993)

India is producing 63.90 percent of the world's mangoes, 11.49 percent of the world's bananas, and 11.72 percent of the world's onions.

Not only does India score in quantity, but also in variety, as the country is blessed with a wide range of agro-climatic zones which enable production of both temperate and tropical fruits and vegetables. Most parts of India, barring the high altitude Himalayan regions, are free from snow cover throughout the year. This enables round-the-year production without recourse to expensive greenhouses.

Unfortunately, due to primitive transport, storage and processing infrastructure, nearly 40 percent of India's horticultural produce goes to waste. The post harvest processing of fruits and vegetables has, till now, been a peripheral activity since India is basically a fresh produce market. Units of the past which make such items as jams, jellies, squashes, purees, pastes, chutneys, and preserves are finding it difficult, as Indians are not inclined, by and large, to spend on these products. The cost of processing and packaging, along with local taxes, makes the processed product too expensive. Perhaps pickles are the only ones having a ready and ever expanding domestic market.

One problem in achieving high capacity utilization is the seasonal availability of the fruits and vegetables. For example, Pepsi Foods has a modern plant at Zaura in Punjab which can process 30 tons of tomato and tomato paste in one hour. But the window of raw material availability for the plant is just about 3 to 6 weeks in the year. During this period, the plant runs at full capacity and then idles for the rest of the year.

Pepsi is now attempting to use part of the capacity by processing chilies. It has set up a facility for aseptic packaging of chili paste (220 to 230 kg per packet). Such packaging enables a shelf life of even 18 months. The company is expecting a good market for chili paste in the Pacific rim countries. Now these countries get their supplies from Thailand and Malaysia, but the chili prices in these countries fluctuate wildly. In India, which grows 50 percent of the world's chilies, the prices are relatively steady.

Pepsi is also planning to install at the Zaura plant a spray drying facility for converting pastes into powders at low temperatures around 50°C. This will enable it to make high value items such as chili and tomato powders. So far, there is no such powder making facility in Asia (including Japan). This facility may cost as much as $2 million.

In the last couple of years, there has been a veritable explosion of entrepreneurial interest in exporting processed fruits and vegetables from India to Europe, West Asia, Australia and Japan. Over 50 projects involving a total investment of Rs. 700 crores and a total foreign equity stake of Rs. 70 crores, have been approved by the Ministry of Food Processing.

A large number of these (22 units) are white button mushroom cultivation and canning projects. Almost all of them are Dutch joint ventures, though there are some with Israeli, Italian, Hong Kong and American tie-ups. A typical project is that of Transchem Ltd., which is located near Pune. This will have a canning capacity of 3,545 tons per year.

Dalsem Veciap of Holland is supplying the technology of growing mushrooms in greenhouses with the help of computers and later processing the harvested mushrooms. Earlier, countries like Taiwan, South Korea and China used to be the major suppliers of button mushrooms to the U.S., but rising labor costs and quality problems have forced the U.S. importers to seek other sources. Holland is still the major producer in Europe, but rising labor costs have made it look to India.

India has been found to be very promising because of the ready availability of cheap skilled labor and high profile professionals and the abundance of raw materials, such as agricultural and poultry wastes. If all the proposed mushroom processing EOUs come on stream, India will be exporting around 30,000 tons per annum compared to the present figure of 2,500 tons.

Among the other products in the pipeline are frozen vegetables and fruits, pulps and concentrates of various fruits, frozen juices, pastes of tomato, chili, guava and mango, fruit juice concentrates, coconut water and coconut cream, dehydrated vegetables such as onions, ground spices, spice oils and oleoresins.

Of the products that show high export promise are vegetables subjected to quick freezing so as to retain their freshness during the long journey overseas. One such plant that has recently come into operation is that of Reddy Foods near Madanpalle in Chittoor District of Andhra Pradesh.

Among the vegetables already processed at Reddy Foods are capsicum, cauliflower, tomato, drumstick, brinjal, okra and chow chow. The capacity of Reddy Foods is 24,000 tons per annum. Two more such projects, Temptation Foods (Pune) and Terai Foods (Rudrapur, U.P.), are on the anvil. Maha Grapes of Maharashtra has used the precooling technique to export grapes to Europe and is to try mangoes and lichie in 1994.

Thanks to these new products, the export of processed fruits and vegetables has shot up from Rs. 82 crores in 1991-92 to Rs. 200 crores in 1992-93 and should touch Rs. 300 crores in 1993-94. The sky is the limit here, provided the farmers are educated on growing the proper types of fruits and vegetables that lend themselves to processing, there is a strong linkage between farm and factory and there is a good transport infrastructure.

Horticulture produce processing can achieve a value-addition of 50 to 500 percent. The existing processing capacity can only handle about 0.5 percent of the total yield. Advanced countries process 60 to 70 percent of their yields. Our inadequate processing capacity results in an annual loss of Rs. 3,000 crores. Our per capita consumption of fruits and vegetables is as low as 60 and 100 grams respectively. Increase in processing capabilities is, therefore, an important national requirement. About Rs. 1,000 crores was allotted in the Eighth Plan for horticulture.

The process of precooling is used for the items fit for table use by the consumer. The fruits are cooled to a low temperature in an environment of high relative humidity. The rate of cooling has to be controlled to avoid injury to the items. Plant and machinery for precooling are available indigenously, except the air handling unit. A plant to precool grapes for export to Europe was commissioned by Alfa Laval for Kalyani Agro at Nasik. Seven tons of grapes are cooled from

30 degrees celsius to 1.2 degrees in six hours at 98-99 percent relative humidity. Precooled grapes were transported to London in refrigerated containers and fetched £6.5 per kg. Many other plants for precooling grapes are coming up in India.

Items not suitable for table use are processed to yield juices, pulps or slices. These can be packed as such or used for jams, jellies, drinks, chutneys, and pickles. The process consists of inspection of the items, washing and dressing, clarification, finishing, refining, peel oil separation (for citrus fruits), aroma recovery, pasteurization, concentration and packing. All the technologies for these processes are available in India. A five ton per hour EOU of Bhilai Engineering Corporation to process papaya, guava, mango and tomato was commissioned by Alfa Laval recently. Another plant of four tons per hour capacity is coming up for Fortune Foods at Nasik.

The technology of dehydration has been upgraded from plain drying in the sun. Majority of capital equipment for dehydration is therefore for thermal drying. Recently, a couple of plants have been planned using vacuum freeze drying. IBP and Alfa Laval are supplying the plant and machinery.

In the latter 1980's, the fruits and vegetables processing industry has expanded considerably. Looking to the trend and envisaging the expected infrastructure improvements, there is an expected annual growth of about 10 percent in the overall production and export of fruit and vegetable products. There is enough potential and good scope for setting up processing units in the concentrated fruit growing areas for fruit juice concentrate as well as fruit pulp plants for subsequent processing.

Areas Identified for Development

It has been observed that fruit processing units in the country remain busy with certain fruits for a limited period because of the seasonal availability. In order to keep the units working for a longer period during the year, they have to evolve a calendar of operations so as to maintain the continuity of operations. In order to materialize this calendar, it is necessary to have tie-up arrangements with the growers of fruits and vegetables for ensuring procurement of right quality, uninterrupted supplies and operational economy. These tie-ups provide an assured market to the growers while ensuring regular supplies to the processor.

With a view to ensure supplies of adequate quantities of raw material at reasonable prices to the processor, it is necessary to develop large scale plantation of the appropriate varieties of fruits and vegetables which are useful for processing and selling in the international market.

The prices of fruits and vegetables should be such that the producer gets adequate remuneration, while the processor is able to produce the product at competitive prices in the international market.

Reduction in the heavy incidence of various duties and taxes on the constituent materials and the finished products of the fruits and vegetables processing industry may provide a boost to domestic as well as export market.

Research and Development (R&D) should evolve ways and means of by-product utilization, fuel efficiency and suitable economic packaging for the fruits and vegetables processing industry so as to augment the returns for the entrepreneurs.

There is vast scope for expanding exports of fresh fruits and vegetables. In order that the potential is tapped, it is necessary to organize export-oriented production so that the domestic market is not affected. The official efforts towards this end need to be speeded up. The commerce industry is making attempts in consultation with the State Governments to identify specific areas where such production can be organized. In addition, the Agricultural and

Processed Food Products Exports Development Authority (APEDA) has been looking for avenues to support related production efforts through provision of production subsidies. In order to strengthen the infrastructure at major ports, APEDA has started developing facilities for export complexes of fresh fruits and vegetables at and near airports at Bombay, Calcutta, Delhi and Trivandrum, transport and warehousing infrastructure and cold chain designed to provide precooling and refrigeration facilities to producers and exporters of fresh fruits and vegetables along with other items of perishable nature according to the *SBP Handbook of Export Oriented Food Processing Projects*.

IIIF. PULP AND PAPER INDUSTRY

1. Introduction

The Indian paper industry is more than 100 years old. India was also the first country in the world to use bamboo as a basic raw material for making paper. Due to limited forest resources, other raw materials like bagasse, straw, jute, etc. were identified and are now extensively used. Waste paper is also being widely used for paper making. Almost all varieties of paper are produced using these materials.

The Indian paper industry can be classified into the following six groups of manufacturing units according to *Chemical Weekly* magazine.

1. Large integrated paper and paperboard units based primarily on conventional raw materials like bamboo, wood, etc., with inhouse pulping facilities.
2. Small paper units based either exclusively on non-conventional raw materials like bagasse, wheat and rice straws, alone or in combination with imported pulp.
3. Small paper units based on waste paper.
4. Paper units set up as a part of large integrated sugar complexes for exploiting the waste products like bagasse.
5. The large integrated newsprint manufacturing units.
6. About 400 hand paper producing units, using cotton rags, jute waste, cotton linters, etc. These units are under the control of the Khadi & Village Industries Commission (KVIC) and produced about 4,000 tons of paper in 1989-90.

2. Cellulose Raw Materials

The requisites for any cellulose raw material for the pulp and paper industry are many:

- Ample supply
- Available to pulp mill throughout the entire year
- Should not deteriorate in storage
- High yield of quality fiber
- Capable of being collected and stored in a small area and transported, if necessary, at low-cost
- Cost of conversion to paper must be low
- Quality of paper is competitive
- Must not have a higher priority use

Unlike the largest paper producing countries which use predominantly wood, India has critical material procurement problems which spread over a number of sources.

Paper production requires a disintegration of the bulky fibrous material to individual or small agglomerate fibers. This is called pulping. The ideal fiber for high grade paper should be long, high in cellulose content, and low in lignin content. Bamboo is an ideal raw material, but its production cannot be greatly expanded to meet increased production requirements. Other sources such as bagasse and hardwoods must be developed and good quality paper pulp made by blending with bamboo fibers.

The following raw materials are used in the paper industry: (i) softwoods: these include coniferous and non-coniferous woods; (ii) grasses and reeds: these include lemon, panni, ulla, siru, munji, etc., others are sabai grass, bamboo, etc.; (iii) straws: these are based on rice, wheat, bagasse, barley, reeds, etc.; (iv) cotton linters; (v) hardwoods: like accacia, lemon, gum, mysore gum, etc., eucalyptus, pinus, patula, paper mulberry and rubber plant wood; (vi) kenaf and mesta, etc.

Taking into consideration the total availability of raw materials, the possible paper production and the gap between demand and supply has been estimated in Table IIIF-1.

Table IIIF-1
Forecast of Raw Material Requirements

(lakh tons)

		Possible Production from Indigenous Raw Material					
Year	Demand	Forest	Bagasse	Straw	Waste Paper	Total	Gap Between Demand and Production
1990	24.58	12.34	1.80	2.00	2.15	18.29	6.29
1995	31.61	12.35	3.60	2.25	2.77	20.97	10.64
2000	41.12	12.35	6.00	2.50	4.75	25.60	15.52
2005	50.45	12.35	7.20	2.50	5.57	27.62	22.83
2010	62.97	12.35	8.40	2.50	8.29	31.54	31.43
2015	79.81	12.35	8.40	2.50	10.00	33.25	46.56

Source: "Kothari's Industrial Directory of India" (1994)

As is obvious from the table, production from available raw material was expected to meet only 74.4% of the demand in 1990 and a meager 40.4% in the year 2015.

Future growth of the industry to meet ultimate demands will require:

(1) Emphasis on planned cultivation of bamboo as the only long-fiber raw material available in India. Large scale "farming" is needed together with improved pulping processes.
(2) Development of eucalyptus as a high-yield tree crop for paper pulp manufacture.
(3) Increased use of bagasse as a raw material.
(4) Better reclamation and reuse of waste paper.
(5) Installation of newer, more efficient, continuous pulping processes.

3. Problems and Plans of the Paper Industry in India

The demand for paper and paperboard by the year 1995-96 in India is likely to be 2.9 million tons/annum and 3.8 million tons/annum by the turn of the century. Total world production of paper and paperboard was 239 million tons in 1990, which is estimated to go up to 320 million tons by the turn of the century.

The Indian paper industry will be constrained by extremely high investment costs and raw material shortfalls, when pitted against foreign competition. Paper is a highly capital intensive industry. The investment cost per annual ton for a paper project is about Rs. 6,000 at present. A 100 TPA plant would require an investment of about Rs. 220 crores and incur an interest of Rs. 45 crores which would not be covered by initial profits.

Despite the recessionary trends faced by the industry in the late 1980's, the demand for paper and paperboard is expected to grow at a compound annual average growth rate of 5.5 to 7% during the next 5 to 7 years, taking the aggregate demand in the country to about 40-45 lakh tons by 2002 AD, including potential export demand of about 4 to 5 lakh tons. The deficit in production is likely to be about 4 to 6 lakh tons by 1996-97 and about 12 to 16 lakh tons by 2001-2002. An additional capacity of nearly 20 to 25 lakh tons may have to be set up in the country to meet this gap in demand. See Tables IIIF-2 and IIIF-3 for trends.

The per capita consumption of paper in India is a meager 3 kg, as against the Asian average of 18 kg, and of 150 to 200 kg in the developed countries. Based on an assumed doubling of per capita consumption from 3 kg in 1990 to 6 kg by 2002, the demand could go up to 60 lakh tons from the present level of 24 lakh tons.

The paper industry performed well in the second half of 1993-94 registering growth of 35.8% over the corresponding period of 1992-93. Still the industry is distraught with problems of sourcing raw materials, high power cost and unremunerative returns in certain segments.

Table IIIF-2
Demand for Paper and Paperboard in India

(figures in lakh tons)

Year	Cultural	Industrial	Total
1991-92	10.5	11.5	22.0
1995-96 (P)	13.2	15.4	28.6
2000-01 (P)	16.8	21.1	37.9

Source: "Kothari's Industrial Directory of India" (1994)

Table IIIF-3
Consumption of Paper and Paperboard in India

(million tons)

Year	Total paper & paperboard	Cultural paper	Wrapping & packing paper	Paperboard	Specialty paper
1989	1.672	0.877	0.465	0.288	0.372
1990	1.748	0.912	0.493	0.303	0.376
1995	2.184	1.103	0.661	0.389	0.397
2000	2.720	1.334	0.887	0.449	0.420

Source: "Kothari's Industrial Directory of India" (1994)

The paper industry finds itself saddled with an acute shortage of raw materials, particularly pulpable wood, combined with a static technology of production. Bamboo and pulpable timber continue to be the basic raw materials for the paper industry. Forests in India occupy 75 million hectares, which is nearly 24 percent of the total land area of the country. This is much below the minimum requirement of forest cover, which is around 33 percent. The yield per hectare in Indian forests is also one of the lowest in the world. The total growth area under bamboo is over 1 lakh sq. km. with an annual potential of 50 lakh tons. Their growth is concentrated mainly in M.P., Orissa, A.P., Karnataka and North Eastern States. The availability of bamboo is getting more scarce day by day due to deforestation and lack of adequate planning.

According to the Expert Committee constituted by the Development Council for the paper industry, the industry would need around 81.5 lakh tons of pulpable wood per annum by 2000 AD. This calls for fresh plantation of pulpable wood over an area of 16.4 lakh hectares in the next years. To augment the diminishing pulpwood, it becomes imperative to create an additional resource base in the form of close spaced plantations of fast growing species with optimum fiber content, located within economic distance of the mills. The Government in consultation with the industry will have to evolve a rational development and exploitation of forest policy, exploit lands by silviculture operations including afforestation, prevention of unauthorized felling of trees and promotion of socio-industrial forestry programs in joint sector.

It is also desirable that the paper industry considers utilizing other alternative sources of raw material. The fibrous materials available for paper making from agricultural resources comprise mainly of bagasse, wheat and rice straw, jute sticks and certain other unconventional grasses. Of these, bagasse has the largest potential for use in paper manufacturing.

India has over 270 major sugar mills providing around 46 lakh tons of bagasse on bone-dry basis every year. The use of bagasse as raw material for paper making has become imperative to save forest wealth and to make better use of this commodity which also goes to waste. The bagasse obtained by gur makers is burnt in their hearths and ovens while that of sugar mills is burnt in the boiler. If the paper manufacturing units could help the sugar mills to convert their boilers from bagasse fired to coal fired, the bagasse thus saved could be spared for use in the manufacture of paper. Ample quantities of coal should be made available to these sugar mills in time, as coal shortage and transportation bottleneck preclude the possibility of switching over to the coal fired boilers.

Waste paper is another secondary source of raw material. Around 38 percent of paper supply in Japan, 31 percent of paper supply in West Germany and 20 percent in the USA is from recycled paper waste, whereas in India it is only 5 percent. Hence, there are great possibilities in this source of raw material for the paper industry.

The industry apart from facing high costs of raw materials and chemicals has also to grapple with the rising cost of effluent treatment (the paper industry is among the 20 highly polluting industries in India), unsatisfactory power and coal supply, non-availability of skilled manpower and lack of professional management.

Pulp

1. Definition

Pulp is a commercial cellulose derived from bamboo, bagasse, wood, etc., by mechanical or chemical methods.

2. Methods of Production

2.1. Groundwood—debarked wood is mechanically shredded to form fibers suitable for the production of newsprint, toweling, toilet tissues, and cheap paperback books where strength and ease of bleaching are not important.

2.2. Chemical—the cellulose from wood is freed from lignins and other non-cellulose ingredients by reaction with chemical reagents. The two important processes are sulfate (Kraft), and sulfite whose characteristics are compared in Table IIIF-4. The non-cellulosic fraction is solubilized with the insoluble pulp consisting of strong fibers of soft texture. These can be bleached to a white or near white. The yield is only about half that from the mechanical groundwood process (40-65%), but the pulp is the only type suitable for chemical grade cellulose (rayon and cellulose derivatives) and for paper of high strength and/or fine texture.

2.3. Semichemical—wood chips are given a mild chemical treatment with dilute mixture: sulfite, sulfate, caustic soda, and/or soda ash reagents. The wood is softened sufficiently to allow mechanical separation of fibers without excess power. A high yield of 65-90% with a somewhat better quality than groundwood pulp is the reason for the increasing interest in semichemical pulp as a substitute for groundwood pulp. The lower yield results from more drastic chemical treatment, but a better grade of fiber is produced.

3. Production Pattern

The production pattern for India is not certain as plants are being changed or modified to yield various types of pulp, depending on the raw material and finished production situation. The lack of sufficient raw material is forcing the production towards a pattern of higher yield, poorer quality pulp via mechanical or semichemical methods than found in other countries.

4. Sulfate (Kraft) Pulp Process

4.1. Reference Flow Sheets: Figures IIIF-1 and IIIF-2; Table IIIF-4

4.2. Chemical Reactions

4.2.1. Digestion—hydrolysis and solubilization of lignin

$$R{-}R' + NaOH \begin{array}{l} \nearrow R''COONa \\ \searrow ROH \end{array}$$

$$R{-}R' + Na_2S \longrightarrow \text{Mercaptans}$$

4.2.2. Chemical recovery from black liquor (wood digestion liquor)

(a) Smelting furnace

$$2NaR\ (\text{lignin salt}) + \text{air} \rightarrow Na_2CO_3 + CO_2$$

$$Na_2SO_4 + 2C\ (\text{from R}) \rightarrow Na_2S + 2CO_2$$

(b) Causticizing

$$Na_2CO_3(aq) + Ca(OH)_2(s) \rightarrow 2NaOH(aq) + CaCO_3(s)$$

$$CaCO_3 \rightarrow CaO + CO_2$$

$$CaO + H_2O \rightarrow Ca(OH)_2$$

4.3. Quantitative Requirements

(a) Basis: 1 ton of pulp (BDS basis)

Bamboo or Wood	2.2-2.5 tons
Lime make-up	18 kg
Salt cake (Na_2SO_4) make-up	50 kg
Sulfur	8 kg

(b) Plant capacities: 100-700 tons/day

Table IIIF-4 Comparison of Chemical Pulping Processes for Cellulose Fibers

Characteristic	Sulfate Pulp	Sulfite Pulp
Trade Name	Kraft	Sulfite; Magnifite, Neutral Sulfate
Type fibrous raw material	All types	Bamboo and hardwoods preferable
Essential chemical reagents used in digestors	60% NaOH 25% Na_2S 15% Na_2CO_3 in 10-15% aqueous solution	Composition depends on process modifications, but all use SO_3 (a) Magnifite process: $Mg(HSO_3)_2$ + free SO_2 in acid media (b) Neutral sulfite: Na_2SO_3, Na_2CO_3, $NaHCO_3$ (c) Acid sulfite: $NaHSO_3$, Na_2SO_3
Type of digestor	Batch or continuous	Batch or continuous
Digestor conditions	Time: 2-5 hours for wood-base materials, 5-6 minutes for bagasse; short time is for paper pulp, longer time for lignin-free chemical cellulosic pulp; Temperature: 170-180°C; Pressure: 10 atms.	Time: 6-10 hours for wood, 20-40 minutes for bagasse Temperature: 120-150°C Pressure: 4-6 atms.
Chemical recovery	Waste disposal laws and economics require a rather complete recovery of all chemicals used in both types of chemical processes; recoveries of 92-98% of Na and S are accepted practice	
Material of construction	Use mild steel or any alloy compatible with caustic liquor; Inconel required for tubes in external heat exchangers	Acid magnifite process requires digestor linings of acid-proof brick; metal components of Type 316 SS, bronze and lead; neutral sulfite process can use same materials as Kraft process
Types of pulp	Brown color; difficult to remove unless ClO_2 used as end bleach; unbleached fibers are very strong	Dull white color; easily bleached; fibers are weaker than those produced in Kraft process
Typical paper products	Strong brown bags, brown paper wrapping, paperboard boxes; strong white paper via bleaching	White grades; book paper sanitary tissues

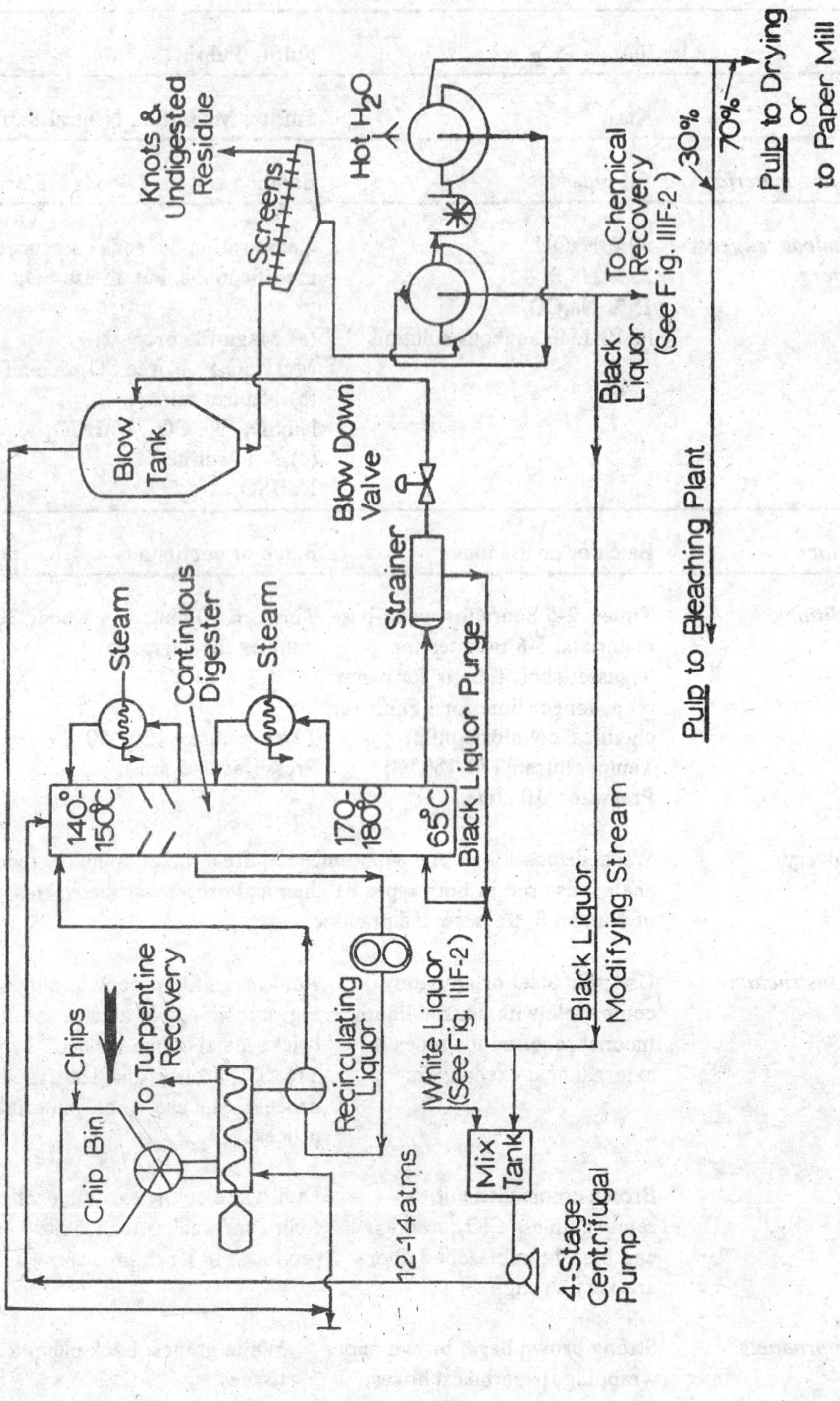

Fig. IIIF-1. Preparation of wood pulp by sulfate process.

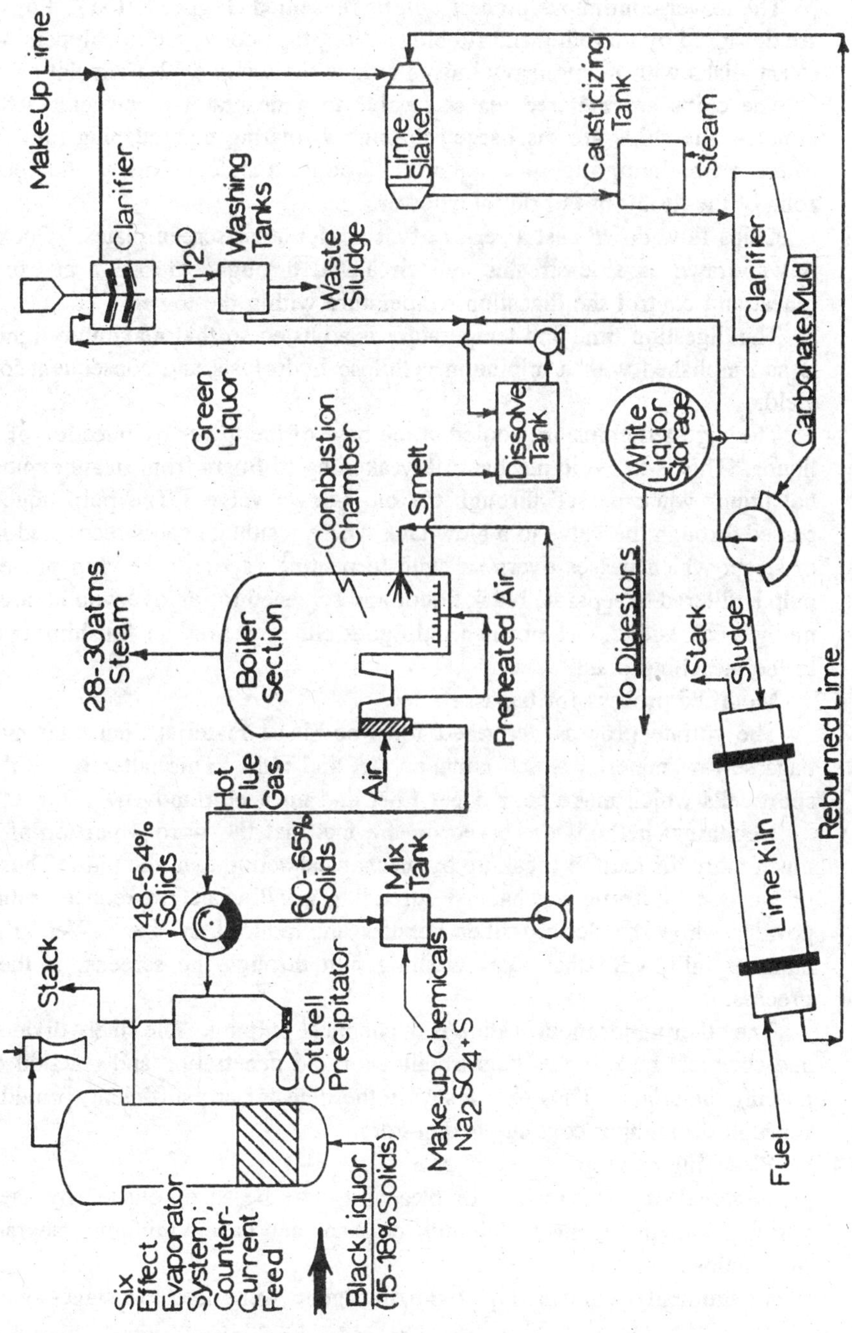

Fig. IIIF-2. Chemical recovery from sulfate pulp digestion liquor.

4.4. Process Description

4.4.1. Digestion of wood-base materials

The newer continuous process will be presented (Figure IIIF-1). Logs with bark are debarked by tumbling and rubbing action, then conveyed to chippers where large rotary disks with many heavy knives reduce the wood to 2-5 cm flat chips.

The chips are metered via star valve to a deaerator-preheater. After several minutes, the chips are discharged through a rotating tapered plug into the lift line where recirculating digestion liquor at 12 atms. transfers chips to the upper soaking zone of the 25-30 m tall digestor tower.

Chips flow down past a series of circumferential screen plates. Cooking liquor is withdrawn as side streams and circulated through external heat exchangers to reheat and control the digestion temperature within the tower.

The digestion time and temperature is adjusted so that maximum lignin removal is accomplished with a minimum cellulose hydrolysis and consequent loss of bulk yield.

The digested chips are cooled at the base of the tower by injection of cold black liquor. This is to avoid mechanical weakening of fibers from steam explosion of the hot liquor when passed through the blow-down valve. The pulp liquor slurry is passed through the valve to a blow tank where residual heat is recovered in the form of steam which passes overhead with turpentine vapor to the chip preheater. The pulp is filtered to separate black liquor and screened to remove wood knots and other undigested residue. The brown pulp goes either to product finishing operations or to the bleaching plant.

4.4.2. Modified process for bagasse

The sulfate process described for wood-base materials must be modified for bagasse raw material which contains dirt and pith. This latter is the thin-walled, short cells which make poor paper fiber and must be removed.

Depithing methods are based on the fact that the fibrous portion of bagasse is much more difficult to break up by mechanical action than the pith. Thus, exposure of bagasse to strong mechanical shredding-grinding action reduces pith to a fine powder while the desired fiber bundles are reduced in size. Wet grinding in a hammer mill, with the water washing pith through the screens, is the preferred process.

The other major modification is in chemical pulping. The finely divided structure and chemical make-up of bagasse allows rapid penetration and reaction by alkaline pulping materials. Thus, 5 minutes in the digestor are sufficient, providing a basis for high throughput continuous digestors.

4.4.3. Bleaching of pulp

Removal of color residue or bleaching may be accomplished by use of one of various oxidizing agents which must be cheap and have a minimum degrading action on cellulose.

Traditionally, chlorine-type oxidizing agents were used in a stage-wise operation.

However, chlorine bleaching has been found to produce dioxins and other undesirable components of the bleacher effluent. Thus, as was described under the uses of chlorine in Section II of this volume, the use of chlorine as a paper mill bleach has steadily been decreasing. Chlorine has been replaced to a substantial extent by hydrogen peroxide.

In the modern and improved bleaching stage, hydrogen peroxide is added together with sodium hydroxide, which activates the peroxide. A stabilizer is necessary, however, to maintain the peroxide concentration at effective levels, and sodium silicate is currently the most commonly used agent. A resulting scale or thin crust that forms on the internal surfaces of the pulp mill equipment, especially on heat-transfer surfaces must be removed in periodic downtime. Replacing the sodium silicate with an organic agent developed by Dow Chemical Co., can eliminate the scale formation and the resultant downtime for cleaning.

It has been estimated that the pulping industry will use about 240 million pounds per year of hydrogen peroxide for bleaching by the year 2001.

4.4.4. Finishing operations of pulp

If the plant is a captive paper type, the wet pulp is conveyed to the beater operations which is the first step in the production of paper (see Figure IIIF-4).

Dewatering is necessary if the pulp is shipped any distance for use in paper or as chemical cellulose. This can be done in several ways:

- Hydraulically pressing pulp at 200-300 atms. to form wet lap sheets which can be dried further
- Vacuum flash drying of mechanically dewatered pulp to produce a dry fluffy material which can be baled
- Extrusion in form of easily-handled noodles or pellets containing 30-40% solids for conveying short distances or dried to 90% solids for longer range shipping

4.4.5. Recovery of chemicals

Black liquor from the blow tank contains 98-99% of the digestion chemicals which must be recovered to avoid water and air pollution problems and to provide a balanced economy of operation. Figure IIIF-2 gives a typical operation of sulfate pulp recovery.

Multiple effect evaporation using 5-6 stages of calandria equipment followed by disk evaporators concentrates the liquor from 15-18% solids to the point where combustion can be sustained in a smelting waste heat boiler. This concentration is around 60% solids. Organic carbon burns in the smelting furnace, supplying the necessary heat and CO_2 to produce an inorganic molten slag or smelt. Make-up alkali is supplied via Na_2SO_4 [chemical reaction 4.2.2 (a)].

The molten smelt falls into a dissolver where it contacts cold H_2O to yield green liquor solution. The insoluble impurities, such as unburned carbon, are settled out and the clear liquor causticized by adding lime. Filtration removes the calcium carbonate sludge while the filtrate (white liquor) is returned to the digestor. The carbonate sludge is calcined to lime for recycle.

5. Major Engineering Problems

5.1. Choice of Processes

In the world market the demand for high-strength-good-quality paper products has reduced the choice to either the chemical sulfite or sulfate process with the latter now moving out in front. One of the great advantages which the sulfate process has over the sulfite process is the fact that raw material quality has less significance in the sulfate process. Moreover, sulfate fibers have superior strength characteristics.

Newer developments in sulfite processing will help to keep this type of pulping from becoming obsolete. Economics and waste disposal laws have virtually eliminated the older calcium sulfite process in favor of modern sodium- or magnesium-based salts (see Table IIIF-4). These processes also provide higher yields, allow more flexibility in raw materials, and produce a type of waste liquor wherein the pentosans can be fermented to ethyl alcohol.

The latest trend in large pulping plants is to integrate operations whereby both processes can be used in the same plant. This is possible with the neutral sulfite process since the only change in black liquor recovery is carbonation of the green liquor followed by oxidation of Na_2S with CO_2 to produce Na_2SO_3. The causticization step is omitted (Figure IIIF-3).

5.2. Use of Soda Process

Small tonnage (25-50 tons/day) plants initially set up in India use a process which involves hydrolysis with NaOH and Na_2CO_3 in 4 : 1 ratio. Advantage is lowest cost if chemicals are not recovered and no sulfur requirement. The soda process produces inferior grade pulp at high cost in batch operations and is not used for modern, large tonnage pulp plants where recovery of chemicals is an economic necessity.

5.3. Pollution and Waste Disposal

The large water requirements of pulp and paper mills, coupled with stringent steam and air pollution laws, forced the pulp manufacturers to undertake a major research and development program for waste disposal and water reuse. As a result, sulfite pulp producers came up with economical chemical recovery processes and now have the advantage over sulfate plants in being able to operate at lower odor levels in both air and water.

5.4. By-product Utilization

The gum, resin, and oil fraction from softwood furnishes the naval stores products of tall oil, rosin, turpentine. These are obtained from the gum flowing from live coniferous trees and from their stumps by steam distillation or naphtha extraction or from chemical pulp processes. The products are in steady demand with vigorous product application research responsible for the favorable picture. Many tall oil products now appear in the resin and plastic field with epoxy resins being a prime example. Camphor is an important derivative of turpentine.

Lignin, available in quantities up to 10 million tons per year, has found little use. It is chemically a complex mixture of polymers starting from a monomer of molecular weight between 850-900. The molecular unit is partially aromatic with phenolic hydroxyl, methoxyl, and carboxyl groups attached.

The only real use for lignin thus far is in a low rupee return as fuel within the pulp and paper plant. Even there, it provides excess steam as seen by the table below.

Heat Duty for Lignin Fuel	*10^6 Kcal/ton Dry Pulp*
Black liquor evaporation	0.89
Pulp digestion	0.82
Causticization	0.11

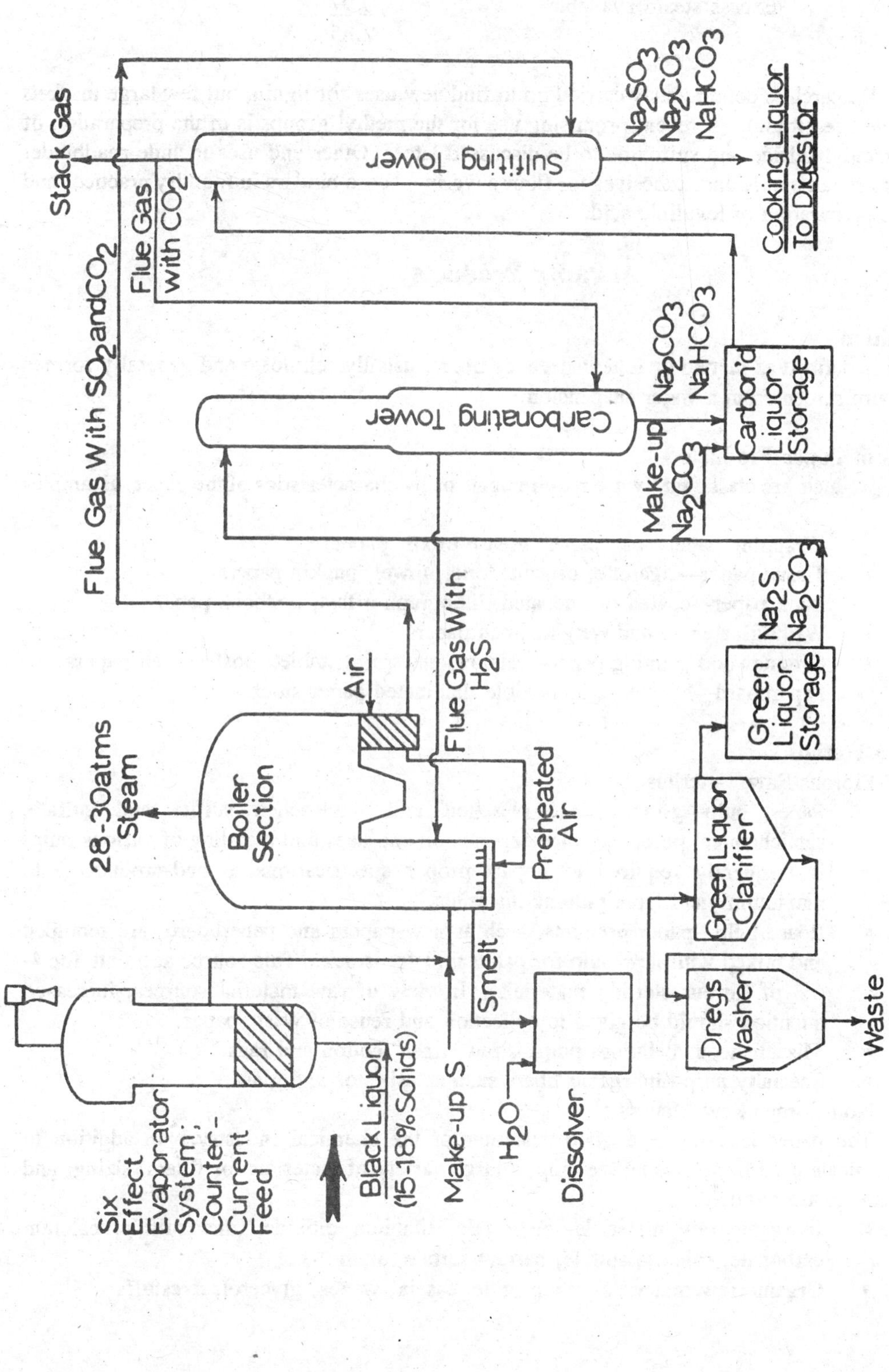

Fig. IIIF-3. Chemical recovery from neutral pulp digestion liquor.

Plant heating, feed water heating	0.06
Excess steam available	0.97
	2.85

Research is continuously carried on to find new uses for lignin, but few large markets have been found. A recent promising use for the methyl groups is in the preparation of dimethyl sulfide and sulfoxide to be discussed later. Other end uses include roadbinder for asphalt emulsions, adhesives for floor coverings, core binders in foundry practice, and the preparation of levulinic acid.

Paper Products

1. Definition

Paper is defined as matted or felted sheets of fibers, usually cellulosic and generally formed on a fine wire screen from a water suspension.

2. Types of Paper Products

Paper products are classified by use requirements or by characteristics of the paper. Examples are:

- Wrapping paper—bag paper, grease-proof paper
- Tissue paper—cigarette, carbon, toilet, towel, napkin papers
- Book paper—coated or uncoated, lithograph offset, textbook paper
- Writing paper—bond weight, linen papers
- Groundwood printing paper—catalog, newsprint, tablet, poster, wall papers
- Paperboard—heavier, less flexible, laminated paper stock

3. Raw Materials

3.1. Fibrous Raw Materials

- Paper pulp—groundwood, bleached and unbleached sulfite and sulfate, semichemical pulps. Choice depends on end uses and blending of various pulps is frequently required to impart proper specifications to end-products with maximum yield from pulping materials.
- Reuse pulp—paper products, such as newspapers and paperboard, are repulped and mixed with new pulp for paper mill feedstock. This source accounts for 4-6% of fibrous starting materials. In view of raw material sources, increased attention should be given to collection and reuse of waste paper.
- Miscellaneous cellulose pulp—straw, linen, cotton and rags.
- Specialty pulp—inorganic fibers such as asbestos and glass.

3.2. Non-fibrous Raw Materials

The paper industry is a good customer of the chemical industry. In addition to chemicals used in producing the pulp, a large variety of materials for fillers, sizing, and coatings are required.

- Inorganic raw materials—clay, talc, titanium dioxide, zinc sulfide, calcium carbonate, calcium sulfate, barium sulfate, alum
- Organic raw materials—rosin, glue, casein, waxes, glycerol, dyestuffs

4. Methods of Production

The commercial method for paper making is to prepare a suitable fiber suspension in water which is fed to a paper machine where the fibers are matted and dried. (See Figure IIIF-4.)

4.1. Preparation of Fiber Suspensions

Pulps are water slurried to ½-¾% fiber content by mechanical disintegrators of various designs. These usually consist of rotating drums with knife attachments or rotating stationary disks to produce viscous shear. Such operations are called beating and refining.

Fillers are added to the slurry to increase brightness, bulk, flexibility, opacity, softness, and weight of finished paper.

Sizing is an important ingredient often added to the slurry to reduce water or other liquid penetration into certain paper products.

Coloring agents are also mixed into the slurry before processing. These are generally synthetic organic dyestuffs, but some coloring is done by water-insoluble pigments.

4.2. Formation of Paper

Conversion of fiber suspension into paper sheet incorporates three principal steps (Reference: Figure IIIF-4):

- Random arrangement of fibers into a wet web
- Removal of free water from wet web by wet pressing and compaction of the sheet
- Progressive removal of additional water by heated rolls

The Fourdrinier process was developed to accomplish all three steps and the extremely complex machine used in the process is termed the Fourdrinier machine. Modifications of this machine produce laminated paperboard stock and fine tissue. Capacity of a single machine is as high as 400-500 tons of paper per day.

4.2.1 Forming a wet web

A wet sheet is formed by running 99½% water-fiber slurry evenly onto a moving endless belt of wire cloth at speeds of 50 m/minute for fine paper to 500 m/minute for newsprint. Water drains by gravity, a part is next removed by a pressure roll and then by a suction roll. The screen also has a side-wise shaking motion to give better interlocking of fibers on the mat.

The water collected in this section of the machine is known as white water and is reused to obtain maximum recovery of fiber, to conserve water and additives, and to prevent stream pollution.

4.2.2. Pressing the wet sheet

The wet paper sheet containing about 80% water is fed via felt roll to the press section where water is removed by mild pressure to reduce content to 60-65% water. Bond or water mark, if needed, is formed on the sheet during the pressing.

4.2.3. Drying the sheet

The sheet from the press section has sufficient strength to carry its own weight. It is passed through smoothing rolls, then a series of steam-heated metal cylinders where heat and moisture are transferred to a felting or canvas belt running on top of the paper. Paperboard is dried directly without a felt.

As the sheet leaves the last drying roll with 5-6% H_2O, it is passed through a final series of pressure or calendering rolls to produce a smooth, well-finished paper. It is wound on large rolls and transferred to the finishing department where it may be cut, coated, and packaged.

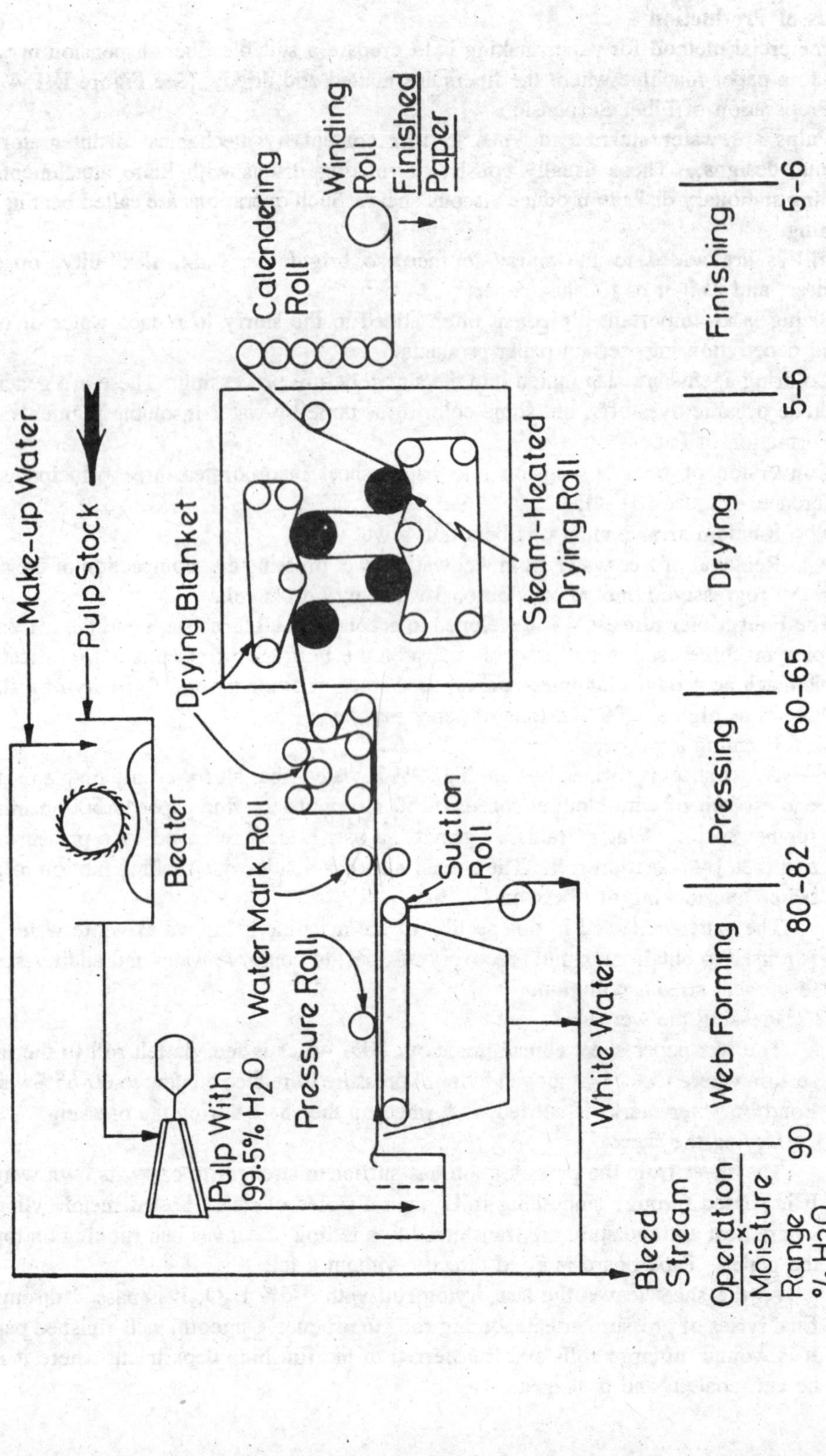

Fig. IIIF-4. Schematic drawing of a paper-making process.

In designing the roll speed in the dryer section, allowance must be made for a 5-10% progressive stretching as the paper is pulled through the dryer. The tendency of paper to shrink on drying, coupled with the machine tendency to stretch, creates a delicate force balance in machine design.

5. Recent Improvements in Paper Making

5.1. Increase in Wet-strength of Paper Products

The sizing of paper with dialdehyde starch and the use of newer types of resin and plastics such as polyethylene, particularly in Kraft-type paperboard, is responsible for the increased use of paper products under varying moisture conditions.

5.2. Modifications in Paper Machines to Improve Properties of Paper

Research is constantly being done to improve the tensile strength of paper. The Klupack process developed by West Virginia Pulp and Paper Company in the USA is one such improvement. It incorporates a rubber belt before the pressing rolls which can be varied in degree of elongation. By changing to a less-stretched condition at the end of the operation, the fibers on the wet web can be compressed and intertwined to give vastly improved strength on the final paper.

6. Economics of the Paper Industry

The paper industry of India is faced with numerous difficulties, some of which are given below.

6.1. Shortage of Fibrous Raw Materials

The lack of forest resources requires long-range planning for development of improved bamboo harvesting, utilization of bagasse, eucalyptus and reed grass, plus more effective collection and reuse of waste paper.

6.2. High Prices and Shortage of Chemicals

Shortages of sulfur, salt cake (Na_2SO_4) and chlorine with corresponding high prices place the Indian paper industry at a great disadvantage in attempting to export paper products to augment the foreign exchange position. This forces a great deal more attention on chemical recovery methods.

6.3. Procurement of Plant and Equipment

Pulping equipment is relatively simple and is being built in India. Paper-making machinery is quite elaborate and expensive so indigenous manufacture has not yet been successfully attempted. Once Indian engineers have mastered all phases of design and construction of continuous high speed processing plants from raw materials to final paper products, the industry should be in a firm position to move ahead.

The present production of kraft paper in the country is estimated at about 6 lakh tons per annum. Its demand in the country is rising at the rate of about 5% per annum.

At present, almost all the large paper mills in our country are manufacturing kraft paper also besides writing and printing and other varieties of paper.

The names and addresses of some of the units engaged in the manufacture of kraft paper are given in Table IIIF-5.

Table IIIF-5
Names and Addresses of Some of the Units Manufacturing Kraft Paper

Aurangabad Paper Mills Ltd.
MIDC, Paithan, Aurangabad (Maharashtra)

Ballarpur Industries Ltd. (Extensible sack kraft paper)
Ashti, Gadchiroli

Cauvery Papers Ltd.
Sathyagala Village, Kollegal Taluk, Mysore Dist. (Karnataka)

Chancellor Paper Mills Ltd.
Arikuzha, Thodupuzha - 685 584, Idukki Dist. (Kerala)

Dhampur Sugar Mills Ltd.
Dhampur, Dist. Moradabad (U.P.)

Mahalaxmi Paper Mills Ltd.
Jawahar Road, Udhna, Surat (Gujarat)

Rama Pulp and Papers Ltd.
Vapi (Gujarat)

R.G. Ispat Ltd.
P.O. Nanauta, Dist. Saharanpur (U.P.)

Shree Acids and Chemicals Ltd.
A-1, Industrial Area, Gajruala, Dist. Moradabad (U.P.)

Sukhna Paper Mills Ltd.
Village Nagla, Dist. Patiala (Punjab)

United Pulp and Paper Mills Ltd.
Asron - 140 001, Tehsil Balchaur, Dist. Hoshiarpur (Punjab)

Universal Paper Mills Ltd.
Jhargram, Dist. Midnapore (W.B.)

Uttar Pradesh Straw and Agro Products Ltd. (corrugating medium)
Aghwanpur, Dist. Moradabad (U.P.)

Yash Paper Ltd.
Faizabad (U.P.)

Source: "SBP Handbook of Projects for Corporate Diversification" (1992)

Cellulose

Cellulose is a polysaccharide used in the chemical industries in the form known as chemical cellulose for preparation of fibers and plastics. It is obtained largely from refined wood pulp.

1. Pertinent Properties of Cellulose

Empirical formula $(C_6H_{10}O_5)_x$

Structural formula

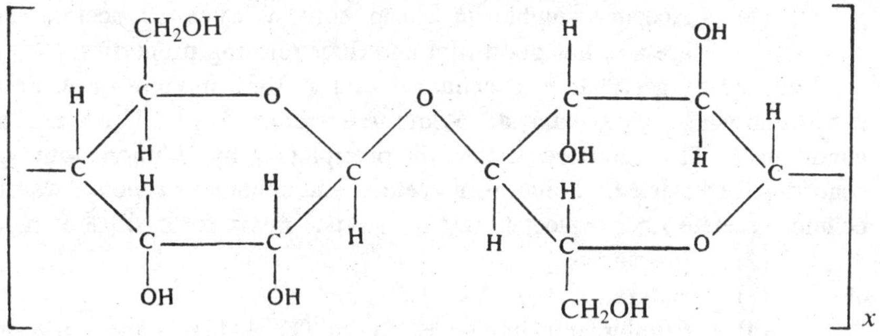

Total glucoside linkages = $2x + 2$

x for chemical cellulose = 250 to 1,500

Density 1.55-1.58 gm/cc

Solubility: Insoluble in water, dilute acid and alkali, ordinary organic solvents; soluble in $Cu(NH_4)_3(OH)_2$ or $NaOH + CS_2$

2. Preparation of Chemical Cellulose

Process choice is either the sulfite pulp process, as summarized in Table IIIF-4, with longer digestion times (9-10 hours) or the sulfate process, modified by subjecting the chips to a prehydrolysis using acidic high temperature conditions. The principal requirement is pulp with better bleachability and less ash, lignin, and pentosans than paper grade pulp. The chemical pulp is bleached with chlorine as with paper pulp, but the caustic bleaching is done at 95°C to increase the insoluble α-cellulose content to 92-95%. This is a major purification step since a very high α-cellulose content is mandatory in chemical cellulose products. Bleaching with hypochlorite, then ClO_2 followed by drying is carried out as in the paper pulp operations described previously.

3. End Uses

3.1. Cellulose Fibers—Rayon

Chemical cellulose can be prepared in the form of fibers called rayon. The principle involved is to solubilize the cellulose using cuprous ammonia or CS_2-NaOH, then reprecipitate the cellulose in acid solution while spinning a filament of regenerated cellulose. Rayon processes will be further discussed in Chapter VB.

3.2. Cellulose Derivatives

All commercial derivatives of cellulose are compounds in which the cellulose has reacted as an alcohol, giving rise to ester and ether linkages. A classification of derivatives is given next.

3.2.1. Cellulose esters

(a) Inorganic

Nitrate (nitrocellulose)—replacement of some of the hydroxyl groups by $—ONO_2$. Low % N nitrocellulose (10.7-11.2% N) is used for lacquers, intermediate (11.2-12.5% N) for films, particularly movie-type film, and high (12.5-13.5% N) for smokeless powder.

(b) Organic

(1) Acetate—soluble in cheap solvents such as acetone and methyl acetate, has good film and fiber forming properties.

Produced by acetylation of cellulose with a 50-50 mixture of acetic acid-acetic anhydride using H_2SO_4 catalyst. Room temperature for 5-8 hours are the reaction conditions. The cellulose acetate is precipitated by dilution with water, then centrifuged and dried. Solution in acetone and spinning in moist, warm air forms cellulose acetate fiber or acetate rayon. Acetate rayon forms 35% of rayon market.

(2) Propionate

(3) Butyrate

(4) Combination of (1) + (2), or (1) + (3) — these are prepared by mixtures of the corresponding acids or anhydrides; have better film forming properties, but are somewhat more costly than the acetate alone.

3.2.2. Cellulose ethers

(a) Soluble in organic solvents

(1) Ethyl cellulose—prepared with ethyl chloride

$$\underset{\text{cellulose}}{R \cdot OH} + NaOH \rightarrow R \cdot ONa + H_2O$$

$$R \cdot ONa + C_2H_5Cl \rightarrow \underset{\text{ethyl cellulose}}{R \cdot OC_2H_5} + NaCl$$

Ethyl cellulose is used in plastic and lacquer compositions because of its compatibility with plasticizers and resins, strength, flexibility and ultraviolet stability.

(2) Benzyl cellulose

(b) Soluble in water or aqueous NaOH

(1) Methyl cellulose—prepared with methyl chloride. Used as paper coating to impart grease-proofness, as a thickening agent in cosmetics, protective colloid in emulsions, and as an adhesive and binder.

(2) Sodium carboxymethyl cellulose

$$R \cdot OH + NaOH \rightarrow R \cdot ONa + H_2O$$

$$R \cdot ONa + \underset{\text{sodium chloroacetate}}{ClCH_2COO \cdot Na} \rightarrow ROCH_2COO \cdot Na$$

Properties: high viscosity in dilute solution, good film-forming, non-toxic, compatible with direct and acid dyes. Used as thickener in foods, emulsion stabilizer, adhesive.

(3) Hydroxyethyl cellulose

$$R{\cdot}OH + \underbrace{CH_2{-}CH_2}_{\substack{\diagdown\,\diagup \\ O}} \longrightarrow R{\cdot}O{\cdot}CH_2CH_2OH$$

ethylene oxide

Used as textile finish by acid precipitation from alkaline solution. Other uses same as sodium carboxymethyl cellulose.

Lignin Chemicals (Dimethyl Sulfide, Dimethyl Sulfoxide)

1. Pertinent Properties of Dimethyl Sulfide

Chemical formula: $(CH_3)_2S$

Mol. wt.	62
M.P.	—83.2°C
B.P.	37°C

Solubility: insoluble in water, miscible with most organic solvents

2. Pertinent Properties of Dimethyl Sulfoxide

Chemical formula: $(CH_3)_2 \cdot S = O$

Mol. wt.	78
M.P.	18.5°C
B.P.	190°C

Solubility: insoluble in water, miscible with nearly all organic molecules except alkanes

3. Consumption Pattern

Dimethyl sulfide is used primarily as an odorant in natural and manufactured gas. It is also an intermediate in preparing many S-containing derivatives including dimethyl sulfoxide. This latter chemical has unique chemical solvent properties, acting as a catalyst also in solution reactions. It has found increasing uses as a solvent for spinning synthetic fibers such as polyacrylonitrile.

4. Methods of Production

4.1. Reference Flow Sheet: Figure IIIF-5

4.2. Chemical Reactions

4.2.1. $\underset{\text{lignin}}{R(CH_3)_2} + S(l) \rightarrow (CH_3)_2S + R'$

4.2.2. $2(CH_3)_2S + N_2O_4 \rightarrow 2(CH_3)_2S{=}O + 2NO$

4.2.3. $2NO + O_2 \rightharpoonup N_2O_4$

4.3. Quantitative Requirements

Basis: 2 tons of $(CH_2)_2S$ or 1 ton of $(CH_3)_2S{=}O$

Black liquor (45% solids)	66-100 tons

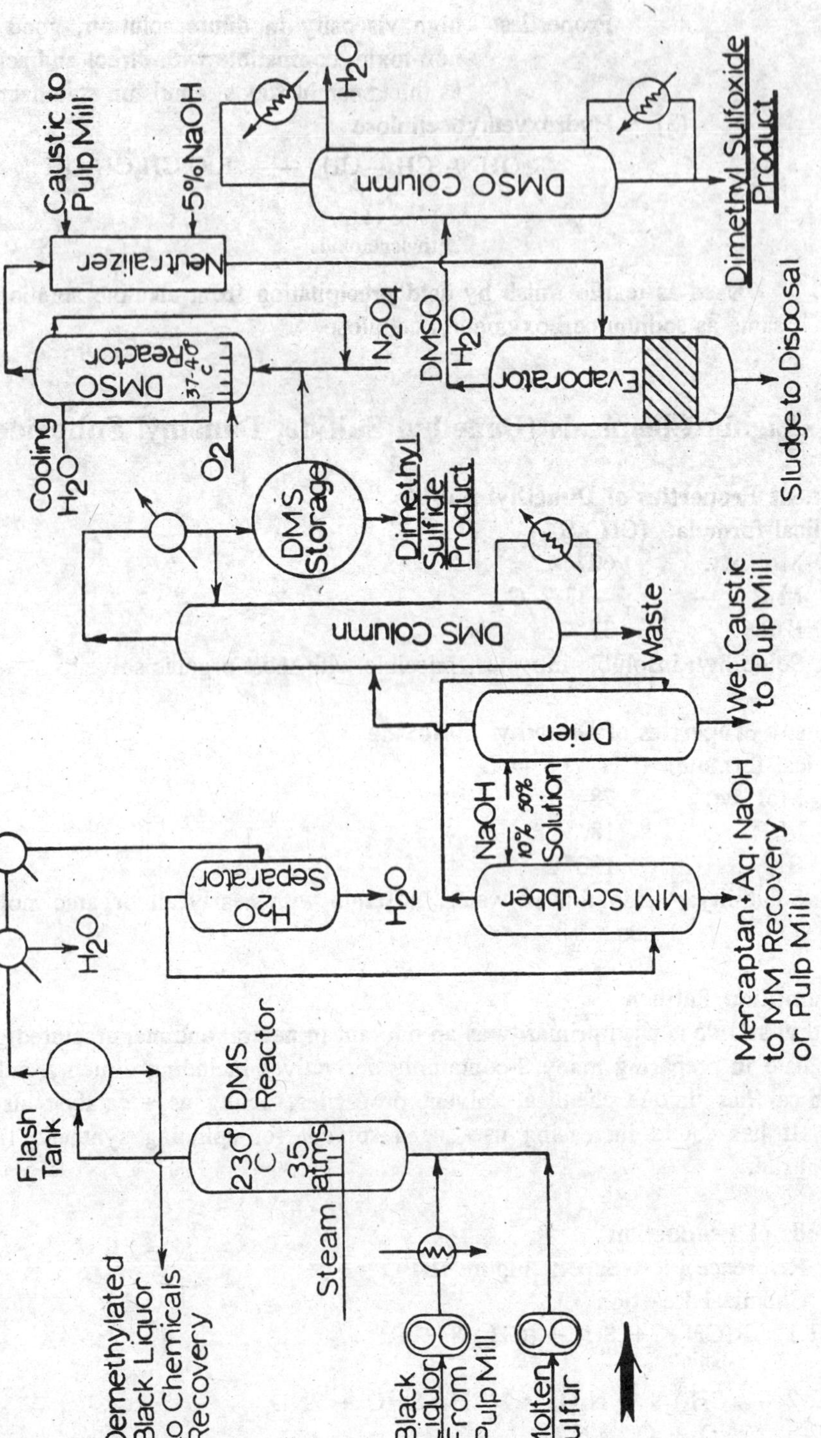

Fig. IIIF-5. Manufacture of dimethyl sulfide and dimethyl sulfoxide from wood liquor.

Sulfur	2.2-2.5 tons
NaOH make-up	25 kg

Plant capacities: 15 tons/day of dimethyl sulfide, 7.5 tons/day of dimethyl sulfoxide

4.4. Process Description

This process is a development of the Crown-Zellerbach Corp. Sulfate pulp black liquor is concentrated to 45-50% solids and pumped to a high pressure reactor along with molten sulfur. Steam spraying in the reactor raises the temperature to 230°C where demethylation of liquor occurs via reaction with sulfur to form dimethyl sulfide (DMS) and methyl mercaptan (MM).

The sulfur-containing products are removed overhead in a flash tank while the demethylated black liquor is returned to the pulp mill for recovery of digestion chemicals. The DMS and MM overheads are condensed with water removal and produce 2-3% yield from the black liquor feed.

Mercaptans and most of the water are removed by concentrated NaOH washings which are returned to the pulp plant. Mercaptans can be separated and purified as a major by-product with a maximum yield of about 5% DMS.

Dimethyl sulfide is finally purified by distillation and sold as a co-product or converted to dimethyl sulfoxide (DMSO).

To make DMSO, the sulfide is line-blended with N_2O_4 and fed into the bottom of the liquid-phase oxidation reactor. (Reference: U.S. Patent 2,702,824.) The nitrogen tetraoxide actually converts DMS to DMSO and the oxygen added serves to reoxidize the nitrogen oxide. The crude liquid DMSO is separated from gases at the top of the column, washed with 5% NaOH solution, stripped by evaporation, with the overhead being fed to a final purification distillation column.

4.5. Major Engineering Problems

4.5.1. Optimization of yield of dimethyl sulfide (DMS)

The cleavage of methoxyl groups and conversion of the methyl groups to DMS depend on the time and temperature of the lignin-sulfur reaction. The conditions shown in Figure IIIF-5 represent a compromise between completeness of demethylation and undesirable condensation of lignin and DMS to produce insoluble products which occur at extreme conditions.

4.5.2. Materials of construction

The high temperature level in many parts of the plant, coupled with the presence of sulfur, requires the use of stainless steel for these conditions.

4.5.3. Explosion hazards in the oxidation step

N_2O_4 catalyzed oxidation of DMS in vapor phase is explosive. A large plant using vapor phase was completely demolished in 1959.

A method for avoiding this hazard has been developed in which a solution of DMS in DMSO is oxidized in liquid phase with a mixture of NO and oxygen. Process is controlled by the presence of excess DMSO and a low temperature of operation (65°C maximum).

5. Economics

The potential DMS production from Kraft liquor in the USA alone is in excess of 1 billion pounds per year. The market for such material is not yet developed and additional work has been concerned with preparing derivatives to increase the market potential.

In addition to sulfur chemicals from lignin, research is constantly going on to cleave and use methoxy groups in other forms (*e.g.*, levulinic acid).

IIIG. COAL AND COAL CHEMICALS

Coal occupies a unique place in the chemical engineer's world. It is both a major energy source for various conversion processes and a major chemical raw material for organic synthesis.

1. Coal as an Energy Source

The economic importance of coal hardly needs to be stressed. As a source of energy it becomes a crucial ingredient of the production process. As a vital raw material to thermal power generation and railway locomotives, it is a key material in keeping the Indian economy's infrastructure alive. Coal has the highest forward linkage effect with steel, cement, fertilizers, electric power and a number of other industries. India continues to be the sixth largest producer of coal in the world, with an annual production of nearly 100 million tons.

Coal mining in India was first started at Ranigunj, West Bengal in 1774 and the industry has made rapid strides since then. The Government of India took over the management of coking coal mines in October 1971 and subsequently nationalized the coal mines and set up the Coal Mines Authority (CMA) in January 1973. Coal India Ltd. was formed in 1975 as a holding company, incorporating Coal Mines Authority, Bharat Coking Coal Ltd., Central Coal Fields Ltd., Eastern Coal Fields Ltd., and Western Coal Fields Ltd. The Central Mine Planning and Design Institute is engaged in the designing of projects in both coal and non-coal sectors. The Singareni Collieries Co. Ltd., a joint public sector undertaking of the Government of India and the Andhra Pradesh Government, is also engaged in coal production. In November 1985, two more producing companies, viz., South Eastern Coal Fields Ltd. (SECL), Bilaspur, and Northern Coal Fields Ltd. (NCL), Singrauli, were carved out of ex-CCL and ex-WCL. Out of total country's production, 90 percent is contributed by CIL with the balance 10 percent by Singareni Collieries Company Ltd., Singareni (SCCL) and the captive mines of TISCO, IISCO and DVC.

2. Nature of Coal

Coal was formed from the remains of trees and ferns which grew in swamps millions of years ago. Initially, bacterial and chemical action on such plant debris produced peat as an intermediate product. The overlying accumulations of debris plus flooding of the areas by sea water followed by deposition of mineral sediments caused the peat to sink and to undergo higher and higher pressures whereupon it was converted to coal.

Coal has the approximate chemical formula $(C_3H_4)_n$ which shows that it is a hydrogen-deficient hydrocarbon, probably consisting of many interlocked aromatic rings.

3. Occurrence of Coal

Coal is widely distributed around the earth with huge reserves in the U.S., Western Europe, Russia, China and India. In terms of duration of supply, most of the major producers have supplies adequate for several hundred years.

The principal centers of coal in India are the Bengal-Bihar coal field at Jharia, Ranigunj, Bokaro and Karanpura; the Madhya Pradesh coal field at Penchkanhan, Bisrampur, Charcha, Jhilmili, Singrauli and Korba; the Maharashtra coal fields at Kamptee; the Orissa coal field at

Talchar; and the Andhra coal fields at Singareni. The Bengal-Bihar belt contributes about 60-65 percent of the country's coal production. Significant deposits of lignite are found in Neyveli in Tamil Nadu, Palana and Khari in Bikaner district of Rajasthan, Nichahom in Jammu and Kashmir and in the Kutch and Bharuch districts in Gujarat.

The proved, indicated and inferred reserves of all types of coal, including lignite in India stand at 86,428 million tons with seams of 1.2 meters and above in thickness and generally up to a depth of 600 meters from the surface. India's reserves of coking coal are placed at around 23,000 million tons. The main problem is that two-thirds of India's coal reserves lie too deep for profitable extraction under present technological conditions. Secondly, the reserve of good quality coal required for industrial purposes is limited. Also poor quality coal cannot be transported economically for long distances. This underlines the need for the establishment of coal washeries and storing as a method of preservation and better utilization.

4. Mining of Coal

Coal is mined both by open cut and underground mining techniques in India as in the rest of the world. Open cut, or strip mines, are used when the coal is 30 meters from the surface or less; the overlying earth and rock are stripped off and the exposed coal is dug or blasted loose. Underground mines use shafts which may penetrate horizontally into hills, at angle into slopes or vertically to hit coal seams.

There are about 850 coal mines in various parts of India.

There is an increasing degree of mechanization being used in the coal mining industry in India; about 90% of the mines use mechanical or electrical power. In the U.S., robot mining machines which dig coal and send it back to the surface in a high-productivity, low-cost/ton, safe operation have been used.

Coal, as mined, contains rock, slate, pyrites and various other impurities, and also a wide range of sizes of coal lumps. Coal is purchased according to rather rigid specifications as to size, ash and sulfur content. Therefore, coal must be screened to size and it must be cleaned by jigging (agitation in water to settle out heavy refuse) or by heavy-media separation. Pneumatic cleaning and froth flotation are other processes which may be used to clean coal.

5. Uses of Coal

Consumption of coal in India stood at 236.70 million tons in 1989-90. India's coal consumption increased by 5.5 percent during the Sixth Plan Period. It was expected to grow at an annual rate of 11.2 percent during the Seventh Plan Period. By the turn of the century, annual coal consumption is likely to touch a level of 417 million tons.

The following table shows the sectorwise coal demand.

Table IIIG-1
Sectorwise Coal Demand of the Consumers

(million tons)

	1984-85	1989-90	1994-95	1999-2000
Steel and coke ovens	24.58	41.10	48.70	57.90
Steel (direct reduction)	0.05	-	2.70	4.60
Power (utilities)	67.98	120.00	177.30	242.90

Power (captive)	3.69	10.00	18.20	18.20
Railways	9.52	8.00	5.00	3.00
Cement	7.07	12.60	17.00	21.60
Fertilizer	3.89	6.50	6.50	6.50
L.T.C.	0.08	5.00	2.60	4.40
Soft coke making	2.16	-	5.40	7.30
Brick burning	22.36	29.00	8.50	9.40
Misc. industries	-	-	27.20	34.70
Export	0.12	0.50	1.00	1.50
Colliery consumption	4.02	4.00	5.00	5.00
Total	145.52	236.70	325.10	417.00

Source: "Kothari's Industrial Directory of India" (1994)

By 1999-2000, the power sector will be the biggest consumer of coal, annually consuming about 261 million tons, followed by steel, consuming 62.5 million tons. There may be a considerable decline in the loco coal demand, because of the steady withdrawal of steam locomotives. The demand of cement and fertilizers will grow from 7.07 million tons and 3.89 million tons in 1984-85 to 21.60 million tons and 6.50 million tons by 1999-2000 respectively.

In India, 50% of energy is produced from coal, 7% from natural gas, 3% from oil, 3% from hydroelectric power and 1% from nuclear energy, according to Investment Research & Information Services Ltd. (IRIS).

One wonders whether there might not be a future for coal-derived chemicals in India akin to the present emphasis on the SASOL process in South Africa. The combination of crude petroleum shortage in India, large coal supplies and huge demand for chemicals due to large population and an expanding middle class of consumers would seem to indicate a big potential for coal as a chemical raw material. The SASOL process was developed in South Africa simply as a source of liquid fuel, but emphasis there is shifting to upgraded hydrocarbon derivatives of higher product value. This would seem to have an obvious application in India.

5.1. Coking of Coal

5.1.1. Reference flow sheet: Figure IIIG-1

5.1.2. Raw materials

The feed materials are coking coals which are distinguished by the fact that they begin to soften at about 300°C. As the temperature rises, the fluidity of the mass reaches a maximum and finally the mass solidifies to form coke. The gases and vapors evolved during the plastic stage swell the mass, causing the coke to have a porous structure. Non-coking coals do not soften during heating and the product, known as char, crumbles easily.

5.1.3. Chemical reaction

The coking of coal may be considered to follow the approximate equation:

$$4(C_3H_4)_n \rightarrow nC_6H_6 + 5nC + 3nH_2 + nCH_4$$

5.1.4. Process description

The high temperature carbonization of coal is carried out at 900°C to 1,150°C in batteries of tall vertical ceramic chambers separated by heating flues. Each

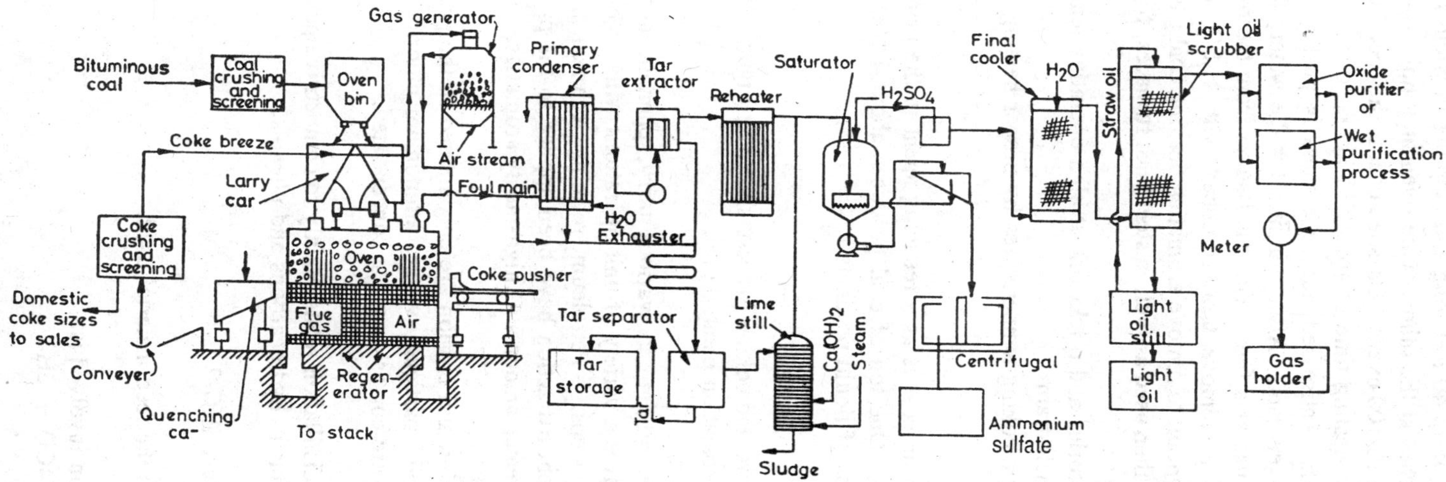

Bituminus coal	1 ton	To produce	10-12.5 cu ft. 550 But gas
Sulfuric Acid (60° Be')	25 lb		1,400 lb coke
Lime	1½-2 lb		10 gal. tar
Water	1,000-2,000 gal.		25 lb ammonium sulfate
Steam	400-600 lb		2.0-4.0 gal. light oil
Electricity	6-9 KWH		
Direct labor	0.7-1.5 man-hr		

Fig. IIIG-1. Co-product coke-oven procedures.

chamber may be 13 feet high, 38 to 40 feet long and tapering in width from 17-18 inches at one end to 15-16 inches at the other. One oven may hold 16-24 tons of coal and a battery may contain 10-100 ovens. Crushed coal is dropped into an oven preheated to 1,100°C. After a heating time of about 17 hours, doors on the ends of the oven are opened and the entire red hot coke mass is pushed out into a quenching car by a power driven ram. After draining off the water, the coke is crushed and screened prior to use as a fuel. The gas issuing from the oven during the coking process is cooled to remove tars, scrubbed with H_2SO_4 to remove ammonia and scrubbed with light oil to remove aromatics, leaving coal gas. The gas is treated to remove sulfur and then used as fuel, in steel blast furnaces, for example.

5.1.5. Major engineering problems

- Maintenance of refractories and brickwork at high operating temperatures, imposing severe thermal strains
- Maintenance of uniform coking temperatures by proper heating and waste-gas recirculations

5.1.6. Economics

The primary use of coke from coal is as a reducing agent in the primary metal industries (iron & steel, *e.g.*). One ton of coal produces about 1,500 pounds of coke, but only about 15 gallons of liquid products.

5.2. Distillation of Coal Tar

5.2.1. Raw materials

The so-called "light oil" from the coking process shown in Figure IIIG-1 is the feed material to a coal "tar" separation plant.

5.2.2. Process description

The separation of the light oil into its various tarry, phenolic and aromatic hydrocarbon constituents involves a variety of unit operations with major emphasis on a number of distillation steps. Petroleum refining techniques, including hydrodesulfurization and solvent extraction have been applied to the processing of coke oven light oils to give greater amounts of high-purity aromatics.

5.2.3. Major engineering problems

Special problems of corrosion and erosion are encountered in the processing of tar due to the presence of solid particles, water, ammonium chloride and other chemicals which can cause severe corrosion when concentrated.

5.2.4. Economics

The economics of coal tar distillation relate mainly to competitive petrochemical routes to such products as aromatic hydrocarbons and phenols.

5.3. Gasification of Coal

5.3.1. Reference flow sheet: Figure IIIG-2

5.3.2. Raw materials

Coke or non-coking coal is the feed material used.

5.3.3. Chemical reaction

The general type of reaction involved is:

$$4C + O_2 + 2H_2O \rightarrow 4CO + 2H_2$$

5.3.4. Process description

Several major processes have been used commercially to produce town gas or synthesis gas from coal.

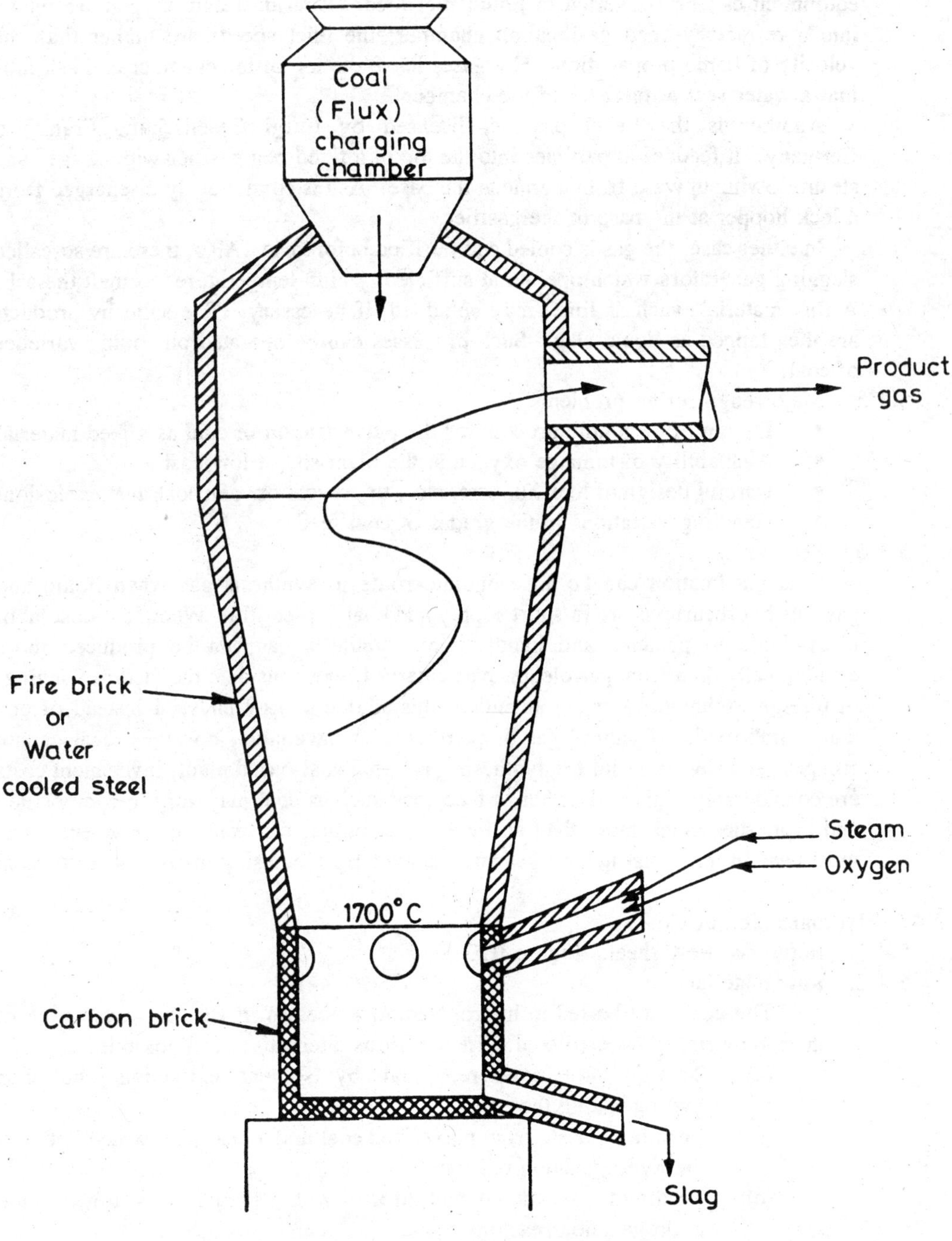

Fig. IIIG-2. Section of coal gasifier.

One of these is the Koppers Totzek process, licensed by Heinrich Koppers G.m.b.H. of Essen, Germany. An important feature of this process is that the equipment can be converted to liquid fuel feed. Coal dust and oxygen are blown into a refractory-lined gasification chamber; the inlet speeds are higher than the velocity of flame propagation. Hot gases leave the top of the chamber and ash falls into a water seal at the base of the chamber.

Another is the Lurgi process, licensed by Lurgi Gesellschaft, Frankfurt, Germany. It feeds coal particles into the top of a fixed-bed gasifier with oxygen and steam flowing upward from a grate at the base. Ash is continuously discharged from a lock hopper at the base of the gasifier.

In either case, the gas is cooled and purified before use. Also, there are so-called slagging generators which operate at sufficiently high temperatures to melt the ash. A flux material, such as lime, may be added, if necessary. The solid by-products are then tapped as liquid slag. Such processes can be operated on coking varieties of coal.

5.3.5. Major engineering problems

- Design of economic process for the pulverization of coal as a feed material
- Availability of tonnage oxygen at the plant site at low-cost
- Careful design of lock hoppers, etc., to prevent oxygen coal dust explosions
- Handling variations in the grades of coal feed

5.3.6. Economics

Coal gasification can be an economic route to synthesis gas when liquid and gaseous hydrocarbons are in short supply and coal is plentiful. When low-cost labor is available to produce and handle coal, synthesis gas can be produced more economically than from petroleum, particularly if one considers the factor of savings in foreign exchange by using an indigenous source of raw material instead of one that is imported. If natural gas or petroleum are available, however, coal cannot compete as a raw material for synthesis gas. In a coal-based plant, investment costs are considerably higher. Further, a feedstock such as coal may vary in composition and properties much more than an imported naphtha, for example. However, one must bear in mind that natural gas and naphtha are increasing in cost, whereas coal is not.

5.4. Hydrogenation of Coal

5.4.1. Reference flow sheet: Figure IIIG-3

5.4.2. Raw materials

The coal may be fed to hydrogenation processes in various ways—each of them requiring powdered coal. Then various alternatives are possible:

(a) Treating the powdered coal by solvent extraction and then hydrogenating the extract.

(b) Forming a paste from pulverized coal and a heavy oil which is fed to the hydrogenation reactor.

(c) Feeding the powdered coal directly with a stream of hydrogen to the hydrogenation reactor.

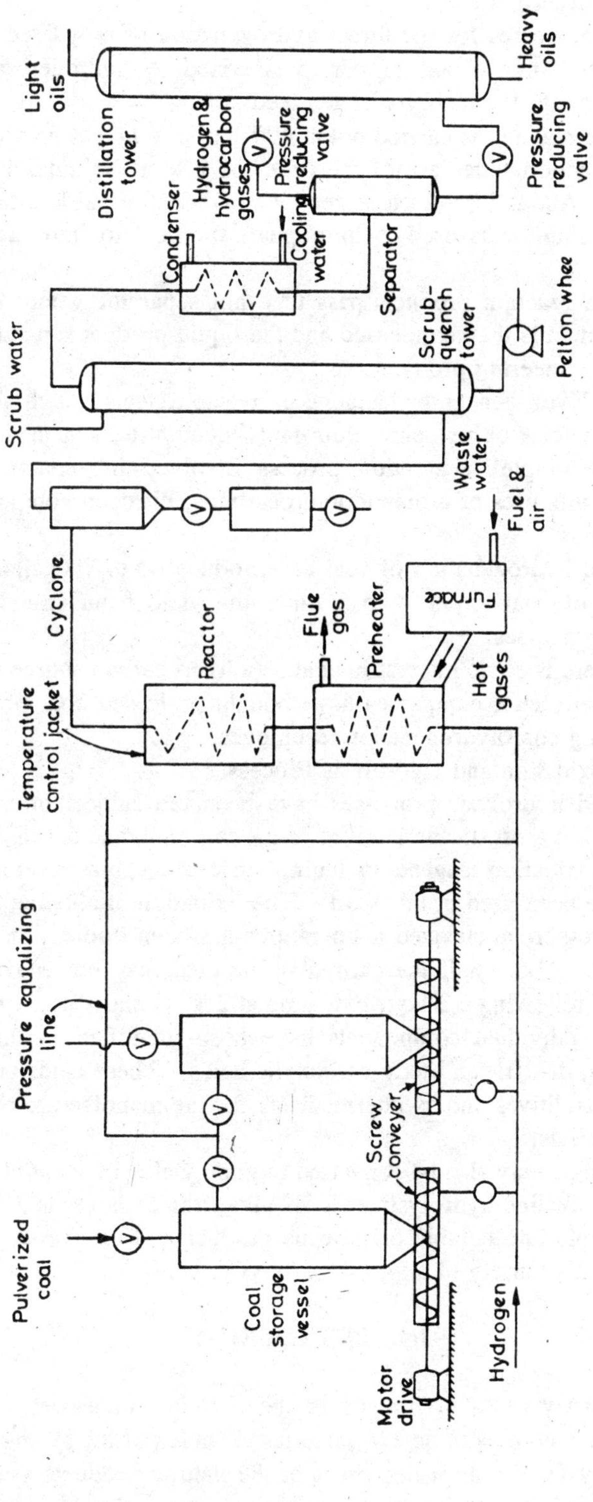

Fig. IIIG-3. Processing of powdered coal to give aromatic liquids.

5.4.3. Process description

In processes for the direct hydrogenation of powdered coal, the powdered coal is fed into a lock hopper, pressurized by hydrogen, and fed by a screw conveyor into the main hydrogen feed stream.

The reaction is carried out at 400-1,000°C and at pressures of 500 to 3,000 psi. Reaction times are of the order of 1 to 10 minutes in a jacketed tubular reactor. About 1% of a tungsten or molybdenum oxide catalyst may be used; a catalyst solution is used to impregnate the coal to introduce it to the reaction zone.

The reaction products pass to a hot separator where solids are removed. The product is then condensed and the liquid product separated by fractionation.

5.4.4. Major engineering problems

- Hydrogen embrittlement of reactor steels which is solved by proper choice of high chromium-molybdenum steels as materials of construction
- Complex separation process involved in separating multicomponent mixtures of aromatic hydrocarbons, nitrogen compounds and phenols

5.4.5. Economics

The hydrogenation of coal can produce 60 to 70 gallons of liquid product per ton of coal—some 4 to 5 times the yield from straight high temperature coking processes.

There is some interest in coal as a hydrocarbon source in the U.S. Several major petroleum companies have bought or leased coal properties and are re-evaluating coal hydrogenation techniques.

5.5. Controlled Oxidation and Hydrolysis Processes

Oxidation and hydrolysis processes have been the subject of much study with the object of producing aromatic derivatives (*e.g.*, carboxylic acids) directly from coal.

A variety of oxidation reagents including nitric acid, potassium permanganate, ozone and oxygen have been used in this work. The oxidation of alkaline slurries of coal with oxygen under pressure at elevated temperatures has been studied, on both laboratory and pilot-plant scale. About half the carbon in the coal may be recovered in the form of carboxylic acids following a 2 hour oxidation at 270°C under an oxygen pressure of 900 psi. Some 35 individual components have been identified in the reaction products including mono-, di-, tri- and tetra-carboxylic acids. These acids are of potential value as drilling mud additives and as intermediates for the manufacture of plasticizers, fibers and similar materials.

Low-grade coals may also be converted in good yields into soluble oxidation products by hydrolysis. Alkaline hydrolysis with 5N alkali for 24 hours at 350°C converted 75% of one coal sample into soluble or gaseous products. These products included phenol, alkyl-phenols and a variety of aliphatic carboxylic acids.

IIIH. PETROLEUM

The petroleum industry ranks highest of all the chemical industries. Since it is a major source of energy and has become a basic raw material for much of the synthetic organic chemical industry, petroleum is by far the most important of the natural products available in the world. Conservation of petroleum will become of increasing concern in the years ahead.

1. Occurrence

Petroleum formed several million years ago from organic matter of marine deposits in a deficiency of oxygen (anaerobic conditions). Selective bacterial attack destroyed proteins and carbohydrates, leaving fats to accumulate as oil reserves, hence the name fossil fuel and the reasons for conservation since the rate of formation compared to present consumption is nil.

2. Chemical Composition

2.1. Open Chain or Aliphatic Compounds

- *n*-paraffin series (C_nH_{2n+2})—comprises largest fraction of petroleum crudes
- isoparaffin series (C_nH_{2n+2})—branched chains are desirable, but not naturally occurring to any extent; must be produced by alkylation, hydroforming, and isomerization

2.2. Ring or Cyclic Compounds

- naphthene series (C_nH_{2n})—same formula as olefins, but completely saturated (methyl cyclohexane, cyclohexane); second most abundantly occurring series in crudes
- aromatic or benzene series (C_nH_{2n-6})—present only in small amounts in crudes; produced by hydroforming

2.3. Asphalts

Complex materials of relatively low value consisting of colloids of asphaltenes and resins in oil.

- Asphaltenes—brownish-black solids soluble in aromatics, but not paraffins; chemically composed of C and H with appreciable quantities of S, O and N
- Resins—highly adhesive, brown semi-solids of lower mol. wt. than asphaltenes, but same chemical composition

3. Refinery Crude Petroleum Classification

3.1. Paraffin Base—predominantly open chain compounds; furnish low grade gasoline and waxy lube oils.

3.2. Naphthene Base—cyclic predominates; lube oils must be solvent refined; asphalt present. Characteristic of most Indian crude oils.

3.3. Intermediate Base—large quantities of both paraffinic and naphthenic compounds; produces both wax and asphalt.

4. The Place of Oil in the Indian Economy

Consumption of energy and petroleum products is a good indicator of the level of a country's economic development. India has one of the lowest rates of per capita energy consumption in the world, at only 217 kgoe (kilograms of oil equivalent). This is only 15% of the global average of 1,478 kgoe. This may be compared with the following values (all in kgoe):

USA	7,804
Canada	7,766
Japan	3,548
Europe	3,202
China	604

Similarly, India's per capita consumption of oil is also very low and is only 11% of the world average.

Development is an energy-intensive process, with rising incomes and improving literacy levels leading to higher consumption of petroleum products. The consumption pattern in growing economies like India is tilted in favor of the light and middle distillates—like LPG and kerosene (SKO—Superior Kerosene Oil) for households, and diesel (HSD—High Speed Diesel) and gasoline for the transportation sector. Further, oil is one of the most important sources of energy because of its excellent combustion properties and convenience of handling, storage and transportation. For these reasons, India's consumption of oil products is expected to grow rapidly over the next few years.

India's consumption of petroleum products for 1992-93 was 58.7 MMT (million metric tons). This may be compared to 4 million tons in 1951 and 16 million tons in 1968. Consumption is projected to go up to 107.90 mt in 2003-04 and to 148.90 mt in 2011-12.

Demand has been sluggish in the last few years largely due to the economic slowdown, but is expected to grow at around 7-8% p.a. over the next few years. The transport sector is the largest consumer of petroleum products, accounting for 47% of total production (diesel alone accounts for around 40% of total consumption). The household sector, which mainly uses LPG and SKO, is the next largest consumer.

India is a petroleum-deficient country. Domestic production of petroleum products, which was 50.9 MMT for 1992-93, was not enough to meet demand, and imported petroleum products accounted for 18% of domestic consumption. The import dependence is much greater in the case of crude; India is a large importer of crude oil and will continue to be so. As much as 54% of the crude processed by Indian refineries has to be imported. The total value of product and crude imports for 1992-93 was Rs. 17,000 crores, nearly 30% of India's total imports; petroleum is the largest item on India's international shopping list. While imports of petroleum products will fall as new refineries come on stream from 1995-96, the crude import bill will only mount unless there are major discoveries of oil in India.

5. Production of Crude Petroleum

Petroleum exploration and development of crude oil production facilities to provide petroleum for the refineries is the lifeblood of the industry. An appreciation of the problems in this sector of the entire petroleum picture is important both for chemical and petroleum engineers.

5.1. Reserves

5.1.1. Reserves are known quantities of crude petroleum, usually expressed in barrels, which are available for further processing. This is similar to inventory of raw materials in other industries. A constant exploration is carried on to find new oil fields.

India has prognosticated hydrocarbon reserves of the order of 17 billion tons about half of which are contained in the three basins of Upper Assam, Cambay and Bombay High. Only 25 percent of the hydrocarbons, that is about 4 billion tons, have been converted into geologically proven reserves. As on January 1, 1991, recoverable crude oil reserves were placed at 8,602 lakh tons: 4,917 lakh tons (61 percent) of Bombay High, 1,583 lakh tons (20 percent) of Gujarat and 1,562 lakh tons (19 percent) of Assam (including Nagaland), Arunachal Pradesh and Tamil Nadu areas. But India's share in the total world reserves is only negligible. It is about half a percent.

As the Plan target for crude output will be inadequate, intensified efforts have to be made to find more oil. The Government has, therefore, taken a decision to expand its search for oil beyond the country's borders and gain access to production from sedimentary basins in other countries. ONGC Videsh Ltd., a subsidiary of ONGC, in collaboration with British Petroleum of the U.K. and Statoil of Norway, is operating an exploration venture in Vietnam. A memorandum of understanding was signed with British Gas in October 1993 for a seven year period for oil exploration in Yemen, Indonesia and Malaysia.

The other way of finding more oil is to step up the recovery of oil from the discovered and existing production fields in India, particularly in the Bombay High offshore. The ONGC's efforts in the Bombay High which were largely responsible for the all-time high output in 1989-90 had also exposed it to the charge that it had caused damage to the reservoirs. See Table IIIH-1.

The Government is, therefore, exploring the possibility of raising more oil from the Bombay High by applying high technology which would avoid any damage to the reservoirs. A number of foreign companies have put forward claims that they have technology which could make this possible and increase the output from recoverable resources. The ONGC has shortlisted some of these companies which include Chevron, Amoco, Arco—all of the U.S. British Gas, Total (France) and BHP of Australia and the ONGC would be giving a presentation to them. The needed data will be given to them and the offers they make will be evaluated for awarding contracts.

Table IIIH-1
Production of Crude Oil & Natural Gas by ONGC

	Crude Oil (In Million Tons)			Natural Gas (In Million Tons)		
Years	Offshore	Onshore	Total	Offshore	Onshore	Total
1980-81	4.98	4.24	9.22	673	937	1,610
1985-86	20.82	6.69	27.51	5,180	1,401	6,581
1986-87	20.62	7.24	27.86	6,705	1,517	8,222
1987-88	20.16	7.75	27.91	8,259	1,641	9,900
1988-89	21.11	8.53	29.64	9,731	1,977	11,708
1989-90	22.32	9.67	31.99	13,088	2,385	15,473
1990-91	20.37	9.83	30.20	14,082	2,398	16,480
1991-92	17.63	9.77	27.40	14,393	E2,425	16,818
1992-93	14.95	10.05	25.00	E14,000	E2,500	E16,500

E = Estimated

Source: "Kothari's Industrial Directory of India" (1994)

A detailed and exhaustive study carried out recently by a team headed by Mr. U. Sundararajan, Chairman and Managing Director of Bharat Petroleum Corporation, has estimated that the country's demand for crude oil would go up from 78 million tons in

1996-97 to 101 mt in 2001-02 and to 164 mt by 2010-11. The corresponding estimate for natural gas in terms of oil equivalent is 27 mt in 1996-97. The prospects of India becoming self-sufficient in hydrocarbons will depend upon major hydrocarbon discoveries and also on further accretions to recoverable oil reserves.

The scene with respect to these right now is very dim. No major discoveries since the Bombay High have been made even after taking into account the strikes in the Cauvery and Krishna Godavari basins as well as in the more extensive Bombay Offshore. The pace of accretion of recoverable hydrocarbon reserves by geophysical prospecting has also slowed down. In the absence of fresh accretions, these reserves will run out in 25 years, even at an annual production rate not exceeding 30 mt according to the *Hindu Survey of Indian Industry* (1995).

5.2. Exploration Methods

From the early days when oil seepage at ground level was used to indicate an oil field, exploration methods have progressed to a highly scientific stage. These can be classified in two phases.

5.2.1. Surface geological methods

The presence of volatile hydrocarbons near the surface is an indication of oil formation at some distance beneath.

- Sensitive gas chromatography used to detect as low as $1x10^{-4}$ vol. % conc.
- Microbiological flora of the hydrocarbon oxidizing type in water wells is usually evidence of hydrocarbon deposits
- Radioactive isotopic exchange of carbon with rock deposits gives lower C-14 assay where gaseous hydrocarbons are seeping

5.2.2. Geophysical methods

Extensive

- Seismic survey measures shock wave patterns and characterizes strata
- Air surveys from 250-300 kph low flying planes with magnetometer for magnetic survey and scintillation counter for radioactivity survey

Intensive

- Sonic and ultrasonic probing during core sampling to measure porosity
- Neutron reflecting measurements with scintillation detector which increase in the vicinity of hydrocarbons

5.3. Methods of Production

5.3.1. Drilling

Making holes in rock faster and cheaper, together with optimum spacing of holes for release of oil from a reservoir, is the constant goal of production research. Holes as deep as 5 miles are often required. Offshore drilling, as on the North American Continental Shelf or in the Persian Gulf, requires entirely new drilling procedures.

5.3.2. Yields

Conservation and use of reservoir energy are the keys to good yields which have increased from as low as 10% to over 80% of the available reservoir hydrocarbons. Methods used now:

- Slower rates of oil withdrawal so water can seep in to maintain pressure
- Recycling and repressurization with natural gas
- Water, air or steam flooding to rework old wells
- Enlargement of drainage channels in limestone-bearing rock by HCl

6. Petroleum Refinery Products

Crude petroleum must be separated into numerous products to achieve maximum economic return. A portion of the separation takes place in the oil fields where natural gas, LPG, and natural petrol are removed before the remainder of crude is put into pipelines or tankers for shipment to the refineries. The flow sheet (Figure IIIH-1) shows the operations to produce all of the products from a typical refinery. A suitable classification of all products is listed:

6.1. Gas Fraction

The gaseous fractions, previously used only for fuel, are now shifting in usage to the preparation of synthesis gas (see Chapter IIB).

- Natural gas, largely methane with some C_2 as separated at the well
- Light gas from distillation of petroleum crudes at the refinery; C_1 and C_2
- Off-gas from petroleum conversion operations at the refinery; H_2, H_2S, SO_2, C_1, C_2
- LPG as propane and butane, liquefied and used for domestic fuel, winterizing gasoline, or for synthesis gas

6.2. Light Ends

6.2.1. Petrol or motor spirits

Petrol is the principal refinery product and most of the chemical conversion at the refinery is aimed at maximizing the yield of various grades of petrol. This fuel, as an energy source for piston engine and gas turbines, is formulated to meet engine combustion requirements.

6.2.2. Combustion characteristics of petrol

- High compression causes violent detonation or knocking
- Antiknock compounds added to slow down the burning rate:

lead tetraethyl	isoparaffins
lead tetramethyl	ring unsaturates

- Antiknock rating in terms of octane number is an arbitrary scale based on percent of isooctane (2,2,4-trimethylpentane) in *n*-heptane which will avoid knocking when tested on an SAE standard engine. Commercial petrol blends, used mainly in airplane piston engines, have better knock resistance than isooctane, *i.e.*, octane number greater than 100. The scale is extended by an arbitrary power number which is proportional to the power extracted from the engine

$$\text{octane number} = \frac{\text{power number} - 100}{3} + 100$$

- Other factors important in petrol blending are:
  engine fouling, ease of starting, warm-up rate, tendency of vapor lock, evaporation losses, and loss of crankcase oil

6.2.3. Production of petrol

- Natural petrol—recovered at the oil fields by absorbing in a gas or straw oil in the stripping of natural gas; used for winter blending
- Refinery motor spirits—produced by blending from various refinery conversion processes to give correct octane number and other characteristics

6.2.4. Solvent naphtha and kerosene—now used for jet fuels and reformate stock in addition to previous requirements for heating and solvents.

6.2.5. Light heating oils

6.3. Intermediate Distillates
- Heavy fuel oils
- Diesel oils
- Gas oil

6.4. Heavy Distillates
- Mineral oil
- Flotation and frothing oil
- Waxes
- Lubricating oil

6.5. Residues
- Lubricants
- Fuel oil
- Greases
- Petrolatum
- Asphalt
- Road oils
- Petroleum coke—used for aluminum plants and electrodes

6.6. By-products
- Detergents
- Ammonia
- Sulfur and derivatives

Table IIIH-2 shows the distribution of petroleum refinery products in various parts of the world.

Table IIIH-2
Distribution of Refinery Products (in wt.%)

	USA			Western Europe			Japan		
	1973	1983	1989	1973	1985	1989	1973	1983	1989
Refinery & liquid gas	9	10	8	4	4	3	6	11	3
Motor gasoline, naphtha	44	49	46	24	26	27	21	24	23
Jet fuel	6	7	11	4	5	7	8	11	14
Light fuel oil, diesel oil	19	20	21	32	38	35	12	17	30
Heavy fuel oil	16	9	9	33	22	20	50	33	25
Bitumen, oil coke	6	5	5	3	5	8	3	4	6
Total refinery products (in 10^6 tons)	825	730	663	730	527	514	260	220	145

Source: "Industrial Organic Chemistry" by Weissermel et al (1993)

Characteristics of Refineries

1. Types of Refineries

1.1. Primary Refinery—simplest refinery consisting only of a distillation unit to produce residual asphalt and sell all of the overhead to another refinery.

1.2. Intermediate Refinery—produces motor fuel, distillate fuels and residuals. Typical of European refineries where petrol demand is low relative to heating fuels.
1.3. Complex Refinery—typical of that shown in Figure IIIH-1.
1.4. Future Refinery Plans in India—refinery plans for the next few years are shown in the following tabulation:

Company and Location	Date Due Online	Capacity
Indian Oil Corp. (IOC)	2000[1]	6,000
Nagapattinam, Tamil Nadu	1998[2]	6,000
Panipat, Haryana	1997[2]	1,440
East Coast Refinery		
Paradeep, Orissa	2001[2]	6,000
Mangalore Refinery & Petrochemicals		
Mangalore, Karnataka	1996[2]	3,000
Hindustan Oman Petroleum Co.		
Deogarh, Maharashtra	2000[1]	6,000
Bharat Petroleum Corp. (BPCL)		
Numaligarh, Assam	1999[2]	3,000
Bharat Oman Refineries		
Bina, Madhya Pradesh	1999[2]	6,000
BPCL-Shell International Co.		
Rae Bareli, Uttar Pradesh	2000[1]	7,000
Reliance Industries Ltd.		
Jamnagar, Gujarat	1998[2]	15,000
Essar Oil Ltd.		
Vadinar, Gujarat	1998[2]	9,000

1 - Proposed
2 - Now being built

Adapted from *Chemical Engineering Magazine* for May 1996

2. Design of Refinery

2.1. Independent Unit Operation—until 1950, all refineries were built with holding capacities between units so that any unit could be operated, shut down, and reconditioned independently.

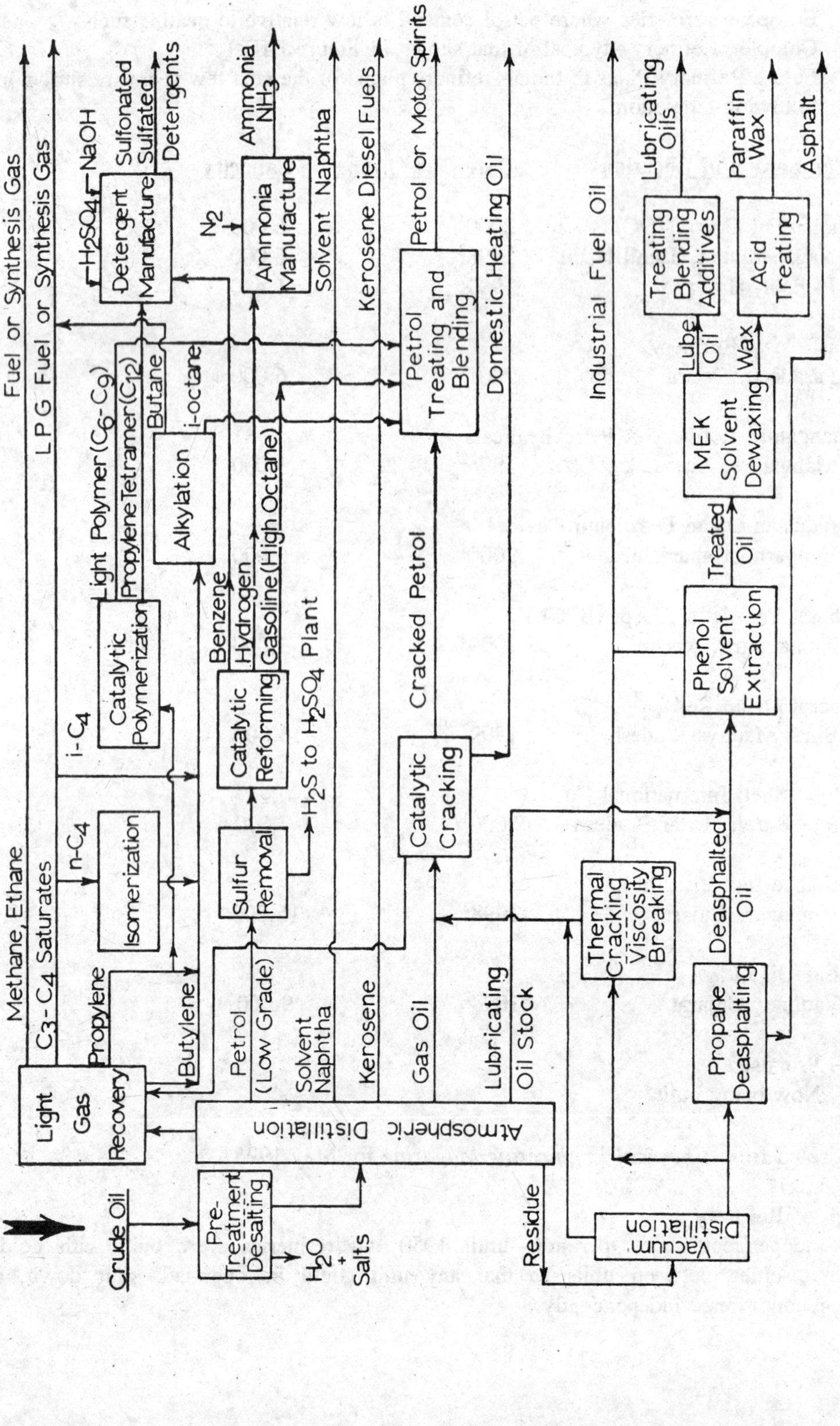

Fig. IIIH-1. Flow sheet of refinery operations.

2.2. Integrated Operation—the integrated refinery can be built with 20-30% investment savings; it is designed with little hold-up capacity between units since refinery maintenance requirements can be reliably scheduled.

3. Choice of Crude Petroleum

Refineries are originally built to handle a certain type of crude oil. The two refineries at Bombay handle Middle East crude. Decision to handle other types of crude involves refinery changes. For example, Venezuela crude has high salt and sulfur impurities which must be removed before conventional refining starts.

A large refinery may use several types of crudes and process them separately. Crude oils which produce superior distillate fuels may be separated from those that yield principally lubricating stocks and asphalts.

4. Refinery Processes

To produce the numerous refinery products, two major divisions of the numerous refinery operations can be set up.

4.1. Physical Changes or Unit Operations

- Distillation—separation based on relative volatilities; most important of all the refinery operations
- Absorption—separation based on relative volatilities; used to scrub out high boiling fractions in low conc. gases
- Extraction—separation based on relative solubilities in different solvents; used primarily in lube oil manufacture
- Adsorption—separation based on relative adherence to surface of solids; color removal, separation of saturates from unsaturates
- Crystallization—separation based on freezing point differences; used in wax preparation
- Heat transfer—energy conservation is primary design requirement with ample use of heat exchangers
- Fluid flow—aside from usual single phase fluid flow of liquids and gases, an important application of two-phase flow is gas-solid catalytic operations of the moving bed and fluidized bed type
- Other unit operations of chemical engineering are used to a lesser degree

4.2. Chemical Changes or Conversion Operations

These are the unit processes (Chapter ID) used by the petroleum industry to produce highest value end-products. For example, the fraction of crude petroleum existing in petrol molecular range (C_5-C_6) is only 25-40%, depending on the grade of crude. Even the arrangement of these molecules is unsatisfactory for current petrol requirements. Since the current refinery output of high quality petrol may be as high as 50% in the U.S., numerous conversion processes are used to accomplish this upgrading. In India, process conditions are set up to maximize kerosene-diesel oil product yield and reduce petrol yields. In addition, excess naphtha which accumulates is being converted by steam cracking to fertilizer and petrochemical starting chemicals. Reforming and hydrodealkylation operations are used to produce primary aromatic chemicals, particularly benzene.

A summary of refinery conversion operations is listed next with details of some given in the sections which follow:

- Pyrolysis and cracking
- Reforming
- Polymerization
- Alkylation
- Isomerization
- Hydrodealkylation
- Hydrogenation
- Sulfur removal

5. Pyrolysis and Cracking

5.1. Background

Pyrolysis is defined as the treatment of hydrocarbons at high temperatures to change their molecular weights. The principal purpose is to crack larger molecules to smaller ones, yet higher molecular weight compounds are produced simultaneously, particularly in thermal, non-catalytic pyrolysis.

Catalysts were developed to permit lower temperatures and pressures and obtain a higher selectivity of cracking with less side reactions.

Commercial thermal pyrolysis started in the U.S. in 1913; fixed bed catalytic cracking was applied in 1936 by Houdry with moving and fluid bed catalytic cracking taking over in 1945.

5.2. Reactions

Different reaction mechanisms are proposed for endothermic thermal pyrolysis and for catalytic cracking. Neither explains all of the experimental results, but constitute the best overall approach.

5.2.1. Thermal pyrolysis mechanism

- Thermal cracking—free radical theory

Free radicals are electrically neutral, highly reactive particles formed by the rupture of C—C or C—H bonds with each particle retaining one of the pair of shared electrons that make up the bond.

(a) $C_4H_{10} \rightarrow H\cdot + C_4H_9\cdot$

(b) $C_4H_9\cdot \rightarrow C_3H_6 + CH_3\cdot$

(c) $CH_3\cdot + RH \rightarrow CH_4 + R\cdot$

If R· is a large alkyl group, it breaks down into an olefin and a small free radical which reacts further as in (c) to produce a chain reaction. It is terminated only when free radical species react with each other or with solids such as coke or the surface of the reactor.

- Thermal polymerization

Larger molecules than present in the feedstock are created by polymerization of the olefins formed above, plus condensation of any aromatics.

- Coke formation

Free carbon always occurs to a degree when hydrocarbons undergo complete degradation.

(d) $RH \rightarrow xC + yH$

5.2.2. Catalytic cracking mechanisms

Catalytic cracking produces no C_1 and C_2 fractions and isomerizes to secondary and tertiary hydrocarbons, desirable components of current petrol. Relatively little free carbon (coke) is formed.

Aromatic rings are stable, but any long alkyl side chains attached to the rings are subject to cracking.

5.3. Reaction Conditions

Optimum time, temperature, pressure and catalyst-feed ratio (if catalytically cracked) are process specifications which depend on feed reactivity, desired product, and coking tendency.

A typical set of conditions for various processes is shown next:

Feed	*Process*	*Reactor Conditions*		
		Contact time, sec	*Temp., °C*	*Pressure atms. gage*
Thermal pyrolysis				
Methane	Acetylene production	0.1	1350	0
Ethane	Ethylene production	1	800	11
Gas oil	Thermal cracking	60	600	20
Residual crude	Coking	—	500	1-3
Catalytic cracking				
Gas oil	High yield of petrol fraction space velocity : 0.5-3/hr catalyst-oil wt. ratio : 5-20	—	480	0.7-1

Several generalizations can be made, based in part on this table.

- Higher molecular weight feeds crack more readily, but have more coking tendency
- Higher pressure increases the rates of polymerization, but increases the throughput
- Catalytic cracking lowers the pressure and temperature requirements
- Quenching to avoid back or side reaction is required where low contact time-high temperature conditions exist (acetylene and ethylene production)

5.4. Catalytic Cracking Process Design and Operation

5.4.1. Background

Cracking on acidic catalysts is an endothermic operation in which tarry materials (coke) deposit gradually and deactivate the catalyst. Reactivation is possible by oxidation of the coke which is exothermic. This is also called regeneration.

Houdry fixed bed units went on stream in 1936, employing a 10 minute make-clean cycle, and using expensive tubular reactors in which molten heat transfer salt was circulated in the shell. The reactors were constructed of expensive alloys to withstand alternate reducing and oxidizing conditions. This design was obsolete within 10 years and was replaced by (1) moving bed reactors with large pellet catalyst or more frequently by (2) fluid bed catalytic reactors. In both of these later designs, the catalyst is moved from the cracking to the regenerating section, thus eliminating the disadvantages of cyclical operation with heat control.

5.4.2. Selection of catalyst

- Composition—acid-treated silica-alumina; natural clays of bentonite and kaolin are being replaced by high purity synthetic oxides (13-25% Al_2O_3, 87-85% SiO_2)
- Form—3-4 mm pellets for moving beds; 20-80 mesh microspherical synthetic catalyst for fluidized bed
- Regenerative properties—burning rate must be high and CO_2/CO rates low for better heat control in fluidized beds
- Poisoning—permanently poisoned by metals, particularly Group III-IV of the reducible-oxide type such as Fe, Ni, Vd, and Cu; have high tolerance to S if steam reactivated
- Aging—reduction in surface area from continued steam reactivation causes catalyst reactivity loss; high SiO_2 compositions more susceptible to aging

5.4.3. Process variables

- Conversion—flexible, depends on petrol/gas oil product rates desired; once-through up to 50%, recycle above 50% is standard to give highest petrol yield
- Temperature—balance between cracking and coking rates, 500°C best average
- Pressure—increasing pressure reduces unsaturation and octane no., increases coke production, but increases reactor throughput; 0.4-1 atm. gage best range
- Catalyst-to-oil ratios—possible to recycle catalyst faster with less coke deactivation, but increasing recirculation costs; 5-20 wt. ratio used with 0.3-0.6% coke levels in reactor
- Catalyst activity—balanced at a constant value dependent on mechanical catalyst losses and additions, dropping to 10-25% of initial value; deliberate additional discard is practiced where cracking capacity is tight

5.4.4. Process characteristics

Distinctive features of catalytic versus thermal cracking as a conversion operation are:

- Produces high quality (80-90 octane no.) petrol from any crude
- More selective cracking and less light ends
- More isomerization
- Greater portion of aromatics
- Less polymerization
- Relatively little coke
- Greater ability to tolerate high sulfur feedstocks
- Uniformity of temperature and pressure control

5.4.5. Equipment design

(a) Fluidized bed (Figure IIIH-2)

By using dense phase (liquid-like) fluidization, a compact design is possible in which regenerative heat is transferred as sensible heat of the clean catalyst to the reactor section. With low rates of dusting in dense phase operation, the cyclones are small enough to place inside the shell as shown. Short lengths of straight standpipes reduce erosion.

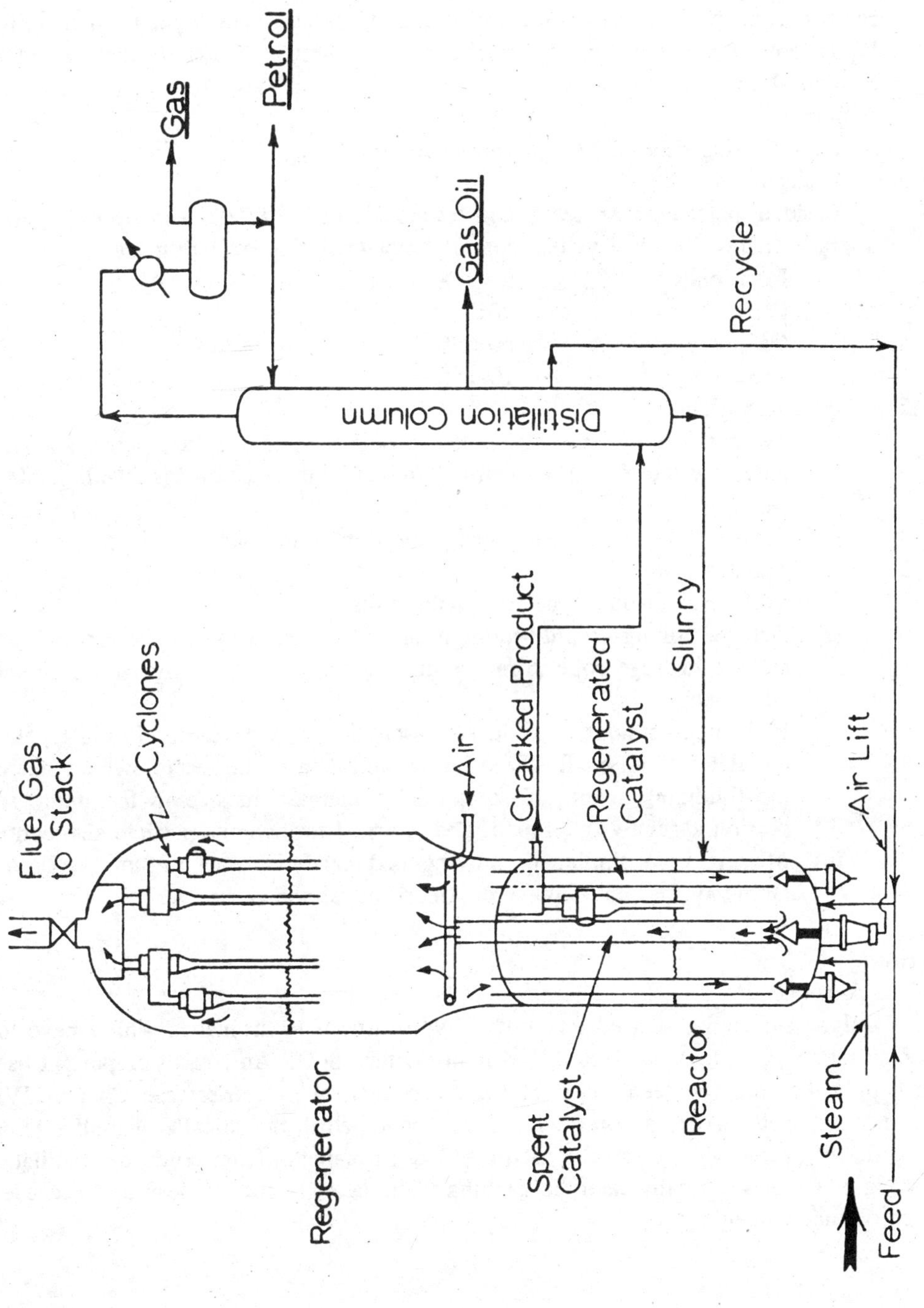

Fig. IIIH-2. Catalytic cracking process—fluidized bed type.

(b) Moving bed (Figure IIIH-3)

Catalyst pellets move at a fixed rate by gravity flow downward through the reactor-regenerator in succession, elevated to the reactor again by a gas lift. Uniform liquid and vapor-liquid feed distribution necessary. Other design drawbacks compared to fluidized units are: excessive steam requirements, poorer heat economy.

5.5. Petroleum Coking Process Design and Operation

5.5.1. Background

Residual petroleum or heavy end fractions from refineries can be pyrolyzed to upgrade values. Typical yields from a complete coking operation are:

Light ends	5 wt.%
Petrol	20%
Gas oil	60-65%
Coke	10-15%

5.5.2. Process variables

- Temperature—increasing results in higher yields of gas, petrol and coke; gases are more olefinic; petrol requires hydrogenation for stability; 500°C best
- Pressure—higher pressure yields more gas and coke; 1-3.5 atms. gage

5.5.3. Equipment design

There are three distinct types of coking units:

(a) Delayed coking—rapid heating in pipe stills followed by coke formation and settling in large coke drums; units are cleaned by cutting with high-speed water jets.

(b) Fluid bed—similar to fluid bed catalytic cracking unit. Product coke is circulated to an air-fluidized burner and then to the reactor where steam is the fluidizing agent. Coke particles increase in size in the units, so a portion is removed, ground, and returned for average particle size control.

(c) Moving bed—similar to moving bed catalytic cracking unit. Used in Germany, but not popular in American refineries.

6. Reforming

6.1. Background

Catalytic reforming is used to convert hydrocarbons to aromatics which have high octane rating (*e.g.*, toluene gives a 104 motor octane no.). An equally important use is to supply the aromatic feedstocks for the petrochemical industries (see Chapter IVF). Feedstocks are the hydrocarbon fractions just above petrol, the so-called naphtha grades. In order of preference, the stocks used are: virgin naphtha from crude oil distillation, coking naphtha, and finally catalytic naphtha. The latter is not too desirable because of high olefinic content.

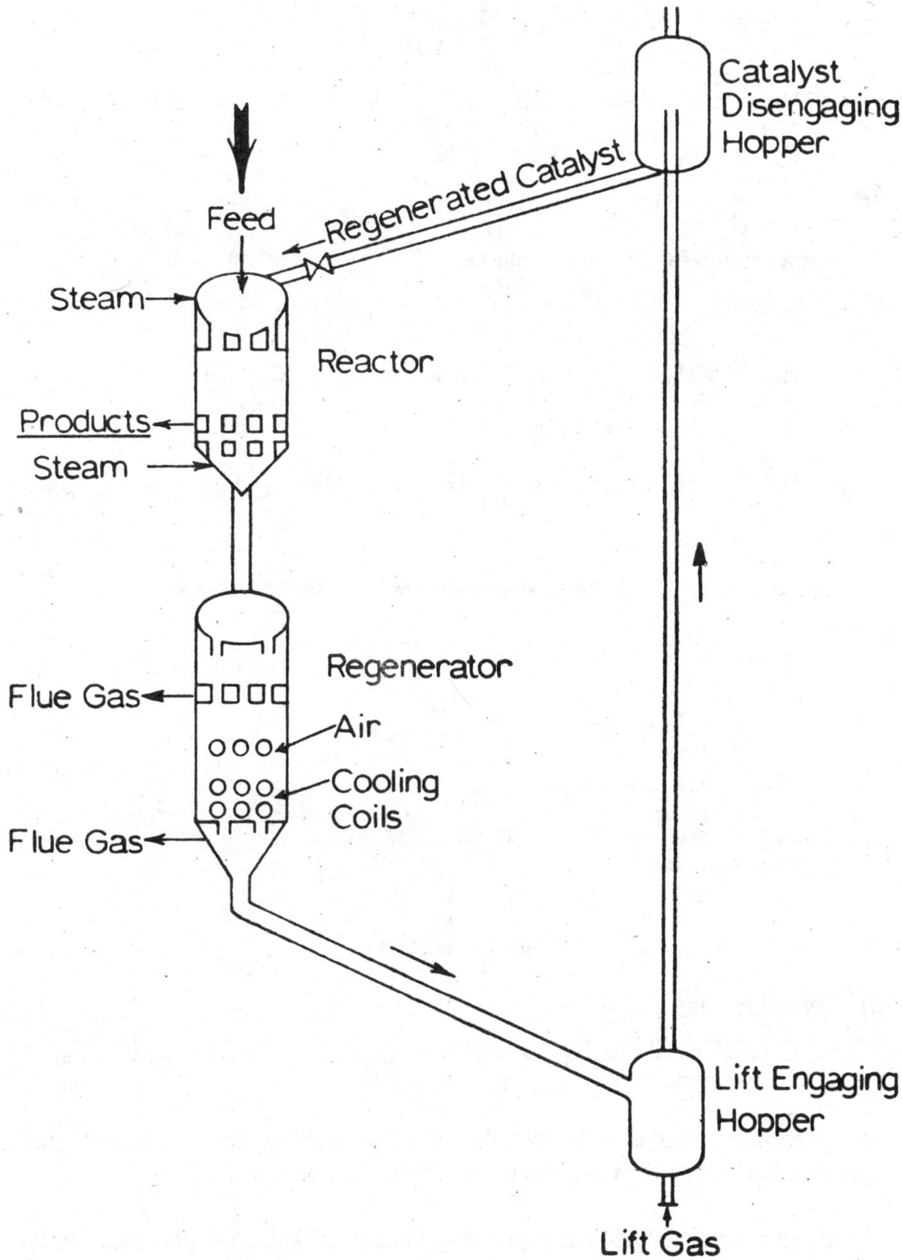

Fig. IIIH-3. Catalytic cracking process—moving bed type.

6.2. Reactions

(a) Dehydrogenation (endothermic)

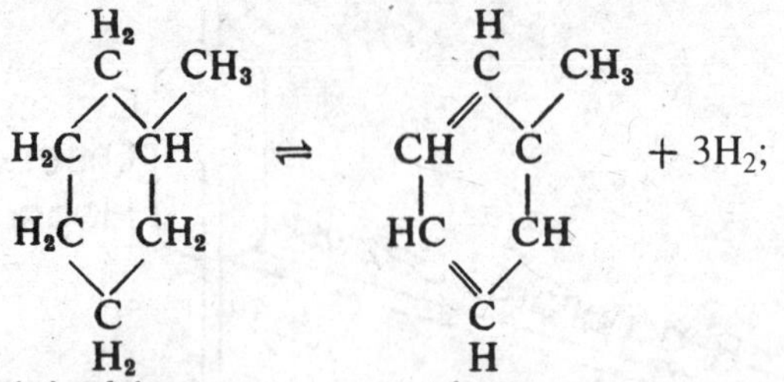

methylcyclohexane toluene

$\Delta H^\circ = +49.0$ Kcal

(b) Cyclization

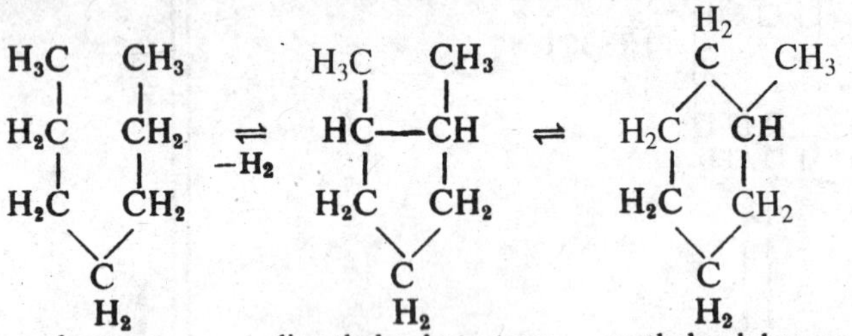

n-heptane dimethylcyclopentane methylcyclohexane

(c) Isomerization

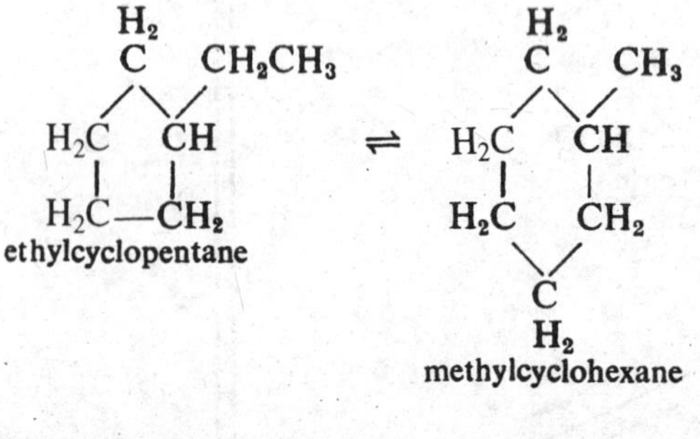

ethylcyclopentane methylcyclohexane

(d) Hydrocracking

$$\underset{n\text{-heptane}}{CH_3(CH_2)_5CH_3} + H_2 \rightarrow \underset{\text{propane}}{C_3H_8} + \underset{\text{butane}}{C_4H_{10}}; \qquad \Delta H^\circ = -9.74 \text{ Kcal}$$

This reaction is undesirable even though lower-boiling paraffins have higher octane numbers, but not as high as toluene produced in reaction 6.2(b).

6.3. Catalysts

Dehydrogenation catalysts are required and can be picked from platinum, molybdenum oxide, chromium oxide, or cobalt molybdate on alumina or silica-alumina base. Platinum is the best in terms of selectivity, lack of hydrocracking, and activity, but is expensive.

Carbon deposits can be removed by steam or air oxidation. Reforming is done under high H_2 pressure so that many possible catalyst poisons, such as S and N, are hydrogenated and consequently removed from the surface. Only the heavy metals such as Pb and As permanently damage Pt catalyst.

6.4. Reaction Conditions

Dehydrogenation at low pressures and high temperatures is predicted thermodynamically. High temperature also favors hydrocracking and carbon deposition. The latter can be suppressed by high hydrogen pressures with use of product hydrogen

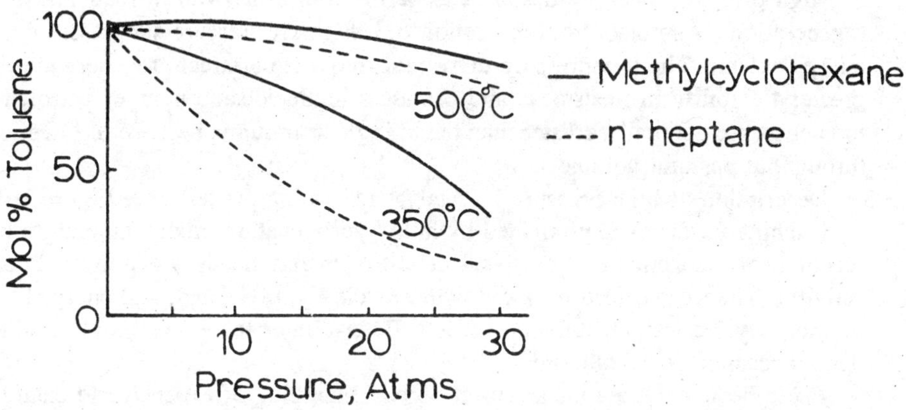

recycle. A compromise is made between catalyst activity and yield of reformate of a given octane number with typical resulting conditions:

Catalyst	platinum
Pressure	15-50 atms.
Temperature	470-525°C
Space velocity	1.5 kg/hr-kg catalyst

6.5. Product Characteristics

Catalytic reformates make excellent blending stocks since they contain no olefins and are oxidation resistant (stable), high in octane no. (>80), and low in sulfur and gum. Boiling point range is broader, thus making good cold weather petrol. They also form the basis for the aromatic petrochemical industry.

6.6. Reforming Process Design and Operation

6.6.1. Choice of process

The factors to consider are comparative petrol yields versus octane no., investment costs, catalyst inventory costs, and operating costs. Platinum catalyst processes are superior to those using less expensive catalysts.

Typical yield curves are shown below:

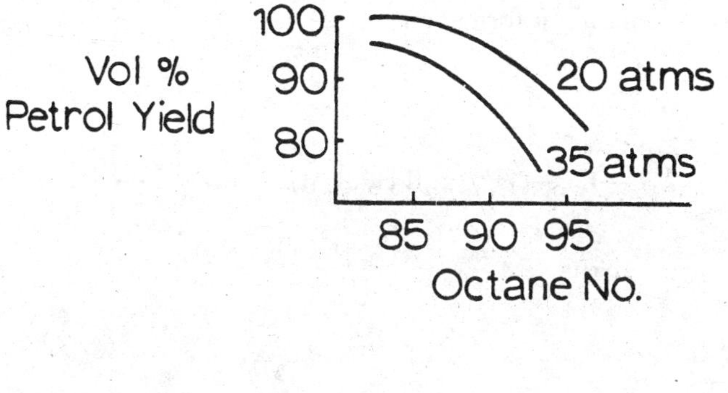

The low pressure platinum catalyst process has a higher octane ceiling, but higher investment cost.

Platinum catalyst inventory costs are high, but non-depreciating with a high salvage value.

6.6.2. Catalyst activity

High pressure units are designed to permit long runs with infrequent off-stream regeneration. As pointed out in Section 6.3, high H_2 pressure suppresses coking to a large extent. The low pressure unit, with frequent on-stream regeneration, allows greater flexibility in feedstocks and produces higher octane number petrol, but the total costs are generally greater than the high pressure units because of lower reactor throughput per unit volume.

6.6.3. Description of high pressure Pt catalyst reforming process (see Figure IIIH-4)

Naphtha feedstock is pretreated by mild hydrogenation, high temperature bauxite reaction, or adsorption to remove sulfur, nitrogen and metals which lower Pt catalyst activity. The treated feed is mixed with recycle H_2, preheated, and charged to three or more cylindrical reactors in series. Reheat interstages are required since the overall reaction is endothermic.

Fixed bed catalytic units are used because handling of expensive Pt catalyst in a fluidized bed would create too high an operating loss via dusting. The catalyst can be regenerated every 2-3 months by burning off the carbonaceous deposit with mixtures of steam, air and flue gas. Non-lubricated compressors are used to recycle H_2, thus avoiding coking of catalyst by lubricating oil.

Reactors operate on downflow with the catalyst particle size of between 1.5-3.0 mm. Smaller particles give higher activity per unit volume, but greater pressure drop in a given-sized reactor. The steel vessel is insulated by monolithic ceramic liners which often crack, causing hot vapor bypassing with resulting high shell temperatures and ultimate rupture. To avoid this, thin alloy liners inside the insulation are now common practice.

7. Polymerization

7.1. Background

Polymerization is defined in the petroleum industry as the combining of two or more olefinic molecules to yield larger molecules. Thus C_3 and C_4 olefins from catalytic cracking can be converted to liquid hydrocarbons of the dimer and trimer type.

7.2. Reactions

(a) Carbonium ion formation

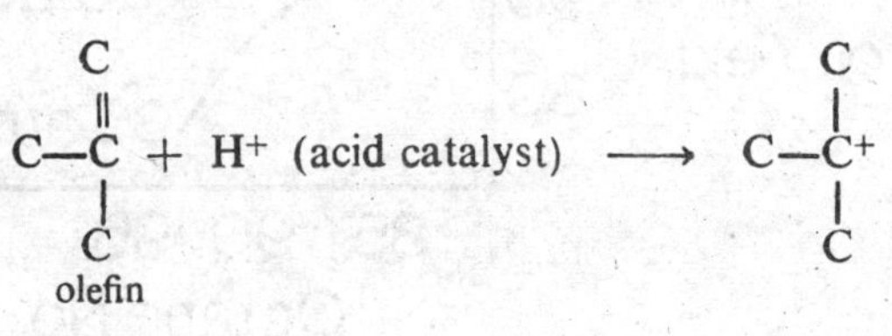

olefin

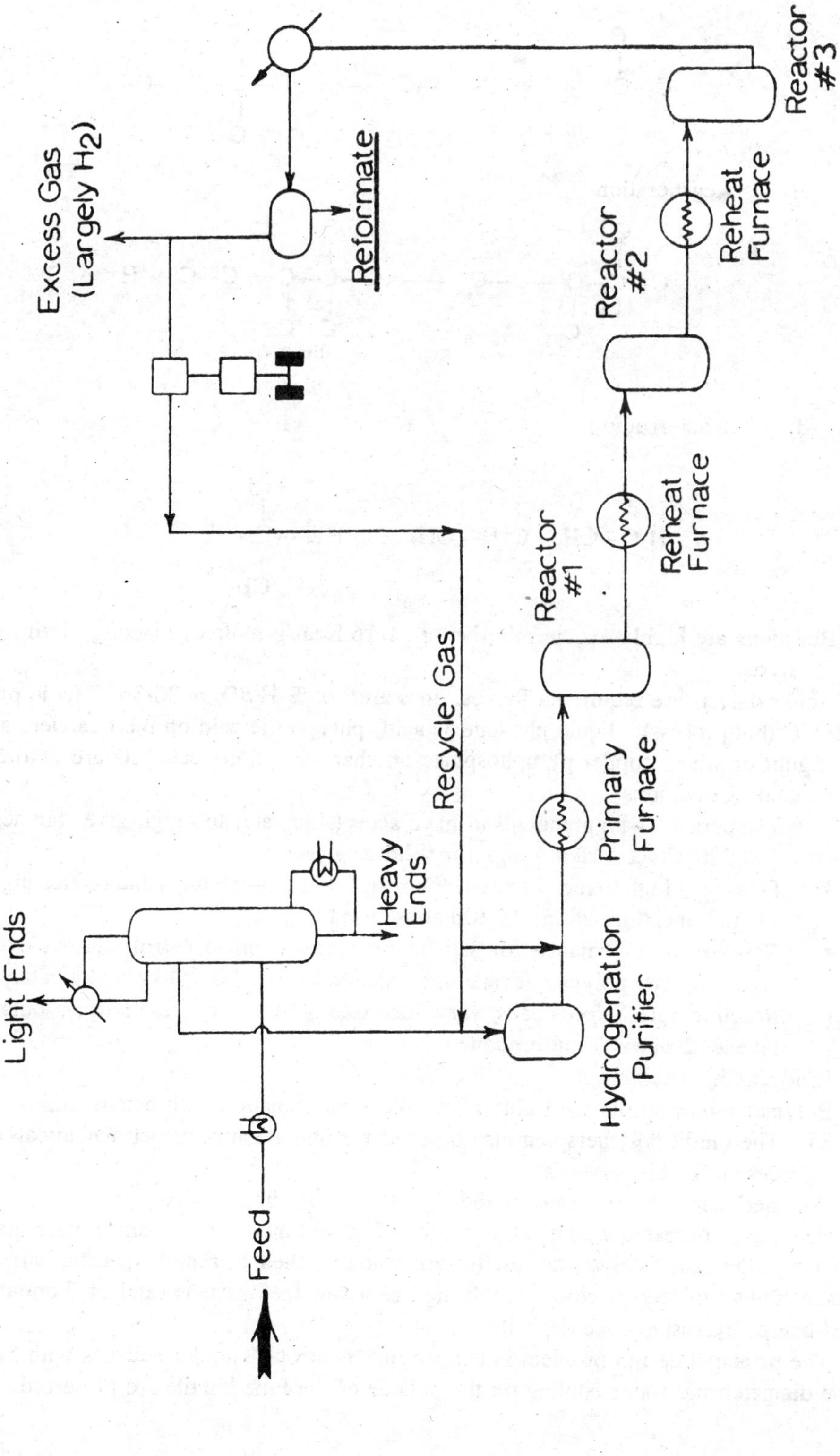

Fig. IIIH-4. High pressure platinum catalyst reforming process.

(b) Addition

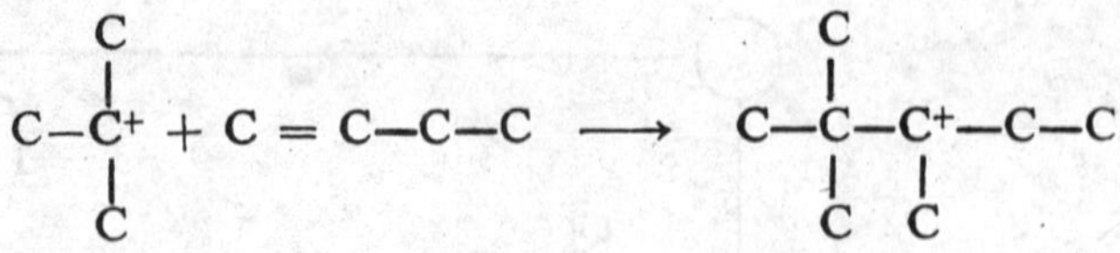

(c) Regeneration

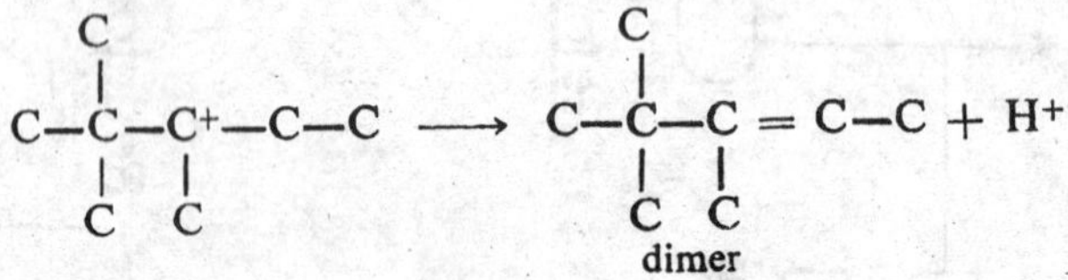

dimer

(d) Isomerization

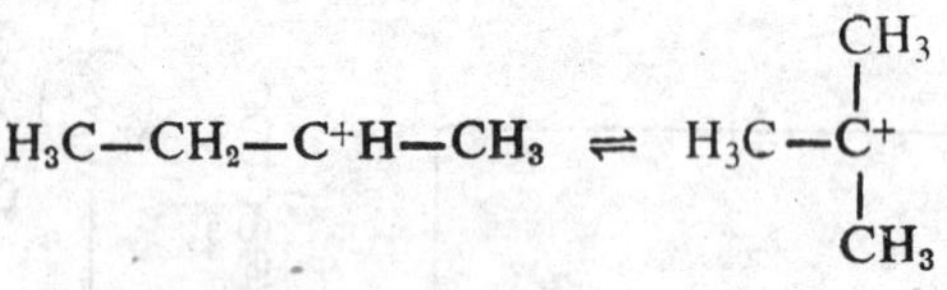

Reactions are highly exothermic, being 11-16 Kcal/g mole of reacting olefin.

7.3. Catalysts

Acid catalysts are required. Typical ones are: 65% H_2SO_4 at 20-36°C (cold process) or 93°C (hot process): liquid phosphoric acid, phosphoric acid on inert carriers such as kieselguhr or silica, copper pyrophosphate on charcoal. Solid catalysts are favored.

7.4. Reaction Conditions

- Temperature—high enough to have acceptable rate; too high gives tar deposits; 150-220°C acceptable range for solid catalyst
- Pressure—high to increase conversion at lower temperatures and reduce high mol. wt. polymer formation; 25-100 atms. used
- Reaction time—balance for satisfactory conversion to petrol without excessive high mol. wt. polymer formation; space velocity of 0.7-3 kg/hr-kg catalyst
- Reaction rates—feedstocks vary; decreasing order of reactivity; *i*-butane, 1-butene, 2-butene, and propane

7.5. Product Characteristics

Polymer motor spirits are stable after mild hydrogenation with octane numbers from 80-85. The olefin polymers can also be used for manufacture of petrochemicals by the Oxo process to be discussed later.

7.6. Polymerization Process Design and Operation (see Figure IIIH-5)

Feeds are pretreated with alkali to remove H_2S and mercaptans. Since basic materials deactivate the acid catalyst, the olefins are water-washed to remove caustic carry-over. Water content of feed is closely controlled as a wet feed softens catalyst; bone-dry gas feed causes excessive coke deposits.

The principal design problem is temperature control. Tubular reactors with 5-15 cm tube diameter and water cooling on the outside of the tube bundle are preferred. The

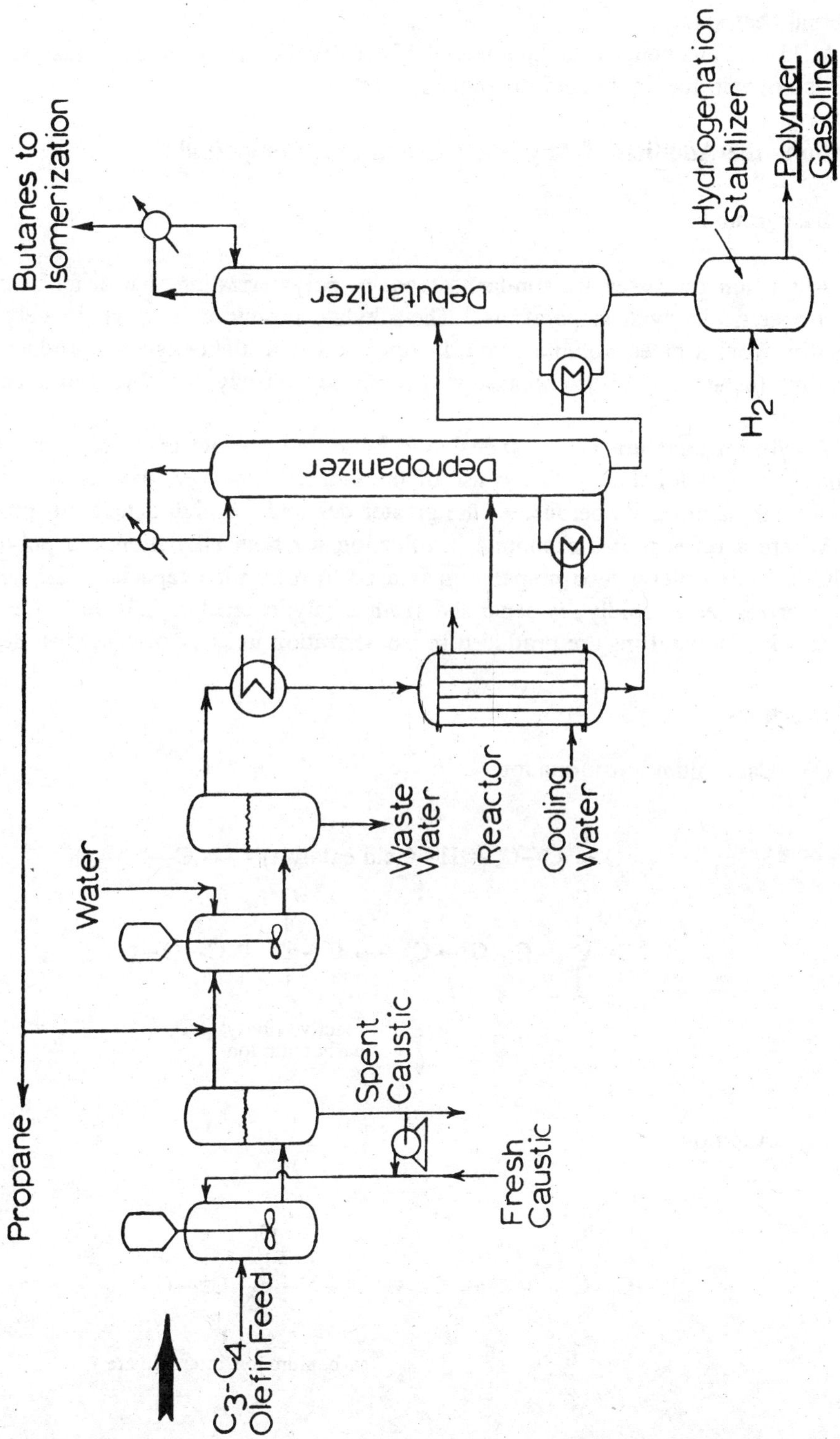

Fig. IIIH-5. Olefin polymerization using phosphoric acid on solid carrier as catalyst.

temperature rise is further reduced by addition of saturated C_3-C_4 recycle to provide an internal heat sink.

Mild steel can be used as the material of construction for solid acid catalyst processes; this is not true for liquid acid operations.

8. Alkylation—the Addition of Any Alkyl Group to a Compound

8.1. Background

Alkylation processes are similar to those of polymerization, but differ in that olefins react specifically with isoparaffins. The alkylate produced is approximately twice the quantity from a given volume of olefin stock. It is a higher quality product for petrol blending (octane no. 85-95) because it is composed entirely of stable, saturated branched paraffins.

Alkylation units are more expensive to build and operate than polymerization units, which accounts for the continued use of the latter. However, new plant additions are usually alkylation units because of the greater demand for high octane no. products.

Where a refinery has economic justification for both alkylation and polymerization units, selective olefin feed preparation is used to maximize capacity. 2-butene, which polymerizes least rapidly, is separated from catalytic cracking distillate for alkylation feedstock. Isoparaffins are produced in isomerization units as discussed in Section 9.

8.2. Reactions

(a) Carbonium ion formation

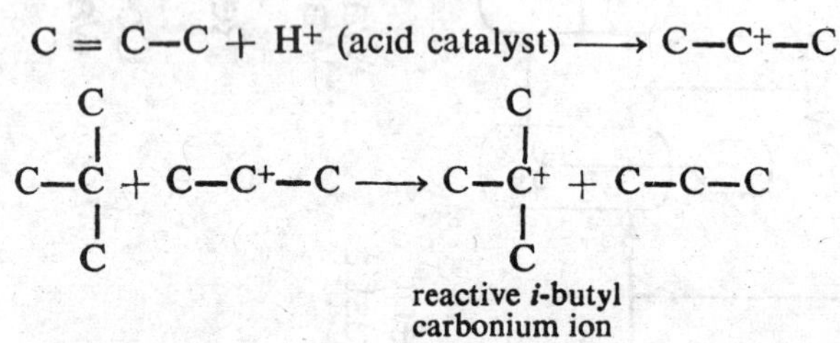

(b) Addition

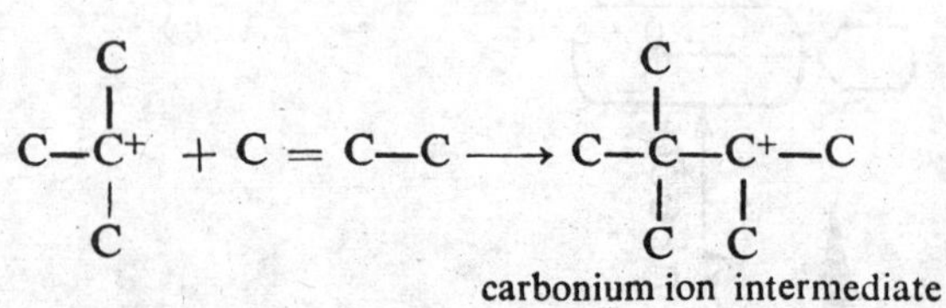

(c) Regeneration

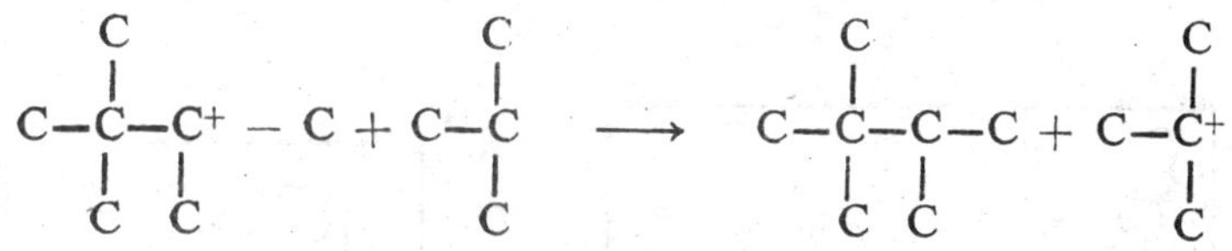

The carbonium ion intermediate isomerizes readily to other structures, thus explaining isomer mixtures in alkylates.

8.3. Catalysts

- Sulfuric acid—85% acidity, circulated at 4-10°C in emulsion form containing 50% acid; acid consumption is 0.05-0.2 ton/ton, requiring H_2SO_4 plant near refinery and spent acid disposal for economical operation.
- Hydrogen fluoride—competitive with H_2SO_4, but consumes only 1/10 the weight of H_2SO_4 used; HF distilled and recycled as compared to H_2SO_4 spent acid disposal: HF requires extreme safety in handling; produces lower grade alkylate; operates at 37°C level, requiring no refrigeration.

8.4. Reaction Conditions

- Temperature—reactions are exothermic, best yield at low temperatures; H_2SO_4 catalyst more temperature sensitive with 0°C lower limit because of viscosity effects and 21°C upper limit because of sulfation reaction; HF has no marked effect from 60°C down to —20°C. Therefore, 37°C is standard for water-cooled units.
- Pressure—just above the bubble point pressure of the mixture of hydrocarbons; no real effect of increasing pressure.
- *i*-butane/olefin—to avoid polymerization of olefins a large excess of *i*-butane is used, ranging from 5 : 1 to 15 : 1.
- Contact time—5 to 40 minutes depending on type of liquid-liquid contact.

8.5. Product Characteristics

Alkylates are denser than the reactants with volumetric shrinkage amounting to 8-15% and varying with feedstock input.

Butene alkylates have octane ratings from 92-97 with those prepared from propene or pentenes somewhat less. All these ratings can be raised by removing 5-10% of the heavy ends which have octane numbers around 80.

8.6. Alkylation Process Design and Operation (see Figure IIIH-6)

Alkylation units have same basic elements: caustic wash to remove sulfur compounds, reactor to contact catalyst acid with fresh feedstock and recycle *i*-butane, fractionators for separating *i*-butane and propane from alkylate.

The HF unit requires additional equipment to dry the feedstock, strip HF from product, a caustic end wash or bauxite adsorption to remove fluoride impurities, and side stream purification of HF from settler to prevent buildup of water, tar and acid soluble fluorinated compounds.

Reactor designs are now limited to two types. The horizontal, baffled tank, cascade reactor is used for the sulfuric acid process—it operates on the mixer-settler principle. Bayonet type heat exchangers with mechanical mixing on the shell side are used for both processes, whereas the simple shell and tube exchanger is used only for HF units because

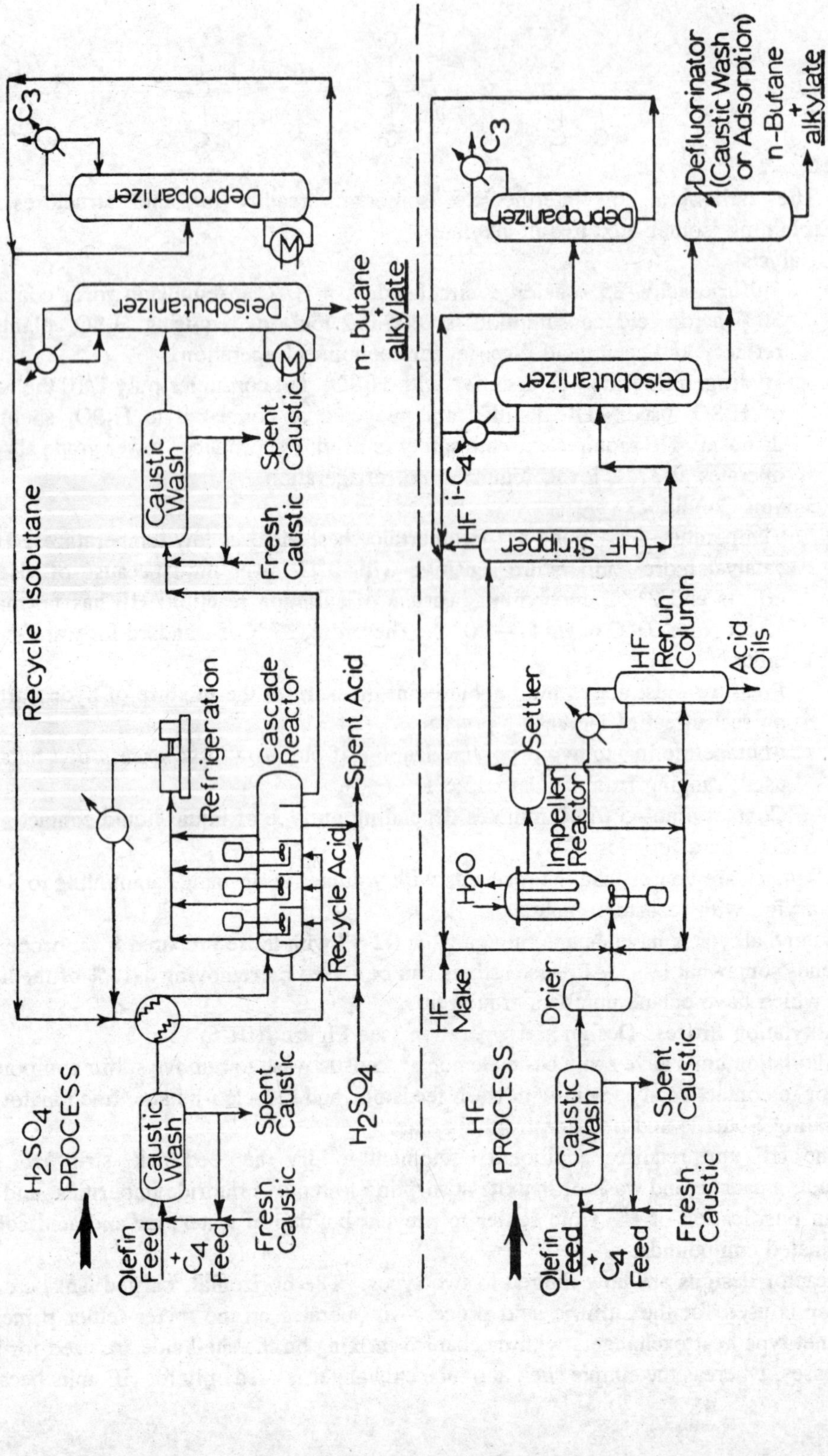

Fig. IIIH-6. Acid alkylation processes.

of the high viscosity, low heat transfer coefficient of the H_2SO_4 emulsion at low temperatures.

9. Isomerization

9.1. Background

Catalytic isomerization of *n*-paraffins to isomers for alkylation feedstock is a necessary refinery operation since *n*-paraffins are of little value as an end-product.

9.2. Reaction

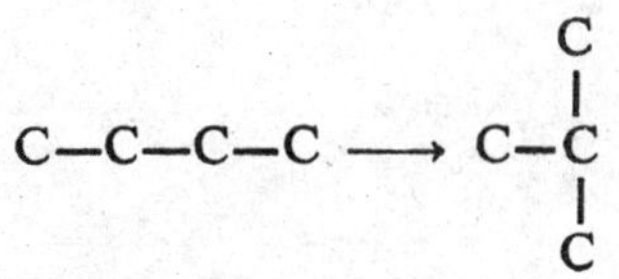

The reaction is mildly exothermic.

9.3. Catalysts

- Aluminum trichloride-HCl promoted—adsorbed on porous carriers or used as a liquid; both vapor and liquid phase reactions are in commercial practice; catalyst life is 0.3-1.5 tons of isomer per kg of catalyst.

9.4. Reaction Conditions

- Temperature—balance between equilibrium which is favored at low temperature (see diagram below) and rates: 100-150°C used with 40-50% conversion and recycle to achieve 98% yield.

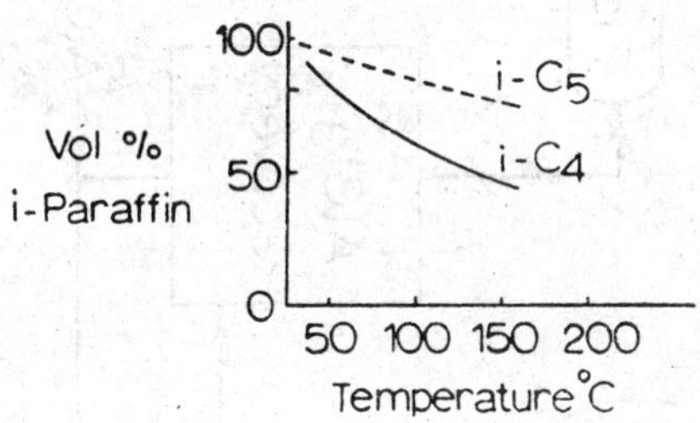

- Pressure—no effect on reaction, 17-27 atms. used as an economic balance between throughput and reactor vessel costs.
- Space velocity—0.5 to 2.5 m^3/hr-m^3 of catalyst.
- Feed purification—must remove water, sulfur compounds and olefins which react with expensive $AlCl_3$ catalyst.

9.5. Isomerization Process Design and Operation (see Figure IIIH-7)

The flow sheet is basic for most of the current refinery isomerization units. Feedstock, mainly from virgin and coking distillate, is dried and preheated, fed to a reactor designed for efficient vapor-solid, vapor-liquid, liquid-liquid or liquid-solid contact, depending on the reactant and catalyst form respectively. HCl and make-up $AlCl_3$ are also added. $AlCl_3$ recovery by distillation or condensation is necessary because it is volatile at reactor conditions and slightly soluble in liquid hydrocarbons. Removal of light ends by flashing, followed by HCl stripping, caustic wash, and fractionation are standard operations.

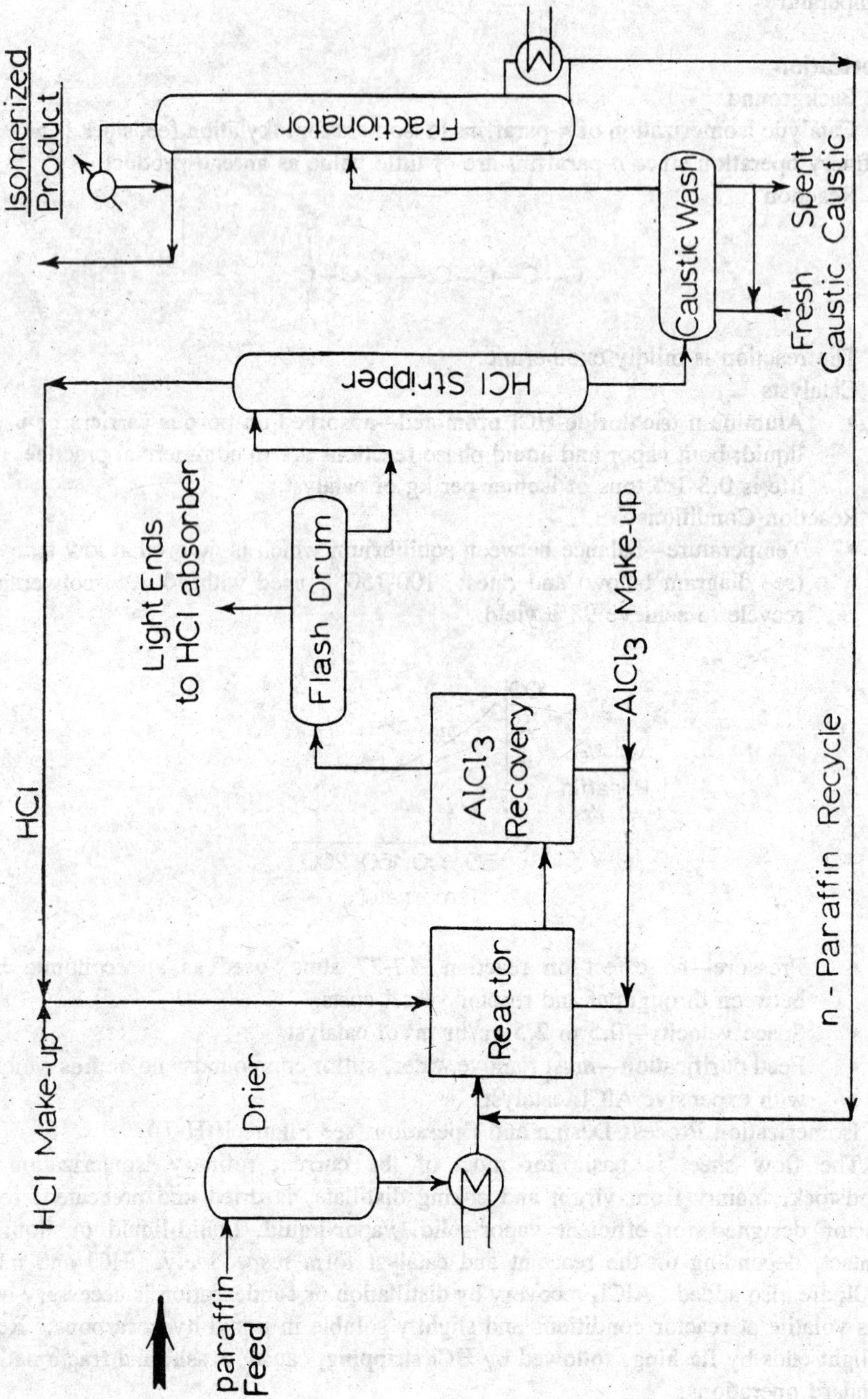

Fig. IIIH-7. Low temperature isomerization process.

10. Hydrodealkylation

Reforming produces about equal yields of benzene, toluene and xylenes. The dominant need is benzene so a combined hydrogenation and dealkylation process is employed. This is discussed in Chapter IVF.

11. Purification of Petroleum End-Products

Before refinery products are marketable, they must be treated with these results in mind:

11.1. Removal of Sulfur and Mercaptan Compounds–accomplished by treating with strong H_2SO_4, sodium plumbite (Na_2PbO_2) or other mild oxidant, catalytic oxidation, or hydrogenation; also improves color and odor.

11.2. Removal of Gums, Color and Odor—use of strong H_2SO_4 and acid clay adsorption.

11.3. Improvement of Stability to Light and Air—use of mild hydrogenation if unsaturation is too high; otherwise the other treatments listed above are satisfactory.

Future Refinery Plans

New refineries with a capacity of six million tons each and another with three million tons will take the total capacity to 83 million tons if they materialize fast enough. The three million ton refinery at Mangalore estimated to cost Rs. 1,160 crores with a foreign exchange component of Rs. 300 crores (June 1990 prices) is being implemented as a joint sector project of Hindustan Petroleum Corporation, Indian Rayon, Grasim, Hindalco and Indo-Gulf Fertilizers. There has already been cost escalation and the revised estimates are Rs. 1,756 crores including a foreign exchange component of Rs. 617 crores.

Three grassroots refineries having a capacity of six million tons each will be coming up in eastern India, central India and western India as joint sector projects. The public sector participants in these projects will be Indian Oil Corporation for the eastern India refinery, Bharat Petroleum Corporation for the central India refinery and Hindustan Petroleum Corporation for the western India refinery. BPCL and HPCL have entered into separate memoranda of understanding with Oman Oil Company for the central and western India refineries according to the *Hindu Survey of Indian Industry* (1994).

Letters of intent have also been given to private parties for setting up refineries. These are: Reliance Petroleum for a 9 million ton refinery in the west coast, International Petroleum SA of Switzerland for a 5 million ton refinery (expandable to 10 million tons) in Gujarat with the refinery being 100 percent export oriented, Ashok Leyland and Gotco (U.S.) for a 6 million ton refinery in Orissa, Essar Investment for a 9 million ton refinery in the west coast and T.R. Datla (Black Gold Refineries) for a 2.5 million ton refinery in Andhra Pradesh.

Apart from the expansion of capacity, the growing demand for lube products has also had to be taken care of. Letters of intent have been granted to set up lube oil refineries to Reliance Industries to set up a 5 lakh ton lube refinery in the West Coast and to Harrisons Malayalam to set up a 2 lakh ton lube refinery for production of lube oil, carbon black, bitumen and slack wax.

Future Natural Gas Plans

The estimated demand for natural gas by 2000-01 in Gujarat, Karnataka, Andhra Pradesh, Maharashtra, Madhya Pradesh, Orissa and Tamil Nadu is 59.2 billion cubic meters a year. The gas will be the feedstock for nine power stations to be commissioned in Maharashtra, Andhra Pradesh, Madhya Pradesh and Gujarat by 2000-01, apart from nine fertilizer plants and 14 sponge iron plants in these States. The much publicized Southern Gas Grid, which has been agreed to in principle, depends very much upon the completion of the Indo-Oman gas project.

Meanwhile, indigenous availability is projected to go up from 18 billion cubic meters a year to between 23 and 30 billion cubic meters by 2001-02. With supplies from Oman and Iran the total availability will go up to between 63 and 70 billion cubic meters a year by 2001-02. As against this, the projected demand will be around 96 million cubic meters a year, with the region-wise break-up as shown in Table IIIH-3.

Table IIIH-3
Regionwise Natural Gas Demand by 2001-02
(in billion cubic meters per year)

Region	*Fertilizer*	*Power Projects*	*Sponge Iron*	*Glass*	*Others*	*Total*
Northern	2.41	7.44	2.89	3.20	4.42	20.36
Eastern	0.36	0.91	0.18	-	1.47	2.92
Western	9.30	10.57	2.94	12.58	5.99	41.38
Southern	7.95	6.60	4.88	6.66	5.27	31.36
Total	**20.02**	**25.52**	**10.89**	**22.44**	**17.15**	**96.02**

The projections imply a shortfall of 26 to 30 billion cubic meters by decade end. While new discoveries can reduce the shortfall, the steps which the GAIL as well as the Oil and Natural Gas Corporation and Oil India have been taking to check wastage are primarily aimed at reduction of flaring. Gas flaring has come down from a high level of 54.90 percent in 1980-81 to 10.4 percent at present.

In order to tide over the difficulties in tying up feedstocks, and to ensure some measure of control over prices at which imports take place, many Indian companies are planning joint ventures in countries where natural/associated gas (the preferred feedstock for urea manufacture) or rock phosphate (the main raw material for phosphatic fertilizer) is available in abundance, and at relatively lower cost. The industry is also looking at the possibility of taking over operations of fertilizer businesses in other parts of the world.

Some of the overseas ventures that are presently under consideration are shown below.

Overseas Ventures under Consideration

Company	Country	Products	Capacity Planned
Indo Jordan Chemicals	Jordan	Phosphoric acid	225,000 TPA
IFFCO, KRIBHCO	Iran	Ammonia/urea	1,350/2,250 TPD
KRIBHCO, RCF	Oman	Ammonia/urea	1,350/2,250 TPD (two plants)

RCF = Rashtriya Chemicals & Fertilizers
IFFCO = Indian Farmers Fertilizer Cooperative
KRIBHCO = Krishak Bharati Cooperative

Source: "Chemical Weekly Annual" (1995)

In addition to those listed above, there have been reports of the Madras-based Southern Petrochemicals Corporation Ltd. (SPIC) setting up a 0.396 million tons per annum urea plant in the United Arab Emirates by relocating a Sri Lankan plant. The Gujarat State Fertilizers Co. Ltd. (GSFC) has also signed a memorandum of understanding with the Ugandan Government for a $120 million phosphatic fertilizer project using Ugandan rock phosphate.

Progress on the project is not yet clear. Discussions are also going on in various other countries such as Abu Dhabi, Brunei, Malaysia, and Qatar for joint venture fertilizer projects in these countries. All these ventures are being planned with a proposal to buy-back a majority, if not all, of the fertilizer produced.

There have also been reports of the KRIBHCO planning to acquire a stake in two Russian plants manufacturing phosphatic fertilizers. If the deal materializes, it will represent a first for the Indian fertilizer industry.

IV

SYNTHETIC ORGANIC CHEMICAL INDUSTRIES

The definition of an organic chemical is a compound containing carbon, oxygen, and hydrogen as principal constituent elements. A synthetic organic chemical, as we shall use it in this chapter, is derived by one or more processes from the low molecular weight compounds in raw materials such as coal, petroleum, or natural gas. A few may also be obtained from natural products as pointed out in Chapter III—for example, ethanol by fermentation, glycerol by hydrolysis. Synthetic organic chemicals usually have a fairly low molecular weight and a relatively simple structure. This is a distinguishing feature when compared with natural product organics.

Synthetic organic chemicals can be categorized as primary, intermediate, or end chemicals according to one of the following definitions:

- Primary chemical—a substance which is first isolated and reasonably pure. Prior to this, it had been present in a raw material or formed therefrom.
- Intermediate chemical—derived from a primary chemical; can be utilized as a product but also undergoes further chemical reactions to produce a variety of other chemicals.
- End chemical—undergoes no further chemical change before usage, but may be either physically modified or used as part of a mixture.

Prior to 1951 Indian organic chemical production was limited to primary chemicals such as alcohol, acetone, benzene, and toluene. Various other chemicals were imported and converted to end-products, principally drugs, dyes, and plastics. By the end of the Second Plan (1961), a number of organic chemical products were indigenously produced, notably DDT, BHC, acetic acid, acetic anhydride, polyethylene and polyvinyl chloride. These were based on industrial alcohol, benzene from coal carbonization, and acetylene derived from calcium carbide.

During the Third Plan (1961-1966), organic chemical industries showed growth prospects and potential target achievements so that the conventional raw materials cited above will no longer suffice. Petroleum feedstocks took over as the major raw material in the Fourth Plan (1969-1974) and thus petrochemicals began to play a major role in Indian economy, a situation which existed in the U.S. and UK after World War II (1946 onwards). The prediction has been made that 65% would be derived from petroleum and the remaining 35% from non-petroleum products (fermentation alcohol, coke oven by-products, and calcium carbide). The success of this prediction will depend on considerations such as:

- Financing—petrochemical industries are large and highly capitalized, hence foreign capital and participation are required as India does not have sufficient foreign exchange resources.

- Technology—petrochemical industries are complex and will require experienced personnel to assist on a foreign investment collaboration scheme.
- Planning—economic-sized plants must be provided to compete on a world market basis for intermediate and end-product sales; planning must be coordinated to provide the long-term requirements for raw materials, machinery and services.

Failure to implement these plans rapidly will result in continued wastage of naphtha fractions, which accumulate in refineries, by use as low value fuel stock and the necessity of importing primary chemicals, a practice which requires valuable foreign exchange. However, the task of formulating a development program for the organic chemical industry in India has not been easy because of the following factors:

- Interprocess competition with the attendant complexity of diverse raw material requirements
- Diversity of end-products with a wide range of tonnage requirements
- Intermediate chemicals competition for consumer goods usage, *e.g.*, competition amongst plastics

IVA. PETROCHEMICALS—THE KEY GROWTH AREA

1. Definition of Petrochemical

A chemical compound or element recovered or derived partially or entirely from petroleum or natural gas hydrocarbons and intended for chemical markets.

2. Reasons for Studying Petrochemical Industries

As pointed out in the previous section, the future organic chemical industry of India will depend more and more on petroleum sources as raw materials.

Aromatic raw materials from coal are geared to steel production which does not have sufficient growth rate to match the organics and ammonia-based fertilizer yearly percentage gain in production.

It is uneconomic to expand the higher cost alcohol supplies.

A second disadvantage of alcohol is the lack of consolidation of producing units with very limited capacity. The availability of large bulk feedstocks at one location, *i.e.*, a refinery to supply a petrochemical-type plant, is a distinct advantage in terms of critical economic plant size. Different products such as ethylene, propylene, etc., being simultaneously produced in one refinery, enable integration of a number of consuming industries utilizing these various raw material streams.

3. Petrochemical Industry Characteristics

3.1. Size and Scope of Petrochemical Industry

The production of basic petrochemicals in India made a modest beginning at a comparatively late stage during the sixties. A rather small capacity naphtha cracker of 20,000 tons per annum (tpa) ethylene capacity was set up in 1966 by Union Carbide in Bombay. In 1968, a larger naphtha cracker of 60,000 tpa ethylene capacity was set up by National Organic Chemical Industries of the Mafatlal Group. Prior to that, small quantities of petrochemicals (mainly plastic resins and intermediates) were being produced based on alcohol, coal tar intermediates and calcium carbide as feedstock.

The major thrust to the industry came when the Indian Petrochemicals Corporation's naphtha cracker of 1.3 lakh tpa ethylene capacity was commissioned at Baroda in 1978. The eighties hardly witnessed any new development except for the Maharashtra Gas Cracker Complex (MGCC) for which official clearance was given in 1984.

The demand for petrochemicals in India rose from 1.4 million tons at the end of the Sixth Plan to nearly three million tons by 1989-90 and is likely to be 5.4 million tons by 1994-95. By 2000 A.D., the demand may soar to eight million tons. Such an increase may appear phenomenal, but in terms of per capita consumption, it is not going to make much difference. Compared to the world average of plastics and synthetic textiles at 15.4 kg and 6.6 kg respectively, India's per capita consumption is 0.67 kg and 2.5 kg respectively. Even if the projected demand is met, the per capita consumption of plastics is expected to rise to only 2 kg in 1994-95 and 2.6 kg by 2000 A.D.

The major problem faced in 1995 by the industry while trying to step up its exports, is that there is a world glut in petrochemicals. When the Government had earlier sanctioned eight large petrochemical complexes with cracker capacities of the order of three to four lakh tons, the emergence of a situation of glut was considered remote. But since then, large complexes have come up in Korea, Saudi Arabia (SABIC) and Europe.

In 1995, the *Chemical Weekly Annual* featured a review of the history and status of the petrochemical industry in India. They stated that with petrochemicals investments pegged at Rs. 50,000 crores, the Indian chemical markets will experience a glut in commodities like ethylene, propylene, PVC, and TPA. With the surge in the polymer and textile sector, growing at 14 and 18% respectively, the capacities being planned seem logical. However, industry experts are skeptical about the performance of the Indian petrochemical sector except for a couple of the majors. The major issue is the ability of the smaller manufacturers to withstand the threat of imports with the markets opening up to international competition. Besides, poor economies of scale of most Indian plants will be a big deterrent to many Indian companies.

In the early 90's, nine huge petrochemical projects were planned at a total investment of Rs. 20,000 crores out of which only two, *i.e.*, IPCL's Gandhar unit and Reliance's Hazira unit, have been on schedule. Other plants are still in planning stages and some are uncertain. This has been due to the 1991 balance of payment crisis and the inflation which followed. The high cost of capital goods made most of the projects unviable. The industry is essentially threatened by imports from West Asia as tariffs are coming down rapidly. Apart from Reliance Industries and IPCL, none of the other players have global size plants and the capability for total integration considering the present structure of the industry. Another notable feature of the petrochemical sector is that unlike oil, finance, and telecom where a number of foreign investments have come in, the petrochemical sector has yet to attract any serious investments.

The sunrise industry in the Indian scene is the polymer industry which has grown at a poor rate of only 4.5% while the demand has shot up by 13%. The rapid growth of the engineering, automobile and consumer durable sector in India is bound to push demand for commodity plastics far beyond the existing capabilities to manufacture them. The transition to value-added polymers which is expected to touch 2.1 lakh tons by 2000 has spurred many firms to shift to engineering and performance plastics. Judging by the present trends, the imports into the country are likely to be as high as 25% until 2000. With the present budget slashing the import duty on many polymer products from 65% to around 40%, the industry faces a constant threat of dumping from its South East Asian competitors.

Reliance Industries has put in motion plans to set up a 15 million ton refinery at Jamnagar to cater to its ethylene demand, and a chlor-alkali plant for its caustic and chlorine needs. With its blueprint for expansion into 2000, it promises to become a completely integrated plant with world size capacities from naphtha to fabrics. The threat of foreign competition has also spurred other petrochemical majors to focus on backward integration in the 90's. If the plans laid down by IPCL are any indication, it is likely to weather the turbulent phase of import threats and tariff rates. It plans to set up a two-phase 300,000 ton gas cracker at Gandhar to produce ethylene and also derived intermediates and commodities. It is also laying emphasis on building its own port to import products and feedstocks from its joint ventures from Middle East. The port which is likely to come up at Dahej, will be the biggest port between Dubai and Singapore.

Petrochemical units are expanding their activities so impressively that the requirements of phthalic anhydride, linear alkyl benzene, polyester staple fiber and nylon filament yarn are available fully from indigenous sources. The staple fiber units have surplus capacity and are obliged to effect exports for maintaining production at the desired rate. The deficit in carbon black supplies is being gradually reduced with the commissioning of new units. Only the output of polyethylene and polyvinyl chloride is not catching up with rising consumption and the situation is expected to be less uncomfortable after the new plants commence production. The output of caprolactam, TPA, DMT and monoethylene glycol will be increasing significantly, when the new projects under implementation take shape. Supply and demand figures are summarized in Table IVA-1.

Table IVA-1
Petrochemicals: Demand/Supply Gap in 1994-95

('000 tons)

Petrochemicals	Demand	Supply	Gap
Thermoplastics:			
LDPE	482	208	274
HDP	375	92	283
Polypropylene	286	92	194
PVC	485	130	355
Polystyrene	82	22	60
Feedstock:			
Ethylene	1,371	424	947
Propylene	600	249	351
Orthoxylene	106	60	46

Intermediates:			
DMT/TPA	393	216	177
LAB	287	173	114
Paraxylene	301	235	66
Other Petrochemicals:			
Benzene	578	298	280
Polyester	390	211	179

Source: "Kothari's Industrial Directory of India" (1994)

The following paragraphs give data on the present and proposed capacities of major petrochemical plants in India, quoting from the *Hindu Survey of Indian Industry* for 1994.

1. **Indian Petrochemicals Corp. Ltd.**
   (Nagothane gas cracker)
   Feedstock: Ethane/propane from ONGC, Uran, 51,000 tons of propane and propylene annually from BPCL.
   Basic capacity ('000 tons): LDPE/HDPE - 135 (commissioned); ethylene oxide - 5; ethylene glycol - 50 and polypropylene - 60. Expansion plans for stepping up cracker capacity by one lakh tons and HDPE by 80,000 tons.

2. **Reliance Industries Ltd., Hazira**
   Feedstock: NGL and naphtha.
   Basic capacity ('000 tons): Ethylene - 750; propylene - 365; butadiene - 275; benzene - 235; toluene - 192; and xylene - 165.
   Proposed downstream ('000 tons): HDPE/LDPE - 440; polypropylene - 250; MEG - 100; ethylene oxide - 110; styrene - 100; polystyrene - 40; synthetic butadiene rubber - 100; acrylonitrile - 70; PVC - 300; terephthalic acid - 350; PSF - 60; and PET chips (bottle grade) - 80 .
   Downstream units of LDPE (160,000 tons)/HDPE (110,000 tons) commissioned. Other downstream units in planning stage.

3. **IPCL's Gandhar Complex (Gujarat)**
   Feedstock: ONGC gas from Gandhar fields.
   Basic capacity ('000 tons): Ethylene - 300; propylene - 20; and butadiene - 10.
   Proposed downstream ('000 tons): EDC - 240; VCM - 158; PVC - 150; EO/MEG - 120; Alpha olefins - 100; and alcohol ethoxylate - 100.
   Remarks: Planning stage.

4. **Auraiya Gas Cracker Complex, U.P. (GAIL)**
Feedstock: HBJ gas.
Basic capacity ('000 tons): Ethylene - 300; propylene - 156; and butadiene - 9.
Proposed downstream ('000 tons): HDPE - 100; HDPE/LDPE 160; styrene - 80; and polystyrene - 40.
Planning stage.

5. **Vizag Cracker**
Feedstock: Naphtha from HPCL.
Basic capacity ('000 tons): Ethylene - 300; propylene - 156; butadiene - 47; C_4 raffinate - 50.4; and benzene - 64.

6. **Haldia Petrochemical Complex, West Bengal**
Basic capacity ('000 tons): Ethylene - 300; propylene - 150; and butadiene - 53.
Proposed downstream ('000 tons): LDPE - 160; HDPE - 100; polystyrene - 75; styrene - 80; polypropylene - 150; benzene - 65; and C_4 - 37.
The project is to be built in two stages. Planning for phase I is on.

7. **National Organic Chemical Industries Ltd. (NOCIL)**
Basic capacity ('000 tons): Ethylene - 300; propylene - 140; butadiene - 47; and benzene and aromatics - 190.
Proposed downstream ('000 tons): Ethylene oxide - 120; polypropylene - 100; synthetic butadiene rubber - 100; polystyrene - 20.
Planning stage.

8. **RPG-Linde Export Oriented Unit**
Basic capacity ('000 tons): Ethylene - 425; propylene - 212.5; butadiene - 75; and benzene - 94.5.
Proposed downstream ('000 tons): HDPE/LDPE - 220; LDPE - 200; and polypropylene - 220.
Planning stage.

9. **Assam Gas Cracker Complex**
Basic capacity ('000 tons): Ethylene - 300; propylene - 51; and butadiene - 16.
Proposed downstream ('000 tons): LDPE - 100; HDPE - 100; C_4 raffinate - 11; pyrolysis gasoline - 44; and acetylene - 1.50.
Planning stage.

10. **Reliance Export Oriented Unit, Hazira**
Proposed downstream ('000 tons): Paraxylene - 270; and terephthalic acid - 200.
Planning stage.

11. **Saleempur Aromatic Complex, Aligarh, U.P.**
Proposed downstream ('000 tons): Benzene - 30; orthoxylene - 30; paraxylene - 136; and terephthalic acid - 200.
Planning stage.

12. **National Aromatics & Petrochemicals Corp. Complex, Manali, Madras**
Proposed downstream ('000 tons): Benzene - 30; orthoxylene - 30; paraxylene - 136; and terephthalic acid - 200.
Preliminary work yet to be completed.

---

4. Principal Raw Materials

4.1. Natural Gas (largely methane)

- Major raw material in U.S., not available in quantity in India. Could be shipped economically by refrigerated tanker from Middle East.
- Ethane (~4% in natural gas) is the most valuable product since ethylene can be produced by thermal cracking

$$\text{Ethane} \xrightarrow[\text{cracking}]{} \text{Ethylene (75\% yield)}$$

However, most of the ethylene comes from refinery gases.

4.2. Liquefied Petroleum Gas (LPG)

- Easily extracted from natural gas
- Can be transported in tank cars or pipelines as a liquid
- Contains propane and butane which can be easily cracked to olefins

4.3. Refinery Off-Gases

- From catalytic and reforming operations
- Paraffinic and olefinic fractions used for petrochemicals
- Hydrogen used for NH_3 production
- Sulfur by-product obtained from H_2S by oxidation process (see Chapter IIA)

4.4. Hydroforming of Petrochemical Stocks

- Produces benzene, toluene, and xylene (BTX)
- Gives large quantities of hydrogen

4.5. Naphtha and Fuel Oil

- Accumulate in large quantities in Indian refineries due to lack of end use
- Used to make (1) synthesis gas by catalytic reforming or partial combustion, (2) petrochemical starting materials such as ethylene, acetylene, and propylene by steam cracking

4.6. Petroleum Coke

- Source of carbon for calcium carbide and acetylene or electrodes for aluminum industry

5. Basis for Study

These raw materials contain one or several predominant hydrocarbons which can be separated so that compounds are synthesized as follows:

A. Chemicals From C_1 Compounds (Methane and Synthesis Gas)
B. Chemicals From C_2 Compounds (Ethylene and Acetylene)
C. Chemicals From C_3 Compounds (Propylene)
D. Chemicals From C_4 Compounds (Butanes and Butenes)
E. Chemicals From Aromatics (Benzene, Toluene and Xylene)
F. Pesticides
G. Pharmaceutical Industry

IVB. CHEMICALS FROM C_1 COMPOUNDS (METHANE AND SYNTHESIS GAS)

This group supplies about 25 wt.% of all petrochemicals produced in the U.S. The processes studied in this section will cover the organic chemicals, particularly methanol, formaldehyde, and halogenated hydrocarbons. See Figure IVB-1.

Methanol

1. Pertinent Properties of Methanol (CH_3OH)

Mol. wt.	32.04
M.P.	−97.8°C
B.P.	64.7°C
Density	0.788 @ 20°C
Explosive limits	Lower = 6.0 vol. % in air
	Upper = 36.5 vol. % in air
Toxicity limits	200 ppm

Grades: pure (99.8%, acetone-free), CP (95%), USP (97%)

2. Consumption Pattern

Formaldehyde, the primary oxidation product of methanol, is the largest outlet for methanol. Formaldehyde is an important monomer in the plastics industry.

The demand for methanol in India is projected to rise to 322,000 tons by 1994-95 and 518,000 tons by 2000 A.D. Approximately 50% of the demand will come from formaldehyde, about 25% from DMT, and the balance from drugs, pesticides, and chemicals such as acetic acid, methyl amines, esters, solvents, etc.

Worldwide demand for methanol is summarized in Table IVB-1.

Table IVB-1
World Consumption of Methanol and Forecasted Demand, 10^6 tons per year

Description	1990	1991	1992	1993	1994	1995
Consumption Total	18.35	19.5	20.5	21.5	22.65	23.9
Formaldehyde	7.03	7.27	7.49	7.73	7.85	7.98
MTBE	2.42	2.95	3.57	4.05	4.70	5.50
Acetic Acid	1.36	1.51	1.55	1.63	1.72	1.87
Solvents	1.34	1.38	1.41	1.45	1.50	1.55
DMT	0.65	0.66	0.67	0.67	0.68	0.68
Methyl Methacrylate	0.49	0.54	0.57	0.59	0.61	0.63
Gasoline	0.26	0.27	0.20	0.23	0.24	0.24
Others	4.80	4.92	5.04	5.15	5.35	5.45

Source: "Global Trends in Chemical Products"—Nandini (1994)

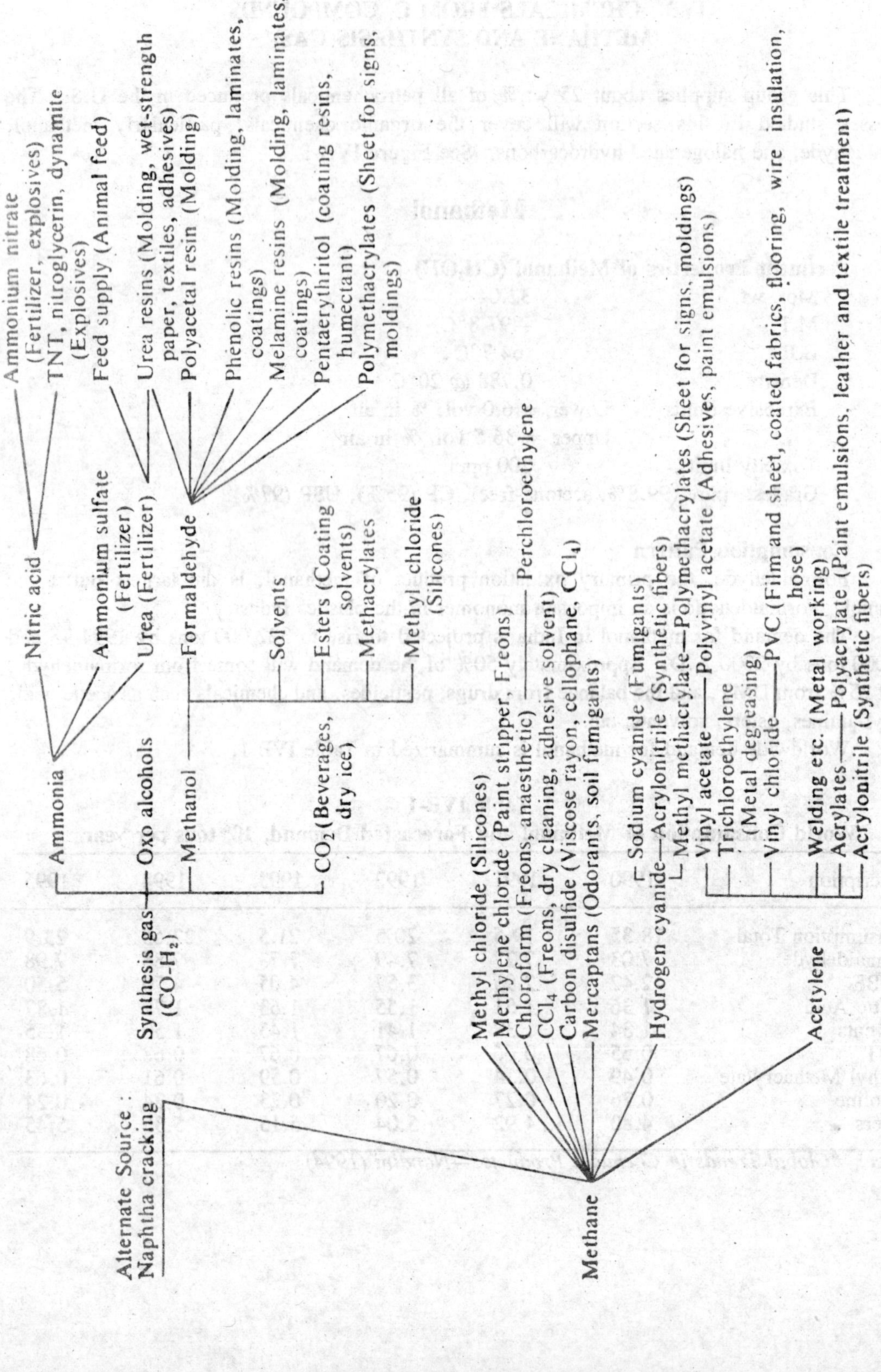

Fig. IVB-1. Synthetic chemical intermediates and products from methane or other sources of synthesis gas.

As per the "Perspective Plan for Chemical Industry (up to the year 2000 A.D.)", the demand for methanol in India is expected to rise to 322,000 M.T. and 518,000 M.T. per annum by 1994-95 and 1999-2000 respectively.

As per the "Report of the Committee for Perspective Planning of Petrochemical Industry (1986-2000 A.D.)" the demand for methanol is expected to rise to 242,000 M.T. and 286,000 M.T. by 1994-95 and 1999-2000 respectively.

If proper incentives are given by the Government, according to the "Perspective Plan for Chemical Industry (up to the year 2000 A.D.)", there is a potential to export 5,000 M.T. and 10,000 M.T. of methanol from India in the years 1994-95 and 1999-2000 respectively.

3. Methods of Production

- Catalytic hydrogenation of carbon monoxide (accounts for ~75% of production)
- Oxidation of LPG to give oxygenated hydrocarbon co-products of which methanol is a major fraction
- Catalytic hydrogenation of carbon monoxide

3.1. Reference Flow Sheet: Figure IVB-2

3.2. Chemical Reactions

(a) $CO + 2H_2 \rightarrow CH_3OH$; $\Delta H = -26.4$ Kcal

(b) Side reactions to methane

$CO + 3H_2 \rightarrow CH_4 + H_2O$; $\Delta H = -50$ Kcal

$2CO + 2H_2 \rightarrow CH_4 + CO_2$; $\Delta H = -60.3$ Kcal

(c) Side reaction to higher mol. wt. compounds

$xCO + yH_2 \rightarrow$ higher mol. wt. alcohols and hydrocarbons

3.3. Quantitative Requirements

(a) Basis: 1 ton of methanol (98% yield)

H_2	0.127 ton or 735 Nm^3
CO	0.89 ton or 650 Nm^3

(b) Plant capacities: 100-800 tons/day of CH_3OH

3.4. Process Description

Hydrogen and carbon monoxide in a mole ratio of 2.25 (12% greater than theoretical) is compressed to 3,000-5,000 psi, mixed with recycle gas, and fed to a high pressure converter. Internal preheat is usually employed. The reactor is copper-lined steel and contains a mixed catalyst of zinc, chromium, manganese, or aluminum oxides. The temperature is maintained at 300-375°C by proper space velocity and heat exchange design.

The exit gases are cooled by heat exchange with reactants, then with water. The methanol condenses under full operating pressure to maximize yields (~50% conversion per pass). The liquid methanol is depressurized, purified by permanganate to remove traces of ketones, aldehydes, and other such impurities, sent to a stripper to remove light ends such as dimethyl ether, and to a fractionator to separate methanol from the higher mol. wt. compounds.

It should be noted that ICI in England have developed a methanol process which operates at only 50 atms. pressure using a copper catalyst.

3.5. Major Engineering Problems

(a) Thermodynamic and kinetic considerations of synthesis gas

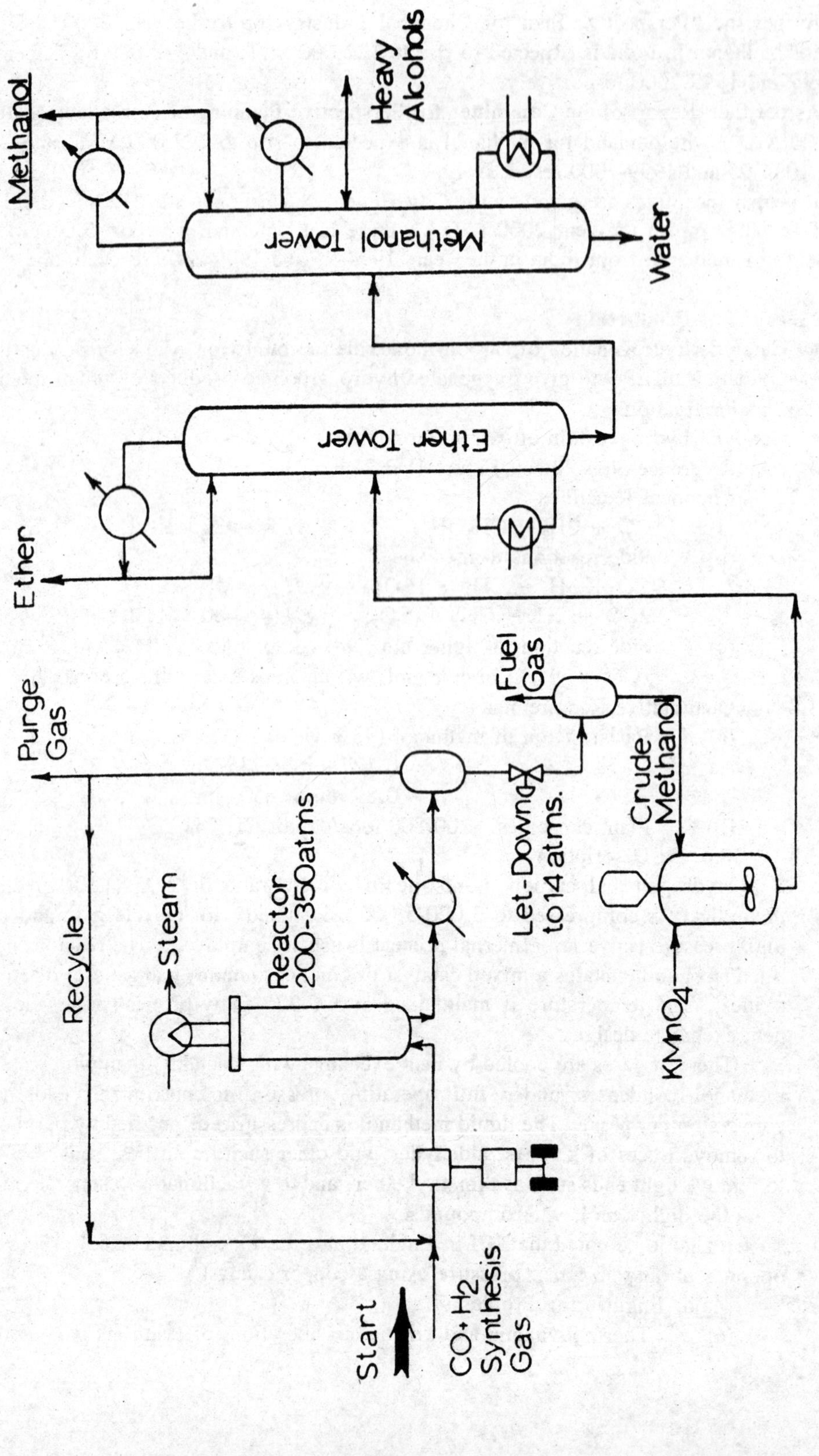

Fig. IVB-2. Methanol via synthesis gas route.

This process is similar to NH_3 in design because of the unfavorable equilibrium constant under normal pressure conditions for an exothermic reaction

$$K_p = \frac{p_{CH_3OH}}{p_{CO} \cdot p_{H_2}^2}$$

Temp., °C	K_p
260	1.5×10^{-3}
300	3.1×10^{-4}
340	8.7×10^{-5}
380	2.7×10^{-6}

For temperatures less than 260°C, reaction rates, even on active catalysts, are too low to be economic. The choice of pressure is also economic, the balance existing between pressurized reactor costs and recycle costs. Under optimum conditions, a 50% conversion per pass at 240 atms. and 300°C is typical.

(b) Reactor design

Thick-walled pressure vessels are constructed of relatively cheap steel, but must be lined with Cu to avoid the formation of iron carbonyl $Fe(CO)_5$, a volatile compound which poisons the catalysts in addition to creating a severe corrosion problem.

Heat exchange to control the highly exothermic reaction is accomplished in several ways. In the Uhde design, the compressed gas enters an annulus along the shell wall which serves to preheat the gas and cool the heat treated steel pressure shell. The gases then move in the opposite direction through the shell side of a tubular array, picking up more heat. The last pass is through the catalyst on the inside of the tubes. The catalyst is placed in zones with further temperature control accomplished by direct bleed of cold reactant gases which bypass the preheat zone.

A second alternate is the simpler Montecatini-Fauser design in which the combination of a circulating high pressure water and waste heat boiler acts as the principal heat control. This is shown in Figure IVB-2.

(c) Catalyst fouling

Excess hydrogen over the minimum theoretical 2:1 H_2/CO ratio is used to avoid fouling the catalyst with higher mol. wt. material which adsorbs on the catalyst under higher CO partial pressures. Synthesis gas from steam reforming has a satisfactory H_2/CO ratio whereas partial combustion gas has about a 2:1 H_2/CO ratio and must be butted up with extra H_2 from the water gas shift reaction ($CO+H_2O$).

(d) Inert gas accumulation

In carrying high recycle loads, the possibility of accumulating inert gas is avoided by maintaining a side-stream purge on the recycle gas.

4. Economics

Table IVB-2 gives the location of principal methanol plants in India.

Table IVB-2
Locations of Major Units for Methanol Manufacture in India

Assam Petrochemicals Ltd.
Namrup, P.O. Parbatpur - 786 623, Dist. Dibrugarh (Assam)

Deepak Fertilizers & Petrochemicals Corp. Ltd.
Taloja (Maharashtra)

Gujarat Narmada Valley Fertilizers Co. Ltd.
P.O. Narmada Nagar - 392 015, Dist: Bharuch (Gujarat)

National Fertilizers Ltd.
Nangal, Dist. Ropar (Punjab)

Orissa Synthetics Ltd.
Lakshmi Nagar, P.O. Baulpur - 754 031, Dist. Dhenkanal (Orissa)

Rama Petrochemicals Ltd.
Village Vashivalli, Patalganga, Dist. Raigad (Maharashtra)

Rashtriya Chemicals & Fertilizers Ltd.
Trombay, Chembur, Bombay (Maharashtra)

Rinki Petrochemicals & Industries Ltd. (under implementation)
Padra (Gujarat)

Source: "SBP Handbook of Projects for Corporate Diversification" (1992)

Most of the plant, equipment and machinery required for the manufacture of methanol is either available or can be fabricated indigenously based on the designs, drawings and specifications worked out by the foreign collaborators and consultants selected for carrying out the detailed engineering work for this project. Typical methanol plant capacities in India are 50,000 tons/yr. or about 200 tons/day.

Formaldehyde

1. Pertinent Properties of Formaldehyde (HCHO)

Mol. wt.	30.03
M.P.	−118°C
B.P.	−19°C
Density	0.815 (−20°C)
Explosive limits:	Lower = 7 vol. % in air
	Upper = 73 vol. % in air

Toxicity limits 10 ppm

Solubility: Soluble in water, alcohol and polar solvents, slightly soluble in hydrocarbons, chloroform, ether

Grades: CP gas, 37% aqueous solutions, trioxane polymer $(CH_2O)_3$, paraformaldehyde, $(CH_2O)_n \cdot nH_2O$, where n=10-50

2. Consumption Pattern

The principal use of formaldehyde is in the manufacture of phenolic, urea, and melamine resins.

2.1. End Uses

Worldwide uses of formaldehyde are summarized in Table IVB-3.

Table IVB-3
Utilization of Formaldehyde (in %)

	World		USA		Western Europe		Japan	
	1984	1988	1984	1989	1984	1989	1984	1989
Urea resins	32	33	27	31	45	47	37	30
Phenolic resins	11	11	23	23	11	8	8	7
Melamine resins	4	4	4	4	6	10	6	6
Pentaerythritol	6	5	7	6	6	6	8	6
1,4-Butandiol	2	2	11	11	6	6	–	–
Methylenediisocyanate	2	3	4	5	3	4	2	4
Others*	43	42	24	20	23	19	39	47
Total use (in 10^6 tonnes)	3.25	3.89	0.71	0.87	1.07	1.22	0.32	0.36

* *e. g.*, trioxane/polyformaldehyde

Source: "Industrial Organic Chemistry" by Weissermel et al (1993)

3. Methods of Production

3.1. Classification

- Catalytic oxidation—dehydrogenation of methanol
- Oxidation of methane or LPG to give oxygenated hydrocarbon co-products in which formaldehyde is separated with difficulty

3.2. Catalytic Oxidation—dehydrogenation

3.2.1. Reference flow sheet: Figure IVB-3

3.2.2. Chemical reactions

(a) Oxidation

$CH_3OH + \frac{1}{2}O_2 \rightarrow HCHO + H_2O$; ΔH = —37 Kcal

(b) Pyrolysis

$CH_3OH \rightarrow HCHO + H_2$; ΔH = +19.8 Kcal

(c) Side reaction—complete combustion

$CH_3OH + 3/2O_2 \rightarrow 2H_2O + CO_2$; ΔH = —162 Kcal

3.2.3. Quantitative requirements

(a) Basis: 1 ton of formaldehyde (90% yield)

Methanol (99+% purity)	1.04 tons
Air	1,760 Nm^3

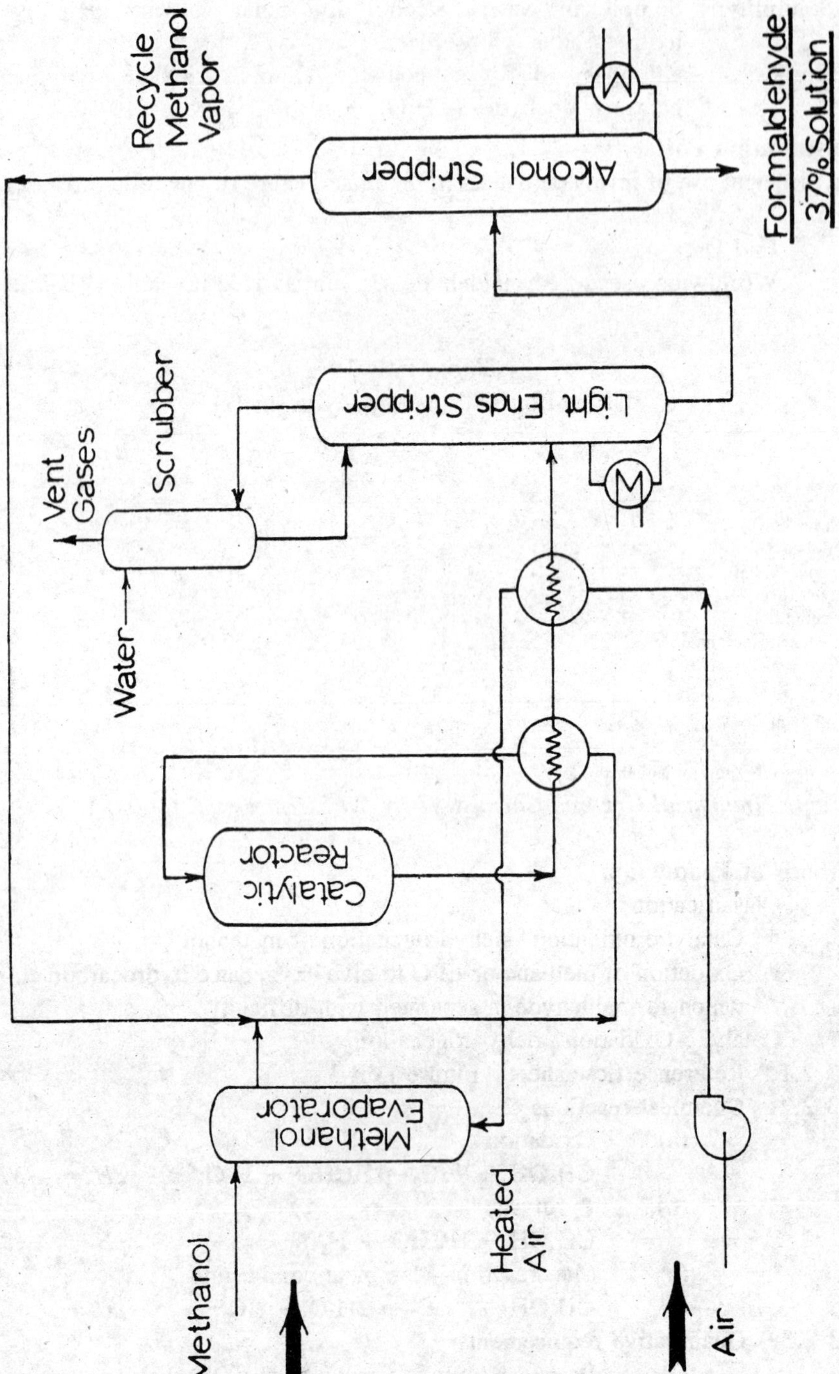

Fig. IVB-3. Formaldehyde from methanol.

(b) Plant capacities: 10-300 tons/day

3.2.4. Process description

Non-purified air, compressed to about 0.2 atm. gage is preheated by heat exchange with reacting gases and then conveyed to a methanol evaporator. Conditions are set to keep the $CH_3OH : O_2$ ratio in the 30-50% range. The mixed gases are preheated, sent to a reactor where silver or copper gauze or their oxides are catalysts. Catalyst activity is controlled to maintain a balance between the endothermic dehydrogenation and exothermic oxidation reactions at reaction conditions of 450-600°C. Some complete combustion takes place.

The product gases are absorbed in a water scrubber which is cooled by external circulation, and then fractionated to recover approximately 15% unreacted methanol for recycle. Ultimate yields of 85-90 wt. % based on methanol are typical.

3.2.5. Major engineering problems

(a) Methanol conversion—specific catalysis

The process described above has a catalyst which provides a heat balance via two reactions [3.2.2 (a) & (b)]. This necessitates some methanol recycle. A process modification using a mixed oxide catalyst of Mo, V, and/or Fe has given > 90% yield with no methanol to be recycled. Higher volume ratios of air to methanol (~ 16 : 1 CH_3OH/O_2) are used with only the oxidation reaction favored. Heat in the tubular reactor is controlled by oil recirculation. Water scrubbing of HCHO gas containing < 1% CH_3OH gives 37% formalin solution directly with no fractionation or recycle requirements.

(b) Choice of space velocity

A balance exists between low space velocities which result in too high a combustion to $CO + CO_2$ and too high a space velocity and low methanol conversion. The compromise finds 4-5% $CO + CO_2$ in the reactor tail gas.

4. Economics

The choice of the hydrocarbon oxidation process (Section 3.1) depends on salability of numerous co-products, *e.g.*, acetic acid, acetone. For this reason, such a process supplies only 25% of the market.

For the air-methanol processes, the sole oxidation process using oxide catalysis is usually preferred, particularly for large-size production plants.

If proper incentives are given by the Government, according to the "Perspective Plan for Chemical Industry (up to the year 2000 A.D.)" there is a potential to export 10,000 M.T. and 25,000 M.T. of formaldehyde from India in the years 1994-95 and 1999-2000 respectively.

As per the "Perspective Plan for Chemical Industry (up to the year 2000 A.D.)" the demand for formaldehyde is estimated at 340,000 M.T. and 480,000 M.T. per annum by 1994-95 and 1999-2000 respectively.

As per the "Report of the Committee for Perspective Planning of Petrochemical Industry (1986-2000 A.D.)" the demand for formaldehyde is expected to rise to 174,000 M.T. and 212,000 M.T. by 1994-95 and 1999-2000 respectively.

Worldwide production trends for formaldehyde are as follows (figures in millions of tons):

	1985	1987	1989
USA	0.70	0.75	0.78
Japan	0.32	0.35	0.36
Western Europe	1.09	1.17	1.30
CIS	0.49	0.55	0.57

Locations of the principal formaldehyde plants in India are given in Table IVB-4.

Table IVB-4
Major Units Manufacturing Formaldehyde

Aegis Chemical Industries Ltd.
National Highway No. 8, Vapi, Dist. Bulsar (Gujarat)

Assam Petrochemicals Ltd.
Namrup, Dist. Dibrugarh (Assam)

Bakelite Hylam Ltd.
P-1/1, Industrial Development Area, Nacharam, Hyderabad - 501 507 (A.P.)

Chemicals & Resins (P) Ltd.
Near Oil Jetty, Kandla (Gujarat)

Cibatul Ltd.
P.O. Atul, Dist. Valsad (Gujarat)

Hindustan Organic Chemicals Ltd.
Rasayani, Dist. Raigad (Maharashtra)

Kanoria Chemicals & Industries Ltd.
3407, GIDC Industrial Estate, P.O. Ankleshwar, Dist. Bharuch (Gujarat)

Konkan Chemicals (P) Ltd.
F-2, MIDC Industrial Area, Badalapur, Dist. Thane (Maharashtra)

Nuchem Ltd.
54, Industrial Area, Faridabad (Haryana)

Pentasia Chemicals Ltd.
B5-B10, SIPCOT Industrial Complex, P.O. Kudikadu - 607005
Dist. Cuddalore (T.N.)

Source: "SBP Handbook of Projects for Corporate Diversification" (1992)

Chloromethanes

The direct chlorination of methane leads to a series of chloromethanes from CH_3Cl to fully chlorinated CCl_4.

1. Properties of Chlorinated Methanes

1.1. Methyl Chloride (CH_3Cl)

Mol. wt.	50.49
M.P.	–97.7°C
B.P.	–24.1°C
Density	0.92 (20°C)
Explosive limits:	Lower = 8 vol. % in air
	Upper = 20 vol. % in air
Toxicity limits	50 ppm

Solubility: Soluble in water, alcohol, acetone, chloroform, and ether

Grades: Technical (99.9%); shipped under pressure in tank cars and cylinders

1.2. Methylene Chloride (CH_2Cl_2)

Mol. wt.	84.95
M.P.	–97.6°C
B.P.	40.1°C
Density	1.33

Solubility: Slightly soluble in water (1.8% @ 20°C); completely miscible with alcohols and ether

1.3. Chloroform ($CHCl_3$)

Mol. wt.	119.4
M.P.	–63.5°C
B.P.	61.2°C
Density	1.49
Toxicity limits	100 ppm

Solubility: Slightly soluble in water (0.8% @ 20°C); completely miscible with alcohols, aromatics, ethers

1.4. Carbon Tetrachloride (CCl_4)

Mol. wt.	153.84
M.P.	–22.6°C
B.P.	76.8°C
Density	1.59
Toxicity limits	25 ppm

Solubility: Slightly soluble in water (0.08% @ 20°C); completely miscible with alcohols, aromatics, and ethers

2. Consumption Pattern

The uses of chlorinated methanes are as follows:

1. Solvents
2. Intermediate products, *e.g.*,

2.1. CH_3Cl for methylations
+ Si (Rochow process) → $(CH_3)_2SiCl_2$ (silicones)

+ Pb → $(CH_3)_4Pb$
(important antiknocking agent) (next to $(C_2H_5)_4Pb$)

+ Na cellulose → methylcellulose

2.2. CCl_4 and $CHCl_3$ for synthesis of hydrocarbons containing F and Cl

3. Methods of Production

3.1. Classification of Processes

3.1.1. Direct thermal methane chlorination—a direct substitution process for making all four chlorinated derivatives depending on mole ratio of CH_4/Cl and reaction conditions.

3.1.2. CH_3Cl by reaction of CH_3OH + HCl—competitive; can be coupled with methane chlorination to use by-product HCl.

3.1.3. CCl_4 by reaction of CS_2 + Cl_2—older process, no longer economic.

3.2. Methane Chlorination

3.2.1. Reference flow sheet: Figure IVB-4

3.2.2. Chemical reactions

$$CH_4 + Cl_2 \rightarrow CH_3Cl + HCl$$
$$CH_3Cl + Cl_2 \rightarrow CH_2Cl_2 + HCl$$
$$CH_2Cl_2 + Cl_2 \rightarrow CHCl_3 + HCl$$
$$CHCl_3 + Cl_2 \rightarrow CCl_4 + HCl$$

Highly exothermic reactions; typical composite value of —24 Kcal/mole CH_4

3.2.3. Quantitative requirements

(a) Basis: depends on mole ratio CH_4/Cl_2

For typical feed ratio of 1.8, the product compositions are:

CH_3Cl—60 wt. %, CH_2Cl_2—28%; $CHCl_3$—9%; CCl_4—3% yields are 99% based on Cl_2 and 85-90% based on CH_4.

For 1 ton production of products listed above:

Chlorine (99% yield) 1.53 tons; Methane (85% yield) 0.305 ton or 385 Nm^3

(b) Plant capacities: 30-120 tons/day

3.2.4. Process description

Thermal chlorination of natural gas is accomplished by different cycles depending on the desired product ratio and the state of by-product HCl (dry gas or 30-32% muriatic acid).

Chlorination is carried out in an adiabatic furnace in which the exothermic heat evolved is recovered for preheating inlet gas to 280°C. The temperature is kept between 370°C and 410°C according to a selected cycle. The CH_4/Cl_2 ratio is fixed by the product ratio desired.

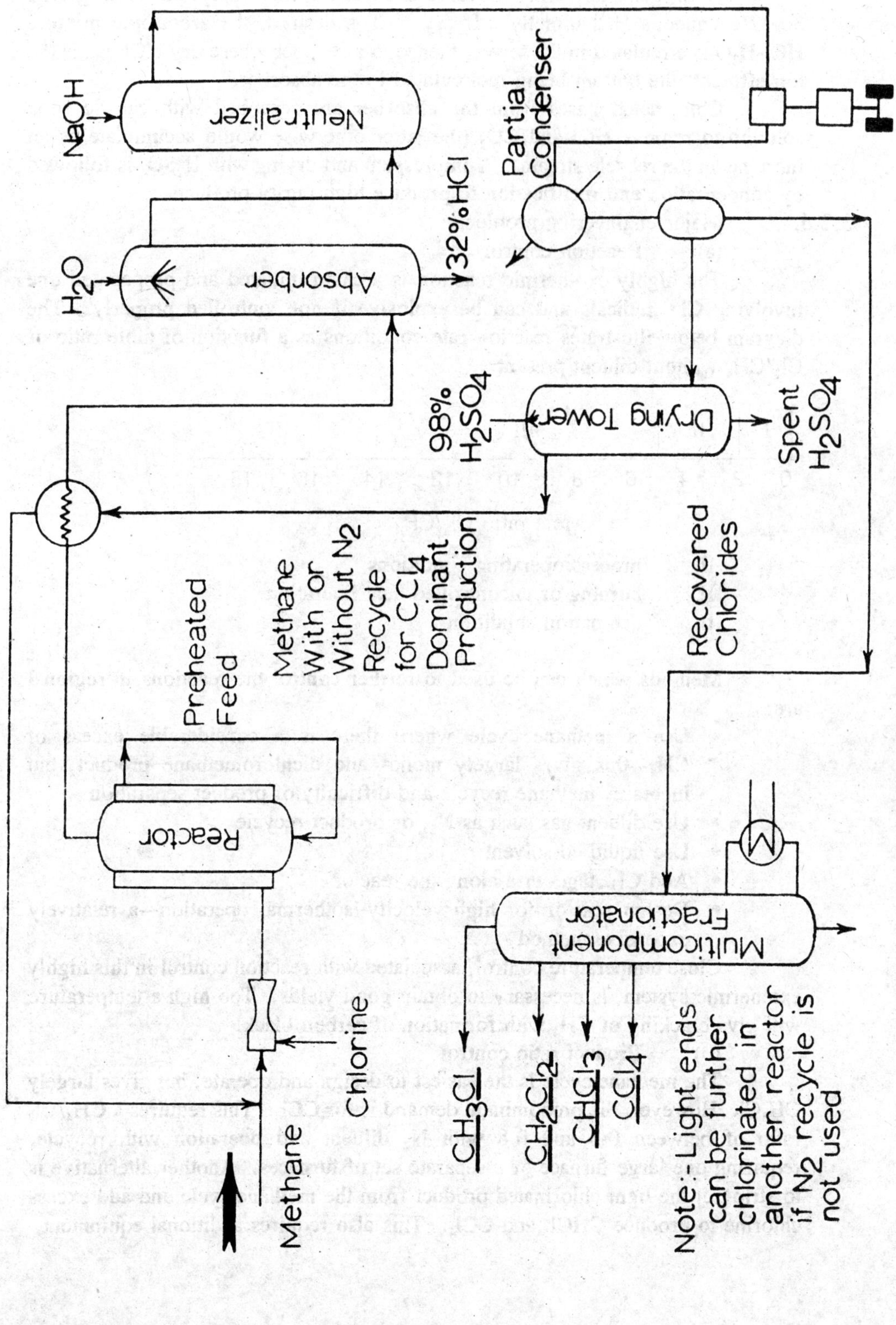

Fig. IVB-4. Direct chlorination of methane to produce methyl chloride, methylene chloride, chloroform, and carbon tetrachloride.

Hydrogen chloride is recovered in a water-spray absorption tower, giving 30-32% aqueous HCl directly. If dry HCl is desired, the azeotropic mixture HCl-H_2O is circulated in the tower, thence to a stripper where dry HCl gas is the top effluent, the bottom being recirculated to the absorber.

Chlorinated gases from the absorber are scrubbed with caustic soda solution to remove HCl and CO_2 (the latter otherwise would accumulate as an inert gas in the recycle stream). Compression and drying with H_2SO_4 is followed by condensation and rectification to produce high purity products.

3.2.5. Major engineering problems

(a) Reaction control

The highly exothermic reaction is a chain initiated and propagated one involving Cl• radicals and can be explosive if not controlled properly. The diagram below illustrates reaction rate conditions as a function of mole ratio of Cl_2/CH_4 without diluent present.

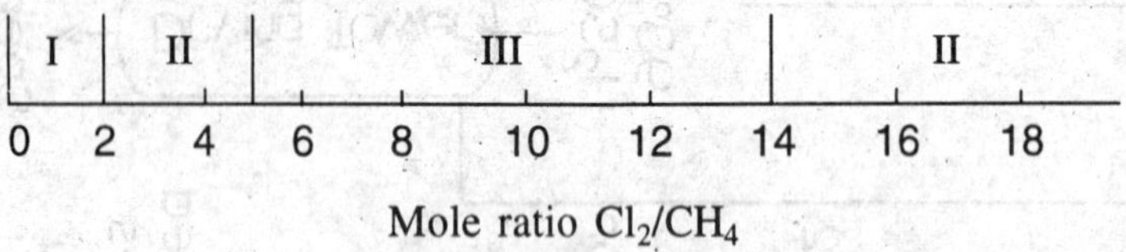

I process operating conditions
II burning or uncontrolled heat liberation
III detonation condition

Methods which can be used to further control the reactions in region I are:

- Use a methane cycle where there is a considerable excess of CH_4—this gives largely mono- and dichloromethane product, but increases methane recycle and difficulty of product separation
- Use diluent gas such as N_2, or product recycle
- Use liquid co-solvent
- Add Cl_2 stage-wise along the reactor
- Design reactor for high velocity-isothermal operation—a relatively expensive method

Close temperature control, associated with reaction control in this highly exothermic system, is necessary to obtain good yields. Too high a temperature will give cracking of CH_4 with formation of carbon black.

(b) Product ratio control

The methane cycle is the easiest to design and operate, but gives largely CH_3Cl. However, the predominant demand is for CCl_4. This requires a CH_4/Cl_2 ratio of between 0.5 and 0.8 with N_2 diluent and operation with recycle, requiring one large furnace or a separate set of furnaces. Another alternative is to strip out the light chlorinated product from the methane cycle and add excess chlorine to produce $CHCl_3$ and CCl_4. This also requires additional equipment.

(c) Utilization of HCl to produce more CH_3Cl

In a plant where methanol is available, it is possible to utilize the replacement reaction

$$CH_3OH + HCl \rightarrow CH_3Cl + H_2O$$

This can be carried out as a vapor phase reaction using alumina or other similar-acting catalyst. In liquid phase, a zinc or aluminum chloride catalyst is employed.

This process is also used in plants when methanol and by-product HCl, not necessarily from methane chlorination, are available.

4. Economics—U.S. Basis

(a) Choice of processes

Analysis of product output from U.S. production capacity of 800 million pounds of chloromethanes shows

CCl_4	-	53%	0.5 via CS_2
			0.5 via methane
CH_2Cl_2	-	18%	(1.0 via methane)
CH_3Cl	-	17%	0.6 via methanol
			0.4 via methane
$CHCl_3$	-	12%	(0.99 via methane)

The process choice for a completely chlorinated set of products is methane chlorination. The high CCl_4 production contribution via CS_2 is due to older plants completely amortized which can still compete.

Methanol process for CH_3Cl still controls unless cheap natural gas and chlorine are available, coupled with a good market for CCl_4 co-product and by-product HCl.

(b) Markets

Carbon tetrachloride is being replaced by perchloroethylene as a dry cleaning solvent. Fortunately, CCl_4 is the starting raw material for production of perchloroethylene. The markets for perfluorochloromethanes are expanding as a refrigerant and aerosol propellant.

Methylene chloride has shown considerable growth, again in the aerosol propellant business, as a diluent for perfluorochloromethanes. On the other hand, methyl chloride has remained static as the perfluorochloromethanes are taking away the refrigeration field.

5. Production

World chloromethane capacity and production figures are as follows:

Chloromethane Capacity, 1988 ('000 tons)

	CH_3Cl	CH_2Cl_2	$CHCl_3$	CCl_4
World	757	752	499	1,081
USA	352	298	218	283
Western Europe	313	380	200	547
Japan	73	63	61	71

Trichloroethylene

Trichloroethylene represents one of the major chemicals produced from acetylene, of which a substantial fraction comes from natural gas (see Chapter IIB). Other chemicals derived from acetylene are acrylonitrile (see Section IVD), and vinyl chloride and acetate monomers (see Section IVC).

1. Pertinent Properties of Trichloroethylene ($ClHC{=}CCl_2$)

Mol. wt.	131.40
M.P.	−73°C
B.P.	87.2°C
Density	1.47
Toxicity limits	200 ppm

Solubility: Slightly soluble in water (0.1% @ 20°C), miscible with alcohols and ethers

Grades: Technical (high purity), extraction (non-acid)

2. Consumption Pattern

Vapor degreasing of metal parts before electroplating or painting is the major end use. As an intermediate, a pyrolysis reaction to perchloroethylene yields an end chemical in high demand as a dry cleaning agent.

2.1. End Uses

	USA
Vapor degreasing	85%
Perchloroethylene	10
Extractant	3

3. Methods of Production

3.1. Classification of Processes

- Vapor phase dehydrochlorination of tetrachloroethane, using $BaCl_2$ catalyst
- Liquid phase dehydrochlorination of tetrachloroethane, using milk of lime

3.2. Vapor Phase Dehydrochlorination

3.2.1. Reference flow sheet: Figure IVB-5

3.2.2. Chemical reactions

(a) $C_2H_2 + 2Cl_2 \xrightarrow{FeCl_3} C_2H_2Cl_4$ (tetrachloroethane)

(b) $C_2H_2Cl_4 \xrightarrow[250\text{-}300°C]{BaCl_2} C_2HCl_3 + HCl$

3.2.3. Quantitative requirements

(a) Basis: 1 ton of trichloroethylene (95% ultimate yield, 90% conversion)

Chlorine	1.15 tons
Acetylene	0.21 ton

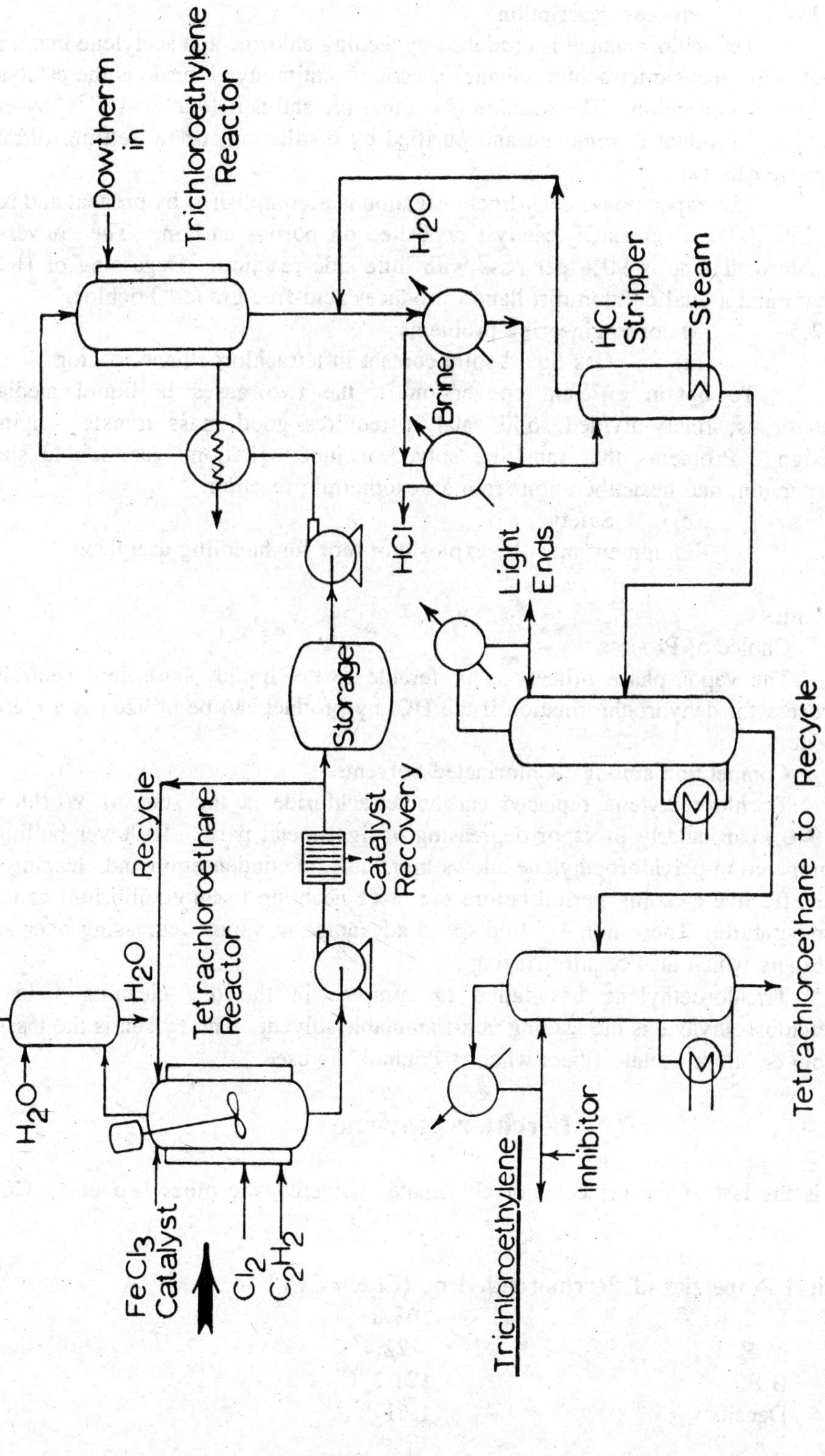

Fig. IVB-5. Trichloroethylene by vapor phase dehydrochlorination of tetrachloroethane via acetylene-Cl_2.

(b) Plant capacities: 50-150 tons/day

3.2.4. Process description

Tetrachloroethane is produced by feeding chlorine and acetylene into a reactor containing recycle tetrachloroethane. Ferric or antimony chloride is the catalyst used in low concentration. The reaction is exothermic and is held at 80-100°C by external cooling. Product is removed and purified by distillation, or by settling-filtration to remove catalyst.

The vapor phase dehydrochlorination is accomplished by preheat and reaction at 250-300°C over $BaCl_2$ catalyst deposited on porous carbon. The conversion to trichloroethylene is 90% per pass with little side reaction. Degassing of HCl with steam and a dual column distillation produces acid-free grade "Trichlor."

3.2.5. Major engineering problems

(a) Gas-liquid-solid contact in tetrachloroethane reactor

To obtain efficient conversion of the two gases in liquid media with anhydrous, finely-divided solid catalyst requires good mass transfer engineering design. Problems that must be solved include agitation, gas bubble size and dispersion, and heat liberation from an exothermic reaction.

(b) Safety

Equipment must be explosion-proof for handling acetylene.

4. Economics

4.1. Choice of Process

The vapor phase process is preferable to the liquid phase-lime neutralization process for dehydrochlorination if the HCl by-product can be utilized at a reasonable value.

4.2. Competition amongst Chlorinated Solvents

Trichloroethylene replaced carbon tetrachloride at the start of World War II (1940), particularly in vapor degreasing of light metal parts. Its lower boiling point compared to perchloroethylene allows more solvent condensation and cleaning during the effective cleaning period before the piece heats up to an equilibrium condensing temperature. There is a 4-5 fold speed advantage in vapor degreasing over alkaline cleaners which also require rinsing.

Trichloroethylene has failed to compete in the dry cleaning field where perchloroethylene is the leading non-flammable solvent. The reason is the loss of dye from cellulose acetate fibers when "Trichlor" is used.

Perchloroethylene

This is the last of the three major chlorinated solvents, the other two being CCl_4 and $CHCl{=}CCl_2$.

1. Physical Properties of Perchloroethylene ($Cl_2C{=}CCl_2$)

Mol. wt.	165.8
M.P.	−22.4°C
B.P.	121.2°C
Density	1.61

Toxicity limits 200 ppm
Solubility: Slightly soluble in water (0.1% @ 20°C), miscible with alcohols and ethers
Grades: Technical

2. Consumption Pattern

Dry cleaning solvent is the principal use, with markets expanding in the coin machine, dry cleaning business.

3. Methods of Production

3.1. Classification of Processes

- Pyrolysis of CCl_4
- Propane chlorination to yield CCl_4 co-product
- Chlorination of trichloroethylene to pentachloroethylene followed by lime dehydrochlorination

3.2. Pyrolysis of CCl_4

3.2.1. Reference flow sheet: Figure IVB-6

3.2.2. Chemical reactions

(a) $2CCl_4 \rightarrow \underset{\text{hexachloroethane}}{Cl_3C \cdot CCl_3} + Cl_2$

(b) $Cl_3C \cdot CCl_3 \rightarrow Cl_2C = CCl_2 + 2Cl_2$

(c) $2CCl_4 \rightarrow Cl_2C = CCl_2 + 2Cl_2$

3.2.3. Quantitative requirements

(a) Basis: 1 ton perchloroethylene (95% yield); 0.86 ton of Cl_2
Carbon tetrachloride 2.0 tons

(b) Plant capacities: 20-50 tons/day

3.2.4. Process description

CCl_4 is vaporized, passed into resistively heated carbon electrode furnace at 800-900°C, and pyrolyzed to perchloroethylene, hexachloroethane, and chlorine. The effluent goes to a partial condenser, held at 80-85°C where Cl_2 plus unreacted CCl_4 are separated from heavy ends. The CCl_4 is stripped of chlorine in a condenser and recycled.

The heavy ends are distilled to separate perchloroethylene from hexachloroethane. The latter can be recycled for further pyrolysis or further purified via crystallization.

In a process modification, propane can be chlorinated to yield CCl_4 which subsequently pyrolyses to "Perchlor."

3.2.5. Major engineering problems

Pyrolysis furnace design. The contact time is a balance between high "Hexachlor" yields at low contact time and destructive formation of carbon and light ends when the contact time is too large.

4. Economics

See Trichloroethylene above.

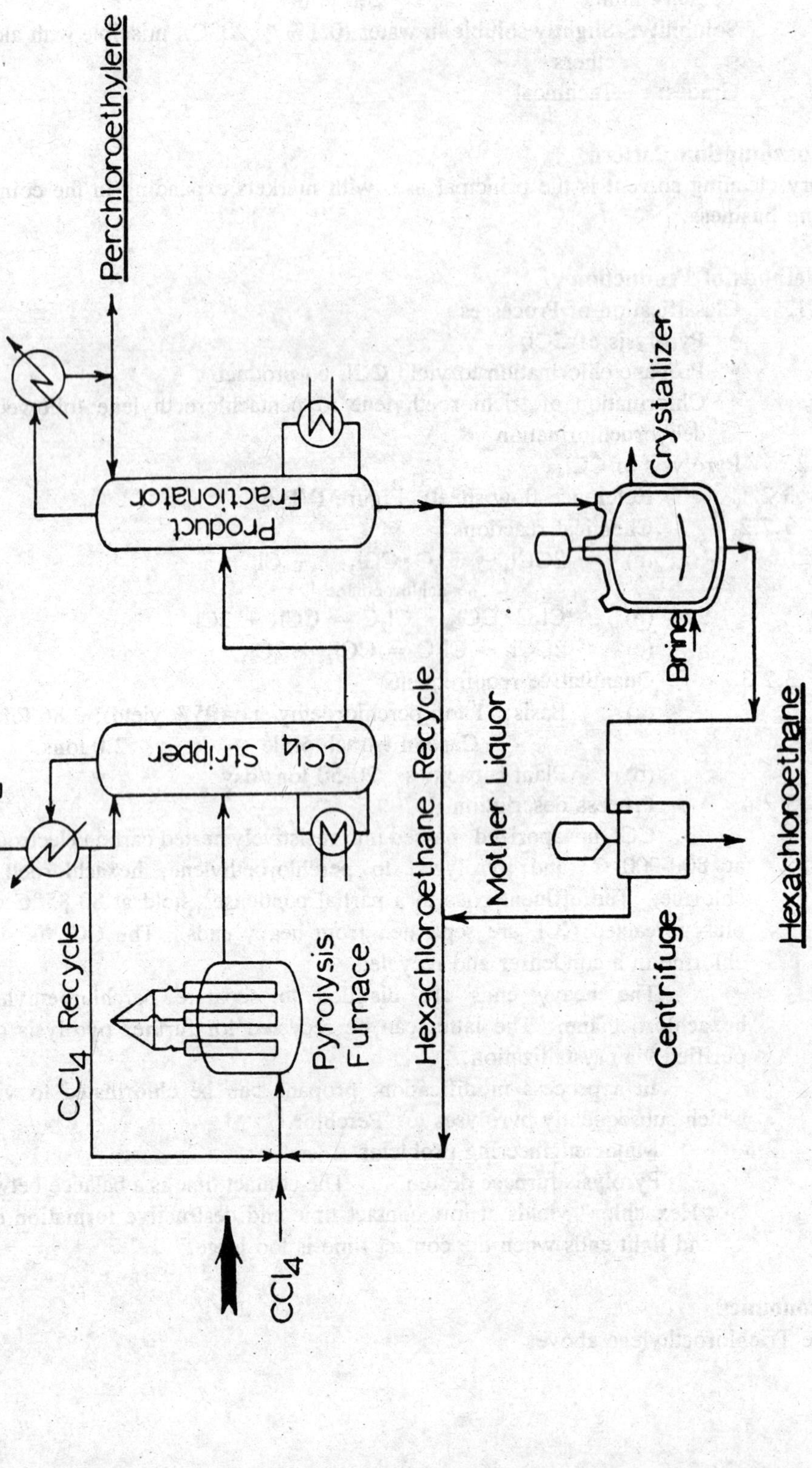

Fig. IVB-6. Perchloroethylene by pyrolysis of carbon tetrachloride.

5. Production

Indian units are shown in Table IVB-5.

Table IVB-5
Major Units Manufacturing Trichloroethylene and Perchloroethylene

Name and Address	Product Range
Ahmedabad Manufacturing & Calico Printing Co. Ltd. Anik Chembur, Bombay (Maharashtra)	Trichloroethylene and perchloroethylene
Chemicals & Plastics India Ltd. Raman Nagar, Mettur Dam R.S., Salem Dist. (T.N.)	Trichloroethylene
DCW Ltd. Sahupuram, P.O. Arumuganeri Dist. Tirunelveli (T.N.)	Trichloroethylene, perchloroethylene and tetrachloroethane
JBF Industries Ltd. GIDC Industrial Estate, Vapi 396105 (Gujarat)	Trichloroethylene and perchloroethylene
Mettur Chemical & Industrial Corp. Ltd. Mettur Dam - 636 404, Dist. Salem (T.N.)	Trichloroethylene

Source: "SBP Handbook of Projects for Corporate Diversification" (1992)

The world breakdown of triclene and perclene plants is as follows:

Tri- and Tetrachloroethylene Production ('000 tons)

	$Cl_2C=CHCl$			$Cl_2C=CCl_2$		
	1985	1987	1990	1985	1987	1990
USA	86	127	107	224	215	174
Japan	73	71	57	72	84	84
Western Europe	205	180	NA	315	305	NA

Source: "Industrial Organic Chemistry" by Weissermel et al (1993)

IVC. CHEMICALS FROM C_2 COMPOUNDS (ETHYLENE AND ACETYLENE)

The C_2 chemicals are the most important of the petrochemicals as reflected by the 1971 projected requirements for India of 165,000 tons of ethylene plus 59,000 tons for acetylene as precursors. These starting materials are obtained from the following sources:

- Ethylene from (1) fermentation alcohol, (2) refinery off-gases, and (3) hydrocarbon-steam cracking
- Acetylene from (1) calcium carbide, (2) partial oxidation of petroleum fractions (see Chapter IIB), and (3) hydrocarbon-steam cracking

The main process is hydrocarbon-steam cracking to be discussed next.

Ethylene and Acetylene via Steam Cracking of Hydrocarbons

The properties and several dominant methods of producing acetylene were given in Chapter IIB. The steam cracking process discussed here produces ethylene/acetylene in ratio of 0.3 to 2.0 depending on operating conditions. Propylene, butadiene and aromatics are obtained in lesser quantities.

1. Pertinent Properties of Ethylene ($CH_2=CH_2$)

Mol. wt.	28.03
M.P.	—169.4°C
B.P.	—103.8°C
Density @ –103.8°C	0.5699

Slightly soluble in water (25.6 cc per 100 g. H_2O at 0°C)

Explosion limits: Lower: 3% in air, 2.9% in O_2
Upper: 29% in air, 79% in O_2

2. Consumption Pattern (see Figure IVC-1)

Use in India will be predominantly for polyethylene, whereas in the U.S. a more diverse end use structure has been developed.

Demand of ethylene for various end uses, as estimated by the Committee for Perspective Planning of Petrochemical Industry, is summarized in Table IVC-1.

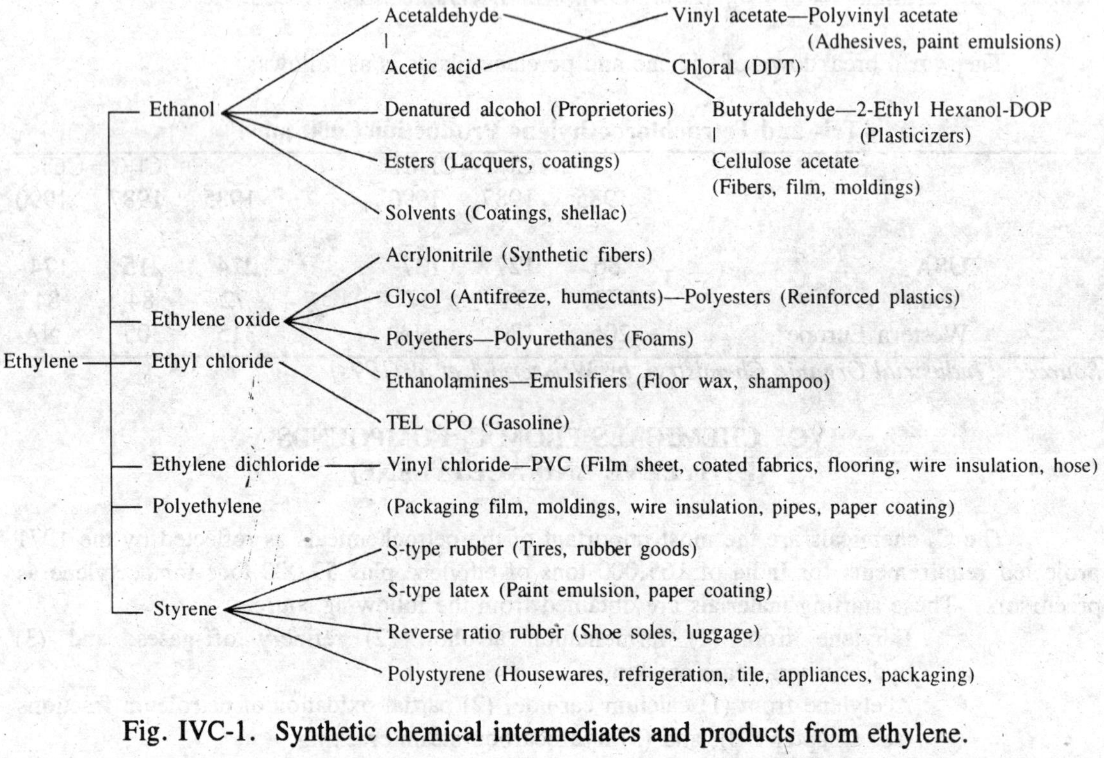

Fig. IVC-1. Synthetic chemical intermediates and products from ethylene.

Table IVC-1
Demand for Ethylene in India
('000 tons)

Product	Demand 1994-95	Demand 1999-2000	Norms of Consumption: Lbs Ethylene / Lbs Product	Ethylene Requirement 1994-95	Ethylene Requirement 1999-2000
Polymers					
LDPE/LLDPE	482	708	1.03	496	729
HDPE	378	555	1.04	393	577
PVC	485	713	0.48	233	342
PS	82	120	0.33	27	40
Styrene (Other than PS)	67	92	0.33	22	30
Petrochemicals					
Ethylene Oxide	24	29.4	0.80	19	24
Ethylene Glycol	165	264	0.65	107	172
Alpha Olefin	60	96	1.03	61	99
Miscellaneous	-	-	-	13	10
Total				**1,371**	**2,023**

Source: *"SBP Handbook of Petrochemical & Downstream Projects" (1991)*

Table IVC-2 summarizes the ethylene use picture worldwide.

Table IVC-2
Ethylene Use Worldwide, in USA, Western Europe, Japan and the CIS
(in wt. %)

Product	World 1991	USA 1984	USA 1989	Western Europe 1984	Western Europe 1990	Japan 1985	Japan 1991	CIS 1989
Polyethylene (LDPE and HDPE)	53	48	51	54	53	52	47	42
Vinyl chloride	16	14	13	19	18	17	18	9
Ethylene oxide and secondary products	13	17	16	10	10	11	9	14
Acetaldehyde and secondary products	2	3	2	3	3	5	4	4
Ethylbenzene/styrene	7	8	7	7	8	9	12	8
Others (*e.g.*, ethanol, vinyl acetate, 1,2-dibromoethane, ethyl chloride, ethylenimine, propionaldehyde, etc.)	9	10	11	7	8	6	8	23
Total use (in 10^6 tonnes)	58.2	13.9	16.6	12.5	15.7	4.05	6.21	3.2

Source: "Industrial Organic Chemistry" by Weissermel et al (1993)

3. Possible Methods of Production

- Steam pyrolysis (cracking) of petroleum from LPG and naphtha feedstocks
- Thermal pyrolysis of ethane and/or propane—not flexible
- Dehydration of ethanol—used in India, but not competitive for large-scale requirements in the long term
- Demand for ethylene will exceed supply in years to come and import of cryogenic ethylene by tankship from Saudi Arabia and Qatar may assume an important place in ethylene supply. It is evident that the Middle Eastern suppliers, Saudi Arabia and Qatar, are low cost producers and have considerable freight advantage to India.

4. Steam Cracking of Petroleum Hydrocarbons

4.1. Reference Flow Sheet: Figure IVC-2

4.2. Chemical Reactions

$$C_xH_{2x+2} + H_2O + O_2 \text{ (optional)} \xrightarrow{700\text{-}800°C} C_2H_4 \text{ (4-15\%)} + C_2H_6$$
$$+ C_2H_2 \text{ (7-13\%)} + H_2 \text{ (25-30\%)} + CO + CO_2 + CH_4 + C_3H_6 + C_3H_8$$
$$+ C_4H_{10} + C_4H_8 + C_4H_6 + C + \text{Heavy oil fraction}$$

4.3. Quantitative Requirements

(a) Basis: 1 ton of ethylene

No figures available (Indian plants will use mostly naphtha)

Co-products: acetylene, propylene, butylene, butadiene, aromatics such as benzene, toluene, xylene heavy oil residues

(b) Plant capacities: 100-600 tons/day of ethylene with current trends to much larger units

4.4. Process Description

The process to be detailed here is high temperature thermal reforming using ethane, propane, butane and/or liquid naphtha. Superheated steam is mixed with the hydrocarbon and fed through the heated coils of a pyrolysis furnace. The C_2-C_4 feed is pyrolyzed in a separate furnace because different residence time-temperature conditions are required. The pyrolyzed gases are quenched in a waste heat steam boiler and then scrubbed with gas oil to remove solids and heavy hydrocarbons before sending to compressors to boost pressure to 35 atms.

The compression station may also handle refinery off-gases which can be separated in the same system. Flash vaporization removes the C_1-C_2 fractions which are caustic-scrubbed to remove CO_2, dried with activated alumina, and then separated into acetylene and ethylene by a combination of absorption, extraction, and fractionation steps. Ethane is recycled for pyrolysis and the CH_4, CO, and H_2 can be further processed to obtain synthesis gas or used for fuel.

The liquid fraction from the flash chamber (C_3 and higher) is split by fractionation into a number of products as indicated on the flow sheet. Extractive distillation is required to separate butane-butylene and butadiene because of the close boiling point range of the three compounds under pressure.

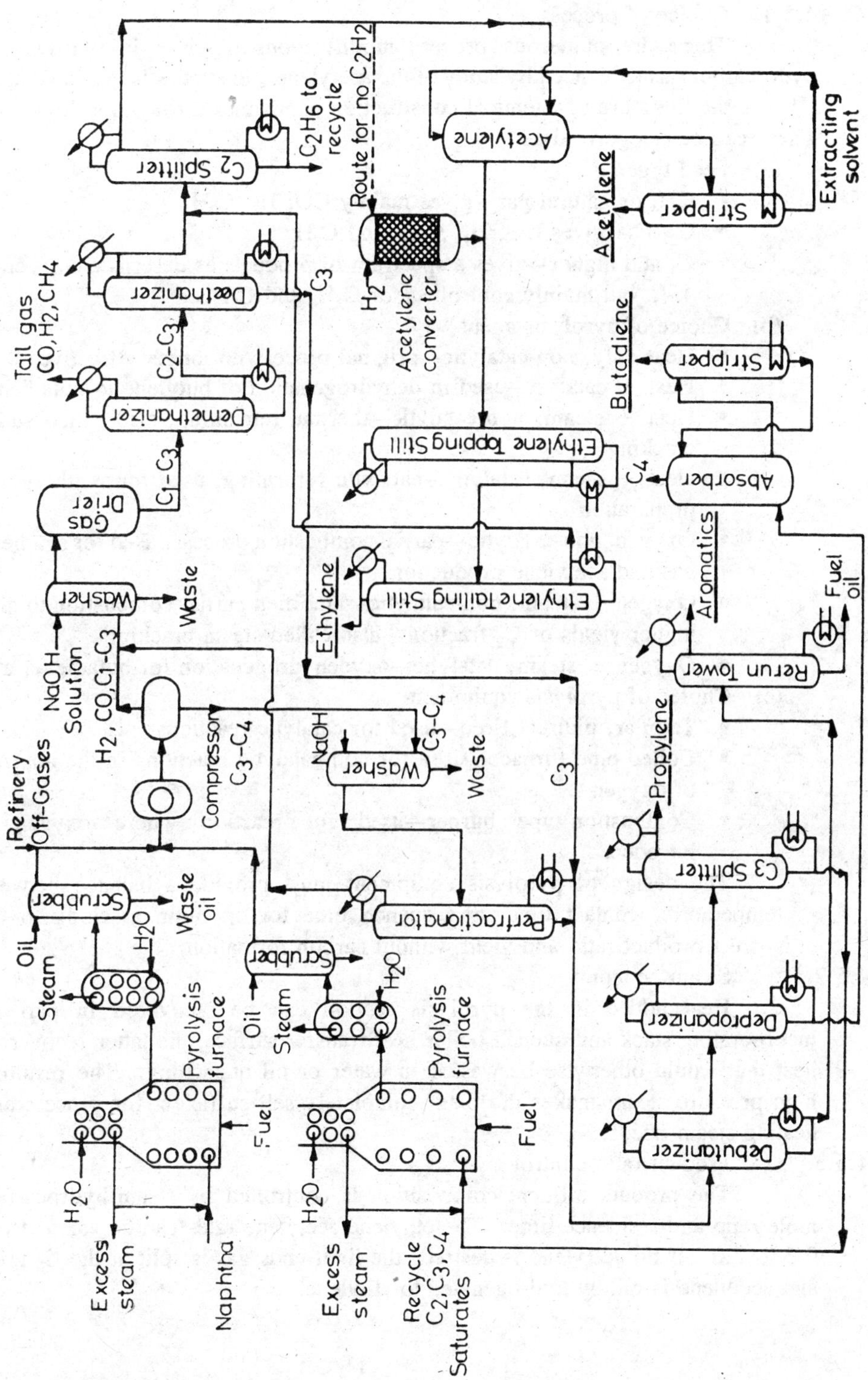

Fig. IVC-2. Ethylene and acetylene production by steam cracking of hydrocarbons.

4.5. Major Engineering Problems

4.5.1. Choice of process

There are numerous process modifications possible in pyrolysis of hydrocarbons as evidenced by study of the acetylene and synthesis gas in Chapter IIB and the literature of chemical construction companies throughout the world. These can be categorized as:

(a) Feed type
- CH_4 or natural gas—gives mainly CO, H_2, C_2H_2
- C_2, C_3—gives CO, H_2, C_2H_2 and C_2H_4
- C_4 and higher—gives a spectrum of products as described in Section 4.4, but mainly controlled for C_2H_4 and C_2H_2

(b) Choice of pyrolysis agent
- Heat only, non-catalytic—original process no longer attractive
- Heat + catalyst—used in dehydrogenation of butylene to butadiene
- Heat + steam, non-catalytic—thermal reforming, also called steam cracking
- Heat + steam, catalytic—catalytic reforming, used for synthesis gas preparation
- Oxygen, non-catalytic—partial combustion process, used for synthesis gas and acetylene production
- Oxygen + steam, non-catalytic—modified partial combustion to give higher yields of C_2 fractions, also called steam cracking
- Oxygen + steam, catalytic—oxydehydrogenation for butadiene, etc.

(c) Choice of pyrolysis equipment
- Tubular, indirect fired—used for catalytic reactions
- Coiled pipe furnace—used for non-catalytic reactions in the absence of oxygen
- Combustion-type burner—used for reaction where oxygen is introduced

The design of pyrolysis equipment must provide a balance between temperature, contact time, and quench time for optimum cracking to the correct product ratio and yield without carbon formation.

4.5.2. Steam economy

Heat added in the pyrolysis section can be recovered in part by incorporating stack and quench boiler heat transfer surface, the latter recovering heat that would otherwise be wasted in water or oil quenching. The resulting high pressure steam makes the plant completely self-sufficient for process and heating steam needs.

4.5.3. Product ratio control

The product effluent composition is controlled by steam-hydrocarbon mole ratio and residence time. The ethylene/acetylene rates can be varied from 0.3 to 2.0. If no acetylene is desired, the light ends gas is split at the C_2 level and acetylene is mildly hydrogenated to ethylene.

Economics

This type of processing is the heart of the petrochemical industry and is responsible for its success. Nearly all chemical construction firms have one type of ethylene plant for sale and competition is keen, thus giving the customer a low-cost plant. The future for this type of process in India is assured as naphtha must be cracked to produce most of the primary C_2-C_5 chemicals needed.

Table IVC-3 shows the world capacity breakdown for ethylene.

Table IVC-3
World Capacity for Ethylene

Region	(Estimated) Capacity in Million Tons (1995)	New Crackers added 1990 through 1995
U.S.	22.2	5
Canada	3.0	1
Latin America	4.4	3
Western Europe	19.7	5
Eastern Europe	7.4	6
Middle East/Africa	5.8	6
Japan	7.1	3
China	2.7	4
Asia/Pacific	8.0	17
Total	80.3	50

Source: "Global Trends in Chemical Products"—Nandini (1994)

Ethanol (Synthetic)

$$CH_2{=}CH_2 + H_2O \rightarrow CH_3{-}CH_2{-}OH$$

Synthetic ethanol is made by the hydration of ethylene over a phosphoric acid-on-celite catalyst and accounts for 18% of all ethanol. The predominant method of ethanol manufacture, at one time, was by fermentation of sugars; this method went out of use in the 1930's. However, corn fermentation is now a source of 82% of all ethanol and is used for gasohol, a 10% alcohol: 90% gasoline blend used for automobile fuel.

Industrial uses for ethanol are shared by synthetic and fermentation alcohol in a 7:3 ratio and include solvents (59%) and chemical intermediates (41%).

See Chapter III on Natural Products Industries for ethanol production by fermentation.

Polyethylene

Polymerized ethylene provides the largest outlet for ethylene, both in India and the other countries. The technology of this product is discussed in Chapter VB.

Ethylene Dichloride (1,2-Dichloroethane)

This compound is of interest as it is one of the intermediates for vinyl chloride monomer which polymerizes to polyvinyl chloride (PVC).

1. Pertinent Properties of Ethylene Dichloride ($ClCH_2 \cdot CH_2Cl$)

Mol. wt.	98.97
M.P.	−35.3°C
B.P.	83.7°C
Density @ 20°C	1.257
Flash point	15.5°C
Ignition temperature	412°C
Explosive limits:	Lower = 6.2%
	Upper = 15.9%
Maximum toxicity limit:	75-100 ppm

2. End Use

	USA
Vinyl chloride	65%
Antiknock agent	30
Solvent	4

3. Methods of Production

3.1. Classification of Processes

3.1.1. Reaction of chlorine with ethylene in liquid or vapor phase

3.1.2. By-product of direct chlorination of ethane to ethyl chloride

3.1.3. By-product of chlorinated hydrocarbons

3.2. Ethylene + Chlorine Reaction

3.2.1. Reference flow sheet: Figure IVC-3

3.2.2. Chemical reaction

$$CH_2 = CH_2 + Cl_2 \rightarrow ClCH_2 \cdot CH_2Cl$$

3.2.3. Quantitative requirements

(a) Basis: 1 ton of $C_2H_4Cl_2$ (95% yield)

Ethylene	0.30 ton
Chlorine	0.75 ton
Ethylene dibromide catalyst—trace	
Cooling water	48 tons

Co-products: HCl, propylene chloride, polychloroethanes

(b) Plant capacities: 30-150 tons/day

3.2.4. Process description

Ethylene (with or without C_2H_6, CH_4 and H_2 diluent) is mixed with chlorine and bubbled through a liquid phase reactor. Ethylene dichloride product serves as the reacting medium. Heat of reaction is controlled by external heat exchange and recycle, or by coil or jacket heat transfer, to hold the reactor at 45-50°C with a pressure of 1.5-2 atms. Traces of ferric chloride or ethylene dibromide as catalyst gives 90-95% yield with little dimer formation. The

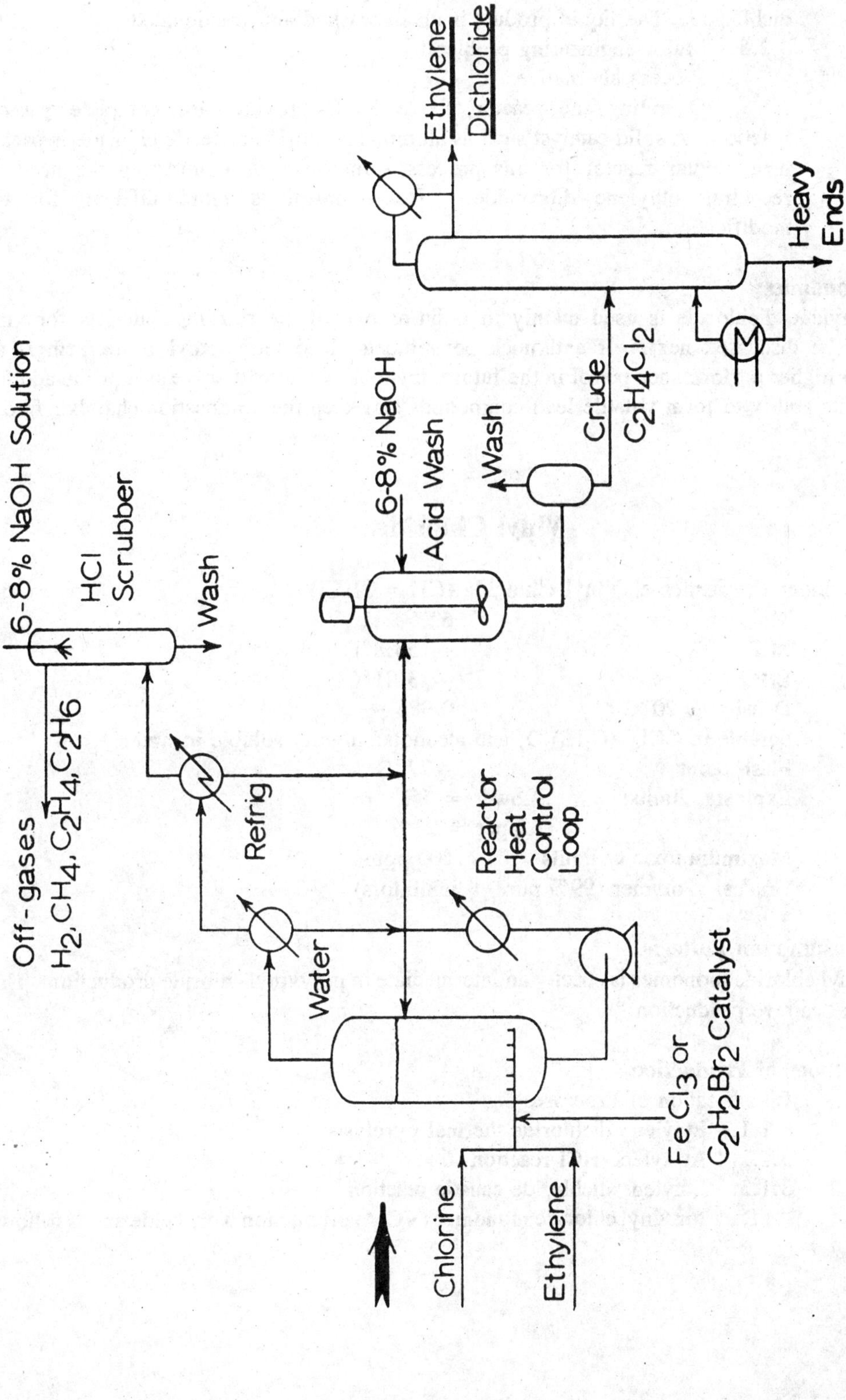

Fig. IVC-3. Ethylene dichloride production.

gaseous products are cooled in two stages to strip the acid gas of ethylene dichloride. The liquid product is alkali washed and fractionated.

3.2.5. Major engineering problems

Process alternative

Operating the reactor above 85°C provides for complete gaseous reaction. A solid catalyst such as aluminum chloride or ferric chloride is packed in a tubular reactor for this process variation, thus eliminating the need for recycling ethylene dibromide. Heat control is more difficult for this modification.

4. Economics

Ethylene dichloride is used mainly in India as one of the starting materials for vinyl chloride to be discussed next. If antiknock constituents (lead tetramethyl or tetraethyl) are required for higher performance petrol in the future, this compound will serve as a prime additive because of its ability to form volatile lead compounds and keep the combustion chamber free of lead deposits.

Vinyl Chloride

1. Pertinent Properties of Vinyl Chloride ($CH_2{=}CHCl$)

Mol. wt. 62.50
M.P. −153.8°C
B.P. −13.81°C
Density @ 20°C 0.983
Soluble in CCl_4, $(C_2H_5)_2O$, and alcohols; slightly soluble in water
Flash point −77°C
Explosive limits: Lower = 5%
Upper = 23%
Maximum toxicity limits 500 ppm
Grades: Polymer (99% pure + inhibitors)

2. Consumption Pattern

Vinyl chloride monomer is strictly an intermediate in polyvinyl chloride production. Thus it is only in "captive production."

3. Methods of Production

3.1. Classification of Processes

3.1.1. Ethylene dichloride thermal pyrolysis
3.1.2. Acetylene-HCl reaction
3.1.3. Ethylene dichloride-caustic reaction

Data for vinyl chloride monomer (VCM) production worldwide are as follows:

VCM Production (in 10^6 tons)

	1987	1989	1991
Western Europe	5.42	5.77	6.11
USA	3.73	4.36	5.35
Japan	1.83	2.16	2.45
CIS	0.50	0.63	0.68

The first two processes will be described since they are often combined to keep a chlorine balance.

3.2. Ethylene Dichloride Thermal Pyrolysis

3.2.1. Reference flow sheet: Figure IVC-4

3.2.2. Chemical reaction

$$CH_2Cl \cdot CH_2Cl \xrightarrow[4\text{ atms.}]{500°C} CH_2{=}CHCl + HCl$$

3.2.3. Quantitative requirements

(a) Basis: 1 ton of vinyl chloride (99.5% pure, 95% yield)

Ethylene dichloride	1.65 tons
Heating steam	2.0 tons
Cooling water	30 tons
Electricity	1.5 KWH
Fuel gas	5.7 Nm^3

Co-product: 0.65 ton HCl

(b) Plant capacities: 30-100 tons/day

3.2.4. Process description

Ethylene dichloride (EDC) vapor at 4 atms. is dried by silica gel and sent to a stainless steel tubular cracking furnace. This is externally flue gas fired and controlled at 480-520°C. The contact surface catalyst within the tubes is pumice or charcoal. The conversion per pass is around 50% and the ultimate yield is 95-96%. Spray quenching with cold EDC prevents back-reaction. Uncondensed gases are sent to a surface heat exchanger to remove the balance of the EDC and vinyl chloride.

The non-condensibles containing HCl are either sent to the acetylene-HCl process in an adjacent process area or water scrubbed to recover HCl as muriatic acid.

The condensate is fractionated with the EDC bottoms returned for recycle and vinyl chloride monomer taken from overhead, stabilized and sent to storage.

3.2.5. Major engineering problems

(a) Carbon formation—this occurs steadily until reactor has too high a pressure drop, thus causing shut down and cleaning periodically. Increasing conversion beyond 50% by longer residence time or higher temperature increases carbon formation and promotes polymerization of monomer. Reactor conditions

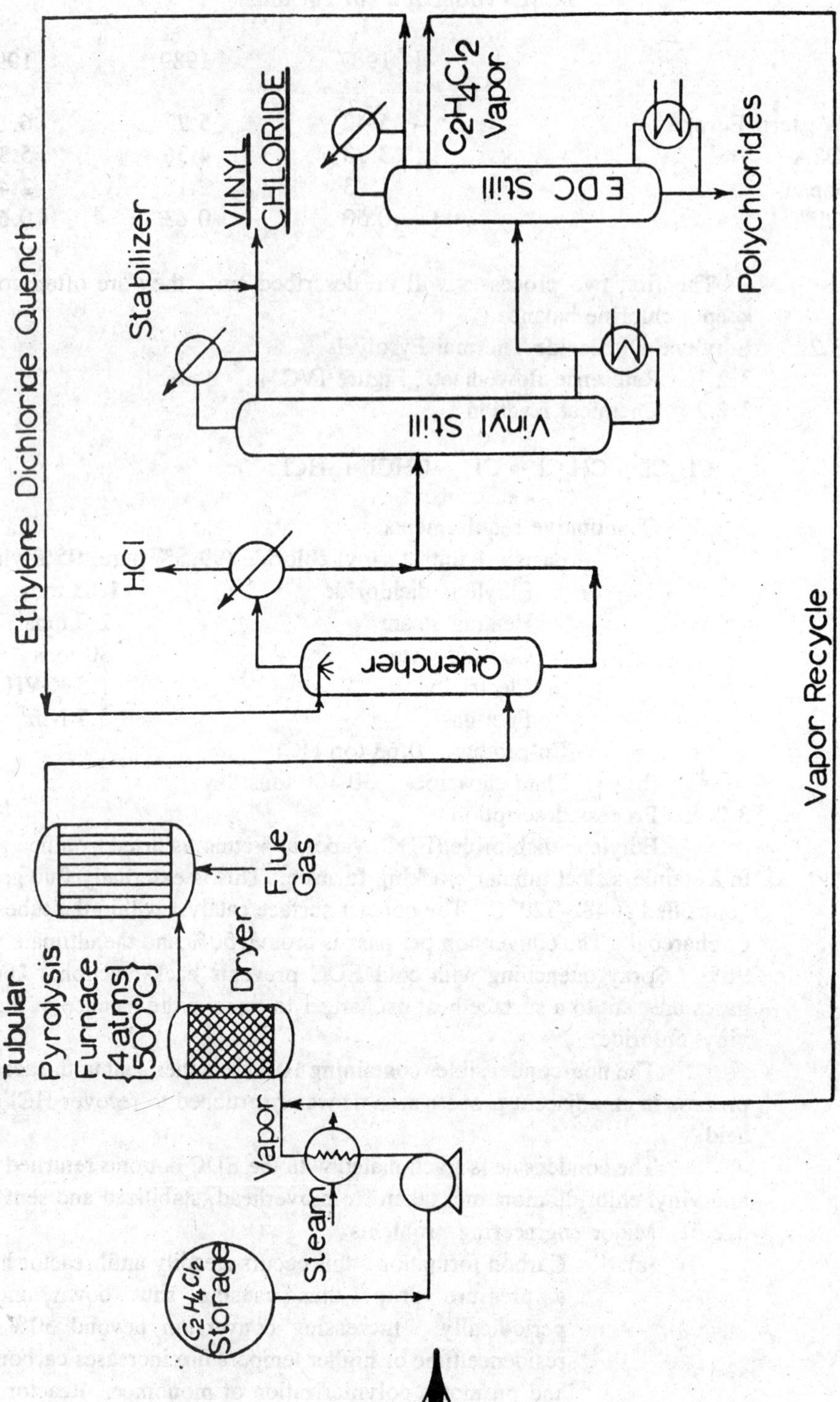

Fig. IVC-4. Vinyl chloride via ethylene dichloride pyrolysis.

had to be worked out to optimize recycle loading versus reactor down time and loss of yield.

(b) Excessive corrosion unless system is kept free of water vapor.

(c) Development of the proper cracking catalyst which prevents polymerization during reaction.

(d) Stabilization of vinyl chloride monomer—antioxidants must be chosen so that no interference will occur later in the polymerization process.

3.3. Acetylene-HCl Reaction

3.3.1. Reference flow sheet: Figure IVC-5

3.3.2. Chemical reaction

$$CH{\equiv}CH + HCl \xrightarrow[1\ atm.]{160\text{-}200^\circ C} CH_2{=}CHCl$$

3.3.3. Quantitative requirements

(a) Basis: 1 ton of vinyl chloride (99.5% pure, 97% yield)

Acetylene	0.462 ton
Hydrogen chloride	0.60 ton

(b) Plant capacities: 30-100 tons/day

3.3.4. Process description

Acetylene and dry HCl in 5-10% molar excess are vapor blended by jet mixing in a pipe and passed through a tubular catalytic reactor containing carbon pellets impregnated with $HgCl_2$. The temperature is maintained at 160°C and is gradually raised to 215°C as the catalyst deteriorates. The effluent gases contain vinyl chloride which is separated from unreacted acetylene plus hydrogen chloride, these unreacted materials being recycled.

3.3.5. Major engineering problems

- Catalyst deterioration and replacement
- Excessive corrosion unless system is dry
- Avoiding polymerization of monomer

4. Economics

The production of vinyl chloride illustrates a unique combination of two processes for minimum cost operation. Hydrogen chloride is difficult to dispose of in the cracking process, but is required for the acetylene reaction. Combining the two processes at the same site location solves this problem of chlorine balance. For the combination, equimolar quantities of acetylene and ethylene are produced by steam cracking. The mixture goes first to the HCl reactor where acetylene reacts; ethylene does not react and is separated from vinyl chloride, HCl, and unreacted acetylene. It then progresses through ethylene dichloride formation and pyrolysis to yield an additional mole of vinyl chloride for each mole made in the acetylene-HCl reactor. Hydrochloric acid is thus available in the correct quantity for hydrochlorination of acetylene in the gas mixture from the naphtha cracking plant. The combination cycle is operable at lowest overall cost under some conditions. An economic disadvantage exists because two smaller plants are required in this set-up, giving rise to a higher capital cost for the total capacity than if one larger plant of either type were specified. Effective chlorine utilization is generally the determining factor.

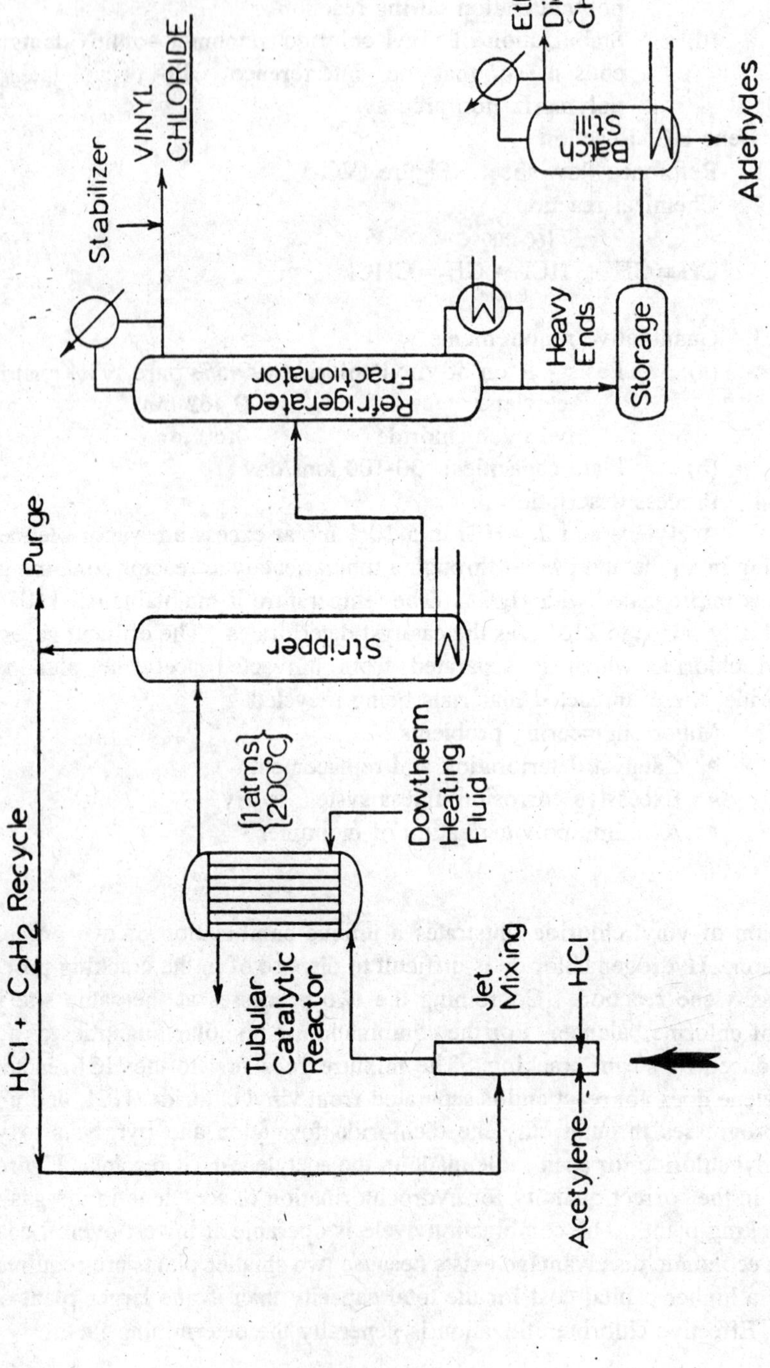

Fig. IVC-5. Vinyl chloride via acetylene-HCl reaction.

Recent developments favor oxychlorination, wherein recycle HCl, air and chlorine react to form ethylene dichloride. New plants will use this process if low-cost ethylene is available.

Ethylene Oxide

1. Pertinent Properties of Ethylene Oxide (CH_2—CH_2)
\ /
O

Mol. wt.	44.05
M.P.	−111.7°C
B.P.	10.7°C
Density @ 0°C	0.896
Flash point	−15°C
Ignition temperature	430°C
Explosive limits:	Lower = 3% in air
	Upper = 80% in air
Maximum toxic limit	25-100 ppm

2. Consumption Pattern

Principal outlet in the U.S. is for production of ethylene glycol, a permanent antifreeze for automobile radiators. India will have very little use for this derivative, but instead will find ethylene glycol polyesters, non-ionic detergents, and ethanolamines useful products derived from ethylene oxide.

2.1. End Uses

Table IVC-4 shows the worldwide pattern for ethylene oxide uses.

Table IVC-4
Utilization of Ethylene Oxide (in wt. %)

	World		USA		Western Europe		Japan	
	1985	1991	1981	1989	1981	1989	1981	1991
Ethylene glycol	59	59	58	57	45	41	62	55
Non-ionic surfactants	13	13	12	12	23	22	17	25
Ethanolamines	6	6	7	8	10	8	7	7
Glycol ethers	6	5	8	8	10	11	5	6
Miscellaneous (*e.g.*, higher ethylene glycols, urethane polyols, etc.)	16	17	15	15	12	18		7
Total use (in 10^6 tonnes)	6.47	8.02	2.31	2.72	1.31	1.57	0.48	0.76

Source: "Industrial Organic Chemistry" by Weissermel et al (1993)

3. Methods of Production

3.1. Classification of Processes

3.1.1. Direct oxidation of ethylene

3.1.2. Chlorohydrination of ethylene

3.2. Direct Oxidation of Ethylene

3.2.1. Reference flow sheet: Figure IVC-6

3.2.2. Chemical reaction

$$CH_2{=}CH_2 + \tfrac{1}{2}O_2 \ \underset{\text{oxygen}}{\overset{\text{air}}{\text{or}}} \ \xrightarrow[\text{250-300°C, 4-5 atms.}]{\text{AgO}} \ \underset{\text{(O bridge)}}{CH_2{-}CH_2} + \underset{\text{side reaction}}{(CO_2 + H_2O)}; \quad \Delta H = -29.2 \text{ Kcal}$$

3.2.3. Quantitative requirements

(a) Basis: 1 ton of ethylene oxide (99% purity, 70% yield)

Ethylene	0.92 ton
Air	9.0 tons
Silver	0.3 kg in fixed bed
	0.7 kg in fluidized bed
Ethylene dichloride suppressor	10-15 kg
Electricity	1,500 KWH
Steam	0.1 ton
Water	180 tons

(b) Plant capacities: 30-300 tons/day

3.2.4. Process description

Ethylene of 95-98% purity and air are compressed separately, mixed together giving 3-10% C_2H_4 volume concentration and passed over a catalyst of silver oxide on a porous inert carrier such as alumina. A side reaction suppressing agent such as ethylene dichloride is added to the feed to reduce the competitive oxidation reaction to CO_2 + H_2O.

The reaction is highly exothermic and is best carried out in a fixed bed tubular reactor in which heat transfer salt or Dowtherm is pumped around the tube within the shell to maintain a 250-300°C temperature. Heat is recovered in a waste-heat steam boiler. A short residence time of 1 sec in plug flow is the design with an ultimate yield of 60-70%.

The effluent gases from the reactor are water-washed under pressure. The absorbed ethylene oxide is sent to a packed bed desorber-fractionator tower and taken overhead. It still contains a large amount of water vapor plus some impurities. This stream is compressed to 4-5 atms., and fractionated twice to remove light ends, water, and high boiling polymers.

3.2.5. Major engineering problems

This process has a large number of alternative flow sheets, depending on customer conditions, patent rights, and the experience of the design-construction firm.

(a) Volume ratio of air-ethylene

The 3% lower explosion limit for C_2H_4 or C_2H_4O in air with a high heat of reaction has caused some designers originally to keep at or below this value in considering process stream concentrations. This is done by recycle inerts from the absorber after side stream purge to remove some CO_2 + H_2O. The conversion is claimed to be improved at low ethylene concentrations of 3-5% in a N_2 carrier stream.

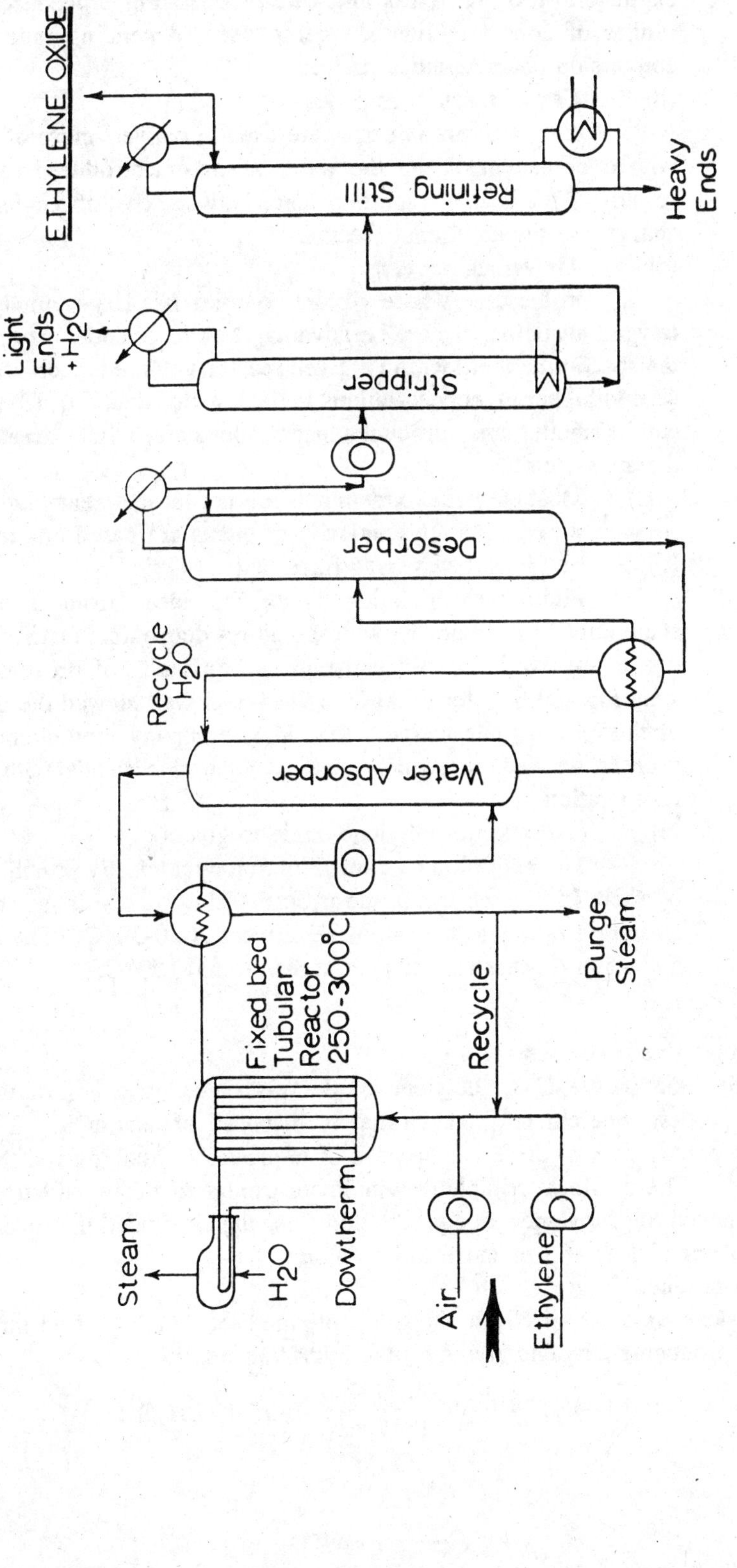

Fig. IVC-6. Ethylene oxide by air oxidation of ethylene.

The explosion hazard has now been minimized by use of explosion-proof standards and careful operating procedures so that all ranges of concentrations are being used, depending more on reactor conversion characteristics desired.

(b) Use of reactors in series

Two reactors in series are used to convert more of the ethylene with overhead gas from the water absorber introduced into a second reactor. This is an economic balance between cost of ethylene and fixed charges on the additional reactor.

(c) Air versus oxygen

In the case where a plant complex has large tonnage, low-cost oxygen available, it may be advantageous to consider oxygen since (1) the space-time yield within a given reactor volume is increased 3-4 times (due to higher O_2 concentrations in the kinetic equation), (2) the absorber can be smaller since product concentrations are 6 times greater than with the air system.

Most ethylene oxide plants are not located near low-cost oxygen sources at present so the majority of plants are based on air oxidation.

(d) Fluidized bed versus fixed bed

Fluid bed operation would be ideal from a heat control standpoint. However, the widespread residence time distribution pattern due to mixing in a fluid bed plus the difficulty of preventing catalyst sintering and transfer of AgO to the vessel wall slowed the development of this process alternative. One U.S. company now claims to have a process worked out which gives comparative yields without catalyst regeneration.

(e) Hydration of ethylene oxide to glycol

The hydration reaction is thermodynamically possible, yet water is used in the absorbing-desorbing train. This is so because the hydration rate constant is not significant at 20-30°C. The commercial hydration process uses temperatures around 150°C.

4. Economics

4.1. Competitive Processes

Until 1955 in the U.S., ethylene oxide was made by a chlorhydrin (HOCl) aqueous process wherein Cl_2 was ultimately disposed of as $CaCl_2$. The catalytic oxidation process is now preferred because of improved technology and the high cost of chlorine. These chlorhydrin plants with lower capital cost than oxidation plants are being switched to propylene oxide production since the air oxidation process is not yet successful for olefins of 3 or more carbon atoms.

4.2. End-product Usage

Ethylene oxide is strictly a chemical intermediate which is used largely in the U.S. for producing ethylene glycol by the hydration reaction:

$$\underset{\diagdown O \diagup}{CH_2-CH_2} + H_2O \xrightarrow[10\text{-}15\ \text{atms.}]{150\text{-}175°C} HOCH_2 \cdot CH_2OH$$

This is done in a continuous reactor-distillation integral unit.

Other end uses are discussed in Section 2. The manufacture of ethanolamines will be given next.

Ethanolamines

1. **Pertinent Properties**

1.1. Monoethanolamine ($HOCH_2 \cdot CH_2 \cdot NH_2$)

Mol. wt.	61.08
M.P.	10.5°C
B.P.	170.5°C
Density @ 20°C	1.02

Appearance: Colorless, moderately viscous oil

Odor: Mild ammoniacal

Soluble in water, alcohol, chloroform, ether; slightly soluble in benzene

Flash point	95°C

Purity: 80-98%, containing higher amines and water; specified on B.P. range

1.2. Diethanolamine [$(HO \cdot CH_2 \cdot CH_2)_2 \cdot NH$]

Mol. wt.	105.2
M.P.	28°C
B.P.	270°C (decomp.)
Density @ 30°C	1.09

Appearance: Colorless crystals @ 20°C

Soluble in water, alcohol; slightly soluble in ether; insoluble in benzene

Flash point	138°C
Ignition temperature	660°C

Purity: 94-95%, containing mono- and triethanolamine

1.3. Triethanolamine [$(HO \cdot CH_2 \cdot CH_2)_3N$]

Mol. wt.	149.2
M.P.	21.2°C
B.P.	360°C (decomp.)
Density @ 20°C	1.13

Appearance: Pale yellow oil

Odor: Slight ammoniacal

Soluble in water, alcohol, chloroform; slightly soluble in ether

Purity: 80% technical grade with approximately 2% mono- and 15% diethanolamine; 98% high purity grade.

2. **Consumption Pattern**

Ethanolamines are valuable products whose main use is in the manufacture of detergents by reaction with fatty acids. Ethanolamine can be used directly in gas purification to remove undesired acidic components. The fatty acid salts of ethanolamines can be used as components of soaps and cosmetic creams. Finally, the ethanolamines may be used as intermediates in the manufacture of morpholine, ethyleneimine and ethylene diamine.

3. Methods of Production

There is only one basic process, namely, reaction of ethylene oxide with ammonia.

3.1. Reference Flow Sheet: Figure IVC-7

3.2. Chemical Reactions

A set of complex series reactions exists:

E + A → M	E = ethylene oxide
E + M → D	A = ammonia
E + D → T	M, D, T = mono-, di-, and triethanolamines respectively

The exact chemical equations are

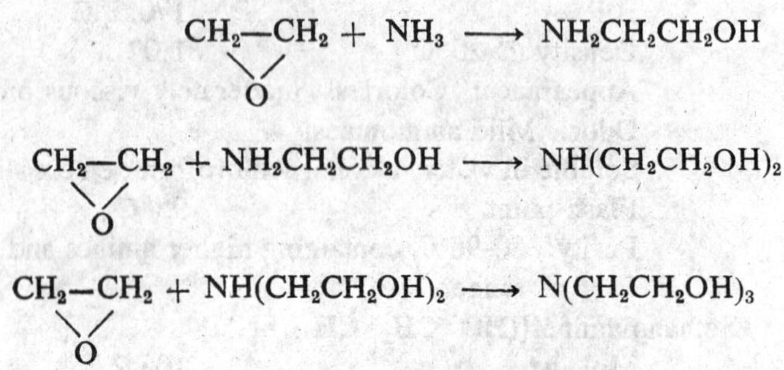

Product ratios depend on conditions used.

3.3. Quantitative Requirements

(a) Basis: 1 ton of mixed ethanolamines (*e.g.*, 70% mono-, 25% di-, and 5% tri- with 95% ethylene oxide utilization)

Ethylene oxide	0.81 ton
Ammonia	0.24 ton

(b) Plant capacities: 15-50 tons/day

3.4. Process Description

Ethylene oxide and aqueous ammonia (25-30% NH_3) are fed to a stirred tank reactor which can be operated under a wide range of conditions depending on product distribution. Ammonolysis is exothermic and heat must be removed. The product stream is flashed to remove NH_3 for recycle. The bottoms contain a water solution of the amines which are separated in four fractionating columns, the last two under vacuum.

3.5. Major Engineering Problems

3.5.1. Kinetics of complex series reactions

Product rates and yield are important in this set of series reactions. The control involves these rate equations:

$$\frac{dC_M}{dt} = k_1 C_E C_A - k_2 C_E C_M$$

$$\frac{dC_D}{dt} = k_2 C_E C_M - k_3 C_E C_D$$

$$\frac{dC_T}{dt} = k_3 C_E C_D$$

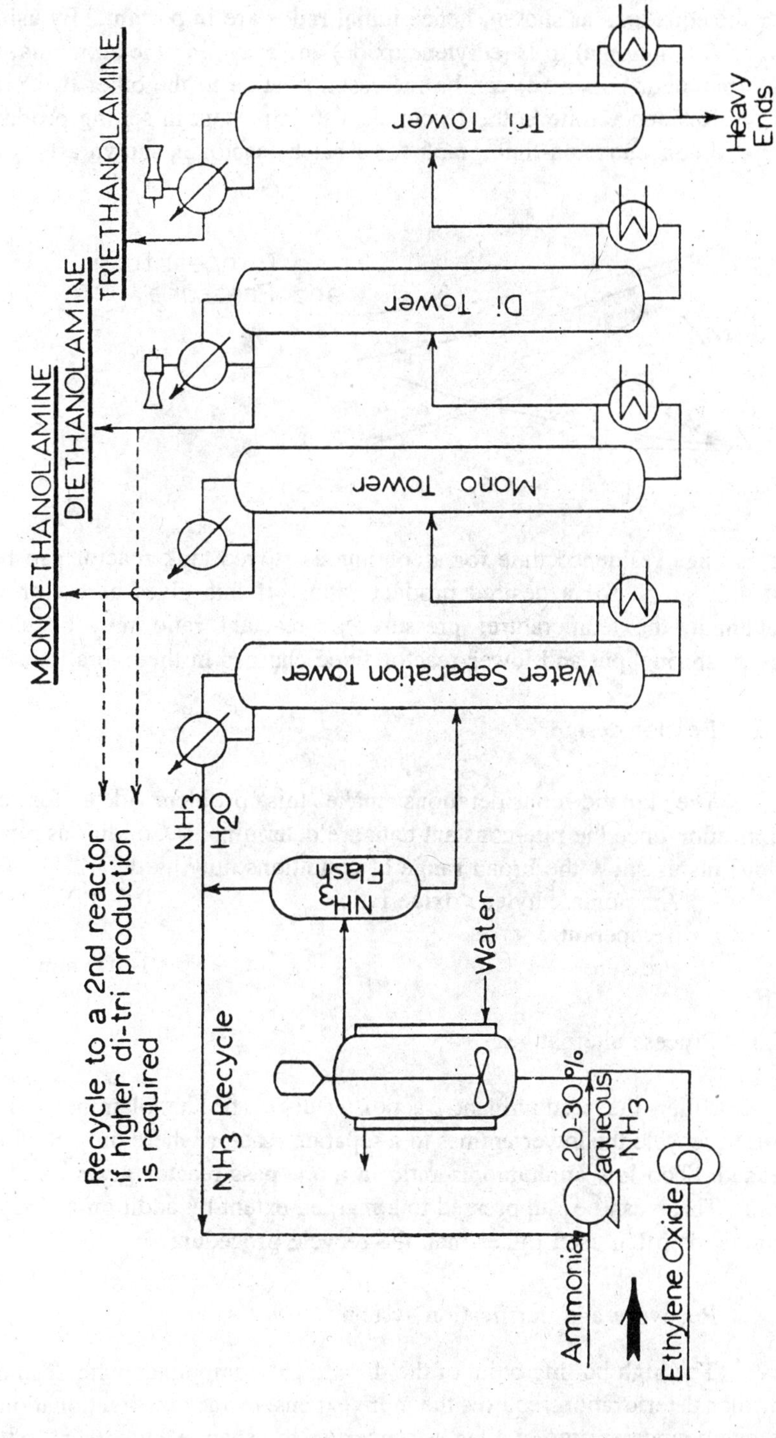

Fig. IVC-7. Ethanolamines from ethylene oxide and ammonia.

Temperature affects the specific rate constants and the reactant conc. C_A and C_M enter the equations as shown, hence initial ratios are important. By using a high ratio of A (ammonia) to E (ethylene oxide) and recycling the ammonia, the yield of M (monoethanolamine) can be increased relative to the other two products.

Residence time in the reactor is also important in setting product ratios. A typical concentration-time graph for a batch reactor is shown as:

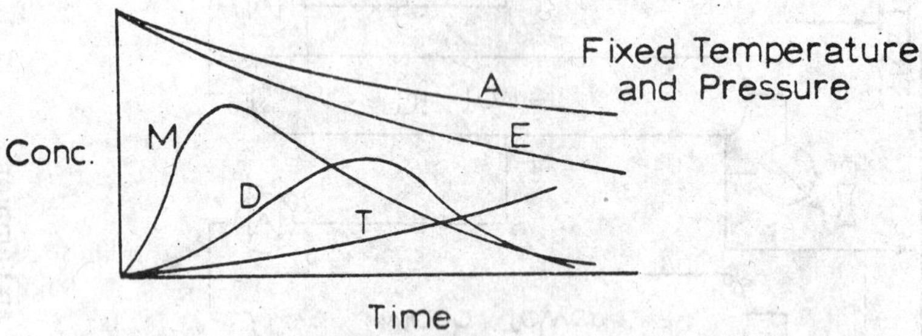

The average residence time for a continuous stirred tank reactor can be picked from this graph for a desired product ratio. If this gives a reactor with low throughput, the temperature, pressure, or reactant ratio may be changed to increase throughput and lower reactor fixed charges in the overall cost picture.

3.5.2. Reactor design

The kinetic considerations make this problem ideal for computer optimization once the rate-constant data are determined. Conditions reported for various plants show the broad range of conditions now used.

Ammonia/ethylene oxide ratio	0.5-3.0
Temperature	35-275°C
Pressure	1-100 atms.

3.5.3. Process alternatives

When the predominant fraction is di- or triethanolamine, it is usually better to recycle the lower amines to a separate reactor where only ethylene oxide is added. Too low an ammonia ratio in a one-pass reactor gives rise to amino-ethers. These can be suppressed to a marked extent by addition of CO_2 and this technique is often used rather than the recycle procedure.

3.5.4. Recovery and purification system

The high boiling point of the di- and tri- compounds with decomposition and color deterioration requires the more expensive vacuum fractionation system. The compounds are too similar in properties to separate by solvent extraction.

4. **Economics**

4.1. Product Demand

These three amines have a variety of end uses and the demand shifts yearly, necessitating good control over product-ratio production.

4.2. Competitive Products

Research and market development for similar homologs made with propylene oxide may displace some of the present uses of ethanolamines. Fortunately, the processes are sufficiently similar so that propanolamines can be produced in the same equipment with minor operating changes.

Acetaldehyde

Acetaldehyde is one of the most important tonnage petrochemicals, being the raw material for acetic acid, acetic anhydride, acetate esters, etc. It was previously made only by the hydration of acetylene in the presence of a liquid $HgSO_4$ catalyst according to the equation

$$C_2H_2 + H_2O \rightarrow CH_3CHO$$

Then, in the early 1960's a new process was announced starting from lower cost ethylene as the raw material and producing acetaldehyde at lower cost according to the equation

$$C_2H_4 + 1/2O_2 \rightarrow CH_3CHO$$

Indeed the new process has been such an economic success that it immediately obsoleted the old process. No more acetylene-based plants have been built while overall acetaldehyde capacity has expanded greatly the world over.

The process operates in the presence of an aqueous liquid copper salt catalyst, promoted by a metal such as palladium. Thus these are really two reactions, a hydration reaction

$$C_2H_4 + 2CuCl_2 + H_2O \rightarrow CH_3CHO + 2CuCl + 2HCl$$

and a catalyst regeneration reaction

$$2CuCl + 2HCl + 1/2O_2 \rightarrow 2CuCl_2 + H_2O$$

which add up to give the net overall reaction

$$C_2H_4 + 1/2O_2 \rightarrow CH_3CHO$$

The process is operated at pressures below 50 atmospheres and at temperatures of 50 to 100°C. Typical reaction times range from 6 to 40 minutes. Tower type reactors are used as shown in Figure IVC-8. Yields of acetaldehyde are very high—about 96%.

Acetaldehyde production (in 10^6 tons) worldwide is as follows:

	1985	1987	1990
Western Europe	0.57	0.58	0.58
Japan	0.27	0.29	0.38
USA	0.31	0.33	0.31

Source: "Industrial Organic Chemistry" by Weissermel et al (1993)

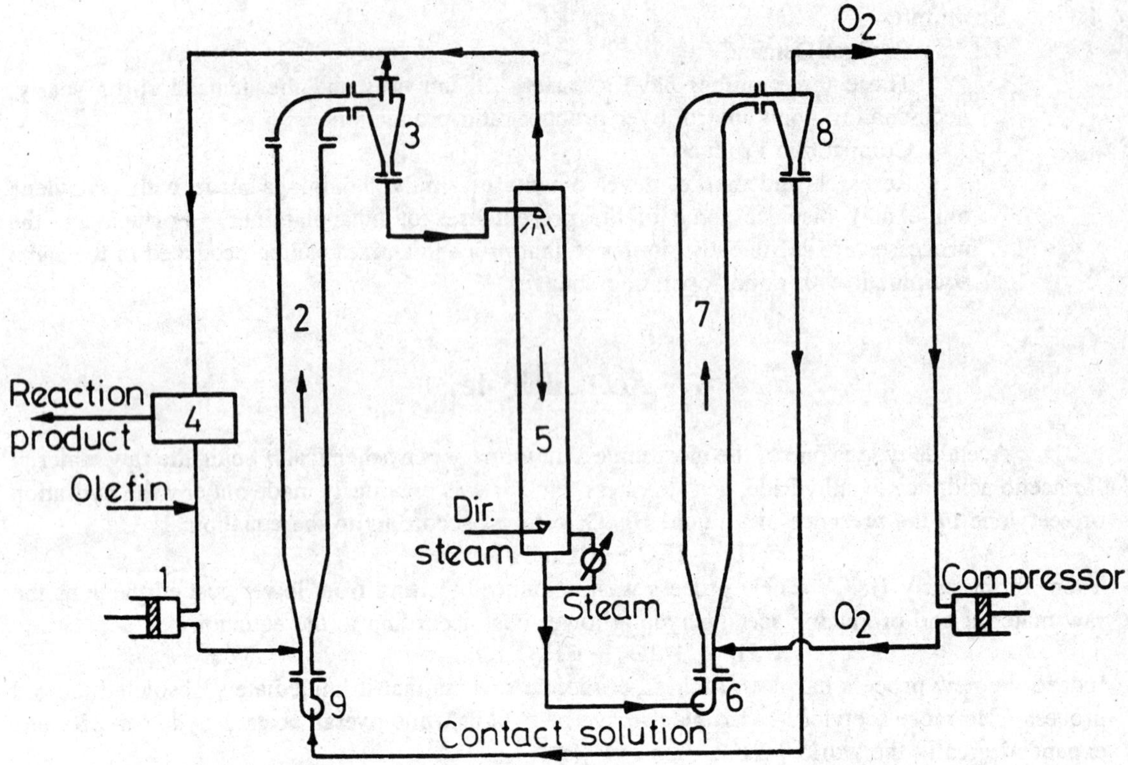

1. Compressor
2. Reactor
3. Cyclone separator
4. Product separator
5. Stripper
6. Pump
7. Regenerator
8. Cyclone separator
9. Pump

Fig. IVC-8. Flow sheet of process for making acetaldehyde directly from ethylene.

Table IVC-5 shows the world pattern for acetaldehyde use.

Table IVC-5
Acetaldehyde Use (in wt. %)

	Western Europe		USA		Japan	
	1980	1990	1980	1990	1978	1990
Acetic acid	60	43	63 (acetic acid and acetic anhydride)	55	69 (acetic acid and acetic anhydride)	34
Acetic anhydride	11	15		—		—
n-Butanol	0.2	—	—	—	2	—
2-Ethylhexanol	0.8	—	—	—	—	—
Ethyl acetate	18	21	—	15	16	42
Miscellaneous (*e.g.*, pyridines, pentaerythritol, peracetic acid)	10	21	37	30	13	24
Total use (in 10^6 tonnes)	0.64	0.56	0.36	0.31	0.59	0.23

Source: "Industrial Organic Chemistry" by Weissermel et al (1993)

Vinyl Acetate

Vinyl acetate is another example of a C_2 petrochemical where ethylene is threatening to displace acetylene as the raw material.

The traditional process involves the reaction of acetylene and acetic acid as follows:

$$C_2H_2 + CH_3COOH \rightarrow CH_3COOCH{=}CH_2$$

A new route which is now being installed commercially involves vinyl acetate manufacture directly from ethylene. In one variant of this process, ethylene and acetic acid are reacted as follows:

$$C_2H_4 + CH_3COOH + 1/2O_2 \rightarrow CH_3COOCH{=}CH_2 + H_2O$$

In a second variant of the new oxyesterification process which is carried out in the presence of a palladium chloride catalyst, ethylene and oxygen are the only reactants, acetaldehyde and then acetic acid being formed during the process. The equations involved are:

$$\begin{array}{l} C_2H_4 + 1/2O_2 \rightarrow CH_3CHO \\ CH_3CHO + 1/2O_2 \rightarrow CH_3COOH \\ C_2H_4 + CH_3COOH + 1/2O_2 \rightarrow CH_3COOCH{=}CH_2 + H_2O \\ \hline 2C_2H_4 + 3/2O_2 \rightarrow CH_3COOCH{=}CH_2 + H_2O \end{array}$$

The production of vinyl acetate monomer in India during the years 1984-85 and 1986-87 was 8,846 M.T. and about 9,000 M.T. respectively. The installed capacity and production of vinyl acetate monomer in 1989 were estimated at 20,000 M.T. and 16,500 M.T. respectively.

Vinyl acetate monomer is used as an intermediate in the manufacture of polyvinyl alcohol, polyvinyl acetate, polyvinyl formal, polyvinyl butyryl, etc.

These polymers are water-white water-soluble resins which find wide application in the manufacture of adhesives, paper coatings, emulsifiers, surface coatings, molding materials, lacquers, textile finishing agents, printing auxiliaries, chemicals, safety glass, etc.

Vinyl acetate production worldwide (in '000 tons) is shown in the following tabulation.

	1987	1989	1991
USA	1,137	1,120	1,145
Western Europe	522	550	575
Japan	425	474	505
CIS	100	115	104

Source: "Industrial Organic Chemistry" by Weissermel et al (1993)

Worldwide data for vinyl acetate use are given in Table IVC-6.

Table IVC-6
Use of Vinyl Acetate (in wt.%)

	World		USA		Japan		Western Europe	
	1984	1991	1984	1990	1984	1990	1984	1990
Polyvinyl acetate (homo- and copolymers)	47	48	55	53	15	15	57	48
Polyvinyl alcohol	29	32	21	19	73	71	16	21
Vinyl chloride/vinyl acetate copolymers	5	3	7	2	1	1	3	9
Ethylene/vinyl acetate resins	6	7	6	9	4	12	5	8
Miscellaneous uses*)	13	10	11	17	7	1	19	14
Total consumption (in 10^6 tonnes)	2.11	2.94	0.71	0.88	0.46	0.52	0.50	0.73

*) *e.g.*, Polyvinyl butyral

Source: "Industrial Organic Chemistry" by Weissermel et al (1993)

Producers of vinyl acetate in India are given in Table IVC-7.

Table IVC-7
Units Manufacturing Vinyl Acetate Monomer in India

Polychem Ltd.
Nimbut Village, Dist. Pune (Maharashtra)

Vam Organic Chemicals Ltd.
Bhartiagram, Gajraula - 244 223, Dist. Moradabad (U.P.)

Vinyl Chemicals (India) Ltd.
Plot No. A-21, MIDC, Mahad, Dist. Raigad (Maharashtra)

Source: "SBP Handbook of Projects for Corporate Diversification" (1992)

Acetic Acid

Acetic acid is a C_2 chemical produced by a variety of routes. The breakdown of various acetic acid processes worldwide is as follows:

Acetic Acid Production Capacity Worldwide (in wt.%)

	1988	1989	1991
CH_3OH carboxylation	47	50	55
CH_3CHO oxidation	27	27	23
C_2H_5OH dehydrogenation/oxidation	6	7	7
Butane/naphtha oxidation	7	12	10
Other methods	13	4	5

Source: "Industrial Organic Chemistry" by Weissermel et al (1993)

Production figures for acetic acid in various areas of the world are as follows:

Acetic Acid Production ('000 tons)

	1987	1989	1991
USA	1,464	1,735	1,630
Western Europe	1,093	1,310	1,290
Japan	377	382	465
CIS	345	370	330

Source: "Industrial Organic Chemistry" by Weissermel et al (1993)

If proper incentives are given by the Government, according to the "Perspective Plan for Chemical Industry (up to the year 2000)" there is a potential to export 10,000 M.T. and 20,000 M.T. of acetic acid from India in the years 1994-95 and 1999-2000 respectively.

The demand for acetic acid is estimated at 200,000 M.T. and 322,000 M.T. per annum by 1994-95 and 1999-2000 respectively.

The breakdown of acetic acid use by product and by world area is shown in Table IVC-8.

Table IVC-8
Use of Acetic Acid (in wt. %)

	World		USA		Western Europe		Japan	
	1988	1991	1984	1990	1985	1991	1984	1991
Vinyl acetate	40	39	52	54	35	36	26	24
Cellulose acetate	4	3	16	-	8	6	18	17
Butyl, isopropyl acetate	9	10	11	10	13	16	5	8
Acetic anhydride, acetanilide, acetyl chloride, acetamide	11	13	4	16	21	21	4	3

Table IVC-8 (cont'd)

	World		USA		Western Europe		Japan	
	1988	1991	1984	1990	1985	1991	1984	1991
Solvent for terephthalic acid and terephthalic dimethyl ester manufacture	8	11	8	12	6	7	11	20
Chloroacetic acids	4	4	2	1	11	10	5	6
Others (e.g., Al, NH_4, alkali metal acetates, etc.)	23	20	6	7	4	4	20	22
Total use (in 10^6 tons)	4.36	4.59	1.41	1.64	0.94	1.18	0.36	0.43

Source: "Industrial Organic Chemistry" by Weissermel et al (1993)

IVD. CHEMICALS FROM C_3 COMPOUNDS (PROPYLENE)

1. Sources of Propylene

The propylene needs of 100,000 tons in 1971 is an evidence that this building block in the organic chemical structure of India has only slightly less importance than ethylene. Unlike ethylene, which can be derived from a second source, fermentation alcohol, propylene must come from petroleum. Processes within a refinery which give propylene are:

- Steam cracking of hydrocarbons
- Direct pyrolysis of propane
- Refinery off-gases

2. Consumption Pattern for Propylene

A study of Figure IVD-1 will give an idea of propylene end uses.

The propylene use picture in India is given in Table IVD-1.

Table IVD-1
Demand for Propylene in India
('000 tons)

Product	Demand		Norms of Consumption	Propylene Requirement	
	1994-95	1999-2000		1994-95	1999-2000
Polymer					
Polypropylene	286	420	1.02	292	428
Fibers/ Intermediates					
Acrylonitrile	139	215	1.10	153	237
Petrochemicals					
Phenol	68.3	92.2	0.60	41	55
Propylene oxide/ Propylene glycol	25.0	36	0.85	21	31
Oxo alcohol	57	84	1.00	57	84
IPA	7	10	0.85	6	9
Acrylates	10.9	15.2	0.65	7	10
Others	-	-	-	23	30
Total				**600**	**884**

Source: "SBP Handbook of Petrochemical & Downstream Projects" (1991)

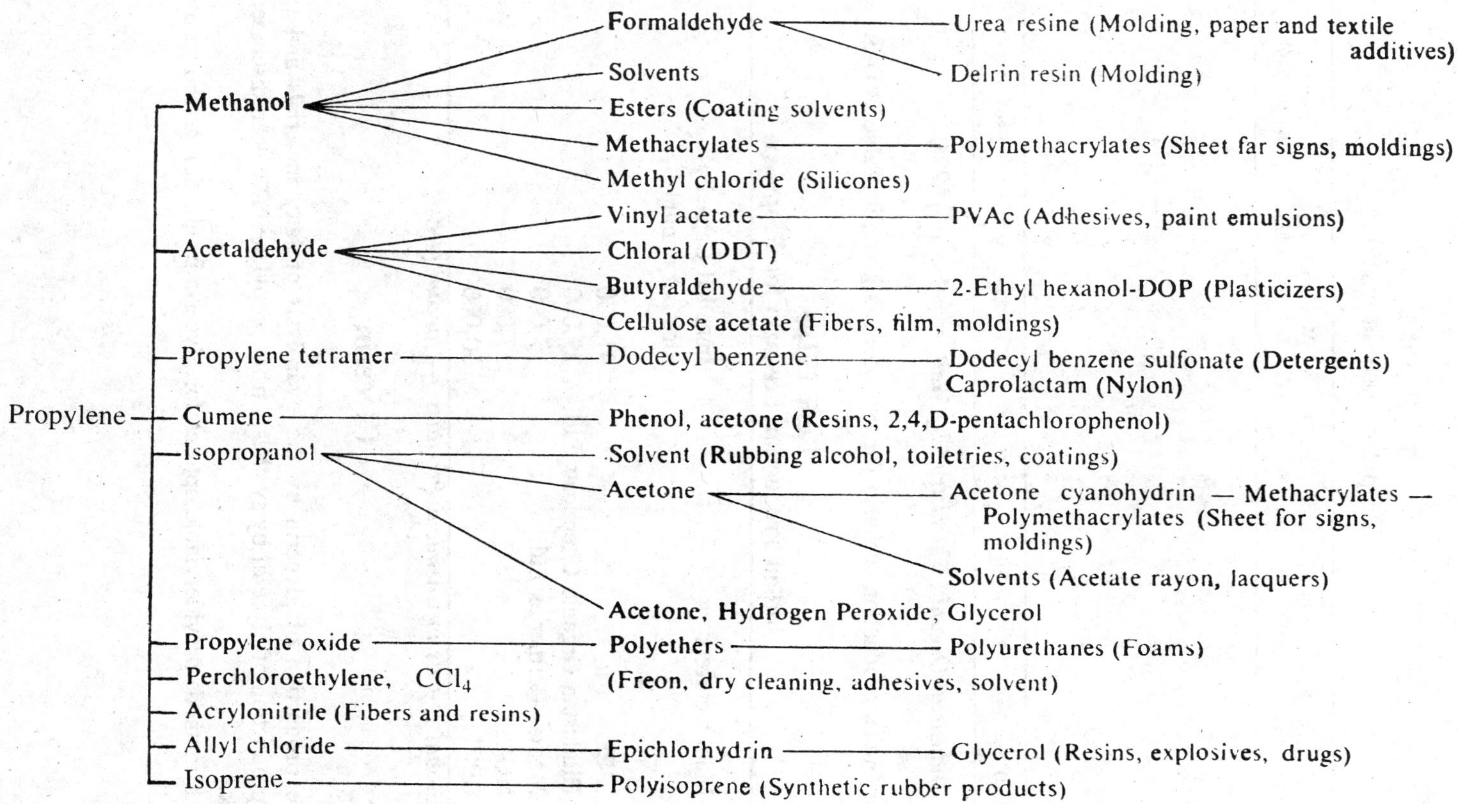

Fig. IVD-1. Synthetic chemical intermediates and products from propylene.

The world propylene use picture is given in Table IVD-2.

Table IVD-2
Propylene Use (in wt.%)

	World		USA		Western Europe		Japan		Germany	
	1988	1991	1986	1990	1986	1991	1985	1989	1986	1989
Polypropylene	41	47	35	39	36	45	45	47	17	20
Acrylonitrile	16	13	16	14	17	11	20	18	18	14
Propylene oxide	9	8	11	11	11	11	7	7	18	19
Isopropanol	6	4	6	5	6	5	3	3	6	5
Cumene	8	8	9	9	8	7	5	6	7	7
Oxo products	11	9	7	8	12	10	11	9	28	27
Oligomers	6	5	8	6	5	5	} 9	} 10	3	3
Miscellaneous	3	6	8	8	5	6			3	5
Total use (in 10^6 tonnes)	2.80	32.0	7.36	9.53	7.45	9.13	2.89	3.72	2.36	2.47

Source: "Industrial Organic Chemistry" by Weissermel et al (1994)

The Indian production scenario for propylene is given in Table IVD-3.

Table IVD-3
Indian Production Scenario for Propylene

Manufacturers	Installed Capacity tons per annum
IPCL	91,000
Hindustan Organic Chemicals Ltd.	29,000
Madras Refineries Ltd.	17,000
NOCIL	37,000
BPCL	50,000

Source: "Global Trends in Chemical Products"—Nandini (1994)

Glycerin

The production of glycerin by the hydrolysis of fatty materials and the question of alternative production of glycerol by synthesis from propylene have been discussed in Section III of this book.

Both methods provide viable options for glycerin production as shown by the following table.

Glycerin Production (% synthetic)

	1975	1980	1988
Western Europe	38	29	18
USA	50	47	33
Japan	54	37	30
World	30	28	21

Source: "Industrial Organic Chemistry" by Weissermel et al (1993)

Isopropanol

1. Pertinent Properties of Isopropanol [$(CH_3)_2 \cdot CHOH$]

Mol. wt.	60.1
M.P.	−89.5°C
B.P.	82.5°C
Density @ 20°C	0.789
Miscible with water, alcohols, ether	
Flash point	11.6°C
Ignition temperature	400°C
Explosive limits (in air)	2-12%
Toxic limit concentration	200-400 ppm

Purity: Absolute grade (99%); technical grade (91% by volume, 88% by weight)

2. Consumption Pattern

Isopropanol (IPA) is used largely as an intermediate for acetone with the next largest use as a multipurpose industrial solvent.

3. Methods of Production

- Direct catalytic hydration of propylene
- Hydration of propylene via sulfation and hydrolysis

3.1. Hydration of Propylene via Sulfation and Hydrolysis

3.1.1. Reference flow sheet: Figure IVD-2

3.1.2. Chemical reactions

(a) Sulfation

$$CH_3CH = CH_2 + H_2SO_4 \longrightarrow \underset{\text{isopropyl acid sulfate}}{(CH_3)_2CH(OSO_3H)}$$

(b) Hydrolysis

$$CH_3\underset{\substack{| \\ H}}{CH} - \underset{\substack{| \\ O-SO_3}}{CH_3} + H_2O \longrightarrow \begin{matrix} CH_3 \diagdown \\ CH_3 \diagup \end{matrix} CHOH + H_2SO_4$$

(c) Ether formation—side reaction

$$\underset{\text{diisopropyl sulfate}}{\begin{matrix} (CH_3)_2CH \diagdown \\ (CH_3)_2CH \diagup \end{matrix} S \begin{matrix} \nearrow O \\ -OH \\ \searrow O \end{matrix}} + H_2O \longrightarrow \underset{\text{diisopropyl ether}}{\begin{matrix} (CH_3)_2CH \diagdown \\ (CH_3)_2CH \diagup \end{matrix} O} + H_2SO_4$$

3.1.3. Quantitative requirements

(a) Basis: 1 ton of isopropanol (88 wt.% purity, 95% yield)

Propylene	0.680 ton
Sulfuric acid (75%)	11 kg
Sodium hydroxide	18 kg

By-products: Isopropyl ether (optional), polymers

(b) Plant capacities: 50-200 tons/day

3.1.4. Process description

Propylene, mixed with other C_2-C_3 hydrocarbons, is absorbed in 70-75% H_2SO_4 in a packed or sieve tray absorption tower or in a series of agitated reactors operating at 20-25 atms. The strongly exothermic sulfation reaction is kept at 20-30°C by refrigerated brine circulation. The solution is hydrolyzed in a steam stripper which removes the organic phase as a vapor. The weak acid bottoms are sent to the H_2SO_4 concentration plant after neutralization in a caustic solution. The product vapor is fractionally condensed, with the non-condensible olefin fraction returned to the sulfation step.

The crude isopropanol is distilled to remove the more volatile isopropyl ether. A portion of the reflux is shunted to a decanter where the ether-rich top layer is pumped back to the sulfation step or dried for product sales. The water-alcohol bottom layer is returned to the reflux-column feed.

Ether column bottoms are pumped to the isopropanol column where an 87% IPA azeotrope is taken off the top. This can be sold as product or sent to a ternary azeotropic distillation column where isopropyl ether removes the water as overhead and the bottoms are 99% absolute isopropanol.

3.1.5. Major engineering problems

(a) Sulfation reaction

Ethylene in the feed gas is not absorbed at the low temperature and acid concentration used. This eliminates a prior fractionation requirement of the light ends. The absorption of propylene depends on keeping the H_2SO_4 content between 70-80%. If C_4 or higher olefins are present, these will show up in the bottoms from the isopropanol column as they are more readily absorbed and come through the system.

(b) Direct hydration reaction

A great deal of research went into direct hydration of propylene as it was not as easy as the commercial process developed for ethanol. The process conditions of higher temperature, acid catalysis, and vapor phase can cause much polymerization of propylene. The ICI now operates a catalytic process where propylene and water are preheated and passed over catalyst pellets (tungsten oxide with zinc or other metal oxide promoters) at 250-300°C and 250 atms. Both liquid and vapor phases are present, thus creating an unusual reactor design problem.

4. Economics

Isopropyl alcohol production is closely related to acetone demands. One phenol process gives acetone as a co-product. The synthetic glycerin process outlined in Chapter IIIA uses isopropanol as a starting raw material and produces acetone as a co-product. The Wacker process

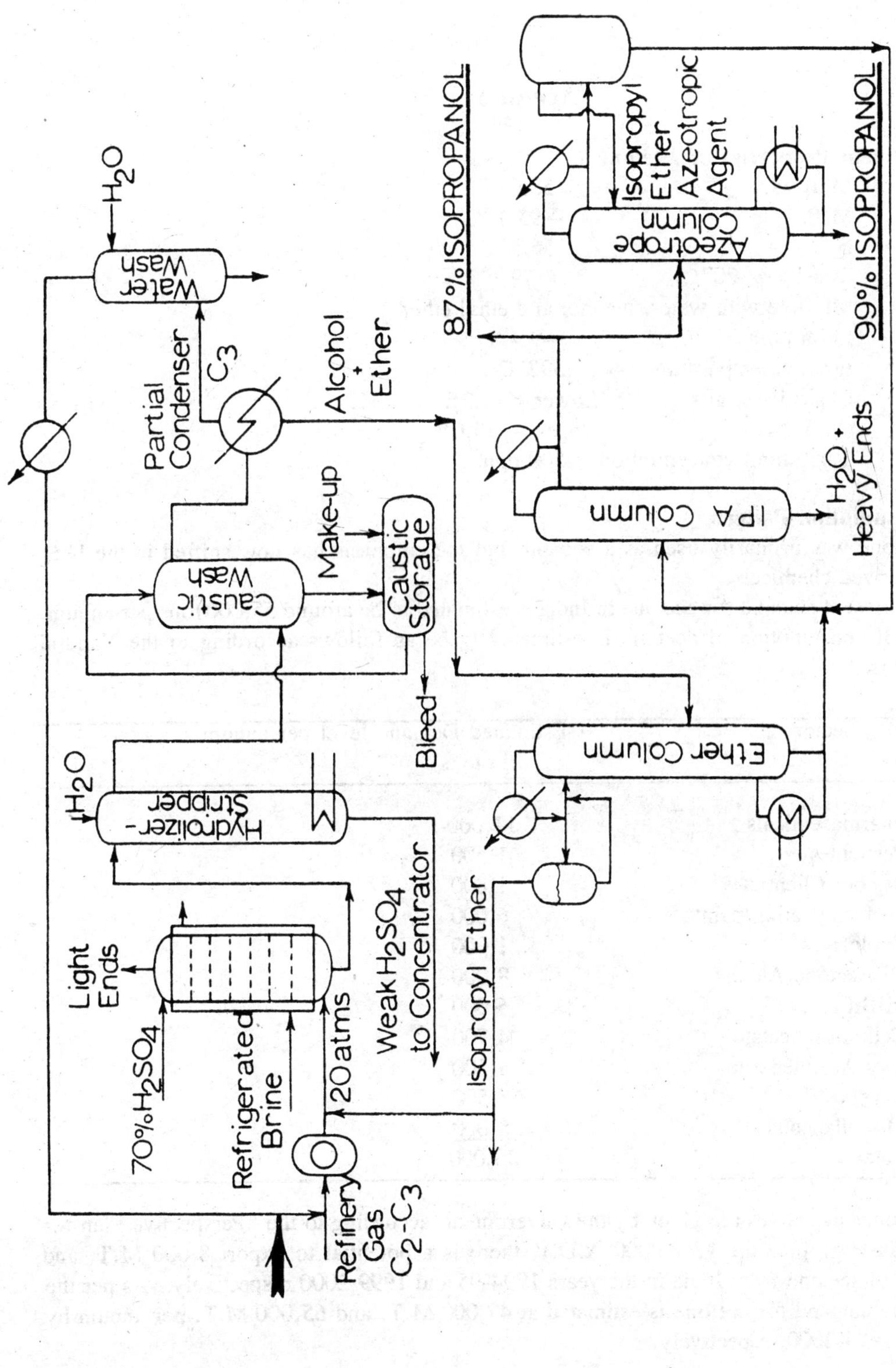

Fig. IVD-2. Isopropyl alcohol by indirect hydration of propylene.

for producing acetone directly from propylene will undoubtedly have an impact on isopropyl alcohol markets.

Acetone

1. Pertinent Properties of Acetone

Mol. wt.	58.08
M.P.	–95.1°C
B.P.	56.5°C
Density @ 20°C	0.79
Miscible with water, alcohol and ethyl ether	
Flash point	–9.4°F
Ignition temperature	592°C
Explosive limits:	Lower = 2.2%
	Upper = 13.0%
Toxic limit concentration	500 ppm

2. Consumption Pattern

Acetone was primarily used as a solvent, but the emphasis has now shifted in the U.S. to acetone-derived chemicals.

The present demand for acetone in India is estimated to be around 55,000 tons per annum. The pattern of consumption of acetone is estimated to be as follows according to the Nandini Chemical Journal:

Sector	Estimated Demand level per annum (in tons)
Pharmaceuticals	11,000
Pesticides	1,500
Rubber Chemicals	1,800
Surface coating/paints	6,000
Explosives	1,000
Di Acetone Alcohol	8,000
MIBK	6,000
Cellulose Acetate	4,700
Oxy Acetylene gas	4,500
Acrylics	5,500
Miscellaneous	5,000
Total	55,000

If proper incentives are given by the Government, according to the "Perspective Plan for Chemical Industry (up to the year 2000 A.D.)" there is a potential to export 8,000 M.T. and 10,000 M.T. of acetone from India in the years 1994-95 and 1999-2000 respectively. As per the same plan, the demand for acetone is estimated at 47,000 M.T. and 65,000 M.T. per annum by 1994-95 and 1999-2000 respectively.

As per the "Report of the Committee for Perspective Planning for Petrochemical Industry (1986-2000 A.D.)" the demand for acetone is expected to rise to 47,100 M.T. and 64,700 M.T. by 1994-95 and 1999-2000 A.D. respectively.

The names and addresses of acetone manufacturers in India are given in Table IVD-4.

Table IVD-4
Names and Addresses of Units Manufacturing Acetone in India

Herdillia Chemicals Ltd.
Plot No. 2, TTC Industrial Area, Thane-Belapur Road, Thane - 400 601 (Maharashtra)

Hindustan Organic Chemicals Ltd.
P.O. Rasayani, Dist. Raigad (Maharashtra)

Krishna Sakahari Sakhar Karkhana Ltd.
P.O. Shivanagar - 415 108, Dist. Satara (Maharashtra)

National Organic Chemical Industries Ltd.
Plot No. 5, TTC Industrial Area, Thane-Belapur Road - 400 601 (Maharashtra)

Shree Chalthan Vibhag Khand Udyog Sakahari Mandli Ltd.
Chalthan, Dist. Surat (Gujarat)

Sirsilk Ltd.
Sirpur, Kaghaz Nagar, Adilabad (A.P.)

Walwa Sakahari Sakhar Karkhana Ltd.
P.O. Sakharale - 415 414, Dist. Sangli (Maharashtra)

Source: "SBP Handbook of Projects for Corporate Diversification" (1992)

The worldwide distribution of acetone production is as follows:

Acetone Production ('000 tons)

	1987	1989	1991
USA	943	1,134	984
Western Europe	867	825	983
CIS	375	323	295
Japan	260	337	354

Source: "Industrial Organic Chemistry" by Weissermel et al (1993)

The breakdown of acetone use worldwide is shown in Table IVD-5.

Table IVD-5
Acetone Use (in wt.%)

	World		USA		Western Europe		Japan	
	1988	1991	1984	1989	1985	1991	1985	1990
Methyl methacrylate	26	29	32	41	32	26	37	32
Methyl isobutyl ketone	10	9	10	14	10	9	23	23
Bisphenol-A	8	10	10	15	10	10	10	13
Miscellaneous	56	52	48	30	48	55	30	32
Total use (in 10^6 tonnes)	2.98	3.10	0.82	1.05	0.83	0.93	0.25	0.30

Source: "Industrial Organic Chemistry" by Weissermel et al (1993)

3. Methods of Production

3.1. Classification of Processes

3.1.1. Catalytic dehydrogenation of isopropanol

3.1.2. Co-product of phenol process utilizing cumene (see Section IVF)

3.1.3. Co-product of glycerin-H_2O_2 process (see Chapter IIIA)

3.1.4. Oxidation of butane

3.1.5. Oxidation of propylene (Wacker process)

3.1.6. Fermentation of molasses

3.2. Catalytic Dehydrogenation of Isopropanol

3.2.1. Reference flow sheet: Figure IVD-3

3.2.2. Chemical reactions

(a) $(CH_3)_2CHOH \rightarrow CH_3COCH_3 + H_2$

(b) $(CH_3)_2CHOH + \frac{1}{2}O_2$ (air) $\rightarrow CH_3COCH_3 + H_2O$

3.2.3. Quantitative requirements

(a) Basis: 1 ton of acetone (99% pure, 90% yield)

Isopropanol (88% grade) 1.30 tons

(b) Plant capacities: 15-60 tons/day

3.2.4. Process description

Isopropanol vapor compressed to 3 atms. is preheated by reactor effluent heat exchange and passed through a tubular catalytic reactor maintained at 500°C with the catalyst consisting of copper or brass deposited on porous carrier. The hot reaction gases pass through a water-cooled condenser and thence into a water scrubber where final traces of isopropanol and acetone are removed from hydrogen. Condensate and water scrub liquor are fractionated to give product grade acetone overhead and dilute isopropanol bottoms. These are further fractionated to give 88% isopropanol recycle with the water recycled to the water scrubber.

3.2.5. Major engineering problems

(a) Process alternative: Combined oxidation-dehydrogenation

A mixture of air and isopropanol vapors is passed through a catalyst containing silver or copper at 400-600°C. Acetone is formed according to reaction 3.2.2(a). The remainder of the process is similar to straight dehyrogenation, with nitrogen released from the top of the scrubber. Yields are equivalent.

(b) Selection of operating pressure

Reaction is favored at low pressures, but is maintained at 3-4 atms. to reduce the size of reactor and water circulation load for a given plant capacity.

(c) Design for hydrogen at high temperature-pressure

High H_2 concentration at 500°C and 4 atms. requires chrome steel in the reactor to avoid embrittlement problems which show up as blistering, cracking and loss of strength of the pressure vessel walls if mild steel were used.

4. Economics

In the planned economic growth, acetone and phenol from cumene will be a serious competitor for the isopropanol dehydrogenation process. One advantage for the latter is flexibility of plant since methyl ethyl ketone, a chemical in large demand as a solvent, can be made from *sec*-butanol in the same equipment.

Cumene (Isopropyl benzene)

1. Pertinent Properties of Cumene [$C_6H_5 \cdot CH \cdot (CH_3)_2$]

Mol. wt.	120.19
M.P.	–96.9°C
B.P.	152.5°C
Density @ 20°C	0.862
Miscible with alcohols, ether, insoluble in water	
Flash point	39°C
Ignition point	138°C
Toxic limit concentration	250 ppm
Purity: Greater than 99.5% for use in phenol-acetone process	

2. Consumption Pattern

Cumene was first developed as a high octane addition for engine fuels. This use has been overshadowed by the phenol process which uses cumene as the starting material and produces acetone as a co-product (see Section IVF under Phenol).

3. Cumene Production by Propylene Alkylation of Benzene

3.1. Reference Flow Sheet: Figure IVD-4

3.2. Chemical Reactions

(a) Main reaction

$$C_6H_6 + CH_3 \cdot CH{=}CH_2 \rightarrow \underset{\text{isopropyl benzene (Cumene)}}{C_6H_5 \cdot C_3H_7}; \quad \Delta H = -23.76 \text{ Kcal}$$

(b) Side reaction

$$C_6H_6 + nCH_3CH{=}CH_2 \rightarrow \underset{\text{polyisopropyl benzene}}{C_6H_{6-n} \cdot (C_3H_7)_n}$$

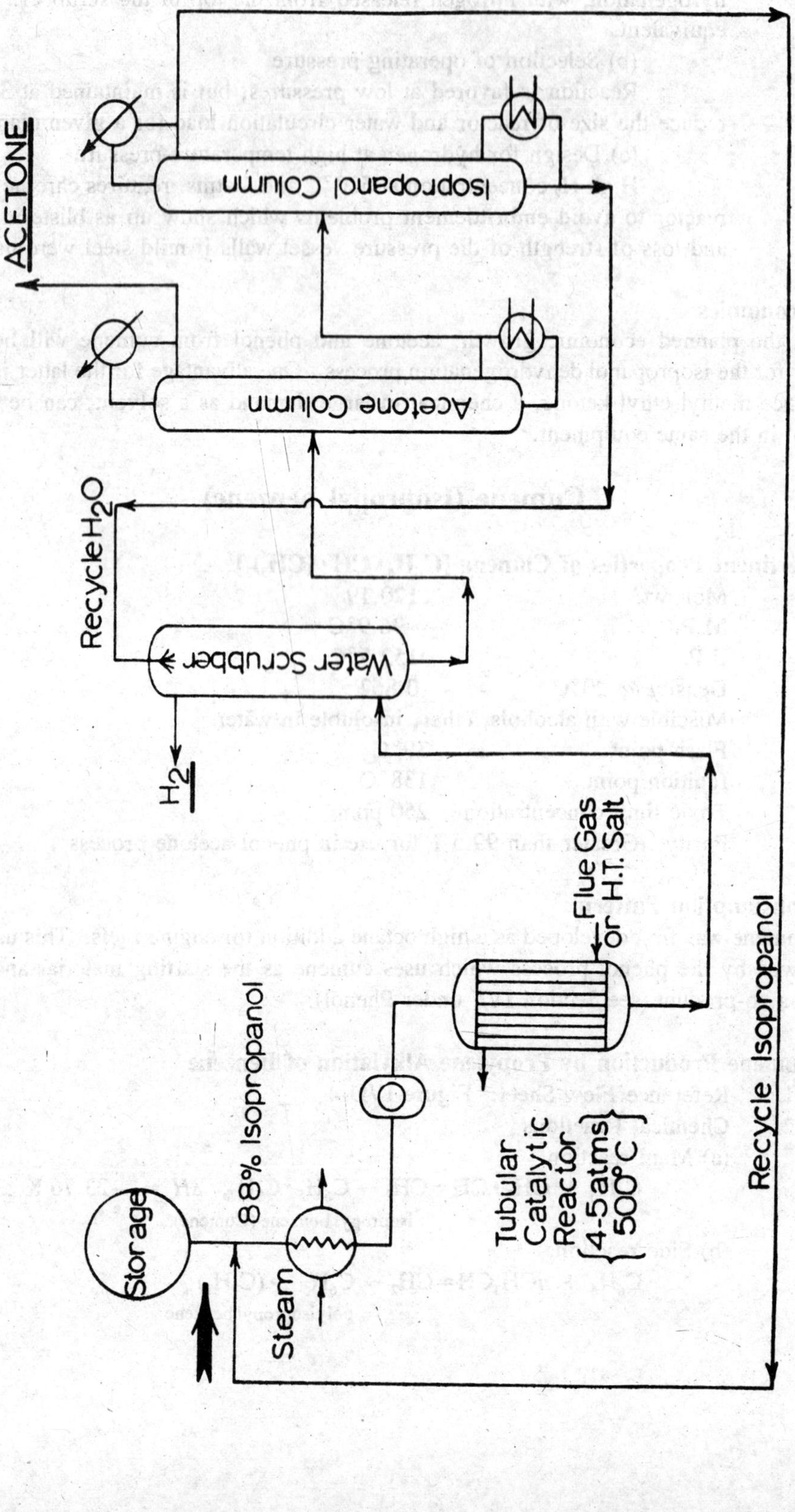

Fig. IVD-3. Acetone by dehydrogenation of isopropanol.

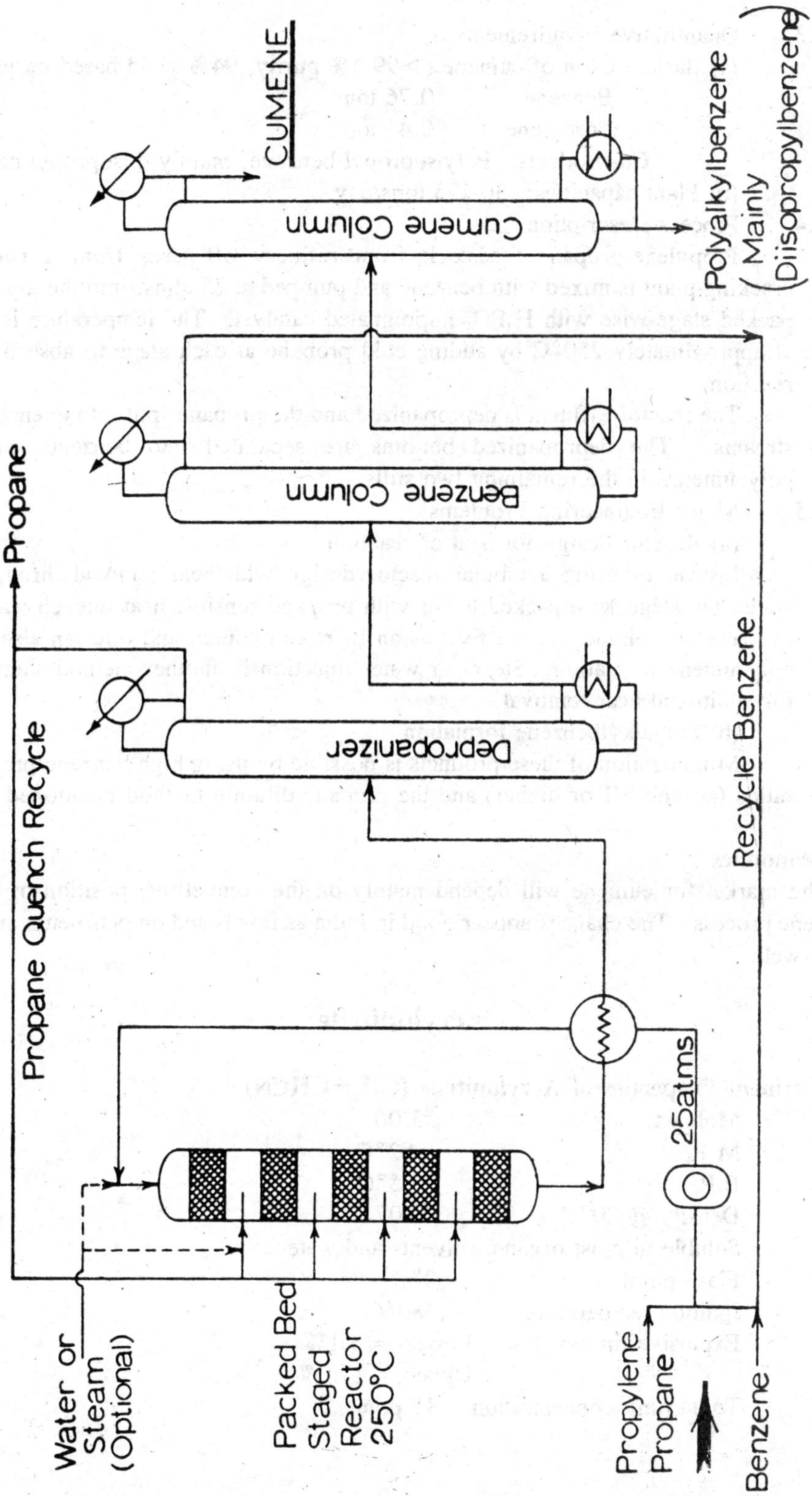

Fig. IVD-4. Cumene (Isopropyl benzene) via propylene alkylation of benzene.

3.3. Quantitative Requirements

(a) Basis: 1 ton of cumene (>99.5% purity, 94% yield based on propylene)

Benzene	0.76 ton
Propylene	0.41 ton

Co-products: Polyisopropyl benzene, mainly diisopropyl benzene

(b) Plant capacities: 30-175 tons/day

3.4. Process Description

Propylene-propane feedstock from refinery off-gases from a naphtha-steam cracking plant is mixed with benzene and pumped at 25 atms. into the top of a reactor packed stage-wise with H_3PO_4 impregnated catalyst. The temperature is maintained at approximately 250°C by adding cold propane at each stage to absorb the heat of reaction.

The reactor effluent is depropanized and the propane split into quench or product streams. The depropanized bottoms are separated into benzene, cumene, and polycumenes in the remaining two stills.

3.5. Major Engineering Problems

(a) Reactor design for heat of reaction

Instead of using a tubular reactor design with heat removal through the tube walls, the stage-wise packed tower with propane sensible heat quench was designed. Propane was already in the feed as an inert component and dilution also minimized polycumene formation. Steam or water injection is another method sometimes used for additional heat removal.

(b) Polyalkylbenzene formation

Minimization of these products is possible by using high benzene/propylene feed ratios (around 5/1 or higher) and the propane dilution method mentioned above.

4. Economics

The market for cumene will depend mainly on the competitive position of the phenol-from-cumene process. The chances appear good in India as it is based on petroleum and produces acetone as well.

Acrylonitrile

1. Pertinent Properties of Acrylonitrile ($CH_2=CHCN$)

Mol. wt.	53.06
M.P.	—82°C
B.P.	78.5°C
Density @ 20°C	0.807
Soluble in most organic solvents and water	
Flash point	0°C
Ignition temperature	480°C
Explosive limits:	Lower = 3.1%
	Upper = 17.0%
Toxic limit concentration	15 ppm

2. Consumption Pattern

Acrylonitrile is the cheapest of the acrylic monomer group and has good reactivity at C≡N bond and the double bond. Its end uses are largely for polymers.

2.1. End Use Pattern

The worldwide pattern of acrylonitrile use is shown in Table IVD-6.

Table IVD-6
Uses of Acrylonitrile (in wt.%)

	World		USA		Western Europe		Japan	
	1984	1991	1984	1990	1985	1991	1984	1990
Acrylic fibers	73	59	52	37	73	60	65	52
ABS and SAN plastics	12	20	21	26	11	16	15	26
Nitrile rubber	3	4	3	3	3	3	4	4
Adiponitrile	6	9	13	22	8	11	4	6
Remaining uses, including acrylamide	6	8	11	18	5	10	12	12
Total use (in 1000 tonnes)	3150	3850	600	659	1133	1145	550	654

Source: "Industrial Organic Chemistry" by Weissermel et al (1993)

3. Methods of Production

3.1. Classification of Processes

3.1.1. Propylene-ammonia-air oxidation reaction
3.1.2. Acetylene-hydrogen cyanide reaction
3.1.3. Ethylene cyanohydrin pyrolysis
3.1.4. Acetaldehyde-hydrogen cyanide reaction

3.2. Propylene-Ammonia-Air Oxidation Process

3.2.1. Reference flow sheet: Figure IVD-5

3.2.2. Chemical reaction

$$CH_2{=}CH{-}CH_3 + NH_3 + 3/2O_2 \rightarrow CH_2{=}CHCN + 3H_2O;\ \Delta H = -136.2 \text{ Kcal}$$

3.2.3. Quantitative requirements

(a) Basis: 1 ton of acrylonitrile (99.0+ %, 80% yield)

Propylene	0.996 ton
Ammonia	0.45 ton
Air	5.2 tons or 4,000 Nm^3

By-products:

Acetonitrile (CH_3CN)	0.09 ton
Hydrogen cyanide (HCN)	0.08 ton

(b) Plant capacities: 50-125 tons/day

3.2.4. Process description

A C_3 refinery stream is introduced along with ammonia and air via spargers into a fluidized bed catalytic reactor. Conditions within the reactor are 1.5-3 atms. pressure, a temperature of 400-500°C, and a contact time of several seconds.

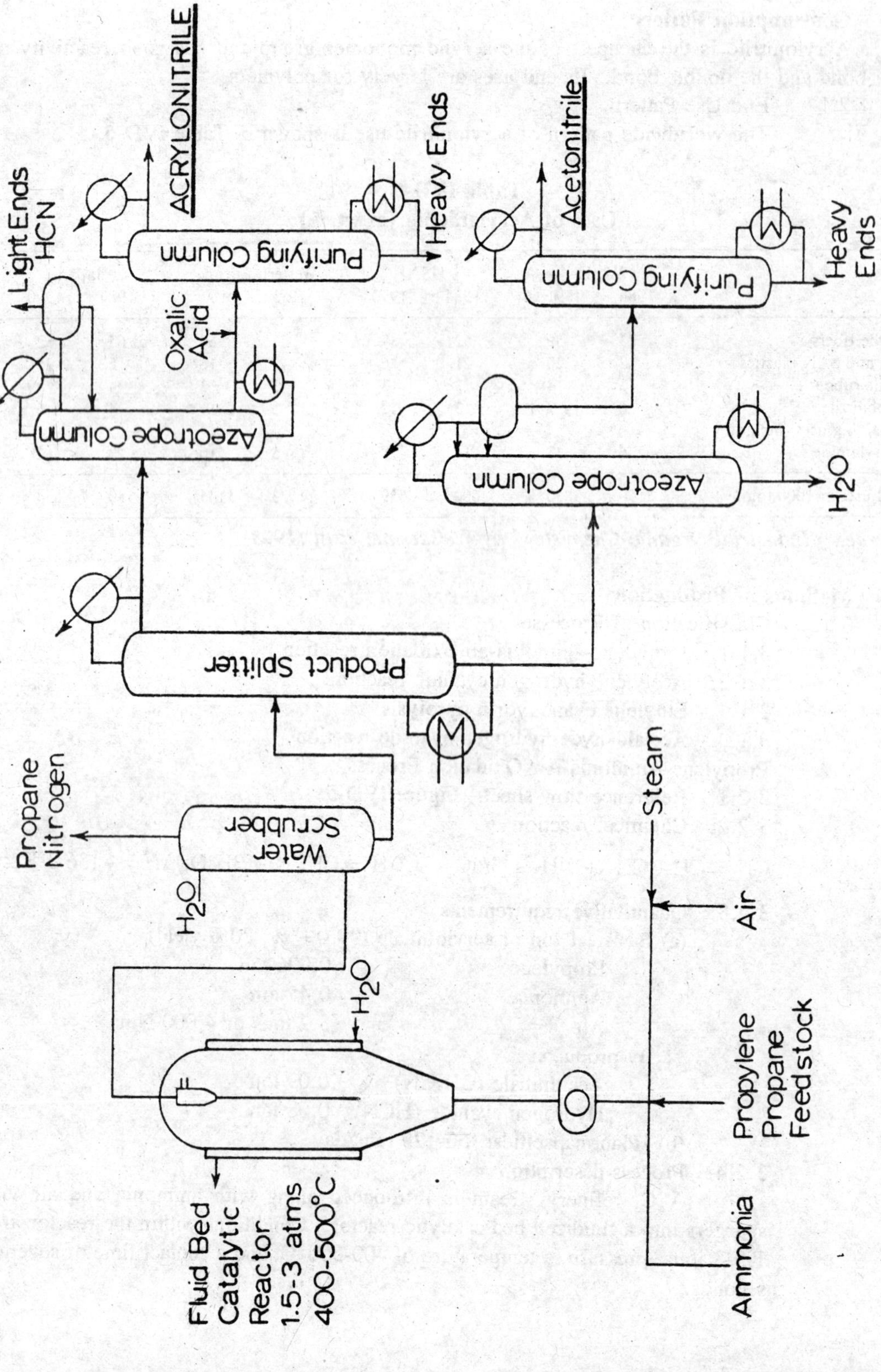

Fig. IVD-5. Acrylonitrile from propylene ammonia oxidation.

The reactor effluent is scrubbed with water to remove the desired products in an aqueous solution which is further fractionated to give wet acrylonitrile and acetonitrile. Both are further purified by azeotropic and conventional distillation.

The world pattern for acrylonitrile production is as follows:

AN Production ('000 tons)

	1987	1989	1991
Western Europe	1,207	1,254	942
USA	1,157	1,184	1,115
Japan	573	576	622

At present there is only one unit manufacturing acrylonitrile in India:

Indian Petrochemicals Corp. Ltd.
P.O. Petrochemicals, Dist. Baroda (Gujarat)

Its present licensed and installed capacity is 30,000 M.T. per annum. Its production of acrylonitrile in 1988-89 and 1989-90 was 20,317 M.T. and 25,211 M.T. respectively.

As per the "Report of the Committee for Perspective Planning of Petrochemical Industry (1986-2000 A.D.)," the demand for acrylonitrile is expected to rise to 140,000 M.T. and 215,000 M.T. by 1994-95 and 1999-2000 respectively.

3.2.5. Major engineering problems

(a) Reaction kinetics

This chemical reaction is one of the few commercialized where three reactants and a solid catalytic surface are all necessarily involved in producing only a single major product with good selectivity. The molybdenum-bismuth catalyst, developed by the Sohio Co. who have patented the process, provides more than an adsorptive surface in furnishing oxygen by surface reaction and transfer.

(b) Catalyst performance

The microspheroidal catalyst in the size range of 0.01-0.03 mm is typical of conventional fluid bed catalytic cracking. Regeneration is not required and activity is stable provided desulfurized feed is used. Sulfur leads to sulfite deposits which mask active sites. The catalyst can be revivified by extended air regeneration.

The catalyst has excellent attrition resistance, but some fines are formed which must be recovered by multiple cyclones to extract the Mo-Bi content for reuse.

(c) Feedstock limitations

Propylene concentration is not critical to the process chemistry with as low as 30% C_3H_6 giving the same high yield. It is better economically to fractionate the propane from propylene ahead of the reactor, for it is more costly to recover unconsumed propane from the water scrubber when it contains a large percentage of air.

(d) Product purification

Impurities in the final acrylonitrile column which give trouble are saturated carbonylic cyanohydrins (HO•R•CN). These dissociate to form volatile contaminants. Oxalic acid complexes these compounds, forcing them into the heavy ends without dissociation. Oxalic acid is effective, economical, less corrosive than the mineral acids and has decreased reboiler fouling.

4. Economics

The Sohio process, which was commercialized in 1960, is more economical than others based on ethylene or acetylene. Its capital cost has been reduced by a factor of 2 and it uses ammonia abundantly available within the petrochemical plant complex. This new development gives the cheapest acrylic monomer, so acrylic fibers such as Orlon and Dynel should capture more of the fabrics market. Acrylonitrile will also enter into more copolymerized products.

Acetonitrile by-product has proven a good solvent competitor for acetone, particularly in the solvent extraction of butadiene and other dienes (see Figure IVC-2).

Isoprene

1. Pertinent Properties of Isoprene ($CH_2=CH-C(CH_3)=CH_2$)

Mol. wt.	68.11
M.P.	−120°C
B.P.	34°C
Density @ 20°C	0.681
Miscible with alcohols, ether	
Flash point	−53°C
Ignition temperature	220°C
Toxic limit concentration	250 ppm

2. Consumption Pattern

Polymerized isoprene (polyisoprene) closely resembles natural rubber chemically and is expected to add flexibility to the synthetic rubber program. This is the only market for the monomer.

3. Methods of Production

3.1. Classification of Processes

3.1.1. Isomerization of propylene dimer

3.1.2. Isobutylene-formaldehyde reaction

3.1.3. Methyl ethyl ketone-formaldehyde reaction

3.1.4. Acetone-acetylene reaction

3.1.5. By-product from isopentane/isopentene dehydrogenation

The propylene dimer process is the most economical of the group and produces the high purity grade isoprene required for polymerization.

3.2. Isomerization of Propylene Dimer

3.2.1. Reference flow sheet: Figure IVD-6

3.2.2. Chemical reactions

(a) Dimerization

$$2CH_3CH{=}CH_2 \xrightarrow[\substack{150\text{-}250^\circ C \\ 200\ \text{atms.}}]{(C_3H_7)_3Al} CH_2{=}\underset{}{C}(CH_3){-}CH_2{-}CH_2{-}CH_3$$

2-methyl-1-pentene

(b) Isomerization

$$CH_2{=}C(CH_3){-}CH_2{-}CH_2{-}CH_3 \xrightarrow[150\text{-}300^\circ C]{\text{acid catalyst}} CH_3{-}C(CH_3){=}CH{-}CH_2{-}CH_3$$

2-methyl-2-pentene

(c) Pyrolysis

$$CH_3{-}C(CH_3){=}CH{-}CH_2{-}CH_3 \xrightarrow[650\text{-}800^\circ C]{HBr} CH_2{=}C(CH_3){-}CH{=}CH_2 + CH_4$$

isoprene

3.2.3. Quantitative requirements

(a) Basis: 1 ton of isoprene (99.0+ % purity, 85% yield)

Propylene 1.46 tons

Minor quantities of tripropyl aluminum and hydrogen bromide catalysts

(b) Plant capacities: 30-60 tons/day

3.2.4. Process description

A compressed propylene refinery cut is mixed with tripropyl aluminum catalyst plus carrier solvent at 200 atms. pressure in a stirred reactor fitted with heat transfer surface to remove the exothermic heat of reaction. A conversion of 60-95% with a temperature range of 150-250°C is possible.

The reactor effluent passes directly to a flash tower which separates the catalyst and carrier solvent (saturated naphtha fraction). The top products, 2-methyl-1-pentene, unreacted propylene, and light hydrocarbons present in the feed are separated by successive distillations.

Isomerization occurs in a packed bed reactor containing an acid type catalyst. Process conditions range from 150°-300°C with liquid hourly space velocities of 15 to 0.5 respectively. Fractionation and recycle of dimer is required to obtain a 98-99% ultimate yield.

The final step involves pyrolysis of 2-methyl-2-pentene to isoprene. This is done in a tubular cracking furnace with HBr as a catalyst and steam as the diluent. Reaction occurs in the range of 650-800°C and residence times of 0.3 to 0.5 second. Acetylenic compounds are avoided under these conditions.

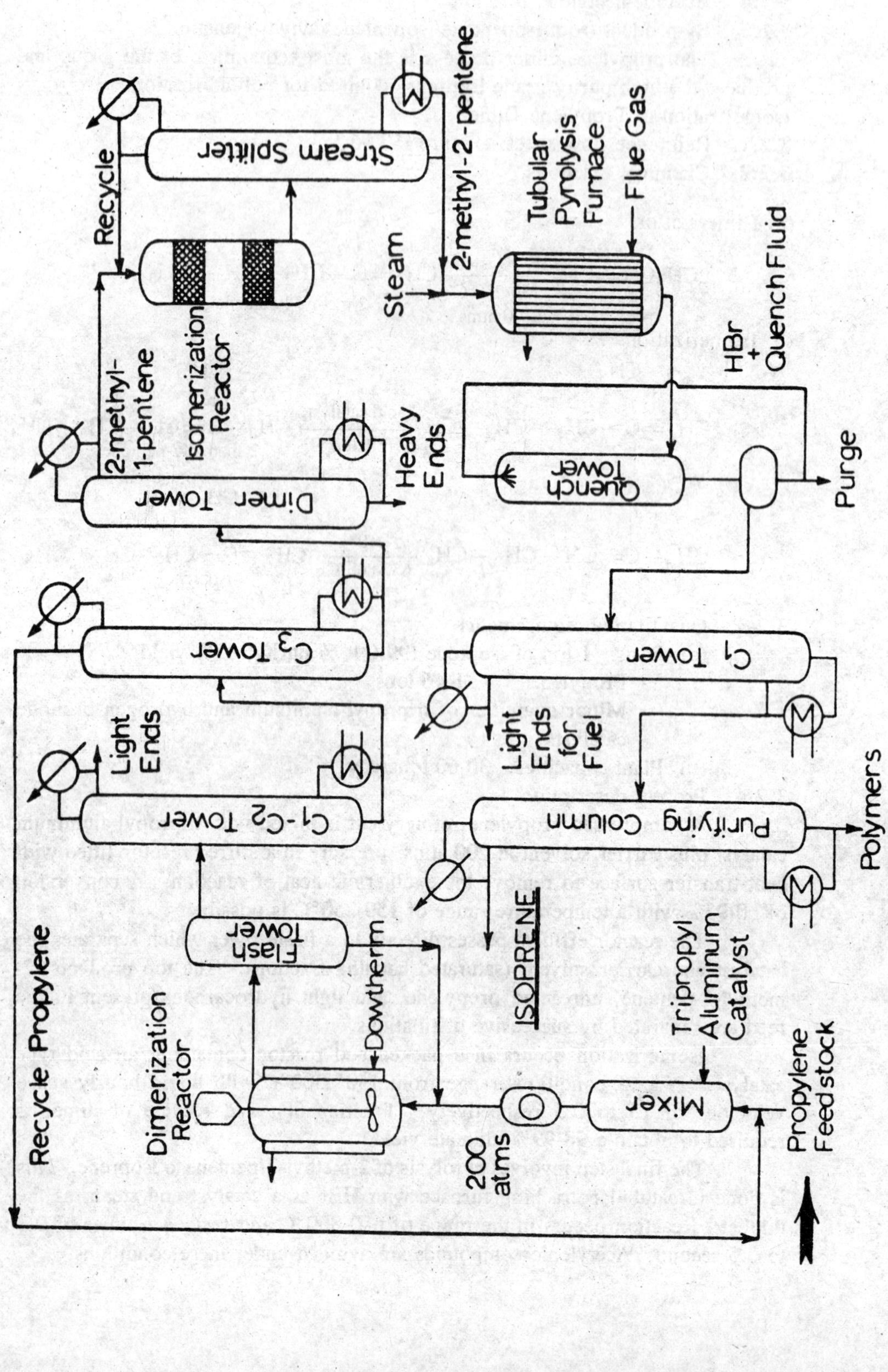

Fig. IVD-6. Isoprene from propylene dimer.

From the pyrolysis furnace, the hot vapors are quenched with a solvent to recover HBr for recycle. The hydrocarbons are fractionated to separate methane and light gases for fuel and recover unreacted 2-methyl-2-pentene for recycle.

3.2.5. Major engineering problems

(a) Dimerization step

Trialuminum alkyl is extremely active towards polar compounds which must be removed from the feed to avoid excessive loss of expensive catalyst. Low concentrations of propylene in the feed will work satisfactorily so there is the economic balance of reactor size versus a prior fractionation step. The high pressure of 200 atms. requires an expensive reactor and it is better to run with high propylene concentrations.

A new vapor-phase dimerization-solid catalyst system has been developed which removes the necessity of highly purifying the feed and recycling a liquid phase catalyst.

(b) Isomerization step

Catalyst deterioration occurs on the acid carrier surface by carbon or polymer formation. Revivification is possible by oxidative regeneration of the fixed bed.

4. Economics

Polyisoprene, the only use for isoprene, has many of the properties of natural rubber, but lacks its good adhesion for tire building.

Use, at present, is limited to rubber specialty items and latex emulsions. The propylene dimer process, a collaborative effort of Goodyear Tire and Rubber Co. and Scientific Design Co., was put on stream in late 1962 with the smallest capital investment of any route to elastomers—natural or synthetic. This low-cost product will boost the use of this type of elastomer.

Both isoprene and butadiene can be polymerized with a stereospecific catalyst in the same equipment and a range of *cis*-4-polybutadiene-polyisoprene elastomer blends can be easily manufactured at the same site (see Chapter VB—Elastomers, for more details on various product possibilities).

Polypropylene

As compared to the dimerization of propylene to propylene dimer which can be converted to isoprene—a more important process today is the production of high polymers of propylene.

Polypropylene will be discussed under polymers in Section V of this book.

As noted there, polypropylene is a rapidly growing product, making considerable inroad into the market for other plastic products.

Epichlorohydrin

Epichlorohydrin, 1-chloro-2,3-epoxypropane is another propylene derivative of industrial importance. Its manufacture involves the following stages:

i) High temperature chlorination of propylene to Allyl chloride
ii) Conversion of allyl chloride to dichlorohydrin with hypochlorous acid in an aqueous medium
iii) Selective dehydrochlorination of dichlorohydrins to epichlorohydrin with an alkali

The worldwide picture of epichlorohydrin production is as follows:

Epichlorohydrin Production ('000 tons)

	1985	1987	1989
USA	196	191	225
Western Europe	168	172	165
Japan	55	85	94

Propylene Oxide

1. Pertinent Properties of Propylene Oxide $(CH_3—CH—CH_2)$ (with O bridging the two CH/CH₂ carbons)

Mol. wt.	58.08
M.P.	−104.4°C
B.P.	33.9°C
Density @ 20°C	0.831
Soluble in water, alcohols, ether	
Flash point	−34°C
Explosive limits:	Lower = 2.1%
	Upper = 22%
Toxic limit concentration	250 ppm

2. Consumption Pattern

Propylene oxide is an interesting chemical to study because of its similarities and differences as compared with ethylene oxide (see Section IVC). For example, the toxic character of ethylene glycol, the hydrate of ethylene oxide, has created markets for propylene glycol in cellophane, food, and drug industries. The largest use for the glycol is in polyester resins.

The worldwide picture for propylene oxide production is as follows:

Propylene Oxide Production (in '000 tons)

	1987	1989	1991
USA	1,184	1,452	1,300
Western Europe	982	1,099	1,251
Japan	250	296	328

Source: "Industrial Organic Chemistry" by Weissermel et al (1993)

Trends in propylene oxide use are summarized in Table IVD-7.

Table IVD-7
Use of Propylene Oxide (in wt.%)

	USA 1986	USA 1990	Western Europe 1985	Western Europe 1991	Japan 1983	Japan 1990	World 1986	World 1991
Polypropylene glycol and propoxylated products for polyurethanes	61	62	66	71	74	66	64	65
Propylene glycol	28	26	22	19	16	21	21	21
Miscellaneous (glycol ethers, glycerin, isopropanolamine, etc.)	11	12	12	10	10	13	15	14
Total use (in 1000 tonnes)	907	1300	926	1326	201	310	2587	3321

Source: "Industrial Organic Chemistry" by Weissermel et al (1993)

3. Methods of Production

3.1. Classification of Processes

3.1.1. Chlorhydrin route

3.1.2. Direct oxidation

3.2. Chlorhydrin Process

3.2.1. Reference flow sheet: Figure IVD-7

3.2.2. Chemical reactions

(a) Chlorhydrination

$$CH_3CH{=}CH_2 + HOCl \rightarrow CH_3\cdot CHCl\cdot CH_2OH$$

(b) Dehydrochlorination

$$2CH_3{\cdot}CHCl{\cdot}CH_2OH + Ca(OH)_2 \longrightarrow 2CH_3CH{-}CH_2\ (\text{epoxide, }{-}O{-}\text{ bridge}) + CaCl_2 + 2H_2O$$

3.2.3. Quantitative requirements

(a) Basis: 1 ton of propylene oxide (99+ % purity, 80% yield)

Propylene	0.91 ton
Chlorine	2.0 tons
Lime (100% CaO)	1.6 tons

Electricity	150 KWH
Steam	12 tons
Water	240 tons

By-products: 0.97 ton of calcium chloride
0.10-0.15 ton of propylene dichloride

(b) Plant capacities: 30-200 tons/day

3.2.4. Process description

Propylene, chlorine and water are introduced into the bottom of a packed tower where reaction forms the chlorhydrin. The reaction mechanism is formation of hypochlorous acid (HOCl or HClO) which reacts rapidly with propylene. The chlorine/propylene ratio of gaseous feed to the tower is chosen so that the liquid effluent contains 4-5% chlorhydrin. The reaction is exothermic and maximum tower temperature is held at 50°C. A conversion of 25-40% is attained, the ultimate yield of chlorhydrin is 87-90% with most of the by-product as propylene dichloride. Unreacted propylene is scrubbed with caustic to remove HCl, which also forms, and then recycled.

3.2.5. Major engineering problems

(a) Corrosion

Wet chlorine system plus calcium chloride in the 50-100°C operating range requires materials of construction such as Duchlor, Durimet, Haveg, ceramic or glass.

(b) Chlorine losses

The relatively high cost of chlorine forces an optimization of the HClO concentration versus tower reaction capacity. The chlorine is ultimately lost as $CaCl_2$ or free Cl_2.

(c) Calcium chloride by-product

The use of lime to neutralize the HCl and aid in rapid dehydrochlorination creates a $CaCl_2$ waste stream. If a way could be found to avoid neutralization and yield only HCl, this acid has more value either by itself or when converted to chlorine for recycle.

3.3. Propylene Oxide by Direct Oxidation

Processes for the direct manufacture of propylene oxide by the single step oxidation of propylene have been the subject of intensive commercial development.

One possible route which is now being commercialized by Scientific Design Co. in the U.S. involves peroxidizing an organic compound, reacting the peroxide with propylene to give propylene oxide and then recovering a useful organic product from the peroxide.

The first commercial plant for direct manufacture of propylene oxide from propylene was built at Bayport, Texas, by Oxirane Chemical Co., a joint venture of Halcon, Inc. (a subsidiary of Scientific Design Co., the engineer-contractor) and Arco Chemical Co. (a subsidiary of Atlantic-Richfield Co., suppliers of propylene feedstock).

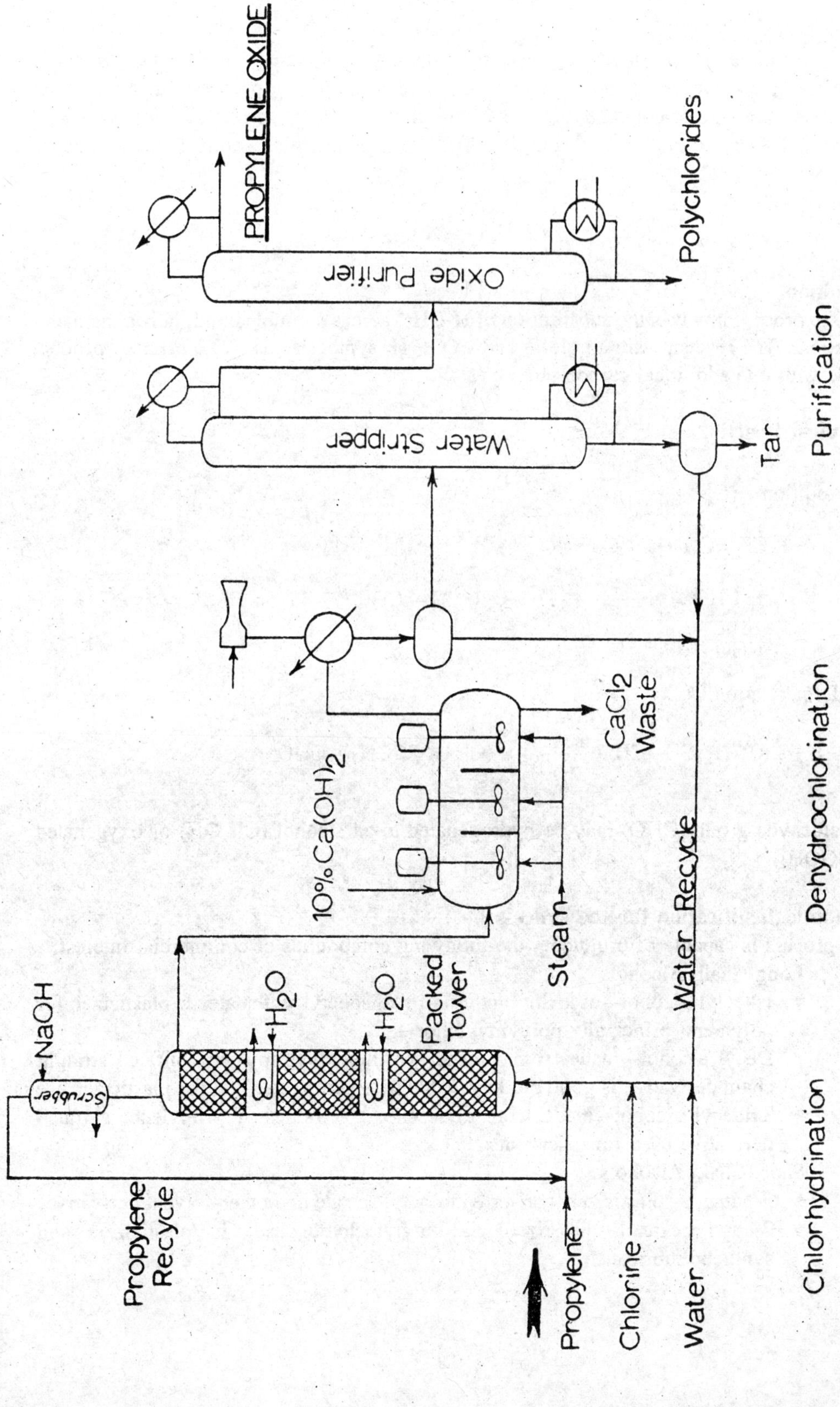

Fig. IVD-7. Propylene oxide via chlorhydrin.

4. Economics

Section 2 points out the increasing new uses for propylene oxide. It is advantageous to adapt units formerly used for making ethylene oxide via chlorhydrin, a process which has been replaced by direct oxidation of ethylene rather than to build new plants specifically for propylene oxide, however. This is an example of complete utilization of facilities within a petrochemical complex.

Oxo Process

1. Definition

An Oxo process involves the substitution of H-CHO across a double bond, hence the name hydroformylation. The reactants are an olefin and $CO + H_2$ synthesis gas. The primary product is an aldehyde with one additional carbon atom.

2. Chemical Reactions

2.1. Addition $(C_n \rightarrow C_{n+1})$

$$\left.\begin{array}{c} R\,CH{=}CH_2 \\ + \\ H\,CHO \\ \text{or} \\ CHO\,H \end{array}\right\} \xrightarrow{\text{Co Salt}} \begin{cases} R\,CH_2 \cdot CH_2 \cdot CHO \\ R \cdot CH{-}CH_3 \\ \quad\;\; | \\ \quad\; CHO \end{cases}$$

2.2. Dimerization $(C_{n+1} \rightarrow C_{2n+2})$

$$2\,R \cdot CH_2 \cdot CH_2 \cdot CHO \xrightarrow[H_2O]{\text{Zn salt}} R\,(CH_2)_3\,R\,(CH_2)_2\,CHO$$

The aldehyde group (CHO) may be hydrogenated to an alcohol (CH_2OH) or oxygenated to an acid (COOH).

3. Economic Justification for the Process

This process is capable of producing the following compounds of commercial interest:

3.1. Long Chain Alcohols

- Isooctyl alcohol—used in synthesis of diisooctyl phthalate, a plasticizer for polymers, principally polyvinyl chloride
- Decyl alcohol—made from nonene, a trimer of propylene; sulfated straight chain derivative is good biodegradable detergent; esterified for plasticizer use
- Tridecyl alcohol—made from dodecene, a tetramer of propylene; sulfated derivative used for detergents

3.2. Short Chain Alcohols

- *n*-butanol—plasticizer; converted to butyl acetate and other solvent derivatives
- 2-ethyl hexanol—dimerized via butyraldehyde; used in plasticizers and synthetic lubricants

3.3. *n*-butyraldehyde

Converted to butyric acid and anhydride for making cellulose acetate butyrate, a high strength thermoplastic; reacts directly with polyvinyl chloride to make polyvinyl butyral film used for safety glass.

4. Thermodynamics

The heat of reaction for hydroformylation is 30-35 Kcal per double bond. For propylene hydroformylation, $\Delta H^\circ = -31.14$ Kcal/mole. The reaction yield should be best at low temperature and high pressure, but the reaction has a favorable equilibrium constant at 200°C and 1 atm. pressure. Higher pressures (100-250 atms.) are used since cobalt carbonyl is involved in the reaction mechanism which can only form at the high pressures.

$$2Co + 8CO \rightarrow Co_2(CO)_8 \rightleftharpoons Co_2(CO)_7 + CO$$

$$Co_2(CO)_8 + RCH{=}CH_2 \rightleftharpoons Co_2(CO)_7 \cdot RCH{=}CH_2 + CO$$

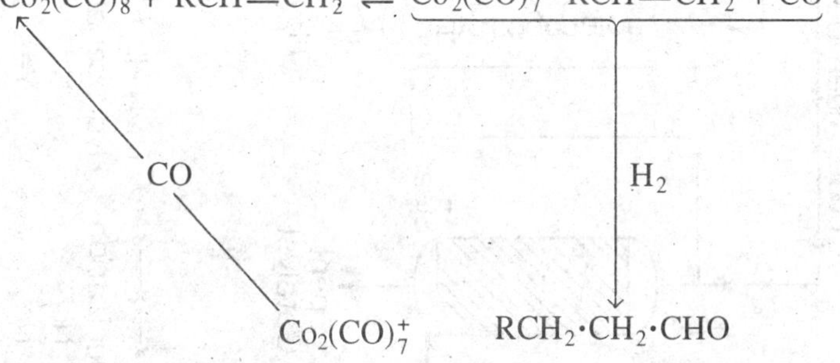

5. Kinetics

The reaction mechanism as postulated was supported by the following kinetic evidence:

5.1. Pressure Effect

Reaction was independent of total pressure from 100-400 atms. with 1 H_2/1 CO ratio within a 100-200°C temperature range. Pressure must be high enough to prevent decomposition of dicobalt octacarbonyl.

5.2. Olefin Concentration—first order dependence

5.3. Cobalt Concentration in Solution—first order dependence

5.4. H_2 Pressure—rate is directly proportional, but not molecularly

5.5. CO Pressure—inversely proportional since CO is a product in the cobalt-hydrocarbon complexing step

5.6. Effect of Olefin Structure—the magnitude of the steric effect caused by the olefin structure is rate determining. Low molecular weight, straight chain olefins give the highest reaction rates

5.7. Effect of Catalyst Structure—cobalt carbonyl solubilizes in the liquid, but reaction requires porous catalyst surface to absorb CO + H_2 and promote the mechanism.

6. Process Description for Butanol Production

An example of Oxo reactions

6.1. Reference Flow Sheet: Figure IVD-8

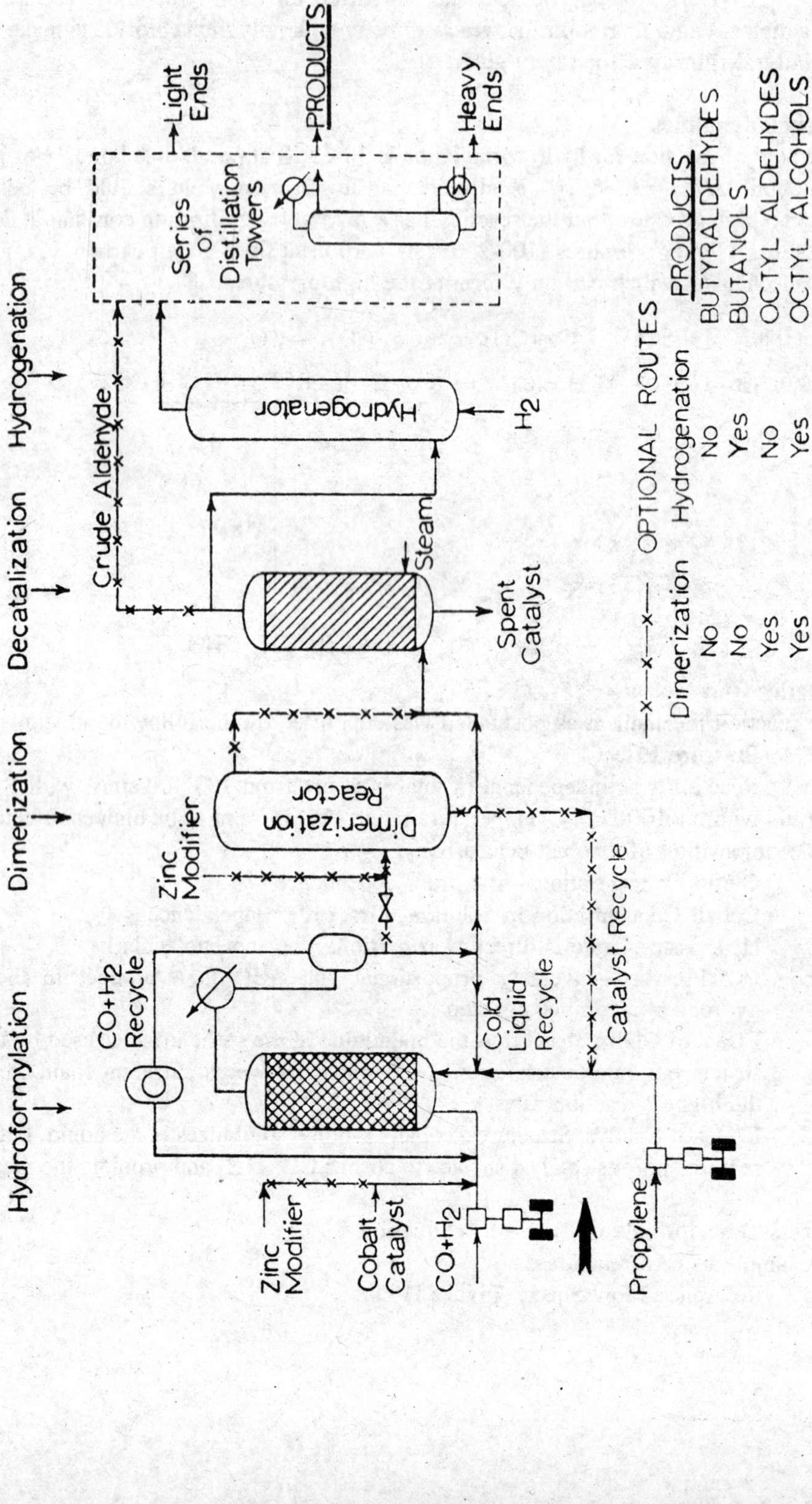

Fig. IVD-8. Oxo processing of olefins and synthesis gas.

6.2. Chemical Reactions

(a) Aldehyde step

$$C_3H_6 + CO + H_2 \begin{matrix} \nearrow CH_3 \cdot CH_2 \cdot CH_2 \cdot CHO & (\sim 50\%) \\ \searrow (CH_3)_2CH \cdot CHO & (\sim 50\%) \end{matrix}$$

(b) Alcohol step

$$C_3H_7CHO + H_2 \xrightarrow[\substack{150°C \\ 100 \text{ atms.}}]{\text{Ni catalyst}} C_3H_7CH_2OH$$

6.3. Quantitative Requirements

(a) **Basis: 1 ton of butanol (99+ % purity and 85% yield)**

Propylene	0.70 ton	equimolar ratio
Hydrogen	0.033 ton	

(b) Plant capacities: 15-75 tons/day

6.4. Process Description

Propylene is compressed to 250 atms. and cobalt naphthenate added to give 0.5-1% Co in solution. This stream is passed co-currently through a packed tower containing a porous carrier with 2% metallic cobalt deposited. The reaction is highly exothermic and the temperature of 170°C is controlled by recycle of a portion of the product stream after cooling.

The liquid fraction is mixed with steam at 180°C and a relatively low pressure of 20 atms. to decompose the cobalt carbonyl and naphthenate, depositing the cobalt on a porous carrier as the oxide. This cobalt is dissolved periodically in an acid wash and converted to the naphthenate for reuse. The unconverted synthesis gas from the Oxo converter is recompressed and recycled.

The crude butyraldehyde can be fractionated for product sales or continuously hydrogenated using a fixed bed nickel catalyst, 100 atms., H_2 pressure, and 150°C. The resulting butanols are fed to a distillation section comprising several fractionating columns in series. Light and heavy ends as by-products are obtained in addition to the purified alcohol.

6.5. Major Engineering Problems

6.5.1. Cobalt balance

Cobalt carbonyl is soluble in the hydrocarbon liquid so the cobalt on the catalyst surface would soon be stripped. This is avoided by adding soluble Co naphthenate, but the metal ion has to be removed in the decobalting unit, otherwise metallic sludge forms in the downstream equipment. A small portion of the carbonyl is carried out of the reactor with unreacted CO + H_2 gas and must be washed out with fresh feed.

6.5.2. Process alternatives

- Heat removal—indirect cooling cycle with heat transfer surface can be substituted for the above-described high recycle rate, sensible heat take-up system
- Decobalting—H_2 gas at low pressure can be used instead of superheated steam to deposit the cobalt

7. Dimerization Process (Humble Oil)

The chemical reaction is shown in Section 2.2 and is promoted by addition of soluble zinc acetylacetonate as well as cobalt naphthenate. The reaction rate is quite slow and a hold-up time of at least two hours is required to obtain a 50% dimerization yield. (See optional route in Figure IVD-8.)

8. Scope of Oxo Process Worldwide

The location and trends of butanol production are as follows:

n-Butanol Production ('000 tons)

	1985	1987	1989
USA	330	424	476
Western Europe	360	400	396
West Germany	274	313	310
Japan	99	93	129

Source: "Industrial Organic Chemistry" by Weissermel et al (1993)

The scope of 2-ethylhexanol production worldwide is as follows:

2-Ethylhexanol Production ('000 tons)

	1985	1987	1989
Western Europe	631	778	760
Germany	446	576	540
Japan	230	257	285
USA	233	300	362

Source: "Industrial Organic Chemistry" by Weissermel et al (1993)

As per the "Report of the Committee for Perspective Planning of Petrochemical Industry (1986-2000 A.D.)" the demand for 2-ethylhexanol in India is expected to rise to 35,700 M.T. and 52,500 M.T. by 1994-95 and 1999-2000 A.D. respectively.

The names and addresses of Oxo alcohol plants in India are given in Table IVD-8.

Table IVD-8
Names and Addresses of Units Manufacturing Oxo Alcohols in India

Name and Address	Product Range
Andhra Petrochemicals Ltd. Visakhapatnam (A.P.)	2-Ethylhexanol, *n*-butanol, iso-butanol

Indu Nissan Oxo Chemical Industries Ltd. Bajwa-Chhani Road, Behind G.S.F.C. Complex, Vadodara (Gujarat)	Iso-octanol, iso-decanol, nonanol
National Organic Chemical Industries Ltd. Thane (Maharashtra)	2-Ethylhexanol
Oswal Agro Mills Ltd. Ludhiana 141 003 (Punjab)	(i) 2-Ethylhexanol (ii) *n*-Butanol

Source: "SBP Handbook of Projects for Corporate Diversification" (1992)

IVE. CHEMICALS FROM C_4 COMPOUNDS (BUTANES AND BUTENES)

See Figure IVE-1 for graphic chart of end-product diversification.

Butadiene

1. Pertinent Properties of Butadiene ($CH_2{=}CH \cdot CH{=}CH_2$)

Mol. wt.	54.09
M.P.	−108.9°C
B.P.	−4.41°C
Density @ 20°C	0.621

Soluble in alcohols, ether; insoluble in water

Explosive limits: Lower = 2.0%
Upper = 11.5%

Toxic limit concentration 5,000 ppm

2. Consumption Pattern

The only major use for butadiene is in the manufacture of synthetic rubber. U.S. manufacture of synthetic rubber from butadiene dates back to the early days of World War II in 1942. Natural rubber supplies were cut off and a styrene-butadiene rubber (SBR) was made. Butadiene was supplied from petroleum refinery operations and by fermentation alcohol dehydrogenation-dehydration. The latter source was not competitive and was dropped after the war in the U.S., although some butadiene is still made from alcohol in India.

3. Methods of Production

3.1. Classification of Processes

3.1.1. Dehydrogenation of butane (Houdry)
3.1.2. Dehydrogenation of butylene
3.1.3. Dehydrogenation-dehydration of ethanol
3.1.4. Steam cracking of hydrocarbons (see Figure IVC-2)

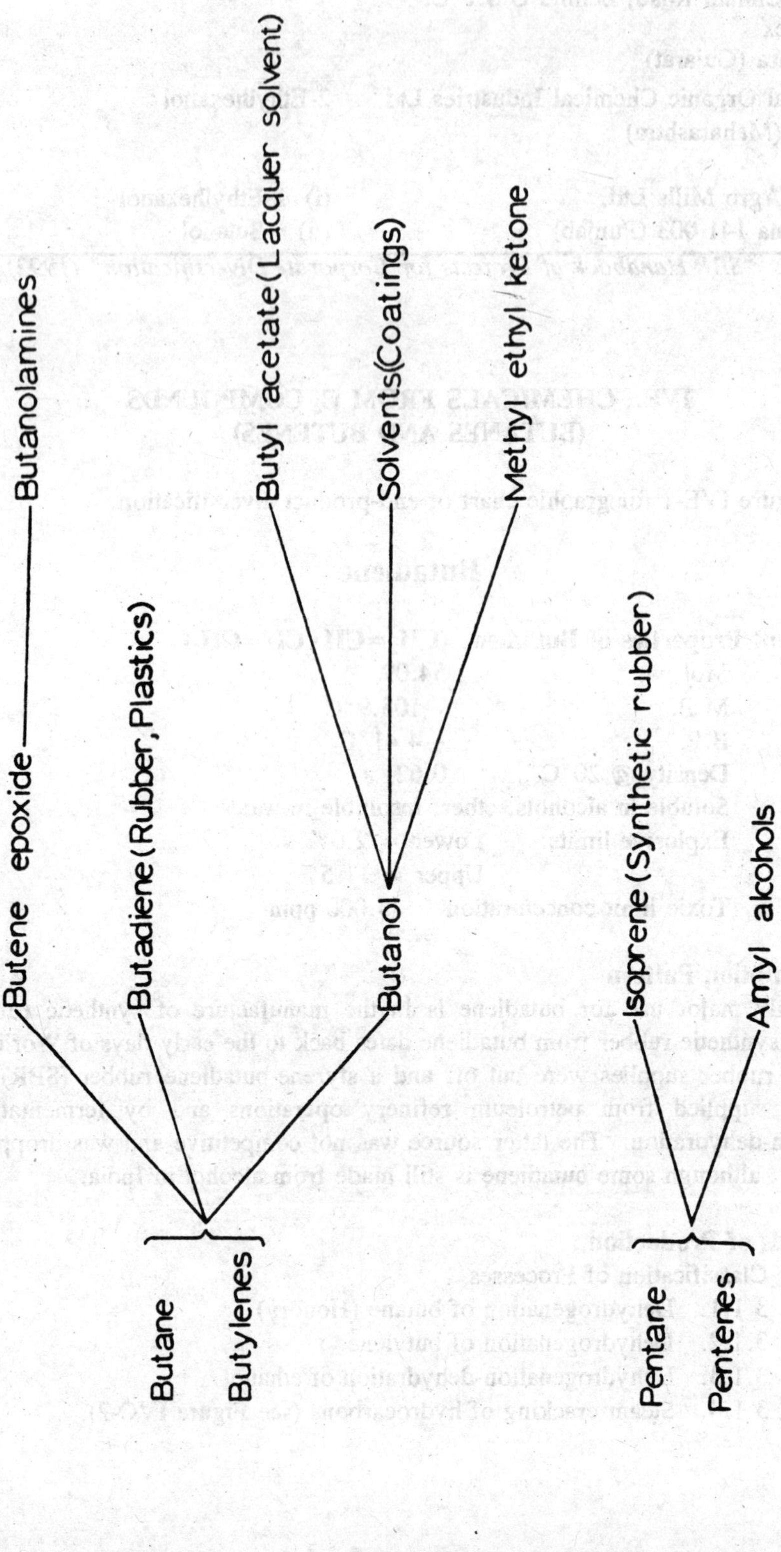

Fig. IVE-1. Synthetic chemical intermediates and products from C_4-C_5 hydrocarbons.

The first process listed has proven more economic in the U.S. if a high yield of butadiene is required. Since the ethanol process is in use in India and is likely to remain so, this will also be discussed.

3.2. Dehydrogenation of Butane

3.2.1. Reference flow sheet: Figure IVE-2

3.2.2. Chemical reactions

(a) Main reaction

$$C_4H_{10} \rightarrow CH_2 = CH \cdot CH = CH_2 + 2H_2; \quad \Delta H = +32.2 \text{ Kcal}$$

(b) Side reaction

$$\underset{n\text{-butylenes}}{C_4H_{10} \rightarrow C_4H_8} + H_2$$

3.2.3. Quantitative requirements

(a) Basis: 1 ton of butadiene (98+ % and 60% yield)

n-butane	1.80 tons
By-products	0.65 ton

(b) Plant capacities: 100-200 tons/day

3.2.4. Process description

A refinery gas of C_4/C_5 cut containing predominantly *n*-butane with some isopentane is mixed with recycle gas and preheated to reaction temperature prior to contact with a catalyst in a fixed bed, regenerative-heating reactor system. A pair of reactors form an adiabatic cycle with the heat of reaction required during the 5-15 minutes "make" period equal to that supplied by the combustion of carbon deposit on the catalyst during the regenerative period. The temperature of reaction at the start of the "make" period is 650°C, dropping to 550°C at the end before switching to regeneration. The pressure is low, 120-150 mm absolute, to force the reaction to the right.

The product gases are oil-quenched, compressed, cooled and separated from the light ends by absorption in naphtha followed by stripping. The overhead is fractionated to yield crude butadiene at the top which is purified by (1) absorption using cuprous ammonium acetate (CAA), (2) extractive distillation with furfural, or (3) azeotropic distillation with ammonia.

The more common absorption process involves contact of the close-boiling butadiene-butene fraction with lean CAA solution which dissolves butadiene. A desorption step at higher temperature is followed by distillation, compression, and liquefaction of butadiene to give 98-99% product purity. Ammonia is recovered in the distillation tower by water addition; it is then separated as substantially anhydrous NH_3 by fractionation.

3.2.5. Major engineering problems

(a) Reactor design

The dual-step adiabatic system operates with valves power operated on a preset cycle time which programs reaction, purging, and regeneration steps. Hydrocarbons are purged from the "make" reactors prior to regeneration with combustion gases swept out just after regeneration.

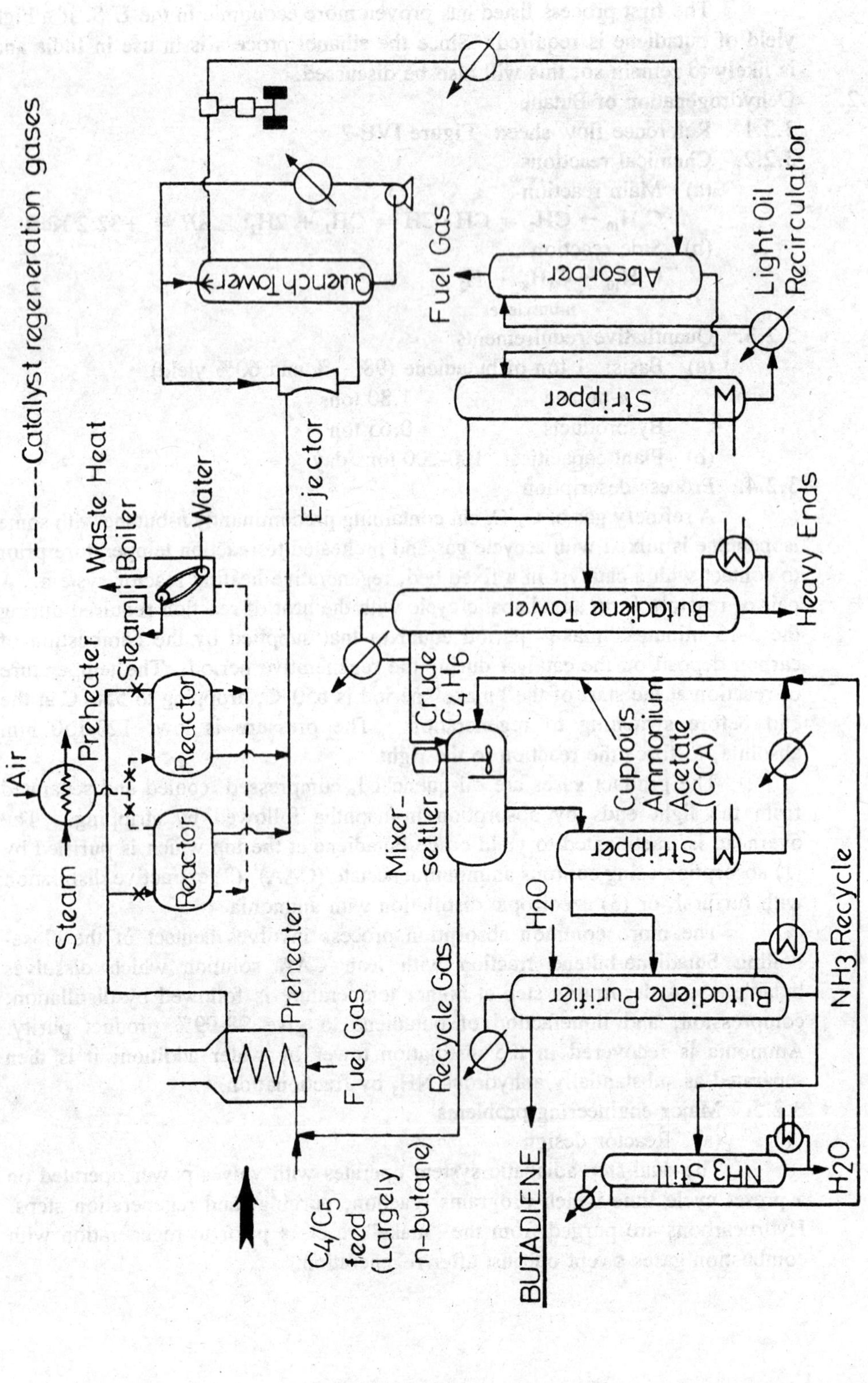

Fig. IVE-2. Butadiene via dehydrogenation of butane.

The reactors are horizontal, steel shell construction lined with ceramic monolith coating or tile. The space velocity is 1-3 Nm^3 of gas charged/m^3 catalyst/hr. The catalyst pellet bed is shallow to avoid excessive pressure drop. A conversion of 11-12% per pass is the usual operating figure.

(b) Catalyst development

The catalyst chosen was chromic oxide impregnated in porous activated alumina. Coke deposits at the end of the cycle are burned off with preheated air. Inert material of high heat capacity is mixed with the catalyst to provide the desired heat capacity during the "make" period. A catalyst life of around two years is quite common.

(c) Effect of feed gas composition

Isopentane can be converted to isoprene with the same ultimate yield as the C_4 homolog (~60%). An additional fractionating tower is required, but this process lends itself quite well to co-products of butadiene and isoprene.

(d) Effect of pressure

Dehydrogenation produces 2 additional moles of gas for each mole of reactant so the forward reaction is favored by the low pressures of 120-150 mm absolute maintained in the reactor. This pressure can be maintained by steam ejector operating from the waste heat steam boiler or by a liquid quench oil jet ejector.

(e) Purification of butadiene

Crude butadiene contains close-boiling hydrocarbons which cannot be separated by ordinary fractionation. Use of polar reagents such as cuprous ammonium acetate markedly alters the solubility and volatility of butadiene by complex formation as compared to mono-olefins. For example, butadiene is several times more soluble in CAA than the butenes. These latter impurities must be removed as they act as chain termination agents in any addition-type polymerization process.

3.3. Butadiene by Oxydehydrogenation

Since the equilibrium in the reaction

$$C_4H_{10} \rightleftharpoons C_4H_6 + 2H_2$$

is reversible, it seems obvious (with the perfect hindsight which we all possess) to add enough oxygen to the reacting mixture to pull the equilibrium far to the right and increase conversions from 20% or so (requiring much expensive recycle) to nearly 100%. Such a process has indeed been developed.

3.3.1. Reference flow sheet: Figure IVE-3 which shows the decrease in plant size for equivalent capacity made possible by adding oxygen to the dehydrogenation process.

3.3.2. Chemical reaction

$$C_4H_{10} + O_2 \rightarrow C_4H_6 + 2H_2O$$

3.3.3. Process description

Butanes or butenes are fed with a carefully controlled amount of oxygen, together with a small amount of a halogen (bromine or iodine) promoter into a reactor containing a heterogeneous catalyst. The higher yields simplify the subsequent product separation step greatly.

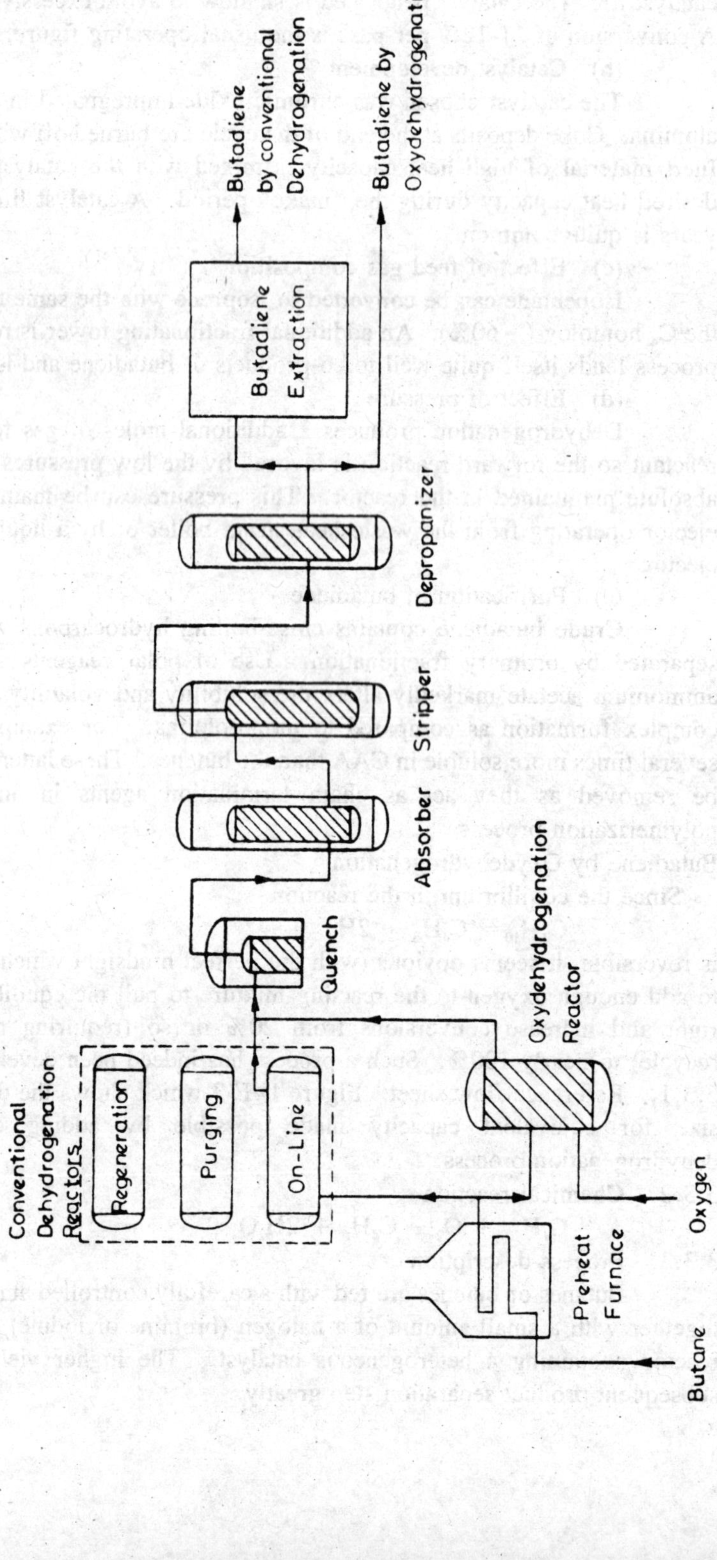

Fig. IVE-3. Comparative plant layout for making butadiene from butane by oxydehydrogenation versus straight dehydrogenation.

3.4. Butadiene from Ethanol

3.4.1. Reference flow sheet: Figure IVE-4

3.4.2. Chemical reactions

(a) Dehydrogenation

$$CH_3CH_2OH \rightarrow CH_3CHO + H_2$$

(b) Dehydration

$$CH_3CH_2OH + CH_3CHO \rightarrow CH_2 = CH \cdot CH = CH_2 + 2H_2O$$

3.4.3. Quantitative requirements

(a) Basis: 1 ton of butadiene (98+ % purity and 70% yield)

Ethanol 2.88 tons

By-products: ethylene, butene, ethyl ether, ethyl acetate, butanol

(b) Plant capacities: 70-100 tons/day

3.4.4. Process description

Ethanol (92-95% grade) is vaporized and passed over a dehydrogenation catalyst at 260-290°C to produce acetaldehyde: 90-94% yield on a 30-50% per pass basis.

Excess alcohol is mixed with acetaldehyde (3 : 1) and fed as a liquid to a fixed bed converter containing tantala-silica catalyst. Pressure is essentially atmospheric, the temperature is 325-350°C and the space velocity is 0.4-0.5/hr on a volume basis. A conversion of 28-30 per cent based on acetaldehyde is obtained with an ultimate yield in this step of 75%.

The reaction gases contain numerous compounds in addition to unreacted ethanol-acetaldehyde. These are separated by a series of fractionating columns with the crude butadiene ultimately being purified as explained in Section 3.2.4.

3.4.5. Major engineering problems

(a) Reactor design

The equipment for both types of reactors are of fixed bed tubular and designed for external heating using Dowtherm. A typical specification calls for 7.5 cm diameter steel tubes, 6 m long, containing 3- to 10-mesh catalyst sealed in headers.

(b) Catalyst specifications

Dehydrogenation catalysts are chromium- or molybdenum-activated copper with no activity decay.

The tantala-silica dehydration catalyst must be regenerated after 100-150 hours by use of air to burn off carbon deposits at about 400°C.

(c) Process alternatives

Oxidation of ethanol to acetaldehyde using air is also a fully commercialized process. It has the disadvantage that H_2 cannot be recovered, but this is offset by not having to supply external heat for this exothermic reaction.

A one-step route is being sought to give butadiene directly from ethanol. So far, the correct dehydrating catalyst has not been found.

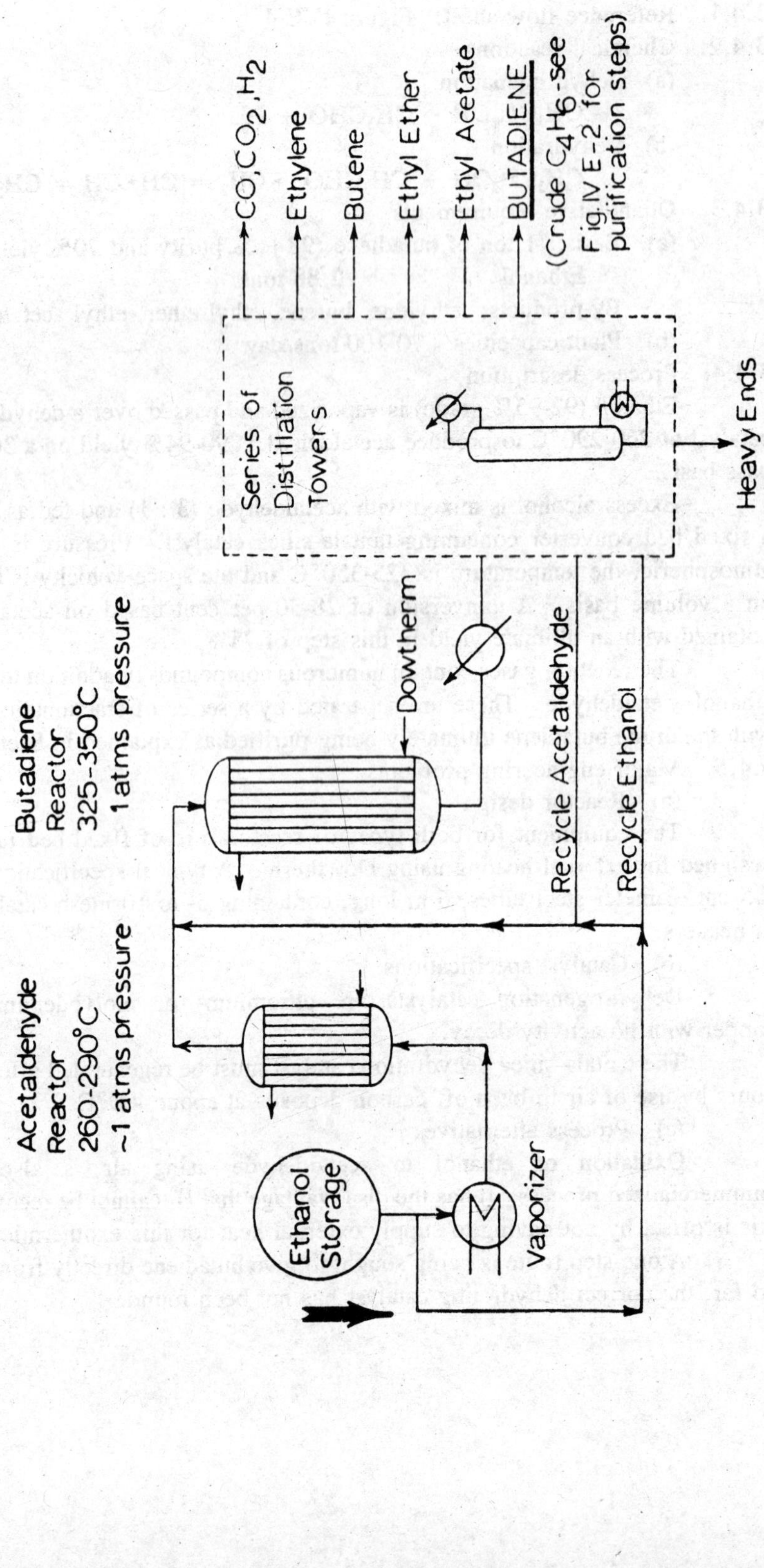

Fig. IVE-4. Butadiene from ethanol.

4. Economics

As pointed out for the consumption pattern, the future of the butadiene business will depend on synthetic rubber production. The SBR plant at Bareilly, started in 1963, is based on butadiene from alcohol, but no further alcohol-based plants are contemplated. This plant may be uneconomic as soon as ethylene, butadiene, and benzene from petroleum raw materials become available at a central petrochemical supply base located closer to end user customers.

The economic position for the Bareilly plant has been improved somewhat by the sale of organic chemical by-products.

Worldwide butadiene production is shown in the following tabulation.

Butadiene Production (in 10^6 tons)

	1987	1989	1991
Western Europe	1.78	1.96	1.81
USA	1.36	1.40	1.41
Japan	0.71	0.83	0.83

Source: "Industrial Organic Chemistry" by Weissermel et al (1993)

World utilization of butadiene is shown in Table IVE-1 and Indian uses are tabulated in Table IVE-2.

Table IVE-1
Utilization of Butadiene (in wt.%)

Product	USA		CIS	Western Europe		Japan		World
	1985	1989	1988	1985	1989	1984	1989	1990
Styrene butadiene rubber (SBR)	46	46	48	49	49	49	44	43
Polybutadiene rubber (BR)	18	23	34	20	21	27	30	23
Adiponitrile	16	12	-	7	6	-	-	8
Chloroprene	7	6	4	6	6	5	4	5
ABS polymers	8	6	3	9	9	11	13	11
Nitrile rubber (NBR)	3	3	4	5	5	6	6	4
Miscellaneous	2	4	7	4	4	2	3	6
Total usage (in 10^6 tons)	1.39	1.62	1.60	1.29	1.47	0.71	0.82	6.26

Source: "Industrial Organic Chemistry" by Weissermel et al (1993)

Table IVE-2
Demand of Butadiene in India
('000 tons)

Product	Demand		Norms of Consumption	Butadiene Requirement	
	1994-95	1999-2000		1994-95	1999-2000
SBR	70	95	0.63	44	60
Polybutadiene rubber (PBR)	43	59	1.1	47	65
Nitrile rubber (NBR)	17	23	0.65	11	15
Total				**102**	**140**

Source: "SBP Handbook of Petrochemical & Downstream Projects" (1991)

The production forecast for butadiene in India is given in Table IVE-3.

Table IVE-3
Butadiene Production during 1994-95 and 1999-2000 for India

Unit	1994-95	1999-2000
IPCL	20	20
MGCC	10	11
NOCIL	8	8
S&C (Alcohol based)	12	12
Total	50	51

Source: "SBP Handbook of Petrochemical & Downstream Projects" (1991)

IVF. CHEMICALS FROM AROMATICS

1. Aromatics as Primary Raw Materials

The principal aromatics for chemical synthesis are benzene (B), toluene (T), xylene (X), and naphthalene. An analysis of source contributions is shown next:

BTX Raw Material Sources (in wt.%)

	Oil		Coal	
	1986	1990	1986	1990
USA	97	98	3	2
Western Europe	96	95	4	5
Japan	90	93	10	7

Coal carbonization is used for metallurgical coke production. The volatiles from the coking operation are stripped of tar by electrostatic precipitators, scrubbed with dilute H_2SO_4 (10-20%) to remove ammonia. The remaining crude benzene fraction is absorbed in a high boiling stable oil such as creosote. This oil has a proximate composition of 60% B, 15% T, 7% X, 4% N, and solvent naphtha 7% and is fractionated to separate these components.

The production of aromatic raw materials from petroleum is derived from (1) solvent extraction of distillate fractions, (2) the reforming process discussed in Chapter IIIE by fractionating the reformate, (3) naphtha cracking as discussed in Section IVC, and (4) hydrodealkylation.

Some principal end uses for aromatic conversion products are given in Figure IVF-1.

1.1. Benzene (C_6H_6 or )

Benzene ranks ahead of toluene, xylene, and naphthalene as seen in the above classification. Except for small amounts used as a solvent and for motor fuels, the major usage of C_6H_6 is for production of phenol and styrene with the remaining approximate 40% divided about equally among other aromatic derivatives such as aniline, sulfonated detergents, DDT, maleic anhydride, chlorobenzene and cyclohexane.

The last chemical, C_6H_{12}, comes from petroleum via two routes: (1) catalytic hydrogenation of benzene, (2) direct fractionation of reforming stock. Cyclohexane is an important intermediate in synthetic fiber preparation. 6,6-Nylon fiber is produced by oxidation of C_6H_{12} to adipic acid, which is then condensed with hexamethylene diamine.

Table IVF-1 shows the various sources of benzene in various parts of the world.

Table IVF-1
Share of Various Sources in Benzene Production (in wt.%)

Product	USA		Western Europe		Japan	
	1985	1990	1986	1990	1984	1990
Pyrolysis gasoline	20	24	59	52	59	44
Reformate gasoline	47	48	15	17	23	39
Hydrodealkylation	28	21	18	22	9	9
Coal and other sources*	5	7	8	9	9	8

* e.g., disproportionation of toluene.

Source: "Industrial Organic Chemistry" by Weissermel et al (1993)

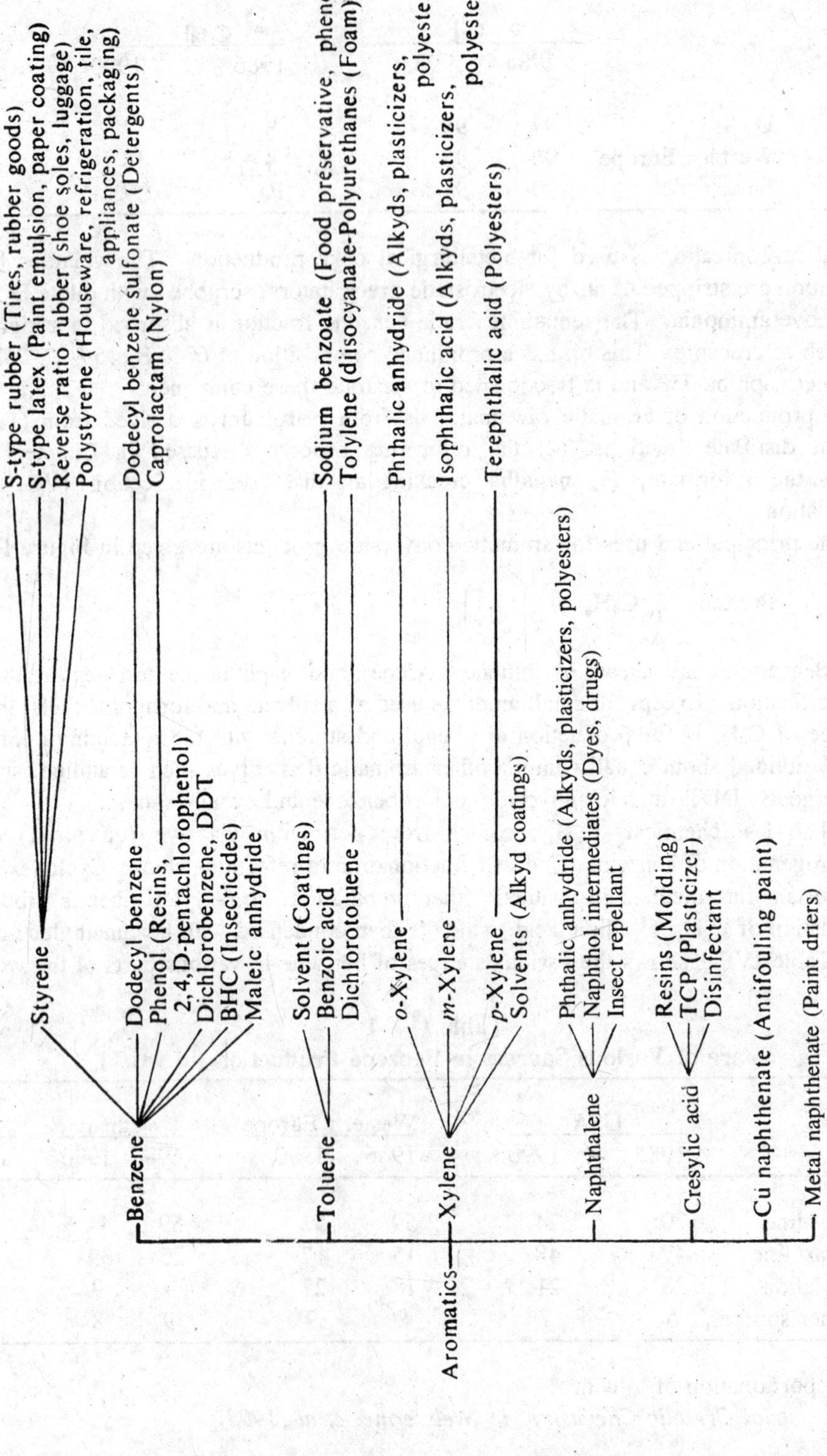

Fig. IVF-1. Synthetic chemicals and intermediates from aromatics.

Table IVF-2 shows the pattern of benzene consumption.

Table IVF-2
Pattern of Benzene Consumption in USA, Western Europe, and Japan (in wt.%)

	USA		Western Europe		Japan	
	1985	1990	1986	1990	1984	1990
Ethylbenzene (styrene)	57	55	46	49	54	57
Cumene (phenol)	20	24	21	21	13	13
Cyclohexane	12	13	16	13	22	20
Nitrobenzene	5	5	8	8	2	3
Maleic anhydride	1	-	3	2	2	2
Alkylbenzenes	3	2	5	3	4	3
Miscellaneous (*e.g.*, chlorobenzene, benzenesulfonic acid)	2	1	1	3	3	2
Total Use (in 10^6 tons)	5.20	5.85	5.18	6.20	2.11	2.99

Source: "Industrial Organic Chemistry" by Weissermel et al (1993)

Table IVF-3 shows the production pattern for benzene in India.

Table IVF-3
Indian Scenario: Major Producers of Benzene

	Installed Capacity tons per annum
Cochin Refinery	87,500
Bharat Petroleum Corp.	85,000
Indian Oil Corporation	33,000
IPCL (Indian Petrochemicals Corp. Ltd.)	23,600
NOCIL	17,000

Source: "Global Trends in Chemical Products"—Nandini (1994)

1.2. Toluene ($C_6H_5 \cdot CH_3$ or 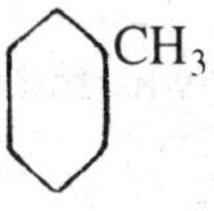)

Toluene is produced in yields about equal to that of benzene and of xylene in petroleum reforming operations. Unfortunately, the demand for toluene is not as prevalent as for benzene.

The major end uses of toluene are:

- Solvents—paints, rubber and plastic cements
- Chemicals—benzyl chloride and its peroxide for polymerization catalysts; benzoic acid; as plasticizer; phenol from benzoic acid; toluene diisocyanate in urethane foams
- Detergents—toluene sulfonates

These uses cannot absorb all of the toluene production; so plans for using up the excess toluene are:

- Blending in motor petrol to upgrade octane number; this produces low income yield as fuel value
- Production of phenol (discussed later in this Chapter)
- Dealkylation with H_2 to yield benzene

The principal source of toluene is catalytic reforming of refinery streams. This source accounts for 87% of the total toluene produced. An additional 9% is separated from pyrolysis of gasoline produced in steam crackers during the manufacture of ethylene and propylene. Other sources are an additional 2% recovered as a by-product from styrene manufacture and 1-2% entering the market from separation from coal tar.

The Indian scenario for toluene is as follows:

Manufacturers	Installed Capacity in TPA
BPCL (Bharat Petroleum Corp. Ltd.)	17,600
Cochin Refineries	12,000
Indian Oil Corp.	14,000

Production—Around 35,000 tons per annum.
Demand level—Around 40,000 tons per annum.

Source: "Global Trends in Chemical Products"—Nandini (1994)

1.3. Xylene $[C_6H_4 \cdot (CH_3)_2]$

A similar story to that of toluene exists for xylene as each is produced in about equal yields from petroleum reforming. Some 60% is used as low-value, high-octane blending fuel; the balance of important high-value products are as follows:

- Solvents—high boiling type, largely for alkyd resins
- Chemicals
  - (a) From orthoxylene—phthalic anhydride and acid competitive with naphthalene oxidation
  - (b) From metaxylene—isophthalic acid which is competitive with phthalic acid for reinforced plastics and plasticizers
  - (c) From paraxylene—dimethyl terephthalate used in polyester fibers and films

The Indian scenario for xylene is as follows:

Manufacturers	Installed Capacity in tons per annum: Ortho & Mixed xylene	Installed Capacity in tons per annum: Paraxylene
IPCL (Indian Petrochemicals Corp. Ltd.)	47,900	46,000
RIL (Reliance Industries Ltd.)		100,000
BRPL (Bongaigaon Ref. & Petrochemicals Ltd.)		(Captive consumption)

Source: "Global Trends in Chemical Products"—Nandini (1994)

Supply/demand scenario of paraxylene in 1992-93:

	Production	Captive Demand (in tons/annum)
RIL (Reliance Industries Ltd.)	140,000	140,000
BRPL (Bongaigaon Ref. & Pet. Ltd.)	26,000	30,600
IPCL (Indian Petrochem. Corp. Ltd.)	44,000	18,750
Bombay Dyeing	-	42,000
Total	210,000	231,350

Source: *"Global Trends in Chemical Products"—Nandini (1994)*

New projects proposed for xylene are as follows:

Company	Product	Capacity Lakh tons
National Aromatics & Petro-chemicals Corp. Ltd.	Paraxylene & Orthoxylene	1.36 & 0.3
BPCL (Bharat Petro. Corp. Ltd.)	Paraxylene & Orthoxylene	1.0 & 0.2
Saleempur Aromatic, M.P.	Paraxylene & Orthoxylene	1.08 & 0.35
Reliance Petrochem. Ltd.	Paraxylene	2.7

Demand for paraxylene: 1.64 lakh tons per annum.
Demand for orthoxylene: 1 lakh tons per annum.

Source: *"Global Trends in Chemical Products"—Nandini (1994)*

1.4. Naphthalene ($C_{10}H_8$ or 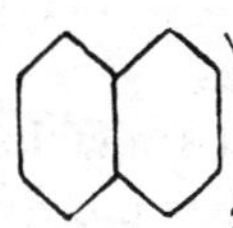)

Over 80% of this naphthalene supply to be derived largely from coal will go into the production of phthalic anhydride. The principal market outlets for phthalic derivatives are in alkyd resins and plasticizers with under 10% to dyestuffs and exports. If coal-supplied naphthalene is insufficient to meet the demand, hydrodealkylation of petroleum from Indian crude oil can be utilized.

Hydrodealkylation

A method of converting toluene and dialkylbenzenes to benzene. Naphthalene can be made from alkyl naphthalenes by the same processes.

1. Chemical Reactions

$$C_6H_5CH_3 + H_2 \rightarrow C_6H_6 + CH_4$$
$$C_6H_4(CH_3)_2 + 2H_2 \rightarrow C_6H_6 + 2CH_4$$

$$C_{10}H_{8-x}(CH_3)_x + XH_2 \rightarrow C_{10}H_8 + XCH_4$$

2. **Competitive Processes**
   2.1. Thermal, non-catalytic
   2.2. Catalytic—run at lower temperature and pressure
   The flow sheets for both types of processes are essentially the same except for the reactor and processing conditions.
   2.3. Reference Flow Sheet: Figure IVF-2
   2.4. Process Description

Hydrogen-rich make-up gas and recycle gas are compressed and mixed with the liquid alkyl aromatic feedstock plus recycle. The combined feed is preheated by means of heat exchange with reactor effluent and finally in a fired preheater for charge to the reactor which contains either a fixed bed catalyst or is tubular, non-catalytic. The effluent is cooled via reactor feed preheater, then with water, and separated in a high pressure stage to gas and liquid fractions. A major portion of the gas is recycled, the balance going to a methane separation unit for H_2 enrichment and make-up. It may also be used for fuel. The liquid fraction is stripped of residual gas at low pressure and fractionated to produce high purity benzene (less than 0.5 ppm thiophene) and recycle alkyl aromatics.

Yields are 95-98% for toluene conversion versus 90-95% for naphthalene.

2.5. Major Engineering Problems

2.5.1. Reactor design

Catalytic processes were utilized first, operating at 600-650°C and pressure of 35-40 atms. A thermal hydrogenation process was next developed to circumvent patent royalty payments. Operating at 800-850°C and 60-70 atms., comparable yields were obtained. Economic balances in the design include: (1) residence time, temperature and recycle rates, (2) pressure, throughput capacity and vessel cost.

2.5.2. Hydrogen problems

Ample hydrogen is available from reformers. The methane composition of charge gas and purge rates are fixed by reactor kinetics. Hydrogen handling requires explosion-proof plant construction and its use in equipment at high temperatures and pressures dictates chrome steel to avoid embrittlement.

2.6. Economics

Hydrodealkylation has proven a low-cost, feasible method to convert unwanted toluene to benzene, thereby avoiding downgrading of toluene to fuel values. The process is readily handled within the refinery operations so that high grade benzene is available to consumer plants in the immediate vicinity.

With this much background on the supply picture for aromatics, the remainder of the chapter will be devoted to important aromatic derivatives, *i.e.*, phenol, styrene, phthalic and maleic anhydrides, nitrobenzene, aniline and dyes.

Phenol

1. **Pertinent Properties of Phenol (C_6H_5OH)**

Mol. wt.	94.11

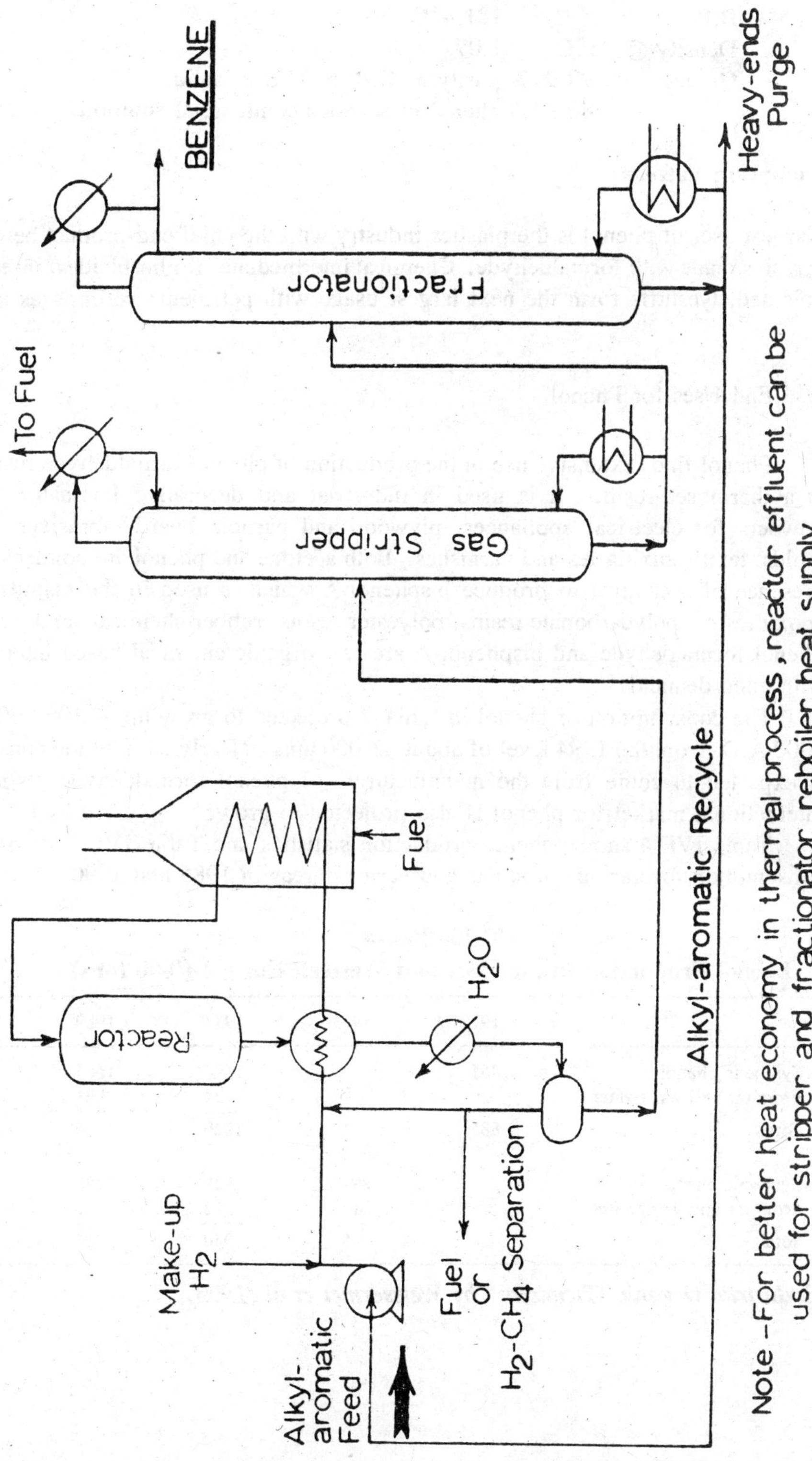

Fig. IVF-2. Hydrodealkylation process to make benzene from alkyl-aromatic (*e.g.*, toluene).

M.P. 42°C
B.P. 181.4°C
Density @ 25°C 1.07
Grades: 98-99% purity as C.P. or U.S.P. solid;
80-92% phenol in aqueous commercial solution

2. Consumption Pattern

The largest user of phenol is the plastics industry with the chief end-product being cheap thermosetting resins made with formaldehyde. Chemical intermediates for herbicides, insecticides, pharmaceuticals and dyestuffs form the next largest usage with petroleum refining as a solvent being next.

2.1. End Uses for Phenol

Phenol finds extensive use in the production of phenol formaldehyde resin which is a thermoset resin. It is used in industrial and decorative laminates, molding powders for electrical appliances, plywood and particle board, abrasives, foundry molds, textile auxiliaries and varnishes. Both acetone and phenol are condensed in the presence of a catalyst to produce bisphenol-A which is used in the manufacture of epoxy resins, polycarbonate resins, polyester resins, rubber chemicals and fungicides. Phenol formaldehyde and bisphenol-A are two organic chemical-based intermediates with good demand.

The consumption of phenol in India is projected to grow up to 105,000 tons by 2000 A.D. from the 1994 level of about 42,000 tons. Nearly 51% of the consumption is expected to come from the manufacturers of phenol formaldehyde resins. The international market for phenol is also projected to grow.

Table IVF-4 shows phenol production statistics and Table IVF-5 shows phenol consumption for various products and various areas in 1985 and 1990.

Table IVF-4
Phenol Production in the USA and Western Europe ('000 tons)

		1972	1973	1983	1989	1991
USA:	Synthetic phenol	865		1196	1665	
	From tar and wastewater	20		24	21	
	Total	885		1220	1686	
Western Europe:	Synthetic phenol		891	928	1288	1460
	From tar and wastewater		14	12	12	28
	Total		905	940	1300	1488

***Source:* "Industrial Organic Chemistry" by Weissermel et al (1993)**

Table IVF-5

Use of Phenol Worldwide, in USA, Japan, and Western Europe (in wt.%)

	World		USA		Japan		Western Europe	
	1989	1991	1985	1990	1986	1990	1985	1991
Phenol resins	36	23	38	40	36	41	41	32
ε-Caprolactam	7	15	18	15	-	-	17	22
Bisphenol-A	20	21	22	30	29	32	22	24
Adipic acid	1	2	1	1	-	-	1	2
Alkylphenols	5	2	4	5	4	4	4	6
Miscellaneous*	21	22	15	13	26	23	24	23
Total use (in 10^6 tons)	4.70	4.60	1.07	1.68	0.25	0.43	1.05	1.33

**e.g.*, aniline, chlorophenols, plasticizers, antioxidants.

Source: "Industrial Organic Chemistry" by Weissermel et al (1993)

3. Methods of Production

There are few chemicals which can be made by so many alternate and commercially feasible routes as is the case of synthetic phenol. When one considers that less than 15% of all phenol production comes as natural phenol from coal carbonization plants, the importance of synthetic phenol is apparent.

Seven processes for synthetic phenol are available of which six are still competitive. A study and comparison of these six processes is a worthwhile experience in process selection.

(a) Competitive processes
- Cumene peroxidation-hydrolysis
- Toluene two-stage oxidation
- Raschig: vapor phase hydrochlorination and hydrolysis
- Chlorobenzene-caustic hydrolysis
- Benzene sulfonate-caustic fusion
- Benzene-direct oxidation

(b) Processes not commercially feasible
- Chlorobenzene-soda ash hydrolysis

3.1. Cumene Process for Phenol Production

3.1.1. Reference flow sheet: Figure IVF-3

3.1.2. Chemical reactions

(a) Peroxidation

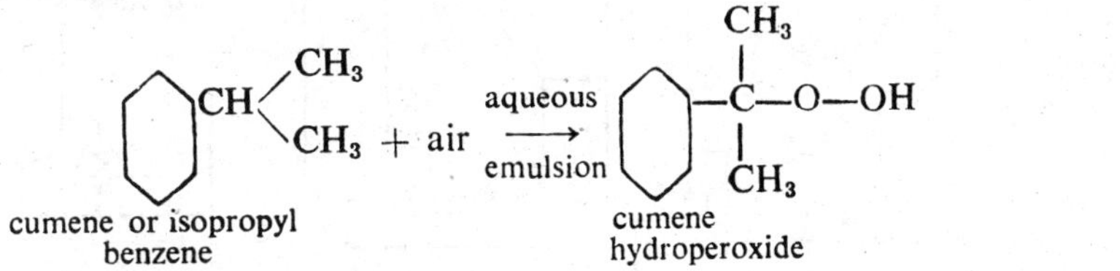

(b) Hydrolysis

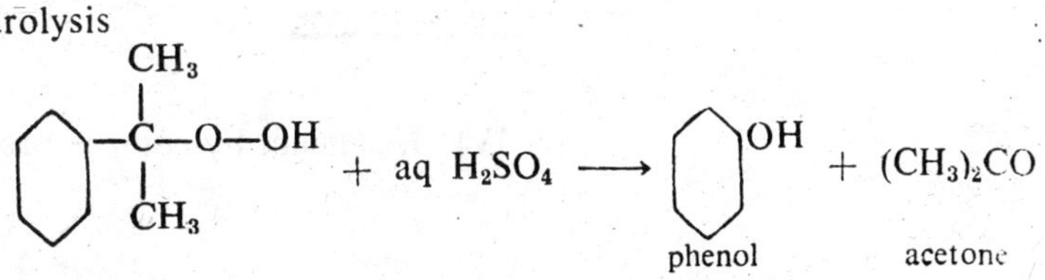

3.1.3. Quantitative requirements

(a) Basis: 1 ton of phenol (92% yield) + 0.6 ton acetone

Cumene	1.40 tons
Air	1.53 tons

Small quantities of sulfuric acid and emulsifying agents

Co-product: Acetone

(b) Plant capacities: 50-125 tons/day

3.1.4. Process description

Cumene (isopropyl benzene) made by alkylation of benzene with propylene is mixed with recycle cumene (1:4 ratio) and sent to the hydrogenator. Unsaturates and α-methyl styrene are converted to saturated materials to avoid undesirable decomposition of the peroxide during the oxidation step. Hydrogen over nickel catalyst at 100°C in a batch reactor is the usual process for purification.

Oxidation is carried out in the presence of air in an aqueous emulsion stabilized by an alkali such as sodium carbonate in the 8.5-10.5 pH range. Vent gases are passed through a condenser to recover hydrocarbons.

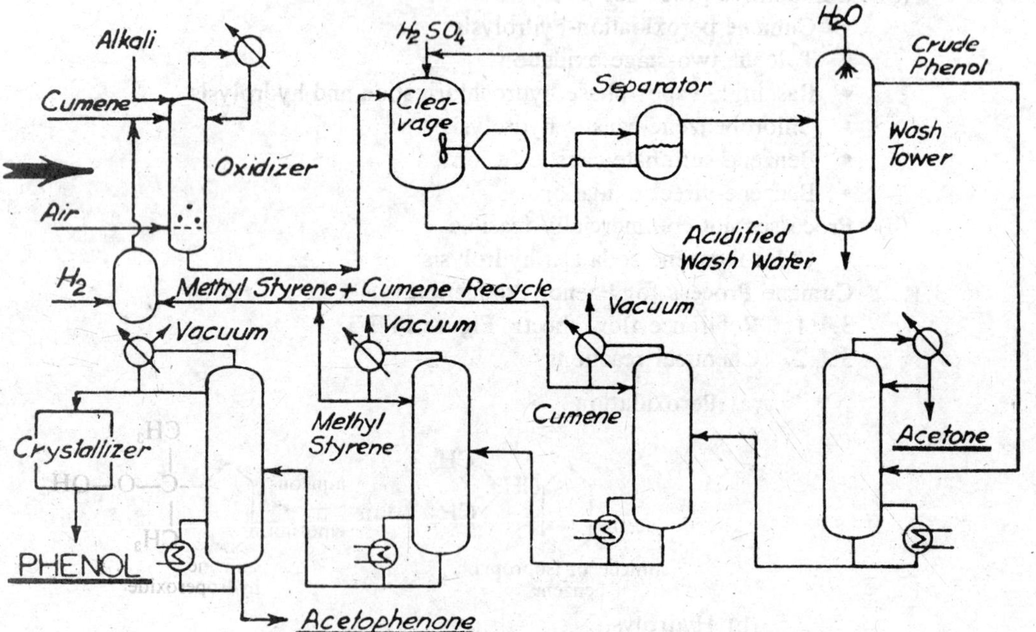

Fig. IVF-3. Phenol by cumene process.

The cumene peroxide thus formed is cleaved in an acidifier containing 10-25% H_2SO_4. This is an agitated vessel at 55-65°C. The reaction products are separated into an aqueous acid layer for recycle to the cleavage vessel and an oil layer containing 76 wt.% cumene, 14% phenol, 8% acetone, and 1-2% α-methyl styrene and acetophenone. This mixture is separated in a series of four distillation steps, the last three of which are under vacuum. Phenol in the overhead of the last vacuum fractionator is purified by crystallization.

3.1.5. Major engineering problems

(a) Gas with two-phase liquid contact

Intimate dispersion of air bubbles with the emulsified hydrocarbon-water mixture is important in attaining good conversion, low loss of hydrocarbons in the vent gases, and explosive limit control.

(b) Peroxide handling to avoid explosions

Cumene hydroperoxide is explosive when allowed to accumulate. Design must be such as to avoid trapping condensed liquid in any large amounts.

3.1.6. Economics of the process

This is a new process which produces 0.6 ton of acetone/ton of phenol as a co-product. The sale of acetone co-product strongly influences the competitive aspects of this process for manufacturing phenol. This dictates plant location and product sales flexibility. Only raw material is the alkylated benzene available within or adjacent to a petrochemical plant.

3.2. Toluene Oxidation Process for Phenol Production

3.2.1. Reference flow sheet: Figure IVF-4

3.2.2. Chemical reactions

(a) Oxidation to benzoic acid

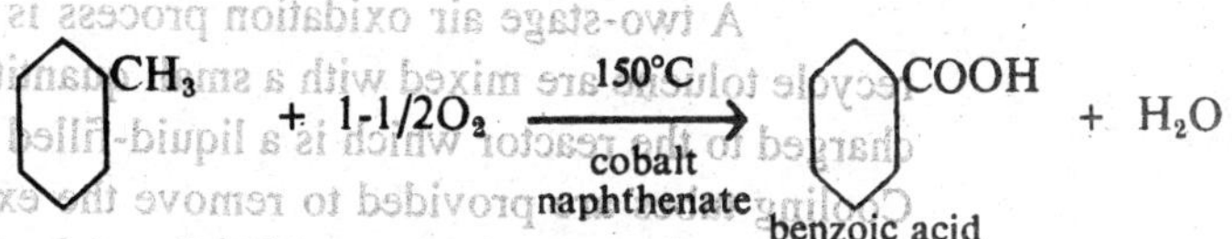

(b) Oxidation of benzoic acid to phenol

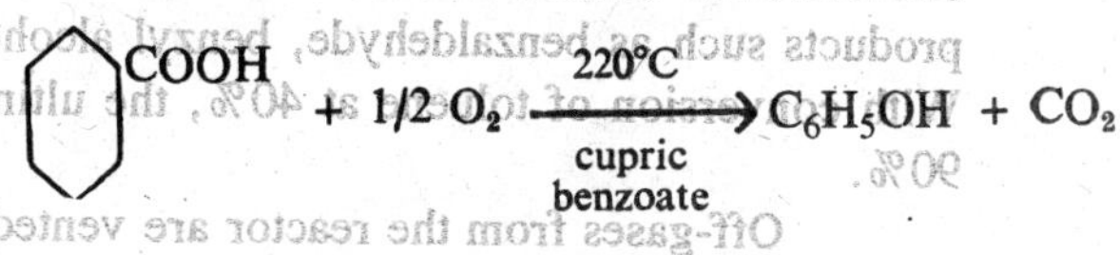

3.2.3. Quantitative requirements

(a) Basis: 1 ton of phenol (80% yield)

Toluene	1.34 tons
Air	8.8 tons

Small quantities of cobalt naphthenate and cupric benzoate catalyst

(b) Plant capacities: 35-75 tons/day

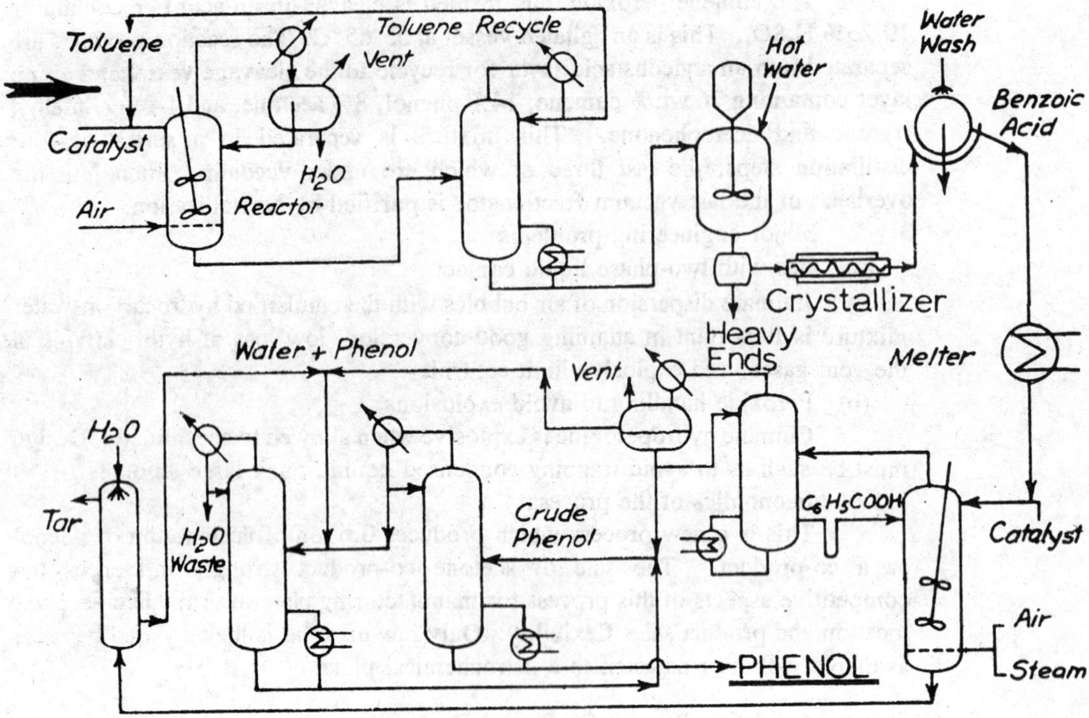

Fig. IVF-4. Phenol from toluene oxidation.

3.2.4. Process description

A two-stage air oxidation process is used. In the first stage, fresh plus recycle toluene are mixed with a small quantity of cobalt naphthenate catalyst and charged to the reactor which is a liquid-filled tower through which air is sparged. Cooling tubes are provided to remove the exothermic heat of reaction.

The reactor is run at 150°C and 3 atms. Excess air is used, but toluene conversion is limited to 40% to avoid excessive side reactions. These give by-products such as benzaldehyde, benzyl alcohol, benzyl benzoate, CO and CO_2. With conversion of toluene at 40%, the ultimate yield of benzoic acid is about 90%.

Off-gases from the reactor are vented through a water-cooled condenser to remove water and to allow return of toluene. Liquid from the reactor continuously passes to a distillation column which strips the toluene and other volatile by-products from the acid fraction in the bottoms. Purified benzoic acid is separated by extracting the bottoms with hot water, then crystallizing and filtering the crude benzoic acid. The latter can be recrystallized to meet USP specifications as a market outlet for benzoic acid.

To make phenol, the crude acid is melted, mixed with cupric benzoate catalyst, then charged to an air-sparged tower containing cooling tubes and mechanical agitation. Reactor conditions are 220°C and 1.3-1.7 atms. Excess air is again necessary to get a 70-80% conversion of benzoic acid with a yield of 90% phenol. The overall process yield for the two steps is about 80%.

Phenol product is obtained by continuously distilling the reactor liquor into a fractionating column where unreacted benzoic acid is returned to the reactor. Non-condensibles such as N_2, O_2 and CO_2 are vented through a condenser along with the condensible fraction of phenol-water. Phenol is withdrawn as the bottom layer in a separator. This crude phenol is again fractionated with purified phenol coming off as bottoms and the overhead phenol-water azeotrope sent to another column for splitting.

The heavy ends in the benzoic acid oxidation tower are water-extracted to recover phenol and benzoic acid which are then recycled, after concentration, to the second stage oxidation tower.

3.2.5. Major engineering problems

Efficient gas-liquid contacting design and economic recovery of organics from the water-containing fractions in the second stage are the two main design problems.

3.2.6. Economics of the process

The incentive for switching to toluene as an aromatic source comes from the oversupply of toluene available at low-cost from petroleum reforming. The major disadvantages of the method are the two-stage oxidation with the handling of solid intermediate and a fairly elaborate process scheme throughout. The development of a simpler, single step oxidation of toluene would indeed be a major breakthrough in synthetic phenol production.

3.3. Raschig Phenol Process Using Hydrochlorination of Benzene

3.3.1. Reference flow sheet: Figure IVF-5

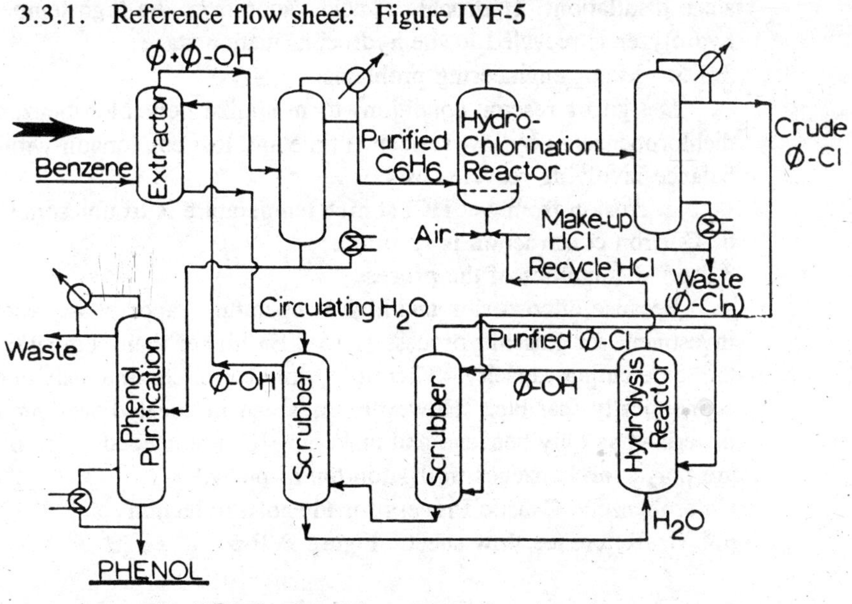

Fig. IVF-5. Raschig process for phenol.

3.3.2. Chemical reactions

(a) Hydrochlorination

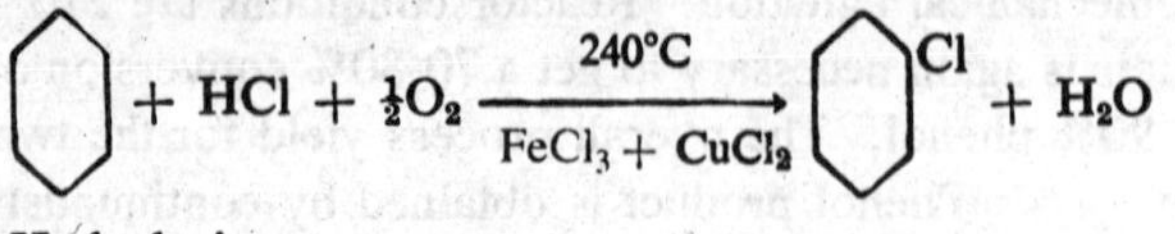

(b) Hydrolysis

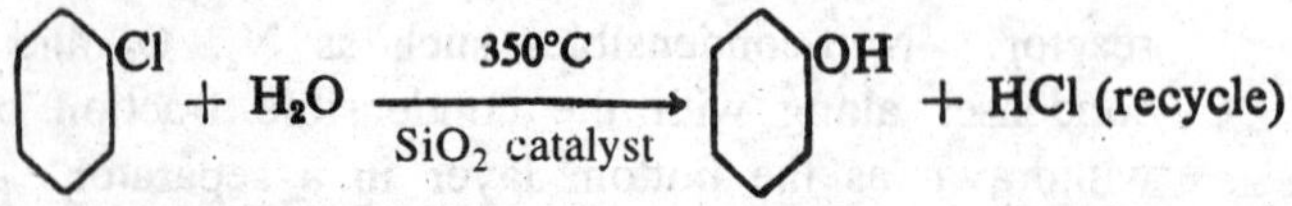

3.3.3. Quantitative requirements

(a) Basis: 1 ton of phenol (75% yield)

Benzene	1.1 tons
HCl	0.19 ton
Air	2.4 tons

(b) Plant capacities: 100-400 tons/day

3.3.4. Process description

The Raschig process has two vapor-phase catalytic stages. Purified benzene is fed to a heated, packed reactor containing ferric chloride and cupric chloride catalyst. Chlorination with HCl-O_2 at 220°C occurs with a short residence time to produce 10-20% conversion of benzene. Fractionation separates unreacted benzene from chlorobenzene and polychlorobenzene.

The crude chlorobenzene is scrubbed with phenol, water-washed, and sent to the second catalytic stage. Here it is hydrolyzed in a tubular, high temperature furnace with either SiO_2 or $Ca_3(PO_4)_2$ as the catalyst. Phenol from the hydrolyzer is washed with water, then extracted by benzene, and finally purified by two-stage distillation. Hydrochloric acid vapor from the high temperature catalytic hydrolyzer is recycled to the hydrochlorination stage.

3.3.5. Major engineering problems

Design of reactor conditions to minimize polychlorobenzenes (principally dichlorobenzene) by low residence time and low conversion within an economic balance involving recycle costs.

Corrosion from wet HCl at high temperature is troublesome so that ceramic or Duriron construction is required.

3.3.6. Economics of the process

Because of corrosion and high-temperature vapor-phase reactions, the plant investment for Raschig process is 15-20% higher than competitive processes at the same output capacity. Therefore, only large, continuously operated units are economically feasible. However, units can be located without regard for raw materials, as only benzene and make-up HCl are needed. The only by-products are polychlorobenzenes in 0.1 ton/ton of phenol.

3.4. Chlorobenzene-Caustic Process for Phenol Production

3.4.1. Reference flow sheet: Figure IVF-6

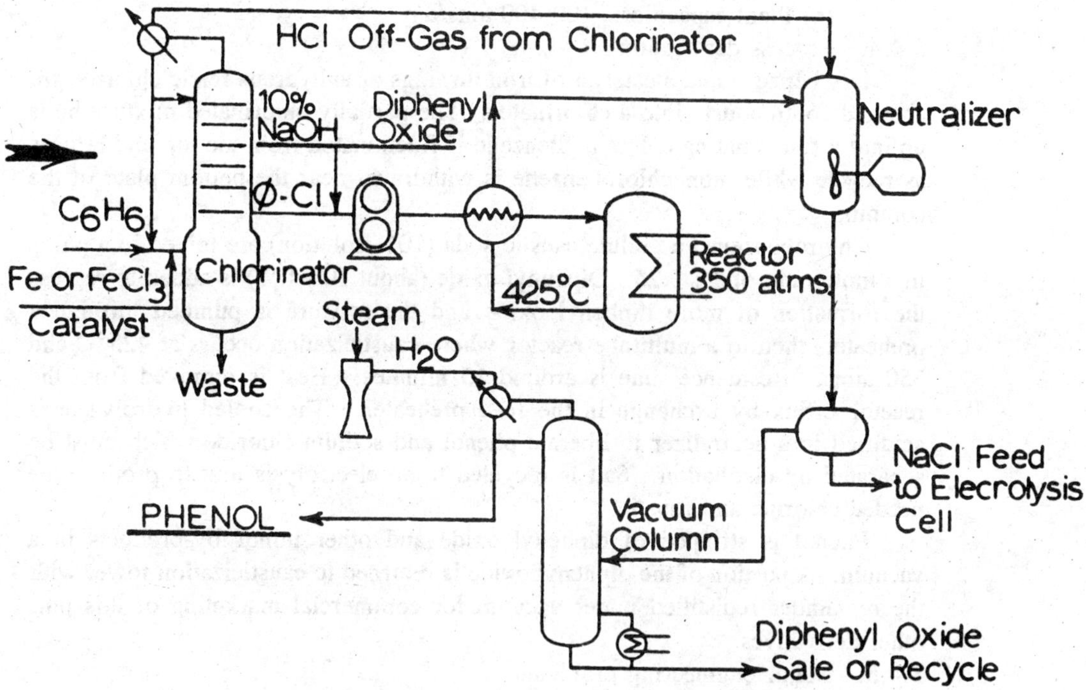

Fig. IVF-6. Phenol by chlorobenzene-NaOH.

3.4.2. Chemical reactions

(a) Chlorination

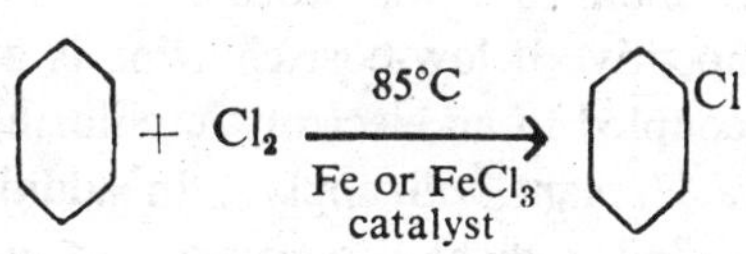

(b) Causticization

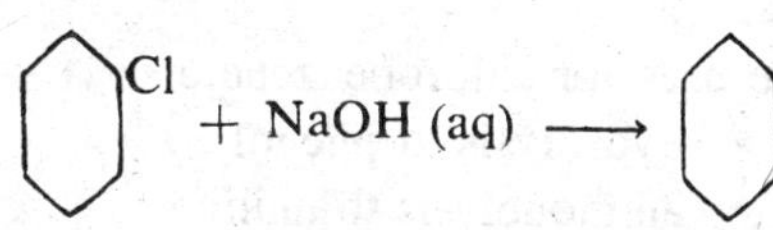

(c) Hydrolysis

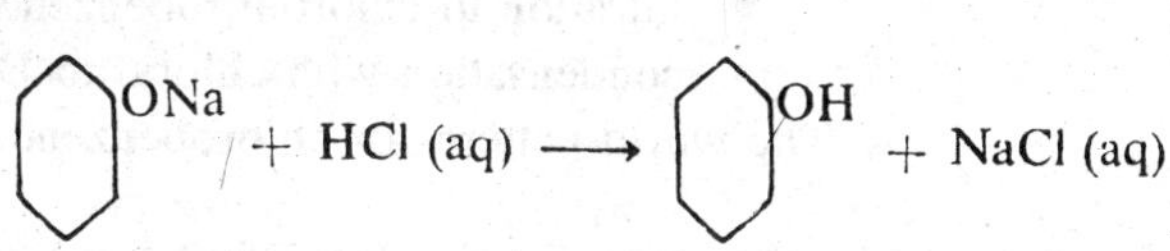

3.4.3. Quantitative requirements

(a) Basis: 1 ton of phenol (95% yield)

Benzene	0.90 ton
Chlorine	0.82 ton
NaOH (100% basis)	0.67 ton
HCl	0.51 ton

(b) Plant capacities: 100-400 tons/day

3.4.4. Process description

Dry benzene and a catalyst of iron turnings or anhydrous ferric chloride are charged continuously into a chlorinator. The partially chlorinated mixture boils up into a fractionating column. Benzene is fractionated from the top and returns as recycle while monochlorobenzene is withdrawn near the bottom plate of the column.

Chlorobenzene and dilute caustic soda (10% solution) are mixed in a pump in a mole ratio of 1 : 1.25. Diphenyl oxide (about 10 wt.%) is added to repress the formation of more diphenyl oxide and the mixture is pumped through a preheater, then to a multitube reactor where causticization occurs at 425°C and 350 atms. Residence time is around 15 minutes. Heat is removed from the reactor efflux by exchange in the feed preheater. The cooled hydrolyzate is acidified in a neutralizer to liberate phenol and sodium chloride which must be separated by distillation. Salt is recycled to an electrolysis unit to produce the needed chlorine and caustic.

Phenol is stripped of diphenyl oxide and other minor by-products in a vacuum. A portion of the diphenyl oxide is returned to causticization tower with the remainder redistilled under vacuum for commercial marketing of this plus other derivatives.

3.4.5. Major engineering problems

- Corrosion from HCl in chlorobenzene unit
- Pressure vessel design for the high temperature-pressure causticization reactor
- Separation of saleable by-products

3.4.6. Economics of the process

Competitive if low-cost chlorine is available. This means that the process must be coupled to an electrolytic chlorine-caustic process so that economics of an integrated plant will apply. In addition, all by-products such as diphenyl oxide, *o*- and *p*-dichlorobenzene and *p*-phenylphenols must be disposed of properly.

The uses for chlorobenzene are:

- hydrolysis to phenol
- ammonolysis to aniline
- nitration to chloronitrobenzenes
- condensation with chloral to DDT

The world pattern for chlorobenzene production is as follows:

Chlorobenzene Production ('000 tons)

	1985	1987	1989
Western Europe	146	135	149
USA	102	112	134
Japan	25	29	33

Source: "Industrial Organic Chemistry" by Weissermel et al (1993)

3.5 Benzene Sulfonate Process for Phenol Production

3.5.1. Reference flow sheet: Figure IVF-7

3.5.2. Chemical reactions

(a) Sulfonation

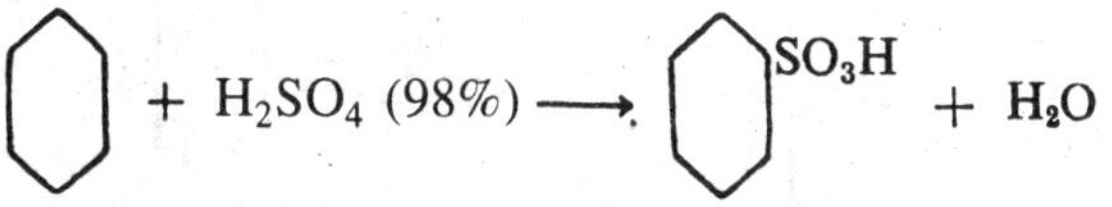

(b) Neutralization

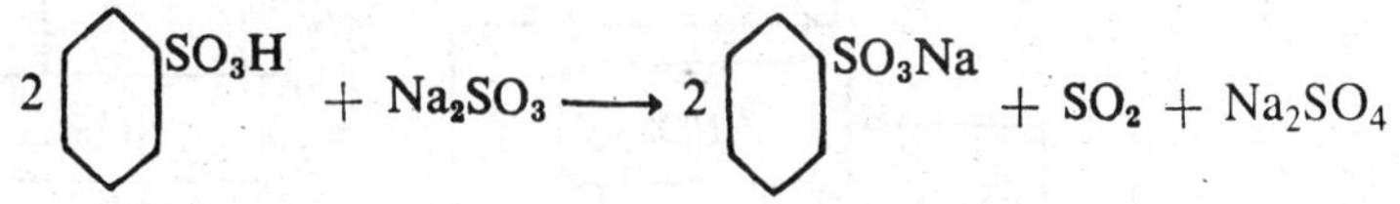

(c) Fusion

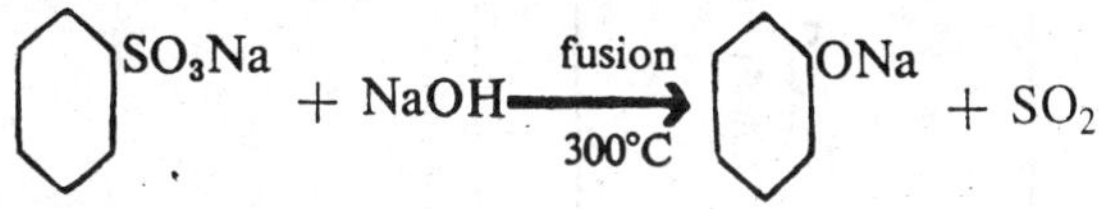

(d) Acidification

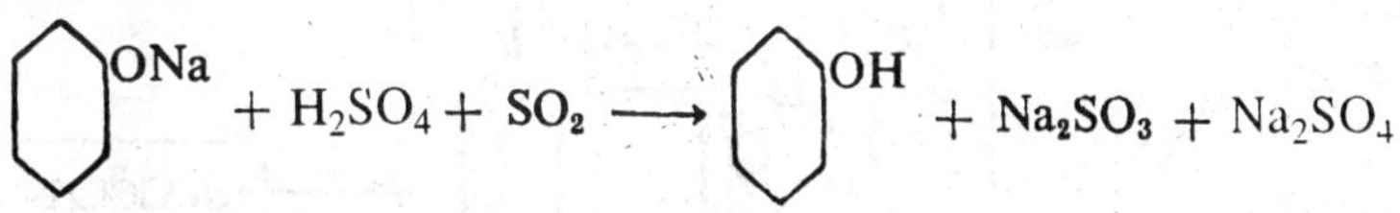

3.5.3. Quantitative requirements

(a) Basis: 1 ton of phenol (87% yield)

Benzene	0.96 ton
H_2SO_4 (98%)	1.70 tons
NaOH (100%)	1.65 tons

(b) Plant capacities: 50-150 tons/day

3.5.4. Process description

Benzene sulfonic acid is formed by contact of benzene vapors with H_2SO_4 liquid in a counter-current reactor. Excess benzene carries off the water formed in the reaction to avoid diluting the acid and slowing down the sulfonation. The sulfonator is designed so that only a few percent of free H_2SO_4 remains before the liquid is discharged to the neutralizer.

Neutralization is accomplished by rapidly adding the reactor liquor to a solution of sodium sulfite. Sulfur dioxide is released and the pot residue contains sodium benzene sulfonate in solution and precipitated Na_2SO_4. This mixture is pressure-filtered at the boiling point with the clear solution moving on to the batch fusion operation. In a process modification some plants centrifuge the hot liquor, concentrate the sulfonate liquor further by evaporation, then remove more sodium sulfate.

A cast iron fusion pot containing molten caustic is kept at 300°C by direct gas or oil fire. The sulfonate is slowly added at the bottom of the pot and the reaction allowed to continue for 5-6 hours. The melt is then diluted with water, acidified with SO_2 from the neutralization step, and the final pH adjusted with dilute H_2SO_4. The released crude phenol floats on an aqueous solution containing sodium sulfate, sodium sulfite and a small percentage of phenol.

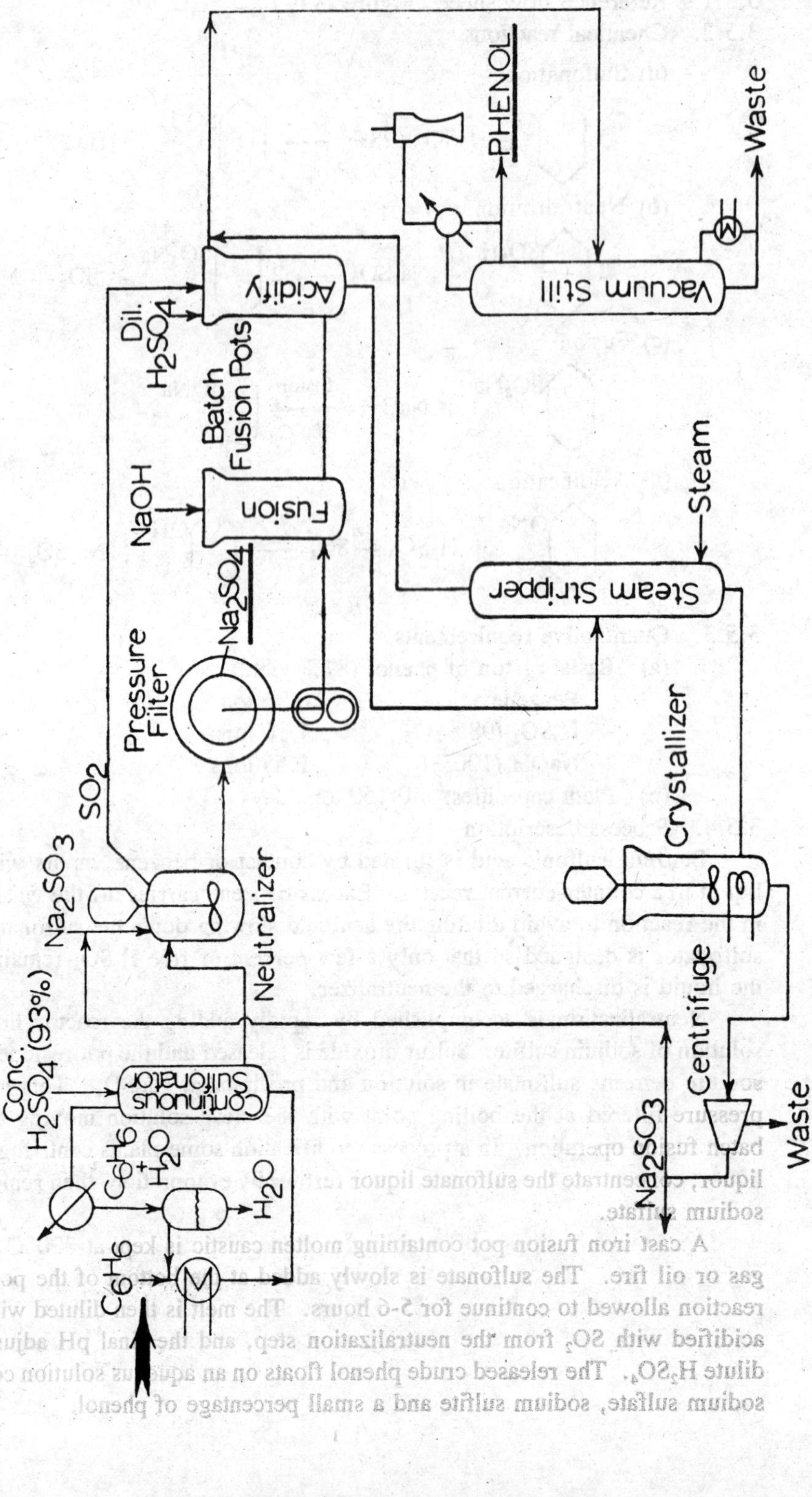

Fig. IVF-7. Phenol via benzene sulfonate process.

Crude phenol is refined in a vacuum distillation column. The aqueous layer is steam distilled to recover more phenol. Part of the salt sludge is used in the neutralization step. The balance is sent directly to a paper mill or crystallized and dried to yield anhydrous sodium sulfite.

3.5.5. Major engineering problems

This process is the oldest of the six and operates on large scale batch cycles for all but the distillation and sulfonation steps. There is no incentive to switch to a completely continuous operation because of the slow reaction rates in the fusion step.

Safety design of the fusion cycle is paramount in both the addition of aqueous sulfonate to molten NaOH and the subsequent water dilution which occurs at the end of the reaction step.

3.5.6. Economics of the process

The presently operating plants are old and fully depreciated and thus cannot compete with more modern processes. Other economic requirements are to have adjacent or captive NaOH and H_2SO_4 plants and be able to utilize or sell all the inorganic by-product salts to nearby plants, such as paper mills.

3.6. Direct Oxidation of Benzene

3.6.1. Reference flow sheet: None

3.6.2. Chemical reactions

(a) $C_6H_6 + 3H_2 \rightarrow C_6H_{12}$

(b) $2C_6H_{12} + 1\frac{1}{2}O_2 \rightarrow C_6H_{11}OH + C_6H_{10}O + H_2O$

(c) $C_6H_{11}OH \rightarrow C_6H_5OH + 3H_2$

3.6.3. Process description

Benzene is hydrogenated to cyclohexane which is oxidized with air, yielding a mixture of cyclohexanol, cyclohexanone, and unreacted cyclohexane. The unreacted cyclohexane is separated and recycled. The oxygenated fraction is then dehydrogenated to phenol over nickel or platinum catalyst.

Though the direct conversion of phenol via air oxidation has been the subject of much research because of its simplicity, the yields were never high enough to warrant full-scale development. The Scientific Design Co. claims that the yields in their process are as high as in any other process; in addition, their process requires lower capital investment and has no by-product disposal problems.

Styrene

1. **Pertinent Properties of Styrene**

Mol. wt.	104.1
M.P.	−30.6°C
B.P.	145.2°C
Density @ 20°C	0.903
Explosive limits:	Lower = 1.1 vol.% air
	Upper = 6.1 vol.% air
Toxicity limit:	400 ppm
Grades:	Technical (99% pure)

2. Consumption Pattern

The impetus to growth of styrene production was the synthetic rubber requirements of World War II. The copolymerized styrene-butadiene rubber (SBR) developed for such process is described in Chapter VB. Demands for styrene in the elastomer field continue to rise. Polystyrene molding resin in solidified form and foamed for insulation is of greater importance.

Table IVF-6 shows trends in styrene uses in the various parts of the world.

Table IVF-6
Styrene Use (in wt.%)

	World	USA		Western Europe		Japan	
	1990	1986	1989	1985	1990	1985	1989
Polystyrene	67	65	65	66	66	63	60
Styrene-butadiene rubber (SBR)	7	6	7	13	12	9	9
Acrylonitrile-butadiene-styrene (ABS)	9	9	9	9	9	14	13
Styrene-acrylonitrile (SAN)	2	1	2	2	2	4	4
Polyester resins (unsaturated)	4	7	7	6	4	4	6
Miscellaneous	11	12	10	4	7	6	8
Total use (in 10^6 tonnes)	13.60	3.04	3.54	2.95	3.76	1.63	2.35

Source: "Industrial Organic Chemistry" by Weissermel et al (1993)

3. Methods of Production

3.1. Classification of Processes

- **Dehydrogenation of ethylbenzene**
- **Hydrogenation-dehydration of acetophenone**

3.2. Dehydrogenation of Ethylbenzene

3.2.1. Reference flow sheet: Figure IVF-8

3.2.2. Chemical reactions

(a) Alkylation of benzene

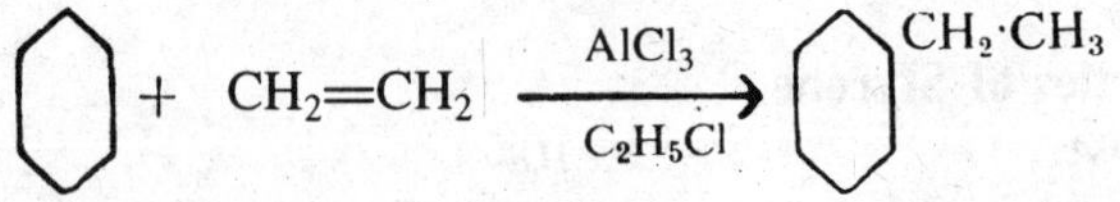

(b) Dehydrogenation of ethylbenzene

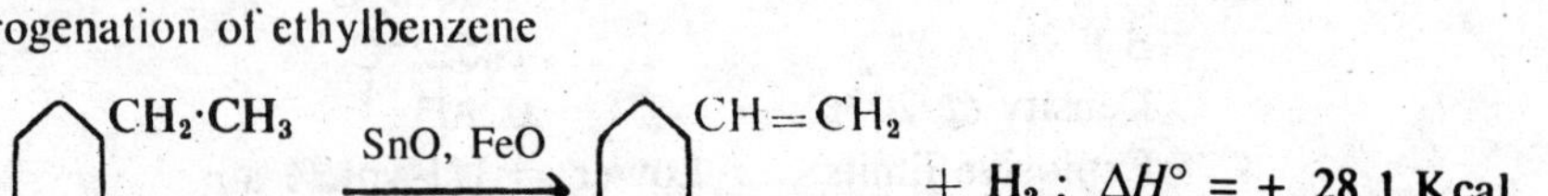

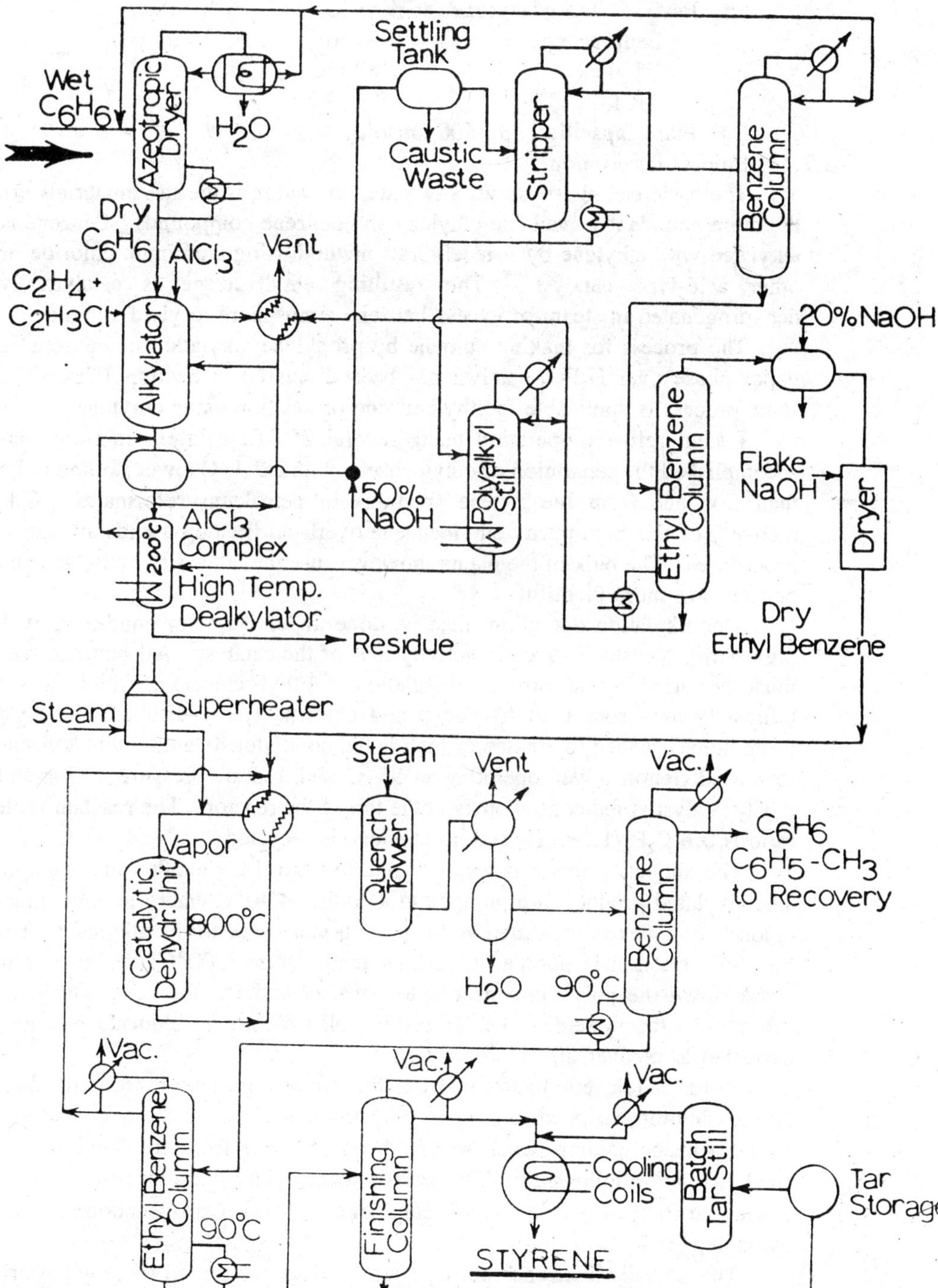

Fig. IVF-8. Styrene from benzene and ethylene.

3.2.3. Quantitative requirements

(a) Basis: 1 ton of styrene (86% yield)

Benzene	0.87 ton
Ethylene	0.32 ton
$AlCl_3$	10-11 kg

(b) Plant capacities: 30-400 tons/day

3.2.4. Process description

The basic chemistry shows a two-step operation if the raw materials are the more abundantly available ethylene and benzene compounds. Benzene is alkylated with ethylene by Friedel-Craft method using aluminum chloride or other acid-type catalyst. The resulting ethylbenzene is catalytically dehydrogenated in steam or excess benzene atmosphere to yield styrene.

The process for making cumene by propylene alkylation of benzene in vapor phase over H_3PO_4 catalyst has been discussed in Section IVD. The same process is applicable to ethylbenzene production using ethylene.

Recent refinery operation using several 250 ft. columns in series has accomplished the separation of ethylbenzene with a 2.1 °C lower boiling point than *p*-xylene from the xylene fractions in petroleum reformates. The recovery of this high purity ethylbenzene overhead fraction avoids alkylation procedures. The bulk of the plants, however, use the latter since ethylene and benzene are more plentiful.

The alkylation operation must be done under very dry conditions with high purity feedstock to avoid activity loss of the catalyst. All benzene feed must be dried by azeotropic distillation. Ethyl chloride, which serves ultimately as a source of hydrogen and chlorine free radicals for catalyst promotion, is added to ethylene which is fed continuously along with benzene to the alkylation tower operating at 95 °C and 1 atm. pressure. Granular $AlCl_3$ catalyst is fed continuously at the top of the reactor. The reactant mole ratio is 0.6 C_2H_4/1.0 C_6H_6 and no ethylene is recycled.

The alkylation tower is water-cooled to control the exothermic reaction. The alkylated products are pumped to a cooler at 40 °C where the aluminum chloride complex is separated and a split stream is fed to the alkylator. The bleed-off fraction is pumped to a high temperature (200 °C) dealkylator to break down the polyethylbenzenes to benzene and ethylbenzene which are returned to the system. The tar residue plus aluminum chloride is water-extracted to recover 80-85% of $AlCl_3$.

Crude acidic ethylbenzene from the coolers is neutralized with 50% NaOH solution, stripped to remove polyethylbenzenes and the overhead sent to the benzene column which separates wet benzene from ethylbenzene. A final distillation followed by 20% caustic wash, then drying by percolation in a flake caustic bed, produces 99% ethylbenzene for dehydrogenation in yields averaging 95%.

The polyalkylbenzenes must be removed as bottoms in the atmospheric stripper to avoid formation of polyfunctional, highly reactive products during the dehydrogenation step. The stripper bottoms fraction is distilled at 50 mm pressure with the overhead combined with bottoms from the ethylbenzene column and returned to the alkylation unit for dealkylation of these higher molecular weight compounds. The highest molecular weight polybenzenes as bottoms from the vacuum still can only be split in the high temperature dealkylator.

Dehydrogenation of ethylbenzene is the step which produces styrene. Steam is injected with the hydrocarbon in a mole ratio of 15 $H_2O/1\ C_6H_5C_2H_5$. The mixed feed passes through the preheater to achieve an input temperature of 500°C to the reactor which operates at 800°C. The dehydrogenation catalyst is promoted zinc, chromium, iron, or MgO on activated carbon, alumina, or bauxite. Conversion is 35-40% with an average yield of 91%.

Reaction product is cooled in the feed preheater, then by steam quenching. A water-cooled condenser and separator operation yields crude styrene-ethylbenzene with impurities of 1% toluene, 0.7% benzene, and 0.3% tar. Sulfur stabilizer is added at this point and the hydrocarbon mixture is passed through a series of vacuum distillation columns to allow the separation of impurities at low enough temperature to avoid styrene polymerization. Benzene and toluene are removed at 160 mm and a reboiler temperature of 90°C. Temperatures higher than this cause autopolymerization of benzene. The second column at 35 mm and 90°C reboiler temperature separates styrene from ethylbenzene. The styrene, stabilized at this point with *p*-tertiary catechol, is vacuum distilled again to remove traces of tar and sulfur. The final overhead (99.8% or better styrene) is refrigerated at 10°C or less and either stored in insulated tanks or used immediately for polymerization.

3.2.5. Major engineering problems

- Production of dry raw materials in the alkylation reaction
- Minimizing loss of aromatics contained in polyalkylbenzenes by high temperature dealkylation
- Reducing losses of $AlCl_3$ catalyst by extracting residues from the high temperature dealkylator
- Control of the dehydrogenation reaction by use of a large mole ratio of superheated steam to ethylbenzene. This accomplishes the following:
  (a) Reduces partial pressure of reacting components and improves the equilibrium conversion
  (b) Supplies endothermic heat of reaction
  (c) Avoids undesirable side reactions
  (d) Controls the temperature of reaction and minimizes coking of catalyst
  (e) Removes carbon deposits by water-gas reaction
- Prevention of undue polymerization of styrene during purification—accomplished by inhibitor plus refrigeration

3.2.6. Economics of styrene

- Marketing

Continued growth in the polymer market is assured as polystyrene resin is cheap, yet furnishes good fabrication and wear characteristics. Synthetic rubber made with styrene-butadiene copolymer (SBR) is not advancing markedly in sales due to competition from other, more recently developed elastomers. The overall marketing picture is quite favorable.

- Competitive process

On the process side, the complex flow sheet described above still provides the most economic route for most producers. The acetophenone process is only economic where co-products of phenylethyl alcohol and acetophenone can be marketed. Any real process change will come by substituting the superfractionation process to recover ethylbenzene directly from petroleum C_8 streams.

- Raw materials

The Synthetics and Chemicals Co. Ltd. operate a 90-ton per day SBR synthetic rubber plant which started in 1963 at Bareilly. Captive ethylene is made from ethanol which comes from a number of small distilleries in U.P. State. Prices are high and ethanol supplies are not reliable. Benzene must be shipped by tank car from coal carbonization plant in Bihar State.

The Polychemicals styrene plant in Trombay is more favorably located. It formerly obtained ethylene from alcohol and benzene from steel plants, but now utilizes petrochemical supplies produced at Trombay.

- Polymer production

While polymerization processes are considered in detail in Chapter V, it is worthy of note that styrene's only use is as a monomer in polymer and copolymer production.

The pattern of styrene production is shown in the following tabulation:

Styrene Production (in 10^6 tons)

	1987	1989	1991
USA	3.67	3.78	3.87
Western Europe	3.16	3.39	3.91
Japan	1.56	1.99	2.59
CIS	0.73	0.77	0.68

Source: "Industrial Organic Chemistry" by Weissermel et al (1993)

At present there are 3 units manufacturing styrene in the organized sector in India. Their names and addresses are given in Table IVF-7.

Table IVF-7
Names and Addresses of Units Manufacturing Styrene in India

Hindustan Polymers (Div. McDowell & Co. Ltd.)
P.O. R.R. Venkatapuram, Visakhapatnam (A.P.)

Polychem Ltd.
Anik Mahul, Chembur, Bombay - 400 074 (Maharashtra)

Synthetics & Chemicals Ltd.
P.O. Bhitaura Rubber Factory, Bareilly - 243 501 (U.P.)

Source: "SBP Handbook of Projects for Corporate Diversification" (1992)

The production of styrene during the past few years in the organized sector in the country is as follows:

Estimated Production of Styrene in India (M.T.)

Year	Production
1987	27,346
1988	29,530
1989	26,511
1990	25,443

Source: "SBP Handbook of Projects for Corporate Diversification" (1992)

The imports of styrene in the country in the past few years were as follows:

Imports of Styrene in India

Year	Quantity (M.T.)	Value (Rs. lakhs)
1985-86	6,797.8	476.82
1986-87	10,519.3	705.43
1987-88	11,792.9	1,649.19

Source: "SBP Handbook of Projects for Corporate Diversification" (1992)

The imports of styrene in 1990-91 were estimated at 15,000 tons. The demand for styrene by 1994-95 and 2000 A.D. was expected to rise to 177,000 tpa and 288,000 tpa respectively.

Phthalic Anhydride

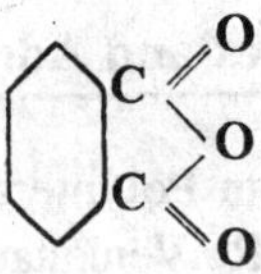

1. Pertinent Properties of Phthalic Anhydride,

Mol. wt.	148.1
M.P.	130.6°C
B.P.	284.5°C
Density @ 4°C	1.53

Slightly soluble in hot water and ether; sublimes below the melting point

Ignition temperature 588°C

Grades: Technical (99-99.8%), pure (>99.8%); as flakes or pellets

2. Consumption Pattern

Major outlets for phthalic anhydride are in alkyd resins and plasticizers. The alkyd industry has been given a boost by the development of solution and emulsion types of alkyd coatings. Phthalate derivatives continue as a standard plasticizer in many resin formulations, particularly vinyl resins.

The consumption pattern for phthalic anhydride in developed countries is as follows:

End Use	Consumption (%)
Phthalate plasticizers	50
Unsaturated polyesters	30
Alkyd resins	17
Others including exports	3

Source: "Global Trends in Chemical Products"—Nandini (1994)

The Indian pattern of consumption is as follows:

End Use Sector	Consumption (%)
Phthalate plasticizers	38
Paints	36
Dyes & Pigments	13
Polyester resins	7.0
Miscellaneous uses	6.0

Source: "Global Trends in Chemical Products"—Nandini (1994)

3. Method of Production

3.1. Oxidation of Naphthalene and/or *o*-xylene

3.1.1. Reference flow sheet: Figure IVF-9

3.1.2. Chemical reactions

(a) Naphthalene oxidation

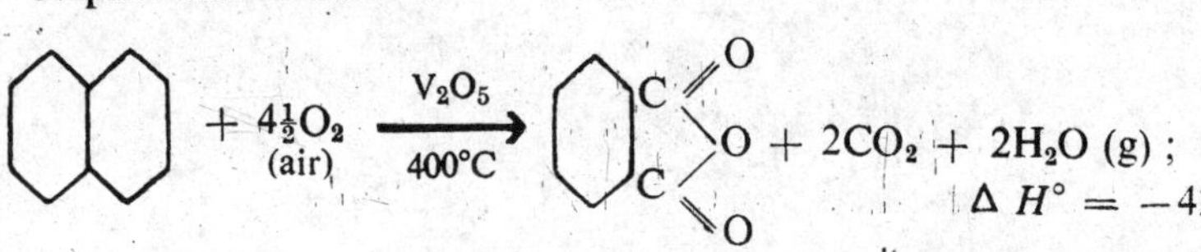

$\Delta H° = -426$ Kcal

(b) *o*-xylene oxidation

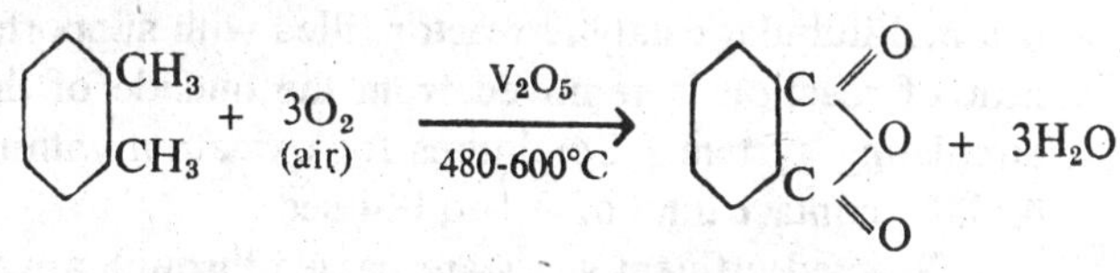

(c) Major side reaction—complete combustion (15-20%)

- $C_{10}H_8 + 12O_2$ (air) → $10CO_2 + 4H_2O$
- $C_8H_{10} + 10\frac{1}{2}O_2$ (air) → $8CO_2 + 5H_2O$

(d) Minor side reaction (3-5% of yield)

- $C_{10}H_8 + 9O_2$ (air) → $C_4H_5O_3$ (maleic anhydride) + $6CO_2 + 3H_2O$
- $C_8H_{10} + 7\frac{1}{2}O_2$ (air) → $C_4H_2O_3$ (maleic anhydride) + $4CO_2 + 4H_2O$

All side reactions are much more endothermic than the principal reaction and a high degree of temperature control is needed to optimize yields.

3.1.3. Quantitative requirements

(a) Basis: 1 ton of phthalic anhydride (75% yield)

Naphthalene	1.15 tons
Air	22.6 tons
o-xylene	0.96 ton
Air	20.1 tons

(b) Plant capacities: 15-150 tons/day

3.1.4. Process description

Naphthalene, *o*-xylene, or mixtures thereof are melted and vaporized by bubbling primary preheated air through the molten material. Secondary air to make up the 22 kg air/kg feed requirement is added downstream and the

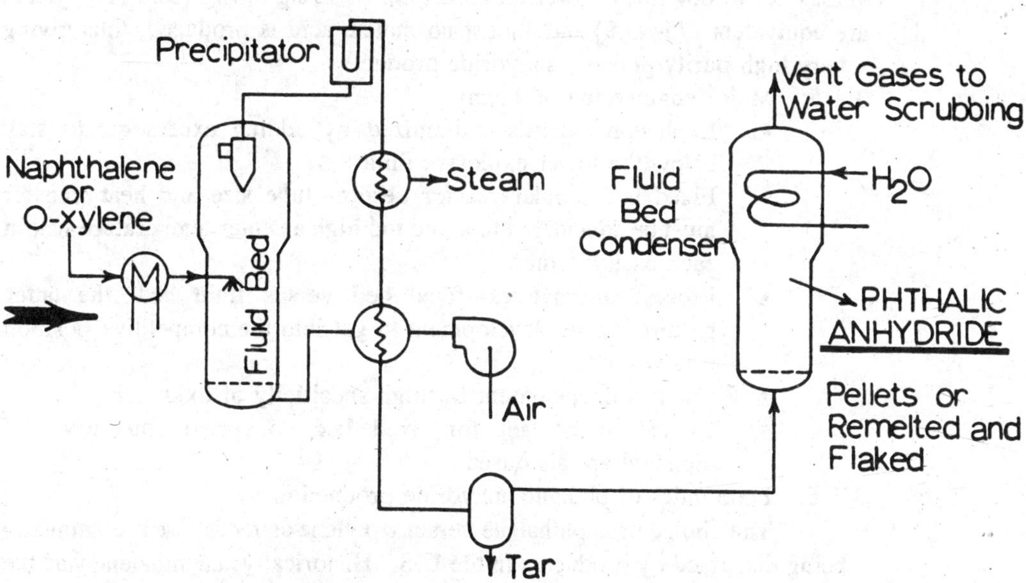

Fig. IVF-9. Phthalic anhydride by air oxidation of naphthalene or ortho-xylene.

reacting mixture is passed through a preheater to a fixed bed converter. This is a multitubular catalytic reactor filled with supported V_2O_5. The exothermic heat of reaction is removed from the outside of the tubes by a molten salt circulating system. Conditions for oxidation within the converter are 380°-450°C, contact time of 0.1 to 0.4 sec.

Reacted effluent gases are passed through a waste-heat steam boiler and thence to a preheater where the final temperature is dropped to a few degrees above the dew point of phthalic anhydride. Condensation of the solid product can be effected by pairs of switching fin-tube condensers, a cyclone, a fluidized bed condenser, or a water scrubber. The crude solid product is melted, distilled under vacuum, and condensed with a flaking or pelletizing operation completing the production scheme. The major impurity is maleic anhydride in 0.2-0.4% quantities.

Maleic anhydride and an easily converted derivative, fumaric acid, can be recovered in 3-5% yield from the off-gas scrubbing liquor of the crude phthalic anhydride condensers.

A process modification which is competitive is the substitution of a fluid bed catalytic reactor for the fixed bed multitubular reactor. Conditions at the head end are somewhat different. The molten naphthalene and/or *o*-xylene is sprayed directly into the air-fluidized catalytic reactor which operates at 600°C. The reacted gases rise upwards through the dense phase into a wider calming-settling zone and thence through the internal cyclone to dust filters. Condensation is the same as above, but no vacuum distillation is required.

A comparison of reactor conditions for the two cases shows that the fluid bed process operates at 140-220°C higher, a longer contact time of 10 sec versus 0.1 to 0.4 sec, a lower air-feed ratio of 15 kg air/kg feed. The yields are equivalent (75-80%) and almost no maleic acid is produced, thus giving a very high purity phthalic anhydride product.

3.1.5. Major engineering problems

- Explosion hazards—minimized by adding excess air to stay below the lower explosive limit
- Fixed bed tubular reactor design—tube size and heat transfer must be considered to avoid too high a center temperature within each catalytic tube
- Process alternatives—fixed bed versus fluid bed, the latter required more development to get into the competitive position it now holds
- Catalyst development for high specificity of oxidation
- Choice of coolant for fixed bed converters—mercury and diphenyl are also used

3.1.6. Economics of phthalic anhydride production

The choice of naphthalene versus *o*-xylene as feedstock is continually being discussed by producers in the U.S. Historically, naphthalene was the sole source from by-product coke. A cheap method for separating *o*-xylene from the more valuable *m*- and *p*-xylene isomers using >100 plate distillation towers brought *o*-xylene into the picture. With petroleum-based naphthalene from a hydrodealkylation process currently in plentiful supply, *o*-xylene has less interest.

The choice between phthalic anhydride feedstocks in various countries is as follows:

		naphthalene	*o*-xylene
World	1960	100	-
	1975	25	75
	1980	15	85
	1989	11	89
Japan	1989	42	58
USA	1989	13	87
Western Europe	1989	6	94
CIS	1989	4	96

Another choice in terms of fixed versus fluid bed is still a toss-up with a slight edge in favor of the latter only on a large-size plant basis unless the co-product of maleic anhydride or fumaric acid can be disposed of profitably.

The plant capacity available in the U.S. of over 1,500 tons/day is nearly double the current requirements. This reflects the success in designing and selling processes with a low break-even point and a confidence by producers of the future of the alkyd resin and plasticizer business.

3.1.7. Production in various countries

Phthalic anhydride production outside India ('000 tons) is as follows:

	1985	1987	1989
Western Europe	620	740	824
USA	379	469	416
Japan	279	307	299
CIS	214	225	230

The first indigenous phthalic anhydride unit in India was put on stream by Herdillia Chemicals Ltd. in a plant on the Thane-Belapur Road near Bombay in early 1968. The plant, using orthoxylene as a feed material, has a capacity of 6,000 tons per year.

If proper incentives are given by the Government, according to the "Perspective Plan for Chemical Industry (up to the year 2000 A.D.)," there is a potential to export 16,000 M.T. and 25,000 M.T. of phthalic anhydride from India in the years 1994-95 and 1999-2000 respectively.

The demand for phthalic anhydride is estimated at 85,700 M.T. and 138,000 M.T. per annum by 1994-95 and 1999-2000 respectively.

As per the "Report of the Committee for Perspective Planning of Petrochemical Industry (1986-2000 A.D.)" the demand for phthalic anhydride is expected to rise to 75,500 M.T. and 113,400 M.T. by 1994-95 and 1999-2000 respectively.

Table IVF-8 shows the units producing phthalic anhydride in India.

Table IVF-8

Names and Addresses of Units Manufacturing Phthalic Anhydride in India

---

Asian Paints (India) Ltd.
Plot No. 2702, GIDC Industrial Area, Ankleshwar - 393 002 (Gujarat)

Durgapur Chemicals Ltd.
Durgapur, Dist. Burdwan (W.B.)

Herdillia Chemicals Ltd.
Thane - 400 601 (Maharashtra)

IG Petrochemicals Ltd., Taloja (Maharashtra) 100% EOU

Indian Dyestuff Industries Ltd.
Near Shahad Station, Kalyan - 421 304 (Maharashtra)

Mysore Petrochemicals Ltd.
Village Hegsanhall, Near Chicksugar, Dist. Raichur (Karnataka)

Shri Ambuja Petrochemicals Ltd.
Plot Nos. 17, 18 & 20, I.D.A. Phase I, Patancheru - 502 319
Dist. Medak (A.P.)

Thirumalai Chemicals Ltd.
Ranipet, Wallajapet Taluk, Dist. North Arcot (T.N.)

Source: "SBP Handbook of Projects for Corporate Diversification" (1992)

Maleic Anhydride

1. Pertinent Properties of Maleic Anhydride,

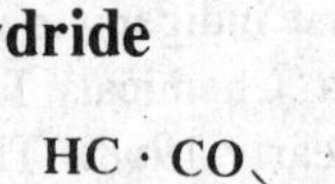

Mol. wt. 98.1
M.P. 53.3°C
B.P. 199.7°C
Density @ 20°C 0.934
Soluble in water (16 wt.% at 30°C), acetone, ether, chloroform, and petroleum
Ignition temperature 475°C
Grades: Commercial (>99%) as flakes, pellets, solidified within containers

2. Consumption Pattern

Most of the maleic anhydride goes into polyesters. It has made some inroad into alkyd resin formulation, but not to the extent that phthalic anhydride has. Agricultural chemicals such as malathion and soil conditioners consume some maleic anhydride, but only a minor amount.

2.1. End Uses

Table IVF-9 shows worldwide maleic anhydride use patterns.

Table IVF-9

Application of Maleic Anhydride in the USA, Western Europe, and Japan (in wt.%)

Product	USA		Western Europe		Japan	
	1986	1989	1986	1989	1986	1989
Unsaturated polyesters	57	58	56	54	41	41
Fumaric/maleic acid	10	7	4	4	14	10
Pesticides	10	5	2	2	3	3
Lubricating oil additives	9	10	5	6	3	3
Miscellaneous	14	20	33	34	39	43
Total Consumption ('000 tons)	164	189	157	196	64	81

Source: "Industrial Organic Chemistry" by Weissermel et al (1993)

3. Method of Production

3.1. Oxidation of Benzene or *n*-butene

3.1.1. Reference flow sheet: Figure IVF-10

3.1.2. Chemical reactions

(a) Benzene oxidation

$$C_6H_6 + 4\frac{1}{2}O_2 \xrightarrow[400\text{-}500°C]{V_2O_5} C_4H_2O_3 + 2H_2O + 2CO_2; \quad \Delta H° = -422 \text{ Kcal}$$

(b) Butene oxidation

$$C_4H_8 + 3O_2 \rightarrow C_4H_2O_3 + 3H_2O; \quad \Delta H° = -271 \text{ Kcal}$$

3.1.3. Quantitative requirements

(a) Basis: 1 ton of maleic anhydride (60% yield)

Benzene 1.33 tons

Air 20-22 tons

(b) Basis: 1 ton of maleic anhydride (50% yield)

Butylene 1.07 tons

Air 38-40 tons

(c) Plant capacities: 8-30 tons/day

3.1.4. Process description

This oxidation process is very similar to the fixed bed catalytic operation just described in making phthalic anhydride. Benzene is vaporized with a large excess of air at 1-1.5 atms. gage in a steam coil to avoid explosive compositions. After preheating, it is fed to a fixed bed converter where the contact time is about 0.1 sec, the temperature is 400-500°C and the pressure 0.8-1 atm. gage.

The exit gases from the reactor are passed successively through a waste heat boiler, feed preheater, tar knock-out drum, and absorbed in water to yield a 40 percent maleic acid solution. This is reconverted to anhydride by a hydrocarbon azeotropic distillation system. The crude product is purified by vacuum distillation.

3.1.5. Major engineering problems

- Hydrocarbon feed alternatives—when the cheaper butene was introduced, a V_2O_5/P_2O_5 on alumina had to be developed.
- Choice of condensation methods—in addition to the water absorbing-dehydration system given above, a partial condenser maintained slightly above the melting point of maleic anhydride followed by final absorption in either aqueous or non-aqueous solvents is used for recovery.
- Fumaric acid production—based on increased demand of this isomer of maleic acid, it was a relatively simple matter to top off a side stream from the water absorption column and isomerize with acid; HCl is a typical acid. (See Figure IVF-10.)
- Choice of reactor design—in this case, in contrast to phthalic anhydride operations, only a short contact time, fixed bed converter will give sufficiently high yield. The inherently higher fluid bed contact time gives rise to more complete oxidation to CO_2-H_2O.

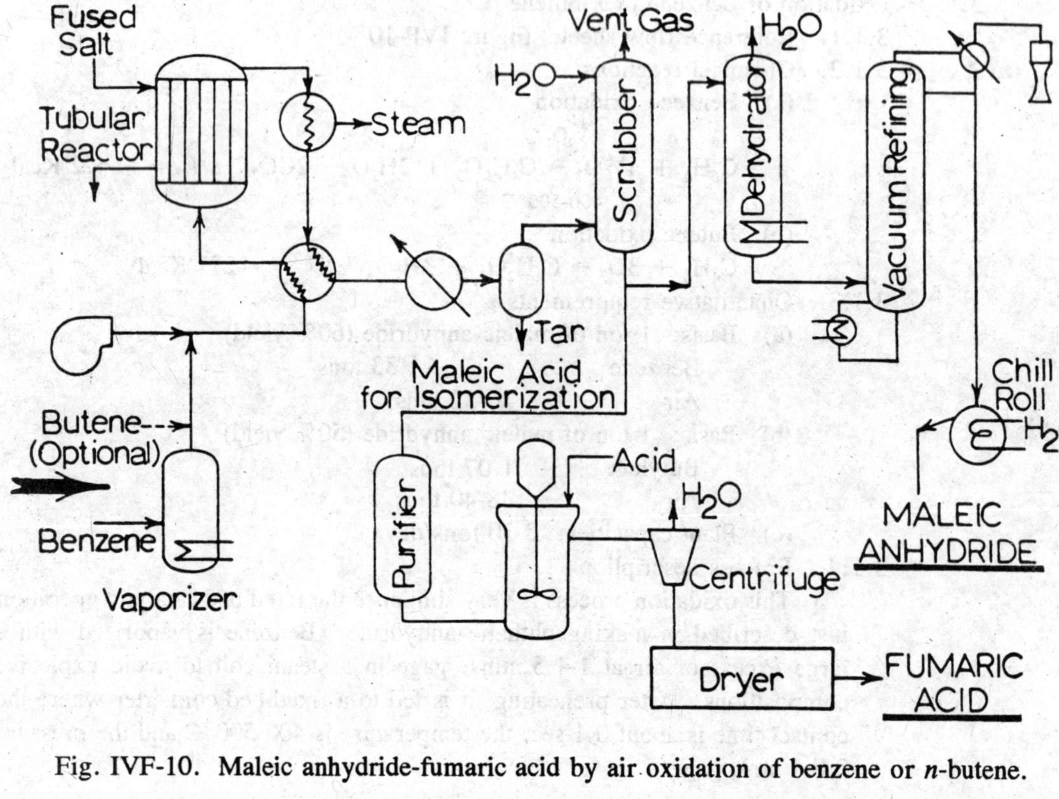

Fig. IVF-10. Maleic anhydride-fumaric acid by air oxidation of benzene or *n*-butene.

3.1.6. Economics of maleic anhydride production—USA

Lower cost butenes are making inroads into the benzene feed situation even though the process yields are lower (an average of 60 versus 50%). Other four- or five-carbon organic chemicals, except paraffins, will yield maleic anhydride by vapor-phase oxidation over vanadium catalysts. Furfural, crotonaldehydes are typical examples, but are too high priced.

The maleic anhydride produced as by-product in phthalic anhydride units does not cause any real economic problem since the total demand is 5-6 times that which can be obtained from the by-product operation.

The increased usage of fumaric acid, the maleic acid isomer, and its production by simple process modification puts the investment in maleic-fumaric plants in a very favorable position. Fumaric acid gives polyester resins with much better heat resistance and strength than those formulated with maleic anhydride.

Maleic anhydride plants, although similar in process scope to phthalic anhydride plants, are 20-25% smaller, requiring a proportionally higher investment per annual kilogram.

4. Maleic Anhydride Production Patterns

4.1. Worldwide picture for maleic anhydride production is as follows (in thousands of tons):

	1985	1987	1989
USA	169	176	193
Western Europe	142	163	181
Japan	71	80	96

At present there are 6 units manufacturing maleic anhydride in the organized sector in India. Their names and addresses, and installed capacities of these units are given in Table IVF-10.

Imports of Maleic Anhydride

Year	Quantity (M.T.)	Value (Rs. lakhs)
1985-86	752.8	105.95
1986-87	428.1	45.27
1987-88	1,037.20	131.60

The exports of maleic anhydride from the country during 1989-90 are estimated at Rs. 18.5 lakhs.

If proper incentives are given by the Government, according to the "Perspective Plan for Chemical Industry (up to the year 2000 A.D.)," there is a potential to export 2,000 M.T. and 3,000 M.T. of maleic anhydride from India in the years 1994-95 and 1999-2000 A.D. respectively.

The demand for maleic anhydride in the country is estimated to rise to about 10,430 M.T. and 18,130 M.T. per annum by 1994-95 and 1999-2000 respectively.

Table IVF-10
Names and Addresses and Installed Capacities of Units Manufacturing Maleic Anhydride

Name and Address	Installed Capacity (M.T./year)
Adarsh Chemicals & Fertilizers Ltd. Udhna - 394 210, Surat (Gujarat)	7,000
Allied Aromatics Ltd. Rampur, 24-Parganas (W.B.)	3,000
Ganesh Anhydride Ltd. G-62, MIDC Industrial Area, Tarapur, Dist. Thane (Maharashtra)	7,000
Mysore Petrochemicals Ltd. Taloja (Maharashtra)	2,400
Niraj Petrochemicals Ltd. Visakhapatnam (A.P.)	5,000
Thirumalai Chemicals Ltd. Ranipet, Wallajapet Taluk, Dist. North Arcot (T.N.)	10,000

Source: "SBP Handbook of Projects for Corporate Diversification" (1992)

Terephthalic Acid & Dimethyl Terephthalate

In the area of dibasic acids and anhydrides from aromatic raw materials, we have touched upon phthalic anhydride and maleic anhydride. An important area which has not yet been covered is that of the terephthalates—terephthalic acid and the ester dimethyl terephthalate which are the basic materials for polyester fibers and films.

1. Production of Terephthalic Acid (TPA)

TPA is produced by the air oxidation of paraxylene in the liquid phase. Making polyester polymer can be thought of as occurring in two stages. First is the production of bis-(β-hydroxyethyl) terephthalate (bis-HET) by causing ethylene glycol to esterify with TPA or DMT:

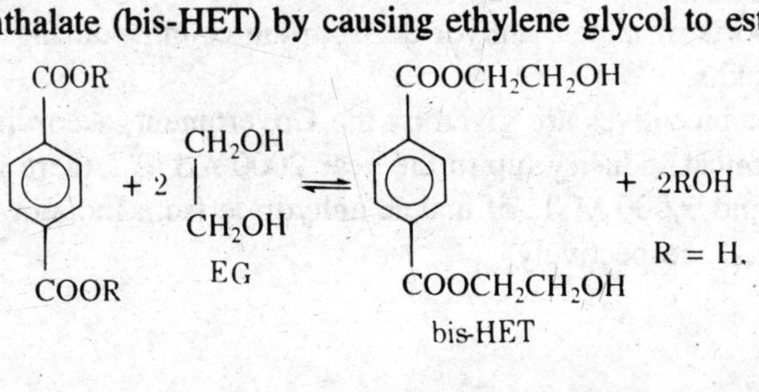

A number of oligomers with varying values of *n* are also formed:

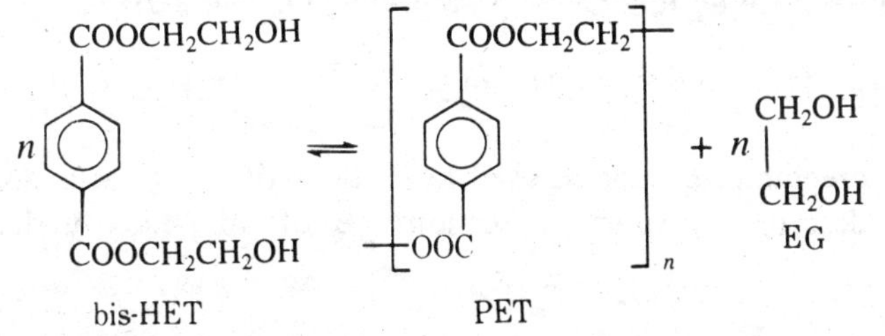

Dimethyl terephthalate (DMT) can be used as a substitute for purified terephthalic acid (TPA) as polyester raw material. All over the world, there has been a clear trend in the preference of TPA to DMT for polyester production.

U.S. xylene consumption for DMT and TPA has been estimated as follows:

	1986	1990	1992	1994	1996
					('000 tons)
Dimethyl terephthalate	983	968	1,028	1,071	1,170
Terephthalic Acid	837	700	842	949	1,059
Total	1,820	1,668	1,870	2,020	2,229

Source: "Global Trends in Chemical Products"—Nandini (1994)

Figures for the world production of TPA and DMT are as follows:

TPA Production ('000 tons)

	1985	1987	1989
USA	1,192	1,569	1,764
Japan	854	1,048	1,200
Western Europe	686	396	913

DMT Production (in '000 tons)

	1985	1987	1989
USA	1,507	1,635	1,776
Japan	358	315	350
Western Europe	1,048	1,002	993

Source: "Industrial Organic Chemistry" by Weissermel et al (1993)

2. Production of Poly(Ethylene) Terephthalate

In the second stage, polycondensation of bis-HET and the mixture of oligomers yield poly(ethylene) terephthalate of high molecular weight and ethylene glycol.

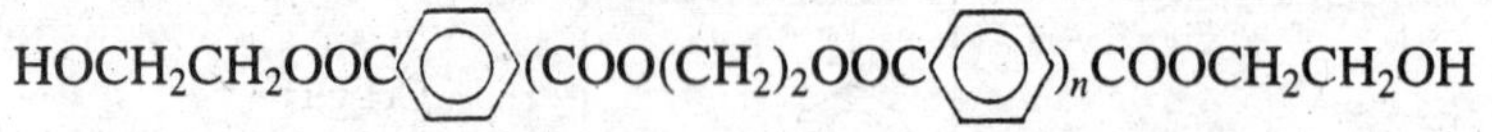

Poly(ethylene) terephthalate may be used to produce filament yarns and staple fiber for textile applications as described further in Section VB of this book under Polymerization Technology.

3. The Indian Production Picture is as Follows:

Indian demand for DMT & TPA	:	Around 360,000 tons per annum
Indian TPA supply level	:	Around 200,000 tons per annum
Indian DMT supply level	:	Around 130,000 tons per annum

The Indian TPA manufacturer is Reliance Industries Ltd. with an installed capacity of 200,000 tons/annum.

DMT manufacturers in India are:

IPCL (Indian Petrochemical Corp. Ltd.)	30,000 tons per annum
Bombay Dyeing & Mfg. Co.	60,000 tons per annum
Bongaigon Refineries & Petrochemical Ltd.	45,000 tons per annum

Nitrobenzene

The production of nitrobenzene by the direct reaction of benzene with nitric acid (usually in the presence of sulfuric acid as a dehydrating agent) is a doubly interesting reaction to the student of chemical engineering processes. In the first place, it is a commercially important method of making nitrobenzene as a raw material for aniline and aniline dyes; also the same technique can be applied to the nitration of toluene to give trinitrotoluene (TNT) as an explosive. The second point of interest in benzene nitration is that this is an old process which has now been subjected to much experimental and theoretical analysis for the determination of kinetic data applicable to reactor design.

Nitrobenzene is made at the rate of 250 million lbs/yr in the USA alone. It is used as a chemical intermediate in the manufacture of aniline, benzidine and many dyestuffs; it is also used widely as an industrial solvent in polishes, etc.

The reaction involved in nitrobenzene manufacture is:

$$C_6H_6 + HNO_3(H_2SO_4) \rightarrow C_6H_5NO_2 + H_2O(H_2SO_4); \quad \Delta H = -27.0 \text{ Kcal}$$

Aniline

Aniline constitutes the bridge between aromatic hydrocarbons and the dye industry. Azo dyes made by the diazotization and coupling of aniline have assumed such importance that many dyes have been referred to as aniline dyes. Actually other types of dyes have grown more in importance proportionately and the consumption of aniline in the manufacture of rubber chemicals (vulcanization accelerators, antioxidants, etc.) has increased. In the USA, as a consequence, some two-thirds of the aniline produced finds its way into rubber chemicals.

The traditional route to aniline was by the reduction of nitrobenzene with iron in the presence of HCl. The reaction, in simplified form, is as follows:

$$4C_6H_5NO_2 + 9Fe + 4H_2O \rightarrow 4C_6H_5NH_2 + 3Fe_3O_4; \; \Delta H = -130 \text{ Kcal}$$

This has now been largely superseded by the continuous catalytic vapor-phase reduction of nitrobenzene according to the reaction

$$C_6H_5NO_2 + 3H_2 \rightarrow C_6H_5NH_2 + 2H_2O; \; \Delta H = -130 \text{ Kcal}$$

This reaction is carried out at 270°C and 20 psi pressure. A three-fold excess of hydrogen is used over the theoretical amount and very short contact times are used. The catalyst used is copper supported on silica.

Aniline is also made, not by reduction as above, but by ammonolysis—the ammonolysis of chlorobenzene according to the equation:

$$C_6H_5Cl + 2NH_3 \text{ (aq)} \rightarrow C_6H_5NH_2 + NH_4Cl$$

This reaction is carried out at 180-220°C and 750 psi pressure. From 4 to 10 times the theoretical amount of ammonia is used.

A process has been developed in the USA for the ammonolysis of phenol to produce aniline. It is claimed that this process presents fewer by-product and waste disposal problems than do the routes based on chlorobenzene and nitrobenzene.

Developers of aniline processes have been summarized as follows:

Sumitomo Chemical Co.'s Process	Vapor phase hydrogenation of nitrobenzene with gaseous hydrogen on a fixed bed catalyst.
Bechamp Process	Reduction of nitrobenzene with iron and hydrochloric acid (outdated).
DuPont Process	Liquid phase hydrogenation of nitrobenzene using palladium/platinum on carbon.

Table IVF-11 summarizes aniline usage worldwide:

Table IVF-11
Aniline Usage in the USA, Western Europe, and Japan (in wt.%)

	USA		Western Europe		Japan	
	1980	1990	1979	1990	1980	1990
Isocyanates (MDI)	62	74	65	79	52	72
Rubber chemicals	22	14	22	21	31	11
Dyes, pigments	4	3	13		9	7
Hydroquinone	3	2			8	11
Miscellaneous (*e. g.*, pharmaceuticals, pesticides)	9	9				
Total consumption (in 10^6 tonnes)	0.29	0.42	0.30	0.56	0.07	0.14

Source: "Industrial Organic Chemistry" by Weissermel et al (1993)

The Indian scenario for aniline production is as follows:

Manufacturers	Installed Capacity, tpa
Hindustan Organic Chemicals Ltd. Maharashtra	15,000
Mardia Chemicals Ltd., Gujarat	6,000
Priya Organics & Chemicals Ltd. Bihar	1,500

Demand is around 20,000 tons per annum.

Source: "Global Trends in Chemical Products"—Nandini (1994)

Dyes

1. Introduction

A dye is a substance imparting color to any material of which it becomes an integral part. The entire dye industry produces high cost chemicals with annual rupee evaluation about half that of the chlor-alkali industry and in much smaller plants. The largest dye plant has a capacity of only 3 tons per day with the smallest at 150 kg per day.

The dye industry on a worldwide basis is one of the oldest chemical businesses. Competition is keen in world trade, and textile manufacturers in India still import dyes despite high tariffs. Like other industries, imports will be reduced as local production costs drop with (1) improved technology, and (2) lower raw material costs.

2. Technical Aspects

The chemistry of dyes is often complex and it is the purpose of this brief introductory section on dyes to merely point the way for further study if time is permitted.

As seen from figures on capacity quoted above, engineering is confined to small-scale operations. In some cases, bench-scale designs using glassware are employed.

2.1. Chemistry of Dyes

The unit process tabulation in Chapter ID lists the important basic reactions which are involved in synthesizing complex organic dyes from intermediates. Aromatic ring structure coupled with side chain construction is nearly always required to give resonance and in turn impart color. One method of classification of dyes is on the basis of their chemical structure.

2.2. Color Phenomena

Resonance structures which cause displacement or appearance of absorption bands in the visible spectrum are responsible for visible colors. For example, a dye which imparts a red color strongly absorbs or suppresses emission of all wavelengths, but those in the red band. Thus, red light is reemitted and/or reflected to the eye of the observer. Correlation of chemical structure with color has been accomplished by a general properties synthesis equation:

Chromogen---chromophore + Auxochrome = Dye

2.2.1. Chromogen

The aromatic structure containing benzene, naphthalene or anthracene rings coupled with chromophoric groups.

2.2.2. Chromophore

This group means color giver and is represented by the following radicals which form a basis for chemical classification of dyes when coupled with the chromogen.

(a) Azo: —N = N—
(b) Carbonyl: = C = O
(c) Carbon: = C = C =
(d) Carbon-nitrogen: > C = NH or —CH = N—
(e) Nitroso: —NO or = N—OH
(f) Nitro: $—NO_2$ or = NO—OH
(g) Sulfur: >C=S, ≡ C—S— ≡ C—S—C ≡ ≡ C—S—S—C≡

2.2.3. Auxochrome

The chromogen: chromophore structure is often not sufficient to impart solubility and to cause adherence of dye to fiber. The auxochrome or bonding affinity groups are $—NH_2$, —OH, COOH, $—SO_3H$ or their derivatives. These auxochromes are important in the use classification of dyes.

2.3. Classification of Dyes

2.3.1. Use classification

A listing of dyes by use classification comprises the following:

- Acetate rayon—dyes developed for cellulose acetate and some synthetic fibers
- Acid—dyes for coloring animal fibers via acidified solution to combine with amphoteric protein
- Azoic—contain azo group and applied especially for cotton
- Basic—amino derivatives used mostly for paper
- Direct—azo dyes employed for cotton-wool or cotton-silk combinations
- Lake or pigment—form insoluble compounds with Al, Ba, Ca, Cr on Mo salts, the precipitates are ground to form pigments used in paint and inks
- Mordant or chrome—metallic salt or lake formed directly on the fiber by use of Al, Cr, or Fe salts which cause precipitation *in situ*
- Sulfur or sulfide—contain S or precipitated from Na_2S bath; furnish dull shades with good fastness to light, washing, and acids, but susceptible to chlorine and light
- Vat—dye is impregnated into fiber under reducing conditions which reoxidizes to an insoluble color

2.3.2. Chemical classification

Based on chromogen. For example, nitro dyes have the chromophore $—NO_2$ under which Naphthol Yellow S, C.I. 10 is classified. Its formula is:

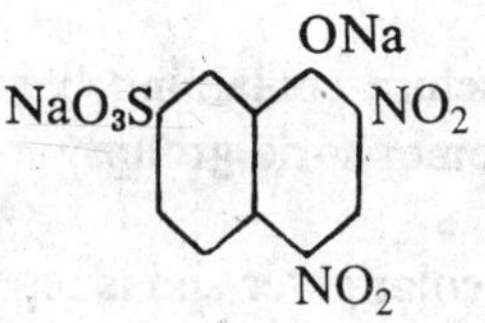

The coding S comes from commercial designations and relates to color or application

B	bluish
G	greenish, often yellowish (*gelbich* in German)
R	reddish
S	sulfur containing or dye for silk
W	wool dye
L	lake forming, easily soluble (*loslich* in German), or for linen

The C.I. number is added to distinguish one specific chemical compound from amongst the many names under which it may be marketed.

3. Economics

The strong position of Indian textiles in the world market is a guarantee of continued usage of dyes. The dyestuffs industry in India is a post independence phenomenon. Right up to the 50's, India depended on the West for supplies of pigments and dyestuffs for its fast growing textile industry. After 1952, a few large units were set up mainly as import substitution projects. Today, the wheel has turned full circle and India exports dyestuffs to the very same countries on which it was dependent till recently.

The number of units in this sector has risen from seven in the 50's to 37 in the organized sector and at least 900 in the small scale sector, manufacturing practically all types of pigments and dyes in the country.

According to the Indian Chemical Manufacturers' Association (ICMA)'s 15 year perspective plan drawn up in December 1976, the total demand for dyes was expected to cross 46,000 tons by 1988-89. The country is absolutely self-sufficient in dyestuffs with total installed capacity of 34,963 tons in the organized sector encompassing a wide range of products, such as direct dyes, acid dyes, basic dyes, sulfur dyes, reactive dyes, disperse dyes, vat dyes, solubilized vat dyes, ingrain dyes and dope dyes, acrylic fiber dyes, metal complex dyes, pigment emulsions, naphthols and bases and organic pigments for paints, printing inks, plastics and rubber industries. Because of lack of reliable data, the extent of installed capacity in the small scale sector has not been accurately established, but it should be of the order of 10,000 tons.

The world distribution of textile dye production is estimated in 1996 to be as follows:

China	19%	Japan	7%
Western Europe	18%	India	5%
North America	17%	Rest of World	34%

The ICMA holds that the dyes and dye intermediates have emerged as the fastest growing sector in the chemical industry. The size of the market has more than doubled from around Rs. 225 crore to around Rs. 500 crore and if the current trends are any guide, the industry will swiftly cross the Rs. 1,000 crore mark by the end of the century.

The total global production of dyestuffs and pigments, estimated at over 1.2 million M.T. (US $20 billion approx.), has been growing at the rate of around 5% per annum. Germany, USA, Japan and UK are the major players, accounting for over 70% of the world production. Germany, with three major manufacturers (BASF, Hoechst and Bayer), enjoys a market share of 22%. However, high cost of manufacture coupled with increasingly stricter environmental laws have forced a number of manufacturers to shut down the plants and shift the production bases to developing countries like India.

IVG. PESTICIDES

Pesticides make up one essential segment of the agro-business complex which is so vital to the future development of countries such as India. The ingredients of the agro-business complex include

- furnishing improved seeds
- development of irrigation
- application of fertilizers
- proper use of pesticides and herbicides
- mechanization of planting and harvesting
- proper crop storage and distribution

To emphasize the vital place of pesticides, it has been estimated that about 20 percent of food production in India may be lost due to destruction caused by various pests including rodents and weeds.

The interrelation of the various agro-business factors listed above is emphasized by the fact that high yielding seeds and increased dosage of fertilizers make plants even more susceptible to destructive attacks by pests.

Some of the raw materials for the pesticide industry are aliphatic hydrocarbons, aromatic hydrocarbons, phosphorus and its derivatives, and halogens such as chlorine. Figure IVG-1 shows some of the interrelations between these basic pesticide raw materials and a few important pesticide products.

The two major categories of synthetic organic pesticides are chlorinated compounds (exemplified by DDT and BHC) and organophosphorus compounds (exemplified by parathion).

BHC was the first organic insecticide produced in India, starting in about 1953. At first, such chlorinated organic materials dominated the pesticide industry, but as time went by, two major problems have developed regarding these materials. The first problem is that insects have developed resistance to these materials. The second is that there has been found a tendency for such pesticides to build up in soils and to wash into rivers and accumulate in larger bodies of water with possible consequent hazard to marine life.

In developed Western countries with stricter environmental regulations on pesticide use, the polychlorinated insecticides such as DDT, 2,4-D and BHC have been pretty much phased out in favor of more biodegradable materials. Where disease control and agricultural pest control are relatively more important and where older processes can utilize existing manufacturing plants, the polychlorinated materials are still being produced and used.

The organophosphorus materials, on the other hand, are much less permanent when exposed to the weather and do not seem to be as prone to the development of resistance on the part of insects. They are, in many cases, however, very powerful materials in concentrated form

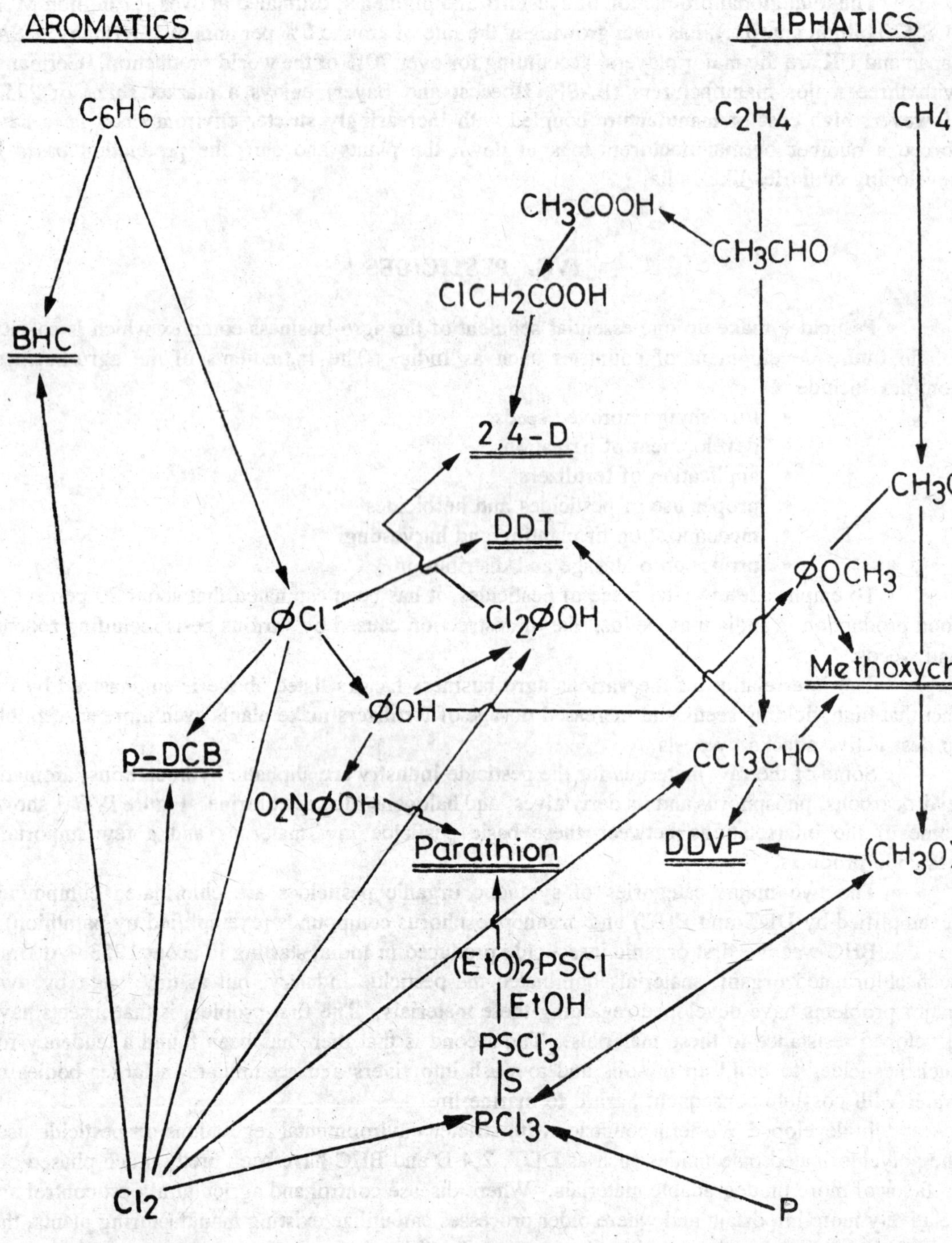

Fig. IVG-1. Some interrelations of pesticide raw materials.

which must be given the same degree of safety attention as chemical warfare agents, to which they are closely related chemically.

Some of the newer organophosphorus compounds act as systemic insecticides which means they can be fed to plants or animals and thus effectively destroy pests at the moment of contact between the pest and the plant or animal; they need not be spread about externally, but are distributed by the inner circulatory systems of the plant or animal.

One important feature of the pesticide industry is that, even though major pesticide chemical manufacturing plants may be located in large installations adjacent to oil refineries, etc., there is much opportunity for small local formulation plants. Thus, the concentrated chemical materials are shipped by road or rail to small formulation plants around the country. There dusts, emulsions and solutions may be made to suit local needs and application conditions.

The pesticide and agrochemical industry has been reviewed statistically in the "Chemical Weekly Annual" for 1995 as follows:

(a) Indigenous demand:

1989-90	71,000 M.T.
2000 A.D.	97,000 M.T.

(b) Industry size:

Producers of tech. grade pesticides	125
Formulators	500

(c) Production:

1993-94	85,500 M.T.
1994-95	85,500 M.T.
1995-96	90,000 M.T. (targeted)

(d) Consumption of pesticides by groups (%)

	India	World
Insecticides	77	44
Herbicides	12	30
Fungicides	8	21
Others	3	5
Total	100	100

As of the 1990's, one can tabulate a number of chlorine-containing pesticides which are manufactured in India as follows:

		Manufacturers Code Numbers (see Manufacturers' listing in text which follows)
A.	Alachlor	18
B.	BHC	8, 10, 14, 20
C.	Butachlor	8, 16, 18, 19, 22
D.	Chlordane	14
E.	DDT	8
F.	Dicofol	8
G.	Endosulfan	5, 8, 21
H.	Lindane	10
I.	Pentachlorophenol	5

Of these, DDT and BHC are described in the process outlines which follow. These are insecticides.

Of the chlorine-containing pesticides, butachlor is perhaps the most widely produced, being made by some 6 manufacturers in India. It is a herbicide with a complex formula:

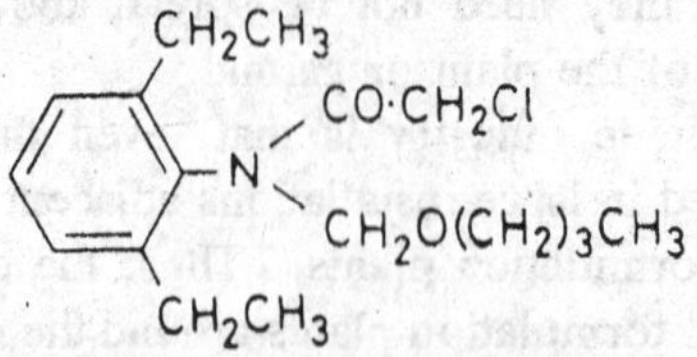

As of the 1990's, when the third edition of this book was produced, a large number of phosphorus-based pesticides were produced in India as follows:

		Manufacturers Code Numbers
J.	Acephate	11
K.	Chlorpyrifos	5, 6, 11, 13, 16, 22
L.	Diazinon	19
M.	Dichlorvos	12, 19
N.	Dimethoate	12, 14, 16, 17
O.	Ethion	14, 17
P.	Fenitrothion	14
Q.	Glyphosate	5
R.	Malathion	8, 12
S.	Methyl Parathion	14
T.	Monocrotophos	3, 7, 8, 12, 14, 16, 19, 21, 22
U.	Phosphamidon	12, 19, 21
V.	Quinalphos	6, 15, 19, 21

Of these, parathion-methyl is the only related material described in the process outlines which follow. It is very similar to parathion.

Of the phosphorus-containing pesticides, monocrotophos is the most widely produced, being made by some 9 manufacturers in India. It is an insecticide which functions as a cholinesterase inhibitor and which is related structurally to materials such as nerve gas. It has the formula:

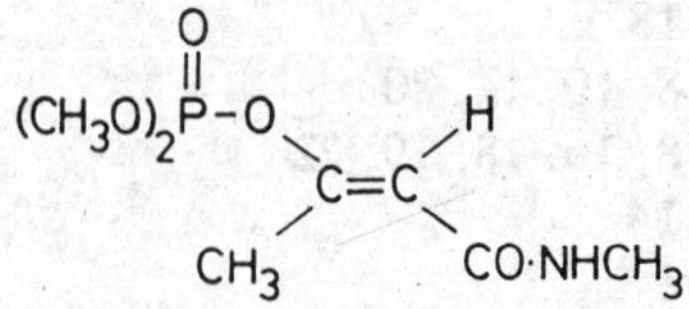

Another phosphorus-containing insecticide is chlorpyrifos, produced by 6 manufacturers in India. It has the formula:

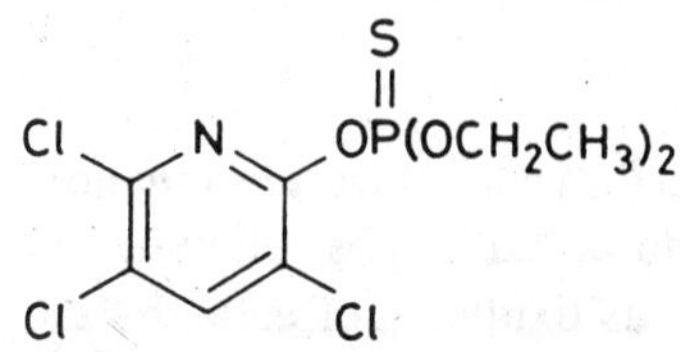

There are a number of pesticide producers in India, among which are:

1. Bayer (India) Ltd.
2. Bharat Rasayan Ltd.
3. Chemagro International Ltd.
4. Colour Chem Ltd.
5. Excel Industries Ltd.
6. Ficom Organics Ltd.
7. Hindustan Ciba Geigy Ltd.
8. Hindustan Insecticides Ltd.
9. I.C.I. India Ltd.
10. Kanoria Chemicals & Industries Ltd.
11. Kedia Chemical Industries Pvt. Ltd.
12. Khatau Junker Ltd.
13. Montari Industries Ltd.
14. Rallis India Ltd.
15. Sandoz (India) Ltd.
16. Searle (India) Ltd.
17. Shaw Wallace & Co. Ltd.
18. Siris Ltd.
19. Sudarshan Chemical Industries Ltd.
20. Tata Chemicals Ltd.
21. Tuticorin Alkali Chemicals & Fertilizers Ltd.
22. Vantech Industry Ltd.

DDT Manufacture

1. **Reference Flow Sheet:** Figure IVG-2

2. **Raw Materials**

The raw materials for DDT manufacture are ethanol and benzene. The ethanol can be converted to chloral by oxidation to acetaldehyde followed by chlorination to chloral, or ethanol can be chlorinated (with simultaneous oxidation effected by the chlorine) directly to chloral. The benzene is chlorinated to monochlorobenzene.

3. **Chemical Reaction**

$$CCl_3CHO + 2C_6H_5Cl \rightarrow (C_6H_4Cl)_2\ CHCCl_3 + H_2O$$

4. **Process Description**

The chloral and chlorobenzene are condensed using strong sulfuric acid (100%) or oleum as a catalyst. A steel reactor, typically of 1,000 gallons capacity, may be used. The reaction takes place at 15-30°C and the reaction time is 5-6 hours.

After condensation, the spent acid is withdrawn, the organic layer is water-washed and then neutralized with soda ash. The mixture of DDT and unreacted chlorobenzene is then dropped into a drier vessel where the DDT is melted and chlorobenzene is distilled overhead. The molten DDT is run into solidifying pans, then ground and bagged for sale.

5. **Major Engineering Problems**

- Temperature must be carefully controlled to prevent sulfonation of the monochlorobenzene by the acid catalyst which is excessive at higher temperatures.
- Contact of the DDT product with iron must be scrupulously avoided since iron catalyzes the decomposition of DDT.

BHC Manufacture

1. **Raw Materials**

The raw materials for BHC manufacture are simply benzene and chlorine.

2. **Chemical Reaction**

$$C_6H_6 + 3Cl_2 \rightarrow C_6H_6Cl_6$$

3. **Process Description**

The crux of the process involves the use of a source of free radicals such as ultraviolet light to produce an addition chlorination reaction (instead of the substitution reaction promoted by iron catalysts in the dark which gives hexachlorobenzene, C_6Cl_6).

Thus benzene and chlorine are passed into a cooled reactor containing a light well or they may be passed through a tubular reactor with a fluorescent lamp mounted on the axis of the reaction tube in a protective glass tube. The reaction products flow to a still from which crude BHC is obtained as a molten bottoms product; benzene is taken overhead and recycled.

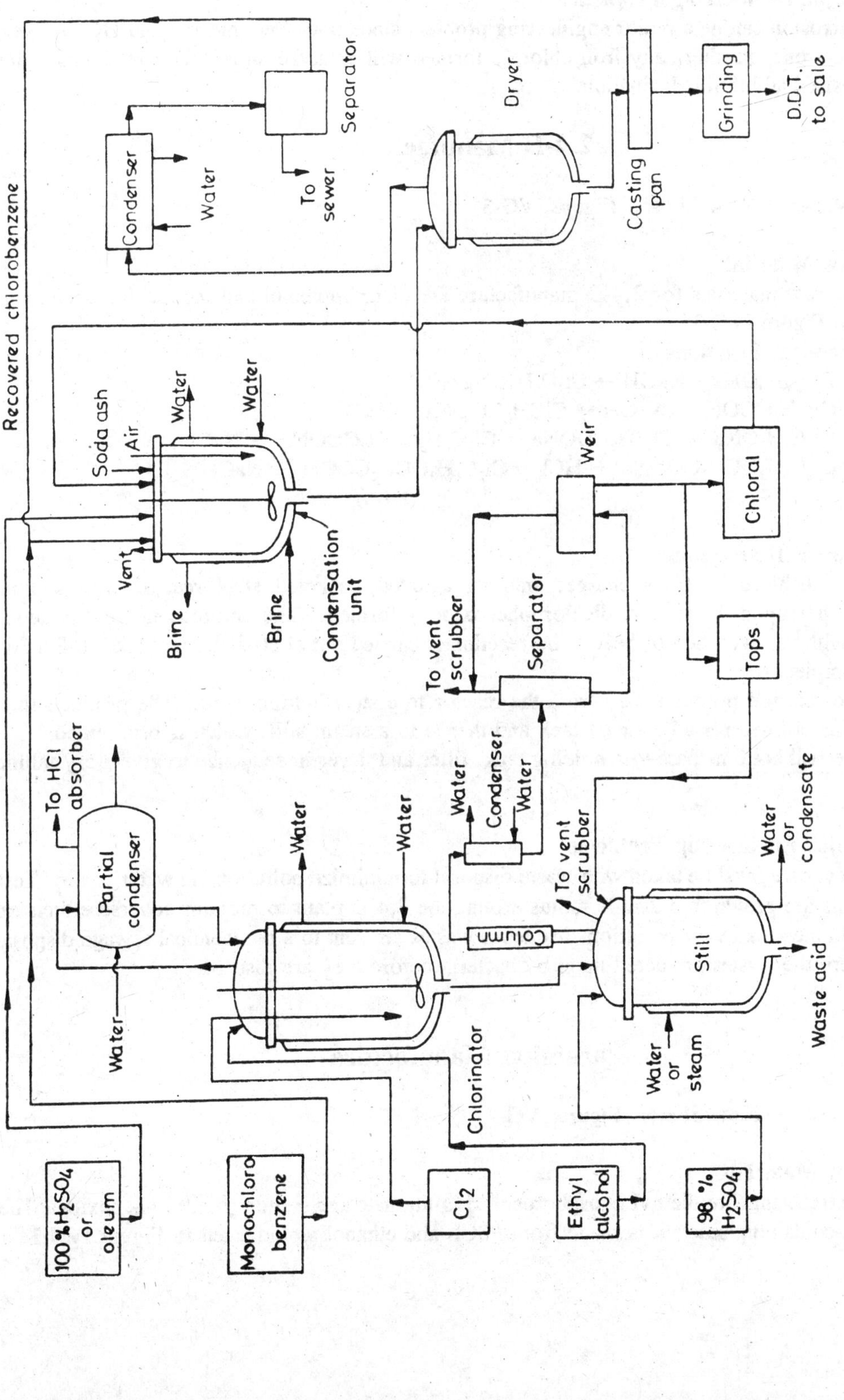

Fig. IVG-2. Flow chart for manufacture of DDT.

4. **Major Engineering Problems**

Corrosion can be a major engineering problem since both wet chlorine and HCl are very corrosive to iron. Further, any iron chloride formed will catalyze substitution reactions rather than the desired addition chlorination.

2,4-D Manufacture

1. **Reference Flow Sheet:** Figure IVG-3

2. **Raw Materials**

The raw materials for 2,4-D manufacture are dichlorophenol and monochloroacetic acid as shown in Figure IVG-3.

3. **Chemical Reactions**

$$Cl_2C_6H_3OH + NaOH \rightarrow Cl_2C_6H_3ONa + H_2O$$
$$ClCH_2COOH + NaOH \rightarrow ClCH_2COONa + H_2O$$
$$Cl_2C_6H_3ONa + ClCH_2COONa \rightarrow Cl_2C_6H_3OCH_2COONa + NaCl$$
$$Cl_2C_6H_3OCH_2COONa + HCl \rightarrow \underset{(2,4\text{-}D)}{Cl_2C_6H_3OCH_2COOH} + NaCl$$

4. **Process Description**

The dichlorophenol is charged into an agitated, jacketed steel reactor with sodium hydroxide whereupon the sodium dichlorophenoxide is formed. The chloroacetic acid is added and reacts with the evolution of heat. The reaction is carried out at 60-80°C and takes 6-8 hours to reach completion.

The reaction products pass from the reactor to a steel holding tank. The products then go to an enamel-lined pH adjustment tank and thence to a steam still, which is brick lined.

The still bottoms pass to a holding tank, filter and dryer in sequence to give a crystalline product.

5. **Major Engineering Problems**

Great care must be taken with waste disposal to minimize pollution via water or air. Test tomato plants are grown in a 2-mile radius around the 2,4-D plant to monitor adverse effects on vegetation in the area by air pollution. Aqueous wastes are sent to a biochemical sewage disposal system where the wastes are acted upon by bacteria before they are discarded.

Parathion Manufacture

1. **Reference Flow Sheet:** Figure IVG-4

2. **Raw Materials**

The reactants are diethyl phosphorochlorido-thionate and sodium *p*-nitro phenoxide. The phosphorus-containing reactant is made from $PSCl_3$ and ethanol as indicated in Figure IVG-1.

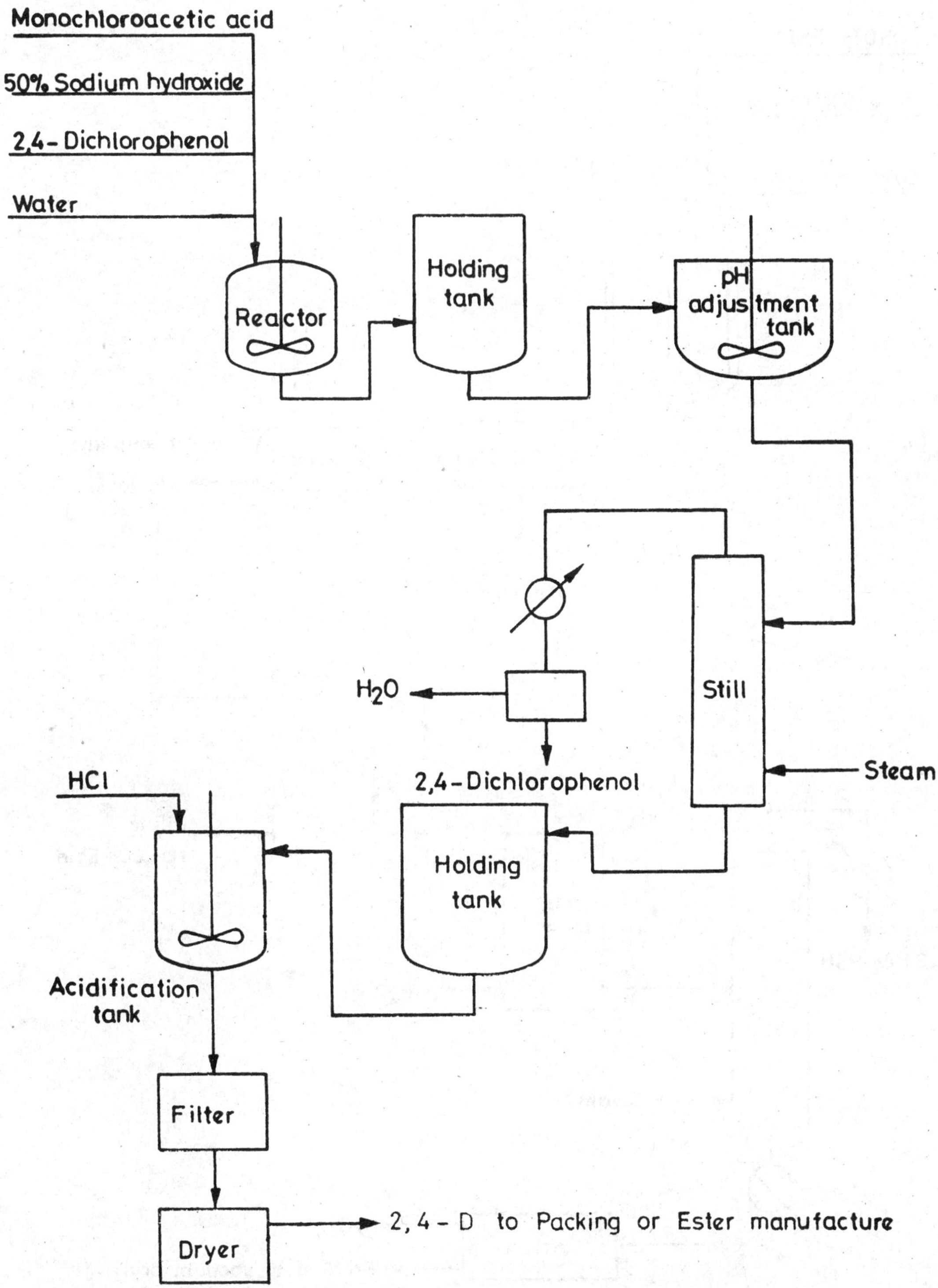

Fig. IVG-3. Flow sheet for 2,4-D manufacture.

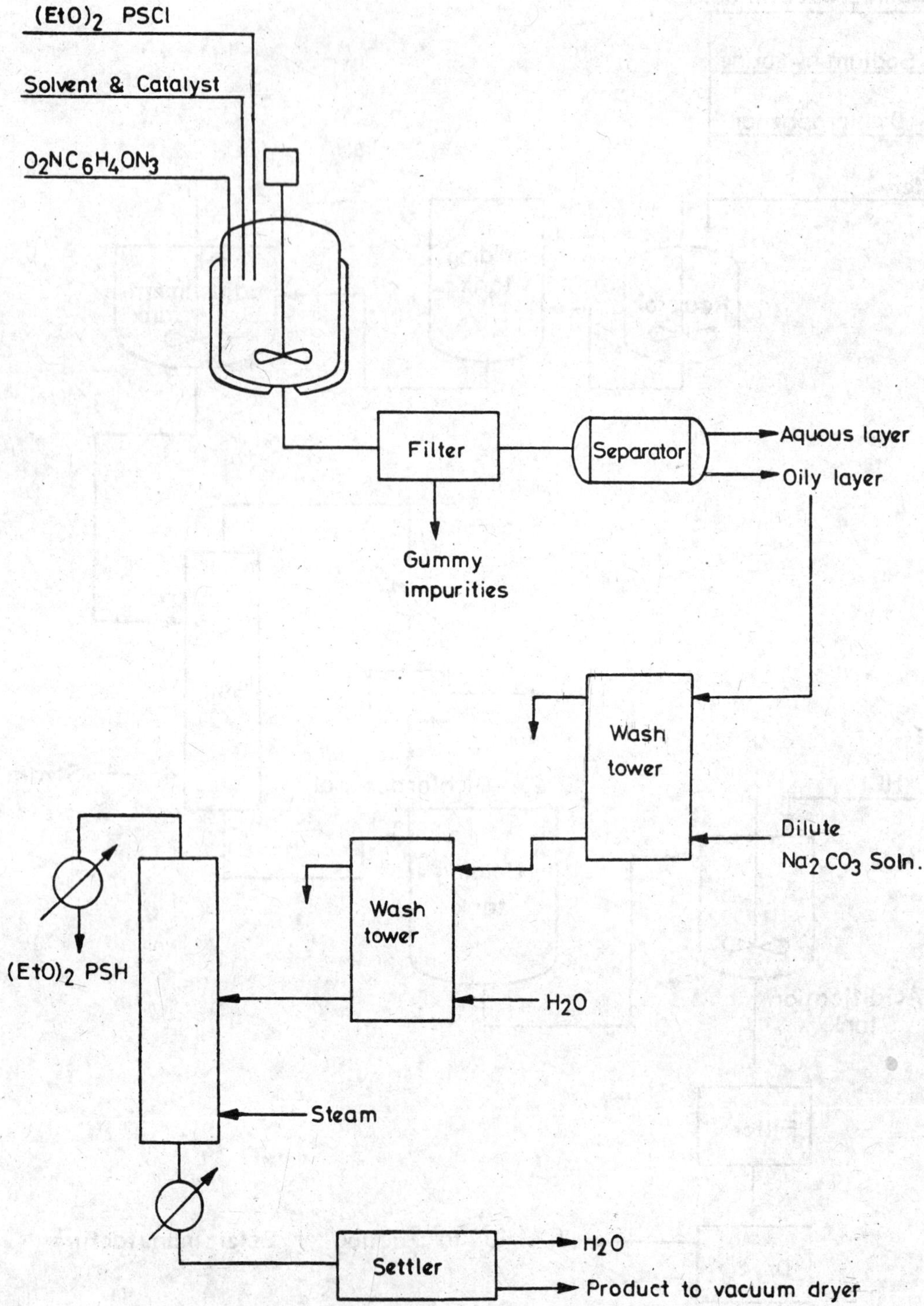

Fig. IVG-4. Flow sheet for parathion manufacture.

3. Chemical Reaction

$$(EtO)_2\overset{S}{\overset{\|}{P}}Cl + NaOC_6H_4NO_2 \rightarrow (EtO)_2\overset{S}{\overset{\|}{P}}OC_6H_4NO_2 + NaCl$$

4. Process Description

The reactants are fed into a stirred, jacketed kettle as shown in Figure IVG-4. The solvent may be an alcohol or benzene or chlorobenzene may be used. Copper powder may be used as a catalyst or the reaction may be conducted in a copper reaction vessel, thereby shortening reaction time appreciably.

Yields of parathion obtained are 90% or higher. The crude reaction products are pumped through a precoated filter to remove gummy impurities. The filtrate is separated into an aqueous layer and a heavier oily layer. The oily layer is washed and distilled to remove unreacted materials. The final product is dried under vacuum; it is a yellowish liquid which is formulated into emulsifiable concentrates or dusts for agricultural application.

5. Major Engineering Problems

- The exothermic reaction can become violently uncontrolled resulting in explosions. Hence an elaborate system of interlocking controls is used to apply full coolant flow in case of reactor agitator failure, and to cut off reactant feed if pressure or temperature rises. Further, the reactors are installed in separate individual concrete cubicles having 3 walls and no roof to direct and not confine the forces in case of explosion.
- Waste disposal is a major problem because of the toxic nature of the materials used. Liquid effluents are subjected to alkali treatment in holding tanks before discharge of public sewers.

IVH. PHARMACEUTICAL INDUSTRY

1. Background and Social Significance

The pharmaceutical industry combines synthetic organic chemical technology and fermentation technology into one of the most powerful tools that modern science possesses for influencing the world around us. Perhaps equally important as the discovery of the potential of nuclear fission (with its joint promise of new power sources and its threat of large scale destruction) is the broad application of drugs or pharmaceuticals to the alleviation of disease and the corresponding extension of man's life span.

The advent and availability of the new life-saving drugs is just an example of a topic where engineers should be aware of the complex social interactions which may result from the use of particular chemical products. It is an area where science and technology have a combined impact on all people, whether within a country or worldwide. It is an area where technology and its application should not be learned alone without a knowledge of the consequences of its use. We are encountering such interactions in various environmental areas; manufacture of a new plastic or pesticide without adequate overall consideration may result in air or stream pollution in a given area with possible consequent damage to animal, plant and even human life. The social consequences of pharmaceutical manufacture and use are a major factor in population growth—in India for example. Whereas the effects of life-saving drugs have been a major cause of longer life expectancy and decreased death rates, the corresponding pharmaceutical industry contribution to decreased birth rates in the form of contraceptive chemicals and devices, has not had an equally dramatic impact due to social reluctance to change in longstanding behavior patterns.

In spite of these interactions, obviously the pharmaceutical industry will continue to grow as it develops new products to improve health and save lives.

2. History and Growth of the Industry

The pharmaceutical industry has made its greatest strides very recently.

- Before 1900, most medicines were produced from natural products of animal, mineral or vegetable origin, such as quinine (for malaria treatment) from cinchona bark. One of the first synthetic pharmaceutical products was chloroform, as an anesthetic, first made in about 1850. Aspirin was first manufactured in 1899.
- In the early 1900's anesthetics such as Novocaine were known. Mercurial compounds were used as antiseptics.
- The 1920's saw the discovery of insulin as an antidiabetic drug.
- The 1930's saw the development of sulfa drugs and vitamins and penicillin.
- The real surge of new products came after World War II with the advent of various vaccines, steroid hormones, tranquillizer drugs and broad-spectrum antibiotics.
- Today research is directed at drugs to cure arthritis, cancer, heart conditions, high blood pressure, hepatitis and various mental and emotional diseases.

One thing which should be mentioned about the pharmaceutical industry is that its products are important for animal as well as for human use. Indeed, veterinary medicine is one of the outstanding growth fields in the pharmaceutical industry. In the U.S., for example, control of disease has changed chicken from a meat for special occasions to one of the cheapest meats available for the everyday diet. Disease losses of growing birds have been cut from 30% to 2%. Modern poultry feeds are carefully compounded products containing vitamins, antibiotics and medicinals.

In the USA and the UK the growth rate of the pharmaceutical industry is high—rating about fourth among the chemical process industries after plastics, petrochemicals and synthetic fibers.

The foundation of the modern Indian Pharmaceutical Industry was laid in the beginning of the current century when, in 1901, a small factory known as the Bengal Chemical and Pharmaceutical Works, was established in Calcutta. Though the two world wars gave a fillip to the development of the industry, the progress made under the British rule was insignificant. The country depended largely on the United Kingdom, France and Germany for its requirements of drugs and medicines.

Among the third world countries, India has been recognized by UNIDO as one of the top ranking countries in terms of production and distribution of pharmaceuticals. At the time of Indian independence, the value of pharmaceuticals output was only Rs. 10 crore for bulk drugs into formulations with no production base. Today, the industry has grown in a gigantic way both in terms of output and product diversification.

At present there are over 15,000 drug manufacturing units in the country with a preponderance of small scale units. The relatively large scale units in the organized sector number about 250 including six FERA companies* and the five units in the public sector. There were 31

FERA companies with direct foreign equity exceeding 40 percent in March 1978 on the eve of the announcement of drug policy (1978). Since then, 25 of them have diluted their foreign equity to 40 percent or below. Hence, now there are only six FERA* companies, viz. Alkali & Chemicals Ltd. (amalgamated with ICI), Bayer India Ltd., Johnson & Johnson Ltd., Roche Products Ltd., Sandoz India Ltd., Wyeth Laboratories.

The public sector units are: Indian Drugs and Pharmaceuticals Ltd. (IDPL), Hindustan Antibiotics Ltd. (HAL), Bengal Chemicals and Pharmaceuticals Ltd. (BCPL), Bengal Immunity Ltd. (BIL), and Smith Stainstreet Pharmaceuticals Ltd. (SSPL).

The organized sector units numbering about 250 (including six FERA and five public sector units) account for nearly 70 percent of the industry's total value of production. The national sector has witnessed a spectacular growth over the last two decades. It now accounts for 90 percent of the production of the industry including that of the small scale sector.

Demand Projections

Year	Rs. Crores
1984-95 (estimated production)	2,204
1989-90	4,112
1994-95	8,300
1999-2000	15,996

Source: "Kothari's Industrial Directory of India" (1994)

Leading Pharmaceutical Companies in India

	Company	*Sales in Rs. crores*
1.	Glaxo	142
2.	Ranbaxy	124
3.	Cadila	122
4.	Alembic Chemical Works	98
5.	Cipla	94
6.	Ambalal Sarabhai	90
7.	Hoechst	89
8.	Pfizer	89
9.	Lupin	82
10.	Boots	76

Source: "Kothari's Industrial Directory of India" (1994)

* FERA = companies covered by the Foreign Exchange Regulations Act (having international financial implications)

Though basically a growth oriented industry, the drug industry is a relatively small industry with a total investment of around Rs. 1,000 crores. About 1/3 of this investment is in the public sector units, which accounts for 10% of the total production. The size of the industry in terms of turnover is also relatively small.

Industry	*Turnover in Crores of Rs.*
Iron & Steel	20,000
Food & Food Products	40,400
Fertilizer & Pesticides	9,200
Cement	9,000
Sugar	10,000
Readymade Garments	6,000
Pharmaceuticals	5,700

Source: "Chemical Industry Digest Fact Book" (1994)

Though India has emerged as the largest pharmaceutical producer among the developing countries, its share in world production is still insignificant at 1.6 percent even though it accounts for 15 percent of the world population. At about Rs. 42 the per capita consumption of drugs in India is among the lowest in the world. Thus the growth potential of the industry in the coming years is obvious.

When one considers per capita expenditure on drugs, according to data from Investment Research & Information Services Ltd., India is near the bottom worldwide. The relative figures are as follows:

Country	Expenditure in $U.S. per capita for drugs
Japan	412
Germany	222
U.S.A.	191
U.K.	97
Brazil	16
Ghana	10
China	7
Pakistan	7
Indonesia	5
India	3

R&D is the pivot on which the progress of any industry depends. Same is the case with the pharmaceutical industry. However, in India, R&D expenditure is less than 2% of sales, which represents more process development work rather than discovery research. On the other hand, in the US, R&D expenditure as percentage of sales for the year 1992 was 16.1% (Aerospace—3.8%, Electronics—5.8%, Office Equipment—8.3%). In the US, the cost of developing a new drug is on an average US $250 million and the average development time is 12 years. Moreover, success is not guaranteed. Reasons for low R&D expenditure in India have been:

(a) Low profitability due to stringent government price controls existing until recently.
(b) Weak patent protection.

Indian law, as it currently stands, does not recognize product patents, but offers patent protection for process of manufacture. This has helped the Indian companies to develop new economical processes for manufacturing newly discovered drugs and market them at a fraction of the price charged by the inventing company in the countries where patent protection is available. The patent laws have helped the Indian companies achieve remarkable growth in the past decades. However, with signing of the GATT Treaty, India has agreed to introduce product patents. A transition period of 10 years (up to 2005 A.D.) is allowed for amending the patents act. This will compel Indian companies to step up R&D expenditure from present 1-2% of sales (compared to 10-12% globally) or tie up with strong research based companies.

3. Economics of the Pharmaceutical Industry

The tonnage production of the pharmaceutical industry is relatively small, but the value of the products is high; the value of pharmaceutical products in the U.S. is well in excess of a billion dollars annually.

The price of pharmaceutical products to the customer is usually high by the usual chemical industry standards. This is due to a variety of special costs peculiar to the pharmaceutical industry:

- Development costs—many different compounds and compositions usually have to be subjected to animal experiments and clinical tests before a saleable product is available. Some 1,700 substances were produced and tested before the first sulfa drug was commercialized, for example.
- The cost of instructing the medical profession as to the availability and optimum handling and application of new drugs is considerable. This is done by "detailers" who contact doctors, their effect supplemented by a considerable volume of expensive instructional and promotional material.

It should be noted, however, that the prices of pharmaceutical products in India are generally well below their sale prices in the rest of the world; this is in marked contrast to the situation for bulk chemicals where Indian prices are well above Western World prices as shown in the introduction to Chapter II of this book.

4. Methods of Production

As noted above, pharmaceutical products are produced by a combination of synthetic organic chemistry and biochemical methods. Before World War II, the major emphasis was on synthetic methods. Now that antibiotics, vitamins and hormones have assumed major importance, more than half of U.S. pharmaceutical production, for example, is by biochemical methods. The relative importance of biochemical methods is growing in other countries as well.

Let us now consider the various specific classes of pharmaceutical products and their manufacture in India. The following sections on specific classes of drugs have been taken from "Indian Pharmaceutical Guide—1994" published (annually) by Pamposh Publications, New Delhi.

4.1. Antibiotics

Antibiotics form roughly more than half in value of the drugs sold in the Indian market.

4.1.1. Penicillin

The major portion of penicillin marketed in India is produced by the Hindustan Antibiotics Ltd., a Government of India undertaking. The factory was started with the monetary and technical assistance of UNICEF and WHO.

It has reached a peak production rate of parenteral penicillin; in addition Alembic Chemical Works and Standard Pharmaceutical each have been licensed for an annual production of 8.5 mmu. of penicillin. One big manufacturing unit in the public sector, Antibiotics Factory at Rishikesh, is producing 230 mmu. of penicillin per year. Some more projects in private sector have entered the manufacture of the antibiotic. On the completion of all the private sector and the public sector projects combined production in 1992-93 was 1,560.23 mmu. In 1975, Hindustan Antibiotics had started commercial production of ampicillin, a plant was set up to manufacture ampicillin from 6-penicilloic acid. Over 253 tons of ampicillin was manufactured in India in 1992-93.

4.1.2. Streptomycin

This antibiotic is of special value in combating TB. A plant to produce streptomycin and dihydrostreptomycin has been installed at Hindustan Antibiotics factory at Pimpri. Under the agreement with the Government of India, Merck & Co., Inc. had provided technical assistance to the factory for the production of this antibiotic. The plant has produced 109 tons of streptomycin and dihydrostreptomycin in 1992-93 from basic raw materials. Synbiotics Ltd. at Vadodara have been issued a license for 60 tons of streptomycin per annum. They are in production of the antibiotics from April 1964.

A streptomycin plant with 275 tons per annum capacity is in production in the public sector antibiotics factory at Rishikesh. On completion of all the schemes the total capacity is expected to move to over 480 tons of this antibiotic per year. Over 243.79 tons of streptomycin was produced in 1988-89.

4.1.3. Tetracyclines

The production of broad spectrum antibiotics of tetracycline group had been started in India long back. Tetracycline and chlortetracycline were produced from imported crude materials and their production in 1958 was 2.4 tons. In 1961, a new plant with a capacity of 1.5 tons of tetracycline was completed at Pimpri. Two U.S. concerns which are main producers, after IDPL, of broad spectrum antibiotics are Pfizer and Cyanamid. A 44 ton capacity plant of Pfizer is in operation for tetracycline at Chandigarh. It is designed to work on the basic raw materials available in India. A 13 ton production plant of Cyanamid started at Vulsad is in full production of antibiotics like Ledermycin, Achromycin, and Aureomycin entirely from indigenous raw materials. India produced 134 tons of tetracycline and 193.15 tons of oxytetracycline in 1992-93.

4.1.4. Chloramphenicol

Chloramphenicol is the only antibiotic produced synthetically. Its manufacture was first established by Parke-Davis in Maharashtra, the initial plant capacity being 3.6 tons per year and the production commencing from imported levo base. The capacity was later expanded to 10 tons per year and the manufacture extended to more basic stage starting with *p*-nitroacetophenone. The capacity of this unit is now licensed for increase to 20 tons which has been implemented. Boehringer-Knoll in the same state has an installed yearly capacity of 30 tons and uses a different process with benzaldehyde as the starting material. The unit started production of chloramphenicol from the year 1960 and is now producing to full capacity. Production in 1992-93 was 109 tons of powder and 17.43 tons of palmitate.

4.2. Other Synthetic Drugs

A wide range of synthetic drugs is being produced in large quantities. Important among these are sulfa drugs, anti-TB drugs, antileprotic drugs, analgesics, anesthetics and antimalarials.

4.2.1. Sulfa drugs

Manufacture of important sulfa drugs such as sulfamethoxazole, sulfathiazole, sulfapyridine, phthalylsulfathiazole is now well established for many years. There are two major units: Rhone-Poulenc in Maharashtra and Cibatul in Gujarat. In both units, the manufacture was initially established from imported penultimate compounds, but the unit in Maharashtra has been for several years using more basic raw materials and is now further extending the manufacture. It produces locally *p*-acetaminobenzene-sulfonyl chloride which is one of the two main intermediates in the manufacture of sulfa drugs. Production of sulfacetamide and phthalylsulfacetamide is established in West Bengal with total capacity of 16 tons per year. Besides the above capacity of 535 tons has been licensed in Andhra Pradesh to Indian Drugs & Pharmaceuticals Ltd. The main production here is intended to be of sulfadimidine, sulfaguanidine, and sulfacetamide sodium.

In 1973, there was an installed capacity of 2,004 tons of sulfa drugs in India, but the actual production in that year was about 1,298 tons. The sulfas (sulfadiazine and sulfathiazole) are produced from the higher intermediates by Atul Products, an associate of American Cyanamid Company. Other producers of sulfa drugs are Rhone-Poulenc, Ciba and German Remedies (sulfasomidine), Haffkine Institute (sulfathiazole), East India Pharmaceutical Works (sulfathiazole, sulfacetamide), Synbiotics, Standard Organics and Nitson Labs (sulfamethoxazole).

Production of sulfa drugs in 1991-93 was sulfamethoxazole 1,592.55 tons, sulfadimidine 41.92 tons, sulfacetamide 38.56 tons, sulfamoxole 52.03 tons, sulfasomidine 0.13 ton, and sulfaguanidine 48.25 tons.

4.2.2. Anti-TB drugs

Isonicotinic acid hydrazide is manufactured from gamma picoline by three firms in the country, present plant capacity being 72 tons per year. Besides this, a capacity of 35 tons per year has been planned in the public sector. Manufacture of *p*-amino salicylic acid was commenced in 1956 with an initial plant capacity of 36 tons a year. Now the manufacturing capacity has expanded to 482 tons per year and further expansion is under implementation. There are about half a dozen firms in India which are producing INH. During 1982-83, the production of this drug was 128 tons, it is estimated that in 1983-84 the requirement went up. In 1960, about 81 tons of PAS were produced by Biochemical and Synthetic Products, which has an installed capacity of 100 tons per year. India's estimated present consumption is about 400 tons per year. Pfizer had erected a unit with a capacity of 80 tons PAS per year. It is estimated that now the country need of PAS has risen to about 560 tons per year. Wander have been licensed for 121 tons capacity per year and Biological Evans to 35.5 tons capacity of PAS.

4.2.3. Antileprotic drugs

Among the synthetic antileprotic drugs, DDS and its derivative (sulphones) are at present produced from the basic stage. Bengal Chemical started production of the drugs on a limited scale before 1952. Burroughs Wellcome in Maharashtra have established a capacity of 11 tons of DDS per year. Further expansion of the total manufacturing capacity in the country to 52.5 tons per year is planned and Biological Evans (10 tons) have been licensed for the production. In 1992-93, 12.56 tons of dapsone were produced. About 2.72 tons of clofazimine were produced in the country in 1992-93.

4.2.4. Analgesics, antipyretics and antirheumatics

Analgin, aspirin, phenylbutazone, oxyphenylbutazone, pethidine, ibuprofen, piroxicam and paracetamol are the synthetics of this group produced at present. For aspirin, manufacturing capacity of 560 tons per year has been established by manufacturers in Maharashtra (97 tons), and Shri Krishna Fine Chemicals & Pharmaceuticals Ltd. in Karnataka has put up a large plant to produce aspirin. Additional annual production of 150 tons is also planned in the public sector. Amongst the other drugs of this group to be taken up all for manufacture in the public sector are metamezol and phenobarbitone.

4.2.5. Anesthetics

Of the different anesthetics, the capacity for production in 1955-56 was limited to some common ones such as ether and ethyl chloride. Other synthetic anesthetics like procaine hydrochloride and xylocaine are now manufactured adequately in the country. Manufacturing capacity of 104.50 tons is available for procaine hydrochloride which is manufactured by Hoechst and Synbiotics. In 1992-93, production of procaine was 53.27 tons and of xylocaine 7.72 tons.

4.2.6. Synthetic antimalarials

Chloroquine and amodiaquin are the only two synthetic antimalarials manufactured so far in the country. Mention may here be made of pyrimethamine, which is produced in small quantity. Manufacturing capacity of 42 tons per year for amodiaquin is established in Maharashtra by Parke-Davis. Chloroquine and its salts are manufactured by Bengal Immunity (80 tons), Bayer Agrochem (24 tons), Ranbaxy Labs (5 tons), and Rhone-Poulenc (12 tons).

In 1992-93, 194.56 tons of chloroquine, 12.80 tons of amodiaquin and 0.13 ton of pyrimethamine were produced in the country.

4.2.7. Gastrointestinal drugs

In 1982-83, India produced 218 tons of halogenated oxyquinolines which is sufficient to meet the demand for the home market of this type of drug. The drugs are produced by Atul Products, Sarabhai Chemicals, East India Pharmaceutical Works, Alembic, Bengal Chemical, Smith Stanistreet, Standard Pharmaceuticals and Rhone-Poulenc. All the firms produce it from phenol hydroxyquinoline. In 1982-83, 1,632 tons of metronidazole were produced and the installed capacity is 137 tons. Unique Chemicals and Rhone-Poulenc are the main firms who are producing the bulk.

The production of anti-dysentery drugs in 1992-93 in the country was metronidazole 559.10 tons, tinidaxole 83.55 tons, diloxanide furoate 3.73 tons, iodochlorohydroxyquinoline 224.41 tons, di-iodohydroxyquinoline 7.16 tons.

4.3. Vitamins

India still imports its requirement of vitamins from foreign countries, excepting for Vitamin A, Vitamin B_1, and Nicotinic acid amide. Glaxo Laboratories and Roche are producing Vitamin A from β-ionone which is extracted from lemon grass oil obtainable locally in abundance. In 1969, Glaxo and Roche produced about 31.5 mmu of Vitamin A. Sarabhai, in collaboration with E. Merck of Germany, had started production of 1,000 kg of Vitamin B_2 from basic raw materials available in the country. The production capacity of Vitamin C of this firm has been increased to 180 tons per year which is obtained from sorbitol and glucose. Jayant Vitamins are also manufacturing Vitamin C. They have produced the country's requirement of Vitamin C to the extent of 60%. Its share was only 30% in 1975-76. Merind, who have a fermentation plant for complete local manufacture of Vitamin B_{12}, is already producing Vitamin B_{12}. Glaxo, Synbiotics and Themis are also producing Vitamin B_{12}. Besides these vitamins, nicotinic acid amide and esters are manufactured by Chemo Pharma and IDPL.

4.4. Synthetic Hormones

Of the various synthetically produced hormones adrenaline, corticosteroids and sex hormones are produced locally, total production in 1991-92 being 7,992 kg. Manufacture of different corticosteroids as cortisone, hydrocortisone, prednisone and prednisolone has been developed in the country based on indigenous raw materials—diosgenin from dioscorea tubers and hecogenin from sisal. Steroid intermediates produced from diosgenin are also exported.

During the year 1958-59, India imported 16 kg of sex hormones and 67 kg of corticosteroids. At present, four plants are being operated, one by Glaxo and the other three by Ciba, Wyeth and Cipla for the production of sex hormones. The firms are licensed to produce these drugs from basic raw materials. Merind and Glaxo Laboratories have set up plants for the production of corticosteroids from basic raw materials. Cipla and John Wyeth have been licensed for the basic manufacture of corticosteroids from diosgenin which is locally available and are the largest for steroid manufacture in India. Cipla is concentrating its efforts on the manufacture of the sex hormones from diosgenin.

Production of corticosteroids in 1992-93 was dexamethasone 488 kg, betamethasone 1,380 kg, prednisolone 2,069 kg, and hydrocortisone 4 kg.

4.5. Drugs of Vegetable Origin

A wide variety of flora and fauna grow in the country because of the varying types of climate and soils. The recorded botanical wealth consists of more than 2,000 types of medicinal and essential oil bearing plants. Several of these plants have been in use for centuries for their medicinal properties.

Most of these plants grow wild in the country. Now that they are being increasingly used as starting material for many of their products, manufacturing units, in furtherance of their self-sufficiency programs, are establishing scientific methods of cultivation and collection.

Scientific cultivation of *Dioscorea*, for the production of synthetic hormones and *Podophyllum* for the extraction of its active principles, has been organized over large areas in the Kulu and Kashmir valleys. Other plants like belladonna, *Digitalis*, *Pyrethrum* and *Mentha arvensis* are also being cultivated extensively for the extraction of their active principles and for export. Experimental cultivation in the plains of *Solanum*, another plant used in the synthesis of hormones, has given promising results.

4.5.1. Quinine

Cinchona is cultivated over large areas totalling about 20,000 acres in Darjeeling (W. Bengal), the Nilgiris and Anamalais, in Tamil Nadu. The factories attached to these plantations have a total production capacity of 61 tons per annum of quinine. Efforts are being made to increase the production of quinine salts to the maximum possible extent for meeting the growing demand from the foreign markets. Although the use of quinine as an antimalarial drug has decreased, it is used increasingly for the production of quinidine and as a bitter for aerated water and in alcoholic beverages.

4.5.2. Strychnine and brucine

Large quantities of nux vomica seeds grow in the forests of Orissa, Andhra Pradesh, Tamil Nadu and other States. The nux vomica alkaloids, strychnine and brucine are now extracted in three factories, one each in Calcutta, Hyderabad, and Amritsar, with a total capacity of 36 tons per annum. Another unit has been established in Cochin. The entire output of these factories is exported.

4.5.3. Emetine

Plantations have been established in Darjeeling to grow ipecac to the extent of 30,000 kg of dry roots and are largely meeting the requirements for the production of emetine. Emetine is being extracted at two factories—one in Calcutta and the other in Bombay, with a total annual capacity of 590 kg.

4.5.4. *Digitalis* glycosides

Two units for the extraction of digoxin from locally grown *Digitalis* leaves have been set up in Bombay. The scientific cultivation of *Digitalis* to obtain a single high constituent of the active principle, digoxin, and the application of modern extraction technology have made possible the indigenous manufacture of this cardiac drug.

4.5.5. Other plant products

A multipurpose plant is being set up to extract the active principles of senna, belladonna, *Podophyllum*, etc. The total active principles of some of these plant products are already being extracted in this country and the new unit envisages, in addition, isolation of the active constituents.

4.6. Vaccines and Sera

India needs approximately diphtheria antitoxin, 4,000 mega units, tetanus antitoxin 30,000 mega units, triple vaccine 20 million doses, BCG vaccine 60 million doses, polio oral vaccine 20 million units and insulin 1,400 mega units. Central Research Council, Kasauli; Haffkine Institute, Bombay; King's Institute, Guindy; and the Pasteur Institute at Coonoor and Shillong have expanded their capacities for producing vaccines and anti-toxins. Some private firms have also been licensed to go into production of triple antigens and antisera.

4.7. Sources of Raw Materials

The organic chemical industry in the private sector now manufactures an increasing variety of items specially suited to the pharmaceutical industry. The petrochemical industry makes available starting materials for synthetic drugs like benzene, phenol, ethylene oxide, phthalic anhydride, monochloro and dichloro acetic acid etc. The downstream units of the petrochemical industry, now under construction, will produce more and more of the starting materials and intermediates of the drugs, dyes, plastics and allied industries.

A pooling of the demands of these chemical-based industries has made possible the planned production of the required starting materials and intermediates.

As the pharmaceutical industry is a section of the chemical industry, integrated development of all the chemical-based industries is vital in any plan for the development of new sources of materials. For example, the manufacture of drugs is interrelated with the manufacture of chemicals, solvents, nutrient media, machinery, etc. As all these industries are being handled by the Directorate General of Technical Development, it has been possible to make an integrated approach to the development of all the connected industries.

Some items like nutrient media, precursors and chemical solvents are now being produced in India almost to the full extent of their requirements in the manufacture of antibiotics. Nutrients like lactose and lard oil have been completely replaced by indigenously available sucrose and corn oil. Soyabean meal has been partially replaced by groundnut and cottonseed meal. Soyabean protein is absolutely essential in the production of streptomycin; this is being obtained by making protein concentrates of soyabean now grown in the country, and used sometimes in combination with cottonseed protein. Imported antifoam compounds and surfactants have now been substituted by those locally produced.

In the field of solvents, butanol, butylacetate, isopropyl alcohol, acetone, methanol, the chloromethanes and chloroethanes have all become indigenous.

Now that the overall production picture has been surveyed, we will turn to a detailed consideration of the manufacture of one specific product—penicillin.

Penicillin

1. Introduction

The antibiotic drugs extracted from microorganism growth under commercial fermentation conditions are sufficiently complex in molecular structure so there is little competition from synthetic methods. This, coupled with high prices, is responsible for the continued growth of the antibiotic drug production by fermentation. Typical of the drugs produced under different processing conditions are:

Penicillin	Terramycin
Streptomycin	Chloromycin
Neomycin	Tetracyclines
Aureomycin	Bacitracin

Antibiotics are chemical substances produced by certain types of microorganisms which will inhibit the growth and even destroy body-harmful microorganisms. Penicillin was the first of this group discovered in 1929 by Fleming in the UK as he observed the inhibiting effect of penicillium mold on *Staphylococcus aureus*, a common infectious bacteria.

2. Properties of Penicillin

2.1. Basic Structure

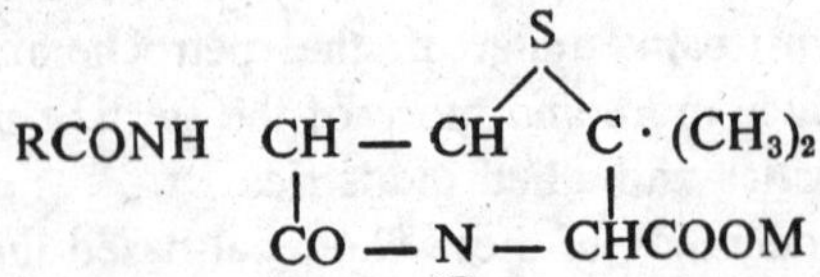

β-lactam-thioazolidine

(I)

Variations in R and M

2.2. Types of Penicillin

Name of derivative	*Designation* *UK*	*USA*	*R in side chain*	*Units/mg of Na salt*
2-Pentenyl-	I	F	$CH_3CH_2CH{=}CHCH_2$—	1,600
n-Amyl	Dihydro I	Dihydro F	*n*-C_5H_{11}—	1,500
Benzyl-	II	G	$C_6H_5CH_2$—	1,667
p-Hydroxy-benzyl	III	X	$HOC_6H_4CH_2$—	900
n-Heptyl	IV	K	*n*-C_7H_{15}	2,300
Phenoxy-methyl	V	Vee	C_6H_5—OCH_2—	1,550

Changes of M in main ring will impart solubility and ingestion rate control:

- Direct rapid action injection: M = Na or K
- Oral tablets: M = K, Ca, Al
- Delayed action oil-base injection: M = procaine or other derivative to impart limited water solubility

Penicillin II and IV are considered clinically most desirable.

3. Consumption Pattern

Used in various forms as indicated above for control of streptococcus and staphylococcus infection in humans and animals. For India the estimated demand in 1993-94 of penicillin and three other antibiotics for which indigenous production is being pushed is:

Penicillin	330 tons
Streptomycin	180 tons
Tetracycline	294 tons
Chloramphenicol	200 tons

4. Methods of Production

4.1. Reference Flow Sheet: Figure IVH-1

4.2. Chemical Reactions

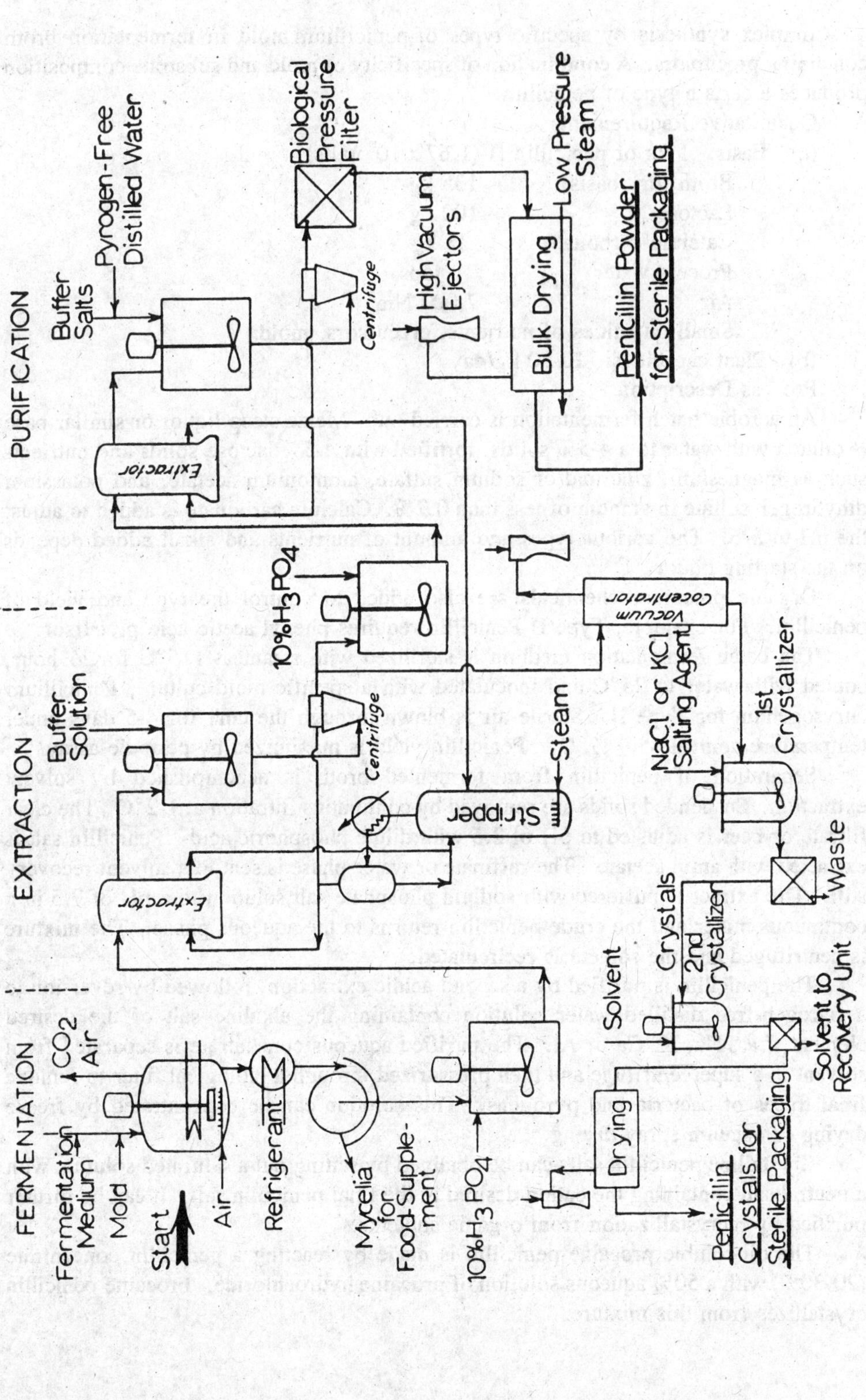

Fig. IVH-1. Penicillin production by fermentation.

Complex synthesis by specific types of penicillium mold in fermentation broth containing precursors. A combination of specificity of mold and substrate composition produces a certain type of penicillin.

4.3. Quantitative Requirements

(a) Basis: 1 kg of penicillin II (1.67 x 10^9 units)

Broth (dry basis)	135 kg
Lactose	100 kg
Calcium carbonate	35 kg
Process water	3 tons
Air	7,000 Nm^3

Small quantities of nutrients, precursors, mold

(b) Plant capacities: 10-50 kg/day

4.4. Process Description

An aerobic batch fermentation is carried out. Maize steep liquor or similar base is diluted with water to a 4-5% solids, fortified with 4-5% lactose solids and nutrients such as magnesium, zinc and/or sodium sulfate, ammonium acetate, and potassium dihydrogen sulfate in amount of less than 0.2%. Calcium carbonate is added to adjust the pH to 5-6. The various types and amount of nutrients and alkali added depends on the starting liquor.

Organic precursor chemicals are also added to control the type and yield of penicillin. For example, Type II Penicillin requires phenyl acetic acid precursor.

The batch fermentation medium is sterilized with steam at 115°C for ½ hour, cooled with water to 25°C and inoculated with a specific mold culture, Penicillium chrysogenum for Type II. Sterile air is blown through the tank for 4-5 days under temperature control of ±½°C. Penicillin yield is maximized by periodic assay.

Separation of penicillin from fermented broth is accomplished by solvent extraction. Suspended solids are removed by continuous filtration at 1-2°C. The clear filtrate or beer is adjusted to pH of 2.5 with dilute phosphoric acid. Penicillin salt is extracted with amyl acetate. The raffinate or water phase is sent to a solvent recovery still. The extract is buffered with sodium phosphate salt solution to a pH of 7.5 in a continuous mixer and the crude penicillin returns to the aqueous phase. The mixture is centrifuged and the solvent is recirculated.

The penicillin is purified by a second acidic extraction, followed by reversion to a pyrogen-free distilled water solution containing the alkaline salt of the desired element, *i.e.*, Na, K, Ca or Al. The purified aqueous concentrate is separated from solvent in a supercentrifuge and then pressurized through a biological filter to remove final traces of bacteria and pyrogens. This solution can be concentrated by freeze drying or vacuum spray drying.

Crystalline penicillin salts can be obtained by salting out a saturated solution with a neutral salt containing the cation desired in the final penicillin salt. It can be further purified by recrystallization from organic solvents.

The oil-soluble procaine penicillin is made by reacting a penicillin concentrate (20-30%) with a 50% aqueous solution of procaine hydrochloride. Procaine penicillin crystallizes from this mixture.

4.5. Major Engineering Problems

- Design of 100-200 m^3 fermenters to provide uniform and efficient air-liquid contact. Tanks are pressurized to 1 atm. gage and air is added just underneath a high speed turbine agitator. Foaming is avoided by addition of small quantities of antifoam agent such as octadecanol.
- Sterile operations as outlined in general discussion of fermentation engineering.
- Recovery of penicillin—solvent extraction method has replaced original activated carbon adsorption-elution procedure.

5. Economics

5.1. Marketing and Sales

Penicillin continues to be a popular reliable antibiotic despite the appearance of at least a dozen competitive products. All of these, except chloramphenicol which is now made synthetically, can be produced with penicillin fermentation equipment with or without minor modifications. The type of antibiotic is controlled by inoculation of species and type of nutrients. Consequently, capital investment in the antibiotics industry is considered safe and the market situation stable.

The problem faced in India is to step up production. This has been undertaken both in the private sector and in the public sector with the aid of Russian experts.

5.2. Raw Materials

The most desirable fermentation base liquor is derived from maize or soyabeans. Both of these products must be imported to a large extent, so emphasis is placed on much larger production in the agricultural sector.

Attempts to use other materials such as mustard and groundnut seed have been only partially successful. Further research along these lines is also desirable.

IVJ. BIOTECHNOLOGY

The discussion of the pharmaceutical industry with its emphasis on fermentation and microbial processes logically leads to a discussion of biotechnology. This is a relatively new science with applications far beyond pharmaceuticals.

1. What is Genetic Engineering?

Genetic engineering is the purposeful manipulation of genetic information within cells, the basic units of all living organisms. For thousands of years man has employed such cells to ferment wine, leaven bread, and ripen cheese. More recently, man has used microorganisms to produce antibiotics, vitamins and a few chemicals.

The central purpose of genetic engineering is to harness the ability of cells to produce chemicals. Each cell, from the simplest bacterial cell to the most complex human cell, contains genes, which are instructions in the molecule deoxyribonucleic acid ("DNA"). The number and arrangement (sequences) of the genes within a cell determine the nature of the instructions given. Genes instruct the productive mechanisms of the cell to assemble particular protein molecules called enzymes. Enzymes, the catalysts of life within the cell, in turn facilitate the cell's chemical reactions. These reactions result in products the cell requires for life, growth and reproduction.

In the reproduction process, a cell creates an identical set of DNA instructions, and then divides. Genetic engineers control, by manipulation and alteration, the information coded in the genes in order to cause the cells to make products useful to man.

2. What is Biotechnology?

Biotechnology is a broader, less well defined field than genetic engineering. It overlaps with bioengineering and centers on industrial fermentation processes and could presumably include blood substitutes and even prosthetic devices such as artificial hearts and limbs.

Usually, however, biotechnology is closely synonymous with industrial microbiology. In any event, that is the sense in which it is used here. The chemical aspect of biotechnology is emphasized here.

Business people and scientists alike predict that the decades ahead will be greatly influenced by a major expansion of the relatively new area of biotechnology. Its potential impact on business and the economy is compared to that of computer technology starting 20 years ago.

Biotechnology uses enzymes (proteins produced by cells), microbes, cells, and tissue (groups or layers of specialized cells) for industrial processes.

Enzymes have long been used as catalysts to speed up chemical reactions in industries as diverse as food and beverages, petrochemicals, agriculture, pharmaceuticals, energy production, leather tanning, and mining.

Tissue cells have been cultured by drug manufacturers to make vaccines. And one example of the use of microbes is in the leaching of valuable metals from ores.

Biotechnical processes are becoming more attractive to many industries when compared with traditional chemical processes, not only due to the increasing cost of petroleum feedstocks, but also due to increasing concerns about pollution and safety.

Petrochemical and many other chemical reactions often operate at extreme temperatures and pressures which require expensive construction materials, elaborate safety devices and high energy needs. These commonly used processes also tend to generate a wide variety of waste materials, sometimes of a toxic nature.

Biological processes, on the other hand, generally operate under moderate or ambient conditions. Furthermore, biological processes are highly specific and seldom generate large amounts of unknown or toxic by-products.

Industrial microbiology, it should be noted, is not just a new field of entrepreneurial activity; it is a well-established factor in the world economy, responsible for a current annual production valued at tens of billions of dollars. Moreover, it is the outgrowth of a pervasive human activity with a rich history that goes back thousands of years.

Commercial fermentation using genetically engineered microorganisms offers several advantages over current chemical production techniques.

- The use of renewable resources: starches, sugars, cellulose, and other components of biomass can serve as the raw material for synthesizing organic chemicals. With proper agricultural management, biomass can assure a continuous renewable supply for the industry.
- The use of physically milder conditions: chemical processes often require high temperatures and extreme pressures. These conditions are energy intensive and pose a hazard in case of accidents. Biological processes operate under milder conditions, which are compatible with living systems.

- One-step production methods: microorganisms can carry out several steps in a synthetic process, eliminating the need for intermediate steps of separation and purification.
- Decreased pollution: because biological processes are highly specific in the reactions they catalyze, they offer control over the products formed and decrease undesirable side-products. As a result, they produce fewer pollutants that require management and disposal.

The impact of this technology will cut across the entire spectrum of chemical groups: plastics and resin materials, flavors and perfumes materials, synthetic rubber, medicinal chemicals, pesticides, and the primary products from petroleum that serve as the raw materials for the synthesis of organic chemicals. Nevertheless, the specific products that will be affected in each group can only be chosen on a case-by-case basis, with the applicability of genetics depending on a variety of factors. Crude estimates of the expected economic impacts are in the billions of dollars per year for dozens of chemicals within 20 years.

3. Pharmaceuticals

For thousands of years moldy cheese, meat and bread had been employed in folk medicine to heal wounds. Thus, biotechnology was unknowingly contributing to pharmaceuticals. Then, this connection became more direct in 1941 when, with the help of the U.S. Department of Agriculture and several American pharmaceutical companies, the production of penicillin by a related mold, penicillium chrysogenum, soon became a reality.

The advent of penicillin, which signaled the antibiotic era, was closely followed by the discoveries of Selman A. Waksman, a soil microbiologist at Rutgers University, who succeeded in obtaining a number of new antibiotics from the class of microorganisms called actinomycetes; the best known of his new "wonder drugs" was streptomycin. From Waksman's time up to the present, there has been a proliferation of economically viable fermentation processes and products.

Now, more recently genetic engineering rather than simply biotechnology promised to be the source of pharmaceuticals.

The gene splicing techniques developed so far can produce purer insulin for diabetics, a growth hormone to treat dwarfism, and interferon—a substance that has been touted for fighting viruses and cancer, but is terribly difficult to obtain in useful quantities without using recombinant DNA techniques.

The pharmaceutical industry has been the first to take advantage of the potentials of applied molecular genetics. Ultimately, it will probably benefit more than any other, with the largest percentage of its products depending on advances in genetic technologies. Already, microorganisms have been engineered to produce human insulin, interferon, growth hormone, urokinase (for the treatment of blood clots), thymosin-α-1 (for controlling the immune response) and somatostatin (a brain hormone).

The products most likely to be affected by genetic engineering in the next 10 to 20 years are non-protein compounds like most antibiotics, and protein compounds such as enzymes and antibodies, and many other hormones and vaccines. Improvements can be made both in the products and in the processes by which they are produced. Process costs may be lowered and even entirely new products developed.

The most advanced applications today are in the field of hormones. While certain hormones have already proved useful, the testing of others had been hindered by their scarcity and high cost. Of 48 human hormones that have been identified so far as possible candidates for production by genetically engineered microorganisms, only 10 are used in current medical practice. The other 38 are not, partly because they have been available in such limited quantities that tests of their therapeutic value have not been possible.

Genetic technologies also open up new approaches for vaccine development for such intractable parasitic and viral diseases as amebic dysentery, trachoma, hepatitis, and malaria. At present, the vaccine most likely to be produced is for foot-and-mouth disease in animals. However, should any one of the vaccines for human diseases become available, the social, economic, and political consequences of a decrease in morbidity and mortality would be significant. Many of these diseases are particularly prevalent in less industrialized countries; the developments of vaccines for them may profoundly affect the lives of tens of millions of people.

For some pharmaceutical products, biotechnology will compete with chemical synthesis and extraction from human and animal organs. Assessing the relative worth of each method must be done on a case-by-case basis. But for other products, genetic engineering offers the only method known that can ensure a plentiful supply; in some instances, it has no competition.

By making a pharmaceutical available, genetic engineering may have two types of effects:

- Drugs that already have medical promise will be available in ample amounts for clinical testing. Interferon, for example, can be tested for its efficacy in cancer and viral therapy, and human growth hormone can be evaluated for its ability to heal wounds.
- Other pharmacologically active substances for which no apparent use now exists will be available in sufficient quantities and at low enough cost to enable researchers to explore new uses. As a result, the potential for totally new therapies exists. Regulatory proteins, for example, which are in an entire class of molecules that control gene activity, are present in the body in only minute quantities. Now, for the first time, they can be recognized, isolated, characterized, and produced in quantity.

The mere availability of a pharmacologically active substance does not ensure its adoption in medical practice. Even if it is shown to have therapeutic usefulness, it may not succeed in the marketplace.

The difficulty in predicting the economic impact is exemplified by interferon. If it is found to be broadly effective against both viral diseases and cancers, sales would be in the tens of billions of dollars annually. If its clinical effectiveness is found to be only against one or two viruses, sales would be significantly lower.

At the very least, even if there are no immediate medical uses for compounds produced by genetic engineering, their indirect impact on medical research is assured. For the first time, almost any biological phenomenon of medical interest can be explored at the cellular level. These molecules are valuable tools for understanding the anatomy and functions of cells. The knowledge gained may lead to the development of new therapies or preventive measures for diseases.

As reviewed in "Chemical Weekly Annual for 1995," genetically engineered products or those based on modern biotechnology are yet to be commercially produced in India and are still at the research stage. Currently, several recombinant (r-DNA based) products like human insulin, interferons, GM-CSF, human growth hormone, streptokinase, erythropoietin, bovine somatotropin, etc., are being produced and marketed globally, with an estimated annual growth of over 25%. In India, five products, namely, insulin, alpha interferon, hepatitis B surface antigen based vaccine, GM-CSF and erythropoietin are approved for marketing. All these products are imported.

The demand for biotech products in the area of human and animal healthcare in the year 2000 is estimated at Rs. 3,500 crores, for industrial products Rs. 1,500 crores and in agriculture about Rs. 385 crores. These are minuscule compared to the sale of biotech products in the US estimated at US $7.7 billion (Rs. 23,000 crores) in 1994. The R&D expenditure in the US for biotechnology was US $7.0 billion (Rs. 21,000 crores) in 1994. There were more than 1,300 biotech companies in 1994 with an employment of over 1,000,000. The R&D expenditure in India for biotechnology based activities was less than Rs. 200 crores during 1994 of which more than 90% was by government, a substantial portion of which was disbursed by the Department of Biotechnology, set up by the Ministry of Science and Technology, in the mid-80's. Two major public sector units, i.e., Indian Vaccines Corporation Ltd. (IVCOL) and Bharath Immunologicals and Biologicals Ltd. (BIBCOL) have been set up by the Department of Biotechnology for production of vaccines for various diseases. The BIBCOL public issue was oversubscribed several times in the summer of 1994. The investments of both these undertakings exceed Rs. 200 crores.

4. Agricultural Applications

Agricultural research into the genetics, physiology and development of plant cells has lagged comparable research on animal cells, because the medical significance of animal work attracted more people and more money. That situation is changing now. Companies and federal agencies have recognized the potential of new biological methods in agriculture, and the action is speeding up.

Two aspects of biotechnology in agriculture have special importance to chemical manufacturers. One is the genetic improvement of crop plants. The other is the genetic improvement or more efficient management of microorganisms that live on or with plants and promote their survival and growth. Efforts in both these areas eventually might alter the need for fertilizers or pesticides in the growing of certain crops, although specific effects on agricultural practices or on chemical market can't be predicted yet.

The American seed trade represents approximately a $4 billion dollar annual market for seeds sold in the U.S. Corn is the biggest seed market today. The world seed trade figure is probably something like 30 billion dollars annually.

Thus, the modification of seed by genetic engineering techniques, to produce increased nitrogen-fixation capabilities, for example, could be a big business in itself and one with huge potential in terms of increased value of the products produced.

In mid-1981, researchers succeeded in transferring a gene that directs the production of a major protein from its location in a bean seed into a sunflower cell, yielding a new plant dubbed a "sunbean."

This accomplishment marks a major step toward the day when scientists will be able to increase the nutritive value of plants, to make plants resistant to disease and environmental stresses and to make them capable of fixing nitrogen from the air. Again, the media recognized the significance of this achievement with major coverage.

Agricultural researchers are obviously at center stage in the pursuit of scientific accomplishments that can produce unparalleled benefits not only for this country but for people throughout the world.

The complexity of plants and animals presents a greater challenge to advances in applied genetics than that posed by microorganisms. Nevertheless, the successful genetic manipulation of microbes has encouraged researchers in the agricultural sciences. The new tools will be used to complement, but not replace, the well-established practices of plant and animal breeding.

5. Metal Extraction and Recovery

Certain microorganisms are the basis of a metallurgical process that is thought to go back to the Romans: the bacterial leaching of low-grade ores to extract metals from them. Today copper and uranium are commercially leached by bacteria, mainly members of the genus Thiobacillus. New approaches to such bacterial leaching are also being made. They include the examination of acid- and heat-resistant microorganisms (including fungi) for their extraction abilities, the investigation of the mechanisms underlying the affinity of bacteria for metals and the genetic manipulation of bacteria to increase their resistance to the toxicity of the metals.

Bacteria have been used to leach metals, such as uranium and copper, from low-grade ores. Although there is reason to believe leaching ability is under genetic control in these organisms, practically nothing is known about the precise mechanisms involved. Therefore, the application of genetic technologies in this area remains speculative. Progress has been slow in obtaining more information, partly because very little research has been conducted.

In addition to leaching, microorganisms can be used to recover valuable metals or eliminate polluting metals from dilute solutions such as industrial waste streams. The process makes use of the ability of microorganisms to bind metals to their surfaces and then concentrate them internally.

The economic competitiveness of biological methods is still unproved, but genetic modifications have been attempted only recently. The cost of producing the microorganisms has been a major consideration. If it can be reduced, the approach might be useful.

6. Petroleum Products

- Enhanced oil field production
- Improved oil spill cleanup techniques using microbes
- Single-cell protein production

are among the possibilities for genetic engineering/bio-engineering applications in the petroleum industry.

Enhanced oil recovery—many methods have been tried in efforts to remove oil from the ground when natural explosive forces alone are no longer effective. Injecting chemicals into a reservoir has, in many cases, aided recovery by changing the oil's flow characteristics.

Microorganisms can produce the necessary chemicals that help to increase flow. Theoretically, they can also be grown in the wells themselves, producing those same chemicals *in situ*. The currently favored chemical, xanthan, is far from ideal for increasing flow. Genetic engineering should be able to produce chemicals with more useful characteristics.

7. Pollution Control

Many microorganisms can consume various kinds of pollutants, changing them into relatively harmless materials before they die. These microorganisms always have had a role in "natural" pollution control.

The usefulness of microorganisms in waste treatment has been recognized since 1914, when the activated-sludge process was first developed. The sludge process depends on a complex population of microorganisms that form naturally because of each organism's ability to degrade a constituent of the waste material and to co-exist with the others in a nutritionally complementary system. The next advance was to enrich the sludge by inoculating it with the desired mixture of microorganisms. Now pure cultures of a single microorganism are being made available to degrade specific compounds in industrial waste, such as polychlorinated biphenyls (PCB's).

Oil spills and the release of ballast and wash waters from oil tankers are other waste problems microbiology may be able to solve. Many microorganisms that can consume components of petroleum have been isolated. Strains of one such bacterial species, *Pseudomonas putida*, carry plasmid genes coding for enzymes that can degrade different components of oil. By genetic engineering the capacity to degrade the various components has been combined in one strain. Such a multiplasmid strain degrades petroleum faster than any of the original strains.

V
POLYMERIZATION INDUSTRIES

Polymeric materials consist of molecules of high molecular weight, varying from 10^3-10^7. All polymers have recurring structural molecular units that comprise the large molecules. Four major industries—plastics, fiber, rubber, paint and varnish—produce and process polymeric materials for different end purposes.

Naturally-occurring polymers in cellulose, lignin, proteins, resins and rubber have been available to man for many centuries. Physical chemical research on these polymers was started at the turn of the 20th century to determine structural properties and to understand their behavior from the standpoint of composition and structure.

By 1928, the concept evolved that these organic products were large molecules built from basic units called monomers which were rather elementary in structure. As soon as this principle was established, systematic efforts were directed to synthesize many types of polymers from well-known organic monomers available in large quantities from the petrochemical, agricultural, and wood industries as discussed in previous chapters.

The art of making and using polymers thus changed to a scientific and engineering achievement which today results in numerous new polymers that satisfy customer demands both at lower costs and in an improved manner; likewise, many new applications are created.

The role of chemistry and chemical engineering is outstanding in these industries. Thus, a study of the polymerization industries is important and extremely interesting to chemical engineers. We shall begin with a section on polymerization fundamentals applicable to all areas and then follow with sections on practice and applications.

Before going to the fundamentals, let us consider the broad picture of the place of plastics in Indian industrial development.

At present, 80 percent of the total requirement of raw materials and almost all types of plastic machines required for the industry are indigenously available. The present investment in all the three segments of the industry, namely, production of raw materials, expansion and diversification of processing capacities, manufacturing or processing machinery and ancillary equipment is Rs. 1,250 crore and it provides employment to more than eight lakh people.

Plastics have been subject to levies not only at the Central level, but also at State and local Government levels. These levies have affected the price of plastic products adversely. The per capita consumption of plastics in India is very low at 0.5 kg (500 grams) as against the world average of 11 kg. The per capita consumption is 68 kg in West Germany, 53 kg in USA, 35 kg in France and 33 kg in UK and even in a developing country like South Korea, 8.5 kg. The level in China is 5.0 kg.

On account of their inherent advantage in properties and versatility in adaptation and use, plastics have come to play a vital role in a variety of applications the world over. In our country, plastics are used in making essential consumer goods of daily use for common man such as baskets, shopping bags, water bottles, school bags, tiffin boxes, hair combs, toothbrushes, spectacle frames and fountain pens. They also find applications in fields like packaging, automobiles and transportation, engineering, electronics, telecommunications, defense, medicine and building and construction. Plastics are growing in importance in agriculture and water management.

Although the employment potential of a basic petrochemical unit is limited, the downstream industries are labor intensive and can create significant job opportunities. The polymer processing industry alone has an employment potential estimated at one technically oriented job for every 10 TPA of polymers.

The scope of value addition in polymers is enormous. For instance, a rupee worth of ethylene can be converted into Rs. 2.5 worth of high density polyethylene which in turn can yield products worth Rs. 5.

Plastics can also play a major role in improving agricultural productivity through new techniques of plastic film use. They are extensively used in water management. The use of LDPE sheets for canal and reservoir lining helps reduce seepage losses. Plastic pipes and fittings find a place in drip irrigation. An important use is in mulching, which seeks to provide protective covering to the roots of plants and trees so that moisture is retained longer.

Packaging is a major outlet for plastics. By providing economic means for packaging, plastics have a role to play in reducing the effective cost of basic items of consumption such as foodgrains, fruits and vegetables, edible oils, milk, sugar, etc. Packaging with conventional materials such as jute, glass, wood and paper is not only expensive, but will also be inadequate to meet the country's demand even for bulk packaging along with the growth in production of basic items of consumption. The packaging needs of the country for these items alone would be enormous by 2000 A.D. The overall need of bulk as well as retail packaging will grow dramatically, particularly as the consumer revolution gathers momentum. Quite apart from fancy packaging for expensive products, the plastic bag is becoming an article of common use for all sorts of articles of daily consumption. There is no way in which this demand can be met by conventional materials.

The sectorwise use of plastics in India is as follows:

Sector	Percent
Agriculture	23
Packaging	21
Electricals	15
Housewares	10
Footwear/Fabrics	9
Building and Construction	9
Others (Transport and medicine)	13

Source: "Hindu Survey of Indian Industry" (1995)

Indian demand for the main commodity polymers (polyethylene, polypropylene, polystyrene and PVC) has tripled every decade since the 1960's, and has now reached 1.5 Mt/a. However, while India has over a fifth of the world's population, its polymer capacity (1.45 Mt/a) is only 1.4% of the world total. This means there is still enormous growth potential for these products according to the British journal "Chemistry & Industry" for 1 April 1996. Plastics consumption will rise from 1.6 Mt/a to 3 Mt/a in 2000, and at least 9 Mt/a by 2010. Capacity will triple by 2000 (see table below) with a more even distribution of plants across the country than at present.

Growth in Polymer Capacity Forecast for India
(in Thousands of Tons/Yr)

	PE	PP	PS	PVC	Total
1995 Capacity	620	115	136	583	1,454
Year 2000 Capacity	1,880	1,410	347	1,223	4,860

VA. POLYMERIZATION FUNDAMENTALS

1. Introduction

- Polymers are composed of molecules of molecular weight from about 10^3-10^7
- A polymer is made up of repeated basic units produced from monomers
- Polymers can be synthesized from various types and combinations of monomers to yield unusual properties, both physical and chemical

2. Classification of Polymers

Polymers are difficult to classify because there are so many interacting relationships among the large number of polymeric materials now in existence.

Four methods of classification are frequently used:

- Physico-chemical structure
- Mode of preparation
- Physical properties
- Technical applications

Physico-chemical structure models are basic and will be discussed first and most fully. Their relationship to preparation methods will be introduced. Physical properties of polymers will only be mentioned briefly in this chapter as it is a subject for design and application engineers and a complete study in itself. Technical preparation and applications will be studied in some detail in Section VB.

3. Physico-Chemical Structure of Polymers

3.1. Functionality

The ultimate result of coupling monomers to produce polymers is wholly dependent on the functionality of the monomer. A molecule is called a mono-, bi-, tri-, or polyfunctional, depending on the number of reactive bonds or groups available for coupling at the beginning or during the course of a polymeric reaction.

- Unifunctional (U—). Example: $CH_3 \cdot COOH$ where carboxyl (COOH) group is the only chemically reactive group. Obviously a polymeric chain cannot be built from this acid alone.

- Bifunctional (—B—). Example: $CH_2 = CH_2$ where the double bond splits to form a coupling with another molecule containing a double bond, not necessarily ethylene. If only ethylene is present, the polymer would be

$$nCH_2 = CH_2 \rightarrow -(CH_2-CH_2)_n-$$

The general schematic for a bifunctional monomer to polymer reaction is

$$n(-B-) \rightarrow (-B-)_n$$

- Trifunctional (—T—). Example: trimethylol phenol made from phenol and formaldehyde

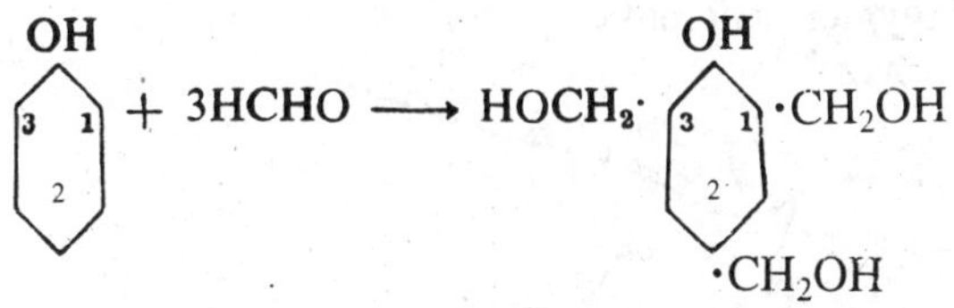

The three OH groups on the methylol linkages are reactive. Note further that a monofunctional and bifunctional monomer can also be made by adding one CH_2OH to the number 1 position and two CH_2OH groups to the number 1 and number 2 positions respectively. The final composition of a phenol-formaldehyde polymer is thus a mixture of bi- and trimethylol phenol monomers structures and depends on reaction conditions maintained.

3.2. Physical Structure and Functionality

- Linear polymers—formed from bifunctional groups only, *i.e.*,

••• — B — B — B — B — B — B — B — B — •••

This type of polymer is normally thermoplastic (creep flow at temperatures >150°C without chemical change), relatively soluble except for very high mol. wt. material.

- Cross-linked polymers—formed from bi- and trifunctional groups, *e.g.*,

```
••• — B — B — T — B — T — B — T — •••
              |       |       |
      ••• — T — B — T — B — T — B — B — •••
```

Cross-linkage in three dimensions via chemical bonding gives elastomeric properties if there are only a few such bonds across linear polymer chains. If bonding is more extensive, solidified thermoset polymers result with high resistance to heat and mechanical deformation.

- Branched-chain polymer—an intermediate case where branches grow from the parent chain without cross-linking

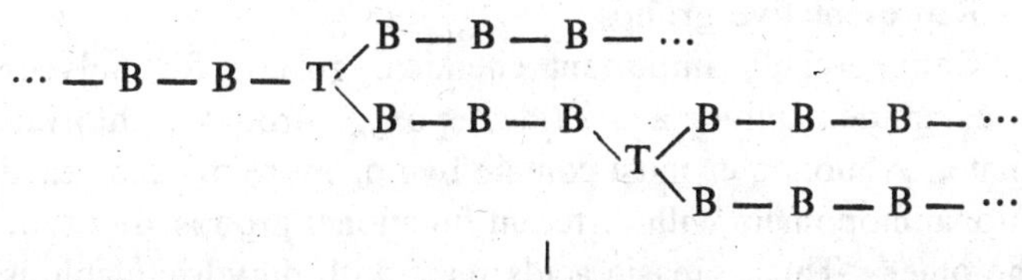

Branching is cased by small amounts of —T— often as impurities, present in a bifunctional monomer formulation. The effect is to lower solubility, increase softening point, and reduce thermoplastic forming properties.

A set of diagrams shown next gives a schematic and comparative view of the structure of solid polymers.

Linear or Chain Polymer Schematic

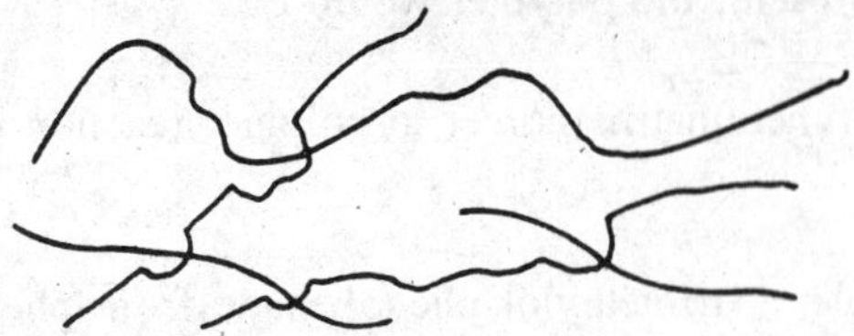

means no chemical bonding but one **chain lying on top of** another

Branched-Chain Polymer Schematic

Cross-linked Polymer Schematic

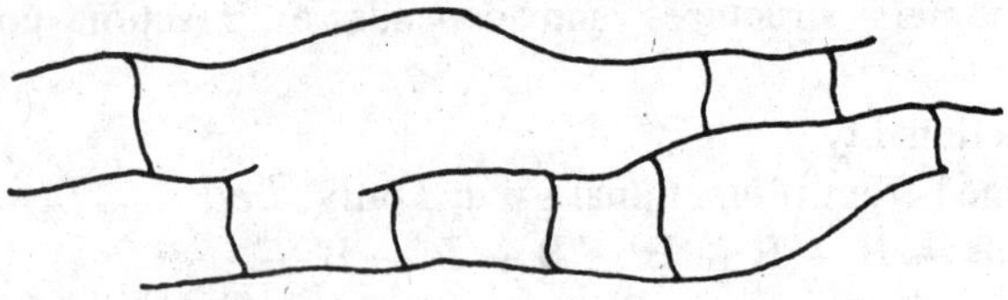

3.3. Polymeric Chemical Reactions

Polymers can be further classified by the type of chemical reactions which the monomers undergo in producing high molecular weight compounds.

- Polycondensation reaction—monomers react by repeatedly splitting off H_2O, NH_3, CH_2O, NaCl, or other small molecules in a step-by-step reaction to build up the molecular size.
- Addition reaction—occurs among molecules containing double or triple bonds or with oxo-ring compounds; no small molecules are liberated and reaction is the rapid chain type.

3.4. Polycondensation Reactions

3.4.1. Representative groups

Commercially important chemical groups for polycondensation reactions are aldehyde, amide, amine, anhydride, epoxy, carboxyl, chloride, hydroxyl, sulfide, and isocyanate. A monomer must contain two or more of such reacting groups. Usually two bifunctional monomers with different functional groups are used, each capable of reacting with the other. Thus, dibasic acids react with dihydric alcohols to give polyesters.

3.4.2. Fundamental reaction mechanism

Same mechanism and chemical activation energies are found in preparing low molecular weight condensation products—for example, the esterification reaction:

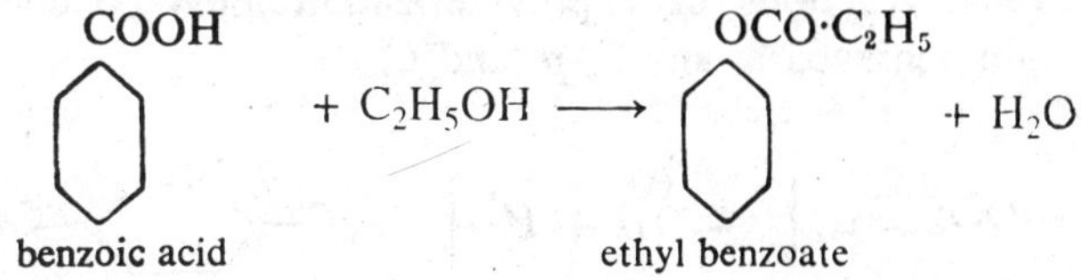

Reacts under given conditions of T, p, and C_i with predictable rates and equilibria.

3.4.3. Complexity of polycondensation reactions

- Functional groups present

Three types of polymer molecules are formed from pairs of bifunctional reactions. Example—terephthalic acid and ethylene glycol.

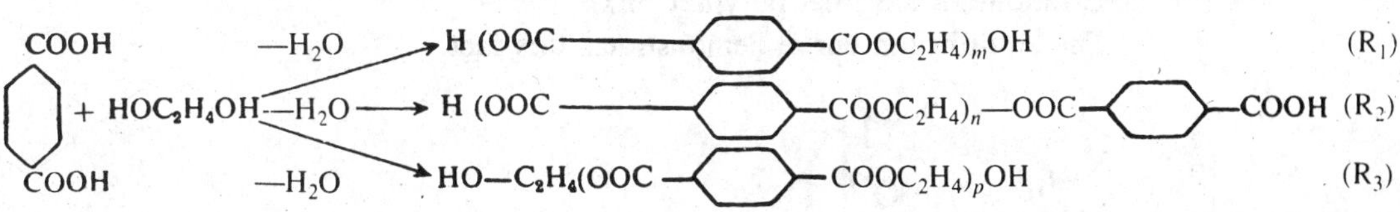

R_1 is a polyester with one terminal hydroxyl and one terminal H, both reactive; occurs only when reactant mole ratio is unity

R_2 is a polyester formed in excess of acid

R_3 is a polyester formed in excess of glycol

The degree of polymerization ($\overline{DP}$) of the reactions above are *m, n,* or *p* respectively.

- Formation of intermediates

In some cases bi- or trifunctional groups are not available from the initial reactants, but must be formed via intermediates. Such is characteristic of phenol-formaldehyde polymerization as shown next.

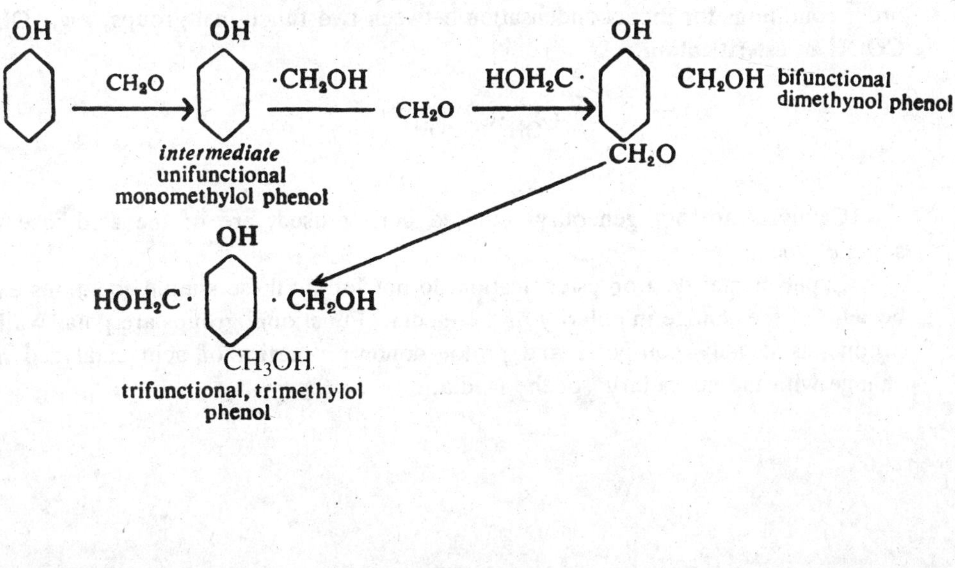

3.4.4. Equilibrium conditions for polycondensation reactions

Reverse reactions or depolymerization must be considered in the final equilibrium achieved at any T, p, and C_i

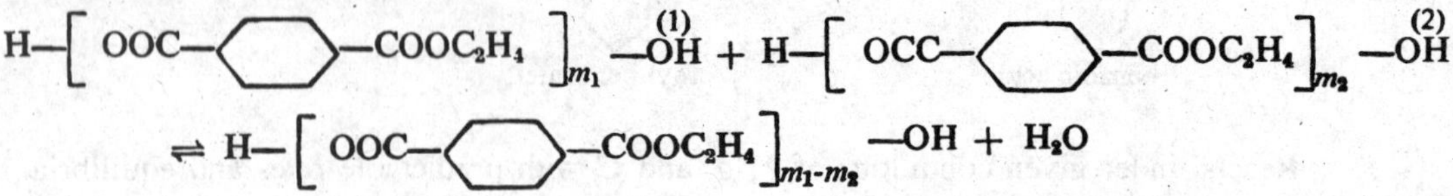

There are only two sites on which the ester bond can be formed—(1) or (2)—but there are $m_1 + m_2$ sites where it may be hydrolyzed. This leads to difficult industrial problems in removing water and maintaining very low water concentrations in the final polymer mix.

The equilibrium curve demonstrates this fact.

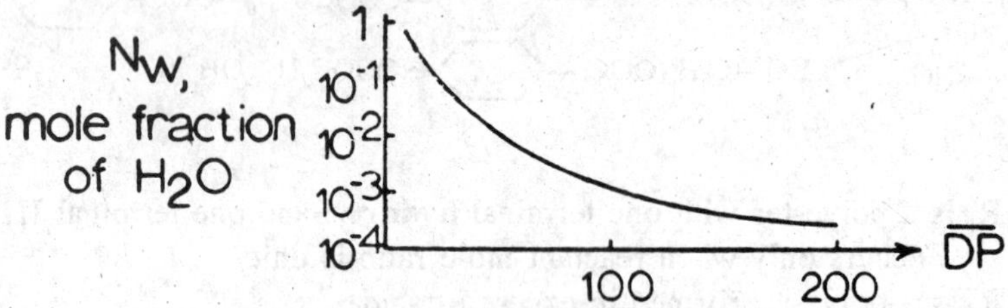

3.4.5. Kinetic considerations for polycondensation reactions

Polycondensations are relatively slow, step-wise reactions in which functional group reactions occur repeatedly to build up a polymer. Since reactions occur between functional groups, the reaction is not restricted to a monomer adding to a multimer of given $\overline{DP}$ but may also occur between two multimers of $\overline{DP}$ m_1 and m_2 as shown in Section 3.4.4. It has further been shown that the rate constants for all functional groups in the condensation are equal, whether on a monomer or multimer.

With this simplification, polycondensation reactions parallel the rate and reaction order conditions for monocondensation between two functional groups, *e.g.*, OH and COOH in esterification.

$$r = k_1 C^a_{\mathrm{OH}} \cdot C^b_{\mathrm{COOH}}$$

Catalysts are not generally required but, if used, are of the acid-base water soluble type.

Experimental data on esterification do not follow these simple equations exactly because of the change in polarity of the media. Functional groups are polar while the product is usually non-polar and proton-donor properties of acid catalyzed media change with the net polarity of the media.

For bulk polymerizations, viscosity increases markedly affect the measured rate constants which change from chemically-controlled to diffusion-controlled values during the polymerization.

A third difficulty is related to the different reactivity of functional groups on the same molecule. For example, different esterification rates exist for the primary and secondary glycerol hydroxyl groups.

The average degree of polymerization, $\overline{DP}$, for polycondensation can be derived from probability statistics as the ratio of the smallest number of reacting groups (N_0) present at the start to the number of the same reacting groups (N) present at time t.

$$\overline{DP} = \frac{N_0}{N} = \frac{1}{1-p}$$

where p = fractional conversion of the reacting group = $\frac{N_0 - N}{N_0}$

3.5. Addition Reactions

3.5.1. General definition

$$\text{R} + \text{R} \rightarrow \text{RR} \rightarrow \overset{\text{R}}{\text{RRR}} \text{ etc.}$$

Note that the monomer always adds to the multimer. Three types of addition polymerization reactions are possible: step reactions, chain reactions, or ionic reactions.

3.6. Step Addition Reactions

Example: ethylene oxide plus trace of methanol

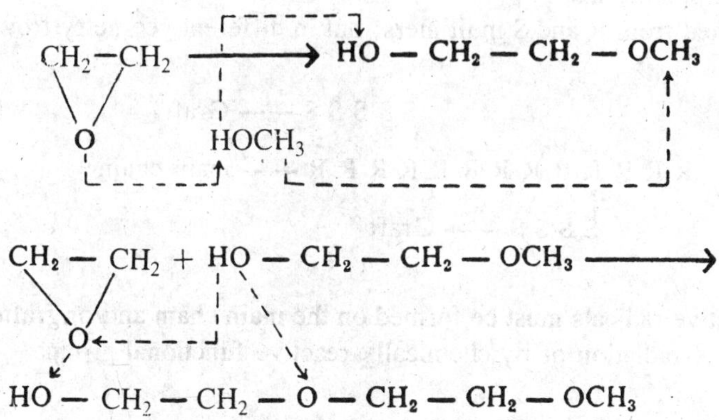

(3) Repeat of (2) to form HO — CH_2 — CH_2 [— O — CH_2 — CH_2]$_n$ — OCH_3

Note that HOH can be used (replace — OCH_3 by —OH). Polymers of the polyethylene oxide type have industrial importance as waxy, resinous, or fibrous products.

3.7. Chain Addition Reactions

These reactions are most prevalent of the three possible types. Characteristics of chain polymerization reactions are:

- Formation of polymer is usually accomplished in a fraction of a second and in a single sweep

- Usual chain kinetics occur—initiation, propagation, transfer, and termination

3.8. Variations of Chain Addition Reactions

Let R and S be two different monomers.

3.8.1. Homopolymerization

R and S present only

$$R \xrightarrow{R} RR \xrightarrow{R} RRR \rightarrow R_n; \text{ or}$$

$$S \xrightarrow{S} SS \xrightarrow{S} SSS \rightarrow S_n$$

3.8.2. Copolymerization

Usual chain kinetics to form these polymers with R and S present together.

- Random type
  RR SR SSS RR S R SS R R...
- Alternating type
  R S R S R S R S R S...

3.8.3. Block polymerization

Start with multimers from straight polymerization, *i.e.*, •RRR•, •SSSS•, etc., then join together in blocks.

•RRR•SSSS•RR•SSSSS•——

3.8.4. Graft polymerization

Formed from R and S multimers, but in different geometry from block polymers

```
                     S S S S S —— Graft
                    /
R R R R R R R R R R R R R R —— main chain
    |
    S S S S —— Graft
```

Reactive radicals must be formed on the main chain and/or grafted section, either by β- or X-radiation or by chemically reactive functional groups.

3.9. Chain Addition Reaction Kinetics

Define species as:

C = source of radicals (benzoyl peroxide, for example)

M = monomer

* = activated

M_m, M_n = growing chains of length of m and n

I = transferable energy species (solvent, impurity, or surface adsorbed)

- Initiation : $nC \xrightarrow{\text{energy}} C^*, 2C^*$, etc. (generally free radicals)
- Propagation : $C^* + M \longrightarrow M^* + C$

$$M^* + M \longrightarrow MM^*$$

$$MM^* + M \longrightarrow MMM^* \longrightarrow M_n^* \text{ (controls } \overline{DP})$$

- Chain transfer : $M_n^* + M \longrightarrow M_n + M^*$ (with monomer)

$$M_n^* + M_m \longrightarrow M_n + M_m^* \text{ (with multimer)}$$

$$M_n^* + I \longrightarrow M_n + I^* \text{ (with other molecules)}$$

- Termination : $2M_m^* \longrightarrow M_{2n}$ (coupling)

$$M_n^* + M_m^* \longrightarrow M_m + M_n \text{ (disproportionation)}$$

$$M_n^* + Y^* \longrightarrow M_n + Y \text{ (loss via other molecules)}$$

3.9.1. Initiation reactions

(a) Energy requirements

Initiation is the relatively slow and rate-controlling step with energy requirements of the bond breaking and forming type important for activation.

Bond	*Dissociation Energy*	*Comments*
C—C	70,000 cal/mole	Unifunctional, will not polymerize
C—N	49,000	
C—S	54,000	
C—O	70,000	
C=C	100,000	Polyfunctional, can be initiated for polymerization
C≡C	123,000	
C=N	94,000	
C=S	103,000	
C=O	149,000	Energy requirement too high for initiation
C=N	150,000	

Initiation energy can be supplied in this form of heat or by radiation with α-, β- or Υ-rays. The activation energy requirements can be considerably lowered by use of catalyst. A comparative example of activation energy requirements for uncatalyzed styrene polymerization which is the C = C type shows:

Reaction	*Activation Energy, cal/mole*
Initiation	30,000
Propagation	7,000
Termination	3,000

(b) Effect of monomer structure

- Substitution—aids reactivity and decreases activation energy if unsymmetrical, *e.g.*,

  $CH_2 = CHX$ has lower activation energy than $CH_2 = CH_2$

- Conjugation or increased unsaturation—aids reactivity; for example:

Compound	*Structure*	*Reactivity*
1-Butene	$CH_2 = CH{-}CH_2{-}CH_3$	non-conjugated, very slow
Butadiene	$CH_2 = CH{-}CH = CH_2$	conjugated, very rapid
Vinylacetylene	$CH \equiv C{-}CH = CH_2$	explosive

3.9.2. Propagation reactions

(a) Energy requirements

Propagation reactions occur between free radicals already formed (M_n^*) and inactive monomer (M). With activation energy of a lower order of magnitude (~7,000 cal/mole), the probability of reaction on collision between these species is high and reactions are rapid to produce a given degree of polymerization.

(b) Reactivity of species

In considering the reaction between M_n^* and M, the reactivity of the monomer is important. For example, styrene monomer has double bond conjugation in resonance form:

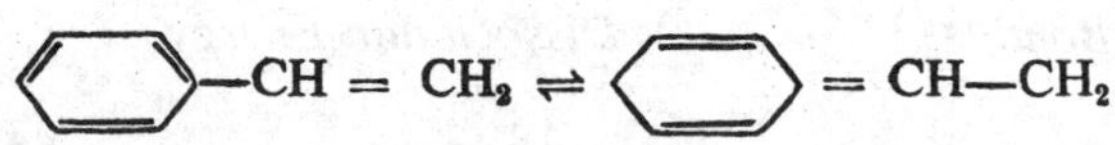

Its activated multimer does not have resonance:

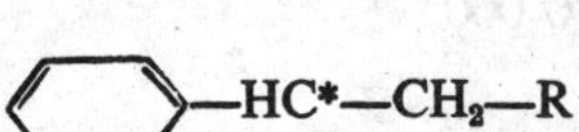

The reaction rate is controlled by the less reactive multimer. In general, more reactive monomers form less reactive multimers and vice versa.

(c) Steric effects

The location of the free radical in the multimer, the size of the multimer, and its electric charge characteristic can seriously reduce the number of successful collisions simply because π-electron of the monomer bond cannot get within reacting distance of the free radical electron.

(d) Type of propagation

This is important in substituted monomers where the unpaired electron is on the C atom coupled to the substituent X.

$$M_n^* + CH_2 = CHX \longrightarrow M_n - CH_2 - CHX$$

Continuous propagation of new multimer in one chain is usually head-to-tail with only 1-2% head-to-head structure.

Predominating head-to-tail structure

$$-CH_2-CHX-CH_2-CHX-CH_2-CHX$$

Minor arrangement in head-to-head structure

$$-CH_2-CHX-CHX-CH_2-CH_2-CHX-CHX-CH_2-$$

3.9.3. Chain transfer reactions

In chain transfer, one radical of a growing chain is terminated and another one started without any reduction in the number of free radicals. Chain transfer reactions are often purposely induced to control $\overline{DP}$ and branching rates of polymers. Solvents such as CCl_4 are good transfer agents for such purposes.

$$R-CH_2-CHX-CH_2-CHX + CCl_4 \rightarrow R-CH_2-CHX-CH_2-CHXCl + CCl_3^*$$

For branching, which occurs mainly at high temperature, reaction of a reactive multimer with a dead chain occurs, followed by successive monomer additions to increase the branch length.

$$\underset{\text{radical}}{R_1-CH_2-CHX^*} + \underset{\text{dead chain}}{R_2-CHX-HCH-CHX-\ldots}$$

$$\downarrow$$

$$R_1-CH_2-CH_2X + R_2-CHX-C^*H-CHX \text{ (branching radical)}$$

$$\downarrow CH_2{=}CHX \text{ (monomer)}$$

$$R_2-CHX-CH(-CH_2-CHX^*)-CHX\ldots \text{ (branched radical)}$$

3.9.4. Chain termination reactions

A termination occurs with a net loss of one free radical by:

(a) collision between growing chains with coupling or disproportionation,

(b) collision of a growing chain with an initiation radical,

(c) collision of a growing chain with inhibition, undesirable impurities, or with the wall of a reaction vessel.

- Coupling—results in an increasing chain length

$$\ldots-CH_2-CHX-CH_2-CHX^* + -CH_2-CHX-CH_2-CHX-\ldots$$

$$\ldots-CH_2-CHX-CH_2-CHX-CH_2-CHX-CH_2-CHX-\ldots$$

- Disproportionation—no change in chain length, but produces one double bond

$$\ldots -CH_2-CHX-CH_2-CHX^* + -CH_2-CHX-CH_2-CHX- \ldots$$

$$\ldots -CH_2-CHX-CH{=}CHX + CH_3-CHX-CH_2-CHX$$

- Initiator termination reaction—high initiator concentrations accelerate polymerization, but also provide for high rates of chain termination with reduction in $\overline{DP}$. In practice, initiator concentrations are controlled to balance the two effects.
- Inhibitor termination reaction—deliberate addition of inhibitor molecules to control chain length and often to avoid any polymerization of monomers during processing, storage and shipment. The inhibitor must be removed before starting the polymerization reaction. Inhibitors often contain nitro, amino, or phenolic hydroxyl groups.

3.9.5. Effect of physical properties on addition polymerization.

An auto-acceleration or gel effect occurs after the start of an addition reaction. The reaction rate increases significantly. The reason is attributed to viscosity effects, wherein the multimers cannot diffuse rapidly for termination collision amongst each other but the monomer can, thus increasing the propagation rate relative to the termination rate.

3.10 Ionic Addition Reactions

Ionic reactions are similar to free radical initiated reactions but have + or — charges instead of neutral, unpaired electrons. An example of ionic polymerization is the preparation of polyisobutylene with boron trifluoride catalyst.

Initiation

$$BF_3 + H_2O\ (\text{Trace}) \longrightarrow F_3BOH^- + H^+$$

$$H^+ + CH_2 = C(CH_3)_2 \longrightarrow (CH_3)_3C^+$$

Propagation

$$(CH_3)_3{\cdot}C^+ + CH_2 = C(CH_3)_2 \longrightarrow (CH_3)_3{\cdot}C-CH_2-\overset{\displaystyle CH_3}{\underset{\displaystyle CH_3}{C^+}}$$

Termination

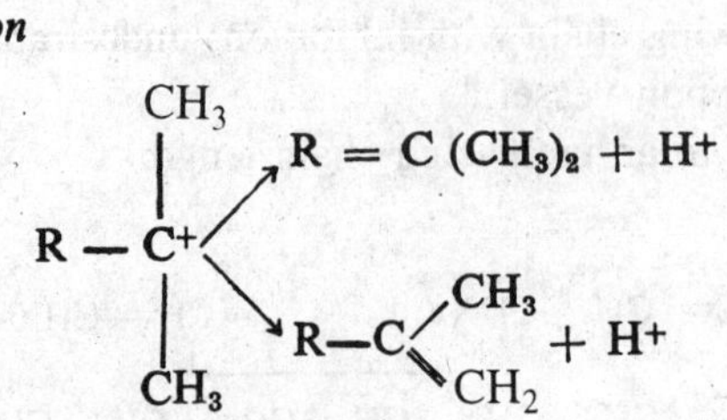

Co-catalyst, as a trace of H_2O, is necessary to produce ionization since no polymerization occurs in absolutely dry conditions.

3.11. Copolymerization

By use of several different monomers, a much greater variety of useful polymers can be obtained. Examples of such monomer combinations are:

butadiene-styrene (GR-S rubber)
styrene-acrylonitrile
vinyl chloride-vinyl acetate
isobutylene-isoprene

The ultimate chemical arrangement of the polymer structure depends on rates of reaction of two types of monomers (R and S). First, there are four possible kinetic rate equations for propagation reactions.

$$R_n^* + R \xrightarrow{k_{rr}} R_{n+1}^*$$

$$R_n^* + S \xrightarrow{k_{rs}} (R_nS)^*$$

$$S_n^* + S \xrightarrow{k_{ss}} S_{n+1}^*$$

$$S_n^* + R \xrightarrow{k_{sr}} (S_nR)^*$$

- If $k_{rs} \gg k_{rr}$ and $k_{sr} \gg k_{ss}$, then radicals of R react preferentially with S and vice-versa with the resulting alternating structure:
  ... — R — S — R — S — R — S — R — S — ...
- If $k_{rr} \gg k_{rs}$ and $k_{ss} \gg k_{sr}$, block copolymers result:
  ... — R — R — R — S — S — S — S — R — R — R — R — R — S — S — S — ...
- When all k's are approximately the same order of magnitude, completely random copolymers are formed:
  ... — R — S — R — R — S — R — S — S — R — S — ...

3.12. Stereospecific Polymerization

3.12.1. Definition

This is a method of tailoring atomic arrangements within chains to produce oriented polymers with unusual properties which include

- Higher density
- Crystallinity
- Higher melting points
- Improved mechanical properties

3.12.2. Stereospecific agents

- Ziegler catalysts—aluminum alkyls plus electro-positive metals in transition groups III-VIII (most common in titanium as $TiCl_4$); used for polyethylene and polypropylene.
- Supported metal oxide catalysts—suboxides of chromium and molybdenum are examples; used for polymerization of ethylene and α-olefins.
- Radiation: X-rays and ϒ-rays are effective.

3.12.3. Examples of stereoisomerization

- **Vinyl H—substituted polymer**

  $\ldots - CH_2 - CHR - CH_2 - CHR - CH_2 - \ldots$

where R = phenyl group in polystyrene or methyl group in polyisopropylene, etc.

- **Random or atactic arrangement—non-stereospecific**

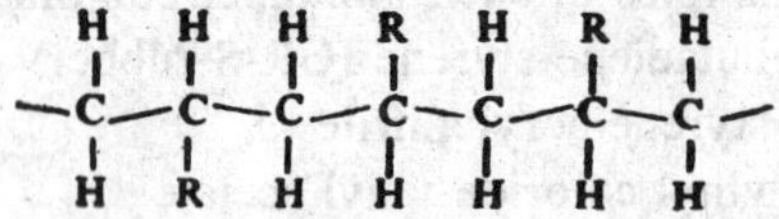

- **Oriented on same side or isotactic arrangement**

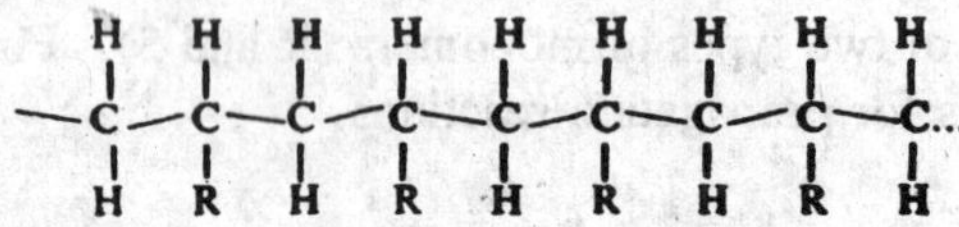

- Oriented on alternating side—syndiotactic arrangement

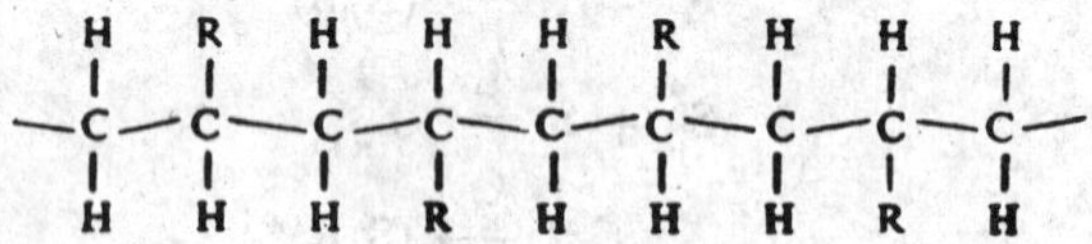

- Polyethylene

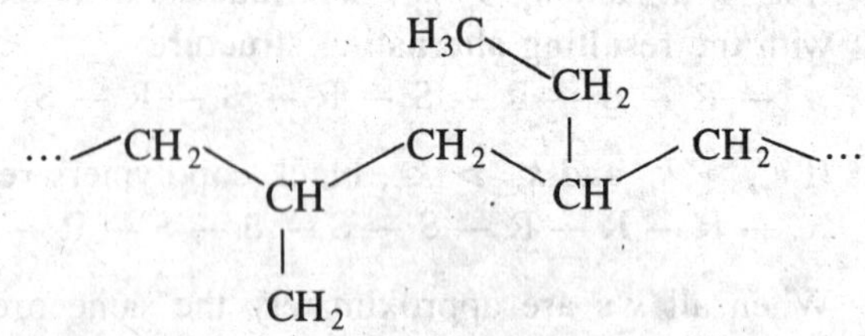

linear or stereospecific polymer

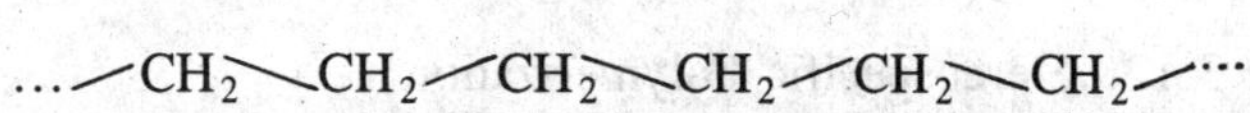

3.13. Addition Polymerization Kinetics

An exact treatment of this subject is beyond the scope of this text. Through use of ordinary kinetic equations for all of the chain processes and probability mathematics, it is possible to predict the rate of disappearance of monomers, the average degree of polymerization $\overline{DP}$, and the distribution of molecular size and weight in a polymer.

4. Modes of Polymerization

Polycondensation methods differ appreciably from those used in addition polymerization and therefore the discussion will be divided into two sections.

4.1. Condensation Polymerization Methods

- Roughly follows procedures used for low molecular weight functional group reactions
- Stoichiometric proportions of reactants chosen for desired final properties
- Can be processed with or without solvent addition

- Mixed in batch reaction vessels with catalyst addition and heat control to avoid premature gelation
- Major problem is to remove condensation products such as H_2O to yield a higher DP; vacuum processing or azeotropic distillation are schemes used
- Tridimensional polymers are often prepared in two states:
  (1) Soluble and fusile polymers with low cross-linkaging are prepared as described above. The reaction is terminated by removal of catalyst, lowering the temperature, or not removing the volatile condensation product.
  (2) Products are shipped to fabricators who convert them by heat curing (time-high temperature) to the final thermosetting products.

4.2. Addition Polymerization Methods

These factors are carried out via controlled heat and catalyst conditions under these classifications:

4.2.1. Homogeneous polymerization

- Bulk—monomer is only feed; can be gas, liquid or solid
- Solution—monomer is completely dissolved in a solvent

4.2.2. Heterogeneous polymerization

- Emulsion—monomer is emulsified in an aqueous media as micelles
- Suspension—monomer is held in an aqueous or other type media as large droplets in suspension

Further explanation of each of these types of addition polymerization is in order.

4.2.3. Bulk polymerization

(a) Gas phase type—ethylene or propylene monomers with BF_3 catalyst
(b) Liquid phase type
- Most common
- Problems of effective heat dissipation of exothermic reactions as viscosity of polymer increases with $\overline{DP}$
- Products are optically clear, pure polymers
- Most frequently a batch-wise process
- Continuous bulk polymerization now being done by carrying out early stages in a tower reactor, then atomization of the liquid polymer in an inert gas spray chamber where polymerization is completed and a solid powder is obtained. Polystyrene powder is made this way.

4.2.4. Solution polymerization

- Has advantage of better heat control
- Solvent slows down reaction and causes considerable chain termination and low molecular weight polymers
- Modification most frequently used is to choose solvent where monomer is soluble, but polymer of given $\overline{DP}$ is not soluble, thus enabling a completely continuous operation with a low solvent recycle

4.2.5. Emulsion polymerization

- Most used method of polymerization
- Overcomes difficulties of two previous methods, *i.e.*, heat control and low $\overline{DP}$
- Monomer + H_2O emulsified with suitable reagent to yield spherical monomer particles in the 1-10 μ range, called micelles

- Heat is controlled by transfer to the aqueous phase with little change in viscosity of the emulsion
- Reaction proceeds rapidly in each particle with some shrinkage to form a stable emulsion or latex
- $\overline{DP}$ depends on droplet size, temperature and catalyst concentration, but is considerably higher than possible with either bulk or solution polymerization
- Disadvantages of emulsion polymerization—occludes emulsifiers, catalyst and product; has poor capacity and low electrical resistance which are sometimes critical properties

4.2.6. Suspension polymerization

- Effective way of controlling bulk polymerization heat release
- Monomer is suspended as spheroids of 0.5-3 mm size in a non-solvent with agitation and no emulsifiers
- Three distinct reaction stages:

(1) Inhibition period—little polymerization, with particle size equilibrium attained from coalescence versus mechanical agitation break-up and dispersion mechanisms

(2) Rapid polymerization—polymer stays dissolved in remaining monomer, particles become sticky and agglomerate; surface coating easily removed by washing later

(3) Polymerization continues to form solidified spheres which do not coalesce

- $\overline{DP}$ is not as high as with emulsion polymerization

4.2.7. Comparison of methods

The advantage of emulsion polymerization in terms of completeness of reaction and highest molecular weight polymer is shown by an example of polystyrene production. The product from suspension had the highest purity and excellent opacity.

Reaction conditions: 2 hours at 85°C

Method	*Catalyst*	*% Conversion*	*Mol. wt.*
Bulk	0.5% benzoyl peroxide	54	40,000
Emulsion	0.5% potassium persulfate	97	370,000
Suspension	0.5% benzoyl peroxide	49	67,000

5. Physical Properties of Polymers

We must keep in mind as engineers that the only real incentive for producing various types of polymers is to satisfy an engineering need for materials of unique physical and chemical properties and/or materials which are competitive with other sources such as wood and metals.

Research scientists are interested in certain of the physical properties of polymers to help explain structural modes. In particular, the colligative behavior of polymers in solvents is important in molecular weight determinations.

Thus, the physical properties of polymers is an important subject, but one which cannot be treated in detail in this brief outline of the entire polymer field.

5.1. List of Important Physical Properties

An evaluation of a polymer for a specific requirement will encompass many of the property measurements listed next.

Optical Properties
- Odor
- Hardness
- Density
- Weatherability

Mechanical Properties
- Tensile strength
- Compressive strength
- Flexural strength
- Shear strength
- Impact resistance
- Rigidity and brittleness
- Ductility
- Creep
- Fatigue
- Dimensional stability
- Sound transmission

Thermal Properties
- Thermal diffusivity
- Heat resistance
- Coefficient of expansion
- Flammability

Electrical Properties
- Resistivity
- Dielectric
- Power factor
- Arcing resistance

Solvent Properties
- Solubility
- Plasticizer compatibility
- Viscosity

Chemical Resistance to:
- Chemical solutions
- Oils and fats
- Solvents

5.2. Classification of Polymers by Physical Properties

This is one of the four general methods of classifying polymers. Further information on certain of these polymers is given in Section VB.

5.2.1. • Thermoplastic—linear or slightly branched molecules; solvent soluble; can be repeatedly melted and useful for melt casting and spinning, injection molding, and extrusion.
- Vinyls
- Cellulose derivatives
- Straight-chain polycondensation products
- Polyethylene and polypropylene, oxides and amines

• Thermosetting—cross-linked or heavily branched molecules, largely solvent insoluble, good heat resistance, but cannot be melted after forming.
- Phenol-formaldehyde
- Urea-aldehydes
- Silicones
- Allyls
- Polycondensation products
- Protein-aldehydes

5.2.2. • Elastomers—resistant solids with high flexural strength
- Butadiene and derivatives
- Butadiene copolymers
- Ethylene-propylene stereospecific copolymers
- Isobutylene and derivatives
- Polycondensation products

Polyisoprene
Polyurethanes
Plasticized vinyl polymers
Silicones
Thiokols

5.2.3. • Fibers—thread-forming solids with high tensile strength
Polyamides
Polyesters
Polyurethanes
Polycarbamides
Cellulose and cellulose derivatives
Polyvinylidine chloride
Polyvinyl derivatives
Protein derivatives

5.3. Outline of Certain Physical Properties of Polymers

5.3.1. Solvent properties

(a) Determination of molecular weight distribution which dictates many of the physical properties. Fractional precipitation from solvents gives most accurate distribution curves.

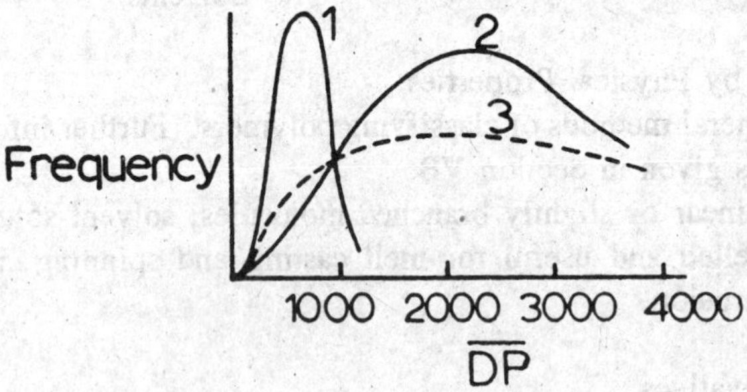

1. Cellulose acetate
2. Polyisobutylene
3. Polystyrene

In general, polymers with narrow band distribution of molecular weights have more predictable physical properties.

(b) Viscosity—average molecular weights can be determined from empirical formula:

$$N = K(M_v)^a,$$

where M_v is somewhere between the number average and weight average molecular weight; this must be considered in solvent polymerization processes.

(c) Plasticizer compatibility—high boiling esters are frequently compounded with polymers to decrease brittleness and increase plastic flow.

5.3.2. Optical properties—luster, clarity, reflectivity, and permanent coloring are real advantages of polymers.

5.3.3. Hardness—most plastics have low scratch resistance, can be improved by lamination with glass fibers.

5.3.4. Density—gravity range from 0.85-2.5 with majority around 1.0; have weight advantage over most materials of construction.

5.3.5. Weatherability—varies, but in general most plastics will darken when exposed to sunlight; moisture resistance excellent.

5.3.6. Mechanical properties

Plastics exhibit a wide variety of mechanical properties and generalities cannot be used safely to predict performance. Polymers should be tested under expected conditions to guarantee performance. It is safe to say that plastics are not as strong as metals and much more sensitive to temperature changes. Improper mechanical design using plastics is largely responsible for the poor service record of polymers, particularly in the early years of the plastics industry.

5.3.7. Thermal properties

(a) Thermal diffusivity—low, giving good thermal insulation characteristics, particularly when gas-foamed.

(b) Heat resistance—poor, ranging from 35-260°C in continuous service.

(c) Flammability—resistance to ignition and burning poorer than for metals and ceramics.

5.3.8. Electrical properties—insulators with high dielectric strength, low dielectric constant and low power factor. The last two minimize power losses; polyethylene, Teflon and polystyrene are superior to glass and ceramics in UHF insulation applications.

5.3.9. Chemical resistance—generalization cannot be used; polymers can be found for each application, but make due allowance for other properties. The most resistant plastic is Teflon (Polytetra-fluorethylene) which is not attacked by highly corrosive chemicals or strong solvents in addition to having the highest heat resistance, but the poorest forming properties.

VB. POLYMERIZATION TECHNOLOGY

Polymeric materials are manufactured by standard chemical engineering methods which cover all types of gas-, liquid- and solid-phase processing. These polymers are used in a vast number and variety of ways. New applications, as well as polymers, are appearing each year.

In studying the technology of the polymerization industries, it is well to look first at the general types of applications for which polymers are useful. This will be followed by a discussion of typical polymer manufacturing processes. Finally, the economics of the polymerization industries will be summarized.

Classification of Polymer Applications

1. Adhesives

Polymers of the resin type are used for bonding where some water resistance is necessary. Plywood laminate gluing is a major use. Cellulose adhesives comprise cellulose derivatives dissolved in a solvent. Duco cement is an example. Vinyls are water-emulsified latex adhesives of the rubber base type. Natural products such as starch, dextrins, proteins, and natural rubber are cheap and effective ingredients of many commercial adhesive formulations.

2. Coatings and Films

This application probably accounts for the largest production of polymers. Free films of the polyethylene and cellulosic types are encountered daily. Protective and decorative coatings such as synthetic resin-solvent mixtures, lacquers, and varnishes are products from a major industry.

Coatings can be formed by:

- Solvent evaporation with or without chemical changes such as oxidation or final polymerization
- Emulsification or dispersion with water evaporation
- Casting or extrusion of free films by mechanical and melting operations

3. Fibers

Synthetic polymeric fibers are linear molecules formed by extrusion or spinning into small diameters (10-50 microns) or thin sections, with weight per unit length an economic criterion. Important mechanical properties of fibers are tensile strength, creep, and resilience. Chemical properties, particularly the ability to retain color dyestuffs, are necessary requirements for textile applications. Natural polymer fibers from cotton and wool are still competitive materials in the textile industry.

4. Solid Shapes

Polymers, as resins, can be molded, cast, laminated or extruded into a variety of shapes rather easily. Finishing operations such as machining, grinding, and polishing require little additional effort and expense. These properties account for the increasing popularity of plastics as structural materials.

Polymerwise consumption in India is shown in the following tabulation.

Polymer	1993-94	1994-95
	(in thousand tons)	
LDPE	260	285
HDPE	245	320
PP	260	300
PVC	415	470
PS	80	85
	1,260	1,460
Other polymers	60	80
	1,320	1,540

Source: "Hindu Survey of Indian Industry" (1995)

U.S. statistics for the production of major types of commercial polymers are shown in the following tabulation for the years 1994/1995:

Resin	In millions of pounds U.S. Production
Low density PE	11,900
High density PE	1,260
Polypropylene	9,500
PVC	9,170
Polystyrene	5,800
ABS Resin	1,160

Polymer Manufacturing Processes

It should be obvious by this time that the number of permutations and combinations of functional monomer groupings make many millions of polymer formulations theoretically possible. This field is a golden opportunity for research and it is heavily supported by the chemical industries. Thus far, the number of commercial polymers is well above a hundred. Evidence of this is seen in the difficulties of polymer classification as discussed in Section VA. A partial list of polymer types was given in the physical properties classification in Section VA.5.

Since the purpose of this book is largely educational, we can only hope to pick several classes of polymers to illustrate the variety of chemical engineering processing techniques which have been utilized in the polymer industries.

An outline of processes to be discussed follows.

1. Plastics
   (a) Ethenic ($\overset{x}{\underset{w}{>}}C = C\overset{y}{\underset{z}{<}}$ monomer addition processes)
      1. Polyethylene
      2. Polypropylene
      3. Polyvinyl chloride and copolymers
      4. Polystyrene
   (b) Polycondensation
      1. Phenol-formaldehyde
      2. Epoxide
      3. Urethane
2. Elastomers
   Rubbers
3. Polymeric Oils
   Silicones
4. Fibers
   (a) Cellulosic
      • Rayon
   (b) Polyamides
      • 6,6-Nylon
   (c) Polyesters
      • Dacron
   (d) Acrylic

(e) Olefin

Note that polymers classified here under one end use frequently are sold for other end uses listed.

Ethenic Polymer Processes

1. Definition

Polymers made from monomers having the bifunctional group are ethenic since ethylene has

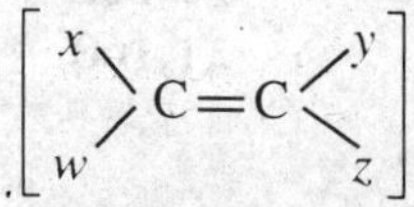

the simplest all-hydrogen atom structure, and others are simply substitutions of other atoms or groups at the *w*, *x*, *y*, and *z* positions.

2. Polyethylene and Polypropylene

2.1. Basic Chemistry

Addition polymerization kinetics with catalysis of purified ethylene

$$n\mathrm{CH_2 = CH_2} \rightarrow -(\mathrm{CH_2 - CH_2})_n -$$

2.2. Pertinent Properties

Mol. formula $-(\mathrm{CH_2 - CH_2})_n-$

Mol. wt. 1,500-100,000

M.P. 85-110°C

Density: 0.91-0.93 by high pressure process; 0.96 by low pressure process

Grades: 1.5 mm to 3 mm pellets, flake or powdered solid sold to extruders

2.3. Methods of Production

2.3.1. High pressure (1,000-2,500 atms.)

This was the original process developed by ICI in the UK using peroxide catalyst at 100-300°C and producing low density random oriented, low M.P. polymer. See Figure VB-1.

2.3.2. Intermediate pressure (30-100 atms.)

Developed by Phillips Petroleum Co. in the USA; uses MoO_3 or Cr_2O_3 on alumina as catalyst, produces high density polymer with accompanying increases in rigidity, crystallinity, tensile strength and softening point. See Figure VB-2.

2.3.3. Low pressure (6-10 atms.)

The original process for preparing high density polyethylene was developed by Dr. Karl Ziegler in Germany. It uses a catalyst consisting of aluminum triethyl activated with heavy metal derivatives such as $TiCl_4$. A similar process developed by Dr. G. Natta in Italy is used for the production of polypropylene.

2.4. Description of Low Pressure Ziegler Process

2.4.1. Reference flow sheet: Figure VB-3

2.4.2. Process description

Very high purity ethylene is prepared by desulfurizing and removing light ends. It is further treated to remove traces of oxygen or its compounds which deactivate the catalyst consisting of aluminum trialkyl (usually triethyl) combined with titanium tetrachloride to produce a finely-divided precipitate in C_5-C_7 saturated paraffin diluent.

The purified ethylene is pumped to a reactor where it is continuously mixed with the catalyst diluent stream. Typical solvent polymerization reaction conditions are 7

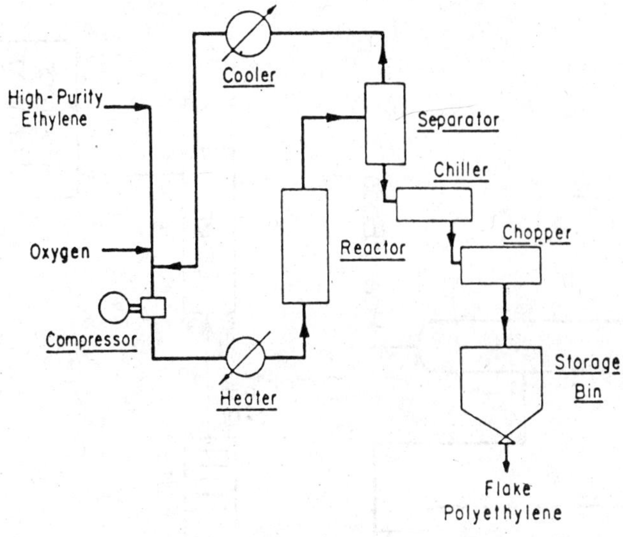

Fig. VB-1. Flow diagram of Imperial Chemical Industries process.

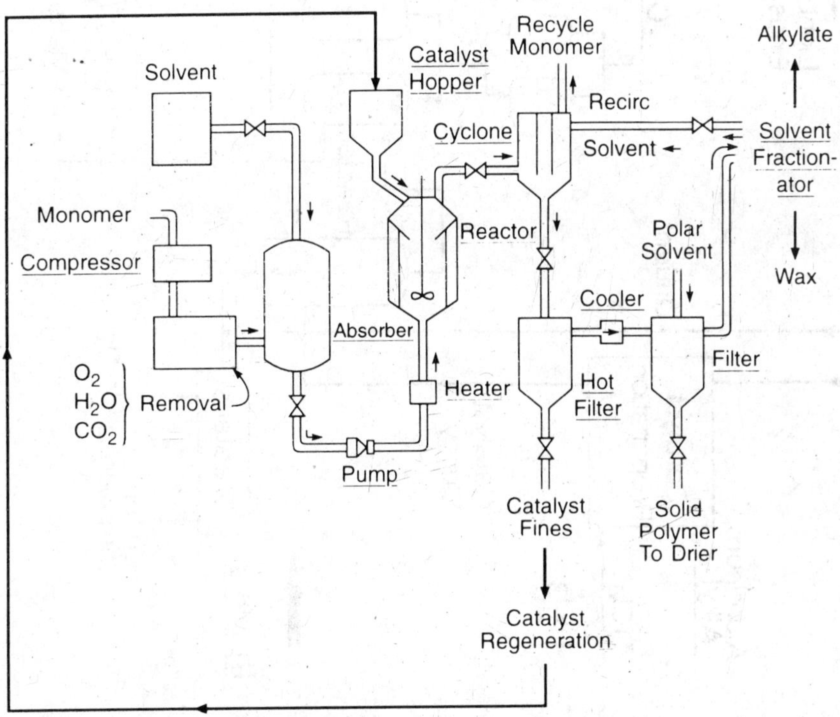

Fig. VB-2. Typical metal oxide-catalyzed process.

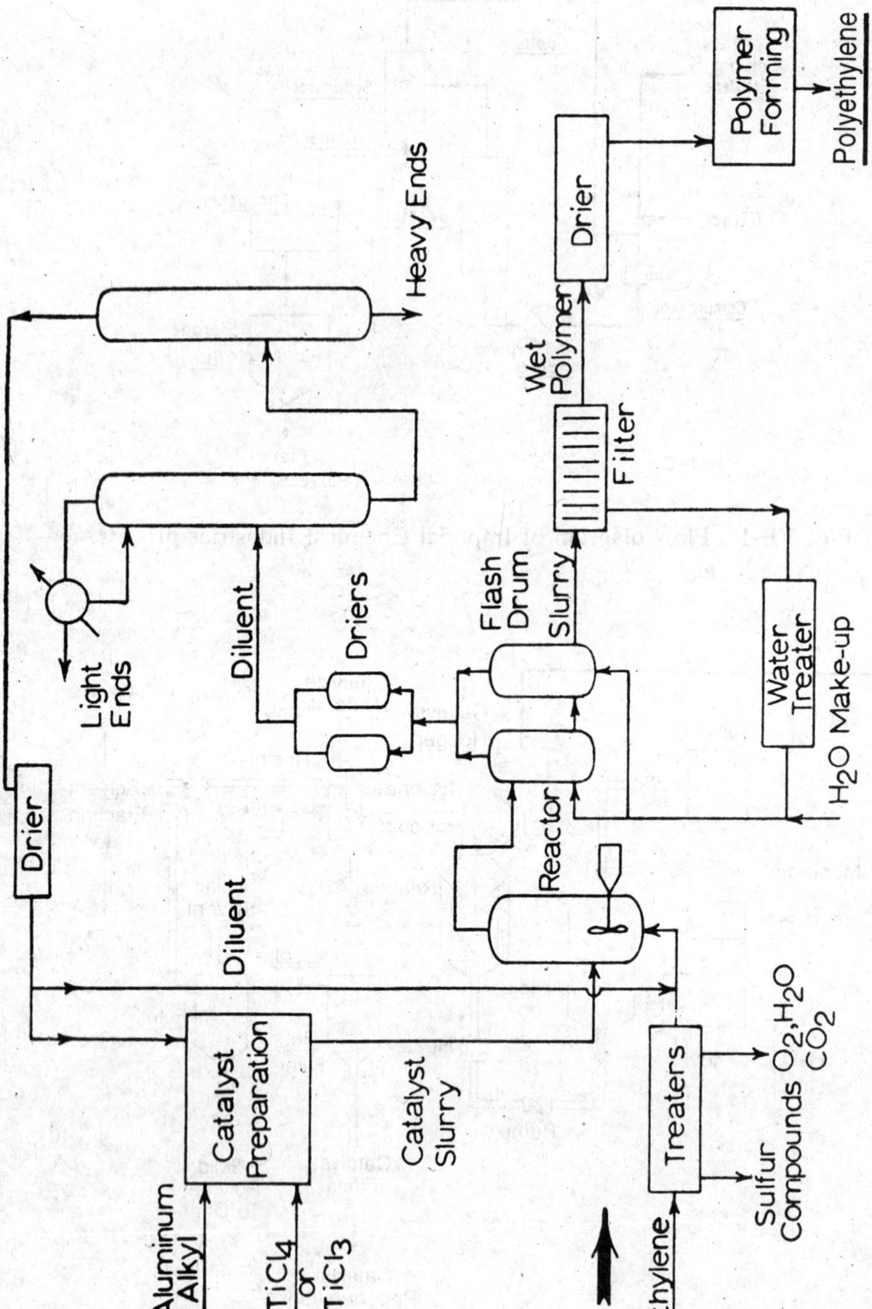

Fig. VB-3. Polyolefins by low pressure Ziegler process.

atms. gage and 70°C. The effluent goes to a series of flash drums to remove the solvent from the catalyst. Water is added at this point to destroy residual catalyst which is highly flammable in the dry condition.

The flashed solvent is dried, redistilled, and recycled to the catalyst make-up unit. Polyethylene slurry is centrifuged to dewater, with the water being treated to remove catalyst before recycle. Polyethylene solids are dried, extruded, and finished to required form (pellets, flakes or powder). The yield based on ethylene is 95-98%.

The same process, with modifications in reaction conditions, can be used for polypropylene.

2.5. Economics of Polyethylene

Ethylene is available either from indigenous alcohol sources from petroleum refinery processes as a potentially large source of supply. Alcohol sources are not always dependable.

The conventional or low density polymer is supplied for about 80% of the market with the balance used as high density product. A large increase for film usage is foreseen as (1) liners for fertilizer and cement jute bags, (2) a seepage barrier in water canals, and (3) packaging material.

Competition exists between low-pressure polyethylene and polypropylene, both of which can be made in the same plant with minor operating changes. Polypropylene marketing efforts have been diverted to (1) textile fibers because of its higher temperature resistance and greater rigidity, and (2) film to replace cellulose acetate.

2.6. Production in India

LDPE (Low Density Polyethylene)

Presently, Indian Petrochemical Corp. Ltd., a public sector enterprise, is the only major manufacturer of low-density polyethylene in India. Installed capacity of its Baroda plant is 80,000 TPA, which was set up with the process know-how from ATO-Chimie, France. Besides IPCL, the Union Carbide plant at Bombay, presently owned by Oswal, has an installed capacity of 20,000 TPA. LDPE in both these units is manufactured from naphtha. Another plant at Rishra, West Bengal, formerly of IEL and presently acquired by Oswal also manufactures LDPE from alcohol route, the installed capacity of this plant is 12,000 TPA production.

It is expected that the installed capacity of LDPE is going to be raised from present level of 80,000 MTA to 4 lakh MTA during the Eighth Plan period.

New LDPE units in the process of setting up and projects under consideration are mentioned below:

Project/Unit	*Location*	*Proposed Capacity (MTA)*
MGCC (IPCL)	Nagothane	80,000
RIL (Reliance)	Hazira	80,000
Auraiya Gas Cracker	Auraiya	160,000
Vam Petrochem Ltd.	Assam	200,000 LDPE/HDPE

Demand projections of LDPE are as follows:

Year	*MTA*
1989-90	2.50 lakhs
1994-95	4.85 lakhs
2000 AD	7.10 lakhs

Source: "SBP Handbook of Petrochemical and Downstream Projects" (1991)

LDPE is always in short supply. Though future production plan as discussed above, if fully implemented in time, will substantially reduce import dependence, import may not be totally eliminated due to two reasons. Firstly, the possibility of setting up the proposed projects as per planned schedule is very rare, and secondly, with the changing scenario of the availability position, there is every likelihood of having a substantial increase in demand.

HDPE (High Density Polyethylene) in India

There is at present only one manufacturer, Polyolefins Industries Ltd., at Bombay having an installed capacity of 50,000 tons per annum. This plant of PIL was set up with process know-how from Hoechst, West Germany.

New projects under implementation and in planning stages are as follows:

Project/Unit	*Location*	*Proposed Capacity (MTA)*
MGCC (IPCL)	Nagothane	55,000
Haldia Petrochem	Haldia	80,000
Reliance Industries	Hazira	100,000
Auraiya Gas Cracker	Auraiya	200,000 LDPE/HDPE
Vam Petrochem Ltd.	Assam	200,000 LDPE/HDPE

Demand projections of HDPE in Eighth and Ninth Plans are indicated below:

Year	*MTA*
1989-90	1.90 lakhs
1994-95	3.78 lakhs
2000 AD	5.55 lakhs

Source: "SBP Handbook of Petrochemical and Downstream Projects" (1991)

Polypropylene

IPCL is the only polypropylene manufacturer at present with a capacity of about 60,000 MTA. Production, imports and consumption of polypropylene during the last three years were as follows:

('000 tons)

Year	Production	Import	Consumption
1986-87	24	26	50
1987-88	26	31	57
1988-89	40	26	66

Initially the capacity of the plant was 30,000 MTA only. After almost doubling the IPCL's polypropylene plant capacity, the production from 1988-89 has increased. To meet the demand indigenous production is not sufficient, it meets nearly 50% of the demand. Due to non-availability of material indigenously, its demand is restricted. Once the new plants under installation and planning start production, the availability position will remarkably improve resulting increase in demand. Following three new projects are very likely to be commissioned during the Eighth Plan:

1. MGCC by IPCL at Nagothane with an installed capacity of 60,000 tons per annum.
2. Reliance Industries Ltd., at Hazira with an installed capacity of 1.2 lakh tons per annum.
3. M.P. Petrochemical Complex by GAIL at Bijalpur with an installed capacity of 1 lakh tons per annum.

Taking these three up-coming projects into consideration along with the existing one, total installed capacity of polypropylene during Eighth Plan is envisaged to be 3.4 lakh tons per annum.

Demand projections for polypropylene during Eighth and Ninth Plan period are given below:

Year	*Demand (MTA)*
1989-90	0.77 lakh
1994-95	2.86 lakhs
2000 AD	4.20 lakhs

3. Polyvinyl Chloride and Copolymers

3.1. Basic Chemistry

Addition type kinetics to produce linear polymers

(a) Polyvinyl chloride (PVC)

$$nCH_2 = CH{\cdot}Cl \longrightarrow -\left[\begin{array}{c} H \quad H \\ | \quad\;\; | \\ C - C \\ | \quad\;\; | \\ H \quad Cl \end{array}\right]_n -$$

(b) Vinyl copolymers

$$m\mathrm{CH_2} = \mathrm{CHCl} + n\mathrm{CH_2} = \mathrm{CH{\cdot}X}$$

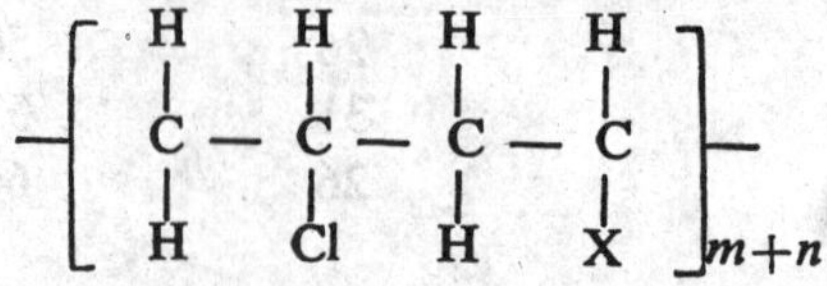

where m is usually greater than n, X is a group on the comonomer such as:

carboxyl (—COOH)—vinyl acetate
hydroxyl (—OH)—vinyl alcohol
carboxyester (—COOR)—methyl methacrylate
nitrile (—CN)—acrylonitrile

Replacing the HX group by chlorine atoms gives the vinylidine monomer.

3.2. Pertinent Properties

PVC has a softening point ranging from 80 °C to 140 °C, increasing with the degree of after-chlorination. It decomposes rapidly at 140 °C, liberating HCl; can be stabilized at lower temperatures with acid neutralizers such as alkali metal salts. Normal PVC is a hard, tough polymer, insoluble in most solvents. It can be softened by plasticizers for mechanical working.

Vinyl chloride copolymers are formulated to overcome some of the disadvantages of PVC, particularly low solvent solubility and poor heat stability.

3.3. Consumption Pattern

PVC with only small concentrations of plasticizer is designated as "rigid" and extruded in heavy structural designs such as pipe and sheets. When heavily plasticized, it can be used for many elastomer-type products.

The copolymers greatly extend the uses for vinyl polymers, particularly where solvent solubility is desirable. Typical uses are latex emulsion and spray coatings, electrical insulation, textile fabric coatings, tubing, clothesline, rainwear, and shower curtains.

This multiplicity of uses places the vinyl polymer group second in annual production, just behind the polyolefins.

3.4. Methods of Production

3.4.1. Reference flow sheet: Figure VB-4

3.4.2. Process description

Emulsion and suspension polymerization methods are used commercially; the latter is used only if high purity polymer is desired.

In emulsion polymerization, a typical formulation is 100 parts of water, 100 parts of vinyl monomers, 1 part of persulfate catalyst, and 1.5 parts of a detergent emulsifier. This is fed to a pressure reactor, either continuous or batch, operating at 50 °C for periods as long as 72 hours. The micellular polymer particles can be further stabilized by addition of more emulsifying agent and sold as vinyl latex. If solid polymer is desired, the mixture is either acid coagulated and dried or spray-dried directly.

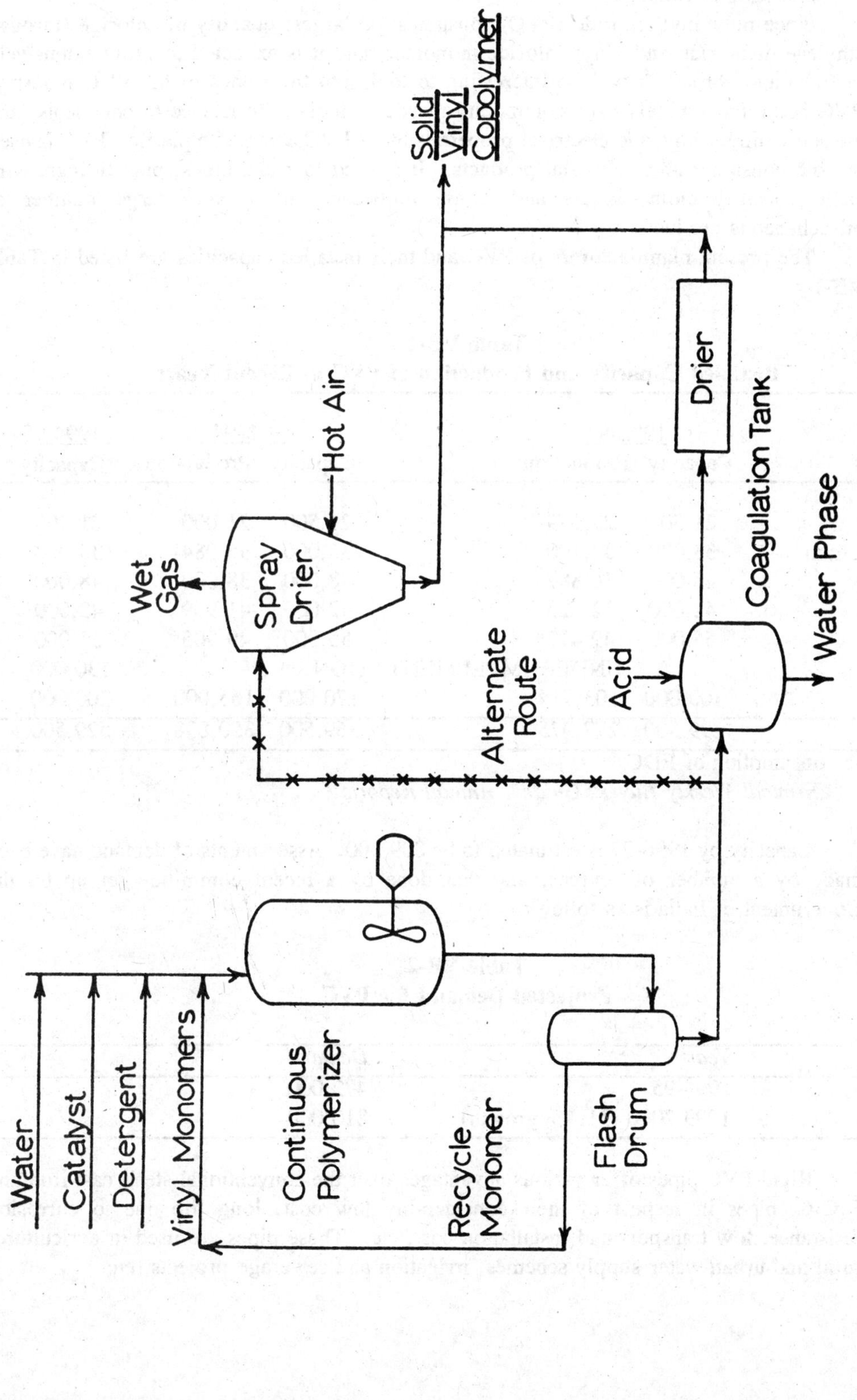

Fig. VB-4. Polymerization process for vinyl polymer.

3.5. Production in India

Since polyvinyl chloride (PVC) consumes the largest quantity of chlorine (through ethylene dichloride and vinyl chloride monomer) and it is expected to grow extensively in India and abroad, it will be interesting to look into the trends of the PVC industry. PVC is the most widely used commodity plastic in India. Resistance to chemicals, and the self-extinguishing and electrical properties make PVC a versatile plastic. PVC is used in both consumer and industrial products. It is used to make pipes, pipe-fittings, wire cables, leather cloth, sheets and films, footwear, and a very large number of miscellaneous products.

The present manufacturers of PVC and their installed capacities are listed in Table VB-1.

Table VB-1
Installed Capacity and Production of PVC in Recent Years

Company	1992-93 Capacity	1992-93 Production	1993-94 Capacity	1993-94 Production	1994-95 Capacity
NOCIL	21,500	23,079	21,500	21,000	21,500
DCM Shriram	33,000	32,100	33,000	35,084	33,000
Chemplast	48,000	36,887	48,000	38,000	48,000
DCW	42,000	32,723	42,000	41,909	42,000
IPCL	55,000	49,472*	55,000	49,905*	55,000
Finolex	UNDER IMPLEMENTATION				130,000
Reliance	100,000	103,714	170,000	165,000	200,000
Total	299,500	277,975	369,500	350,898	529,500

*Based on consumption of EDC

Sources: "Chemical Weekly Buyer's Guide" Annual Reports

Capacity by 1996-97 is estimated to be 809,500. Assessments of demand have been made by a number of sources, and that done by a recent committee set up by the Government of India is as follows:

Table VB-2
Projected Demand for PVC

Year	*Demand*
1994-95	472,000
1999-2000 (11.4% growth)	810,000

Rigid PVC pipes offer various advantages over the conventional steel, cast iron and R.C.C. pipes in respect of their considerably low cost, long life due to corrosion resistance, low transport and installation cost, etc. These pipes are used in agriculture, rural and urban water supply schemes, irrigation and sewerage projects, etc.

A plant may manufacture rigid PVC pipes of 125 mm to 400 mm diameter. The manufacture of rigid PVC pipes up to 110 mm diameter is reserved for the small scale sector as per the present industrial policy of the Government.

Scope and Prospects

At present there are a number of units manufacturing rigid PVC pipes and fittings in the organized sector in the country. Their names and addresses are given in Table VB-3. The present (1991-92) production of rigid PVC pipes in the country, including the production in the small scale sector, is estimated at about 2.5 lakh tons per annum.

Table VB-3
Names and Addresses of Major Units Manufacturing Rigid PVC Pipes in India

Ajanta Tubes Ltd.
Jain Industrial Estate, 36 KM, Delhi-Hapur Road, Ghaziabad (U.P.)

Finolex Pipes Ltd.
Block D1, Plot No. 10, MIDC, Chinchwad, Pune (Maharashtra)

Grandlay Plastics Ltd.
73B, Murthal Industrial Area, Phase 1, Dist. Bhind (M.P.)

Gwalior Polypipes Ltd.
Malanpur Industrial Area, Malanpur, Dist. Bhind (M.P.)

Prakash Industries Ltd.
(i) 15 KM Stone, Delhi Road, Village Mayar, Hissar - 125 005 (Haryana)
(ii) 5 KM Stone, Village Gangapur, Kashipur - 244 713, Nainital (U.P.)
(iii) Pithampur (M.P.)

Supreme Industries Ltd.
(i) Plot D-101, MIDC Additional Industrial Area, Jalgaon (Maharashtra)
(ii) Taloja, Raigad (Maharashtra)

Uniplas India Ltd.
(i) F-129/130, Sector VII, NOIDA, Dist. Ghaziabad (U.P.)
(ii) B-189, Phase 1, NOIDA, Dist. Ghaziabad (U.P.)
(iii) Village Kedaiya, Nani Daman, Dist. Daman

Usha Rectifier Corp. (India) Ltd.
11/2, Delhi-Mathura Road, Faridabad (Haryana)

Wavin India Ltd.
(i) Ambattur, Madras (T.N.)
(ii) Nagpur (Maharashtra)
(iii) Ghaziabad (U.P.)

Source: "SBP Handbook of Projects for Corporate Diversification" (1992)

4. Polystyrene

Installed capacity of PS at present is only 26,000 tons per annum from two manufacturers.

Polychem - Bombay	16,000 MTA
Hind Polymers - Vizag	10,000 MTA

Polychem plant has been set up with the process know-how from Dow, USA and that of Hind Polymers is from BX Plastics, UK.

To increase the indigenous production capacity, new projects and capacity enhancement of existing units are under consideration.

New projects being planned are as follows:

1. BASF has proposed to set up a plant with 15,000 MTA capacity.
2. Reliance Industries Ltd. is to set up following capacity plants at Hazira.

Styrene	0.8 lakh TPA
Polystyrene	0.5 lakh TPA

3. The Rs. 85.70 crore Supreme Industries, which manufactures flexible packaging films and plastics industrial components, is planning not only to increase the scope of its current operations, but also to integrate backwards. An application for Rs. 140 crore project to manufacture 80,000 tons per annum of styrene monomers and 40,000 tons per annum of polystyrene was given the green signal in August 1989.
4. Polychem, presently a leading producer of styrene monomer and polystyrene, has sought permission to set up an integrated plant to produce 80,000 tons per annum of polystyrene.

Of the above mentioned proposed projects RIL, Supreme and Hind Polymers projects are likely to come up in the near future. Thus, a total capacity of 98,000 tons per annum is likely to be added during the Eighth Plan, raising the installed capacity of polystyrene in the country from 26,000 MTA to 1.24 lakh MTA.

Demand projections of polystyrene in the terminal years of the Eighth and Ninth Plan are indicated below:

Year	*Demand*
1989-90	4.8 lakhs
1994-95	8.2 lakhs
2000 AD	12.0 lakhs

Projecting a large demand-supply gap, it will be necessary to expedite the other projects for production of polystyrene.

5. ABS Resins

ABS resin (acrylonitrile, butadiene & styrene copolymer), generally classified as an engineering plastic, is used in various industries like refrigerator liners, automobile components, molded and thermoformed parts of telephone, intercoms, mixers, computer cabinets, cameras, vacuum cleaners, molded luggage, toys, etc. There are about 109 grades of ABS resins available internationally. In India, the present availability is only about 10 grades of ABS.

A monomer-soluble polybutadiene rubber or butadiene copolymer is dissolved in the styrene and acrylonitrile with initiators and modifiers. This mixture is polymerized through phase conversion. Several types of bulk polymerizers may be used interchangeably for high impact ABS. The raw materials for the manufacture of ABS resins are styrene, butadiene and acrylonitrile.

The market potential has been summarized as follows in "SBP Handbook of Petrochemical & Downstream Projects," SBP Consultants (1991).

Demand-Supply Situation

The present estimated demand	10,000 TPA
Present supply position	Largely matches the demand
Gap in supply position	Small quantity
Estimated growth rate in demand	15% per annum
Estimated demand by 2000 AD	23,500 tons
Total Production capacity to be created by 2000 AD	29,000 TPA

Present manufacturers of ABS along with their installed capacities are mentioned below:

1. Polychem, Bombay	2,000 MTA
2. ABS Plastics, Baroda	2,000 MTA
3. Gujarat Binil Chemicals Ltd.	2,200 MTA
4. Synthetics & Chemicals, Bareilly	1,200 MTA
Total Installed Capacity	7,400 MTA

ABS resins enjoy several advantages, as compared to other substitutes like metals, since it is light in weight, easy to process and will have lower maintenance. The current demand for ABS resins is expected to increase as a result of growth in user industries, such as automobiles and telecommunications.

High level of import duty on raw materials for ABS resin has made the price of the product high in the country. If ABS were to be available today at the price of around Rs. 40 per kilogram, the present demand for the product would be at least two times more than the prevailing level. Higher plant capacity of around 15,000 TPA can contribute to lower the production cost of the product.

Demand projections for ABS resin at the end of the Eighth and Ninth Plan are indicated below:

Year	*Demand (MTA)*
1989-90	12,000
1994-95	24,000
2000 AD	35,000

Polycondensation Processes

Polycondensation has been defined previously as the step-wise reaction of monomers with functional grouping which often eliminates small molecules such as H_2O. Both linear and tridimensional polymers are made; the latter are more prevalent.

1. Phenol-Formaldehyde

1.1. Basic Chemistry

(a) Methylol monomer formation

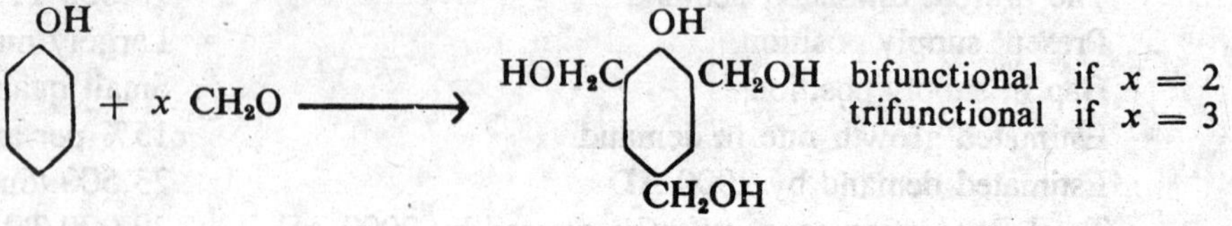

(b) Linear polymer

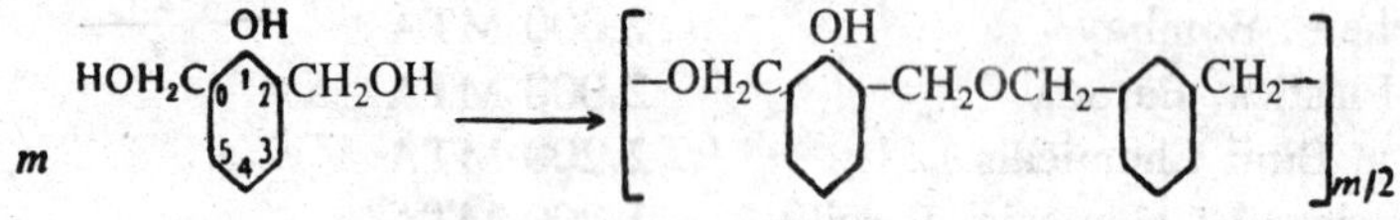

Substitution of non-functional group in the 4 position will block the cross-linking possibilities shown next.

(c) Cross-linked tridimensional polymer

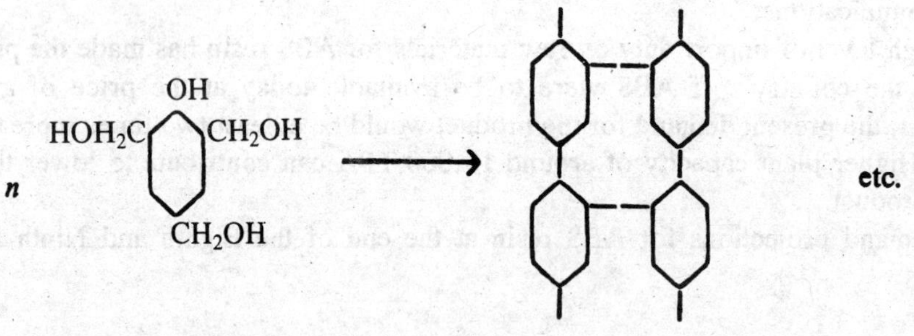

1.2. Pertinent Properties

Phenol-formaldehyde polymers can be prepared in such a wide variety of forms, based on bi- and trifunctional group reaction possibilities, that it is impossible to give specific properties in this brief outline. General resin characteristics can be controlled by:

(a) Acid solution catalyst with excess phenol—produces linear soluble thermoplastics.

(b) Alkaline catalysts

- one-stage process—correct ratio of phenol to formaldehyde is reacted with proper control of time and heat to yield a thermosetting or heat reactive powder which can later be heated to an infusible, insoluble state via further cross-linking.

- two-stage process—thermoplastic material from the acid catalysis process is mixed with hexamethylene tetramine, a white solid which breaks down to CH_2O and NH_3. The formaldehyde combines with the resin to form a thermosetting product with ammonia as catalyst. Both one- and two-stage resins are used as commercial molding materials with the final cross-linked polymer having good resistance to all chemicals except alkalies.

(c) A strictly linear polymer with good heat fusion and solvent solubility properties for varnishes and adhesives is made by substituting cresol ($HO \cdot C_6H_4 \cdot CH_3$) for phenol with the methyl group blocking the trifunctional position.

1.3. Consumption Pattern

Phenolics are low-cost polymers with excellent physical and electrical properties and fast curing characteristics. Their poor color characteristic can be partially overcome by adding pigments, dyes and fillers.

The main uses fall into three classes:

- Resins in solvents—coatings, varnishes, and laminated structures
- Resins in water solutions—adhesive bonding
- Solid resin—all types of thermoset molded solid forms

For a number of years phenolic resins ranked first in U.S. production as they were the first commercial polymers. They have decreased in relative importance as thermoplastics have forged ahead.

1.4. Methods of Production

1.4.1. Reference flow sheet: Figure VB-5

1.4.2. Process description

Polymerization is an exothermic reaction which must be controlled by batch reaction as the material rapidly changes viscosity.

Phenol, formaldehyde, and catalyst are mixed together in a jacketed autoclave (resin kettle) and heated with steam. After reaction starts, the heat of reaction is removed by refluxing and water cooling. In the early stages of reaction, the heavier viscous resin separates as a bottom layer with an aqueous layer at the top. Dehydration is next completed in the kettle by a combination of heat and vacuum. The fused resin at 130-150°C is removed from the kettle, cooled and ground to a fine powder.

The heat reactive molding powder prepared above can be mixed with fillers, coloring agent, lubricants, and catalyst in a ribbon blender or ball mill. It is then heated further on a pair of differential heating rolls to prepare fast curing commercial phenolic molding powder.

2. Epoxy Polymers

2.1. Basic Chemistry

(a) Epoxidation is the addition of an oxygen atom across a C = C to give

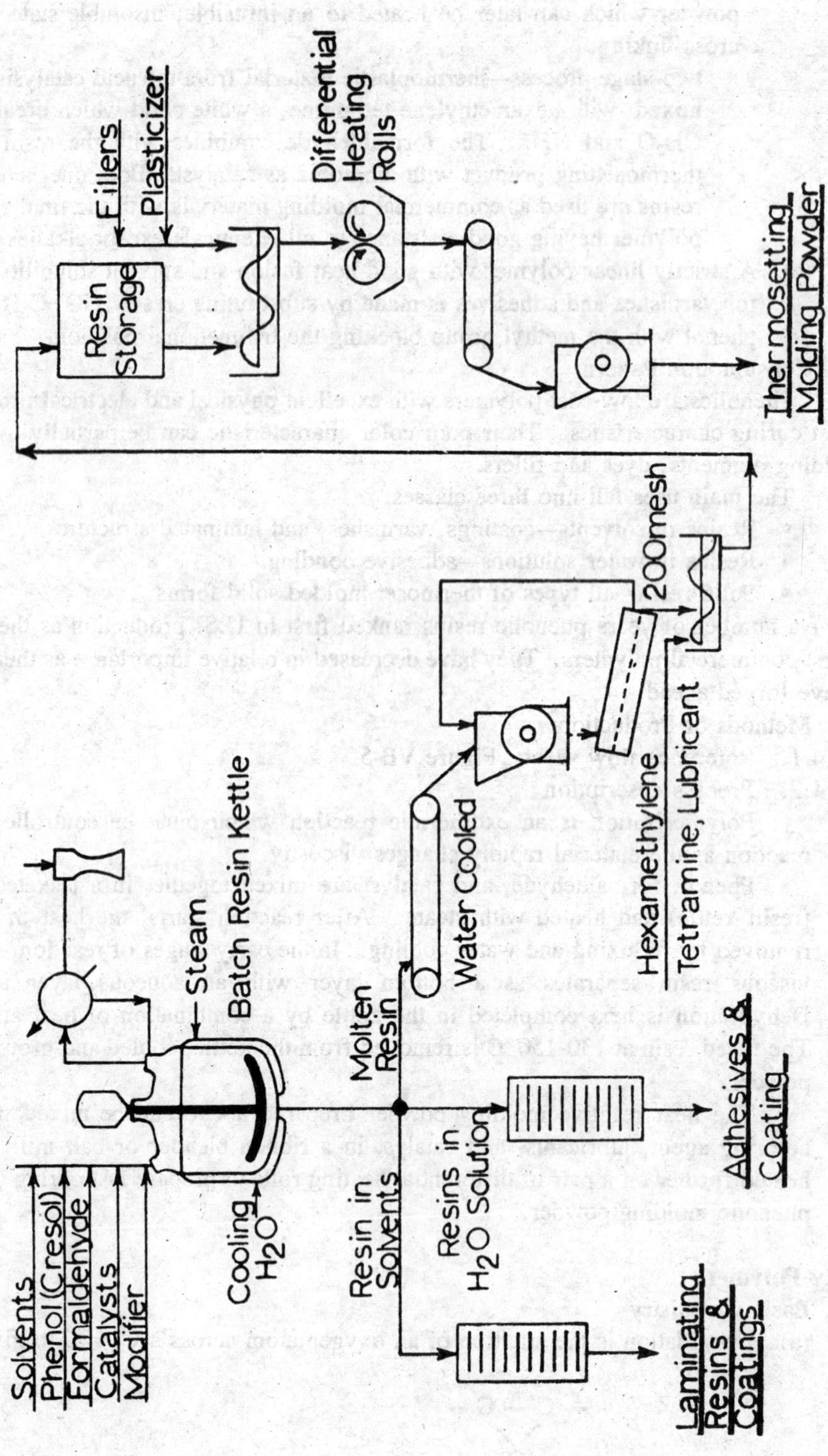

Fig. VB-5. Phenol-formaldehyde resin products production.

The oxygen transfer agent can be peracids such as peracetic acid ($CH_3 \cdot CO \cdot O \cdot O \cdot CO \cdot CH_3$), hydrogen peroxide, or chlorhydrin (HOCl) followed by HCl removal. The latter gives epichlorhydrin.

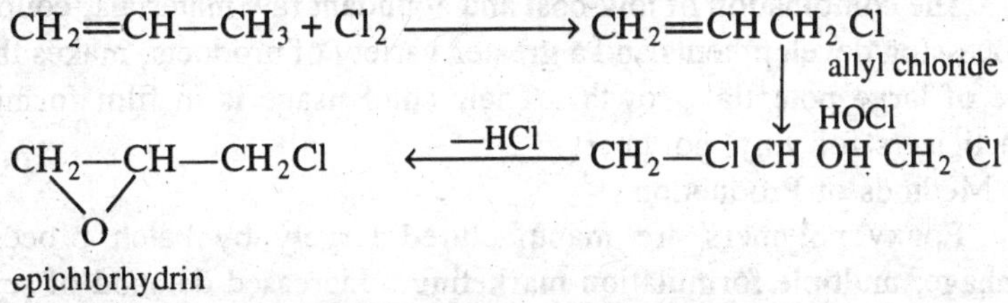

(b) Epoxide polymers contain an epoxy group at the ends of the polymer. For example, the reaction of epichlorhydrin with bisphenol-A (prepared by condensation of acetone with phenol) is a condensation with loss of HCl:

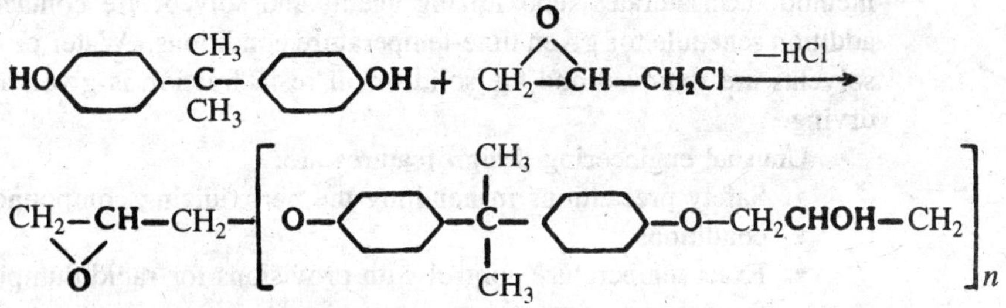

Epichlorhydrins are also condensed with other hydroxyl groups in compounds such as resorcinol, hydroquinone, ethylene glycol, and glycerol.

(c) Epoxy monomers can be obtained from unsaturated natural products such as vegetable oils, particularly soybean oil, and tall oil from wood pulping. The molecular structure of polymers from epoxidized natural product monomers is extremely complex. Both linear and cross-linked polymers are possible.

(d) Synthetic epoxy monomers are obtained via butadiene cyclization and peroxidation

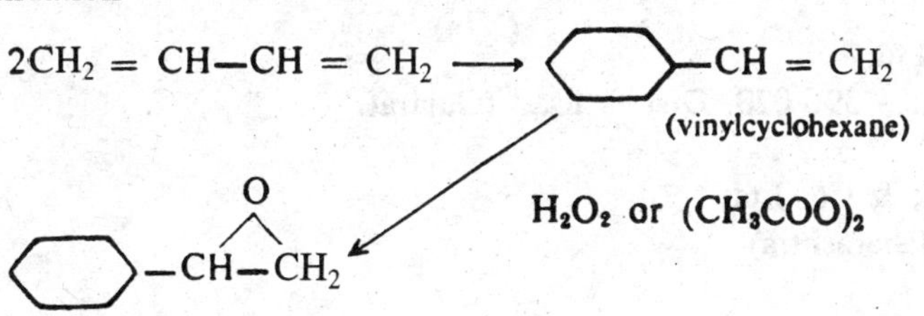

2.2. Pertinent Properties

Epoxy resins exhibit extreme versatility because of possible combinations of properties such as:

- Chemical stability from ether linkages
- Chemical reactivity from residual epoxy and hydroxy groups
- Excellent adhesion to a variety of surfaces
- Good abrasion resistance
- Curing and molding without evolution of gas and with low shrinkage
- Outstanding electrical properties
- Ability to form copolymers with unusual properties

The molecular structure, purity and residual saturation in the product are the chief criteria for suitability in most applications.

2.3. Consumption Pattern

The combination of low-cost and abundant raw materials, coupled with continual new processing developments and a greater variety of products, makes the epoxy resin industry one of large potential growth. Their chief usage is in film forming, adhesives, and as plasticizers for vinyl polymers.

2.4. Methods of Production

Epoxy polymers are manufactured largely by batch processing because of low tonnage, multiple formulation marketing. Increased demand of several epoxy resins has led to the development of continuous processing, using two or more mixing reactors in series.

Epoxy polymer processes are relatively simple and use the solvent polymerization method. Unsaturates, epoxidizing agent, and solvent are contacted on a programmed addition schedule for given time-temperature conditions. Water or other condensibles and solvents are removed and the solid or oil resin fraction is given a final purification and drying.

Unusual engineering design features are:

- Safety precautions in handling the peroxidizing compounds to avoid detonating conditions
- Exact temperature control with provisions for rapid dumping and water flushing for a runaway reaction

2.5. Production of Epoxy Resins in India

At present there are four units manufacturing epoxy resins in the organized sector in India as shown in Table VB-4. The installed capacity totals about 16,000 tons/yr and the production about 10,000 tons/yr.

Table VB-4
Names and Addresses of Units Manufacturing Epoxy Resins in India

Cibatul Ltd.
P.O. Atul - 396 020, Dist. Valsad (Gujarat)

Dr. Beck & Co. Ltd.
Pune (Maharashtra)

Inter Polymers Ltd.
6-3-1219/6, Uma Nagar, Begumpet, Hyderabad - 500 016 (A.P.)

Mittal Fertilizers Ltd. (Unit SIP Resins Ltd.)
Plot No. 46, SIPCOT Industrial Complex, Ranipet - 632 403 (T.N.)

Source: "SBP Handbook of Projects for Corporate Diversification" (1992)

Polyurethanes

Another type of condensation polymer to be considered here is polyurethanes.

Organic isocyanate compounds have been known for a long time, but first became commercially interesting in the last decades based on development work by O. Bayer (1937). It was shown that the reaction of di-and polyisocyanates with di- and polyols formed polyurethanes with many uses. The preferred use of polyurethanes in the automobile industry, in construction, and in refrigeration technology led to a considerable increase in the production capacity for feedstock diisocyanates.

Polyols are used as main raw materials (along with methylene di-phenyl diisocyanate and/or toluene diisocyanate) in the manufacture of polyurethane foams (flexible-rigid/rigid).

These foams have extensive application in industrial insulation, refrigeration, manufacture of mattresses, furniture and automobile seats, footwear and wood components replacement.

Propylene glycol is used in pharmaceuticals, cosmetics, food flavors, tobacco processing and in the manufacture of unsaturated polyester resins for FRP (fiber reinforced plastics). It has many other applications also.

At present there are four units manufacturing polyols and/or propylene glycol in the organized sector in the country. Their names and addresses are given in Table VB-5.

Until recently, the production of polyols and propylene glycol in the country has been practically nil. The present demand for polyols is estimated at more than 10,000 TPFA and that for propylene glycol at more than 8,000 TPA in the country.

There are good prospects for their exports, also. Demand for these products has been growing at the rate of about 15% per annum in the past few years.

As per the "Perspective Plan for Chemical Industry (up to the year 2000 A.D.)," the demand for polyols is estimated at 18,000 M.T. and 30,000 M.T. per annum by 1994-95 and 1999-2000 respectively.

If proper incentives are given by the Government, according to the above-cited report there is a potential to export 500 M.T. and 5,000 M.T. of polyols from India in the years 1994-95 and 1999-2000 respectively.

Table VB-5
Names and Addresses of Units Manufacturing Polyols in India

Dai-Ichi Karkaria Pvt. Ltd. Bombay (Maharashtra)
Castrol (India) Ltd. White House, 91, Walkeshwar Road, Bombay - 400 006
Manali Petrochemicals Ltd. Ponneri High Road, Manali, Madras - 600 068 (T.N.)
UB Petrochemicals Ltd. Village Sathangadu, Manali, Madras (T.N.)

Source: "SBP Handbook of Projects for Corporate Diversification" (1992)

Toluene diisocyanate (TDI), in the form of its 2,4- and 2,6-isomers, has been the most significant diisocyanate. TDI production in the USA, Western Europe, and Japan is given in the adjacent table.

In the last few years, however, 4,4'-diphenylmethane diisocyanate (methane diphenyldiisocyanate, MDI), whose precursor 4,4'-diaminodiphenylmethane is obtained from the condensation of aniline with formaldehyde, has overtaken TDI. In 1990, capacities in Western Europe, the USA, and Japan for MDI were 600,000, 530,000, and 19,000 tons, respectively; for TDI, they were 400,000, 360,000, and 110,000 tons.

Another important component of polyurethanes is hexamethylene-1,6-diisocyanate (HDI, formerly HMDI).

The following figures show trends in isocyanate production:

TDI Production (in '000 tons)

	1985	1987	1989
USA	294	368	333
Western Europe	286	316	331
Japan	84	91	109

MDI Production (in '000 tons)

	1985	1987	1989
USA	347	379	436
Western Europe	358	410	510
Japan	94	129	165

Toluene diisocyanate is generally manufactured in a continuous process involving three steps:

1. Nitration of toluene to dinitrotoluene
2. Hydrogenation of dinitrotoluene to toluenediamine
3. Phosgenation to toluene diisocyanate

Manufacturing Process

MDI is produced by reacting aniline with formaldehyde to get methylene bis-dianiline. The diamine is reacted with phosgene to yield MDI.

TDI is manufactured by the reduction of dinitrotoluene to diamine with hydrogen and reacting the diamine with phosgene to yield TDI.

Indian Scenario

TDI and MDI are not produced in the country and entire demand is met by imports.

The combined demand of MDI and TDI in the country is estimated to be around 9,000 tons per annum.

New Projects

Narmada Chematur Petrochemicals, a joint venture of Gujarat Narmada Valley Fertilizers Co. Ltd., Chematur AB of Sweden and IBI Chematur, Bombay propose to set up a 10,000 tons per annum TDI plant.

Hindustan Organic Chemicals Ltd. is negotiating with Chematur AB of Sweden for its TDI/MDI project of capacity 15,000 tons per annum.

Other organizations considering project proposal for TDI/MDI include Manali Petrochemicals Ltd., ICI India Ltd., Thirumalai Chemicals Ltd.

Manufacturing Process for Polyurethanes

Thermoplastic Polyurethanes are formed by linking three basic components.

i) A linear hydroxyl terminated polyol with molecular weight of 500-3,500.

ii) A diisocyanate, which may be aromatic such as MDI, TDI or non-aromatic, as dicyclo hexyl methane diisocyanates. The preferred isocyanate is MDI.

iii) A low molecular weight glycol such as 1,4 butanediol, ethylene glycol or 1,4 phenylene bis b-hydroxyl ethyl ether to serve as chain extender.

Indian Scenario

Manufacturers	Installed capacity (in tons)
Urethane India Ltd.	2,500
Kaso Chemie India Ltd.	600

Note: Indian units are operating at low capacity utilization level due to low demand.

New Projects

Hans Polyurethanes has entered into technical collaboration with Imperial Chemical Industries (ICI) of the UK to manufacture TPU and TPU-based products.

Table VB-6
Polyurethane Use in the USA, Western Europe, and Japan (in wt.%)

	USA 1990	Western Europe 1987	Western Europe 1990	Japan 1990
Flexible foams	52	41	43	32
Rigid foams	27	25	24	17
Integral-skin and filling foams		8		
Paint raw materials		7		
Elastomers	21	6	33	51
Thermoplastic polyurethanes				
Artificial leathers		6		
Others		8		
Total use (in 10^6 tonnes)	1.54	1.35	1.40	0.60

(The values 21, 33 and 51 are bracketed together for Integral-skin and filling foams through Others.)

Source: "Industrial Organic Chemistry" by Weissermel et al (1993)

Elastomer Polymerization Processes

Elastomer is an elastic polymer which returns to original dimensions when stretched considerably from its original shape. Under the broad classification is the rubber group. A true rubber, whether natural or synthetic, must elongate at least 200 percent and return to its original dimensions rapidly and forcibly. Where a rapid retraction is not needed, elastic polymer formulations often outperform rubber. Such materials are derived from vinyl polymers and copolymers, polystyrene and acrylates.

1. Rubber Polymers

Natural rubber (70% indigenous) still supplies about 65% of the needs in the rubber products industry of India as against 30% for the U.S. where, during World War II, synthetic rubber polymers, particularly from butadiene-styrene copolymerization, were substituted, often to advantage. There are now a number of types of rubber polymers and an ASTM classification gives letter abbreviations. A summary of structural formulae, raw materials and trade names is given in Table VB-7. Two of these polymer processes will be discussed further.

1.1. Pertinent Properties of Rubber Polymers

Physical properties important for rubber products are:

- Tensile strength
- Hardness
- Tear resistance
- Resilience
- Flex failure
- Abrasion
- Repeated stress failure
- Permanent set
- Aging
- Ozone and oxygen reactivity
- Oil and solvent resistance
- Thermal and electrical

Such properties are dependent, not only on the original polymer molecular structure, but on additional processing which includes:

- Compounding—addition of fillers, coloring agents, plasticizers, antioxidants, vulcanizing agents
- Mixing—homogeneous distribution of compounding ingredients into solid elastomeric polymer; rubber mill is used which has one of the two rolls running at slower speed, giving kneading action
- Vulcanization—optical cross-linking process at C = C in polymer units of Table VB-7; sulfur is common vulcanizing agent with accelerators (catalysts) of the organic or inorganic type
- Forming—production of final shapes by molding, calendering, extrusion

2. Butadiene-Styrene Copolymer (SBR)

2.1. Basic Chemistry—see Table VB-7

2.2. Properties and Uses

SBR is a general purpose rubber widely used for tires either by itself or as a high percentage blend with natural rubber. It is superior to natural rubber in all properties except tensile strength, resistance and heat build-up under heavy loading. SBR is also used for mechanical goods and electrical insulation.

2.3. Methods of Production

2.3.1. Reference flow sheet: Figure VB-6

2.3.2. Process description

Butadiene and styrene are copolymerized by emulsion polymerization in about 3:1 weight ratio. The original World War II government plants were designed for batch polymerization, but later plants were well-integrated continuous units.

Properties of SBR rubber can be modified by the temperature of polymerization. "Hot" rubber is prepared at 50°C. Superior quality "cold" rubber is made at 5°C by refrigeration techniques with slightly higher operating costs. The development of improved catalysts of the redox type more than offset the decrease in reaction rate with temperature, thus allowing successful commercialization of a continuous cold rubber process.

The process involves 20% aqueous caustic purification of the fresh plus recycle monomers, followed by consecutive passage through 6 to 12 glass-lined or stainless steel reactors. The total residence time ranges from 5-15 hours and reactors are equipped for steam heating, water cooling, and refrigeration. The reactors can thus produce cold SBR (5°C, 1 atm. gage) or hot SBR (50°C, 3-4 atms. gage).

Latex from the reactors is collected in blow-down tanks after stripping the polymerization with chemical inhibitors and then fed to a falling film stripper to remove butadiene. The bottoms are passed to a perforated plate column to strip out styrene.

The monomer-free emulsion is pumped to blend tanks for addition of certain compounding ingredients. The latex is coagulated to rubber "crumbs" which float onto shaker screens where wash water removes catalyst, emulsifiers and other solubles. The crumbs are dried with hot air in continuous-belt dryers, then pressed into bales for shipping to compounding and fabricating plants.

2.4. Production in India

The manufacture of SBR at Bareilly takes place at a plant, the only one in India, which was built in 1963 by Kilachand Deepchand and Co. Pvt. Ltd. of Bombay in collaboration with Firestone Tire and Rubber Co. of USA. Both the ethylene for styrene manufacture and the butadiene are made from alcohol.

3. Polymeric Oils and Rubbers Based on Silicon

The use of synthetic lubricants of a polymeric composition is synonymous with silicones. While silicone polymers have found use as high temperature rubbers and resin coatings, their unusual physical properties as fluid polymers account for much of the marketing efforts in silicone polymers.

3.1. Basic Chemistry

Silicones differ structurally from other polymers in that the main chain is a recurring sequence of tetravalent silicon and oxygen atoms with varying properties depending on the group substitutions on the two free silicon bonds.

- Linear silicone polymer

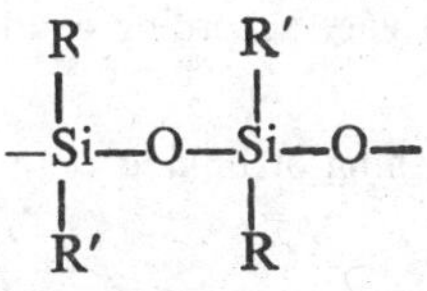

Table VB-7 Rubber Polymers

Chemical Name (type of monomer)	*ASTM Abbrev.*	*Trade Name*	*Polymer Unit**
Polyisoprene	NR IR	Natural Synthetic	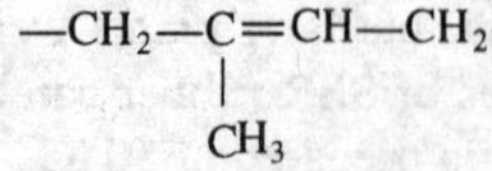
Ethylene-propylene copolymer	EPR EPT	 Terpolymer	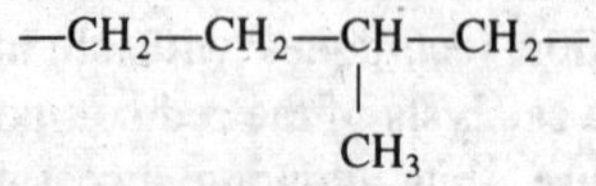
Polybutadiene	BR	*cis*-4-Butadiene Buna	$—CH_2—CH=CH—CH_2—$
Butadiene + styrene copolymer	SBR	GRS, Buna-S	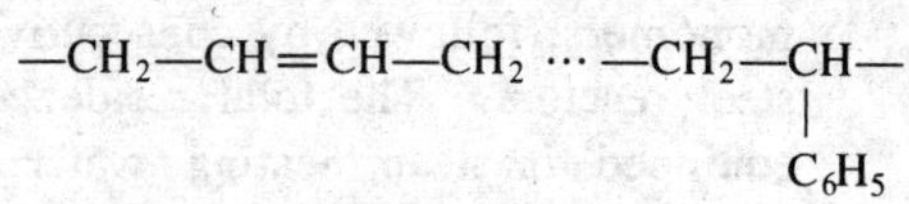
Butadiene + acrylonitrile	NBR	Nitrile rubber Buna-N	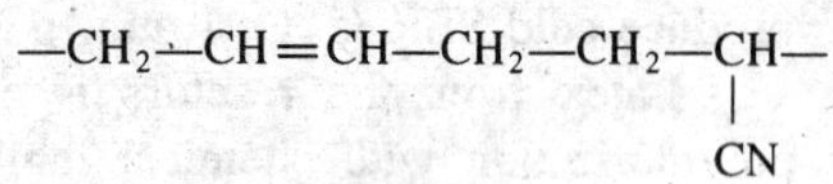
Polychloroprene	CR	Neoprene	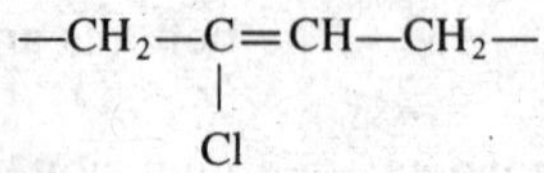
Isobutylene-isoprene copolymer	IIR	Butyl	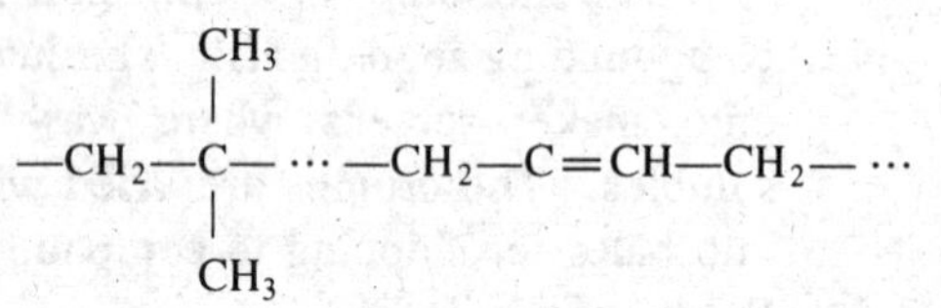
Polysulfide	—	Thiokols	$—CH_2—CH_2—S—S—$
Chlorosulfonated polyethylene	—	Hypalon	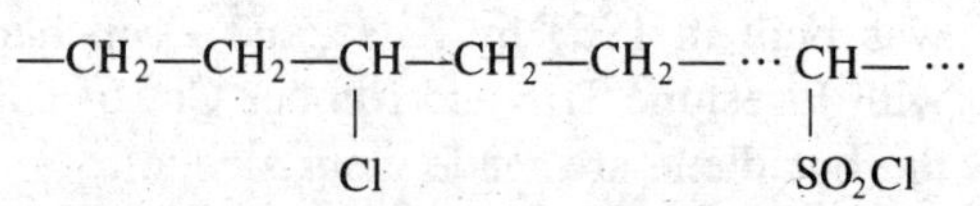
Polyurethane (polyhydroxy-polyisocyanate polymers)	—	—	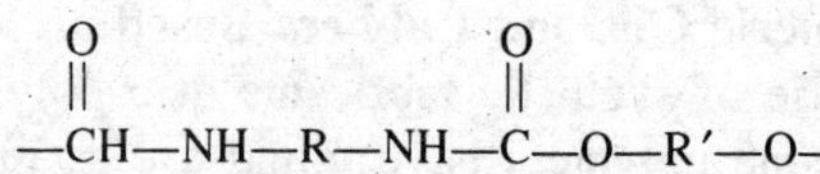
Silicone (dimethyl siloxane)		Silicone	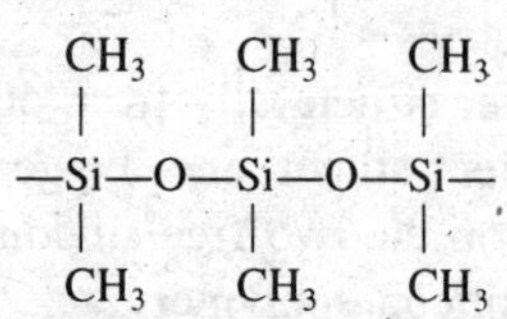

*Units containing ... are not alternately repeating units, but vary according to the ratio of monomers used in copolymerization.

Units containing double bond (=) are subject to chain branching or linking.

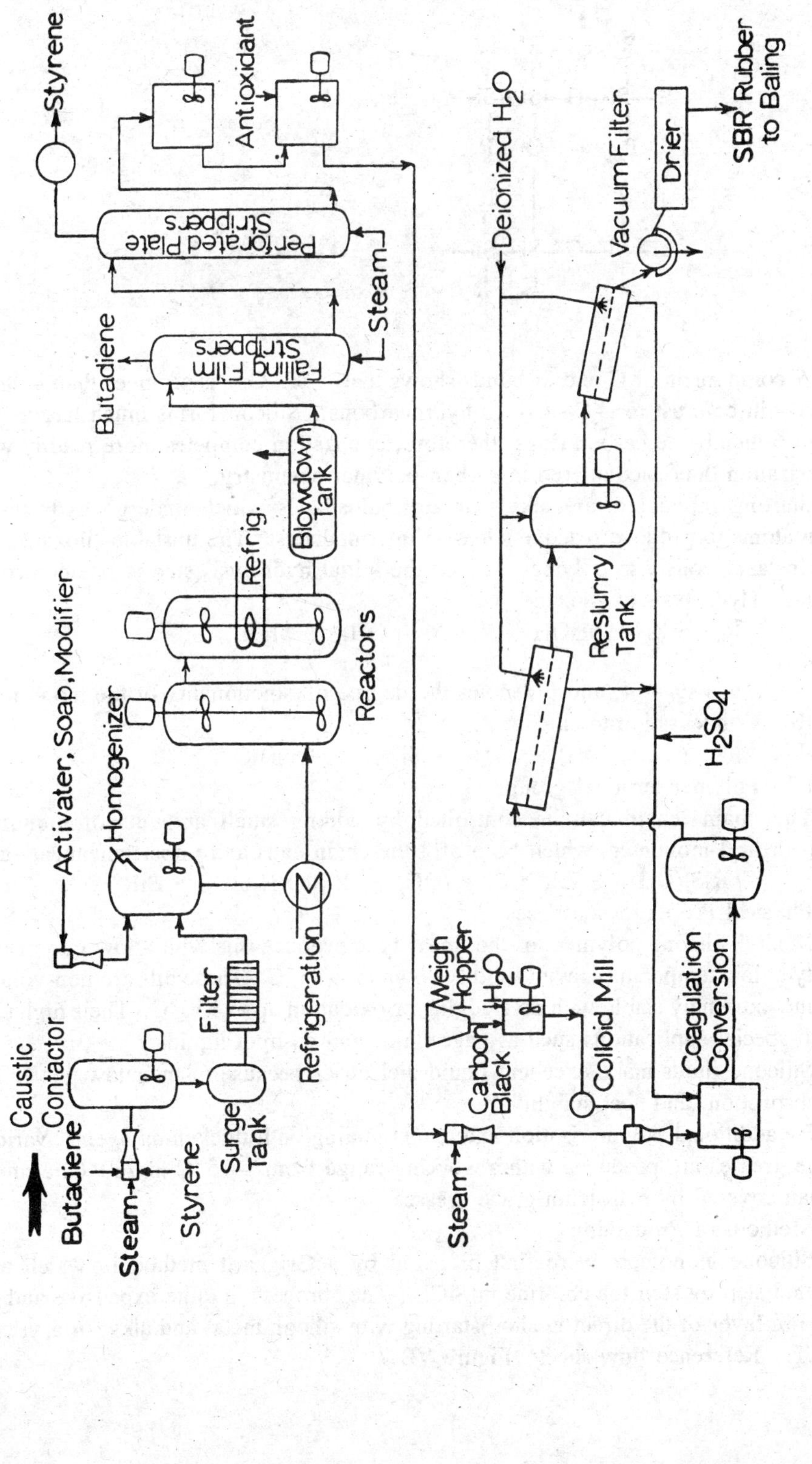

Fig. VB-6. Butadiene-styrene (SBR) rubber process.

- Cross-linked silicone polymer

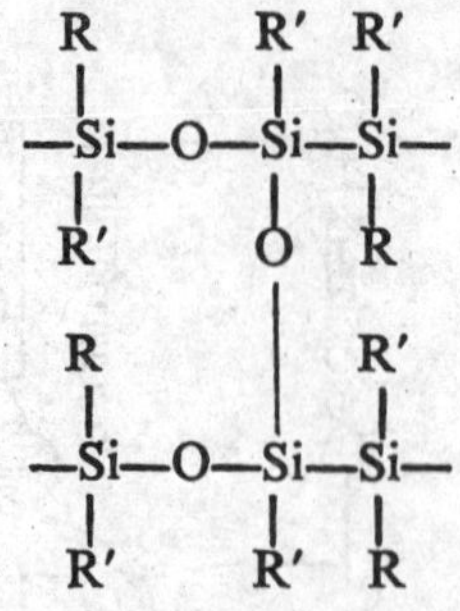

A comparison of C and Si bonds shows that —Si—O— is stronger than —Si—Si— or —Si—C— in contrast to —C—C— in hydrocarbons. Silicon forms much larger rings than the 5- to 6-membered carbon rings; therefore, cyclization competes more readily with chain polymerization than encountered in carbon-polymer chemistry.

Starting monomers are alkyl- or aryl-halosilanes which undergo hydrolysis of the halogen atoms to produce reactive siloxane intermediates. The unstable siloxanes condense almost instantaneously to polymers so that the initial hydrolysis step is rate-controlling.

(a) Hydrolysis to siloxane

$$R_a \cdot SiX_b + bHOH \rightarrow \underset{\text{siloxane}}{R_a \cdot Si \cdot (OH)_b} + bHX$$

$a + b = 4$, and b denotes the degree of functionality of the monomer.

(b) Condensation to silicone ($b = 2$)

$$nR_2 \cdot Si \cdot (OH)_2 \rightarrow -(R_2 \cdot SiO)_n - + nH_2O$$

(c) Polymer terminal groups

The chain length can be controlled by adding small amounts of monofunctional trialkyl- or aryl-monomers which "can off" the chain ends and impart chemical stability.

$$nR_2Si(OH)_2 + 2R_3 \cdot Si \cdot (OH)_2 \rightarrow R_3SiO(R_2SiO)_n \cdot SiR_3$$

3.2. Physical Properties and Uses

Methyl silicone polymers of the linear type produce oils with a low rate of change of viscosity at low temperatures with fluidity down to —85°C. These oils are non-volatile, non-toxic, and extremely stable with no sludging or oxidation up to 150°C. Their high cost limits usage to special applications such as gage fluids and dashpot liquids.

Silicone fluids make excellent liquid dielectrics because of their low power loss, low water absorption, and heat stability.

By additional polymerization and compounding with thickening agents, various types of stable greases are produced with a working range from —75°C to 260°C, a much wider span than covered by petroleum grade greases.

3.3. Methods of Production

Silicone monomers were first prepared by a Grignard method in which alkyl was substituted step by step for chlorine in $SiCl_4$. The process is quite expensive and has been dropped in favor of the direct method starting with silicon metal and alkyl or aryl chlorides.

3.3.1. Reference flow sheet: Figure VB-7

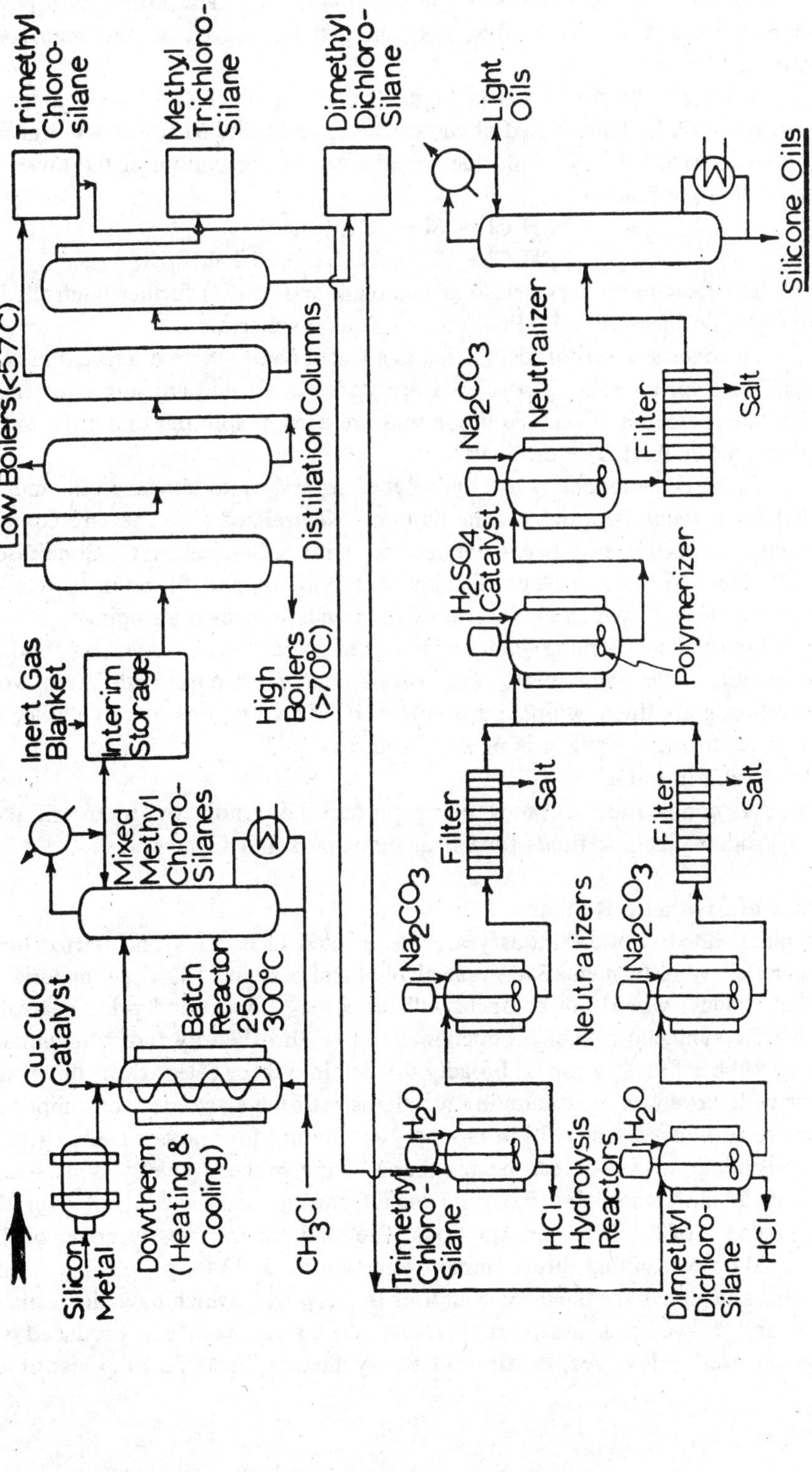

Fig. VB-7. Silicone oils via direct monomer process.

3.3.2. Process description

Silicon metal of low purity (98-99%) is crushed and milled to a powder. It is mixed with a Cu-CuO catalyst and charged batch-wise to the methylating tower reactor.

A typical reactor is 4.5 m high x 0.6 m diameter, fitted with a vertical screw conveyor-stirrer, constructed of carbon steel, and jacketed for Dowtherm heat control at about 300°C. Methyl chloride vapor is fed to the bottom of the tower to produce an exothermic reaction.

$$2CH_3Cl + Si \rightarrow (CH_3)_2SiCl_2$$
$$6CH_3Cl + 3Si \rightarrow 2(CH_3)_3SiCl + SiCl_4$$

The Dowtherm serves also as a coolant and heat is further controlled by rate of methyl chloride addition. Pressure is 1-2 atmospheres.

The overhead gas product is fed to a fractionator where unreacted methyl chloride is stripped for recycle. The silanes are stored in air and moisture-free conditions for distillation column feeds. Four columns are used to split out dimethyl- and trimethyl-chlorosilanes from side products.

These two monomers are hydrolyzed separately to siloxane oils and an aqueous HCl layer which is drawn off the bottom. Neutralized siloxanes are combined in the correct proportion in a batch polymerizer with H_2SO_4 catalyst. Conditions are 100-200°C for 2-3 hours. Neutralization with Na_2CO_3 and filtration to remove Na_2SO_4 yields a clear oil which can be rid of light ends by steam stripping.

Unusual engineering features include maintenance of anhydrous conditions in the formation of the monomers. Hydrolysis units must cope with corrosive wet HCl; therefore glass-lined equipment is specified. The monomers are volatile, flammable often explosive if oxygen is present, and toxic.

3.4. Production in India

Silicone compounds are now being produced in India by Metroark Pvt. Ltd. of Calcutta. Products include fluids for use as defoamers and varnishes.

4. Economics of Synthetic Rubber

An SBR plant, rated at 30,000 tons/year, was erected in Bareilly and started production in 1963. Raw materials were fermentation-grade alcohol and benzene. The raw material costs were too high so that product would not compete with imports. Import and price control had to be enforced so that the synthetic rubber production could be absorbed by Indian manufacturers.

The Indian Rubber Industry can be broadly divided into three categories: the well-organized auto tire sector with eleven units, accounting for almost half the elastomer consumption, followed by the medium scale units, about 150 in number, accounting for another twenty-five percent of the polymer consumption. However, the backbone of the rubber industry is its small and tiny sector consisting of more than five thousand manufacturing units spread all over the country accounting for balance of the 25% consumption. The total annual sales turnover of the industry is about Rs. 6,500 crores, giving direct employment to over 300,000 people.

India, China and Brazil are the three countries in the world, which have domestic production facilities for natural as well as synthetic rubbers, and the entire quantity so produced is consumed within the country itself. However, Brazil produces synthetic rubbers far in excess of its domestic needs which it exports. India and China depend on import of NR and SR as well, indigenous production being either insufficient in certain areas, or not being available in certain other areas to meet the industry's demand in full. The present per capita consumption of rubber in India is lowest at 0.63 kg in contrast to 14 kg of Japan which is the highest or against 1 kg of China and about 2.5 kg of the world average.

The prediction for the use of natural rubber versus synthetic rubber in India has been given in "Chemical Weekly Annual" for 1995 as follows in terms of percentage of the total market:

Year	*NR*	*SR*	*Total*
1994-95	80	20	100
2000	75	25	100
2005	72	28	100
2010	70	30	100

The position of natural rubber in India is unique. In the Western World, the availability of low-cost hydrocarbon raw materials combines with the relative unavailability of natural rubber due to large labor requirements and relatively undesirable climate. In India, however, desirable climate and land availability combine with the availability of low-cost labor to produce an attractive supply of natural rubber.

In India, among the plantation crops, natural rubber has maintained one of the fastest growth rates, vigorous in nature and vibrant in character. India obtains its bulk requirements of natural rubber from domestic resources. Competition from synthetic rubber to natural rubber is practically non-existent in India and economically insignificant. Thus the natural rubber scene in India is entirely different from that obtaining in other producing countries.

The rubber goods manufacturing industry in India has done remarkably well in the recent past. With the rapid development of transport, agriculture, defense, etc., the rubber products manufacturing industry is called upon to meet the needs of these sectors, as indeed of other sectors.

Kerala, Tamil Nadu and Karnataka are traditionally the leading rubber producing states in the country. Kerala accounts for nearly four-fifths of the annual natural rubber production and the area under its cultivation. The Northeastern States, particularly Tripura, Assam and Meghalaya, are emerging as major rubber producing states.

India is the fourth largest producer of natural rubber, accounting for about six percent of the global output. Production of natural rubber was estimated to be 365,000 tons in 1991-92 compared to 330,000 tons in 1990-91. Consumption was likely to increase from 364,000 tons in 1990-91 to around 380,000 tons in 1991-92. Imports were placed at around 31,700 tons in 1990-91 as against 26,500 tons in 1989-90.

Synthetic rubber supplements natural rubber in tires for two wheelers, other automobiles and animal drawn vehicles. The annual demand of synthetic rubber in the transportation sector is 35,000 tons and this may grow to 1.8 lakh tons by the year 2000.

Table VB-8
Rubber Use by 1999 Worldwide
(figures in thousands of metric tons)

Thousands of metric tons	Synthetic rubber 1993	1994	1999	Average annual change, % 1994–99	Natural rubber 1993	1994	1999	Average annual change, % 1994–99	Total rubber Average annual change, % 1994–99
North America	2,773	2,935	3,080	1.0%	1,058	1,106	1,103	0 %	0.7%
Western Europe	2,028	2,164	2,413	2.2	845	900	1,010	2.3	2.2
Asia & Oceania	1,888	2,020	2,443	3.9	1,990	2,070	2,340	2.5	3.2
China[a]	453	485	680	7.0	750	803	1,125	7.0	7.0
Latin America	531	561	705	4.7	247	254	280	2.0	3.9
Central Europe	230	250	351	7.0	60	65	91	7.0	7.0
C.I.S.[b]	944	480	1,140	18.9	50	40	100	20.0	19.0
Mideast & Africa	120	128	151	3.4	183	188	215	2.7	3.0
TOTAL	8,967	9,023	10,963	4.0%	5,183	5,426	6,264	2.9%	3.6%

a includes North Korea and Vietnam. b Commonwealth of Independent States.
Source: International Institute of Synthetic Rubber Producers quoted in August 14, 1995 C&EN

Table VB-9
Pattern of Synthetic Rubber Production (in wt.%)

Product	World 1984	World 1987	USA 1986	USA 1991	Western Europe 1984	Western Europe 1987	Japan 1986	Japan 1990
Styrene butadiene rubber (SBR)	59	51	43	38	56	48	49	49
Polybutadiene rubber (BR)	15	18	19	19	14	18	19	18
Chloroprene rubber (CR)	5	6	6	5	5	8	7	6
Olefin rubber (EPR, EPTR[1)])	6	7	7	10	8	9	9	10
Butyl rubber (IIR)	7	10	7	9	8	7	4	3
Polyisoprene rubber (IR)	5	2	4	3	2	4	5	3
Nitrile rubber (NBR)	4	5	3	3	5	5	5	5
Others	1	1	11	13	2	1	2	6
Total production (in 10^6 tonnes)	9.0	9.5	2.0	2.2	1.8	2.4	1.2	1.4

[1)] also abbreviated EPDM (ethylene propylene diene monomer)
EP = ethylene propene
EPT = ethylene propene terpolymer
II = isobutene isoprene
NB = acrylonitrile butadiene

Source: "Industrial Organic Chemistry" by Weissermel et al (1993)

The following table shows the consumption pattern of natural and synthetic rubber in India for the period 1984 to 1989 and the projection for 1990-2000.

Table VB-10
Consumption Pattern of Natural and Synthetic Rubber in India

	Consumption		Growth rate %	
	Natural Rubber	(Tons) Synthetic Rubber	Natural Rubber	Synthetic Rubber
1984-85	217510	65400	3.83	4.98
1985-86	237440	70035	9.16	7.09
1986-87	257305	71785	8.37	2.50
1987-88	287480	76410	11.73	6.44
1988-89	312000	81147	8.53	6.20
(Estimated)				
Projected				
1990-91	345938	102905	-	-
1994-95	470645	140000	-	-
1999-2000	691533	205707	-	-

Source: "Kothari's Industrial Directory of India" (1994)

A more detailed breakdown of rubber uses in India is given in "Chemical Weekly Annual" for 1995 as is shown in Table VB-11.

Table VB-11
Projected Demand for NR and Major Grades of Synthetic Rubber under Gradually Changing Consumption Pattern in India

Year	*NR*	*SBR*	*PBR*	*Butyl*	*Other SR*	*Total SR*	*Total New Rubbers* (natural + synthetic)
1945-95	486000	48000	33000	20000	16000	117080	603000
1999-2000	664505	120495	48730	29240	23035	221500	886005
2000 AD	704375	127725	51655	30990	24420	234790	939165
2005 AD	993660	229070	75895	45540	35880	386385	1379945
2010 AD	1419315	377130	111515	66910	52720	608275	2027590

Source: "Chemical Weekly Annual" (1995)

The Indian rubber industry is of great importance to the national economy. This industry is servicing the precision requirements of defense, transport sector, railway transport system, air services, mechanical and consumer requirements. This requires development of scientific and technical man power with an estimated annual turnover of Rs. 2,750 crore, producing 35,000 items. The rubber goods industry comprises 3,500 manufacturers and provides employment to more than two lakh people.

The rubber goods industry is the third largest contributor to the nation's exchequer by way of duties and taxes at over Rs. 800 crore. The major items produced by the industry are tires, tubes, belts, hoses, rubber footwear, waterproofed fabrics, etc. As the products are of vastly different nature, the industry can be broadly classified into tire and non-tire sectors. The non-tire sector is mostly dominated by small scale and medium sized units.

There are about 20 large and medium sized tire companies, with a total capacity of over 21 million tires. The production of tires in 1988-89 is estimated to be 17.8 million. It is reckoned that by the turn of the next decade, the demand for tires may reach 20 million. The demand for various tires by the year 2000 is estimated as follows:

Demand for Tires (Million Nos.)

Type	*Demand*
Giant tires	7.30
Two-wheeler tires	9.4
Tractor	1.95
Aero	0.03
Car/jeep	2.2

Source: "SBP Handbook of Projects for Corporate Diversification" (1992)

The tire industry is essentially a processing industry, with raw materials accounting for about 70% of cost of production of tires. The raw materials used in the manufacture of tires include nylon tire cord (36% of raw material cost in value terms), natural rubber (25%), carbon black (16%), synthetic rubber (11%), and rubber chemicals (12%). However, prices of domestic raw material are 50% to 100% higher than that in the world markets. Imported raw materials attract an average duty of 65%, but are of better quality. A point to note in the profile of raw material consumption is the 22 : 78 ratio of synthetic and natural rubber consumption (in quantity terms) in the case of Indian tires as against the 64 : 36 ratio abroad. This is primarily on account of the larger production of truck tires, wherein natural rubber is the preferred choice by virtue of being cheaper and more rugged. In an over supply situation, tire companies may not be able to fully pass on the cost increase in inputs such as nylon tire cord and natural rubber, according to Investment Research & Information Services Ltd.

At present there are about 25 units manufacturing automobile tires and tubes in the organized sector in the country. Their names and addresses are given in Table VB-12.

The main raw materials required for the manufacture of automobile tires and tubes are natural and synthetic rubber, carbon black, nylon tire cord, bead wire and certain rubber chemicals, all of which are available indigenously. However, for the manufacture of radial tires, the unit may also have to import special steel cord fabric from some reputed company abroad.

Table VB-12
Names and Addresses and Products of Some Units Manufacturing Automobile Tires

Name and Address	Product Range
Apollo Tyres Ltd.	Tires, tubes (giant, tractor,
(i) Perambra, Dist. Trichur (Kerala)	passenger car, scooter,
(ii) Village Limda, Waghodra, Baroda (Gujarat)	motorcycle)
(iii) Vadodara (Gujarat)	

Company	Products
Balkrishna Industries Ltd. B-66, MIDC, Waluj, Aurangabad (Maharashtra)	Tires and tubes for 2/3/4 wheelers
Bombay Tyres International Ltd. Hay Bunder Road, Bombay (Maharashtra)	Tires (giant, tractor, passenger car, scooter, motorcycle)
Ceat Tyres of India Ltd. (i) Bhandup, Bombay (Maharashtra) (ii) Mehboobnagar, Near Hyderabad (A.P.) (iii) Satpur, Nasik (Maharashtra) (iv) Waluj, Dist. Aurangabad (Maharashtra)	Tires, tubes and flaps (giant, tractor, passenger car, scooter, motorcycle)
Dunlop India Ltd. (i) Sahaganj, Dist. Hooghly (W.B.) (ii) Ambattur, Dist. Madras (T.N.)	Tires, tubes (giant, tractor, passenger car, scooter, motorcycle)
Falcon Tyres Ltd. KRS Road, Mysore (Karnataka)	Scooter, motorcycle tires and tubes
Goodyear India Ltd. Mathura Road, Ballabhgarh, Dist. Faridabad (Haryana)	Tires, tubes (giant, tractor, car, scooter, motorcycle)
Hindustan Cycle & Tubes (P) Ltd. G-3, Industrial Area, Ludhiana (Punjab)	Scooter, motorcycle tires and tubes
Inchek Tyres Ltd. Kankinara, Dist. 24-Parganas (W.B.)	Tires, tubes (car, scooter, motorcycle)
Jaysree Tyres (P) Ltd. IDA, Nacharam, Hyderabad (A.P.)	Scooter, motorcycle tires and tubes
J.K. Industries Ltd. (i) Jaykaygram, P.O. Tyre Factory, Kankroli Dist. Udaipur (Rajasthan) (ii) Banmore (M.P.) (iii) Gajraula (U.P.)	Tires, tubes (giant, tractor, passenger car, scooter, motorcycle)
Kesoram Industries Ltd. Balasore (Orissa)	Tires (giant, tractor, passenger car, scooter, motorcycle)
KTC Tyres (India) Ltd. KTC Nagar, Ayikkerpaddi - 673 637 Malappuram Dist. (Kerala)	Closed

Metro Tyres (P) Ltd. B-27, Focal Point, Dhandari Kalan, Ludhiana (Punjab)	Scooter, motorcycle tires and tubes
Modi Rubber Ltd. Modipuram, Dist. Meerut (U.P.)	Tires, tubes (giant, tractor, passenger car, scooter, and motorcycle)
MRF Ltd. (i) Thiruvottiyur, Madras - 600 002 (T.N.) (ii) Arkonam, Dist. North Arcot (T.N.) (iii) Kandepar, Taluk Ponda (Goa) (iv) Vadavathoor, Dist. Kottayam (Kerala)	Tires, tubes (giant, tractor, passenger car, scooter, and motorcycle)
Premier Tyres Ltd. Kalamassery - 683 104, Dist. Ernakulam (Kerala)	Tires, tubes and flaps (giant, tractor, passenger car, scooter, motorcycle)
S. Kumar Tyre Mfg. Co. Ltd. Pithampur, Dist. Dhar (M.P.)	
Srichakra Tyres Ltd. Vellaripatti Village, Melur Taluk, Dist. Madurai (T.N.)	Scooter, motorcycle tires and tubes
Stallion Tyres Ltd. P-9, Industrial Estate, Macharan, Rangareddy Dist. (A.P.)	Tires for cars and 2-3 wheelers
Tanfort Tyres Ltd. 9, Doddanekkundi Industrial Area, Bangalore (Karnataka)	Scooter, motorcycle tires and tubes
Tyre Corporation of India Ltd. Kankinara, 24-Parganas (W.B.)	
Unicorn Tyres Ltd. Plot E-7, MIDC, Chikalthana, Dist. Aurangabad (Maharashtra)	Scooter, motorcycle tires and tubes
U.P. Tyres & Tubes Ltd. Rae Bareli (U.P.)	Scooter, motorcycle tires and tubes

Vikrant Tyres Ltd.
K.R.S. Road, Metagalli P.O., Mysore - 570 002
(Karnataka)

Source: "SBP Handbook of Projects for Corporate Diversification" (1992)

5. Compounding Ingredients for Elastomers

An essential aspect of the production of a finished part from any elastomer, whether it be natural rubber or SBR or silicone rubber, is the addition of compounding ingredients. As Shreve has put it, "Pure rubber is as useless as pure gold. The desirable properties of

- plasticity
- elasticity
- hardness
- softness
- abrasion resistance
- impermeability

and various combinations thereof are achieved by the art of the rubber compounder."

Perhaps the most important compounding ingredient is carbon black which is used to improve wearing qualities of both natural rubber and SBR by imparting toughness. The following tabulation shows the status of carbon black manufacture in India as reviewed in *Chemical Weekly Annual* for 1995.

Name	Plant Location	Corporate Abbreviation	Remarks
1. Carbon & Chemicals Ltd.	Cochin	CACIL	
2. Gujarat Carbon and Chemicals Ltd.	Palej (near Baroda)	GCIL	Originally Gujarat Carbon, changed to Consolidated Petrotech, and then changed to present name mid-1994.
3. HiTech Carbon	Renukoot	HiTech	A Division of Indian Rayon (A.V. Birla)
4. Oriental Carbon and Chemicals Ltd.	Ghaziabad	OCCL	Also makes soluble sulfur, sulfuric acid and fertilizer.
5. Phillips Carbons Black Ltd.	Durgapur	PCBL	
6. Ralson Carbon	Ludhiana	Ralson	A Division of Ralson Tires
7. United Carbon India Ltd.	Thane	UCIL	Controlled by Cabot of Boston, USA, the largest Carbon Black manufacturer in the world.

Fibers

A fiber filament is a thread-like structure of varying length, capable of being woven or spun into larger units. Natural fibers such as cotton, wool, silk, and linen are being replaced to an appreciable extent by synthetic fibers. These synthetics are prepared from molten linear polymers or a solution of polymers by extrusion through a die containing 20 to 15,000 small holes, solidifying, and collecting a group of threads as a filament. This process is called spinning.

Statistics on consumption of fibers show that cotton, a natural cellulose product, is still predominant in India, although synthetics are in first place in the USA.

Fiber	*India*	*USA*
Cotton	89.9%	42%
Synthetic	8.8%	54%
Wool	1.3%	4%
Annual per capita consumption, kg/yr	2.4	22.7

The price of synthetic fibers is over four times that of cotton, but less than the cost per kg for wool. All of the synthetic fibers have one or more advantages in terms of high tensile strength, good temperature stability, and excellent resistance to chemicals, abrasion, solvents and moisture.

Fibers and the Overall Textile Industry

Fibers, by which one usually thinks of synthetic fibers in the context of this book on chemical technology, are but a part of the overall textile industry and it is worthwhile to consider that overall industry at this point.

The textile industry is one of India's oldest. Virtually all India's leading business families started in textiles. However, the ups and downs of the industry are amply reflected in the fact that most of these families consolidated their fortunes outside textiles.

A second feature of the industry is its complex structure and diversity. Textile manufacturers range from modern industrial plants and urban mills to rural handloom weavers. Some manufacturers are integrated, directly using a wide variety of natural and synthetic raw materials—cotton, polyester, wool, viscose, nylon, acrylic, silk; others purchase intermediate products like yarn and tops to make fabric. Still others make garments. The industry caters to the huge range of buyers in the domestic market as well as the international market—it is India's largest industry as well as its biggest foreign exchange earner. Not unsurprisingly, each constituent group has conflicting interests. Finally, the State is an interested constituent of the industry because, among other reasons, the millions of cotton farmers and handloom weavers in the country are politically important groups.

There are three interlinked themes in the industry. One is the dominance of the decentralized sector in the domestic mass market, a trend which has led to a complete transformation in the strategies and operations of the organized sector. The second theme is India's re-emergence as a large exporter of textiles, for the first time since the Industrial Revolution of the late 18th century. The third is the arrival of polyester, initially as a substitute for other synthetic fibers, but now as challenger to cotton itself, according to Investment Research & Information Services Ltd.

The worldwide production of synthetic fibers is shown in Table VB-13.

Table VB-13
World Manmade Fiber Production ('000 tons)

Fiber	*1993*	*1994*
Synthetic Fibers		
Polyester	10,350	11,048
Polyamide	3,710	3,858
Acrylic	2,323	2,447
Polypropylene	2,962	3,116
Others	445	505
Total Synthetic	**19,790**	**20,974**
Cellulosic Manmade Fibers		
Viscose	2,152	2,187
Others	688	695
Total Cellulosic Manmade Fibers	**2,840**	**2,882**
Total Manmade Fibers	**22,630**	**23,856**

Source: TECNON (UK) Ltd.

The following table projects the growth of the synthetic fiber (polyester, polyamide, acrylic, and polypropylene) production in the Asia-Pacific region as a percentage of world production.

Synthetic Fibers: Demand Growth in the Asia-Pacific Region

Country	*1995* %	*2002* %
Japan	7.4	6.2
China	9.7	13.3
Taiwan	11.1	12.1
South Korea	8.3	9.2
India	3.4	2.9
ASEAN	4.5	6.4

The Indian textile industry has a vital role to play in the Nation's economy. This is the single largest industry in the country as it accounts for 20 to 25 percent in the total industrial production index. It employs about 20 million people and earns as much as 27 percent of the country's total export earnings. It is the base on which the pyramid of the industrial sector of the country has been built. What started largely as a spinning enterprise a century ago has now gradually developed into a mature composite industry.

The main raw materials of the industry are natural fibers like silk, cotton, wool and manmade fibers like cellulosic (viscose acetate, etc.). The Indian textile industry is today at the crossroads having reached a stage which requires appropriate restructuring. The process of restructuring is taking place with the installation of sophisticated shuttleless looms.

Cotton

One competitive advantage enjoyed by the textile industry is also a source of continuing uncertainty. Unlike countries like China and Pakistan which grow only coarse varieties of cotton, India grows the entire range of cotton. However, the availability and price of cotton, the most important raw material, are highly variable. Of late, however, restrictions on import of cotton are being slowly relaxed.

Cotton is one of the major cash crops in the country. India has the largest harvested area of 7.68 million hectares under cotton, almost twice that of the US and works out to nearly one-fourth of the world cotton area. Despite this, India ranks as the fourth largest producer of cotton in the world, after China, the US and the CIS.

The fortunes of the textile industry in India are looking up now and at the heart of this turn around is the sea change occurring in cotton production. In recent years, the crisis shortage syndrome in cotton has been overcome, thanks to the development of hybrid varieties, larger coverage of the crop under irrigation and improved management practices. A succession of good cotton crop has ensured abundant availability of this fiber and favorable prices have encouraged a brisk off take and good demand for yarn both from the mill and decentralized weaving sectors. The overseas markets have facilitated optimum utilization of spindles in the spinning sector.

Wool

This sector of the textile industry is better known as the worsted industry, as its main product is suitings—all-wool (AW), polyester-wool (PW) and polyester-viscose (PV). Unlike in cotton, where price is the most important selling point, suitings sell on brand image and quality. Competition from the powerloom sector is therefore limited, and the leading manufacturers can charge a premium for their products. The leading suiting manufacturers have all been building their brands for decades now.

The worsted business differs from the cotton textile industry in other respects also. The variety of fabrics in suitings is much larger than in cotton, and the manufacturers have to produce two collections a year. The larger producers put out over 1,000 new varieties of suitings each year.

Demand for suitings is growing at over 10% p.a. in line with rising disposable incomes and increasing urbanization and westernization. Demand in India picks up during the marriage and festival seasons, both of which coincide with winter. Further, sales of suitings rise in winter as they are still considered suitable for cold climates. The second half of the year is therefore better for the manufacturers. Demand for suitings is expected to boom for the rest of this decade, and all leading manufacturers of suitings are expanding capacities rapidly. Apart from the domestic market, manufacturers are finding the export markets lucrative, and India does have a competitive advantage in worsted fabrics also due to its lower labor costs.

Virtually, the entire requirement of wool is imported from Australia, the world's largest producer of wool.

Polyester

The Indian market holds tremendous latent demand for polyester (both PFY—polyester filament yarn and PSF—polyester stable fiber) as India adjusts its fiber consumption pattern away from cotton and in favor of synthetics. Demand has been growing at fairly high rates of over 10% p.a. for polyester, but has been held back by high excise and imports duties. Apart from high prices on account of high duties, most manufacturers suffer from small, uneconomical capacities because of capacity restrictions imposed before liberalization. In order to be able to compete effectively, most players are expanding capacities to become competitive, especially in PFY. A number of new players, attracted by the industry's prospects, are also coming in. The total consumption of PFY for 1993-94 was around 290,000 tons with negligible imports; total capacity by 1997 is likely to be in excess of 750,000 tons. Overcapacity is virtually certain in the case of PFY by 1996, and there will be pressure on margins.

The PSF industry, which had been suffering from overcapacity for the last few years, is now looking up after a phase of consolidation. A number of players have announced new plants, and a fresh round of overcapacity looks a distinct possibility.

Viscose Rayon

Viscose is known as the poor man's silk. The industry is dying out worldwide due to material constraints and adverse environmental effects. The main raw material is wood pulp, a forest-based material, and the production process generates toxic effluents. Viscose itself suffers from some deficiencies—it is a weak fiber, especially when wet. The industry has hardly grown over the last few years, as many weavers have switched over to newer fibers like polyester.

There are only eight manufacturers of viscose in India (both VFY—viscose filament yarn and VSF—viscose staple fiber). The most recent plant came up in 1983, and new entrants are not expected because of the limited availability of raw materials and the very high capital cost of new projects. Capacities will rise only marginally as existing manufacturers debottleneck their facilities, but these expansions will be small.

The industry is doing well today, largely because of the closure of viscose plants abroad due to environmental reasons. The industry can therefore look forward to exporting a significant proportion of its output.

Nylon

The main uses of nylon are in garments and as tire cord for tires. Nylon is a dying fiber in India, being rapidly overtaken by superior materials like polyester. Between 1982-83 and 1992-93, production of nylon filament yarn (NFY) rose by 27%. Over the same period, production of PFY rose ninefold—by 900%. Apart from being a superior fiber, PFY is also cheaper than NFY and will remain so. No new nylon plants for textile applications are expected, according to Investment Research & Information Services Ltd.

1. Cellulosic Fibers

The chemistry, production, and uses of cellulose and its derivatives were given in Chapter IIIF. One of the main uses is in production of rayon and acetate fibers. Most of the regenerated cellulose or rayon is produced by the viscose or xanthate process, with the cuprammonium produced contributing only minor production.

1.1. Basic Chemistry of Viscose Process

(a) Alkali conversion

$$\underset{\text{cellulose}}{(C_6H_9O_4\cdot OH)_x} + xNaOH \rightarrow \underset{\text{alkali cellulose}}{(C_6H_9O_4\cdot ONa)_x} + xH_2O$$

(b) CS_2 solubilization

$$(C_6H_9O_4\cdot ONa)_x + xCS_2 \rightarrow \underset{\text{sodium cellulose xanthate}}{\left(C_6H_9O_4{-}O{-}\overset{\overset{S}{\|}}{C}{-}SNa\right)_x}$$

(c) Acid regeneration

$$\left(C_6H_9O_4\cdot O\cdot \overset{\overset{S}{\|}}{C}{-}SNa\right)_x + xH_2SO_4 \rightarrow \underset{\text{rayon or regenerated cellulose}}{(C_6H_9O_4\cdot OH)_x} + xCS_2 + xNaHSO_4$$

1.2. Consumption Pattern

Rayon yarn is used for many purposes in the textile weaving industry. A second major use is in the production of rayon cord for rubber tire casings. Nylon is giving strong competition in this latter usage.

1.3. Method of Production

1.3.1. Reference flow sheet: Figure VB-8

1.3.2. Process description

Cellulose wood pulp sheets or cotton linters are placed in a steeping press and contacted with 18% aqueous NaOH for 2-4 hours at room temperature. The excess alkali is pressed out with a hydraulic ram, the sheets are shredded to crumbs and aged for 2-3 days, depending on temperature (20-25°C). Aging has a direct bearing on the viscosity of the xanthate solution.

CS_2 is added in a rotating drum mixer (barratte) over a three-hour period. The orange cellulose xanthate is transferred to the solubilizer where it is mixed into dilute caustic to produce an orange-colored viscous solution containing 7-8% cellulose and 6.5-7% NaOH. After digesting for 4-5 days at room temperature, the solution is filtered and fed to spinning machines.

For spinning viscose rayon, the extrusion spinnerettes are made of platinum or gold alloys with anywhere from 20-1,500 orifices of 0.1-0.2 mm diameter for continuous filament yarns and 3,000-15,000 holes of 0.05-0.1 mm diameter for staple or short fiber shapes.

As the solution is extruded from the spinnerette, it contacts the acid bath which precipitates the filaments without causing them to stick together or break. The filament group is wound and transferred to a series of plastic reels where processing treatments of washing, desulfurizing, bleaching, and conditioning take place continuously and in that order.

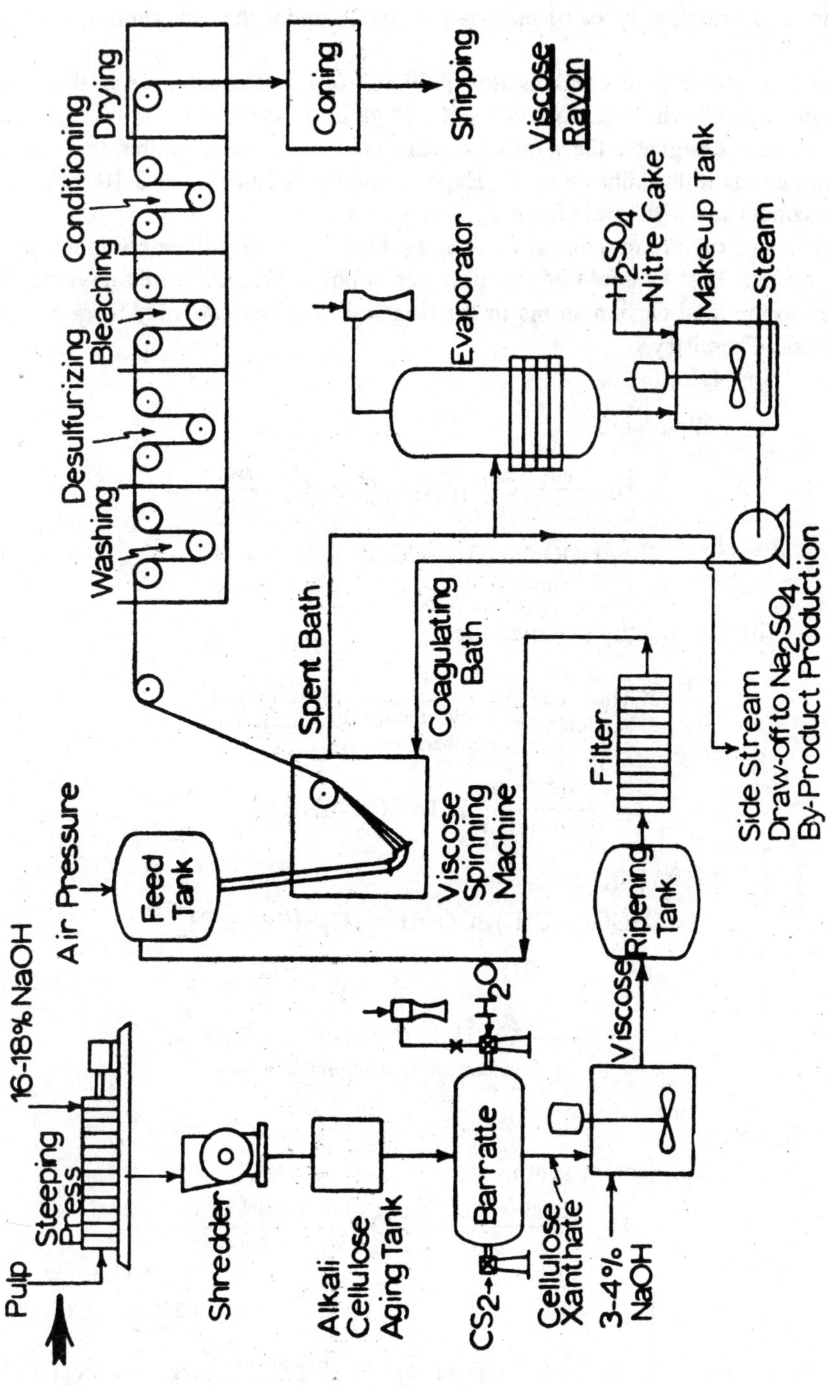

Fig. VB-8. Viscose rayon production.

2. Polyamides

There are two principal types of materials included under the polyamides, each type having a number of polymers.

- Diamine—dibasic acid condensation polymers—a prime example is the first and well-known "nylon" which is now called 6,6-Nylon or Nylon 66. In this nomenclature the first number designates the number of carbon atoms in the diamine, the second is for the carbon atoms in the dibasic acid. Experimentally, amines from 2-10 carbon atoms have been condensed with acids from 2-18 carbon atoms.
- Single ring structure monomers containing the NH-group—linear polymers form when the ring opens. Best example of this polymer is polycaprolactam or 6-Nylon. The number refers to the total carbon atoms in the ring; this number can vary from 5 to 12.

2.1. Basic Chemistry

2.1.1. 6,6-Nylon

(a) Adipic acid

$$C_6H_{12} \xrightarrow{\text{air}} C_6H_{11}OH + C_6H_{10}O \xrightarrow[\text{aq } HNO_3]{80°C}$$

$$\underset{\text{adipic acid}}{HOOC{\cdot}(CH_2)_4{\cdot}COOH} + xNO + yN_2O$$

(b) Hexamethylene diamine

$$\underset{\text{acrylonitrile}}{2CH_2{=}CHCN} \xrightarrow[\text{low pressure dimerization}]{H_2} \underset{\text{adiponitrile}}{NC(CH_2)_4{\cdot}CN}$$

$$\xrightarrow[\text{high pressure}]{H_2 + NH_3} H_2N(CH_2)_6NH_2$$

(c) 6,6-Nylon

$$xHOOC{\cdot}(CH_2)_4{\cdot}COOH + xH_2N(CH_2)_6NH_2$$

$$\rightarrow (-\overset{\overset{O}{\|}}{C}(CH_2)_4{\cdot}\overset{\overset{O}{\|}}{C}{\cdot}NH{\cdot}(CH_2)_6{\cdot}NH-)_x$$

polyhexamethylene adipimide or 6,6-Nylon

2.1.2. 6-Nylon

(a) Caprolactam synthesis

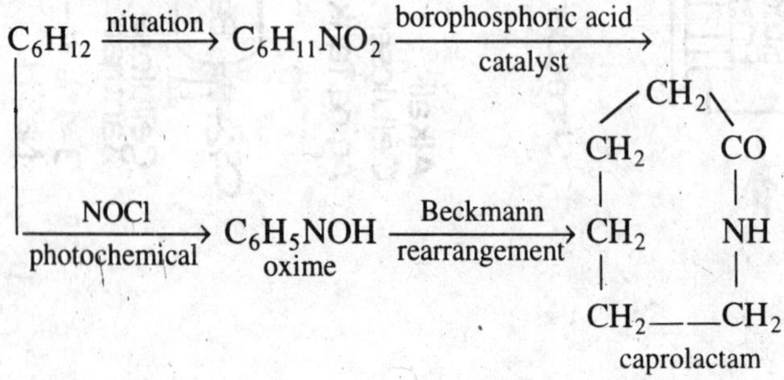

(b) Stage condensation of caprolactam

$$n\underline{OC—(CH_2)_5—NH} + H_2O \rightarrow nH_2N—(CH_2)_5—COOH$$

$$\rightleftharpoons -H_2O$$

$$H[—HN\cdot(CH_2)_5\cdot C]_n—OH$$

polycaprolactam or 6-Nylon

2.2. Properties and Uses

Both nylons have very similar properties and find use as thin films, and in plastics for extrusion and injection molding, in addition to fiber applications previously discussed. Principal differences in properties are: 6,6-Nylon melts 40-45 °C higher than 6-Nylon; it is also harder, more rigid and less abrasive-resistant than 6-Nylon.

Larger diameter monofilaments are produced for bristles, strings, fishing leaders and similar products where combination of strength, toughness, and elasticity are required.

2.3. Method of Production of 6,6-Nylon

2.3.1. Reference flow sheet: Figure VB-9

2.3.2. Process description

Nylon salt is first prepared by mixing the amine and acid in aqueous solution and adjusting the pH to 7.8. The salt is concentrated under vacuum and then charged to an autoclave. Here the rest of the water is removed and the temperature gradually is raised to 280 °C to complete polymerization and remove water of condensation.

The final product with a molecular weight range of 12,000-16,000 is extruded as a ribbon onto chilling rolls, then to a chipper for producing small chips suitable for storage and rehandling.

When nylon fibers are produced, the chips are melted, metered through high pressure pumps, filtered and passed through a melt spinnerette. The extruded filaments harden immediately on air cooling and can be wound on bobbins at speeds of 750 meters per minute or higher. The thread is stretched to about 4 times its original length in cold drawing to give the fiber desirable textile properties.

2.4. Method of Production of 6-Nylon

The photochemical route developed in Japan by Toyo Rayon avoids the conventional oxidation-nitration step with a simplified process. The success of the latter was largely due to development of 20 KW mercury lamps with power consumption of less than 4.5 KWH per kg of oxime.

The polymerization process differs from that for 6,6-Nylon by the nature of the polymerization. The step-wise condensation of caprolactam with no net water removal is a similar process. The difficulty arises, however, in the thermal equilibrium between monomer and polymer at the melting and spinning temperatures. As much as 10% monomer is retained, so the fibers have to be water-washed to remove the soluble caprolactam monomer. Molecular weight is controlled by addition of monofunctional acid.

In other respects, the two Nylon processes are essentially the same with little difference in manufacturing costs.

2.5. Production in India

The following tabulations summarize nylon and nylon intermediate production over recent years (from "Industrial Organic Chemistry" by Weissermel et al (1993)):

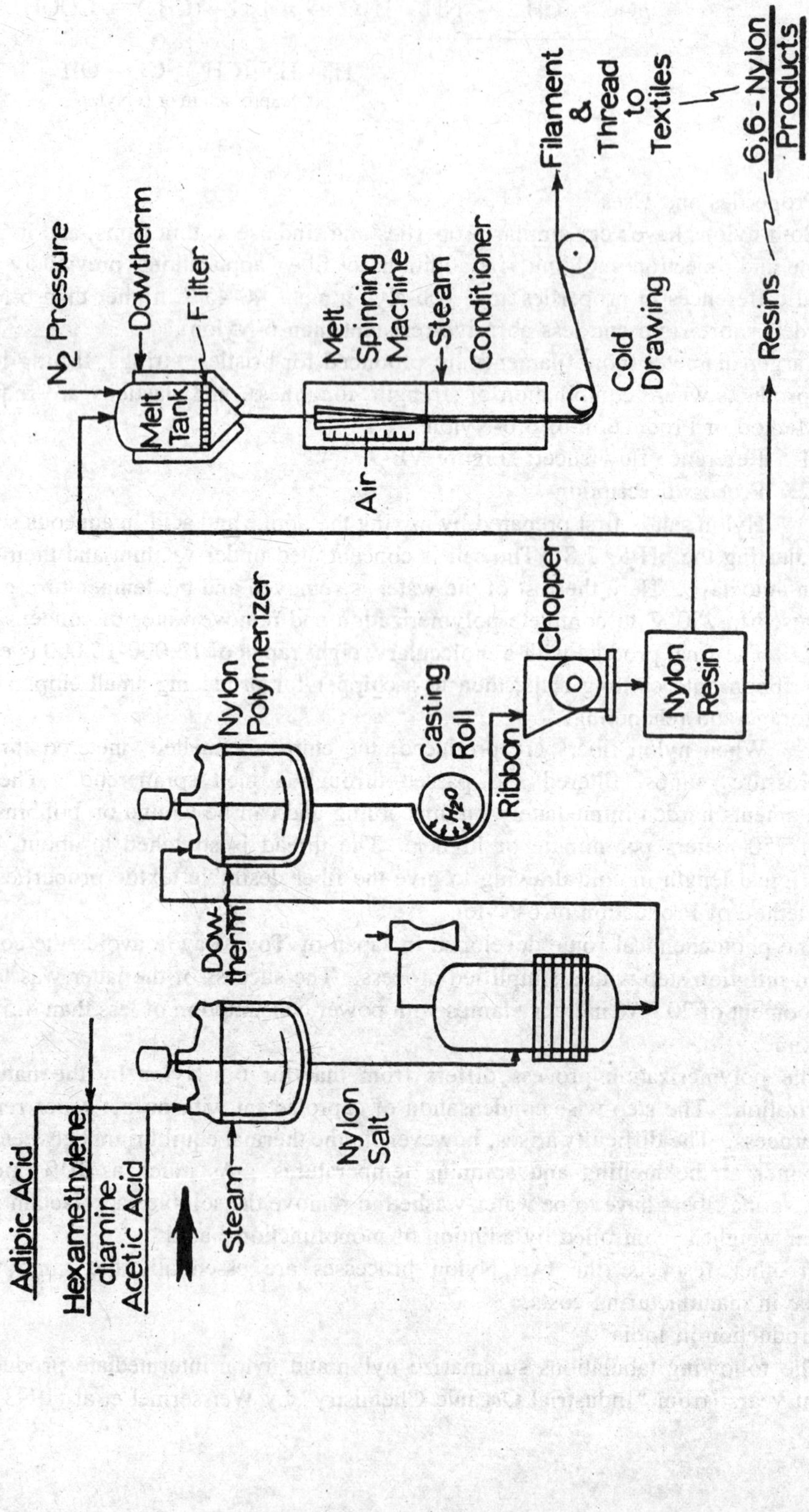

Fig. VB-9. Nylon resin and fiber production (6,6-nylon).

Production of Polyamides (in '000 tons):

	1986	1988	1990
USA	1,141	1,211	1,208
Western Europe	625	617	680
Japan	280	273	260

Adipic Acid Production (in '000 tons):

	1987	1989	1991
USA	712	744	713
Western Europe	653	680	600
Japan	67	88	95

Production of HMDA (in '000 tons):

	1987	1989	1991
USA	526	546	556
Western Europe	289	301	330
Japan	39	52	64

ε-Caprolactam Production (in '000 tons):

	1985	1987	1989
Western Europe	663	808	775
USA	491	526	595
CIS	479	530	580
Japan	455	470	469

About 70% of the total nylon filament yarn produced in India is used for the manufacture of sarees, socks and other knitted garments. Its use in the manufacture of fishnet ropes and industrial filter fabrics is also increasing.

At present there are several units manufacturing nylon filament yarn in the organized sector in the country. Their names and addresses are given in Table VB-14.

The production of nylon filament yarn in the past few years in the country was as follows:

Production of Nylon Filament Yarn (M.T.)

Year	Production
1987-88	34,100
1988-89	35,800
1989-90	38,000
1990-91	41,500
1991-92	30,682

As per the Report of the Committee for Perspective Planning of Petrochemical Industry (1986-2000 A.D.), the demand for nylon filament yarn in the country is expected to rise to about 122,000 M.T. and 197,000 M.T. respectively by 1994-95 and 1999-2000. The demand for nylon tire cord by 2000 AD is expected to rise to 68,500 M.T.

Table VB-14
Names and Addresses of Some Units Manufacturing Nylon Filament Yarn in India

Baroda Rayon Corporation Ltd.
394 220, Dist. Surat (Gujarat)

Century Enka Ltd.
Bhosari, Pune (Maharashtra)

Garware Nylons Ltd.
Bombay-Pune Road, Pimpri, Pune - 411 018
(Maharashtra)

Gujarat Nylons Ltd.
Village Kuwarda, Taluk Mangrol, Dist. Surat (Gujarat)

JCT Ltd.
Village Chohal, Hoshiarpur Dist. (Punjab)

J.K. Synthetics Ltd.
Jay Kay Nagar, Kota - 324 003 (Rajasthan)

LML Fibres Ltd.
C-17, Panki Industrial Estate, 60 B, Dadanagar, Kanpur - 208 022 (U.P.)

Modipon Ltd.
Hapur Road, Modinagar, Dist. Ghaziabad (U.P.)

Nirlon Ltd.
Goregaon (East), Bombay (Maharashtra)

Shree Synthetics Ltd.
Naulakhi Maksi Road, Ujjain (M.P.)

Source: "SBP Handbook of Projects for Corporate Diversification" (1992)

3. Polyesters

Polymers formed by condensation of polyfunctional acids or esters with polyfunctional alcohols are called polyesters. When monomer acids and alcohols are used and some trifunctional groups are present, the polymers produced are termed alkyd resins for use largely in high grade paints and varnishes. The linear polyesters are formed from bifunctional groups and are suitable for fibers and films. Outstanding examples of this group are the Dacron fiber-Mylar film products formed from condensation of dimethyl terephthalate and ethylene glycol.

3.1. Basic Chemistry of Dacron-Mylar Polyesters

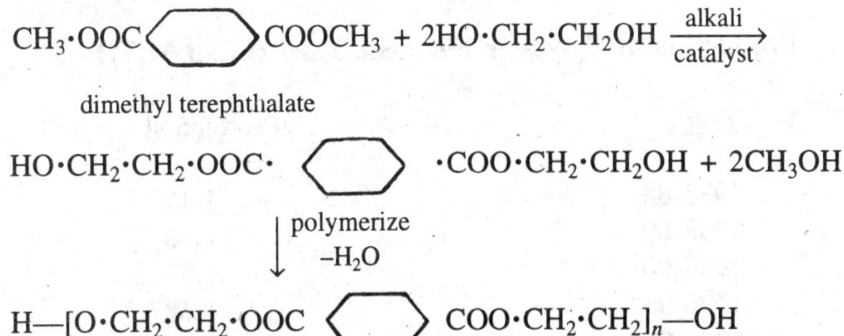

3.2. Properties and Uses of Dacron-Mylar

The chief advantage of Dacron polyester fiber is its high wrinkle resistance relative to other fibers, particularly when wet. Dacron textiles retain creases and pleats when washed and dried and are the principal ingredient of "wash and wear" clothing. Blends of 65% Dacron with wool, cotton, or rayon are used to prevent excessive build-up of static electricity and to allow moisture absorption and diffusion needed for wearing comfort.

Mylar film has extreme toughness when given a two-dimensional stretch, which makes it ideal for photographic film and recording tape.

3.3. Methods of Production

Dimethyl terephthalate is the ester prepared from crude terephthalic acid which comes from oxidizing *p*-xylene. The ester allows for easier control of the polymerization with glycol as it is more soluble in ethylene glycol.

The ester interchange reaction prior to polymerization proceeds smoothly in the presence of alkali. Methanol is removed continuously in a fractionating column. The reaction starts rapidly at 160°C and rises to 230°C before all of the methyl groups are removed. Polymerization then proceeds at 275°C and vacuum is applied to remove water of condensation. The formation of diethylene glycol and its condensation is an undesirable side reaction which will affect polymer properties if present to any extent.

The polymer is melt spun to produce Dacron fiber and roll-extruded to give Mylar film. Dye or coloring for the finished product must be done in the melting stage because of the chemical inertness of the polyester.

3.4. Production in India

Polyester filament yarn is used in the manufacture of all polyester, polyester-viscose, polyester-cotton and polyester-viscose-cotton suitings and shirtings, sarees, bedsheets, and other dress materials. The easy washability, wrinkle resistance, no need of frequent ironing, longer life, and better look and feel have made polyester filament the most sought after yarn all over the world for the production of all types of fabrics.

The texturizing and twisting process, by which partially oriented polyester filament yarn can be texturized and twisted, has resulted in the production of a yarn which possesses almost all the good properties of cotton (including feel) as well as polyester. Almost 90% of polyester filament produced is twisted or texturized before it is used in weaving of any fabrics.

At present about 20 units are manufacturing polyester filament yarn in India. Their names and addresses are given in Table VB-15.

The production of polyester filament yarn in the country during the past few years in the organized sector has been as follows:

Production of Polyester Filament Yarn (Lakh M.T.)

Year	Production
1987-88	1.12
1988-89	1.43
1989-90	1.57
1990-91	1.68
1991-92	2.05

In the recent years, India has started exporting polyester filament yarn. In 1992-93, India is expected to export about 30,000 tons (Rs. 250 crores) of polyester filament yarn.

As per the Report of the Committee for Perspective Planning of Petrochemical Industry (1986-2000 A.D.), the demand for polyester filament yarn is expected to rise to about 220,000 M.T. and 352,000 M.T. by 1994-95 and 1999-2000 respectively.

Table VB-15
Names and Addresses of Units Manufacturing Polyester Filament Yarn

Century Enka Ltd.
Bhosari, Pune (Maharashtra)

DCL Polyesters Ltd.
Dahali, Mouda Taluq, Dist. Nagpur (Maharashtra)

Ester Industries Ltd.
P.O. Charubeta, Pilibhit Road, Khatima - 262 308
Dist. Nainital (U.P.)

Garware Nylons Ltd.
Bombay-Pune Road, Pimpri, Pune - 411 018
(Maharashtra)

Haryana Petrochemicals Ltd.
55-59, HUDA Industrial Area, Delhi-Rewari Road, Rewari (Haryana)

Indian Organic Chemicals Ltd.
Bombay-Pune Road, Khopoli - 410 203
Dist. Raigad (Maharashtra)

JCT Ltd.
Village Chohal, Dist. Hoshiarpur (Punjab)

J.K. Synthetics Ltd.
Jay Kay Nagar, Kota -324 003 (Rajasthan)

LML Fibres Ltd.
C-17, 18, & 20 Panki Industrial Estate, Kanpur - 208 022 (U.P.)

Modipon Ltd.
Hapur Road, Modinagar, Dist. Ghaziabad (U.P.)

Orissa Synthetics Ltd.
Lakshmi Nagar, P.O. Baulpur - 759 031, Dist. Dhenkanal (Orissa)

Orkay Silk Mills Ltd.
A-41, MIDC Industrial Area, Patalganga, Kolaba (Maharashtra)

Parasrampuria Industries Ltd.
SP 145, D&G Rico Industrial Area, Bhiwadi, Dist. Alwar (Rajasthan)

Petrofils Co-Operative Ltd.
P.O. Petrochemicals, Dist. Baroda (Gujarat)

Prag Bosimi Synthetics Ltd.
Sipajhar, Dist. Darrang (Assam)

Raymond Synthetics Ltd.
Naini, Allahabad (U.P.)

Reliance Textile Industries Ltd.
B-4, MIDC Industrial Area, Patalganga, Kolaba (Maharashtra)

Sanghi Polyesters Ltd.
Anajpur, Dist. Rangareddy (A.P.)

Shree Synthetics Ltd.
Naulakhi, Maksi Road, Ujjain - 456 001 (M.P.)

Source: "SBP Handbook of Projects for Corporate Diversification" (1992)

Polyester staple is a synthetic fiber used in the manufacture of synthetic blended yarn in combination with cotton and/or viscose. The synthetic blended yarn is used in the manufacture of blended fabrics, widely known as terrycot fabrics, for suitings and shirtings, bedsheets, sarees, etc.

At present there are 10 units manufacturing polyester staple fiber in the organized sector in the country. Their names and addresses are given in Table VB-16.

The production of polyester staple fiber in the past few years in the organized sector in the country has been as follows:

Production of Polyester Staple Fiber (M.T.)

Year	No. of Units	Installed Capacity	Production
1986	6	85,400	59,019
1987	10	-	79,319
1988	9	-	98,022
1989	9	-	122,667
1990	9	-	138,493

The production of polyester staple fiber in 1989-90, 1990-91, and 1991-92 was 111,805 M.T., 122,507 M.T. and 136,379 M.T. respectively.

India was expected to export about 60,000 tons of polyester staple fiber in 1990-91.

India imported about 25,000 tons of polyester staple fiber in 1986-87. In 1987-88, its imports and exports nearly matched. From 1988-89, it has become a net exporter of this fiber.

In the international market, while Taiwan, South Korea, Japan, and India are the exporters of this fiber, UK, Italy, Belgium, Netherlands, the UAE, Saudi Arabia and Oman are the importers.

The demand for polyester staple fiber is expected to go up to 160,000 to 200,000 tons per year by 1994-95.

Table VB-16
Names and Addresses of Units Manufacturing Polyester Staple Fiber

Ahmedabad Mfg. & Calico Ptg. Co. Ltd.
Opp. Railway Colony, Near IPCL
P.O. Petrochemicals, Ahmedabad (Gujarat)

Bongaigaon Refinery & Petrochemicals Ltd.
P.O. Dhaligaon - 783 385, Dist Bongaigaon (Assam)

ICI India Ltd.
Kalwa-Belapur Road, Thane - 400 601 (Maharashtra)

India Polyfibers Ltd.
Dewa Road, Barabanki - 225 123 (U.P.)

Indian Organic Chemicals, Ltd.
Chinnasekadu, Manali, Chinglepet (T.N.)

JCT Ltd.
Dist. Hoshiarpur (Punjab)

J.K. Synthetics Ltd.
Jay Kay Nagar, Kota - 324 003 (Rajasthan)

Orissa Synthetics Ltd.
Lakshmi Nagar, P.O. Baulpur - 754 031
Dist. Dhenkanal (Orissa)

Reliance Industries Ltd.
Patalganga, Off Bombay-Pune Road, Near Panvel
Dist. Raigad (Maharashtra)

Swadeshi Polytex Ltd.
New Kavi Nagar, Ghaziabad (U.P.)

Source: "SBP Handbook of Projects for Corporate Diversification" (1992)

4. Acrylic Fibers

Acrylics constitute one of the four major classes of synthetic fibers—the classes being polyamides, polyesters, acrylic, and polyolefin (polypropylene).

Polyacrylonitrile—$(CH_2CHCN)_x$—is the major component of the acrylic fibers. A comonomer is usually incorporated to improve such fiber properties as dyeability. When large amounts (over 15%) of such comonomers are incorporated, the fibers are referred to as modified acrylics or "modacrylics." Thus Union Carbide's Dynel contains 40% acrylonitrile units and 60% vinyl chloride units in the polymer chain.

The first of the acrylic fibers was DuPont's Orlon. It is made by first polymerizing acrylonitrile in a manner similar to that used for other vinyl polymers (see Figure VB-4). The ivory-white polymer is then dissolved in an organic solvent (such as dimethyl formanide) or an inorganic solvent (such as concentrated zinc chloride or sodium thiocyanate solutions). The solution is filtered and then dry spun (into warm air) or wet spun (into a coagulating solution). The fiber is then stretched to several times its original length to orient the polymer molecules into long parallel chains for strength.

The acrylic fibers feature good weather resistance and resistance to chemical attack. They have a texture resembling that of wool. They are used in making sweaters, carpets and blankets. They may be used in blends with wool.

Acrylic fiber consists of copolymers with at least 85% by weight of acrylonitrile. Modacrylic fibers contain at least 30-80% acrylonitrile. The main characteristics of acrylic fiber are warmth, lightweight, ease in washing and low flammability which makes it suitable for use in the manufacture of woolen and worsted fabrics, sweaters, pullovers, blankets, furnishings, carpets, rugs, curtains, draperies, knitted garments, etc.

At present there are 5 units manufacturing acrylic fiber in the organized sector in the country. Their names and addresses are given in Table VB-17.

The production of acrylic fiber in the past few years in the organized sector in the country was as follows:

Production of Acrylic Fiber (M.T.)

Year	Installed Capacity	Production
1985-86	22,500	22,105
1986-87	22,500	23,081
1987-88	22,500	22,191
1989-90	39,000	28,518
1990-91	51,000	31,239

The present installed capacity for the manufacture of acrylic fiber in the country is about 51,000 tons per annum. The demand in 1995 is estimated at 94,000 tpa.

Table VB-17
Names and Addresses of Units Manufacturing Acrylic Fiber (M.T.) in India

Name and Address	Lic./Reg. Capacity	Installed Capacity
Indian Acrylics Ltd. Sangrur Dist. (Punjab) (Was due to commission in 1992-93)	20,000	20,000
Consolidated Fibers & Chemicals Ltd. Industrial Zone (Southeast), Haldia, Dist. Midnapore (W.B.) (Was due to commission in 1992-93)	20,000	12,000

Indian Petrochemicals Corp. Ltd.	24,000	12,000
P.O. Petrochemicals, Dist. Vadodara (Gujarat)	24,000	12,000
J.K. Synthetics Ltd.	16,000	10,500
Jay Kay Nagar, Kota - 324 003 (Rajasthan)	16,000	10,500
	24,000	12,000
	24,000	24,000
	24,000	24,000
Pasupati Acrylon Ltd.		
Kashipur Road, Thakur Dwara,	20,000	15,000
Dist. Moradabad (U.P.)		
(Production commenced in 1990-91)		

Source: "SBP Handbook of Projects for Corporate Diversification" (1992)

5. Olefin (Polypropylene) Fibers

Polypropylene multifilament yarn is used in various industrial applications like manufacture of fish nets, twines, cordages, ropes, sewing threads, synthetic furnishings and upholstery, tapestry, carpets, etc. It is much cheaper than nylon and other synthetic and natural fiber yarns.

This yarn, when produced from isotactic polypropylene, has high strength and durability, low density, rich woolen texture and excellent resistance to all types of chemicals, acids and alkalies. Its low density yields higher length of yarn as compared to other textile yarns of same weight and thickness.

At present there are several units manufacturing polypropylene multifilament yarn in the organized sector in the country. Their names and addresses are given in Table VB-18.

The present demand for polypropylene multifilament yarn in the country is estimated at about 1 lakh tons per annum.

5.1 Manufacturing Process

Polypropylene resin is fed into an extruder in which it is heated and melted. The melt is forced through a filter screen and an electrically heated tube into a spinning head. From the spinning head, the polymer is metered and forced through a spinnerette assembly. It is cooled by a blast of air and is passed through an antistatic unit for proper spin finish.

To impart strength and stability, the filaments are stretched longitudinally by a pair of godets. During stretching, the filaments are slightly heated for molecular re-orientation. On slow cooling, after stretching, the yarn shrinks to predetermined extent. This imparts desired tensile and thermal characteristics to the yarn. The stabilized and set yarn is again passed through another antistatic unit for final dressing with antistatic oil. The treated yarn is then wound on a winding unit.

Table VB-18

Names and Addresses of Units Manufacturing Polypropylene Multifilament Yarn

Alembic Chemical Works Ltd.
Neomar Division, Dist. Panchmahal (Gujarat)

Chandra Synthetics Ltd.
Sikandrabad, Dist. Bulandshahr (U.P.)

Gujarat Filaments Ltd.
2502, GIDC Industrial Estate, Halol - 389 350 (Gujarat)

Parasrampuria Synthetics Ltd.
SP-145, D&G Rico Industrial Area,
Bhiwadi, Dist. Alwar (Rajasthan)

Rajasthan Petro Synthetics Ltd.
F-210-213, Udyog Vihar, RIICO Industrial Area, Village Sukher
Dist. Udaipur (Rajasthan)

Source: "SBP Handbook of Projects for Corporate Diversification" (1992)

Composite Materials

Composite materials really constitute a bridge between polymers which we have been discussing and metals which are to be discussed in the section which follows.

Composite materials are really reinforced plastics in which a strong ceramic or other fiber is positioned in a plastic matrix. The original material in this category was glass fiber reinforced resins which have been applied to a variety of uses requiring high mechanical strength such as automobile fenders or sailboat hulls. See Tables VB-19 and VB-20.

Composite materials have evolved into more and more sophisticated materials such as resins reinforced by carbon or graphite fibers to give materials suitable for aircraft and aerospace use in areas ranging from aircraft wing surfaces to heat-resistant blocks suitable for use in aircraft brakes to nose cones for missiles.

Automobile tires can even be considered as an example of composite materials in that the rubber matrix and the textile reinforcing fibers are interdependent, neither one being able to function without the other in a tire.

Asbestos has been used as the reinforcing fiber in a variety of composite materials, but the carcinogenic properties of fine asbestos fibers have decreased its use very markedly. At one time, asbestos-reinforced phenolee resins were the material of choice for automotive brake linings, but the constant sluffing off of asbestos particles during high-speed braking has been judged a serious health hazard and has resulted in virtual abandonment of asbestos in favor of fluorinated fibers and other substitutes.

Table VB-19
Survey of the Application Fields of Inorganic Fibers

Application Field	Foremost Requirements	Fibers Utilized
Plastics reinforcement	High tensile strength, high elasticity modulus, low density	Asbestos, glass fibers, carbon fibers, SiC fibers, boron fibers, oxide fibers (Al_2O_3)

Seals, frictional linings	Compression strength, elastic deformation behavior, thermal stability, abrasion resistance	Asbestos, glass fibers, steel fibers
Tire cord	Stability to alternating mechanical stress	Steel fibers and very short metal fibers
Cement reinforcement	Chemical resistance to cement, mechanical stability	Asbestos, cement-resistant glass fibers, steel fibers

Source: "Industrial Inorganic Chemistry" by Buchner et al (1989)

Table VB-20
Applications Spectrum of Glass Fiber Reinforced Plastics in 1983

	Europe (%)	USA (%)
Transportation	17	25
Electrical Industry	15	9
Construction Industry	20	20
Industry and Agriculture	25	21
Sport and Leisure Activities	12	15
Consumer Goods	3	6
Miscellaneous	8	4

Source: "Industrial Inorganic Chemistry" by Buchner et al (1989)

The industrial manufacture of carbon fibers is based on the thermal degradation of non-melting organic polymers such as polyacrylonitrile (PAN).

The level of mechanical properties attainable with carbon fibers is dependent upon the crystallinity and structure of the carbon formed. These, in turn, are critically dependent both on the quality and composition of the fiber starting material and on the manufacturing technology used.

The PAN-fibers utilized as starting materials are first clamped to prevent shrinkage of the fibers during the subsequent oxidative pretreatment at temperatures below 300°C. This clamping also produces preorientation in the direction of the fiber axis in the subsequently formed graphite crystals. In the second stage (carbonization stage) at ca. 1,600°C, high strength carbon fibers of the HT-type are formed, which are converted in a third stage by graphization at temperatures up to 3,000°C into high modulus carbon fibers. Significant improvements in the properties have been recently achieved by mutual fine tuning of the raw materials and the carbonization process.

Reinforcing carbon fibers are relatively recent industrial products which are currently being introduced. Since about 1970, they have been utilized in the field of military aircraft, spacecraft and, more recently, in the sports article sector (golf clubs, fishing rods, tennis rackets, skis, boots, yachts, masts, sports cars, etc.). Its breakthrough into civil aviation came in 1980 (1 ton carbon fiber per Boeing 767!, side tail units of the Airbus representing the first fiber-reinforced primary structural component) and in the event of further price reduction, this could be extended to industrial fields to achieve, for example, weight savings in motor vehicles, lighter engine components and lightweight components for machines and robots.

VI

METALLURGICAL INDUSTRIES

The topic of metallurgical industries is not usually included in books on chemical technology, but a brief survey chapter is presented here because of the importance of the metallurgical industries to industrial development in India and the interrelation of the chemical and metallurgical industries. The metallurgical industries are major consumers of chemical industry products (lime, coke, oxygen, etc.). Also, the metallurgical industries are major producers of chemical by-products (notably sulfur dioxide from smelting operations). Further, chemical engineering techniques of process design and process control are more and more being applied to old-line metallurgical operations to give high output continuous operations.

Process coverage will be given here to

- Iron and steel manufacture
- Aluminum manufacture
- Copper production
- Lead and zinc production

Non-ferrous metals like aluminum, zinc, tin, lead, etc., are used to make alloys, castings, forgings, extrusions, wires, cables, pipes, etc., which are used in vital infrastructure facilities like power plants, automobiles, railways, telecommunications, engineering and chemical plants, as well as for the agricultural sector and domestic use.

VIA. IRON AND STEEL

Iron ore takes the form of Fe_2O_3 (hematite) or $Fe_2O_3 \cdot FeO$ which is Fe_3O_4 (magnetite) as a rule. Other iron ores are $FeCO_3$ (siderite) and FeS_2 (pyrites). Hematite is, in fact, the principal ore used for the production of iron and steel.

India is fortunate in having extensive iron ore deposits estimated at 21,000 million tons or about 5% of total world reserves. Further, the average iron content of Indian ores is about 60%. Also most Indian ores are low in phosphorus content and hence are ideally suited for smelting to iron and steel.

Iron ore production in India is currently 50 million tons and is expected to go up to 72 million tons by the end of the Eighth Plan. See Table VIA-1.

Table VIA-1

Indian Production, Consumption and Export of Iron Ore (Millions of Tons)

	1991-92	1996-97
Production	56.50	72.00
Consumption	24.50	40.00
Export	32.00	32.00

Source: "Economic Times"

The recoverable reserves of iron ore, hematite and magnetite are 9.58 billion tons and 3.14 billion tons, respectively. Hematite was mainly found in Bihar, Goa, Karnataka, and Madhya Pradesh, while magnetite was in Andhra Pradesh, Goa, Karnataka, and Kerala. Iron ore is produced through a combination of large mechanized mines in the State-owned sector and smaller mines operated on a manual or semi-manual basis in the private-owned sector.

Ore, as mined, must be dried. Further, when the fines content of the ore is high, it must be sintered (in admixture with coke breeze and flux) to give lumps which can be charged to the blast furnace without excessive fines losses resulting from blowing powdered ore out of the blast furnace with the flue gases.

The first step in steel manufacture is the production of pig iron by reduction of iron ore in a blast furnace. The next step is the production of the iron-carbon alloy known as steel in an open hearth furnace or in one of various types of convertor vessels. Finally, high-alloy steels may be made in electric furnaces.

1. Production of Pig Iron

1.1. Reference Flow Sheet: Figure VIA-1

1.2. Raw Materials

Ore in lump form, coke and limestone flux are the raw materials.

1.3. Chemical Reactions

The essential chemical reaction is

$$Fe_2O_3 + 3C \rightarrow 2Fe + 3CO$$

although a variety of chemical reactions take place in the different temperature zones of the blast furnace.

1.4. Process Description

The charge materials of ore coke and limestone are introduced by conveyors (called skips) in the proper portions for the reaction in the furnace. A layer of ore is intermixed with layers of coal and limestone as the furnace is charged. Simultaneously a hot air blast is introduced to the base of the furnace at 600-800°C from recuperator stoves which are steel vessels filled with checkerworks of refractory brick. These stoves are alternatively heated by blast furnace off-gas and used to preheat incoming air to the blast furnace using the sensible heat in the checkerwork as the heat source.

As the air reacts with the coke generating carbon monoxide and heat, and as the iron oxide is reduced, molten iron gathers at the base of the furnace. It is periodically tapped and the molten pig iron run into cars from which in turn it is poured into long blocks called "pigs."

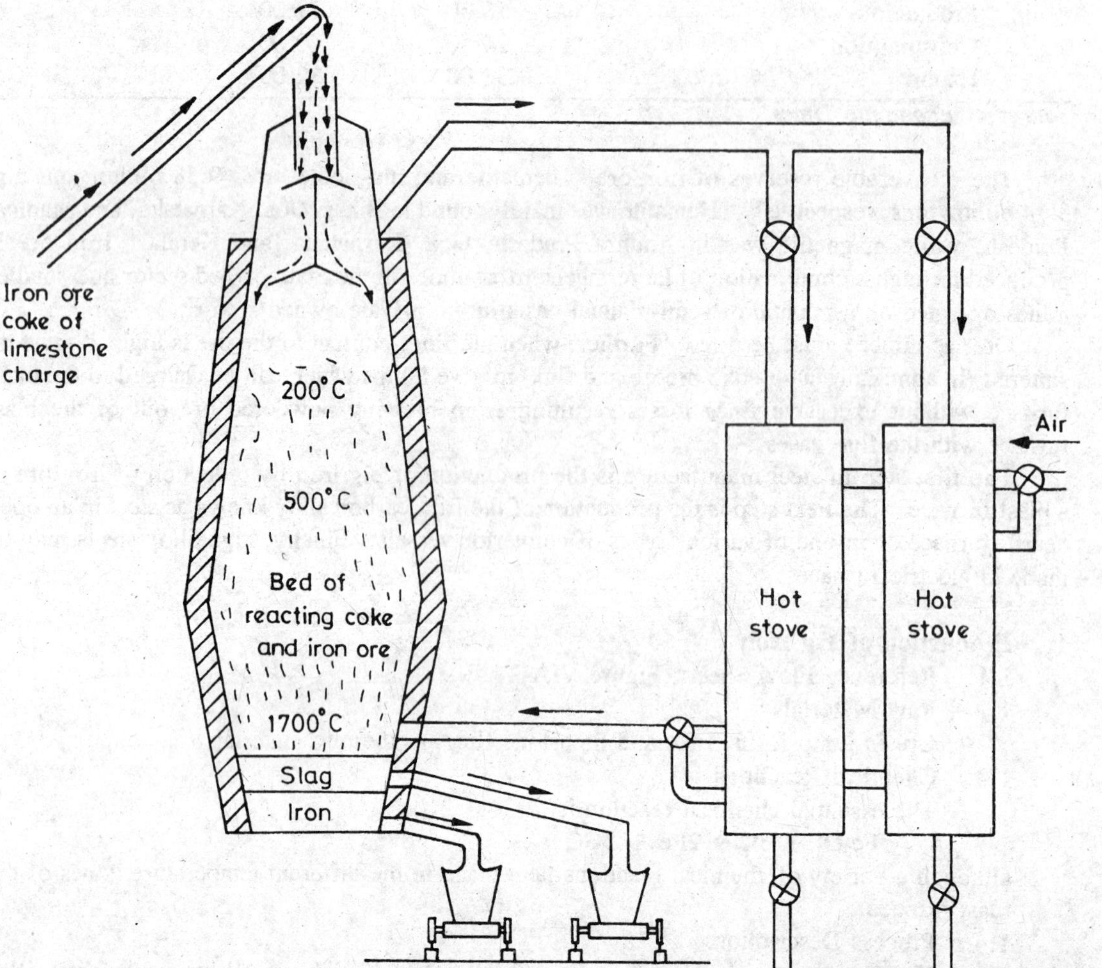

Fig. VIA-1. Flow sheet for pig iron production.

1.5. Major Engineering Problems

- The structure itself is considerable in size and may weigh 10,000 tons; so careful structural design is necessary.
- The furnace lining is subjected to intense heat so that water cooling of walls must be used in the lower zone of the furnace to counteract the destructive effects of the heat.
- Cleaning of waste gas from blast furnaces before discharge to the atmosphere is increasingly important to prevent adverse effects on vegetation and local population.
- Increased production may be achieved by pressure operation. This reduces dust carry over and permits higher operating rates.
- Reduced coke consumption is desirable and 20% savings may be made using supplementary oil injection.
- Improved furnace operating efficiency can be effected by enriching the air blast with oxygen.

2. Production of Steel

2.1. Reference Flow Sheet: Figure VIA-2

2.2. Raw Materials

The raw materials for steel manufacture are pig iron and air or oxygen.

2.3. Chemical Reactions

The chemical reactions involved are primarily oxidation of such impurities as phosphorus to give oxides which end up in the slag in open hearth furnaces or in converters. Also carbon is oxidized to CO & CO_2 and removed in the exit gases.

2.4. Process Description

Steel making, in brief, involves the removal of undesirable elements from pig iron by oxidation followed by the addition of the necessary ingredients to make the type of steel required. It should be noted that pure iron is relatively useless as it is soft and has a high melting point; it is used for magnet ores, but structural and machine parts require alloy steels.

Carbon, sulfur and phosphorus, as the major undesirable elements, are removed by oxidation, the carbon and sulfur as gases and the phosphorus by combination of the oxide with basic oxides from the furnace lining or flux addition.

More than 50% of the steel made today is made by the open hearth process. In this process, several hundred tons of molten pig iron, steel scrap, limestone and iron ore are charged; the limestone reacts with the phosphorus and the iron ore furnishes oxygen. As the reaction proceeds, the molten mass "boils" as a result of CO evolution. The reaction may take 4 to 20 hours. Oxygen lances inserted in the furnace roof are used in newer furnaces to supplement the oxygen supply. (See Figure VIA-2.)

Various types of converters in which air and/or oxygen are blown onto or through molten iron are also used which require no external heating and permit much shorter process times. The earliest of these was the Bessemer converter which however contaminated the steel with nitrides from the nitrogen in the air which was blown through the charge. Blowing oxygen through the charge would result in excessive temperature rise so surface blowing of oxygen (which may contain powdered lime flux) is used in newer converters such as the Austrian-developed LD converter. (See Figure VIA-2.)

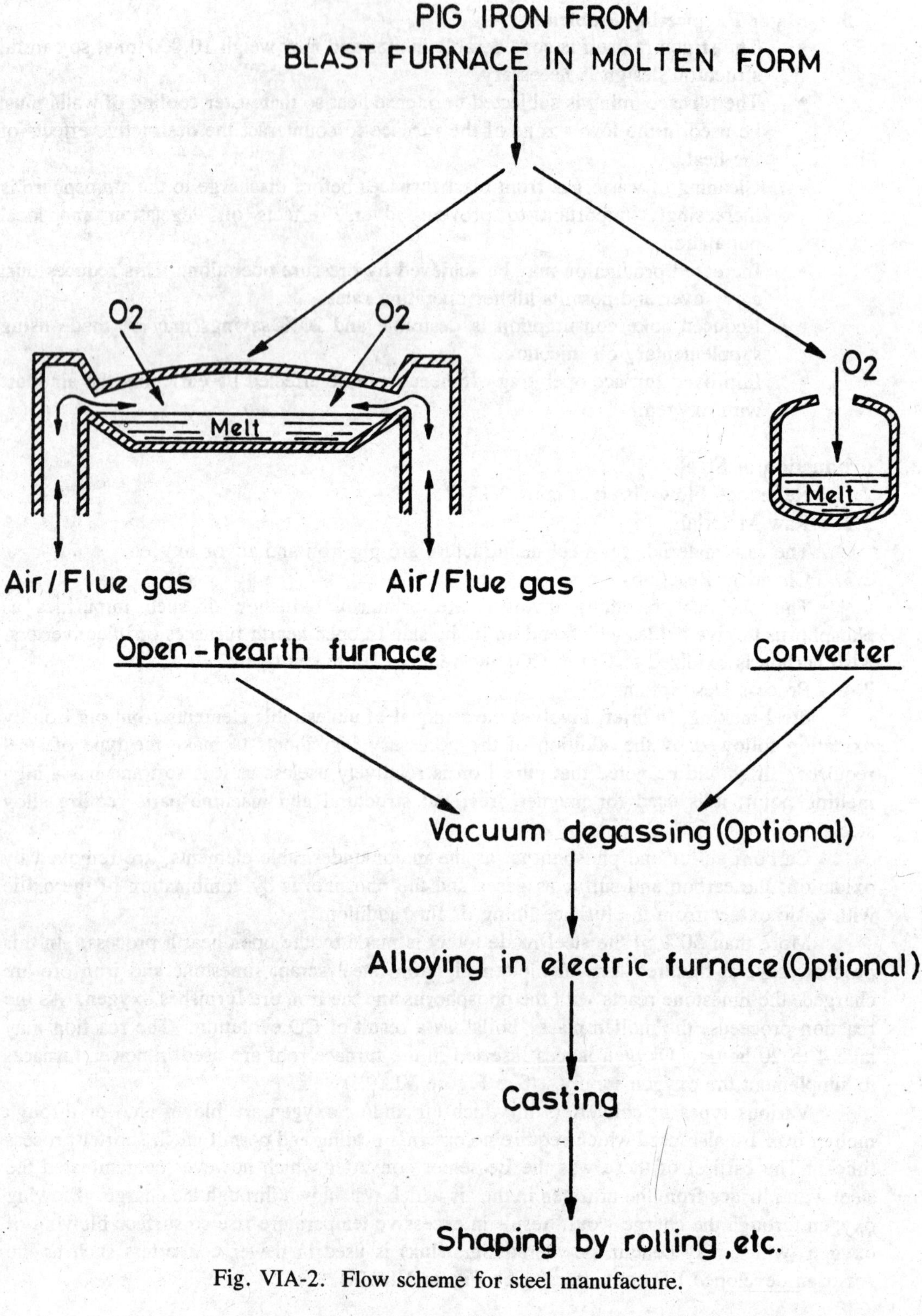

Fig. VIA-2. Flow scheme for steel manufacture.

2.5. Major Engineering Problems

- Minimization of nitrogen content of the steel produced by using oxygen-steam mixtures in place of air is desirable. The nitrogen content, if present, causes embrittlement of the steel product.
- Mixing of the oxygen with the slag which can be improved by using a rotating horizontal or tilted converter. This also permits the lining of the converter to operate at a lower average temperature, lengthening its life.

2.6. Economics

The total output of the Indian steel industry in 1993-94 was approximately Rs. 250 billion, which comprised roughly 15% of value added by the Indian manufacturing sector. India now has an installed capacity of around 24 million tons of steel, and produces around 16 million tons of saleable steel. The growth rate of the industry in 1994-97 is likely to be around 5%, with 10% growth for flat products and 3% growth for long/round products.

Steel is a core industry, tightly linked to the state of the local economy. Currently, there is a glut in the industry worldwide, with total installed capacity far exceeding demand. However, transportation costs being very high, local production is cheaper and greenfield sites are still coming up in the developing world. The developed world is moving towards customized production even at lower overall capacity utilization. In terms of production, plants in the USA, UK (British Steel) and France (Usinor) produce less than those in Japan (23 million tons Nippon Steel) and Korea (18 million tons POSCO). China, with new plants in Baoshan and Shenzen, may soon be the world's largest producer.

India today ranks tenth among the steel producing countries of the world. This is a tremendous improvement from the 16th position a decade ago. But India's per capita consumption at 24 kg is still one of the lowest in the world. Our presence in the global steel trade is barely one percent. On the other hand, India's natural advantage for steel making is well-known. The country has abundant basic raw materials such as iron ore and fluxes; a vast pool of skilled manpower and an established expertise in steel production. The moot question is, "can India become a global leader in the steel industry in the next century?" according to the "Hindu Survey of Indian Industry" (1995).

The currently available projection of domestic demand for finished steel is 23 million tons in 1996-97, 31 million tons in 2001-02 and 42 million tons in 2006-07. Compared to the 1993-94 consumption level of around 15 million tons, this represents a fairly high growth. The steel market will be characterized by low import tariff rates and relatively free trade flows. The magnitude of the demand projection also signifies the expected penetration of the steel market in the rural areas.

The Indian steel industry can be divided into two phases—preliberalization and post. Preliberalization saw the government owned Joint Plant Committee (JPC) controlling licensing of facilities, price of end products, freight-equalization and establishment of the Steel Development Fund for upgradation/expansion of facilities. The major players were Steel Authority of India Limited (SAIL), and Tata Iron and Steel Company Limited (TISCO), with a host of secondary steel makers and rerollers who processed their products. The government fully decontrolled the industry in January 1992. The steel sector now comprises 7 integrated plants and around 180 mini-mills and rerollers, 77 of which are listed on the country's stock exchanges.

The production of saleable pig iron by various units in the past few years in the country was as follows:

Production of Saleable Pig Iron (Lakh M.T.)

Name of Unit	Production During the Year			
	1986-87	1987-88	1988-89	1989-90
Bhilai Steel Plant	3.14	2.02	2.91	3.21
Durgapur Steel Plant	1.53	1.79	1.29	2.07
Rourkela Steel Plant	0.60	0.97	0.68	0.72
Bokaro Steels Ltd.	6.42	6.41	3.45	3.90
Indian Iron & Steel	0.92	0.84	1.70	2.43
Others	1.13	1.21	1.24	NA
Total	*13.74*	*13.24*	*11.27*	*12.33*

Source: "SBP Handbook of Projects for Corporate Diversification" (1992)

According to the Economic Survey 1990-91, the production of saleable pig iron decreased from 1.23 million tons in 1989-90 to 0.87 million tons in 1990-91, whereas the demand for pig iron increased from 1.75 million tons to 1.85 million tons. The shortfall of 0.98 million tons was only slightly covered with imports of 0.17 million tons of pig iron in 1990-91.

There are at present about 4,200 foundries in the country with an annual installed capacity of about 2.4 million tons of castings. The demand for pig iron for the manufacture of castings, etc., in 1991-92 was estimated at about 1.9 million tons out of which about 1.4 million tons was available from indigenous sources including 0.3 million tons from IISCO and 0.5 million tons may have been imported.

According to industry circles, the demand for pig iron is expected to rise at about 20% per annum. It is expected to rise from 19.00 lakh tons in 1991-92 to 22.00 lakh M.T., 28.00 lakh M.T. and 35.70 lakh M.T. in 1994-95, 1999-2000 and 2004-2005 respectively.

The imports of pig iron in 1989-90 and 1990-91 were 0.36 million tons and 0.17 million tons respectively. The imports were lower because of a stiffer import duty.

The availability of pig iron from the integrated steel plants, however, is expected to decrease because most of the units would like to convert the hot metal into steel to the maximum extent possible for value-added steel products.

Taking into account, the indigenous availability of pig iron at 1.7 million tons in 1995 and 1.1 million tons in 2000 from the integrated steel plants, there is scope for creating capacity for the production of 2.3 million tons pig iron in 1995 and 2.9 million tons pig iron in 2000.

Indeed the worldwide trend is away from large integrated steel plants to so-called mini-steel plants. These mini-mills do not require huge and expensive hot blast furnaces and do require a much smaller work force to monitor and adjust the newer type of equipment. Not only are the new mills less capital-intensive, but they have production cycles measured in hours rather than days, allowing them to meet changing market demands more easily. The new mills require less than one half a man hour per ton of steel produced, whereas even the most efficient integrated mills require more than two man hours per ton. Mini-mills in 1995 represent 25% of U.S. steel making capacity and the trend is upward worldwide. The new mini-mills are fed with direct-reduced ore plus scrap.

In India, at the end of 1988, there were 163 mini-steel units in the country with an installed capacity of 46 lakh tons of steel ingots/billets per annum. A further capacity of 20 lakh tons was approved through issue of new letters of intent/industrial licenses.

The total production of steel by mini-steel plants in 1988-89 was only 3.0 million tons against their installed capacity of about 4.6 million tons and a production target of 3.85 million tons. This was due to acute shortage of steel scrap. Against an annual requirement of 5.5 million tons of scrap, the indigenous availability was only about 2 million tons.

The total production of finished steel increased from 10.5 million tons in 1985-86 to 12.85 million tons in 1989-90. Of this production, SAIL accounted for around 6.97 million tons and the rest was by TISCO and the mini-steel plants. In 1989-90, the mini-steel plants produced about 4 million tons of steel.

In India, the per capita consumption of steel is about 20 kg as against 60 kg in China and 600 to 700 kg in developed countries.

The mini-steel sector is expected to produce about 11.03 million tons of steel and the integrated steel plants about 13.06 million tons.

Mini-steel plants are fed with a mixture of sponge iron and scrap iron. Sponge iron is made by using either coal or gas as the reducing agent for iron ore. The producers of sponge iron in India include the following:

Essar Gujarat in Hazira, Gujarat
Usha Ispat at Redi, Maharashtra
Grasim Industries in Raigad District, Maharashtra

The producers of iron and steel in India are:

Iron Ore & Concentrate	Company	Location
	Chowgule & Co. Pvt. Ltd.	Goa
	Dempo Mining Corp. Ltd.	do
	V.M. Salgaocar & Bros. Pvt. Ltd.	do
	Indian Iron & Steel Co. Ltd.	Singhbhum Dist., Bihar
	Kudremukh Iron Ore Co. Ltd.	Chikmagalur Dist., Karnataka
	National Mineral Dev. Corp. Ltd.	Bellary Dist., Karnataka
	Steel Authority of India Ltd.	Singhbhum Dist., Bihar
	do	Bastar and Durg Dist., M.P.
	do	Keonjhar Dist., Orissa
	Tata Iron & Steel Co. Ltd.	Singhbhum Dist., Bihar
	do	Keonjhar Dist., Orissa

Primary Steel	Company	Location
	Steel Authority of India Ltd.	Bhilai, Durg Dist., M.P.
	do	Bokaro, Bihar
	Tata Iron & Steel Co. Ltd.	Jamshedpur, Singhbhum Dist., Bihar
	Rashtriya Ispat Nigam Ltd.	Visakhapatnam, Andhra Pradesh
	159 private mini-steel plants	Countrywide

Source: "Mineral Industries of Asia & the Pacific," U.S. Bureau of Mines (1992)

The Visakhapatnam Steel Plant (VSP) was the first to be implemented by Steel Authority of India Ltd. (SAIL). In 1982, Rashtriya Ispat Nigam Ltd. (RINL) was incorporated in the public sector and became a sole correspondent for the establishing VSP. The plant design adopted the most modern technology, including a 3,200-m^3 blast furnace, dry quenching of coke with auxiliary power generation facilities, torpedo ladle for steel melt shop, in addition to conventional mixer, cast house slag granulation for blast furnace, and 100% continuous casting of liquid steel. VSP was dedicated on August 1, 1992.

The plant of Rashtriya Ispat Nigam Ltd. is an interesting new development in the Indian steel industry in many ways. It includes involvement by Ispat International which is based in Jakarta, Indonesia. It also includes involvement by the Mittal family who have a large interest in Ispat International which is one of the largest private steel producers in Indonesia.

The Vizag or VSP plant as it is variously designated is more modern than the plants of SAIL and TISCO. For example, the entire steel output is produced through the continuous casting process which consumes less energy per ton than the open hearth-ingot casting route. The modern design permits employment levels of only 17,000 compared to nearly thrice that number for similar capacity plants at SAIL and TISCO according to the Hindu Survey of Indian Industry for 1995.

VIB. ALUMINUM

Aluminum is a non-ferrous metal with unique applications. Its application is growing in the recent times. The long term growth potentials for aluminum are excellent. The aluminum, because of its inherent strengths, is going to become as one of the most economical and versatile means for multi-faceted applications. Aluminum has emerged as a substitute and complementary material in the following market segments: electric power transmission, electrical power generation, transport by air, rail, road and water, architecture, engineering, construction, communication, canning, packaging, alloys, explosives, defense, utensils and as a substitute for wood, tinplate, etc. Aluminum has made inroads into all of these applications with varying level of market penetrations.

1. Alumina Production as a Raw Material for Aluminum Manufacture

The major source of aluminum oxide (alumina or Al_2O_3) used in electrolytic reduction cells is bauxite, a 50-60% Al_2O_3 ore with the balance as silica and iron ore. The purification process for electrolytic cell-grade alumina will be discussed first.

1.1. Reference Flow Sheet: Figure VIB-1

1.2. Chemical Reactions

(a) $6NaOH\ (aq) + Al_2O_3\ (s) \rightarrow 2Na_3AlO_3 + H_2O$

(b) $Na_3AlO_3 + 3H_2O \rightarrow 3NaOH + Al(OH)_3$

(c) $2Al(OH)_3 \rightarrow Al_2O_3\ (purified) + 3H_2O$

1.3. Raw Materials

The only major raw material is bauxite which is transported from nearby Indian deposits. Minor quantities of make-up sodium hydroxide are required.

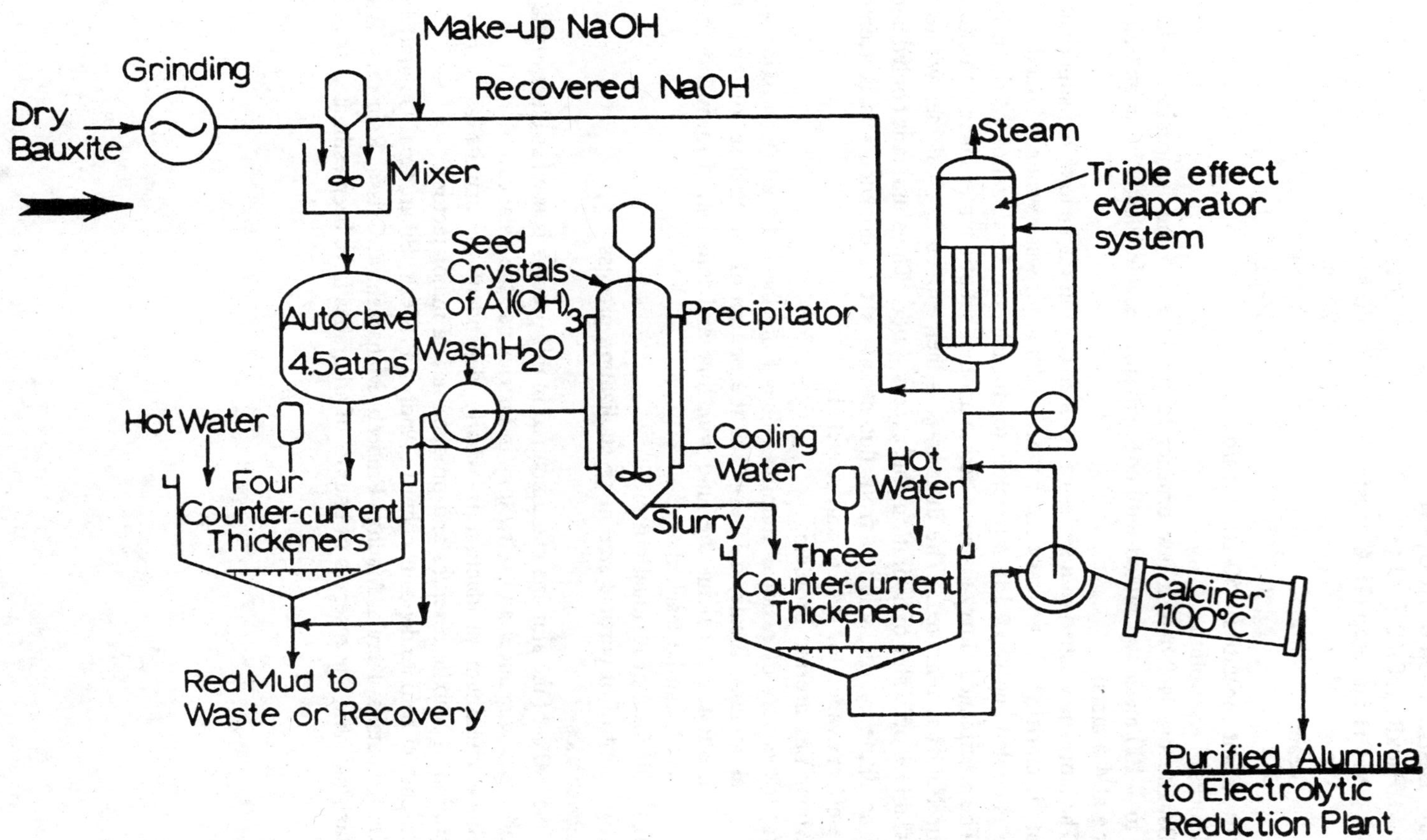

Fig. VIB-1. Purification of alumina from bauxite by Bayer process.

1.4. Quantitative Requirements

(a) Basis: 1 ton of $Al_2O_3 \cdot 3H_2O$

Bauxite (50-60% Al_2O_3)	1.3 tons
NaOH make-up (76% caustic)	40 kg
Water	24 tons
Steam	6 tons
Power	160 KWH

(b) Plant capacities: 50-200 tons/day

1.5. Process Description

Bauxite ore is fed to a jaw crusher to produce 2-5 cm lump size. These are wet ground to —100 mesh and mixed with concentrated recycle caustic in an autoclave-digestor operating at 4.5 atms.

The slurry is washed in a series of counter-current thickeners; the supernatant sodium aluminate is clarified via a rotary filter where additional wash water is added. The diluted mixture is cooled and seeded in a precipitator to induce crystallization of the trihydrate.

The precipitated slurry matrix is fed to another set of counter-current thickeners where all of the NaOH is removed. The underpass is then moved to a calciner where heating to 1,100°C drives off water of hydration plus excess water. The alumina is cooled and shipped.

The dilute caustic solution from this second set of thickeners is concentrated in a multiple-effect evaporator system and recycled.

1.6. Major Engineering Problems

(a) Recovery of residual alumina values from the red mud (iron oxide and sodium aluminum silicate) discharged at the bottom of the first set of thickeners. One method is to calcine the mud with lime and soda ash to form sodium aluminate which can be leached.

(b) Disposal of residual red mud

(c) Control of particle size in crystallization process

1.7. Economics

Over 90% of the alumina manufactured in this process is used as electrolytic reduction plant cell feed. Chemical and refractory industries use the balance.

Since aluminum production is wholly dependent on bauxite as a raw material, consideration of bauxite reserves and production is a major factor.

Important bauxite deposits occur in Andhra Pradesh, Bihar, Goa, Gujarat, Jammu and Kashmir, Karnataka, Kerala, Madhya Pradesh, Maharashtra, Orissa, Rajasthan, Tamil Nadu and Uttar Pradesh. The reserves of bauxite of all grades have been estimated at 265.37 crore tons.

Table VIB-1
Production of Bauxite
(Tons)

Year	BALCO	NALCO	INDAL	HINDALCO	MALCO
1988-89	350,816 (164,133)	1,748,450	720,585	681,636	N.A.
1989-90	246,965 (253,035)	2,230,041	752,767	723,945	66,584
1990-91	250,729 (280,731)	1,920,000	693,073	504,771	89,816
1991-92 (April-Dec. '91)	156,389 (261,108)	1,226,620	354,139	600,264	N.A.

Figures in brackets indicate purchases from outside sources.
Source: "Economic Times"

Table VIB-2
Bauxite Reserves
(Million Tons)

States	Total	Metallurgical grade
Orissa	1,501	1,252
Andhra Pradesh	597	499
Madhya Pradesh	166	99
Bihar	56	41
Maharashtra	82	68
Gujarat	14	10
Karnataka & Goa	19	13
TN, UP, Kerala & Rajasthan	9	5

Source: "Economic Times"

The producers of bauxite in India are:

		Annual Capacity in Metric Tons
Bharat Aluminum Co. Ltd.	Asansol, W.B.	200
do	Bilaspur, Madhya Pradesh	600
Bombay Mineral Supply Co. (Pvt.) Ltd	Jamnagar, Gujarat	150
Hindustan Aluminum Co. Ltd.	Ranchi, Bihar	300
do	Shandol, Madhya Pradesh	300
Indian Aluminum Co. Ltd.	Kalharpur, Maharashtra	250
do	Ranchi, Bihar	250
Madras Aluminum Co. Ltd.	Salem, Mettur Dam Tamil Nadu	150
Minerals & Minerals Ltd.	Ranchi, Bihar	200
National Aluminum Co. Ltd.	Panchpatmali, Orissa	2,400

2. Aluminum

2.1. Reference Flow Sheet: Figure VIB-2

2.2. Chemical Reactions

(a) $2Al_2O_3$ (s) + 3C (s) → 4Al (1) + $3CO_2$ (g); $\Delta H = +470$ Kcal

(b) C + CO_2 → 2CO

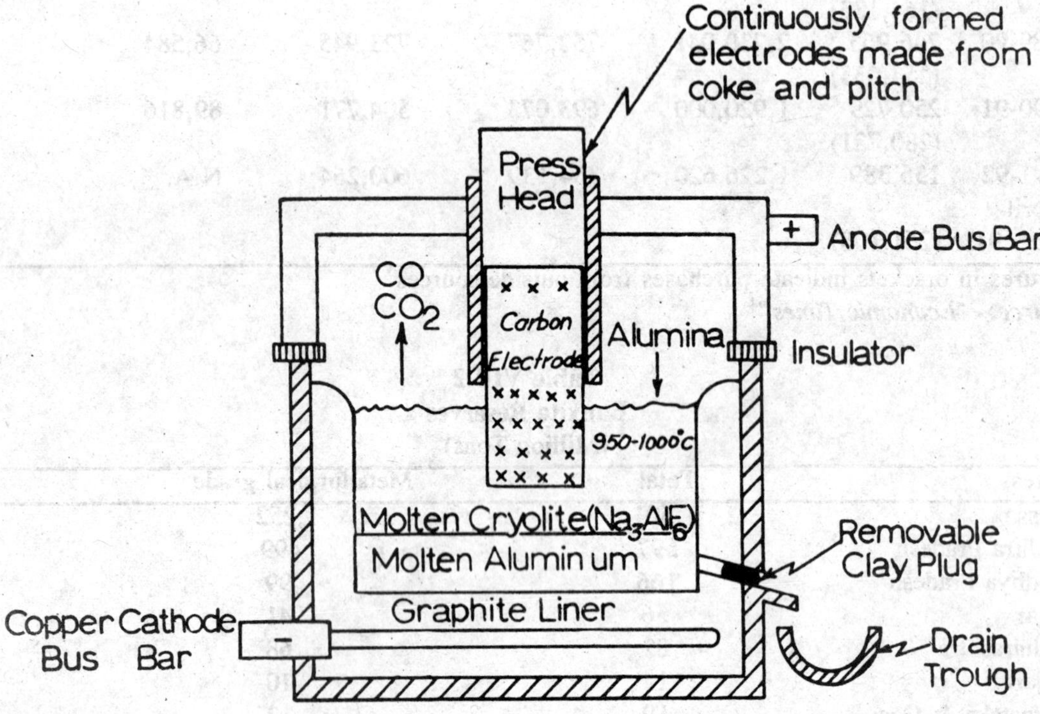

Fig. VIB-2. Electrolytic aluminum smelting cell.

2.3. Raw Materials

Purified bauxite as per Figure VIB-1, electrode materials (coke, pitch, and tar), cryolite flux ($AlF_3 \cdot 3NaF$).

2.4. Quantitative Requirements

Basis: 1 ton of aluminum

Alumina (99% Al_2O_3)	2.25 tons
Coke	0.5-0.6 ton
Tar and Pitch	20-30 kg
Cryolite	40 kg
Electricity (DC)	22,000 KWH

2.5. Electrolytic Cell Designation

$$\underset{\text{Anode}}{\overset{}{C}}\ \Big|\ Al_2O_3 \cdot AlF_3 \cdot 3NaF\ \vdots\ Al\ (l)\ \Big|\ \underset{\text{Cathode}}{C}\ ;\ E_r = 2.8 \text{ volts}$$

+ Anode ⟶ − Cathode

2.6. Process Description

A molten cryolite bath is maintained at 950-1,000°C and alumina is dumped periodically into each cell to keep a 3-5% Al_2O_3 concentration.

Reduction takes place at the graphite anodes. These are either fed continuously or replaced batch-wise as they erode. The aluminum drops to the bottom of the cell and is periodically tapped off.

The purity of this aluminum is not greater than 99.7% which is poor quality for electric conductor usage. It is refined in a similar type electrolytic cell with this designation:

$$\mathrm{C} \;\Big|\; \text{Al-Cu (1), } AlF_3 \cdot 3NaF \cdot BaF_2 \;\; Al_2O_3 \;\vdots\; \text{Al (1)} \;\Big|\; \mathrm{C}$$

$$\overset{+}{\text{Anode}} \longrightarrow \overset{-}{\text{Cathode}}$$

The aluminum-copper alloy on the bottom of the cell is tapped periodically and replenished with low purity aluminum. The high purity (99.9%) aluminum floats to the top and is drained off under $CO\text{-}CO_2$ atmosphere.

The normal operating voltage per cell is 5-7 volts with 40-100 cells in series, using direct current of 8,000 to 50,000 amperes, depending on the cell size.

The power supply for these systems is AC converted to DC by mercury arc rectifiers, or semiconductor converters such as silicon rectifiers.

2.7. Major Engineering Problems

(a) Scale-up of cells to get more capacity per unit.
(b) Minimizing of voltage and current losses to increase energy efficiency, η_E which should be 85-87%.
(c) Devising more effective ways to feed and remove materials from the high temperature cells.
(d) Development of better cell liners.
(e) Minimize loss of cell liquids by gas carry-off.

2.8. Economics

There are four major primary producers and around twenty secondary producers. The two public sector undertakings are Bharat Aluminum Company Limited (Balco) & National Aluminum Company Limited (Nalco). The private sector companies are Indian Aluminum Company Limited (Indal) & Hindalco Industries Limited (Hindalco).

Power is the single most critical cost element, constituting around 40% of the total cost of production. Thus, consumption efficiency and unit cost of power are critical to operating efficiency. All the primary producers have captive power generation facilities. However, only Hindalco & Nalco are nearly self-sufficient. Indal is largely dependent on State Electricity Boards (SEB). Nalco is reputed to be the world's cheapest producer of bauxite at \$7/ton. Hindalco & Nalco compare favorably with the efficient international manufacturers having cost of production of around \$1,000-\$1,100/ton.

The Indian aluminum industry consisting of two major units in the public sector and three units in the private sector has an aggregate installed capacity of 4.71 lakh tons. The total availability of aluminum metal was expected to rise from 362,000 tons in 1986 to 580,000 tons in 1990.

	Aluminum Production	(Thousand tons)
1985-86		264.8
1986-87		257.3
1987-88		290.0
Projected Figures		
1988-89		400.00
1989-90		470.00
1994-95		580.00*
1999-2000		580.00*

*If no additional capacity is created

	Imports of Aluminum	(Thousand tons)
1985-86		31
1986-87		65
1987-88		55
1988-89		10
Projected		
1994-95		35
1999-2000		2,70

	Installed Capacity	(Thousand tons)
1987-88		362
1988-89		580
1989-90		610
1994-95		610
1999-2000		610

Source: "Kothari's Industrial Directory of India" (1994)

The per capita consumption of aluminum in India is a paltry 400 gm. This compares unfavorably with 10 kg in Canada, 11 kg in the U.K., 11.5 kg in West Germany and 17 kg in the U.S.A. The per capita consumption of South Asian countries has also been placed at between 5 to 7 kg. The total consumption of aluminum which was 2.53 lakh tons in 1985 was likely to be 4 lakh tons in 1990. The demand for aluminum is expected to reach 6.42 lakh tons in 1995 and 10.13 lakh tons in 2000.

The consumption of aluminum in electrical sector is likely to go down from 42.27 percent in 1990 to 37.35 percent in 1995 and 32.07 percent in 2000 since many states have nearly completed rural electrification. The demand for alumina in packaging is placed at 31,600 tons in 1995 put at a modest level. In building and structure, the demand for aluminum is likely to be 54,200 tons in 1995 and 119,300 tons in 2000. In consumer durables, the demand for aluminum is expected to reach 112,750 tons in 2000. The actual use and pace of consumption of aluminum could further be enhanced by intensifying research and development, application, engineering and other necessary programs. The sectors like aerospace, defense, exports also offer exciting potentials for the growth of aluminum.

Projected Demand for Aluminum (1990-2000) in tons

Sector	1985	1990	1995	2000
Electrical	120,000 (47.34)	170,000 (42.27)	240,000 (37.35)	325,000 (32.07)
Transport	43,570 (17.19)	81,790 (20.34)	142,000 (22.10)	232,000 (22.89)
Utensils	24,700 (9.74)	39,800 (9.90)	64,100 (9.98)	103,250 (10.90)
Consumer Durables	19,150 (7.55)	35,600 (8.55)	62,750 (9.76)	112,750 (11.13)
Packaging	18,900 (7.45)	25,050 (6.23)	31,600 (4.91)	39,950 (3.94)
Building and Structure	12,050 (4.75)	22,150 (5.51)	54,200 (8.43)	119,300 (11.77)
Coinage	765 (0.30)	1,065 (0.26)	1,445 (0.22)	2,000 (0.19)
Others	14,350 (5.66)	26,700 (6.64)	46,300 (7.26)	78,950 (7.79)
Total	253,485 (100)	402,155 (100)	642,395 (100)	1,013,200 (100)

Figures in brackets refer to the percentage share in respective applications.
Source: "Kothari's Industrial Directory of India" (1994)

The producers of aluminum metal in India are:

		Capacity Thousand Metric Tons/Year
Bharat Aluminum Co. Ltd.	Korba, Madhya Pradesh	100
Hindalco Aluminum Co. Ltd.	Renukoot, Uttar Pradesh	150
Indian Aluminum Co. Ltd.	Alipuram, Kerala	20
do	Belgaum, Karnataka	73
do	Hirakud, Orissa	24

Madras Aluminum Co. Ltd.	Salem, Mettur Dam, Tamil Nadu	25
National Aluminum Co. Ltd.	Angul, Dhenkanal Dist., Orissa	218

Indian Aluminum Co. (INDAL) suspended operations at its Belgaum plant in Karnataka because of a steep increase in the cost of power in 1992. Bharat Aluminum Co. (BALCO) and INDAL were plagued by power shortages. The Public Investment Board approved National Aluminum Co.'s (NALCO) $370 million plan to expand its bauxite mines and alumina refinery at Damanjodi in District Koraput of Orissa. The mining capacity will be doubled to 4.8 Mmt/a and the refinery capacity expanded from 860,000 mt/a to 1,35 Mmt/a. It will take more than 4 years to complete the expansion. The Government of India scrubbed plans for a 600,000-mt/a bauxite mine at Gandhmardan in Orissa in the wake of local agitation against its environmental impact.

NALCO, India's largest aluminum producer, exported 423,000 tons of alumina and 85,496 tons of aluminum of its output of 800,000 tons and 192,000 tons, respectively, in fiscal 1992-93. The Government estimated that the demand of aluminum would be 575,000 tons in 1994-95 and 855,000 tons in the year 2000. BALCO and NALCO have plans to raise their respective capacities by 50,000 tons and 115,000 tons to 150,000 tons and 333,000 tons in 1995, respectively.

VIC. COPPER

Copper is one of the most important non-ferrous metals and has wide domestic and industrial applications. It is used in the electrical industry as well as other industries like non-ferrous castings, heat transfer equipment and bearing material. It is estimated that nearly half of the total annual world production is consumed by the electrical industry. The other half is either alloyed with other metals for diverse uses like fans and coolers or used in making pots, utensils and domestic wares.

Copper occurs in nature in the form of various oxide and sulfide ores. In India, the predominant ore is chalcopyrite, $CuFeS_2$. The ore concentration step is shown in Figure VIC-1.

1. Copper Ores and Scrap Sources

Integrated development of copper reserves in Singhbhum (Bihar) and expansion of Malanjkhand (Madhya Pradesh) copper project will be the two major projects during the Eighth Plan period to double copper production in the country. Once these projects are completed, copper production is expected to increase to 97,000 tons by 1994-95. A long term strategy has been proposed for the integrated development of Singhbhum Copper reserves. Expansion of Malanjkhand project involves setting up of a complex for mining, smelting, and refining of copper. At present, the ore from the mine is converted into concentrates and transported to Khetri smelter in Rajasthan for smelting. Schemes are afoot to re-operationalize the Khetri and Ghatsila smelters to enable them to produce according to their actual installed capacities of 31,000 tons and 16,500 tons respectively.

More than 90 percent of the copper resources of the country are confined in three states, namely, Bihar 46 percent, Rajasthan 20 percent and Madhya Pradesh 25 percent. Assuming a sustained three percent growth of demand after 2000 A.D., the total quantity of copper needed for the next 30 years would be 11 million tons. The satisfaction of demand based on prospective hypothetical resources would be from 38 percent to 44 percent provided prospective ore is available.

The lead, zinc and copper frequently are associated in ores. These are commonly mixed sulfide ores.

Copper scrap consumption in India is about 15 percent of the total copper consumption. With a view to encourage the use of scrap, the import of scrap has been liberalized over the years. Since there is an appreciable gap between demand and indigenous production of copper, increased availability of scrap would reduce imports of copper metal. By 1999-2000, copper requirement is expected to be around 292,400 MT.

2. Copper Production

Hindustan Copper Ltd. was incorporated in November, 1976, and is presently the sole indigenous producer of primary copper in the country. In 1972, management of Indian Copper Corp. Ltd., a company incorporated in England, was taken over by the Government of India and entrusted to Hindustan Copper Ltd., thus bringing under its control the copper mines and the smelter at Ghatsila in Bihar.

Hindustan Copper Ltd. has smelters and refineries at Khetri in Rajasthan and at Ghatsila in Bihar, an open cast mine and concentrator at Malanjkhand in Madhya Pradesh and a continuous cast copper wire rod plant at Taloja in Maharashtra.

A. Khetri Copper Complex

The four projects under this complex at Khetri, Kolihan, Chandmani and Dariba were commissioned between 1973 and 1975. Khetri and Kolihan mines have matching concentrator plant and smelter and electrolytic refinery and wire bar casting plant with a designed capacity of 31,000 tons per annum. The company proposes to expand its smelter and refinery from 31,000 tons per annum to 1 lakh tons per annum at cost of Rs. 200 crores.

The estimated production of ore, metal in concentrate, and refined copper (cathode) at Khetri complex during the year 1993-94 was 1,816 lakh tons, 15,433 tons and 25,200 tons respectively.

B. Indian Copper Complex (ICC)

Indian copper complex has a copper smelter of 16,500 tons per annum capacity with supporting mines at Mosabani, Pathargora, Surda, Kendadih and Rakha in district Singhbhum of Bihar. In addition to the concentrator plant, the complex consists of a 16,500 tons per annum refinery plant, 8,400 tons per annum wire bar casting plant and 54,000 tons per annum sulfuric acid plant, and brass rolling mill. There is also a precious metal recovery plant for gold, silver, selenium, tellurium and nickel sulfate. Copper sulfate is also produced by copper dust generated in the smelter. With the objective of expanding the Kendadih mine in Singhbhum belt from 200 tons per day to 700 tons per day, the main winder for the mine has already been commissioned. The interconnected development is in progress and commercial production is expected during 1994-95.

The producers of copper in India are:

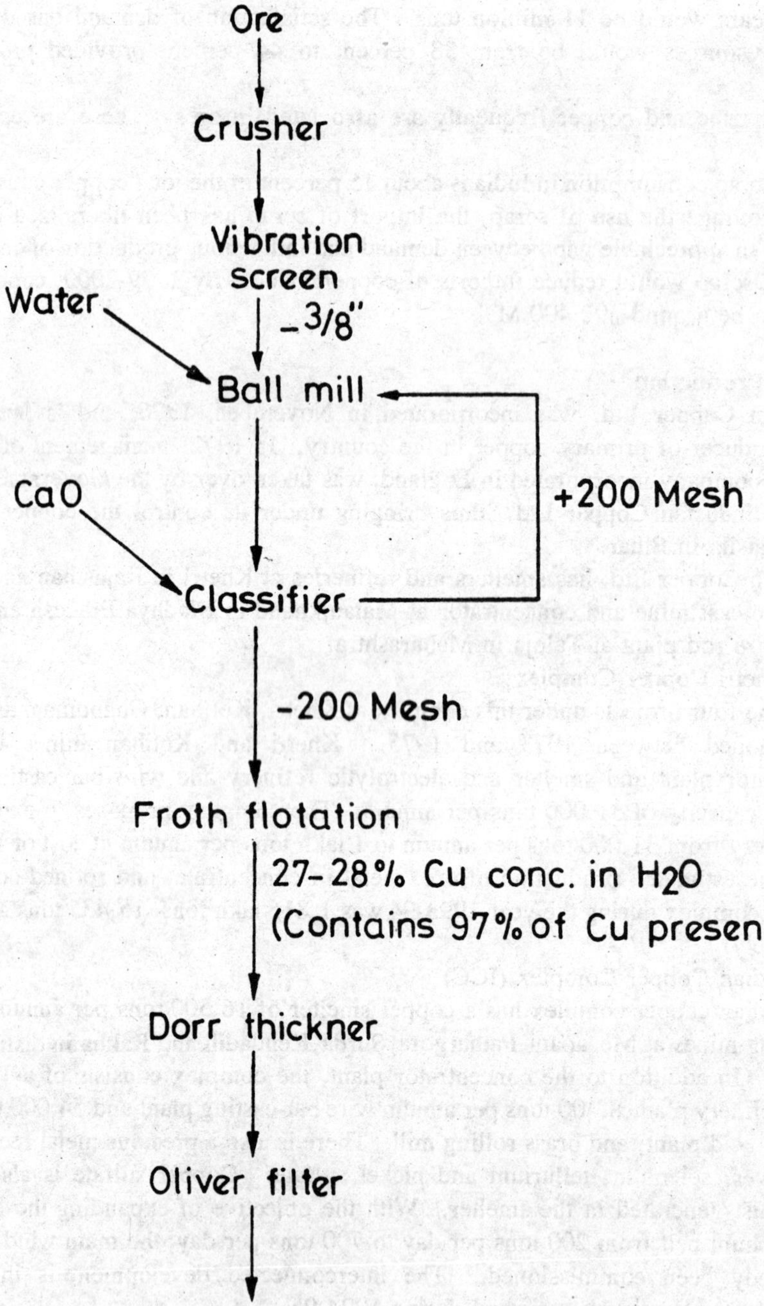

Fig. VIC-1. Flow scheme for copper ore concentrate.

	Location	Annual capacity thousand metric tons
Copper Ore		
	Khetri Copper Complex, Jhunjhunu District, Rajasthan:	
	Khetri Mine	825
	Kolihan Mine	825
	Chandmani Mine	330
	Indian Copper Complex, Singhbhum District, Bihar:	
	Mosabani Mine	
	Pathargora Mine	1,800
	Surda Mine	
	Kendadih Mine	
	Rakha Mine	
	Malanjkhand, Balahhar District, Madhya Pradesh	2,000
Copper Metal	Khetri Smelter, Rajasthan	31
	Maubhandar Smelter, Ghatsila District, Bihar	20

Source: "Mineral Industries of Asia & the Pacific," U.S. Bureau of Mines (1992)

VID. LEAD

Lead is an important strategic metal because it has got both civil and military applications. In terms of tonnage used, lead ranks fourth among the non-ferrous metals. Its main use is in automobile batteries. The largest use of lead is in batteries. Consumer preference, environmental regulation and energy conservation innovations have brought about a number of changes. The increasing use of electric trucks at airports, hospitals, warehouses and for delivery purposes, will certainly increase demand for lead batteries. Lead-acid traction batteries in railway applications will continue to be in demand.

Lead has been used as a sheathing material on cables to prevent ingress of moisture. Lead antimony alloy bricks are used in nuclear power plants to protect human beings from radiation. Lead is also used in the disposal of nuclear wastes. Lead-tin solders are used for joining purposes in electronics, computers, etc. Architects have been using lead in construction, for insulating sound. Lead compounds have been used in the ceramic industry. They impart low surface tension and low viscosity over a wide temperature range, which results in smoothness and adds luster and brilliance to the object. Lead is used as a lining on steel tanks and vessels that store acids because it is chemically corrosion resistant. Lead-based paints are used extensively in structural, marine and industrial application.

1. Production

Mines under production are Mochia, Balania, Zawarmala, Rajpura-Dariba, Agnigundala, Sargipalli and Rangpo, which have a plant capacity of 7,840 TPD ore. With existing ore reserves of 54.54 million tons, these mines have lives from 9 to 27 years.

Deposits under formulation at Ambmata and Rampura-Agucha have demonstrated ore reserves of 58.21 million tons. With a projected plant capacity of 3,700 TDP ore, these mines will have lives between 13 and 69 years. Mochia, Rajpura, Dariba and Sargipalli mines have a projected life of 9 to 10 years, based on existing ore reserves and 90 percent capacity utilization. The production of lead in 1986-87 was 19,929 tons which increased to 33,140 tons in 1991-92.

The following table brings out demand, production and imports of lead from 1986-87 to 1999-2000.

Demand, Production and Imports of Lead (in Tons)

	Demand	Production	Imports
1986-87	65,000	19,929	46,000
1987-88	49,000	20,164	29,000
1989-90 (Estimated)	80,000	65,000	15,000
1994-95	102,100	65,000	37,100
1999-2000 (Estimated)	130,300	65,000	65,300

Source: Financial Express

The producers of lead in India are:

Lead Concentrate	Hindustan Zinc Ltd.	Guntur District, Andhra Pradesh	10
Do	do	Udaipur District, Rajasthan	20
Lead Metal, Primary	do	Visakhapatnam, Andhra Pradesh	22
Do	do	Tundoo, near Ghatsila, Bihar	8

2. Consumption

The per capita consumption of lead in India has continued to be low at 0.07 kg. It is 5.14 kg in the USA, 5.12 kg in West Germany, 1.08 kg in the Republic of Korea and 0.219 kg in China. The world average is around 1.3 kg of lead. According to the Applied Economic Research Studies, the per capita consumption of lead is expected to go up to 1.7 kg by the turn of the century.

Break Up of Lead Consumption in India

	(percent)
Batteries	42
Cables	22
Paints	10
Sheets/Pipes	10
Industrial Alloys	8
Miscellaneous	8

Source: "Kothari's Industrial Directory of India" (1994)

VIE. ZINC

Zinc is the third most extensively used non-ferrous metal next to aluminum and copper. Since zinc tends to lose its identity in the end-product, it fails to attract the public awareness. Zinc is mainly used in coatings and castings. The future of zinc coating depends on the steel industry. Electrogalvanizing, the name given to zinc plating, when applied continuously to steel has been in use for many years. Automobile manufacturers have been using zinc coated steel more extensively on their newer models. It has been estimated that the amount of zinc coated materials in cars will increase by 70 percent between now and the end of the decade, mainly using electrogalvanizing.

The construction industry requires the zinc coating to be much thicker than in automotive applications. Thus, a construction boom is bound to give an impetus to total zinc consumption. Zinc is used in casting. The zinc die casting industry depends a lot on the automotive industry. Computers and other electronic items provide a splendid opportunity for zinc.

The identified resources in the country are estimated at 383 million tons, primarily in Rajasthan. Most of the country's mines have very low metal content compared to international norms and consequently high cost of concentrate production.

India has been a substantial importer of zinc. However, with the commissioning of the Rampura-Agucha mining complex and zinc-lead smelter at Chanderiya, Rajasthan by Hindustan Zinc Limited (HZL), an additional capacity of 70,000 TPA has been added. With this, India has become nearly self-sufficient in zinc and imports have fallen substantially.

Primary zinc production in India is being carried on by Hindustan Zinc Ltd. in the public sector (see Figure VIE-1) and Cominco Binani Zinc Ltd. in the private sector. The principal objectives of Hindustan Zinc Ltd. are mining and smelting of lead zinc metal and production of allied products. The company owns seven mines and operates three smelters. The mines are: (1) The Zawar group of mines in Rajasthan; (2) Matan rockphosphate mine also in Rajasthan; (3) Agnigundala lead mines in Andhra Pradesh; (4) the Rajpura-Dariba mines in Rajasthan which are under development; (5) Gangipalli lead mines in Orissa, also under development; (6) Rampura-Agucha deposits under exploration in Rajasthan; and (7) Baroi deposits in Rajasthan which are also in exploration stage. The corporation also operates a zinc smelter in Debari in Rajasthan, a lead smelter in Tundoo in Bihar and a zinc-lead smelter complex in Visakhapatnam in Andhra Pradesh.

The following table shows the zinc production, imports and demand:

Zinc Production, Imports and Demand (in tons)

Year	Production	Imports	Demand
1980-81	45,526	52,000	97,526
1986-87	76,367	61,920	138,287
1987-88	60,557	91,000	151,557
1988-89 (Estimated)	89,000	66,800	155,800
1989-90 (Estimated)	99,000	63,800	162,800
1999-2000 (Estimated)	99,000	142,000	241,000

Source: Financial Express

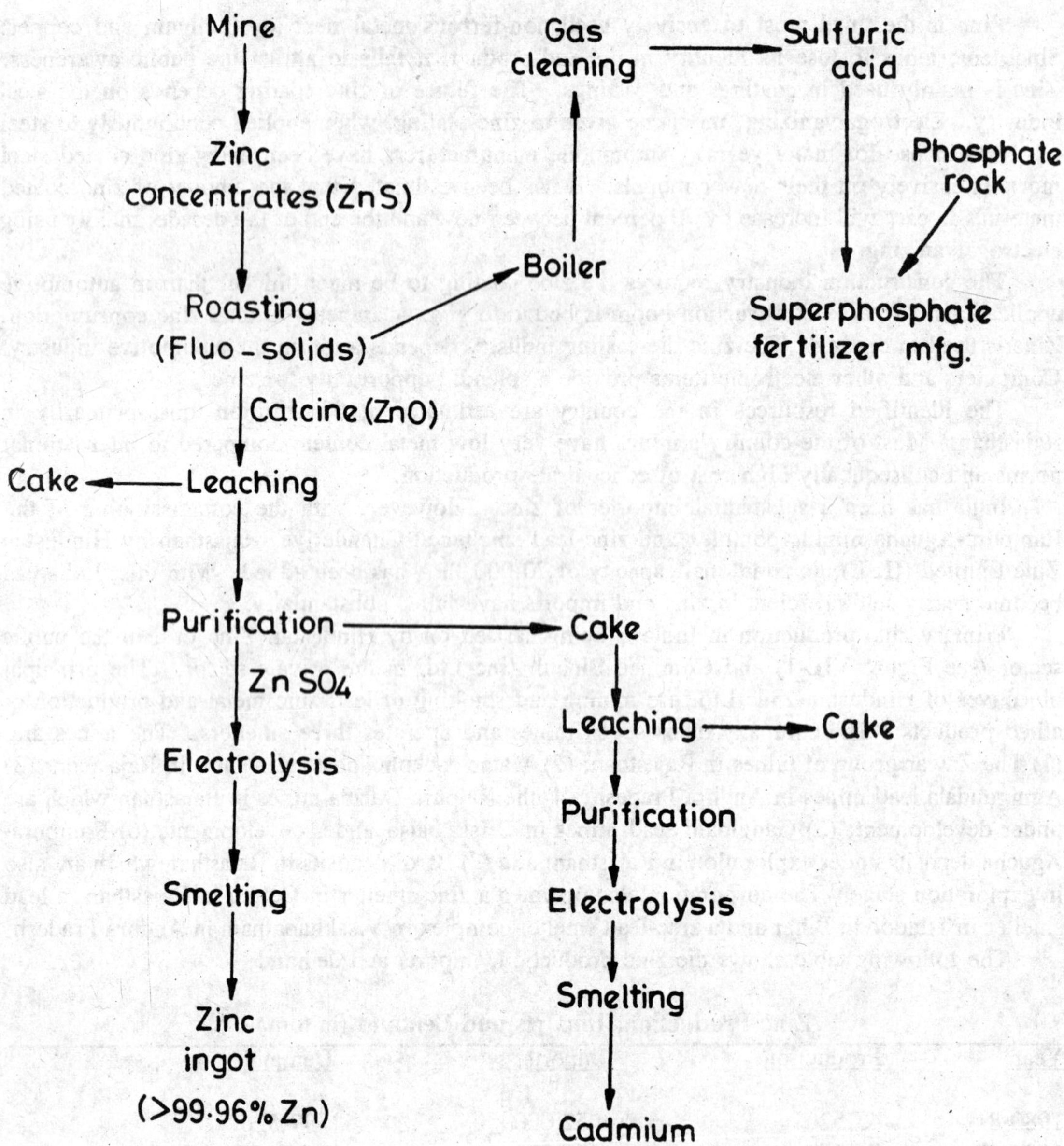

Fig. VIE-1. Flow scheme of Hindustan Zinc Plant.

In the private sector, Binani Zinc Ltd. produced zinc from imported concentrates at the Alwaye plant in Kerala. The company modernized and expanded the plant to increase its capacity to 20,000 mt/a. Indian Lead Ltd., which has two plants at Thane in Maharashtra and at Kalipara in West Bengal with a total installed capacity of 24,500 mt/a, produced secondary lead from indigenous and imported lead scrap and lead concentrates.

The producers of zinc in India are:

	Company	Location	Production in Tons
Zinc Concentrate	Hindustan Zinc Ltd.	Zawar, Udaipur District, Rajasthan	34,000
Do	do	Rajpura-Dariba, Udaipur District, Rajasthan	42,000
Zinc Metal	Cominco Binani Zinc Ltd.	Binanipuram, near Alwaye, Kerala	17,000
Do	Hindustan Zinc Ltd.	Debari, Udaipur District, Rajasthan	49,000
Do	do	Visakhapatnam, Andhra Pradesh	30,000

Source: "Mineral Industries of Asia and the Pacific," U.S. Bureau of Mines (1992)

VII
POLLUTION CONTROL & TOXIC CHEMICALS

The manufacture of chemicals, of necessity, produces many discharges of gaseous liquid and solid materials. Some of these are merely nuisances, some have adverse effects on streams and marine life and some cause direct toxic effects.

Exposures to toxic substances are linked to a variety of health problems. The immediate effects of high level exposures for a short time include burns, rashes, nausea, loss of eyesight, and fatal poisoning. Prolonged exposure to low doses can cause chronic lung disease (e.g., from coal or cotton dust), heart disease (from exposure to cadmium or carbon monoxide), sterility (from dibromochloropropane-DBCP), and kidney, liver, brain, nerve, and other damage. Exposure to industrial solvents can cause depression, and carbon disulfide workers are associated with a higher suicide rate than the general population. Although most chemicals do not cause cancers, exposure to some has been linked to cancer. Some workers exposed to asbestos, even for a short time, have developed a rare cancer of the chest and stomach linings 30 to 40 years after initial exposure. Vinyl chloride gas is linked to a rare liver cancer, to a brain cancer, and possibly to lung cancer. Diethylstilbestrol (DES), when taken by pregnant women to prevent miscarriages, led to increased risk of vaginal cancer in their daughters and abnormal sexual organs in their sons. Methylmercury, formed by the action of bacteria in sediments on mercury metal and on mercuric ions, can cause acute poisoning, deafness, brain damage, and a range of birth defects.

A single substance can have several kinds of adverse effects, depending on the route and level of exposure. Some effects of exposure to chemicals which are produced in substantial quantities are shown in Table VII-1. Chemicals listed in the National Occupational Hazard Survey were preselected for all chemicals to which more than 100,000 workers are potentially exposed. The Toxicology Data Bank of the National Library of Medicine was then searched for evidence (human and animal) of chronic or acute effects for all targets, and the 19 substances were chosen to illustrate the multiple target effects. Other data bases could suggest different target specificity.

Table VII-1
Selected High Volume Substances and Effects of Exposure

Substance	Kidney	Liver	Central Nervous System	Reproductive System	Pulmonary System	Skin
Acetone	x	x			x	x
Acrylonitrile					x	x
Ammonia	x	x			x	x
Asbestos					x	
Cresol	x	x	x		x	x
Dichloromethane	x	x	x		x	x
Diethylene glycol	x	x	x	x	x	x
2-Ethoxyethanol	x	x	x	x	x	x
Ethylene glycol	x	x			x	
Lead	x	x	x	x		
Methyl ethyl ketone	x	x	x		x	x
2-Methyl-2, 4-Pentanediol	x	x			x	x
Oxalic acid	x		x	x	x	x
Phenol	x	x	x		x	x
Sodium hydroxide					x	x
Sulfuric acid	x	x			x	x
Talc					x	x
1,1,1-Trichloroethane	x	x	x		x	x
Trichlorethyiene	x	x	x		x	

Source: "National Institute for Occupational Safety and Health" (U.S.A.), 1979

Corporate managements have now reoriented their environmental strategies towards development of eco-friendly products. These products are conceived to reduce the burden on the environment both during use and disposal while ensuring the desired product performance with environmental compatibility. A very good example of a common household commodity is synthetic detergents. Alkyl benzene sulfonate (ABS) used initially as the active ingredient in detergent formulations has been replaced by linear alkyl benzene sulfonate (LABS) during the past decade and more recently by alpha olefin sulfonate (AOS) in an effort to offer biodegradable detergents, to overcome the problem of persistent residual pollutants in the receiving water bodies. Likewise, phosphate used as builders to promote detergency ultimately affects aquatic life in rivers and lakes through eutrophication. Phosphate is now being replaced by silicates, carbonates and zeolites in some premium grade zero-phosphate detergents.

Water or air serves the purpose of a medium for the transport of the pollutants in the biosphere. The quantum of pollutants generated needs to be reduced by appropriate changes in process conditions and manufacturing sequences. Industries must evaluate available options to adopt alternate raw materials, process chemicals, catalysts, new designs of reactors and separation equipment all targeted to improve the conversion efficiencies at various stages thereby reducing/eliminating side products which are otherwise released as pollutants.

The United Nations has made a series of recommendations concerning chemical pollution in general as follows:

1. In view of the increasing worldwide use and dispersal of chemical substances, governments should establish institutional procedures at the national level specializing in chemical safety and coordinating their response through regional and international cooperation. These procedures should deal with human health and environmental consequences of industrial processes and chemical use. The priority listing of hazardous chemicals at the national level should be encouraged. Industrialized countries should assist developing countries to establish and to implement such proposals.
2. Industries should be called upon to further develop and implement the concept of product stewardship, taking into account the entire life cycle of chemicals.
3. Governments should monitor exposure of people and the environment to chemical substances and evaluate the results using existing information systems and modelling as a basis for setting guidelines and establishing legislation designed to reduce such exposure.
4. Risk reduction programs should be implemented by governments and industries through the use of cleaner products and technologies; the development of alternatives, restrictions on marketing, effective product labeling and phasing out of specific chemicals.
5. The use of dispersion of heavy metals, such as lead, mercury and cadmium, should be curtailed and alternatives introduced. New uses of heavy metals should be limited and recycling of such substances encouraged by all possible means.
6. Human and environmental exposure to persistent and toxic organic chemicals, such as PCBs, dioxins, pentachlorophenol and others, should be markedly reduced by product substitution, use in enclosed systems and by universal banning except for specified uses.
7. Education programs should discuss the benefits gained from industrial activities and chemical usage alongside actual and potential environmental and human health effects. The concept of risk perception should be further developed in this regard.

VIIA. AIR POLLUTION

Gaseous and particulate emissions are released to the atmosphere from various ferrous and non-ferrous metallurgical process industries, fertilizers, cement and thermal power plants.

The use of enriched air or pure oxygen will improve the efficiency of thermal processes during combustion, roasting, calcination, etc., with consequent reduction of atmospheric emissions.

Apart from specific emissions of nuisance or toxic substances into the air from industrial processes, there are many other broad scale influences on the atmosphere which must be considered, including

- acid rain from sulfur dioxide emissions from industrial and power plants, often several hundred miles away
- effect of carbon dioxide emissions from power plants causing an elevation of CO_2 content of the atmosphere and possible "global warming" with consequent adverse effects on agriculture and on sea levels worldwide
- effect of emissions of fluorocarbon spray propellants and refrigerants into the atmosphere causing depletion of the ozone in the atmosphere with consequent ultraviolet ray damage to humans.

The United Nations has made several recommendations as to control methods for air pollution as follows:

1. Strategies for reducing SO_2 emissions include the use of low sulfur coal, fuel desulfurization, flue gas scrubbing and fluidized-bed combustion. Particulate control technologies should be introduced in all existing and future fossil fuel boilers. Relatively simple and inexpensive methods are often very effective.
2. The introduction of high-efficiency generators (e.g., combined cycle power plants), cogeneration (e.g., combined heat and power plants) and fuel cells should be encouraged to reduce all stationary source emissions (including CO_2). Improved combustion and fuel management systems also need to be developed.
3. In transportation greater use and research into the use of alternative fuels, such as compressed natural gas, liquid petroleum gas and alcohol and also the development of electrically-powered vehicles (using fuel cells or rechargeable batteries) should be encouraged, particularly in captive fleets. The use of public transport should be encouraged, especially in cities.
4. Greater energy efficiency and conservation would cut consumption and therefore emissions. Energy efficiency is the most effective way of reducing all emissions, including CO_2.

Another aspect of the air pollution question, aside from minimization of emissions, is the control of emissions and the chemical engineering design of pollution control equipment.

The air pollution equipment used may consist of fans/blowers, cyclones, scrubbers, bag filters, electrostatic precipitators, pneumatic conveyors, classifiers, machine hoods, spray booths, cooling towers, fume extractors, ventilation towers, air washers, etc.

They are used for dust and ash collection, dust handling and control, gas recovery and absorption, etc. These equipment are mainly used for above purposes in the cement, steel, mineral processing, petrochemical and chemical industries and thermal power plants.

With stringent emission standards that are enforced for the various industries under the Environmental Control Act, the manufacture and use of efficient air pollution control equipment have assumed great significance in India.

At present there are 22 units manufacturing air pollution control equipment in the organized sector in India.

One of the major producers is Flakt India Ltd. according to Kothari's Industrial Directory of India.

VIIB. WATER POLLUTION

While several industries in the large and medium scale sectors have put up adequate treatment facilities to combat pollution, the costs of environmental compliance are rather high with no tangible benefits in many cases. Further, in multi-product complexes like refineries, petrochemical or fertilizer units with frequent inherent upsets in the various process units, the limitations of the central wastewater treatment facility are quite obvious. In such cases, the normal options for augmentation of capacity and restabilization of operations require add-on retrofit equipment or special bacterial cultures to achieve desired results. The complex wastewater is treated sequentially by: (a) physico-chemical primary methods, (b) secondary biological processes, and (c) advanced tertiary treatment methods, to achieve progressive improvement of the treated water quality. Any degree of upgradation is feasible by prudent sequencing of treatment techniques, avoiding redundancy and in-house measures to reduce the quantum of wastewater generation. It is evident that end-of-pipe treatment as normally adopted by many industries presently can tackle the major pollutants. Several residual pollutants like non-biodegradable organic compounds, inorganic salts, color, etc., present in the effluent discharged will tend to contaminate the rivers, streams, and groundwater resources. Most of these pollutants are formed as a result of the multiple reactions at various stages of the process operations and not desired in the final products. Consequently, they are released with the process waste streams. It is necessary to review present water use patterns with the objective of curtailing the total volume of wastewater.

Apart from point source effluents from industrial process, there are a number of other water pollution effects including fertilizers, runoff from agricultural lands and oil spill pollution resulting from marine disasters involving oil tankers. This last problem involves complex engineering solutions including contaminant removal and disposal of marine oil spills.

Waste treatment, in general, comprises of screening and grit removal, sedimentation, biological treatment, sludge digestion and disposal.

Screening and Grit Removal

Large solid matters and heavy sediments are removed by screening and grit removal process. This is essential to protect and safeguard the subsequent treatment units.

Sedimentation

Organic matter, present in the waste in the form of suspended solids, is removed in the sedimentation tanks. It is a physical method of separation achieved by allowing the waste to remain in more or less quiescent condition.

Biological Treatment

This is the most important stage of treatment. This stage can be achieved by two processes—activated sludge process or spray aeration. The former is carried out by mechanical surface aeration process or by injecting air or oxygen, and the latter by rotary sprinklers.

In both the above processes, the organic matter present in the settled waste is converted into insoluble substances.

Sludge Digestion and Disposal

The sludge digestion and disposal of sludge from a wastewater plant is the most complicated process and therefore requires skill and experience. Sludge digestion can be carried out aerobically or anaerobically. Anaerobic digestion plants are more common and some companies like Batliboi have some good designs for digester. Aerobic digester was also first introduced in India by the same company.

Several distilleries are benefitting by deriving the total energy requirement as biogas by end-of-pipe anaerobic treatment of spentwash in novel bioreactor systems with an attractive pay back period of three years. These plants recover only 50% of the energy potential and options for downstream treatment to tackle the residual pollutants appear to be quite expensive. Interestingly, a distillery near Madras utilizes the biologically treated spentwash in a full scale aqua-culture fish farm. A prototype commercial size plant has been commissioned recently in a distillery in the South based on indirect gasification technology in a fluidized bed reactor. The energy potential of spentwash in organic constituents is recovered as a gaseous fuel and the potassium rich inorganics as fertilizer, with no residual or secondary pollutants.

A mini-paper mill in the north, based on sugar cane bagasse, is putting up a fluidized bed chemical recovery system for reclaiming valuable caustic soda from the spent pulping liquors with major benefits of pollution prevention, energy recovery, chemical recovery and water conservation. A paper mill near Pune is actively pursuing the use of solvents like alcohol for pulping bagasse to produce special papers and recovering value-added polymeric products based on lignin. Other commercial developments include energy recovery as biogas by anaerobic treatment of spent pulping liquors to reduce the pollutant load by 15-20%. Recent developments in environmental biotechnology using special microbial cultures are also being considered by the industry to prevent pollution as a cost-effective alternative to physicochemical methods requiring significant recurring expenses.

The potential for biotech applications in the area of environmental management is quite substantial. In the US, the major areas for biotreatment have been focussed on tackling hydrocarbon based pollution problems. The use of bioremediation is increasing at an accelerated pace and is expected to pick up even more, as companies isolate new organisms, using r-DNA techniques, to degrade such hazardous waste streams as polychlorinated biphenyls (PCBs) and tetrachlorinated ethylenes (TCEs). The market for biodegradable processes, currently around US $200 million annually, is expected to grow annually at 40% over the next three years and at higher rates after 1996, when genetically engineered microorganisms become commercially available.

VIIC. EXAMPLES OF POLLUTION CONTROL PRACTICES

As one example of the importance of pollution control, a recent edition of the "Chemical Weekly Buyer's Guide" gives "pollution control measures adopted" as one of the important criteria for the chemical producers listed in that directory.

Several examples of companies and "pollution control measures adopted" are taken at random and reproduced here :

Albright Morarji & Pandit Ltd.

Pollution control measures adopted: (1) Liquid effluent treatment facility is put up for equalization, neutralization and settling as well as recycle of treated effluent water. Treated liquid effluents meeting the Maharashtra Pollution Control Board (MPCB)'s consent conditions are discharged; (2) Gaseous emissions are scrubbed, cyclones and filters are provided to control dust emissions. Emissions through stack are as per MPCB's consent; (3) Solid waste sold to users as by-product; (4) Noise level is controlled as per MPCB's requirements; (5) Efficiency of pollution control facilities provided is reviewed intermittently and improved.

Colour-Chem Ltd.

Pollution control measures adopted: Effluent treatment plants at factories render liquid waste harmless. Sophisticated pollution control equipment keeps emissions within tolerance limits. R&D develops environment friendly products, searches for ways to recycle wastes and constantly evaluates the effectiveness of their own pollution prevention and control efforts.

Deepak Fertilizers & Petrochemicals Corporation Ltd.

Pollution control measures adopted: Adequate safeguards have been incorporated in the plants at the design stage itself and these have proved effective in ensuring that pollution is controlled. An environment audit exercise has confirmed adequacy of the installed pollution control devices and revealed that pollution levels are well below the statutory limits.

E.I.D. Parry (India) Ltd.

Pollution control measures adopted: The conventional type single absorption contact process sulfuric acid plant was scrapped and a double absorption plant installed. The SO_2 emission is now 0.025% which is below the standard. While expanding the superphosphate plant, they propose to modify the scrubbing system to abate pollution. The liquid effluent of superphosphate plant is reused (partly) and sold.

Madras Refineries Ltd.

Pollution control measures adopted: With a view to maintain the water pollution levels at the minimum, modernization and upgradation of the treatment facilities in the effluent treatment plants were taken up and completed during 1992-93. Ambient air is being continuously monitored using stationary ambient air monitor and also using the mobile air monitor at the R&D wing. The development of a green belt around the new Cauvery Basin Refinery near Nagapattinam is also in progress.

Shriram Fertilizers & Chemicals (Unit of DCM Shriram Consolidated) Ltd.

Pollution control measures adopted: The company has spent over Rs. 15 crores towards modernization and updating environmental protection and preservation measures including installation of bag house, electrostatic precipitators, ammonia treatment/recovery system, mercury, bearing effluent treatment systems, conservation of water and development of green belts. Around 1.5 lakh lush green plants flourish at Kota complex.

Southern Petrochemical Industries Corporation Ltd.

Pollution control measures adopted: As a pollution abatement feature, fluorine from phosphoric acid was recovered and finally converted into aluminum fluoride, an important chemical used in aluminum extraction from its ore. All solid, liquid and gaseous wastes are periodically tested and let out only when they are meeting the relevant specifications laid down by the pollution control authorities.

SPIC Fine Chemicals Ltd.

Pollution control measures adopted: The plant has been designed and operated on zero effluent concept. No liquid effluent will be discharged outside due to unique concept of effluent treatment. Green belt is being developed around the plant as per the pollution control norms. A state-of-the-art aspiration system ensures that there is no dust emission inside the plant.

Sree Krishna Drugs Pvt. Ltd.

Pollution control measures adopted: Effluents coming out are first collected in the equalization tank and then pumped into neutralization tank, then with the help of the paddle mixer, the total effluent is thoroughly mixed, adding sufficient quantity of lime solution to bring the effluent to neutral pH, followed by settling after the addition of alum. After settling for a few hours, the sediment settles down and a clear supernatant liquid is transferred to solar evaporation ponds for drying and the bottom sludge is allowed into sludge drying beds, where the water content in the sludge is removed. The cake residue is dried for a few days, then removed and transported to a far off dumping ground.

VIIID. THE FOOD INDUSTRY AS A SAMPLE INDUSTRY DEALING WITH POLLUTION CONTROL PROBLEMS

In the food processing industry huge amounts of waste and effluents are released, particularly in the fruits and vegetables processing industry wherein the proportion of waste materials to be handled is often more than the preserved edible material itself. Safe disposal of the waste effluents is very important to prevent pollution of atmosphere and water supplies. These wastes are generally biodegradable.

During the processing of fruits and vegetables, peels, cores and unsuitable portions of edible materials are obtained which are solids and some of them get mixed with water also. By-products may be recovered from them, the remaining material may be spread out thinly on agricultural land, and cattle and pigs allowed to graze. The dried material may be disposed of by burning.

Besides fruits and vegetables processing, other manufacturing processes relevant in this context are:

(a) Meat and meat products manufacture
(b) Milk and milk products manufacture
(c) Fish and fish products manufacture
(d) Poultry and poultry products manufacture

The following text is drawn from the "SBP Handbook of Export Oriented Food Processing Projects" (1993) and summarizes the overall pollution problems faced by the food industry.

Contaminants

In the overall food industry, dairies and meat processing units contribute most to liquid wastes which must be effectively treated prior to their discharge to streams or other waterways. The quantity and quality of effluents discharged depend upon the process in operation and, of course, on the size of the plant. The main types of the wastewater in a dairy plant are water borne milk solids from various sources, detergents, lubricants and domestic waste. As a thumb rule, a plant of 200,000 liters bottling capacity will discharge about three to four times the quantity of effluents to be treated.

The high B.O.D. of dairy effluent is due to the presence of rich biodegradable organic matter, which is mostly contributed by direct milk spoilage and bottle washings. Dairy effluents are treated by biological process with an aeration period of 15 to 40 hours, depending on the B.O.D. Slaughterhouse effluents also contain a large amount of organic matter along with other greasy material. Blood and other wastes from the slaughterhouse can also be treated by biological process.

Water Pollution

Wastewater generally contains large quantities of inorganic impurities from fruit/vegetable washing process, and various organic substances in dissolved and suspended particles form, which give them a high biochemical oxygen demand (BOD). Small doses of pesticide residue may also occur. The wastewater may also contain nitrates and nitrites formed out of residual protein and ammoniacal compounds during processing, which may increase nitrate levels in surface and groundwaters, used for drinking purposes.

The liquid waste disposal is a serious problem. To reduce liquids, amount of water used in the plant should be kept to a minimum, and the liquid and solid wastes handled separately. All coarse particles are screened on rotary or vibrating screen and the wastewater is allowed to flow directly to the sewerage system or to agriculture lands or may be settled in a tank before allowing to overflow. Settling sludge method removes the fine solids (with lowered BOD). Sediment is periodically removed and disposed of. If the tank is large enough, the overflow shall have very low BOD, due to the microbiological treatment, and pollution shall be controlled. Incorporation of air, nitrogen and phosphorus compounds gives a very good result. A clear, problem-free effluent shall be obtained which can be simply drained.

For very large quantities of wastewater disposal, land treatment is the cheapest and the best. In any case, as far as possible, by-products are recovered from the waste and then the wastes and the effluents disposed of to reduce the pollution problem and to reduce the cost of the main food products. But all these are only viable in practice if the processing plants are sufficiently big in capacity.

Air Pollution

The major source of air pollution is fuel burning in boilers which mainly emits smoke/particulates/dust, sulfur oxides and oxides of nitrogen. The intensity of emission varies with the type of fuel and boilers used and the boiler-firing practice adopted. Minor discharge of benz pyrenes and trace metals contained in coal may also be present.

Provision of inadequate smokestacks (e.g., lower height) and/or existence of unfavorable meteorological conditions, may result in increased ground level concentration of pollutants which can result in discomfort and respiratory complaints initially and impairment of lung functions in the long run.

VIIE. GOVERNMENTAL AUTHORITIES FOR ENVIRONMENTAL CLEARANCE IN INDIA

It is necessary to establish and maintain contact with environmental boards in the geographic jurisdiction in which chemical plants are located.

The following is a listing of specified authorities of states for environmental clearance.

Andhra Pradesh Pollution Control Board
6/6/115-124, Kavadiaguda, Secunderabad - 500 003

Assam State Board for Prevention and Control of Water Pollution
Piyali Phokan Road, Rohaba, Gauhati - 781 001

Bihar State Water Pollution Control Board
Rudra Bhavan, East Boring Canal Road, Patna - 800 001

Gujarat Water and Air Pollution Control Board
Patnagar, Old Assembly Building, 2nd Floor, Sec. No. 17, Gandhinagar - 382 017

Haryana State Board for Prevention and Control of Water Pollution
Kothi No. 661, Sector 8, Chandigarh 160 008

Himachal Pradesh State Board for Prevention and Control of Water Pollution
Jaksal House, Kasumpti, Simla - 171 002

Jammu & Kashmir State Board for Environmental Improvement & Ecology Development
Div. Planning and Development Department, New Secretariat, Jammu/Srinagar

Karnataka State Pollution Control Board
7th and 8th Floors, Public Utility Building, Mahatma Gandhi Road, Bangalore - 560 001

Kerala State Pollution Control Board
Keston Road, Kawdiar (P.O.), Trivandrum - 695 003

Madhya Pradesh State Pollution Prevention Board
Paryavacan Parisar, Sector E-5, Arera Colony, Bhopal

Maharashtra Pollution Control Board
Army and Navy Building, 148, M.G. Road, Fort, Bombay - 400 001

Orissa State Pollution Control Board
Gautam Nagar, Bhubaneshwar - 751 014

Punjab State Board for the Prevention and Control of Water Pollution
11-A, The Mall, Patiala

Rajasthan State Board for Prevention and Control of Water Pollution
J-2/35, Mahaveer Marg, Jaipur-1

Department of Environment (Sikkim)
Mahatma Gandhi Road, Gangtok, Sikkim

Tamil Nadu Pollution Control Board
80, Kamarajar Salai, Ramakrishna Nagar, R.A. Puram, Madras - 28

Uttar Pradesh Pollution Control Board
B-159, Nirala Nagar, Lucknow - 226 007

West Bengal Prevention and Control of Water Pollution Board
Industry House, 10, Camac Street, Calcutta - 700 017

Directorate of Smoke Nuisance
60-B, Chowringhee Road, Calcutta - 700 020

Department of Environment (Delhi)
Government of India, Bikaner House, New Delhi

Central Board for the Prevention and Control of Water Pollution (Goa)
Dhavali Mal, Ponda, Goa - 403 408

Central Board for the Prevention and Control of Water Pollution (Delhi)
A-1, Chandra House, Dr. Mukherjee Nagar, Delhi 110 009

Board for the Prevention and Control of Water Pollution (Pondicherry)
"Ballamalyayam" 42, Sellam Nagar, Pondicherry 605 011

VIIF. SPECIMEN APPLICATION FORM FOR OBTAINING N.O.C. FROM POLLUTION ANGLE

The following shows the data which needs to be supplied to get a "No Objection Certificate" (NOC) from the pertinent agencies. *Source: Central Board for the Prevention and Control of Water Pollution, 5th and 6th Floor, Skylark Building, 60, Nehru Place, New Delhi - 110 019*

1. General:
   Name of the Industry and its location.
   Address for correspondence.
   Name and address of applicant with telephone number.
   Name and address of the consultant appointed if any.
   Name, designation, address and telephone No. of the official authorized to deal with the questionnaire.
   Date on which letter of intent was issued (Form "C" & "D" of...)
2. Process Details:
   a. Production Schedule
      List of the main products proposed to be produced with designed daily capacity.
      List of the by-products produced with designed daily capacity.
      Time phasing for achieving full production.

   b. Raw Material Consumption
      List of all raw material with monthly consumption (full capacity).
      List of all processing chemicals/materials consumed with approximate quantities per month.
      Is any material from the waste of your industry or any other industry used in the process?
      Is any portion salvaged from your waste stream reusable economically for any other purpose?

   c. Source of Process Know-how
      Have you considered less polluting process alternatives?
      If yes, the reason for adopting the present process.
      Give brief description of the process technology utilized with a flow chart.
      Have you any foreign collaboration?

d. Energy Consumption
Source of Energy
Inplant generation
Public supply
If energy is generated in plant, type and quantity of the fuel used daily.

Fuel LPG Diesel

3. Residential Accommodation:
Do you propose to build residence within the factory premises for your employment?
Area allotted for above.
Population to be accommodated.
Total No. of persons proposed to be employed (full production).

4. Water Requirement:
Source of supply of water.
Is any pretreatment required for *the water before use? If yes,* please specify.
Average daily quantities likely to be consumed (full production).
(a) for industrial use
(b) for domestic use
Is adequate quantity of water available?
(a) at present
(b) for future

5. Wastewater Discharges:
Total quantity of the wastewater expected to be discharged from the industry per day:
(a) Industrial wastewater
(b) Domestic wastewater
How do you propose to discharge the wastewater?
Type of wastewater treatment proposed to be adopted. Give details and flow chart.
What standards for the quality of treatment effluent have you proposed to adopt?
Point of final discharge (work clearly in attached sewer plan).
What methods you propose to adopt for handling and disposal of sludge from wastewater treatment plant?
Indicate available information on industrial wastewater characterization as below:
a. Physical
Temperature (°C)
pH
Color
Odor
Total spent solids (in mg/1)
b. Chemical
B.O.D. (mg/1)
C.O.D. (mg/1)
Oil & Grease (mg/1)
Sulfates
Metals: like Nickel, Chromium, Zinc, Tin, Cyanide
Is there any specific toxic substance discharged?

6. Solid Wastes:
Total quantity of solid wastes per day.
Nature of waste.
Approximate composition.

Methods proposed for disposal.
Have you considered the possibility of recovery and reutilization of any portion of the solid waste?
Are there any problems of subsequent pollution of air, water or soil likely at the place of solid wastes?
Have you any problem regarding collection, handling and transportation of solid wastes?

7. Atmospheric Emissions:
Emissions from fuel burning.
Expected quantity of stack emissions.
Composition of emissions.
Emissions from process/plant other than fuel burning.
Height of stacks.
Proposed air pollution control devices, if any.
Proposed method of handling and disposal of dust, ash, etc., trapped.
Is any standard of emissions prescribed for or adopted by the industry?

8. Other Sources of Pollution:
Is your industry likely to cause pollution? If yes, what noise abatement measures you have planned?
Is there any odor problems likely to occur from your industry?
Is there any thermal pollution of surface water likely to occur from the industrial discharges?

9. Pollution Control Management:
Give details of the organ proposed to be set up by you for the control of the pollution.
What is the level of expenditure of the person in charge of the control?
Do you propose to monitor the pollution from your industry?
What laboratory facilities you propose to have?
Give details of the operation and maintenance of the facilities you propose to have (pollution control equipment/treatment plant).

10. Cost of Pollution Control:
Total expenditure proposed for pollution monitoring and control
Amount
Capital
Recurring

Any other additional information about beneficial or adverse environmental impact from your industry.

Signature of Applicant

Enclosures: (I) Copy of Letter of Intent issued by S.I.A., (II) Copy of Foreign Collaboration Approval issued by S.I.A., (III) Copy of Letter from our collaborators. (IV) (i) Brief description of processes for setting up this industry. (ii) Process Flow Chart. (V) Permission letter of the State Government for setting up this industry. (VI) Land Sale Deed. (VII) Land N.A. approval letter. (VIII) (i) Approved Building Plan. (ii) Layout of sewer line and water supply line.

VIII

APPLICATION OF THE COMPUTER TO THE CHEMICAL INDUSTRY*

VIIIA. COMPUTERS AS ENGINEERING TOOLS

Computer hardware and software are tools-of-the-trade for engineers. The capabilities provided by computers for fast calculation, large storage, and logical decisions, plus the available technical and mathematical software, permit engineers to solve large problems much more rapidly than ever before. The engineers' emphasis can therefore shift from problem solving to planning, conceiving, interpreting, and implementing with the information made available. Design is one of the engineering functions that has been impacted by computers.

VIIIB. CHEMICAL ENGINEERING/TECHNOLOGY

Chemical engineering stresses the processes for manufacturing chemicals and/or the chemical-based products. In this effort, the emphasis of the chemical engineer tends to be on the process rather than on the product.

VIIIC. HISTORY OF COMPUTERS

Mathematics has long been one of the basic tools of engineering. Now as the 21st century approaches, computers are the major channels for the application of mathematics to engineering.

Digital computers became available in the early 1950's, but not until the development of the FORTRAN programming language in 1957 did chemical engineers begin to become seriously involved. In 1973, a collection of 97 stand-alone FORTRAN computer programs written by almost 100 chemical engineering educators was distributed. In the 1980's, large computer-aided process design packages became available for installation on computers. Most recently, the use of spreadsheets and interactive programs which make use of color graphics on personal computers is emerging.

The use of digital computers, because of their ability to manipulate numbers, text, and symbols at blinding speeds, offers for the first time a tool that can involve engineers efficiently

---

* This chapter represents contributions by several individuals. Thus, pages 699-706 inclusive were contributed by M.A. Tayyabkhan of Princeton, New Jersey and most of the illustrations in this chapter, as well as the text on pages 706-721 inclusive, were furnished by Subhash Mehta, Computer Consultant, New Delhi, formerly Project Manufacturing Engineer, Burroughs Corporation, Pasadena, California.

in all aspects of problem solving, including comprehension, application, analysis, synthesis, and evaluation. Cost-effective computer hardware is readily available to cover at least a 5,000-fold range in computational speed. Well-tested software is readily available for application to almost all areas of chemical engineering and additional useful software continues to become available at an ever-increasing rate.

Trends in Computer Hardware

Since 1951, the characteristics of digital computing have changed drastically. From the mid-1950's to the mid-1960's, computing was done mainly at computer centers on large mainframe computers (see Figure VIIIC-1) in a batch mode from punched cards. The user could not interact with the computer, but simply submitted a deck of punched cards and received, after some period of time (perhaps hours, or overnight), the printed results.

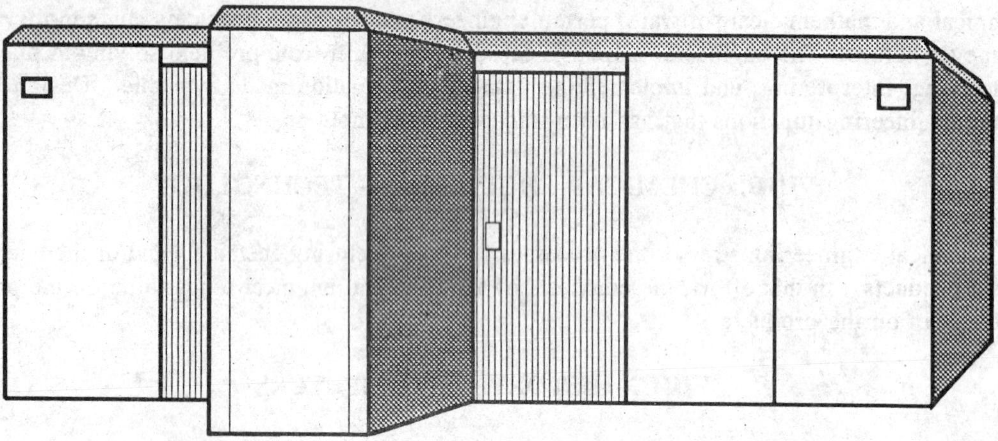

Fig. VIIIC-1. A mainframe computer.

In the 1960's, two very significant developments occurred. The first was the replacement of the batch operating system with a time-sharing operating system so that a number of users could simultaneously and interactively access a large mainframe computer from CRT (cathode-ray tube) or printing terminals, equipped with typewriter keyboards to input commands, programs, and data. The terminals could be located in close or remote vicinity to the computer by hard wiring or by use of existing telephone lines. Turnaround time was now drastically reduced and persons who had never used a computer were now stimulated to use one.

The other significant development, which did not begin to gain momentum until the late 1960's, was the introduction of minicomputers. These scaled-down versions of mainframe computers were made possible by the miniaturization of logic and storage circuitry to the degree that it could all be placed on a single circuit board. The minicomputer was, therefore, sometimes referred to as a "computer on a board." Although less powerful than the mainframes, minicomputers were far less expensive, making it feasible for departments that were heavy computer users to have their own computer. But, perhaps more importantly, it made possible new uses for computers, particularly in experimental laboratory research and other areas where real-time data acquisition, control of experiments, and interactive computer graphics were essential.

Further development of miniaturization and integration of circuitry resulted in the microprocessor (computer logic on a single small silicon chip). In 1974, powerful 8-bit microprocessors were announced. By 1977, the first inexpensive microcomputers ("computer on a chip"), such as the Apple II, were available. Relatively inexpensive peripherals quickly followed. Individuals could now justify the ownership of a computer and the microcomputer became known as the Personal Computer or PC (Figure VIIIC-2).

The widespread recognition and acceptance of microcomputers by businesses and universities did not begin until August 12, 1981, when IBM announced the PC, based on the Intel microprocessor. This unit had 10 times the internal memory capacity of the first microcomputers, could process 16 bits, and an Intel co-processor chip could be added to greatly speed up scientific calculations. By the end of 1983, IBM had shipped an estimated 500,000 machines and the PC was the business standard. Readily available and relatively inexpensive software permitted owners

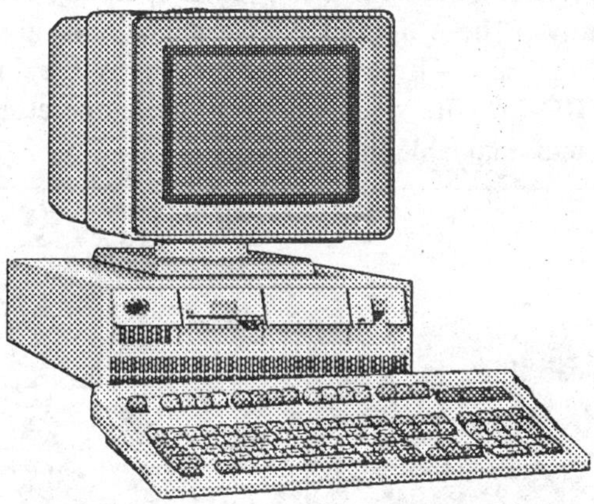

Fig. VIIIC-2. IBM PC—Personal Computer system.

of the IBM PC to use their machines for a very wide range of applications, including word processing, spreadsheet calculations, database management, communications, data processing, and graphics. While decentralization of computing on campuses began with minicomputers, complete decentralization was now possible with the microcomputer.

It has been stated that the microcomputer is the most powerful learning device since the printed textbook. If the computer is used properly, individualized interactive learning is economically possible for the first time.

At their present state of development, the microcomputers are capable of efficiently performing all tasks required. They can, to a large extent, also perform tasks that demand the use of superminicomputers, mainframes, or supercomputers, including applications requiring: (1) databases that are large, are accessed by many users, and/or need frequent updates; (2) huge number-crunching on mathematical, scientific, or engineering modeling problems; and (3) very sophisticated graphics, such as computer-aided design (CAD).

VIIID. THE PLACE OF SOFTWARE

The computer hardware on its own cannot make the computer system perform a particular function without software. Every computer system must be provided with an operating system program that is automatically loaded into the computer memory when the computer is turned on. This program manages all the activities going on in the computer, including coordination of the flow of information among the keyboard or other input device, video monitor, random-access memory (RAM), read-only memory (ROM), floppy disk drives, hard disk drives, printers, and every other peripheral device. The user directs the operating system by issuing, from the keyboard or some other input device, commands that are interpreted by the operating system. Even though an operating system is a very complex piece of software, two computers with different operating systems are usually not compatible in the sense that they cannot execute each other's software. However, recent advances have introduced operating systems which tend to be universally applicable to all sorts of hardware. Many such operating systems have visual options, thus making them user-friendly. These options enable the user to give commands by a simple click of a device, called a mouse. These operating systems are known as Windows-based operating systems (Figure VIIID-1). The visual appeal of these operating systems makes working with computers both fruitful and enjoyable.

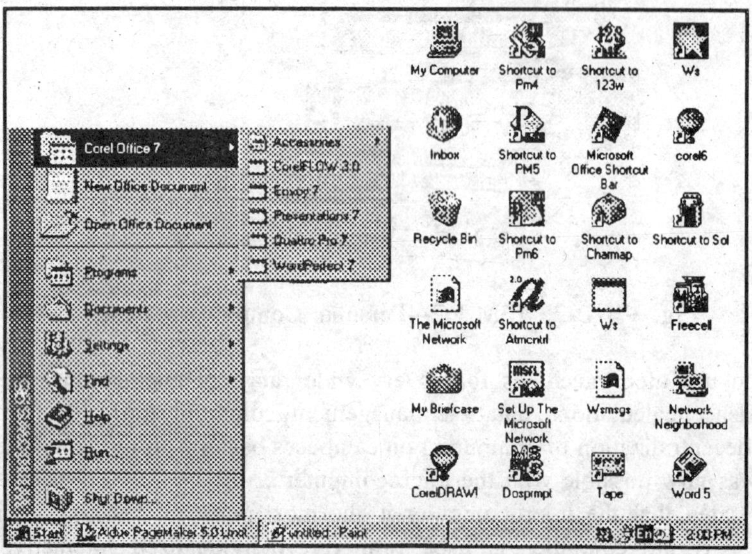

Fig. VIIID-1. Windows 95 operating system.

To significantly increase the use of computer programming by scientists and engineers, IBM began in 1954 and completed in 1957 the first high-level procedural programming language, called FORTRAN, for formula translation. The purpose of this language was to allow the user to write a concise mathematics-like statement of the problem to be solved. A compiler translator would then convert the program into machine language and assign storage locations. The success of FORTRAN stimulated the development of other high-level procedural languages, such as COBOL. Today, many application programs are written in these third-generation languages, such as C, C++, etc.

Of perhaps the greatest interest to users of computers are application programs. Thousands of such programs are available from more than one thousand software development companies, both in India and abroad. The cost of applications software packages for supercomputers, mainframes, and minicomputers can run from thousands to hundreds of thousands of dollars. The cost of personal computer software ranges from less than \$100 to more than \$2,000, but most packages can be obtained for less than \$400. It is best to standardize as much as possible on a few good software packages for efficiency in providing training and ease of establishment of expertise and support.

Word processing is the most popular type of applications software (Figure VIIID-2) for microcomputers. In fact, the early popularity of microcomputers for office use was due mainly to the full-featured word processor. The second most popular type of software for microcomputers is the spreadsheet (Figure VIIID-3). While a word processor works mainly with text, a spreadsheet works mainly with rows and columns of numbers and formulas to perform rapid calculations in tabular form. Spreadsheets are widely used in business, science, and engineering applications. They are of particular value in making rapid studies of the effect of changing certain assumed values or parameters (so-called "what if" problems); for example, determining the effect of reactor conversion on product distribution. So popular are spreadsheets that some claim that they alone are responsible for the tremendous acceptance of personal computers by the business community.

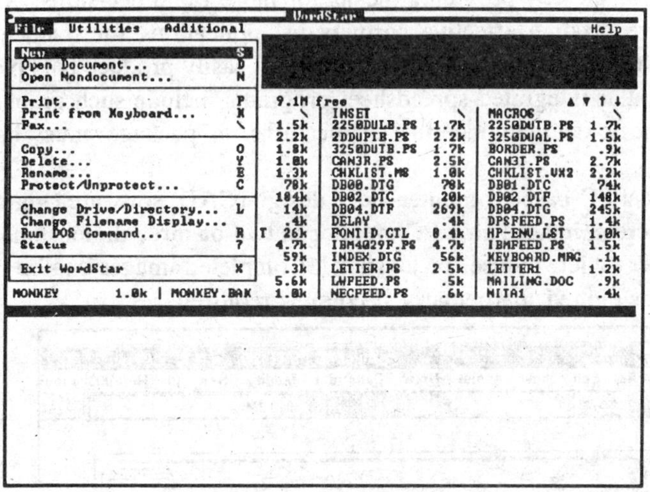

Fig. VIIID-2. A popular word processing software—WordStar.

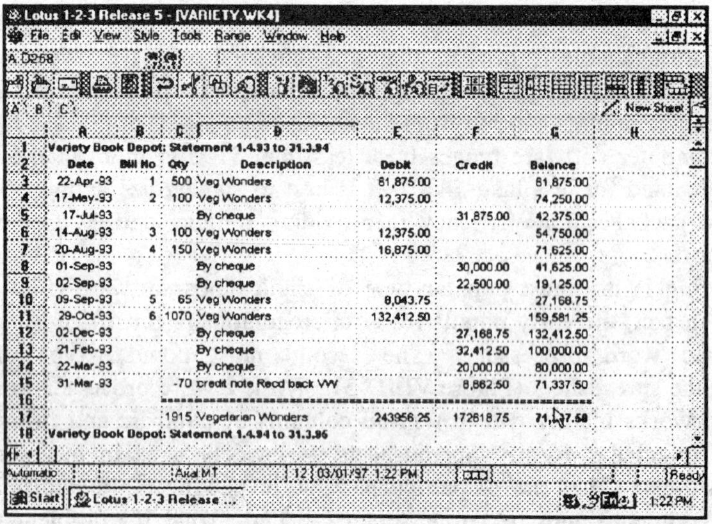

Fig. VIIID-3. A popular spreadsheet software—Lotus 1-2-3.

Graphics is a rapidly growing area of applications software for microcomputers, because of the ability of a graph or chart to represent a large amount of data in a manner that permits trends to be quickly discerned, thereby providing means for more rapid decisions. Graphics combined with spreadsheets have become effective partners in applications for science and engineering. Graphics packages differ widely in capability. Many can easily produce bar, pie, line, and scatter charts and plots. Popular integrated spreadsheet programs include such graphics capability. To be suitable for scientific and engineering applications, a package must have capability for logarithmic scales.

Relatively low-cost PC-based computer-aided design (CAD) software (Figure VIIID-4) is now available to develop screen images on a PC monitor in two or three dimensions. Data are usually entered with a digitizer tablet, mouse, or joystick. Completed images can be printed, preferably with a laser printer, or plotted, particularly if color is required.

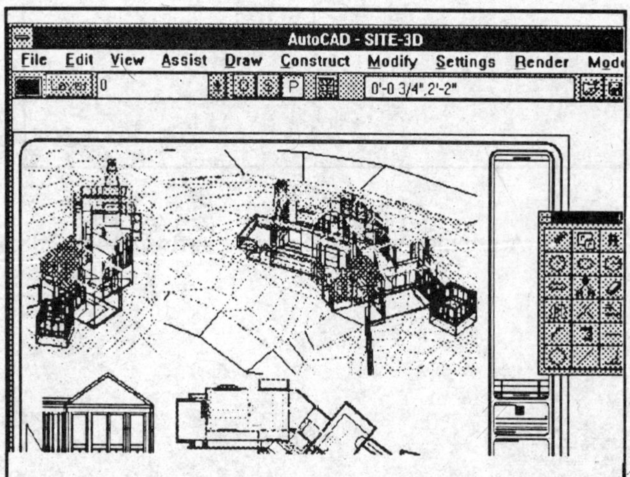

Fig. VIIID-4. A popular CAD software—AutoCAD.

VIIIE. COMPUTERS AND ENGINEERING EDUCATION

Higher education is rapidly becoming involved in mankind's fourth information revolution. The first revolution, "speech," made possible the exchange of ideas and concepts. The revolutions of "writing" and "printing" greatly facilitated education, making it available to all who could read. These first three revolutions depended strongly on the capabilities of the human memory. The fourth information revolution, "computers," barely 40 years old, appears to offer something very different from the first three revolutions. Computers, as the name applies, are well known for their ability, once programmed, to perform numerical calculations at blinding speed. What is not well known is that computers, especially those equipped with large amounts of memory, can also store, give rapid access to, and quickly manipulate huge amounts of textual and symbolic information. Thus, computers can greatly reinforce the human memory in all disciplines of knowledge. For this reason, it is believed that computers are destined to have a strong impact on every aspect of human endeavor.

From the beginning of digital computers, universities have pioneered their development and application. The first large-scale operational electronic digital computer, the ENIAC, was completed in 1946 by John Eckert and John Mauchly of the Moore School of Electrical Engineering at the University of Pennsylvania in Philadelphia.

In the early 1950's, U.S. colleges and universities began to establish computer centers. By 1960, 125 of an estimated 2,000 campuses in the United States had computer centers; by 1970, the number had grown considerably to some 1,700 of an estimated 2,800 campuses. Today, it is hard to conceive of a campus without some kind of computing facilities that are accessible to students, staff, and faculty. The I.I.T.'s in India have led the way in computer applications in India.

Computer Education for Chemical Engineers

The Computer Aids for Chemical Engineering (CACHE) Corporation makes available several programs intended mainly for educational use, but provides them at modest cost to anyone. CACHE is a not-for-profit organization whose purpose is to promote computer-and-technology-based aids for chemical engineering education. CACHE has addressed the current question of the competence of chemical engineering graduates in the use of computing technology in a position paper. CACHE proposes that all chemical engineering graduates: (1) be familiar with at least one computer operating system; (2) be competent in the use of at least one scientific programming language; (3) have experience in computer-aided acquisition and processing of information; (4) be able to conduct information-retrieval searches from electronic data bases; (5) be able to use word processors and graphics programs for the generation of reports; (6) be experienced, within the next few years, in the use of electronic mail and external data bases. Already, the use of digital computers throughout the curriculum is required for accreditation in the U.S.

In order to take full advantage of the computer hardware and software currently available, chemical engineering educators might consider the following time table for student computing. In the Freshman year, the emphasis might be on personal computers, with students becoming skilled in the use of a computer operating system, computer programming, word processing, spreadsheets, graphics, database management, and communications. In the Sophomore year, students could be introduced to numerical methods; flowsheeting by spreadsheets; drawing of flow sheets; writing small computer codes in FORTRAN, PASCAL, or C; using numerical methods software; and equation solving. In the Junior year, students would be ready for computer applications in thermodynamic and transport properties; separators, heat exchangers, and reactors; small open-ended design problems; and heat exchanger network synthesis. Computer applications in the Senior year could be extended to computer-controlled experiments, process synthesis, optimization, process simulation, second-law analysis, and computer-aided report writing. Following such a time table should ensure that even students would view the computer as a very valuable tool for many aspects of chemical engineering.

Chemical engineering has always been a problem-solving discipline. First, the student is taught a large number of scientific and engineering laws, principles, and facts, which are applied to short, well-defined problems, each of which may involve the solution of only one equation. Later in the curriculum, more comprehensive problems are assigned which may involve the solution of a number of equations. Finally, the student is introduced to open-ended problems involving synthesis and/or optimization as well as analysis. An open-ended capstone process design problem often is the culminating educational experience.

Before digital computers, problems were tackled by graphical construction or manually by solving one or two equations at a time. Few chemical engineering students received training in the handling of matrices and, thus, never attempted to solve linear algebraic equations simultaneously except by reduction or determinants. Sets of non-linear equations were purposely avoided by making assumptions so as to linearize all or all but one or two of the equations in the set. The one or two non-linear equations resulting from manual reduction of the set or problems involving just one or two non-linear equations were then solved by a primitive trial-and-error method, often involving graphical construction. Numerous examples of this approach may be found in the well-written textbook on material and energy balances by Hougen, Watson, and Ragatz, which was widely used before computers.

Another class of problems found in chemical engineering textbooks written before digital computers involved integral equations or initial-value problems in first-order ordinary differential equations. The former were solved by analytical or graphical integration; the latter usually by simplification so as to permit separation of variables and subsequent integration. The text by Hougen et al includes numerous examples to illustrate this approach. Additional examples appear in the popular pre-digital-computer textbooks by Brown et al, on unit operations, Smith on thermodynamics and Hougen and Watson on reactor engineering. The latter textbook included a classical treatment of the linear least squares method for determining constants in kinetic rate equations and graphical finite-difference methods for solving a few problems involving partial differential equations.

The personal computer, with its easy-to-program color graphics and large base of relatively inexpensive software, is attracting the attention of many educators. Recent increases in addressable main memory are making it possible to execute programs of a substantial size. At some schools in the U.S., students are required to purchase a personal computer. At other schools, even though students are provided with access to hundreds of personal computers scattered throughout the campus in microcomputer labs, many students elect to purchase their own computer, often at a substantial discount. More and more chemical engineering departments are encouraging or requiring their students to use word processing, spreadsheets, database, and graphics programs to prepare laboratory reports, design reports and solutions to comprehensive problems. Personal computers are revolutionizing the senior laboratory course because of availability of low-cost, analog-to-digital converters to interface computers to various laboratory measurement devices. No longer is the computer simply a device for rapid computations.

VIIIF. COMPUTERS AND CHEMICAL ENGINEERING

The computers have found use with chemical engineers for designing the process rather than the product. One of the popular application areas of computers is known as CAD/CAM (computer-aided design/computer-aided manufacturing). The CAD/CAM software is usually concerned with product-as-object and is highly graphical and spatial. Chemical process computer-aided design, on the other hand, is much less graphical. It is more concerned with the performance of process units (such as the classical unit operations of chemical engineering) and the integration of these units into complete, consistent, efficient process to produce chemical products. This section introduces you to computer software useful for process and plant design and to approaches in design that take advantage of the capabilities of computers and software.

An engineer may write a programming language code to solve a particular design problem. Before the explosive growth of software, this was commonly done. There is still a place for it when appropriate software is not available, or as a learning technique. For example, specific code may be written to solve a chemical-reactor-design problem, in different programming languages. Chemical reactors, because of the great variety of reactor types, reaction kinetics, and specific design requirements, constitute a process unit type for which available software may not be appropriate. However, the program writing and debugging are usually quite time consuming. It is, therefore, recommended that the available ready-made software be used, as far as possible. A specific design program may be written only after determining that the appropriate software is not available. Many ready-to-use programs useful for chemical engineers are available.

VIIIG. READY-MADE PROGRAMS/SOFTWARE PACKAGES

One of the most ready-made software packages belongs to the spreadsheet variety. The spreadsheet has become an indispensable tool to engineers because of its availability on personal computers, ease of use and adaptability to many types of problems. A little later we discuss an example of spreadsheet application to a problem typical of chemical process design.

Hundreds, even thousands, of programs have been written to solve problems commonly encountered by chemical engineers. Many of these have become available for purchase. In turn, many of these programs are for the design of individual units of chemical process equipment. Design programs are available for virtually every unit operation and every type of common process equipment.

Availability of Ready-Made Software

The USA-based magazine Chemical Engineering provides a feature, "Chemputer," in each issue reporting on computer hardware and software developments and periodically publishes a comprehensive list of programs useful to chemical engineers. The "Software" department of Chemical Engineering Progress likewise reports on software of interest to chemical engineers.

Perhaps the newest development in software for chemical engineers is the application of artificial intelligence (AI) and expert systems. The use of AI in the chemical engineering curriculum could involve such things as plant design, molecule design, process synthesis, discrete-event planning and analysis, troubleshooting and alarm analysis, symbolic computation, and selection of physical property estimation methods. The development of artificial intelligence could give substantial momentum towards an alteration in the curriculum to include training in process operations, including planning, scheduling, monitoring, diagnosis, control, and optimization. This would be, perhaps, the major curriculum change caused directly by the capability of the digital computer.

VIIIH. COMPUTERS AND PROCESS DESIGN

In the late 1950's, it was well understood by industry that the use of digital computers could have an enormous impact on solving design problems. What was needed was an effort to assist engineering design teachers in making the transition from pre-computer design techniques to computer-aided design. Starting in 1964, the University of Michigan initiated a project, supported by the National Science Foundation, to: (1) train engineering design teachers in computer-aided design; (2) study the role of the computer in design; and (3) generate representative computer-oriented design problems. Many of the conclusions reached by the study still hold true today. The study recommended that engineering schools: (1) give introductory courses on programming and digital computation, (2) teach model building, numerical methods, and optimization, (3) integrate computer work into engineering science and design course, (4) stress open-ended problems, (5) provide time-shared interactive computing, and (6) train engineering teachers to use computers. The project produced five comprehensive chemical engineering design problems solved with a digital computer and suitable for the senior design course.

This effort was followed, in 1972, by the CACHE (Computer Aids for Chemical Engineering) Committee, under the direction of E.J. Henley and with financial support by the National Science Foundation, with a seven-volume set of books entitled "Computer Programs for Chemical Engineering Education." These volumes, which were distributed to all departments in the U.S. and Canada, covered the curriculum areas of stoichiometry, kinetics, control, transport phenomena, thermodynamics, design, and stagewise computations with 97 debugged and tested FORTRAN programs, written by almost 100 chemical engineering educators. Now, for the first time, educators had at their disposal a large set of examples which cut across all of the standard chemical engineering courses. Most of the programs amounted to no more than 500 lines of FORTRAN code.

Starting in the late 1950's and early 1960, at universities and in industry, chemical engineers, often with the assistance of mathematicians and computer scientists, began to write process simulation programs for computer-aided process design and analysis of continuous steady-state vapor-liquid and liquid-liquid processes. With built-in libraries of subroutines for equipment and thermodynamic property models and techniques for converging interactive computations when non-linear equations and/or recycle loops were involved, these so-called flowsheeting programs performed material and energy balance calculations and, in some cases, sized and costed equipment. Before using the program, the user was required to develop a flow sheet and a set of design specifications.

In 1974, the FLOWTRAN simulator of Monsanto, consisting of 160 subroutines and 60,000 lines of FORTRAN code and data was made available through CACHE for educational use by departments of chemical engineering via a national computer network. During the period from 1971 to 1982, FLOWTRAN was used in this manner mainly in senior design courses, by 57 schools, mainly in the United States. Many of the FORTRAN subroutines in the FLOWTRAN program involved sophisticated numerical methods especially suited for digital computation.

The following paragraphs give more detail as to the applications of the CACHE program in chemical technology.

PIP (Process Invention Procedure) is an interactive computer code for the conceptual design of petrochemical processes. The user supplies a production rate, the reaction chemistry, the raw materials, and some product distribution information. Then the code identifies the decisions necessary to develop a flow sheet and suggests appropriate decisions for a first design based on heuristics. After a design has been completed, the user can go back and change the decisions and generate process alternatives. An experienced user can complete a design in about one hour (material balances, energy balances, equipment sizes and costs).

Following the "invention" of the process as just described, one can pursue process simulation as described in the following examples:

- AMOCO RESID HYDROTREATER SIMULATION
  - Conduct "simulated experiments" of up to three reactors in series to deduce reaction and catalyst deactivation model parameters.
  - Simulate plant start-up and manual control at steady state.

- DOW STYRENE/BUTADIENE EMULSION CO-POLYMERIZATION SIMULATION
  - Conduct "simulated experiments" of a 20 gallon batch polymerization to obtain propagation and chain transfer reaction rate constants.
  - Study heat transfer requirements (additional heat-transfer area/refrigeration needs) in a 20,000 gallon scale-up.

- EASTMAN CHEMICALS REACTIVE DISTILLATION PROCESS
  - Conduct "simulated experiments" of a batch reactor (to deduce kinetic constant of the formation of methyl acetate) and an equilibrium cell (to deduce two-component VLE model parameters).
  - Simulate individual trays of a reactive distillation column to confirm efficacy of conversion separation.

- MOBIL CATALYTIC REFORMING PROCESS SIMULATION
  - Conduct "simulated experiments" of a plug-flow reactor to study catalyst deactivation kinetics.
  - Simulate a reformer to optimize gasoline yield and catalyst deactivation.

Several examples of alternative process designs are given in the following paragraphs from a program in "Computer Applications in Chemical Engineering" prepared by a number of American Universities. For further details, one can contact:

CACHE Corporation
P.O. Box 7939
Austin, Texas 78713-7939
(512) 295-4933
FAX (512) 295-4498
Email: cache@uts.cc.utexas.edu

1. Design of an Ammonia Synthesis Plant

The objective of the case is the design of an ammonia synthesis plant that was to be built in 1990 and uses hydrogen and nitrogen feedstocks from a coal gasification plant. All stages of the design procedure from preliminary calculations down to detailed flow sheet calculations are described. The following steps are emphasized: screening of key flow sheet decisions (pressure of synthesis loop, ammonia recovery synthesis of gas recycle, hydrogen recovery from purge stream), selection of reactor configuration, cost minimization, and synthesis of heat exchanger network.

2. Design of an Ethanol Dehydrogenation Plant

The objective of this case study is the preliminary design of an acetaldehyde synthesis process by ethanol dehydrogenation. The project covered all stages of the design procedure from consideration of qualitative aspects of the flow sheet and preliminary calculation to detailed process simulations and final economic evaluations. Emphasis is placed on synthesizing a workable flow sheet and justifying its configuration, simulating the design using a commercial process simulator and deriving a heat recovery network for the final process.

The main reaction in this process is the endothermic dehydrogenation of ethanol to acetaldehyde. However, under the specified reactor conditions, a number of by-products are produced and their presence determines a number of interesting alternatives for separation.

3. Alternative Fermentation Processes for Ethanol Production

The objective of this case study is the preliminary technical and economic evaluation of a fermentation process for the production of ethanol from a molasses feedstock. The intent is to expose the student to some non-traditional chemical engineering processes and to the rapidly expanding field of biotechnology. Groups of 2-3 students should be able to complete the design in about 30 days. The major focus of this design study is the creation and rational development of a suitable process flow sheet, simulation of the flow sheet by a commercial process simulator and economic evaluation and cost minimization of the final process.

The problem begins with the specification of the plant operating requirements. The type of fermenter to be used as well as plant conditions are left open. Suggested fermenters include a novel extractive fermenter based on the use of hollow fiber membranes, the Hollow Fiber Extractive Fermenter (HFEF). The choice of fermenter will affect the nature of the flow sheet and lead to several design alternatives. Given the time constraints, the student will have to rationally screen these alternatives before arriving at a workable flow sheet ready for simulation. A kinetic expression describing the production of ethanol from glucose is provided as well as a program for evaluating the performance of the fermenters. Performance characteristics are also provided for the batch fermenter and the HFEF.

4. Retrofit of a Heat Exchanger Network and Design of a Multi-Product Batch Plant

The first problem deals with the retrofit of a heat exchanger network consisting of 8 exchangers with 5 hot and 3 cold processing streams as well as steam and cooling water. The layout of the network and areas of the exchangers are also given. The objective is to determine a retrofit design that can reduce the energy consumption within specified limits for the capital investment and payout times. This problem requires examination of alternatives for the level of energy recovery, matching of streams, addition of area, and removal or reassignment of existing exchangers and piping. This problem can be used to illustrate basic concepts of heat integration, as well as the application of computer software. The second design problem deals with the design of a batch processing plant that has to manufacture 4 different products, all of which require 5 similar processing steps (reaction, product recovery, purification, crystallization and centrifuge). An important aspect of this problem is that the production schedule and inventory must be anticipated at the design stage. Furthermore, this problem also requires analyzing alternatives for merging processing tasks into single units, and using parallel units with and without intermediate storage.

In addition to the general questions of process design there can be computer applications to specific plant design questions as follows:

5. Pump Selection

This case study is an exercise in heuristic classification of pumps and the selection of the most appropriate for given specifications. In addition to the problem statement and the outline of the selection approach, this volume contains a detailed list of the heuristic rules used and of the reasoning strategy employed. This knowledge allows the direct implementation of the case study in any development software environment.

6. Plastics Selection

This is also a case study in heuristic classification for the selection of plastics satisfying a set of desired properties. This provides a complete description of the knowledge employed and allows the reproduction of the case study in any software environment.

7. Other Aspects of CAD

Today's CAD systems are capable of building complete three-dimensional data models of plants. Each user can have a different view of the data—say, as a piping isometric—but the views can be overlaid to give the whole picture. And the model is smart, including specifications along with graphic data. When modeling is done, any view can be drawn automatically—complete with dimensions. Specifications, too, can be viewed differently, and used to generate lists of equipment, piping, valves, materials, instruments, etc.

A CAD system, which replaced a drafting-oriented system, generates process flow diagrams, P&IDs, wiring diagrams, instrumentation loops, plot plans, exchanger setting plan drawings, mechanical details, and data sheets.

Thus, at one time, conventional design calculations were able to help to produce three-dimensional models of chemical plants which could foresee, for example, problems of interference between pipe and structures. Now computer modeling has replaced such models.

Further, business and economic input can be inserted into process design to produce an optimum plant from the standpoint of safety, economy, and environmental impact and regulatory compliance as well as maximum economic benefit.

VIIIJ. OTHER PROGRAMS

CACHE has PC programs available for the following operations: slurry flow in pipes, supercritical fluid extraction, gas absorption with chemical reaction, design of flash vessels and distillation towers, heterogeneous reaction kinetics, and CSTR (chemical stirred tank reactor) dynamics and stability. Also available from CACHE are instructional modules for binary distillation, material balances, and flow sheet drawing. CACHE has the programs THEN and TARGET II that are useful in the design of heat-exchange networks.

Property Data Programs

The property data program developed by the Design Institute for Physical Properties of the American Institute of Chemical Engineers, known as DIPPR, is widely known and used. The PC version of DIPPR contains 26 constant and 13 temperature-dependent, pure-component properties for 766 common industrial chemicals.

There are at least 20 physical databases commercially available as on-line data services. Five of the databases listed include vapor-liquid-equilibrium calculations for mixtures.

COADE/Chemstations, Inc. provides PREDICT™ and ISI Software offers ChemSmart™ for property estimation on personal computers.

Chemical process flowsheeting programs include property data and prediction methods for pure components and mixtures. Property data can be retrieved from these programs for use in flowsheeting, or such a program can be used as a property database without using the flowsheeting capability.

Process Synthesis

The first task in plant design is to define a process, namely, the chemical and physical processing steps to convert raw materials into desired products. The number of choices and combinations of unit operations, reactor designs, and ancillary processes that might be used for even a simple process can be quite large. Perry's Chemical Engineers' Handbook shows 15 different ways just to separate a solid from a liquid.

Chemical engineers have traditionally synthesized process flow sheets using experience, insight, invention, and sequential evaluation of alternatives. Recently, there has been some analysis and computerization of process synthesis.

Flowsheeting Software

Flowsheeting has been defined as "the use of the computer aids to perform steady-state heat and mass balancing, sizing, and costing calculation for a chemical process." Flowsheeting and process design are analogous activities. The process flow sheet defines the reactors, unit operations, and utilities needed, along with the streams of material and energy put into and out of the process and between all the process units. Sufficient information is specified so that a unique solution exists to the posed problem. Feed and product compositions, temperatures, and pressures typically are specified, as are performance requirements and some operating characteristics of the process equipment.

Flowsheeting is applied to steady-state conditions. The unsteady-state features of normally steady-state processes—start-up, shut-down, disturbances, control actions—are usually analyzed separately from the process-design task. This results in a major simplification of the design problem, because time variations and integration, with respect to time, need not be considered (although integration, with respect to space, may still be required in models for particular operations, such as that of a plug-flow chemical reactor). The flowsheeting language SPEED-UP is an exception, in that it includes unsteady-state capability in its code.

The solution of the problem is obtained by solving mass and energy balances to yield the quantity and state (i.e., composition, temperature, pressure) of all the streams and the utility requirements. Additional parameters for the process equipment, sufficient so that stream specifications are met and the cost of the equipment can be estimated, are calculated. The cost of equipment, raw materials, and utilities is estimated and an economic analysis is carried out. Methods of cost estimation and economic analysis are presented later in this text. This entire procedure may be repeated many times to examine modifications of the process flow sheet or to find optimal values of key process variables. Computer software can greatly simplify these repetitive calculations for the engineer. But even without the need for repetition, the software may simplify the calculations and provide detail and accuracy that would have been impossible otherwise.

Certain features of chemical design lead to difficult and complex calculations, and therefore pose a challenge. These include: large sets of non-linear algebraic equations, the need for large amounts of physical and chemical property data, the presence of operations that require very complex models, and the occurrence of recycle streams.

The flowsheeting program FLOWTRAN is available to universities through CACHE. This program was developed by the Monsanto Company in the 1960's and made available for university use in 1974. FLOWTRAN is well documented with a manual and examples. It can be installed on many mainframe computers, but not on personal computers. FLOWTRAN is available through Chemical Engineering Departments at most universities. CHEMCAD II™ is a flowsheeting program for personal computers offered by COADE/Chemstations, Inc. PROCESS™, the product of Simulation Sciences, Inc., is available in mainframe and personal computer versions; many universities utilize PROCESS. ASPEN PLUS™, by Aspen Technology, Inc., is available for mainframe and personal computers.

The ASPEN system was developed to handle solid-liquid-gas processes (such as coal conversions) and is probably the most versatile of the generally available flowsheeting programs. ChemShare Corporation offers DESIGN II™ in a personal computer version. HYSIM™ is a personal computer flowsheeting program from Hyprotech Ltd. In addition to the foregoing commercially available programs, there are many proprietary flowsheeting programs such as Exxon's COPE, DuPont's CPES, and Union Carbide's IPES.

Process Simulation

The specific examples described in Section VIIIH are illustrative of the many models of processes that have been developed in processing companies and engineering contracting companies. The general technique of computer modeling, as applied to chemical processes, is known as *process simulation*. It is a technique used in process design as well as in process plant operation and control.

General purpose programs that can be used to simulate any process are called *process simulation systems*. FLOWTRAN is one such system. At the same time that Monsanto was developing FLOWTRAN, other companies, including Kellogg, Exxon, Mobil, DuPont, and Union Carbide, were developing their own process simulation systems.

All process calculations are based on stoichiometry and the physical properties of compounds and mixtures, including their thermodynamic properties. Process simulation systems generally include physical property databases and methods of estimating parameters and properties. Most process simulation systems have a software component, known as the *physical properties service*, which manages these databases and methods of estimating.

In choosing a process simulation system, the quality of the physical properties service is an important consideration. The service has to provide many parameters and properties, the most useful of which are:

<u>Thermodynamic</u>

Equations of State	Heats of formation
Density	Entropy of formation
Compressibility	Heat of reaction
Thermal expansion coefficients	Free energy of reaction
Heat capacity	K-values (vapor/liquid equilibrium)
Enthalpy	Activity coefficients
Heat of mixing	Fugacity coefficients
Entropy	Chemical potential
Gibbs free energy	Fugacity

<u>Transport</u>

Viscosity
Thermal conductivity
Diffusion coefficients
Surface tension

For a process flow sheet, the stoichiometric calculations (or material energy balances) can be carried out sequentially for each process unit, one after another, or they can be modeled as a set of simultaneous equations. These two methods of dealing with such calculations provide the technical bases for characterizing modern process simulators. Both techniques tackle the important problem of handling recycle computations. For any specific application, one or the other may turn out to be more appropriate, efficient and useful.

A process simulation calculation is not complete until the calculation of the recycle has converged to a value within a narrow tolerance. Similar convergence is required for some other calculations such as multi-component distillation and also for a set of simultaneous equations. All simulation systems may not be able to arrive at a satisfactory answer for a specific problem. Hence, it is generally necessary for a user to evaluate the quality of the results of any simulation.

Computers and Operations of Process Plants

The demarcation between computers and instruments has become fuzzy. Computers are used for direct data acquisition wherein electronic signals from instruments are fed into a computer system. If a signal is an analog, electrical signal, it is converted into a digital signal by interface hardware. The process data is thus directly acquired by the computer, and it can then be stored, summarized, and used to activate alarms and initiate process control actions.

Hardware and software are set up to sample process data such as temperatures, pressures, and flow rates. This is done at desired frequencies, for example, once a second or once every 20 seconds. These readings are digitally filtered to eliminate spurious spikes in the instrument's signals and then are stored in the computer system. The readings are checked against predetermined limits; exceptions are reported and alarms are activated by the computer system.

Computer-acquired data are averaged as desired to produce, for example, hourly or daily averages. These process data are logged to provide production records.

Plant operation information systems (sometimes known as *plant management information systems*) store and report plant-wide production records. Some of the necessary data for the information system may also be input into the computer by operators, engineers or chemists. Occasionally, a plant information system may not have any computerized direct data acquisition. Additional process variables, such as catalyst activities, heat exchanger fouling factors, and internal refluxes in distillation columns, may be calculated periodically (such as hourly or daily) from the operating data in the computer. Similarly, material balances and yields may be calculated periodically. Such calculations and their reporting are included in plant operation information systems.

The operators and technical staff of a plant exercise control of plant operations, using the plant information system. In addition, computers can be used for process control directly. At the lowest level, there is *direct digital control*, wherein the values that regulate the flow streams for material or energy flows are manipulated directly by the computer hardware. When an increase or decrease in flow rate is required, the computer sends out a digital signal. It goes to special hardware that converts it into a pressure pulse in a pneumatic control system, which opens or closes the flow stream valve. More frequently, the digital signal goes to a stepping motor, which directly manipulates the flow stream valve.

In direct digital control, commonly known as *DDC*, the set points for the control valve are entered manually into the computer at a higher level in the control systems hierarchy, which is known as *supervisory control*. The computer determines the set point required to achieve an objective, such as a yield or another indirect variable. In such a system, once the computer calculations have determined the set point, the computer hardware may move the set point of an analog control system or it may, using DDC, move the flow valves directly. In any case, such a use of computers is known as *closed loop control*.

Many different control schemes can be designed to control any process or processing unit. Each control system will affect the behavior of the process differently. In order to choose among possible control systems, the behavior of the process needs to be evaluated with a control system in operation. *Dynamic simulation* of the process is carried out with the help of a computer.

Mathematically speaking, a process simulation model consists of a set of variables (stream flows, stream conditions and compositions, conditions of process equipment, etc.), which can be equalities and inequalities. Simulation of steady-state processes assumes that the values of all the variables are independent of time; a mathematical model results in a set of algebraic equations.

If, on the other hand, many of the variables were to be time-dependent (in the case of simulation of batch processes, shut-downs and start-ups of plants, dynamic response to disturbances in a plant, etc.), then the mathematical model would consist of a set of differential equations or a mixed set of differential and algebraic equations.

Dynamic simulation deals with this problem. For the past 30 years, engineers have been developing general purpose dynamic simulation systems, spurred by applications in the design and control of aircraft and spacecraft. Many of the process simulation systems described above have been or are being extended to carry out dynamic simulation of processes. Besides analyses of control systems, dynamic simulations are also used for developing start-up and shut-down procedures and for analyzing the safety of operating conditions.

Another very common use of dynamic simulators is in *operator training systems* (also known as *training simulators*). A process plant is simulated on a computer and simulated temperatures, pressures and flow rates are displayed on a panel that looks like the normal instrument panel of the plant. The computer then simulates disturbances in the plant and the dynamic model of the plant produces variations in the temperatures, pressures and flow rates reflected on the panel. An operator trainee initiates control actions in response to these changes, and these actions are input directly into the computer. The panel then displays the effects of the actions the trainee has taken.

Operator training simulators have been developed for many specific processes such as ammonia plants, cement kilns, blast furnaces, petroleum refinery gas plants and crude units, offshore oil and gas platforms, distillation towers, heat exchanger networks, and others.

Optimization

Finding the "best" solution when a large number of variables are involved is a fundamental engineering activity. The optimal solution is with respect to some critical resource, most often the cost (or profit) as measured in dollars. For some problems the optimum may be defined as minimum solvent recovery, etc. The calculated variable that is maximized or minimized is called the *objective* or the *objective function*.

Exhaustive enumeration is the most straightforward method of finding an optimum when the number of possibilities is limited and is manageable with the computer power available to an engineer. Many times certain pieces of equipment such as heat exchanger, reactor vessels, etc., come in discrete sizes. In such cases the objective function can be calculated for each combination of possible variables and the optimum can be found. The computer makes it possible to consider many more combinations than otherwise possible. Many stand-alone design programs and most process simulators have a way of making and recording case studying, varying certain parameters so that the user can find the optimum conveniently.

In the design of a distillation column for a given separation, increasing the reflux ratio would reduce column height and increase its diameter and the operating cost for the column. An optimum reflux ratio can be found for the minimum total cost. In designing or developing a process with a reactor, separator and recycle of unreacted materials, the design can be optimized and the optimal size of the reactor, the size of the separator and the recycle constraints can be determined.

Many process simulators come with optimizers that vary an arbitrary set of stream variables and operating conditions and optimize an objective function. Such optimizers start with an initial set of values of those variables, carry out the simulation for the entire flow sheet, determine the steady-state values of all the other variables, compute the value of the objective function, and develop a new guess for the variables for the optimization so as to produce an improvement in the objective function.

There are several mathematical methods for producing new values of the variables in this iterative optimization process. The relation between a simulation and an optimization is depicted in Figure VIIIJ-1.

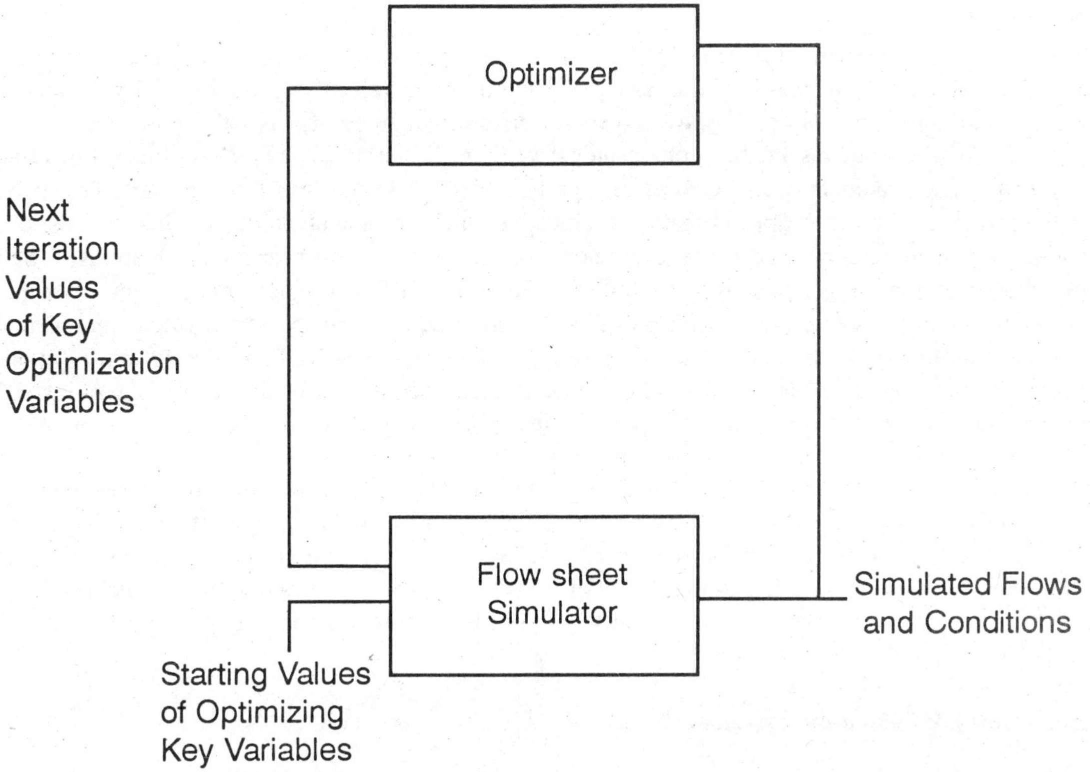

Fig. VIIIJ-1. Relation between simulation and optimization.

Mountain climbing is a method that is common, general, and intuitive. In this method, one solution for the entire flow sheet is obtained for a given set of the variables to be optimized, and the value of the objective function is determined. The values of the variables are then perturbed or changed by either a small amount in their absolute value or by a small percentage of the values. The flow sheet is calculated for this new set of values and the objective function is recalculated. If the changes in the values and the objective function are an improvement in the objective function, then the new values are taken as a starting point and perturbation in the same direction as that made in the last step is made again. The process is continued as long as the objective function keeps improving. If the perturbation, on the other hand, reduces the value of the objective function, then new perturbations are made in the direction opposite to the previous ones. If this perturbation produces an improvement in the objective function, then the process is continued. When an optimum is reached, the perturbation in any direction would reduce the value of the objective function. Such an optimum, however, does not guarantee a global optimum, and the mountain climbing process stops at a local optimum.

Linear programming is a very powerful and computer-efficient method for finding an optimum for linear objective functions and linear constraints. When a situation can be modeled approximately as a linear model, then computer codes available for general linear programming can be used and the optimum can be found very readily. For a special case of linear objective function and for the variables, all of which have linear equalities and inequalities (known as constraints), very efficient methods of linear programming have been developing for finding an optimum.

For continuous variables without constraints, optimum values can be found mathematically by using advanced calculus. Numerically, such optimum values can be found by computer programs, a number of which are available with different degrees of sophistication.

In real-life problems in the process industry, there is nearly always a non-linear objective function. The gradients determined at any particular point in the space of the variables to be optimized can be used to approximate the objective function at that point as a linear function; similar techniques can be used to represent non-linear constraints as linear approximations. Then the linear programming code can be used to find an optimum for the linearized problem. At this optimum point, the objective can be reevaluated, the gradients can be recomputed, and a new linearized program can be generated. The new problem can be solved and the optimum found. If the new optimum is the same as the previous one, then the computations are terminated. Otherwise, the iterations consisting of formulation of linear approximations and the solution of the linear programming problem are continually repeated.

Optimization techniques can be used both in the design and operation of process plants. Mechanical designs of shell and tube heat exchangers and heat exchange networks have been optimized in industry. Naphtha reforming cycles have been optimized in the operation of petroleum refineries. Blending of raw materials or intermediate products to produce final products has been optimized in food processing, petroleum refining, paints production, and pharmaceutical, metallurgical, and other industries.

Laboratory Information Systems

All sophisticated laboratory instruments come with a computer, which is integrated with the instrument. Examples are chromatographs, mass spectrometers, and instruments for nucleomagnetic resonance and X-ray defraction. The sensors from the instrument send data to the computer, just as in the digital data acquisitions systems described earlier. The computer filters and smooths the instrument's signal. It often identifies special features of the signal, such as peaks in a chromatograph or mass spectrometer; it identifies and sometimes calculates the quantity of chemicals and then reports the results as laboratory data.

In many plants and laboratories, comprehensive and integrated *laboratory information systems* are organized, wherein data from sophisticated instruments, as well as other data such as wet chemical analyses, are stored in a computer system. Laboratory technicians continually enter data in the system as their work progresses. In their technology and design, such systems are analogous to plant information systems, and at times they are considered a part of those systems.

Fault Tree Analysis

Fault tree analysis (FTA) is a widely used computer-aided tool for plant and process safety analysis. One of the primary strengths of the method is the systematic, logical development of the many contributing factors that might result in an accident. This type of analysis requires that the analyst have a complete understanding of the system/plant operation and the various equipment failure modes.

FTA breaks down an accident or potential accident into its contributing equipment failures and human errors. The method therefore is a "reverse-thinking" technique; that is, the analyst begins with an accident or undesirable event that is to be avoided and identifies its possible immediate causes. Each of these possible causes is examined in turn until the analyst has identified the root causes of the event. The fault tree is a diagram that displays the logical interrelationships between those root causes and the accident.

The result of the FTA is a list of different combinations of equipment and human failures that are sufficient to result in the accident. These combinations are known as *minimal cut sets*. Each minimal cut set is the smallest set of equipment and human failures that are sufficient to cause the accident if all the failures in that minimal set exist simultaneously. Thus, a minimal cut set is logically equivalent to the undesired accident, stated in terms of equipment failures and human errors.

Fault tree construction begins with the accident under study as the *top event* and proceeds, level by level, until all fault events have been traced to their root contributing causes. The analyst begins with the top event and, for the next level, determines the immediate, necessary and sufficient causes that result in the top event. Normally, these are not the root causes but are intermediate faults that require additional tracing. If the analyst can immediately determine the root causes of the top event, the problem is not suitable (too simple) for fault tree analysis and can be evaluated by other methods such as Failure Modes, Effects, and Criticality Analysis (FMECA). Figure VIIIJ-2 shows a representative fault tree structure.

The immediate causes of the top event are shown in the fault tree with their relationship to the top event. If any one of the immediate causes results directly in the top event, the causes are connected to the top event with an OR logic gate. If all the immediate causes are required for the top event to occur, then the causes are connected to the top event with an AND logic gate. Each of the immediate causes is then treated in the same manner as the top event, and its immediate, necessary, and sufficient causes are determined and shown on the fault tree with the appropriate logic gate. This diagramming continues until all intermediate fault events have been traced to their root causes.

Solving the fault tree means obtaining the *minimal cut sets*. The minimal cut sets are all the combinations of equipment failures that can result in the fault tree top event. Computer programs are required to determine the minimal cut sets for large fault trees.

Minimal cut sets are ranked. Two factors are considered in the ranking procedure. The first considers structure, i.e., a one-event minimal cut set is more important than a two-event minimal cut set. The implication is that one event is more likely to occur than two events; two events are more likely than three events; and so on. The second factor considers ranking within equal-size minimal cut sets. The general ranking rule considers the probability of:

1. Human error
2. Active equipment failure
3. Passive equipment failure

This ranking implies that human errors are more likely to occur than active equipment failures (functioning equipment, such as a running pump) and that active equipment failures are more likely to occur than passive equipment failures (static, non-functioning equipment, such as a storage tank).

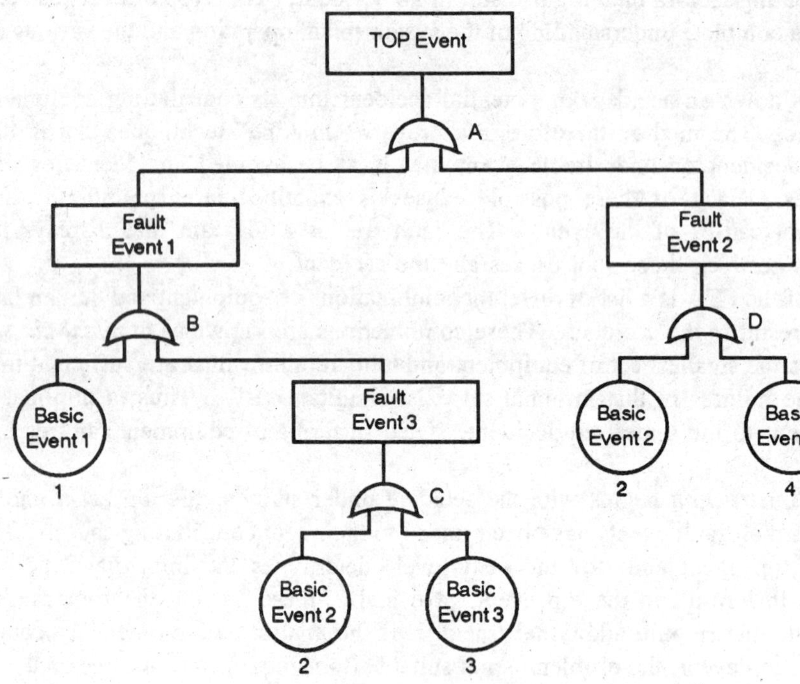

Fig. VIIIJ-2. Fault tree structure.

Fault tree analysis can be applied to the design and operation of a plant. It has been applied extensively to analyzing the Bhopal accident that occurred in 1984. It is used routinely during the design of nuclear power plants and for ensuring the safety of their operation.

VIIIK. SOFTWARE AND SYSTEM VENDORS

In the 'sixties and 'seventies, most engineers (and their companies) in the chemical industry developed their own computing software. As the use of computers has spread and the software systems have become more and more complex, the business of providing engineering applications software and installing data acquisitions, process control, and laboratory systems has become a separate industry in its own right.

Today no chemical company writes its own software for process simulation. They rely on vendors like Aspen Technology, Simulation Sciences, and Hypertech. Vendors such as AAA Technology and B-Jac specialize in specific process units like heat exchangers. Joint industry groups such as HTRI and PFR also provide software to their members. OLI Systems supplies software to analyze environmental systems. Chesapeake, Numetrix, Stone and Webster, and CAPS, Inc. market production scheduling software.

Systems vendors who provide data acquisition and process control systems have come into existence. Almost all of the instrument vendors, such as Honeywell, Foxboro, Bailey, and Taylor, provide data acquisitions, process control, and plant information systems. Vendors like Technion and Lim supply laboratory information systems. Organizations such as Set Point Systems and

DMC have grown up solely to provide computer systems for plant operations (including process control).

The majority of the software and systems vendors that provide services to the process industry are in the U.S.A. However, there are some in Europe and a few in other countries.

VIIIL. SPREADSHEETS

Most people do budgets and calculations manually on large worksheets containing many rows and columns. As a matter of fact, an accountant uses such a worksheet to carry out much of his routine tasks. An electronic spreadsheet (Figure VIIIL-1) is a computerized version of your manual worksheet. Thus, it too contains a grid of rows and columns that define "cells" for entering data, reports, titles, and certain other things.

You can program a spreadsheet to display and print output in many appealing ways. You can have an output that displays numbers with decimal places properly aligned. You can even have **bold** or *italic* entries highlighting specific characteristics or data. The result is a professional looking document to prepare which you may otherwise spend much effort and money.

Another reason for using a spreadsheet is computational accuracy. For example, you can enter a formula into a cell that adds a column of numbers together, and the spreadsheet will display the resultant answer automatically. As long as the formula is correct, you're assured of accurate answers because the spreadsheet uses the computer to perform the computations.

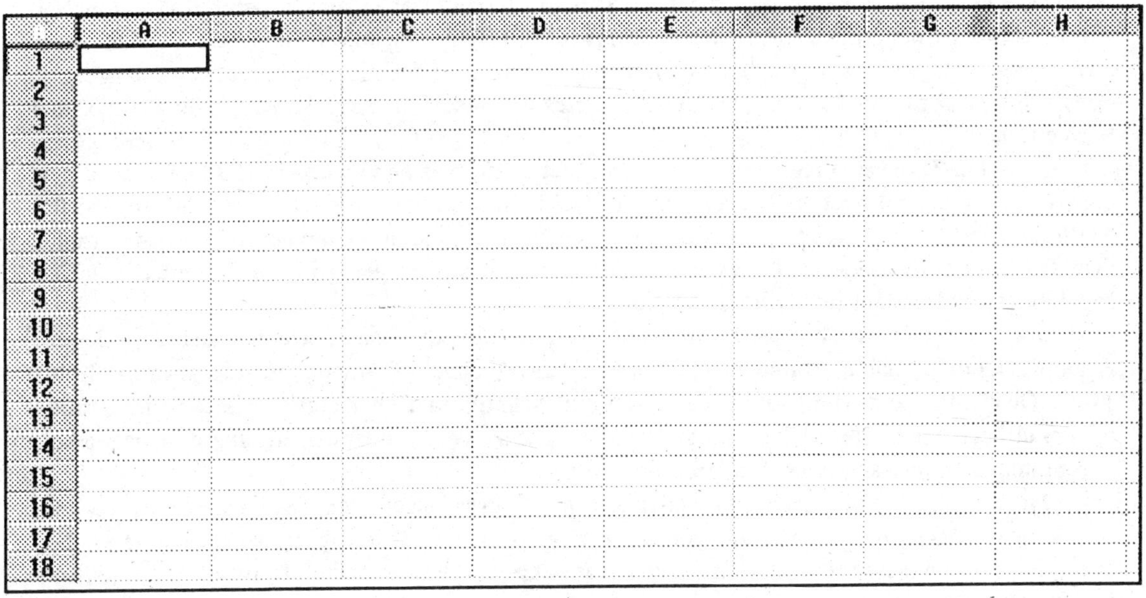

Fig. VIIIL-1. Electronic spreadsheet.

On manual worksheets, correcting a simple mistake often requires you to recalculate many other values. With electronic spreadsheets, all you do is change the one data value that's wrong. The spreadsheet automatically recalculates everything else.

One of the most important uses of electronic spreadsheets is "what-if" analysis. You can see what changes occur in results with the change you make to some numbers—parameter values on which the results are based.

Most modern spreadsheets are actually integrated software packages that enable you to embed spreadsheet models in word-processing reports, create graphs from spreadsheet data, or use spreadsheets as database managers. This list goes on and on.

Electronic Spreadsheets Defined

Electronic spreadsheets are grids of rows and columns that are displayed on terminal or microcomputer screens and that store data or formulas. Thus, electronic spreadsheets are remarkably versatile tools, enabling anyone to plan a budget, a manager to forecast corporate sales, an instructor to maintain students grades, or a scientist to simulate an experiment. You use spreadsheets to keep the periodic table, tabulate important chemical and other design data and also perform numerical calculations lightning fast.

Spreadsheet Basics

The development of electronic spreadsheets has occurred in phases, or generations. The first electronic spreadsheet, VisiCalc, was developed in 1979 by Visicorp. Look-alikes that soon followed had similar names (e.g., CalcStar, PlannerCalc, and LogicCalc), capabilities, and prices. All of these earlier spreadsheets were designed primarily for microcomputers. With time, developers improved on the earlier versions and began to offer more features, e.g., large grid sizes and therefore space for more data. Examples included Enhanced VisiCalc, SuperCalc, and PerfectCalc.

Lotus 1-2-3, the all-time winner in spreadsheet sales, was announced in 1982 and was a new generation of spreadsheet software. Lotus 1-2-3 and similar products, such as SuperCalc, Multiplan, and Context MBA, possessed advanced features, including the ability to create graphic displays from spreadsheet data, faster execution speeds, still larger grid sizes, limited database capabilities, and certain text-editing functions.

Most recent spreadsheet software programs, as already stated, are integrated packages. Examples include Enable, Framework, Symphony, Javelin and, of course, the old stalwarts—Lotus 1-2-3, QuattroPro and Microsoft Excel. Their most important characteristic is their integration of spreadsheet capabilities with such other applications as word processing, database management, telecommunications, and computer programming.

Over the years, the working procedures in most spreadsheet packages have converged and, if you have worked in one of them, you can easily adapt your working towards the others. For example, if you have been working in Lotus 1-2-3 and you wish to switch to Excel, there will not be much of a problem.

Spreadsheet Cells

An electronic spreadsheet can be visualized as a large, computerized worksheet that has been divided into rows and columns.

However, because the CRT screen of a terminal or microcomputer cannot display all the rows and columns of large arrays, you can see only a small portion of the spreadsheet at any one time. Figure VIIIL-2 thus shows eight columns A through H and twenty rows.

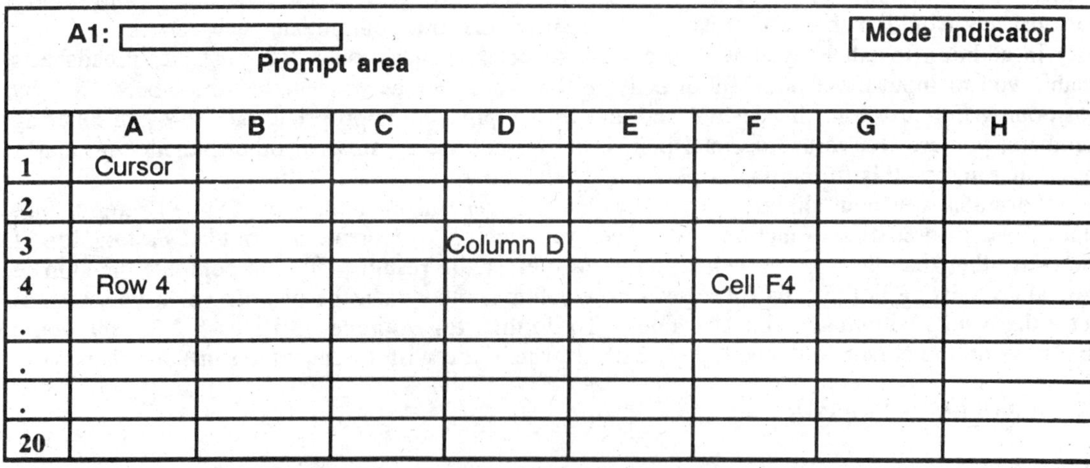

Fig. VIIIL-2. A view of a spreadsheet as seen on the monitor.

You can also think of an electronic spreadsheet as a large grid of blocks conventionally called cells. These cells are similar to those of a manual worksheet—blank areas that can be filled with data. The exact number of cells is equal to the number of rows times the number of columns—dimensions that vary with the software. Array sizes in excess of 13,000 cells are common, although the number is misleading. You can run out of microcomputer memory before running out of potential cells.

Electronic spreadsheets reference cells by their row and column coordinates, e.g., column A, row 4. This referencing differs slightly from spreadsheet to spreadsheet, e.g., "A4" in Lotus 1-2-3, but "R4C1" (for row 4 and column 1) in Multiplan.

Most spreadsheets allow you to input three distinct types of entries: (1) alphabetic text, (2) numeric data, and (3) formulas. Some spreadsheets allow you to store macro instructions in data cells. These "macros" are miniprograms or sets of spreadsheet instructions that enable you to avoid repetitive keystrokes when constructing or manipulating a spreadsheet. Macros are not discussed in detail here.

With spreadsheets, the screen cursor indicates the current cell for data entry. However, you can reposition the cursor to any other cell using the arrow keys of your PC. If you move the cursor continuously to the right, for example, the screen "window" automatically realigns itself, enabling you to see new portions of the spreadsheet. When beginning your work, the starting data-entry cell is one in the upper left-hand corner. This is called the home position However, you are free to enter data wherever you wish.

The spreadsheet also has a prompt area. This area typically indicates the position of the cursor (e.g., "A1") as well as one or more menus of spreadsheet options. These menus assist you in constructing, formatting, printing, saving, or retrieving spreadsheet data by listing what options are available and how they may be invoked. On PerfectCalc, Lotus 1-2-3, and VisiCalc, the prompt area appears at the top of the grid. With other spreadsheets, such as Multiplan and SuperCalc, this area appears at the bottom of the grid.

Almost all spreadsheet models require headings and alphabetic text to identify rows and columns, i.e., names of the parameters or categories whose values are to be filled for a given problem. These are called labels. Labels are entered by typing the letters, or by first selecting "label entry" option, on the electronic spreadsheet. If your label entries are long, most spreadsheets would enable you to expand column widths to accommodate such entries.

In addition to labels, you will also want to enter numeric data. Almost all spreadsheets enable you to input these numbers directly in the same way as you entered the labels, i.e., by positioning the cursor to the desired cell and then typing the appropriate data. When entering numbers, you are free to use decimal points, but do not use commas or other punctuation marks and dollar signs—this formatting is performed separately.

Formulas are input slightly differently, but two general methods are: (1) cell referencing, and (2) use of predefined functions. With cell referencing, you create a formula as a function of the cells other than the one on which you wish to enter the result. Thus, to compute the sum of the values existing in the cells (of a given row/column) other than the one on which you wish to enter the result, you must add such values. To do this, for example, in Lotus 1-2-3, you would first position the cursor to the cell, say, B10, in which you wish to enter the sum, and then type:

+B5+B6+B7+B8+B9

Here, the initial plus sign begins the formula. In a similar fashion, the formula for totalling the values in any other column/row can be obtained.

An alternative to creating formulas with cell referencing is to use predefined functions. Table VIIIL-1 provides a sample list of predefined functions which Lotus 1-2-3 offers:

Table VIIIL-1 Lotus 1-2-3 Functions

Mathematical Functions	
@ABS(x)	Absolute value
@ACOS(x)	Arc cosine
@ASIN(x)	Arc sine
@ATAN(x)	Two-quadrant arc tangent
@ATAN2(x,y)	Four-quadrant arc tangent
@COS(x)	Cosine
@EXP(x)	Exponential
@INT(x)	Integer component
@LN(x)	Log base *e*
@LOG(x)	Log base 10
@MOD(x,y)	*x* mod *y*
@PI	Pi
@RAND	Random number between 0 and 1
@ROUND(x,n)	Round *x* to *n* decimal places
@SIN(x)	Sine
@SQRT(x)	Square root
@TAN(x)	Tangent

Financial Functions	
@IRR(guess, range)	Internal rate of return
@NPV(x, range)	Net present value
@FV(payment, interest, term)	Future value of an annuity
@PV(payment, interest, term)	Present value of an annuity
@PMT(principal, interest, term)	Payment
Statistical Functions	
@COUNT(list)	Returns the number of items in a list
@SUM(list)	Sums the values of all items in a list
@AVG(list)	Averages the values of all items in a list
@MIN(list)	Returns the minimum value in a list
@MAX(list)	Returns the maximum value in a list
@STD(list)	Returns standard deviation of values in a list
@VAR(list)	Returns variance of all items in a list
Date Functions	
@DATE(year, month, day)	Returns number of days since 31/12/1989 (e.g., @DATE(96,1,8) = 35072 and @DATE(96,2,15) = 35110
@DAY(date)	Returns the day number of a date
@MONTH(date)	Returns the month number of a date
@YEAR(date)	Returns the year number of a date
@TODAY	Returns number of today's date

Spreadsheet Application Packages

There are a number of spreadsheet packages available, each having its unique features, advantages and drawbacks. Two of the leading branded spreadsheet packages are:

1. Microsoft Excel for DOS and Windows and
2. Lotus 1-2-3 for DOS and Windows

Although Microsoft Excel has made a significant improvement in its market share, Lotus 1-2-3 still maintains its market share in the world spreadsheet market. Both spreadsheet packages are however similar to work with. You can select either of these to use with our case study.

Earlier versions were developed to work with DOS, which was the de facto operating system for PCs. These versions of Lotus 1-2-3 or Excel provided interface which was text-oriented. The latest versions are developed to work under the Windows environment. The interface is attractive and fun to work with as the spreadsheets displayed are WYSIWYG (what you see is what you get). However, the Windows-based spreadsheets (see Figures VIIIL-3 and VIIIL-4) require a bigger system. If you wish to use Lotus 1-2-3 for Windows 5 or Microsoft Excel 5 for Windows 3.1 or Excel 7 for Windows 95, you will need a system based on at least the following configuration: A personal computer with an Intel-80486 or a Pentium microprocessor, 4 to 8 megabytes of RAM (random access memory) and 300 megabytes of hard disk.

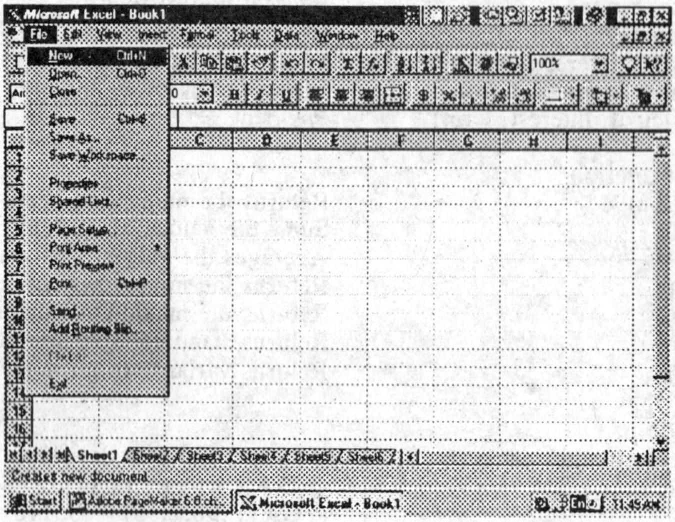

Fig. VIIIL-3. Microsoft Excel for Windows.

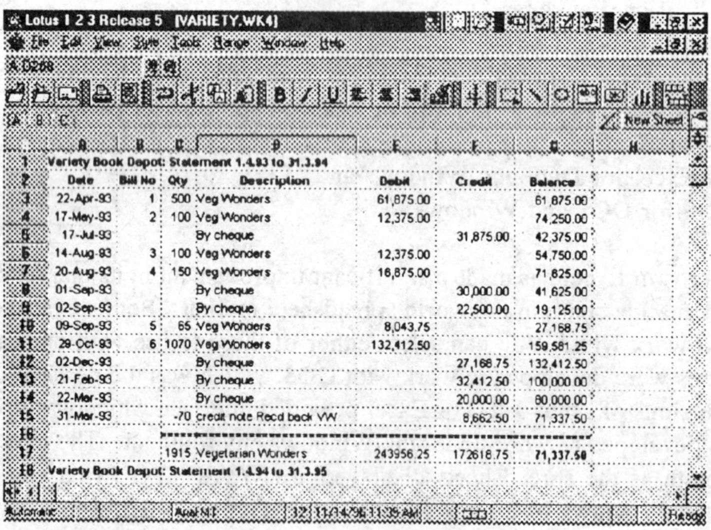

Fig. VIIIL-4. Lotus 1-2-3 for Windows.

The DOS versions, on the other hand, especially versions 2.x, require just a PC to work with. Barring the WYSIWYG feature and attractive report generation, versions 2.x can be used to be functionally effective. You can perform "what-if" analysis, make and print graphs and perform numerical calculations fast.

If you wish to take advantage of the advanced computer hardware technology, you may select Windows-based versions. The DOS-based versions, on the other hand, serve you adequately for most of your work in chemical process design.

Applying Spreadsheets to Chemical Engineering Processes: A Case Study

The critical need for chemical and physical property data is apparent to anyone who has worked on process-design projects.

Consider a hypothetical methanol process in which the feed consists of a hydrogen-to-carbon monoxide molar ratio 2:1, the same ratio in which they react; therefore the hydrogen-carbon monoxide ratio remains constant throughout the process. Thus, it is sufficient to calculate the flow rates of only one of the reactants; carbon monoxide flow rates are calculated here. The hydrogen flow rate in any stream is twice that of carbon monoxide. Perfect separation between reactants and products is assumed.

Spreadsheet columns are labeled with letters and rows with numbers (see Figure VIIIL-2). A combination of a letter and a number, say, A1, identifies a cell in the spreadsheet and represents the number stored in that cell; for example, B3 indicates the cell at the intersection of column B and row 3 and, when used in an equation, B3 stands for the numerical value stored in the cell.

Mol balances for the reactor (see Table VIIIL-2) are (the symbol * is used as a multiplication operator in computers)

B6 = (1—B3)*A3

where A3 is the carbon monoxide feed flow rate (100 mol/h in this example), B3 is the fractional conversion of carbon monoxide through the reactor (0.3), and B6 is the carbon monoxide flow rate out of the reactor. Thus,

C6 = B3*A3

where C6 is the methanol flow rate out of the reactor. Mol balances for the separation unit are

B7 = B6

where B7 is the carbon monoxide flow rate out of the separator and

C8 = C6

where C8 is the methanol product flow rate.

The data and equations are entered into locations in the spreadsheet as follows:

The first five rows are used for labels and constants; the first column is used for labels and stream numbers. Each location that will contain a number is initialized to zero. The value 100, the carbon monoxide feed rate in mol/h, is entered into location A3, and the value 0.3, the fractional conversion, is entered into location B3. The right-hand side of each equation is entered into the cell representing the variable on the left-hand side of the equation. Table VIIIL-2 shows all the entries into the spreadsheet.

Table VIIIL-2 Formula and Label Entries

	A	B	C	D
1	Mass balances			
2	Reaction	CO + 2H2		CH3OH
3	100	0.3		
4	Flow rates, mol/h			
5	Stream no	CO	CH3OH	
6	2	(1—B3)*A3	B3*A3	
7	3	B6	0.0	
8	4	0.0	C6	

The results of computation by the spreadsheet (omitting titles) are as given in Table VIIIL-3. This solution for the process is without recycle.

Table VIIIL-3 Computational Results

	A	B	C	
3	100	0.3		
5	Stream no	CO	CH3OH	
6	2	70	30	
7	3	70	0.0	
8	4	0.0	30	

Now suppose the recycle of the unreacted products is added to the reactor and the reactor balance equations become

B6 = (1—B3)*(A3+B7)
C6 = B3(A3+B7)

These new equations are substituted in place of the previous ones in the spreadsheet. The separation-step equations are unchanged. The calculations are now circular, because B6 depends upon B7, which in turn depends upon B6. These equations will be solved iteratively, that is, the calculations will be repeated until the values in Table VIIIL-2 stop changing (without limits). The calculations can be performed automatically by the spreadsheet software. It is recommended, however, that the calculations be made utilizing the manual option of the software, at least initially, until it is clear that the calculations are converging. The manual option has another advantage: It keeps the software from attempting to calculate as the equations are being entered (such calculations would result in errors because of the circularity).

If the case without the recycle were solved first, the calculations then for the case with recycle can utilize the values from Table VIIIL-3 for the same feed rate and conversion. The result of the first iteration is then

	B	C
6	119	51
7	119	0.0
8	0.0	51

Clearly the values have changed since the previous calculation; convergence has not been attained. The user requests another calculation with the result

	B	C
6	153.3	65.7
7	153.3	0.0
8	0.0	65.7

Again the values have changed, so the calculations are repeated. Calculations are continued until the user is satisfied that no further significant change has occurred (the definition of "significant" is up to the user; a maximum change in values of 0.01 percent between iterations is a reasonable criterion).

The final results (to 0.01 percent) for this example are

	B	C
6	233.31	99.99
7	333.31	0.0
8	0.0	99.99

The exact values for this problem (by algebraic solution) are 233 1/3, 100, and 333 1/3, respectively.

If, after several manual trials, the calculations appear to be converging, it is advisable to switch from manual to automatic iteration. It is strongly recommended that the calculations be always checked by a simple hand calculation. In this example, for instance, the user may add the feed and recycle carbon monoxide flow rates, multiply the sum by the conversion, and compare the result with the tabulated value for the methanol product rate C8.

Scratch Pad

A scratch pad can be very useful for a spreadsheet user. A scratch pad (Figure VIIIL-5) is an area (columns to the right of the main spreadsheet) set aside for doing side calculations of parameters or constants for the main spreadsheet, writing comments, locating macros, and other uses. A scratch pad would be useful in the foregoing example if the user needed mass balances for a particular product flow rate rather than a specified feed rate. The problem has been solved

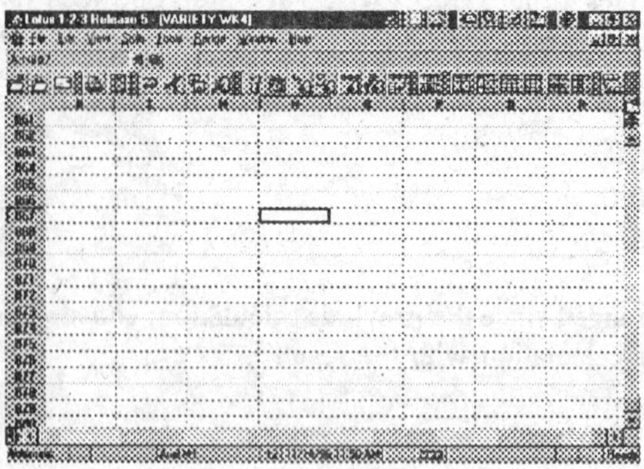

Fig. VIIIL-5. Scratch pad.

for a carbon dioxide feed rate of 100 mol/h, but suppose it is desired to know the feed rate required to produce 880 mol/h of methanol product, the problem then might intentionally be solved first for a specified feed rate as done, because it is often more convenient to write the mass-balance equations for known process feed rates rather than known product rates. The results thus obtained may be converted to the basis of the new product flow rate. Mass-balance equations are linear, so that if the product flow rate is doubled, for example, all flow rates in the process are doubled. In this example then, the new flow rates are obtained by multiplying the previously calculated values by the ratio of the new-to-previous product-stream flow rates, i.e., by (880/99.99 =) 8.801. This ratio can be calculated in the scratch pad (say location E3), the new CO feed rate, .8801, entered into A3, and the iterative calculations repeated until convergence is attained. The iteration could be avoided, however, if each mass balance had been entered after multiplying it by a coefficient E3 (the scratch-pad location). Initially, E3 would have been set equal to 1 and the calculations would have proceeded. The user then enters 880/C8 for location E3, repeats the calculation, and obtains the final flow rates without iteration.

VIIIM. RECENT ADVANCES IN COMPUTERS AND COMMUNICATIONS

Internet

The Internet originated in 1969 as an experiment by the Advanced Research Project Agency (ARPA, originally called ARPANET) of the U.S. Department of Defense. This experiment was designed to enable scientists to communicate among themselves. ARPANET consisted of four computers, but by 1972 grew to 50 university and military research sites.

Now the Internet is here. A 24-lane interstate of the Information Superhighway, it's growing, expanding, evolving, and changing the ways we deliver and receive facts and figures. Right now, as you read this, hundreds of thousands of people around the world are communicating with one another and exchanging ideas without leaving their desks. The resources which are available to each one of them are expanding at breathtaking speed.

But what is the Internet (or just "Net")? Simply put, the Net is thousands of computers "talking" to thousands of others. Each computer on the Net is a potential storage place for information. Each of these storage places is called a "site." These sites may have files which can be retrieved, databases which can be searched, or people with whom you can "talk" in real-time. Whether you want to do a full-text search through the Uniform Commercial Code, download the newest upgrade of that software you bought a week ago, send electronic messages (or email) to someone at another university, or play a game against a hundred other people from twenty different countries, the Internet has got *something* that you'll find interesting. And, odds are, while you're searching for that one site you've heard of from the guy next door, you'll find five others that will interest you just as much.

The *World Wide Web (WWW)* is part of the Internet that you can think of as an accessible network of networks across the globe. Because of the Web's unique hypertext link system, you can easily navigate through and access information on virtually any subject from a potentially unlimited number of sources. Using a Web browser, you simply click on a word or phrase of interest that leads to other related subjects and so on. This hypertext method of navigation allows you to hop from information on a computer in one part of the world to information on a computer that could be nearby or thousands of miles away.

If you have the Internet connection you can look for information on chemical engineering and computers by logging on to the relevant website. The following information was received by the use of a search engine and querying for the computer engineering and chemical engineering topics. Wherever available, the site addresses are also given.

1) Computer Engineering Technology, Bachelor of Science Computer Engineering Technology, Mostafa Mortezai, Ph.D., Chair Computer Engineering
http://www.cogswell.edu/academics/cet/cet.html (2k)

2) The Chemical Engineering Computer Center
http://virginia.eng.auth.gr/info/comput.html

3) RIT - Computer Engineering Technology, George Zion, Coordinator
http://www.rit.edu/RIT/COMD/UGradCat/Colleges/CAST/EngTech/comptech.html

4) Rochester Institute of Technology (Computer Engineering) Institute of Technology (Computer Engineering)
http://zoo.cs.umass.edu/~kaplan/jobs/rit-ce.html (2k)

5) An International Journal of Computers & Chemical Engineering
http://www.elsevier.nl/catalogue/SA2/210/06300/06325/349/349.editors.html

6) HOME CATALOGUE UP SEARCH HELP, ContentsDirect now available Computers & Chemical Engineering
http://www.elsevier.nl/catalogue/SAA/210/06300/06325/349/349.html

7) Chemical Engineering and Chemical Engineers
http://www.tuns.ca/che/aboutche.html

8) Engineering Technology B.S. in Engineering Technology, Guttenberg Information Technologies Center, Room 2100.
http://www.njit.edu/njIT/catalog/undergraduate/94/28.html

9) Chemical Engineering Principles
http://www.chemeng.ed.ac.uk/course/ceplh/notes/www.html

10) Engineering and Science Curtin Online Handbook, Bachelor of Engineering (Chemical Engineering)
http://www.curtin.edu.au/curtin/handbook/engsci/ch9616.html

You can log on to any of the addresses given above to obtain information on a wide variety of topics, including the following:

Process Simulation

- Capacity Expansion of a Specialty Plant Using BATCHES - Mike Liguori, Rhone Poulenc, Inc., and Paul Travis, Batch Process Technologies

- The Design of Complex Azeotropic Distillation Systems Using Geometric Methods - Stanley Wasylkiewicz, Leo Kobylka, Marco Satyro, Hyprotech

- PROTISS: An Example of Open Simulation Integration - Stu Goldfarb, Simulation Sciences, Inc.

- Intelligent Data Transfer - Process Simulation Tool - Tim Howley, AEA Technology Engineering Software

- Optimization of Pharmaceutical and Food Process Development - Demetri Petrides and John Calandranis, Intelligen, Inc.

- Dynamic Process Simulation - Chris Sowa, Hyprotech International

Intelligent Systems

- Advanced Control and Optimization of Manufacturing Processes Using Neural Networks - James D. Keeler, Pavilion Technologies, Inc.

- Visualization, Modeling and Troubleshooting Batch Manufacturing

- Processes Using Neural Networks - Stephen Piche, Pavilion Technologies, Inc.

- Applications of Neural Networks and Genetic Algorithms for Process Monitoring and Optimization - Ed Wilson, AI Ware, Inc.

Manufacturing Execution Systems

- The Chemical Industry: Lessons Learned in Implementing SAP R/3 - David Dodge, SAP Consulting and Services, IBM
- MES at a Bulk Pharmaceutical Chemical Research Site - Kim Conklin and Geoffrey Netto, Rhone Poulenc Rorer
- MES Solutions for Batch Process Industries - Robert Black, ABB Industrial Systems
- Flexible Production at Hybrid Manufacturers - Jeffrey Kissling, Wonderware Corp.

Enterprise Computing

- Plant Information System and Software Integration - Pat Kennedy, OSI Software, Inc.
- Technology's Role in Managing Environmental Health and Safety - Richard Freeborn, Datalogix International, Inc.
- Closing the Information Gap with Advanced Process Execution - Pradeep Amladi, Hewlett-Packard Co.

Computational Fluid Dynamics

- CFD Analysis Improves Cooling Pumps - Gene Sabini, Goulds Pumps, Inc., Glenn Smith, Advanced Scientific Computing
- Troubleshooting Chemical Process Equipment with FLUENT CFD Software - S. Subbiah, Ph.D., Fluent, Inc.
- Numerical Simulation of Stirred Reactors - Dr. Vanchi Gurumoorthy, AEA Technology

CAD and Process Design Tools

- New Trends in Software for Concurrent Engineering - Rick Geritz, ICARUS Corp.
- The Design Envelope as a Powerful Aid to Sizing Shell-and-Tube Exchangers - David Butterworth, Sr. HTFS Consultant, and Ian Kirk, AEA Technology
- New Wave Plant Design and Data Management Software - Buddy Cleveland, Jacobus Technology, Inc.

Productivity Tools for Process Systems

- The Management of Change of Instrumentation and Control Systems - Michael Spenser, QIC Systems

- SYNAPSE: A Molecular Design Tool for Engineering Chemicals - Kevin G. Joback, Molecular Knowledge Systems, Inc.

- Use Software to Reduce the Costs of Field Tests - Nicholas Capik, ABZ, and Ron Chasteen, Echlin Technical Center

Computer-Based Training

- Compliance Through Knowledge Transfer—A Case for PROCEDUREWARE - Rick Bawcum, HTG

- The Silver Bullet for Control Software Verification - Michael Sullivan, Cape Software

- Process Simulators for Training Plant Operators - Ray Froeschle, Sun Refining, Donald Glaser, Atlantic Simulation, Inc.

Information Technology

- Enterprise-Wide Security and Auditing - Rebecca Duncan, Senior Analyst

- Corporate High-Speed LANs and Virtual LANs: Current Practices - Christopher Baum, Managing Senior Analyst

- Operating System Interoperability - Deborah Hess, Senior Analyst

Environmental Design

- AEA Toolkit: A New Approach in the Application of Conceptual Design Tools - Nick Hallas, AEA Technology

- Modeling of Wastewater Treatment Processes - Demetri Petrides and John Calandranis, Intelligen, Inc.

- Low-Cost Power Generation That Meets Environmental Requirements - Jerry Howard, Ultramax Corp.

- Flow and Transport Modeling in Remediation Systems - Carlo San Giovanni and Brent Dell, Geraghty & Miller, Inc.

Environmental Data and Process Safety

- Data Handling Systems for Economical Emissions Monitoring - Joseph Larusso, Contec Systems

- Integrated Computer Programs for Environmental Data Management - Allen Hatfield, Mitchell Scientific, Inc.

- The Next Generation of EHS Management Programs - Gabriele Crognale, MCG/Roux Associates

- Pressure-Relief System Documentation: Key to OSHA 1910 Compliance - Aman Ahmad, Berwanger, Inc.

VIIIN. COMPUTERS & CHEMICAL ENGINEERING—A JOURNAL

For information about the application of the computer to the chemical industry, you can read regularly the journal, "Computers & Chemical Engineering, An International Journal of Computer Applications in Chemical Engineering," designed for the chemical engineers and engineers in the chemical process industries, especially those of a process systems orientation.

"Computers & Chemical Engineering" is primarily a journal of record for new developments in the application of computing and systems technology to chemical engineering problems. Several major areas of chemical engineering study are represented in the journal, including:

- Process synthesis, analysis and design,
- Dynamic analysis and control of chemical processes.
- Design methods for chemical engineering equipment, including chemical reactors, distillation columns, extractors, etc.
- Applications of computing and numerical analysis in chemical engineering science.
- Process operations (e.g., integrated manufacturing systems, reliability, safety, scheduling).

Articles published cover different aspects of the application of computing to one or more of these various areas, including new applications of established methods, comparisons of alternative methodologies, descriptions of state-of-the-art industrial applications and significant computing developments targeted at training/education.

"Computers & Chemical Engineering" publishes full-length articles, survey papers, journal reviews, Short Notes and Letters to the Editor, and the annual proceedings of ESCAPE—the European Symposium on Computer Aided Process Engineering.

The table of contents of this journal is now available pre-publication, via e-mail, as part of the free ContentsDirect service from Elsevier Science. You may send an e-mail message to cdhelp@elsevier.co.uk for further information about this service.

VIIIO. OBJECT-ORIENTED PROGRAMMING AND CHEMICAL ENGINEERING

Programming for computers and the development of programming languages for computers are an evolutionary process. The evolution of programming languages from the first generation machine language to the fourth generation high-level languages has shown a gradual shift from machine-oriented languages to user-friendly languages which offer easier interface to work with. There has been also a shift from the procedure-oriented languages like FORTRAN, COBOL, Pascal, C to the object-oriented languages like Smalltalk and the much hyped C++ with its visual version.

The object-oriented programming (OOP) languages are not magical, not even unfamiliar, to anyone with a scientific programming background. Indeed, they only extend the rigorously logical beauty of very familiar languages such as FORTRAN. Nevertheless, these clever extensions provide elegant mechanisms for managing engineering data.

Offering a richer set of tools for building logical models than FORTRAN, the OOP languages can be used to create your own data types (called **classes**); you can declare as many parameters as you like for each user-defined data type (called **objects** or **instances**); you write functions that are tied to specific data type (called **functions**); you can hide data and executable code within a data type (called **private members** and **member functions**); and you can declare functions to be subordinate to other functions (called **inheritance** and **refinement**).

A language like FORTRAN provides a fixed set of data types, including real numbers, integers, character strings, etc. FORTRAN does not provide a mechanism for combining these primitives into higher-level data structures. The C++ class facility enables you to assemble a variety of primitive types into a structure that can be named and understood as a type in itself.

As an example, for a chemical equipment design, a programmer may wish to implement a conceptual model of a line segment as a part of pointers to 3D vertices, which are themselves represented as three real values denoting the (x,y,z) coordinates of each vertex. C++ enables the programmer to create a "vertex" class which contains three real values describing its coordinates. A "line" class can then be created that points to two vertices. In contrast, this simple conceptual model may be surprisingly "complex" when mapped to FORTRAN primitives.

The three real coordinates of the vertex class described above are called its attributes. Likewise, the pointers to two vertices comprise the attributes of the line class. In general, attributes capture the data that is essential to defining the class.

Let us take another example encountered frequently in chemical process and equipment design. Consider a class written to store an array of temperatures. Assume the array of real numbers representing temperatures is declared to be private to this class. The user of the class then could not directly access these members. Instead, the user might be provided with eight public member functions. The first might be designed to store a Celsius temperature in one element of the array. The next three might store temperatures provided in Fahrenheit, Kelvin, or Rankine. The last four would return an element of the temperature array in any of the four possible unit systems. The calling format for these member functions comprises the specification.

The real numbers representing temperatures stored within the private array would be in one of the four possible unit systems. Thus, one of the four member functions written to store a temperature could simply insert the value of the input temperature directly into the designated location of the private array. The remaining three would have to convert the input temperature to the unit system used in the private array before the insertion. The return member functions would be coded in a parallel fashion.

The implementation consists of the real numbers stored in the private array and the executable code within the member functions described above. Note that the user of the class need only know the specification, of calling format for the public member functions, to take full advantage of the functionality of the class. The user probably will not know, and does not need to know, the implementation. For example, the user does not have to know the units corresponding to the real numbers inserted in the private array. Only the authors of the class need deal with the implementation.

High modularity is achieved by declaring all data stored within an object to be private. All interactions with the data are then decoupled through member functions. This strictly separates the specification from the implementation.

Now assume that the initial implementation for the temperature array class is written to store each temperature in the private array in Kelvin. However, when the software is put into production, the implementor of the temperature class discovers the temperatures are being stored in Fahrenheit in 90% of the applications where the class is used. The implementor can then increase the efficiency of the class by actually storing Fahrenheit temperatures in the private array. The efficiency would improve because the numerical operations required to perform unit conversions would be eliminated most of the time.

The executable code of the member functions could be changed to actually store Fahrenheit temperatures as private data without changing the specifications, i.e., the calling format for the public member functions could be left untouched. Thus, changing the implementation to the more efficient temperature storage scheme would be invisible to the user of the class, except that the performance would improve. This compresses "reverse tuning" of the class.

While artificially simplistic, this example introduces high degree of software modularity that is made possible by hiding data within classes. This modularity can be used to great advantage in large-scale computer-aided engineering software development and maintenance.

The object-oriented programming languages offer three benefits to the engineer over conventional programming languages:

- The code development time can be reduced and quality increased through the use of inheritance and refinement.
- The improved modeling capabilities of an object language reduce the amount of abstraction that the programmer must apply to convert a real-world system to a computer model.
- The software modularity improves by separating the specification from the implementation.

VIIIP. CHEMICAL ENGINEERING AND COMPUTER HARDWARE

Another aspect of computer interaction with the chemical industry lies in the manufacture of semiconductors which are the heart of computers. The scrupulously clean production of silicon, gallium arsenide and the like, together with the automated fabrication of semiconductor devices, represents the application of chemical technology at its most sophisticated level. Further, the pollution control of such emissions as arsenic in air and water presents another challenge for the chemical engineer.

IX

PERTINENT REFERENCES

1. Associated Chambers of Commerce & Industry of India, "India—A Sound Business Proposition," New Delhi, Assocham (1994).

2. Bazaz, M.C., "Indian Pharmaceutical Guide 1994," New Delhi, Pamposh Publications (1994).

3. Buchner, W., Schliebs, R., Winter, G. & Buchel, K.H., "Industrial Inorganic Chemistry," New York, VCH Publishers (1989).

4. Chenier, P.J., "Survey of Industrial Chemistry," New York, VCH Publishers (1992).

5. Fertilizer Association of India, "Handbook on Fertiliser Technology," New Delhi (1992).

6. Fertilizer Association of India, "Fertiliser Statistics," New Delhi, F.A.I. (1994).

7. Hargeaves, D., Eden-Green, M. & Devaney, J., "World Index of Resources & Population," Aldershot, U.K., Dartmouth Publishing Co. (1994).

8. Investment Research & Information Services, Ltd. (IRIS), "The Investor's Guide to Indian Corporates," Bombay, I.R.I.S. (1994).

9. Kothari Enterprises, "Kothari's Industrial Directory of India 1994," Madras, Kothari Enterprises (1994).

10. Matthews, Vinoo, "Chemical Industry Digest Fact Book 1994," Bombay, Blockdale Publishers (1994).

11. Nandini Consultancy Centre Private Limited, "Global Trends in Chemical Products," Madras, Nandini Centre (1994).

12. Nandini Consultancy Centre Private Limited, "Performance Appraisal of 244 Chemical Companies & Their Share Prospects in 1995," Madras, Nandini Centre (1995).

13. National Press, "The Hindu Survey of Indian Industry 1994," Madras (1994).

14. National Press, "The Hindu Survey of Indian Industry 1995," Madras (1995).

15. Planning Commission, "Energy Modelling for India," New Delhi (1993).

16. Raghavan, R., "Chemical Weekly Buyer's Guide 1994," Bombay, Sevak Publications (1994).

17. Raghavan, R., "Chemical Weekly Annual 1995," Bombay, Sevak Publications (Aug. 15, 1995).

18. SBP Consultants & Engineers Pvt. Ltd., "SBP Handbook of Petrochemical & Downstream Projects," New Delhi, S.B.P. (1991).

19. SBP Consultants & Engineers Pvt. Ltd., "SBP Handbook of Projects for Corporate Diversification," New Delhi, S.B.P. (1992).

20. SBP Consultants & Engineers Pvt. Ltd., "SBP Handbook of Export Oriented Food Processing Projects," New Delhi, S.B.P. (1993).

21. Small Industry Research Institute, "S.I.R.I. Directory of Industries in India," New Delhi, S.I.R.I. (1995).

22. Technology Information, Forecasting & Assessment Council (TIFAC), "Manufacturing Technologies for High Volume Industrial Air Gases," Publication No. S-044, New Delhi (1993).

23. United Nations Environment Programme, "Chemical Pollution: A Global Overview," Geneva, U.N.E.P. (1992).

24. United States Department of the Interior, Bureau of Mines, "Mineral Industries of Asia & the Pacific," Wash., D.C. (1992).

25. Weissermel, K. & Arpe, H.J., "Industrial Organic Chemistry," New York, VCH Publishers (1993).

X

LEADING CHEMICAL PRODUCERS AND RELATED COMPANIES IN INDIA

You have now had a panoramic view of the chemical process industries with particular reference to conditions in the Indian chemical industry.

You may be a college or university student about to embark on an industrial career. You may be in the business of manufacturing or selling chemical raw materials or chemical plant equipment. You may be a businessman interested in investment in the chemical industry. In any event, it is the hope of the authors that going through this book has made you better prepared for your next step.

A list of leading chemical producers and related companies in India is now appended to give you additional entree to the Indian chemical industry.

Good luck!

ABS Industries Ltd.

Office: P.O. Box No. 74
11th Floor, Kirthi Towers
Tilak Road, Baroda 390 001 (Gujarat)

Factory: 51, GIDC Industrial Estate
Nandesari 391 340
Dist. Baroda (Gujarat)

Product: ABS Resins

Adarsh Chemicals & Fertilizers Ltd.

Office: Udhna, Surat 394 210 (Gujarat)

Factory: Same Location

Products: Sulfuric Acid, Superphosphate Fertilizers, Maleic Anhydride

Aegis Chemical Industries Ltd.

Office: Baldota Bhavan 117
Maharshi Karva Road
Bombay 400 020 (Maharashtra)

Factories: (1) Petrochemical Works
National Highway No. 8
Vapi, Dist. Bulsar (Gujarat)

(2) Oleochemical Division
Plot No. E-11, Additional Jalgaon Industrial Area
Jalgaon 425 001 (Maharashtra)

Products: Formaldehyde, Hexamine, Pentaerythritol

Ahmedabad Manufacturing and Calico Printing Co. Ltd.

Office: Outside Jamalpur Gate
Ahmedabad 380 022 (Gujarat)

Factory: Anik Chembur, Bombay (Maharashtra)

Products: Trichloroethylene and Perchloroethylene, Caustic Soda

Albright, Morarji & Pandit Ltd.

Office: Raj Mahal
3rd Floor, 84 Veer Nariman Road
Bombay 400 020 (Maharashtra)

Factories: (1) Plots F-2 & F-3, MIDC Chemical Zone
Ambarnath 421 501, Dist. Thane (Maharashtra)
(2) Plot Nos. 103 & 104, MIDC Industrial Area
Dhatay, Roha Taluk, Dist. Raigad (Maharashtra)

Products: Sulfuric Acid, Phosphoric Acid, Sodium Phosphates

Alchemie Organics Ltd.

Office: 74 Matru Smruti, Road No. 4, Scheme No. 6
Sion East, Bombay 400 022 (Maharashtra)

Factory: B-39, MIDC, Kalyan Shill Road
Near Police Station, Dombivli East
Dist. Thane (Maharashtra)

Products: Aromatic Intermediates

Alembic Chemical Works Co. Ltd.

Office: Alembic Road, Baroda 390 003 (Gujarat)

Factories: (1) Same address as above
(2) Panelev, Tal. Halol, Dist. Panchmahal 390 003 (Gujarat)

Products: Drugs (fourth largest producer in India), Polypropylene Fiber and Yarn

Alkyl Amines Chemicals Ltd.

Office: 401-407 Nirman Vyapar Kendra
Plot No. 10, DBC, Vashi, New
Bombay 400 705 (Maharashtra)

Factory: Plot No. A-7, MIDC Patalganga
Industrial Area, Village Khaire
Taluka Khalapur, Raigad 410 220 (Maharashtra)

Product: Alkyl Amines

Allied Resins & Chemicals Ltd.

Office: 13, Camac St.
Calcutta 700 017 (W.B.)
Factories: Calcutta (2 locations)
Product: Formaldehyde

Alpine Solvex Ltd.

Office: Industrial Area, Pithampur, Dist. Thar 453 001 (M.P.)
Factory: 10-11, Yeshwant Niwas Road
Indore 452 003, M.P.
Products: Soybean Oil & Cake

Ambalal Sarabhai Enterprises Ltd.

Office: Wadi, Baroda (Gujarat)
Factories: (1) Same as above
(2) Ahmedabad (Gujarat)
Products: Pharmaceuticals (sixth largest producer in India)

Aminex Chemicals Ltd.

Office: D-4, MIDC Industrial Area
Kurkumbh, Tal Daund
Dist. Pune (Maharashtra)
Factory: Same location as above
Product: Sulfuric Acid

Amit Alcohol Ltd.

Office: 8, National Highway
Vapi, Dist. Valsad (Gujarat)
Factory: Same location
Products: Ethanol, Acetaldehyde, Pentaerythritol

Andhra Petrochemicals Ltd.

Office: Venkatarayapuram, Tanuku
West Godavari Dist. 534 215 (A.P.)
Factory: Opposite Naval Dry Dock,
Beside Dhanireddy Godowns
Visakhapatnam 530 014 (A.P.)
Products: 2-Ethylhexanol, Other Oxo Products

Andhra Pradesh Paper Mills Ltd.

Office: 501-509 Swapnalok Complex
92/93 Sarojini Devi Road
Secunderabad 500 003 (A.P.)
Factory: Rajahmundry (A.P.)
Products: Paper and Paper Board

Andhra Pradesh Rayons Ltd.

Office: 31-A Sarojini Devi Road, Secunderabad 500 003 (A.P.)
Factory: Warangal (A.P.)
Product: Rayon-Grade Cellulose Pulp

Andhra Sugars Ltd.

Office: Venkatarayapuram, Tanuku 534 215
West Godavari Dist. (A.P.)
Factory: Same location as above
Products: Sulfuric Acid, Alcohol, Acetic Acid, Caustic Soda, Sugar

Anil Chemicals Ltd.

Office: J-18, MIDC Area, Chikalthana
Aurangabad 431 210 (Maharashtra)
Factory: Waidhan Sidhi (M.P.)
Product: Ammonium Nitrate

Anil Starch Products Ltd.

Office: Anil Road, P.O. No. 10009, Ahmedabad 380 025 (Gujarat)
Factories: (1) Same as above
(2) Nava Bunder Road
Bhavnagar (Gujarat)
Products: Sulfuric Acid, Fertilizers, Starch Derivatives

Apollo Tyres Ltd.

Office: 6th Floor, Cherupushopam Building
Shanmugham Road, Cochin 682 031 (Kerala)
Factories: (1) Perambra, Dist. Trichur (Kerala)
(2) Baroda (Gujarat)
(3) Vadodara (Gujarat)
Products: Automobile Tires

Armour Polymers Ltd.

Office: 54-A, M. Vassanji Road
Andheri East, Bombay 400 093 (Maharashtra)
Factory: T-140, MIDC Industrial Area, Tarapore 401 506 (Maharashtra)
Product: Pyridine

Aruna Sugars & Enterprises Ltd.

Office: Aruna Centre, 145 Sterling Road
Madras 600 034 (T.N.)
Factory: Aruna Puram, Pennadam R.S.
South Arcot Dist. 606 111 (T.N.)
Products: Sugar, Ethanol

Ashok Organic Industries Ltd.

Office: 406, Sharda Chambers
33, New Marine Lines,
Bombay 400 020 (Maharashtra)
Factory: Plot 71-A, GIDC Industrial Estate
Nandesari, Dist. Baroda 391 340 (Gujarat)
Products: Caustic, Chlorine, Chloracetic Acid, Ethanol, Acetic Acid, Acetic Anhydride

Asian Paints (India) Ltd.

Office: 2702, GIDC Industrial Area
Ankleshwar 393 002 (Gujarat)
Factory: Plot No. 5, Gaiwadi Industrial Estate
Goregaon (W) Bombay 400 062 (Maharashtra)
Products: Phthalic Anhydride, Paints

Asian Peroxides Ltd.

Office: 69, Armenian Street
Madras 600 001 (T.N.)
Factory: G.N.T. Road, Kota Polor Village
Nellore District 524 121 (A.P.)
Product: Hydrogen Peroxide

Assam Petrochemicals Ltd.

Office: Lamb Road, Ambari
Guwahati 781 001 (Assam)
Factory: Namrup, P.O. Parbatpur 786 623
Dist. Dibrugarh, Assam
Products: Methanol, Formaldehyde, Urea-Formaldehyde Resins

Associated Cement Ltd.

Office: Cement House, 121 Maharshi Karve Road, Bombay 400 020 (Maharashtra)
Factories: (1) Chanda (Maharashtra)
(2) Gagal (M.P.)
(3) Madukkarai (T.N.)
(4) Wadi (A.P.)
(5) Jamul (M.P.)
(6) Kymore (M.P.)
Product: Cement (largest producer in India)

Astra IDL Ltd.

Office: 32/1-2 Crescent Towers, Crescent Road
P.O. Box 5039, Bangalore 560 001 (Karnataka)
Factory: 12th Mile on Bellary Road
Yellahanka, Venkatala Kattigenahalli Village
Bangalore 560 003 (Karnataka)
Products: Pharmaceuticals

Atic Industries Ltd.

Office: Crescent House
19 Walchand Hirachand Marg
Ballard Estate, Bombay 400 038 (Maharashtra)
Factory: Post Atul 396 020
Dist. Valsad (Gujarat)
Products: Dyestuffs

Atul Products Ltd.

Office: P.O. Atul 396 020
Dist. Valsad (Gujarat)
Factory: Same as above
Products: Dye Intermediates

Aurangabad Paper Mills Ltd.

Office: 171/B Mittal Tower
Nariman Point, Bombay 400 021 (Maharashtra)
Factory: MIDC, Paithan, Dist. Aurangabad (Maharashtra)
Product: Kraft Paper

Bajaj Hindustan Ltd.

Office: Bajaj Bhawan
2nd Floor, 226 Nariman Point
Jamnalal Bajaj Marg
Bombay 400 021 (Maharashtra)
Factory: Kheri (U.P.)
Products: Sugar, Alcohol, Cement

Bakelite Hylam Ltd.

Office: Surya Towers, 3rd Floor
104 Sardar Patel Road
Secunderabad 500 003 (A.P.)
Factory: 7-2-1669 Sanathnagar
P.B. 1908, Hyderabad 500 018 (A.P.)
Products: Formaldehyde, Phenolic Resins

Balaji Amines Ltd.

Office: E-93, Sholapur 413 006 (Maharashtra)
Factory: Gate No. 197, Tamalwadi
Tal. Tuljapur, Dist. Osmanabad 413 623
(Maharashtra)
Products: Methylamines

Balkrishna Industries Limited

Office: 106, Sardar Patel Road, Secunderabad 500 003 (A.P.)
Factory: B-66, MIDC, Waluj, Aurangabad (Maharashtra)

Products: Automobile Tires and Tubes, Paper

Ballarpur Industries Ltd.

Office: P.O. Ballarpur 442 901
Dist. Chandrapur (Maharashtra)
Factories: (1) Same as above
(2) P.O. Binaga (Karnataka)
(3) Yamunanagar (Haryana)
(4) Singach, Dist. Jamnagar (Gujarat)
Products: Caustic, Chlorine, Phosphoric Acid, Paper

Balmer, Lawrie & Co. Ltd.

Office: 21 Netaji Subhas Road
Calcutta 700 001 (W.B.)
Factories: (1) Calcutta (W.B.)
(2) Madras (T.N.) (leather chemicals)
(3) Grease Div., 149 Jackeria Bdr Road, Sewree, Bombay (Maharashtra)
Products: Greases, Leather Chemicals

Balrampur Chini Mills Ltd.

Office: FMC Fortuna, 234/3A A.J.C. Bose Road
Calcutta 700 020 (W.B.)
Factory: Balrampur (U.P.)
Product: Sugar

Baroda Rayon Corporation Ltd.

Office: Hoechst House
193 Backbay Reclamation
Nariman Point, Bombay 400 021 (Maharashtra)
Factory: Surat 394 220 (Gujarat)
Products: Nylon Yarn, Polyester Filament Yarn, Nylon Tire Cord, Sulfuric Acid

B.A.S.F. India Ltd.

Office: Rhone Poulenc House
S.K. Alire Marg
Bombay 400 025 (Maharashtra)
Factory: 12, T.T.C. Area
Thane-Belapur Road
Turbhe, Thane 400 613 (Maharashtra)
Products: Polystyrene, Leather Chemicals, Pesticides

Bayer (India) Ltd.

Office: Express Towers
Nariman Point, Bombay 400 021 (Maharashtra)
Factory: Kolshet Road
Thane 400 607 (Maharashtra)

Products: Pesticides, Rubber Chemicals, Pharmaceuticals

Bengal Chemicals & Pharmaceuticals Ltd.
Office: 6, Ganesh Chunder Ave.
Calcutta 700 013 (W.B.)
Factory: 164, Maniktala Main Road
Calcutta 700 054 (W.B.)
Products: Sulfuric Acid, Pharmaceuticals

Bengal Immunity Ltd.
Office: Immunity House
153 Lenin Sarani
Calcutta 700 013 (W.B.)
Factory: 44 Gopal Lal Tagore Road, Calcutta 700 036 (W.B.)
Products: Pharmaceuticals

Berger Paints India Ltd.
Office: Berger House
129, Park Street
Calcutta 700 017 (W.B.)
Factory: Howrah (West Bengal)
Products: Paints

Beta Naphthol Ltd.
Office: World Trade Center Arcade
Unit No. 16, Ground Floor, Cuffe Parade
Bombay 400 005 (Maharashtra)
Factory: 411, Vikram Tower, III Floor
Sapna-Sangeeta Main Road, Indore 452 001 (M.P.)
Products: Dye Intermediates

Bharat Aluminum Co. Ltd.
Office: Aluminum Sadan, Core-6
Scope Office Complex, 7 Lodi Road, New Delhi 110 003
Factories: (1) Balco Township, Korba via Champa
Dist. Bilaspur (M.P.)
(2) Bidhanbag, Asansol, Dist. Burdwan (W.B.)
Products: Bauxite and Aluminum Metal

Bharat Commerce & Industries Ltd.
Office: Surya Kiran
5th Floor, 19, Kasturba Gandhi Marg, New Delhi 110 001
Factories: (1) Nagda (M.P.)
(2) Rajpura (Punjab)
(3) Thane (Maharashtra)
(4) Nanjangud (Karnataka)

Products: Cement, Viscose Rayon Yarn

Bharat Petroleum Corp. Ltd.

Office: Bharat Bhavan
Ballard Estate, Bombay 400 038 (Maharashtra)
Factory: Mahul, Bombay 400 074 (Maharashtra)
Products: Benzene, Toluene, Hexane, Kerosene, LPG, Naphtha

Bharat Rasayan Ltd.

Office: 211, Samuel Street
1st Floor, Vadgadi
Bombay 400 003 (Maharashtra)
Factory: E 117, MIDC, Tarapur, Boisar
Dist. Thane 401 501 (Maharashtra)
Products: Agrochemicals including Fenvalerate, Isoproturon, DDVP

Bihar Caustic & Chemicals Ltd.

Office: Ghanshyam Kunj
Garhwa Road
P.O. Rehla 822 124
Dist. Palamau (Bihar)
Factory: Same as above
Products: Caustic, Chlorine

Binani Zinc Ltd.

Office: Mercantile Chambers
12, J.N. Heredia Marg
Ballard Estate, Bombay 400 038 (Maharashtra)
Factory: Binanipuram 683 502 (Kerala)
Products: Zinc, Sulfuric Acid, Cadmium

Bindal Agro Chem Ltd.—Now Oswal Chemicals & Fertilizers Ltd.

Office: 12th Floor, Gopala Tower
25 Rajendra Place
New Delhi 110 008
Factories: (1) Shahjahanpur (U.P.)
(2) Rishra (West Bengal)
(3) Mandideep (M.P.)
(4) Dewas (M.P.)
Products: Urea, LDPE

Birla Jute & Industries Ltd.

Office: Birla Building
9/1 R.N. Mukherjee Road
Calcutta 700 001 (W.B.)

Factories: (1) Birlapur (W.B.)
(2) Satna (M.P.)
(3) Chittor (M.P.)
(4) Durgapur (W.B.)
(5) Howrah (W.B.)
Products: Cement, Jute Goods, PVC Coated Fabrics, Calcium Carbide

Birla Salt & Chemicals Ltd.
Office: Birlanagar, Gwalior 474 004 (M.P.)
Factory: See above
Products: Salt, Gypsum

BOC India Ltd. (formerly IOL Limited or Indian Oxygen)
Office: Oxygen House
P43 Taratala Road
Calcutta 700 088 (W.B.)
Factories: (1) Calcutta (W.B.)
(2) Jamshedpur (Bihar)
(3) Tarapur (Maharashtra)
(4) Taloja (Maharashtra)
Products: Oxygen, Nitrogen, Argon

Boehringer Mannheim (India) Ltd.
Office: United India Building
Sir Ferozeshah Mehta Road
Fort, Bombay 400 001 (Maharashtra)
Factory: Kolshet Road, Thane 400 607 (Maharashtra)
Products: Pharmaceutical Intermediates

Bombay Dyeing & Mfg. Co. Ltd.
Office: Neville House
J.N. Heredia Marg
Ballard Estate
Bombay 400 038 (Maharashtra)
Factories: (1) MIDC Patalganga, Rasayani
Dist. Raigad (Maharashtra)
(2) 18/1 MIDC Dhatav, Roha (Maharashtra)
Products: Xylene, Dimethyl Terephthalate

Bombay Oxygen Corp. Ltd.
Office: L.B.S. Marg
Mulund (West), Bombay 400 080 (Maharashtra)
Factories (all in Maharashtra):
(1) Mulund
(2) Kalwe
(3) Khopoli

(4) Pune
(5) Nira
(6) Tarapur
Products: Oxygen, Nitrogen, Acetylene

Bombay Paints Ltd.
Office: Corridor Road
Gavanpada, Chembur, Bombay 400 074 (Maharashtra)
Factory: See above
Products: Paints, Enamels and Varnishes

Bombay Tyres International Ltd.
Office: Hay Bunder Road, Bombay 400 033 (Maharashtra)
Factory: Same location as office
Products: Tires, Tubes

Bongaigaon Refinery & Petrochemicals Ltd.
Office: P.O. Dhaligaon, Dist. Bongaigaon (Assam)
783 385
Factory: Same address
Products: Xylenes, Methanol, Dimethyl Terephthalate, Polyester Fiber

Boots Pharmaceuticals Ltd.
Office: 17, R. Kamani Road
Ballard Estate
Bombay 400 038 (Maharashtra)
Factories (all in Maharashtra):
(1) 107, Sion (E), Bombay 400 022
(2) Admednagar, Pune
(3) Jejuri
Products: Pharmaceuticals

Borax Morarji Ltd.
Office: Jolly Bhajan No. 2, First Floor
Sir Vithaldas Thackersey Marg
New Marine Lines, Bombay 400 020 (Maharashtra)
Factories: (1) Mahatma Gandhi Road, Ambernath 421 501
Dist. Thane (Maharashtra)
(2) Nedumangad Road, Shenbagaraman Puthur 629 304
Dist. Kanyakumari (T.N.)
Products: Borax, Boric Acid

Burroughs Wellcome (India) Ltd.
Office: 16, NGN Vaidya Marg
Bombay 480 023 (Maharashtra)

Factory: Plot 91, Lal Bahadur Shastri Marg
Mulund West, Bombay 400 080 (Maharashtra)
Products: Drugs

Calcutta Chemical Co. Ltd.
Office: 28, S. Roy Road
Calcutta 700 039 (W.B.)
Factory: See above
Products: Soap, Detergents, Glycerin

Camphor & Allied Products Ltd.
Office: Plot No. 3, GIDC Industrial Estate
Nandesari 391 340, Vadodara (Gujarat)
Factory: See above
Products: Camphor, Terpene Chemicals

Carbon & Chemicals India Ltd.
Office: XXXIX/137-A Krishnaswamy Cross Road
Cochin 682 035 (Kerala)
Factory: Karimugal, Brahmapuram, P.O. Cochin 682 303 (Kerala)
Product: Carbon Black

Castrol India Ltd.
Office: White House
91, Walkeshwar Road, Bombay 400 006 (Maharashtra)
Factories: (1) Patalganga (Maharashtra)
(2) Bombay (Maharashtra)
(3) Madras
(4) Calcutta (W.B.)
Products: Lubricating Oil, Grease

Cauvery Papers Ltd.
Office: 168 A, 8th B Main Road
Rajamahal Vilas, Bangalore 560 080
Factory: Sathyagala Village
Kollegal Taluk, Mysore Dist. (Karnataka)
Product: Kraft Paper

Ceat Tyres of India Ltd.
Office: 463, Dr. Annie Besant Road
Bombay 400 025 (Maharashtra)
Factories: (1) Bhandup, Bombay (Maharashtra)
(2) Mehboobnagar, Near Hyderabad (A.P.)
(3) Satpur, Nasik (Maharashtra)
(4) Waluj, Dist. Aurangabad (Maharashtra)
(5) Thane (Maharashtra)

(6) Gwalior (M.P.)
(7) Gandhinagar (Gujarat)
Products: Automobile Tires and Tubes, Nylon Tire Fabric

Cellulose Products of India Ltd.
Office: National Chambers, Office Nos. 7 & 5, 2nd Floor
Near Dipali Theater, Ashram Road
Ahmedabad 380 009 (Gujarat)
Factories: (1) Kathwada (Dist. Ahmedabad) (Gujarat)
(2) Ramol (Dist. Ahmedabad) (Gujarat)
(3) Kappalpur, Dist. Madurai (T.N.)
(4) Pungam, Dist. Bharuch, Ankleshwar (Gujarat)
Products: Carboxymethyl Cellulose, Ethanol, Acetic Acid

Century Enka Ltd.
Office: 9 Waterloo Street, 2nd Floor
Calcutta 700 069 (W.B.)
Factories: (1) Bhosari, Pune 411 026 (Maharashtra)
(2) Mahad Dist., Raigad 402 301 (Maharashtra)
Products: Nylon Yarn, Polyester Yarn, Nylon Tire Cord, Methanol

Century Textiles & Industries Ltd.
Office: Century Bhavan
Dr. Annie Besant Road
Bombay 400 025 (Maharashtra)
Factories: (1) Textile Mills: Pandurang Budhkar Marg, Bombay 400 025 (Maharashtra)
(2) Century Rayon: Rayon, Tyrecord and Chemical Plants,
Murbad Road, Kalyan (Maharashtra)
(3) Century Minerals & Chemicals, Jamnagar (Gujarat)
(4) Century Cement, Baikunth, Raipur (Madhya Pradesh)
(5) Maihar Cement, Sarlanagar, Maihar (M.P.)
(6) Century Pulp and Paper, Lalkua, Dist. Nainital (U.P.)
(7) Manikgarh Cement, Gadchandur, Dist. Chandrapur (Maharashtra)
Products: Caustic, Cement, Rayon Yarn, Sulfuric Acid

Cetex Petrochemicals Ltd.
Office: 12, Bishop Wallers Ave. (E)
Mylapore, Madras 600 004 (T.N.)
Factory: Manali, Madras 600 068 (T.N.)
Product: Methy Ethyl Ketone

Chambal Fertilizers & Chemicals Ltd.
Office: Devika Tower (Ground Floor), 6, Nehru Place, New Delhi 110 019
Factory: Village Gadepan
Dist. Kota
P.O. Simlia 325 203 (Rajasthan)

Products: Ammonia, Urea

Chemagro International Ltd.

Office: Plot 51, Nagarjuna Hills
Hyderabad 500 482 (A.P.)
Factory: Plot 117, Allinagaram
Etcherla Mandal, Srikakrulam 532 403 (A.P.)
Products: Pesticides including Monocrotophos

Chemfab Alkalies Ltd.

Office: Temple Tower, 4th Floor
576 Anna Salai, Madras 600 035 (T.N.)
Factory: Gnanananda Place
Kalapet, Pondicherry 605 104 (T.N.)
Products: Caustic, Chlorine

Chemicals & Plastics India Ltd.

Office: 8, Cathedral Road
Madras 600 086 (T.N.)
Factories: (1) Caustic Soda Division
Raman Nagar, Mettur Dam
R.S. 636 402 (Tamil Nadu)
(2) Salt Works
Sethu Rastha, Vedaranyam 614 810, Thanjavur Dist. (T.N.)
(3) PVC Division
Marigampalli Village, P.B. No. 16, Krishnagiri, 635 001
Dharmapuri Dist. (T.N.)
(4) Industrial Alcohol Plant
P.O. Box 16, Krishnagiri 635 001 (T.N.)
Products: Chlorine, Trichloroethylene, Perchloroethylene, PVC

Cheminor Drugs Ltd.

Office: 7-1-27 Ameerpet, Hyderabad 500 016 (A.P.)
Factories: (1) Jeedimetla (A.P.)
(2) Nalgonda (A.P.)
(3) Srikakulam (A.P.)
Products: Drugs

Chemox Chemical Industries Ltd.

Office: 317, Pooran Asha Building
Narsi Natha Street
Bombay 400 009 (Maharashtra)
Factory: Plot 620/3 GIDC
Panoli, Ankleshwar (Gujarat)
Products: Drugs

Chettinad Cement Corp. Ltd.

Office: Rani Seethai Hall Building
No. 603 Anna Salai, Madras 600 006 (T.N.)
Factory: Trichy (Tamil Nadu)
Product: Cement

Chloride Industries Ltd.

Office: Exide House
59E Chowringhee Road
Calcutta 700 020 (W.B.)
Factories: (1) Shamnagar (West Bengal)
(2) Chinchwad (Maharashtra)
(3) Haldia (West Bengal)
Product: Storage Batteries

Cibatul Ltd.

Office: Atul, Dist. Valsad 396 020 (Gujarat)
Factory: Same location
Products: Formaldehyde, Hexamine, Bisphenol-A, Drug Intermediates, Epoxy Resins

Cipla Ltd.

Office: 289 Dimtikar Road
Bombay Central (Maharashtra)
Factory: A-33/2 MIDC Patalganga 410 220 Dist. Raigad (Maharashtra)
Products: Pharmaceuticals (5th largest producer in India)

Citurgia Biochemicals Ltd.

Office: Neville House, J.N. Heredia Marg
Ballard Estate, Bombay 400 038 (Maharashtra)
Factories: (1) 237/3 GIDC Notified Area
P.O. Pandesara, Udhna, Dist. Surat 394 221 (Gujarat)
(2) Rishikesh 249 021 (U.P.)
Products: Citric Acid, Dibutyl Phthalate, Calcium Carbonate

Claro India Ltd.

Office: 161, Mount Road
Madras 600 002 (T.N.)
Factory: Gummidipoondi
B-7, Sipcot Industrial Complex
Gummidipoondi 601 201 (T.N.)
Products: Formaldehyde, Paraformaldehyde

Coal India Ltd.

Office: Coal Bhawan
10 Netaji Subhas Road
Calcutta 700 001 (West Bengal)

Mines: Bharat Coking Coal Ltd.
105 mines in Bihar, Orissa, and Uttar Pradesh

Eastern Coalfields Ltd.
187 mines in Bihar and West Bengal

Northern Coalfields Ltd.
61 mines in Madhya Pradesh and Uttar Pradesh

Southeastern Coalfields Ltd.
44 mines in Andhra Pradesh and Orissa

Western Coalfields Ltd.
55 mines in Madhya Pradesh, Maharashtra, and Orissa

Products: Coal, Cresol, Ammonium Sulfate

Cochin Refineries Ltd.

Office: P.O. Box No. 2
Abalamnugal, Ernakulam Dist. 682 302 (Kerala)
Factory: Same location
Products: Benzene, Toluene, LPG

Colgate-Palmolive (India) Ltd.

Office: Apeejay House, 3 Dinshaw Vachha Road
Bombay 400 020 (Maharashtra)
Factories: (1) Sewree Fort Road, Bombay 400 015 (Maharashtra)
(2) Waluj Industrial Area, MIDC, Aurangabad 431 133 (Maharashtra)
Products: Soaps

Colour Chem. Ltd.

Office: Ravindra Annexe
194, Churchgate Reclamation
Bombay 400 020 (Maharashtra)
Factories: (1) Balkum (Dist. Thane)
(2) Roma (Dist. Raigad) (both in Maharashtra)
Products: Dyes, Pigments, Pesticides

Cominco Binani Zinc Ltd.

See Binani Zinc Ltd.

Consolidated Fibres & Chemicals Ltd.

Office: Haldia (West Bengal)
Factory: Haldia (West Bengal)
Product: Acrylic Fibers

Consolidated Petrotech Industries Ltd.

Office: Offtel Towers, 6th Floor
R.C. Dutt Road, Vadodara 390 005 (Gujarat)
Factory: National Highway No. 8
Palej, Dist. Bharuch (Gujarat)
Product: Carbon Black

Coromandel Fertilizers Ltd.

Office: Coromandel House
1-2-10 Sardar Patel Road
Secunderabad 500 003 (A.P.)
Factory: Visakhapatnam (A.P.)
Products: Sulfuric Acid, Fertilizers

Cyanamid India Ltd.

Office: Nyloc House
254-D2 Dr. Annie Besant Road
P.O. Box No. 9109
Bombay 400 025 (Maharashtra)
Factory: Atul (Gujarat)
Products: Drugs, Agrochemicals

Dai-Ichi Karkaria Ltd.

Office: Liberty Building
Sir Vithaldas Marg
Bombay 400 020 (Maharashtra)
Factory: 105th Milestone
Bombay-Pune Road
P.O. Kasarwadi, Pune 411 034 (Maharashtra)
Products: Polyols for Polyurethanes, Textile Chemicals

Dalmia Cement (Bharat) Ltd.

Office: 11th & 12th Floors, Hansalaya Building
15 Barakhamba Road, New Delhi 110 001
Factory: Trichy (T.N.)
Products: Cement, Iron Ore

DCL Polyesters Ltd.

Office: Usha Complex, 3rd Floor
345 R, Kingsway, Nagpur 440 001 (Maharashtra)
Factory: Dahali, Mouda Taluq, Nagpur Dist. (Maharashtra)
Product: Polyester Filament Yarn

DCM Shriram Consolidated Ltd.

Office: Kanchenjunga Building
18 Barakhamba Road
New Delhi 110 001

Factory: Kota (Rajasthan)

Products: Caustic, Chlorine, PVC, Cement

DCW Ltd.

Office: Nirmal, 3rd Floor
Nariman Point, Bombay 400 021 (Maharashtra)

Factories:
(1) Caustic Soda/PVC Division
Sahupuram, Arumuganeri, P.O. Chidambaranar 628 202 (T.N.)
(2) Soda Ash Division
Dhrangadhra 363 315 (Gujarat)
(3) Salt Works
Kuda (Gujarat)

Products: Caustic Soda, Chlorine, Trichloroethylene, PVC Resins, Sodium Bicarbonate, Bromine

Deepak Fertilizers & Petrochemicals Corp. Ltd.

Office: Opposite Golf Course, Shastri Nagar
Jail Road, Yerawada, Pune (Maharashtra)

Factory: Plot K-1, MIDC Industrial Area
Taloja A.V. 410 208, Dist. Raigad
P.B. No. 26 (Maharashtra)

Products: Ammonia, Nitric Acid, Ammonium Nitrate, Methanol

Deepak Nitrite Ltd.

Office: Shiv Shakthi
B.G. Kher Road
Worli, Bombay 400 018 (Maharashtra)

Factory: Opposite Golf Course
Jail Road, Yerawada
Pune 411 006 (Maharashtra)

Products: Nitric Acid, Dye Intermediates, Dyes

Detergents India Ltd.

Office: Industrial Development Area
Kodur R.S. 516 101, Cuddapah D.L. (A.P.)

Factory: See above

Products: Detergent Cakes, Bars and Powders

Dhampur Sugar Mills Ltd.

Office: Dhampur (N.R.) District Bijnor (U.P.)

Factories:
(1) Dhampur (U.P.)
(2) Bulandshahr (U.P.)

(3) Barabanki (U.P.)
(4) Moradabad (U.P.)

Products: Kraft Paper, Sugar

Dharamsi Morarji Chemical Co. Ltd.

Office: Prospect Chambers
317/21 Dr. Dadabhoy Naoroji Road
Fort, Bombay 400 001 (Maharashtra)

Factories: (1) Ambernath (Maharashtra)
(2) Roha (Maharashtra)
(3) Kumhari (M.P.)
(4) Jhar (Gujarat)

Product: Sulfuric Acid

Diamines & Chemicals Ltd.

Office: Bharat Vijay Mills Ltd.
Seven Garval
Kalol 382 721 (Gujarat)

Factory: Plot No. 13, P.O. Petrofils, Vadodara 391 347 (Gujarat)

Products: Piperazine and Polyamines

Dr. Beck & Co. Ltd.

Office: Construction House
796/189-B Bhandarkar Road
Pune 411 004 (Maharashtra)

Factories: (1) 147 Bombay-Pune Road
Pimpri, Pune 411 018 (Maharashtra)
(2) Plot No. 1 (A, B & C)
GIDC, Ankleshwar 393 002 (Gujarat)

Products: Epoxy Resins

Dr. Reddy's Laboratories Ltd.

Office: 71-1027 Ameerpet
Hyderabad 500 016 (A.P.)

Factory: Plot No. 108/11, S.V. Coop. Industrial Estate
Bollaram, Narsapur Taluk
Medak Dist. (A.P.)

Products: Bulk Drugs

Dunlop India Ltd.

Office: 57B, Mirza Ghalib Street, Calcutta 700 016 (W.B.)

Factories: (1) Sahaganj, Dist. Hooghly (W.B.)
(2) Ambattur, Dist. Madras (T.N.)

Products: Tires, Tubes, Industrial Belting

Durgapur Chemicals Ltd.

Office: 6 Little Russell Street
Calcutta 700 071 (W.B.)

Factory: Dr. Manemann Sarani
Durgapur 713 215 (West Bengal)

Products: Phthalic Anhydride, Caustic Soda, Chlorine, Chlorobenzene, Phenol, Pentachlorophenol

E.I.D. Parry (India) Ltd.

Office: 234, Dare House, P.O. Box 12, Madras 600 001 (T.N.)

Factories:
(1) Ranipet, N. Arcot Dist. (T.N.)
(2) Ennore (T.N.)
(3) Nellikuppam, S. Arcot Dist. (T.N.)
(4) Tadepalli, Guntur Dist. (A.P.)
(5) Bangalore (Karnataka)

Products: Sugar, Ethanol, Fertilizers

E. Merck (India) Ltd.

Office: Shiva Sagar Estate "A"
Dr. Annie Besant Road
Worli, Bombay 400 018 (Maharashtra)

Factories:
(1) Taloja (Maharashtra)
(2) Usgaon (Goa)

Products: Bulk Drugs

Essar Gujarat Ltd.

Office: Post Hazira
Pin 394 270
Dist. Surat (Gujarat)

Factory: Hazira (Gujarat)

Product: Sponge Iron

Ester Industries Ltd.

Office: 75-76 Amrit Nagar
(Behind N.D.S.E.-I)
New Delhi 110 003

Factory: 10, Charubeta, Pilibhit Road, Khatima Dist.
Nainital 262 308 (U.P.)

Products: Polyester Chips, Film and Filaments

Excel Industries Ltd.

Office: 184-87 S.V. Road, Jogeshwari (W)
Bombay 400 102 (Maharashtra)

Factories:
(1) Veera Desai Road, Amboli Hill
Andheri (W), Bombay 400 058 (Maharashtra)

(2) Plot No. 112, MIDC Industrial Area
Dhatan, Rota, Dist. Raigad (Maharashtra)

Products: Phosphorus and Phosphorus Halides, Pesticides including Endosulfan, Glyphosate, Malathion and Pentachlorophenol

Falcon Tyres Ltd.

Office: Mohan Towers, 50 Residency Road
Bangalore 560 025 (Karnataka)

Factory: Metagalli, K.R.S. Road 571 016 (Karnataka)

Products: Tires, Tubes, Industrial Belting

Fertilizer Corp. of India Ltd.

Office: Madhuban
55 Nehru Place
New Delhi 110 019

Factories: (1) Sindri (Bihar)
(2) Gorakhpur (U.P.)
(3) Ramagundam (A.P.)
(4) Talcher (Orissa)
(5) Korba Project (M.P.)

Products: Ammonia, Nitric Acid, Urea, Argon, Ammonium Salts

Fertilizers & Chemicals Travancore Ltd.

Office: Eloor, Udyogamandal, Cochin 683 501 (Kerala)

Factories: (1) Udyogamandal (Kerala)
(2) Ambalamedu (Kerala)

Products: Ammonia, Urea, Caprolactam, Soda Ash, Sulfuric Acid

Ficom Organics Ltd.

Office: 162, Maker Chambers No. III, 15th Floor
223, Nariman Point, Bombay 400 021 (Maharashtra)

Factory: 3024, GIDC Industrial Area
Ankleshwar, Dist. Bharuch (Gujarat)

Products: Malathion, Quinalphos, Chlorpyrifos and Alkyl Phenols

Finolex Pipes Ltd.

Office: Block D-1, Plot No. 10, MIDC
Chinchwad, Pune 411 019 (Maharashtra)

Factory: Same location as above

Product: PVC Pipes

Flakt India Ltd.

Office: 6 Poonam Building
5/2 Russell Street
Calcutta 700 071 (W.B.)

Factories: (1) Budge Budge Trunk Road, Village Jalkura
24-Parganas (W.B.)
(2) Poonamallee High Road, P.O. Tiruvedaku
Dist. Chingleput (T.N.)
Product: Air Pollution Control Equipment

Gammon Fer-Chems
Office: Gammon House
Veer Savarkar Marg
Prabhadevi, Bombay 400 025 (Maharashtra)
Factory: Refer to above
Products: Sulfuric Acid, Superphosphate Fertilizer

Ganesh Anhydride Ltd.
Office: 191-H, Dr. Viegas Street
9th Cavel Lane
Kalbadevi, Bombay 400 002 (Maharashtra)
Factory: G61/62 MIDC, Tarapur, Boisar (Maharashtra)
Products: Maleic Anhydride, Fumaric Acid, Tetrahydrophthalic Anhydride, Dibutyl Maleate, Dioctyl Maleate

Ganesh Benzoplast Ltd.
Office: 145-A, Dr. Viegas Street, 9th Cavel Lane
Kalbadevi, Bombay 400 002 (Maharashtra)
Factory: G-5/2, MIDC, Tarapur, Boisar (Maharashtra)
Products: Benzoic Acid, Sodium Benzoate, Benzoate Plasticizers

Garware Paints Ltd.
Office: 401, Marine Chambers
43, Sir V. Thackersey Marg
Bombay 400 020 (Maharashtra)
Factory: Refer to above
Products: Paints

Garware Plastics & Polyester Ltd.
Office: Western Express Highway
Vile Parle (East), Bombay 400 057 (Maharashtra)
Factories: (1) Aurangabad (Maharashtra)
(2) Nasik (Maharashtra)
Products: Polyester Chips and Films

German Remedies Ltd.
Office: Shiva Sagar Estate, Block A
Dr. Annie Besant Road
Worli, Bombay 400 018 (Maharashtra)

Factories: (1) M. Vasamji Road (Andheri-Kurla Road), Bombay 400 093 (Maharashtra)
(2) Plot A-2, MIDC, Patalganga, Dist. Raigad (Maharashtra)
(3) Kundaim Industrial Estate, Ponda 403 401 (Goa)
Products: Pharmaceuticals and Intermediates

Glaxo (India) Ltd.
Office: Dr. Annie Besant Road
Worli, Bombay 400 025 (Maharashtra)
Factories: (1) Same address as above
(2) 2nd Pokhran Road, P.B. No. 26, Thane 400 607 (Maharashtra)
(3) Mazughari, P.O. No. 1, Aligarh 202 001 (U.P.)
(4) 3109 GIDC, P.B. No. 64, Ankleshwar (Gujarat)
Products: Pharmaceuticals (#1 manufacturer in India)

Godavari Fertilizers & Chemicals Ltd.
Office: Vani Nilayam
50 Sebastian Road
Secunderabad 500 003 (A.P.)
Factory: Beach Road, Kakinada 533 001 (A.P.)
Products: Diammonium Phosphate, Urea

Godrej Foods Ltd.
Office: Administration Building
Godrej Soaps Ltd.
Eastern Express Highway
Vikhroli (East), Bombay 400 079 (Maharashtra)
Factories: (1) Raisen (M.P.)
(2) Wadala (Maharashtra)
Product: Vegetable Oils

Godrej Soaps Ltd.
Office: Pirojshanagar, Vikhroli, Bombay 400 079 (Maharashtra)
Factories: (1) As above
(2) U-30, Industrial Area, Malanpur, Dist. Bhind 477 116 (M.P.)
Products: Soaps, Detergents, Fatty Acids, Glycerin

Goodlass Nerolac Paints Ltd.
Office: Nerolac House
Ganpatrao Kadam Marg
Lower Parel, Bombay 400 013 (Maharashtra)
Factories: (1) Same as above
(2) Kavesar, Ghodbunder Road, Thane Dist. (Maharashtra)
Products: Paints, Varnishes, Enamels, Pigments

Goodyear India Ltd.

Office: Godrej Bhavan
Mathura Road, New Delhi 110 085
Factory: Mathura Road, Ballabhgarh, Dist. Faridabad 121 004 (Haryana)
Products: Automobile Tires and Tubes, Industrial Belting

Graphite India Ltd.

Office: 31, Chowringhee Road, Calcutta 700 016 (W.B.)
Factory: Durgapur (W.B.)
Product: Graphite Electrodes

Grasim Industries Ltd.

Office: Birlagram, Nagda 456 331 (M.P.)
Factories: (1) Nagda (M.P.)
(2) Gwalior (M.P.)
(3) Jawad (M.P.)
(4) Jaipur (Rajasthan)
(5) Mavoor (Kerala)
(6) Bhiwani (Punjab)
(7) Harihar (Karnataka)
(8) Raigad (Maharashtra)
Products: Caustic Soda, Rayon Grade Pulp, Viscose Fiber, Sponge Iron

Gujarat Alkalies & Chemicals Ltd.

Office: Yashkamal, Sayajigunj
P.O. Box No. 2505, Vadodara 390 005 (Gujarat)
Factory: P.O. Petrochemicals, Vadodara 391 346 (Gujarat)
Products: Soda Ash, Caustic, Chlorine

Gujarat Ambuja Cements Ltd.

Office: 122, Maker Chambers III
Nariman Point, Bombay 400 021 (Maharashtra)
Factory: Kodinar (Gujarat)
Product: Cement

Gujarat Apar Polymers Ltd.

Office: Opposite "D" Cabin,
Dharamsinh Desai Marg
Chhani Road, Baroda 390 002 (Gujarat)
Factory: See above
Product: Acrylonitrile-Butadiene Rubber

Gujarat Binil Chemicals Ltd.

Office: 3rd Floor, Rawal Building No. 1
Opera House, Bombay 400 004 (Maharashtra)

Factory: Plot No. 2701-A GIDC, Ankleshwar, 393 002
Dist. Bharuch (Gujarat)
Products: ABS Resins, Polystyrene

Gujarat Filaments Ltd.
Office: Krishna Krupa
3, Bhawanipura Society
Nizampura, Baroda 390 002 (Gujarat)
Factory: 2502, GIDC Industrial Estate
Halol 389 350, Dist. Panchmahal (Gujarat)
Product: Polypropylene Multifilament Yarn

Gujarat Heavy Chemicals Ltd.
Office: International Trade Tower
F Block, 2nd Floor, Nehru Place
New Delhi 110 019
Factory: Prakash Commercial Complex
Rajmahal Road, Veraval 362 265 (Gujarat)
Product: Soda Ash

Gujarat Narmada Valley Fertilizers Co. Ltd.
Office: P.O. Narmadanagar
Bharuch 392 015 (Gujarat)
Factory: Same location as office
Products: Urea, Methanol, Formic Acid, Butachlor, Nitric Acid,
Ammonium Nitrophosphate, Isocyanates

Gujarat Sidhee Cement Ltd.
Office: Sidheegram
Off Veraval-Kodinar Highway 362 276
Dist. Junagadh (Gujarat)
Factory: Same as above
Product: Cement

Gujarat State Fertilizers Co. Ltd.
Office: Giriraj Apartments, Race Course Circle
Vadodara 390 007 (Gujarat)
Factory: P.O. Petrofils
Dist. Vadodara 391 347 (Gujarat)
Products: Ammonia, Urea, Sulfuric Acid, Caprolactam, LPG

Harshvardan Chemicals & Minerals Ltd.
Office: A-4, Motilal Atal Road, Jaipur 302 001 (Rajasthan)
Factory: Antravalia, Meghnagar, Dist. Jhabhua (M.P.)
Products: Fertilizers, Sulfuric Acid

Haryana Petrochemicals Ltd.

Office: B-18, Adhitam Kendra
Qutab Institutional Area
New Delhi 110 016

Factory: 55-59, HUDA Industrial Area
Delhi-Rewari Road
Rewari 123 401 (Haryana)

Product: Polyester Filament Yarn

HEG Ltd.

Office: Bhilwara Bhawan, 40-41 Community Centre
New Friends Colony, New Delhi 110 065

Factories: (1) Mandideep (M.P.)
(2) Raisen (M.P.)
(3) Bari Brahmana (J&K)
(4) Udaipur (Rajasthan)
(5) Borai (M.P.)
(6) Durg (M.P.)
(7) Ankleshwar (Gujarat)
(8) Rajamundary (A.P.)

Products: Sponge Iron, Graphite Anodes, Cotton Yarn

Herdillia Chemicals Ltd.

Office: Air India Building
13th Floor, Nariman Point, Bombay 400 021 (Maharashtra)

Factories: Thane-Belapur Road
Thane 400 601 (Maharashtra)

Products: Phenol, Acetone, Phthalic Anhydride, Cumene

Hikal Chemical Industries Ltd.

Office: 202, Standard House
83, M. Karve Road
Bombay 400 002 (Maharashtra)

Factory: A-18, MIDC
Mahed, Dist. Raigad 402 301 (Maharashtra)

Products: Aromatic Intermediates, Herbicides

Himadri Chemicals & Industries Ltd.

Office: Howrah (W.B.)

Factories: (1) Liluah, Howrah (W.B.)
(2) Vizag (A.P.)

Product: Coal Tar Pitch

Hindalco Industries Ltd.

Office: Century Bhavan, 3rd Floor, Dr. Annie Besant Road
Bombay 400 025 (Maharashtra)

Factory: P.O. Renukoot, Dist. Sonebhadra (U.P.)
Product: Aluminum Metal

Hindustan Antibiotics Ltd.
Office: Pimpri, Pune 411 018 (Maharashtra)
Factory: Same as above
Products: Penicillin and other Antibiotics

Hindustan Ciba Geigy Ltd.
Office: Royal Insurance Building, 14 J. Tata Road
Bombay 400 020 (Maharashtra)
Factory: Esplanade House
29H Somani Marg
Bombay 400 001 (Maharashtra)
Products: Pesticides (including Phosphamidon and DDVP), Drugs and Dyes

Hindustan Copper Ltd.
Office: Industry House
13th & 14th Floors, 10 Camac Street
Calcutta, 700 017 (W.B.)
Factories: (1) Khetri Copper Complex
P.O. Khetrinagar 333 504 (Rajasthan)
(2) Ghatsila (Bihar) (Smelter and Refinery)
(3) Malanjkhand (M.P.) (Mine and Ore Concentrator)
(4) Taloja (Maharashtra) (Copper Casting Plant)
Products: Phosphoric Acid, Sulfuric Acid, Copper

Hindustan Fertilizer Corp. Ltd.
Office: Madhuban
55 Nehru Place
New Delhi 110 019
Factories: (1) Durgapur (W.B.)
(2) Barauni (W.B.)
(3) Namrup (Assam)
Products: Ammonia, Urea, Ammonium Sulfate

Hindustan Fluorocarbons Ltd.
Office: 1401, Babukhan Est.
Basheerbagh, Hyderabad 500 001 (A.P.)
Factory: P.O. Rudraram, Tal. Sangareddy
Dist. Medak, 502 319 (A.P.)
Products: Fluorinated Refrigerants, Teflon Resins

Hindustan Heavy Chemicals Ltd.
Office: Globe Building, 7E Lindsay Street
Calcutta 700 087 (W.B.)

Factory: 19 B.T. Road
Khardah, P.O. Balaram Darma
Dist. Sopan 743 121 (W.B.)
Products: Caustic, Chlorine, Sulfuric Acid

Hindustan Insecticides Ltd.
Office: 2nd Floor, Core-6 Scope Complex
7, Lodi Road, New Delhi 110 003
Factories: (1) Guru Gobind Singh Marg
Rohtak Road, New Delhi 110 015
(2) Rasayani, Raigad Dist. 410 207 (Maharashtra)
(3) Udyogamandal
P.O. Alwaye 683 501 (Kerala)
Products: DDT, BHC, Endosulfan, Malathion, Butachlor, Dicofol, Monocrotophos

Hindustan Lever Ltd.
Office: Hindustan Lever House
165/166 Backbay Reclamation
Bombay 400 020 (Maharashtra)
Factories: (1) 63, Garden Beach Road, Calcutta 700 024 (W.B.)
(2) Haji Bunder, Sewree, Bombay 400 033 (Maharashtra)
(3) P.O. Durgachak, Haldia 721 602 (W.B.)
Products: Soaps, Detergents, Glycerin, Sulfuric Acid, Phosphoric Acid

Hindustan Organic Chemicals Ltd.
Office: Rasayani, Dist. Raigad 410 207 (Maharashtra)
Factory: Same location
Products: Formaldehyde, Sulfuric Acid, Nitrobenzenes, Aniline, BHC,
Acetic Acid, Propylene, Phenol, Acetone

Hindustan Petroleum Corp. Ltd.
Office: 17, Jamshedji Tata Road, Bombay 400 020 (Maharashtra)
Factories: (1) Bombay (Maharashtra)
(2) Visakhapatnam (A.P.)
Products: Bulk Petroleum including Lube Oils

Hindustan Polymers Ltd.
See entry under McDowell & Co. Ltd.

Hindustan Zinc Ltd.
Office: Yashad Bhawan
Udaipur 313 001 (Rajasthan)
Factory: Zinc Smelter
Debari 313 024
Udaipur (Rajasthan)
Products: Sulfuric Acid, Lead, Zinc, Silver

Hoechst India Ltd.

Office: Hoechst House
193 Backbay Reclamation
Nariman Point, Bombay 400 021 (Maharashtra)
Factories: (1) Bombay (Maharashtra)
(2) Ankleshwar (Gujarat)
Products: Pharmaceuticals, Agrochemicals

Hukumchand Jute & Industries Ltd.

Office: 15, India Exchange Place
Calcutta 700 001 (W.B.)
Factory: P.O. Amlai Paper Mills
Dist. Shahdol 484 117 (M.P.)
Products: Caustic, Chlorine

IBP Co. Ltd.

Office: Gilander House
8, Netaji Subhas Road
Calcutta 700 001 (W.B.)
Factories: (1) Pankagrant (Assam)
(2) Korba (M.P.)
(3) New Bombay (Maharashtra)
Products: Explosives, Petroleum Products

I.C.I. India Ltd.

Office: 34, Chowringhee Road, Calcutta 700 071 (W.B.)
Factories: (1) Post Box No. 5, Ennore Post Office
Madras 600 057 (T.N.)
(2) Kalwa-Belapur Road, Box No. 87
Thane 400 601 (Maharashtra)
(3) Kanpur (U.P.)
Products: Pesticides, Explosives, Rubber Chemicals, Dyestuffs, Pharmaceuticals, Paints

IDL Chemicals Ltd.

Office: Kukatpally, P.O. Bag No. 1
Sanatnagar (IE) P.O.
Hyderabad 500 018 (A.P.)
Factories: (1) Rourkela 769 016 (Orissa)
(2) Bhiwandi 421 302 (Maharashtra)
(3) Singrauli 486 886 (M.P.)
Product: Explosives

IG Petrochemicals Ltd.

Office: 401/404 Raheja Centre
Nariman Point, Bombay 400 021 (Maharashtra)
Factory: Taloja (Maharashtra)

Product: Phthalic Anhydride

India Castor Ltd.

Office: 10, Wellington Estate
24, Commander-in-Chief Road
Madras 600 105 (T.N.)
Factory: Gummidipoondi (T.N.)
Product: Castor Oil

India Cements Ltd.

Office: Dhun Building
827 Anna Salai
Madras 600 002 (T.N.)
Factories: (1) Sankarnagar (T.N.)
(2) Salem (T.N.)
(3) Cuddapah (A.P.)
Product: Cement

India Glycols Ltd.

Office: C-124, Okhla Industrial Area
Phase 1, New Delhi 110 020
Factory: A-1, Industrial Area
Bazpur Road, Kaslipur
Dist. Nainital 244 713 (U.P.)
Products: Ethylene Oxide, Monoethylene Glycol

Indian Aluminum Co. Ltd. (INDALCO)

Office: 1 Middleton Street, Calcutta 700 071 (W.B.)
Factories: (1) Belur (W.B.)
(2) Belgaum (Karnataka)
(3) Mun (Bihar)
(4) Kalwa (Maharashtra)
(5) Taloja (Maharashtra)
(6) Hirakud (Orissa)
(7) Nanjangud (Karnataka)
Products: Alumina, Aluminum Metal, Carbon Electrode Paste

Indian Drugs & Pharmaceuticals Ltd. (IDPL)

Office: IDPL Complex
Dundahera-Gurgaon Road
Gurgaon 122 016 (Haryana)
Factories: (1) P.O. Virbhadra 249 202 Rishikesh (U.P.)
(2) P.O. Balanagar Township, Hyderabad 500 037 (A.P.)
(3) Nandambakkam, Madras 600 089 (T.N.)
(4) Dundahera Industrial Complex, Delhi-Gurgaon Road, Gurgaon 122 016 (Haryana)

(5) Industrial Area, P.O. Ramakrishna Ashram, P.O. Box 76, Muzaffarpur 842 001 (Bihar)
Products: Pharmaceuticals

Indian Dyestuff Industries Ltd.
Office: Mafatlal Centre
Nariman Point, Bombay 400 021 (Maharashtra)
Factories: (1) Murbad Road, Shahad, Kalyan
Dist. Thane 421 304 (Maharashtra)
(2) MIDC, Plot No. D-16, Tarapur, Boisar Railway Station,
Dist. Thane 401 506 (Maharashtra)
(3) Opposite Ranoli Station (W. Rly.), Dist. Baroda 391 350 (Gujarat)
Products: Phthalic Anhydride, Sulfuric Acid

Indian Farmers Fertilizer Cooperative Ltd. (IFFCO)
Office: 34 Nehru Place
New Delhi 110 019
Factories: (1) Phulpur Unit, Ghiyanagar, Allahabad 212 404 (U.P.)
(2) Kalol (Gujarat)
(3) Kandla (Gujarat)
(4) Aonla (U.P.)
Products: Ammonia, Urea, Nitrogenous Fertilizers, Phosphate Fertilizers, Malathion

Indian Iron & Steel Co. Ltd.
Office: IISCO House
50 Chowringhee Road
Calcutta 700 071 (W.B.)
Factories: (1) Burnpur Works, Burnpur 713 325 (W.B.)
(2) Kulti Works, Kulti 713 343 (W.B.)
Products: Iron and Steel

Indian Oil Corporation Ltd.
Office: Indian Oil Bhavan G-9
Ali Yavar Jung Marg
Bandra (E), Bombay 400 051 (Maharashtra)
Factory: Guwahati Refinery
P.O. Noonmati (Assam)
Products: Benzene, Toluene

Indian Organic Chemicals Ltd.
Office: New Excelsior Building
Wallace Street, Fort, Bombay 400 001 (Maharashtra)
Factories: (1) Bombay-Pune Road
Khopoli, Dist. Raigad 410 203 (Maharashtra)
(2) Chinnasekadu, Manali, Chinglepet (T.N.)
Products: Polyester Staple Fiber, Plasticizers

Indian Petrochemicals Corp. Ltd. (IPCL)

Office: P.O. Petrochemicals Township
Dist. Vadodara 391 346 (Gujarat)

Plants: (1) Vadodara Complex
P.O. Petrochemicals
Dist. Vadodara 391 346 (Gujarat)
(2) Nagothane Complex
Nagothane, Tal. Roha
Dist. Raigad 402 106 (Maharashtra)
(3) Gandhar Complex
Dist. Bharuch (Gujarat)

Products: Polyethylene, Polypropylene, PVC, Polybutadiene Rubber (1), Terephthalic Acid, Acrylic Fiber, Polyester Fiber (2), Chlor-Alkali, PVC (3)

Indian Rayon & Industries Ltd.

Office: Junagadh-Veraval Road
Veraval 362 266 (Gujarat)

Factories: (1) Veraval (Gujarat)
(2) Renukoot (U.P.)
(3) Malkhed (Maharashtra)
(4) Gulbarga (Karnataka)
(5) Rishra (West Bengal)
(6) Midnapore (West Bengal)
(7) Halol (Gujarat)
(8) Jodhpur (Rajasthan)

Products: Portland Cement, Viscose Yarn

India Polyfibres Ltd.

Office: 9, Laxmibai Marg
Lucknow 226 001 (U.P.)

Factory: Dewa Road, Barabanki 225 123 (U.P.)

Product: Polyester Staple Fiber

Indo Gulf Fertilizers & Chemicals Corp. Ltd.

Office: P.O. Jagdishpur Industrial Area
Dist. Sultanpur 227 817 (U.P.)

Factory: Same as above

Products: Ammonia, Urea, Pesticides

Indo Rama Synthetics (India) Ltd.

Office: 903 Mohan Dev
13 Tolstoy Marg
New Delhi 110 001

Factories: (1) 51 A, Sector III, Pithampur, Dist. Dhar (M.P.)
(2) Nagpur (Maharashtra)

Products: Polyester Fiber and Yarn

Indu Nissan Oxo Chemical Industries Ltd.

Office: Maker Bhavan No. 2
18 New Marine Lines
Bombay 400 020 (Maharashtra)

Factory: Bajwa-Chhani Road
Behind G.S.F.C. Complex
Dist. Vadodara 391 310 (Gujarat)

Products: Oxo Alcohols

Insilco Ltd.

Office: Hemkunt Chambers
III Floor, 89 Nehru Place
New Delhi 110 019

Factory: A-5, UPSIDC LTD Industrial Estate
Bhartiagram, Gajraula 244 223 (U.P.)

Product: Precipitated Silica

IOL Ltd.

See under new name of BOC India Ltd.

IPCA Laboratories

Office: 142-AB Kandivli Industrial Estate
Kandivli (W.), Bombay 400 067 (Maharashtra)

Factory: See above

Products: Pharmaceuticals

ITC Agro-Tech Ltd.

Office: 31 Sarojini Devi Road
Secunderabad 500 003 (A.P.)

Factory: Mantralayam (A.P.)

Product: Vegetable Oils

ITC Bhadrachalam Paperboards Ltd.

Office: 106, Sardar Patel Road
Secunderabad 500 003 (A.P.)

Factory: Khammam (A.P.)

Products: Paper and Paperboard

IVP Ltd.

Office: Shashikant N. Rediji Marg
Ghorupdeo, Bombay 400 033 (Maharashtra)

Factories:
(1) Bombay (Maharashtra)
(2) Aurangabad (Maharashtra)
(3) Thane (Maharashtra)
(4) Hyderabad (M.P.)
(5) Jamshedpur (Bihar)

(6) Bangalore (Karnataka)
Product: Vegetable Oils

Jaiprakash Industries Ltd.
Office: JA House
63 Basant Lok
Vasant Vihar
New Delhi 110 057
Factory: Rewa (M.P.)
Product: Cement

Jayant Agro Organics Ltd.
Office: 13 Sitafalwadi
Off Dr. Mascarenhas Road
Mazgaon, Bombay 400 010 (Maharashtra)
Factory: 480/81/82/83/84 G.I.D.C.
Makarpura, Baroda (Gujarat)
Product: Castor Oil

Jayant Vitamins Ltd.
Office: Raheja Centre, I Floor
Nariman Point, Bombay 400 021 (Maharashtra)
Factory: Dosigaon Industrial Area
Ratlam 457 001 (M.P.)
Products: Vitamin C, Sorbitol

Jayshree Chemicals Ltd.
Office: 14 Netaji Subhas Road
Calcutta 700 001 (W.B.)
Factory: Ganjam (Orissa)
Products: Caustic, Chlorine, Sulfuric Acid

Jay Shree Tea & Industries Ltd.
Office: Industry House, 10 Camac Street, Calcutta 700 017 (W.B.)
Factories: (1) Andaman Islands
(2) Darjeeling (W.B.)
(3) Jorhat (Assam)
(4) Cachar (Assam)
(5) Mariani (Assam)
(6) Coimbatore (T.N.)
(7) Unnao (U.P.)
(8) Gurgaon (Haryana)
Products: Sulfuric Acid, Superphosphate Fertilizers, Tea

Jaysynth Dyechem Ltd.

Office: E-16 Everest, Tardeo Road
Bombay 400 034 (Maharashtra)
Factory: D-55 Trans-Thane Creek Industrial Area
Dist. Thane (Maharashtra)
Products: Dyes and Dye Intermediates

J.B. Chemicals & Pharmaceuticals Ltd.

Office: Neelam Centre
4th Floor, B-Wing
Hind Cycle Road
Worli, Bombay 400 025 (Maharashtra)
Factory: Plot No. P-10 & 10-P, P.O. Gansoli, Dist. Thane (Maharashtra)
Products: Pharmaceuticals

JBF Industries Ltd.

Office: 12th Floor, Arcadia
NCPA Marg, Nariman Point, Bombay 400 021 (Maharashtra)
Factory: Plot No. 6301/6312, GIDC Industrial Estate
Vapi 396 195 (Gujarat)
Products: Trichlorethylene and Perchlorethylene, Bulk Drugs, such as Ampicillin, Polyester Yarn

JCT Ltd.

Office: Thapar House, 124 Janpath
New Delhi 110 001
Factories: (1) Sriganganagar (Rajasthan)
(2) Phagwara (Punjab)
(3) Hoshiarpur (Punjab)
Products: Nylon Filament Yarn, Polyester Filament Yarn, Acrylic Staple Fiber, Portland Cement

Jenson & Nicholson (India) Ltd.

Office: 225 Acharya Jagdish Bose Road
Calcutta 700 020 (W.B.)
Factories: (1) Naihati, 24 Parganas Dist. (W.B.)
(2) Panvel, Raigad Dist. (Maharashtra)
(3) Tupudana, Ranchi (Bihar)
Products: Paints

Jindal Iron & Steel Co. Ltd.

Office: Jindal Mansion
5A G. Deshmukh Marg
Bombay 400 026 (Maharashtra)
Factory: Thane (Maharashtra)
Products: Steel Ingots and Shapes

Jindal Strips Ltd.

Office: Delhi Road, Hissar 125 005 (Haryana)
Factories: (1) Hissar (Haryana)
(2) Vasind (Maharashtra)
(3) Raigarh (M.P.)
Products: Sponge Iron, Rolled Steel

J.K. Corp. Ltd.

Office: Jaykaypur 765 017, Rayaguda (Orissa)
Factories: (1) Baulpur (Orissa)
(2) Rayaguda (Orissa)
(3) Sirohi (Rajasthan)
(4) Ghaziabad (U.P.)
Products: Cement, Paper & Board, Polyester staple fiber

J.K. Industries Ltd.

Office: 7 Council House Street
Calcutta 700 001 (W.B.)
Factories: (1) Jaykaygram, P.O. Tyre Factory, Kankroli
Dist. Udaipur (Rajasthan)
(2) Banmore (M.P.)
(3) Gajraula (U.P.)
Products: Automobile Tires and Tubes

J.K. Pharmaceuticals Ltd.

Office: Sipcot Industrial Complex
Cuddalore 607 003
South Arcot Vallalar Dist. (Tamil Nadu)
Factory: Same address
Product: Penicillin

J.K. Synthetics Ltd.

Office: Kamla Tower
Kanpur 208 001 (U.P.)
Factories: (1) Kota (Rajasthan)
(2) Jhalawar (Rajasthan)
(3) Nimbahera (Rajasthan)
(4) Gotan (Rajasthan)
(5) Kanpur (U.P.)
(6) Chittorgarh (Rajasthan)
Products: Nylon, Polyester and Acrylic Yarns, Portland Cement

Kalyani Steels Ltd.

Office: Mundhwa, Pune 411 036 (Maharashtra)
Factories: (1) See above
(2) Baramati (Maharashtra)

Product: Steel Ingots

Kamar Chemicals and Industries Ltd.

Office: No. 5-C, 2nd Street
Dr. Radhakrishnan Salai
Mylapore, Madras 600 004 (T.N.)
Factory: See above
Product: Sulfuric Acid

Kanoria Chemicals & Industries Ltd.

Office: Park Plaza, 71 Park Street, Calcutta 700 016 (W.B.)
Factories: (1) Renukoot Chemical Works Division
P.O. Renukoot, Dist. Sonebhadra 231 117 (U.P.)
(2) Ankleshwar Chemical Works Division
3407, GIDC Industrial Estate
Ankleshwar 393 002 (Gujarat)
Products: (1) Caustic and chlorine Chlorine, BHC, Lindane
(2) Acetaldehyde, Formaldehyde, Hexamine, Pentaerythritol

Karnataka Soaps & Detergents Ltd.

Office: Bangalore-Pune Highway
P.B. 5531, Bangalore 560 055 (Karnataka)
Factory: See above
Products: Soaps and Detergents

Kaso Chemie India Ltd.

Office: 205, Padma Palace
86, Nehru Place
New Delhi 110 019
Factory: A-594, RIICO Industrial Area
Bhiwadi (Rajasthan)
Product: Polyurethane Resins

K.C.P. Ltd.

Office: Ramakrishna Building
2, Dr. P.V. Cherian Crescent
Madras 600 105 (T.N.)
Factories: (1) Vuyyuru (A.P.)
(2) Lakshmipuram (T.N.)
(3) Macheria (A.P.)
(4) Tiruvottiyur (T.N.)
Products: Sugar, Alcohol, Cement

Kedia Chemical Industries Pvt. Ltd.

Office: 53 B, Mittal Court
224 Nariman Point, Bombay 400 021 (Maharashtra)

Factory: D-267, TTC Industrial Area
Thane-Belapur Road
New Bombay 400 706 (Maharashtra)
Products: Pesticide Intermediates and Pesticides

Kerala Chemicals & Proteins Ltd.
Office: Post Bag 1688, XXVII/972
Pampilly Nagar, Ernakulam
Kochi 682 015 (Kerala)
Factory: Kathikudam P.O. (Via) Koratty
Trichur District 680 308 (Kerala)
Products: Ossein and Dicalcium Phosphate

Kerala Minerals & Metals Ltd.
Office: Post Bag No. 4
Chavara, Quilon Dist., 691 583 (Kerala)
Factory: See above
Product: Rutile Pigment Grade Titanium Dioxide

Kesoram Industries Ltd.
Office: 9/1 R.N. Mukherjee Road, Calcutta 700 001 (W.B.)
Factories: (1) 42, Garden Beach Road, Calcutta 700 024 (W.B.)
(2) Tribeni, Dist. Hooghly (West Bengal)
(3) Bansbaria (W.B.)
(4) Kulti, Dist. Burdwan (W.B.)
(5) Basant Nagar, Dist. Karimnagar (A.P.)
(6) Sedam, Dist. Gulbarga (Karnataka)
(7) Balasore (Orissa)
Products: Cement, Viscose Yarn, Tires and Tubes

Khaitan Chemicals & Fertilizers Ltd.
Office: B-1, Satkar Building
79/80 Nehru Place
New Delhi 110 019
Factory: AB Road, Village Nimrani
Dist. Khargone 451 659 (M.P.)
Products: Superphosphate and Sulfuric Acid

Khatau Junker Ltd.
Office: Udyog Mandir Compound
Mahim, Bombay 400 016 (Maharashtra)
Factory: Plot #3000, GIDC
Ankleshwar 393 002, Dist. Bharuch (Gujarat)
Products: Pesticides including Malathion, Dimethoate, Monocrotophos,
Phosphamidon, and DDVP; Dyestuffs

Kilburn Chemicals Ltd.

Office: Shantiniketan
16th Floor, 8 Camac Street
Calcutta 700 017 (W.B.)
Factory: A-80/81 SIPCOT Industrial Estate
Milavittan, Tuticorin 628 002 (T.N.)
Products: Titanium Dioxide, Anatase Grade

Kolmak Chemicals Ltd.

Office: 21 A, Shakespeare Sarani
Calcutta 700 017 (W.B.)
Factory: Kulia Kanchrapara Road
WBIIDC Area
P.O. Gayaspur
Nadia 731 234 (W.B.)
Product: Titanium Dioxide

Kopran Ltd.

Office: Parijat House
1676, Dr. E. Moses Road
Worli, Bombay 400 011 (Maharashtra)
Factories: (1) Savroli Village, Khopoli, Dist. Raigad (Maharashtra)
(2) Mehra Industrial Estate, Saki Naka, Bombay 400 072 (Maharashtra)
Product: Penicillin

Kothari Industrial Corp. Ltd.

Office: 114-117, Nungambakkam High Road, Madras 600 034 (T.N.)
Factory: Ennore 600 057 (Madras)
Products: Fertilizers, Sulfuric Acid

Kothari Phytochemicals Plantations & Industries Ltd.

Office: 766, Anna Nagar, Madurai 625 020 (T.N.)
Factory: Nagari, P.O. Thanichchiyam 624 121 Madras District (T.N.)
Products: Pharmaceutical Intermediates

Kothari Sugars & Chemicals Ltd.

Office: Kothari Building
115 Mahatma Gandhi Salai
Madras 600 034 (T.N.)
Factory: PNCB Project
Melavanjoor Village
Nagore Post 611 002, U.T. of Pondicherry
Product: Maleic Anhydride

Krishak Bharati Cooperative Ltd. (KRIBHCO)

Office: Red Rose House, 49-50 Nehru Place, New Delhi 110 019

Factory: P.O. Kribhco Nagar, Surat 394 515 (Gujarat)
Products: Ammonia, Urea

Krishna Industrial Corp. Ltd.
Office: Ramakrishna Building
183 Mount Road, Madras 600 006 (T.N.)
Factory: Nidadavole, Kouvurtaluk
W. Godavari Dist. (A.P.)
Products: Sulfuric Acid, Superphosphate Fertilizer

Krishna Sakahari Sakhar Karkhana Ltd.
Office: Rethare Budruk
P.O. Shivanagar, Tal. Karad, Dist. Satara
415 108 (Maharashtra)
Factory: Same address
Products: Acetone, Ethanol

Kusum Products Ltd.
Office: Bombay Mutual Building
9, Biplabi Trailokya Maharaj Sarani
Calcutta 700 001 (W.B.)
Factory: Panchugopal Bhaduri Sarani
Rishra, Dist. Hooghly (W.B.)
Products: Vegetable Oils, Paints, Varnishes

Lactose India Ltd.
Office: 10 Shah & Nahar Industrial Estate
Dr. E. Moses Road
Worli Naka, Worli, Bombay 400 018 (Maharashtra)
Factory: Survey No. 6, Village Poicha
Taluka Savli, Dist. Vadodara (Gujarat)
Product: Lactose

Larsen & Toubro Ltd.
Office: L&T House
Ballard Estate
Bombay 400 038 (Maharashtra)
Factories: (1) Ankleshwar (Gujarat)
(2) Bombay (Maharashtra)
(3) Ahmednagar (Maharashtra)
(4) Bangalore (Karnataka)
(5) Faridabad (U.P.)
(6) Madras (T.N.)
Products: Cement, Chemical Plant Machinery

Link Pharma Chem Ltd.

Office: B2, Ramakrishna Chamber
Productivity Road, Alkapure, Baroda 390 001 (Gujarat)
Factory: Plot Nos. 7112, 7213
GIDC Industrial Estate
Ankleshwar 393 002 (Gujarat)
Products: Thionyl Chloride, Other Sulfur Chemicals

LML Fibres Ltd.

Office: C-17, Panki Industrial Estate
Kanpur 208 022 (U.P.)
Factory: Same as above
Products: Nylon and Polyester Yarn

Lupin Laboratories Ltd.

Office: 159, CST Road, Kalina
Santacruz (E), Bombay 400 098 (Maharashtra)
Factories: (1) 202 New Industrial Area No. 2, P.B. No. 4622
Manideep, Dist. Raisen (M.P.)
(2) Plot No. 2A-28-1, MIDC Area, Chikalthana
Aurangabad 431 120 (Maharashtra)
(3) Plot Nos. 124, 125, 126/1, GIDC Estate
Ankleshwar, Dist. Bharuch 393 002 (Gujarat)
(4) T-142, MIDC Industrial Area, Tarapur (Maharashtra)
(5) Agrochemicals Division
24 1/2 GIDC Estate, Panoli, Dist. Bharuch (Gujarat)
Products: Pharmaceuticals, Pesticides (in top 10 drug cos. in India)

Lyka Labs Ltd.

Office: 77, Nehru Road, Ville Parle (E), Bombay 400 099 (Maharashtra)
Factory: 4801/B & 4802/A, GIDC Industrial Estate
Ankleshwar 393 002 (Gujarat)
Products: Pharmaceuticals

Madras Cements Ltd.

Office: 98-A, Dr. Radhakrishnan Salai
V Floor, Mylapore, Madras 600 004 (T.N.)
Factories: (1) Tulukapatti (T.N.)
(2) Jayantipuram (T.N.)
Product: Cement

Madras Fertilizers Ltd.

Office: Manali, Madras 600 068 (T.N.)
Factory: See above
Products: Ammonia, Urea, NPK Mixed Fertilizers

Madras Petro-Chem Ltd.

Office: Nariman Bhavan
No. 16, 1st Floor
Plot 227, Nariman Point, Bombay 400 021 (Maharashtra)
Factory: Ponneri High Road, Manali, Madras 600 068 (T.N.)
Product: Sulfuric Acid

Madras Refineries Ltd.

Office: 480 Anna Salai, Nandanam, Madras 600 018 (T.N.)
Factory: Manali, Madras 600 068 (T.N.)
Products: Various Petroleum Products including Propylene, Hexane and Wax

Mafatlal Dyes & Chemicals Ltd.

Office: Hoechst House
193 Backbay Reclamation
Nariman Point, Bombay 400 021 (Maharashtra)
Factory: Lal Bahadur Shastri Marg
Bombay 400 080 (Maharashtra)
Products: Polyester Staple Fiber, Dyestuffs

Mafatlal Industries Ltd.

Office: Mafatlal House
Backbay Reclamation
Bombay 400 020 (Maharashtra)
Factories: (1) Ahmedabad (Gujarat)
(2) Gandhinagar (Gujarat)
(3) Nadiad (Gujarat)
(4) Dewas (M.P.)
Products: Dyes and Intermediates

Manali Petrochemicals Ltd.

Office: SPIC Annexe, 7th Floor, 97 Mount Road
Guindy, Madras 600 032 (T.N.)
Factory: Ponneri High Road
Manali, Madras 600 068 (T.N.)
Products: Polyols for Polyurethanes

Mangalore Chemicals & Fertilizers Ltd.

Office: 10/2 Kasturba Road
Bangalore 560 001 (Karnataka)
Factory: Panambur (Karnataka)
Products: Ammonia, Urea

Mangalore Refinery & Petrochemicals Ltd.

Office: 7, Magadi Road, Bangalore 560 023 (Karnataka)
Factory: See above

Product: Petroleum Products

Mardia Chemicals Ltd.

Office: 85/1 GIDC Estate, Phase I
Vatva, Ahmedabad 382 445 (Gujarat)
Factory: Mardia Nagar, Sitagadh, Taluka Sayla
Dist. Surendranagar (Gujarat)
Products: Aniline, Dyes and Intermediates

Mark Omega Organic Industries Ltd.

Office: 502 Jyoti Chambers
372 Narsi Natha Street, Masji
Bunder, Bombay 400 009 (Maharashtra)
Factory: Plot No. 44/45, MIDC Road
Dhatav, Roma, District Raigad (Maharashtra)
Product: Benzaldehyde

Max India Ltd.

Office: Devika Tower, 12th Floor
6 Nehru Place, New Delhi 110 019
Factory: Bhai Mohan Singh Nagar
Village Toansa, Dist. Ropar 144 533 (Punjab)
Products: Pharmaceuticals, Polypropylene Film

McDowell & Co. Ltd.

Office: McDowell House
3 Second Line Beach
Madras 600 001 (T.N.)
Factory: Hindustan Polymers Plant, Vizag (A.P.)
Products: Styrene, Polystyrene, Ethanol

Metrochem Industries Ltd.

Office: Village Umraiya
Taluka Padra, Dist. Baroda 391 440 (Gujarat)
Factory: GIDC, Phase II, Vatva
Ahmedabad (Gujarat)
Products: Dyestuff Intermediates

Mettur Chemical & Industrial Corp. Ltd.

Office: 2/1-64-A, TCM Colony
Gonur Road, Mettur Dam 636 402, Salem Dist. (T.N.)
Factory: Same location
Products: Trichloroethylene, Textile Chemicals

Mittal Fertilizers Ltd.

Office: 5/1 Roop Nagar
Delhi 110 007
Factory: Industrial Area, Phase II
Amawan Road, Rae Bareli 229 001 (U.P.)
Products: Sulfuric Acid, Superphosphate Fertilizers

Modi Alkalies & Chemicals Ltd.

Office: 18, Community Centre
New Friends Colony
New Delhi 110 065
Factory: SP-460 Matsya Industrial Area
Alwar 301 030 (Rajasthan)
Products: Caustic, Chlorine

Modi Cement Ltd.

Office: 32, Community Centre
New Friends Colony
New Delhi 110 065
Factory: Raipur (M.P.)
Product: Cement

Modipon Ltd.

Office: 426, Thapar Chambers II
Opposite Kalindi Colony
Ring Road, New Delhi 110 014
Factory: Modinagar 201 204, Dist. Ghaziabad (U.P.)
Products: Nylon Yarn, Fungicides, Synthetic Tanning Agents

Modi Rubber Ltd.

Office: 4/7 C, DDA Shopping Centre
New Friends Colony
New Delhi 110 065
Factories: (1) Modipuram 250 110
Dist. Meerut (U.P.)
(2) Modinagar 201 204
Dist. Ghaziabad (U.P.)
Products: Automobile Tires and Tubes

Montari Industries Ltd.

Office: 78, Nehru Place, New Delhi 110 019
Factory: Bhai Mohan Singh Nagar, Toansa, Dist. Ropar 144 533 (Punjab)
Products: Pesticides including Chlorpyrifos and Isoproturon

Morepen Laboratories Ltd.

Office:	416-418 Antriksh Bhawan 22 K.G. Marg New Delhi 110 001
Factory:	Village and P.O. Masulkhana Parwanoo, Dist. Solan (H.P.)
Product:	Antibiotics

MRF Ltd.

Office:	124, Greames Road Madras 600 006 (T.N.)
Factories:	(1) Thiruvottiyur, Madras 600 002 (T.N.) (2) Arkonam, Dist. North Arcot (T.N.) (3) Kandepar, Taluk Ponda (Goa) (4) Vadavathoor, Dist. Kottayam (Kerala)
Products:	Automobile Tires and Tubes, Finished Leather, Conveyor Belting

Munak Chemicals Ltd.

Office:	SCO (1-2), First Floor, Sector 26 Madhya Marg, Chandigarh 160 026
Factory:	A-9 to A-15, Industrial Area Focal Point, Dabwali Road Bhatinda 151 001 (Punjab)
Products:	Sulfuric Acid, Superphosphate Fertilizer

Mysore Acetate & Chemicals Co. Ltd.

Office:	Mysugar Buildings, Sri Jaya Chamaraja Wadiyar Road Bangalore 560 002 (Karnataka)
Factory:	Acetate Town, Sathnur Farm Mandya 571 404 (Karnataka)
Products:	Acetic Acid, Acetic Anhydride, Cellulose Triacetate

Mysore Cements Ltd.

Office:	Industry House 45 Race Course Road Bangalore 560 001 (Karnataka)
Factories:	(1) Ammasandra (Karnataka) (2) Damoh (M.P.) (3) Jhansi (U.P.)
Product:	Cement

Mysore Petrochemicals Ltd.

Office:	1/4 Jyothi Complex 134/1 Infantry Road Bangalore 560 001 (Karnataka)

Factories: (1) Maleic Anhydride Plant
T-1, MIDC Industrial Area
Taloja (Maharashtra)
(2) Phthalic Anhydride Plant
Near Chicksugar Railway Station
P.B. No. 34, Raichur, 584 101 (Karnataka)
Products: Maleic Anhydride, Phthalic Anhydride

Nagarjuna Fertilizers & Chemicals Ltd.
Office: Nagarjuna Hills
Hyderabad 500 482 (A.P.)
Factory: Nagarjuna Road
Kakinada 533 033
East Godavari Dist. (A.P.)
Products: Ammonia, Urea, Fertilizers, Pesticides

Narmada Cement Co. Ltd.
Office: 2-C, Phoenix Mill Compound
462 Senapati Bapat Marg
Lower Parel, Bombay 400 093
Factories: (1) Magdalla (Gujarat)
(2) Ratnagiri (Maharashtra)
(3) Jafrabad (Gujarat)
Product: Cement

National Aluminum Co. Ltd.
Office: IDCO Tower
Bhubaneswar 751 007 (Orissa)
Factories: (1) Koraput (Orissa)
(2) Dhenkanal (Orissa)
(3) Visakhapatnam (A.P.)
Products: Alumina and Aluminum Metal

National Aromatics & Petrochemicals Corp. Ltd.
Office: 480 Anna Salai
Nandanam, Madras 600 035 (T.N.)
Factory: See above address
Products: Xylenes, Benzene, Terephthalic Acid

National Fertilizers Ltd.
Office: SCO No. 76-79, Sector 17-D
Chandigarh 160 017
Factories: (1) Nangal, Dist. Ropar (Punjab)
(2) Panipat (Haryana)
(3) Bhatinda (Punjab)
(4) Vijaipur, Dist. Guna (M.P.)

Products: Methanol, Urea

National Organic Chemical Industries Ltd. (NOCIL)

Office: Mafatlal Centre
Nariman Point, Bombay 400 021 (Maharashtra)

Plants: (1) Petrochemicals Plant
5, Trans-Thane Creek Industrial Area
Thane-Belapur Road, Thane (Maharashtra)
(2) Agrochemicals Plant
A-1, Lote-Parshuram Industrial Area
Taluka Khed, Dist. Ratnagiri (Maharashtra)

Products: Ethylene, Propylene, Benzene, Butadiene, Acetone, Oxo Alcohols, Ethylene Oxide and Glycols, Vinyl Chloride & PVC @ (1)
Monocrotophos, Cypermethrin, Phosphamidon, DDVP @ (2)

National Peroxides Ltd.

Office: Neville House, J.N. Heredia Marg
Ballard Estate
Bombay 400 038 (Maharashtra)

Factories: (1) NRC Road, P.O. Atali, Via Mohone
Kalyan, Thane 421 002 (Maharashtra)
(2) Plot No. 2, Industrial Area, AB Road, Rewas (M.P.)

Products: Hydrogen Peroxide, Sodium Perborate

National Rayon Corp. Ltd.

Office: Eros Theatre Building
1 Jamshedji Tata Road
Bombay 400 023 (Maharashtra)

Factory: Mohone 421 102 (Kalyan, Thane, Maharashtra)

Products: Caustic, Chlorine, Rayon Yarn, Nylon Tirecord, Sulfuric Acid

Neyveli Lignite Corp. Ltd.

Office: Temple View Apartments
5th Floor, 89/8 Santhome High Road
Madras 600 028 (T.N.)

Factory: Neyveli, S. Arcot Dist. 607 807 (T.N.)

Products: Ammonia, Urea, Lignite

NGL-Fine Chem Ltd.

Office: 101, Kohinoor Apartment
Bandlivi Village
Jogeshwari (W), Bombay 400 102 (Maharashtra)

Factory: W-142 (C), T.T.C.
MIDC Industrial Area, Pawane
Thane-Belapur Road
New Bombay 400 705 (Maharashtra)

Product: Antibiotics

Niraj Petrochemicals Ltd.

Office: 6-3-883/6/D
Second Floor, Ponjagutta, Hyderabad 500 482 (A.P.)
Factories: (1) Wadechipurapalli, Parvada Mandal
Anakapalli Taluk, Vizag Dist. (A.P.)
(2) Brahmanpalli Road, Bibi Nagar Mandal
Nalgonda Dist. (A.P.)
Products: Maleic Anhydride, Calcium Carbonate

Nirlon Ltd.

Office: Pahadi Village
Goregaon (East)
Bombay 400 063 (Maharashtra)
Factories: (1) Tarapur (Maharashtra)
(2) Roha (Maharashtra)
Products: Nylon and Polyester Fibers

Nirma Ltd.

Office: Nirma House, Ashram Road
Ahmedabad 380 009 (Gujarat)
Factory: Block No. 16/B
Ahmedabad-Mehsana Highway
P.O. Mandali, Tal Dist. Mehsana (Gujarat)
Products: Soap, Detergents, Sulfuric Acid, Glycerin

Nuchem Ltd.

Office: 54, Industrial Area
Faridabad 121 001 (Haryana)
Factory: Same location
Products: Formaldehyde, Hexamine, Urea - Formaldehyde & Melamine - Formaldehyde Molding Powders

Oil India Ltd.

Office: Duliajan, Dibrugarh District 786 602 (Assam)
Factory: See above
Products: Crude Oil, Refined Products and LPG

Orchid Chemicals & Pharmaceuticals Ltd.

Office: 6th Floor, Crown Court
34 Cathedral Road
Madras 600 086 (T.N.)
Factory: 139-46, Sidco Industrial Estate
Alathur, Chengal
MGR District 603 110 (T.N.)

Product: Antibiotics

Orient Paper & Industries Ltd.

Office: Brajrajnagar
Dist. Sambalpur (Orissa)

Factories: (1) Brajrajnagar (Orissa)
(2) Amlai (M.P.)
(3) Dharuhera (Haryana)

Products: Cement, Pulp, Paper, Caustic Soda

Oriental Carbon & Chemicals Ltd.

Office: 31, Netaji Subhas Road, Calcutta 700 001 (W.B.)

Factories: (1) Carbon Black Division
A-14, Industrial Area No. 1, South Side of G.T. Road
Ghaziabad 201 001 (U.P.)
(2) Fertilizer & Chemical Division
Plot Nos. 3 & 4, Dharuhera Industrial Estate, P.O. Dharuhera
Dist. Rewari (Haryana)

Products: Sulfuric Acid, Superphosphate Fertilizer, Carbon Black

Orissa Cement Ltd.

Office: B-47, Connaught Place
New Delhi 110 001

Factory: Rajgangpur (Orissa)

Products: Cement, Soda Ash

Orissa Synthetics Ltd.

Office: Link House
3, Bahadur Shah Zafar Marg
New Delhi 110 002

Factory: Lakshmi Nagar
P.O. Baulpur 759 031
Dist. Dhenkanal (Orissa)

Products: Methanol, Polyester Fibers

Orkay Industries Ltd.

Office: N.K.M. International House
Babubhai Chinai Marg 178
Backbay Reclamation, Bombay 400 020 (Maharashtra)

Factories: (1) Sakinaka, Marol, Andheri East, Bombay (Maharashtra)
(2) MIDC Industrial Estate, Patalganga (Maharashtra)

Products: Polyester Chips and Yarn

Oswal Agro Furane Ltd.

Office: 434, Sector 37-A, Chandigarh

Factory: Sangrur (Punjab)

Products: Furfural, Rice Bran Oil

Oswal Agro Mills Ltd.
Office: G.T. Road, Sherpur
Ludhiana 141 033 (Punjab)
Factory: Same location
Products: Oxo Alcohols, Sugar, Ethanol, Polyethylene

Oswal Chemicals & Fertilizers Ltd.
See data under former name of Bindal Agro Chem Ltd.

Oswal Fats & Oils Ltd.
Office: 1107, 11th Floor, Ashoka Estate
24 Barakhamba Road, New Delhi 110 001
Factory: Ludhiana (Punjab)
Products: Vegetable Oils, Fatty Acids, Soap, Glycerin

Oudh Sugar Mills Ltd.
Office: Industry House
159 Churchgate Reclamation
Bombay 400 020 (Maharashtra)
Factories: (1) Hargoan/Rosa (U.P.)
(2) Sitapur (U.P.)
(3) Narkatiaganj (Bihar)
Products: Sugar, Ethanol, Vegetable Oils

Paam Pharmaceuticals (Delhi) Ltd.
Office: 13 Alipur Road
The Exchange Stores
Civil Lines, Delhi 110 054
Factory: 29 Bhargava Lane
Civil Lines, Nityanand Marg
New Delhi 110 054
Products: Pharmaceuticals

Panyam Cements & Mineral Industries Ltd.
Office: Cementnagar 518 206, Kurnool (A.P.)
Factories: (1) Kurnool (A.P.)
(2) Bellary (Karnataka)
(3) Bangalore (Karnataka)
Products: Cement, Calcium Carbide, Acetylene Black

Paradeep Phosphates Ltd.
Office: 2nd Floor, Mansarovar, 90 Nehru Place
New Delhi 110 019
Factory: Paradeep, Cuttack District 754 145 (Orissa)

Products: Phosphoric Acid, Sulfuric Acid

Parasrampuria Industries Ltd.

Office: 103, Surya Mansion, 1 Kaushalaya Park
Hauz Khas, New Delhi 110 016

Factories: (1) S.P. 145, D&G Rico Industrial Area
Bhiwadi, Dist. Alwar (Rajasthan)
(2) Khushkhera (Rajasthan)
(3) Pithampur (M.P.)

Products: Polyester Chips & Yarn, Nylon Yarn, Polypropylene Yarn

Parke-Davis (India) Ltd.

Office: Sion-Trombay Road
Deonar, Bombay 400 088 (Maharashtra)

Factories: (1) Thane (Maharashtra)
(2) Pithampur (M.P.)
(3) Tarsadi (Gujarat)

Products: Pharmaceuticals

Pasupati Acrylon Ltd.

Office: M-14, Connaught Circus (Middle Circle), New Delhi 110 001

Factory: Thakurdwara
Moradabad-Kashipur Road
Moradabad 244 601 (U.P.)

Product: Acrylic Fiber

Paushak Ltd.

Office: Alembic Road, Baroda 390 003 (Gujarat)

Factory: Post Panelav, Taluka Halol, Dist. Panchmahals 381 350 (Gujarat)

Products: Sulfuric Acid, Mixed Fertilizers, Pesticides

Pentasia Chemicals Ltd.

Office: East Coast Chambers
92 G.N. Chetty Road, T. Nagar
Madras 600 017 (T.N.)

Factory: B5-B10 SIPCOT Industrial Complex
Cuddalore 607 003 (T.N.)

Products: Formaldehyde, Sodium Formate, Pentaerythritol

Pfizer Ltd.

Office: Express Towers, Nariman Point, Bombay 400 021 (Maharashtra)

Factories: (1) D-35, Industrial Area
Kalyani, Dist. Nadia 741 235 (West Bengal)
(2) 178 Industrial Area, Chandigarh 160 002
(3) Thane-Belapur Road
Turbhe, New Bombay 400 705 (Maharashtra)

Products: Pharmaceuticals (in top 10 in India)

Phillips Carbon Black Ltd.

Office: 31 Netaji Subhas Road
Calcutta 700 001 (W.B.)
Factory: R.N. Mukherjee Road
Durgapur District, Burdwan (W.B.)
Product: Carbon Black

Phosphate Co. Ltd.

Office: 14, Netaji Subhas Road
Calcutta 700 001 (W.B.)
Factory: Rishra, Dist. Hooghly (W.B.)
Products: Superphosphates, Sulfuric Acid

Pidilite Industries Ltd.

Office: Regent Chambers, 7th Floor
Nariman Point, Bombay 400 021 (Maharashtra)
Factory: Ramkrishna Mandir Road
P.B. No. 17411, Andheri (E), Bombay 400 059 (Maharashtra)
Products: Textile Chemicals

Polychem Ltd.

Office: Oriental House, 7 Jamshedji Tata Road
Churchgate, Bombay 400 020 (Maharashtra)
Factories:
(1) Polystyrene Plant
45 A, S.V. Road, Goregaon (W), Bombay 400 062 (Maharashtra)
(2) Monomer Plant
Anik Mahul, Chembur, Bombay 400 074 (Maharashtra)
(3) Vinyl Acetate Monomer Plant & PV Alcohol Plant
Nimbut Village, Dist. Pune 412 102 (Maharashtra)
(4) Alcohol Distillery
Nira, Taluka, Baramati, Dist. Pune (Maharashtra)
(5) ABS Polymer Plant
14, PCC Area, P.O. Petrofils, Vadodara 391 347 (Gujarat)
Products: Vinyl Acetate Monomer, Styrene, Polystyrene, Alcohol, ABS Resin, Acetic Acid

Polyolefins Industries Ltd.

Office: Mafatlal Centre
11th Floor, Nariman Point
Bombay 400 021 (Maharashtra)
Factories:
(1) Thane-Belapur Road
P.O. Ghansoli, Thane 400 701 (Maharashtra)
(2) C-37, T.T.C. Industrial Area, Thane (Maharashtra)
(3) C-1, MIDC Industrial Area, Akola (Maharashtra)
Products: Polyethylenes, Catalysts, Polypropylene

Polyplex Corp. Ltd.
Office: 75 Amrit Nagar, 2nd Floor
Behind N.D.S.E.-1, New Delhi 110 003
Factory: Lohia Head Road, Khatima 262 308, Dist. Nainital (U.P.)
Products: Polyester Chips and Film

Prakash Industries Ltd.
Office: 7th Floor, Padma Tower-1
5 Rajendra Place
New Delhi 110 008
Factories: (1) Kashipur (U.P.)
(2) Pithampur (M.P.)
(3) Rayya (Punjab)
(4) Koira (Orissa)
Products: Sponge Iron, Steel, PVC Pipes & Fittings

PRAXAIR (was Linde Division of Union Carbide formerly)
Office: Not yet established. Construction underway at Jindal (Karnataka) and Haldia (W.B.)
Factories: Not yet established
Products: Oxygen and Nitrogen

Premier Tyres Ltd.
Office: Merchant Chamber
41 Sir V. Thackersey Marg
Bombay 400 020 (Maharashtra)
Factory: Kalamassery 683 104, Dist. Ernakulam (Kerala)
Products: Tires and Tubes for Cars, Trucks, Buses and Scooters

Priya Organics & Chemicals Ltd.
Office: Lords, 3rd Floor, 7/1 Lord Sinha Road
Calcutta 700 071 (W.B.)
Factory: P.O. Govindpur, Dhanbad 832 195 (Bihar)
Products: Nitrobenzene, Aniline

Priyadarshini Cement Co. Ltd.
Office: 6-3-1092 Shantisikhara Complex
Raghavan Road, Hyderabad 500 482 (A.P.)
Factory: Ramapuram Village, Kodad Taluk, Nalagonda Dist. (A.P.)
Product: Cement

Procter & Gamble India Ltd.
Office: Tiecicon House, Dr. E. Moses Road
Bombay 400 011 (Maharashtra)

Factories: (1) Kalwe (Maharashtra)
(2) Annaram (A.P.)
(3) Mandideep (M.P.)
Products: Soaps and Detergents

Pudumjee Pulp & Paper Mills Ltd.
Office: Thergaon, Pune 411 033 (Maharashtra)
Factory: Same as above
Products: Pulp and Paper

Punjab Alkalies & Chemicals Ltd.
Office: S.C.O. 125-127, Sector 17-B
Chandigarh 160 017
Factory: Nangal-Una Road
Naya Nangal 140 126, Dist. Ropar (Punjab)
Products: Caustic, Chlorine, Hypochlorites

Punjab Chemicals & Pharmaceuticals Ltd.
Office: 417-418, Sector 35-C, Chandigarh 160 022 (Punjab)
Factory: Milestone 18, Ambala-Kalka Road
P.O. Bhankharpur 140 201, Dist. Patiala (Punjab)
Products: Oxalic Acid, Oxalates

Punjab National Fertilizers & Chemicals Ltd.
Office: S.C.O. 119-120, Sector 17-B
Chandigarh 160 017
Factory: Naya Nangal, Tehsil Anandpur Sahib, Dist. Ropar (Punjab)
Products: Fertilizers, Chemicals

Raasi Cement Ltd.
Office: 5th Floor, Minerva House
94 Sarojini Devi Road
Secunderabad 500 003 (A.P.)
Factory: Vishnupuram, Wadapalli 508 355
Maryalguda Tq., Nalagonda Dist. (A.P.)
Product: Cement

Radico Khaitan Ltd.
Office: Bareilly Road, Rampur 244 901 (U.P.)
Factories: (1) Same as above
(2) Ratlam (M.P.)
Products: Alcohol, Superphosphate

Rajasthan Petro Synthetics Ltd.

Office: 4, Community Centre
East of Kailash
New Delhi 110 065

Factory: F-210-233, Udyog Vihar
RIICO Industrial Area
Village Sukher
Udaipur 313 001 (Rajasthan)

Product: Polypropylene Filament Yarn

Rajasthan Spinning & Weaving Mills Ltd.

Office: Bhilwara Bhawan
40-41 Community Centre
New Friends Colony
New Delhi 110 065

Factories: (1) Bhilwara (Rajasthan)
(2) Banswara (Rajasthan)
(3) Gulabpur (Rajasthan)

Product: Viscose Yarn

Rallis India Ltd.

Office: Ralli House, 21 Damodardas Sukhadvala Marg
Bombay 400 001 (Maharashtra)

Factories: (1) Belapur Unit, P.O. 62, K.U.
Bazar P.O. Turbhe, New Bombay 400 705 (Maharashtra)
(2) Plot 3301, GIDC Estate
Ankleshwar 393 002 (Gujarat)
(3) Devinagar, Dera Bassi (Punjab)
(4) Plot 21 & 22, Phase 2, Peenya Industrial Area
Bangalore 560 058 (Karnataka)

Products: Agrochemicals including Dimethoate, Ethion, Captan, Fenitrothion

Rama Petrochemicals Ltd.

Office: 51/52 Free Press House
215 Nariman Point
Bombay 400 021 (Maharashtra)

Factory: Savroli Kharpada Road
Village Vashivalli
Patalganga, Dist. Raigad 410 220 (Maharashtra)

Product: Methanol

Rama Phosphates Ltd.

Office: 812, Raheja Chambers
Nariman Point, Bombay 400 021 (Maharashtra)

Factory: 20/4 KM Stone, Ujjain Road, Indore 452 004 (M.P.)

Products: Superphosphate and Sulfuric Acid

Rama Pulp & Papers Ltd.

Office:	Chateau Windsor 86 Veer Nariman Road Churchgate, Bombay 400 020 (Maharashtra)
Factory:	Plot Nos. 292-294 & 309, GIDC Industrial Estate Vapi 396 195 (Gujarat)
Product:	Kraft Paper

Ranbaxy Laboratories Ltd.

Office:	19, Nehru Place New Delhi 110 019
Factories:	(1) A-2, Phase 1, Okhla Industrial Area New Delhi 110 020 (2) Industrial Area 3 Dewas 455 001 (M.P.) (3) Mohali (Punjab) (4) Toansa (Punjab)
Products:	Pharmaceuticals (second largest manufacturer in India)

Rashtriya Chemicals & Fertilizers Ltd.

Office:	Priyadarshini, Eastern Express Highway Bombay 400 022 (Maharashtra)
Factories:	(1) Thal Unit Tal, Alibag, Dist. Raigad 402 208 (Maharashtra) (2) Mahul Unit Mahul Road, Chembur, Bombay 400 074 (Maharashtra) (3) Trombay (Maharashtra)
Products:	Methanol, Methylamines, Nitric Acid, Urea, Sulfuric Acid, Phosphoric Acid

Rashtriya Ispat Nigam Ltd. (Vizag Steel)

Office:	Visakhapatnam 530 031 (A.P.)
Factory:	Visakhapatnam Steel Plant Visakhapatnam (A.P.)
Products:	Pig Iron and Steel

Raymond Synthetics Ltd.

Office:	USIDC Industrial Area Kailashnagar, Karchana, Dist. Allahabad 212 301 (U.P.)
Factory:	Same as above location
Products:	Polyester Filament Yarn and Chips

Reliance Industries Ltd.

Office:	Maker Chambers IV 3rd Floor, 222 Nariman Point Bombay 400 021 (Maharashtra)

Plants: (1) Patalganga, P.O. Rasayani
Dist. Raigad 410 207 (Maharashtra)
(2) Mora Village P.O. Batha
Surat-Hazira Road
Dist. Surat 394 510 (Gujarat)
(3) Naroda Industrial Estate, #103/106
Naroda, Ahmedabad 382 330 (Gujarat)
Products: Terephthalic Acid, Xylene, Polyester Fibers @ Plant #1
PVC, Polyethylenes, Ethylene Oxide and Glycols @ Plant #2

R.G. Ispat Ltd.
Office: 118-120, Road No. 9, V.K.I. Area, Jaipur 302 013 (U.P.)
Factory: See above
Product: Kraft Paper

Rinki Petrochemicals & Industries Ltd.
Office: 67 Race Course Circle
Near Bombay Shopping Centre
Baroda 390 007 (Gujarat)
Factory: Padra (Gujarat)
Products: Methanol, Formaldehyde

Ruchi Soya Industries Ltd.
Office: 214, Tulsiani Chambers
Nariman Point
Bombay 400 021 (Maharashtra)
Factories: (1) Indore (M.P.)
(2) Noida (U.P.)
Product: Soybean Oil

Sadhana Nitrochem Ltd.
Office: 207, Kakad Chambers
132 Dr. A.B. Road
Worli, Bombay 400 018 (Maharashtra)
Factory: 47, MIDC, Roha 402 116
Dist. Raigad (Maharashtra)
Product: Nitrobenzene

Sakthi Sugars Ltd.
Office: Sakthi Nagar
638 315, Periyar (T.N.)
Factories: (1) Same as above
(2) Pallagoundenpaiayam (T.N.)
(3) Sunpai (Orissa)
Products: Sugar, Ethanol

Sandoz (India) Ltd.

Office: Sandoz House, Dr. A.B. Road
Worli, P.O. Box 6596, Bombay 400 018 (Maharashtra)
Factories: (1) P.O. Sandoz Baug
Thane 400 607 (Maharashtra)
(2) Kandla Free Trade Zone
Gandhidham, Ahmedabad, 370 230 (Gujarat)
(3) Plots 629/630 GIDC
Panoli 394 115 (Gujarat)
Products: Pharmaceuticals, Leather Chemicals, Pesticides

Sanghi Polyesters Ltd.

Office: Sanghi Nagar
P.O. Hayatnagar
Mandal, Koheda 501 511 (A.P.)
Factory: Same as above
Products: Polyester Chips and Yarn

Saraswati Industrial Syndicate Ltd.

Office: Yamunanagar (Haryana)
Factory: Same as above
Products: Sugar, Steel

Saurashtra Cement & Chemical Industries Ltd.

Office: Near Railway Station, Ranavav 360 560 (Gujarat)
Factory: Junagadh (Gujarat)
Products: Cement, Soda Ash, Bauxite

Searle (India) Ltd.

Office: 21, Damodardas Sukhadvaia Marg
Bombay 400 001 (Maharashtra)
Factories: (1) Plot No. 25
MIDC, Thane-Belapur Road
Thane 400 613 (Maharashtra)
(2) Shed No. 2403/A, Ankleshwar Industrial Estate
Ankleshwar, Bharuch (Gujarat)
(3) Plots 3102/A & 2703/A, Ankleshwar Industrial Estate (Gujarat)
Products: Drugs, Pesticide Intermediates & Pesticides

Sesa Goa Ltd.

Office: Altinho, Panjim 403 001 (Goa)
Factory: See above
Products: Iron Ore, Pig Iron

Shalimar Paints Ltd.

Office: 13, Camac Street
Calcutta 700 017 (W.B.)
Factory: See above
Products: Paints, Enamels and Varnishes

Shasun Chemicals & Drugs Ltd.

Office: A1/B SIPCOT Industrial Complex
Kudikadu Village, Cuddacore (T.N.)
Factory: Same address
Products: Ibuprofen, Ranitidine

Shaw Wallace & Co. Ltd.

Office: 3, Walchand Hirachand Marg
Bombay 400 038 (Maharashtra)
Factories: (1) Aurangabad (Maharashtra)
(2) Durgachak, Haldia 721 602
Dist. Midnapore (West Bengal)
(3) Madras (T.N.)
Products: Sulfuric Acid, Fertilizers, Pesticides

Shree Acids & Chemicals Ltd.

Office: Delhi Cold Storage Building
15, New Subzi Mandi
Azadpur, Delhi 110 033
Factory: A-1, Industrial Area, Gajruala
Dist. Moradabad (U.P.)
Products: Kraft Paper, Sulfuric Acid, Superphosphate

Shree Cement Ltd.

Office: 21, Strand Road
Calcutta 700 001 (W.B.)
Factory: Beawar Masuda Road
Near Village Andheri Deori, Beawar 395 901
Dist. Ajmer (Rajasthan)
Product: Cement

Shree Digvijay Cement Co. Ltd.

Office: Digvijaygram (Gujarat)
Factories: (1) Cement: Digvijaygram, (Gujarat)
(2) Clinter grinding: Sewree, Bombay (Maharashtra)
(3) Asbestos Cement Products: Digvijaynagar, Ahmedabad (Gujarat)
(4) Rishra (West Bengal)
(5) Konnagar (West Bengal)
Product: Cement

Shree Synthetics Ltd.

Office: Naulakhi, Maksi Road, Ujjain (M.P.)
Factory: Same as above
Products: Nylon and Polyester Filament Yarn

Shri Ambuja Petrochemicals Ltd.

Office: 7-C Surya Towers
105 S.P. Road
Secunderabad 500 003 (A.P.)
Factory: Plot Nos. 17, 18 and 20
IDA Phase I
Patencheru 502 319
Medak District (A.P.)
Products: Phthalic Anhydride, Fumaric Acid

Shriram Fertilizers & Chemicals Ltd.

Office: Kanchenjunga Building
18 Barakhamba Road
New Delhi 110 001
Factory: Shriram Nagar, Kota 324 004 (Rajasthan)
Products: Caustic Soda, Ammonia, Urea

Shriram Industrial Enterprises Ltd.

Office: Surya Kiran Building
18 Kasturba Gandhi Marg
New Delhi 110 001
Factories: (1) Mawana (U.P.)
(2) Titawi (U.P.)
(3) Hyderabad (A.P.)
Products: Sugar, Caustic, Chlorine

SIP Resins Ltd.

Office: 116, Dr. Radhakrishnan Salai
3rd Floor, Mylapore, Madras 600 004 (T.N.)
Factory: Plot No. 46, SIPCOT Industrial Complex
Ranipet 632 403 (T.N.)
Product: Epoxy Resins

Siris Ltd.

Office: L.B. Nagar, Hyderabad 500 963 (A.P.)
Factories: (1) Hyderabad (A.P.)
(2) Gopanapalli (A.P.)
Products: Pharmaceuticals

Sirpur Paper Mills Ltd.

Office: 5-9-22/1/1, First Floor
Adarsh Nagar, Hyderabad 500 463 (A.P.)
Factory: Sirpur, Kaghaz Nagar 504 296 (A.P.)
Products: Caustic, Chlorine, Pulp, Paper and Paperboard

Sirsilk Ltd.

Office: Sirpur, Kaghaz Nagar 504 296 (A.P.)
Factory: Same location
Products: Acetic Acid, Acetic Anhydride, Acetone

SIV Industries Ltd.

Office: 1977-A Trichy Road
Singallur, Coimbatore 641 005 (T.N.)
Factory: Sirumugai (T.N.)
Products: Viscose Yarn, Vegetable Oils, Sulfuric Acid

SM Dye Chem Ltd.

Office: SM Centre
Andheri Kurla Road
Maro-Naka, Andheri (E), Bombay 400 059 (Maharashtra)
Factories: (1) Rabale, Thane (Maharashtra)
(2) Wagle, Thane (Maharashtra)
(3) Taloja (Maharashtra)
(4) Vidisha (M.P.)
(5) Kurkumbh, Pune (Maharashtra)
Products: Ethylene Oxide, Glycols

SOL Pharmaceuticals Ltd.

Office: 5-9-88/2 Sapphire Building
Fateh Maidan, Nacharam, Hyderabad 501 507 (A.P.)
Factories: (1) K-4 & 9-9/7, Road No. 5, Nacharam, Hyderabad 501 507 (A.P.)
(2) Plot No. 86-B, IDA, Jeedimetla, Hyderabad 500 855 (A.P.)
(3) Plot No. 73, B & C Kolhar Industrial Area (Bihar)
Products: Pharmaceuticals

Southern Petrochemical Industries Corp. Ltd.

Office: SPIC Centre
2nd Floor, 97 Mount Road
Guindy, Madras 600 032 (T.N.)
Factories: (1) Heavy Chemicals Division
Express Highway
Manali, Madras 600 068 (T.N.)

(2) Fertilizer Division
SPIC Nagar
Tuticorin 628 005
Chidambaranar District (T.N.)

Products: Ammonia, Chlorine, Caustic, Urea, Sulfuric Acid, Phosphoric Acid

SPIC Fine Chemicals Ltd.

Office: 6, Nungambakkam High Road
Madras 600 034 (T.N.)

Factory: Peralam Main Road
Sorarudy Post
Thirunallar
Karaikal 609 607 (T.N.)

Products: Zeolite builders for detergents

Sree Rayalaseema Alkalies & Allied Chemicals Ltd.

Office: Vasant Nagar
Gondiparla Village
518 004 Kurnool Dist. (A.P.)

Factory: Same location

Products: Caustic, Chlorine

Sree Rayalaseema Petrochemicals Ltd.

Office: 1-1-290, First Floor, A Block
Ashoknagar, Hyderabad 500 020 (A.P.)

Factories: (1) Chloromethanes Plant
Nemam Village, Kakinada (A.P.)
(2) Bromine Plant
Thiruporur, Old Mahabalipuram, Madras (T.N.)

Products: Chloromethanes, Bromine

SRF Ltd.

Office: Express Building
9-10 Bahadur Shah Zafar Marg
New Delhi 110 002

Factories: (1) Manali Industrial Area, Manali, Madras 600 068 (T.N.)
(2) Viralimalai, Pudukottai Dist. (T.N.)
(3) Jhiwana, Tehsil Tijara, Dist. Alwar (Rajasthan)
(4) Doddaballapura (Karnataka)

Products: Nylon Yarn, Tire Cord, Fluorocarbons

Srichakra Tyres Ltd.

Office: TVS Building
7-B West Veli Street
Madurai 625 001 (T.N.)

Factory: Vellaripatti Village, Melur Taluk, Dist. Madurai (T.N.)
Products: Tires and Tubes

Sriman Organic Petrochemicals Ltd.
Office: 710 Dalamal Towers
Nariman Point
Bombay 400 021 (Maharashtra)
Factory: A-171, Phase 1, MIDC, Dombivli (E)
Thane (Maharashtra)
Products: Dye Intermediates

Standard Industries Ltd.
Office: Mafatlal Centre
6th Floor, Nariman Point
Bombay 400 021 (Maharashtra)
Factories: (1) New Prabhadevi Road, Bombay 400 025
(2) Tokersi Jivraj Road, Bombay 400 015 (Maharashtra)
(3) Balgarh, Dewas (M.P.)
(4) Chemicals: Standard Alkali,
Thane-Belapur Road, Thane (Maharashtra)
(5) Nawabwadi, Begumpura, Surat (Gujarat)
Products: Caustic Soda, Chlorine

Star Paper Mills Ltd.
Office: 27, Biplabi Trailokya Maharaj Sarani
Calcutta 700 001 (W.B.)
Factory: Saharanpur (U.P.)
Product: Paper

Steel Authority of India Ltd. (SAIL)
Office: Ispat Bhawan
Lodi Road, New Delhi 110 003
Factories: (1) Durgapur (W.B.)
(2) Burnpur (W.B.)
(3) Rourkela (Orissa)
(4) Bokaro (Bihar)
(5) Bhilai (M.P.)
(6) Salem (T.N.)
Products: Pig Iron, Steel, Fertilizers

Stepan Chemicals Ltd.
Office: Dakshna, Sector 11, Central Business District
New Bombay 400 614 (Maharashtra)
Factory: Rajpura (Punjab)
Products: Detergents

Sudarshan Chemical Industries Ltd.

Office:	162, Wellesley Road Sangam Bridge, Pune 411 001 (Maharashtra)
Factory:	Same location
Products:	Pigments, Pesticides

Sukhna Paper Mills Ltd.

Office:	S.C.O. 116-117 Sector 8-C Madhya Marg, Chandigarh
Factory:	Village Nagla Dist. Patiala (Punjab)
Product:	Kraft Paper

Sumitra Pharmaceuticals & Chemicals Ltd.

Office:	5-9-30 Basheerbagh, Palace Colony Road No. 4, Basheerbagh, Hyderabad 500 029 (A.P.)
Factory:	See above
Products:	Pharmaceuticals

Supreme Petrochem Ltd.

Office:	17/18 Shah Industrial Estate Veera Desai Road Andheri (W), Bombay 400 058 (Maharashtra)
Factory:	See above
Products:	Styrene and Polystyrene

Swadeshi Polytex Ltd.

Office:	6th Floor, Hotel Samrat Chanakyapuri New Delhi 110 021
Factory:	New Kavi Nagar Ghaziabad 201 002 (U.P.)
Product:	Polyester Staple Fiber

Synthetics & Chemicals Ltd.

Office:	Oriental House 7 Jamshedji Tata Road Bombay 400 020 (Maharashtra)
Factory:	P.O. Bhitaura Rubber Bareilly 243 501 (U.P.)
Products:	Styrene, ABS Resins, Ethanol

Tamil Nadu Chemical Products Ltd.

Office:	TCP Sapthagiri Bhavan 10, Karpagamal Nagar Mylapore, Madras 600 004 (T.N.)

Factory: Karaikudi-Kundrakudi Road
Kovilur 623 307, P.M.T. District (T.N.)
Product: Sodium Hydrosulfite

Tamil Nadu Petroproducts Ltd.
Office: 6, Nungambakkam, High Road
Madras 600 034 (T.N.)
Factory: See above
Products: Linear Alkylbenzenes, Epichlorohydrin

Tanfac Industries Ltd.
Office: Plot No. 14, SIPCOT Industrial Complex
Cuddalore 607 005 (T.N.)
Factory: Same location
Products: Sulfuric Acid, HF

Tata Chemicals Ltd.
Office: Bombay House, 24 Homi Mody Street, Fort
Bombay 400 001 (Maharashtra)
Factories: (1) Mithapur, Okhamandal 361 345 (Gujarat)
(2) Babrala (U.P.)
(3) Badaun (U.P.)
(4) Pithampur (M.P.)
(5) Dhar (M.P.)
Products: Soda Ash, Chlorine, BHC, Caustic, Detergents

Tata Iron & Steel Co. Ltd. (TISCO)
Office: 24 Homi Mody Street, Fort
Bombay 400 001 (Maharashtra)
Factories: (1) Jamshedpur (Bihar)
(2) Kharagpur (W.B.)
Products: Iron and Steel

Tata Oil Mills Co. Ltd.
Office: Bombay House
24 Homi Mody Street, Fort, Bombay 400 001
Factories: (1) Tatapuram (Maharashtra)
(2) Bombay (Maharashtra)
(3) Calcutta (W.B.)
(4) Ghaziabad (U.P.)
(5) Madras (T.N.)
(6) Calicut (Kerala)
(7) Aurangabad (Maharashtra)
(8) Kandla (A.P.)
Products: Soaps, Detergents, Glycerin, Vegetable Oils

Tata Vashisti Detergents Ltd.

Office: P.B. No. 6, Lote, Plot No. 7, Lote Parshuram
MIDC Area, Villa-Awashi Tal Khed
Ratnagiri 415 722 (Maharashtra)
Factory: See above
Products: Detergents

Thirumalai Chemicals Ltd.

Office: B Wing, 8th Road, Mittal Tower
Nariman Point, Bombay 400 021 (Maharashtra)
Factory: 25-B, SIPCOT Industrial Complex
Ranipet 632 403, North Arcot District (Tamil Nadu)
Products: Phthalic Anhydride, Maleic Anhydride

Tide Water Oil Co. (India) Ltd.

Office: Yule House, 8 Dr. Rajendra Prasad Sarani
Calcutta 700 001 (W.B.)
Factory: Calcutta (W.B.)
Products: Oils and Greases

Tinplate Co. of India Ltd.

Office: 4, Bankshall Street, Calcutta 700 001 (W.B.)
Factory: Golmuri, Jamshedpur 831 003 (Bihar)
Products: Tinplate, Sulfuric Acid

Torrent Pharmaceuticals Ltd.

Office: Torrent House
Ashram Road
Ahmedabad 380 009 (Gujarat)
Factory: See above
Products: Pharmaceuticals

Transpek Industry Ltd.

Office: Karan Road, Atladra
Vadodara 390 012 (Gujarat)
Factories: (1) Atladra (Gujarat)
(2) Ekalbara (Gujarat)
Product: Sulfur Chemicals

Travancore Cochin Chemicals Ltd.

Office: Udyogmandal, P.O. Cochin, 683 501 (Kerala)
Factory: Same location
Products: Caustic, Chlorine

Travancore Rayons Ltd.

Office: Rayonpuram, 683 543 (Kerala)
Factory: Same location as above
Products: Sulfuric Acid, Carbon Disulfide, Rayon Yarn

Trichy Distilleries & Chemicals Ltd.

Office: Mahalakshmi Mansion
No. 14, Main Road, Gandhi Nagar
Adyar, Madras 600 020 (T.N.)
Factory: Tiruchirapalli (T.N.)
Products: Alcohol, Acetic Acid, Acetates

Trimurtee Fertilizers Ltd.

Office: 12/11 Tilak Marg
Dalibagh, Lucknow 226 001 (U.P.)
Factory: Village Gaur Pathok
P.O. Pokhrayan, Tehsil Bhognipur
Dist. Kanpur Dehat (U.P.)
Products: Sulfuric Acid, Superphosphate

Triveni Engineering Works Ltd.

Office: Kailash, 2nd Floor, Kasturba Gandhi Marg
New Delhi 110 001
Factories: (1) Khatauli (U.P.)
(2) Muzaffar Nagar (U.P.)
(3) Nain (U.P.)
(4) Peenya (Karnataka)
(5) Belagola (Karnataka)
Product: Sugar

Tuticorin Alkali Chemicals & Fertilizers Ltd.

Office: East Coast Centre
553 Anna Salai
Teynampet, Madras 600 018 (T.N.)
Factory: D-3, Developed Plot
Tuvakudi, Tiruchirapalli
620 015 (Tamil Nadu)
Products: Soda Ash, Ammonium Chloride (fertilizer grade), Pesticides

UB Petroproducts Ltd.

Office: McDowell House
3, Second Line Beach
Madras 600 001 (T.N.)
Factory: Sathangadu Village
Manali, Madras 600 068 (T.N.)
Products: Polyols for Polyurethanes

Ultramarine & Pigments Ltd.
Office: Mittal Tower, B. Wing, 8th Floor
Nariman Point, Bombay 400 021 (Maharashtra)
Factory: Ambattur, Madras 600 053 (T.N.)
Products: Dye Intermediates, Detergents, Soap

Union Carbide India Ltd.
Office: 1, Middleton Street
Calcutta 700 071 (W.B.)
Factories: (1) Turbhe (Maharashtra)
(2) Lucknow (U.P.)
(3) Srinagar (J&K)
(4) Hyderabad (A.P.)
Product: Batteries

United Carbon India Ltd.
Office: NRM International House
178 Babubhai M. Chinai Marg
Backbay Reclamation, Bombay 400 020 (Maharashtra)
Factory: MIDC Plot No. 3, Trans Thane Creek Area
Thane-Belapur Road, Post Ghansoli, Thane 400 701 (Maharashtra)
Product: Carbon Black

United Phosphorus Ltd.
Office: 167, Dr. Annie Besant Road
Worli, Bombay 400 018 (Maharashtra)
Factories: (1) 11, GIDC Estate
Vapi, Dist. Bulsar 396 195 (Gujarat)
(2) 117, GIDC, Ankleshwar 393 002 (Gujarat)
Products: Phosphorus, Pesticides

United Pulp & Paper Mills Ltd.
Office: Asron-140 001, Tehsil Balchaur
Dist. Hoshiarpur (Near Ropar) (Punjab)
Factory: Same location
Product: Kraft Paper

Universal Paper Mills Ltd.
Office: 75C Park Street, Calcutta 700 016 (W.B.)
Factory: P.O. Jhargram, Dist. Midnapore (W.B.)
Product: Kraft Paper

Usha Ispat Ltd.
Office: Terekhoi Road, Post Redi, Taluka Venguria
Dist. Sindhudurg 516 517 (Maharashtra)

Factories: (1) As above
(2) Pithampur (M.P.)
Products: Pig Iron and Steel

Uttar Pradesh Straw & Agro Products Ltd.
Office: Aghwanpur 244 502
Dist. Moradabad (U.P.)
Factory: Same location
Product: Kraft Paper

Vam Organic Chemicals Ltd.
Office: Skyline House
85 Nehru Place, New Delhi 110 019
Factory: Bhartiagram, Gajraula
Dist. Moradabad 244 223 (U.P.)
Products: Vinyl Acetate Monomer, Acetaldehyde, Acetic Acid, Acetic Anhydride

Vantech Industry Ltd.
Office: 6-3-778/A/12 Durganagar Colony
Ameerpet, Hyderabad 500 016 (A.P.)
Factory: See above
Product: Pesticides

VBC Industries Ltd.
Office: A-4 Unit Industrial Estate
Visakhapatnam 530 007 (A.P.)
Factory: P.O. Box No. 67, Ponnada, Srikakulam 532 408 (A.P.)
Products: Nitric Acid, Ammonium Nitrate

Vidula Chemicals & Manufacturing Industries
Office: 7-E Neelamber Building
28-B Shakespeare Sarani, Calcutta 700 017 (W.B.)
Factory: Gopalpur Chandigar, P.O. Ganganagar, Parganas (N) 743 250 (W.B.)
Product: Sulfuric Acid

Vikrant Tyres Ltd.
Office: Vikrant House
1, Main Road, V.V. Mohalla
Mysore 570 002 (Karnataka)
Factory: Metagalli (Karnataka)
Products: Automobile Tires and Tubes

Vinyl Chemicals (India) Ltd.
Office: 7th Floor, Regent Chambers
Jamnalal Bajaj Marg
Nariman Point, Bombay 400 021 (Maharashtra)

Factories: (1) Ramakrishna Road
P.B. No. 17411, Andheri (E), Bombay 400 059
(2) Plot A-21, MIDC, Mahad, Dist. Raigad (Maharashtra)
Product: Vinyl Acetate Monomer

Vizag Steel
See entry under Rashtriya Ispat Nigam Ltd.

VXL India Ltd.
Office: Saurashtra Chemicals
Aerodrome Road, Jamnagar 361 006 (Gujarat)
Factories: (1) Birlasagar, Porbandar 360 576 (Gujarat)
(2) Amritsar (Punjab)
(3) Jamnagar (Gujarat)
Products: Soda Ash, Caustic Soda

Welspun Polyester (India) Ltd.
Office: Plot 112, Achhad Industrial Estate
Talasari, Dist. Thane 401 606 (Maharashtra)
Factories: (1) Palghar (Maharashtra)
(2) Valsad (Gujarat)
(3) Nagar Haveli (Gujarat)
Product: Polyester Yarn

West Coast Paper Mills Ltd.
Office: Shreeniwas House, Hazarimal Marg
Bombay 400 001 (Maharashtra)
Factory: Bangur Nagar (Karnataka)
Products: Paper and Paperboard

Wipro Ltd.
Office: Bakhtawar
229 Nariman Point
Bombay 400 021 (Maharashtra)
Factory: Bangalore (Karnataka)
Products: Vegetable Oils and Soaps

Wockhardt Ltd.
Office: Ready Money Terrace
Dr. A.B. Road
Worli, Bombay 400 018 (Maharashtra)
Factories: (1) L-1, MIDC Chikalthana
Jalgaon Road, Aurangabad 431 210 (Maharashtra)
(2) 2-B, GIDC Estate, Ankleshwar
Dist. Bharuch 393 002 (Gujarat)

(3) Kalol-Halol Road, Opposite Kalbhairav Mandir
Alindra Village, Kalol 389 330 (Gujarat)

Products: Pharmaceuticals

Zuari Agro Chemicals Ltd.

Office: Jai Kisan Bhavan
Zuarinagar 403 726 (Goa)

Factory: Zuarinagar (Goa)

Products: Ammonia, Urea, Cement

INDEX